Prentice Hall Canada Series in Accounting

Financial Accounting

Canadian Second Edition

Charles T. Horngren
Stanford University

Walter T. Harrison, Jr.
Baylor University

W. Morley Lemon
University of Waterloo

With
Johan P. de Rooy
University of British Columbia

Prentice Hall Canada Inc., Scarborough, Ontario

Canadian Cataloguing in Publication Data

Horngren, Charles T., 1926–
 Financial accounting
Canadian 2nd ed.
First published as part of: Horngren, Charles T.,
1926– . Accounting. Canadian ed. (1991).
1. Accounting. I. Harrison, Walter T.
II. Lemon, W. Morley, 1939– . III. Title.

HF5635.H67 1993   657   C93-093279-X

Prentice-Hall, Inc., Englewood Cliffs, New Jersey
Prentice-Hall International (UK) Limited, London
Prentice-Hall of Australia, Pty. Limited, Sydney
Prentice-Hall Hispanoamericana, S.A., Mexico City
Prentice-Hall of India Private Limited, New Delhi
Prentice-Hall of Japan, Inc., Tokyo
Simon & Schuster Asia Private Limited, Singapore
Editora Prentice-Hall do Brasil, Ltda., Rio de Janeiro

ISBN 0-13-106170-4

Photo Credits

1 Dave Starrett—Cove Studios; **44** Price Club of Canada; **93** Photograph
courtesy of Communications Canada; **137** Canada Mortgage & Housing
Corporation; **198** Courtesy: *The Evening Telegram*; **255** Dave Starrett—
Cove Studios; **259** Courtesy of IBM Canada; **301** Dave Starrett—Cove
Studios; **351** Kathleen Bellesiles—Little Apple Studios; **392** Dave Starrett—
Cove Studios; **431** Courtesy: Bank of Montreal; **473** National Film Board
Photograph; **524** *The Financial Post*; **568** Prentice Hall Archives; **610** Dave
Starrett—Cove Studios; **650** Prentice Hall Archives; **690** Dave Starrett—
Cove Studios; **735** McCain Foods; **777** Joe McNally—Sygma; **838** Women
Inventors project.

Acquisitions Editor: Suzanne Tyson
Developmental Editor: David Jolliffe
Production Editor: Dawn du Quesnay
Permissions/Photo Research: Angelika Baur
Cover Design: Monica Kompter
Cover Image: © Hans Neleman/Image Bank Canada
Page Layout: Olena Serbyn

1 2 3 4 5 BG   97 96 95 94 93

Printed and bound in Canada

Original U.S. edition published by Prentice-Hall, Inc.
Englewood Cliffs, New Jersey. Copyright 1992, 1989 Prentice-Hall, Inc.

This edition for sale in Canada only.

Brief Contents

Part One

The Basic Structure of Accounting

1 Accounting and Its Environment   1

2 Recording Business Transactions   44

3 Measuring Business Income: The Adjusting Process   93

4 Completing the Accounting Cycle   137

5 Merchandising and the Accounting Cycle   198

Part Two

Introduction to Accounting Systems

6 Accounting Information Systems   255

7 Internal Control and Cash Transactions   301

Part Three

Accounting for Noncash Assets and Liabilities

8 Accounts and Notes Receivable   351

9 Merchandise Inventory   392

10 Capital Assets, Intangibles, and Related Expenses   431

11 Current Liabilities and Payrol Accounting   473

Part Four

Generally Accepted Accounting Principles

12 The Foundation for Generally Accepted Accounting Principles   524

Part Five

Accounting for Partnerships and Corporations

13 Accounting for Partnerships   568

14 Corporations: Organization, Capital Stock, and the Balance Sheet   610

15 Corporations: Retained Earnings, Dividends, and the Income Statement   650

16 Corporations: Long-Term Liabilities   690

17 Corporations: Investments and Accounting for International Operations   735

Part Six

Using External Accounting Information

18 Statement of Changes in Financial Position   777

19 Using Accounting Information to Make Business Decisions   838

Appendices

A Accounting for the Effects of Changing Prices   A-1

B Present-Value Tables and Future-Value Tables   A-11

C Published Financial Statements   A-19

Glossary   G-1

Index   I-1

Contents

Part One

The Basic Structure of Accounting

1   Accounting and Its Environment   1

Accounting and Decisions   2
What Is Accounting?   2
Users of Accounting Information: The Decision-Makers   2
The Development of Accounting Thought   4
The Accounting Profession   4
Accounting Organizations and Designations   5
Ethical Considerations in Accounting and Business   7
Specialized Accounting Services   9
Types of Business Organizations   10
Accounting Concepts and Principles   11
The Accounting Equation   14
Accounting for Business Transactions   14
Evaluating Business Transactions   19
Financial Statements   19
Summary Problem for Your Review   22
Summary   24
Self-Study Questions   25
Accounting Vocabulary   26
Assignment Material*   26
Extending Your Knowledge**   41

2   Recording Business Transactions   45

The Account   45
Double-Entry Bookkeeping   47
The T-Account   48

Increases and Decreases in the Accounts   48
The Debit-Credit Language of Accounting   50
Recording Transactions in Journals   50
Posting from the Journal to the Ledger   52
Flow of Accounting Data   53
Illustrative Problem   53
Summary Problem for Your Review   56
Details of Journals and Ledgers   58
Posting   60
Chart of Accounts   60
Normal Balances of Accounts   61
Additional Owner's Equity Accounts: Revenues and Expenses   62
Typical Account Titles   62
Illustrative Problem   64
Analytical Use of Accounting Information   68
Computers and Accounting   69
Summary Problem for Your Review   70
Summary   73
Self-Study Questions   74
Assignment Material   75
Extending Your Knowledge   90

3   Measuring Business Income: The Adjusting Process   93

Accrual-Basis Accounting versus Cash-Basis Accounting   94
The Accounting Period   95
Revenue Principle   96
Matching Principle   96
Time-Period Concept   97
Adjustments to the Accounts   98
Posting the Adjusting Entries   106
Adjusted Trial Balance   108
Preparing the Financial Statements from the Adjusted Trial Balance   108
Relationships among the Three Financial Statements   111
Computers and the Accounting Process   111

*In each chapter, Assignment Material includes Questions, Exercises, and Problems (Group A and Group B).
**Extending Your Knowledge includes Decision Problems, an Ethical Issue, and Financial Statement Problems.

Summary Problem for Your Review   112
Summary   116
Self-Study Questions   116
Accounting Vocabulary   117
Assignment Material   117
Extending Your Knowledge   133

4   Completing the Accounting Cycle   137

Overview of the Accounting Cycle   138
The Accountant's Work Sheet   138
Computer Spreadsheets   146
Summary Problem for Your Review   148
Using the Work Sheet   149
Reversing Entries   155
Classification of Assets and Liabilities   158
Formats of Balance Sheets   160
Use of Accounting Information in Decision-Making   161
Detecting and Correcting Accounting Errors   162
Summary Problem for Your Review   163
Summary   166
Self-Study Questions   167
Accounting Vocabulary   168
Assignment Material   168
Extending Your Knowledge   185

Appendix: Prepaid Expenses, Unearned Revenues, and Reversing Entries   188

Prepaid Expenses   188
Unearned (Deferred) Revenues   191
Summary   194
Appendix Assignment Material   194

5   Merchandising and the Accounting Cycle   198

The Operating Cycle for a Merchandising Business   200
Purchase of Merchandise Inventory   200
Sale of Inventory   205
Cost of Goods Sold   206
Summary Problem for Your Review   210
The Adjusting and Closing Process for a Merchandising Business   211
Financial Statements of a Merchandising Business   214

Income Statement Format   216
Use of Accounting Information in Decision-Making   219
Computers and Inventory   220
Summary Problem for Your Review   221
Summary   226
Self-Study Questions   226
Accounting Vocabulary   227
Assignment Material   228
Extending Your Knowledge   242

Appendix: The Adjusting and Closing Process for a Merchandising Business: Adjusting-Entry Method   246

The Adjusting and Closing Process   246
Alternate Solution to Review Problem   251
Comprehensive Problem for Part One   253

Part Two

Introduction to Accounting Systems

6   Accounting Information Systems   255

Accounting System Design and Installation   256
Basic Model of Information Processing   257
An Effective Information System   257
Computer Data Processing   258
Overview of an Accounting Information System   261
Special Accounting Journals   261
Summary Problem for Your Review   267
The Credit Memorandum: A Basic Business Document   273
The Debit Memorandum: A Basic Business Document   275
Sales Tax   275
Balancing the Ledgers   277
Documents as Journals   277
Computers and Special Journals   277
Summary Problem for Your Review   278
Summary   278

Self-Study Questions 279
Accounting Vocabulary 280
Assignment Material 280
Extending Your Knowledge 299

7 Internal Control and Cash Transactions 301

Effective Internal Control 304
Limitations of Internal Control 307
The Bank Account as a Control Device 308
Summary Problem for Your Review 315
Reporting of Cash 316
Internal Control over Cash Receipts 317
Internal Control over Cash Disbursements 318
Computers, Internal Control, and Cash 326
Summary Problem for Your Review 327
Summary 328
Self-Study Questions 328
Accounting Vocabulary 330
Assignment Material 330
Extending Your Knowledge 346
Comprehensive Problem for Part Two 348

Part Three

Accounting for Noncash Assets and Liabilities

8 Accounts and Notes Receivable 351

Different Types of Receivables 352
The Credit Department 353
Uncollectible Accounts (Bad Debts) 353
Credit Balances in Accounts Receivable 360
Credit Card Sales 360
Internal Control over Collections of Accounts Receivable 361
Summary Problem for Your Review 362

Notes Receivable 363
Receivables Reporting and Allowances: Actual Reports 369
Use of Accounting Information in Decision-Making 370
Computers and Accounts Receivable 371
Summary Problem for Your Review 372
Summary 373
Self-Study Questions 373
Accounting Vocabulary 374
Assignment Material 375
Extending Your Knowledge 389

9 Merchandise Inventory 392

Figuring the Cost of Inventory 394
Inventory Costing Methods 395
Income Effects of FIFO, LIFO, and Average Cost 396
Generally Accepted Accounting Principles: A Comparison of the Inventory Methods 397
Consistency Principle 399
Summary Problem for Your Review 399
Accounting Conservatism 401
Effect of Inventory Errors 403
Methods of Estimating Inventory 404
Periodic and Perpetual Inventory Systems 406
Internal Control over Inventory 409
Computerized Inventory Records 410
Summary Problems for Your Review 410
Summary 412
Self-Study Questions 412
Accounting Vocabulary 413
Assignment Material 414
Extending Your Knowledge 428

10 Capital Assets, Intangibles, and Related Expenses 431

The Cost of Property, Plant and Equipment 433
Amortization of Capital Assets 434
Determining the Useful Life of Property, Plant and Equipment 435
Measuring Depreciation 435
Depreciation Methods 436

Comparison of the Depreciation
   Methods *440*
Summary Problem for Your Review *441*
Depreciation and Income Taxes *442*
Special Issues in Depreciation
   Accounting *443*
Using Fully Depreciated Assets *445*
Disposal of Property, Plant and
   Equipment *445*
Selling a Capital Asset *445*
Accounting for Intangible Assets and
   Amortization *449*
Computers and Amortization *451*
Betterments versus Repairs *452*
Summary Problems for Your Review *453*
Summary *454*
Self-Study Questions *454*
Accounting Vocabulary *456*
Assignment Material *456*
Extending Your Knowledge *470*

11 **Current Liabilities and Payroll
Accounting** **473**
Current Liabilities of Known Amount *474*
Goods and Services Tax and Sales Tax
   Payable *476*
Current Liabilities That Must Be
   Estimated *480*
Contingent Liabilities *482*
Summary Problem for Your Review *484*
Accounting for Payroll *485*
Gross Pay and Net Pay *485*
Payroll Entries *492*
The Payroll System *493*
Recording Cash Disbursements for
   Payroll *496*
Internal Control over Payroll *500*
Reporting Payroll Expense and
   Liabilities *501*
Computer Accounting Systems for Current
   Liabilities *501*
Summary Problem for Your Review *502*
Summary *504*
Self-Study Questions *504*
Accounting Vocabulary *505*
Assignment Material *505*

Extending Your Knowledge *520*
**Comprehensive Problem for Part
Three** **522**

Part Four

Generally Accepted Accounting Principles

12 **The Foundation for Generally
Accepted Accounting
Principles** **524**
Objective of Financial Reporting *529*
Underlying Concepts *529*
Accounting Principles *532*
Constraints on Accounting *544*
Financial Statements and Their
   Elements *546*
Accounting Standards Throughout the
   World *547*
Summary Problem for Your Review *548*
Summary *549*
Self-Study Questions *550*
Accounting Vocabulary *551*
Assignment Material *551*
Extending Your Knowledge *565*

Part Five

Accounting for Partnerships and Corporations

13 **Accounting for
Partnerships** **568**
Characteristics of a Partnership *569*
Initial Investments by Partners *572*
Sharing Partnership Profits and
   Losses *573*
Partner Drawings *577*
Dissolution of a Partnership *578*
Summary Problem for Your Review *581*

Withdrawal of a Partner   *583*
Death of a Partner   *586*
Liquidation of a Partnership   *586*
Partnership Financial Statements   *590*
Summary Problem for Your Review   *592*
Summary   *594*
Self-Study Questions   *595*
Accounting Vocabulary   *597*
Assignment Material   *597*
Extending Your Knowledge   *608*

14 Corporations: Organization, Capital Stock, and the Balance Sheet   *610*

Characteristics of a Corporation   *611*
Organization of a Corporation   *613*
Capital Stock   *614*
Shareholders' Equity   *614*
Shareholder Rights   *616*
Classes of Stock   *616*
Issuing Stock   *618*
Summary Problem for Your Review   *622*
Donated Capital   *623*
Incorporation of a Going Business   *623*
Organization Cost   *624*
Dividend Dates   *624*
Dividends on Preferred and Common
    Stock   *625*
Convertible Preferred Stock   *627*
Rate of Return on Total Assets and Rate of
    Return on Shareholders' Equity   *628*
Different Values of Stock   *629*
Summary Problems for Your Review   *631*
Summary   *633*
Self-Study Questions   *634*
Accounting Vocabulary   *635*
Assignment Material   *635*
Extending Your Knowledge   *647*

15 Corporations: Retained Earnings, Dividends, and the Income Statement   *650*

Retained Earnings and Dividends   *651*
Stock Dividends   *653*
Stock Splits   *655*
Repurchase of Capital Stock   *656*
Summary Problem for Your Review   *659*

Restrictions on Retained Earnings   *661*
Variations in Reporting Shareholders'
    Equity   *662*
Corporation Income Statement   *662*
Statement of Retained Earnings   *668*
Summary Problem for Your Review   *670*
Summary   *672*
Self-Study Questions   *672*
Accounting Vocabulary   *674*
Assignment Material   *674*
Extending Your Knowledge   *687*

16 Corporations: Long-Term Liabilities   *690*

The Nature of Bonds   *691*
Types of Bonds   *691*
Bond Prices   *692*
Issuing Bonds Payable   *694*
Adjusting Entries for Interest
    Expense   *698*
Summary Problem for Your Review   *699*
Effective-Interest Method of
    Amortization   *701*
Bond Sinking Fund   *705*
Retirement of Bonds Payable   *705*
Convertible Bonds and Notes   *706*
Current Portion of Long-Term Debt   *707*
Mortgage Notes Payable   *707*
Advantage of Financing Operations with
    Debt versus Stock   *707*
Lease Liabilities   *709*
Off-Balance-Sheet Financing   *711*
Pension Liabilities   *711*
Computers and Corporate Financial
    Planning   *713*
Summary Problem for Your Review   *713*
Summary   *715*
Self-Study Questions   *716*
Accounting Vocabulary   *717*
Assignment Material   *717*
Extending Your Knowledge   *727*

Appendix: Present Value   *729*

Present Value Tables   *730*
Present Value of an Annuity   *730*
Present Value of Bonds Payable   *732*
Capital Leases   *733*
Appendix Assignment Material   *733*

17 Corporations: Investments and Accounting for International Operations 735

ACCOUNTING FOR INVESTMENTS 736
Stock Prices 736
Investments in Stock 737
Classifying Stock Investments 737
Accounting for Stock Investments 738
Investments in Bonds and Notes 748
Summary Problem for Your Review 751
ACCOUNTING FOR INTERNATIONAL OPERATIONS 753
Economic Structures and Their Impact on International Accounting 754
Foreign Currencies and Foreign-Currency Exchange Rates 754
Accounting for International Transactions 755
Hedging: A Strategy to Avoid Foreign-Currency Transaction Losses 757
Consolidation of Foreign Subsidiaries 757
International Accounting Standards 758
Computers and Consolidations 758
Summary Problem for Your Review 759
Summary 760
Self-Study Questions 760
Accounting Vocabulary 762
Assignment Material 762
Extending Your Knowledge 773
Comprehensive Problem for Part Five 775

Part Six

Using External Accounting Information

18 Statement of Changes in Financial Position 777

Purposes of the Statement of Changes in Financial Position 778
Basic Concept of the Statement of Changes in Financial Position 779
Operating, Financing and Investing Activities 779
Interest and Dividends 782
Preparing the Statement of Changes in Financial Position: The Direct Method 782
Focus of the Statement of Changes in Financial Position 785
Summary Problem for Your Review 786
Computing Individual Amounts for the Statement of Changes in Financial Position 788
Noncash Financing and Investing Activities 795
Preparing the Statement of Changes in Financial Position: The Indirect Method 795
An Actual Statement of Changes in Financial Position 798
Computers and the Statement of Changes in Financial Position 799
Summary Problem for Your Review 800
Summary 801
Self-Study Questions 802
Accounting Vocabulary 803
Assignment Material 803
Extending Your Knowledge 824

Appendix: The Work-Sheet Approach to Preparing the Statement of Changes in Financial Position 827

Preparing the Work Sheet: Direct Method for Operating Activities 828
Preparing the Work Sheet: Indirect Method for Operating Activities 832
Appendix Assignment Material 835

19 Using Accounting Information to Make Business Decisions 838

Financial Statement Analysis 839
Horizontal Analysis 841
Vertical Analysis 844
Common-Size Statements 845
Industry Comparisons 846
Information Sources 847
The Statement of Changes in Financial Position in Decision-Making 848
Summary Problem for Your Review 849
Using Ratios to Make Business Decisions 850
Measuring the Ability to Pay Current Liabilities 851

Measuring the Ability to Sell Inventory and
   Collect Receivables   852
Measuring the Ability to Pay Long-Term
   Debt   855
Measuring Profitability   856
Analyzing Stock as an Investment   859
The Complexity of Business Decisions   860
Efficient Markets, Management Action, and
   Investor Decisions   861
Computers and Financial Statement
   Analysis   861
Summary Problem for Your Review   862
Summary   864
Self-Study Questions   866
Accounting Vocabulary   867
Assignment Material   867
Extending Your Knowledge   883
Comprehensive Problem for Part Six   885

Appendices

**A   Accounting for the Effects of
   Changing Prices   A-1**

**B   Present-Value Tables and
   Future-Value Tables   A-11**

**C   Published Financial
   Statements   A-19**

Glossary   G-1

Index   I-1

Charles T. Horngren is the Edmund W. Littlefield Professor of Accounting at Stanford University. A graduate of Marquette University, he received his M.B.A. from Harvard University and his Ph.D. from the University of Chicago. He is also the recipient of honorary doctorates from Marquette University and DePaul University.

A Certified Public Accountant, Horngren served on the Accounting Principles Board for six years, the Financial Accounting Standards Board Advisory Council for five years and the Council of the American Institute of Certified Public Accountants for three years. He is currently serving as a trustee of the Financial Accounting Foundation.

A member of the American Accounting Association, Horngren has been its President and its Director of Research. He received the Outstanding Accounting Educator Award in 1973, when the association initiated an annual series of such awards.

The California Certified Public Accountants Foundation gave Horngren its Faculty Excellence Award in 1975 and its Distinguished Professor Award in 1983. He is the first person to have received both awards.

In 1985 the American Institute of Certified Public Accountants presented its first Outstanding Educator Award to Horngren. Professor Horngren is also a member of the National Association of Accountants, where he was on its research planning committee for three years. He was a member of the Board of Regents, Institute of Management Accounting, which administers the Certified Management Accountant examinations.

Horngren is the author of three other books published by Prentice Hall: *Cost Accounting: A Managerial Emphasis*, Seventh Edition, 1991 (with George Foster); *Introduction to Financial Accounting*, Fourth Edition, 1990 (with Gary L. Sundem); and *Introduction to Management Accounting*, Eighth Edition, 1990 (with Gary L. Sundem).

Charles T. Horngren is the Consulting Editor for the Prentice Hall Series in Accounting.

Walter T. Harrison, Jr., is Professor of Accounting and holds the Peat Marwick-Thomas L. Holton Chair in Accounting at the Hankamer School of Business, Baylor University. He received his B.B.A. degree from Baylor University, his M.S. from Oklahoma State University and his Ph.D. from Michigan State University.

Professor Harrison, recipient of numerous teaching awards from student groups as well as from university administrators, has also taught at Cleveland State Community College, Michigan State University, the University of Texas and Stanford University.

A member of the American Accounting Association and the American Institute of Certified Public Accountants, Professor Harrison has served as Chairperson of the Financial Accounting Standards Committee of the American Accounting Association and on the Program Advisory Committee for Accounting Education and Teaching.

Professor Harrison has published research articles in numerous journals, including *The Accounting Review*, *Journal of Accounting Research*, *Journal of Accountancy*, *Journal of Accounting and Public Policy* and *Economic Consequences of Financial Accounting Standards*. He has received scholarships, fellowships and research grants from Price Waterhouse & Co., Deloitte Haskins & Sells and the Ernst & Young Tax Research Program.

W. Morley Lemon is Associate Professor of Accounting at the School of Accountancy, University of Waterloo. He received his B.A. from the University of Western Ontario, his M.B.A. from the University of Toronto and his Ph.D. from the University of Texas at Austin.

Professor Lemon has taught at the University of Texas, the University of Illinois, McMaster University and the University of Waterloo. In addition, he has taught and prepared courses for professional accountants and accounting students in Canada and the United States.

A member of the Institute of Chartered Accountants of Ontario, Professor Lemon was elected a Fellow by that body. He is also a member of the Canadian Academic Accounting Association and the American Accounting Association, and has served as Chairperson of and on committees for all three organizations. He is Director of the Centre for Accounting Ethics, University of Waterloo.

Professor Lemon is the author of *Auditing: An Integrated Approach*, Canadian Fifth Edition, 1992 (with Alvin A. Arens and James K. Loebbecke), published by Prentice Hall Canada, Inc. He has co-authored a monograph published by the Canadian Academic Accounting Association, and has published articles in *CAMagazine*, *Contemporary Accounting Research*, and other professional and academic publications. He has received scholarships, fellowships and research grants from the Canadian Academic Accounting Association, Peat Marwick, and Ernst and Whinney.

Johan P. de Rooy is a lecturer with the Accounting Division of the Faculty of Commerce and Business Administration, University of British Columbia. He earned his B.Ed. from the University of British Columbia and his M.B.A. from Queen's University. He is both a Chartered Accountant and a Certified Management Accountant.

Mr. de Rooy is an active educator in all three professional accounting programs, having taught introductory and advanced levels of financial accounting, management accounting and auditing. He has been the national examiner for the CGA accounting theory course and the course co-author for the CGA introductory financial accounting course. Mr. de Rooy is the author of *The Uniform Final Examination, A Systematic Study Approach (Fourth Edition)*, published by Clarence Byrd Inc.

Mr. de Rooy has served on the governing council of the Chartered Accountants of British Columbia for five years and acted as chairperson for numerous provincial committees for this institute. Currently he is president-elect of the Canadian Cancer Society, B.C. and Yukon Division and sits on several provincial and national committees for the Canadian Cancer Society.

Preface

Financial Accounting provides full introductory coverage of financial accounting. In content and emphasis, instructors will find that the book is in the mainstream for courses in introductory accounting. This book focuses on the most widely used accounting theory and practice. This text and its supplements supply the most effective tools available for learning fundamental accounting concepts and procedures.

Clarity and Accuracy

Two themes have directed our writing of this text — *clarity* and *accuracy*. We believe that we have produced the clearest prose, learning objectives, exhibits, definitions, and assignment material for courses in principles of accounting. Students will find this book easy to study. We have assumed that students have no previous education in accounting or business.

The contributions of users of the first edition and their students and reviewers of this Canadian Second Edition have guided us in writing an accurate text. We and the publishers have sought input on our work from an unprecedented number of accounting educators and students in order to publish a book that meets your strict demands for accuracy.

This demand for accuracy did not stop with the test. The authors and publisher have taken extraordinary care and incurred extraordinary cost to ensure that the supplements are accurate.

The Business Context of Accounting

To enhance our presentation of accounting, we set out in the Canadian First Edition to create a business context for the student. As often as possible, we have integrated actual companies and their business data into our text narrative and assignment material. Students reading about companies familiar to them find the material interesting and also develop a deeper appreciation for accounting's importance in today's business world. When information drawn from real companies would be too advanced for introductory students, we illustrated the accounting point at hand by using realistic examples, building a framework of relevance that makes learning the topic more inviting to the students.

We have expanded on this approach in the Canadian Second Edition. Each chapter now opens with a description of an actual business situation. We call these vignettes, and most are drawn from the business press.

Distinctive Features of the Second Edition

Increased Assignment Material

Financial Accounting, Canadian Second Edition, has increased assignment material. We have added more exercises and problems, which are now referenced to chapter learning objectives. In addition, chapters now conclude with a special feature called Extending Your Knowledge. This section includes two Decision

Problems, an Ethical Issue case (new this edition), and two Financial Statement problems (double from the first edition). Parts 1, 2, 3, 5, and 6 end with a Comprehensive Problem (also new to this edition).

Chapter-Opening Vignettes

Each chapter opens with an actual business situation. We found in the first edition that emphasis on the real-world environment of business promotes student interest and learning. Our new second-edition chapter-opening vignettes build on what we learned from the first edition.

Recommendations of the Accounting Education Change Commission

The recommendations of this important group have inspired us in several ways.

* Chapter 1 includes a discussion of ethics in business, and, as we mentioned, all chapters include an Ethical Issue case for student analysis.
* To sharpen students' decision-making skills, financial ratios are interspersed throughout the text. For example, Chapter 4 introduces the current ratio and the debt ratio, Chapter 5 covers the gross margin percentage and inventory turnover, and Chapter 8 discusses the acid-test ratio and days' sales in receivables. Other ratios appear throughout the book as appropriate. (Chapter 19, Using Accounting Information to Make Business Decisions, presents all important financial ratios, including those discussed elsewhere in the text.)
* International accounting receives more emphasis and now appears as the second half of Chapter 17.
* To meet the challenge of improving students' communications skills, we include in all chapters new assignment material that requires essay answers.

End-of-Chapter Appendices

For maximum flexibility, several chapters have their own appendices, enabling instructors to give expanded coverage to certain topics. The Chapter 4 appendix is Prepaid Expenses, Unearned Revenues, and Reversing Entries.

The Chapter 5 appendix is The Adjusting and Closing Process for a Merchandising Business: Adjusting Entry Method. The Chapter 16 appendix is Present Value. The Chapter 18 appendix is The Work-Sheet Approach to Preparing the Statement of Changes in Financial Position.

End-of-Book Appendices

Three appendices are presented at the end of the book:

Appendix A: Accounting for the Effects of Changing Prices
Appendix B: Present-Value and Future-Value Tables. This appendix complements the present-value coverage in Chapter 16.
Appendix C: The Financial Statements of the Schneider Corporation.

Chapter Organization _____

1. Each chapter begins with a vignette, as we have described. Learning objectives also appear at the start of every chapter. These objectives are keyed to the relevant chapter material and are also referenced to the exercises and problems.

2. Most chapters offer two Summary Problems for Your Review. Each Summary Problem includes its fully worked-out solution. These features, which generally appear at the halfway point and at the end of each chapter, provide students with immediate feedback and serve as key review aids.

3. Each chapter presents three important tools for student review. A text Summary recaps the chapter discussion. Self-Study Questions allow students to test their understanding of the chapter. The text that supports the answer is referenced by page number, and the answers appear at the end of the Extending Your Knowledge section. Accounting Vocabulary presents the key terms introduced in the chapter, with page references. A full Glossary, keyed by page number, appears at the end of the book.

4. Assignment Material is more varied and plentiful than in completing texts. Questions (covering the major definitions, concepts, and procedures) may be assigned as homework or used to promote discussion in class. Exercises, identified by topic area and learning objectives, cover the full spectrum of the chapter text. Problems, also identified by topic area and learning objectives, come in A and B sets. The two sets allow instructors to vary assignments from term to term and to solve the A or B problem in class and assign the related problem for homework. Some exercises and problems can be solved using the Lotus R 1-2-3 templates.

5. Each chapter ends with an Extending Your Knowledge section. Under this heading are presented:

   * two Decision Problems, which help students to develop critical thinking skills. Analysis, interpretation, and determining a course of action are ordinarily required.

   * an Ethical Issue case, which presents a business scenario that challenges the ethical conduct of the accountant and asks the student to resolve the dilemma. Many of these cases also challenge students' accounting skills.

   * two Financial Statement Problems (for most chapters). The first problem links the chapter's subject matter directly to the actual financial statements in the annual report of the Schneider Corporation which appears in Appendix C. Students answer the second financial statement problem using data taken from the annual report of another company.

The Supplements Package

We have a far-reaching package of teaching and learning tools to supplement the text. A team of contributors devoted hundreds of hours to perfecting the supplements. Our supplements coordinator, who is a professional accounting teacher, together with a full-time editor worked with the contributors to ensure maximum instructional value, accuracy, and consistency with the text and within the supplements package.

Resources for the Instructor

Instructor's Manual	Test Item File
Solutions Manual	Computerized Test Item File
Solutions Transparencies	Instructor's manuals to the Practice Sets
Teaching Transparencies	

Resources for the Student

Study Guide with Demonstration Problems	PHACTS Tutorial Videos
Working Papers	Lotus Templates
Practice Sets	

Acknowledgements to the Canadian Second Edition _____

I would like to thank Chuck Horngren and Tom Harrison for their encouragement and support.

Special thanks to Johan de Rooy for all his work. Thanks to Jack Hanna, University of Waterloo, for his help with the material in Appendix A on inflation accounting. Thanks also to Bob Beam, University of Waterloo and Van Hall, C.A. for their help with Chapter 11. Thanks to Carrie Mace, Julie Robson, and especially to Lynn Miske, for their work on the Solutions Manual. The work of Melanie E. Russell on the Test Item File and other supplements, and Don Rogazynski on the Working Papers is also appreciated.

I would also like to thank the following individuals for the invaluable assistance they provided in reviewing the text and supplements and for providing so many helpful suggestions:

Wayne A. Campbell, Seneca College
Ray Carrol, Mount St. Vincent University
Randy Dickson, Red Deer College
Janet E. Falk, Fraser Valley College
Harvey C. Freedman, Humber College
John Glendenning, Centennial College
Maureen Labonte, Algonquin College
Robert F. Madden, St. Francis Xavier
   University

Allen McQueen, Grant MacEwan
   Community College
Michael A. Perretta, Sheridan College
Gordon Rice, Mohawk College
Al Scherbluk, Ryerson Polytechnical
   Institute
Ralph H. Sweet, Durham College
Nora Wilson, Humber College
Leroy Wright, Fanshawe College

Many people gave very useful feedback on the first edition, including Sylvia Brown, Ian Wells, and the accounting faculty of Fanshawe College, members of the accounting faculty of Conestoga College, and the many focus group participants.

Thanks are extended to Douglas Dodds, Schneider Corporation, for permission to use the Schneider Corporation annual report. Thanks are also due to John Labatt Limited and National Trust for permission to use as exhibits a bond and a stock certificate, respectively issued by their companies.

Publications from the Canadian Institute of Chartered Accountants, the Butterworths series on Financial Statement Presentation prepared by the partners of Price Waterhouse and edited by Christina Drummond, *The Financial Post*, *The Globe and Mail*, and financial statements issued by a large number of Canadian companies have been very helpful in the writing of this book.

I would like especially to acknowledge the people of Prentice Hall Canada, especially the editorial work of David Jolliffe and the support of Yolanda de Rooy and Suzanne Tyson over the past months as the Canadian Edition took shape. I would also like to acknowledge the editorial support of Amy Lui-Ma, Dawn du Quesnay, Maryrose O'Neill and Marta Tomins. And I would like to thank Lu Mitchell, who was there at the start.

This book is dedicated to Margie, whose life and spirit have been my inspiration.

W. Morley Lemon
Waterloo, Ontario
1993

Chapter 1

Accounting and Its Environment

"Recession made discounting the norm. Now, as recovery dawns and retailers look to fortify starving (profit) margins, how do you swing bargain-hardened customers back to regular-priced goods?"

During the late 1980s and early 1990s, Craig Scott, owner of an upscale men's and women's clothing shop in London, Ontario, Scott's of London Ltd., faced the above challenge, and successfully overcame it.

But what does this have to do with accounting? Everything. It was accounting information that afforded Craig the insights to meet this challenge. His records indicated a large investment in inventories of slow-moving items, suppliers expecting payments for items ordered, little cash in the bank, and high overhead costs. Craig's response to these problems was to move to a smaller location, reduce the amount of goods held in inventory, extend the opening hours, and generally reduce prices. Accounting-derived data helped isolate these problems, which were undermining his profitability —

another accounting-determined amount. While the accounting information alone did not solve Craig's problems, it did recommend the actions he took to help his clothing store adjust to the recession and new competitive environment. Without such information, he would have had no idea he was experiencing problems until it was too late to do anything about them other than go out of business.

As you read Chapter 1 and the rest of the book, always remember that the accounting process is extensively concerned with recording and reporting the results of past transactions to assist users of the information in making decisions about *future* courses of action. Accounting is the language that records what happens between businesses or individuals and the environment with which they interact.

Source: Pat Morden: "Retailers Rebound from Margins of Terror," *Profit* (November 1991), pp. 46, 48.

LEARNING OBJECTIVES

After studying this chapter, you should be able to

1 Develop a working vocabulary for decision-making

2 Identify different aspects of the accounting profession

3 Apply accounting concepts and principles to the analysis of business situations

4 Use the accounting equation to describe an organization's financial position

5 Use the accounting equation to analyze business transactions

6 Prepare three financial statements

Accounting and Decisions

Accounting has been called "the language of business." Perhaps a better term is "the language of financial decisions." The better you understand the language, the better you can manage the financial aspects of living. Personal financial planning, investments, loans, car payments, income taxes, and many other aspects of daily life are based on accounting. Scott's of London is facing some of these decisions.

A recent survey indicates that business managers believe it is more important for college students to learn accounting than any other subject. Other surveys show that persons trained in accounting and finance make it to the top of their organizations in greater numbers than persons trained in any other field. Indeed, accounting is an important subject.

Regardless of your roles in life — student, head of household, investor, manager, politician — you will find a knowledge of accounting helpful. The major purpose of this book is to help you learn to use accounting information to make informed decisions. Individuals who can do so have a great advantage over those who cannot.

What Is Accounting?

OBJECTIVE 1

Develop a working vocabulary for decision-making

Accounting is the system that measures business activities, processes that information into reports and financial statements, and communicates these findings to decision-makers. **Financial statements** are the documents that report on an individual's or an organization's business in monetary amounts.

Is our business making a profit? Should we start up a new line of women's clothing? Are sales strong enough to warrant opening a new branch outlet? The most intelligent answers to business questions like these are based on accounting information. Decision-makers use the information to develop sound business plans. As new programs affect the business's activities, accounting takes the company's financial pulse rate. The cycle continues as the accounting system measures the results of activities and reports the results to the decision-makers.

Bookkeeping is a procedural element of accounting as arithmetic is a procedural element of mathematics. Increasingly, people are using computers to do much of the detailed bookkeeping work at all levels — in households, business, and organizations of all types. Exhibit 1-1 illustrates the role of accounting in business.

Users of Accounting Information: The Decision-Makers

Decision-makers need information to make decisions. The more important the decision, the greater the need for relevant information. Virtually all businesses and most

EXHIBIT 1-1 *The Accounting System: the Flow of Information*

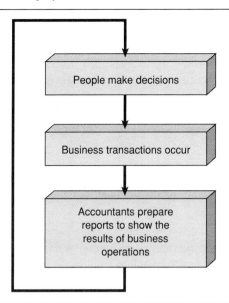

individuals keep accounting records to aid decision-making. Most of the material in this book describes business situations, but the principles of accounting apply to to the financial considerations of individuals as well. The following sections discuss the range of people and groups who use accounting information and the decisions they make.

Individuals   People use accounting information in day-to-day affairs to manage their bank accounts, evaluate job prospects, make investments, and decide whether to rent or buy a house.

Businesses   Managers of businesses like Craig Scott use accounting information to set goals for their organizations, evaluate their progress toward those goals, and take corrective action if necessary. Decisions based on accounting information may include which building and equipment to purchase, how much merchandise inventory to keep on hand, and how much cash to borrow.

Investors and Creditors   Investors provide the money that businesses need to begin operations. To decide whether to help start up a new venture, potential investors evaluate what return they can reasonably expect on their investment. This means analyzing the financial statements of the new business. Those people who do invest monitor the progress of the business by analyzing the company's financial statements and by keeping up with its developments in the business press, for example, *The Financial Post*, *The Financial Times of Canada* and *Report on Business* published by *The Globe and Mail*. Accounting reports are a major source of information for the business press.

Before making a loan, potential lenders determine the borrower's ability to meet scheduled payments. This evaluation includes a projection of future operations, which is based on accounting information.

Government Regulatory Agencies   Most organizations face government regulation. For example, the provincial securities commissions in British Columbia, Alberta, Saskatchewan, Manitoba, Ontario, and Quebec see that businesses, which sell their shares or borrow money from the public, disclose certain financial information to the investing public. The securities commissions, like many government agencies, base their regulatory activity in part on the accounting information they receive from the firms that they watch over.

Taxing Authorities   Local, provincial and federal governments levy taxes on individuals and businesses. The amount of the tax is figured using accounting information. Businesses determine their goods and services tax and sales tax based on their accounting records that show how much they have sold. Individuals and businesses compute their income tax based on how much money their records show they have earned.

Nonprofit Organizations   Nonprofit organizations such as churches, hospitals, government agencies and colleges, which operate for purposes other than to earn a profit, use accounting information in much the same way that profit-oriented businesses do, that is, to manage and control their operations. Both profit organizations and nonprofit organizations deal with budgets, payrolls, rent payments, and the like — all from the accounting system.

Other Users   Employees and labor unions may make wage demands based on the accounting information that shows their employer's reported income. Consumer groups and the general public are also interested in the amount of income that businesses earn. For example, during times of fuel shortages, consumer groups have charged that oil companies have earned "obscene profits." On a more positive note, newspapers may report "improved profit pictures" of major companies as the nation emerges from an economic recession. Such news, based on accounting information, is of widespread interest because it covers the economic activity that affects our standard of living.

The Development of Accounting Thought

Accounting has a long history. Some scholars claim that writing arose in order to record accounting information. Account records date back to the ancient civilizations of China, Babylonia, Greece, and Egypt. The rulers of these civilizations used accounting to keep track of the cost of labor and materials used in building structures like the great pyramids.

Accounting developed further as a result of the information needs of merchants in the city-states of Italy during the 1400s. In that busy commercial climate, the monk Luca Pacioli, a mathematician and friend of Leonardo da Vinci, published the first known description of double-entry bookkeeping in 1494.

The pace of accounting development increased during the Industrial Revolution of the eighteenth and nineteenth centuries as the economies of developed countries moved from handcraft industries to the factory system and mass-produced goods. Until this time, merchandise had been priced by merchants based on their hunches about cost, but the increased competition in the Industrial Revolution required merchants to adopt more sophisticated accounting systems.

In the nineteenth century, the growth of corporations, especially those in the railroad and steel industries, spurred the continuing development of accounting. The corporation owners — the shareholders — were no longer necessarily the managers of their business. Managers had to create accounting systems to report to the owners how well their businesses were doing.

The role of government has led to still more accounting developments. When the federal government started collecting income tax, accounting supplied the concept "income." Also, government at all levels has assumed expanded roles in health, education, labor and economic planning. To ensure that the information that it uses to make decisions is reliable, government has required strict accountability in the business community.

OBJECTIVE 2

Identify different aspects of the accounting profession

The Accounting Profession

Positions in the field of accounting may be divided into several areas. Two general classifications are *public accounting* and *private accounting*.

In Canada, most accountants, both public and private, belong to one of three accounting bodies, which set the standards for admission of and deal with matters like the rules of professional conduct followed by their members: The Canadian Institute of Chartered Accountants (CICA), whose members are called *Chartered Accountants (CA)*; the Certified General Accountants Association of Canada (CGAAC), whose members are called *Certified General Accountants (CGA)*; and the Society of Management Accountants of Canada (SMAC), whose members are called *Certified Management Accountants (CMA)*. The role and activities of each of these bodies are discussed below.

Private accountants work for a single business, such as a local department store, the Swiss Chalet restaurant chain or ATCO Ltd. Charitable organizations, educational institutions and government agencies also employ private accountants. The chief accounting officer usually has the title of controller, treasurer or chief financial officer. Whatever the title, this person usually carries the status of vice-president.

Public accountants are those who serve the general public and collect professional fees for their work, much as doctors and lawyers do. Their work includes auditing, income tax planning and preparation of returns, management consulting, and various accounting services. These specialized accounting services are discussed in the next section. Public accountants represent about a quarter of all professional accountants.

Some public accountants pool their talents and work together within a single firm. Public accounting firms are called CA firms, CGA firms, or CMA firms, depending on the accounting body from which the partners of the firm come. Public accounting firms vary greatly in size. Some are small businesses, and others are medium-sized partnerships. The largest firms are worldwide partnerships with over 2,000 partners. The six largest accounting firms in the world are often called the Big Six. They represent the first five and eighth largest CA firms in Canada and are, in alphabetical order:

Arthur Anderson
Coopers & Lybrand
Deloitte & Touche (Samson Belair/
   Deloitte & Touche in Quebec)
Ernst & Young (formerly
   Clarkson Gordon)
KPMG Peat Marwick Thorne
Price Waterhouse

Although these firms employ less than 25 percent of the more than 50,000 CAs in Canada, they audit more than 80 percent of the 1,000 largest corporations in Canada. The top partners in large accounting firms earn about the same amount as the top managers of other large businesses.

Exhibit 1-2 shows the accounting positions within public accounting firms and other organizations. Of special interest in the exhibit is the upward movement of accounting personnel, as the arrows show. In particular, note how accountants may move from positions in public accounting firms to similar or higher positions in industry and government. This is a frequently traveled career path. Because accounting deals with all facets of an organization, such as purchasing, manufacturing, marketing and distribution, it provides an excellent basis for gaining broad business experience.

Accounting Organizations and Designations

The importance of accounting in today's business world has created the need for control over the professional, educational and ethical standards of accountants. Through statutes passed by provincial legislatures, the three accounting organizations in Canada have received the authority to set educational requirements and professional standards for their members and to discipline members who fail to adhere to their codes of conduct. The acts make them self-regulating bodies, just as provincial associations of doctors and lawyers are.

The Canadian Institute of Chartered Accountants (CICA), whose members are chartered accountants or CAs, is the senior accounting organization in Canada.

EXHIBIT 1-2   *Accounting Positions within Organizations*

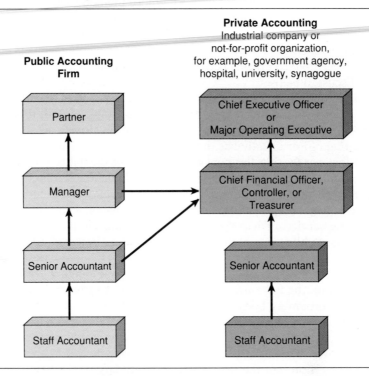

Experience and education requirements for becoming a CA vary among the provinces. Generally, the educational requirement includes a university degree. All provinces, however, require that an individual, to qualify as a CA, pass a national four-day uniform final examination administered by the CICA. The province grants the right to use the professional designation CA.

CAs in Canada must earn their practical experience by working for a public accounting firm; subsequently, about half the CAs in Canada leave public practice for jobs in industry, government or education. A small number of CAs meet their experience requirements working for the federal or provincial governments. CAs in public accounting have the right to perform audits and issue opinions on the audited financial statements in all provinces in Canada.

CAs belong to a provincial institute (*Ordre* in Quebec) and through that body to the CICA. The provincial institutes have the responsibility for developing and enforcing the code of professional conduct which guides the actions of the CAs in that province.

The CICA, through the Accounting Standards Board and the Auditing Standards Board respectively, promulgates accounting standards (**Generally Accepted Accounting Principles** or **GAAP** which are discussed later in this chapter and Chapter 12) and auditing standards (Generally Accepted Auditing Standards or GAAS). These standards are enunciated in the *CICA Handbook*. Specific standards are italicized and called *Recommendations*. Accounting Recommendations are the standards or regulations that govern the preparation of financial statements in Canada. The Accounting Standards Board and the Auditing Standards Board publish Accounting Guidelines and Auditing Guidelines respectively; these do not have the force of Recommendations, but simply provide guidance on specific issues. A third body, the Public Sector Accounting and Auditing Committee (PSAAC), issues standards pertaining to public sector accounting and auditing. The CICA supports and publishes research relating primarily to financial reporting and auditing, and publishes a monthly professional journal *CA Magazine*.

The Certified General Accountants Association of Canada (CGAAC) is also regulated by provincial law. The experience and education requirements for becoming a CGA vary from province to province, but in all provinces the individual must either pass national examinations administered by the CGAAC in the various subject areas, or gain exemption by taking specified university courses. Certain subjects may only be passed by taking a national examination.

CGAs may gain their practical experience through work in public accounting, industry or government. They are employed in public practice, industry and government. Some provinces license CGAs in public practice, which gives them the right to conduct audits and issue opinions on financial statements, while some other provinces do not require a license for them to perform audits.

The association supports research in various areas pertaining to accounting through the Canadian CGA Research Foundation. CGAAC publishes a professional journal entitled *CGA Magazine*.

The Society of Management Accountants of Canada (SMAC) administers the Certified Management Accountant program which leads to the Certified Management Accountant (CMA) designation. The use of this designation is similarly controlled by provincial law. Students generally must have a university degree. The SMAC administers an admission or entrance examination which students must pass before embarking on a two year professional program and completing two years of required work experience. After completing the professional program and the work experience, they write a final examination in order to obtain the CMA designation. The SMAC also administers the professional program and the final examination. CMAs earn their practical experience in industry or government, and are generally employed in industry or government although some CMAs are in public accounting. The Society promulgates standards relating to management accounting through the SMAC. The SMAC conducts and publishes research relating primarily to management accounting, and publishes a professional journal entitled *Cost and Management*.

The Financial Executives Institute (FEI) is an organization composed of senior financial executives from many of the larger corporations in Canada, who meet on a regular basis with a view to sharing information on how they can better manage their organizations. Most of these executives have one of the three designations just discussed. It supports and publishes research relating to management accounting, and also publishes a journal, the *Financial Executive*.

The Institute of Internal Auditors (IIA) is a world-wide organization of internal auditors. It administers the examinations leading to and grants the Certified Internal Auditor (CIA) designation. Internal auditors are employees of an organization whose job is to review the operations, including financial operations, of the organization with a view to making it more economical, efficient, and effective. Many Canadian internal auditors are members of Canadian chapters of the IIA. It supports and publishes research and conducts courses related in internal auditing. The IIA journal is *The Internal Auditor*.

The Canadian Academic Accounting Association (CAAA) directs its attention toward the academic and research aspects of accounting. A high percentage of its members are professors. The CAAA publishes a journal devoted to research in accounting and auditing, *Contemporary Accounting Research*.

Revenue Canada enforces the tax laws and collects the revenue needed to finance federal the government.

Ethical Considerations in Accounting and Business _____

Ethical considerations pervade all areas of accounting and business. Consider a situation that challenges the ethical conduct of the accountant.

A company is being sued by a competitor over an alleged patent infringement by the company. Loss of the lawsuit will impose significant financial hardship on the company, jeopardize the company's relationships with its customers and creditors, and likely cause the price of the company's stock to fall. Should the company disclose this sensitive information in its financial statements? Generally accepted accounting principles require the company to describe the lawsuit in its financial statements and the company's auditor to indicate if he or she thinks the company's disclosure is inadequate.

By what criteria do accountants address questions that challenge their ethical conduct? The three accounting bodies described above all have rules of conduct that govern their members' professional behavior. In addition, many companies have codes of conduct that bind their management and employees to high levels of ethical conduct. For example, see the last paragraph of Management's Report in the financial statements of Schneider Corporation in Appendix C.

The Professional Accounting Bodies and Their Rules of Conduct

CAs, CGAs, and CMAs are all governed by rules of conduct promulgated by their respective organizations. Many of the rules apply whether the members are public accountants working in public practice or private accountants working for a single business, while other rules are applicable only to those members in public practice.

The rules of conduct serve both the members of the body promulgating them and the public. The rules serve members by setting standards that they must meet, and providing a benchmark against which they will be measured by their peers. The public is served because the rules of conduct provide it with a list of the standards to which the members of the body adhere. This helps it determine its expectations of members' behavior. However, the rules of conduct should be considered a minimum standard of performance; ideally, the members should continually strive to exceed them.

There are certain rules that are fundamental to the practice of accounting and common to the rules of conduct of all three bodies. They concern the confidentiality of information the accountant is privy to, maintenance of the reputation of the profession, integrity and due care, competence, refusal to be associated with false and misleading information, and compliance by the accountant with professional standards such as the accounting standards found in the *CICA Handbook*.

There are other rules that are fundamental to the practice of public accounting. They deal with the public accountant's need for independence, and with the rules governing advertising and solicitation and the conduct of practice.

Codes of Business Conduct of Companies

Many companies have codes of conduct that apply to their employees in their dealings with each other and with the companies' suppliers and customers. Some of these companies mention their code in the report of management section of the annual report. For example, the Spar Aerospace Limited 1990 annual report stated:

> Management also recognizes its responsibility for ensuring that Spar's business is conducted with integrity. This responsibility is reflected in the Spar business conduct policy to which designated employees are required to make a commitment.

Xerox Canada's 1990 annual report stated in the report of management:

> The company has established its intent to maintain the highest standards of ethical conduct in all its business activities. A business ethics policy is communicated to employees annually.

> Both companies indicate to their employees how management expects employees to behave.

Specialized Accounting Services ──────────────

As accounting affects so many people in so many different fields, public accounting and private accounting include specialized services.

Public Accounting

Auditing is the most significant service that public accountants perform. An audit is the independent examination that adds credibility to the accounting reports that management prepares and submits to investors, creditors, and others outside the business. In carrying out an audit, public accountants from outside a business examine the business's financial statements. If the public accountants believe that these documents fairly represent the business's operations, they offer a professional opinion stating that the firm's financial statements are in accordance with generally accepted accounting principles, which is the standard used by the profession. Why is the audit so important? Creditors considering loans want assurance that the facts and figures the business submits are reliable. Shareholders, who have invested in the business, need to know that the financial picture management shows them is complete. Government agencies need information from businesses.

Tax accounting has two aims: complying with the tax laws and minimizing taxes to be paid. Because combined federal and provincial income tax rates range as high as 51 percent for individuals and 46 percent for corporations, reducing income tax is an important management consideration. Tax work by accountants consists of preparing tax returns and planning business transactions in order to minimize taxes. In addition, since the imposition of the goods and services tax, public accountants have been involved in advising their clients how to properly collect and account for it. Public accountants advise individuals on what types of investments to make, and on how to structure their estates and design their transactions.

Management consulting is the catchall term that describes the wide scope of advice public accountants provide to help managers run a business. As they conduct audits, public accountants look deep into a business's operations. With the insight they gain, they often make suggestions for improvements in cost accounting, budgeting, and information systems design. (We discuss these areas of accounting in the next section.) Management consulting is the fastest-growing service provided by accountants.

Accounting services is also a catchall term used to describe the wide range of services related to accounting provided by public accountants. These services include bookkeeping, write-up work and preparation of financial statements on a monthly or annual basis. Some small companies have all their accounting done by a public accounting firm.

Private Accounting

Cost accounting analyzes a business's costs to help managers control expenses. Good cost accounting records guide managers in pricing their products to achieve greater profits. Also, cost accounting information shows management when a product is not profitable and should be dropped.

Budgeting sets sales and profit goals, and develops detailed plans — called budgets — for achieving those goals. Some of the most successful companies in Canada have been pioneers in the field of budgeting, for example, London Life Insurance Co., and J.M. Schneider Inc., the meat packing company whose statements are in Appendix C.

Information systems design identifies the organization's information needs, both internal and external. Using flow charts and manuals, designers develop and implement the system to meet those needs.

Internal auditing is performed by a business's own accountants. Many large organizations, Ontario Hydro, Hudson's Bay Co., and the Toronto-Dominion Bank among them, maintain a staff of internal auditors. These accountants evaluate the firm's own accounting and management systems to improve operating efficiency, and to ensure that employees follow management's policies.

Summary

Exhibit 1-3 summarizes these accounting specializations. They may also be grouped under the headings "financial accounting" and "management accounting."

Financial accounting provides information to people outside the firm. Creditors and shareholders, for example, are not part of the day-to-day management of the company. Likewise, government agencies, such as Revenue Canada, and the Alberta Securities Commission, and the general public are external users of a firm's accounting information. Chapters 2 through 19 of this book deal primarily with financial accounting.

Management accounting generates confidential information for internal decision-makers, such as top executives, department heads, college deans and hospital administrators. Chapters 20 through 26 cover management accounting.

Types of Business Organizations

Businesses take one of three forms of organization, and in some cases the accounting procedures depend on the organizational form. Therefore you should understand the differences between a proprietorship, a partnership, and a corporation.

A **proprietorship** has a single owner, called the proprietor, who is usually also the manager. Proprietorships tend to be small retail establishments and individual professional businesses, such as those of physicians, lawyers and accountants. From the accounting viewpoint, each proprietorship is distinct from its proprietor. Thus the accounting records of the proprietorship do *not* include records of the proprietor's personal affairs.

A **partnership** joins two or more individuals together as co-owners. Each owner is a partner. Many retail establishments, as well as some professional organiza-

EXHIBIT 1-3   *Accounting*

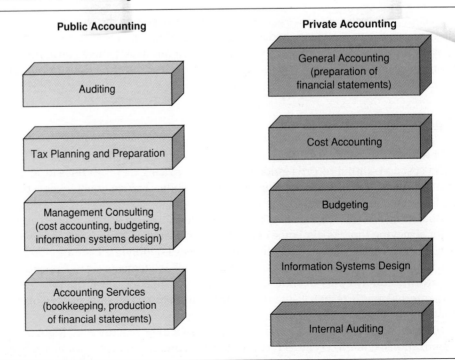

tions of physicians, lawyers and accountants, are partnerships. Most partnerships are small and medium-sized, but some are quite large; there are public accounting firms in Canada with more than 500 partners and law firms with more than 100 partners. Accounting treats the partnership as a separate organization, distinct from the personal affairs of each partner.

A **corporation** is a business owned by **shareholders**. The business becomes a corporation when the federal or provincial government approves its articles of incorporation. A corporation is a legal entity, an "artificial person" that conducts its business in its own name. Like the proprietorship and partnership, the corporation is also an organization with existence separate from its owners.

From a legal standpoint, however, corporations differ significantly from proprietorships and and partnerships. If a proprietorship or a partnership cannot pay its debts, lenders can take the owner(s)'s personal assets to satisfy the business's obligations. But if a corporation goes bankrupt, lenders cannot take the personal assets of the shareholders. This limited personal liability of shareholders for corporate debts partially explains why corporations are the dominant form of business organization: people can invest in corporations with limited personal risk.

Another factor in corporate growth is the division of ownership into individual shares. Companies such as BCE, Inc., the parent company of Bell Canada, the Bank of Montreal, and Canadian Pacific Limited have millions of shares of stock outstanding and tens of thousands of shareholders. An investor with no personal relationship either to the corporation or to any other shareholder can become an owner by buying 30, 100, 5,000, or any number of shares of its stock. For many corporations, the investor can sell the stock whenever he or she wishes. It is usually harder to sell out of a proprietorship or a partnership.

Accounting for corporations includes some unique complexities. For this reason, we initially focus on proprietorships. Partnerships are covered in Chapter 13, and corporations begin in Chapter 14.

Accounting Concepts and Principles _____

> **OBJECTIVE 3**
>
> Apply accounting concepts and principles to the analysis of business situations

Accounting practices rest on certain guidelines. The rules that govern how accountants measure, process and communicate financial information fall under the heading GAAP, which stands for generally accepted accounting principles.

The term *accounting principles* is broader than you might at first think. Generally accepted accounting principles include not only principles but also concepts and methods that identify the proper way to produce accounting information. Generally accepted accounting principles are are very much like the law — a set of rules for conducting behavior in a way acceptable to the majority of people. Unfortunately, also like the law, there are people who violate generally accepted accounting principles or who provide their own unique interpretations of them.

GAAP in Canada rests on Section 1000, "Financial Statement Concepts," of the *CICA Handbook*. The primary objective of financial reporting is to provide information useful for making investment and lending decisions and for assessing management's stewardship. To be useful, information must be understandable, relevant, reliable, and comparable. Accountants strive to meet these goals in the information they produce. Your study of this course will expose you to the generally accepted methods of accounting. First, however, you need to understand the *entity concept*, the *reliability principle*, the *cost principle*, the *going-concern concept*, and the *stable-monetary-unit concept*. These are basic to your first exposure to accounting.

The Entity Concept

The most basic concept in accounting is that of the **entity**. An accounting entity is an organization or a section of an organization that stands apart from other organizations and individuals as a separate economic unit. From an accounting perspective, sharp boundaries are drawn around each entity so as not to confuse its affairs with those of other entities.

Consider Mazzio, a pizzeria owner whose bank account shows a $20,000 balance at the end of the year. Only half of that amount — $10,000 — grew from the business's operations. The other $10,000 arose from the owner's sale of the family motorboat. If Mazzio follows the entity concept, he will keep separate the money generated by the business — one economic unit — from the money generated by the sale of an item belonging not to the business but to himself — a second economic unit. This separation makes it possible to view the business's operating result clearly.

Suppose Mazzio disregards the entity concept and treats the full $20,000 amount as income from the pizzeria's operations. He will be misled into believing that the business has performed twice as well as it has. He will not be able to correctly assess the business and its operations.

Consider Canadian Pacific Ltd. (CP), the fifth largest company in Canada with revenues exceeding $10 billion and assets exceeding $20 billion. CP has five divisions: Transportation (which includes Laidlaw Inc.), Energy (which includes PanCanadian Petroleum), Forest Products (which includes Canadian Pacific Forest Products), Real Estate and Hotels (which includes Marathon Realty and Canadian Pacific Hotels), and Manufacturing (which includes United Dominion Industries). Management of CP considers each company in each division to be a separate accounting entity. The divisions and the companies in them produce financial data so that the management of CP will know how each division and each company in that division is doing. Suppose all the revenue data were combined in a lump-sum amount — if Canadian Pacific Hotels were doing badly, management of CP would not know that was the case. And because management would not know what Canadian Pacific Hotels' situation was, they would not be able to suggest a solution to the problem. However, because separate financial statements are prepared, CP management would know immediately if Canadian Pacific Hotels or any other company in the group were having problems.

Other accounting entities include professional organizations such as a law firm, a doctor's practice, a hospital, a church or synagogue, a college or university, and a family household. Each entity may have a number of subentities. For example, family accounting for a household can be organized by expenditures. The household may break overall costs down into payments for food, housing, utilities, clothing, insurance and recreation. To control these costs, the household may consider each category a subentity in its accounting.

In summary, business transactions should not be confused with personal transactions. Similarly, the transactions of different entities should not be accounted for together. Each entity should be evaluated separately.

The Reliability (or Objectivity) Principle

Accounting records and statements are based on the most reliable data available so that they will be as accurate and useful as possible. This is the *reliability principle*. Reliable data are verifiable. They may be confirmed by any independent observer. Ideally, then, accounting records are based on information that flows from activities that are documented by objective evidence. Without the reliability principle, also called the objectivity principle, accounting records would be based on whims and opinions and would be subject to dispute.

Suppose you start a stereo shop, and in order to have a place for operations, you transfer a small building to the business. You believe the building is worth $55,000. To confirm its value, you hire two real estate professionals, who appraise the building at $47,000. Is $55,000 or $47,000 the more reliable estimate of the building's value? The real estate appraisal of $47,000 is, because it is supported by independent, objective observation.

The Cost Principle *Historical*

The *cost principle* states that assets and services that are acquired should be recorded at their actual cost, also called historical cost. Even though the purchaser may believe the price paid is a bargain, the item is recorded at the price paid in the transaction.

Suppose your stereo shop purchases some stereo equipment from a supplier who is going out of business. Assume you get a good deal on this purchase and pay only $2,000 for merchandise that would have cost you $3,000 elsewhere. The cost principle requires you to record this merchandise at its actual cost of $2,000, not the $3,000 that you believe the equipment to be worth.

The cost principle also holds that the accounting records maintain the historical cost of an asset for as long as the business holds the asset. Why? Suppose your store holds the stereo equipment for six months. During that time, stereo prices increase, and the equipment can be sold for $3,500. Should its accounting value — the figure "on the books" — be the actual cost of $2,000 or the current market value of $3,500? According to the cost principle, the accounting value of the equipment remains at actual cost, $2,000.

The Going-Concern Concept

Another reason for measuring assets at historical cost is the *going-concern concept*, which holds that the entity will remain in operation for the forseeable future. Most assets, such as supplies, land, buildings, and equipment, are acquired for use rather than to sell. Under the going-concern concept, accountants assume the business will remain in operation long enough to use existing assets for their intended purpose. The market value of an asset — the price for which the asset can be sold — may change many times during the asset's life. Therefore, an asset's current market value may not be relevant for decision making. Moreover, historical cost is a more reliable measure for assets.

To better understand the going-concern concept, consider the alternative, which is to *go out of business*. You have probably seen stores advertise a Going Out of Business Sale. The entity is trying to sell its assets. In that case, the relevant measure of the assets is their current market value. However, going out of business is the exception rather than the rule, and for this reason accounting records list assets at historical cost.

The Stable-Monetary-Unit Concept $

We think of a loaf of bread , a suit of clothes, and a month's apartment rent in terms of its dollar value. In Canada, accountants record transactions in dollars because the dollar is the medium of exchange. French accountants record transactions in terms of the franc, and in Japan transactions are recorded in yen.

Unlike a litre, a kilometre or a tonne, the value of a dollar changes over time. A rise in prices is called inflation, and during inflation a dollar will purchase less milk, less toothpaste, and less of other necessities. When prices are relatively stable — when there is little inflation — a dollar's purchasing power is also stable. Most periods of Canadian history have experienced low rates of inflation.

Accountants assume that the dollar's purchasing power is relatively stable. The *stable-monetary-unit concept* is the basis for ignoring the effect of inflation in the accounting records. It allows accountants to add and subtract dollar amounts as though each dollar had the same purchasing power.

Accountants have devised ways to take inflation into account. When inflation accelerates, the CICA's Accounting Standards Board can issue Recommendations that require companies to show inflation-adjusted amounts in reports.

As we continue to explore accounting, we will discuss other principles that guide accountants.

The Accounting Equation

Financial statements tell us how a business is performing and where it stands. We will see several financial statements in this course of study. But how do accountants arrive at the items and amounts that make up the financial statements?

The most basic tool of the accountant is the accounting equation. This equation presents the assets of the business and the claims to those assets. **Assets** are the economic resources of a business that are expected to be of benefit in the future. Cash, office supplies, merchandise, furniture, land, and buildings are examples. Claims to those assets come from two sources. **Liabilities** are "outsider claims," which are economic obligations — debts— payable to outsiders. These outside parties are called *creditors*. For example, a creditor who has loaned money to a business has a claim — a legal right — to a part of the assets until the business pays the debt. "Insider claims" are called **owner's equity** or **capital**. These are the claims held by the owners of the business. An owner has a claim to the entity's assets because he or she has invested in the business. Owner's equity is measured by subtracting liabilities from assets.

The accounting equation shows the relationship among assets, liabilities, and owner's equity. Assets appear on the left-hand side of the equation. The legal and economic claims against the assets — the liabilities and owner's equity — appear on the right-hand side of the equation:

$$\text{ASSETS} = \text{LIABILITIES} + \text{OWNER'S EQUITY}$$

Let us take a closer look at the elements that make up the accounting equation. Suppose you run a business that supplies meat to fast-food restaurants. Some customers may pay you in cash when you deliver the meat. Cash is an asset. Other customers may buy on credit and promise to pay you within a certain time after delivery. This promise is also an asset because it is an economic resource that will benefit you in the future when you receive cash from the customer. This promise is called an **account receivable**. If the promise that entitles you to receive cash in the future is written out, it is called a **note receivable**. All receivables are assets.

The fast-food restaurant's promise to pay you in the future for the meat it purchases on credit creates a debt for the restaurant. This liability is an **account payable**, which means the debtor (restaurant) usually does not give the creditor (meat seller) a written promise to pay. Instead it is backed up by the reputation and credit standing of the restaurant and its owner. A written promise of future payment is called a **note payable**. All payables are liabilities.

Owner's equity is the amount of the assets that remains after subtracting liabilities. We often write the accounting equation to show that the owner's claim to business assets is a residual:

$$\text{ASSETS} - \text{LIABILITIES} = \text{OWNER'S EQUITY}$$

Accounting for Business Transactions

In accounting terms, a **transaction** is any event that *both* affects the financial position of the business entity *and* may be reliably recorded. Many events may affect a company, including (1) elections, (2) economic booms and recessions, (3) purchases and sales of merchandise inventory, (4) payment of rent, (5) collection of cash from customers, and so on. However, the accountant records only events with effects that can be measured reliably as transactions.

Which of the above five events would the accountant record? The answer is events (3), (4) and (5) because their dollar amounts can be measured reliably. Dollar effects of elections and economic trends cannot be measured reliably, so they would not be recorded even though they may affect the business more than events (3), (4) and (5).

To illustrate accounting for business transactions, let us assume that Gary Lyon has recently become a lawyer and opens his own law practice. Because the business has a single owner, it is called a proprietorship.

We now consider eleven events and analyze each in terms of its effect on the accounting equation of Gary Lyon's law practice. Transaction analysis is the essence of accounting.

> ## OBJECTIVE 5
> Use the accounting equation to analyze business situations

Transaction 1   Gary Lyon invests $50,000 of his money to begin the business. Specifically, he deposits $50,000 in a bank account entitled Gary Lyon, Lawyer. The effect of this transaction on the accounting equation of the business entity is

Assets	=	Liabilities	+	Owner's Equity	Type of Owner's Equity Transaction
Cash				Gary Lyon, Capital	
(1) +50,000				+50,000	Owner investment

The first transaction increases both the assets, in this case Cash, and the owner's equity of the business, Gary Lyon, Capital. The transaction involves no liabilities of the business because it creates no obligation for Lyon to pay an outside party. To the right of the transaction we write "Owner investment" to keep track of the reason for the effect on owner's equity.

Note that the amount on the left side of the equation equals the amount on the right side. This equality must hold for every transaction.

Transaction 2   Lyon purchases land for a future office location, paying cash of $40,000. The effect of this transaction on the accounting equation is

Assets		=	Liabilities	+	Owner's Equity	Type of Owner's Equity Transaction
Cash	+ Land				Gary Lyon, Capital	
(1) 50,000					50,000	Owner investment
(2) − 40,000	+ 40,000					
Bal. 10,000	40,000				50,000	
	50,000				50,000	

The cash purchase of land increases one asset, Land, and decreases another asset, Cash, by the same amount. After the transaction is completed, Lyon's business has cash of $10,000, land of $40,000, no liabilities, and owner's equity of $50,000. Note that the sums of the balances (which we abbreviate "Bal.") on each side of the equation are equal. This equality must always exist.

Transaction 3   Lyon buys stationery and other office supplies, agreeing to pay $500 within thirty days. This transaction increases the assets and liabilities of the business. Its effect on the accounting equation is

Assets			=	Liabilities	+	Owner's Equity
Cash	+ Office Supplies	+ Land		Accounts Payable	+	Gary Lyon, Capital
Bal. 10,000		40,000				50,000
(3)	+500			+500		
Bal. 10,000	500	40,000		500		50,000
	50,500				50,500	

The asset affected is Office Supplies, and the liability is called an account payable. The term *payable* signifies a liability. Since Lyon is obligated to pay $500 in the future, but signs no formal promissory note, we record the liability as an Account Payable, not as a Note Payable. We say that purchases supported by the general credit standing of the buyer but not by written evidence are made on *open account*.

Transaction 4   The purpose of business is to increase assets and owner's equity through **revenues**, which are amounts earned by delivering goods or services to customers. Revenues increase owner's equity because they increase the business's assets but not its liabilities. As a result, the owner's interest in the assets of the business increases.

Exhibit 1-4 shows that owner investments and revenues increase the owner's equity of the business. The exhibit also indicates the type of transactions that decrease owner's equity. Owner withdrawals are those amounts that are removed from the business by the owner. Withdrawals are the opposite of owner investments. Expenses are the cost of doing business and are the opposite of revenues. Our illustration will also show how to account for expenses and withdrawals. Gary Lyon earns service revenue by providing legal services to his clients. Assume he earns $5,500 for providing services to several clients and collects this amount in cash. The effect on the accounting equation is an increase in the asset Cash and an increase in Gary Lyon, Capital, as follows:

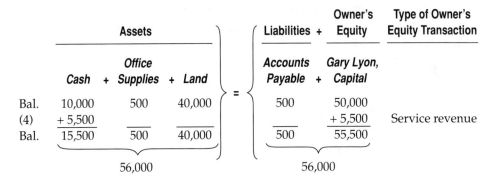

This revenue transaction caused the business to grow, as shown by the increase in total assets and total equities.

Transaction 5   Lyon performs services for a client who does not pay immediately. In return for his legal services, Lyon receives the client's promise to pay the $3,000 amount within one month. This promise is an asset, an account receivable to Lyon because he expects to collect the cash in the future. In accounting, we say that Lyon performed this service on account; that is, the client does not pay cash but has

EXHIBIT 1-4   *Transactions that Increase and Decrease Owner's Equity*

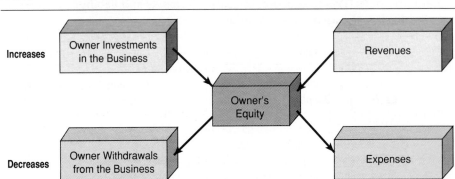

Lyon charge the fee for the service to the client's account receivable. When the business performs service for a client or a customer, the business earns revenue regardless of whether it receives cash immediately or expects to collect cash later. This $3,000 of service revenue is as real to Lyon's business as the $5,500 of revenue that he collected immediately in the preceding transaction. Lyon records an increase in the asset accounts receivable and an increase in owner's equity as follows:

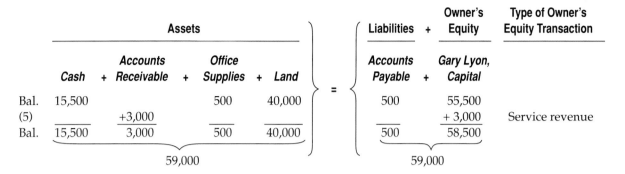

		Assets					Liabilities	+	Owner's Equity	Type of Owner's Equity Transaction
	Cash	+ Accounts Receivable	+	Office Supplies	+ Land	=	Accounts Payable	+	Gary Lyon, Capital	
Bal.	15,500			500	40,000		500		55,500	
(5)		+3,000							+ 3,000	Service revenue
Bal.	15,500	3,000		500	40,000		500		58,500	
			59,000					59,000		

Again, this revenue transaction caused the business to grow.

Transaction 6   In earning revenue a business incurs expenses. Expenses are decreases in owner's equity that occur in the course of delivering goods or services to clients. Expenses decrease owner's equity because they use up the business's assets. Expenses include office rent, salaries paid to employees, newspaper advertisements, and utility payments for light, electricity, gas, and so forth.

This transaction shows that during the month Lyon pays $2,700 in cash expenses: office rent, $1,100; employee salary, $1,200 (for a part-time assistant); and total utilities, $400. The effect on the accounting equation is

		Assets					Liabilities	+	Owner's Equity	Type of Owner's Equity Transaction
	Cash	+ Accounts Receivable	+	Office Supplies	+ Land	=	Accounts Payable	+	Gary Lyon, Capital	
Bal.	15,500	3,000		500	40,000		500		58,500	
(6)	– 2,700								– 1,100	Rent expense
									– 1,200	Salary expense
									– 400	Utilities expense
Bal.	12,800	3,000		500	40,000		500		55,800	
			56,300					56,300		

Because expenses have the opposite effect of revenues, they cause the business to shrink, as shown by the smaller amounts of total assets and total equities.

Each expense can be recorded in a separate transaction or together, as shown here. Note that even though the figure $2,700 does not appear on the right-hand side of the equation, the three individual expenses add up to a $2,700 total. As a result, the "balance" of the equation holds, as we know it must.

Business people, Gary Lyon included, run their businesses with the objective of taking in more revenues than they pay out in expenses. An excess of total revenues over total expenses is called **net income**, **net earnings** or **net profit**. If total expenses are greater than total revenues, the result is called a **net loss**.

Transaction 7   Lyon pays $400 to the store from which he purchased $500 worth of office supplies in Transaction 3. In accounting, we say that he pays $400 on account, or on his account payable to the store (while the store receives the money on its account receivable). The effect on the accounting equation is a decrease in the asset Cash and a decrease in the liability Accounts Payable, as follows:

		Assets				=	Liabilities +	Owner's Equity
	Cash	+ Accounts Receivable +	Office Supplies +	Land			Accounts Payable +	Gary Lyon, Capital
Bal.	12,800	3,000	500	40,000			500	55,800
(7)	– 400						– 400	
Bal.	12,400	3,000	500	40,000			100	55,800
		55,900						55,900

The payment of cash on account has no effect on the asset Office Supplies because the payment does not increase or decrease the supplies available to the business.

Transaction 8   Lyon remodels his home at a cost of $30,000, paying cash from his personal funds. This event is a nonbusiness transaction. It has no effect on Lyon's law practice and therefore is not recorded by the business. It is a transaction of the Gary Lyon *personal* entity, not the Gary Lyon, Lawyer, *business* entity. We are focusing now solely on the business entity, and this event does not affect it. This transaction illustrates an application of the entity concept.

Transaction 9   In Transaction 5, Gary Lyon performed service for a client on account. Lyon now collects $1,000 from the client. We say that Lyon collected the cash on account. Lyon will record an increase in the asset Cash. Should he also record an increase in service revenue? No, because Lyon already recorded the revenue when he earned it in Transaction 5. The phrase "collect cash on account" means to record an increase in Cash and a decrease in the asset Accounts Receivable. The effect on the accounting equation is

		Assets				=	Liabilities +	Owner's Equity
	Cash	+ Accounts Receivable +	Office Supplies +	Land			Accounts Payable +	Gary Lyon, Capital
Bal.	12,400	3,000	500	40,000			100	55,800
(9)	+ 1,000	– 1,000						
Bal.	13,400	2,000	500	40,000			100	55,800
		55,900						55,900

Total assets are unchanged from the preceding transaction's total. Why? It is because Lyon merely exchanged one asset for another. Also, total equities are unchanged.

Transaction 10   An individual approaches Lyon about selling a parcel of the land owned by the Gary Lyon, Lawyer, entity. Lyon and the other person agree to a sale price of $22,000, which is equal to Lyon's cost of the land. Lyon's business sells the land and receives $22,000 cash, and the effect on the accounting equation is

		Assets				=	Liabilities +	Owner's Equity
	Cash	+ Accounts Receivable +	Office Supplies +	Land			Accounts Payable +	Gary Lyon, Capital
Bal.	13,400	2,000	500	40,000			100	55,800
(10)	+22,000			–22,000				
Bal.	35,400	2,000	500	18,000			100	55,800
		55,900						55,900

Transaction 11   Lyon withdraws $2,100 cash from the business for personal use. The effect on the accounting equation is

	Cash	+	Accounts Receivable	+	Office Supplies	+	Land	=	Accounts Payable	+	Gary Lyon, Capital	Type of Owner's Equity Transaction
Bal.	35,400		2,000		500		18,000		100		55,800	
(11)	− 2,100										− 2,100	Owner withdrawals
Bal.	33,300		2,000		500		18,000		100		53,700	

Assets: 53,800

Liabilities + Owner's Equity: 53,800

Lyon's withdrawal of $2,100 in cash decreases the asset Cash and also the owner's equity of the business.

Does this withdrawal decrease the business entity's holdings? The answer is yes because the cash withdrawn is no longer available for business use after Lyon spends it on food, clothing, home mortgage payments, and so on. The withdrawal does not represent a business expense, however, because the cash is used for personal affairs unrelated to the business. We record the decrease in owner's equity in an account called Withdrawals. Another acceptable title is Drawing.

Evaluating Business Transactions

Exhibit 1-5 summarizes the eleven preceding transactions. Panel A of the exhibit lists the details of the transactions, and Panel B presents the analyses. As you study the exhibit, note that every transaction maintains the equality:

$$\text{ASSETS} = \text{LIABILITIES} + \text{OWNER'S EQUITY}$$

Financial Statements

The analysis of the transactions complete, what is the next step in the accounting process? How does an accountant present the results of the analysis? We now look at the financial statements, which are the formal reports of financial information about the entity. The primary financial statements are the (1) balance sheet, (2) income statement, (3) statement of owner's equity, and (4) statement of changes in financial position. In this chapter, we discuss and illustrate the first three statements. We cover the statement of changes in financial position in Chapter 18.

The **balance sheet** lists all the *assets, liabilities,* and *owner's equity* of an *entity* as of a specific date, usually the end of a month or a year. The balance sheet is like a snapshot of the entity. For this reason, it is also called the **statement of financial position**.

The **income statement** presents a summary of the revenues and expenses of an entity for a specific period, such as a month or a year. The income statement, also called the **statement of earnings** or **statement of operations**, is like a moving picture of the entity's operations during the period. The income statement holds perhaps the most important single piece of information about a business — its net income, which is revenues minus expenses. If expenses exceed revenues, the result is a net loss for the period.

The **statement of owner's equity** presents a summary of the changes that occurred in the owner's equity of the entity during a specific period, such as a month or a year. Exhibit 1-4 shows how owner's equity may be changed in any of four

OBJECTIVE 6

Prepare three financial statements

EXHIBIT 1-5 *Analysis of Transactions of Gary Lyon*

Panel A: Details of Transactions

1. Lyon invested $50,000 cash in the business.
2. Paid $40,000 cash for land.
3. Purchased $500 office supplies on account payable.
4. Received $5,500 cash from clients being revenue for legal services performed.
5. Performed legal service for a client on account, $3,000.
6. Paid cash expenses: rent, $1,100; employee salary, $1,200; utilities, $400.
7. Paid $400 on the account payable created in Transaction 3.
8. Remodeled his personal residence. This is not a business transaction.
9. Received $1,000 on the account receivable created in Transaction 5.
10. Sold land for cash equal to its cost of $22,000.
11. Withdrew $2,100 cash for personal living expenses.

Panel B: Analysis of Transactions

							Assets			=	Liabilities	+	Owner's Equity	Type of Owner's Equity Transaction
	Cash	+	Accounts Receivable	+	Office Supplies	+	Land				Accounts Payable	+	Gary Lyon, Capital	
(1)	+50,000												+50,000	Owner investment
Bal.	50,000												50,000	
(2)	−40,000						+40,000							
Bal.	10,000						40,000						50,000	
(3)					+500						+ 500			
Bal.	10,000				500		40,000				500		50,000	
(4)	+ 5,500												+ 5,500	Service revenue
Bal.	15,500				500		40,000				500		55,500	
(5)			+3,000										+ 3,000	Service revenue
Bal.	15,500		3,000		500		40,000				500		58,500	
(6)	− 2,700												− 1,100	Rent expense
													− 1,200	Salary expense
													− 400	Utilities expense
Bal.	12,800		3,000		500		40,000				500		55,800	
(7)	− 400										− 400			
Bal.	12,400		3,000		500		40,000				100		55,800	
(8)	Not a business transaction													
(9)	+ 1,000		−1,000											
Bal.	13,400		2,000		500		40,000				100		55,800	
(10)	+22,000						−22,000							
Bal.	35,400		2,000		500		18,000				100		55,800	
(11)	− 2,100												− 2,100	Owner withdrawal
Bal.	33,300		2,000		500		18,000				100		53,700	

53,800 = 53,800

ways. Increases in owner's equity arise from investments by the owner and net income earned during the period. Decreases result from withdrawals by the owner and from a net loss for the period. Net income or net loss comes directly from the income statement. Investments and withdrawals by the owner are capital transactions between the business and its owner, so they do not affect the income statement.

Each financial statement has a heading, which gives the name of the business — in our discussion, Gary Lyon, Lawyer — the name of the particular statement, and the date or period covered by the statement. A balance sheet taken at the end of year 19X4 would be dated December 31, 19X4. A balance sheet prepared at the end of March 19X7 is dated March 31, 19X7.

An income statement or a statement of owner's equity covering an annual period ending in December 19X5 is dated "for the year ended December 31, 19X5." A monthly income statement or statement of owner's equity for September 19X9 has in its heading "for the month ended September 30, 19X9" or simply "for the month of September 19X9." Income is meaningless unless identified with a particular time period.

Exhibit 1-6 illustrates all three statements. Their data come from the transaction analysis in Exhibit 1-5. We are assuming the transactions occurred during the month of April 19X1. Study the exhibit carefully, because it shows the relationships among the three financial statements.

EXHIBIT 1-6 *Financial Statements of Gary Lyon, Lawyer*

Gary Lyon, Lawyer
Income Statement
for the month ended April 30, 19X1

Revenues		
Service revenue		$8,500
Expenses		
Salary expense	$ 1,200	
Rent expense	1,100	
Utilities expense	400	
Total expenses		2,700
Net income		$5,800

Gary Lyon, Lawyer
Statement of Owner's Equity
for the month ended April 30, 19X1

Gary Lyon, capital, April 1, 19X1	$ 0
Add: Investment by owner	50,000
Net income for the month	5,800
	55,800
Less: Withdrawals by owner	2,100
Gary Lyon, capital, April 30, 19X1	$53,700

Gary Lyon, Lawyer
Balance Sheet
April 30, 19X1

Assets		Liabilities	
Cash	$33,300	Accounts payable	$ 100
Accounts receivable	2,000		
Office supplies	500	**Owner's Equity**	
Land	18,000	Gary Lyon, capital	53,700
		Total liabilities and	
Total assets	$53,800	owner's equity	$53,800

Observe the following in Exhibit 1-6:

1. The *income statement* for the month ended April 30, 19X1
   a. Reports all *revenues* and all *expenses* during the period. Revenues and expenses are reported only on the income statement.
   b. Reports *net income* of the period if total revenues exceed total expenses, as in the case of Gary Lyon's law practice for April. If total expenses exceed total revenues, the result is a net loss.

2. The *statement of owner's equity* for the month ended April 30, 19X1
   a. Opens with owner's capital balance at the beginning of the period.
   b. Adds *investments by the owner* of the business and also adds *net income* (or subtracts *net loss*, as the case may be). Net income (or net loss) comes directly from the income statement, which includes the effect of all the revenues and all the expenses for the period (see the first arrow in the exhibit).
   c. Subtracts *withdrawals by the owner*.
   d. Ends with owner's capital balance at the end of the period.

3. The *balance sheet* at April 30, 19X1, the end of the period
   a. Reports all *assets*, all *liabilities*, and *owner's equity* of the business at the end of the period. No other statement reports assets and liabilities.
   b. Reports that total assets equal the sum of total liabilities plus total owner's equity. This balancing feature gives the balance sheet its name. It is based on the accounting equation.
   d. Reports the owner's ending capital balance, taken directly from the statement of owner's equity (see the second arrow).

Summary Problem for Your Review

Jill Smith opens an apartment-locator business in Regina. She is the sole owner of the proprietorship, which she names Fast Apartment Locators. During the first month of operations, May 19X1, Smith engages in the following transactions:

a. Smith invests $35,000 of personal funds to start the business.

b. She purchases on account office supplies costing $350.

c. Smith pays cash of $30,000 to acquire a lot. She intends to use the land as a future building site for her business office.

d. Smith locates apartments for clients and receives cash of $1,900.

e. She pays $100 on the account payable she created in transaction b.

f. She pays $2,000 of personal funds for a vacation for her family.

g. She pays cash expenses for office rent, $400, and utilities, $100.

h. The business sells office supplies to another business for its cost of $150.

i. Smith withdraws cash of $1,200 for personal use.

2. Prepare the income statement, statement of owner's equity and balance sheet of the business after recording the transactions. Use Exhibit 1-6 as a guide.

Required

1. Analyze the preceding transactions in terms of their effects on the accounting equation of Fast Apartment Locators. Use Exhibit 1-5 as a guide but show balances only after the last transaction.

SOLUTION TO REVIEW PROBLEM

1.   **Panel A: Details of Transactions**

a. Smith invested $35,000 cash to start the business.

b. Purchased $350 in office supplies on account.

c. Paid $30,000 to acquire land as a future building site.

d. Earned service revenue and received cash of $1,900.

e. Paid $100 on account.

f. Paid for a personal vacation, which is not a business transaction.

g. Paid cash expenses for rent, $400, and utilities, $100.

h. Sold office supplies for cost of $150.

i. Withdrew $1,200 cash for personal use.

Panel B: Analysis of Transactions

		Assets				Liabilities +	Owner's Equity	Type of Owner's Equity Transaction
	Cash	+	Office Supplies +	Land		Accounts Payable +	Jill Smith, Capital	
(a)	+35,000						+35,000	Owner investment
(b)			+350			+350		
(c)	−30,000			+30,000				
(d)	+ 1,900						+ 1,900	Service revenue
(e)	− 100				=	−100		
(f)	Not a business transaction							
(g)	− 500						− 400	Rent expense
							− 100	Utilities expense
(h)	+ 150		−150					
(i)	− 1,200						− 1,200	Owner withdrawal
Bal.	5,250		200	30,000		250	35,200	

35,450   35,450

2. *Financial Statements of Fast Apartment Locators*

Fast Apartment Locators
Income Statement
for the month ended May 31, 19X1

Revenues		
Service revenue		$1,900
Expenses		
Rent expense	$400	
Utilities expense	100	
Total expenses		500
Net Income		$1,400

Fast Apartment Locators
Statement of Owner's Equity
for the month ended May 31, 19X1

Jill Smith, capital, May 1, 19X1	$ 0
Add: Investment by owner	35,000
Net income for the month	1,400
	36,400
Less: Withdrawals by owner	1,200
Jill Smith, capital, May 31, 19X1	$35,200

(1)

Fast Apartment Locators
Balance Sheet
May 31, 19X1

(2)

Assets		**Liabilities**	
Cash	$ 5,250	Accounts payable	$ 250
Office Supplies	200		
Land	30,000	**Owner's Equity**	
		Jill Smith, capital	35,200
		Total liabilities and	
Total assets	$35,450	owner's equity	$35,450

Summary

Accounting is a system for measuring, processing and communicating financial information. As the "language of business," accounting helps a wide range of decision-makers.

Accounting dates back to ancient civilizations, but its importance to society has been greatest since the Industrial Revolution. Today, accountants serve as CAs, CGAs or CMAs in all types of organizations. They offer many specialized services for industrial companies, including general accounting, cost accounting, budgeting, system design and internal auditing. Accountants in public practice deal with auditing, tax planning and preparation, management consulting and accounting services.

The three basic forms of business organizations are the *proprietorship*, the *partnership*, and the *corporation*. Whatever the form, accountants use the entity concept to keep the business's records separate from the personal records of the people who run it. Accountants at all levels must be ethical to serve their intended purpose.

Generally accepted accounting principles (GAAP) guide accountants in their work. Among these guidelines are the *entity concept*, the *reliability principle*, the *cost principle*, the *going-concern concept*, and the *stable-monetary-unit concept*.

In its most common form, the accounting equation is

$$\text{ASSETS} = \text{LIABILITIES} + \text{OWNER'S EQUITY}$$

Transactions affect a business's assets, liabilities and owner's equity. Therefore, transactions are analyzed in terms of their effect on the accounting equation.

The *financial statements* communicate information for decision-making by the entity's managers, owners, employees and creditors and by government agencies. The *income statement* presents a moving picture of the entity's operations in terms of revenues earned and expenses incurred during a specific period. Total revenues minus total expenses equal *net income*. Net income or net loss answers the question: How much income did the entity earn, or how much loss did it incur during the period? The *statement of owner's equity* reports the changes in owner's equity during the period. The *balance sheet* provides a photograph of the entity's financial standing in terms of its assets, liabilities, and owner's equity at a specific time. It answers the question: What is the entity's financial position?

Self-Study Questions

Test your understanding of the chapter by marking the correct answer for each of the following questions:

1. Accounting information is used by *(pp. 2–4)*
   a. Businesses
   b. Governments and government agencies
   c. Household members
   d. All of the above

2. The organization that formulates generally accepted accounting principles is *(p. 6)*
   a. Ontario Securities Commission
   b. Public Accountants Council of Canada
   c. Canadian Institute of Chartered Accountants (CICA)
   d. Revenue Canada

3. Which of the following forms of business organization is an "artificial person" and must obtain legal approval from the federal government or a province to conduct business? *(p. 11)*
   a. Law firm   c. Partnership
   b. Proprietorship   d. Corporation

4. The economic resources of a business are called *(p. 14)*
   a. Assets   c. Owner's equity
   b. Liabilities   d. Receivables

5. A business has assets of $140,000 and liabilities of $60,000. How much is its owner's equity? *(p. 14)*
   a. $0   c. $140,000
   b. $80,000   d. $200,000

6. The purchase of office supplies (or any other asset) on account will *(p. 16)*
   a. Increase an asset and increase a liability
   b. Increase an asset and increase owner's equity
   c. Increase one asset and decrease another asset
   d. Increase an asset and decrease a liability

7. The performance of service for a customer or client and immediate receipt of cash will *(p. 16)*
   a. Increase one asset and decrease another asset
   b. Increase an asset and increase owner's equity
   c. Decrease an asset and decrease a liability
   d. Increase an asset and increase a liability

8. The payment of an account payable (or any other liability) will *(p. 17)*
   a. Increase one asset and decrease another asset
   b. Decrease an asset and decrease owner's equity
   c. Decrease an asset and decrease a liability
   d. Increase an asset and increase a liability

9. The report of assets, liabilities, and owner's equity is called the *(p. 19)*
   a. Financial statement   c. Income statement
   b. Balance sheet   d. Statement of owner's equity

10. The financial statements that are dated for a time period (rather than a specific time) are the *(p. 19)*
    a. Balance sheet and income statement
    b. Balance sheet and statement of owner's equity
    c. Income statement and statement of owner's equity
    d. All financial statements are dated for a time period.

Answers to the Self-Study Questions are at the end of the chapter.

Accounting Vocabulary

Accounting, like many other subjects, has a special vocabulary. It is important that you understand the following terms. They are explained in the chapter and also in the glossary at the end of the book.

accounting *(p. 2)*
account payable *(p. 14)*
account receivable *(p. 14)*
assets *(p. 14)*
auditing *(p. 9)*
balance sheet *(p. 19)*
budgeting *(p. 9)*
capital *(p. 14)*
Certified General Accountant (CGA) *(p. 5)*
Certified Management Accountant (CMA) *(p. 5)*
Chartered Accountant (CA) *(p. 5)*
corporation *(p. 11)*
cost accounting *(p. 9)*
entity *(p. 11)*

expenses *(p. 16)*
financial accounting *(p. 9)*
financial statements *(p. 2)*
generally accepted accounting principles (GAAP) *(p. 6)*
income statement *(p. 19)*
information systems design *(p. 9)*
internal auditing *(p. 9)*
liabilities *(p. 14)*
management accounting *(p. 10)*
net earnings *(p. 17)*
net income *(p. 17)*
net loss *(p. 17)*
net profit *(p. 17)*
note payable *(p. 14)*

note receivable *(p. 14)*
owner's equity *(p. 14)*
partnership *(p. 10)*
private accountant *(p. 5)*
proprietorship *(p. 10)*
public accountant *(p. 5)*
revenues *(p. 16)*
shareholders *(p. 11)*
statement of earnings *(p. 19)*
statement of financial position *(p. 19)*
statement of operations *(p. 19)*
statement of owner's equity *(p. 19)*
transaction *(p. 14)*

ASSIGNMENT MATERIAL _____

Questions

1. Distinguish between accounting and bookkeeping.
2. Identify five users of accounting information and explain how they use it.
3. Where did accounting have its beginning? Who wrote the first known description of bookkeeping? In what year?

4. Name two important reasons for the development of accounting thought.

5. Name three professional titles of accountants. Also give their abbreviations.

6. What organization formulates generally accepted accounting principles? Is this organization a government agency?

7. Name the four principal types of services provided by public accounting firms.

8. How do financial accounting and management accounting differ?

9. Give the name(s) of the owner(s) of a proprietorship, a partnership, and a corporation.

10. Why do ethical standards exist in accounting? Which organizations direct their standards more toward independent auditors? Which organizations direct their standards more toward management accountants?

11. Why is the entity concept so important to accounting?

12. Give four examples of accounting entities.

13. Briefly describe the reliability principle.

14. What role does the cost principle play in accounting?

15. If assets = liabilities + owner's equity, then how can liabilities be expressed?

16. Explain the difference between an account receivable and an account payable.

17. What role do transactions play in accounting?

18. What is a more descriptive title for the balance sheet?

19. What feature of the balance sheet gives this financial statement its name?

20. What is another title of the income statement?

21. Which financial statement is like a snapshot of the entity at a specific time? Which financial statement is like a moving picture of the entity's operation during a period of time?

22. What information does the statement of owner's equity report?

23. Give two synonyms for the owner's equity of a proprietorship.

24. What piece of information flows from the income statement to the statement of owner's equity? What information flows from the statement of owner's equity to the balance sheet?

Exercises

Exercise 1-1   *Explaining the income statement and the balance sheet*   **(L.O. 1,2)**

Felix and Charlotte Jiminez want to open a Mexican restaurant in Alberta. In need of cash, they ask the Bank of Montreal for a loan. The bank's procedures require borrowers to submit financial statements to show likely results of operations for the first year and likely financial position at the end of the first year. With little knowledge of accounting, Felix and Charlotte don't know how to proceed. Explain to them the information provided by the statement of operations (the income statement) and the statement of financial position (the balance sheet). Indicate why a lender would require this information.

Exercise 1-2   *Business transactions*   **(L.O. 3)**

For each of the following items, give an example of a business transaction that has the described effect on the accounting equation:

a. Increase one asset and decrease another asset.

b. Decrease an asset and decrease owner's equity.

c. Decrease an asset and decrease a liability.

d. Increase an asset and increase owner's equity.

e. Increase an asset and increase a liability.

Exercise 1-3   *Transaction analysis*   **(L.O. 3)**

Kreitze Contractors, a proprietorship, or Darren Kreitze, the owner, experienced the following events. State whether each event (1) increased, (2) decreased, or (3) had no effect on the total assets of the business. Identify any specific asset affected.

a. Borrowed money from the bank.

b. Cash purchase of land for a future building site.

c. Kreitze increased his cash investment in the business.

d. Paid cash on accounts payable.

e. Purchased machinery and equipment for a manufacturing plant; signed a promissory note in payment.

f. Performed service for a customer on account.

g. Kreitze withdrew cash from the business for personal use.

h. Received cash from a customer on account receivable.

i. Kreitze used personal funds to purchase a swimming pool for his home.

j. Sold land for a price equal to the cost of the land; received cash.

Exercise 1-4   *Accounting equation*   **(L.O. 4)**

Compute the missing amount in the accounting equation of each of the following three entities:

	Assets	Liabilities	Owner's Equity
Entity A	$?	$41,800	$34,400
Entity B	65,900	?	34,000
Entity C	61,700	29,800	?

Exercise 1-5   *Accounting equation* **(L.O. 3,4)**

Oriole Travel Agency balance sheet data, at May 31, 19X2 and June 30, 19X2, were as follows:

	May 31, 19X2	June 30, 19X2
Total assets	$150,000	$195,000
Total liabilities	109,000	131,000

Required

Below are three assumptions about investments and withdrawals by the owner of the business during June. For each assumption, compute the amount of net income or net loss of the business during June 19X2.

a. The owner invested $30,000 in the business and made no withdrawals.

b. The owner made no additional investments in the business but withdrew $6,000 for personal use.

c. The owner invested $8,000 in the business and withdrew $6,000 for personal use.

Exercise 1-6   *Transaction analysis* **(L.O. 5)**

Indicate the effects of the following business transactions on the accounting equation. Transaction *a* is answered as a guide.

a. Invested cash of $1,800 in the business.
   Answer: Increase asset (Cash)
              Increase owner's equity (Capital)

b. Performed legal service for a client on account, $650.

c. Purchased on account office furniture at a cost of $500.

d. Received cash on account, $400.

e. Paid cash on account, $250.

f. Sold land for $12,000, which was our cost of the land.

g. Paid $90 cash to purchase office supplies.

h. Performed legal service for a client and received cash of $2,000.

i. Paid monthly office rent of $700.

Exercise 1-7 *Transaction analysis, accounting equation* **(L.O. 3,5)**

Allison LaChappelle opens a veterinary medicine practice to specialize in small animals. During her first month of operation, January, her practice, entitled Allison LaChappelle, D.V.M., experienced the following events:

Jan.   6   LaChappelle invested $120,000 in the business by opening a bank account in the name of Allison LaChappelle, D.V.M.

         9   LaChappelle paid cash for land costing $90,000. She plans to build an office building on the land.

        12   She purchased medical supplies for $2,000 on account.

        15   On January 15, LaChappelle officially opened for business.

     15–31   During the rest of the month she treated patients and earned service revenue of $6,000, receiving cash from their owners.

     15–31   She paid cash expenses: employee salaries, $1,400; office rent, $1,000; utilities, $300.

        28   She sold supplies to another physician for cost of $500.

        31   She paid $1,500 on account.

Required

Analyze the effects of these events on the accounting equation of the medical practice of Allison LaChappelle, D.V.M. Use a format similar to that of Exhibit 1-5 in the chapter with headings for Cash; Medical Supplies; Land; Accounts Payable; and Allison LaChappelle, Capital.

Exercise 1-8 *Business organization, transactions, and net income* **(L.O. 3,4,5)**

The analysis of the transactions that Allied Leasing engaged in during its first month of operations follows. The company buys equipment that it leases out to earn revenue. The owners of the business made only one investment to start the business and no withdrawals.

	Cash +	Accounts Receivable +	Lease Equipment =	Accounts Payable +	Partners' Capital
a.	+46,000				+46,000
b.			+80,000	+80,000	
c.	+ 1,600				+ 1,600
d.		+500			+ 500
e.	−10,000			−10,000	
f.		+850			+ 850
g.	+ 150	−150			
h.	− 2,000				− 2,000

Required

1. What type of business organization is Allied Leasing? How can you tell?
2. Describe each transaction.
3. If these transactions fully describe the operations of Allied Leasing during the month, what was the amount of net income or net loss?

Exercise 1-9   *Business organization, balance sheet* **(L.O. 3,6)**

Presented below are the balances of the assets and liabilities of Long-Gone Delivery Service as of September 30, 19X2. Also included are the revenue and expense figures of the business for September.

Delivery service revenue........	$4,100	Delivery equipment.........	$15,500
Accounts receivable	900	Supplies	600
Accounts payable	750	Note payable.....................	8,000
D. Joliffe, capital	?	Rent expense	500
Salary expense	2,000	Cash....................................	650

Required

1. What type of business organization is Long-Gone Delivery Service? How can you tell?
2. Prepare the balance sheet of Long-Gone Delivery Service as of September 30, 19X2. Not all amounts are used.

Exercise 1-10   *Income statement* **(L.O. 3,6)**

Presented below are the balances of the assets, liabilities, owner's equity, revenues and expenses of Technical Consultants at December 31, 19X3, the end of its first year of business. During the year, K. Toshi, the owner, invested $15,000 in the business.

Note payable	$ 30,000	Office furniture	$ 40,000
Utilities expense....................	5,800	Rent expense........................	21,000
Accounts payable..................	3,300	Cash	3,600
K. Toshi, capital.....................	27,100	Office supplies.....................	4,800
Service revenue	131,000	Salary expense.....................	39,000
Accounts receivable..............	8,000	Salaries payable	2,000
Supplies expense...................	10,000	Property tax expense...........	1,200

Required

1. Prepare the income statement of Technical Consultants for the year ended December 31, 19X3. Not all amounts are used.
2. What was the amount of the proprietor's withdrawals during the year?

Problems   (Group A)

Problem 1-1A   *Analyzing a loan request* **(L.O. 1, 3)**

As an analyst for the Bank of Nova Scotia, it is your job to write recommendations to the bank's loan committee. Sigma Enterprises has submitted these summary data to support the company's request for a $300,000 loan:

Income Statement Data	19X5	19X4	19X3
Total revenues............................	$790,000	$730,000	$720,000
Total expenses............................	640,000	570,000	540,000
Net income	$150,000	$160,000	$180,000

Statement of Owner's Equity Data	19X5	19X4	19X3
Beginning capital........................	$280,000	$300,000	$290,000
Add: Net income	150,000	160,000	180,000
	430,000	460,000	470,000
Less: Withdrawals	190,000	180,000	170,000
Ending capital............................	$240,000	$280,000	$300,000

Balance Sheet Data	19X5	19X4	19X3
Total assets.................................	$630,000	$600,000	$560,000
Total liabilities............................	$390,000	$320,000	$260,000
Total owner's equity	240,000	280,000	300,000
Total liabilities and			
owner's equity	$630,000	$600,000	$560,000

Required

Should the bank lend $300,000 to Sigma Enterprises? Write a one-paragraph recommendation to the loan committee.

Problem 1-2A   *Entity concept, transaction analysis, accounting equation* **(L.O. 3,5)**

Kathy Wood practised law with a large firm, a partnership, for ten years after graduating from law school. Recently she resigned her position to open her own law office, which she operates as a proprietorship. The name of the new entity is Kathy Wood, Barrister & Solicitor.

Wood recorded the following events during the organizing phase of her new business and its first month of operations. Some of the events were personal and did not affect the law practice. Others were business transactions and should be accounted for by the business.

July 1 Wood sold 5,000 shares of Dofasco stock, which she had owned for several years, receiving $88,000 cash from her stockbroker.

2 Wood deposited the $88,000 cash from sale of the Dofasco stock in her personal bank account.

3 Wood received $135,000 cash from her former partners in the law firm from which she resigned.

5 Wood deposited $130,000 cash in a new business bank account entitled Kathy Wood, Barrister & Solicitor.

6 A representative of a large company telephoned Wood and told her of the company's intention to transfer its legal business to the new entity of Kathy Wood, Barrister & Solicitor.

7 Wood paid $550 cash for letterhead stationery for her new law office.

9 Wood purchased office furniture for the law office, agreeing to pay the account payable, $11,500, within three months.

23 Wood finished court hearings on behalf of a client and submitted her bill for legal services, $2,100. She expected to collect from this client within one month.

30 Wood paid office rent expense, $1,900.

31 Wood withdrew $3,500 cash from the business for personal living expenses.

Required

1. Classify each of the preceding events as one of the following:
   a. Business transaction to be accounted for by the proprietorship of Kathy Wood, Barrister & Solicitor.
   b. Business-related event but not a transaction to be accounted for by the proprietorship of Kathy Wood, Barrister & Solicitor.
   c. Personal transaction not to be accounted for by the proprietorship of Kathy Wood, Barrister & Solicitor.

2. Analyze the effects of the above events on the accounting equation of the proprietorship of Kathy Wood, Barrister & Solicitor. Use a format similar to Exhibit 1-5.

Problem 1-3A *Balance sheet* *(L.O. 3,6)*

The bookkeeper of Glass Travel Agency prepared the balance sheet of the company while the accountant was ill. The balance sheet contains numerous errors. In particular, the bookkeeper knew that the balance sheet should balance, so she plugged in the owner's equity amount needed to achieve this balance. However, the owner's equity amount is not correct. All other amounts are accurate.

<table>
<tr><td colspan="4" align="center">Glass Travel Agency
Balance Sheet
for the month ended October 31, 19X7</td></tr>
<tr><td>Assets</td><td></td><td>Liabilities</td><td></td></tr>
<tr><td>Cash</td><td>$ 1,400</td><td>Notes receivable</td><td>$ 11,000</td></tr>
<tr><td>Advertising expense</td><td>300</td><td>Interest expense</td><td>2,000</td></tr>
<tr><td>Land</td><td>30,500</td><td>Office supplies</td><td>800</td></tr>
<tr><td>Salary expense</td><td>3,300</td><td>Accounts receivable</td><td>1,600</td></tr>
<tr><td>Office furniture</td><td>4,700</td><td>Note payable</td><td>20,000</td></tr>
<tr><td>Accounts payable</td><td>3,000</td><td></td><td></td></tr>
<tr><td>Utilities expense</td><td>1,100</td><td>Owner's Equity</td><td></td></tr>
<tr><td></td><td></td><td>Owner's equity</td><td>8,900</td></tr>
<tr><td>Total assets</td><td>$44,300</td><td>Total liabilities</td><td>$44,300</td></tr>
</table>

Required

1. Prepare the correct balance sheet as of October 31, 19X7. Compute total assets and total liabilities. Then take the difference to determine correct owner's equity.

2. Identify the accounts listed above that should not be presented on the balance sheet and state why you excluded them from the correct balance sheet you prepared for requirement 1.

Problem 1-4A *Balance sheet, entity concept* *(L.O. 3,4,6)*

Matt Thomas is a realtor. He buys and sells properties on his own, and he also earns commission as a real estate agent for buyers and sellers. He organized his business as a proprietorship on March 10, 19X2. Consider the following facts as of March 31, 19X2:

a. Thomas had $5,000 in his personal bank account and $9,000 in his business bank account.

b. Office supplies on hand at the real estate office totaled $1,000.

c. Thomas's business had spent $15,000 for an Electronic Realty Associates (ERA) franchise, which entitled him to represent himself as an ERA agent. ERA is a national affiliation of independent real estate agents. This franchise is a business asset.

d. Thomas owed $48,000 on a note payable for some undeveloped land that had been acquired by his business for a total price of $90,000.

e. Thomas owed $65,000 on a personal mortgage on his personal residence, which he acquired in 19X1 for a total price of $90,000.

f. Thomas owed $950 on a personal charge account with Sears Canada Inc.

g. He had acquired business furniture for $12,000 on March 26. Of this amount, Thomas's business owed $6,000 on open account at March 31.

Required

1. Prepare the balance sheet of the real estate business of Matt Thomas, Realtor at March 31, 19X2.

2. Identify the personal items given in the preceding facts that would not be reported on the balance sheet of the business.

Problem 1-5A *Transaction analysis for an actual company* **(L.O. 4,5)**

A recent balance sheet of Copy Canada Inc., the manufacturer of copiers and other office equipment, is summarized as follows.

Copy Canada Inc.
Balance Sheet
December 31, 19XX

Assets		Liabilities	
Cash	$ 266,600	Notes payable	$ 1,985,500
Accounts receivable	1,466,900	Accounts payable	390,300
Merchandise inventories	1,469,800	Other liabilities	2,107,600
Land, buildings, and		Total liabilities	4,483,400
equipment	2,659,700		
Other assets	3,953,700	**Owners' Equity**	
		Owners' Equity	5,333,300
		Total liabilities and	
Total assets	$9,816,700	owners' equity	$9,816,700

Suppose the company had the following transactions and events during January:

a. Received cash investment from owners, $160.

b. Purchased inventories on account, $400.

c. Paid cash on account (to reduce accounts payable), $136.

d. Sold inventory to another company on account, $670. The equipment had cost $670.

e. Learned that a CBC Television news program would show members of the House of Commons using Copy's copiers as part of a Commons investigation. The value of this advertisement to the company is estimated to be $1,000.

f. Borrowed cash, signing a note payable, $550.

g. Purchased equipment for cash, $380.

h. Collected cash on account from customers, $289.

i. Received special equipment from an owner as an investment in the company. The value of equipment was $119.

Required

1. Showing all amounts, analyze the January 19X5 transactions of Copy Canada. Use a format similar to Exhibit 1-5.
2. Prove that assets = liabilities + owner equity after analyzing the transactions.

Problem 1-6A *Business transactions and analysis* **(L.O. 5)**

Amalfi Ltd. was recently formed. The balance of each item in the company's accounting equation is shown below for February 8 and for each of nine following business days.

	Cash	Accounts Receivable	Supplies	Land	Accounts Payable	Owner's Equity
Feb. 8	$3,000	$7,000	$ 800	$11,000	$3,800	$18,000
12	2,000	7,000	800	11,000	2,800	18,000
14	6,000	3,000	800	11,000	2,800	18,000
17	6,000	3,000	1,100	11,000	3,100	18,000
19	3,000	3,000	1,100	11,000	3,100	15,000
20	1,900	3,000	1,100	11,000	2,000	15,000
22	7,900	3,000	1,100	5,000	2,000	15,000
25	7,900	3,200	900	5,000	2,000	15,000
26	7,700	3,200	1,100	5,000	2,000	15,000
28	2,600	3,200	1,100	10,100	2,000	15,000

Required

Assuming a single transaction took place on each day, describe briefly the transaction that was most likely to have occurred, beginning with February 12. Indicate which accounts were affected and by what amount. No revenue or expense transactions occurred on these dates.

Problem 1-7A *Income statement, statement of owner's equity, balance sheet* **(L.O. 6)**

Presented below are the amounts of (a) the assets and liabilities of Coleman Delivery Service as of December 31, and (b) the revenues and expenses of the company for the year ended on that date. The items are listed in alphabetical order.

Accounts payable	$ 14,000	Note payable	$ 31,000
Accounts receivable	6,000	Property tax expense	2,000
Building	13,000	Rent expense	14,000
Cash	4,000	Salary expense	38,000
Equipment	21,000	Service revenue	100,000
Interest expense	4,000	Supplies	13,000
Interest payable	1,000	Utilities expense	3,000
Land	8,000		

The beginning amount of Jane Coleman, Capital, was $12,000. During the year Coleman withdrew $32,000 for personal use.

Required

1. Prepare the income statement of Coleman Delivery Service for the year ended December 31 of the current year.

2. Prepare the statement of owner's equity of the company for the year ended December 31.
3. Prepare the balance sheet of the company at December 31.

– Problem 1-8A *Transaction analysis, accounting equation, financial statements* **(L.O. 5,6)**

Kathy Starr owns and operates an interior design studio called Starr Designers. The following amounts summarize the financial position of her business on April 30, 19X5:

	Assets				=	Liabilities	+	Owner's Equity
	Cash +	Accounts Receivable +	Supplies +	Land	=	Accounts Payable +		Kathy Starr, Capital
Bal.	720	2,240		23,100		4,400		21,660

During May 19X5, the following events occurred:

a. Starr received $12,000 as a gift and deposited the cash in the business bank account.
b. Paid off the beginning balance of accounts payable.
c. Performed services for a client and received cash of $1,100.
d. Collected cash from a customer on account, $750.
e. Purchased supplies on account, $120.
f. Consulted on the interior design of a major office building and billed the client for services rendered, $5,000.
g. Invested personal cash of $1,700 in the business.
h. Recorded the following business expenses for the month:
   1. Paid office rent — $1,200.
   2. Paid advertising — $860.
i. Sold supplies to another interior designer for $80 cash, which was the cost of the supplies.
j. Withdrew cash of $2,400 for personal use.

Required

1. Analyze the effects of the above transactions on the accounting equation of Starr Designers. Adapt the format of Exhibit 1-5. You need to add a column for Supplies.
2. Prepare the income statement of Starr Designers for the month ended May 31, 19X5. List expenses in decreasing order by amount.
3. Prepare the statement of owner's equity of Starr Designers for the month ended May 31, 19X5.
4. Prepare the balance sheet of Starr Designers at May 31.

(Group B)

Problem 1-1B *Analyzing a loan request* **(L.O. 1,3)**

As an analyst for The Royal Bank, it is your job to write recommendations to the bank's loan committee. Lomoni Ltd. has submitted these summary data to support its request for a $100,000 loan:

Income Statement Data	19X5	19X4	19X3
Total revenues	$850,000	$760,000	$720,000
Total expenses	640,000	570,000	540,000
Net income	$210,000	$190,000	$180,000

Statement of Owner's Equity Data	19X5	19X4	19X3
Beginning capital	$440,000	$390,000	$330,000
Add: Net income	210,000	190,000	180,000
	650,000	580,000	510,000
Less: Withdrawals	160,000	140,000	120,000
Ending Capital	$490,000	$440,000	$390,000

Balance Sheet Data	19X5	19X4	19X3
Total assets	$730,000	$660,000	$590,000
Total liabilities	$240,000	$220,000	$200,000
Total owner's equity	490,000	440,000	390,000
Total liabilities and owner's equity	$730,000	$660,000	$590,000

Required

Should the bank lend $100,000 to Lomoni Ltd.? Write a one-paragraph recommendation to the loan committee.

Problem 1-2B *Entity concept, transaction analysis, accounting equation* **(L.O. 3,5)**

Melvin Dexter practised law with a large firm, a partnership, for five years after graduating from law school. Recently he resigned his position to open his own law office, which he operates as a proprietorship. The name of the new entity is Melvin Dexter, Lawyer.

Dexter recorded the following events during the organizing phase of his new business and its first month of operations. Some of the events were personal and did not affect his law practice. Others were business transactions and should be accounted for by the business.

May   4   Dexter received $50,000 cash from his former partners in the law firm from which he resigned.

      5   Dexter deposited $50,000 cash in a new business bank account, entitled Melvin Dexter, Lawyer.

      6   Dexter paid $300 cash for letterhead stationery for his new law office.

      7   Dexter purchased office furniture for his law office. He agreed to pay the account payable, $6,000, within six months.

    10   Dexter sold 800 shares of IBM stock, which he and his wife had owned for several years, receiving $80,000 cash from his stockbroker.

    11   Dexter deposited the $80,000 cash from sale of the IBM stock in his personal bank account.

    12   A representative of a large company telephoned Dexter and told him of the company's intention to transfer its legal business to the new entity of Melvin Dexter, Lawyer.

    29   Dexter finished court hearings on behalf of a client and submitted his bill for legal services, $3,000. Dexter expected to collect from this client within two weeks.

May 30   Dexter paid office rent expense, $1,000.
     31   Dexter withdrew $2,000 cash from the business for personal living expenses.

Required

1. Classify each of the preceding events as one of the following:
   a. Business transaction to be accounted for by the proprietorship of Melvin Dexter, Lawyer.
   b. Business-related event but not a transaction to be accounted for by the proprietorship of Melvin Dexter, Lawyer.
   c. Personal transaction not to be accounted for by the proprietorship of Melvin Dexter, Lawyer.

2. Analyze the effects of the above events on the accounting equation of the proprietorship of Melvin Dexter, Lawyer. Use a format similar to Exhibit 1-5.

Problem 1-3B   *Balance sheet* **(L.O. 3,6)**

The bookkeeper of Getz Auction Co. prepared the balance sheet of the company while the accountant was ill. The balance sheet contains numerous errors. In particular, the bookkeeper knew that the balance sheet should balance, so he plugged in the owner's equity amount needed to achieve this balance. However, the owner's equity amount is not correct. All other amounts are accurate.

Getz Auction Co.
Balance Sheet
for the month ended July 31, 19X3

Assets		**Liabilities**	
Cash	$ 2,000	Accounts receivable	$ 3,000
Office supplies	1,000	Service revenue	35,000
Land	20,000	Property tax expense	800
Advertising expense	2,500	Accounts payable	8,000
Office furniture	10,000	**Owner's Equity**	
Note payable	16,000	Owner's equity	8,700
Rent expense	4,000	Total liabilities and owner's	
Total assets	$55,500	equity	$55,500

Required

1. Prepare the correct balance sheet as of July 31, 19X3. Compute total assets and total liabilities. Then take the difference to determine correct owner's equity.

2. Identify the accounts listed above that should not be presented on the balance sheet and state why you excluded them from the correct balance sheet you prepared for requirement 1.

Problem 1-4B   *Balance sheet, entity concept* **(L.O. 3,4,6)**

Sue Kerault is a realtor. She buys and sells properties on her own, and she also earns commission as a real estate agent for buyers and sellers. She organized her business as a proprietorship on November 24, 19X4. Consider the following facts as of November 30, 19X4:

a. Kerault owed $80,000 on a note payable for some undeveloped land that had been acquired by her business for a total price of $140,000.

b. Kerault's business had spent $15,000 for a Century 21 real estate franchise, which entitled her to represent herself as a Century 21 agent. Century 21 is a national affiliation of independent real estate agents. This franchise is a business asset.

c. Kerault owed $120,000 on a personal mortgage on her personal residence, which she acquired in 19X1 for a total price of $170,000.

d. Kerault had $10,000 in her personal bank account and $12,000 in her business bank account.

e. Kerault owed $1,800 on a personal charge account with Holt-Renfrew.

f. Kerault acquired business furniture for $17,000 on November 25. Of this amount, her business owed $6,000 on open account at November 30.

g. Office supplies on hand at the real estate office totaled at $1,000.

Required

1. Prepare the balance sheet of the real estate business of Sue Kerault, Realtor, at November 30, 19X4.

2. Identify the personal items given in the preceding facts that would not be reported on the balance sheet of the business.

Problem 1-5B *Transaction analysis for an actual company* **(L.O. 4,5)**

A recent balance sheet of Scott, Boyle & Company, one of Canada's larger sellers of jeans and casual pants, is summarized as follows.

Scott, Boyle & Company
Balance Sheet
November 25, 19XX

Assets		Liabilities	
Cash	$ 263,389	Notes payable	$ 83,361
Accounts receivable	339,798	Accounts payable	229,453
Merchandise inventories	387,660	Other liabilities	300,847
Property, plant, and		Total liabilities	613,661
equipment	330,455		
Other assets	99,800	**Owner's Equity**	
		Owner's Equity	807,441
		Total liabilities and	
Total assets	$1,421,102	owner's equity	$1,421,102

Suppose that the company had the following transactions and events (amounts in thousands) during December:

a. Received cash investments from owners, $18,000.

b. Received special equipment from an owner as an investment in the company. The value of the equipment was $40,000.

c. Borrowed cash, signing a note payable, $10,000.

d. Purchased equipment for cash, $12,500.

e. Purchased inventories on account, $9,000.

f. Paid cash on account (to reduce accounts payable), $54,000.

g. Sold equipment to another company on account, $14,000. The equipment had cost $14,000.

h. Discovered that the prime minister of Canada was going to wear Scott blue jeans while performing the ceremonial kick-off at the 19X1 Grey Cup.

i. Collected cash on account from customers, $84,000.

Required

1. Analyze the December transactions of Scott, Boyle & Company. Use a format similar to Exhibit 1-5.
2. Prove that assets = liabilities + owner's equity after analyzing the transactions.

Problem 1-6B   *Business transactions and analysis* **(L.O. 5)**

Cardinale Corp. was recently formed. The balance of each item in the company's accounting equation is shown below for May 10 and for each of nine following business days.

		Cash	Accounts Receivable	Supplies	Land	Accounts Payable	Owner's Equity
May	10	$ 8,000	$4,000	$1,000	$ 8,000	$4,000	$17,000
	11	11,000	4,000	1,000	8,000	4,000	20,000
	12	6,000	4,000	1,000	13,000	4,000	20,000
	15	6,000	4,000	3,000	13,000	6,000	20,000
	16	5,000	4,000	3,000	13,000	5,000	20,000
	17	7,000	2,000	3,000	13,000	5,000 .	20,000
	18	16,000	2,000	3,000	13,000	5,000	29,000
	19	13,000	2,000	3,000	13,000	2,000	29,000
	22	12,000	2,000	4,000	13,000	2,000	29,000
	23	8,000	2,000	4,000	13,000	2,000	25,000

Required

Assuming a single transaction took place on each day, describe briefly the transaction that was most likely to have occurred beginning with May 11. Indicate which accounts were affected and by what amount. No revenue or expense transactions occurred on these dates.

Problem 1-7B   *Income statement, statement of owner's equity, balance sheet* **(L.O. 6)**

Presented below are the amount of (a) the assets and liabilities of Petoski Theater as of December 31, and (b) the revenues and expenses of the company for the year ended on that date. The items are listed in alphabetical order.

Accounts payable	$ 19,000	Note payable	$ 85,000
Accounts receivable	12,000	Property tax expense	4,000
Advertising expense	11,000	Rent expense	23,000
Building	170,000	Salary expense	63,000
Cash	10,000	Salaries payable	1,000
Furniture	20,000	Service revenue	200,000
Interest expense	9,000	Supplies	3,000
Land	65,000		

The beginning amount of Jean Petoski, Capital, was $150,000. During the year Petoski withdrew $65,000 for personal use.

Required

1. Prepare the income statement of Petoski Theater for the year ended December 31 of the current year.
2. Prepare the statement of owner's equity of the company for the year ended December 31.
3. Prepare the balance sheet of the company at December 31.

Problem 1-8B *Transaction analysis, accounting equation, financial statements* **(L.O. 5,6)**

Lisa Reed owns and operates an interior design studio called Reed Interiors. The following amounts summarize the financial position of her business on August 31, 19X2:

			Assets			=	Liabilities	+	Owner's Equity
	Cash	+	Accounts Receivable	+ Supplies +	Land	=	Accounts Payable	+	Lisa Reed, Capital
Bal.	1,250		1,500		12,000		8,000		6,750

During September 19X2, the following events occurred:

a. Reed inherited $15,000 and deposited the cash in the business bank account.
b. Performed services for a client and received cash of $700.
c. Paid off the beginning balance of accounts payable.
d. Purchased supplies on account, $500.
e. Collected cash from a customer on account, $1,000.
f. Invested personal cash of $1,000 in the business.
g. Consulted on the interior design of a major office building and billed the client for services rendered, $2,400.
h. Recorded the following business expenses for the month:
   1. Paid office rent — $900.
   2. Paid advertising — $100.
i. Sold supplies to another business for $150 cash, which was the cost of the supplies.
j. Withdrew cash of $1,800 for personal use.

Required

1. Analyze the effects of the above transactions on the accounting equation of Reed Interiors. Adapt the format of Exhibit 1-5.
2. Prepare the income statement of Reed Interiors for the month ended September 30, 19X2. List expenses in decreasing order by amount.
3. Prepare the statement of owner's equity of Reed Interiors for the month ended September 30, 19X2.
4. Prepare the balance sheet of Reed Interiors at September 30, 19X2.

Extending Your Knowledge

Decision Problems

1. Using financial statements to evaluate a request for a loan (L.O. 1,3)

The proprietors of two businesses, Dillard's Hardware Store and Leslie Falco Home Decorators, have sought business loans from you. To decide whether to make the loans, you have requested their balance sheets.

Dillard's Hardware Store
Balance Sheet
August 31, 19X4

Assets		Liabilities	
Cash..	$ 1,000	Accounts payable.................	$ 12,000
Accounts receivable	14,000	Note payable	18,000
Merchandise inventory.........	85,000	Total liabilities.......................	30,000
Store supplies........................	500		
Furniture and fixtures...........	9,000	**Owner's Equity**	
Building	90,000	Jack Dillard, capital	183,500
Land	14,000	Total liabilities and	
Total assets............................	$213,500	owner's equity	$213,500

Leslie Falco Home Decorators
Balance Sheet
August 31, 19X4

Assets		Liabilities	
Cash	$11,000	Accounts payable..................	$ 3,000
Accounts receivable..............	4,000	Note payable	18,000
Office supplies.......................	1,000	Total liabilities	21,000
Office furniture	6,000		
Land..	19,000	**Owner's Equity**	
		Leslie Falco, capital................	20,000
		Total liabilities and	
Total assets.............................	$41,000	owner's equity...................	$41,000

Required

1. Based solely on these balance sheets, which entity would you be more comfortable loaning money to? Explain fully, citing specific items and amounts from the balance sheets.

2. In addition to the balance sheet data, what other financial statement information would you require? Be specific.

2. *Using accounting information (L.O. 1,3,4,5,6)*

A friend learns that you are taking an accounting course. Knowing that you do not plan a career in accounting, the friend asks why you are "wasting your time." Explain to the friend:

1. Why you are taking the course.
2. How accounting information is used or will be used:
   a. In your personal life.
   b. In the business life of your friend, who plans to be a farmer.
   c. In the business life of another friend, who plans a career in sales.

Ethical Issue

An ethical issue of current importance is the nature of the work that accounting firms perform. Accounting firms audit the financial statements of companies to express a professional opinion on the reliability of those statements. For this audit opinion to be objective and unbiased, it is critical that the auditors be entirely independent of their clients. However, accounting firms also perform management advisory (consulting) services for clients, which often include designing accounting systems. In many cases, the same accounting firm audits the financial statements of a company for which it has designed the accounting system.

Required

Discuss the ethical issue in this situation. Propose a solution.

Financial Statement Problems

1. *Identifying items from a company's financial statements (L.O. 4)*

This and similar problems in succeeding chapters focus on the financial statements of an actual company: Schneider Corporation. As you study each problem, you will gradually become confident that you can understand and use actual financial statements.

   Refer to the Schneider financial statements in Appendix C, and answer the following questions:

1. How much did Schneider's customers owe the company at October 26, 1991?
2. What were total assets at October 26, 1991? At October 27, 1990?
3. Write the company's accounting equation at October 26, 1991, by filling in the dollar amounts:

ASSETS = LIABILITIES + SHAREHOLDERS' EQUITY

4. Identify sales for the year ended October 26, 1991.
5. How much net income (net earnings) or net loss did Schneider experience for the year ended October 16, 1991? Was 1991 a good year or bad year compared to 1990?

2. *Identifying items from an actual company's financial statements (L.O. 4)*

Obtain the annual report of an actual company of your choosing. Annual reports are available in various forms including the original document in hard copy, microfiche, and computerized data bases.

Answer the following questions about the company. Concentrate on the current year in the annual report you select, except as directed for particular questions.

1. How much in cash (which may include cash equivalents) did the company have at the end of the current year? At the end of the preceding year? Did cash increase or decrease during the current year? By how much?

2. What were the total assets at the end of the current year? At the end of the preceding year?

3. Write the company's accounting equation at the end of the current year by filling in the dollar amounts:

Assets = Liabilities + Owner's equity

4. Identify net sales revenue for the current year. The company may label this as Net Sales, Sales, Revenue, or other title. How much was the corresponding revenue for the preceding year?

5. How much net income or net loss did the company experience for the current year? For the preceding year?

Answers to Self-Study Questions

1. d	3. d	5. b	7. b	9. b
2. c	4. a	6. a	8. c	10. c

Chapter 2

Recording Business Transactions

During December, 1991, Price Club's Mississauga, Ontario store averaged about 100 shoppers lining up at their check-outs during the evening hours. It was not unusual for this Price Club outlet to rake in close to $1 million a day during the Christmas selling season. Can you imagine the number of transactions this must translate to!

In your day-to-day affairs, you likely use some form of record-keeping system, perhaps a combination of keeping receipts and recording cheques and deposits in your cheque book. Or, you might rely extensively on memory — or a hope and a prayer — that there is money in your bank account. Clearly, Price Club cannot use such a system as it could not efficiently keep track of the volume of its daily transactions.

Since the 15th century, accountants have used the double-entry, debit-credit bookkeeping system to record business transactions. Amazingly, after 500 years, this system is still the fundamental basis of all accounting procedures. Arguably, without the ability to keep track of thousands or millions of transactions a day efficiently and accurately, business, the economy, and our way of life would not be possible. And it is all because *Debits equal Credits*.

As you read Chapter 2, consider the importance of keeping accurate business records, and how the double-entry, debit-credit system meets this need.

Source: Anne Bokma, "Raking in the Dough," *The Financial Post Magazine* (January 1992), pp. 32-35.

Chapter 1 illustrates how to account for business transactions by analyzing their effects on the accounting equation. That approach emphasizes accounting analysis, but it becomes unwieldy in day-to-day business if many transactions occur. In practice, accountants use a different approach to record accounting information. This chapter focuses on processing accounting information as it is actually done in the business.

The Account

The basic summary device of accounting is the **account**. This is the detailed record of the changes that have occurred in a particular asset, liability or owner's equity during a period of time. Each account appears on its own page. For convenient access to the information in the accounts, the pages are grouped together in a single book called the **ledger**. When you hear reference to "keeping the books" or "auditing the books," the word *books* refers to the ledger. The ledger may be a bound book, a loose-leaf set of pages or a computer record.

In the ledger, the accounts are grouped in three broad categories, based on the accounting equation:

ASSETS = LIABILITIES + OWNER'S EQUITY

Assets

Those economic resources that will benefit the business in the future are assets. The following asset accounts are common to many firms.

Cash   The Cash account shows the cash effects of a business's transactions. Cash means money and any medium of exchange that a bank accepts at face value. Cash includes currency, coins, money orders, certificates of deposit and cheques. The Cash account covers these items whether they are kept on hand, in a safe, in a cash register or in a bank.

Accounts Receivable   A business may sell its goods or services in exchange for an oral or implied promise of future cash receipt. Such sales are made on credit (on account). The Accounts Receivable account includes these amounts.

Notes Receivable   A business may sell its goods or services in exchange for a promissory note, which is a written pledge that the customer will pay the business a fixed amount of money by a certain date. The Notes Receivable account is a record of the promissory notes that the business expects to collect in cash.

Prepaid Expenses   A business often pays certain expenses in advance. A prepaid expense is an asset because the business avoids having to pay cash in the future for the specified expense. The ledger holds a separate asset account for each prepaid expense. Prepaid Rent and Prepaid Insurance are prepaid expenses that occur often in business. Office Supplies are also accounted for as prepaid expenses.

Land   The Land account is a record of the land that a business owns.

Building   The buildings (office, warehouse, garage, and the like) that a business owns and uses in its operations appear in the Building account.

Equipment, Furniture and Fixtures   A business has a separate asset account for each type of equipment — Office Equipment and Store Equipment, for example. The Furniture and Fixtures account shows the cost of this asset.

Other asset categories and accounts will be discussed as needed. For example, many businesses have an Investments account for their investments in other companies.

Liabilities

Recall from Chapter 1 that a *liability* is a debt. A business generally keeps fewer liability accounts than asset accounts because a business's liabilities can be summarized under relatively few categories.

Accounts Payable   This account is the opposite of the Accounts Receivable account. The oral or implied promise to pay off debts arising from credit purchases of goods appears in the Accounts Payable account. Such purchases are said to be made on acount. Other liability categories and accounts are added as needed. Taxes Payable, Wages Payable, Goods and Services Tax Payable, and Salary Payable are accounts that appear in many ledgers.

Notes Payable   Notes Payable records the amounts that the business must pay because it signed promissory notes to purchase goods or services.

Owner's Equity

The claim that the owner has on the assets of the business is called *owner's equity*. In a proprietorship or a partnership, owner's equity is often split into separate accounts for the owner's capital balance and the owner's withdrawals.

Capital   This account shows the owner's claim to the assets of the business. After total liabilities are subtracted from total assets, the remainder is the owner's capital. The balance of the capital account equals the owner's investments in the business plus its net income and minus net losses and owner withdrawals. In addition to the capital account, the following accounts also appear in the owner's equity section of the ledger.

Withdrawals   When the owner withdraws cash or other assets from the business for personal use, its assets and its owner's equity both decrease. The amounts taken out of the business appear in a separate account entitled Withdrawals or Drawing. If withdrawals were recorded directly in the Owner's Equity account, the amount of owner withdrawals would not be highlighted. To separate these two amounts for decision-making, businesses use a separate account for Withdrawals. This account shows a *decrease* in owner's equity.

Revenues   The increase in owner's equity from delivering goods or services to customers or clients is called *revenue*. The ledger contains as many revenue accounts as needed. Gary Lyon's law practice would have a Service Revenue account for amounts earned by providing legal service for clients. If the business loans money to an outsider, it will also need an Interest Revenue account for interest earned on the loan. If the business rents a building to a tenant, it will need a Rent Revenue account. Increases in revenue accounts are *increases* in owner's equity.

EXHIBIT 2-1   *The Ledger (Asset, Liability, and Owner's Equity Accounts)*

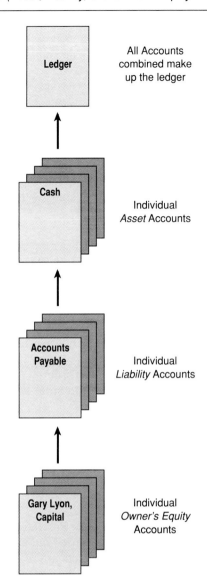

Expenses   The cost of operating a business is called *expense*. Expenses have the opposite effect of revenues, so they decrease owner's equity. A business needs a separate account for each category of its expenses, such as Salary Expense, Rent Expense, Advertising Expense, and Utilities Expense. Expense accounts are decreases in owner's equity.

Exhibit 2-1 shows how asset, liability and owner's equity accounts can be grouped into the ledger. Typically, each account occupies a separate sheet.

Double-Entry Bookkeeping _____

Accounting is based on double-entry bookkeeping, which means that accountants record the dual effects of a business transaction. We know that each transaction affects at least two accounts. For example, Gary Lyon's $50,000 cash investment in his law practice increased both the Cash account and the Owner's Equity account of the business. It would be incomplete to record only the increase in the entity's cash without recording the increase in its owner's equity.

Consider a cash purchase of supplies. What are the dual effects of this transaction? The purchase (1) decreases cash and (2) increases supplies. A purchase of supplies on credit (1) increases supplies and (2) increases accounts payable. A cash payment on account (1) decreases cash and (2) decreases accounts payable. All transactions have at least two effects on the entity.

The T-Account

How do accountants record business transactions in the accounts? The account format used for most illustrations in this book is called the T-account. It takes the form of the capital letter "T". The vertical line in the letter divides the account into its left and right sides. The account title rests on the horizontal line. For example, the Cash account of a business appears in the following T-account format:

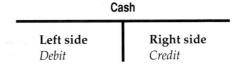

The left side of the account is called the **debit** side, and the right side is called the **credit** side. Often beginners in the study of accounting are confused by the words debit and credit. To become comfortable using them, simply remember this:

> debit = left side
> credit = right side

Even though left side and right side may be more convenient, debit and credit are too deeply entrenched in accounting to avoid using.[1]

Increases and Decreases in the Accounts

The type of an account determines how increases and decreases in it are recorded. For any given account, all increases are recorded on one side, and all decreases are recorded on the other side. Increases in assets are recorded in the left (the debit) side of the account. Decreases in assets are recorded in the right (the credit) side of the account. Conversely, increases in liabilities and owner's equity are recorded by credits. Decreases are recorded by debits.

This pattern of recording debits is based on the accounting equation:

ASSETS = LIABILITIES + OWNER'S EQUITY

Notice that assets are on the opposite side from liabilities and owner's equity. This explains why increases and decreases in assets are recorded in the opposite manner from liabilities and owner's equity. It also explains why liabilities and owner's equity are treated in the same way: they are on the same side of the equal sign. Exhibit 2-2 shows the relationship between the accounting equation and the rules of debit and credit.

---

[1] The words debit and credit have a Latin origin (debitum and creditum). Pacioli, the Italian monk who wrote about accounting in the fifteenth century, used them.

EXHIBIT 2-2   *Accounting Equation and the Rules of Debit and Credit*

Accounting Equation	Assets		=	Liabilities		+	Owner's Equity	
Rules of Debit and Credit	Debit for Increase	Credit for Decrease		Debit for Decrease	Credit for Increase		Debit for Decrease	Credit for Increase

To illustrate the ideas diagrammed in Exhibit 2-2, reconsider the first transaction from the preceding chapter. Gary Lyon invested the $50,000 he inherited in cash to begin his law practice. What accounts are affected? By what amounts? On what side (debit or credit)? The answer is that Assets and Owner's Equity would increase by $50,000, as the following T-accounts show:

ASSETS   =   LIABILITIES   +   OWNER'S EQUITY

Cash				Gary Lyon, Capital	
Debit for Increase, 50,000					**Credit for Increase, 50,000**

Notice that Assets = Liabilities + Owner's Equity, and that total debits = total credits.

The amount remaining in an account is called its balance. This initial transaction gives Cash a $50,000 debit balance and Gary Lyon, Capital, a $50,000 credit balance.

The second transaction is a $40,000 cash purchase of land. This transaction affects two assets: Cash and Land. It decreases (credits) Cash and increases (debits) Land, as shown in the T-accounts:

OBJECTIVE 2

Apply the rules of debit and credit

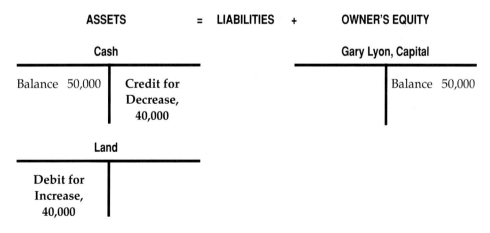

ASSETS   =   LIABILITIES   +   OWNER'S EQUITY

Cash				Gary Lyon, Capital	
Balance 50,000	**Credit for Decrease, 40,000**				Balance 50,000

Land	
Debit for Increase, 40,000	

After this transaction, Cash has a $10,000 debit balance ($50,000 debit amount — $40,000 credit amount), Land's debit balance is $40,000, and Capital has a $50,000 credit balance.

Transaction 3 is a $500 purchase of office supplies on account. This transaction increases the asset Office Supplies and the liability Accounts Payable, as shown in the following accounts:

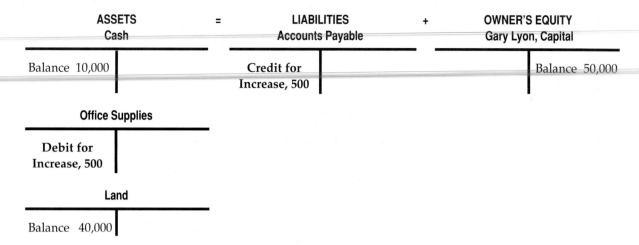

Accountants create accounts as needed. The process of writing a new T-account in preparation for recording a transaction is called *opening the account*. For Transaction 1, we opened the Cash account and the Gary Lyon, Capital account. For Transaction 2, we opened the Land account, and for Transaction 3, Office Supplies and Accounts Payable.

Accountants could record all transactions directly in the accounts as we have shown for the first three transactions. However, that way of accounting is not practical because it does not leave a clear record of each transaction. Suppose you need to know what account was debited and what account was credited in a particular transaction. Looking at each account in the ledger does not answer this question because double-entry accounting always affects at least two accounts. Therefore, you may have to search through all the accounts in the ledger to find both sides of a particular transaction. To avoid this waste of time, accountants keep a record of each transaction and then transfer this information into the accounts.

The Debit-Credit Language of Accounting

As we have seen, *debit* means "left side" and *credit* means "right side." We say "Debit Cash for $1,000," which means to place $1,000 on the left side of the cash account. We record "a $500 debit to Accounts Payable" by entering the $500 in the left side of this account, which signals a decrease in a liability. When we speak of "crediting a liability account for $750," we mean to increase the account's balance by recording $750 on the right side of the account.

In everyday conversation, we sometimes use the word credit in a sense that is different from its technical accounting meaning. For example, we may praise someone by saying, "She deserves credit for her good work." In your study of accounting forget this general use. Remember that debit means left side and credit means right side. Whether an account is increased or decreased by a debit or credit depends on the type of account (see Exhibit 2-2).

Recording Transactions in Journals

In actual practice, accountants record transactions first in a book called the **journal**. A journal is a chronological record of the entity's transactions. In this section, we describe the recording process and illustrate how to use the journal and the ledger.

The recording process follows these five steps:

1. Identify the transactions from source documents, such as bank deposit slips, sales receipts, and cheque stubs.

2. Specify each account affected by the transaction and classify it by type (asset, liability, or owner's equity).

3. Determine whether each account is increased or decreased by the transaction.

4. Using the rules of debit and credit, determine whether to debit or credit the account.

5. Enter the transaction in the journal, including a brief explanation for the journal entry. Accountants write the debit side of the entry first and the credit side next.

We have discussed steps 1, 2, 3, and 4. Step 5, "Enter the transaction in the journal," means to write the transaction in the journal. This step is also called "making the journal entry," "preparing the journal entry," or "journalizing the transaction." A major part of learning accounting is learning how to prepare journal entries.

Let us apply the five steps to journalize the first transaction of the accounting practice of Gary Lyon, Lawyer — the $50,000 cash investment in the business.

Step 1. The source documents are the bank deposit slip and Lyon's $50,000 cheque, which is drawn on his personal bank account.

Step 2. Cash and Gary Lyon, Capital are the accounts affected by the transaction. Cash is an asset account, and Gary Lyon, Capital is an owner's equity account.

Step 3. Both accounts increase by $50,000. Therefore, debit Cash: it is the asset account that is increased. Also, credit Gary Lyon, Owner's Equity: it is the owner's equity account that is increased.

Step 4. Debit Cash to record an increase in this asset account. Credit Gary Lyon, Capital; it is the owner's equity account that is increased.

Step 5. The journal entry is

> **OBJECTIVE 3**
>
> Record transactions in the journal

Date	Accounts and Explanation	Debit	Credit
Apr. 2	Cash	50,000	
	Gary Lyon, Capital		50,000
	Initial investment by owner.		

Note that the journal entry includes (1) the date of the transaction, (2) the title of the account debited (placed flush left) and the title of the account credited (indented slightly), (3) the dollar amounts of the debit (left) and credit (right)—dollar signs are omitted in the money columns—and (4) a short explanation of the transaction.

A helpful hint: To get off to the right start when analyzing a transaction, you should first pinpoint its effects (if any) on cash. Did cash increase or decrease? Then find its effect on other accounts. Typically, it is much easier to identify the effect of a transaction on cash than to identify the effect on other accounts.

The journal offers information that the ledger accounts do not provide. Each journal entry shows the complete effect of a business transaction. Let us examine Gary Lyon's initial investment. The Cash account shows a single figure, the $50,000 debit. We know that every transaction has a credit, so in what account will we find the corresponding $50,000 credit? In this simple illustration, we know that the Capital account holds this figure. But imagine the difficulties an accountant would face trying to link debits and credits for hundreds of daily transactions without a separate record of each transaction. The journal answers this problem and presents the full story for each transaction.

The journal can be a loose-leaf notebook, a bound book, or a printout of a computer file. Exhibit 2-3 shows how a journal page might look with the first transaction entered.

In these introductory discussions we temporarily ignore the date of each transaction in order to focus on the accounts and their dollar amounts.

EXHIBIT 2-3   *The Journal*

	Journal		Page 8
Date	**Accounts and Explanation**	**Debit**	**Credit**
Apr. 2	Cash	50,000	
	Gary Lyon, Capital		50,000
	Initial investment by owner.		

Posting from the Journal to the Ledger

Posting means transferring the amounts from the journal to the appropriate accounts in the ledger. Debits in the journal are posted as debits in the ledger, and credits in the journal as credits in the ledger. The initial investment transaction of Gary Lyon is posted to the ledger as shown in Exhibit 2-4.

EXHIBIT 2-4 *Journal Entry and Posting to the Ledger*

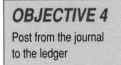

OBJECTIVE 4

Post from the journal to the ledger

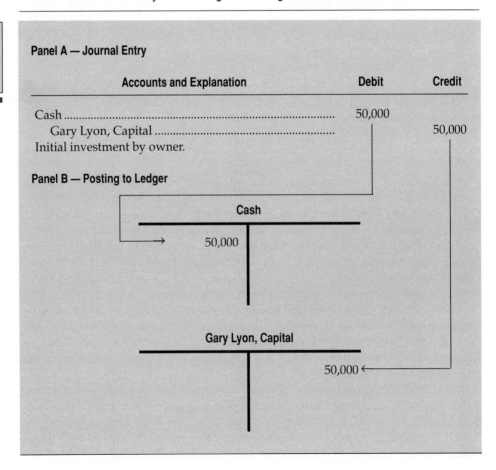

Panel A — Journal Entry

Accounts and Explanation	Debit	Credit
Cash	50,000	
Gary Lyon, Capital		50,000
Initial investment by owner.		

Panel B — Posting to Ledger

Cash

50,000

Gary Lyon, Capital

50,000

EXHIBIT 2-5 *Flow of Accounting Data*

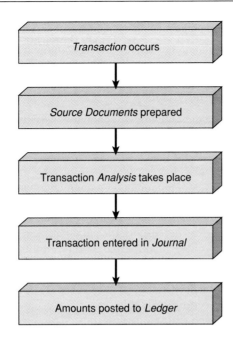

Flow of Accounting Data

Exhibit 2-5 summarizes the flow of accounting data from the business transaction to the ledger.

Illustrative Problem

In this section, we illustrate transaction analysis, journalizing and posting. We continue the example of Gary Lyon, Lawyer, and account for six of his early transactions first described in pages 15–17. Transactions that affect cash are the easiest to analyze. Therefore, when a transaction affects cash, we account for the cash effect first.

Transaction Analysis, Journalizing and Posting

1. *Transaction:* Lyon invested $50,000 to begin his law practice.

   Analysis: Lyon's investment in the business increased its asset cash; to record this increase, debit Cash. His investment also increased the owner's equity of the entity; to record this increase, credit Gary Lyon, Capital.

   Journal Entry:
   Cash 50,000
       Gary Lyon, Capital..............   50,000
   Initial investment by owner.

   Ledger Accounts:

Cash	Gary Lyon, Capital
(1) 50,000	(1) 50,000

2.   *Transaction:*   He paid $40,000 cash for land as a future office location.

    Analysis: The purchase increased the entity's asset land; to record this increase, debit Land.

The purchase decreased cash; therefore, credit Cash.

    Journal   Land 40,000
Entry: Cash   40,000
Paid cash for land.

Ledger
Accounts:

Cash				Land	
(1)	50,000	(2)	40,000	(2)	40,000

3.   *Transaction:*   He purchased $500 office supplies on account.

    Analysis: The credit purchase of office supplies increased this asset; to record this increase, debit Office Supplies.
The purchase also increased the liability accounts payable; to record this increase, credit Accounts Payable.

    Journal   Office Supplies 500
Entry: Accounts Payable   500
Purchased office supplies on account.

Ledger
Accounts

Office Supplies		Accounts Payable	
(3)	500	(3)	500

4.   *Transaction:*   He paid $400 on the account payable created in the preceding transaction.

    Analysis: The payment decreased the asset cash; therefore, credit Cash.
The payment also decreased the liability, accounts payable; to record this decrease, debit Accounts Payable.

    Journal   Accounts Payable 400
Entry: Cash   400
Paid cash on account.

Ledger
Accounts:

Cash				Accounts Payable			
(1)	50,000	(2)	40,000	(4)	400	(3)	500
		(4)	400				

5.   *Transaction:*   He remodeled personal residence. This is not a business transaction of the law practice, so no journal entry is made.

6.   *Transaction:*   Lyon withdrew $2,100 cash for personal living expenses.

    Analysis: The withdrawal decreased the entity's cash; therefore, credit Cash. The transaction also decreased the owner's equity of the entity and must be recorded by a debit to an owner's equity account. Decreases in the owner's equity of a proprietorship that result from owner withdrawals are debited to a separate owner's equity account entitled Withdrawals. Therefore, debit Gary Lyon, Withdrawals.

    Journal   Gary Lyon, Withdrawals 2,100
Entry: Cash   2,100
Withdrawal of cash by owner.

Ledger Accounts:

		Cash			Gary Lyon, Withdrawals	
(1)	50,000	(2)	40,000	(6)	2,100	
		(4)	400			
		(6)	2,100			

As each journal entry is posted to the ledger, it is keyed by date or by transaction number. In this way, a trail is provided through the accounting records so that any transaction can be traced from the journal to the ledger, and, if need be, back to the journal. This linking allows the accountant to locate efficiently any information needed.

Ledger Accounts after Posting

We next illustrate how the accounts look when the amounts of the preceding transactions have been posted. The accounts were grouped under the accounting equation's headings.

Note that each account has a balance figure. This amount is the difference between the account's total debits and its total credits. For example, the balance in the Cash account is the difference between the debits, $50,000 and the credits, $42,500 ($40,000 + $400 + $2,100). Thus the balance figure is $7,500. The balance amounts are not journal entries posted to the accounts, so we set an account balance apart by horizontal lines.

If the sum of an account's debits is greater than the sum of its credits, that account has a debit balance, as the Cash account does here. If the sum of its credits is greater, that account has a credit balance, as Accounts Payable does.

Assets				**=**	**Liabilities**			**+**	**Owner's Equity**	
	Cash				**Accounts Payable**				**Gary Lyon, Capital**	
(1)	50,000	(2)	40,000	(4)	400	(3)	500		(1)	50,000
		(4)	400			Bal.	100		Bal.	50,000
		(6)	2,100							
Bal.	7,500									

	Office Supplies				**Gary Lyon, Withdrawals**	
(3)	500			(6)	2,100	
Bal.	500			Bal.	2,100	

	Land	
(2)	40,000	
Bal.	40,000	

Trial Balance

A **trial balance** is a list of all accounts with their balances. It provides a check on accuracy by showing whether the total debits equal the total credits. A trial balance may be taken at any time the postings are up to date. Exhibit 2-6 is the trial balance of the general ledger of Gary Lyon's law practice after the first six transactions have been journalized and posted.

The word *trial* is well chosen. The list is prepared as a test of the accounts' amounts. The trial balance shows the accountant whether the total debits and total credits are equal. In this way it may signal accounting errors. For example, if only the debit (or only the credit) side of a transaction is posted, the total debits will

EXHIBIT 2-6 Trial Balance

Gary Lyon, Lawyer
Trial Balance
April 30, 19X1

Account Titles	Balance	
	Debit	Credit
Cash..	$ 7,500	
Office supplies...	500	
Land	40,000	
Accounts payable...		$ 100
Gary Lyon, capital...		50,000
Gary Lyon, withdrawals	2,100	
Total..	$50,100	$50,100

not equal the total credits. If a debit is posted as a credit or vice versa, debits and credits will be out of balance. For example, if the $500 debit in Office Supplies is incorrectly posted as a credit, total debits will be $49,600 and total credits will be $50,600. The trial balance alerts the accountant to such errors in posting.

Some errors may not be revealed by the trial balance. For example, a $1,000 cash payment for supplies may be debited to Office Furniture instead of to Office Supplies. This error would cause Office Furniture to be overstated and Office Supplies to be understated, each by $1,000. But these errors would offset each other (they are both asset accounts) so the trial balance would still show debits equal to credits. Also, if an accountant erroneously recorded a $5,000 transaction at only $500, the trial balance would show no error. However, total debits and total credits would both be understated by $4,500 (that is, $5,000 – $500).

Do not confuse the trial balance with the balance sheet. Accountants prepare a trial balance for their internal records. The company reports its financial position — both inside and outside the business — on the balance sheet, a formal financial statement.

Summary Problem for Your Review

On August 1, 19X5, Liz Shea opens a business that she names Shea's Research Service. She will be the sole owner of the business, so it will be a proprietorship. During the entity's first ten days of operations, the following transactions take place:

a. To begin operations, Shea deposits $50,000 of personal funds in a bank account entitled Shea's Research Service.

b. Shea pays $40,000 cash for a small house to be used as an office. (Debit an asset account entitled Building.)

c. Shea purchases $250 in office supplies on credit (that is, on account).

d. Shea pays cash of $6,000 for office furniture. (Debit Office Furniture.)

e. Shea pays $150 on the account payable she created in transaction *c*.

f. Shea withdraws $1,000 cash for personal use.

Required

1. Prepare the journal entries to record these transactions. Key the journal entries by transaction number.
2. Post the entries to the ledger.
3. Prepare the trial balance of Shea's Research Service at August 10, 19X5.

SOLUTION TO REVIEW PROBLEM

Requirement 1

Accounts and Explanation	Debit	Credit
a. Cash	50,000	
Liz Shea, Capital		50,000
Initial investment by owner.		
b. Building	40,000	
Cash		40,000
Purchased building for an office.		
c. Office Supplies	250	
Accounts Payable		250
Purchased office supplies on account.		
d. Office Furniture	6,000	
Cash		6,000
Purchased office furniture.		
e. Accounts Payable	150	
Cash		150
Paid cash on account.		
f. Liz Shea, Withdrawals	1,000	
Cash		1,000
Withdrew cash for personal use.		

Requirement 2

ASSETS

	Cash					Office Supplies		
(a)	50,000	(b)	40,000		(c)	250		
		(d)	6,000		Bal.	250		
		(e)	150					
		(f)	1,000					
Bal.	2,850							

	Office Furniture				Building	
(d)	6,000			(b)	40,000	
Bal.	6,000			Bal.	40,000	

LIABILITIES			OWNER'S EQUITY				

Accounts Payable				Liz Shea, Capital		Liz Shea, Withdrawals	
(e)	150	(c)	250	(a) 50,000		(f) 1,000	
		Bal.	100	Bal. 50,000		Bal. 1,000	

Requirement 3

Shea's Research Service
Trial Balance
August 10, 19X5

	Balance	
Account Titles	**Debit**	**Credit**
Cash	$ 2,850	
Office supplies	250	
Office furniture	6,000	
Building	40,000	
Accounts payable		$ 100
Liz Shea, capital		50,000
Liz Shea, withdrawals	1,000	
Total	$50,100	$50,100

Details of Journals and Ledgers

To focus on the main points of journalizing and posting, we purposely omitted certain essential data. In actual practice, the journal and the ledger provide additional details that create a "trail" through the accounting records for future reference. For example, an accountant may need to verify the date of a transaction or to determine whether a journal entry has been posted to the ledger. Let us take a closer look at the journal and the ledger.

Journal In Exhibit 2-7, Panel B presents the journal format most often used by accountants. Note that the journal page number appears in the upper-right corner.
As the column headings indicate, the journal displays the following information:

1. The date, which is most important because it indicates when the transaction occurred. The year appears first. It is not necessary to repeat it for each journal entry. The year appears only when the journal is started or when the year has changed. Note that the year appears with an X in the third column. We present the year in this way because the dates we choose are for illustration only. Thus 19X1 is followed by 19X2, and so on. We will use this format throughout the book. Like the year, the month is entered only once. The second date column holds the day of the transaction. This column is filled in for every transaction.

2. The account title and explanation of the transaction. You are already familiar with this presentation from Exhibit 2-3.

3. The posting reference, abbreviated Post. Ref. How this column helps the accountant becomes clear when we discuss the details of posting.

4. The debit column, which shows the amount debited.

5. The credit column, which shows the amount credited.

EXHIBIT 2-7 *Details of Journalizing and Posting*

Panel A: Illustrative Transactions

Date	Transaction
Apr. 2, 19X1	Gary Lyon invested $50,000 in his law practice.
3	Paid $500 cash for office supplies.

Panel B: Journal

Page 1

Date	Accounts and Explanation	Post. Ref.	Debit	Credit
19X1				
Apr. 2	Cash	11	50,000	
	Gary Lyon, Capital	31		50,000
	Initial investment			
3	Office Supplies	13	500	
	Cash	11		500
	Purchased office supplies			

① ② ③ ④

Panel C: Ledger

Cash   Account No. 11

Date	Item	Jrnl. Ref.	Debit	Date	Item	Jrnl. Ref.	Credit
19X1				19X1			
Apr. 2		J.1	50,000	Apr. 3		J.1	500

Office Supplies   Account No. 13

Date	Item	Jrnl. Ref.	Debit	Date	Item	Jrnl. Ref.	Credit
19X1							
Apr. 3		J.1	500				

Gary Lyon, Capital   Account No. 31

Date	Item	Jrnl. Ref.	Debit	Date	Item	Jrnl. Ref.	Credit
				19X1			
				Apr. 2		J.1	50,000

Ledger   In Exhibit 2-7, Panel C presents the ledger in T-account format. Each account has its own page in the illustrative ledger. Our example shows Gary Lyon's Cash account. This account maintains the basic format of the T-account but offers more information.

The account title appears at the top of the page. Note also the account number at the upper-right column. Each account has its own identification number. We will look later at how accountants assign account numbers.

The column headings identify the ledger account's features as follows:

1. The date.
2. The item column. This space is used for any special notation.
3. The journal reference column, abbreviated Jrnl. Ref. The importance of this column becomes clear when we discuss the mechanics of posting.
4. The debit column, with the amount debited.
5. The credit column, with the amount credited.

Posting

We know that posting means moving information from the journal to the ledger accounts. But how do we handle the additional details that appear in the journal and the ledger formats that we have just seen? Exhibit 2-7 illustrates the steps in full detail. Panel A lists the first two transactions of Gary Lyon, Lawyer; Panel B presents the journal; and Panel C shows the ledger.

Since the flow of accounting data moves from the journal to the ledger, the accountant first records the journal entry, as shown in Panel B. The transaction data are given in Panel A, except for the Post. Ref. number. Let us trace the arrows to follow the details of posting.

Arrow 1 traces the date, Apr. 2, 19X1, from the journal to the ledger account Cash.

Arrow 2 begins at the journal's page number, Page 1, and ends in the journal reference column, Jrnl. Ref. of the ledger. The J.1 entry in that column stands for "Journal (page) 1." Why bother with this detail? If an accountant is using the Cash account and needs to locate the original journal entry, the journal page number tells where to look.

Arrow 3 indicates that the accountant records the debit figure, $50,000 in this journal entry, as a debit figure in the account.

Arrow 4 points to a posting detail. Once the accountant has recorded a dollar figure to the appropriate account, that account's number is entered in the journal's Post. Ref. column. This step indicates that all the information for that account has been posted from the journal to the ledger. A blank Post. Ref. column for an entry means that the entry has not yet been posted to the ledger account.

Having performed these steps for the debit entry, the accountant then posts the credit entry to the ledger. After posting, the accountant draws up the trial balance, as we discussed earlier.

Chart of Accounts

As you know, the general ledger contains the business's accounts grouped under the headings Assets, Liabilities, Owner's Equity, Revenues and Expenses. To keep track of their accounts, organizations have a **chart of accounts**, which lists all the accounts and their account numbers. These account numbers are used as posting references, as illustrated by arrow 4 in Exhibit 2-7. It is easier to write the account number, 11, in the posting reference column of the journal than to write the account title, Cash. Also, this numbering system makes it easy to locate individual accounts in the ledger.

EXHIBIT 2-8 *Chart of Accounts: Law Practice of Gary Lyon, Lawyer*

Balance Sheet Accounts

Assets	Liabilities	Owner's Equity
11 Cash	21 Accounts Payable	31 Gary Lyon, Capital
12 Accounts Receivable	22 Notes Payable	32 Gary Lyon, Withdrawals
13 Office Supplies		
17 Office Furniture		
19 Land		

Income Statement Accounts

	Revenues	Expenses
	41 Service Revenue	51 Rent Expense
		52 Salary Expense
		53 Utilities Expense

Assets are usually numbered beginning with 1, liabilities with 2, owner's equity with 3, revenues with 4, and expenses with 5. The second digit in an account number indicates the position of the individual account within the category. For example, Cash may be account number 11, which is the first asset account. Accounts Receivable may be account number 12, the second asset account. Accounts Payable may be account number 21, the first liability account. All accounts are numbered using such a system.

Many organizations have so many accounts that they use three- or four-digit account numbers. For example, account number 101 may be Cash on Hand, account number 102 may be Cash on Deposit in the Huron Bank, and account number 103 may be Cash on Deposit in the Bank of Manitoba.

The chart of accounts for Gary Lyon, Lawyer, appears in Exhibit 2-8. Notice that the account numbers jump from 13 to 17. Gary Lyon realizes that later on he may want to add other supplies accounts, for example, Legal Forms Supplies. Any additional supplies account would logically appear next to Office Supplies, and Legal Forms Supplies might be account number 14.

Normal Balances of Accounts

Accountants speak of an account's normal balance, which refers to the side of the account — debit or credit — on which increases are recorded. This term also refers to the usual balance — debit or credit — in the account. For example, Cash and all other assets usually have a debit balance, so assets are debit-balance accounts. On the other hand, liabilities and owner's equity usually have a credit balance, so they are credit-balance accounts. Exhibit 2-9 illustrates the normal balances of assets, liabilities, and owner's equity.

EXHIBIT 2-9 *Normal Balances of Balance Sheet Accounts*

Assets	=	Liabilities	+	Owner's Equity
Normal Bal. Debit		Normal Bal. Credit		Normal Bal. Credit

An account that normally has a debit balance may occasionally have a credit balance. This indicates a negative amount of the item. For example, Cash will have a temporary credit balance if the entity overdraws its bank account. Similarly, the liability Accounts Payable (normally a credit balance account) will have a debit balance if the entity overpays its account. In other instances, the shift of a balance amount away from its normal column indicates an accounting error. For example, a credit balance in Office Supplies, Office Furniture or Buildings indicates an error because negative amounts of these assets cannot exist.

As we have explained, owner's equity usually contains several accounts. In total, these accounts show a normal credit balance for the owner's equity of the business. Each individual owner's equity account has a normal credit balance if it represents an increase in owner's equity, for example, the Capital account. However, if the individual owner's equity account represents a decrease in owner's equity, the account will have a normal debit balance, for example, the Withdrawals account.

Additional Owner's Equity Accounts: Revenues and Expenses

The owner's equity category includes two additional types of accounts: revenues and expenses. As we have discussed, revenues are increases in owner's equity that result from delivering goods or services to customers. Expenses are decreases in owner's equity due to the cost of operating the business. Therefore, the accounting equation may be expanded as follows:

$$\text{ASSETS} = \text{LIABILITIES} + \text{OWNER'S EQUITY}$$

$$\text{(CAPITAL} - \text{WITHDRAWALS)}$$
$$+ \text{(REVENUES} - \text{EXPENSES)}$$

Revenues and expenses appear in parentheses because their impact on the accounting equation arises from their effect on owner's equity. If revenues exceed expenses, the net effect — revenues minus expenses — is net income, which increases owner's equity. If expenses are greater, the net effect is a net loss, which decreases owner's equity.

We can now express the rules of debit and credit in final form as shown in Panel A of Exhibit 2-10. Panel B shows the normal balances of the five types of accounts: (1) assets, (2) liabilities, (3) capital minus withdrawals, (4) revenues, and (5) expenses. Note that owner's equity is normally a credit because capital must exceed withdrawals (an owner of a company cannot withdraw more than the capital that has been put in) and revenues normally exceed expenses.

All of accounting is based on these five types of accounts. You should become very familiar with the related rules of debit and credit and the normal balances of accounts.

Typical Account Titles

Thus far we have dealt with a limited number of transactions and accounts to introduce key concepts. Businesses engage in more transactions, requiring more accounts. Additional transactions are recorded in the same manner, with accounts added to the analysis as needed. The following summary describes some of the more common accounts grouped by financial statement and account category. As you answer the exercises and problems in this and future chapters, you will find these descriptions useful.

EXHIBIT 2-10 *Rules of Debit and Credit and Normal Balances of Accounts*

Panel A: Rules of Debit and Credit

Assets			=	Liabilities			+	Capital	
Debit for Increase	Credit for Decrease			Debit for Decrease	Credit for Increase			Debit for Decrease	Credit for Increase

Withdrawals

Debit for Increase	Credit for Decrease

Revenues

Debit for Decrease	Credit for Increase

Expenses

Debit for Increase	Credit for Decrease

Panel B: Normal Balances

Assets	Debit	
Liabilities		Credit
Owner's equity — overall		Credit
Capital		Credit
Withdrawals	Debit	
Revenue		Credit
Expenses	Debit	

Balance Sheet: Assets, Liabilities, and Owner's Equity

Assets

Cash: Money on hand and in the bank.

Accounts receivable: Claim on open account against the cash of a client or a customer. (Open account means that no written promise exists to support the receivable.)

Note receivable: Claim against the cash of another party, supported by a promissory note signed by the other party. (All receivables are assets and any account with receivable in its title is an asset.)

Merchandise inventory: Merchandise that an entity sells in its business (such as clothing by a department store, stereos by a stereo shop).

Office supplies: Stationery, stamps, paper clips, staples, and so forth.

Office furniture: Desks, chairs, file cabinets, and so forth.

Office equipment: Computers and related equipment such as printers, typewriters, fax machines, calculators and other equipment used in a business office.

Building: Building used in a business.

Land: Land on which a business building stands.

Liabilities

Account payable: Liability to pay cash to another party on open account.

Note payable: Liability to pay cash to another party, supported by a signed promissory note.

Salary payable: Liability to pay an employee for work. (Most liabilities have the word payable in the account title, and any account with payable in its title is a liability.)

Goods and services tax payable: Liability (net) to pay goods and services tax collected.

Owner's Equity

Gary Lyon, Capital: The interest of the owner of the business in its assets. (This account title bears the name of the owner.)

Gary Lyon, Withdrawals: The owner's withdrawals of assets from the business for personal use.

Income Statement: Revenues and Expenses

Revenues

Service revenue: Revenue earned by performing a service (accounting service by a public accounting firm, laundry service by a laundry).

Sales revenue: Revenue earned by selling a product (sales of hardware by a hardware store, food by a grocery store).

Expenses

Rent expense: Expense for office rent and the rental of office equipment or any other business asset.

Salary expense: Expense of having an employee work for the business.

Employee benefits expense: Expense of employee benefits such as Unemplyment Insurance and Workers' Compensation.

Utilities expense: Expense of using electricity, water, gas, and other items provided by utility companies.

Supplies expense: Expense of using supplies such as stationery, stamps, paper clips, staples, and so forth.

Advertising expense: Expense of advertising the business.

Interest expense: Expense of using borrowed money.

Property tax expense: Expense for property tax on business land and buildings.

Illustrative Problem

Let us account for the revenues and expenses of the veterinary practice of Sally Gunz for the month of July 19X1. We follow the same steps illustrated earlier: analyze the transaction, journalize, post to the ledger, and prepare the trial balance. Revenue accounts and expense accounts work just like asset, liability, and owner's equity accounts. Each revenue and each expense account has its own page in the ledger and its own identifying account number.

Transaction Analysis, Journalizing, and Posting

1. *Transaction*:   Sally Gunz invested $10,000 cash in a business bank account to open her veterinary practice.

    Analysis: The asset cash is increased; therefore debit Cash.

The owner's equity of the business increased; therefore, credit
Sally Gunz, Capital

Journal   Cash   10,000
Entry: Sally Gunz, Capital   10,000
             Invested cash in the business.

Ledger
Accounts:

Cash		**Sally Gunz, Capital**	
(1) 10,000			(1) 10,000

2.   *Transaction:* Gunz performed veterinarian services for a number of patients
             and received $3,000 from their owners.

      Analysis: The asset cash is increased; therefore, debit Cash.
             The revenue service revenue is increased; credit Service Revenue.

      Journal   Cash   3,000
      Entry: Service Revenue   3,000
             Performed service and received
             payment.

      Ledger
      Accounts:

Cash		**Service Revenue**	
(1) 10,000			(2) 3,000
(2) 3,000			

3.   *Transaction:* Gunz performed services for a local kennel and billed the ken-
             nel for $500 on account receivable. This means the kennel owes
             the business $500 even though the kennel signed no formal
             promissory note.

      Analysis: The asset accounts receivable is increased; therefore, debit
             Accounts Receivable.
             The revenue service revenue is increased; credit Service Revenue.

      Journal   Accounts Receivable   500
      Entry: Service Revenue   500
             Performed service on account.

      Ledger
      Accounts:

Accounts Receivable		**Service Revenue**	
(3) 500			(2) 3,000
			(3) 500

4.   *Transaction:* Gunz performed veterinary services of $700 for a farmer, who
             paid $300 cash immediately. Gunz billed the remaining $400 to
             the farmer on account receivable.

      Analysis: The assets cash and accounts receivable are increased; there-
             fore, debit both of these asset accounts.
             The revenue service revenue is increased; credit Service Revenue
             for the sum of the two debit amounts.

      Journal   Cash   300
      Entry: Accounts Receivable   400
                   Service Revenue   700
             Performed service for cash and
             on account.

Note: Because this transaction affects more than two accounts at the same time, the entry is called a compound entry. No matter how many accounts a compound entry affects (there may be any number), total debits must equal total credits.

*Ledger
Accounts:*

Cash

(1)	10,000	
(2)	3,000	
(4)	**400**	

Accounts Receivable

| (3) | 500 | |
| (4) | 400 | |

Service Revenue

		(2)	3,000
		(3)	500
		(4)	**700**

5. *Transaction:* Gunz paid the following cash expenses: office rent, $900; employee salary, $1,500; and utilities, $500.

Analysis: The following expenses are increased: Rent Expense, Salary Expense, and Utilities Expense. They should each be debited. The asset cash is decreased; therefore, credit Cash for each of the three expense amounts.

*Journal
Entry:*

(a) Rent Expense 900
    Cash 900
(b) Salary Expense 1,500
    Cash 1,500
(c) Utilities Expense 500
    Cash 500
Issued three cheques to pay cash expenses.

*Ledger
Accounts:*

Cash

(1)	10,000	(5a)	900
(2)	3,000	(5b)	1,500
(4)	400	(5c)	500

Rent Expense

| (5a) | 900 | |

Salary Expense

| (5b) | 1,500 | |

Utilities Expense

| (5c) | 500 | |

6. *Transaction:* Gunz received a telephone bill for $120 and will pay this expense next week.

Analysis: Utilities expense is increased; therefore, debit this expense. The liability accounts payable is increased; credit this account.

*Journal
Entry:*

Utilities Expense 120
    Accounts Payable 120
Received utility bill.

*Ledger
Accounts:*

Accounts Payable

| | | (6) | 120 |

Utilities Expense

| (5c) | 500 | |
| (6) | 120 | |

7.   *Transaction*:   Gunz collected $200 cash from the farmer established in transaction 3.

   Analysis: The asset cash is increased; therefore, debit Cash.
   The asset accounts receivable is decreased; therefore, credit Accounts Receivable.

   Journal Entry:

   Cash   200
       Accounts Receivable   200
   Received cash on account.

   Note: This transaction has no effect on revenue; the related revenue is accounted for in transaction 3.

   Ledger Accounts:

Cash				Accounts Receivable			
(1)	10,000	(5a)	900	(3)	500	**(7)**	**200**
(2)	3,000	(5b)	1,500	(4)	400		
(4)	400	(5c)	500				
(7)	**200**						

8.   *Transaction*:   Gunz paid the telephone bill that was received and recorded in transaction 6.

   Analysis: The liability accounts payable is decreased; therefore, debit Accounts Payable.
   The asset cash is decreased; credit Cash.

   Journal Entry:

   Accounts Payable   120
       Cash   120
   Paid cash on account.

   Note: This transaction has no effect on expense because the related expense was recorded in transaction 6.

   Ledger Accounts:

Cash				Accounts Payable			
(1)	10,000	(5a)	900	**(8)**	**120**	(6)	120
(2)	3,000	(5b)	1,500				
(4)	400	(5c)	500				
(7)	200	**(8)**	**120**				

9.   *Transaction*:   Gunz withdrew $1,100 cash for personal use.

   Analysis: The withdrawal decreased owner's equity; therefore, debit Sally Gunz, Withdrawals.
   The asset cash decreased; credit Cash.

   Journal Entry:

   Sally Gunz, Withdrawals   1,100
       Cash   1,100
   Withdrew for personal use.

   Ledger Accounts:

Cash				Sally Gunz, Withdrawals			
(1)	10,000	(5a)	900	**(9)**	**1,100**		
(2)	3,000	(5b)	1,500				
(4)	400	(5c)	500				
(7)	200	(8)	120				
		(9)	**1,100**				

Ledger Accounts After Posting

ASSETS	LIABILITIES	OWNER'S EQUITY

Cash

(1)	10,000	(5a)	900
(2)	3,000	(5b)	1,500
(4)	400	(5c)	500
(7)	200	(8)	120
		(9)	1,100
Bal.	9,380		

Accounts Receivable

(3)	500	(7)	200
(4)	400		
Bal.	700		

Accounts Payable

| (8) | 120 | (6) | 120 |
| | | Bal. | 0 |

Sally Gunz, Capital

| | | (1) | 10,000 |
| | | Bal. | 10,000 |

Sally Gunz, Withdrawals

| (9) | 1,100 | |
| Bal. | 1,100 | |

REVENUE	EXPENSES

Service Revenue

		(2)	3,000
		(3)	500
		(4)	700
		Bal.	4,200

Rent Expense

| (5a) | 900 | |
| Bal. | 900 | |

Salary Expense

| (5b) | 1,500 | |
| Bal. | 1,500 | |

Utilities Expense

(5c)	500	
(6)	120	
Bal.	620	

Trial Balance

Sally Gunz, Veterinarian
Trial Balance
July 31, 19X1

	Balance	
Account Title	Debit	Credit
Cash	$ 9,380	
Accounts receivable	700	
Accounts payable		$ 0
Sally Gunz, capital		10,000
Sally Gunz, withdrawals	1,100	
Service revenue		4,200
Rent expense	900	
Salary expense	1,500	
Utilities expense	620	
Total	$14,200	$14,200

Analytical Use of Accounting Information

OBJECTIVE 6

Analyze transactions without a journal

What dominates the accountant's analysis of transactions: the accounting equation, the journal, or the ledger? The accounting equation is most fundamental. In turn, the ledger is more useful than the journal in providing an overall model of the organization. Accountants and other business persons must often make quick decisions without the benefit of a complete accounting system: journal, ledger, accounts and trial balance. For example, the owner of a company may be negotiating the purchase price of another business. For quick analysis of the effects of transactions, accountants often skip the journal and go directly to the ledger. They compress transaction analysis, journalizing and posting into one step. This type of analysis saves time that may be the difference between a good business decision and a lost opportunity.

Let us take an example to see how it works. For instance, the first revenue transaction — Sally Gunz performed veterinarian services for patients and collected cash of $3,000 from their owners — may be analyzed by debiting the Cash account and crediting the Service Revenue account directly in the ledger in the following manner:

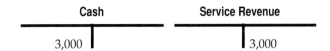

Cash	Service Revenue
3,000	3,000

With this shortcut, the accountant can see immediately the effect of the transaction on both the entity's cash and its service revenue. Or you can take the quick analysis one step further — go straight to the financial statements. This transaction increased cash on the balance sheet by $3,000. It also increased Service Revenue on the income statement, and the owner's capital on the balance sheet, by $3,000. Modern computer-assisted accounting systems often have this "journal-less" feature.

Computers and Accounting

Computers have revolutionized accounting. Two decades ago, big and expensive computers were available only to the large companies that could afford them. Today, prices for increasingly powerful microcomputers continue to drop, enabling smaller businesses to take advantage of accounting with computers. Microcomputers —also known as personal computers — such as IBM, Apple, Compaq, Zenith, Tandy, and Dell electronically handle much of the work done by hand in the past.

Just what benefits does a computer offer? An accountant must analyze every business transaction, whether the accounting system is manual, as we are presenting in these opening chapters, or computerized. Once the transaction has been analyzed, a computerized accounting package performs much the same actions as accountants do in a manual system. The computer automatically makes a journal entry, capturing the necessary information in a consistent format. A computer's ability to perform routine tasks and mathematical operations fast and without error frees accountants for decision-making. On the market today is a wide variety of specialized computer programs — known as *software* — that require almost no computer programming expertise.

You may be wondering about the role of debits and credits in a computerized accounting system. The computer interprets debits and credits as increases or decreases by account type. For example, a computer reads a debit to cash as an increase to that account. Debits and credits actually need not be used in a computerized system. They were originally designed to ensure accuracy in manual accounting systems.

In addition to helping with accounting itself, microcomputers assist with many financial applications of accounting information and in business correspondence. Also, thanks to telecommunications, microcomputers can tap into the information stored in larger computers across the globe. As we progress through the study of accounting, we will consider computer applications that fit the topics under discussion.

Summary Problem for Your Review

The trial balance of Tomassini Computer Service Center on March 1, 19X2, lists the entity's assets, liabilities and owner's equity on that date.

	Balance	
Account Titles	**Debit**	**Credit**
Cash	$26,000	
Accounts receivable	4,500	
Accounts payable		$ 2,000
L. Tomassini, capital..		28,500
Total..	$30,500	$30,500

During March the business engaged in the following transactions:

1. Tomassini borrowed $45,000 from the bank. He signed a note payable in the name of the business.
2. Paid cash of $40,000 to a real estate company to acquire land.
3. Performed service for a customer and received cash of $5,000.
4. Purchased supplies on credit, $300.
5. Performed customer service and earned revenue on account, $2,600.
6. Paid $1,200 on account.
7. Paid the following cash expenses: salaries, $3,000; rent, $1,500; and interest, $400.
8. Received $3,100 on account.
9. Received a $200 utility bill that will be paid next week.
10. Tomassini withdrew $1,800 for personal use.

Required

1. Open the following accounts, with the balances indicated, in the ledger of Tomassini Computer Service Center. Use the T-account format.
   Assets: Cash, $26,000; Accounts Receivable, $4,500; Supplies, no balance; Land, no balance
   Liabilities: Accounts Payable, $2,000; Note Payable, no balance
   Owner's Equity: Larry Tomassini, Capital, $28,500; Larry Tomassini, Withdrawals, no balance
   Revenues: Service Revenue, no balance
   Expenses: Salary Expense, Rent Expense, Utilities Expense, Interest Expense, (none have balances)
2. Journalize the preceding transactions. Key journal entries by transaction number.
3. Post to the ledger.

4. Prepare the trial balance of Tomassini Computer Service Center at March 31, 19X2.

5. Compute the net income or net loss of the entity during the month of March. List expenses in order from the largest to the smallest.

SOLUTION TO REVIEW PROBLEM

Requirement 1

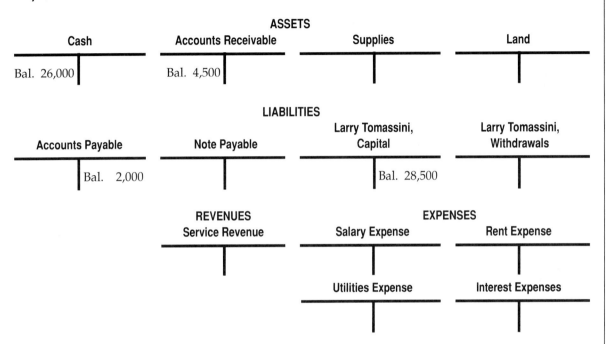

ASSETS

Cash	Accounts Receivable	Supplies	Land
Bal. 26,000	Bal. 4,500		

LIABILITIES

Accounts Payable	Note Payable	Larry Tomassini, Capital	Larry Tomassini, Withdrawals
Bal. 2,000		Bal. 28,500	

REVENUES

Service Revenue

EXPENSES

Salary Expense	Rent Expense
Utilities Expense	Interest Expenses

Requirement 2

	Accounts and Explanation	Debit	Credit
1.	Cash	45,000	
	Note Payable		45,000
	Borrowed cash on note payable.		
2.	Land	40,000	
	Cash		40,000
	Purchased land for cash.		
3.	Cash	5,000	
	Service Revenue		5,000
	Performed service and received cash.		
4.	Supplies	300	
	Accounts Payable		300
	Purchased supplies on account.		
5.	Accounts Receivable	2,600	
	Service Revenue		2,600
	Performed service on account.		
6.	Accounts Payable	1,200	
	Cash		1,200
	Paid on account.		

7.	(a) Salary Expense	3,000	
	Cash		3,000
	(b) Rent Expense	1,500	
	Cash		1,500
	(c) Interest Expense	400	
	Cash		400
	Issued three cheques to pay cash expenses.		
8.	Cash	3,100	
	Accounts Receivable		3,100
	Received on account.		
9.	Utilities Expense	200	
	Accounts Payable		200
	Received utility bill.		
10.	Larry Tomassini, Withdrawals	1,800	
	Cash		1,800
	Withdrew for personal use.		

Requirement 3

ASSETS

Cash

Bal.	26,000	(2)	40,000
(1)	45,000	(6)	1,200
(3)	5,000	(7a)	3,000
(8)	3,100	(7b)	1,500
		(7c)	400
		(10)	1,800
Bal	31,100		

Accounts Receivable

Bal.	4,500	(8)	3,100
(5)	2,600		
Bal.	4,000		

Supplies

| (4) | 300 | |
| Bal. | 300 | |

Land

| (2) | 40,000 | |
| Bal. | 40,000 | |

LIABILITIES

Accounts Payable

(6)	1,200	Bal.	2,000
		(4)	300
		(9)	200
		Bal.	1,300

Note Payable

| | (1) | 45,000 |
| | Bal. | 45,000 |

OWNER'S EQUITY

Larry Tomassini, Capital

| | Bal. | 28,500 |

Larry Tomassini, Withdrawals

| (10) | 1,800 | |
| Bal. | 1,800 | |

REVENUES

Service Revenue

	(3)	5,000
	(5)	2,600
	Bal.	7,600

EXPENSES

Salary Expense

| (7a) | 3,000 | |
| Bal. | 3,000 | |

Rent Expense

| (7b) | 1,500 | |
| Bal. | 1,500 | |

Utilities Expense

| (9) | 200 | |
| Bal. | 200 | |

Interest Expense

| (7c) | 400 | |
| Bal. | 400 | |

Requirement 4

Tomassini Computer Service Center
Trial Balance
March 31, 19X2

Account Title	Balance Debit	Balance Credit
Cash	$31,200	
Accounts Receivable..	4,000	
Supplies..	300	
Land	40,000	
Accounts Payable...		$ 1,300
Note Payable...		45,000
Larry Tomassini, Capital.................................		28,500
Larry Tomassini, Withdrawals........................	1,800	
Service Revenue		7,600
Salary Expense	3,000	
Rent Expense	1,500	
Interest Expense	400	
Utilities Expense	200	
Total	$82,400	$82,400

Requirement 5   Net income for the month of March

Revenues		
Service Revenue...		$7,600
Expenses		
Salary Expense	$3,000	
Rent Expense..	1,500	
Interest Expense...	400	
Utilities Expense	200	
Total expenses		5,100
Net income..		$2,500

Summary

The *account* can be viewed in the form of the letter "T." The left side of each account is its *debit* side. The right side is its *credit* side. The *ledger*, which contains a record for each account, groups and numbers accounts by category in the following order: assets, liabilities, owner's equity, and its subparts: revenues and expenses.

Assets and *expenses* are increased by debits and decreased by credits. *Liabilities, owner's equity,* and *revenues* are increased by credits and decreased by debits. The side — debit or credit — of the account in which increases are recorded is that account's normal balance. Thus the normal balance of assets and expenses is a debit, and the normal balance of liabilities, owner's equity, and revenues is a credit. The Withdrawals account, which decreases owner's equity, normally has a debit balance. *Revenues,* which are increases in owner's equity, have a normal credit balance. *Expenses,* which are decreases in owner's equity, have a normal debit balance.

The accountant begins the recording process by entering the transaction's information in the *journal*, a chronological list of all the business's transactions. The information is then posted (transferred) to the ledger accounts. Posting references are used to trace amounts back and forth between the journal and the ledger. Businesses list their account titles and numbers in a chart of accounts.

The *trial balance* is a summary of all the account balances in the ledger. When *double-entry accounting* has been done correctly, the total debits and the total credits in the trial balance are equal.

We can now trace the flow of accounting information through these steps:

Business Transaction ⟶ Source Documents ⟶ Journal Entry ⟶ Posting to Ledger ⟶ Trial Balance

Self-Study Questions

Test your understanding of the chapter by marking the correct answer for each of the following questions:

1. An account has two sides called the *(p. 48)*
   a. Debit and credit
   b. Asset and liability
   c. Revenue and expense
   d. Journal and ledger

2. Increases in liabilities are recorded by *(p. 48)*
   a. Debits
   b. Credits

3. Why do accountants record transactions in the journal? *(p. 50)*
   a. To ensure that all transactions are posted to the ledger
   b. To ensure that total debits equal total credits
   c. To have a chronological record of all transactions
   d. To help prepare the financial statements

4. Posting is the process of transferring information from the *(p. 52)*
   a. Journal to the trial balance
   b. Ledger to the trial balance
   c. Ledger to the financial statements
   d. Journal to the ledger

5. The purchase of land for cash is recorded by a *(p. 54)*
   a. Debit to Cash and a credit to Land
   b. Debit to Cash and a debit to Land
   c. Debit to Land and a credit to Cash
   d. Credit to Cash and a credit to Land

6. The purpose of the trial balance is to *(p. 55)*
   a. Indicate whether total debits equal total credits
   b. Ensure that all transactions have been recorded
   c. Speed the collection of cash receipts from customers
   d. Increase assets and owner's equity

7. What is the normal balance of the Accounts Receivable, Office Supplies, and Rent Expense accounts? *(p. 62)*
   a. Debit
   b. Credit

8. A business has Cash of $3,000, Notes Payable of $2,500, Accounts Payable of $4,300, Service Revenue of $7,000 and Rent Expense of $1,800. Based on these data, how much are its total liabilities? *(p. 64)*
   a. $5,500
   b. $6,800
   c. $9,800
   d. $13,800

9. The earning of revenue on account is recorded by a *(pp. 64, 65)*
   a. Debit to Cash and a credit to Revenue
   b. Debit to Accounts Receivable and a credit to Revenue
   c. Debit to Accounts Payable and a credit to Revenue
   d. Debit to Revenue and a credit to Accounts Receivable

10. The account credited for a receipt of cash on account is *(p. 66)*
    a. Cash
    b. Accounts Payable
    c. Service Revenue
    d. Accounts Receivable

Answers to the Self-Study Questions are at the end of the chapter.

Accounting Vocabulary

account *(p. 45)*   debit *(p. 48)*   posting *(p. 52)*
chart of accounts *(p. 60)*   journal *(p. 50)*   trial balance *(p. 55)*
credit *(p. 48)*   ledger *(p. 45)*

ASSIGNMENT MATERIAL _____

Questions

1. Name the basic summary device of accounting. What letter of the alphabet does it resemble, and what are its two sides called?

2. Is the following statement true or false? Debit means decrease and credit means increase. Explain your answer.

3. Write two sentences that use the term *debit* in different ways.

4. What are the three *basic* types of accounts? Name two additional types of accounts. To which one of the three basic types are these two additional types of accounts most closely related?

5. Suppose you are the accountant for Smith Courier Service. Keeping in mind double-entry bookkeeping, identify the dual effects of Mary Smith's investment of $10,000 cash in her business.

6. Briefly describe the flow of accounting information.

7. To what does the *normal balance* of an account refer?

8. Complete the table by indicating the normal balance of the five types of accounts.

Account Type	Normal Balance
Assets	_____
Liabilities	_____
Capital	_____
Revenues	_____
Expenses	_____

9. What does posting accomplish? Why is it important? Does it come before or after journalizing?

10. Label each of the following transactions as increasing owner's equity (+), decreasing owner's equity (–), or as having no effect on owner's equity (0). Write the appropriate symbol in the space provided.

    ___ Investment by owner   ___ Cash payment on account
    ___ Revenue transaction   ___ Withdrawal by owner
    ___ Purchase of supplies   ___ Borrowing money on a note
        on credit   payable
    ___ Expense transaction   ___ Sale of services on account

11. What four steps does posting include? Which step is the fundamental purpose of posting?

12. Rearrange the following accounts in their logical sequence in the ledger:

    Notes Payable   Cash
    Accounts Receivable   Jane East, Capital
    Sales Revenue   Salary Expense

13. What is the meaning of the statement, Accounts Payable has a credit balance of $1,700?

14. Jack Brown Campus Cleaners launders the shirts of customer Bobby Baylor, who has a charge account at the cleaners. When Bobby picks up his clothes and is short on cash, he charges it. Later, when he receives his monthly statement from the cleaners, Bobby writes a cheque on Dear Old Dad's bank account and mails the cheque to Jack Brown. Identify the two business transactions described here. Which transaction increases Jack Brown's owner's equity? Which transaction increases Jack Brown's cash?

15. Explain the difference between the ledger and the chart of accounts.

16. Why do accountants prepare a trial balance?

17. What is a compound journal entry?

18. The accountant for Bower Construction mistakenly recorded a $500 purchase of supplies on account as a $5,000 purchase. He debited Supplies and credited Accounts Payable for $5,000. Does this error cause the trial balance to be out of balance? Explain your answer.

19. What is the effect on total assets of collecting cash on account from customers?

20. What is the advantage of analyzing and recording transactions without the use of a journal? Describe how this "journal-less" analysis works.

Exercises

Exercise 2-1   *Using accounting vocabulary (L.O. 1)*

The trial balance of Auditron, Inc. lists Cash of $62,100. Write a short memo to explain the accounting process that produced this listing on the trial balance. Mention debits, credits, journals, ledgers, posting, and so on.

Exercise 2-2   *Analyzing and journalizing transactions (L.O. 2,3)*

Analyze the following transactions in the manner shown for the December 1 transaction. Also, record each transaction in the journal.

Dec.   1   Paid monthly rent expense of $1,000. (Analysis: The expense, rent expense, is increased; therefore, debit Rent Expense. The asset, cash, is decreased; therefore credit Cash.)

1	Rent Expense	1,000	
	Cash		1,000

    4   Received $600 cash on account from a customer.
    8   Performed service on account for a customer, $1,100.
    12   Purchased office furniture on account, $810.
    19   Sold for $69,000 land that had cost this same amount.
    24   Purchased building for $140,000; signed a note payable.
    27   Paid the liability created on December 12.

Exercise 2-3   *Journalizing transactions (L.O. 3)*

Vines Consulting Service engaged in the following transactions during March 19X3, its first month of operations:

Mar.   1   John Vines invested $65,000 of cash to start the business.
    2   He purchased supplies of $200 on account.
    4   He paid $25,000 cash for land to use as a future building site.
    6   He performed service for customers and received cash, $2,000.

9   He paid $100 on accounts payable.
17   He performed service for customers on account, $1,600.
23   He received $1,200 cash from a customer on account.
31   He paid the following expenses: salary, $1,200; rent, $500.

Required

Record the preceding transactions in the journal of Vines Consulting Service. Key transactions by date and include an explanation for each entry, as illustrated in the chapter. Use the following accounts: Cash; Accounts Receivable; Office Supplies; Land; Accounts Payable; John Vines, Capital; Service Revenue; Salary Expense; Rent Expense.

Exercise 2-4   *Posting to the ledger and preparing a trial balance* **(L.O. 4,5)**

1. After journalizing the transactions of Exercise 2-3, post the entries to the ledger, using T-account format. Key transactions by date as in the following example. Date the ending balance of each account Mar. 31.

John Vines, Capital

	Mar. 1 65,000

2. Prepare the trial balance of Vines Consulting Service at March 31, 19X3.

Exercise 2-5   *Describing transactions and posting* **(L.O. 3,4)**

The journal of Scholes Company is as follows:

Journal   **Page 5**

Date	Accounts and Explanation	Post Ref.	Debit	Credit
Aug. 5	Cash..		530	
	Sales Revenue....................................			530
9	Supplies		270	
	Accounts Payable			270
11	Accounts Receivable.............................		2,100	
	Sales Revenue....................................			2,100
14	Rent Expense		1,200	
	Cash...			1,200
22	Cash..		1,400	
	Accounts Receivable			1,400
25	Advertising Expense		350	
	Cash...			350
27	Accounts Payable.................................		270	
	Cash...			270
31	Utilities Expense...................................		220	
	Accounts Payable			220

Required

1. Describe each transaction. Example: Aug. 5 — Cash sale.
2. Post the transactions to the ledger using the following account numbers: Cash, 11; Accounts Receivable, 12; Supplies, 13; Accounts Payable, 21; Sales Revenue, 41; Rent Expense, 51; Advertising Expense, 52; Utilities Expense, 53. Use dates, journal references and posting references as illustrated in Exhibit 2-7. You may

write the account numbers as posting references directly in your book unless directed otherwise by your instructor.

3. Compute the balance in each account after posting. The first debit amount of $530 is posted to Cash as an example:

Cash

Aug. 5 J.5 530

Exercise 2-6 *Journalizing transactions (L.O. 4)*

The first five transactions of Rosenthal Security have been posted to the company's accounts as follows:

Cash				**Supplies**		**Equipment**	
(1)	45,000	(3)	42,000	(2)	400	(5)	6,000
(4)	7,000	(5)	6,000				

Land		**Accounts Payable**		**Note Payable**	
(3)	42,000	(2)	400	(4)	7,000

Stu Rosenthal, Capital

(1) 45,000

Required

Prepare the journal entries that served as the sources for the five transactions. Include an explanation for each entry as illustrated in the chapter.

Exercise 2-7 *Preparing a trial balance (L.O. 5)*

Prepare the trial balance of Rosenthal Security at September 30, 19X4, using the account data from the preceding exercise.

Exercise 2-8 *Preparing a trial balance (L.O. 5)*

The accounts of Japra Realty are listed below with their normal balances at September 30, 19X4. The accounts are listed in no particular order.

Account	Balance
Lia Japra, capital	$48,800
Advertising expense	650
Accounts payable	4,300
Sales commission revenue	16,000
Land	23,000
Note payable	25,000
Cash	7,000
Salary expense	6,000
Building	45,000
Rent expense	2,000
Lia Japra, withdrawals	4,000
Utilities expense	400
Accounts receivable	5,500
Supplies expense	300
Supplies	250

[handwritten margin note: List expense Alphabeticaly.]

Required

Prepare the company's trial balance at September 30, 19X4, listing accounts in proper sequence, as illustrated in the chapter. Supplies comes before Building and Land. List the expense with the largest balance first, the expense with the next largest balance second, and so on.

Exercise 2-9   *Correcting errors in a trial balance* **(L.O. 5)**

The trial balance of Thai Enterprises at November 30, 19X9, does not balance.

Cash	$ 4,200	
Accounts receivable	2,000	
Supplies	600	
Land	46,000	
Account payable		$ 3,000
Emily Thai, capital		42,000
Service revenue		4,700
Salary expense	1,700	
Rent expense	800	
Utilities expense	300	
Total	$55,600	$49,700

Investigation of the accounting records reveals that the bookkeeper

a. Recorded a cash revenue transaction by debiting Cash for the correct amount of $5,000 but failed to record the credit to Service Revenue.

b. Posted a $1,000 credit to Accounts Payable as $100.

c. Did not record utilities expense or the related account payable in the amount of $200.

d. Understated Cash and Emily Thai, Capital, by $400 each.

Required

Prepare the correct trial balance at November 30, complete with a heading. Journal entries are not required.

Exercise 2-10   *Recording transactions without a journal* **(L.O. 6)**

Open the following T-accounts: Cash; Accounts Receivable; Office Supplies; Office Furniture; Accounts Payable; Albert Peña, Capital; Albert Peña, Withdrawals; Service Revenue; Salary Expense; Rent Expense.
  Record the following transactions directly in the T-accounts without using a journal. Use the letters to identify the transactions.

a. Albert Peña opened an accounting firm by investing $8,800 cash and office furniture valued at $7,400.

b. Paid monthly rent of $1,500.

c. Purchased office supplies on account, $800.

d. Paid employee salary, $1,800.

e. Paid $400 of the account payable credited in c.

f. Performed accounting service on account, $1,700.

g. Withdrew $2,000 for personal use.

Exercise 2-11   *Preparing a trial balance (L.O. 5)*

After recording the transactions in Exercise 2-10, prepare the trial balance of Albert Peña, CGA, at May 31, 19X7.

Problems   (Group A)

Problem 2-1A   *Analyzing a trial balance (L.O. 1)*

The owner of Wang Service Co. is selling the business. He offers the following trial balance to prospective buyers:

Wang Service Company Trial Balance December 31, 19XX		
Cash	$ 18,000	
Accounts receivable	27,000	
Prepaid expenses	4,000	
Land	81,000	
Accounts payable		$ 41,000
Note payable		32,000
Li-Ping Wang, capital		30,000
Li-Ping Wang, withdrawals	18,000	
Sales revenue		104,000
Rent expense	26,000	
Advertising expense	3,000	
Wage expense	23,000	
Supplies expense	7,000	
Total	$207,000	$207,000

Your best friend is considering buying Wang Service Company. He seeks your advice in interpreting this information. Specifically, he asks whether this trial balance is the same as a balance sheet and an income statement. He also wonders whether Wang is a sound company. He thinks it must be; after all, the accounts are in balance.

Required

Write a short note to answer your friend's questions. To help him decide, state how he can use the information on the trial balance to determine whether Wang has earned a net income or experienced a net loss for the current period.

Problem 2-2A   *Analyzing and journalizing transactions (L.O. 2,3)*

Good Times Theater Company owns movie theaters in the shopping centers of a major metropolitan area. Its owner, Jill Mead, engaged in the following business transactions:

Dec. 1 Mead invested $75,000 personal cash in the business by depositing this amount in a bank account entitled Good Times Theater Company.
    2 Paid $55,000 cash to purchase land for a theater site.
    5 Borrowed $250,000 from the bank to finance the construction of the new theater. Mead signed a note payable to the bank in the name of Good Times Theater Company.
    7 Received $20,000 cash from ticket sales and deposited this amount in the bank. (Label the revenue as Sales Revenue.)
   10 Purchased supplies for the older theaters on account, $1,700.

15   Paid theater employee salaries, $2,800, and rent on a theater building, $1,800.
15   Paid property tax expense on theater building, $1,200.
16   Paid $800 on account.
17   Withdrew $3,000 from the business to take her family to a nearby resort.

Good Times uses the following accounts: Cash; Supplies; Land; Accounts Payable; Notes Payable; Jill Mead, Capital; Jill Mead, Withdrawals; Sales Revenue; Salary Expense; Rent Expense; Property Tax Expense.

Required

1. Prepare an analysis of each business transaction of Good Times Theater Company, as shown for the December 1 transaction:

   Dec. 1   The asset Cash is increased. Increases in assets are recorded by debits; therefore, debit Cash.
   The owner's equity of the entity is increased. Increases in owner's equity are recorded by credits; therefore, credit Jill Mead, Capital.

2. Prepare the journal entry for each transaction. Explanations are not required.

Problem 2-3A   *Journalizing transactions, posting to T-accounts, and preparing a trial balance*
(L.O. 2,3,4,5)

Oliver Goldsmith opened a law office on September 3 of the current year. During the first month of operations, he completed the following transactions:

Sept. 3   Goldsmith transferred $20,000 cash from his personal bank account to a business account entitled Oliver Goldsmith, Lawyer.
       4   Purchased supplies, $200, and furniture, $1,800, on account.
       6   Performed legal services for a client and received $1,000 cash.
       7   Paid $15,000 cash to acquire land for a future office site.
      10   Defended a client in court, billed the client, and received her promise to pay the $900 within one week.
      14   Paid for the furniture purchased September 4 on account.
      15   Paid secretary salary, $600.
      16   Paid the telephone bill, $120.
      17   Received partial payment from client on account, $700.
      20   Prepared legal documents for a client on account, $800.
      24   Paid the water and electricity bills, $110.
      28   Received $1,500 cash for helping a client sell real estate.
      30   Paid secretary salary, $600.
      30   Paid rent expense, $500.
      30   Withdrew $2,000 for personal use.

Required

Open the following T-accounts: Cash; Accounts Receivable; Supplies; Furniture; Land; Accounts Payable; Oliver Goldsmith, Capital; Oliver Goldsmith, Withdrawals; Service Revenue; Salary Expense; Rent Expense; Utilities Expense.

1. Record each transaction in the journal, using the account titles given. Key each transaction by date. Explanations are not required.
2. Post the transactions to the ledger, using transaction dates as posting references in the ledger. Label the balance of each account Bal., as shown in the chapter.
3. Prepare the trial balance of Oliver Goldsmith, Lawyer at September 30 of the current year.

Problem 2-4A   *Journalizing transactions, posting to ledger accounts, and preparing a trial balance* **(L.O. 2,3,4,5)**

The trial balance of the accounting practice of Elizabeth Vanza, CMA is dated February 14, 19X3.

Elizabeth Vanza, CMA
Trial Balance
February 14, 19X3

Account Number	Account	Debit	Credit
11	Cash...	$ 4,000	
12	Accounts Receivable	11,000	
13	Supplies...	800	
14	Land...	18,600	
21	Accounts Payable		$ 3,000
31	Elizabeth Vanza, capital......................		31,000
32	Elizabeth Vanza, withdrawals	1,200	
41	Service revenue.....................................		7,200
51	Salary expense.......................................	3,600	
52	Rent expense	800	
53	Utilities expense....................................	200	
	Total..	$40,200	$40,200

During the remainder of February, Vanza completed the following transactions:

Feb.	15	Vanza collected $2,000 cash from a client on account.
	16	Performed tax services for a client on account, $900.
	18	Paid utilities, $300.
	20	Paid on account, $1,000.
	21	Purchased supplies on account, $100.
	21	Withdrew $1,200 for personal use.
	21	Paid for a swimming pool for private residence, using personal funds, $13,000.
	22	Received cash of $2,100 for consulting work just completed.
	28	Paid rent, $800.
	28	Paid employees' salaries, $1,600.

Required

1. Record the transactions that occurred during February 15 through 28 in page 3 of the journal. Include an explanation for each entry.

2. Open the ledger accounts listed in the trial balance, together with their balances at February 14. Use the account format illustrated below. Enter Bal. (for previous balance) in the Item column, and place a check mark (✓) in the journal reference column for the February 14 balance, as illustrated for Cash:

Account	Cash					Account No. 11	
Date	Item	Jrnl. Ref.	Debit	Credit		Balance	
Feb. 14	Bal.	✓				4,000	Dr.

Post the transactions to the ledger, using dates, account numbers, journal references and posting references.

3. Prepare the trial balance of Elizabeth Vanza, CMA at February 28, 19X3.

Problem 2-5A   *Journalizing, posting to T-accounts and preparing a trial balance* **(L.O. 2,3,4,5)**

Dwyer Delivery Service completed the following transactions during its first month of operations:

a. Paul Dwyer, the proprietor of the business, began operations by investing in the business $5,000 cash and a truck valued at $10,000.

b. Paid $200 cash for supplies.

c. Used a company credit card to purchase $50 fuel for the delivery truck. (Credit Accounts Payable).

d. Performed delivery services for a customer and received $600 cash.

e. Completed a large delivery job, billed the customer $2,000, and received a promise to be paid the $2,000 within one week.

f. Paid employee salary, $800.

g. Received $900 cash for performing delivery services.

h. Purchased fuel for the truck on account, $40.

i. Received $2,000 cash from a customer on account.

j. Paid for advertising in the local newspaper, $170.

k. Paid utility bills, $100.

l. Purchased fuel for the truck, paying $30 with a company credit card.

m. Performed delivery services on account, $800.

n. Paid for repairs to the delivery truck, $110.

o. Paid employee salary, $800, and office rent, $200.

p. Paid $120 on account.

q. Withdrew $1,900 for personal use.

Required

1. Record each transaction in the journal, using the account titles given. Key each transaction by letter. Explanations are not required.

2. Open the following T-accounts: Cash; Accounts Receivable; Supplies; Delivery Truck; Accounts Payable; Paul Dwyer, Capital; Paul Dwyer, Withdrawals; Delivery Service Revenue; Salary Expense; Rent Expense; Advertising Expense; Fuel Expense; Repair Expense; Utilities Expense. Post the transactions to the ledger, keying transactions by letter. Label the balance of each account Bal., as shown in the chapter.

3. Prepare the trial balance of Dwyer Delivery Service, using the current date.

Problem 2-6A   *Correcting errors in a trial balance* **(L.O. 2,5)**

The following trial balance does not balance:

Samaritan Counseling Services
Trial Balance
June 30, 19X2

Cash	$ 2,000
Accounts receivable	10,000
Supplies	900

Office furniture...	3,600	
Land...	26,000	
Accounts payable....................................		$4,000
Note payable..		14,000
Carmen Cathay, capital..........................		22,000
Carmen Cathay, withdrawals.................	2,000	
Counseling service revenue		6,500
Salary expense...	1,600	
Rent expense..	1,000	
Advertising expense...............................	500	
Utilities expense.....................................	300	
Property tax expense	100	
Total...	$48,000	$46,500

The following errors were detected:

a. The cash balance is understated by $300.

b. A property tax payment of $500 was not recorded.

c. Land should be listed in the amount of $24,000.

d. A $200 purchase of supplies on account was neither journalized nor posted.

e. A $2,800 credit to Counselling Service Revenue was not posted.

f. Rent Expense of $200 was posted as a credit rather than a debit.

g. The balance of Advertising Expense is $600, but it was listed as $500 on the trial balance.

h. A $300 debit to Accounts Receivable was posted as $30.

i. The balance of Utilities Expense is overstated by $70.

j. A $900 debit to the Withdrawal account was posted as a credit to Carmen Cathay, Capital.

Required

Prepare the correct trial balance at June 30. Journal entries are not required.

Problem 2-7A   *Recording transactions directly in the ledger; preparing a trial balance* **(L.O. 2,5,6)**

Diana Flori started a consulting service and during the first month of operations completed the following selected transactions:

a. Flori began the business with an investment of $15,000 cash and a building valued at $60,000.

b. Borrowed $30,000 from the bank; signed a note payable.

c. Purchased office supplies on account, $1,300.

d. Paid $18,000 for office furniture.

e. Paid employee salary, $2,200.

f. Performed consulting service on account for client, $2,100.

g. Paid $800 of the account payable created in c.

h. Received a $900 bill for advertising expense that will be paid in the near future.

i. Performed consulting service for customers and received cash, $1,600.

j. Received cash on account, $1,200.

k. Paid the following cash expenses:

    (1) Rent on land, $700.

    (2) Utilities, $400.

l. Withdrew $3,500 for personal use.

Required

1. Open the following T-accounts: Cash; Accounts Receivable; Office Supplies; Office Furniture; Building; Accounts Payable; Note Payable; Diana Flori, Capital; Diana Flori, Withdrawals; Service Revenue; Salary Expense; Advertising Expense; Rent Expense; Utilities Expense.

2. Record each transaction directly in the T-accounts without using a journal. Use the letters to identify the transactions.

3. Prepare the trial balance of Flori Consulting Service at June 30, 19X3.

(Group B)

Problem 2-1B   *Analyzing a trial balance* **(L.O. 1)**

The owner of McBee Service Company is selling the business. She offers the following trial balance to prospective buyers.

McBee Service Company Trial Balance December 31, 19XX		
Cash	$ 4,000	
Accounts receivable	11,000	
Prepaid expenses	4,000	
Land	31,000	
Accounts payable		$ 31,000
Note Payable		20,000
Laura McBee, capital		30,000
Laura McBee, withdrawals	21,000	
Sales revenue		47,000
Rent expense	14,000	
Advertising expense	3,000	
Wage expense	33,000	
Supplies expense	7,000	
Totals	$128,000	$128,000

Your best friend is considering buying McBee Service Company. He seeks your advice in interpreting this information. Specifically, he asks whether this trial balance is the same as a balance sheet and an income statement. He also wonders whether McBee is a sound company. He thinks it must be; after all, the accounts are in balance.

Required

Write a short note to answer your friend's questions. To help him decide, state how he can use the information on the trial balance to determine whether McBee has earned a net income or experienced a net loss for the current period.

Problem 2-2B   *Analyzing and journalizing transactions* **(L.O. 2,3)**

Lee Quinius practices dentistry under the business title Lee Quinius, D.D.S. During April his dental practice engaged in the following transactions:

Apr. 1   Quinius deposited $75,000 cash in the business bank account.
      5   Paid monthly rent on dental equipment, $700.
      9   Paid $42,000 cash to purchase land for an office site.

10	Purchased supplies on account, $1,200.
19	Paid $1,000 on account.
30	Revenues earned during the month included $6,000 cash and $5,000 on account.
30	Paid employee salaries ($2,400), office rent ($1,500), and utilities ($400).
30	Borrowed $20,000 from the bank for business use. Quinius signed a note payable to the bank in the name of the business.
30	Withdrew $4,000 from the business to take his family on a trip.

Quinius's business uses the following accounts: Cash; Accounts Receivable; Supplies; Land; Accounts Payable; Notes Payable; Lee Quinius, Capital; Lee Quinius, Withdrawals; Service Revenue; Salary Expense; Rent Expense; Utilities Expense.

Required

1. Prepare an analysis of each business transaction of Lee Quinius, D.D.S., as shown for the April 1 transaction;

> Apr. 1   The asset Cash is increased. Increases in assets are recorded by debits; therefore, debit Cash.
> The owner's equity is increased. Increases in owner's equity are recorded by credits; therefore, credit Lee Quinius, Capital.

2. Prepare the journal entry for each transaction. Explanations are not required.

Problem 2-3B   *Journalizing transactions, posting to T-accounts, and preparing a trial balance*
    (L.O. 2,3,4,5)

Marie Haley opened a law office on January 2 of the current year. During the first month of operations the business completed the following transactions:

Jan.	2	Haley deposited $40,000 cash in a business bank account entitled Marie Haley, Lawyer.
	3	Purchased supplies, $500, and furniture, $2,600, on account.
	4	Performed legal services for a client and received cash, $1,500.
	7	Paid cash to acquire land for a future office site, $22,000.
	11	Defended a client in court, billed the client, and received his promise to pay the $800 within one week.
	15	Paid secretary salary, $650.
	16	Paid for the furniture purchased January 3 on account.
	17	Paid the telephone bill, $110.
	18	Received partial payment from client on account, $400.
	19	Prepared legal documents for a client on account, $600.
	22	Paid the water and electricity bills, $130.
	29	Received $1,800 cash for helping a client sell real estate.
	31	Paid secretary salary, $650.
	31	Paid rent expense, $700.
	31	Withdrew $2,200 for personal use.

Required

Open the following T-accounts: Cash; Accounts Receivable; Supplies; Furniture; Land; Accounts Payable; Marie Haley, Capital; Marie Haley, Withdrawals; Service Revenue; Salary Expense; Rent Expense; Utilities Expense.

1. Record each transaction in the journal, using the account titles given. Key each transaction by date. Explanations are not required.

2. Post the transactions to the ledger, using transaction dates as posting references in the ledger. Label the balance of each account Bal. as shown in the chapter.

3. Prepare the trial balance of Marie Haley, Lawyer at January 31 of the current year.

Problem 2-4B *Journalizing transactions, posting to ledger accounts, and preparing a trial balance* **(L.O. 2,3,4,5)**

The trial balance of the accounting practice of William Pittenger, CA at November 15, 19X3 is shown below.

William Pittenger, CA
Trial Balance
November 15, 19X3

Account Number	Account	Debit	Credit
11	Cash	$ 5,000	
12	Accounts receivable.............................	8,000	
13	Supplies...	600	
14	Land..	35,000	
21	Accounts payable.................................		$ 4,400
31	William Pittenger, capital....................		42,000
32	William Pittenger, withdrawals..........	2,100	
41	Service revenue		7,100
51	Salary expense......................................	1,800	
52	Rent expense..	700	
53	Utilities expense...................................	300	
	Total	$53,500	$53,500

During the remainder of November, Pittenger completed the following transactions:

Nov. 16	Collected $4,000 cash from a client on account.
17	Performed tax services for a client on account, $1,700.
19	Paid utilities, $200.
21	Paid on account, $2,600.
22	Purchased supplies on account, $200.
23	Withdrew $2,100 for personal use.
23	Paid for the renovation of private residence, $55,000.
24	Received $1,900 cash for audit work just completed.
30	Paid rent, $700.
30	Paid employees' salaries, $1,800.

Required

1. Record the transactions that occurred during November 16 through 30 in page 6 of the journal. Include an explanation for each entry.

2. Post the transactions to the ledger, using dates, account numbers, journal references and posting references. Open the ledger accounts listed in the trial balance together with their balances at November 15. Use the account format illustrated below. Enter Bal. (for previous balance) in the Item column, and place a check mark (✓) in the journal reference column for the November 15 balance, as illustrated for Cash:

Account	Cash					Account No. 11	
Date	Item	Jrnl. Ref.	Debit	Credit		Balance	
Nov. 15	Bal.	✓				5,000	Dr.

3. Prepare the trial balance of William Pittenger, CA at November 30, 19X3.

Problem 2-5B   *Journalizing, posting to T-accounts, and preparing a trial balance* **(L.O. 2,3,4,5)**

Steakley Delivery Service began operations during May of the current year. During a short period thereafter, the entity engaged in the following transactions:

a. Lou Steakley, the owner, deposited $3,500 cash in a bank account entitled Steakley Delivery Service and also invested in the business a delivery truck valued at $8,000.
b. Purchased $40 fuel for the delivery truck, using a business credit card.
c. Paid $100 cash for supplies.
d. Completed a delivery job and received cash, $700.
e. Performed delivery services on account, $3,200.
f. Purchased advertising leaflets for cash, $200.
g. Paid the office manager salary, $950.
h. Received $1,000 cash for performing delivery services.
i. Received cash from customer on account, $1,800.
j. Purchased used office furniture on account, $600.
k. Paid office utility bills, $120.
l. Purchased $70 fuel on account for the truck.
m. Completed a delivery job and received the customer's promise to pay the amount due, $100, within ten days.
n. Paid cash to creditor on account, $200.
o. Paid $250 for repairs to the delivery truck.
p. Paid office manager the salary of $950 and office rent of $250.
q. Withdrew $1,900 for personal use.

Required

1. Record each transaction in the journal, using the account titles given. Key each transaction by letter. Explanations are not required.
2. Open the following T-accounts: Cash; Accounts Receivable; Supplies; Delivery Truck; Office Furniture; Accounts Payable; Lou Steakley, Capital; Lou Steakley, Withdrawals; Delivery Service Revenue; Salary Expense; Rent Expense; Repair Expense; Advertising Expense; Utilities Expense; Fuel Expense. Post the transactions to the ledger, keying transactions by letter. Label the balance of each account Bal. as shown in the chapter.
3. Prepare the trial balance of Steakley Delivery Service using the current date.

Problem 2-6B   *Correcting errors in a trial balance* **(L.O. 2,5)**

The trial balance in this problem, shown on the next page, does not balance. The following errors were detected:

a. The cash balance is understated by $400.

b. Office maintenance expense of $200 is omitted from the trial balance.

c. Rent expense of $200 was posted as a credit rather than a debit.

d. The balance of Advertising Expense is $300, but it is listed as $400 on the trial balance.

e. A $600 debit to Accounts Receivable was posted as $60.

f. The balance of Utilities Expense is understated by $60.

g. A $500 debit to the withdrawal account was posted as a credit to Laura Hewitt, Capital.

h. A $100 purchase of supplies on account was neither journalized nor posted.

i. A $5,600 credit to Service Revenue was not posted.

j. Office furniture should be listed in the amount of $1,300.

Hewitt Speed & Marine		
Trial Balance		
October 31, 19X1		
Cash	$ 3,800	
Accounts receivable	2,000	
Supplies	500	
Office furniture	2,300	
Land	46,800	
Accounts payable		$ 2,000
Note payable		18,300
Laura Hewitt, capital		32,100
Laura Hewitt, withdrawals	3,700	
Service revenue		4,900
Salary expense	1,000	
Rent expense	600	
Advertising expense	400	
Utilities expense	200	
Property tax	100	
Total	$61,400	$57,300

Required

Prepare the correct trial balance at October 31. Journal entries are not required.

Problem 2-7B *Recording transactions directly in the ledger; preparing a trial balance* **(L.O. 2,5,6)**

Ken Mazanec started a cable television service and during the first month of operations completed the following selected transactions:

a. Mazanec began the business with an investment of $30,000 cash and a building valued at $50,000.

b. Borrowed $25,000 from the bank; signed a note payable.

c. Paid $32,000 for transmitting equipment.

d. Purchased office supplies on account, $400.

e. Paid employee salary, $1,300.

f. Received $500 for cable TV service performed for customers.

g. Sold cable service to customers on account, $2,300.

h. Paid $100 of the account payable created in d.

    i. Received a $600 bill for utility expense that will be paid in the near future.

    j. Received cash on account, $1,100.

    k. Paid the following cash expenses:

        (1) Rent on land, $1,000.

        (2) Advertising, $800.

    l. Withdrew $2,600 for personal use.

Required

1. Open the following T-accounts: Cash; Accounts Receivable; Office Supplies; Transmitting Equipment; Building; Accounts Payable; Note Payable; Ken Mazanec, Capital; Ken Mazanec, Withdrawals; Service Revenue; Salary Expense; Rent Expense; Advertising Expense; Utilities Expense.

2. Record the following transactions directly in the T-accounts without using a journal. Use the letters to identify the transactions.

3. Prepare the trial balance of Mazanec Cable TV Service at January 31, 19X7.

Extending Your Knowledge

Decision Problems

1. Recording transactions directly in the ledger, preparing a trial balance, and measuring net income or loss (L.O. 2,5,6)

You have been requested by a friend named Charles Sligh to give advice on the effects that certain business transactions will have on the entity he plans to start. Time is short, so you will not be able to do all the detailed procedures of journalizing and posting. Instead, you must analyze the transactions without the use of a journal. Sligh will continue in the business only if he can expect to earn monthly net income of $3,500. Assume the following transactions have occurred:

    a. Sligh deposited $6,000 cash in a business bank account.

    b. Borrowed $4,000 cash from the bank and signed a note payable due within one year.

    c. Paid $300 cash for supplies.

    d. Purchased advertising in the local newspaper for cash, $800.

    e. Purchased office furniture on account, $1,500.

    f. Paid the following cash expenses for one month: secretary salary, $1,400; office rent, $400; utilities, $300; interest, $50.

    g. Earned revenue on account $4,300.

    h. Earned revenue and received $2,500 cash.

    i. Collected cash from customers on account, $1,200.

    j. Paid on account, $1,000.

    k. Withdrew $900 for personal use.

Required

1. Open the following T-accounts: Cash; Accounts Receivable; Supplies; Furniture; Accounts Payable; Notes Payable; Charles Sligh, Capital; Charles Sligh,

Withdrawals; Service Revenue; Salary Expense; Advertising Expense; Rent Expense; Utilities Expense; Interest Expense.

2. Record the transactions directly in the accounts without using a journal. Key each transaction by letter.

3. Prepare a trial balance at the current date. List expenses with the largest amount first, the next largest second, and so on. The business name will be Sligh Apartment Locators.

4. Compute the amount of net income or net loss for this first month of operations. Would you recommend Sligh continue in business?

2. Using the accounting equation (L.O. 2)

Although all the following questions deal with the accounting equation, they are not related:

1. Explain the advantages of double-entry bookkeeping over single-entry book-keeping to a friend who is opening a used-book store.

2. When you deposit money in your bank account, the bank credits your account. Is the bank misusing the word credit in this context? Why does the bank use the term credit to refer to your deposit, and not debit?

3. Your friend asks, "When revenues increase assets and expenses decrease assets, why are revenues credits and expenses debits and not the other way around?" Explain to your friend why revenues are credits and expenses are debits.

Ethical Issue

Community Charities, a charitable organization in Sudbury, Ontario, has a stand-ing agreement with Canada Trust. The agreement allows Community Charities to overdraw its cash balance at the bank when donations are running low. In the past, Community Charities managed funds wisely and rarely used this privilege. Greg Osborn has recently become the president of Community Charities. To expand op-erations, Osborn is acquiring office equipment and spending large amounts for fund-raising. During his presidency, Community Charities has maintained a neg-ative bank balance of approximately $1,000.

Required

What is the ethical issue in this situation? State why you approve or disapprove of Osborn's management of Community Charities funds.

Financial Statement Problems

1. Journalizing transactions (L.O. 2,3)

This problem helps to develop skill in recording by using an actual company's ac-count titles. Refer to the Schneider Corporation's financial statements in Appendix C. Assume Schneider completed the following selected transactions during August, 1991:

Aug. 5 Earned sales revenues on account, $1,500,000.
     9 Borrowed $5,000,000 by signing a note payable (debentures and loans).
    12 Purchased equipment on account, $9,000,000.
    17 Paid $1,200,000, which represents payment of $1,000,000 on deben-tures and loans plus interest expense of $200,000.
    19 Earned sales revenues and immediately received cash of $500,000.

22 Collected the cash on account that was earned on August 5.

24 Paid operating lease rental of $1,300,000, for three months in advance.

29 Received a home-office electricity bill for $150,000, which will be paid in September. (This is a selling, marketing, and administrative expense.)

30 Paid half the account payable created on August 12.

Required

Journalize these transactions using the following account titles taken from the financial statements of Schneider: Accounts Receivable; Inventories; Other (which includes Prepaid Expenses); Property, Plant and Equipment Bank Advances (Instead of showing Cash as an asset, Schneider has netted [deducted] the balance of Cash [a debit] from Bank Advances [a credit] to show a smaller balance in the latter: note that no Cash account appears on the Balance Sheet); Accounts Payable; Debentures and Loans; Sales; Cost of Products Sold, Selling, Marketing and Administrative; Interest. Explanations are not required.

2. Journalizing transactions (L.O. 2,3)

Obtain the annual report of an actual company of your choosing. Assume the company completed the following selected transactions during May of the current year:

May 3 Borrowed $350,000 by signing a short-term note payable (may be called short-term debt or other account title).

5 Paid rent for six months in advance, $4,600.

9 Earned revenue on account, $74,000.

12 Purchased equipment on account, $33,000.

17 Paid a telephone bill, $300 (this is a Selling Expense).

19 Paid $90,000 of the money borrowed on May 3.

26 Collected one half of the cash on account from May 9.

30 Paid the account payable from May 12.

Required

Journalize these transactions using account titles from the financial statements in the annual report you have chosen. If no account title is suggested, develop an appropriate title yourself.

Answers to Self-Study Questions

1. a	6. a
2. b	7. a
3. c	8. b ($6,800 = $2,500 + $4,300)
4. d	9. b
5. c	10. d

Chapter 3

Measuring Business Income:
The Adjusting Process

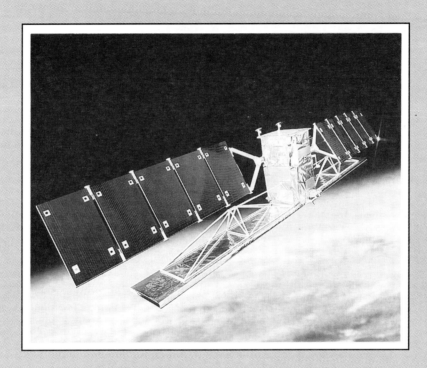

Dipix Systems Ltd., an Ottawa based manufacturer of satellite remote-sensing systems, is a classic example of how a business's income can go from boom to bust (but fortunately recover again).

In 1984, Dipix had sales of $4.2 million. Over the next two years annual sales rocketed to $10.2 million, but in 1987 they fell to $3 million. Similarly, income varied substantially over the years; even while sales were rocketing, in 1985 it reported a $700,000 loss, and in 1986, an income of only $200,000. By October, 1987, without the funds to repay creditors, Dipix was in receivership. Two of the original executives were able to buy most of the assets of Dipix from the receivers for $1 million, and changed the company's name to Dipix Technologies Inc. By 1990, the new Dipix was back on its feet; sales were $4.3 million, and the company showed a profit of $500,000.

Every day in the newspaper there is mention of the income (or loss) of some company. However, the way we use the term "income" for our personal affairs differs somewhat from the financial accounting determination of income. We tend to consider income relative to money-in-the-bank, or cash flow. Accountants, as you will see, use a different method.

As you read this chapter, ensure that you appreciate why your personal cash basis of accounting is appropriate for your purposes, but that the accrual basis is the only correct method, in the long run, for measuring a business's income. The immediate cause of Dipix's problems in 1987 was not so much the absence of income, but the absence of cash.

Source: John Southerst, "Curse of the Vanishing Contracts," *Profit* (October 1991), p. 24.

The primary goal of business is to earn a profit. Many companies such as Dipix Systems expect to earn increasing amounts of profit each year. When they do, they expand the business, hire more employees, and make their owners happy. When profits fail to meet goals, the results can be layoffs, idle facilities, and unhappy owners.

Gary Lyon, the lawyer whose law practice we discussed in the earlier chapters, earns business income by providing legal services for clients. Regardless of the type of activity, the profit motive increases the owner's drive to carry on the business. As you read Chapter 3, consider how important accounting procedures are in measuring income.

At the end of each accounting period, the accountant prepares the entity's financial statements. The period may be a month, three months, six months or a full year. Whatever the length of the period, the end accounting product is the same — the financial statements. A very important amount in these statements insofar as owners, managers, employees, creditors, Revenue Canada, and all the other users of the financial statements are concerned is the net income or net loss — the profit or loss — for the period. A double-entry accounting system produces not only the income statement but the other financial statements as well.

An important step in financial statement preparation is the trial balance that we discussed in Chapter 2. The trial balance includes the effects of the transactions that occurred during the period: the cash collections, purchases of assets, payments of bills, sales of assets and so on. To measure its income properly, however, a business must do some additional accounting at the end of the period to bring the records up to date before preparing the financial statements. This process is called *adjusting the books*. It consists of making special entries called *adjusting entries*. This chapter focuses primarily on these adjusting entries to help you better understand the nature of business income.

Accountants have devised concepts and principles to guide the measurement of business income. Chief among these are the concepts of accrual accounting, the accounting period, the revenue principle and the matching principle. In this chapter, we apply these concepts and principles to measure the income and prepare the financial statements of Gary Lyon's business for the month of April.

Accrual-Basis Accounting versus Cash-Basis Accounting

OBJECTIVE 1

Distinguish accrual-basis accounting from cash-basis accounting

There are two widely used bases of accounting: the accrual basis and cash basis. In **accrual-basis accounting**, an accountant recognizes the impact of a business event as it occurs. When the business performs a service, makes a sale or incurs an expense, the accountant enters the transaction into the books, whether or not cash has been received or paid. In **cash-basis accounting**, however, the accountant does not record a transaction until cash is received or paid. Cash receipts are treated as revenues and cash disbursements are handled as expenses.

GAAP requires that a business use the accrual basis. This means that the accountant records revenues as they are earned and expenses as they are incurred — not necessarily when cash changes hands.

Using accrual-basis accounting, Gary Lyon records revenue when he performs services for a client on account. Lyon has earned the revenue at that time because his efforts have generated an account receivable, a legal claim against the client for whom he did the work. By contrast, if Gary Lyon used cash-basis accounting, he would not record revenue at the time he performed the service. He would wait until he received cash.

Why does GAAP require that businesses use the accrual basis? What advantage does accrual-basis accounting offer? Suppose Gary Lyon's accounting period ends after he has earned the revenue, but before he has collected the money due him. If he used the cash-basis method, his financial statements would not include this revenue or the related account receivable. As a result, the financial statements would be misleading. Revenue and the asset Accounts Receivable would be understated, and thus his business would look less successful than it actually is. If he wants to get a bank loan to expand his practice, the understated revenue and asset figures might hurt his chances.

Gary Lyon, using accrual-basis accounting, treats expenses in a like manner. For instance, salary expense includes amounts paid to employees plus any amount owed to employees but not yet paid. Lyon's use of the employee's service, not the payment of cash to the employee, brings about the expense. Under cash-basis accounting, Lyon would record the expense only when he actually paid the employee.

Suppose Gary Lyon owes his secretary a salary payment, and the financial statements are drawn up before Lyon pays. Expenses and liabilities would be understated, so that the business would look more successful than it really is. This incomplete information would not provide an accurate accounting to potential creditors.

As these examples show, accrual accounting provides more complete information than does cash-basis accounting. This is important because the more complete the data, the better equipped decision-makers are to reach intelligent conclusions about the firm's financial health and future prospects. Three concepts used in accrual accounting are the accounting period, the revenue principle and the matching principle.

The Accounting Period

The only way to know for certain how successfully a business has operated is to close its doors, sell all its assets, pay the liabilities, and return any leftover cash to the owner. This process, called *liquidation*, is the same as going out of business. Obviously, it is not practical for accountants to measure business income in this manner. Instead, businesses need periodic reports on their progress. Accountants slice time into small segments and prepare financial statements for specific periods. Until a business liquidates, the amounts reported in its financial statements must be regarded as estimates.

The most basic accounting period is one year, and virtually all businesses prepare annual financial statements. For about 60 percent of companies in a recent Canadian survey, the annual accounting period or *fiscal year* runs the calendar year from January 1 through December 31. The other companies in the survey use a fiscal year ending on some date other than December 31. The year-end date is usually the low point in business activity for the year. Depending on the type of business, the fiscal year may end on April 30, July 31 or some other date. Retailers are a notable example. Traditionally, they have used a fiscal year ending on January 31, because the low point in their business activity has followed the after-Christmas sales during January; Woodward's Ltd. of Vancouver and Hudson's Bay Co. of Toronto are two examples.

Companies cannot wait until the end of the year to gauge their progress. The manager of a business wants to know how well the business is doing each month, each quarter and each half year. Outsiders such as lenders also demand current information about the business. So companies also prepare financial statements for *interim* periods, which are less than a year. Monthly financial statements are common, and a series of monthly statements can be combined for quarterly and semiannual periods. Most of the discussions in this book are based on an annual accounting period. However, the procedures and statements can also be applied to interim periods as well.

Revenue Principle

The **revenue principle** tells accountants (1) *when* to record revenue, and (2) the *amount* of revenue to record. When we speak of "recording" something in accounting, the act of recording the item naturally leads to posting to the ledger accounts and preparing the trial balance and the financial statements. Although the financial statements are the end product of accounting and what accountants are most concerned about, our discussions often focus on recording the entry in the journal because that is where the accounting process starts.

The general principle guiding when to record revenue is that revenue should be recorded as it has been earned — but not before. In most cases, revenue is earned when the business has delivered a completed good or service to the customer. The business has done everything required by the agreement, including transferring the item to the customer. Two situations that provide guidance on when to record revenue follow. The first situation illustrates when *not* to record revenue, and the second situation illustrates when revenue should be recorded.

Situation 1: Do not record revenue.   A client of one public accounting firm expresses her intention to transfer her tax work to another firm. Should the second firm record any revenue based on this intention? The answer is no because no transaction has occurred.

OBJECTIVE 2

Apply the revenue and matching principles

Situation 2: Record revenue.   Next month the second public accounting firm consults with this client and tailors a business plan to her goals. After transferring the business plan to the client, the firm should should record revenue. If the client pays for this service immediately, the firm will debit Cash. If the service is performed on account, the firm will debit Accounts Receivable. In either case, the second public accounting firm should record revenue by crediting the Service Revenue account.

The general principle guiding the amount of revenue to record is record revenue equal to the cash value of the goods or the service transferred to the customer. Suppose that in order to obtain a new client, Gary Lyon performs legal service for the cut-rate price of $500. Ordinarily, Lyon would have charged $600 for this service. How much revenue should Lyon record? The answer is $500 because that was the cash value of the transaction. Lyon will not receive the full value of $600, so that is not the amount of revenue to record. He will receive only $500 cash, and that pinpoints the amount of revenue earned.

Matching Principle

The **matching principle** is the basis for recording expenses. Recall that expenses, such as rent, utilities, and advertising, are the costs of operating a business. Expenses are the costs of assets and services that are used up in the earning of revenue. The matching principle directs accountants (1) to identify all expenses incurred during the accounting period, (2) to measure the expenses, and (3) to "match" them against the revenues earned during that same span of time. To "match" expenses against revenues means to subtract the expenses from the revenues in order to compute net income or net loss.

There is a natural link between revenues and some types of expenses. Accountants follow the matching principle by first identifying the revenues of a period and the expenses that can be linked to particular revenues. For example, a business that pays sales commissions to its sales persons will have commission expense if the employees make sales. If they make no sales, the business has no commission expense. Cost of goods sold is another example. When merchandise is sold, there must also be a cost — the cost incurred by the seller — assigned to the goods sold. If there are no sales, there can be no cost of goods sold.

Other expenses are not so easy to link with particular sales. Monthly rent expense occurs, for example, regardless of the revenues earned during the period. The matching principle directs accountants to identify these types of expenses with a particular time period, such as a month or a year. If Gary Lyon employs a secretary at a monthly salary of $1,900, the business will record salary expense of $1,900 each month. Because financial statements appear at definite intervals, there must be some cutoff date for the necessary information. Most entities engage in so many transactions that some are bound to spill over into more than a single accounting period. Gary Lyon prepares a monthly statement for his business at April 30. How does he handle a transaction that begins in April but ends in May? How does he bring the accounts up to date for preparing the financial statements? To answer these questions, accountants use adjusting entries.

Time-Period Concept

Managers, investors and creditors make decisions daily and need periodic readings on the business's progress. To meet this need for information, accountants prepare financial statements at regular intervals. Virtually all companies report net income for an annual period and their assets, liabilities, and owner's equity at the end of the year. Most companies also prepare monthly and quarterly financial statements.

The **time-period concept** ensures that accounting information is reported at regular intervals. It interacts with the revenue principle and matching principle to underlie the use of accruals. To measure income accurately, companies update the revenue and expense accounts immediately prior to the end of the period. For example, Finning Ltd., who sells Caterpillar earthmoving equipment, has a December 31 year end. When December 31 falls during a pay period (say, December 31, 1992 is on a Thursday, and Finning pays its employees weekly on Friday), the company must record the employee compensation owed to the workers for unpaid services performed up to and including December 31. Assume weekly salary and wages expense for Finning is $2,300,000; the entry would be ($\frac{4}{5} \times $2,300,000 = $1,840,000):

1992			
Dec. 31	Salary and Wages Expense	1,840,000	
	Salary and Wages Payable.....................		1,840,000

This entry serves two purposes. It assigns the expense to the proper period. Without the accrual entry at December 31, total expenses for 1992 would be understated, and as a result, net income would be overstated. Incorrectly, the expense would fall in 1993 when Finning makes the next payroll disbursement. The accrual entry also records the liability for reporting on the balance sheet at December 31, 1992. Without the accrual entry, total liabilities would be understated.

At the end of the accounting period, companies also accrue revenues that have been earned but not collected. The remainder of the chapter discusses how to make the necessary adjustments to the accounts.

Adjustments to the Accounts

At the end of the period, the accountant prepares the financial statements. This end-of-the-period process begins with the trial balance that lists the accounts and their balances after the period's transactions have been recorded in the journal and posted to the accounts in the ledger. Exhibit 3-1 is the trial balance of Gary Lyon's law practice at April 30, 19X1.

This *unadjusted* trial balance includes some new accounts that will be explained in this section. It lists most, but not all, of the revenue accounts and the expenses of Lyon's legal practice for the month of April. These trial balance amounts are incomplete because they omit certain revenue and expense transactions that affect more than one accounting period. That is why it is called an *unadjusted* trial balance. In most cases, however, we refer to it simply as the trial balance, without the "unadjusted" label.

Under the cash basis of accounting, there would be no need for adjustments to the accounts because all April cash transactions would have been recorded. The accrual basis requires adjusting entries at the end of the period in order to produce correct balances for the financial statements. To see why, consider the Supplies account in Exhibit 3-1.

Lyon's law practice uses supplies in providing legal services for clients during the month. This reduces the quantity of supplies on hand and thus constitutes an expense, just like salary expense or rent expense. Gary Lyon does not bother to record his daily expense, and it is not worth his while to record supplies expense more than once a month. It is time-consuming to make hourly, daily or even weekly journal entries to record the expense incurred by the use of supplies. So how does he account for supplies expense?

By the end of the month, the Supplies balance is not correct. The balance represents the amount of supplies on hand at the start of the month plus any supplies purchased during the month. This balance fails to take into account the supplies used

EXHIBIT 3-1 *Unadjusted Trial Balance*

Gary Lyon, Lawyer Unadjusted Trial Balance April 30, 19X1		
Cash	$24,800	
Accounts receivable	2,250	
Supplies	700	
Prepaid rent	3,000	
Furniture	16,500	
Accounts payable		$13,100
Unearned service revenue		450
Gary Lyon, capital		31,250
Gary Lyon, withdrawals	3,200	
Service revenue		7,000
Salary expense	950	
Utilities expense	400	
Total	$51,800	$51,800

(supplies expense) during the accounting period. It is necessary, then, to subtract the month's expenses from the amount of supplies listed on the trial balance. The resulting new adjusted balance measures the cost of supplies that are still on hand at April 30. This is the correct amount of supplies to report on the balance sheet. Adjusting entries in this way brings the accounts up to date.

Adjusting entries assign revenues to the period in which they are earned and expenses to the period in which they are incurred. They are needed (1) to measure properly the period's income, and (2) to bring related asset and liability accounts to correct balances for the financial statements. For example, an adjusting entry is needed to transfer the amount of supplies used during the period from the asset account Supplies to the expense account Supplies Expense. The adjusting entry updates both the Supplies asset account and the Supplies Expense account. This achieves accurate measures of assets and expenses. Adjusting entries, which are the key to the accrual basis of accounting, are made before preparing the financial statements.

The end-of-period process of updating the accounts is called *adjusting the accounts, making the adjusting entries,* or *adjusting the books.* Adjusting entries can be divided into five categories:

1. Prepaid expenses
2. Depreciation
3. Accrued expenses
4. Accrued revenues
5. Unearned revenues

Some accountants would combine categories 1 and 2, and have only four categories of adjusting entries. They would argue that a fixed asset is a form of prepaid expense, and that depreciation expense reflects the depletion of prepaid expense.

Prepaid Expenses

Prepaid expenses is a category of miscellaneous assets that typically expire or are used up in the near future. Prepaid rent, prepaid insurance, and supplies are examples of prepaid expenses. They are called prepaid expenses because they are expenses that are paid in advance. Salary expense and utilities expense, among others, are *not* prepaid expenses because they are not paid in advance.

Prepaid Rent Landlords usually require tenants to pay rent in advance. This prepayment creates an asset for the renter, because that person has purchased the future benefit of using the rented item. Suppose Gary Lyon prepays three months' rent on April 1, 19X1, after negotiating a lease for the office of his law practice. If the lease specifies monthly rental amounts of $1,000 each, the entry to record the payment for three months is a debit to the asset account, Prepaid Rent, as follows:

Apr. 1	Prepaid Rent ($1,000 × 3)	3,000	
	Cash		3,000
	Paid three months' rent in advance.		

After posting, Prepaid Rent appears as follows:

Prepaid Rent

Apr. 1	3,000

The trial balance at April 30, 19X1 lists Prepaid Rent as an asset with a debit balance of $3,000. Throughout April, the Prepaid Rent account maintains this beginning balance, as shown in Exhibit 3-1.

At April 30, Prepaid Rent should be adjusted to remove from its balance the amount of the asset that has expired, which is one month's worth of the prepayment. By definition, the amount of an asset that has expired is *expense*. This adjusting entry transfers one third, or $1,000 ($3,000 × ⅓), of the debit balance from Prepaid Rent to Rent Expense. The debit side of the entry records an increase in Rent Expense and the credit records a decrease in the asset Prepaid Rent.

OBJECTIVE 3

Make the typical adjusting entries at the end of the accounting period

Apr. 30	Rent Expense ($3,000 × ⅓)	1,000
	Prepaid Rent	1,000
	To record rent expense.	

After posting, Prepaid Rent and Rent Expense appear as follows:

Prepaid Rent					**Rent Expense**		
Apr. 1	3,000	Apr. 30	1,000	⟷	Apr. 30	1,000	
Bal.	2,000				Bal.	1,000	

Correct asset amount, $2,000	→	Total accounted for, $3,000	←	Correct expense amount, $1,000

The full $3,000 has been accounted for: two thirds measures the asset, and one third measures the expense. This is correct because two thirds of the asset remains for future use, and one third of the prepayment has expired. Recording this expense illustrates the matching principle. The same analysis applies to a prepayment of three months' insurance premiums. The only difference is in the account titles, which would be Prepaid Insurance and Insurance Expense instead of Prepaid Rent and Rent Expense.

Supplies

On April 2, Gary Lyon paid cash of $700 for office supplies.

Apr. 2	Supplies	700	
	Cash		700
	Paid cash for supplies.		

Assume that Lyon purchased no additional supplies during April. The April 30 trial balance, therefore, lists Supplies with a $700 debit balance, as shown in Exhibit 3-1.

During April, Lyon used supplies in performing services for clients. The cost of the supplies used is the measure of *supplies expense* for the month. Lyon does not keep a continuous record of supplies used each day or each week during April. To keep detailed records for so insignificant an asset would be impractical. Instead, to measure his firm's supplies expense during April, Gary Lyon counts the supplies on hand at the end of the month. This is the amount of the asset still available to the business. Assume the count indicates that supplies costing $400 remain. Subtracting the entity's $400 of supplies on hand at the end of April from the cost of supplies available during April ($700) measures supplies expense during the month ($300).

Cost of asset available during the period		Cost of asset on hand at the end of the period		Cost of asset used (expense) during the period
	−		=	
$700	−	$400	=	$300

The April 30 adjusting entry to update the Supplies account and to record the supplies expense for the month debits the expense and credits the asset, as follows:

Apr. 30   Supplies Expense ($700 – $400)   300
           Supplies..   300
          To record supplies expense.

After posting, the Supplies and Supplies Expense accounts appear as follows:

Supplies				**Supplies Expense**	
Apr. 2	700	Apr. 30	300	Apr. 30	300
Bal.	400			Bal.	300

Correct asset amount, $400 → Total accounted for, $700 ← Correct expense amount, $300

The Supplies account enters the month of May with a $400 balance, and the adjustment process is repeated each month.

Depreciation and Capital Assets

The logic of the accrual basis is best illustrated by how businesses account for capital assets. **Capital assets** are long-lived assets, such as land, buildings, furniture, machinery and equipment. As one accountant said, "All assets but land are on a march to the junkyard." That is, all capital assets but land decline in usefulness as they age. This decline is an *expense* to the business. Accountants systematically spread the cost of each capital asset, except land, over the years of its useful life. This process is called the recording of **depreciation** or **amortization**. The concept underlying accounting for capital assets and depreciation expense is the same as for prepaid expenses. In both cases the business purchases an asset that wears out or is used up. As the asset becomes less and less useful, more and more of its cost is transferred from the asset account to the expense account. The major difference between prepaid expenses and capital assets is the length of time it takes for the asset to lose its usefulness. Prepaid expenses usually expire within a few months. Most capital assets remain useful for a number of years.

Consider Gary Lyon's law practice. Suppose on April 3, Lyon purchased furniture on account for $16,500.

Apr. 3   Furniture   16,500
          Accounts Payable...   16,500
          Purchased office furniture on account.

After posting, the Furniture account appears as follows:

Furniture	
Apr. 3 16,500	

Using cash-basis accounting, Gary Lyon would enter in the ledger the entire $16,500 as an expense for April. As a result, his financial statements for that month would be extremely misleading. Income would be significantly understated. Also, the cash-basis approach fails to take into consideration that the asset will be of benefit to Lyon's business in future accounting periods. After all, his furniture will remain useful for quite some time.

In accrual-basis accounting, an asset is recorded when the furniture is acquired. Then, a portion of the asset's cost is transferred from the asset account to

Depreciation Expense each period that the asset is used. This method matches the asset's expense to the revenue of the period, which is an application of the matching principle.

Lyon believes the furniture will remain useful for five years and be virtually worthless at the end of its life. One way to compute the amount of depreciation for each year is to divide the cost of the asset ($16,500 in our example) by its useful life (5 years). This procedure gives annual depreciation of $3,300 ($16,500/5 years = $3,300 per year). Depreciation for the month of April is $275 ($3,300/12 months = $275 per month). Chapter 10 covers depreciation in more detail.

Depreciation expense for April is recorded by the following entry:

Apr. 30	Depreciation Expense	275	
	Accumulated Depreciation — Furniture.......		275
	To record depreciation expense on furniture.		

You may be wondering why Accumulated Depreciation is credited instead of Furniture. The reason is that the original cost of the capital asset is an objective measurement, and that figure remains in the original asset account as long as the business uses the asset. Accountants may refer to that account if they need to know how much the asset costs. This information is useful in a decision about whether to replace the furniture and the amount to pay. The amount of depreciation, however, is an *estimate*. Accountants use the **Accumulated Depreciation** account to show the cumulative sum of all depreciation expense from the date of acquiring the asset. Therefore, the balance in this account increases over the life of the asset.

Accumulated Depreciation is a **contra asset** account, which means an asset account with a credit balance. A **contra account** has two distinguishing characteristics: (1) it always has a companion account, and (2) its normal balance is opposite that of the companion account. In this case, Accumulated Depreciation accompanies Furniture. It appears in the ledger directly after Furniture. Furniture has a debit balance, and therefore Accumulated Depreciation, a contra asset, has a credit balance. All contra asset accounts have credit balances.

A business carries an accumulated depreciation or amortization account for each depreciable asset. If a business has a building and a machine, for example, it will carry the accounts Accumulated Depreciation — Building, and Accumulated Depreciation — Machine.

After posting the depreciation entry, the Furniture, Accumulated Depreciation and Depreciation Expense accounts are

Furniture		Accumulated Depreciation — Furniture			Depreciation Expense		
Apr. 3 16,500			Apr. 30	275	Apr. 30	275	
Bal. 16,500			Bal.	275	Bal.	275	

The balance sheet shows the relationship between Furniture and Accumulated Depreciation. The balance of Accumulated Depreciation is subtracted from the balance of Furniture. This net amount of a capital asset (cost minus accumulated depreciation) is called its **book value**, as shown below for Furniture:

Capital Assets

Furniture...	$16,500
Less: Accumulated Depreciation	275
Book Value...	$16,225

Suppose Lyon's law practice owns a building that cost $48,000, on which annual depreciation is $2,400. The amount of depreciation for one month would be $200 ($2,400/12), and the entry to record depreciation for April is

Apr. 30   Depreciation Expense — Building 200
             Accumulated Depreciation — Building   200
           To record depreciation on building.

The balance sheet at April 30 would report Lyon's capital assets as shown in Exhibit 3-2. Now, however, let's return to Gary Lyon's actual situation.

EXHIBIT 3-2 *Capital Assets on the Balance Sheet, April 30*

Capital Assets		
Furniture..	$16,500	
Less: Accumulated Depreciation	275	$16,225
Building	48,000	
Less: Accumulated Depreciation	200	47,800
Book Value of Capital Assets...		$64,025

Accrued Expenses

Businesses often incur expenses before they pay cash. Consider an employee's salary. The employer's salary expense and salary payable grow as the employee works, so the liability is said to *accrue*. Another example is interest expense on a note payable. Interest accrues as the clock ticks. The term **accrued expense** refers to an expense that the business has incurred but has not yet paid.

It is time-consuming to make hourly, daily or even weekly journal entries to accrue expenses. Consequently, the accountant waits until the end of the period. Then an adjusting entry brings each expense (and related liability) up to date just before the financial statements are prepared.

Salary Expense   Most companies pay their employees at set times. Suppose Gary Lyon pays his employee a monthly salary of $1,900, half on the 15th and half on the last day of the month. Here is a calendar for April that has paydays circled:

APRIL

S	M	T	W	T	F	S
					1	2
3	4	5	6	7	8	9
10	11	12	13	14	(15)	16
17	18	19	20	21	22	23
24	25	26	27	28	29	(30)

Assume that if either payday falls on a weekend, Lyon pays the employee on the following Monday. During April, Lyon paid his employee's first half-month salary of $950 on Friday, April 15 and recorded the following entry:

Apr. 15   Salary Expense... 950
            Cash   950
           To pay salary.

After posting, the Salary Expense account is

Salary Expense	
Apr. 15 950	

The trial balance at April 30 (Exhibit 3-1) includes Salary Expense, with its debit balance of $950. As April 30, the second payday of the month, falls on a Saturday, the second half-month amount of $950 will be paid on Monday, May 2. Without an adjusting entry, this second $950 amount is not included in the April 30 trial balance amount for Salary Expense. Therefore, at April 30, Lyon adjusts for additional *salary expense* and *salary payable* of $950 by recording an increase in each of these accounts as follows:

Apr. 30	Salary Expense	950	
	Salary Payable		950
	To accrue salary expense.		

After posting, the Salary Expense and Salary Payable accounts appear as follows:

Salary Expense			Salary Payable	
Apr.15	950		Apr. 30	950
Apr. 30	**950**		Bal.	950
Bal.	1,900			

The accounts at April 30 now contain the complete salary information for the month. The expense account has a full month's salary, and the liability account shows the portion that the business still owes.

Lyon will record the payment of this liability on May 2 by debiting Salary Payable and crediting Cash for $950. This payment entry does not affect April or May expenses, because the April expense was recorded on April 15 and April 30. May expense will be recorded in a like manner. All accrued expenses are recorded with similar entries — a debit to the appropriate expense account and a credit to the related liability account.

Accrued Revenues

Businesses often earn revenue before they receive the cash because payment is not due until later. A revenue that has been earned but not yet received in cash is called an **accrued revenue**. Assume Gary Lyon is hired on April 15 by Guerrero Construction Co. Ltd. to perform legal services on an as-needed basis. Under this agreement, Guerrero will pay Lyon $500 monthly, with the first payment on May 15. During April, Gary Lyon will earn half a month's fee, $250. On April 30, he makes the following adjusting entry to record an increase in Accounts Receivable and Service Revenue:

Apr. 30	Accounts Receivable ($500 × ½)	250	
	Service Revenue		250
	To accrue service revenue.		

Recall that Accounts Receivable has an unadjusted balance of $2,250 and the Service Revenue unadjusted balance is $7,000 (Exhibit 3-1). Posting this adjustment has the following effects on these two accounts:

Accounts Receivable			Service Revenue	
	2,250			7,000
Apr. 30	**250**		**Apr. 30**	**250**
Bal.	2,500		Bal.	7,250

This adjusting entry illustrates accrual accounting and the revenue principle in action. Without the adjustment, Lyon's financial statements would be misleading. All accrued revenues are accounted for similarly — by debiting a receivable and crediting a revenue.

Unearned Revenues

Some businesses collect cash from customers in advance of doing work for the customer. This creates a liability called **unearned revenue**, which is an obligation arising from receiving cash in advance of providing a product or service. Only when the job is completed will the business have earned the revenue. Suppose Baldwin Computer Service Center engages Lyon's services, agreeing to pay him $450 monthly, beginning immediately. If Baldwin makes the first payment on April 21, Lyon records this increase in the business's liabilities as follows:

Apr. 20	Cash	450	
	Unearned Service Revenue.............................		450
	Received revenue in advance.		

After posting, the liability account appears as follows:

Unearned Service Revenue

	Apr. 20 450

Unearned Service Revenue is a liability because it represents Lyon's obligation to perform service for the client. The April 30 unadjusted trial balance (Exhibit 3-1) lists this account with a $450 credit balance prior to the adjusting entries. During the last 10 days of the month, Lyon will have earned one third (10 days divided by April's total 30 days) of the $450, or $150. Therefore, he makes the following adjustments to decrease the liability, Unearned Service Revenue, and to record an increase in Service Revenue:

Apr. 30	Unearned Service Revenue ($450 × ⅓).................	150	
	Service Revenue..		150
	To record service revenue that was collected in advance.		

This adjusting entry shifts $150 of the total amount from the liability account to the revenue account. After posting, the balance of Service Revenue is increased by $150 and the balance of Unearned Service Revenue has been reduced to $300.

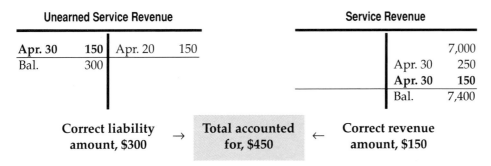

Accounting for all types of revenues that are collected in advance follows the same pattern.

EXHIBIT 3-3 *Summary of Adjusting Entries*

Adjusting Entry	Type of Account Debited	Type of Account Credited
Prepaid expense, supplies	Expense	Prepaid expense, supplies (Asset)
Depreciation	Expense	Accumulated depreciation (Contra asset)
Accrued expenses	Expense	Payable (Liability)
Accrued revenues	Receivable (Asset)	Revenue
Unearned revenues	Unearned revenue (Liability)	Revenue

Adapted from Beverly Terry.

Summary of the Adjusting Process

Since one purpose of the adjusting process is to measure business income properly, each adjusting entry affects at least one income statement account — a revenue or an expense. The other side of the entry, a debit or a credit, as the case may be, is to a balance sheet account — an asset or a liability. This step updates the accounts for preparation of the balance sheet, which is the second purpose of the adjustments. No adjusting entry debits or credits Cash, because the cash transactions are recorded earlier in the period. The end-of-period adjustment process is reserved for the noncash transactions that are required by accrual accounting. Exhibit 3-3 summarizes the adjusting entries.

Posting the Adjusting Entries

Exhibit 3-4 summarizes the adjusting entries of Lyon's business at April 30. Panel A of the exhibit briefly describes the data for each adjustment, Panel B gives the adjusting entries, and Panel C shows the accounts. The adjustments are keyed by letter.

EXHIBIT 3-4 *Journalizing and Posting the Adjusting Entries*

Panel A: Information for Adjustments at April 30, 19X1

a. Accrued service revenue, $250.
b. Supplies on hand, $400.
c. Prepaid rent expired, $1,000.
d. Depreciation on furniture, $275.
e. Accrued salary expense, $950.
f. Amount of unearned service revenues that has been earned, $150.

Panel B: Adjusting Entries

a. Accounts Receivable	250	
Service Revenue		250
To accrue service revenue.		
b. Supplies Expense	300	
Supplies		300
To record supplies used.		
c. Rent Expense	1,000	
Prepaid Rent		1,000
To record rent expense.		

d. Depreciation Expense...	275	
Accumulated Depreciation..		275
To record depreciation on furniture.		
e. Salary Expense	950	
Salary Payable		950
To accrue salary expense.		
f. Unearned Service Revenue...	150	
Service Revenue		150
To record unearned revenue that has been earned.		

Panel C: Ledger Accounts

ASSETS

Cash				Accounts Receivable				Supplies		
Bal.	24,800				2,250				700	(b)	300
				(a)	250			Bal.	400	
				Bal.	2,500					

Prepaid Rent				Furniture				Accumulated Depreciation — Furniture		
	3,000	(c)	1,000	Bal.	16,500				(d)	275
Bal.	2,000								Bal.	275

LIABILITIES

Accounts Payable			Salary Payable			Unearned Service Revenue		
	Bal.	13,100		(e)	950	(f)	150	450
				Bal.	950		Bal.	300

OWNER'S EQUITY

Gary Lyon, Capital			Gary Lyon, Withdrawals			REVENUES Service Revenue		
	Bal.	31,250	Bal.	3,200				7,000
							(a)	250
							(f)	150
							Bal.	7,400

EXPENSES

Rent Expense			Salary Expense			Supplies Expense		
(c)	1,000			950		(b)	300	
Bal.	1,000		(e)	950		Bal.	300	
			Bal.	1,900				

Depreciation Expense			Utilities Expense		
(d)	275		Bal.	400	
Bal.	275				

Adjusted Trial Balance

This chapter began with the trial balance before any adjusting entries — the unadjusted trial balance (Exhibit 3-1). After the adjustments are journalized and posted, the accounts appear as shown in Panel C, Exhibit 3-4. A useful step in preparing the financial statements is to list the accounts, along with their adjusted balances, on an **adjusted trial balance**. This document has the advantage of listing all the accounts and their adjusted balances in a single place. Exhibit 3-5 shows the preparation of the adjusted trial balance.

The format of Exhibit 3-5 is called a *work sheet*. We will take a long look at the accounting work sheet in the next chapter. For now, simply note how clearly this format presents the data. The information in the account title column and in the Trial Balance columns is drawn directly from the trial balance. The two Adjustments columns list the debit and credit adjustments directly across from the appropriate account title. Each adjusting debit is identified by a letter in parentheses that refers back to the adjusting entry. For example, the debit labeled *a* on the work sheet refers back to the debit adjusting entry of $250 to Accounts Receivable in Panel B of Exhibit 3-4. Likewise for credit adjusting entries, the corresponding credit, labeled *a*, refers back to the $250 credit to Service Revenue.

OBJECTIVE 4

Prepare an adjusted trial balance

The Adjusted Trial Balance columns give the adjusted account balances. Each amount on the adjusted trial balance of Exhibit 3-5 is computed by combining the amounts from the unadjusted trial balance plus or minus the adjustments. For example, Accounts Receivable starts with a debit balance of $2,250. Adding the $250 debit amount from adjusting entry *a* gives Accounts Receivable an adjusted balance of $2,500. Supplies begins with a debit balance of $700. After the $300 credit adjustment, its adjusted balance is $400. More than one entry may affect a single account, as is the case for Service Revenue. If accounts are unaffected by the adjustments, they show the same amount on both trial balances. This is true for Cash, Furniture, Accounts Payable, and the Owner's Equity accounts.

Preparing the Financial Statements from the Adjusted Trial Balance

The April financial statements of Gary Lyon, Lawyer, can be prepared from the information on the adjusted trial balance.

Exhibit 3-6 shows how the accounts are distributed from the adjusted trial balance to these three financial statements. The income statement (Exhibit 3-7) comes from the revenue and expense accounts. The statement of owner's equity (Exhibit 3-8) shows the reasons for the change in the owner's capital during the period. The balance sheet (Exhibit 3-9) reports the assets, liabilities, and owner's equity.

Financial Statements

The accounts and amounts for the income statement and balance sheet may be taken from the adjusted trial balance. The adjusted trial balance also provides the data for the statement of owner's equity. Exhibits 3-7, 3-8, and 3-9 illustrate these three financial statements, best prepared in the order shown: the income statement first, followed by the statement of owner's equity and last, the balance sheet. The essential features of all financial statements are (1) the name of the entity, (2) the title of the statement, (3) the date or the period covered by the statement and (4) the body of the statement.

It is customary to list expenses in descending order by amount, as shown in Exhibit 3-7. However, Miscellaneous Expense, a catch-all account for expenses that do not fit another category, is usually reported last regardless of its amount.

EXHIBIT 3-5 *Preparation of Adjusted Trial Balance*

Gary Lyon, Lawyer
Preparation of Adjusted Trial Balance
April 30, 19X1

Account Title	Trial Balance Debit	Trial Balance Credit	Adjustments Debit	Adjustments Credit	Adjusted Trial Balance Debit	Adjusted Trial Balance Credit
Cash	24,800				24,800	
Accounts receivable	2,250		(a) 250		2,500	
Supplies	700			(b) 300	400	
Prepaid rent	3,000			(c)1,000	2,000	
Furniture	16,500				16,500	
Accumulated depreciation				(d) 275		275
Accounts payable		13,100				13,100
Salary payable				(e) 950		950
Unearned service revenue		450	(f) 150			300
Gary Lyon, capital		31,250				31,250
Gary Lyon, withdrawals	3,200				3,200	
Service revenue		7,000		(a) 250		7,400
				(f) 150		
Rent expense			(c)1,000		1,000	
Salary expense	950		(e) 950		1,900	
Supplies expense			(b) 300		300	
Depreciation expense			(d) 275		275	
Utilities expense	400				400	
	51,800	51,800	2,925	2,925	53,275	53,275

EXHIBIT 3-6 *Preparing the Financial Statements from the Adjusted Trial Balance*

Account Title	Adjusted Trial Balance Debit	Adjusted Trial Balance Credit	
Cash	24,800		
Accounts receivable	2,500		
Supplies	400		
Prepaid rent	2,000		
Furniture	16,500		Balance Sheet
Accumulated depreciation		275	
Accounts payable		13,100	
Salary payable		950	
Unearned service revenue		300	
Gary Lyon, capital		31,250	Statement of
Gary Lyon, withdrawals	3,200		Owner's Equity
Service revenue		7,400	
Rent expense	1,000		
Salary expense	1,900		Income Statement
Supplies expense	300		
Depreciation expense	275		
Utilities expense	400		
	53,275	53,275	

OBJECTIVE 5

Prepare the financial
statements from the
adjusted trial balance

EXHIBIT 3-7 *Income Statement*

Gary Lyon, Lawyer Income Statement for the month ended April 30, 19X1		
Revenue		
Service revenue		$7,400
Expenses		
Salary expense...	$1,900	
Rent expense...	1,000	
Utilities expense...	400	
Supplies expense...	300	
Depreciation expense...	275	
Total expenses		3,875
Net income..		$3,525

EXHIBIT 3-8 *Statement of Owner's Equity*

Gary Lyon, Lawyer Statement of Owner's Equity for the month ended April 30, 19X1	
Gary Lyon, capital, April 1, 19X1	$31,250
Add: Net income	3,525
	34,775
Less: Withdrawals	3,200
Gary Lyon, capital, April 30, 19X1	$31,575

EXHIBIT 3-9 *Balance Sheet*

Gary Lyon, Lawyer Balance Sheet April 30, 19X1					
Assets			**Liabilities**		
Cash............................		$24,800	Accounts payable		$13,100
Accounts receivable		2,500	Salary payable...................		950
Supplies......................		400	Unearned service		
Prepaid rent..............		2,000	revenue		300
Furniture...................	$16,500		Total liabilities..................		14,350
Less: Accumulated					
depreciation	275	16,225	**Owner's Equity**		
			Gary Lyon, capital		31,575
			Total liabilities and		
Total assets...............		$45,925	owner's equity...............		45,925

Relationships among the
Three Financial Statements _____

The arrows in Exhibits 3-7, 3-8, and 3-9 illustrate the relationship among the income statement, the statement of owner's equity, and the balance sheet.

1. The income statement reports net income or net loss, figured by subtracting expenses from revenues. Because revenues and expenses are owner's equity accounts, their net figure is then transferred to the statement of owner's equity. Note that net income in Exhibit 3-7, $3,525, increases owner's equity in Exhibit 3-8. A net loss would decrease owner's equity.

2. Capital is a balance sheet account, so the ending balance in the statement of owner's equity is transferred to the balance sheet. This amount is the final balancing element of the balance sheet. To solidify your understanding of this relationship, trace the $31,575 figure from Exhibit 3-8 to Exhibit 3-9.

You may be wondering why the total assets on the balance sheet ($45,925 in Exhibit 3-9) do not equal the total debits on the adjusted trial balance ($53,275 in Exhibit 3-6). Likewise, the total liabilities and owner's equity do not equal the total credits on the adjusted trial balance. The reason for these differences is that Accumulated Depreciation and Owner Withdrawals are *subtracted* from their related accounts on the balance sheet, but *added* in their respective columns on the adjusted trial balance.

Computers and the Accounting Process _____

How would adjusting entries be handled in a computerized system that a large company like Nova Corp. of Alberta might use? A company's general ledger accounting software package would print out a trial balance. The accountants would then analyze the account balances on the trial balance, testing them for reasonableness, and tracing the balances back to the general ledger and, if necessary, back to the individual transactions and the supporting documents that first generated the transactions. This analysis results in the adjusting entries.

Once the adjusting entries are posted (that is, entered into the computer) the general ledger accounts are automatically updated. The trial balance now becomes the adjusted trial balance.

Computerized accounting packages also print out financial statements. These statements include the income statement, the statement of owner's equity, and the balance sheet. Also the computer package may give the company the flexibility to print out selected data in a specialized presentation to meet a particular company's information needs.

For example, an owner may want a forecast of the year's net income. The accountant can make several sets of estimates for the ending quantities, accrued salaries, unearned revenues, and all the other items that will be adjusted. The computer can produce several different sets of financial statements — one for each set of estimated data. Using these data the owner may identify a lagging division in the business immediately, rather than at the end of the period when the routine financial statements are issued. The owner would then be able to take steps quickly to help the lagging division before its operations grew worse. Alternatively, the company's bank may require forecasted financial statements before making a loan. Without a computer these forecasts may be very difficult to prepare.

Summary Problem for Your Review

The trial balance of O'Malley's Service Company pertains to December 31, 19X1, which is the end of its year-long accounting period.

O'Malley's Service Company		
Trial Balance		
December 31, 19X1		
Cash	$ 198,000	
Accounts receivable	370,000	
Supplies	6,000	
Furniture and fixtures	100,000	
Accumulated depreciation — furniture and fixtures		$ 40,000
Building	250,000	
Accumulated depreciation — building		130,000
Accounts payable		380,000
Salary payable		
Unearned service revenue		45,000
Trish O'Malley, capital		293,000
Trish O'Malley, withdrawals	65,000	
Service revenue		286,000
Salary expense	172,000	
Supplies expense		
Depreciation expense — furniture and fixtures		
Depreciation expense — building		
Miscellaneous expense	13,000	
Total	$1,174,000	$1,174,000

Data needed for the adjusting entries include:

a. Supplies on hand at year's end, $2,000.

b. Depreciation on furniture and fixtures, $20,000.

c. Depreciation on building, $10,000.

d. Salaries owed but not yet paid, $5,000.

e. Accrued service revenue, $12,000.

f. Of the $45,000 balance of unearned service revenue, $32,000 was earned during the year.

Required

1. Open the ledger accounts with their unadjusted balances. Show dollar amounts in thousands, as shown for Accounts Receivable.

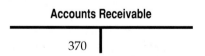

Accounts Receivable

370

2. Journalize O'Malley's Service Company's adjusting entries at December 31, 19X1. Key entries by letter as in Exhibt 3-4.

3. Post the adjusting entries.

4. Write the trial balance on a sheet of paper, enter the adjusting entries, and prepare an adjusted trial balance, as shown in Exhibit 3-5.

5. Prepare the income statement, the statement of owner's equity, and the balance sheet. Draw the arrows linking the three statements together.

SOLUTION TO REVIEW PROBLEM

Requirements 1 and 3

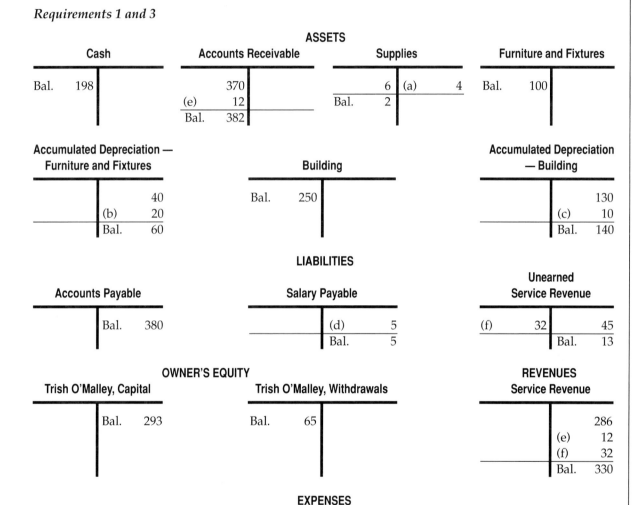

Requirement 2

	19X1			
a.	Dec. 31	Supplies Expense ($6,000 – $2,000)	4,000	
		Supplies...		4,000
		To record supplies used.		
b.	31	Depreciation Expense — Furniture and Fixtures....	20,000	
		Accumulated Depreciation — Furniture and Fixtures..		20,000
		To record depreciation expense on furniture and fixtures.		
c.	31	Depreciation Expense — Building	10,000	
		Accumulated Depreciation — Building..............		10,000
		To record depreciation expense on building.		
d.	31	Salary Expense	5,000	
		Salary Payable...		5,000
		To accrue salary expense.		
e.	31	Accounts Receivable	12,000	
		Service Revenue..		12,000
		To accrue service revenue.		
f.	31	Unearned Service Revenue	32,000	
		Service Revenue..		32,000
		To record unearned service revenue that has been earned.		

Requirement 4

O'Malley's Service Company
Preparation of Adjusted Trial Balance
December 31, 19X1
(amounts in thousands)

Account Title	Trial Balance Debit	Trial Balance Credit	Adjustments Debit	Adjustments Credit	Adjusted Trial Balance Debit	Adjusted Trial Balance Credit
Cash	198				198	
Accounts receivable	370		(e) 12		382	
Supplies	6			(a) 4		2
Furniture and fixtures	100				100	
Accumulated depreciation — furniture and fixtures		40		(b) 20		60
Building	250				250	
Accumulated depreciation — building		130		(c) 10		140
Accounts payable		380				380
Salary payable				(d) 5		5
Unearned service revenue		45	(f) 32			13
Trish O'Malley, capital		293				293
Trish O'Malley, withdrawals	65				65	
Service revenue		286		(e) 12 (f) 32		330
Salary expense	172		(d) 5		177	
Supplies expense			(a) 4		4	
Depreciation expense — furniture and fixtures			(b) 20		20	
Depreciation expense — building			(c)10		10	
Miscellaneous expense	13				13	
	1,174	1,174	83	83	1,221	1,221

Requirement 5

O'Malley's Service Company
Income Statement
for the year ended December 31, 19X1
(amounts in thousands)

Revenues		
Service revenue..		$330
Expenses		
Salary expense	$177	
Depreciation expense — furniture and fixtures	20	
Depreciation expense — building	10	
Supplies expense..	4	
Miscellaneous expense	13	
Total expenses..		224
Net income		$106

O'Malley's Service Company
Statement of Owner's Equity
for the year ended December 31, 19X1
(amounts in thousands)

Trish O'Malley, capital, January 1, 19X1..	$293
Add: Net income	106
	399
Less: Withdrawals	65
Trish O'Malley, capital, December 31, 19X1	$334

①

O'Malley's Service Company
Balance Sheet
December 31, 19X1
(amounts in thousands)

---

②

Assets			**Liabilities**		
Cash...		$198	Accounts payable.......................		$380
Accounts receivable		382	Salary payable		5
Supplies		2	Unearned service revenue.........		13
Furniture and fixtures	$100		Total liabilities		398
Less: Accumulated					
depreciation..............	60	40	**Owner's Equity**		
Building	250		Trish O'Malley, capital		334
Less: Accumulated					
depreciation..............	140	110	Total liabilities and		
Total assets		$732	owner's equity........................		$732

Summary

In *accrual-basis accounting*, business events are recorded as they affect the entity. In *cash-basis accounting*, only those events that affect cash are recorded. The cash basis omits important events such as purchases and sales of assets on account. It also distorts the financial statements by labeling as expenses those cash payments that have long-term effects, like the purchases of buildings and equipment. Some small organizations use cash-basis accounting, but the generally accepted method is the accrual basis.

Accountants divide time into definite periods, such as a month, a quarter and a year, to report the entity's financial statements. The year is the basic *accounting period*, but companies prepare financial statements as often as they need the information. Accountants have developed the *revenue principle* to guide them in when to record revenue and the amount of revenue to record. The *matching principle* guides the accounting for expenses. *Adjusting entries* are a result of the accrual basis of accounting. These entries, made at the end of the accounting period, update the accounts for preparation of the financial statements. One of the most important pieces of accounting information is net income or net loss, and the adjusting entries help measure the *net income* of the period.

Adjusting entries can be divided into five categories: *prepaid expenses, depreciation, accrued expenses, accrued revenues,* and *unearned revenues.*

To prepare the *adjusted trial balance*, enter the adjusting entries next to the *unadjusted trial balance*. The adjusted trial balance can be used to prepare the *income statement*, the *statement of owner's equity*, and the *balance sheet*.

These three statements are related as follows: Income, shown on the income statement, increases owner's equity, which also appears on the statement of owner's equity. The ending balance of owner's equity is the last amount reported on the balance sheet.

Computers can aid the accounting process in a number of ways, chiefly by performing routine operations. Many adjusting entries, however, require analysis that is best done manually, without the computer.

Self-Study Questions

Test your understanding of the chapter by marking the correct answer for each of the following questions:

1. Accrual-basis accounting *(p. 95)*
   a. Results in higher income than cash-basis accounting
   b. Leads to the reporting of more complete information than does cash-basis accounting
   c. Is not acceptable under GAAP
   d. Omits adjusting entries at the end of the period

2. Under the revenue principle, revenue is recorded *(p. 96)*
   a. At the earliest acceptable time
   b. At the latest acceptable time
   c. After it has been earned, but not before
   d. At the end of the accounting period

3. The matching principle provides guidance in accounting for *(p. 97)*
   a. Expenses   c. Assets
   b. Revenues   d. Liabilities

4. Adjusting entries *(p. 99)*
   a. Assign revenues to the period in which they are earned
   b. Help to properly measure the period's net income or net loss
   c. Bring asset and liability accounts to correct balances
   d. All of the above

5. A law firm began November with supplies of $160. During the month, the firm purchased supplies of $290. At November 30, supplies on hand total $210. Supplies expense for the period is *(p. 100)*
   - a. $210
   - b. $240
   - c. $290
   - d. $450

6. A building that cost $120,000 has accumulated depreciation of $50,000. The book value of the building is *(p. 102)*
   - a. $50,000
   - b. $70,000
   - c. $120,000
   - d. $170,000

7. The adjusting entry to accrue salary expense *(p. 104)*
   - a. Debits Salary Expense and credits Cash
   - b. Debits Salary Payable and credits Salary Expense
   - c. Debits Salary Payable and credits Cash
   - d. Debits Salary Expense and credits Salary Payable

8. A business received cash of $3,000 in advance for revenue that will be earned later. The cash receipt entry debited Cash and credited Unearned Revenue for $3,000. At the end of the period, $1,100 is still unearned. The adjusting entry for this situation will *(pp. 104–105)*
   - a. Debit Unearned Revenue and credit Revenue for $1,900
   - b. Debit Unearned Revenue and credit Revenue for $1,100
   - c. Debit Revenue and credit Unearned Revenue for $1,900
   - d. Debit Revenue and credit Unearned Revenue for $1,100

9. The links between the financial statements are *(p. 110)*
   - a. Net income from the income statement to the statement of owner's equity
   - b. Ending capital from the statement of owner's equity to the balance sheet
   - c. Both of the above
   - d. None of the above

10. Accumulated Depreciation is reported on the *(p. 110)*
    - a. Balance sheet
    - b. Income statement
    - c. Statement of owner's equity
    - d. Both a and b

Answers to the Self-Study Questions are at the end of the chapter.

Accounting Vocabulary

accrual-basis accounting *(p. 94)*
accrued expense *(p. 103)*
accrued revenue *(p. 104)*
accumulated depreciation *(p. 102)*
adjusted trial balance *(p. 108)*

adjusting entry *(p. 99)*
amortization *(p. 101)*
book value of a capital asset *(p. 102)*
capital asset *(p. 101)*
cash-basis accounting *(p. 95)*
contra account *(p. 102)*

contra asset *(p. 102)*
depreciation *(p. 101)*
matching principle *(p. 96)*
prepaid expense *(p. 99)*
revenue principle *(p. 96)*
time-period concept *(p. 97)*
unearned revenue *(p. 105)*

ASSIGNMENT MATERIAL _____

Questions

1. Distinguish the accrual basis of accounting from the cash basis.
2. How long is the basic accounting period? What is a fiscal year? What is an interim period?
3. What two questions does the revenue principle help answer?
4. Briefly explain the matching principle.

5. What is the purpose of making adjusting entries?

6. Why are adjusting entries made at the end of the accounting period, not during the period?

7. Name five categories of adjusting entries and give an example of each.

8. Do all adjusting entries affect the net income or net loss of the period? Include in your answer the definition of an adjusting entry.

9. Why does the balance of Supplies need to be adjusted at the end of the period?

10. Manning Supply Company pays $1,800 for an insurance policy that covers three years. At the end of the first year, the balance of its Prepaid Insurance account contains two elements. What are the two elements, and what is the correct amount of each?

11. The title Prepaid Expense suggests that this type of account is an expense. If so, explain why. If not, what type of account is it?

12. What is a contra account? Identify the contra account introduced in this chapter, along with the account's normal balance.

13. The manager of a Quickie-Pickie convenience store presents his entity's balance sheet to a banker to obtain a loan. The balance sheet reports that the entity's capital assets have a book value of $135,000 and accumulated depreciation of $65,000. What does book value of a capital asset mean? What was the cost of the capital assets?

14. Give the entry to record accrued interest revenue of $800.

15. Why is an unearned revenue a liability? Use an example in your answer.

16. Identify the types of accounts (assets, liabilities, and so on) debited and credited for the five types of adjusting entries.

17. What purposes does the adjusted trial balance serve?

18. Explain the relationship among the income statement, the statement of owner's equity, and the balance sheet.

19. Bellevue Company failed to record the following adjusting entries at December 31, the end of its fiscal year: (a) accrued expenses, $500; (b) accrued revenues, $850; and (c) depreciation, $1,000. Did these omissions cause net income for the year to be understated or overstated and by what overall amount?

20. Identify several accounting tasks for which it is efficient to use a computer. What is the basic limitation on the use of a computer?

Exercises

Exercise 3-1   *Cash-basis versus accrual-basis accounting* **(L.O. 1)**

The Oak Lodge had the following selected transactions during August:

Aug.	1	Prepaid damage and liability insurance for the year, $6,000.
	5	Paid electricity expenses, $700.
	9	Received cash for the day's room rentals, $1,400.
	31	Purchased six television sets, $3,000.
	31	Served a banquet, receiving a note receivable, $1,200.
	31	Made an adjusting entry for insurance expense (from Aug. 1).

Show how each transaction would be handled using the cash basis and the accrual basis of accounting. Under each column give the amount of revenue or expense for August. Journal entries are not required. Use the following format for your answer, and show your computations:

Amount of Revenue or Expense for August		
Date	**Cash Basis**	**Accrual Basis**

Exercise 3-2 *Applying accounting concepts and principles (L.O. 2)*

Identify the accounting concept or principle that gives the most direction on how to account for each of the following situations:

a. Expenses of $2,600 must be accrued at the end of the period to properly measure income.

b. A customer states her intention to shift her business to a travel agency. Should the travel agency record revenue based on this intention?

c. The owner of a business desires monthly financial statements to measure the progress of the entity on an ongoing basis.

d. Expenses of the period total $6,100. This amount should be subtracted from revenue to compute the period's income.

Exercise 3-3 *Applying accounting concepts (L.O. 2)*

Write a short paragraph to explain in your own words the concept of depreciation as it is used in accounting.

Exercise 3-4 *Allocating prepaid expense to the asset and expense (L.O. 2)*

Compute the amounts indicated by question marks for each of the following Prepaid Rent situations. Consider each situation separately.

	Situation			
	1	**2**	**3**	**4**
Beginning Prepaid Rent	$ 300	$ 500	$ 600	$ 900
Payments for Prepaid Rent during the year	900	?	?	1,100
Total amount to account for	?	?	1,500	2,000
Ending Prepaid Rent	200	600	500	?
Rent Expense	$?	$ 300	$1,000	$1,600

Exercise 3-5 *Journalizing adjusting entries (L.O. 3)*

Journalize the entries for the following adjustments at December 31, the end of the accounting period:

a. Interest revenue accrued, $4,100.

b. Unearned service revenue earned, $800.

c. Depreciation, $6,200.

d. Employee salaries owed for two days of a five-day workweek; weekly payroll, $9,000.

e. Prepaid insurance expired, $450.

Exercise 3-6 *Analyzing the effects of adjustments on net income (L.O. 3)*

Suppose the adjustments required in Exercise 3-5 were not made. Compute the overall overstatement or understatement of net income as a result of the omission of these adjustments.

Exercise 3-7   *Recording adjustments in T-accounts* **(L.O. 3)**

The accounting records of Lucca Galvez, Artist include the following unadjusted balances at May 31: Accounts Receivable, $1,200; Supplies, $600; Salary Payable, $0; Unearned Service Revenue, $400; Service Revenue, $5,100; Salary Expense, $1,200; and Supplies Expense, $0.

Galvez's accountant develops the following data for the May 31 adjusting entries:

a. Supplies on hand, $100.

b. Salary owed to employee, $400.

c. Service revenue accrued, $350.

d. Unearned service revenue that has been earned, $250.

Open the foregoing T-accounts and record the adjustments directly in the accounts, keying each adjustment amount by letter. Show each account's adjusted balance. Journal entries are not required.

Exercise 3-8   *Adjusting the accounts* **(L.O. 3,4)**

Preparation of the Pack-n-Mail Service adjusted trial balance is incomplete. Enter the adjustment amounts directly in the adjustment columns of the text. Service Revenue is the only account affected by more than one adjustment.

Pack-n-Mail Service
Preparation of Adjusted Trial Balance
October 31, 19X2

Account Title	Trial Balance		Adjustments		Adjusted Trial Balance	
	Debit	Credit	Debit	Credit	Debit	Credit
Cash	3,000				3,000	
Accounts receivable	6,500		600		7,100	
Supplies	1,040			240	800	
Office furniture	19,300				19,300	
Accumulated depreciation		11,060		260		11,320
Salary payable						600
Unearned revenue		900	210			690
Capital		16,340				16,340
Owner's withdrawals	6,200				6,200	
Service revenue		11,830				12,640
Salary expense	2,690				3,290	
Rent expense	1,400				1,400	
Depreciation expense			260		260	
Supplies expense					240	
	40,130	40,130			41,590	41,590

Exercise 3-9   *Journalizing adjustments* **(L.O. 3,4)**

Make journal entries for the adjustments that would complete the preparation of the adjusted trial balance in Exercise 3-8. Include explanations.

Exercise 3-10   *Preparing the financial statements* **(L.O. 5)**

Refer to the adjusted trial balance in Exercise 3-8. Prepare Pack-n-Mail Service's income statement and statement of owner's equity for the three months ended

October 31, 19X2 and its balance sheet on that date. Draw the arrows linking the three statements.

Exercise 3-11 *Preparing the financial statements* **(L.O. 5)**

The accountant for Artie Sudan, M.D., has posted adjusting entries a through e to the accounts at September 30, 19X2. Selected balance sheet accounts and all the revenues and expenses of the entity are listed in the following T-accounts:

Accounts Receivable		Supplies		Accumulated Depreciation — Furniture	
23,000		4,000 | (a) 2,000			5,000
(e) 4,500					(b) 3,000

Accumulated Depreciation — Building		Salaries Payable		Service Revenue	
	33,000		(d) 1,500		135,000
(c) 4,000					(e) 4,500

Salary Expense		Supplies Expense		Depreciation Expense — Furniture		Depreciation Expense — Building	
28,000		(a) 2,000		(b) 3,000		(c) 4,000	
(d) 1,500							

Required

Prepare the income statement of Artie Sudan, M.D. for the year ended September 30, 19X2. List expenses in order from the largest to the smallest.

Exercise 3-12 *Preparing the statement of owner's equity* **(L.O. 5)**

J.C. Norris Company began the year with capital of $85,000. On July 9, the owner invested $12,000 cash in the business. On September 26, he transferred to the company land valued at $70,000. The income statement for the year ended September 30, 19X5 reported a net loss of $28,000. During this fiscal year, the owner withdrew $1,500 monthly for personal use. Prepare the company's statement of owner's equity for the year ended September 30, 19X5.

Problems   (Group A)

Problem 3-1A *Cash-basis versus accrual-basis accounting* **(L.O. 1,2)**

Temporary Manpower Services experienced the following selected transactions during January:

Jan. 1 Prepaid insurance for January through March, $600.
    4 Purchased office equipment for cash, $1,400.
    5 Received cash for services performed, $900.
    8 Paid gas bill, $300.
    12 Performed services on account, $1,000.
    14 Purchased office equipment on account, $300.
    28 Collected $500 on account from January 12.
    31 Paid salary expense, $1,100.

31   Paid account payable from January 14.
31   Recorded adjusting entry for January insurance expense (see Jan. 1)

Required

1. Show how each transaction would be handled using the cash basis and the accrual basis of accounting. Under each column give the amount of revenue or expense for January. Journal entries are not required. Use the following format for your answer, and show your computations:

Amount of Revenue or Expense for January

Date	Cash Basis	Accrual Basis

2. Compute January net income or net loss under each method.
3. Indicate which measure of net income or net loss is preferable. Give your reason.

Problem 3-2A   *Applying accounting principles (L.O. 2)*

Write a short memo to contrast the cash basis of accounting with the accrual basis. Mention the roles of the revenue principle and the matching principle in accrual accounting.

Problem 3-3A   *Journalizing adjusting entries (L.O. 3)*

Journalize the adjusting entry needed on December 31, end of the current accounting period, for each of the following independent cases affecting Windsor Contractors:

a. Windsor pays its employees each Friday. The amount of the weekly payroll is $2,100 for a five-day workweek, and the daily salary amounts are equal. The current accounting period ends on Monday.

b. Windsor has loaned money, receiving notes receivable. During the current year the entity has earned accrued interest revenue of $737 which it will receive next year.

c. The beginning balance of Supplies was $2,680. During the year the entity purchased supplies costing $6,180, and at December 31 the inventory of supplies on hand is $2,150.

d. Windsor is servicing the air-conditioning system in a large building, and the owner of the building paid Windsor $12,900 as the annual service fee. Windsor recorded this amount as Unearned Service Revenue. Ralph Windsor, the owner, estimates that the company has earned one fourth of the total fee during the current year.

e. Depreciation for the current year includes: Office Furniture, $650; Equipment, $3,850; and Trucks, $10,320. Make a compound entry.

f. Details of Prepaid Rent are shown in the account:

Prepaid Rent

Jan. 1	Bal. 600	
Mar. 31	1,200	
Sept. 30	1,200	

Windsor pays office rent semiannually on March 31 and September 30. At December 31, $600 of the last payment is still an asset.

Problem 3-4A *Analyzing and journalizing adjustments* **(L.O. 3)**

Patricia Wood Court Reporting Company unadjusted and adjusted trial balances at April 30, 19X1 are as follows:

Patricia Wood Court Reporting Company
Adjusted Trial Balance
April 30, 19X1

Account Title	Trial Balance		Adjusted Trial Balance	
	Debit	Credit	Debit	Credit
Cash	8,180		8,180	
Accounts receivable	6,360		6,540	
Interest receivable			300	
Note receivable	4,100		4,100	
Supplies	980		290	
Prepaid rent	1,440		720	
Building	66,450		66,450	
Accumulated depreciation		14,970		16,070
Accounts payable		6,920		6,920
Wages payable				320
Unearned service revenue		670		110
Patricia Wood, capital		60,770		60,770
Patricia Wood, withdrawals	3,600		3,600	
Service revenue		9,940		10,680
Interest revenue				300
Wage expense	1,600		1,920	
Rent expense			720	
Depreciation expense			1,100	
Insurance expense	370		370	
Supplies expense			690	
Utilities expense	190		190	
	93,270	93,270	95,170	95,170

Required

Journalize the adjusting entries that account for the differences between the two trial balances.

Problem 3-5A *Journalizing and posting adjustments to T-accounts; preparing the adjusted trial balance* **(L.O. 3,4)**

The trial balance of Insurers of Saskatchewan at October 31, 19X2 and the data needed for the month-end adjustments are as follows:

Adjustment data:

a. Prepaid rent still in force at October 31, $400.

b. Supplies used during the month, $440.

c. Depreciation for the month, $700.

d. Accrued advertising expense at October 31, $320. Credit Accounts Payable.

e. Accrued salary expense at October 31, $180.

f. Unearned commission revenue still unearned at October 31, $2,000.

Insurers of Saskatchewan
Trial Balance
October 31, 19X2

Cash	$ 1,460	
Accounts receivable	14,750	
Prepaid rent	3,100	
Supplies	780	
Furniture	22,370	
Accumulated depreciation		$11,640
Accounts payable		1,940
Salary payable		
Unearned commission revenue		2,290
Peggy Bailes, capital		24,140
Peggy Bailes, withdrawals	2,900	
Commission revenue		8,580
Salary expense	2,160	
Rent expense		
Utilities expense	340	
Depreciation expense		
Advertising expense	730	
Supplies expense		
Total	$48,590	$48,590

Required

1. Open T-accounts for the accounts listed in the trial balance, inserting their October 31 unadjusted balances.

2. Journalize the adjusting entries and post them to the T-accounts. Key the journal entries and the posted amounts by letter.

3. Prepare the adjusted trial balance.

Problem 3-6A   *Preparing the financial statements from an adjusted trial balance* **(L.O. 5)**

The adjusted trial balance of Tradewinds Travel Designers at December 31, 19X6 follows:

Tradewinds Travel Designers
Adjusted Trial Balance
December 31, 19X6

Cash	$ 3,320	
Accounts receivable	11,920	
Supplies	2,300	
Prepaid rent	600	
Office equipment	21,180	
Accumulated depreciation		
— office equipment		$ 4,350
Office furniture	17,680	
Accumulated depreciation		
— office furniture		4,870
Accounts payable		3,640
Property tax payable		1,100
Interest payable		830

Unearned service revenue		620
Note payable		27,500
Monica Gillen, capital		6,090
Monica Gillen, withdrawals	44,000	
Service revenue		127,880
Depreciation expense — office equipment	6,680	
Depreciation expense — office furniture	2,370	
Salary expense	39,900	
Rent expense	14,400	
Interest expense	3,100	
Utilities expense	2,670	
Insurance expense	3,810	
Supplies expense	2,950	
Total	$176,880	$176,880

Required

Prepare Tradewinds' 19X6 income statement, statement of owner's equity, and balance sheet. List expenses in decreasing order on the income statement and show total liabilities on the balance sheet. Draw the arrows linking the three financial statements.

Problem 3-7A   *Preparing an adjusted trial balance and the financial statements* **(L.O. 3,4,5)**

The unadjusted trial balance of Joe Heider, Lawyer, at July 31, 19X2 and the related month-end adjustment data are as follows:

Joe Heider, Lawyer		
Trial Balance		
July 31, 19X2		
Cash	$14,600	
Accounts receivable	11,600	
Prepaid rent	3,600	
Supplies	800	
Furniture	16,800	
Accumulated depreciation		$ 3,500
Accounts payable		3,450
Salary payable		
Joe Heider, capital		38,650
Joe Heider, withdrawals	4,000	
Legal service revenue		8,750
Salary expense	2,400	
Rent expense		
Utilities expense	550	
Depreciation expense		
Supplies expense		
Total	$54,350	$54,350

Adjustment data:

a. Prepaid rent expired during the month. The unadjusted prepaid balance of $3,600 relates to the period July through October.

b. Supplies on hand at July 31, $500.

c. Depreciation on furniture for the month. The estimated useful life of the furniture is four years.

d. Accrued salary expense at July 31 for one day only. The five-day weekly payroll is $1,000.

e. Accrued legal service revenue at July 31, $700.

Required

1. Write the trial balance on a sheet of paper similar to Exhibit 3-5 and prepare the adjusted trial balance of Joe Heider, Lawyer, at July 31, 19X2. Key each adjusting entry by letter.

2. Prepare the income statement, the statement of owner's equity, and the balance sheet. Draw the arrows linking the three financial statements.

Problem 3-8A   *Journalizing and posting adjustments to ledger accounts; preparing the adjusted trial balance and the financial statements* **(L.O. 3,4,5)**

The trial balance of Foster Cleaning Service at July 31, 19X3, and the data needed to make the year-end adjustments are as follows:

Foster Cleaning Service
Trial Balance
July 31, 19X3

Account No.			
101	Cash	$ 1,010	
121	Accounts receivable	6,200	
131	Supplies	3,400	
133	Prepaid rent	1,890	
141	Cleaning equipment	37,300	
151	Accumulated depreciation		$ 14,360
201	Accounts payable		6,410
211	Salary payable		
221	Unearned service revenue		3,110
301	J.B. Foster, capital		14,310
302	J.B. Foster, withdrawals	40,100	
401	Service revenue		91,060
501	Salary expense	32,150	
504	Depreciation expense		
506	Supplies expense		
509	Rent expense	6,000	
511	Utilities expense	1,200	
	Total	$129,250	$129,250

Adjustment data:

a. At July 31, the business has earned $1,420 service revenue that has not yet been recorded.

b. Supplies used during the year totaled $3,060.

c. Prepaid rent still in force at July 31 is $1,040.

d. Depreciation for the year is based on cleaning equipment costing $37,300 and an estimated useful life of 10 years.

e. The entity cleans the carpets of a large apartment complex that pays in advance. At July 31 the entity has earned $2,210 of the unadjusted balance of Unearned Service Revenue.

f. At July 31, the business owes its employees accrued salaries for two thirds of a four-week payroll. Total payroll for the four weeks is $2,670.

Required

1. Open the accounts listed in the trial balance, inserting their July 31 unadjusted balances. The following accounts have experienced no activity during the month, so their balances should be dated July 31: Supplies, Prepaid Rent, Accumulated Depreciation, and Unearned Service Revenue.
2. Journalize the adjusting entries, using page 4 of the journal.
3. Post the adjusting entries to the ledger accounts, using all posting references.
4. Prepare the adjusted trial balance at July 31.
5. Prepare the income statement, the statement of owner's equity, and the balance sheet. Draw the arrows linking the three financial statements.

(Group B)

Problem 3-1B   *Cash-basis versus accrual-basis accounting (L.O. 1,2)*

Samaritan Counseling Service had the following selected transactions during October:

Oct.		
	1	Prepaid insurance for October through December, $450.
	4	Purchased office equipment for cash, $800.
	5	Performed counseling services and received cash, $700.
	8	Paid advertising expense, $100.
	11	Performed counseling service on account, $1,200.
	19	Purchased office furniture on account, $150.
	24	Collected $400 on account for the October 11 service.
	31	Paid account payable from October 19.
	31	Paid salary expense, $600.
	31	Recorded adjusting entry for October insurance expense (see Oct. 1).

Required

1. Show how each transaction would be handled using the cash basis and the accrual basis. Under each column give the amount of revenue or expense for October. Journal entries are not required. Use the following format for your answer, and show your computations:

Amount of Revenue or Expense for October

Date	Cash Basis	Accrual Basis

2. Compute October net income or net loss under each method.
3. Indicate which measure of net income or net loss is preferable. Give your reason.

Problem 3-2B   *Applying accounting principles (L.O. 2)*

As the controller of Hillsborough Auto Glass Company, you have hired a new bookkeeper, whom you must train. Write a memo to explain why adjusting entries are needed to measure net income properly. Mention the accounting principles underlying the use of adjusting entries.

Problem 3-3B   *Journalizing adjusting entries (L.O. 3)*

Journalize the adjusting entry needed on December 31, end of the current accounting period, for each of the following independent cases affecting Randolph Engineering Consulting Company:

a. Each Friday Randolph pays its employees for the current week's work. The amount of the payroll is $2,500 for a five-day work week. The current accounting period ends on Thursday.

b. Randolph has received notes receivable from some clients for professional services. During the current year, Randolph has earned accrued interest revenue of $8,575, which will be received next year.

c. The beginning balance of Engineering Supplies was $3,800. During the year the entity purchased supplies costing $12,530, and at December 31 the inventory of supplies on hand is $2,970.

d. Randolph is conducting tests of the strength of the steel to be used in a large building, and the client paid Randolph $27,000 at the start of the project. Randolph recorded this amount as Unearned Engineering Revenue. The tests will take several months to complete. Randolph executives estimate that the company has earned two thirds of the total fee during the current year.

e. Depreciation for the current year includes: Office Furniture, $4,500; Engineering Equipment, $6,360; and Building, $3,790. Make a compound entry.

f. Details of Prepaid Insurance are shown in the account:

Prepaid Insurance

Jan. 1 Bal. 2,400	
Apr. 30 3,600	
Oct. 31 3,600	

Randolph pays semiannual insurance premiums (the payment for insurance coverage is called a *premium*) on April 30 and October 31. At December 31, $2,400 of the last payment is still in force.

Problem 3-4B   *Analyzing and journalizing adjustments (L.O. 3)*

Ahmed Rashad Company unadjusted and adjusted trial balances at December 31, 19X0, are shown in the following.

Ahmed Rashad Company
Adjusted Trial Balance
December 31, 19X0

Account Title	Trial Balance		Adjusted Trial Balance	
	Debit	Credit	Debit	Credit
Cash	3,620		3,620	
Accounts receivable	11,260		14,090	
Supplies	1,090		780	
Prepaid insurance	2,200		1,330	
Office furniture	21,630		21,630	
Accumulated depreciation		8,220		10,500
Accounts payable		6,310		6,310

Salary payable				960
Interest payable				280
Note payable		12,000		12,000
Unearned commission revenue		1,440		960
Ahmed Rashad, capital		13,010		13,010
Ahmed Rashad, withdrawals	29,370		29,370	
Commission revenue		72,890		76,200
Depreciation expense			2,280	
Supplies expense			310	
Utilities expense	4,960		4,960	
Salary expense	26,660		27,620	
Rent expense	12,200		12,200	
Interest expense	880		1,160	
Insurance expense			870	
	113,870	113,870	120,220	120,220

Required

Journalize the adjusting entries that account for the differences between the two trial balances.

Problem 3-5B   *Journalizing and posting adjustments to T-accounts; preparing the adjusted trial balance and the financial statements* **(L.O. 3,4)**

The trial balance of Conrad Realty at August 31 of the current year and the data needed for the month-end adjustments follow:

Conrad Realty
Trial Balance
August 31, 19XX

Cash	$ 2,200	
Accounts receivable	23,780	
Prepaid rent	2,420	
Supplies	1,180	
Furniture	19,740	
Accumulated depreciation		$ 3,630
Accounts payable		2,410
Salary payable		
Unearned commission revenue		2,790
Tom Griffin, capital		39,510
Tom Griffin, withdrawals	4,800	
Commission revenue		11,700
Salary expense	3,800	
Rent expense		
Utilities expense	550	
Depreciation expense		
Advertising expense	1,570	
Supplies expense		
Total	$60,040	$60,040

Adjustment data:

a. Prepaid rent still in force at August 31, $620.

b. Supplies used during the month, $300.

   c. Depreciation for the month, $400.

   d. Accrued advertising expense at August 31, $110. Credit Accounts Payable.

   e. Accrued salary expense at August 31, $550.

   f. Unearned commission revenue still unearned at August 31, $1,670.

Required

1. Open T-accounts for the accounts listed in the trial balance, inserting their August 31 unadjusted balances.

2. Journalize the adjusting entries and post them to the T-accounts. Key the journal entries and posted amounts by letter.

3. Prepare the adjusted trial balance.

Problem 3-6B   *Preparing the financial statements from an adjusted trial balance* **(L.O. 5)**

The adjusted trial balance of Blaine Delivery Services at December 31, 19X8 follows:

Blaine Delivery Services Adjusted Trial Balance December 31, 19X8		
Cash	$ 8,340	
Accounts receivable	41,490	
Prepaid rent	1,350	
Supplies	970	
Equipment	70,690	
Accumulated depreciation — equipment		$ 22,240
Office furniture	24,100	
Accumulated depreciation — office furniture		18,670
Accounts payable		13,600
Unearned service revenue		4,520
Interest payable		2,130
Salary payable		930
Note payable		40,000
Ray Blaine, capital		32,380
Ray Blaine, withdrawals	48,000	
Service revenue		201,790
Depreciation expense — equipment	11,300	
Depreciation expense — office furniture	2,410	
Salary expense	102,800	
Rent expense	12,000	
Interest expense	4,200	
Utilities expense	3,770	
Insurance expense	3,150	
Supplies expense	1,690	
Total	$336,260	$336,260

Required

Prepare Blaine's 19X8 income statement, statement of owner's equity, and balance sheet. List expenses in decreasing order on the income statement and show total liabilities on the balance sheet. Draw the arrows linking the three financial statements.

Problem 3-7B   *Preparing an adjusted trial balance and the financial statements* **(L.O. 3,4,5)**

Consider the unadjusted trial balance of Terri Peterson, Audio Therapist, at October 31, 19X2 and the related month-end adjustment data.

Terri Peterson, Audio Therapist		
Trial Balance		
October 31, 19X2		
Cash	$16,300	
Accounts receivable	8,000	
Prepaid rent	4,000	
Supplies	600	
Furniture	15,000	
Accumulated depreciation		$ 3,000
Accounts payable		2,800
Salary payable		
Terri Peterson, capital		36,000
Terri Peterson, withdrawals	3,600	
Consulting service revenue		7,400
Salary expense	1,400	
Rent Expense		
Utilities expense	300	
Depreciation expense		
Supplies expense		
Total	$49,200	$49,200

Adjustment data:

a. Prepaid rent expired during the month. The unadjusted prepaid balance of $4,000 relates to the period October through January.

b. Supplies on hand at October 31, $400.

c. Depreciation on furniture for the month. The furniture's expected useful life is five years.

d. Accrued salary expense at October 31 for one day only. The five-day weekly payroll is $1,500.

e. Accrued consulting service revenue at October 31, $1,000.

Required

1. Write the trial balance on a sheet of paper, using as an example Exhibit 3-5, and prepare the adjusted trial balance of Terri Peterson, Audio Therapist, at October 31, 19X2. Key each adjusting entry by the letter.

2. Prepare the income statement, the statement of owner's equity, and the balance sheet. Draw the arrows linking the three financial statements.

Problem 3-8B   *Journalizing and posting adjustments to ledger accounts; preparing the adjusted trial balance and the financial statements* **(L.O. 3,4,5)**

The trial balance of Air-Tite Security Service at May 31, 19X3 is shown on the next page. The data needed to make the year-end adjustments follow:

Adjustment data:

a. At May 31 the business has earned $1,000 service revenue that has not yet been recorded.

b. Supplies used during the year totaled $5,650.

c. Prepaid rent still in force at May 31 is $330.

d. Depreciation for the year is based on tools and installation equipment costing $27,900 and having an estimated useful life of 9 years.

e. Air-Tite installs locks in a large apartment complex that pays in advance. At May 31 the entity has earned $3,600 of the unadjusted balance of Unearned Service Revenue.

f. At May 31, the business owes its employees accrued salaries for half of a four-week payroll. Total payroll for the four weeks is $2,600.

<table>
<tr><td colspan="3" align="center">**Air-Tite Security Service**
Trial Balance
May 31, 19X3</td></tr>
<tr><td>**Account**
No.</td><td></td><td></td></tr>
<tr><td>101</td><td>Cash ....</td><td>$ 3,260</td><td></td></tr>
<tr><td>112</td><td>Accounts receivable.......................................</td><td>4,700</td><td></td></tr>
<tr><td>127</td><td>Supplies..</td><td>7,700</td><td></td></tr>
<tr><td>129</td><td>Prepaid rent ....</td><td>1,430</td><td></td></tr>
<tr><td>143</td><td>Equipment..</td><td>27,900</td><td></td></tr>
<tr><td>154</td><td>Accumulated depreciation ....</td><td></td><td>$ 12,150</td></tr>
<tr><td>211</td><td>Accounts payable...</td><td></td><td>4,240</td></tr>
<tr><td>221</td><td>Salary payable ....</td><td></td><td></td></tr>
<tr><td>243</td><td>Unearned service revenue ....</td><td></td><td>5,810</td></tr>
<tr><td>301</td><td>Thomas King, capital.....................................</td><td></td><td>7,080</td></tr>
<tr><td>311</td><td>Thomas King, withdrawals ....</td><td>34,800</td><td></td></tr>
<tr><td>401</td><td>Service revenue ....</td><td></td><td>80,610</td></tr>
<tr><td>511</td><td>Salary expense..</td><td>28,800</td><td></td></tr>
<tr><td>513</td><td>Depreciation expense ....</td><td></td><td></td></tr>
<tr><td>515</td><td>Supplies expense..</td><td></td><td></td></tr>
<tr><td>519</td><td>Rent expense...</td><td></td><td></td></tr>
<tr><td>521</td><td>Utilities expense...</td><td>1,300</td><td></td></tr>
<tr><td></td><td>Total..</td><td>$109,890</td><td>$109,890</td></tr>
</table>

Required

1. Open the accounts listed in the trial balance, inserting their May 31 unadjusted balances. The following accounts have experienced no activity during the month, so their balances should be dated May 1: Supplies, Prepaid Rent, Accumulated Depreciation, and Unearned Service Revenue.

2. Journalize the adjusting entries, using page 7 of the journal.

3. Post the adjusting entries to the ledger accounts, using all posting references.

4. Prepare the adjusted trial balance at May 31.

5. Prepare the income statement, the statement of owner's equity, and the balance sheet. Draw the arrows linking the three financial statements.

Extending Your Knowledge

Decision Problems

1. Valuing a business based on its net income (L.O. 4,5)

Ace Black has owned and operated Black Biomedical Systems, a management consulting firm for physicians, since its beginning 10 years ago. From all appearances the business has prospered. Black lives in the fast lane — flashy car, home located in an expensive suburb, frequent trips abroad, and other signs of wealth. In the past few years, you have become friends with him and his wife through weekly rounds of golf at the country club. Recently, he mentioned that he has lost his zest for the business and would consider selling it for the right price. He claims that his clientele is firmly established, and that the business "runs on its own." According to Black, the consulting procedures are fairly simple, and anyone could perform the work.

Assume you are interested in buying this business. You obtain its most recent monthly trial balance, which follows. Assume that revenues and expenses vary little from month to month and April is a typical month.

Your investigation reveals that the trial balance does not include the effects of monthly revenues of $1,100 and expenses totaling $2,100. If you were to buy Black Biomedical Systems, you would hire a manager so you could devote your time to other duties. Assume that this person would require a monthly salary of $2,000.

Black Biomedical Systems		
Trial Balance		
April 30, 19XX		
Cash	$ 7,700	
Accounts receivable	4,900	
Prepaid expenses	2,600	
Capital assets	241,300	
Accumulated depreciation		$189,600
Land	138,000	
Accounts payable		11,800
Salary payable		
Unearned consulting revenue		56,700
Ace Black, capital		137,400
Ace Black, withdrawals	9,000	
Consulting revenue		12,300
Salary expense	3,400	
Rent expense		
Utilities expense	900	
Depreciation expense		
Supplies expense		
Total	$407,800	$407,800

Required

1. Is this an unadjusted or adjusted trial balance? How can you tell?

2. Assume that the most you would pay for the business is 30 times the monthly net income you could expect to earn from it. Compute this possible price.

3. Black states that the least he will take for the business is his ending capital. Compute this amount.

4. Under these conditions, how much should you offer Black? Give your reasons.

2. *Understanding the concepts underlying the accrual basis of accounting (L.O. 1,2)*

The following independent questions relate to the accrual basis of accounting:

1. It has been said that the only time a company's financial position is known for certain is when the company is wound up and its only asset is cash. Why is this statement true?

2. A friend suggests that the purpose of adjusting entries is to correct errors in the accounts. Is your friend's statement true? What is the purpose of adjusting entries if the statement is wrong?

3. The text suggested that furniture (and each other capital asset that is depreciated) is a form of prepaid expense. Do you agree? Why do you think some accountants view capital assets this way?

Ethical Issue

The net income of Christopher's, a department store, decreased sharply during 1991. Matthew Christopher, owner of the store, anticipates the need for a bank loan in 1992. Late in 1991 he instructed the accountant to record a $4,500 sale of furniture to the Christopher family, even though the goods will not be shipped from the manufacturer until January 1992. Christopher also told the accountant not to make the following December 31, 1991 adjusting entries:

Salaries owed to employees	$1,800
Prepaid insurance that has expired..................	670

Required

1. Compute the overall effect of these transactions on the store's reported income for 1991.

2. Why did Christopher take this action? Is this action ethical? Give your reason, identifying the parties helped and the parties harmed by Christopher's action.

3. As a personal friend, what advice would you give the accountant?

Financial Statement Problems

1. *Journalizing and posting transactions, and tracing account balances to the financial statements (L.O. 3,4,5)*

Schneider Corporation, like all other businesses, makes adjustments prior to year end in order to measure assets, liabilities, revenues, and expenses properly. Examine Schneider's balance sheet in Appendix C, paying particular attention to "Other" in the current asset section. Assume that the Current Asset account "Other" is a prepaid expense account; call it Prepaid Expenses for the purposes of this question. Also, identify the Accounts Payable and Accrued Liabilities accounts, in the current liability section of the balance sheet. Further, assume that the Accounts Payable and Accrued Liabilities include Selling, Marketing and Administrative Expenses Payable of $27 million on October 27, 1990, and Interest Payable of $4,109,000 on October 27, 1990; use those names as account titles.

Required

1. Open T-accounts for: Prepaid Expenses; Selling, Marketing and Administrative Expenses Payable; and Interest Payable. For each account, insert Schneider's actual October 27, 1990 balance.

2. Journalize the following for fiscal 1991. Key entries by letter. Explanations are not required.

Cash transactions:

   a. Paid prepaid expenses of $6,515,000

   b. Paid the October 27, 1990 Selling, Marketing and Administrative Expenses Payable.

   c. Paid the October 27, 1990 Interest Payable.

   d. Paid Selling, Marketing and Administrative expenses of $8,242,000 during the fiscal year.

   e. Paid Interest expenses of $3,142,000 during the fiscal year.

   Adjustments at October 26, 1991:

   f. Prepaid expenses expired, $6,849,000 Debit Selling, Marketing and Administrative Expenses.

   g. Accrued Selling, Marketing and Administrative Expenses Payable of $31,000,000.

   h. Accrued Interest Payable of $3,808,000.

3. After these entries are posted, show that the balances in the three accounts opened in requirement 1 agree with the corresponding amounts reported in the October 26, 1991 balance sheet.

2.   *Adjusting the accounts of an actual company (L.O. 2)*

Obtain the annual report of an actual company of your choosing. Assume the company accountants failed to make four adjustments at the end of the current year. For illustrative purposes, we shall assume that the amounts reported for the related assets and liabilities are incorrect.

Adjustments omitted:

a. Depreciation of equipment, $800,000.

b. Salaries owed to employees but not yet paid, $230,000.

c. Prepaid rent used up during the year, $100,000.

d. Accrued sales (or service) revenue, $140,000.

Required

1. Compute the correct amounts for the following balance sheet items:
   a. Book value of capital assets
   b. Total liabilities
   c. Prepaid expenses
   d. Accounts receivable

2. Compute the amount of net income or net loss that the company would have reported if the accountants had recorded these transactions properly. Ignore income tax.

Answers to Self-Study Questions

1. b

2. c

3. a

4. d

5. b ($160 + $290 − $210 = $240)

6. b ($120,000 − $50,000 = $70,000)

7. d

8. a ($3,000 received − $1,100 unearned = $1,900 earned)

9. c

10. a

Chapter 4

Completing the Accounting Cycle

"Homer, if you don't get those invoices and cheque stubs to the office in Winnipeg this week, you can just hang it up."

Ed Simpson, the owner of a Winnipeg, Manitoba construction company, was talking to his construction superintendent, Homer Huntley.... By the time Simpson left the small construction shack, Homer was furious. Muttering under his breath, "Bookkeepers! Don't they have anything better to do than ruin my day?" He started yanking invoices, cheque stubs, handwritten notes, and other papers off the nails he had driven into the shack's walls as a haphazard filing system for job records.

Homer stuffed the papers into a brown grocery bag he'd been using as a trash container, folded the bag's top, and fastened it with a nail pulled from the wall.... On his way home later that night, Homer stuffed the bag into a mail box outside the local post office.

Homer was understandably surprised when the company's bookkeeper called a few days later to say that he had received the bag. For years after that, the bag hung on the wall in the accounting office at Simpson Construction Company.

As you read this chapter, consider how the bookkeeper was able to use these scraps of paper and other loose ends to prepare a complete set of financial statements for the project Homer was supervising.

Source: adapted from Arthur Sharplin, "Brown Bag Bookkeeping," *Journal of Accountancy* (July 1986), p. 122.

LEARNING OBJECTIVES

After studying this chapter, you should be able to

1 Prepare a work sheet

2 Explain how a microcomputer spreadsheet can be used in accounting

3 Use the work sheet to complete the accounting cycle

4 Close the revenue, expense and withdrawal accounts

5 Use reversing entries to save time

6 Classify assets and liabilities as current or long-term

7 Correct typical accounting errors

Our humorous real-life example illustrates how some small businesses keep their accounting records. As you study Chapter 4, consider the advantages that a more formal way of keeping records and completing the accounting cycle offers a business.

You have studied how accountants journalize transactions, post to the ledger accounts, prepare the trial balance and the adjusting entries, and draw up the financial statements. One major step remains to complete the accounting cycle — closing the books. This chapter illustrates the closing process for Gary Lyon's law practice at April 30, 19X1. It also shows how to use two additional accounting tools that are optional. One of these optional tools is the accountant's work sheet. Building upon the adjusted trial balance, the work sheet leads directly to the financial statements, which are the focal point of financial accounting. The chapter also presents an example of an actual balance sheet to show how companies classify assets and liabilities in order to provide meaningful information for decision-making.

Overview of the Accounting Cycle _____

The **accounting cycle** is the process by which accountants produce an entity's financial statements for a specific period of time. For a new business, the cycle begins with setting up (opening) the ledger accounts. Gary Lyon started his law practice from scratch on April 1, 19X1, so the first step in the cycle was to open the accounts. After a business has operated for one period, however, the account balances carry over from period to period. Therefore, the accounting cycle usually starts with the account balances at the beginning of the period, as shown in Exhibit 4-1. The exhibit highlights the new steps that we will be discussing in this chapter.

The accounting cycle is divided into work that is performed during the period (journalizing transactions and posting to the ledger) and work performed at the end of the period to prepare the financial statements. A secondary purpose of the end-of-period work is to get the accounts ready for recording the transactions of the next period. The greater number of individual steps at the end of the period may seem to suggest that most of the work is done at the end. Nevertheless, the recording and posting during the period takes far more time than the end-of-period work. Some of the terms in Exhibit 4-1 may be unfamiliar, but they will become clear by the end of the chapter.

The Accountant's Work Sheet _____

Accountants often use a **work sheet**, a columnar document that is designed to help move data from the trial balance to the finished financial statements. The work

EXHIBIT 4-1   *The Accounting Cycle*

During the period
1. Start with the account balances in the ledger at the beginning of the period.
2. Analyze and journalize transactions as they occur.
3. Post journal entries to the ledger accounts.

End of the period
4. Compute the unadjusted balance in each account at the end of the period.
5. **Enter the trial balance on the work sheet, and complete the work sheet.***
6. Using the work sheet as a guide,
   a. Prepare the financial statements.
   b. Journalize and post the adjusting entries.
   c. **Journalize and post the closing entries.**
7. **Prepare the postclosing, or afterclosing, trial balance. This trial balance becomes step 1 for the next period.**

_____
*Optional

sheet provides an orderly way to compute net income and arrange the data for the financial statements. By listing all the accounts and their unadjusted balances, it helps the accountant identify the accounts needing adjustment. Although it is not essential, the work sheet is helpful because it brings together in one place the effects of all the transactions of a particular period. The work sheet aids the closing process by listing the adjusted balances of all the accounts. It also helps the accountant discover potential errors.

OBJECTIVE 1
Prepare a work sheet

The work sheet is not part of the ledger or the journal, nor is it a financial statement. Therefore, it is not part of the formal accounting system. Instead, it is a summary device that exists for the accountant's convenience.

Exhibits 4-2 through 4-6 illustrate the development of a typical work sheet for the business of Gary Lyon, Lawyer. The heading at the top names the business, identifies the document, and states the accounting period. A step-by-step description of its preparation follows. Observe that steps 1 through 3 use the adjusted trial balance that was introduced in Chapter 3. Only steps 4 and 5 are entirely new.

Steps introduced in Chapter 3 to prepare the adjusted trial balance:

1. Write the account titles and their unadjusted ending balances in the Trial Balance columns of the work sheet and total the amounts.

2. Enter the adjustments in the Adjustments columns and total the amounts.

3. Compute each account's adjusted balance by combining the trial balance and adjustment figures. Enter the adjusted amounts in the Adjusted Trial Balance columns.

New steps introduced in this chapter:

4. Extend the asset, liability, and owner's equity amounts from the Adjusted Trial Balance to the Balance Sheet columns. Extend the revenue and expense amounts to the Income Statement columns. Total the statement columns.

5. Compute net income or net loss as the difference between total revenues and total expenses on the income statement. Enter net income or net loss as a balancing amount on the income statement and the balance sheet, and compute the adjusted column totals. After completion, total debits equal total credits in the income statement columns and in the balance sheet columns.

EXHIBIT 4-2

Gary Lyon, Lawyer
Work Sheet
for the month ended April 30, 19X1

Account Title	Trial Balance		Adjustments		Adjusted Trial Balance		Income Statement		Balance Sheet	
	Debit	Credit	Debit	Credit	Debit	Credit	Debit	Credit	Debit	Credit
Cash	24,800									
Accounts receivable	2,250									
Supplies	700									
Prepaid rent	3,000									
Furniture	16,500									
Accumulated depreciation										
Accounts payable		13,100								
Salary payable										
Unearned service revenue		450								
Gary Lyon, capital		31,250								
Gary Lyon, withdrawals	3,200									
Service revenue		7,000								
Rent expense										
Salary expense	950									
Supplies expense										
Depreciation expense										
Utilities expense	400									
	51,800	51,800								

} Write the account titles and their unadjusted ending balances in the Trial Balance columns of the work sheet, and total the amounts.

EXHIBIT 4-3

Gary Lyon, Lawyer
Work Sheet
for the month ended April 30, 19X1

Account Title	Trial Balance Debit	Trial Balance Credit	Adjustments Debit	Adjustments Credit	Adjusted Trial Balance Debit	Adjusted Trial Balance Credit	Income Statement Debit	Income Statement Credit	Balance Sheet Debit	Balance Sheet Credit
Cash	24,800									
Accounts receivable	2,250		(a) 250							
Supplies	700			(b) 300						
Prepaid rent	3,000			(c) 1,000						
Furniture	16,500									
Accumulated depreciation				(d) 275						
Accounts payable		13,100								
Salary payable				(e) 950						
Unearned service revenue		450	(f) 150							
Gary Lyon, capital		31,250								
Gary Lyon, withdrawals	3,200									
Service revenue		7,000		(a) 250						
				(f) 150						
Rent expense			(c) 1,000							
Salary expense	950		(e) 950							
Supplies expense			(b) 300							
Depreciation expense			(d) 275							
Utilities expense	400									
	51,800	51,800	2,925	2,925						

Enter the adjusting entries in the Adjustments columns, and total the amounts.

1. Write the account titles and their unadjusted ending balances in the Trial Balance columns of the work sheet and total the amounts. Of course, total debits should equal total credits as shown in Exhibit 4-2. The account titles and balances come directly from the ledger accounts before the adjusting entries. If the business uses a work sheet, there is no need for a separate trial balance. It is written directly onto the work sheet, as shown in the exhibit. Accounts are grouped on the work sheet by category and are usually listed in the order they appear in the ledger. By contrast, their order on the financial statements follows a different pattern. For example, the expenses on the work sheet in Exhibit 4-2 indicate no particular order. But on the income statement, expenses are ordered by amount with the largest first (see Exhibit 4-7).

Accounts may have zero balances (for example, Depreciation Expense). All accounts are listed on the trial balance because they appear in the ledger. Electronically prepared work sheets list all the accounts, not just those with a balance.

2. Enter the adjusting entries in the Adjustments columns and total the amounts. Exhibit 4-3 includes the April adjusting entries. These are the same adjustments that were illustrated in Chapter 3 to prepare the adjusted trial balance.

How does the accountant identify the accounts that need to be adjusted? By scanning the trial balance. Cash needs no adjustment because all cash transactions are recorded as they occur during the period. Consequently, Cash's balance is up to date.

Accounts Receivable is listed next. Has Gary Lyon earned revenue that he has not yet recorded? The answer is yes. Lyon provides professional service for a client who pays a $500 fee on the 15th of each month. At April 30, Lyon has earned half of this amount, $250, which must be accrued. To accrue this service revenue, Lyon debits Accounts Receivable and credits Service Revenue on the work sheet in Exhibit 4-3. A letter is used to link the debit and the credit of each adjusting entry. By moving down the trial balance, Lyon identifies the remaining accounts needing adjustment. Supplies is next. The business has used supplies during April, so Lyon debits Supplies Expense and credits Supplies. The other adjustments are analyzed and entered on the work sheet as shown in the exhibit.

The process of identifying accounts that need to be adjusted is aided by listing the accounts in their proper sequence. However, suppose one or more accounts is omitted from the trial balance. It can always be written below the first column totals, $51,800. Assume that Supplies Expense was accidentally omitted and thus did not appear on the trial balance. When the accountant identifies the need to update the Supplies account, he or she knows that the debit in the adjusting entry is to Supplies Expense. In this case, the accountant can write Supplies Expense on the line beneath the amount totals and enter the debit adjustment, $300, on the Supplies Expense line. Keep in mind that the work sheet is not the finished version of the financial statements, so the order of the accounts on the work sheet is not critical. When the accountant prepares the income statement, Supplies Expense can be listed in its proper sequence.

3. Compute each account's adjusted balance by combining the trial balance and adjustment figures; enter the adjusted amounts in the Adjusted Trial Balance columns. After the adjustments are entered on the work sheet, the amount columns should be totaled to ensure that total debits equal total credits. This provides some assurance that each debit adjustment is accompanied by an equal credit. Exhibit 4-4 shows the work sheet with the adjusted trial balance added.

This step is performed as it was in Chapter 3. For example, the Cash balance is up to date, so it receives no adjustment. Accounts Receivable's adjusted balance of $2,500 is computed by adding the trial balance amount of $2,250 to the $250

EXHIBIT 4-4

Gary Lyon, Lawyer
Work Sheet
for the month ended April 30, 19X1

Account Title	Trial Balance Debit	Trial Balance Credit	Adjustments Debit	Adjustments Credit	Adjusted Trial Balance Debit	Adjusted Trial Balance Credit	Income Statement Debit	Income Statement Credit	Balance Sheet Debit	Balance Sheet Credit
Cash	24,800				24,800					
Accounts receivable	2,250		(a) 250		2,500					
Supplies	700			(b) 300	400					
Prepaid rent	3,000			(c) 1,000	2,000					
Furniture	16,500				16,500					
Accumulated depreciation				(d) 275		275				
Accounts payable		13,100				13,100				
Salary payable				(e) 950		950				
Unearned service revenue		450	(f) 150			300				
Gary Lyon, capital		31,250				31,250				
Gary Lyon, withdrawals	3,200				3,200					
Service revenue		7,000		(a) 250		7,400				
				(f) 150						
Rent expense			(c) 1,000		1,000					
Salary expense	950		(e) 950		1,900					
Supplies expense			(b) 300		300					
Depreciation expense			(d) 275		275					
Utilities expense	400				400					
	51,800	51,800	2,925	2,925	53,275	53,275				

Compute each account's adjusted balance by combining the trial balance and adjustment figures. Enter the adjusted amounts in the Adjusted Trial Balance columns.

EXHIBIT 4-5

Gary Lyon, Lawyer
Work Sheet
for the month ended April 30, 19X1

Account Title	Trial Balance		Adjustments		Adjusted Trial Balance		Income Statement		Balance Sheet	
	Debit	Credit	Debit	Credit	Debit	Credit	Debit	Credit	Debit	Credit
Cash	24,800				24,800				24,800	
Accounts receivable	2,250		(a) 250		2,500				2,500	
Supplies	700			(b) 300	400				400	
Prepaid rent	3,000			(c) 1,000	2,000				2,000	
Furniture	16,500				16,500				16,500	
Accumulated depreciation				(d) 275		275				275
Accounts payable		13,100				13,100				13,100
Salary payable				(e) 950		950				950
Unearned service revenue		450	(f) 150			300				300
Gary Lyon, capital		31,250				31,250				31,250
Gary Lyon, withdrawals	3,200				3,200				3,200	
Service revenue		7,000		(a) 250		7,400		7,400		
				(f) 150						
Rent expense			(c) 1,000		1,000		1,000			
Salary expense	950		(e) 950		1,900		1,900			
Supplies expense			(b) 300		300		300			
Depreciation expense			(d) 275		275		275			
Utilities expense	400				400		400			
	51,800	51,800	2,925	2,925	53,275	53,275	3,875	7,400	49,400	45,875

Extend the asset, liability, and owner's equity amounts from the the the Adjusted Trial Balance to the Balance Sheet columns. Extend the revenue and expense amounts to the Income Statement columns. Total the statement columns.

EXHIBIT 4-6

Gary Lyon, Lawyer
Work Sheet
for the month ended April 30, 19X1

Account Title	Trial Balance Debit	Trial Balance Credit	Adjustments Debit	Adjustments Credit	Adjusted Trial Balance Debit	Adjusted Trial Balance Credit	Income Statement Debit	Income Statement Credit	Balance Sheet Debit	Balance Sheet Credit
Cash	24,800				24,800				24,800	
Accounts receivable	2,250		(a) 250		2,500				2,500	
Supplies	700			(b) 300	400				400	
Prepaid rent	3,000			(c) 1,000	2,000				2,000	
Furniture	16,500				16,500				16,500	
Accumulated depreciation				(d) 275		275				275
Accounts payable		13,100				13,100				13,100
Salary payable				(e) 950		950				950
Unearned service revenue		450	(f) 150			300				300
Gary Lyon, capital		31,250				31,250				31,250
Gary Lyon, withdrawals	3,200				3,200				3,200	
Service revenue		7,000		(a) 250		7,400		7,400		
				(f) 150						
Rent expense			(c) 1,000		1,000		1,000			
Salary expense	950		(e) 950		1,900		1,900			
Supplies expense			(b) 300		300		300			
Depreciation expense			(d) 275		275		275			
Utilities expense	400				400		400			
	51,800	51,800	2,925	2,925	53,275	53,275	3,875	7,400	49,400	45,875
Net income							3,525			3,525
							7,400	7,400	49,400	49,400

Compute net income or net loss as the difference between total revenues and total expenses on the income statement. Enter net income or net loss as a balancing amount on the income statement and on the balance sheet, and compute the adjusted column totals.

debit adjustment. Supplies' adjusted balance of $400 is determined by subtracting the $300 credit adjustment from the debit balance of $700. An account may receive more than one adjustment, as does Service Revenue. The column totals should maintain the equality of debit and credits.

4. Extend the asset, liability and owner's equity amounts from the Adjusted Trial Balance to the Balance Sheet columns. Extend the revenue and expense amounts to the Income Statement columns. Total the statement columns. Every account is either a balance sheet account or an income statement account. The asset, liability and owner's equity accounts go to the balance sheet, and the revenues and expenses go to the income statement. Debits on the adjusted trial balance remain debits in the statement columns, and likewise for credits. Each account's adjusted balance should appear in only one statement column, as shown in Exhibit 4-5.

The income statement indicates total expenses in the debit column ($3,875) and total revenues ($7,400) in the credit column. The balance sheet shows total debits of $49,400 and total credits of $45,875. At this stage, the column totals should not necessarily be equal.

5. Compute net income or net loss as the difference between total revenues and total expenses on the income statement. Enter net income or net loss as a balancing amount on the income statement and on the balance sheet and compute the adjusted column totals. Exhibit 4-6 presents the completed work sheet, which shows net income of $3,525, computed as follows:

Revenue (total credits on the income statement)	$7,400
Expenses (total debits on the income statement)	3,875
Net income	$3,525

Net income of $3,525 is entered in the debit column of the income statement, and the income statement columns are totaled at $7,400. The net income amount is then extended to the credit column of the balance sheet. This is because an excess of revenues over expenses increases capital, and increases in capital are recorded by a credit. In the closing process, which we discuss later, net income will find its way into the capital account.

If expenses exceed revenue, the result is a net loss. In that event, the accountant writes the words *Net loss* on the work sheet. The loss amount should be entered in the credit column of the income statement and in the debit column of the balance sheet. This is because an excess of expenses over revenue decreases capital, and decreases in capital are recorded by a debit.

The balance sheet columns are totaled at $49,400. An out-of-balance condition indicates an error in preparing the work sheet. Common mistakes include arithmetic errors and carrying an amount to the wrong column — to the incorrect statement column, or extending a debit as a credit or vice versa. Columns that balance offer some, but not complete, assurance that the work sheet is correct. For example, it is possible to have offsetting errors. Fortunately, that is unlikely.

Computer Spreadsheets

Computerized general ledger packages, which we discussed in the last chapter, have a disadvantage. With most general ledger packages, the trial balance, adjustments, and adjusted trial balance cannot appear on the computer screen at the same time. To counter this disadvantage, some software programs create an electronically prepared work sheet, also called a **spreadsheet** or an **electronic spreadsheet**. Lotus 1-2-3® and Supercalc® are popular electronic spreadsheets.

An electronic spreadsheet is a grid of information *cells* named by row and column. Columns are designated alphabetically from left to right, rows numerically from top to bottom. For example, the cell in the third row from the top and fourth column from the left is labeled D3. Spreadsheets typically have thousands of rows and hundreds of columns. Accountants skilled in using electronic spreadsheets can use them for work sheet analysis.

An electronic spreadsheet has three types of information: numbers, labels, and formulas. For example, the title of an account on an electronic spreadsheet formatted as a work sheet would be entered in, say, cells A3 and A4 as a label: Accounts Receivable. The unadjusted debit balance of $2,250 debit (see the work sheet in Exhibits 4-4 through 4-6) would be entered as a number in the next column, B4. A credit balance for an account would appear in column C. Column D would hold an adjustment if a debit ($250 in our example), and column E would hold an adjustment if a credit. Column F would hold the adjusted trial balance for this account if a debit, and column G would hold the adjusted trial balance, if a credit.

How does the accountant get the correct amount displayed in column F or column G? Let us use a simplified example to illustrate. A formula is entered cell F4 as follows: @ SUM(B4 + D4) – E4. The formula itself would not appear in the cell. It would appear in the upper-left corner of the spreadsheet when the cursor (the electronic marker) is in that cell. Notice this formula on the sample screen below. What would appear in F4 is the numerical result of that formula, which is 2,500 (2,250 + 250 – 0).

The spreadsheet can be programmed to complete the entire work sheet after the accountant has entered the trial balance and the adjustment amounts. This is a big time-saver because once the spreadsheet program is set up, it can be saved as a spreadsheet template. This can be used over and over again without the user having to rewite the account titles or the cell formulas and do the arithmetic by hand. The spreadsheet can also be programmed to journalize and post the adjusting and closing entries, and prepare the financial statements directly from the data on the work sheet.

```
F4: @SUM(B4+D4)-E4                                                    READY

              A          B         C        D        E        F        G
    1                   TRIAL BALANCE       ADJUSTMENT     ADJUSTED TRIAL BALANCE
    2                   Debit   Credit    Debit   Credit    Debit   Credit
    3    Accounts
    4    receivable     2250              250               2500
    5
    6
    7
    8
    9
   10
   11
   12
   13
   14
   15
   16
   17
   18
   19
   20
   28-Aug-92 09:10 AM                                            NUM CAPS
```

Summary Problem for Your Review

The trial balance of O'Malley's Service Company at December 31, 19X1, the end of its fiscal year, is presented below:

O'Malley's Service Company
Trial Balance
December 31, 19X1

Cash	$ 198,000	
Accounts receivable	370,000	
Supplies	6,000	
Furniture and fixtures	100,000	
Accumulated depreciation		
— furniture and fixtures		$ 40,000
Building	250,000	
Accumulated depreciation — building		130,000
Accounts payable		380,000
Salary payable		
Unearned service revenue		45,000
Trish O'Malley, capital		293,000
Trish O'Malley, withdrawals	65,000	
Service revenues		286,000
Salary expense	172,000	
Supplies expense		
Depreciation expense		
— furniture and fixtures		
Depreciation expense — building		
Miscellaneous expense	13,000	
Total	$1,174,000	$1,174,000

Data needed for the adjusting entries include:

a. Supplies on hand at year end, $2,000

b. Depreciation on furniture and fixtures, $20,000

c. Depreciation on building, $10,000

d. Salaries owed but not yet paid, $5,000

e. Accrued service revenue, $12,000

f. Of the $45,000 balance of Unearned Service Revenue, $32,000 was earned during the year.

Required

Prepare the work sheet of O'Malley's Service Company for the year ended December 31, 19X1. Key each adjusting entry by the letter corresponding to the data given.

SOLUTION TO REVIEW PROBLEM

O'Malley's Service Company
Work Sheet
for the year ended December 31, 19X1

Account Title	Trial Balance Debit	Trial Balance Credit	Adjustments Debit	Adjustments Credit	Adjusted Trial Balance Debit	Adjusted Trial Balance Credit	Income Statement Debit	Income Statement Credit	Balance Sheet Debit	Balance Sheet Credit
Cash	198,000				198,000					198,000
Accounts receivable	370,000		(e) 12,000		382,000					382,000
Supplies	6,000			(a) 4,000	2,000				2,000	
Furniture and fixtures	100,000				100,000				100,000	
Accumulated depreciation										
— furniture and fixtures		40,000		(b) 20,000		60,000				60,000
Building	250,000				250,000				250,000	
Accumulated depreciation										
— building		130,000		(c) 10,000		140,000				140,000
Accounts payable		380,000				380,000				380,000
Salary payable				(d) 5,000		5,000				5,000
Unearned service revenue		45,000	(f) 32,000			13,000				13,000
Trish O'Malley, capital		293,000				293,000				293,000
Trish O'Malley, withdrawals	65,000				65,000				65,000	
Service revenue		286,000		(e) 12,000		330,000		330,000		
				(f) 32,000						
Salary expense	172,000		(d) 5,000		177,000		177,000			
Supplies expense			(a) 4,000		4,000		4,000			
Depreciation expense										
—furniture and fixtures			(b) 20,000		20,000		20,000			
Depreciation expense — building			(c) 10,000		10,000		10,000			
Miscellaneous expense	13,000				13,000		13,000			
	1,174,000	1,174,000	83,000	83,000	1,221,000	1,221,000	224,000	330,000	997,000	891,000
Net income							106,000			106,000
							330,000	330,000	997,000	997,000

Using the Work Sheet

OBJECTIVE 3

Use the work sheet
to complete the
accounting cycle

As illustrated thus far, the work sheet helps organize accounting data and compute the net income or net loss for the period. It also aids in preparing the financial statements, recording the adjusting entries and closing the accounts.

Preparing the Financial Statements

Even though the work sheet shows the amount of net income or net loss for the period, it is still necessary to prepare the financial statements. The sorting of accounts to the balance sheet and income statement eases the preparation of the statements. The work sheet also provides the data for the statement of owner's equity. Exhibit 4-7 presents the April financial statements for the law practice of Gary Lyon, Lawyer (based on the data from the work sheet in Exhibit 4-6).

The financial statements can be prepared directly from the adjusted trial balance as shown in Chapter 3. That is why completion of the work sheet is optional.

EXHIBIT 4-7 April Financial Statements of Gary Lyon, Lawyer

Gary Lyon, Lawyer
Income Statement
for the month ended April 30, 19X1

Revenues		
Service revenue		$7,400
Expenses		
Salary expense	$1,900	
Rent expense	1,000	
Utilities expense	400	
Supplies expense	300	
Depreciation expense	275	
Total expenses		3,875
Net income		$3,525

Gary Lyon, Lawyer
Statement of Owner's Equity
for the month ended April 30, 19X1

Gary Lyon, capital, April 1, 19X1	$31,250
Add: Net income	3,525
	34,775
Less: Withdrawals	3,200
Gary Lyon, capital, April 30, 19X1	$31,575

Gary Lyon, Lawyer
Balance Sheet
April 30, 19X1

Assets			Liabilities	
Cash		$24,800	Accounts payable	$13,100
Accounts receivable		2,500	Salary payable	950
Supplies		400	Unearned service revenue	300
Prepaid rent		2,000	Total liabilities	14,350
Furniture	$16,500			
Less: Accumulated			**Owner's Equity**	
depreciation	275	16,225	Gary Lyon, capital	31,575
			Total liabilities and	
Total assets		$45,925	owner's equity	$45,925

Recording the Adjusting Entries

The adjusting entries are a key element of accrual-basis accounting. The work sheet helps identify the accounts that need adjustments, which may be conveniently entered directly on the work sheet as shown in Exhibits 4-2 through 4-6. However, these work sheet procedures do not adjust the accounts in the ledger itself. Recall that the work sheet is neither a journal nor a ledger. Actual adjustment of the accounts requires journal entries that are posted to the ledger accounts. Therefore, the adjusting entries must be recorded in the journal as shown in Panel A of Exhibit 4-8. Panel B of the exhibit shows the postings to the accounts, with Adj. denoting an

EXHIBIT 4-8 *Journalizing and Posting the Adjusting Entries*

Panel A: Journalizing Adjusting Entries

Page 4

Apr. 30	Accounts Receivable	250	
	Service Revenue		250
30	Supplies Expense	300	
	Supplies		300
30	Rent Expense	1,000	
	Prepaid Rent		1,000
30	Depreciation Expense	275	
	Accumulated Depreciation		275
30	Salary Expense	950	
	Salary Payable		950
30	Unearned Service Revenue	150	
	Service Revenue		150

Panel B: Posting the Adjustments to the Revenue and Expense Accounts

REVENUE

EXPENSES

Service Revenue

		7,000
Adj.		250
Adj.		150
Bal.		7,400

Rent Expense

Adj.	1,000
Bal.	1,000

Salary Expense

	950
Adj.	950
Bal.	1,900

Depreciation Expense

Adj.	275
Bal.	275

Utilities Expense

	400
Bal.	400

Supplies Expense

Adj.	300
Bal.	300

Adj. = Amount posted from an adjusting entry
Bal. = Balance

---

amount posted from an adjusting entry. Only the revenue and expense accounts are presented here in order to focus on the closing process, which is discussed in the next section.

The adjusting entries could have been recorded in the journal as they were entered on the work sheet. However, it is not necessary to journalize them at that time. Most accountants prepare the financial statements immediately after completing the work sheet. They can wait to journalize and post the adjusting entries before they make the closing entries.

Delaying the journalizing and posting of the adjusting entries illustrates another use of the work sheet. Many companies journalize and post the adjusting entries (as in Exhibit 4-8) only once annually, at the end of the year. The need for monthly and quarterly financial statements, however, requires a tool like the work sheet. The entity can use the work sheet to aid in preparing interim statements without entering the adjusting entries in the journal and posting them to the ledger.

Closing the Accounts

Accountants use the term **closing the accounts** to refer to the step at the end of the period that prepares the accounts for recording the transactions of the next period. Closing the accounts consists of journalizing and posting the closing entries. Closing sets the balances of the revenue and expense accounts back to zero in order to measure the net income of the next period. Closing is a clerical procedure devoid of any accounting theory. Recall that the income statement reports only one period's income. For example, net income for Journey's End Corp., owner of Journey's End motels, for the year ended July 31, 1993 relates exclusively to the twelve months ended on that date. At July 31, 1993, Journey's End accountants close the company's revenues and expense accounts for that year. Because these accounts' balances relate to a particular accounting period and are therefore closed at the end of the period, the revenue and expense accounts are called **temporary (nominal) accounts**. The owner's withdrawal account (although not a revenue or an expense) is also a temporary account, because it is important to measure withdrawals for a specific period. The closing process applies only to temporary accounts.

To better understand the closing process, contrast the nature of the temporary accounts with the nature of the **permanent (real) accounts** — the assets, liabilities, and capital. The permanent accounts are *not* closed at the end of the period because there balances are not used to measure income. Consider Cash, Supplies, Buildings, Accounts Payable, Notes Payable, and Gary Lyon, Capital. These accounts do not represent increases and decreases for a single period as do revenues and expenses, which relate only to one accounting period. Instead the permanent accounts represent assets, liabilities, and capital that are on hand at a specific time. This is why their balances at the end of one accounting period carry over to become the beginning balances of the next period. For example, the Cash balance at December 31, 19X1 is also the beginning balance for 19X2.

Briefly, **closing entries** transfer the revenue, expense and owner withdrawal balances from their respective accounts to the capital account. As you know, revenues increase owner's equity, and expenses and owner withdrawals decrease it. It is when we post the closing entries that the capital account absorbs the impact of the balances in the temporary accounts. As an intermediate step, however, the revenues and the expenses are transferred first to an account entitled **Income Summary**, which collects in one place the total debit for the sum of all expenses and the total credit for the sum of all revenues of the period. The Income Summary account is like a temporary "holding tank" used only in the closing process. Then the balance of Income Summary is transferred to capital. The steps in closing the accounts of a proprietorship like Gary Lyon, Lawyer, are as follows:

1. Debit each revenue account for the amount of its credit balance. Credit Income Summary for the sum of the revenues. This entry transfers the sum of the revenues to the credit side of the Income Summary.

2. Credit each expense account for the amount of its debit balance. Debit Income Summary for the sum of the expenses. This entry transfers the sum of the expenses to the debit side of the Income Summary.

3. Debit Income Summary for the amount of its credit balance (revenues minus expenses) and credit the Capital account. If Income Summary has a debit balance, then credit Income Summary for this amount and debit Capital. This entry transfers the net income or loss from Income Summary to the Capital account.

4. Credit the Withdrawals account for the amount of its debit balance. Debit the Capital account of the proprietor. Withdrawals are not expenses and do not affect net income or net loss. Therefore this account is not closed to the Income Summary. This entry transfers the withdrawal amount to the debit side of the Capital account.

To illustrate, suppose Gary Lyon closes the books at the end of April. Exhibit 4-9 presents the complete closing process for Lyon's business. Panel A gives the closing journal entries, and Panel B shows the accounts after the closing entries have been posted.

OBJECTIVE 4

Close the revenue, expense, and withdrawal accounts

EXHIBIT 4-9 *Journalizing and Posting the Closing Entries*

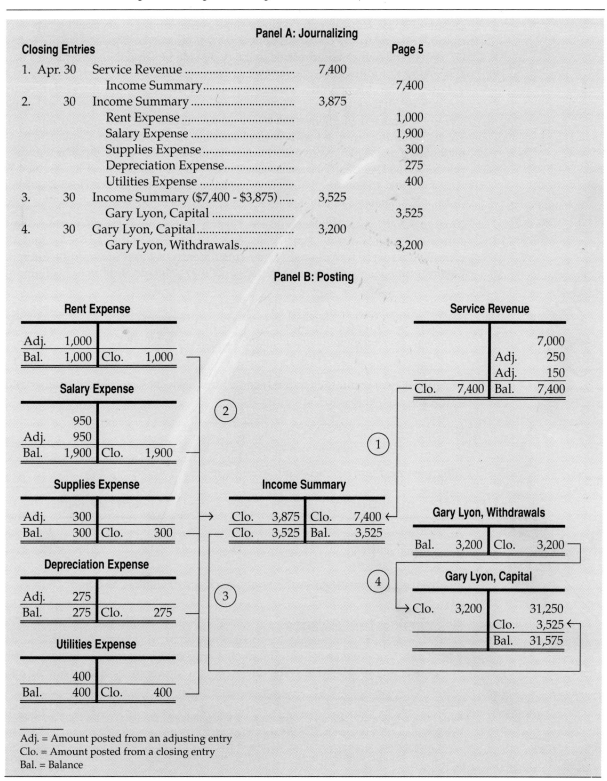

Panel A: Journalizing

Closing Entries   Page 5

1.	Apr. 30	Service Revenue	7,400	
		Income Summary.............................		7,400
2.	30	Income Summary..................................	3,875	
		Rent Expense.....................................		1,000
		Salary Expense...................................		1,900
		Supplies Expense...............................		300
		Depreciation Expense.......................		275
		Utilities Expense		400
3.	30	Income Summary ($7,400 - $3,875)	3,525	
		Gary Lyon, Capital		3,525
4.	30	Gary Lyon, Capital..............................	3,200	
		Gary Lyon, Withdrawals.................		3,200

Panel B: Posting

Rent Expense

Adj.	1,000		
Bal.	1,000	Clo.	1,000

Salary Expense

	950		
Adj.	950		
Bal.	1,900	Clo.	1,900

Supplies Expense

Adj.	300		
Bal.	300	Clo.	300

Depreciation Expense

Adj.	275		
Bal.	275	Clo.	275

Utilities Expense

	400		
Bal.	400	Clo.	400

② ① ③ ④

Income Summary

Clo.	3,875	Clo.	7,400
Clo.	3,525	Bal.	3,525

Service Revenue

			7,000
		Adj.	250
		Adj.	150
Clo.	7,400	Bal.	7,400

Gary Lyon, Withdrawals

Bal.	3,200	Clo.	3,200

Gary Lyon, Capital

Clo.	3,200		31,250
		Clo.	3,525
		Bal.	31,575

Adj. = Amount posted from an adjusting entry
Clo. = Amount posted from a closing entry
Bal. = Balance

The amount in the debit side of each expense account is its adjusted balance. For example, Rent Expense has a $1,000 debit balance. Also note that Service Revenue has a credit balance of $7,400 before closing. These amounts come directly from the adjusted balances in Panel B, Exhibit 4-8.

Closing entry 1, denoted in the Service Revenue account Clo., transfers Service Revenue's balance to the Income Summary account. This entry zeroes out Service Revenue for April and places the revenue on the credit side of Income Summary. Closing entry 2 zeroes out the expenses and moves their total ($3,875) to the debit side of Income Summary. At this point, Income Summary contains the impact of April's revenues and expenses; hence Income Summary's balance is the month's net income ($3,525). Closing entry 3 closes the Income Summary account by transferring net income to the credit side of Gary Lyon, Capital.[1] The last closing entry, (4), moves the owner withdrawals to the debit side of Capital, leaving a zero balance in the Withdrawals account.

After all the closing entries, the revenues, the expenses, and the Withdrawals account are set back to zero to make ready for the next period. The owner's Capital account includes the full effects of the April revenues, expenses, and withdrawals. These amounts, combined with Capital's beginning balance, give Capital an ending balance of $31,575. Note that this Capital balance agrees with the amount reported on the statement of owner's equity and on the balance sheet in Exhibit 4-7. Also note that the ending balance of Capital remains. We do not close it out because it is a balance sheet account.

Closing a Net Loss   What would the closing entries be, if Lyon's business had suffered a net *loss* during April? Suppose April expenses totaled $7,700 and all other factors were unchanged. Only closing entries 2 and 3 would be altered. Closing entry 2 would transfer expenses of $7,700 to Income Summary, as follows:

Income Summary

Clo.	7,700	Clo.	7,400
Bal.	300		

Closing entry 3 would then credit Income Summary to close its debit balance and to transfer the net loss to Capital:

3.	Apr. 30	Gary Lyon, Capital..	300	
		Income Summary..		300

After posting, these two accounts would appear as follows:

Income Summary

Clo.	7,700	Clo.	7,400
Bal.	300	Clo.	300

Gary Lyon, Capital

Clo.	300	31,250

Finally, the Withdrawals balance would be closed to Capital, as before.

Postclosing Trial Balance

The accounting cycle ends with the **postclosing trial balance** (see Exhibit 4-10). The postclosing trial balance is the final check on the accuracy of journalizing and

---

[1] The Income Summary account is a convenience for combining the effects of the revenues and expenses prior to transferring their income effect to Capital. It is not necessary to use the Income Summary account in the closing process. Another way of closing the revenues and expenses makes no use of this account. In this alternative procedure, the revenues and expenses are closed directly to Capital.

EXHIBIT 4-10   *Postclosing Trial Balance*

Gary Lyon, Lawyer		
Postclosing Trial Balance		
April 30, 19X1		
Cash	$24,800	
Accounts receivable	2,500	
Supplies	400	
Prepaid rent	2,000	
Furniture	16,500	
Accumulated depreciation		$ 275
Accounts payable		13,100
Salary payable		950
Unearned service revenue		300
Gary Lyon, capital		31,575
Total	$46,200	$46,200

posting the adjusting and closing entries. Like the trial balance that begins the work sheet, the postclosing trial balance is a list of the ledger's accounts and balances. This step ensures that the ledger is in balance for the start of the next accounting period. The postclosing trial balance is dated as of the end of the accounting period for which the statements have been prepared.

Note that the postclosing trial balance resembles the balance sheet. It contains the ending balances of the permanent accounts — the balance sheet accounts: the assets, liabilities and capital. No temporary accounts (revenues, expenses, or withdrawal accounts) are included because their balances have been closed. The ledger is up to date and ready for the next period's transactions.

Reversing Entries

Reversing entries are special types of entries that ease the burden of accounting after adjusting and closing entries have been made at the end of a period. Reversing entries are used most often in conjunction with accrual-type adjustments such as accrued salary expense and accrued service revenue. GAAP does not require reversing entries. They are used only for convenience and to save time.

Reversing Entries for Accrued Expense   Accrued expenses accumulate with the passage of time and are paid at a later date. At the end of the period, the business makes an adjusting entry to record the expense that has accumulated up to that time.

To see how reversing entries work, return to the adjusting entries (Exhibit 4-8) that Gary Lyon used to update his accounting records for the April financial statements. At April 30 (prior to the the the adjusting entries), Salary Expense has a debit balance of $950 from salaries paid during April. At April 30, the business owes employees an additional $950 for their service during the last part of the month. Assume for the purpose of this illustration that on May 5, the next payroll date, Lyon will pay $950 of accrued salaries plus $100 in salaries that employees have earned in the first few days of May. The next payroll payment will be $1,050 ($950 + $100). However, to present the correct financial picture, the $950 in salaries incurred in April must be included in the April statements, not in the May statements. Accordingly, Lyon makes the following adjusting entry on April 30:

OBJECTIVE 5
Use reversing entries to save time

Adjusting Entries

April 30   Salary Expense   950
                    Salary Payable   950

After posting, the Salary Payable and Salary Expense accounts appear as follows:

Salary Payable

| | Apr. 30 Adj.*   950 |
| | Apr. 30 Bal.   950 |

Salary Expense

Paid	
during	
April CP 950	
Apr. 30 Adj. 950	
Apr. 30 Bal. 1,900	

---

*Entry explanations used throughout this discussion are

Adj. = Adjusting entry	CP = Cash payment entry
Bal. = Balance	CR = Cash receipt entry
Clo. = Closing entry	Rev. = Reversing entry

After the adjusting entry, the April income statement reports Salary Expense of $1,900, and the balance sheet at April 30 reports Salary Payable, a liability, of $950. The $1,900 debit balance of Salary Expense is eliminated by a closing entry at April 30, 19X1, as follows:

Closing Entries

April 30   Income Summary   1,900
                    Salary Expense   1,900

After posting, Salary Expense appears as follows:

Salary Expense

Paid	
during	
April CP 950	
Apr. 30 Adj. 950	
Apr. 30 Bal. 1,900	Apr. 30 Clo. 1,900

In the normal course of recording salary payments during the year, Gary Lyon makes the standard entry, as follows:

Salary Expense..   XXX
        Cash   XXX

In our example, however, payday does not land on the day the accounting period ends, and Lyon has made an adjusting entry to accrue salary payable of $950, as we have just seen. On May 5, the next payday, assume the total payroll is $1,050. Lyon credits Cash for $1,050, but what account (or accounts) should he debit? The cash payment entry is

May 5   Salary Payable   950
                Salary Expense   100
                        Cash   1,050

This method of recording the cash payment is correct, but inefficient because Lyon must refer back to the adjusting entries of April 30. Otherwise, he does not know the amount of the required debit to Salary Payable (in this example, $950). Searching through the preceding period's adjusting entries takes time, and in business, time is money. To avoid having to separate the debit of a later cash payment entry into two accounts, accountants have devised a technique called *reversing* entries.

Making a Reversing Entry   A **reversing entry** switches the debit and the credit of a previous adjusting entry. A reversing entry, then, is the exact opposite of an adjusting entry. The reversing entry is dated the first day of the period following the adjusting entry.

Let us continue with our example of the May 5 cash payment of $1,050 in salaries. On April 30, 19X1, Lyon made the following adjusting entry to accrue Salary Payable:

Adjusting Entries

Apr. 30	Salary Expense	950	
	Salary Payable...		950

The reversing entry simply reverses the position of the debit and the credit:

Reversing Entries

May 1	Salary Payable..	950	
	Salary Expense		950

Notice that the reversing entry is dated the first day of the new period. It is the exact opposite of the April 30 adjusting entry. Ordinarily, the person who makes the adjusting entry also prepares the reversing entry at the same time. Lyon postdates the reversing entry to the first day of the next period, however, so that it affects only the new period. Note how the accounts appear after Lyon posts the reversing entry:

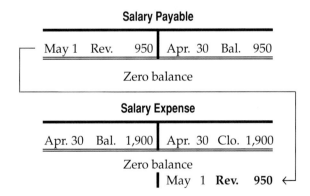

The arrow shows the transfer of the $950 credit balance from Salary Payable to Salary Expense. This credit balance in Salary Expense does not mean that the entity has negative salary expense, as might be suggested by a credit balance in an expense account. Instead, the odd credit balance is merely a temporary result of the reversing entry. The credit balance is eliminated on May 5 when the $1,050 cash payment for salaries is debited to Salary Expense in the customary manner:

May 5	Salary Expense..	1,050	
	Cash...		1,050

Then this cash payment entry is posted:

Salary Expense

May 5	CP	1,050	May 1 Rev.	950
May 5	Bal.	100		

Now Salary Expense has its correct debit balance of $100, which is the amount of salary expense incurred thus far in May. The $1,050 cash disbursement also pays the liability for Salary Payable. Thus the Salary Payable account has a zero balance which is correct, as shown on the previous page.

The adjusting and reversing process is repeated period after period. Cash payments for salaries are debited to Salary Expense, and these amounts accumulate in that account. At the end of the period, the accountant makes an adjusting entry to accrue salary expense incurred but not yet paid. At the same time, the accountant also makes a reversing entry, which allows him or her to record all payroll entries in the customary manner by routinely debiting Salary Expense. Even in computerized systems, making reversing entries is more efficient than writing a program to locate the amount accrued from the preceding period and making the more complicated journal entry. Reversing entries may be made for all types of accrued expenses.

Reversing Entries for Accrued Revenues   Certain revenues, such as services performed on a continuous basis and interest earned on notes receivable, accrue with the passage of time, just as expenses do. However, a business usually does not record accrued revenues daily, weekly or even monthly. Thus at the end of the accounting period, the business may have to accrue revenue that will be collected later. Then, when cash is received, a second entry is needed.

To illustrate reversing entries for accrued revenue, recall that Gary Lyon performs services for clients on a monthly basis. At April 30, Lyon has earned $250 of service revenue that he will collect on May 15, along with an additional $250 for services performed in the first half of May. On April 30, Lyon made this adjusting entry:

Adjusting Entries

Apr. 30	Accounts Receivable	250	
	Service Revenue		250

At the same time, Lyon can make the following reversing entry, postdated to May 1:

Reversing Entries

May 1	Service Revenue	250	
	Accounts Receivable		250

The net effect of the reversing entry is that Lyon need not refer back to the April 30 adjusting entry when recording the May cash transaction. On May 15, when he receives $500 from the client, Lyon can record the cash receipt as follows:

May 15	Cash	500	
	Service Revenue		500

After this entry is posted, the accounts have their correct balances.

The appendix at the end of this chapter discusses the use of reversing entries for prepaid expenses and unearned revenues.

Classification of Assets and Liabilities _____

On the balance sheet, assets and liabilities are classified as either *current* or *long-term* to indicate their relative *liquidity*. **Liquidity** is a measure of how quickly an item may be converted to cash. Therefore, cash is the most liquid asset. Accounts receivable is a relatively liquid asset because the business expects to collect the amount in cash in the near future. Supplies are less liquid than accounts receivable, and furniture and buildings are even less so.

Users of financial statements are interested in liquidity because business difficulties often arise owing to a shortage of cash. How quickly can the business convert an asset to cash and pay a debt? How soon must a liability be paid? These are questions of liquidity. Balance sheets list assets and liabilities in the order of their relative liquidity.

> **OBJECTIVE 6**
> Classify assets and liabilities as current or long-term

Current Assets   **Current assets** are assets that are expected to be converted to cash, sold or consumed during the next 12 months or within the business's normal operating cycle if longer than a year. The **operating cycle** is the time span during which (1) cash is used to acquire goods and services, and (2) those goods and services are sold to customers, who in turn pay for their purchases with cash. For most businesses, the operating cycle is a few months. A few types of business have operating cycles longer than a year. Cash, Accounts Receivable, Notes Receivable due within a year or less, and Prepaid Expenses are current assets. Merchandising entities such as Eaton's, The Bay, and Woodwards have an additional current asset, Inventory. This account shows the cost of goods that are held for sale to customers.

Long-Term Assets   **Long-term assets** are all assets other than current assets. They are not held for sale, but rather they are used to operate the business. One category of long-term assets is capital assets or fixed assets. Land, Buildings, Furniture and Fixtures, and Equipment are examples of capital assets.

Financial statement users such as creditors are interested in the due dates of an entity's liabilities. The sooner a liability must be paid, the more current it is. Liabilities that must be paid on the earliest future date create the greatest strain on cash. Therefore, the balance sheet lists liabilities in the order in which they are due. Knowing how many of a business's liabilities are current and how many are long-term helps creditors assess the likelihood of collecting from the entity. Balance sheets usually have at least two liability classifications, *current liabilities* and *long-term liabilities*.

Current Liabilities   **Current liabilities** are debts that are due to be paid within one year or one of the entity's operating cycles if the cycle is longer than a year. Accounts Payable, Notes Payable due within one year, Salaries Payable, Unearned Revenue, Goods and Services Tax Payable and Interest Payable owed on notes payable are current liabilities.

Long-Term Liabilities   All liabilities that are not current are classified as **long-term liabilities**. Many notes payable are long-term. Other notes payable are paid in installments, with the first installment due within one year, the second installment due the second year, and so on. In this case, the first installment would be a current liability and the remainder a long-term liability.

An Actual Classified Balance Sheet

Exhibit 4-11 is a classified balance sheet of John Labatt Limited. John Labatt Limited combines all its capital assets under the title Fixed Assets.

As you study the balance sheet, you will be delighted at how much of it you understand. You have been exposed to the more common assets and liabilities reported by this actual company. You will note, however, that there are other accounts, such as Net Assets of Discontinued Operations, Deferred Income Taxes, and Cumulative Translation Adjustment, with which you will not be familiar. These accounts will become familiar to you as your study of financial accounting progresses.

EXHIBIT 4-11 *Classified Balance Sheet*

John Labatt Limited	
Balance Sheet	
April 30, 1992	

	(dollar amounts in millions)
Assets	
Current assets	
Cash and securities	$ 766
Accounts receivable (note 7)*	406
Inventories (note 8)	359
Prepaid expenses	103
	1,634
Fixed assets (note 9)	1,027
Other assets (note 10)	520
Net assets of discontinued operations (note 5)	139
	$ 3,320
Liabilities and Shareholders' Equity	
Current liabilities	
Accounts payable and accrued charges	$ 759
Taxes payable	36
Long-term debt due within one year	41
	836
Non-convertible long-term debt (note 11)	646
Deferred income taxes	90
	$ 1,572
Convertible debentures and shareholders' equity	
Convertible debentures (note 12)	$ 255
Shareholder's equity	
Share capital (note 13)	
Preferred shares	300
Common shares	337
Retained earnings	844
Cumulative translation adjustment	12
	1,493
	1,748
	$ 3,320

* The references to notes are to the notes to the financial statements, not included in this text.

Formats of Balance Sheets

The balance sheet of John Labatt Limited shown in Exhibit 4-11 lists the assets at the top, with the liabilities and owner's equity (called Shareholder's Equity in Exhibit 4-11) below. This is the **report format**. The balance sheet of Gary Lyon, Lawyer presented in Exhibit 4-7 lists the assets at the left, with the liabilities and the owner's equity at the right. That is the **account format**.

Either format is acceptable. A recent survey of 600 companies indicated that slightly more than half use the account format and the remainder use the report format.

Use of Accounting Information in Decision-Making _____

The purpose of accounting is to provide information for decision-making. Chief users of accounting information include managers, investors, and creditors; other users include employees, the government (for example, Revenue Canada) and regulatory bodies (for example, the Alberta Securities Commission for companies that are listed on the Alberta Stock Exchange).

A creditor considering lending money must predict whether the borrower can repay the loan. If the borrower already has lots of debt, the probability of repayment is lower than if the borrower has a small amount of liabilities. To asssess financial position, decision-makers use ratios of various items drawn from a company's financial statements.

You will discover in Chapter 19 that there are no hard-and-fast rules as to what an acceptable or good ratio is, but rather that each ratio has to be considered in the context of the company and financial statements being examined.

One of the most common ratios is the **current ratio**, which is the ratio of an entity's current assets to its current liabilities. The current ratio measures the ability to pay current liabilities with current assets. It is computed as follows:

$$\text{Current Ratio} = \frac{\text{Total current assets}}{\text{Total current liabilities}}$$

A company prefers a high current ratio, which means the business has plenty of current assets to pay current liabilities. An increasing current ratio from period to period generally indicates improvement in financial position.

A rule of thumb: A strong current ratio would be in the range of 2.00; it would indicate that the company has approximately $2.00 in current assets for every $1.00 in current liabilities. As you will see in Chapter 19, most successful businesses operate with current ratios in the range between 1.10 and 2.00.

John Labatt has a current ratio of 1.95 (1.95 = $1,634,000,000/$836,000,000). The ratio indicates that John Labatt is in a fairly strong liquidity position.

How would a decision-maker use the current ratio? A low current ratio would worry managers of a company because it indicates to them, and to the users of the company's financial statements, that the company is having trouble paying its debts as they come due. The company would have trouble making purchases on account and borrowing money. Creditors might want cash in advance or on delivery and lenders would want higher than normal interest rates from the company. This trouble would make the managers' jobs even more difficult, and would likely worsen the company's liquidity position. In contrast, lenders and other users would view a corporation that had a current ratio approaching 2.00 as substantially less risky. Such a company would probably be able to arrange better credit terms and lower borrowing rates; the company would be more attractive to investors.

A second aid to decision-making is the **debt ratio**, which is the ratio of total liabilities to total assets. The debt ratio indicates the proportion of a company's assets that are financed with debt. This ratio measures a business' ability to pay both current and long-term debts — total liabilities. It is calculated as follows:

$$\text{Debt ratio} = \frac{\text{Total liabilities}}{\text{Total assets}}$$

A low debt ratio is safer than a high debt ratio. Why? Because a company with a small amount of liabilities has low required payments. Such a company is less likely to get into financial difficulty. By contrast, a company with a high debt ratio may have trouble paying its liabilities, especially when sales are low and cash is scarce. When a company fails to pay its debts on a timely basis, the creditors could put the company into bankruptcy.

John Labatt has a debt ratio of .55 [(.55 = ($836,000,000 + $646,000,000 + $90,000,000 + $255,000,000)/$3,320,000,000)]. The norm for a debt ratio is about .50 or lower. When it is higher than that, lenders are likely to place restrictions on a borrower with respect to such cash flow items as dividends and non-routine purchases, and are likely to demand a much higher interest rate than normal. Potential investors are not likely to invest in a company with a higher than average debt ratio.

In general, a high current ratio is preferred over a low current ratio. Increases in the current ratio indicate improving financial position. By contrast, a low debt ratio is preferred over a high debt ratio. Improvement is indicated by a decrease in the debt ratio.

Financial ratios are an important aid to decision-makers. However, it is unwise to place too much confidence in a single ratio or group of ratios. For example, a company may have a high current ratio, which indicates fiancial strength. It may also have a high debt ratio, which suggests weakness. Which ratio gives the more reliable signal about the company? Experienced managers, lenders and investors evaluate a company by examining a large number of ratios over several years to spot trends and turning points. These people also consider other facts, such as the company's cash position and its trend in net income. No single ratio gives the whole picture about a company.

As you progress through the study of accounting, we will introduce key ratios used in decision-making. Chapter 19, Using Accounting Information to Make Business Decisions, summarizes all the ratios discussed throughout this book. This chapter provides a good overview of ratios used in decision-making.

Detecting and Correcting Accounting Errors _____

You have now learned all the steps that an accountant takes from opening the books and recording a transaction in the journal through closing the books and the postclosing trial balance. Along the way, errors may occur. Accounting errors include incorrect journal entries, mistakes in posting, and transpositions and slides. This section discusses their detection and correction.

> **OBJECTIVE 7**
>
> Correct typical accounting errors

Incorrect Journal Entries   When a journal entry contains an error, the entry can be erased and corrected if the error is caught immediately. Other accountants prefer to draw a line through the incorrect entry to maintain a record of all entries to the journal. After the incorrect entry is crossed out, the accountant can make the correct entry.

If the error is detected after posting, the accountant makes a *correcting entry.* Suppose Gary Lyon paid $5,000 cash for furniture and erroneously debited Supplies as follows:

Incorrect Entry

May 13	Supplies...	5,000	
	Cash		5,000
	Bought supplies.		

The debit to Supplies is incorrect, so it is necessary to make a correcting entry as follows:

Correcting Entry

May 15	Office Furniture	5,000	
	Supplies..		5,000
	To correct May 13 entry.		

The credit to Supplies in the second entry offsets the incorrect debit of the first entry. The debit to Furniture in the correcting entry places the purchase amount in the correct account.

Incorrect Posting Sometimes an accountant posts a debit as a credit or a credit as a debit. Such an error shows up in the trial balance — total debits do not equal total credits.

Suppose a $100 debit to Cash is posted as a $100 credit. The trial balance's total debits are $200 too low. Total credits are correct. The difference is $200. Whenever a debit or credit has been misplaced, the resulting difference is evenly divisible by 2, as is the $200 figure in our example. Dividing that difference by 2 yields the amount of the incorrect posting, which in this case we know to be $100. The accountant may then search the journal for the misplaced $100 entry and make the corrections.

Transpositions and Slides A **transposition** occurs when digits are flip-flopped. For example, $85 is a transposition of $58. Transpositions cause errors that are evenly divisible by 9. In this particular case, the transposition causes a $27 error ($85 – $58), which is evenly divisible by 9 ($27/9 = $3).

A **slide** results from adding one or more zeroes to a number or from dropping off a zero, for example, writing $500 as $5,000, or vice versa. The difference of $4,500 ($5,000 – $500) is evenly divisible by 9 ($4,500/9 = $500).

Transpositions and slides occur in the transfer of numbers, for example, from the journal to the ledger or from the ledger to the trial balance.

Incorrect postings, transpositions and slides can be corrected by crossing out the incorrect amount and then inserting the correct amount in its appropriate place.

Summary Problem for Your Review

Refer to the data in the earlier Summary Problem for Your Review, presented on pp. 148–49

Required

1. Journalize and post the adjusting entries. (Before posting to the accounts, enter their balances as shown in the trial balance. For example, enter the $370,000 balance in the Accounts Receivable account before posting its adjusting entry.) Key adjusting entries by *letter*, as shown in the work sheet solution to the first review problem. You can take the adjusting entries straight from the work sheet on p. 149.

2. Journalize and post the closing entries. (Each account should carry its balance as shown in the trial balance.) To distinguish closing entries from adjusting entries, key the closing entries by *number*. Draw the arrows to illustrate the flow of data, as shown in Exhibit 4-9, p. 153. Indicate the balance of the Capital account after the closing entries are posted.

3. Prepare the income statement for the year ended December 31, 19X1. List Miscellaneous Expense last among the expenses, a common practice.

4. Prepare the statement of owner's equity for the year ended December 31, 19X1. Draw the arrow that links the income statement to the statement of owner's equity.

5. Prepare the classified balance sheet at December 31, 19X1. Use the report form. All liabilities are current. Draw the arrow that links the statement of owner's equity to the balance sheet.

SOLUTION TO REVIEW PROBLEM

Requirement 1

a. Dec. 31	Supplies Expense	4,000	
		Supplies		4,000
b.	31	Depreciation Expense — Furniture and Fixtures	20,000	
		Accumulated Depreciation — Furniture and Fixtures		20,000
c.	31	Depreciation Expense — Building	10,000	
		Accumulated Depreciation — Building		10,000
d.	31	Salary Expense	5,000	
		Salary Payable		5,000
e.	31	Accounts Receivable	12,000	
		Service Revenue		12,000
f.	31	Unearned Service Revenue	32,000	
		Service Revenue		32,000

Accounts Receivable

	370,000		
(e)	12,000		

Supplies

	6,000	(a)	4,000

Accumulated Depreciation — Furniture and Fixtures

			40,000
		(b)	20,000

Accumulated Depreciation — Building

			130,000
		(c)	10,000

Salary Payable

		(d)	5,000

Unearned Service Revenue

(f)	32,000		45,000

Service Revenue

			286,000
		(e)	12,000
		(f)	32,000
		Bal.	330,000

Salary Expense

	172,000		
(d)	5,000		
Bal.	177,000		

Supplies Expense

(a)	4,000		
Bal.	4,000		

Depreciation Expense — Furniture and Fixtures

(b)	20,000		
Bal.	20,000		

Depreciation Expense — Building

(c)	10,000		
Bal.	10,000		

Requirement 2

1.	Dec. 31	Service Revenue...	330,000	
		Income Summary		330,000
2.	31	Income Summary	224,000	
		Salary Expense..		177,000
		Supplies Expense...		4,000
		Depreciation Expense		
		— Furniture and Fixtures......................		20,000
		Depreciation Expense — Building.............		10,000
		Miscellaneous Expense...............................		13,000
3.	31	Income Summary ($330,000 – $224,000).........	106,000	
		Trish O'Malley, Capital..............................		106,000
4.	31	Trish O'Malley, Capital.....................................	65,000	
		Trish O'Malley, Withdrawals.....................		65,000

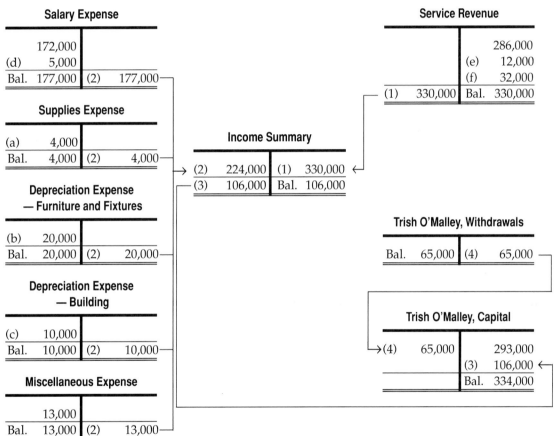

Requirement 3

O'Malley's Service Company
Income Statement
for the year ended December 31, 19X1

Revenues		
Service revenue		$330,000
Expenses		
Salary expense	$177,000	
Depreciation expense — furniture and fixtures	20,000	
Depreciation expense — building	10,000	
Supplies expense	4,000	
Miscellaneous expense	13,000	
Total expenses		224,000
Net Income		$106,000

Requirement 4

O'Malley's Service Company
Statement of Owner's Equity
for the year ended December 31, 19X1

Trish O'Malley, Capital, January 1, 19X1	$293,000
Add: Net income	106,000
	399,000
Less: Withdrawals	65,000
Trish O'Malley, Capital, December 31, 19X1	$334,000

Requirement 5

O'Malley's Service Company
Balance Sheet
December 31, 19X1

Assets		
Current assets		
Cash		$198,000
Accounts receivable		382,000
Supplies		2,000
Total current assets		582,000
Capital assets		
Furniture and fixtures	$100,000	
Less: Accumulated depreciation	60,000	40,000
Building	250,000	
Less: Accumulated depreciation	140,000	110,000
Total assets		$732,000
Liabilities		
Current liabilities		
Accounts payable		$380,000
Unearned service revenue		13,000
Salary payable		5,000
Total current liabilities		398,000
Owner's Equity		
Trish O'Malley, Capital		334,000
Total liabilities and owner's equity		$732,000

Summary _____

The *accounting cycle* is the process by which accountants produce the financial statements for a specific period of time. The cycle starts with the beginning account balances. During the period, the business journalizes transactions and posts them to the ledger accounts. At the end of the period, the trial balance is prepared, and the accounts are adjusted to measure the period's net income or net loss.

Completion of the accounting cycle is aided by the use of a *work sheet*. This columnar document summarizes the effects of all the activity of the period. It is neither a journal nor a ledger but merely a convenient device for completing the accounting cycle.

The work sheet has columns for the trial balance, adjustments, adjusted trial balance (optional), income statement and balance sheet. It aids the adjusting process, and it is the place where the period's net income or net loss is first computed. The work sheet also provides the data for the financial statements and the *closing entries*. While the work sheet is not necessary, it does facilitate completion of the accounting cycle and preparation of the financial statements.

Computer *spreadsheets* are extremely useful for tasks such as completing the accounting cycle. Their main advantage is that they can be programmed to perform repetitive tasks without error and print documents such as the work sheet.

Revenues, expenses and withdrawals represent increases and decreases in owner's equity for a specific period. At the end of the period, their balances are closed out to zero and, for this reason, they are called *temporary accounts*. Assets, liabilities and owner's equity are not closed, because they are the *permanent accounts*. Their balances at the end of one period become the beginning balances of the next period. The final accuracy check of the period is the *postclosing trial balance*. *Reversing entries*, the opposite of adjusting entries from the previous period end, ease the accountant's work.

Four common accounting errors are: incorrect journal entries, incorrect postings, transpositions, and slides. Techniques exist for detecting and correcting these errors.

The balance sheet reports *current* and *long-term assets,* and *current* and *long-term liabilities,* and can be presented in *report* or *account* format. Two decision-making aids are: the *current ratio* (total current assets divided by total current liabilities), and the *debt ratio* (total liabilities divided by total assets).

Self-Study Questions

Test your understanding of the chapter by marking the correct answer to each of the following questions:

1. The focal point of the accounting cycle is the *(p. 138)*
   a. Financial statements
   b. Trial balance
   c. Adjusted trial balance
   d. Work sheet

2. Arrange the following accounting cycle steps in their proper order *(p. 139)*
   a. Complete the work sheet
   b. Journalize and post adjusting entries
   c. Prepare the postclosing trial balance
   d. Journalize and post cash transactions
   e. Prepare the financial statements
   f. Journalize and post closing entries

3. The work sheet is a *(p. 139)*
   a. Journal
   b. Ledger
   c. Financial statement
   d. Convenient device for completing the accounting cycle

4. The usefulness of the work sheet is *(p. 139)*
   a. Identifying the accounts that need to be adjusted
   b. Summarizing the effects of all the transactions of the period
   c. Aiding the preparation of the financial statements
   d. All of the above

5. Which of the following accounts is not closed? *(pp. 150–151)*
   a. Supplies Expense   c. Interest Revenue
   b. Prepaid Insurance   d. Owner Withdrawals

6. The closing entry for Salary Expense, with a balance of $322,000, is *(pp. 152–153)*

   a. Salary Expense 322,000
         Income Summary   322,000

   b. Salary Expense 322,000
         Salary Payable   322,000

   c. Income Summary 322,000
         Salary Expense   322,000

   d. Salary Payable 322,000
         Salary Expense   322,000

7. The purpose of the postclosing trial balance is to *(p. 154)*
   a. Provide the account balances for preparation of the balance sheet
   b. Ensure that the ledger is in balance for the start of the next period
   c. Aid the journalizing and posting of the closing entries
   d. Ensure that the ledger is in balance for completion of the work sheet

8. Reversing entries are used to *(p. 155)*
   a. Avoid having to refer back to a preceding period's adjusting entry when recording a cash transaction of a later period
   b. Prepare the financial statements
   c. Close the accounts
   d. Bring the accounts to their correct balances at the beginning of a new period

9. The classification of assets and liabilities as current or long-term depends on *(p. 158)*
   a. Their order of listing in the general ledger
   b. Whether they appear on the balance sheet or the income statement
   c. The relative liquidity of the item
   d. The format of the balance sheet — account format or report format

10. Posting a $300 debit as a credit causes an error *(p. 163)*
    a. That is evenly divisible by 9
    b. That is evenly divisible by 2
    c. In the journal
    d. Known as a transposition

Answers to the Self-Study Questions are at the end of the chapter.

Accounting Vocabulary

account format of the
  balance sheet *(p. 160)*
accounting cycle *(p. 138)*
closing entry *(p. 152)*
closing the accounts
  (p. 152)
current assets *(p. 159)*
current liabilities *(p. 159)*
current ratio *(p. 161)*
debt ratio *(p. 161)*
income summary *(p. 152)*

liquidity *(p. 158)*
long-term assets *(p. 159)*
long-term liabilities
  (p. 159)
nominal account *(p. 152)*
operating cycle *(p. 159)*
permanent account
  (p. 152)
postclosing trial balance
  (p. 154)
real account *(p. 152)*

report format of the
  balance sheet *(p. 160)*
reversing entry *(p. 157)*
slide *(p. 163)*
spreadsheet *(p. 146)*
temporary account
  (p. 152)
transposition *(p. 163)*
work sheet *(p. 139)*

ASSIGNMENT MATERIAL _____

Questions

1. Identify the steps in the accounting cycle, distinguishing those that occur during the period from those that are performed at the end.
2. Why is the work sheet a valuable accounting tool?
3. Name two advantages the work sheet has over the adjusted trial balance.
4. Briefly explain how a microcomputer spreadsheet can be programmed to complete the work sheet.
5. Why must the adjusting entries be journalized and posted if they have already been entered on the work sheet?
6. Why should the adjusting entries be journalized and posted before making the closing entries?
7. Which types of accounts are closed?
8. What purpose is served by closing the accounts?
9. State how the work sheet helps with recording the closing entries.
10. Distinguish between permanent accounts and temporary accounts, indicating which type is closed at the end of the period. Give five examples of each type of account.
11. Is Income Summary a permanent account or a temporary account? When and how is it used?
12. Give the closing entries for the following accounts (balances in parentheses): Service Revenue ($4,700), Salary Expense ($1,100), Income Summary (credit balance of $2,000), Rhonda McGill, Withdrawals ($2,300).
13. Briefly describe a reversing entry by stating what it is, when it is dated, and what it accomplishes.
14. Why are assets classified as current or long-term? On what basis are they classified? Where do the classified amounts appear?
15. Indicate which of the following accounts are current assets and which are long-term assets: Prepaid Rent, Building, Furniture, Accounts Receivable, Merchandise Inventory, Cash, Note Receivable (due within one year), Note Receivable (due after one year).
16. In what order are assets and liabilities listed on the balance sheet?
17. Name an outside party that is interested in whether a liability is current or long-term. Why is this party interested in this information?
18. A friend tells you that the difference between a current liability and a long-term liability is that they are payable to different types of creditors. Is your friend correct? Include in your answer the definitions of these two categories of liabilities.
19. Show how to compute the current ratio and the debt ratio. Indicate what ability each ratio measures, and state whether a high value or a low value is safer.
20. Give the name of the following accounting errors:
    a. Posted a $300 debit from the journal as a $300 credit in the ledger.
    b. Posted a $300 debit from the journal as a $3,000 debit in the ledger.
    c. Recorded a transaction by debiting one account for $3,100 and crediting the other account for $1,300.
21. How would you detect each of the errors in the preceding question?
22. Capp Company purchased supplies of $120 on account. The accountant debited Supplies and credited Cash for $120. A week later, after this entry has been posted to the ledger, the accountant discovers the error. How should he correct the error?

Exercises

Exercise 4-1   *Preparing a work sheet (L.O. 1)*

The trial balance of Makovic Pest Control Service follows.

Additional information at September 30, 19X6:

a. Accrued salary expense, $200
b. Prepaid rent expired, $900
c. Supplies used, $2,250
d. Accrued service revenue, $210
e. Depreciation, $40

	Makovic Pest Control Service Trial Balance September 30, 19X6	
Cash	$ 1,560	
Accounts receivable	2,840	
Prepaid rent	1,200	
Supplies	3,390	
Equipment	12,600	
Accumulated depreciation		$ 2,240
Accounts payable		1,600
Salary payable		
Lee Makovic, capital		16,030
Lee Makovic, withdrawals	3,000	
Service revenue		7,300
Depreciation expense		
Salary expense	1,800	
Rent expense		
Utilities expense	780	
Supplies expense		
Total	$27,170	$27,170

Required

Complete Makovic's work sheet for September 19X6.

Exercise 4-2   *Journalizing adjusting and closing entries (L.O. 3)*

Journalize the adjusting and closing entries in Exercise 4-1.

Exercise 4-3   *Posting adjusting and closing entries (L.O. 3)*

Set up T-accounts for those accounts affected by the adjusting and closing entries in Exercise 4-1. Post the adjusting and closing entries to the accounts, denoting adjustment amounts by Adj., closing amounts by Clo., and balances by Bal. Double rule the accounts with zero balances after closing and show the ending balance in each account.

Exercise 4-4   *Preparing a postclosing trial balance (L.O. 3)*

Prepare the postclosing trial balance in Exercise 4-1.

Exercise 4-5   *Identifying and journalizing closing entries* **(L.O. 4)**

From the following selected accounts that Langefeld Catering Service reported in its June 30, 19X4 annual financial statements, prepare the entity's closing entries.

P. Langefeld, capital............	$45,600	Interest expense......................	$ 2,200
Service revenue...................	92,100	Accounts receivable..............	26,000
Unearned revenues.............	1,350	Salary payable	850
Salary expense.....................	12,500	Depreciation expense	10,200
Accumulated depreciation	35,000	Rent expense..........................	5,900
Supplies expense.................	1,400	P. Langefeld, withdrawals	40,000
Interest revenue..................	700	Supplies	1,100

Exercise 4-6   *Identifying and journalizing closing entries* **(L.O. 4)**

The accountant for Damon Reed, Lawyer, has posted adjusting entries a through e to the accounts at December 31, 19X2. All the revenue, expense, and owner's equity accounts of the entity are listed here in T-account form.

Accounts Receivable		Supplies		Accumulated Depreciation — Furniture	
23,000		4,000	(a) 2,000		5,000
(e) 3,500					(b) 1,100

Accumulated Depreciation — Building		Salary Payable		Damon Reed, Capital	
	33,000		(d) 700		49,400
	(c) 6,000				

Damon Reed, Withdrawals		Service Revenue		Salary Expense	
52,400			103,000	28,000	
			(e) 3,500	(d) 700	

Supplies Expense		Depreciation Expense — Furniture		Depreciation Expense — Building	
(a) 2,000		(b) 1,100		(c) 6,000	

Required

Journalize Reed's closing entries at December 31, 19X2.

Exercise 4-7   *Preparing a statement of owner's equity* **(L.O. 4)**

From the following accounts of Overhead Door Company, prepare the entity's statement of owner's equity for the year ended December 31, 19X5.

Debra Ringle, Capital				Debra Ringle, Withdrawals			
Dec. 31 41,000	Jan. 1 52,000			Mar. 31 8,000	Dec. 31 41,000		
	Mar. 9 28,000			Jun. 30 8,000			
	Dec. 31 43,000			Sept. 30 8,000			
				Dec. 31 17,000			

Income Summary			
Dec. 31 85,000	Dec. 31 128,000		
31 43,000			

Exercise 4-8   *Identifying and recording adjusting and closing entries (L.O. 3,4)*

The trial balance and income statement amounts are presented from the March work sheet of Bigelow Electric Company are presented in the following.

Account Title	Trial Balance		Income Statement	
Cash	$ 3,100			
Supplies	2,400			
Prepaid rent	1,100			
Office equipment	30,800			
Accumulated depreciation		$ 6,900		
Accounts payable		4,600		
Salary payable				
Unearned service revenue		4,400		
Bernard Bigelow, capital		14,800		
Bernard Bigelow, withdrawals	1,000			
Service revenue		12,700		$16,000
Salary expense	3,000		$ 3,800	
Rent expense	1,200		1,400	
Depreciation expense			400	
Supplies expense			500	
Utilities expense	800		800	
	$43,400	$43,400	$ 6,900	$16,000
			9,100	
Net income			$16,000	$16,000

Required

Journalize the adjusting and closing entries of Bigelow Electric Company at March 31.

Exercise 4-9   *Journalizing reversing entries (L.O. 5)*

Return to Exercise 4-6. Identify the two adjustments for which reversing entries would be most useful. Journalize those reversing entries.

Exercise 4-10   *Journalizing and posting an accrued expense and the related reversing entry (L.O. 5)*

During 19X2, London Sales Company pays wages of $44,200 to its employees. At December 31, 19X2, the company owes accrued wages of $900 that will be included in the $1,200 weekly payroll payment on January 4, 19X3.

Required

1. Open T-accounts for Wage Expense and Wage Payable.
2. Journalize all wage transactions for 19X2 and 19X3, including adjusting, closing, and reversing entries. Record the $44,200 amount by a single debit to Wage Expense.
3. Post amounts to the two T-accounts, showing their balances at January 4, 19X3. Denote cash payment entries by CP, adjusting entries by Adj., closing entries by Clo., reversing entries by Rev., and balances by Bal.

Exercise 4-11   *Preparing a classified balance sheet (L.O.6)*

1. Use the data in Exercise 4-8 to prepare Bigelow Electric's classified balance sheet at March 31 of the current year. Use the report format.
2. Compute Bigelow's current ratio and debt ratio at March 31. One year ago, the current ratio was 1.20 and the debt ratio was .30. Indicate whether Bigelow's ability to pay its debts has improved or deteriorated during the current year.

Exercise 4-12 *Correcting accounting errors* **(L.O. 7)**

Prepare a correcting entry for each of the following accounting errors:

a. Adjusted prepaid rent by debiting Prepaid Rent and crediting Rent Expense for $700. This adjusting entry should have debited Rent Expense and credited Prepaid Rent for $700.

b. Debited Salary Expense and credited Cash to accrue salary expense of $500.

c. Recorded the earning of $3,200 service revenue collected in advance by debiting Accounts Receivable and crediting Service Revenue.

d. Accrued interest revenue of $800 by a debit to Accounts Receivable and a credit to Interest Revenue.

e. Recorded a $600 cash purchase of supplies by debiting Supplies and crediting Accounts Payable.

f. Debited Supplies and credited Accounts Payable for a $2,300 credit purchase of office equipment.

Problems   *(Group A)*

Problem 4-1A *Preparing a work sheet* **(L.O. 1)**

The trial balance of Agape Counseling Center at May 31, 19X2 follows:

Agape Counseling Center
Trial Balance
May 31, 19X2

Cash	$ 1,670	
Notes receivable	10,340	
Interest receivable		
Supplies	560	
Prepaid insurance	1,790	
Furniture	27,410	
Accumulated depreciation — furniture		$ 1,480
Building	55,900	
Accumulated depreciation — building		33,560
Land	13,700	
Accounts payable		14,730
Interest payable		
Salary payable		
Unearned service revenue		6,800
Note payable, long-term		18,700
Rex Jennings, capital		34,290
Rex Jennings, withdrawals	3,800	
Service revenue		9,970
Interest revenue		
Depreciation expense — furniture		
Depreciation expense — building		
Salary expense	2,170	
Insurance expense		
Interest expense		
Utilities expense	490	
Property tax expense	640	
Advertising expense	1,060	
Supplies expense		
Total	$119,530	$119,530

Additional data at May 31, 19X2:

a. Accrued salary expense, $600.

b. Supplies on hand, $410.

c. Prepaid insurance expired during May, $390.

d. Accrued interest expense, $220.

e. Unearned service revenue earned during May, $4,400.

f. Accrued advertising expense, $60. Credit Accounts Payable.

g. Accrued interest revenue, $170.

h. Depreciation: furniture, $380; building, $160.

Required

Complete Agape's work sheet for May.

Problem 4-2A *Preparing financial statements from an adjusted trial balance; journalizing adjusting and closing entries (L.O. 3, 6)*

The adjusted trial balance of Lopez Tailoring Service at April 30, 19X2, the end of the company's fiscal year, follows:

Lopez Tailoring Service
Adjusted Trial Balance
April 30, 19X2

Cash	$ 2,370	
Accounts receivable	25,740	
Supplies	3,690	
Prepaid insurance	2,290	
Equipment	63,930	
Accumulated depreciation — equipment		$ 28,430
Building	74,330	
Accumulated depreciation — building		18,260
Accounts payable		19,550
Interest payable		2,280
Wage payable		830
Unearned service revenue		3,660
Note payable, long-term		69,900
Maria Lopez, capital		46,200
Maria Lopez, withdrawals	47,500	
Service revenue		99,550
Depreciation expense — equipment	6,700	
Depreciation expense — building	3,210	
Wage expense	29,800	
Insurance expense	5,370	
Interest expense	8,170	
Utilities expense	5,670	
Property tax expense	3,010	
Supplies expense	6,880	
Total	$288,660	$288,660

Additional data at April 30, 19X2:

a. Supplies used during the year, $6,880.

b. Prepaid insurance expired during the year, $5,370.

c. Accrued interest expense, $2,280.

d. Accrued service revenue, $2,200.

e. Depreciation for the year: equipment, $6,700; building, $3,210.

f. Accrued wage expense, $830.

g. Unearned service revenue earned during the year, $5,180.

Required

1. Journalize the adjusting and closing entries.

2. Prepare Lopez's income statement and statement of owner's equity for the year ended April 30, 19X2 and the classified balance sheet on that date. Use the account format for the balance sheet.

3. Compute Lopez's current ratio and debt ratio at April 30, 19X2. One year ago, the current ratio stood at 1.21, and the debt ratio was .82. Did Lopez's ability to pay debts improve or deteriorate during 19X2?

Problem 4-3A *Taking the accounting cycle through the closing entries* **(L.O. 3, 4)**

The unadjusted T-accounts of Dave Laufenberg, M.D., at December 31, 19X2, and the related year-end adjustment data follow:

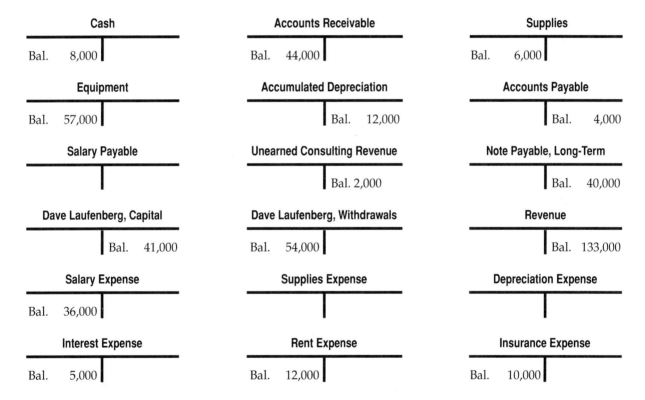

Adjustment data at December 31, 19X2 include:

a. Supplies on hand, $2,000.

b. Depreciation for the year, $6,000.

c. Accrued salary expense, $3,000.

d. Accrued revenue, $4,000.

e. Unearned consulting revenue earned during the year, $2,000, from the University of Manitoba; revenue from medical practice and consulting revenue are combined for accounting purposes.

Required

1. Write the trial balance on a work sheet and complete the work sheet. Key each adjusting entry by the letter corresponding to the data given.

2. Prepare the income statement, the statement of owner's equity, and the classified balance sheet in account format.

3. Journalize the adjusting and closing entries.

Problem 4-4A *Completing the accounting cycle (L.O. 3, 4)*

This problem should be used only in conjunction with Problem 4-3A. It completes the accounting cycle by posting to T-accounts and preparing the postclosing trial balance.

Required

1. Using the Problem 4-3A data, post the adjusting and closing entries to the T-accounts, denoting adjusting amounts by Adj., closing amounts by Clo., and account balances by Bal., as shown in Exhibit 4-9. Double underline all nominal accounts with a zero ending balance.

2. Prepare the postclosing trial balance.

Problem 4-5A *Completing the accounting cycle (L.O. 3, 4, 6)*

The trial balance of Hubby Insurance Agency at October 31, 19X0, and the data needed for the month-end adjustments are as follows:

Hubby Insurance Agency
Trial Balance
October 31, 19X0

Account Number	Account Title	Debit	Credit
11	Cash	$ 2,900	
12	Accounts receivable	12,310	
13	Prepaid rent	2,200	
14	Supplies	840	
15	Furniture	26,830	
16	Accumulated depreciation — furniture		$ 3,400
17	Building	68,300	
18	Accumulated depreciation — building		9,100
21	Accounts payable		7,290
22	Salary payable		
23	Unearned commission revenue		5,300
31	Erin Hubby, capital		85,490
32	Erin Hubby, withdrawals	3,900	
41	Commission revenue		9,560
51	Salary expense	1,840	
52	Rent expense		
53	Utilities expense	530	
54	Depreciation expense — furniture		
55	Depreciation expense — building		
56	Advertising expense	490	
57	Supplies expense		
	Total	$120,140	$120,140

Adjustment data:

a. Prepaid rent still in force at October 31, $2,000.

b. Supplies used during the month, $570.

c. Depreciation on furniture for the month, $250.

d. Depreciation on building for the month, $280.

e. Accrued salary expense at October 31, $310.

f. Unearned commission revenue still unearned at October 31, $4,700.

Required

1. Open the accounts listed in the trial balance, inserting their October 31 unadjusted balances. Also open the Income Summary account, number 33. Date the balances of the following accounts October 1: Prepaid Rent, Supplies, Building, Accumulated Depreciation — Building, Furniture, Accumulated Depreciation — Furniture, Unearned Commission Revenue, and Erin Hubby, Capital.

2. Write the trial balance on a work sheet and complete the work sheet of Hubby Insurance Agency for the month ended October 31, 19X0.

3. Prepare the income statement, the statement of owner's equity, and the classified balance sheet in report format.

4. Using the work sheet data, journalize and post the adjusting and closing entries. Use dates and posting references. Use 12 as the number of the journal page.

5. Prepare a postclosing trial balance.

Problem 4-6A   *Using reversing entries* **(L.O. 5)**

Refer to the data in Problem 4-5A.

Required

1. Open accounts for Salary Payable and Salary Expense. Insert their unadjusted balances at October 31, 19X0.

2. Journalize adjusting entry e and the closing entry for Salary Expense at October 31. Post to the ledger accounts.

3. On November 3, Hubby Insurance Agency paid the next payroll amount of $470. Journalize this cash payment, and post to the accounts. Show the balance in each account.

4. Repeat requirements 1-3 using a reversing entry. Compare the balances of Salary Payable and Salary Expense computed (a) using a reversing entry, and (b) without using a reversing entry (as in your answer to requirement 3).

Problem 4-7A   *Journalizing adjusting and reversing entries* **(L.O. 5)**

The accounting records of Conner Company reveal the following information before adjustments at December 31, 19X6, the end of the accounting period.

a. On July 31, Conner deposited $25,000 in a savings account. The bank will pay Conner interest of $1,200 on January 31, 19X7. Of this amount, five sixths is earned in 19X6.

b. On November 29, Conner Company received a property tax bill from the city. The total amount, due on January 15, 19X7, is $3,900. Three fourths of this amount is property tax expense for 19X6.

c. Commissions owed to sales employees at December 31 are $2,565, and salaries owed to home office employees are $1,870.

Required

1. Journalize the adjusting entry needed for each situation at December 31, 19X6, identifying each entry by its corresponding letter.

2. Journalize reversing entries as needed. Use the corresponding letters for references. Date the entries.

3. Use the first situation that calls for a reversing entry to explain the practical value of the reversal.

Problem 4-8A   *Preparing a classified balance sheet in report format*   **(L.O. 6)**

The accounts of Louise Pinkoff, CA, at March 31, 19X3 are listed in alphabetical order.

Accounts payable................	$12,700	Interest receivable..................	$ 800
Accounts receivable............	11,500	Louise Pinkoff, capital,	
Accumulated depreciation		March 31, 19X2	42,800
— building......................	47,300	Louise Pinkoff, withdrawals	31,200
Accumulated depreciation		Note payable, long-term.......	3,200
— furniture.....................	7,700	Note receivable, long-term...	6,900
Advertising expense...........	900	Other assets	1,300
Building..............................	55,900	Other current assets	900
Cash	1,400	Other current liabilities.........	1,100
Current portion of		Prepaid insurance.................	600
note payable	800	Prepaid Rent..........................	4,700
Current portion of		Salary expense	17,800
note receivable	3,100	Salary payable.......................	1,400
Depreciation expense.........	1,900	Service revenue.....................	71,100
Furniture	43,200	Supplies.................................	3,800
Insurance expense	600	Supplies expense	4,600
Interest payable..................	200	Unearned service revenue....	2,800

Required

1. All adjustments have been journalized and posted, but the closing entries have not yet been made. Prepare the company's classified balance sheet in report format at March 31, 19X3. Use captions for total assets, total liabilities, and total liabilities and owner's equity.

2. Compute Pinkoff's current ratio and debt ratio at March 31, 19X3. At March 31, 19X2, the current ratio was 1.28, and debt ratio was .32. Did Pinkoff's ability to pay debts improve or deteriorate during 19X3?

Problem 4-9A   *Analyzing and journalizing corrections, adjustments, and closing entries*   **(L.O. 4, 7)**

The auditors of Polanski Catering Service, a proprietorship, encountered the following situations while adjusting and closing the books at February 28. Consider each situation independently.

a. The company bookkeeper made the following entry to record a $950 credit purchase of supplies:

Feb. 26 Equipment 950
            Accounts Payable 950
Prepare the correcting entry, dated February 28.

b. A $390 credit to Accounts Receivable was posted as $930.
   (1) At what stage of the accounting cycle will this error be detected?
   (2) Describe the technique for identifying the amount of the error.

c. The $1,620 balance of Utilities Expense was entered as $16,200 on the trial balance.

(1) What is the name of this type of error?

(2) Assume this is the only error in the trial balance. Which will be greater, the total debits or the total credits, and by how much?

(3) How can this type of error be identified?

d. The accountant failed to make the following adjusting entries at February 28:

(1) Accrued service revenue, $700.

(2) Insurance expense, $460.

(3) Accrued interest expense on a note payable, $520.

(4) Depreciation of building, $3,300.

(5) Earned service revenue that had been collected in advance, $2,700.

Compute the overall net income effect of these omissions.

e. Record each of the adjusting entries identified in item d.

f. The revenue and expense accounts after the adjusting entries had been posted were Service Revenue, $95,330; Wage Expense, $29,340; Depreciation Expense, $6,180; Interest Expense, $4,590; Utilities Expense, $1,620; and Insurance Expense, $740. Two balances prior to closing were Eva Polanski, Capital, $75,150, and Eva Polanski, Drawing, $48,000. Journalize the closing entries.

(Group B)

Problem 4-1B *Preparing a work sheet* **(L.O. 1)**

The trial balance of Ross Family Painting Contractors at July 31, 19X3 appears below.

Ross Family Painting Contractors Trial Balance July 31, 19X3		
Cash	$ 4,200	
Accounts receivable	37,820	
Supplies	17,660	
Prepaid insurance	2,300	
Equipment	32,690	
Accumulated depreciation — equipment		$ 26,240
Building	36,890	
Accumulated depreciation — building		10,500
Land	28,300	
Accounts payable		22,690
Interest payable		
Wage payable		
Unearned service revenue		10,560
Note payable, long-term		22,400
Peter Ross, capital		62,130
Peter Ross, withdrawals	4,200	
Service revenue		17,190
Depreciation expense — equipment		
Depreciation expense — building		
Wage expense	6,200	
Insurance expense		
Interest expense		
Utilities expense	270	
Property tax expense	840	
Advertising expense	340	
Supplies expense		
Total	$171,710	$171,710

Additional data at July 31, 19X3:

a. Accrued wage expense, $440.

b. Supplies on hand, $14,740.

c. Prepaid insurance expired during July, $500.

d. Accrued interest expense, $180.

e. Unearned service revenue earned during July, $4,770.

f. Accrued advertising expense, $100. Credit Accounts Payable.

g. Accrued service revenue, $1,100.

h. Depreciation: equipment, $430; building, $270.

Required

Complete Ross's worksheet for July.

Problem 4-2B   *Preparing financial statements from an adjusted trial balance; journalizing adjusting and closing entries* **(L.O. 3,6)**

The adjusted trial balance of Armoured Car Security Couriers at June 30, 19X1, the end of the company's fiscal year, follows:

Armoured Car Security Couriers		
Adjusted Trial Balance		
June 30, 19X1		
Cash	$ 18,350	
Accounts receivable.......................................	26,470	
Supplies..	1,290	
Prepaid insurance	1,700	
Equipment...	55,800	
Accumulated depreciation — equipment...		$ 16,480
Building..	144,900	
Accumulated depreciation — building		16,850
Accounts payable..		36,900
Interest payable		1,490
Wage payable...		770
Unearned service revenue		2,300
Note payable, long-term		97,000
Ramon DeSoto, capital....................................		67,390
Ramon DeSoto, withdrawals	45,300	
Service revenue		108,360
Depreciation expense — equipment............	6,300	
Depreciation expense — building	3,470	
Wage expense	18,800	
Insurance expense...	3,100	
Interest expense..	11,510	
Utilities expense	4,300	
Property tax expense	2,670	
Supplies expense...	3,580	
Total...	$347,540	$347,540

Additional data at June 30, 19X1:

a. Supplies used during the year, $3,580.

b. Prepaid insurance expired during the year, $3,100.

c. Accrued interest expense, $680.

d. Accrued service revenue, $940.

e. Depreciation for the year: equipment, $6,300; building, $3,470.

f. Accrued wage expense, $770.

g. Unearned service revenue earned during the year, $6,790.

Required

1. Journalize the adjusting and closing entries.

2. Prepare Armoured Car's income statement and statement of owner's equity for the year ended June 30, 19X1 and the classified balance sheet on that date. Use the account format for the balance sheet.

3. Compute Armoured Car's current ratio and debt ratio at June 30, 19X1. One year ago, the current ratio stood at 1.01, and the debt ratio was .71. Did Armoured Car's ability to pay debts improve or deteriorate during 19X1?

Problem 4-3B   *Taking the accounting cycle through the closing entries* **(L.O. 3,4)**

The unadjusted T-accounts of Christine Ciancia, Psychologist, at December 31, 19X2 and the related year-end adjustment data follow:

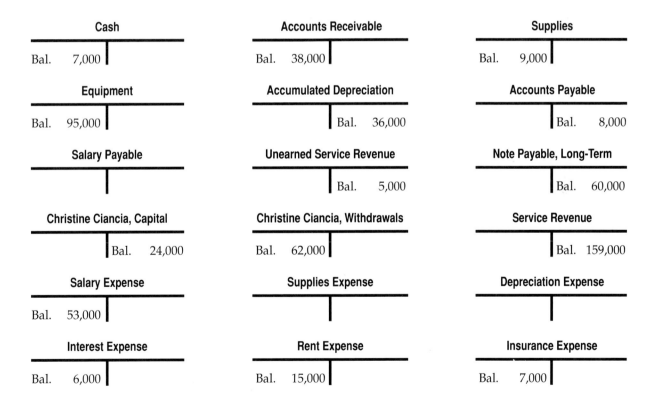

Adjustment data at December 31, 19X2 include:

a. Supplies on hand, $1,000.

b. Depreciation for the year, $9,000.

c. Accrued salary expense, $2,000.

d. Accrued service revenue, $1,000.

e. Unearned service revenue earned during the year, $5,000.

Required

1. Write the trial balance on a work sheet, and complete the work sheet. Key each adjusting entry by the letter corresponding to the data given.

2. Prepare the income statement, the statement of owner's equity, and the classified balance sheet in account format.

3. Journalize the adjusting and closing entries.

Problem 4-4B   *Completing the accounting cycle (L.O. 3,4)*

This problem should be used only in conjunction with Problem 4-3B. It completes the accounting cycle by posting to T-accounts and preparing the postclosing trial balance.

Required

1. Using the Problem 4-3B data, post the adjusting and closing entries to the T-accounts, denoting adjusting amounts by Adj., closing amounts by Clo., and account balances by Bal., as shown in Exhibit 4-9. Double underline all nominal accounts with a zero ending balance.

2. Prepare the postclosing trial balance.

Problem 4-5B   *Completing the accounting cycle (L.O. 3,4,6)*

The trial balance of Nix Insurance Agency at August 31, 19X9, and the data needed for the month-end adjustments follow.

<table>
<tr><td colspan="4" align="center">**Nix Insurance Agency**
Trial Balance
August 31, 19X9</td></tr>
<tr><td>**Account
Number**</td><td align="center">**Account Title**</td><td align="center">**Debit**</td><td align="center">**Credit**</td></tr>
<tr><td>11</td><td>Cash</td><td>$ 6,800</td><td></td></tr>
<tr><td>12</td><td>Accounts receivable</td><td>17,560</td><td></td></tr>
<tr><td>13</td><td>Prepaid rent</td><td>1,290</td><td></td></tr>
<tr><td>14</td><td>Supplies</td><td>900</td><td></td></tr>
<tr><td>15</td><td>Furniture</td><td>15,350</td><td></td></tr>
<tr><td>16</td><td>Accumulated depreciation — furniture</td><td></td><td>$ 12,800</td></tr>
<tr><td>17</td><td>Building</td><td>89,900</td><td></td></tr>
<tr><td>18</td><td>Accumulated depreciation — building</td><td></td><td>28,600</td></tr>
<tr><td>21</td><td>Accounts payable</td><td></td><td>6,240</td></tr>
<tr><td>22</td><td>Salary payable</td><td></td><td></td></tr>
<tr><td>23</td><td>Unearned commission revenue</td><td></td><td>8,900</td></tr>
<tr><td>31</td><td>L.M. Nix, capital</td><td></td><td>74,920</td></tr>
<tr><td>32</td><td>L.M. Nix, withdrawals</td><td>4,800</td><td></td></tr>
<tr><td>41</td><td>Commission revenue</td><td></td><td>7,800</td></tr>
<tr><td>51</td><td>Salary expense</td><td>1,600</td><td></td></tr>
<tr><td>52</td><td>Rent expense</td><td></td><td></td></tr>
<tr><td>53</td><td>Utilities expense</td><td>410</td><td></td></tr>
<tr><td>54</td><td>Depreciation expense — furniture</td><td></td><td></td></tr>
<tr><td>55</td><td>Depreciation expense — building</td><td></td><td></td></tr>
<tr><td>56</td><td>Advertising expense</td><td>650</td><td></td></tr>
<tr><td>57</td><td>Supplies expense</td><td></td><td></td></tr>
<tr><td></td><td>Total</td><td>$139,260</td><td>$139,260</td></tr>
</table>

Adjustment data:

a. Prepaid rent still in force at August 31, $1,050.

b. Supplies used during the month, $140.

c. Depreciation on furniture for the month, $370.

d. Depreciation on building for the month, $130.

e. Accrued salary expense at August 31, $460.

f. Unearned commission revenue still unearned at August 31, $7,750.

Required

1. Open the accounts listed in the trial balance, inserting their August 31 unadjusted balances. Also open the Income Summary account, number 33. Date the balances of the following accounts as of August 1: Prepaid Rent, Supplies, Furniture, Accumulated Depreciation — Furniture, Building, Accumulated Depreciation — Building, Unearned Commission Revenue, and L.M. Nix, Capital.

2. Write the trial balance on a work sheet and complete the work sheet of Nix Insurance Agency for the month ended August 31, 19X9.

3. Prepare the income statement, the statement of owner's equity, and the classified balance sheet in report format.

4. Using the work sheet data, journalize and post the adjusting and closing entries. Use dates and posting references. Use page 7 as the number of the journal page.

5. Prepare a postclosing trial balance.

Problem 4-6B *Using reversing entries (L.O. 5)*

Refer to the data in Problem 4-5B.

Required

1. Open accounts for Salary Payable and Salary Expense. Insert their unadjusted balances at August 31, 19X9.

2. Journalize adjusting entry e and the closing entry for Salary Expense at August 31. Post to the accounts.

3. On September 5, Nix Insurance Agency paid the next payroll amount of $580. Journalize this cash payment, and post to the accounts. Show the balance in each account.

4. Repeat requirements 1-3 using a reversing entry. Compare the balances of Salary Payable and Salary Expense computed (a) using a reversing entry, and (b) without using a reversing entry (as appear in your answer to requirement 3).

Problem 4-7B *Journalizing adjusting and reversing entries (L.O. 5)*

Vidmar Company's accounting records reveal the following information before adjustments at December 31, 19X3, the end of the accounting period:

a. Wages owed to hourly employees total $3,400. Total salaries owed to salaried employees are $2,790. These amounts will be paid on the next scheduled payday in January 19X4.

b. On October 31, Vidmar loaned $40,000 to another business. The loan agreement requires the borrower to pay Vidmar interest of $2,400 on April 30, 19X4. One third of this interest is earned in 19X3.

c. On December 23, Vidmar received a property tax bill from the city. The total amount, due on February 1, 19X4, is $4,600. Half of this amount is property tax expense for 19X3.

Required

1. Journalize the adjusting entry needed for each situation at December 31, 19X3, identifying each entry by its corresponding letter.

2. Journalize reversing entries as needed. Use the corresponding letters for references. Date the entries appropriately.

3. Use the first situation that calls for a reversing entry to explain the practical value of the reversal.

Problem 4-8B   *Preparing a classified balance sheet in report format* **(L.O. 6)**

The accounts of Hankins Travel Agency at December 31, 19X6 are listed in alphabetical order.

Accounts payable	$ 3,100	Interest receivable	200
Accounts receivable	4,600	Barry Hankins, capital,	$50,300
Accumulated depreciation		December 31, 19X5	
— building	37,800	Barry Hankins, withdrawals	47,400
Accumulated depreciation		Note payable, long-term	27,800
— furniture	11,600	Note receivable, long-term	4,000
Advertising expense	2,200	Other assets	3,600
Building	104,400	Other current assets	1,700
Cash	4,500	Other current liabilities	4,700
Commission revenue	93,500	Prepaid insurance	1,100
Current portion of		Prepaid Rent	6,600
note payable	2,200	Salary expense	22,600
Current portion of		Salary payable	1,900
note receivable	1,000	Supplies	2,500
Furniture	22,700	Supplies expense	5,700
Insurance expense	800	Unearned commission	
Interest payable	600	revenue	3,400
Depreciation expense	1,300		

Required

1. All adjustments have been journalized and posted, but the closing entries have not yet been made. Prepare the company's classified balance sheet in report format at December 31, 19X6. Use captions for total assets, total liabilities, and total liabilities, and owner's equity.

2. Compute Hankins' current ratio and debt ratio at December 31, 19X6. At December 31, 19X5, the current ratio was 1.52 and the debt ratio was .37. Did Hankins' ability to pay debts improve or deteriorate during 19X6?

Problem 4-9B   *Analyzing and journalizing corrections, adjustments, and closing entries* **(L.O. 4, 7)**

Accountants for Osaka Catering Service, a proprietorship, encountered the following situations while adjusting and closing the books at December 31. Consider each situation independently.

a. The company bookkeeper made the following entry to record a $400 credit purchase of office equipment:

Nov. 12	Office Supplies	400	
	Accounts Payable		400

Prepare the correcting entry, dated December 31.

b. A $750 debit to Cash was posted as a credit.
   (1) At what stage of the accounting cycle will this error be detected?
   (2) Describe the technique for identifying the amount of the error.

c. The $35,000 balance of Equipment was entered as $3,500 on the trial balance.
   (1) What is the name of this type of error?
   (2) Assume this is the only error in the trial balance. Which will be greater, the total debits or the total credits, and by how much?
   (3) How can this type of error be identified?

d. The accountant failed to make the following adjusting entries at December 31:
   (1) Accrued property tax expense, $200.
   (2) Supplies expense, $1,390.
   (3) Accrued interest revenue on a note receivable, $950.
   (4) Depreciation of equipment, $4,000.
   (5) Earned service revenue that had been collected in advance, $5,300.
   Compute the overall net income effect of these omissions.

e. Record each of the adjusting entries identified in item d.

f. The revenue and expense accounts, after the adjusting entries had been posted, were Service Revenue, $55,800; Interest Revenue, $2,000; Salary Expense, $13,200; Rent Expense, $5,100; Depreciation Expense, $5,550; Supplies Expense, $1,530; and Property Tax Expense, $1,190. Two balances prior to closing were Mitsuo Osaka, Capital, $58,600, and Mitsuo Osaka, Withdrawals, $30,000. Journalize the closing entries.

Extending Your Knowledge

Decision Problems

1. Completing the accounting cycle to develop the information for a bank loan (L.O. 4,6)

One year ago, your friend Grant Thornton founded Thornton Computing Service. The business has prospered. Thornton, who remembers that you took an accounting course while in college, comes to you for advice. He wishes to know how much net income his business earned during the past year. He also wants to know what the entity's total assets, liabilities, and capital are. His accounting records consist of the T-accounts of his ledger, which were prepared by an accountant who moved to another city. The ledger at December 31 of the current year is

Cash	Accounts Receivable	Prepaid Rent
Dec. 31 6,830	Dec. 31 12,360	Jan. 2 2,800

Supplies	Equipment	Accumulated Depreciation
Jan. 2 2,600	Jan. 2 23,600	

Accounts Payable	Unearned Service Revenue	Salary Payable
Dec. 31 19,540	Dec. 31 4,130	

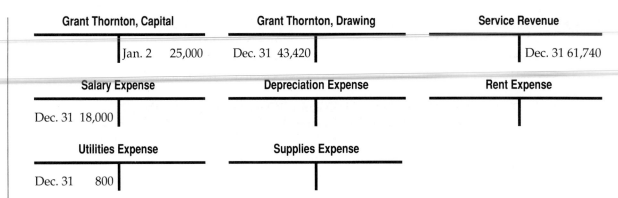

Grant Thornton, Capital	Grant Thornton, Drawing	Service Revenue
Jan. 2 25,000	Dec. 31 43,420	Dec. 31 61,740

Salary Expense	Depreciation Expense	Rent Expense
Dec. 31 18,000		

Utilities Expense	Supplies Expense
Dec. 31 800	

Thornton indicates that at the year's end customers owe him $1,600 accrued service revenue, which he expects to collect early next year. These revenues have not been recorded. During the year he collected $4,130 service revenue in advance from customers, but he earned only $1,190 of that amount. Rent expense for the year was $2,400, and he used up $2,100 in supplies. Thornton estimates that depreciation on his equipment was $5,900 for the year. At December 31, he owes his employee $1,200 accrued salary.

At the conclusion of your meeting, Thornton expresses concern that his withdrawals during the year might have exceeded his net income. To get a loan to expand the business, Thornton must show the bank that his capital account has grown from its original $25,000 balance. Has it? You and Thornton agree that you will meet again in one week. You perform the analysis and prepare the financial statements to answer his questions.

2. Finding an error in the work sheets (L.O. 1,7)

You are preparing the financial statements for the year ended October 31, 19X5 for Woodside Publishing Company, a weekly newspaper. You began with the trial balance of the ledger, which balanced, and then made the required adjusting entries. To save time, you omitted preparing an adjusted trial balance. After making the adjustments on the work sheet, you extended the balances from the trial balance, adjusted for the adjusting entries, and computed amounts for the income statement and balance sheet columns.

a. You added the debits and credits on the income statement and found that the credits exceeded the debits by $X. Did Woodside Publishing have a profit or a loss based on your finding?

b. You entered the balancing amount from the income statement columns in the balance sheet columns and found the total debits exceeded total credits in the balance sheet. The difference between the debits and credits is twice the amount ($2X) you calculated in question a. What is the likely cause of the difference? What assumption have you made in your answer?

Ethical Issue

McBride Associates, a management consulting firm, is in its third year of operations. The company was initially financed by owner's equity as the three partners each invested $30,000. The first year's slim profits were expected because new businesses often start slowly. During the second year, McBride Associates landed a large contract with a paper mill, and referrals from that project brought in several other large jobs. To expand the business, McBride borrowed $100,000 from the Bank of British Columbia. As a condition for making this loan, the bank required McBride to maintain a current ratio of at least 1.50 and a debt ratio of no more than .50.

Business during the third year has been good, but slightly below the target for the year. Expansion costs have brought the current ratio down to 1.47 and the debt ratio up to .51 at December 15. Glenda McBride and her partners are considering the implication of reporting this current ratio to the Bank of British Columbia. One course of action that the partners are considering is to record in December of the third year some revenue on account that McBride Associates will earn in January of their fourth year of operations. The contract for this job has been signed, and McBride will perform the management consulting services for the client during January.

Required

1. Journalize the revenue transaction, and indicate how recording this revenue in December would affect the current ratio and the debt ratio.
2. State whether it is ethical to record the revenue transaction in December. Identify the accounting principle relevant to this situation.
3. Propose an ethical course of action for McBride Associates.

Financial Statement Problems

1. Using an actual balance sheet (L.O. 6)

This problem, based on Schneider's balance sheet in Appendix C, will familiarize you with some of the assets and liabilities of this actual company. Answer these questions, using Schneider's balance sheet:

1. Which balance sheet format does Schneider use?
2. Name the company's largest current asset and largest current liability at October 26, 1991?
3. How much were total current assets and total current liabilities at October 27, 1990? Which had decreased by the greater percentage during the year ended October 26, 1991: total current assets or total current liabilities?
4. Compute Schneider's current ratio at October 26, 1991 and October 27, 1990. Also compute the debt ratios at these dates. Did the ratio values improve or deteriorate during 1991?
5. What is the cost of company's property, plant and equipment at October 26, 1991? What is the book value of these assets? To answer this question, refer to the Property, plant and equipment note.

2. Using an actual balance sheet (L.O. 6)

Obtain the annual report of an actual company of your choosing. Answer these questions about the company:

1. Which balance sheet format does the company use?
2. Name the company's largest asset and largest liability at the end of the current year and at the end of the preceding year. Name the largest current asset and the largest current liability at the end of the current year and at the end of the preceding year.
3. Compute the company's current ratio at the end of the current year and the current ratio at the end of the preceding year. Also compute the debt ratio at the end of the current year and at the end of the preceding year. Did these ratio values improve or deteriorate during the current year? Does the income statement help to explain why the ratios improved or deteriorated? Give your reason.

Appendix

Prepaid Expenses, Unearned Revenues, and Reversing Entries

Chapters 1 through 4 illustrate the most popular way to account for prepaid expenses and unearned revenues. This appendix expands that coverage by illustrating an alternate approach to handling prepaid expenses and unearned revenues — equally appropriate — that calls for reversing entries.

Prepaid Expenses

Prepaid expenses are advance payments of expenses. Prepaid Insurance, Prepaid Rent, Prepaid Advertising and Prepaid Legal Cost are prepaid expenses. Supplies that will be used up in the current period or within one year are also accounted for as prepaid expenses.

When a business prepays an expense (rent, for example) it can debit an *asset* account (Prepaid Rent) as follows:

Prepaid Rent	XXX	
Cash		XXX

Alternatively, the accountant can debit an *expense* account in the entry to record this cash payment, as follows:

Rent Expense	XXX	
Cash		XXX

Regardless of the account debited, the business must adjust the accounts at the end of the period. Making the adjustment allows the business to report the correct amount of expense for the period and the correct amount of asset at the period's end.

Prepaid Expense Recorded Initially as an Asset

Prepayments of expenses provide a future benefit to the business, so it is logical to record the prepayment by debiting an asset account. Suppose on August 1, 19X6, the business prepays one year's rent of $6,000 ($500 per month). The cash payment is recorded:

19X6			
Aug. 1	Prepaid Rent	6,000	
	Cash		6,000

On December 31, the end of the accounting period, five months' prepayment has expired and must be accounted for as *expense*. The adjusting entry is

Adjusting Entries

19X6			
Dec. 31	Rent Expense ($6,000 × $\frac{5}{12}$)	2,500	
	Prepaid Rent		2,500

The adjusting entry transfers $2,500 of the original $6,000 prepayment from Prepaid Rent to Rent Expense. This leaves a $3,500 debit balance in Prepaid Rent, which is seven months' rent still prepaid. After posting, the accounts appear as follows:

Prepaid Rent

19X6			19X6		
Aug. 1	CP	6,000	Dec. 31	Adj.	2,500
Dec. 31	Bal.	3,500			

Rent Expense

19X6				
Dec. 31	Adj.	2,500		
Dec. 31	Bal.	2,500		

CP = Cash payments; Adj. = Adjusting entry; Bal. = Balance

The $2,500 balance of Rent Expense is closed to Income Summary, along with all other expenses and revenues, at the end of the accounting period.

No reversing entry is used under this approach. The asset account Prepaid Rent has a debit balance to start the new period. This is consistent with recording prepaid expenses initially as assets.

The balance sheet at December 31, 19X6, reports Prepaid Rent of $3,500 as an asset. The 19X6 income statement reports Rent Expense of $2,500 as an expense, which is the expired portion of the initial $6,000 rent prepayment. Keep this reporting result in mind as you study the next section.

Prepaid Expense Recorded Initially as an Expense

Prepaying an expense creates an asset. However, the asset may be so short-lived that it will expire in the current accounting period (one year or less). Thus the accountant may decide to debit the prepayment to an expense account at the time of payment. Continuing with the rent example, the $6,000 cash payment on August 1 may be debited to Rent Expense:

19X6			
Aug. 1	Rent Expense	6,000	
	Cash		6,000

At December 31, only five months' prepayment has expired, leaving seven months' rent still prepaid. In this case, the accountant must transfer $7/12$ of the original prepayment of $6,000, or $3,500, to Prepaid Rent. The adjusting entry decreases the balance of Rent Expense to $5/12$ of the original $6,000, or $2,500. The December 31 adjusting entry is

Adjusting Entries

19X6			
Dec. 31	Prepaid Rent ($6,000 × $7/12$)	3,500	
	Rent Expense		3,500

After posting, the two accounts appear as follows:

Prepaid Rent

19X6				
Dec. 31	Adj.	3,500		
Dec. 31	Bal.	3,500		

Rent Expense

19X6			19X6		
Aug. 1	CP	6,000	Dec. 31	Adj.	3,500
Dec. 31	Bal.	2,500			

The balance sheet for 19X6 reports Prepaid Rent of $3,500, and the income statement for 19X6 reports Rent Expense of $2,500. Whether the business initially debits the prepayment to an asset account or to an expense account, the financial statements report the same amounts for prepaid rent and rent expense. The Rent Expense's balance is closed at the end of the period.

During the next accounting period, the $3,500 balance in Prepaid Rent will expire and become expense. It is efficient on the beginning date of the new year to make a reversing entry that transfers the ending balance of Prepaid Rent back to Rent Expense:

Reversing Entries

19X7			
Jan. 1	Rent Expense..	3,500	
	Prepaid Rent...		3,500

This reversing entry avoids later worry about what prepayments become expenses. The arrow shows the transfer of the debit balance from Prepaid Rent to Rent Expense after posting:

Prepaid Rent

19X6				19X7		
Dec. 31	Bal.	3,500		Jan.	**Rev.**	**3,500**

Zero balance

Rent Expense

19X6				19X6		
Aug. 1	CP	6,000		Dec. 31	Adj.	3,500
Dec. 31	Bal.	2,500		Dec. 31	Clo.	2,500
19X7						
Jan. 1	**Rev.**	**3,500**				

Clo. = Closing entry

After the reversing entry, the $3,500 amount is lodged in the expense account. This is consistent with recording prepaid expenses initially as expenses. Because this $3,500 amount will become expense during 19X7, no additional adjustment is needed. Subsequent expense prepayments are debited to Rent Expense and then adjusted at the end of the period as outlined here. Reversing entries ease the work of the accounting process for all types of prepaid expenses that are recorded initially as expenses. Reversing entries are not used for prepaid expenses that are recorded initially as assets.

Comparing the Two Approaches to Recording Prepaid Expenses

In summary, the two approaches to recording prepaid expenses are similar in that the asset amount reported on the balance sheet and the expense amount reported on the income statement are the same. They differ, however, in the prepayment entries and the adjusting entries. When a prepaid expense is recorded initially as an asset, (1) the adjusting entry transfers the used portion of the asset to the expense account, and (2) no reversing entry is used. When a prepaid expense is recorded initially as an expense, (1) the adjusting entry transfers the unused portion of the expense to the asset account, and (2) a reversing entry transfers the amount of the asset account back to the expense account to start the new accounting period.

Unearned (Deferred) Revenues

Unearned (deferred) revenues arise when a business collects cash in advance of earning the revenue. The recognition of revenue is *deferred* until later when it is earned. Unearned revenues are liabilities because the business that receives cash owes the other party goods or services to be delivered later.

Recall the prepaid expense examples listed on p. 188: insurance, rent, advertising, and so on. Prepaid expenses create assets for the business that pays the cash. The business that receives the cash in advance, however, faces a liability. For example, the landlord who receives a tenant's rent in advance must provide future service to the tenant. This is a liability, and the cash the landlord receives is unearned rent revenue. Similarly, unearned revenue arises as magazine publishers sell subscriptions, colleges collect tuition, airlines sell tickets, and lawyers accept advance fees.

When a business receives cash before earning the related revenue, the business debits Cash. It can credit either a *liability* account or a *revenue* account. In either case, the business must make adjusting entries at the end of the period to report the correct amounts of liability and revenue on the financial statements.

Unearned (Deferred) Revenue Recorded Initially as a Liability

Receipt of cash in advance of earning revenue creates a liability, so it is logical to debit Cash and credit a liability account. Assume a lawyer receives a $7,200 fee in advance from a client on October 1, 19X2. The lawyer will earn this amount at the rate of $800 per month during the nine-month period ending June 30, 19X3. The lawyer's cash receipt entry is

```
19X2
Oct. 1   Cash.........................................................   7,200
            Unearned Revenue..................................              7,200
```

On December 31, 19X2, the end of the law firm's accounting period, three months of the fee agreement have elapsed. The lawyer has earned ⅜ of the $7,200, or $2,400. The adjusting entry to transfer $2,400 to the revenue account is

Adjusting Entries
```
19X2
Dec. 31   Unearned Revenue ($7,200 × ⅜) ...........................   2,400
             Revenue ...............................................              2,400
```

After posting, the liability and revenue accounts are

Unearned Revenue

19X2			19X2		
Dec. 31 Adj.	2,400		Oct. 1 CR	7,200	
			Dec. 31 Bal.	4,800	

Revenue

			19X2		
			Dec. 31 Adj.	2,400	
			Dec. 31 Bal.	2,400	

CR = Cash Receipt

The law firm's 19X2 income statement reports revenue of $2,400, while its balance sheet reports unearned revenue of $4,800 as a liability. During 19X3, the lawyer will earn the remaining $4,800, and will then make an adjusting entry to transfer $4,800 to the Revenue account. No reversing entry is used. The balance in the liability account is consistent with recording the unearned revenue initially as a liability.

Unearned (Deferred) Revenue Recorded Initially as a Revenue

Receipt of cash in advance of earning the revenue can be credited initially to a revenue account. If the business has earned all the revenue within the period during which it received the cash, no adjusting entry is necessary. However, if the business earns only a part of the revenue at the end of the period, it must make adjusting entries.

Suppose on October 1, 19X2, the law firm records the nine-month advance fee of $7,200 as revenue. The cash receipt entry is

19X2			
Oct. 1	Cash...	7,200	
	Revenue		7,200

After December 31, the lawyer has earned only ⅓ of the $7,200, or $2,400. Accordingly, the firm makes an adjusting entry to transfer the unearned portion (⅔ of $7,200, or $4,800) from the revenue account to a liability account.

Adjusting Entries

19X2			
Dec. 31	Revenue ($7,200 × ⅔)	4,800	
	Unearned Revenue..................................		4,800

The adjusting entry leaves the earned portion (⅓, or $2,400) of the original amount in the revenue account. After posting, the total amount ($7,200) is properly divided between the liability account ($4,800) and the revenue account ($2,400), as follows:

Unearned Revenue

		19X2		
		Dec. 31	Adj.	4,800
		Dec. 31	Bal.	4,800

Revenue

19X2				19X2		
Dec. 31	Adj.	4,800		Oct. 1	CR	7,200
				Dec. 31	Bal.	2,400

The lawyer's 19X2 income statement reports revenue of $2,400, and the balance sheet at December 31, 19X2 reports as a liability the unearned revenue of $4,800. Whether the business initially credits a liability account or a revenue account, the financial statements report the same amounts for unearned revenue and revenue.

The law firm will earn the $4,800 during 19X3. On January 1, 19X3, it is efficient to make a reversing entry in order to transfer the liability balance back to the revenue account. By making the reversing entry, the accountant avoids having to reconsider the situation one year later, when the 19X3 adjusting entries will be made. The reversing entry is

Reversing Entries

19X3			
Jan. 1	Unearned Revenue..................................	4,800	
	Revenue		4,800

After posting, the liability account has a zero balance. The $4,800 credit is now lodged in the revenue account because it will be earned during 19X3. The arrow in the following example shows the transfer from the liability account to the revenue account:

Unearned Revenue

				19X2			
				Dec. 31	Adj.	4,800	
19X3				19X2			
Jan. 1	**Rev.**	**4,800**		Dec. 31	Bal.	4,800	

Zero balance

Revenue

				19X2			
19X2				19X2			
Dec. 31	Adj.	4,800		Oct. 1	CR	7,200	
Dec. 31	Clo.	2,400		Dec. 31	Bal.	2,400	
				19X3			
				Jan. 1	**Rev.**	**4,800**	

Subsequent advance receipts of revenue are credited to the Revenue account. The year-end adjusting process is the same for every period.

Comparing the Two Approaches to Recording Unearned (Deferred) Revenues

The two approaches to recording unearned revenue are similar in that the liability amount reported on the balance sheet and the revenue amount reported on the income statement are the same. The approaches differ, though, in how adjustments are handled. When unearned revenues are recorded initially as liabilities, (1) the adjusting entry transfers to the revenue account the amount of the advance collection that has been earned during the period, and (2) no reversing entry is used. When unearned revenues are recorded initially as revenue, (1) the adjustment transfers to the liability account the amount of the advance collection that is still unearned, and (2) a reversing entry transfers the balance of the liability account to the revenue account to begin the next accounting period.

Summary

Prepaid expenses may be recorded initially in an *asset* account or an *expense* account. When prepaid expenses are recorded initially as an asset, no need exists for a reversing entry because the asset account balance will be adjusted at the end of the next period. However, when prepaid expenses are recorded initially as an expense, a reversing entry eases accounting for the expense of the new period. Regardless of the approach taken, the financial statements should report the same amount of asset and expense.

Unearned (deferred) revenues may be recorded initially as a *liability* or a *revenue*. Recording unearned revenues initially as liabilities causes no need for a reversing entry. However, when recording them initially as revenues, a reversing entry eases accounting. Either recording approach is acceptable as long as the *financial statements* report the *correct* amounts.

APPENDIX ASSIGNMENT MATERIAL _____

Exercises

Exercise 4A-1   *Recording supplies transactions two ways*

At the beginning of the year, supplies of $1,490 were on hand. During the year, the business paid $3,300 cash for supplies. At the end of the year, the count of supplies indicates the ending balance is $1,260.

Required

1. Assume the business records supplies by initially debiting an asset account. Therefore, place the beginning balance in the Supplies T-account, and record the above entries directly in the accounts without using a journal.
2. Assume the business records supplies by initially debiting an expense account. Therefore, place the beginning balance in the Supplies Expense T-account, and record the above entries directly in the accounts without using a journal.
3. Compare the ending account balances under the two approaches. Are they the same or different? Why?

Exercise 4A-2   *Recording unearned revenue two ways*

At the beginning of the year, the company owed customers $6,450 for unearned sales collected in advance. During the year, the business received advance cash receipts of $10,000. At year end, the unearned revenue liability is $3,900.

Required

1. Assume the company records unearned revenues by initially crediting a liability account. Open T-accounts for Unearned Sales Revenue and Sales Revenue, and place the beginning balance in Unearned Sales Revenue. Journalize the cash collection and adjusting entries, and post their dollar amounts. As references in the T-accounts, denote a balance by Bal., a cash receipt by CR, and an adjustment by Adj.
2. Assume the company records unearned revenues by initially crediting a revenue account. Open T-accounts for Unearned Sales Revenue and Sales Revenue and place the beginning balance in Sales Revenue. Journalize the cash collection and adjusting entries, and post their dollar amounts. As references in the T-accounts, denote a balance by Bal., a cash receipt by CR, and an adjustment by Adj.
3. Compare the ending balances in the two accounts. Explain why they are the same of different.

Exercise 4A-3   *Using reversing entries to account for unearned revenues*

One approach to recording unearned revenue in Exercise 4A-2 calls for a reversing entry. Identify that approach. Journalize and post the entries required in Exercise 4A-2 and also the closing and reversing entries. The end of the current period is December 31, 19X1. Use dates for all entries and postings except the cash collection, which is a summary of the year's transactions. As references in the ledger accounts, denote a balance by Bal., cash receipts by CR, adjusting entries by Adj., closing entries by Clo., and reversing entries by Rev.

Exercise 4A-4   *Identifying transactions from a ledger account*

McGraw Company makes its annual insurance payment on June 30. Identify each of the entries (a) through (e) to the Insurance Expense account as a cash payment, an adjusting entry, a closing entry, or a reversing entry. Also give the other account debited or credited in each entry.

Insurance Expense

Date		Item	Debit	Credit	Balance
19X4	Jan. 1	(a)	800		800 (Dr)
	June 30	(b)	1,240		2,040 (Dr)
	Dec. 31	(c)		410	1,630 (Dr)
	Dec. 31	(d)		1,630	—
19X5	Jan. 1	(e)	410		410 (Dr)

Problems   (Group A)

Problem 4A-1   *Recording prepaid rent and rent revenue collected in advance two ways*

Denman Sales and Service completed the following transactions during 19X4:

Aug. 31   Paid $9,000 store rent covering the six-month period ending February 28, 19X5.

Dec.   1   Collected $2,200 cash in advance from customers. The service revenue will be earned $550 monthly over the period ending March 30, 19X5.

Required

1. Journalize these entries by debiting an asset account for Prepaid Rent, and by crediting a liability account for Unearned Service Revenue. Explanations are unnecessary.
2. Journalize the related adjustments at December 31, 19X4.
3. Post the entries to the ledger accounts and show their balances at December 31, 19X4. Posting references are unnecessary.
4. Repeat requirements 1 through 3. This time debit Rent Expense for the rent payment and credit Service Revenue for the collection of revenue in advance.
5. Compare the account balances in requirements 3 and 4. They should be equal.

Problem 4A-2   *Journalizing adjusting and reversing entries*

The accounting records of Mimico Company reveal the following information before adjustments at December 31, 19X7, end of the accounting period:

a. Mimico routinely debits Sales Supplies when it purchases supplies. At the beginning of 19X7 supplies of $800 were on hand, and during the year the company purchased supplies of $6,700. At year end, the count of sales supplies on hand indicates the ending amount is $950.

b. Mimico collects revenue in advance from customers, and credits such amounts to Sales Revenue because the revenue is usually earned within a short time. At December 31, 19X7, however, the company has a liability of $6,840 to customers for goods they paid for in advance.

c. Rentals cost the company $1,000 per month. The company prepays rent of $6,000 each May 1 and November 1, and debits Rent Expense for such payments.

d. The company prepaid $3,500 for television advertising that will run daily for two weeks, December 27, 19X7 through January 9, 19X8. Mimico debited Prepaid Advertising for the full amount on December 1.

Required

1. Journalize the adjusting entry needed for each situation at December 31, 19X7, identifying each entry by its corresponding letter.

2. Journalize reversing entries as needed. Use the corresponding letters for references. Date the entries appropriately.

Problem 4A-3   *Recording supplies and unearned revenue transactions two ways*

The accounting records of Stone Company reveal the following information about sales supplies and unearned sales revenue for 19X5:

Sales Supplies

19X5			
Jan. 1	Beginning amount on hand	$	420
Mar. 16	Cash purchase of supplies		3,740
Dec. 31	Ending amount on hand		290

Unearned Sales Revenue

19X5			
Jan. 1	Beginning amount on advance collections	$	6,590
July 22	Advance cash collection from customer		16,480
Nov. 4	Advance cash collection from customer		38,400
Dec. 31	Advance collections earned during the year		52,160

Required

1. Assume Stone Company records (a) supplies by initially debiting an asset account, and (b) advance collections from customers by initially crediting a liability account.

   a. Open T-accounts for Sales Supplies, Sales Supplies Expense, Unearned Sales Revenue, and Sales Revenue. Insert the beginning balances in the appropriate accounts.
   b. Record the cash transactions during 19X5 directly in the accounts.
   c. Record the adjusting and closing entries at December 31, 19X5 directly in the accounts.
   d. If appropriate, record the reversing entries at January 1, 19X6 directly in the accounts.

2. Assume Stone Company records (a) supplies by initially debiting an expense account, and (b) advance collections by initially crediting a revenue account. Perform steps a through d as in requirement 1.

3. Using the following format, compare the amounts that would be reported for the above accounts in the 19X5 balance sheet and income statement under the two recording approaches of requirements 1 and 2. Explain any similarity or difference.

	Requirement 1	Requirement 2
Balance sheet at December 31, 19X5 reports:		
Sales supplies	$ _____	$ _____
Unearned sales revenue	_____	_____
Income statement for year ended December 31, 19X5 reports:		
Sales revenue	_____	_____
Sales supplies expense	_____	_____

Answers to Self-Study Questions

1. a	2. d, a, e, b, f, c
3. d	4. d
5. b	6. c
7. b	8. a
9. c	10. b

Chapter 5

Merchandising
and the Accounting Cycle

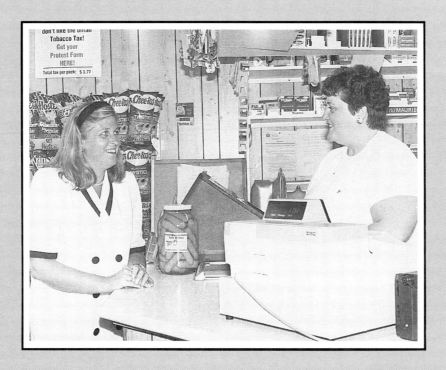

"*Your local supermarket or convenience store hardly looks like a war-zone. But in the bitter battle for retail display space, every store, shelf, and product facing counts. The lengths to which manufacturers will go to get their product on the shelf became vividly public when snack giant Hostess Frito-Lay Co. was caught last year fighting dirty. To stymie a move into Ontario by Winnipeg potato-chip champ Old Dutch Food Co., Hostess's sales reps were buying up retailers' entire stock of the new product. Their aim: to make sure that the consumers hooked by the newcomer's launch campaign couldn't find any Old Dutch chips to sample.*

The trick — an old one, by all accounts — might have worked, but retailers blew the whistle.... The media fried Hostess in the headlines, but the food industry merely yawned. When defending your turf, it seems, what Hostess did was small potatoes."

The merchandising industry is a very competitive and occasionally ruthless business to be in, whether you are selling potato chips, cars, computers, or any other product. Furthermore, fierce competition occurs not only at the consumer level, but also at the manufacturing and wholesale stages in the distribution chain.

Accounting information is critical to effective competition in the merchandising industry. Accountants determine three of the most fundamental figures that all merchants monitor closely: sales revenue, cost of goods sold, and gross profit. Small percentage changes in any of these accounts can mean the difference between a profitable and an unprofitable year.

In the potato chip battle described above, Hostess is estimated to have spent $200,000 buying up the Old Dutch stock. But the market Hostess was defending is worth $300 million a year!

Source: Richard Wright, "Dirty Work at the Corner Store," *Profit* (March 1992), pp. 38, 40, 41.

LEARNING OBJECTIVES

After studying this chapter, you should be able to

1 Explain the operating cycle of a merchandising business

2 Account for the purchase and sale of inventory

3 Compute cost of goods sold and gross margin

4 Prepare a merchandiser's financial statements

5 Adjust and close the accounts of a merchandising business

6 Recognize different formats of the income statement

How do the operations of Hostess Frito-Lay Co. differ from the businesses we have studied so far? In the first four chapters, Gary Lyon, Lawyer provided an illustration of a business that earns revenue by selling its services. Service enterprises include Four Seasons Hotels, Canadian Airlines, physicians, lawyers, public accountants, the Edmonton Oilers hockey team, and the twelve-year-old who cuts lawns in your neighborhood. A *merchandising entity* earns its revenue by selling products, called *merchandise inventory* or, simply, *inventory*. Hostess Frito-Lay Co., a Canadian Tire store, a Loblaws grocery, a Woodwards department store, and an ice-cream shop are merchandising entities. Exhibit 5-1 shows the income statement for a merchandising business. You will notice that this income statement differs from those shown earlier.

The amount that a merchandiser earns from selling its inventory is called **net sales revenue**, often abbreviated as **sales revenue**. The income statement in Exhibit 5-1 reports sales revenue of $680,000. The major revenue of a merchandising entity, sales revenue, represents the increase in owner's equity from delivering inventory to customers. The major expense of a merchandiser is *Cost of Goods Sold*. This expense's title is well chosen, because its amount represents the entity's cost of the goods (inventory) it has sold to customers. As long as inventory is held, it is an asset. When the inventory is sold to the customer, the inventory's cost becomes an expense. The excess of Sales Revenue over Cost of Goods Sold is called **gross margin** or **gross profit**. This important business statistic is often mentioned in the busi-

EXHIBIT 5-1 *A Merchandiser's Income Statement*

Foothills Supply Company Income Statement for the year ended December 31, 19X6		
Net sales revenue		$680,000
Cost of goods sold		370,000
Gross margin		310,000
Operating expenses		
Salary expense	$130,000	
Rent expense	60,000	
Insurance expense	18,000	
Depreciation expense	14,000	
Supplies expense	8,000	230,000
Net income		$ 80,000

ness press because it helps measure a business's success. A sufficiently high gross margin is often vital to success.

The following illustration will clarify the nature of gross margin. Consider a concession stand at a junior hockey game. Assume the business sells a soft drink for $1.00, and the vendor's cost is $.20. Gross margin per unit is $.80 ($1.00 – $.20), and the overall gross margin is $.80 multiplied by the number of drinks sold. If the concession stand sells 400 drinks on a Saturday night, its gross margin on drink sales is $320 (400 × $.80). The gross margin on all sales, including hot dogs, popcorn and candy, is the sum of the gross margins on all the items sold. Petro-Canada's gross margin (and that of a Red and White grocery store, a neighborhood drug store, and every other merchandiser) is computed in exactly the same way: Sales – Cost of Goods Sold = Gross Margin.

Margin in gross margin refers to the excess of revenue over expense. *Gross* indicates that the operating expenses (rent, depreciation, advertising, and so on) have not yet been subtracted. After subtracting all the expenses we have *net income*. Gross margin and net income are *not* accounts in the ledger, so we cannot make journal entries to them. Instead, we compute these amounts by subtracting one amount from another: Gross Margin - Operating Expenses = Net Income. Study Exhibit 5-1, focusing on the sales revenue, cost of goods sold, and gross margin. Note the separate category for operating expenses.

The Operating Cycle for a Merchandising Business _____

OBJECTIVE 1

Explain the operating cycle of a merchandising business

A merchandising entity buys inventory, sells the inventory to its customers and uses the cash to purchase more inventory to repeat the cycle. Exhibit 5-2 diagrams the operating cycle for *cash sales* and for *sales on account*. For a cash sale (item a in the exhibit), the cycle is from cash to inventory, which is purchased for resale and back to cash. For a sale on account (item b), the cycle is from cash to inventory to accounts receivable and back to cash.

Purchase of Merchandise Inventory _____

The cycle of a merchandising entity begins with the purchase of inventory, as Exhibit 5-2 shows. **Purchases**, in the accounting sense, are only those items of in-

EXHIBIT 5-2   *Operating Cycle of a Merchandiser*

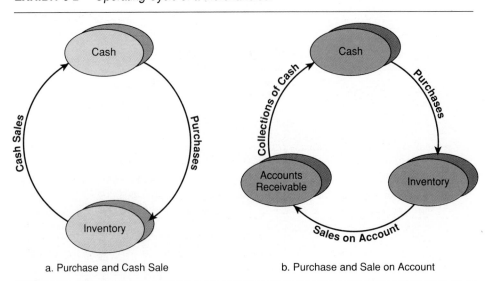

a. Purchase and Cash Sale   b. Purchase and Sale on Account

ventory that a firm buys to resell to customers in the normal course of business. For example, a stereo center records in the Purchases account the price it pays for tape decks, turntables, and other items of inventory acquired for resale. A bicycle shop records Purchases when it buys ten-speeds and mountain bikes for its inventory. A grocery store debits Purchases when it buys canned goods, meat, frozen food, and other inventory. A $500 purchase on account is recorded as follows:

June 14 Purchases	500	
Accounts payable		500
Purchased inventory on account.		

The Purchase Invoice: A Basic Business Document

Business documents are the tangible evidence of transactions. As we trace the steps that Austin Sound Stereo Center, an actual business, takes in ordering, receiving and paying for inventory, we point out the roles that documents play in carrying on business.

1. Suppose Austin Sound wants to stock JVC brand turntables, cassette decks, and speakers. Austin prepares a *purchase order* and mails it to JVC.
2. On receipt of the purchase order, JVC scans its warehouse for the inventory that Austin Sound ordered. JVC ships the equipment and mails the invoice to Austin on the same day. The **invoice** is the seller's request for payment from the purchaser. It is also called the *bill*.
3. Often the purchaser receives the invoice before the inventory arrives. Austin Sound does not pay immediately. Instead, Austin waits until the inventory arrives in order to ensure that it is (1) the correct type, (2) the quantity ordered, and (3) in good condition. After the inventory is inspected and approved, Austin Sound pays JVC the invoice amount.

Exhibit 5-3 is a copy of an actual invoice from JVC Canada Inc. to Austin Sound Stereo Center. From Austin Sound's perspective, this document is a purchase invoice, whereas to JVC it is a sales invoice. The circled numbers on the exhibit correspond to the following numbered explanations:

1. The seller is JVC Atlantic Branch, JVC Canada Inc.
2. The invoice date is 05/27/92. The date is needed for determining whether the purchaser gets a discount for prompt payment (see item 5 below).
3. The purchaser is Austin Sound Stereo Center. The inventory is invoiced (billed) and shipped to the same address, 305 Robie St., Halifax, Nova Scotia B3H 4K7.
4. Austin Sound's purchase order (P.O.) date was 05/25/92.
5. Credit terms of the transaction are 3% 15, NET 30 DAYS. This means that Austin Sound may deduct 3 percent of the total amount due if Austin pays within 15 days of the invoice date, not the purchase order date. Otherwise, the full amount (net) is due in 30 days. (A full discussion of discounts appears in the next section.)
6. Austin Sound ordered 6 turntables, 3 cassette decks, and 2 speakers.
7. JVC shipped 5 turntables, no cassette decks, and no speakers.
8. The cost of the stereo equipment is $660, and the goods and services tax (see p. 209) is $47 ($660 × .07); total invoice amount is $707.
9. Austin Sound paid on 6-10-92. How much did Austin Sound pay?
10. Payment occurred 14 days after the invoice date (within the discount period). Therefore, Austin Sound paid $685.79 ($707 minus the 3 percent discount).

EXHIBIT 5-3   *Business Invoice*

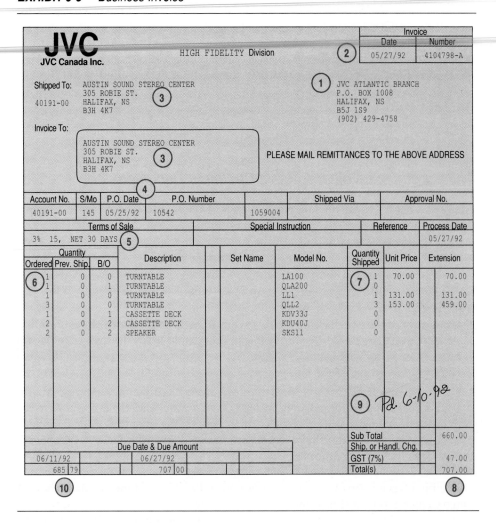

Discounts from Purchase Prices

There are two major types of discounts from purchase prices: quantity discounts and cash discounts (called purchase discounts).

Quantity Discounts   A **quantity discount** works this way: the larger the quantity purchased, the lower the price per item. For example, JVC may offer no trade discount for the purchase of only one or two cassette decks, and charge the list price (the full price) of $200 per unit. However, JVC may offer the following quantity discount terms in order to persuade customers to buy a larger number of cassette decks:

Quantity	Quantity Discount	Net Price Per Unit
Buy minimum quantity, 3 cassette decks	5%	$190 [$200 − .05($200)]
Buy 4–9 decks	10	$180 [$200 − .10($200)]
Buy more than 9 decks	20	$160 [$200 − .20($200)]

Suppose Austin Sound purchases five cassette decks from this manufacturer. The cost of each unit is, therefore, $180. Purchase of five units on account would be recorded by debiting Purchases and crediting Accounts Payable for the total price of $900 ($180 × 5).

There is no quantity discount account and no special accounting entry for a quantity discount. Instead, all accounting entries are based on the net price of a purchase after subtracting the quantity discount.

Purchase Discounts   Many businesses offer purchase discounts to their customers. A **purchase discount** is a reward for prompt payment. If a quantity discount is also offered, the purchase discount is computed on the net purchase amount after subtracting the quantity discount.

JVC's credit terms of 3% 15 NET 30 DAYS can also be expressed as 3/15 n/30. Terms of simply n/30 indicate that no discount is offered, and that payment is due 30 days after the invoice date. Terms of *eom* mean that payment is due by the end of the current month. However, a purchase after the twenty-fifth of the current month on terms of *eom* can be paid at the end of the next month.

Let us use the Exhibit 5-3 transaction to illustrate accounting for a purchase discount. Austin Sound records this purchase on account as follows:

May 25	Purchases	707.00	
	Accounts Payable		707.00
	Purchased inventory on account.		

Since Austin Sound paid within the discount period, its cash payment entry is

June 10	Accounts Payable	707.00	
	Cash ($707.00 × .97)		685.79
	Purchase Discounts ($707.00 × .03)		21.21
	Paid on account within discount period.		

> **OBJECTIVE 2**
> Account for the purchase and sale of inventory

Purchase Discounts, which has a credit balance, is a contra account to Purchases. We show how to report Purchase Discounts on the income statement later in the chapter.

Alternatively, if Austin Sound pays this invoice after the discount period, it must pay the full invoice amount. In this case, the payment entry is

June 29	Accounts Payable	707.00	
	Cash		707.00
	Paid on account after discount period.		

Purchase Returns and Allowances

Most businesses allow their customers to *return* merchandise that is defective, damaged in shipment or otherwise unsuitable. Or if the buyer chooses to keep damaged goods, the seller may deduct an *allowance* from the amount the buyer owes. Because returns and allowances are closely related, they are usually recorded in a single account, **Purchase Returns and Allowances**. This account, a contra account to Purchases, gives a record of the amount of returns and allowances for the period. Later in the chapter, we show how to report this account on the income statement.

Suppose the $70 turntable purchased by Austin Sound (in Exhibit 5-3) was not the turntable ordered. Austin returns the merchandise to the seller and records the purchase return as follows:

June 3	Accounts Payable	70.00	
	Purchase Returns and Allowances		70.00
	Returned inventory to seller.		

Now assume that one of the JVC turntables is damaged in shipment to Austin Sound. The damage is minor, and Austin decides to keep the turntable in exchange for a $10 allowance from JVC. To record this purchase allowance, Austin Sound makes this entry:

June 4	Accounts Payable	10.00	
	Purchase Returns and Allowances		10.00
	Received a purchase allowance.		

Observe that the return and the allowance had two effects: (1) they decreased Austin Sound's liability, which is why we debit Accounts Payable, and (2) they decreased the net cost of the inventory, which is why we credit Purchase Returns and Allowances. It would be incorrect to credit Purchases because Austin Sound did in fact make the purchase. Changes due to returns and allowances are recorded in the contra account.

During the period, the business records the cost of all inventory bought in the Purchases account. The balance of Purchases is a *gross* amount because it does not include subtractions for purchase discounts, returns or allowances. **Net purchases** is the remainder that is computed by subtracting the contra accounts as follows:

> **Purchases (*debit* balance account)**
> **−Purchase discounts (*credit* balance account)**
> **−Purchase returns and allowances (*credit* balance account)**
>
> =**Net purchases (a *debit* subtotal, not a separate account)**

Transportation Costs

The transportation cost of moving inventory from seller to buyer can be significant. The purchase agreement specifies FOB terms to indicate who pays the shipping charges. The term *FOB* stands for *free on board* and governs when the legal title to the goods passes from seller to buyer. Under FOB *shipping point* terms, title passes when the inventory leaves the seller's place of business, the shipping point. The buyer owns the goods while they are in transit, and therefore pays the transportation cost. Under FOB *destination* terms, title passes when the goods reach the destination, so the seller pays transportation cost.

	FOB Shipping Point	FOB Destination
When does title pass to buyer?	Shipping point	Destination
Who pays transportation cost?	Buyer	Seller

FOB shipping point terms are the more common, so generally, the buyer bears the shipping cost. The buyer debits Freight In (sometimes called Transportation In), and credits Cash or Accounts Payable for the amount. Suppose the buyer receives a shipping bill directly from the freight company. The buyer's entry to record payment of the freight charge is

March 3	Freight In	190	
	Cash		190
	Paid a freight bill.		

Under FOB shipping point terms, the seller sometimes prepays the transportation cost as a convenience, and lists this cost on the invoice. The buyer would *not* debit Purchases for the combined cost of the inventory and the shipping cost. Rather, the buyer would debit Purchases for the cost of the goods and Freight In separately. A $5,000 purchase of goods, coupled with a related freight charge of $400, would be recorded as follows:

March 12	Purchases	5,000	
	Freight In	400	
	Accounts Payable		5,400
	Purchased inventory on account plus freight.		

Quantity discounts and Purchase discounts are computed only on the cost of the inventory, *not* on the freight charges. Suppose the $5,000 credit purchase allows a $100 discount for early payment. The cash payment within the discount period would be $5,300 [net payment of $4,900 on the inventory ($5,000, less the $100 purchase discount), plus the freight charges of $400].

Sale of Inventory

The sale of inventory may be for cash or on account, as Exhibit 5-2 shows.

Cash Sale   Sales of retailers such as drug stores, gift shops, and restaurants are often for cash. A $50.00 cash sale is recorded by debiting Cash and crediting the revenue account, Sales Revenue, as follows:

Jan. 9	Cash..	50
	Sales Revenue	50
	Cash sale.	

Sale on Account   Many sales by department stores, furniture stores, and other consumer goods stores are made on account using either the store's credit card or some other credit card such as Visa or Mastercard. To simplify the discussion, we will assume the seller records the receivable as a regular account receivable rather than a special receivable from the credit card company.

Most sales by wholesalers and manufacturers are made on account or on credit. A $5,000 sale on account is recorded by a debit to Accounts Receivable and a credit to Sales Revenue, as follows:

Jan. 11	Accounts Receivable..	5,000
	Sales Revenue	5,000
	Sale on account.	

The related cash receipt on account is journalized by the following entry:

Jan. 19	Cash..	5,000
	Accounts Receivable.....................................	5,000
	Collection on account.	

Sales Discounts, Sales Returns and Allowances

Sales Discounts and **Sales Returns and Allowances** are contra accounts to Sales Revenue, just as Purchase Discounts, and Purchase Returns and Allowances are contra accounts to Purchases. Let us take a sequence of the sale transactions of JVC. Suppose JVC uses one account for Sales Returns and Allowances.

On July 7, JVC sells stereo components for $7,200 on credit terms of 2/10 n/30. JVC's entry to record this credit sale follows:

July 7	Accounts Receivable	$7,200
	Sales Revenue	$7,200
	Sale on account.	

Assume the buyer returns goods that cost $600. JVC records the sales return and the related decrease in Accounts Receivable as follows:

July 12	Sales Returns and Allowances	600
	Accounts Receivable.....................................	600
	Received returned goods.	

JVC grants a $100 sales allowance for damaged goods. JVC journalizes this transaction by debiting Sales Returns and Allowances and crediting Accounts Receivable as follows:

July 15	Sales Returns and Allowances	100	
	Accounts Receivable...		100
	Granted a sales allowance for damaged goods.		

After the preceding entries are posted, Accounts Receivable has a $6,500 debit balance as follows:

Accounts Receivable

July 7	7,200	July 12	600
		15	100
Bal.	6,500		

On July 17, the last day of the discount period, JVC collects half ($3,250) of this receivable ($6,500 × ½ = $3,250). The cash receipt is $3,185 [$3,250 − (.02 × $3,250)], and the collection entry is

July 17	Cash..	3,185	
	Sales Discounts (.02 × $3,250)	65	
	Accounts Receivable......................................		3,250
	Cash collection with the discount period.		

Suppose JVC collects the remainder on July 28 (after the discount period) so there is no sales discount. To record this collection on account, JVC debits Cash and credits Accounts Receivable for the same amount as follows:

July 28	Cash..	3,250	
	Accounts Receivable......................................		3,250
	Cash collection after the discount period.		

Net sales is computed in a manner similar to net purchases. We subtract the contra accounts as follows:

> **Sales revenue (*credit* balance account)**
> − **Sales discounts (*debit* balance account)**
> − **Sales returns and allowances (*debit* balance account)**
> = **Net sales (a *credit* subtotal, not a separate account)**

Cost of Goods Sold

Cost of goods sold is the largest single expense of most merchandising businesses. It is the cost of the inventory that the business has sold to customers. Another name for cost of goods sold is **cost of sales**. How is it computed?

Recall from Chapter 3 that supplies expense is computed as follows:

> **Beginning supplies**
> + **Supplies purchased during the period**
> = **Supplies available for use during the period**
> − **Supplies on hand at the end of the period**
> = **Supplies expense**

Cost of goods sold is computed this same way, as shown in Exhibit 5-4.

Exhibit 5-4 *Measurement of Cost of Goods Sold*

Computation

OBJECTIVE 3

Compute cost of goods
sold and gross margin

> **Beginning inventory**
> **+ Net purchases**
> **+ Freight in**
> _____
> **= Cost of goods available for sale**
> **– Ending inventory**
> _____
> **= Cost of goods sold**

Diagram

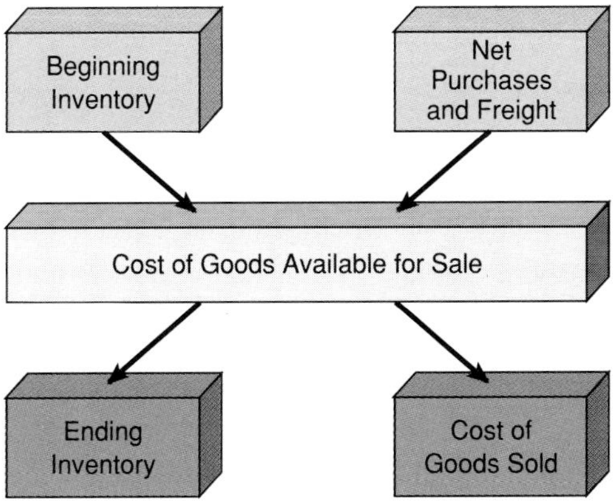

By studying the exhibit, you will see that the computation and the diagram tell the same story. That is, a company's goods available for sale during a period come from beginning inventory and the period's net purchases and freight costs. Either the merchandise is sold during the period or it remains on hand at the end. The merchandise that remains is an asset, Inventory. The cost of the inventory that has been sold is an expense, Cost of Goods Sold.

Two main types of inventory accounting systems exist: the periodic system and the perpetual system. The periodic system is used by businesses that sell relatively inexpensive goods. A grocery store without an optical-scanning cash register does not keep a daily running record of every loaf of bread and package of Schneider's bacon that it buys and sells. The cost of record keeping would be overwhelming. Instead, the grocer would count his or her inventory periodically (at least once a year) to determine the quantities on hand. The inventory amounts are used to prepare the annual financial statements. Other businesses such as office supply outlets, restaurants, and variety stores also use the periodic inventory system. The key is that detailed inventory records are not necessary in the ledger for controlling merchandise and managing day-to-day operations. In small businesses, the owner can visually inspect the goods on hand for control purposes.

Under the perpetual inventory system, the business maintains a running record of inventory on hand. The system achieves control over expensive goods such as automobiles, jewellery, and furniture. The loss of one item would be significant, and this justifies the cost of a perpetual system. More and more businesses are using the perpetual system as computers become more flexible and less expensive. Even under a perpetual system the business counts the inventory annually. The physical count establishes the correct amount of inventory on hand, and permits a check of the perpetual records.

In this chapter, we illustrate the periodic inventory system because it highlights the relationship between inventory and cost of goods sold, as shown in Exhibit 5-4. This model for computing expense is used throughout accounting and is extremely useful for analytical purposes. Furthermore, the periodic system is used by many small businesses, such as the proprietorships we use as illustrations in the early chapters of this book. Chapter 9 discusses the perpetual system.

Under the periodic system, as we have noted, the business does not keep a running record of the cost of its inventory on hand. Instead, it counts the goods on hand at the end of each period to determine the inventory to be reported on the balance sheet. This ending inventory amount becomes the beginning inventory of the next period, and is used to compute cost of goods sold for the income statement. In the periodic inventory system, entries to the Inventory account are made only at the end of the period.

In this inventory system, cost of goods sold is *not* a ledger account like Salary Expense, Rent Expense, and the other operating expenses. Instead, it is the cost left over when we subtract the cost of ending inventory from the cost of goods available for sale. Cost of goods sold is computationally more complex than the other expenses.

Exhibit 5-5 summarizes the first half of the chapter by showing Austin Sound's net sales, cost of goods sold (including net purchases), and gross margin on the income statement.

Note that arithmetic operations, addition and subtraction, move across the columns from left to right. For example, the figures for Sales Discounts and for Sales Returns and Allowances appear in a separate column. Their sum, $3,400, appears to the right, where it is subtracted from Sales Revenue. The net sales amount of $135,900 appears in the right-most column.

Contra accounts (discounts, returns and allowances, and the like) are frequently netted against their related accounts parenthetically. Thus many accountants would report sales in our example as follows:

Net sales revenue (net of sales discounts, $1,400,
    and returns and allowances, $2,000) $135,900

EXHIBIT 5-5 *Partial Income Statement*

Austin Sound Income Statement for the year ended December 31, 19X6			
Sales revenue		$139,300	
Less: Sales discounts	$ 1,400		
Sales returns and allowances	2,000	3,400	
Net sales revenue			$135,900
Cost of goods sold			
Beginning inventory		$40,500	
Purchases	$89,300		
Less: Purchase discounts	$3,000		
Purchase returns and allowances ..	1,200	4,200	
Net purchases		85,100	
Freight in		5,200	
Cost of goods available for sale		130,800	
Less: Ending inventory		42,000	
Cost of goods sold			88,800
Gross margin			$ 47,100

Purchases can also be reported at its net amount in the following manner:

Cost of goods sold	
Beginning inventory	$ 40,500
Net purchases (net of purchase discounts, $3,000,	
and returns and allowances, $1,200)	85,100
Freight in	5,200
Cost of goods available for sale	$130,800
Less: Ending inventory	42,000
Cost of goods sold	$ 88,800

These presentations of *net* sales and *net* purchases underscore an important fact: published financial statements usually report only *net* amounts for these items, because discounts and returns and allowances are relatively small in amount. For most businesses, these contra items are details of primary interest only to managers, and therefore are not highlighted in the financial statements. For example, Dofasco Inc. recently reported:

	1991	1990
Net sales	$2,055,800,000	$2,349,300,000
Cost of sales	1,842,400,000	1,905,700,000
Gross profit	$ 213,400,000	$ 443,600,000

Goods and Services Tax

This topic is introduced here to make you aware of the goods and services tax because most goods and services sold today in Canada have the goods and services tax (GST) levied on them by the federal government at the time of sale. However, it was decided to omit consideration of the GST from the discussion and examples in the early chapters to avoid making the material overly complicated. The following discussion provides a brief introduction to the topic; GST is dealt with more fully in Chapter 11.

The manufacturer, wholesaler, and retailer pay the GST on the cost of their purchases, and then pass it on to the next link in the economic chain by collecting it on their respective sales. The consumer, the last link in the chain, pays the final tax. Each entity that collects the GST remits the tax collected to the Receiver General.

The GST is designed to be a consumption tax and, as was suggested above, the entity ultimately paying the tax is the final purchsaser of the product or service. Earlier links in the chain (for example, the retailer) pay tax on their purchases, but are then allowed to deduct that tax from the tax they themselves collect on their sales. Therefore the GST paid on purchases does not really affect the cost of the purchase. For example, Austin Sound paid the GST of 7 percent, or $4.90 ($70 × .07), on the LA100 turntable purchased on Exhibit 5-3. The entry to record the purchase of the single turntable would have been

May 27	Purchases..	70.00	
	GST on purchases	4.90	
	Accounts payable..		74.90
	Purchased JVC LA100 turntable on account.		

Assume Austin Sound Stereo Center sold the JVC LA100 turntable for $110.00 to a customer; the GST on the sale would be $7.70 ($110.00 × .07). The entry to record the sale would be

June 10	Cash	117.70	
	GST payable..		7.70
	Net sales		110.00
	Sold turntable for cash.		

Subsequently, Austin Sound would have to remit the GST collected. The entry would be

July 31	GST payable..	7.70	
	GST on purchases		4.90
	Cash		2.80
	Payment of GST collected net of GST paid on purchases.		

Summary Problem for Your Review

Brun Sales Company engaged in the following transactions during June of the current year:

June	3	Purchased inventory on credit terms of 1/10 net eom (end of month), $1,610.
	9	Returned 40 percent of the inventory purchased on June 3. It was defective.
	9	Sold goods for cash, $920.
	15	Purchased merchandise of $5,100, less a $100 quantity discount. Credit terms were 3/15 n/30.
	16	Paid a $260 freight bill on goods purchased.
	18	Sold inventory on credit terms of 2/10 n/30, $2,000.
	22	Received damaged merchandise from the customer to whom the June 18 sale was made, $800.
	24	Borrowed money from the bank to take advantage of the discount offered on the June 15 purchase. Signed a note payable to the bank for the net amount.
	24	Paid supplier for goods purchased on June 15, less all discounts.
	28	Received cash in full settlement of the account from the customer who purchased inventory on June 18.
	29	Paid the amount owed on account from the purchase of June 3.
	30	Purchased inventory for cash, $900, less a trade discount of $35.

Required

1. Journalize the above transactions.

2. Assume the note payable signed on June 24 requires the payment of $95 interest expense. Was the decision wise or unwise to borrow funds to take advantage of the cash discount?

SOLUTION TO REVIEW PROBLEM

Requirement 1

June	3	Purchases...	1,610	
		Accounts Payable		1,610
	9	Accounts Payable ($1,610 × .40)	644	
		Purchase Returns and Allowances		644
	9	Cash...	920	
		Sales Revenue		920

15	Purchases ($5,100 – $100)	5,000	
	Accounts Payable		5,000
16	Freight In	260	
	Cash...		260
18	Accounts Receivable	2,000	
	Sales Revenue		2,000
22	Sales Returns and Allowances	800	
	Accounts Receivable.................................		800
24	Cash [$5,000 – .03($5,000)]..............................	4,850	
	Note Payable...		4,850
24	Accounts Payable	5,000	
	Purchase Discounts ($5,000 × .03)		150
	Cash ($5,000 × .97)		4,850
28	Cash [($2,000 – $800) × .98]	1,176	
	Sales Discounts [($2,000 – $800) × .02]............	24	
	Accounts Receivable ($2,000 – $800)		1,200
29	Accounts Payable ($1,610 – $644)....................	966	
	Cash...		966
30	Purchases ($900 – $35)	865	
	Cash...		865

Requirement 2

The decision to borrow funds was wise, because the discount earned ($150) exceeded the interest paid on the amount borrowed ($95). Thus the entity was $55 better off as a result of its decision.

The Adjusting and Closing Process for a Merchandising Business

A merchandising business adjusts and closes the accounts much as a service entity does. The steps of this end-of-period process are the same. If a work sheet is used, enter the trial balance, and complete the work sheet to determine net income or net loss. The work sheet provides the data for preparing the financial statements and journalizing the adjusting and closing entries. After these entries are posted to the ledger, a post-closing trial balance can be prepared.

The Inventory account affects the adjusting and closing entries of a merchandiser. At the end of the period, before any adjusting or closing entries, the Inventory balance is still the cost of the inventory that was on hand at the beginning date. It is necessary to remove this beginning balance and replace it with the cost of the ending inventory. Various acceptable bookkeeping techniques might be used to bring the inventory records up to date. In this chapter, we illustrate the closing-entry method. In the chapter appendix we present an alternative approach, the adjusting-entry method.

To illustrate a merchandiser's adjusting and closing process, let us use Austin Sound's December 31, 19X6 trial balance in Exhibit 5-6. All the new accounts — Inventory, Freight In, and the contra accounts — are highlighted for emphasis. However, Inventory is the only account that is affected by the new closing procedures. Note that additional data item g gives the ending inventory of $42,000.

Work Sheet of a Merchandising Business

The Exhibit 5-7 work sheet is similar to the work sheets we have seen so far, but a few differences appear. Note that this work sheet does not include adjusted trial balance columns. In most accounting systems, a single operation combines trial balance

EXHIBIT 5-6 *Trial Balance*

Austin Sound
Trial Balance
December 31, 19X6

Cash	$ 2,850	
Accounts receivable	4,600	
Note receivable, current	8,000	
Interest receivable		
Inventory	**40,500**	
Supplies	650	
Prepaid insurance	1,200	
Furniture and fixtures	33,200	
Accumulated depreciation		$ 2,400
Accounts payable		47,000
Unearned sales revenue		2,000
Interest payable		
Note payable, long-term		12,600
E. Boritz, capital		25,900
E. Boritz, withdrawals	34,100	
Sales revenue		**138,000**
Sales discounts	**1,400**	
Sales returns and allowances	**2,000**	
Interest revenue		600
Purchases	**89,300**	
Purchase discounts		**3,000**
Purchase returns and allowances		**1,200**
Freight in	**5,200**	
Rent expense	8,400	
Depreciation expense		
Insurance expense		
Supplies expense		
Interest expense	1,300	
Total	$232,700	$232,700

Additional data at December 31, 19X6:

a. Interest revenue earned but not yet collected, $400.

b. Supplies on hand, $100.

c. Prepaid insurance expired during the year, $1,000.

d. Depreciation, $600.

e. Unearned sales revenue earned during the year, $1,300.

f. Interest expense incurred but not yet paid, $200.

g. Inventory on hand, $42,000.

amounts with the adjustments and extends the adjusted balances directly to the income statement and balance sheet columns. Therefore, to reduce clutter, the adjusted trial balance columns are omitted. A second difference is that the merchandiser's work sheet includes inventory and purchase amounts (which are highlighted here). Let us examine the entire work sheet.

Account Title Columns The trial balance lists a number of accounts without balances. Ordinarily, these accounts are affected by the adjusting process. Examples include Interest Receivable, Interest Payable, and Depreciation Expense. The ac-

EXHIBIT 5-7 *Work Sheet*

Austin Sound
Work Sheet
for the year ended December 31, 19X6

Account Title	Trial Balance Debit	Trial Balance Credit	Adjustments Debit	Adjustments Credit	Income Statement Debit	Income Statement Credit	Balance Sheet Debit	Balance Sheet Credit
Cash	2,850						2,850	
Accounts receivable	4,600						4,600	
Note receivable, current	8,000						8,000	
Interest receivable			(a) 400				400	
Inventory	**40,500**				**40,500**	**42,000**	**42,000**	
Supplies	650			(b) 550			100	
Prepaid insurance	1,200			(c)1,000			200	
Furniture and fixtures	33,200						33,200	
Accumulated depreciation		2,400		(d) 600				3,000
Accounts payable		47,000						47,000
Unearned sales revenue		2,000	(e)1,300					700
Interest payable				(f) 200				200
Note payable, long-term		12,600						12,600
E. Boritz, capital		25,900						25,900
E. Boritz, withdrawals	34,100						34,100	
Sales revenue		138,000		(e)1,300		139,300		
Sales discounts	1,400				1,400			
Sales returns and allowances	2,000				2,000			
Interest revenue		600		(a) 400		1,000		
Purchases	**89,300**				**89,300**			
Purchase discounts		**3,000**				**3,000**		
Purchase returns and allowances		**1,200**				**1,200**		
Freight in	**5,200**				**5,200**			
Rent expense	8,400				8,400			
Depreciation expense			(d) 600		600			
Insurance expense			(c)1,000		1,000			
Supplies expense			(b) 550		550			
Interest expense	1,300		(f) 200		1,500			
	232,700	232,700	4,050	4,050	150,450	186,500	125,450	89,400
Net income					36,050			36,050
					186,500	186,500	125,450	125,450

counts are listed in the order they appear in the ledger. This eases the preparation of the work sheet. If additional accounts are needed, they can be written in at the bottom of the work sheet before net income is determined. Simply move net income down to make room for the additional accounts.

Trial Balance Columns   Examine the Inventory account, $40,500 in the trial Balance. This $40,500 is the cost of beginning inventory. The work sheet is designed to replace this outdated amount with the new ending balance, which in our example is $42,000 (additional data item g in Exhibit 5-6). As we shall see, this task is accomplished later in the columns for the income statement and the balance sheet.

Adjustments Columns   The adjustments are similar to those discussed in Chapters 3 and 4. They may be entered in any order desired. The debit amount of each entry should equal the credit amount, and total debits should equal total credits.

Income Statement Columns The income statement columns contain adjusted amounts for the revenues and expenses. Sales Revenue, for example, is $139,300, which includes the $1,300 adjustment.

You may be wondering why the two inventory amounts appear in the income statement columns. The reason is that beginning inventory and ending inventory are part of the computation of cost of goods sold. Recall that beginning inventory is added to cost of goods amount sold, and ending inventory is subtracted. Even though the resulting cost of goods sold does not appear on the work sheet, all the components of cost of goods sold are evident there. Placement of beginning inventory ($40,500) in the work sheet's income statement debit column has the effect of adding beginning inventory in computing cost of goods sold. Placing ending inventory ($42,000) in the credit column has the opposite effect.

Purchases and Freight In appear in the debit column because they are added in computing cost of goods sold. Purchase Discounts and Purchase Returns and Allowances appear as credits because they are subtracted. Together, all these items are used to compute cost of goods sold, $88,800 on the income statement in Exhibit 5-5.

The income statement column subtotals on the work sheet indicate whether the business earned net income or incurred a net loss. If total credits are greater, the result is net income, as shown in the exhibit. Inserting the net income amount in the debit column brings total debits into agreement with total credits. If total debits are greater, a net loss has occurred. Inserting a net loss amount in the credit column would equalize total debits and total credits. Net income or net loss is then extended to the opposite column of the balance sheet.

Balance Sheet Columns The only new item on the balance sheet is inventory. The balance listed is the ending amount of $42,000, which is determined by a physical count of inventory on hand at the end of the period, since Austin Sound is using the periodic system.

OBJECTIVE 4

Prepare a merchandiser's financial statements

Financial Statements of a Merchandising Business _____

Exhibit 5-8 presents Austin Sound Stereo Center's financial statements. The *income statement* through gross margin repeats Exhibit 5-5. This information is followed by the **operating expenses**, which are those expenses incurred in the entity's major line of business — merchandising. Rent is the cost of obtaining store space for Austin Sound's operations. Insurance is necessary to protect the inventory. The business's store furniture and fixtures wear out, and that expense is depreciation. Supplies expense is the cost of stationery, mailing, computer supplies, and the like, used in operations.

Many companies report their operating expenses in two categories. *Selling expenses* are those expenses related to marketing the company's products: sales salaries; sales commissions; advertising; depreciation, rent, utilities and property taxes on store buildings; depreciation on store furniture; delivery expense, and the like. *General expenses* include office expenses, such as the salaries of the company president and office employees who are not engaged in selling, depreciation, rent, utilities, property taxes on the home office building, and supplies.

Gross margin minus operating expenses equals **income from operations**, or **operating income**, as it is also called. Many businesspeople view operating income as the most reliable indicator of a business's success because it measures the entity's major ongoing activities.

The last section of Austin Sound's income statement is **other revenue and expense**. This category reports revenues and expenses that are outside the main operations of the business. Examples include gains and losses on the sale of capital assets (not inventory), and unusual and nonrecurring writedowns of assets such as accounts receivable or inventory. Accountants have traditionally viewed Interest Revenue and Interest Expense as "other" items, because they arise from loaning

EXHIBIT 5-8 *Financial Statements of Austin Sound Stereo Center*

Austin Sound
Income Statement
for the year ended December 31, 19X6

Sales revenue			$139,300
Less: Sales discounts		$ 1,400	
Sales returns and allowances		2,000	3,400
Net sales revenue			$135,900
Cost of goods sold			
Beginning inventory		40,500	
Purchases		89,300	
Less: Purchase discounts	$3,000		
Purchase returns and allowances	1,200	4,200	
Net purchases		85,100	
Freight in		5,200	
Cost of goods available for sale		130,800	
Less: Ending inventory		42,000	
Cost of goods sold			88,800
Gross margin			47,100
Operating expenses			
Rent expense		8,400	
Insurance expense		1,000	
Depreciation expense		600	
Supplies expense		550	10,550
Income from operations			36,550
Other revenue and expense			
Interest revenue		1,000	
Interest expense		(1,500)	(500)
Net income			$ 36,050

Austin Sound
Statement of Owner's Equity
for the year ended December 31, 19X6

E. Boritz, capital, January 1, 19X6	$ 25,900
Add: Net income	36,050
	61,950
Less: Withdrawals	34,100
E. Boritz, capital, December 31, 19X6	$ 27,850

Austin Sound
Balance Sheet
December 31, 19X6

Assets			**Liabilities**		
Current			Current		
Cash		$ 2,850	Accounts payable		$47,000
Accounts receivable		4,600	Unearned sales revenue		700
Note receivable		8,000	Interest payable		200
Interest receivable		400	Total current liabilities		47,900
Inventory		42,000	Long-term		
Prepaid insurance		200	Note payable		12,600
Supplies		100	Total liabilities		60,500
Total current assets		58,150			
Capital			**Owner's Equity**		
Furniture and fixtures	$33,200				
Less: Accumulated			E. Boritz, capital		27,850
depreciation	3,000	30,200	Total liabilities and		
Total assets		$88,350	owner's equity		$88,350

money and borrowing money — financing activities that are outside the operating scope of selling merchandise or, for a service entity, rendering services.

The bottom line of the income statement is net income, which includes the effects of all the revenues and gains less all the expenses and losses. We often hear the term *bottom line* used to refer to a final result. The term originated in the position of net income on the income statement.

A merchandiser's *statement of owner's equity* looks exactly like that of a service business. In fact, you cannot determine whether the entity is merchandising or service oriented from looking at the statement of owner's equity.

If the business is a merchandiser, the *balance sheet* shows inventory as a major asset. In contrast, service businesses usually have minor amounts of inventory.

Adjusting and Closing Entries for a Merchandising Business

OBJECTIVE 5

Adjust and close the accounts of a merchandising business

Exhibit 5-9 presents Austin Sound's adjusting entries, which are similar to those you have seen previously.

The closing entries in the exhibit include two new effects. The first closing entry debits Inventory for the ending balance of $42,000 and debits the temporary accounts that have credit balances. For Austin Sound, these accounts are Sales Revenue, Interest Revenue, Purchase Discounts, and Purchase Returns and Allowances. The offsetting credit of $186,500 transfers their sum to Income Summary. This amount comes directly from the credit column of the income statement on the work sheet (Exhibit 5-7).

The second closing entry includes a credit to Inventory for its beginning balance and credits to the revenue and expense accounts with debit balances. These are Sales Discounts, Sales Returns and Allowances, Purchases, Freight In, and the expense accounts. The offsetting $150,450 debit to Income Summary comes from the debit column of the income statement on the work sheet.

The last two closing entries close net income from Income Summary, and also close owner Withdrawals, into the Capital account.

The entries to the Inventory account deserve additional explanation. Recall that before the closing process, Inventory still has the period's beginning balance. At the end of the period, this balance is one year old and must be replaced with the ending balance in order to prepare the financial statements at December 31, 19X6. The closing entries give Inventory its correct ending balance of $42,000, as shown below:

Inventory

Jan. 1 Bal.	40,500		Dec. 31 Clo.	40,500
Dec. 31 Clo.	42,000			
Dec. 31 Bal.	42,000			

The inventory amounts for these closing entries are taken directly from the income statement columns of the work sheet. The offsetting debits and credits to Income Summary in these closing entries also serve to record the dollar amount of cost of goods sold into the accounts. Income Summary contains the cost of goods sold amount after Purchases, and its related contra accounts and Freight In are closed.

Study Exhibits 5-7, 5-8 and 5-9 carefully because they illustrate the entire end-of-period process that leads to the financial statements. As you progress through this book, you may want to refer to these exhibits to refresh your understanding of the adjusting and closing process for a merchandising business.

Income Statement Format _____

OBJECTIVE 6

Recognize different formats of the income statement

We have seen that the balance sheet appears in two formats: the account format and report format. There are also two basic formats for the income statement: *multiple step* and *single step*.

EXHIBIT 5-9A *Journalizing and Posting the Adjusting and Closing Entries*

		Journal		
		Adjusting Entries		
a.	Dec. 31	Interest Receivable..	400	
		Interest Revenue		400
b.	31	Supplies Expense ($650 - $100)	550	
		Supplies..		550
c.	31	Insurance Expense..	1,000	
		Prepaid Insurance.......................................		1,000
d.	31	Depreciation Expense......................................	600	
		Accumulated Depreciation		600
e.	31	Unearned Sales Revenue	1,300	
		Sales Revenue..		1,300
f.	31	Interest Expense...	200	
		Interest Payable...		200
		Closing Entries		
	Dec. 31	Inventory (ending balance)	42,000	
		Sales Revenue	139,300	
		Interest Revenue..	1,000	
		Purchase Discounts......................................	3,000	
		Purchase Returns and Allowances	1,200	
		Income Summary		186,500
	31	Income Summary	150,450	
		Inventory (beginning balance)		40,500
		Sales Discounts		1,400
		Sales Returns and Allowances		2,000
		Purchases..		89,300
		Freight In		5,200
		Rent Expense..		8,400
		Depreciation Expense		600
		Insurance Expense...................................		1,000
		Supplies Expense.....................................		550
		Interest Expense.......................................		1,500
	31	Income Summary ($186,500 - $150,450)	36,050	
		E. Boritz, Capital..		36,050
	31	E. Boritz, Capital..	34,100	
		E. Boritz, Withdrawals..............................		34,100

[handwritten margin notes: "Sales & Inventory go with Expenses   purchases go with Revenue"]

Multiple-Step Income Statement

The income statements presented thus far in this chapter have been multiple-step income statements. Austin Sound's multiple-step income statement for the year ended December 31, 19X6 appears in Exhibit 5-8. The **multiple-step format** contains subtotals to highlight significant relationships. In addition to net income, it also presents gross margin and income from operations. This format communicates a merchandiser's results of operations especially well, because gross margin and income from operations are two key measures of operating performance.

Single-Step Income Statement

The **single-step format** groups all revenues together, and then lists and deducts all expenses together without drawing any sub-totals. The single-step format has

EXHIBIT 5-9B Ledger Accounts of Austin Sound Stereo Center

ASSETS

Cash	Accounts Receivable	Note Receivable	Interest Receivable
2,850	4,600	8,000	(A) 400

Inventory	Supplies	Prepaid Insurance	Furniture and Fixtures
40,500 | (C) 40,500	650 | (A) 650	1,200 | (A) 1,000	33,200
(C) 42,000	100	200	

Accumulated Depreciation

	2,400
(A)	600
	3,000

LIABILITIES

Accounts Payable	Unearned Sales Revenue	Note Payable	Interest Payable
47,000	(A) 1,300 | 2,000	(A) 200	12,600
	700		

OWNER'S EQUITY

E. Boritz, Capital	E. Boritz, Withdrawals	Income Summary
(C) 34,100 | 25,900	34,100 | (C) 34,100	(C) 150,450 | (C) 186,500
(C) 36,050		(C) 36,050
27,850		

REVENUES

Sales Revenue	Sales Discounts	Sales Returns and Allowances	Interest Revenue
| 138,000	1,400 | (C) 1,400	2,000 | (C) 2,000	| 600
(A) 1,300			(A) 400
(C) 139,300 | 139,300			(C) 1,000 | 1,000

EXPENSES

Purchases	Purchase Discounts	Purchase Returns and Allowances	Freight In
89,300 | (C) 89,300	(C) 3,000 | 3,000	(C) 1,200 | 1,200	5,200 | (C) 5,200

Rent Expense	Depreciation Expense	Insurance Expense	Supplies Expense
8,400 | (C) 8,400	(A) 600 | (C) 600	(A) 1,000 | (C) 1,000	(A) 550 | (C) 550

Interest Expense

1,300	
(A) 200	
1,500 | (C) 1,500	

A= Adjusting entry   C= Closing entry

EXHIBIT 5-10 *Single-Step Income Statement*

Austin Sound Income Statement for the year ended December 31, 19X6		
Revenues		
Net sales (net of sales discounts, $1,400, and returns and allowances, $2,000).......	$135,900	
Interest revenue...	1,000	
Total revenues..	136,900	
Expenses		
Cost of goods sold...	$ 88,800	
Rent expense...	8,400	
Interest expense...	1,500	
Insurance expense..	1,000	
Depreciation expense....................................	600	
Supplies expense..	550	
Total expenses..	100,850	
Net income..	$ 36,050	

the advantage of listing all revenues together and all expenses together, as shown in Exhibit 5-10. Thus it clearly distinguishes revenues from expenses. The income statements in Chapters 1 through 4 were single-step. This format works well for service entities because they have no gross margin to report. Slightly more reporting entities use the single-step format. Single-step income statements may become even more popular as Canada moves to a more service-oriented economy.

Most published financial statements are highly condensed. Of course, condensed statements can be supplemented with desired details. For example, in Exhibit 5-10, the single-step income statement could be accompanied by a supporting schedule that gives the detailed computation of cost of goods sold.

Use of Accounting Information in Decision-Making _____

Merchandise inventory is the most important asset to a merchandising business because it captures the essence of the entity. To manage the firm, owners and managers focus their energies on the best way to sell the inventory. They use several ratios to evaluate operations.

A key decision tool for a merchandiser relates to gross margin, which is net sales minus cost of goods sold. Merchandisers strive to increase the *gross margin percentage*, which is computed as follows:

For Austin Sound
(Exhibit 5-8)

$$\text{Gross margin percentage} = \frac{\text{Gross margin}}{\text{Net sales revenue}} = \frac{\$47,100}{\$135,900} = .347$$

The gross margin (or gross profit) percentage is one of the most carefully watched measures of profitability because it is fundamental to a merchandiser. For most firms, the gross margin percentage changes little from year to year, and a small downturn may signal an important drop in income. A small increase in the gross margin percentage usually indicates an increase in profitability.

Austin Sound's gross margin percentage of 34.7 percent compares favorably with the industry average for electronic retailers, which is 34.9 percent. By contrast, the average gross margin percentage is 14.1 percent for automobile dealers, 22.8 percent for grocery stores, and 55.7 percent for restaurants.

Owners and managers strive to sell inventory as quickly as possible because unsold merchandise drains profits. The faster the sales occur, the higher the income. The slower the sales, the lower the income. Ideally, a business could operate with zero inventory. Most businesses, however, including retailers such as Austin Sound, must keep goods on hand for customers. Successful merchandisers purchase carefully to keep the goods moving through the business at a rapid pace. **Inventory turnover**, the ratio of cost of goods sold to average inventory, indicates how rapidly inventory is being sold or *turned over*. Its computation follows:

For Austin Sound
(Exhibit 5-8)

$$\text{Inventory turnover} = \frac{\text{Cost of goods sold}}{\text{Average inventory}} = \frac{\text{Cost of goods sold}}{(\text{Beginning inventory} + \text{ending inventory})/2} = \frac{\$88,000}{(\$40,500 + \$42,000)/2}$$

$$= \textbf{2.2 times per year}$$

Inventory turnover is usually computed for an annual period, and the relevant cost-of-goods sold figure is the amount from the entire year. Average inventory is computed from the beginning and ending amounts. The resulting inventory turnover statistic shows how many times inventory was sold during the year. A high rate of turnover is preferred over a low rate of turnover. An increase in turnover usually means higher profits.

Inventory turnover varies from industry to industry. Grocery stores, for example, turn their goods over faster than automobile dealers do. Drug stores have a higher turnover than furniture stores do. Retailers of electronic products, such as Austin Sound Stereo Center, have an average turnover of 3.6 times per year. What does Austin Sound's turnover rate of 2.2 per year indicate about its ability to sell inventory? It suggests that Austin Sound is not very successful. The lower one fourth of electronics retailers average a turnover rate of 2.7, so Austin Sound's turnover rate of 2.2 looks rather bad.

Financial analysis is complex. For Austin Sound, we see an acceptable gross margin percentage but a poor rate of inventory turnover. These two ratios do not provide enough information to yield an overall conclusion about the firm, but the illustration shows how owners and managers may apply ratios to evaluate a company.

Computers and Inventory

Inventory record keeping is a demanding manual accounting task, from the paperwork required in purchasing and selling inventory to the job of periodically counting it. Computers have dramatically reduced the time required to manage inventory, and have greatly increased a company's ability to control its inventory.

A computerized system enhances accounting control over inventory because the computer can keep accurate and up-to-the-minute records of the number of units purchased, the number of units sold, and the quantities on hand. The computer can also issue purchase-order forms automatically when inventory on hand falls below the minimum amount.

Computerized inventory systems are now integrated with accounts receivable and sales. For example, once a prospective customer's order is entered into the computer, the computer checks warehouse records to see if the requested units are in stock. If so, the details of the shipment are entered into the computer, which then multiplies the number of units shipped by the unit price. The computer then prints an invoice for the customer, and calculates the debit to Accounts Receivable (for that specific customer), the credit to Sales, and the reduction in inventory units.

The computer can keep up-to-the-minute records, so managers can call up current inventory information at any time. This type of inventory system is explored in more detail in Chapter 9.

Summary Problem for Your Review

The trial balance of Jan King Distributing Company follows:

Jan King Distributing Company
Trial Balance
December 31, 19X3

Cash	$ 5,670	
Accounts receivable	37,100	
Inventory	60,500	
Supplies	3,930	
Prepaid rent	6,000	
Furniture and fixtures	26,500	
Accumulated depreciation		$ 21,200
Accounts payable		46,340
Salary payable		
Interest payable		
Unearned sales revenue		3,500
Note payable, long-term		35,000
Jan King, capital		23,680
Jan King, withdrawals	48,000	
Sales revenue		346,700
Sales discounts	10,300	
Sales returns and allowances	8,200	
Purchases	175,900	
Purchases discounts		6,000
Purchase returns and allowances		7,430
Freight in	9,300	
Salary expense	82,750	
Rent expense	7,000	
Depreciation expense		
Utilities expense	5,800	
Supplies expense		
Interest expense	2,900	
Total	$489,850	$489,850

Additional data at December 31, 19X3:

a. Supplies used during the year, $2,580.

b. Prepaid rent in force, $1,000.

c. Unearned sales revenue still not earned, $2,400. The company expects to earn this amount during the next few months.

d. Depreciation. The furniture and fixtures' estimated useful life is 10 years, and they are expected to be worthless when they are retired from service.

e. Accrued salaries, $1,300.

f. Accrued interest expense, $600.

g. Inventory on hand, $65,800.

Required

1. Make a single-summary journal entry to record King's
   a. Unadjusted sales for the year, assuming all sales were made on credit.
   b. Sales returns and allowances for the year.
   c. Sales discounts for the year, assuming the cash collected on account was $329,000.
   d. Purchases of inventory for the year, assuming all purchases were made on credit.
   e. Purchase returns and allowances for the year.
   f. Purchase discounts for the year, $6,000. Cash paid on account was $188,400.
   g. Transportation costs for the year, assuming a cash payment in a separate entry.

2. Enter the trial balance on a work sheet and complete the work sheet.

3. Journalize the adjusting and closing entries at December 31. Post to the Income Summary account as an accuracy check on the entries affecting that account. The credit balance closed out of Income Summary should equal net income computed on the work sheet.

4. Prepare the company's multiple-step income statement, statement of owner's equity, and balance sheet in account format.

5. Compute the inventory turnover for 19X3. Turnover for 19X2 was 2.1. Would you expect Jan King Distributing Company to be more profitable in 19X3 than in 19X2? Give your reason.

Note: If your instructor assigned the appendix to this chapter, which illustrates the adjusting-entry method, turn to p. 251 for the Alternate Solution to Review Problem. If you were not assigned this appendix, then study the Solution to Review Problem that follows.

SOLUTION TO REVIEW PROBLEM

Requirement 1

Sale, purchase, and related return and discount entries

19X3

a.	Accounts Receivable.................................	346,700	
	Sales Revenue.......................................		346,700
b.	Sales Returns and Allowances.................	8,200	
	Accounts Receivable............................		8,200
c.	Cash	329,000	
	Sales Discounts..	10,300	
	Accounts Receivable............................		339,300
d.	Purchases	175,900	
	Accounts Payable.................................		175,900
e.	Accounts Payable.......................................	7,430	
	Purchase Returns and Allowances.....		7,430
f.	Accounts Payable.......................................	194,400	
	Purchase Discounts		6,000
	Cash		188,400
g.	Freight In...	9,300	
	Cash		9,300

Requirement 2

Jan King Distributing Company
Work Sheet
for the year ended December 31, 19X3

Account Title	Trial Balance Debit	Trial Balance Credit	Adjustments Debit	Adjustments Credit	Income Statement Debit	Income Statement Credit	Balance Sheet Debit	Balance Sheet Credit
Cash	5,670						5,670	
Accounts receivable	37,100						37,100	
Inventory	60,500				60,500	65,800	65,800	
Supplies	3,930			(a) 2,580			1,350	
Prepaid rent	6,000			(b) 5,000			1,000	
Furniture and fixtures	26,500						26,500	
Accumulated depreciation		21,200		(d) 2,650				23,850
Accounts payable		46,340						46,340
Salary payable				(e) 1,300				1,300
Interest payable				(f) 600				600
Unearned sales revenue		3,500	(c) 1,100					2,400
Note payable, long-term		35,000						35,000
Jan King, capital		23,680						23,680
Jan King, withdrawals	48,000						48,000	
Sales revenue		346,700		(c) 1,100		347,800		
Sales discounts	10,300				10,300			
Sales returns and allowances	8,200				8,200			
Purchases	175,900				175,900			
Purchase discounts		6,000				6,000		
Purchase returns and allowances		7,430				7,430		
Freight in	9,300				9,300			
Salary expense	82,750		(e) 1,300		84,050			
Rent expense	7,000		(b) 5,000		12,000			
Depreciation expense			(d) 2,650		2,650			
Utilities expense	5,800				5,800			
Supplies expense			(a) 2,580		2,580			
Interest expense	2,900		(f) 600		3,500			
	489,850	489,850	13,230	13,230	374,780	427,030	185,420	133,170
					52,250			52,250
Net income					427,030	427,030	185,420	185,420

Requirement 3

Adjusting entries

19X3

Dec. 31	Supplies Expense...	2,580	
	Supplies..		2,580
31	Rent Expense..	5,000	
	Prepaid Rent...		5,000
31	Unearned Sales Revenue..................................	1,100	
	Sales Revenue...		1,100
31	Depreciation Expense ($26,500/10)...............	2,650	
	Accumulated Depreciation		2,650
31	Salary Expense..	1,300	
	Salary Payable...		1,300
31	Interest Expense..	600	
	Interest Payable...		600

Closing entries

19X3

Dec. 31	Inventory (ending balance)..........................	65,800	
	Sales Revenue...	347,800	
	Purchase Discounts	6,000	
	Purchase Returns	7,430	
	Income Summary.......................................		427,030
31	Income Summary...	374,780	
	Inventory (beginning balance)................		60,500
	Sales Discounts		10,300
	Sales Returns and Allowances................		8,200
	Purchases		175,900
	Freight In...		9,300
	Salary Expense		84,050
	Rent Expense		12,000
	Depreciation Expense		2,650
	Utilities Expense		5,800
	Supplies Expense.......................................		2,580
	Interest Expense...		3,500
31	Income Summary ($427,030 – $374,780).....	52,250	
	Jan King, capital..		52,250
31	Jan King, Capital...	48,000	
	Jan King, Withdrawals..............................		48,000

Income Summary

Clo.	374,780	Clo.	427,030
Clo.	52,250	Bal.	52,250

Requirement 4

Jan King Distributing Company
Income Statement
for the year ended December 31, 19X3

Sales revenue			$347,800
Less: Sales discounts		$ 10,300	
Sales returns and allowances		8,200	18,500
Net sales revenue			$329,300
Cost of goods sold			
Beginning inventory			60,500
Purchases		175,900	
Less: Purchase discounts	$6,000		
Purchase returns and allowances	7,430	13,430	
Net purchases			162,470
Freight in			9,300
Cost of goods available for sale			232,270
Less: Ending inventory			65,800
Cost of goods sold			166,470
Gross margin			162,830
Operating expenses			
Salary expense			84,050
Rent expense			12,000
Utilities expense			5,800
Depreciation expense			2,650
Supplies expense			2,580	107,080
Income from operations			55,750
Other expense			
Interest expense			3,500
Net income			$ 52,250

Jan King Distributing Company
Statement of Owner's Equity
for the year ended December 31, 19X3

Jan King, capital, December 31, 19X2	$23,680
Add: Net income	52,250
	75,930
Add: Withdrawals	48,000
Jan King, capital, December 31, 19X3	$27,930

Jan King Distributing Company
Balance Sheet
December 31, 19X3

Assets			**Liabilities**		
Current			Current		
Cash	$ 5,670		Accounts payable	$ 46,340	
Accounts receivable	37,100		Salary payable	1,300	
Inventory	65,800		Interest payable	600	
Supplies	1,350		Unearned sales revenue	2,400	
Prepaid Rent	1,000		Total current liabilities	50,640	
Total current assets	110,920		Long-term		
Capital			Note payable	35,000	
Furniture and fixtures	$26,500		Total liabilities	85,640	
Less: Accumulated					
depreciation	23,850	2,650	**Owner's Equity**		
			Jan King, capital	27,930	
			Total liabilities and		
Total assets		$113,570	owner's equity	$113,570	

Requirement 5

$$\text{Inventory turnover} = \frac{\text{Cost of goods sold}}{\text{Average inventory}} = \frac{\$166,470}{(\$60,500 + \$65,800)/2} = 2.6$$

The increase in the rate of inventory turnover from 2.1 to 2.6 suggests higher profits in 19X3 than in 19X2.

Summary

The major revenue of a merchandising business is *sales revenue* or *sales*. The major expense is *cost of goods sold*. Sales minus cost of goods sold is called *gross margin,* or *gross profit*. This amount measures the business's success or failure in selling its products at a higher price than it paid for them.

The merchandiser's major asset is *inventory*. In a merchandising entity, the accounting cycle is from cash to inventory as the inventory is purchased for resale, and back to cash as the inventory is sold.

Cost of goods sold is unlike the other expenses in that it is not an account in the ledger. Instead, cost of goods sold is the remainder when beginning inventory and net purchases are added, and ending inventory is subtracted from that sum.

The *invoice* is the business document generated by a purchase/sale transaction. Most merchandising entities offer *discounts* to their customers and allow them to *return* unsuitable merchandise. They also grant *allowances* for damaged goods that the buyer chooses to keep. Discounts and Returns and Allowances are *contra* accounts to Purchases and Sales.

The end-of-period adjusting and closing process of a merchandising business is similar to that of a service business. In addition, a merchandiser makes inventory entries at the end of the period. These closing entries replace the period's beginning balance with the cost of inventory on hand at the end. A by-product of these closing entries is the computation of cost of goods sold for the income statement.

The income statement may appear in the *single-step format* or the *multiple-step format*. A single-step income statement has only two sections — one for revenues and the other for expenses —and a single income amount for net income. A multiple-step income statement has subtotals for gross margin and income from operations. Both formats are widely used in practice.

Two key decision aids for a merchandiser are the *gross margin percentage* and the *rate of inventory turnover*. Increases in these measures usually signal an increase in profits.

Self-Study Questions

Test your understanding of the chapter by marking the correct answer for each of the following questions:

1. The major expense of a merchandising business is *(p. 199)*
   a. Cost of goods sold   c. Rent
   b. Depreciation   d. Interest

2. Sales total $440,000, cost of goods sold is $210,000, and operating expenses are $160,000. How much is gross margin? *(pp. 199–200)*
   a. $440,000   c. $210,000
   b. $230,000   d. $70,000

3. A purchase discount results from *(p. 203)*
   a. Returning goods to the seller
   b. Receiving a purchase allowance from the seller
   c. Buying a large enough quantity of merchandise to get the discount
   d. Paying within the discount period

4. Which one of the following pairs includes items that are the most similar? *(pp.206–207)*
   a. Purchase discounts and purchase returns
   b. Cost of goods sold and inventory
   c. Net sales and sales discounts
   d. Sales returns and sales allowances

5. Which of the following is *not* an account? *(pp. 207–208)*
   a. Sales revenue
   b. Net sales
   c. Inventory
   d. Supplies expense

6. Cost of goods sold is computed by adding beginning inventory and net purchases and subtracting X. What is X? *(p. 207)*
   a. Net sales
   b. Sales discounts
   c. Ending inventory
   d. Net purchases

7. Which account causes the main difference between a merchandiser's adjusting and closing process and that of a service business? *(p. 211)*
   a. Purchases
   b. Sales revenue
   c. Inventory
   d. Sales returns and allowances

8. The major item on a merchandiser's income statement that a service business does not have is *(p. 215)*
   a. Cost of goods sold
   b. Inventory
   c. Net purchases
   d. Net sales

9. The closing entry for Sales Discounts is *(p. 216)*
   a. Sales Discounts
       Income Summary
   b. Sales Discounts
       Sales Revenue
   c. Income Summary
       Sales Discounts
   d. Not used because Sales Discounts is a permanent account, which is not closed.

10. Which income statement format reports income from operations? *(p. 217)*
    a. Account format
    b. Report format
    c. Single-step format
    d. Multiple-step format

Answers to the Self-Study Questions are at the end of the chapter.

Accounting Vocabulary

cost of goods sold
   (p. 206)
cost of sales *(p. 206)*
gross margin *(p. 199)*
gross profit *(p. 199)*
income from operations
   (p. 214)
inventory turnover
   (p. 220)
invoice *(p. 201)*
multiple-step income
   statement *(p. 217)*

net purchases *(p. 204)*
net sales *(p. 206)*
net sales revenue *(p. 199)*
operating expenses
   (p. 214)
operating income
   (p. 214)
other expense *(p. 214)*
other revenue *(p. 214)*
purchase discount
   (p. 203)

purchase returns and
   allowances *(p. 203)*
purchases *(p. 200)*
quantity discount
   (p. 202)
sales discount *(p. 205)*
sales returns and
   allowances *(p. 205)*
sales revenue *(p. 199)*
single-step income
   statement *(p. 217)*

ASSIGNMENT MATERIAL

Questions

1. Gross margin is often mentioned in the business press as an important measure of success. What does gross margin measure, and why is this important?

2. Describe the operating cycle for (a) the purchase and cash sale of inventory, and (b) the purchase and sale of inventory on account.

3. Identify 10 items of information on an invoice.

4. What is the similarity and what is the difference between purchase discounts and quantity discounts?

5. Indicate which accounts are debited and credited for (a) a credit purchase of inventory and the subsequent cash payment, and (b) a credit sale of inventory and the subsequent cash collection. Assume no discounts, returns, allowances, or freight.

6. Inventory costing $1,000 is purchased and invoiced on July 28 under terms of 3/10 n/30. Compute the payment amount on August 6. How much would the payment be on August 8? What explains the difference? What is the latest acceptable payment date under the terms of sale?

7. Inventory listed at $35,000 is sold subject to a quantity discount of $3,000 and under payment terms of 2/15 n/45. What is the net sales revenue on this sale, if the customer pays within 15 days?

8. Name four contra accounts introduced in this chapter.

9. Briefly discuss the similarity in computing supplies expense and computing cost of goods sold.

10. Why is the title of cost of goods sold especially descriptive? What type of <u>item</u> is cost of goods sold?

11. Beginning inventory is $5,000, net purchases total $30,000 and freight in is $1,000. If ending inventory is $8,000, what is cost of goods sold?

12. Identify two ways that cost of goods sold differs from operating expenses such as Salary Expense and Depreciation Expense.

13. Suppose you are evaluating two companies as possible investments. One entity sells its services and the other entity is a merchandiser. How can you identify the merchandiser by examining the two entities' balance sheets and their income statements?

14. You are beginning the adjusting and closing process at the end of your company's fiscal year. Does the trial balance carry the beginning or the ending amount of inventory? Will the balance sheet that you prepare report the beginning or the ending inventory?

15. Give the two closing entries for inventory (using no specific amount).

16. During the closing process, what accounts contain the amount of cost of goods sold for the period? Where is the final resting place of cost of goods sold?

17. What is the identifying characteristic of the "other" category of revenues and expenses? Give an example of each.

18. Name and describe the two income statement formats and identify the type of business to which each format best applies.

19. List eight different operating expenses.

20. Which financial statement reports sales discounts, sales returns and allowances, purchase discounts, and purchase returns and allowances? Show how they are reported, using any reasonable amounts in your illustration.

21. Does a merchandiser prefer a high or low rate of inventory turnover? Give your reason.

Exercises

Exercise 5-1 *Journalizing purchase and sale transactions* **(L.O. 2)**

Journalize, without explanations, the following transactions of Gonzaga, Inc. during July:

July 3   Purchased $2,000 of inventory under terms of 2/10 n/eom (end of month) and FOB shipping point.

7   Returned $300 of defective merchandise purchased on July 3.

9   Paid freight bill of $110 on July 3 purchase.

10   Sold inventory for $2,200, collecting cash of $400. Payment terms on the remainder were 2/15 n/30.

12   Paid amount owed on credit purchase of July 3, less the discount and the return.

16   Granted a sales allowance of $800 on the July 10 sale.

23   Received cash from July 10 customer in full settlement of her debt, less the allowance and the discount.

Exercise 5-2 *Journalizing transactions from a purchase invoice* **(L.O. 2)**

As the proprietor of Kendrick Tire Company, you receive the accompanying invoice from a supplier.

ABC TIRE WHOLESALE DISTRIBUTORS, INC.
2600 Victoria Avenue
Regina, Saskatchewan S4P 1B3

Invoice date: May 14, 19X3   **Payment terms:** 2/10 n/30

Sold to: Davidson Tire Co.
4219 Cumberland Avenue
Saskatoon, SK S7M 1X3

Quantity Ordered	Description	Quantity Shipped	Price	Amount
6	P135-X4 Radials.........	6	$37.14	$222.84
8	L912 Belted-bias........	8	41.32	330.56
14	R39 Truck tires........	10	50.02	500.20
	Total..$1,053.60			

Due date: **Amount:**
May 24, 19X3 $1,032.53
May 25 through June 13, 19X3 $1,053.60

Paid:

Required

1. Record the May 14 purchase on account.
2. The R39 truck tires were ordered by mistake and therefore were returned to ABC. Journalize the return on May 19.
3. Record the May 22 payment of the amount owed.

Exercise 5-3 *Journalizing purchase transactions (L.O. 2)*

On April 30, Feldman Jewelers purchased inventory of $4,300 on account from a wholesale jewelry supplier. Terms were 3/15 n/45. On receiving the goods Feldman checked the order and found $800 worth of items that were not ordered. Therefore, Feldman returned this amount of merchandise to the supplier on May 4.

To pay the remaining amount owed, Feldman had to borrow from the bank because of a temporary cash shortage. On May 14 Feldman signed a short-term note payable to the bank and immediately paid the borrowed funds to the wholesale jewelry supplier. On May 31 Feldman paid the bank the net amount of the invoice, which was the amount borrowed, plus $30 interest.

Required

Record the indicated transactions in the journal of Feldman Jewelers. Explanations are not required.

Exercise 5-4 *Journalizing sale transactions (L.O. 2)*

Refer to the business situation in Exercise 5-3. Journalize the transactions of the wholesale jewelry supplier. Explanations are not required.

Exercise 5-5 *Computing the elements of a merchandiser's income statement (L.O. 3)*

Supply the missing income statement amounts in each of the following situations:

Sales	Sales Discounts	Net Sales	Beginning Inventory	Net Purchases	Ending Inventory	Cost of Goods Sold	Gross Margin
$98,300	(a)	$92,800	$32,500	$66,700	$39,400	(b)	$33,000
82,400	$2,100	(c)	27,450	43,000	(d)	$44,100	36,200
91,500	1,800	89,700	(e)	54,900	22,600	59,400	(f)
(g)	3,000	(h)	40,700	(i)	48,230	62,500	36,600

Exercise 5-6 *Computing cost of goods sold for an actual company (L.O. 3)*

For the year ended December 31, 19X9, House of Fabrics, a retailer of home-related products, reported net sales of $338 million and cost of goods sold of $154 million. The company's balance sheet at December 31, 19X8 and 19X9 reported inventories of $133 million and $129 million, respectively. What were House of Fabrics' net purchases during 19X9?

Exercise 5-7 *Preparing a merchandiser's multiple-step income statement (L.O. 3, 4, 6)*

Selected accounts of Home Hardware are listed in alphabetical order.

Accounts receivable..........	$ 48,300	Purchases	$ 71,300
Accumulated depreciation	18,700	Purchase discounts...............	3,000
Freight in............................	2,200	Purchase returns	2,000
General expenses..............	23,800	Sales discounts	9,000
Interest revenue	1,500	Sales returns	4,600
Inventory, June 30.............	21,870	Sales revenue.........................	201,000
Inventory, May 31..............	19,450	Selling expenses....................	37,840
Owner's equity, May 31...	126,070	Unearned sales revenue.......	6,500

Required

Prepare the business's multiple-step income statement for June of the current year. Compute the rate of inventory turnover. Last year the turnover was 2.8 times. Does this two-year trend suggest improvement or deterioration in profitability?

Exercise 5-8   *Preparing a single-step income statement for a merchandising business (L.O. 3, 4, 6)*

Prepare Home Hardware's single-step income statement for June, using the data from the preceding exercise. In a separate schedule, show the computation of cost of goods sold.

Exercise 5-9   *Using work sheet data to prepare a merchandiser's income statement (L.O. 5, 6)*

The trial balance and adjustments columns of the work sheet of Midway Auto Supply include the following accounts and balances at March 31, 19X2:

Account Title	Trial Balance		Adjustments	
	Debit	Credit	Debit	Credit
Cash	$ 2,000			
Accounts receivable	8,500		(a) 2,100	
Inventory	36,070			
Supplies	13,000			(b) 8,600
Store fixtures	22,500			
Accumulated depreciation		$ 11,250		(c) 2,250
Accounts payable		9,300		
Salary payable				(d) 1,200
Note payable, long-term		7,500		
K. Brownlee, Capital		33,920		
K. Brownlee, Withdrawals	45,000			
Sales revenue		213,000		(a) 2,100
Sales discounts	2,000			
Purchases	114,200			
Purchase returns		2,600		
Selling expense	21,050		(b) 5,200	
			(d) 1,200	
General expense	10,500		(b) 3,400	
			(c) 2,250	
Interest expense	2,750			
Total	$277,570	$277,570	$14,150	$14,150

Ending inventory at March 31, 19X2 is $34,500.

Prepare the company's multiple-step income statement for the year ended March 31, 19X2. Compute the gross margin percentage and the inventory turnover for the year. Compare these figures with the gross margin percentage of .43 and the inventory turnover of 3.16 for 19X1. Does the two-year trend suggest improvement or deterioration in profitability?

Exercise 5-10   *Use work sheet data to prepare the closing entries of a merchandising business (L.O. 5)*

Use the data from Exercise 5-9 to journalize Midway Auto Supply's closing entries at March 31, 19X2.

Problems   *(Group A)*

Problem 5-1A   *Explaining the operating cycle of a retailer (L.O. 1)*

Eaton's is one of the most famous retailers in the world. The women's sportswear department of Eaton's purchases clothing from many well-known manufacturers. Eaton's advertising department is promoting end-of-year sales.

Required

You are the manager of the Eaton's store in Vancouver. Write a memo to a new employee in the women's sportswear department explaining how the company's operating cycle works.

Problem 5-2A   *Accounting for the purchase and sale of inventory (L.O. 2)*

The following transactions occurred between Supply and Services Canada and Transport Canada during June of the current year.

June   8   Supply and Services Canada sold $3,900 worth of merchandise to Transport Canada on terms of 2/10 n/30, FOB shipping point. Supply and Services prepaid freight charges of $200 and included this amount in the invoice total. (Supply and Services' entry to record the freight payment debits Accounts Receivable and credits Cash.)

11   Transport Canada returned $600 of the merchandise purchased on June 8. Supply and Services issued a credit memo for this amount.

17   Transport Canada paid $2,000 of the invoice amount owed to Supply and Services for the June 8 purchase. This payment included none of the freight charge.

26   Transport Canada paid the remaining amount owed to Supply and Services for the June 8 purchase.

Required

Journalize these transactions, first on the books of Transport Canada, and second on the books of Supply and Services Canada.

Problem 5-3A   *Journalizing purchase and sale transactions (L.O. 2)*

Davis Book Store engaged in the following transactions during July of the current year:

July   2   Purchased inventory for cash, $800, less a quantity discount of $150.

3   Purchased store supplies on credit terms of net eom (end of month), $2,300.

8   Purchased inventory of $3,000 less a quantity discount of 10 percent, plus freight charges of $230. Credit terms are 3/15 n/30.

9   Sold goods for cash, $1,200.

11   Returned $200 (net amount after the quantity discount) of the inventory purchased on July 8. It was damaged in shipment.

12   Purchased inventory on credit terms of 3/10 n/30, $3,330.

14   Sold inventory on credit terms of 2/10 n/30, $9,600, less a $600 quantity discount.

16   Paid the electricity and water bills, $275.

20   Received returned inventory from July 14 sale, $400 (net amount after the quantity discount). Davis shipped the wrong goods by mistake.

21   Borrowed the amount owed on the July 8 purchase. Signed a note payable to the bank for $2,655, which takes into account the return of inventory on July 11.

21 Paid supplier for goods purchased on July 8 less the discount and the return.
23 Received $6,860 cash in partial settlement of his account from the customer who purchased inventory on July 14. Granted the customer a 2 percent discount and credited his account receivable for $7,000.
30 Paid for the store supplies purchased on July 3.

Required

1. Journalize the above transactions.
2. Compute the amount of the receivable at July 31 from the customer to whom Davis sold inventory on July 14. What amount of cash discount applies to this receivable at July 31?

Problem 5-4A   *Computing cost of goods sold and gross margin (L.O. 3)*

Selected accounts of Montpelier Supply Company had these balances at June 30, 19X9.

Purchases	$ 98,100
Selling expenses	29,800
Equipment	44,700
Purchase discounts	1,300
Accumulated depreciation — equipment	6,900
Note payable	30,000
Sales discounts	3,400
General expenses	16,300
Accounts receivable	22,600
Accounts payable	23,800
Cash	13,600
Freight in	4,300
Sales revenue	173,100
Purchases returns and allowances	1,400
Salary payable	1,800
John Wilfong, capital	36,000
Sales returns and allowances	12,100
Inventory: May 31	33,800
June 30	32,500

Required

1. Show the computation of Montpelier Supply's net sales, cost of goods sold, and gross margin for the year ended June 30, 19X9.
2. John Wilfong, owner of Montpelier Supply, strives to earn a gross margin percentage of 40 percent. Did he achieve this goal?
3. Did the rate of inventory turnover reach the industry average of 2.8?

Problem 5-5A   *Preparing a merchandiser's financial statements (L.O. 3, 4, 6)*

The accounts of Frieda Super Store are listed in alphabetical order.

Accounts payable	$ 27,380	Purchases	$273,100
Accounts receivable	31,200	Purchase discounts	4,670
Accumulated depreciation ..		Purchase returns and	
— office equipment	9,500	allowances	10,190
Accumulated depreciation ...		Salary payable	6,120
— store equipment	6,880	Sales discounts	8,350
Capital, June 30	73,720	Sales returns and	
Cash	12,320	allowances	17,900

General expenses	75,830	Sales revenue	531,580
Interest expense	7,200	Selling expenses	84,600
Interest payable	3,000	Store equipment	47,500
Inventory: June 30	190,060	Supplies	4,350
July 31	187,390	Unearned sales revenue	9,370
Note payable, long-term	160,000	Withdrawals	11,000
Office equipment	79,000		

Required

1. Prepare the entity's multiple-step income statement for July of the current year.
2. Prepare the income statement in single-step format.
3. Prepare the balance sheet in report format at July 31 of the current year. Show your computation of the July 31 balance of Capital.

Problem 5-6A   Using work sheet data to prepare financial statements **(L.O. 3, 4, 6)**

The trial balance and adjustments columns of the work sheet of Lawson Coffee Company include the following accounts and balances at September 30, 19X5:

	Trial Balance		Adjustments	
Account Title	**Debit**	**Credit**	**Debit**	**Credit**
Cash	$ 7,300			
Accounts receivable	4,360		(a)1,800	
Inventory	31,530			
Supplies	10,700			(b) 7,640
Equipment	79,450			
Accumulated depreciation		$ 29,800		(c) 9,900
Accounts payable		13,800		
Salary payable				(e) 200
Unearned sales revenue		3,780	(d) 2,600	
Note payable, long-term		10,000		
Leslie Lawson, capital		58,360		
Leslie Lawson, drawing	35,000			
Sales revenue		242,000		(a) 1,800
				(d) 2,600
Sales returns	3,100			
Purchases	127,400			
Purchase discounts		3,700		
Selling expense	40,600		(b) 7,640	
			(e) 200	
General expense	21,000		(c) 9,900	
Interest expense	1,000			
Total	$361,440	$361,440	$22,140	$22,140

Required

1. Inventory on hand at September 30, 19X5 is $32,580. Without entering the preceding data on a formal work sheet, prepare the company's multiple-step income statement for the year ended September 30, 19X5 and its September 30, 19X5 balance sheet. Show your computation of the ending balance of Leslie Lawson, Capital.

2. Compute the gross margin percentage and the inventory turnover for 19X5. For 19X4, Lawson's gross margin percentage was .57 and the rate of inventory turnover was 4.2. Does the two-year trend in these ratios suggest improvement or deterioration in profitability?

Problem 5-7A   *Preparing a merchandiser's work sheet* **(L.O. 5)**

Gideon Paint Company trial balance relates to December 31 of the current year.

Gideon Paint Company **Trial Balance** **December 31, 19XX**		
Cash	$ 2,910	
Accounts receivable......................................	6,560	
Inventory...	101,760	
Store supplies	1,990	
Prepaid insurance	3,200	
Store fixtures...	63,900	
Accumulated depreciation		$ 37,640
Accounts payable...		29,770
Salary payable		
Interest payable...		
Note payable, long-term		37,200
Carole Gideon, capital..................................		63,120
Carole Gideon, withdrawals	36,300	
Sales revenue		286,370
Purchases..	161,090	
Salary expense...	46,580	
Rent expense..	14,630	
Utilities expense	6,780	
Depreciation expense		
Insurance expense...	5,300	
Store supplies expense		
Interest expense...	3,100	
Total...	$454,100	$454,100

Additional data at December 31, 19XX:

a. Insurance expense for the year, $6,090.
b. Store fixtures have an estimated useful life of 10 years, and are expected to be worthless when they are retired from service.
c. Accrued salaries at December 31, $1,260.
d. Accrued interest expense at December 31, $870.
e. Store supplies on hand at December 31, $760.
f. Inventory on hand at December 31, $99,350.

Required

Complete Gideon's work sheet for the year ended December 31 of the current year.

Problem 5-8A   *Journalizing the adjusting and closing entries of a merchandising business* **(L.O. 5)**

Required

1. Journalize the adjusting and closing entries for the data in Problem 5-7A.
2. Determine the December 31 balance of Carole Gideon, Capital.

Problem 5-9A   *Preparing a merchandiser's work sheet, financial statements, and adjusting and closing entries (L.O. 3, 4, 5)*

The year-end trial balance of Wang Sales Company relates to July 31 of the current year.

Wang Sales Company **Trial Balance** **July 31, 19XX**		
Cash	$ 3,120	
Notes receivable, current	6,900	
Interest receivable		
Inventory..	104,000	
Prepaid insurance	2,810	
Notes receivable, long-term	19,300	
Furniture	16,000	
Accumulated depreciation		$ 12,000
Accounts payable..		14,360
Salary payable		
Sales commission payable		
Unearned sales revenue................................		4,090
Ken-Hsi Wang, capital...................................		102,270
Ken-Hsi Wang, withdrawals	59,000	
Sales revenue		337,940
Sales discounts	3,440	
Sales returns and allowances	8,900	
Interest revenue...		1,910
Purchases..	163,200	
Purchase discounts		2,100
Purchase returns and allowances		5,760
Freight in	11,100	
Salary expense..	39,030	
Sales commission expense...........................	31,500	
Rent expense...	10,000	
Utilities expense	2,130	
Insurance expense..		
Depreciation expense		
Total...	$480,430	$480,430

Additional data at July 31, 19XX:

a. Accrued interest revenue, $350.

b. Prepaid insurance still in force, $310.

c. Furniture has an estimated useful life of eight years. Its value is expected to be zero when it is retired from service.

d. Unearned sales revenue still unearned, $1,900.

e. Accrued salaries, $1,640.

f. Accrued sales commissions, $1,430.

g. Inventory on hand, $102,600.

Required

1. Enter the trial balance on a work sheet, and complete the work sheet for the year ended July 31 of the current year.

2. Prepare the company's multiple-step income statement and statement of owner's equity for the year ended July 31 of the current year. Also prepare its balance sheet at that date. Long-term notes receivable should be reported on the balance sheet between current assets and plant assets in a separate section labeled Investments.

3. Journalize the adjusting and closing entries at July 31.

4. Post to the Ken-Hsi Wang, Capital account and to the Income Summary account as an accuracy check on the adjusting and closing process.

(Group B)

Problem 5-1B   *Explaining the operating cycle of a retailer* **(L.O. 1)**

Claire Vision is a regional chain of optical shops in Manitoba. They specialize in offering a large selection of eyeglass frames, and they provide while-you-wait service. Claire Vision carries frames made by Logo Paris, Liz Claiborne, Ralph Lauren, and others. Claire Vision has launched a vigorous advertising campaign promoting its two-for-the-price-of-one frame sales.

Required

You are the president of this company. Write a memo to your store manager explaining how the company's operating cycle works.

Problem 5-2B   *Accounting for the purchase and sale of inventory* **(L.O. 2)**

The following transactions occurred between Allcare Medical Supply and Greenview Clinic during February of the current year.

Feb.   6   Allcare Medical Supply sold $5,300 worth of merchandise to Greenview Clinic on terms of 2/10 n/30, FOB shipping point. Allcare prepaid freight charges of $300 and included this amount in the invoice total. (Allcare's entry to record the freight payment debits Accounts Receivable and credits Cash.)

  10   Greenview returned $900 of the merchandise purchased on February 6. Allcare issued a credit memo for this amount.

  15   Greenview paid $3,000 of the invoice amount owed to Allcare for the February 6 purchase. This payment included none of the freight charge.

  27   Greenview paid the remaining amount owed to Allcare for the February 6 purchase.

Required

Journalize these transactions, first on the books of Greenview Clinic, and second on the books of Allcare Medical Supply.

Problem 5-3B   *Journalizing purchase and sale transactions* **(L.O. 2)**

Monarch Paper Company engaged in the following transactions during May of the current year:

May   3   Purchased office supplies for cash, $300.

  7   Purchased inventory on credit terms of 2/10 net eom (end of month), $1,100.

  8   Returned half the inventory purchased on May 7. It was not the inventory ordered.

  10   Sold goods for cash, $450.

13 Sold inventory on credit terms of 2/15 n/45, $3,900, less $600 quantity discount offered to customers who purchased in large quantities.

16 Paid the amount owed on account from the purchase of May 7, less the discount and the return.

17 Received defective inventory returned from May 13 sale, $900, which is the net amount after the quantity discount.

18 Purchased inventory of $4,000 on account. Payment terms were 2/10 net 30.

26 Borrowed $3,920 from the bank to take advantage of the discount offered on May 18 purchase. Signed a note payable to the bank for this amount.

26 Paid supplier for goods purchased on May 18, less the discount.

28 Received cash in full settlement of his account from the customer who purchased inventory on May 13, less the discount and the return.

29 Purchased inventory for cash, $2,000, less a quantity discount of $400, plus freight charges of $160.

Required

1. Journalize the above transactions.

2. Assume the note payable signed on May 26 requires the payment of $30 interest expense. Was the decision wise or unwise to borrow funds to take advantage of the cash discount?

Problem 5-4B *Computing cost of goods sold and gross margin* (L.O. 3)

Selected accounts of Cargill Coin Collectors had these balances at November 30 of the current year.

Accumulated depreciation — furniture and fixtures	$ 13,600
Note payable	14,000
Purchase discounts	600
Sales discounts	2,100
General expenses	19,300
Accounts receivable	7,200
Purchases	132,000
Selling expenses	8,800
Furniture and fixtures	37,200
Purchase returns and allowances	900
Salary payable	300
Gretchen Cargill, capital	52,800
Sales Revenue	184,600
Sales returns and allowances	3,200
Inventory: October 31	41,700
November 30	39,500
Accounts payable	9,500
Cash	3,700
Freight in	1,600

Required

1. Show the computation of Cargill's net sales, cost of goods sold, and gross margin for the year ended November 30 of the current year.

2. Gretchen Cargill, owner of Cargill Coin Collectors, strives to earn a gross margin percentage of 25 percent. Did she achieve this goal?

3. Did the rate of inventory turnover reach the industry average of 3.4?

Problem 5-5B   *Preparing a merchandiser's financial statements* (L.O. 3, 4, 6)

The accounts of Pure Milk Company are listed in alphabetical order.

Accounts payable.................	$ 16,950	Office equipment..................	$ 58,680
Accounts receivable.............	43,700	Purchases..............................	364,000
Accumulated depreciation		Purchase discounts	1,990
— office equipment...........	22,450	Purchase returns	
Accumulated depreciation		and allowances	3,400
— store equipment............	16,000	Salary payable.......................	2,840
Capital, April 30	74,620	Sales revenue	731,000
Cash	7,890	Sales discounts......................	10,400
General expenses	116,700	Sales returns and allowances	18,030
Interest expense....................	5,400	Selling expenses....................	132,900
Interest payable	1,100	Store equipment	88,000
Inventory: April 30	69,350	Supplies	5,100
May 31	71,520	Unearned sales revenue	13,800
Note payable, long-term	45,000	Withdrawals..........................	9,000

Required

1. Prepare the business's multiple-step income statement for May of the current year.
2. Prepare the income statement in single-step format.
3. Prepare the balance sheet in report format at May 31 of the current year. Show your computation of the May 31 balance of Capital.

Problem 5-6B   *Using work sheet data to prepare financial statements* (L.O. 3, 4, 6)

The trial balance and adjustments columns of the work sheet of Scarlatti Development Company include the following accounts and balances at November 30, 19X4:

	Trial Balance		Adjustments	
Account Title	**Debit**	**Credit**	**Debit**	**Credit**
Cash	$ 4,000			
Accounts receivable...........................	14,500		(a) 6,000	
Inventory..	47,340			
Supplies..	2,800			(b) 2,400
Furniture	39,600			
Accumulated depreciation		$ 4,900		(c) 2,450
Accounts payable...............................		12,600		
Salary payable				(e) 1,000
Unearned sales revenue.....................		13,570	(d) 6,700	
Note payable, long-term....................		15,000		
C. Scarlatti, capital		60,310		
C. Scarlatti, drawing..........................	42,000			
Sales revenue.......................................		164,000		(a) 6,000
				(d) 6,700
Sales returns...	6,300			
Purchases	73,200			
Purchase discounts		2,040		
Selling expense....................................	28,080		(e) 1,000	
General expense...................................	13,100		(b) 2,400	
			(c) 2,450	
Interest expense...................................	1,500			
Total	$272,420	$272,420	$18,550	$18,550

Required

1. Inventory on hand at November 30, 19X4, is $52,650. Without entering the preceding data on a formal work sheet, prepare the company's multiple-step income statement for the year ended November 30, 19X4, and its November 30, 19X4, balance sheet. Show your computation of the ending balance of C. Scarlatti, Capital.

2. Compute the gross margin percentage and the rate of inventory turnover for 19X4. For 19X3, Scarlatti's gross margin percentage was .58, and inventory turnover was 1.1. Does the two-year trend in these ratios suggest improvement or deterioration in profitability?

Problem 5-7B *Preparing a merchandiser's work sheet* **(L.O. 5)**

Randall Apparel's trial balance relates to December 31 of the current year.

	Randall Apparel Trial Balance December 31, 19XX	
Cash	$ 1,270	
Accounts receivable	4,430	
Inventory	73,900	
Prepaid rent	4,400	
Store fixtures	22,100	
Accumulated depreciation		$8,380
Accounts payable		6,290
Salary payable		
Interest payable		
Note payable, long term		18,000
Roberta Randall, capital		55,920
Roberta Randall, withdrawals	39,550	
Sales revenue		170,150
Purchases	67,870	
Salary expense	24,700	
Rent expense	7,700	
Advertising expense	4,510	
Utilities expense	3,880	
Depreciation expense		
Insurance expense	2,770	
Interest expense	1,660	
Total	$258,740	$258,740

Additional data at December 31, 19XX:

a. Rent expense for the year, $10,200.

b. Store fixtures have an estimated useful life of 10 years, and are expected to be worthless when they are retired from service.

c. Accrued salaries at December 31, $900.

d. Accrued interest expense at December 31, $360.

e. Inventory on hand at December 31, $80,200.

Required

Complete Randall's work sheet for the year ended December 31 of the current year.

Problem 5-8B   *Journalizing the adjusting and closing entries of a merchandising business* **(L.O. 5)**

Required

1. Journalize the adjusting and closing entries for the data in Problem 5-7B.
2. Determine the December 31 balance of Roberta Randall, Capital.

Problem 5-9B   *Preparing a merchandiser's work sheet, financial statements and adjusting and closing entries* **(L.O. 3, 4, 5)**

The year-end trial balance of Weisner Sales Company pertains to March 31 of the current year.

Weisner Sales Company Trial Balance March 31, 19XX		
Cash..	$ 7,880	
Notes receivable, current.............................	12,400	
Interest receivable...		
Inventory	130,050	
Prepaid insurance...	3,600	
Notes receivable, long-term.........................	62,000	
Furniture...	6,000	
Accumulated depreciation...........................		$ 4,000
Accounts payable		12,220
Sales commission payable............................		
Salary payable..		
Unearned sales revenue		9,610
Ed Weisner, capital.......................................		172,780
Ed Weisner, withdrawals..............................	66,040	
Sales revenue...		440,000
Sales discounts..	4,800	
Sales returns and allowances......................	11,300	
Interest revenue		8,600
Purchases..	233,000	
Purchase discounts..		3,100
Purchase returns and allowances................		7,600
Freight in..	10,000	
Sales commission expense	78,300	
Salary expense	24,700	
Rent expense	6,000	
Utilities expense..	1,840	
Depreciation expense....................................		
Insurance expense		
Total...	$657,910	$657,910

Additional data at March 31, 19XX:

a. Accrued interest revenue, $1,030.

b. Insurance expense for the year, $3,000.

c. Furniture has an estimated useful life of 6 years. Its value is expected to be zero when it is retired from service.

d. Unearned sales revenue still unearned, $8,200.

e. Accrued salaries, $1,200.

f. Accrued sales commissions, $1,700.

g. Inventory on hand, $133,200.

Required

1. Enter the trial balance on a work sheet, and complete the work sheet for the year ended March 31 of the current year.

2. Prepare the company's multiple-step income statement and statement of owner's equity for the year ended March 31 of the current year. Also prepare its balance sheet at that date. Long-term notes receivable should be reported on the balance sheet between current assets and capital assets in a separate section labeled Investments.

3. Journalize the adjusting and closing entries at March 31.

4. Post to the Ed Weisner, Capital account and to the Income Summary account as an accuracy check on the adjusting and closing process.

Extending Your Knowledge

Decision Problems

1. Using the financial statements to decide on a business expansion (L.O. 4, 6)

David Wheelis owns Heights Pharmacy, which has prospered during its second year of operation. In deciding whether to open another pharmacy in the area, David has prepared the current financial statements of the business.

Heights Pharmacy
Income Statement
for the year ended December 31, 19X1

Sales revenue		$175,000
Interest revenue		24,600
Total revenue		199,600
Cost of goods sold		
Beginning inventory	$ 27,800	
Net purchases	87,500	
Cost of goods available for sale	115,300	
Less: Ending inventory	30,100	
Cost of goods sold		85,200
Gross margin		114,400
Operating expenses		
Salary expense	18,690	
Rent expense	12,000	
Interest expense	6,000	
Depreciation expense	4,900	
Utilities expense	2,330	
Supplies expense	1,400	
Total operating expense		45,320
Income from operations		69,080
Other expense		
Sales discounts ($3,600) and returns ($7,100)		10,700
Net income		$ 58,380

Heights Pharmacy
Statement of Owner's Equity
for the year ended December 31, 19X1

D. Wheelis, capital, January 1, 19X1	$40,000
Add: Increases in owner's equity	
Net income	58,380
D. Wheelis, capital, December 31, 19X1	$98,380

Heights Pharmacy
Balance Sheet
December 31, 19X1

Assets

Current	
Cash	$ 5,320
Accounts receivable..	9,710
Inventory...	30,100
Supplies...	2,760
Store fixtures...	63,000
Total current assets..	110,890
Other	
Withdrawals	45,000
Total assets...	$155,890

Liabilities

Current	
Accumulated depreciation — store fixtures	$ 6,300
Accounts payable...	10,310
Salary payable	900
Total current liabilities...	17,510
Other	
Note payable due in 90 days..	40,000
Total liabilities..	57,510

Owner's Equity

D. Wheelis, capital...	98,380
Total liabilities and owner's equity..	$155,890

David recently read in an industry trade journal that a successful pharmacy meets all of these criteria:

a. Gross margin is at least one half of net sales.

b. Current assets are at least two times current liabilities.

c. Owner's equity is at least as great as total liabilities.

Basing his opinion on the entity's financial statement data, David believes the business meets all three criteria. He plans to go ahead with his expansion plan, and asks your advice on preparing the pharmacy's financial statements in accordance with generally accepted accounting principles. He assures you that all amounts are correct.

Required

1. Prepare a correct multiple-step income statement, a statement of owner's equity, and a balance sheet in report format.

2. Based on the corrected financial statements, compute correct measures of the three criteria listed in the trade journal.

3. Assuming the criteria are valid, make a recommendation about whether to undertake the expansion at this time.

2. *Understanding the operating cycle of a merchandiser (L.O. 1, 3)*

A. Gayle Yip-Chuk has come to you for advice. Earlier this year, she opened a record store in a plaza near the university she had attended. The store sells records, cassettes and compact discs for cash and on credit cards and, as a special feature, on credit to certain students. Many of the students at the university are co-op students who alternate school and work terms. Gayle allows co-op students to buy on credit while they are on a school term, with the understanding that they will pay their account shortly after starting a work term.

  Business has been very good. Gayle is sure it is because of her competitive prices and the unique credit terms she offers. Her problem is that she is short of cash, and her loan with the bank has grown significantly. The bank manager has indicated that he wishes to reduce Gayle's line of credit because he is worried that Gayle will get into financial difficulties.

Required

1. Explain to Gayle why you think she is in this predicament.

2. Gayle has asked you to explain her problem to the bank manager and to assist in asking for more credit. What might you say to the bank manager to assist Gayle?

B. The employees of Oscar Ltd. made an error when they performed the periodic inventory count at year end, October 31, 19X2. Part of one warehouse was not counted and therefore was not included in inventory.

Required

1. Indicate the effect of the inventory error on cost of goods sold, gross margin, and net income for the year ended October 31, 19X2.

2. Will the error affect cost of goods sold, gross margin, and net income in 19X3? If so, what will the effect be?

Ethical Issue

Kingston & Barnes, a partnership, makes all sales of industrial conveyor belts under terms of FOB shipping point. The company usually receives orders for sales approximately one week before shipping inventory to customers. For orders received late in December, Lisa Kingston and Meg Barnes, the owners, decide when to ship the goods. If profits are already at an acceptable level, they delay shipment until January. If profits are lagging behind expectations, they ship the goods during December.

Required

1. Under Kingston & Barnes' FOB policy, when should the company record a sale?

2. Do you approve or disapprove of Kingston & Barnes' means of deciding when to ship goods to customers? If you approve, give your reason. If you disapprove, identify a better way to decide when to ship goods. (There is no accounting rule against the Kingston & Barnes practice.)

Financial Statement Problems

1. *Closing entries for a merchandising corporation; evaluating ratio data (L.O. 5)*

This problem uses both the income statement (statement of earnings) and the balance sheet of Schneider in Appendix C. It will aid your understanding of the closing process of a business with inventories.

Assume that the inventory and closing procedures outlined in this chapter are appropriate for Schneider. Further, use the amounts of inventories reported on the balance sheet, and assume net purchases for the year ended October 26, 1991 totaled $554,118,000 and net purchases for the year ended October 27, 1990 totaled $561,050,000.

1. Using Net Purchases and amounts from the income statement, journalize Schneider's closing entries for the year ended October 26, 1991. You will be unfamiliar with certain costs and expenses, but you should treat them all similarly. Corporations such as Schneider, close Income Summary into an account called Retained Earnings (instead of Capital). Also, corporations have no Withdrawals account to close.
2. What amount was closed to Retained Earnings? How is this amount labeled on Schneider's income statement?
3. Compute Schneider's gross margin percentages and inventory turnover rates during 1991 and 1990. (In addition to the information in the Schneider's report in Appendix C, you will also need the October 28, 1989 Inventories balance, which was $50,524,000) Did these ratio values of Schneider's improve or deteriorate during 1991? Summarize these results in a sentence.

2. *Identifying items from an actual company's financial statements (L.O. 5)*

Obtain the annual report of an actual incorporated company of your choosing. Make sure that the company's balance sheet reports Inventories, Merchandise Inventories, or a similar asset category. Answer these questions about the company:

1. What was the balance of total inventories reported on the balance sheet at the end of the current year? At the end of the preceding year? (If you selected a manufacturing company, you may observe more than one category of inventories. If so, name these categories and briefly explain what you think they mean.)
2. Corporations, such as the one you are analyzing, close Income Summary to an account called Retained Earnings (instead of Capital). Give the company's journal entry to close Income Summary to Retained Earnings.
3. Compute the company's gross margin percentage for the current year and for the preceding year. Did the gross margin percentage increase or decrease during the current year? Is this a favorable or an unfavorable signal about the company?
4. Compute the rate of inventory turnover for the current year. Would you expect your company's rate of inventory turnover to be higher or lower than that of a grocery chain such as Safeway or IGA? Higher or lower than that of an aircraft manufacturer such as Boeing or Canadair? State your reasoning.

Appendix

The Adjusting and Closing Process for a Merchandising Business:
Adjustng-Entry Method

This appendix illustrates the adjusting-entry method for completing the accounting cycle of a merchandising business. In this approach we record the end-of-period inventory entries as adjustments rather than as closing entries. Except for this difference in handling inventory entries, the adjusting-entry method and the closing-entry method are identical. No other adjusting or closing entries are affected by the approach taken, and the financial statements that result from both methods are the same. Because of the way computers operate, computerized systems use the adjusting-entry method.

The Adjusting and Closing Process

To illustrate a merchandiser's adjusting and closing process, let's use Austin Sound Stereo Center's December 31, 19X6, trial balance in Exhibit 5-6, p. 212. All the new accounts — Inventory, Freight In, and the contra accounts — are highlighted for emphasis. Inventory is the only new account that is affected by the adjusting procedures. Note that additional item g gives the ending inventory of $42,000.

Work Sheet of a Merchandising Business

The Exhibit 5A-1 work sheet is similar to the work sheets that we have seen so far, but a few differences appear. Note that this work sheet does not include adjusted trial balance columns. In most accounting systems, a single operation combines trial balance amounts with adjustments and extends the adjusted balances directly to the income statement and balance sheet columns. Therefore, to reduce clutter, the adjusted trial balance columns are omitted. A second difference is that the merchandiser's work sheets include inventory and purchase amounts (which are highlighted). Let us examine the entire work sheet.

Account Title Columns   The trial balance lists a number of columns without balances. Ordinarily, these accounts are affected by the adjusting process. Examples include Interest Receivable, Interest Payable, and Depreciation Expense. The accounts are listed in the order that they appear in the ledger. This eases the preparation of the work sheet. Note that the Income Summary, used for the inventory adjustments, is listed between the owner withdrawals and sales revenue. If additional accounts are needed, they can be written in at the bottom of the work sheet before net income is determined. Simply move net income down to make room for the additional accounts.

Trial Balance Columns   Examine the Inventory account, $40,500 in the trial balance. The $40,500 is the cost of beginning inventory. The work sheet is designed to replace this outdated amount with the new ending balance, which in our example is $42,000 (additional data item *g* in Exhibit 5-6). As we shall see, this task is accomplished through the adjusting process.

Adjustments Columns   The adjustments are similar to those discussed in Chapters 3 and 4. They may be entered in any order desired. The debit amount of each entry should equal the credit amount, and total debits should equal total credits.

　　The inventory adjustments are new. At the end of the period, accountants replace the beginning Inventory balance with the ending Inventory balance. Entry g1 removes the beginning balance ($40,500) by crediting the Inventory account. the debit portion of entry g1 transfers the beginning inventory amount to the Income

Exhibit 5A-1   *Work Sheet*

Austin Sound
Work Sheet
For the Year Ended December 31, 19X6

Inventory set up

Account Title	Trial Balance Debit	Trial Balance Credit	Adjustments Debit	Adjustments Credit	Income Statement Debit	Income Statement Credit	Balance Sheet Debit	Balance Sheet Credit
Cash	2,850						2,850	
Accounts receivable	4,600						4,600	
Not receivable, current	8,000						8,000	
Interest receivable			(a) 400				400	
Inventory	**40,500**		**(g2) 42,000**	**(g1) 40,500**			**42,000**	
Supplies	650			(b) 550			100	
Prepaid insurance	1,200			(c) 1,000			200	
Furniture and Fixtures	33,200						33,200	
Accumulated depreciation		2,400		(d) 600				3,000
Accounts payable		47,000						47,000
Unearned sales revenue		2,000	(e) 1,300					700
Interest payable				(f) 200				200
Note payable, long-term		12,600						12,600
E. Boritz, capital		25,900						25,900
E. Boritz, withdrawls	34,100						34,100	
Income summary			**(g1) 40,500**	**(g2) 42,000**	40,500	42,000		
Sales revenue		138,000		(e) 1,300		139,300		
Sales discounts	1,400				1,400			
Sales returns and allowances	2,000				2,000			
Interest revenue		600		(a) 400		1,000		
Purchases	**89,300**				89,300			
Purchase discounts		**3,000**				3,000		
Purchase returns and allowances		**1,200**				1,200		
Freight in	**5,200**				5,200			
Rent expense	8,400				8,400			
Depreciation expense			(d) 600		600			
Insurance expense			(c) 1,000		1,000			
Supplies expense			(b) 550		550			
Interest expense	1,300		(f) 200		1,500			
	232,700	232,700	86,550	86,550	150,450	186,500	125,450	89,400
Net income					36,050			36,050
					186,500	186,500	125,450	125,450

Summary. This is done because beginning inventory becomes part of cost of goods sold during the year. Entry g2 places the ending inventory balance ($42,000) in the Inventory account with a debit. The credit to Income Summary signifies that the ending inventory amount is subtracted in computing cost of goods sold. Therefore, the two inventory adjustments prepare Inventory for the balance sheet, and aid in computing cost of goods sold for the income statement.

Income Statement Columns   The income statement columns contain adjusted amounts for the revenues and expenses. Sales Revenue, for example, is $139,300, which includes the $1,300 adjustment.

The two inventory amounts appear in the income statement columns alongside Income Summary because beginning inventory and ending inventory enter the computation of cost of goods sold. Recall that beginning inventory is added to purchases and ending inventory is subtracted. Even though the resulting cost-of-goods-sold amount does not appear on the work sheet, all the components of cost of goods sold are evident there. Placement of beginning inventory ($40,500) in the work sheet's income statement debit column has the effect of adding beginning inventory in computing cost of goods sold. Placing ending inventory ($42,000) in the credit column has the opposite effect.

Purchases and Freight In appear in the debit column because they are added in computing cost of goods sold. Purchase Discounts and Purchase Returns and Allowances appear as credits because they are subtracted. Together, all these items are used to compute cost of goods sold — $88,800 on the income statement in Exhibit 5-5 on p. 208.

The income statement columns subtotals on the work sheet indicate whether the business earned net income or incurred a net loss. If total credits are greater, the result is net income, as shown in Exhibit 5A-1. Inserting the net income amount in the debit column brings total debits into agreement with total credits. If total debits are greater, a net loss has occurred. Inserting a net loss amount in the credit column would equalize total debits and total credits. Net income or net loss is then extended to the opposite column of the balance sheet.

Balance Sheet Columns   The only new item on the balance sheet is inventory. The balance listed is the ending amount of $42,000, which is determined by a physical count of inventory on hand at the end of the period (periodic system). On the work sheet this amount comes from the $42,000 amount in the Adjustments Debit column.

Recall that the financial statements for a company are the same whether the adjusting-entry method or the closing-entry method is used. Exhibit 5-8 on p. 215, presents Austin Sound's financial statements, which are based on the information in the work sheet. The text on p. 214 discusses these financial statements in detail.

Adjusting and Closing Entries for a Merchandising Business

Exhibit 5A-2 presents Austin Sound's adjusting entries, which are similar to those you have seen previously. Adjustment g1 transfers the beginning Inventory balance to the Income Summary. Entry g2 sets up the ending Inventory balance.

The first closing entry debits the revenue and expenses accounts that have credit balances. For Austin Sound Stereo Center, these accounts are Sales Revenue, Interest Revenue, Purchase Discounts, and Purchase returns and Allowances. The offsetting credit of $144,500 transfers their sum to the Income Summary.

The second closing entry credits the revenue and expense accounts with debit balances. These are Sales Discounts, Sales Returns and Allowances, Purchases, Freight In, and the expense accounts.

The last two closing entries close net income from the Income Summary and also close Owner Withdrawals into the Capital account.

The entries to the Inventory account deserve additional explanation. Recall that before the adjusting process. Inventory still has the period's beginning balance. At the end of the period, this balance is one period old, and must be replaced with the ending balance in order to prepare the financial statements at December 31, 19X6. The adjusting entries give Inventory its correct ending balance of $42,000, as shown below.

Inventory

Jan. 1 Bal.	40,500	Dec. 31 Adj. 40,500
Dec. 31 Adj.	42,000	
Dec. 31 Bal.	42,000	

The inventory amounts for these adjusting entries are taken directly from the Adjustments column of the work sheet. The offsetting debits and credits to Income Summary in these adjusting entries also serve to record the dollar amount of cost

Exhibit 5A-2A *Journalizing and Posting the Adjusting and Closing Entries*

Journal

Adjusting Entries

a.	Dec. 31	Interest Receivable.....................................	400	
		Interest Revenue		400
b.	31	Supplies Expense ($650-$100)	550	
		Supplies...		550
c.	31	Insurance Expense......................................	1,000	
		Prepaid Insurance.............................		1,000
d.	31	Depreciation Expense.................................	600	
		Accumulated Depreciation..............		600
e.	31	Unearned Sales Revenue	1,300	
		Sales Revenue....................................		1,300
f.	31	Interest Expense	200	
		Interest Expense		200
g1.	31	Income Summary...	40,500	
		Inventory..		40,500
g2.	31	Inventory...	42,000	
		Income Summary...............................		42,000

Closing Entries

	Dec. 31	Sales Revenue...	139,300	
		Interest Revenue	1,000	
		Purchase Discounts	3,000	
		Purchase Returns and Allowances...........	1,200	
		Income Summary		144,500
	31	Income Summary	109,950	
		Sales Discounts		1,400
		Sales Returns and Allowances........		2,000
		Purchases...		89,300
		Freight In		5,200
		Rent Expenser		8,400
		Depreciation Expense		600
		Insurance Expense............................		1,000
		Supplies Expense..............................		550
		Interest Expense................................		1,500
	31	Income Summary ($186,500-$150,450)*...	36,050	
		E. Boritz, Capital..............................		36,050
	31	E. Boritz, Capital..	34,100	
		E. Boritz, Withdrawls......................		34,100

---

* The $186,500 amount is the sum of the $144,500 credit in the closing entry and the $42,000
credit in the g2 adjusting entry. The $150,450 amount is the sum of the $109,950 debit in the
closing entry and the $40,500 debit in the g1 adjusting entry.

of goods sold in the accounts. Income Summary contains the cost-of-goods-sold
amount after Purchases, and its related contra accounts and Freight In are closed.

Study Exhibits 5A-1, 5A-2, and 5-8 carefully because they illustrate the entire
end-of-period process that leads to the financial statements. As you progress through
this book, you may want to refer to these exhibits to refresh your understanding of
the adjusting and closing process for a merchandising business.

Return to the heading Income Statement Format on p. 219.

Exhibit 5A-2B   *Ledger Accounts of Austin Sound*

ASSETS

Cash		Accounts Receivable		Note Receivable		Interest Receivable	
2,850		4,600		8,000		(A) 400	

Inventory		Supplies		Prepaid Insurance		Furniture and Fixtures	
40,500	(A) 40,500	650	(A) 550	1,200	(A) 1,000	33,200	
(A) 42,000		100		200			

Accumulated Depreciation	
	2,400
	(A) 600
	3,000

LIABILITIES

Accounts Payable		Unearned Sales Revenue		Interest Payable		Note Payable	
	47,000	(A) 1,300	2,000		(A) 200		12,600
			700				

OWNER'S EQUITY

E. Boritz Capital		E. Boritz, Withdrawals		Income Summary	
	34,100	34,100	(C) 34,100	(A) 40,500	(A) 42,000
	25,900			(C)109,950	(C)144,500
	(C) 36,050			(C) 36,050	
	27,850				

REVENUES

Sales Revenue		Sales Discounts		Sales Returns and Allowances		Interest Revenue	
	138,100	1,400	(C) 1,400	2,000	(C) 2,000		600
	(A) 1,300						(A) 400
(C)139,300	139,300					(C) 1,000	1,000

EXPENSES

Purchases		Purchase Discounts		Purchase Returns and Allowances		Freight In	
89,300	(C) 89,300	(C) 3,000	3,000	(C) 1,200	1,200	5,200	(C) 5,200

Rent Expense		Depreciation Expense		Insurance Expense		Supplies Expense	
8,400	(C) 8,400	(A) 600	(C) 600	(A) 1,000	(C) 1,000	(A) 550	(C) 550

Interest Expense	
1,300	
(A) 200	
1,500	(C) 1,500

(A) = Adjusting entry; (C) = Closing entry

ALTERNATE SOLUTION TO REVIEW PROBLEM

Requirement 1   **(Problem is on pages 221–22)**

Sales, purchases, and related discount and return and allowance entries:

19X3

a.	Accounts Receivable	346,700	
	Sales Revenue		346,700
b.	Sales Returns and Allowances	8,200	
	Accounts Receivable		8,200
c.	Cash	329,000	
	Sales Discounts	10,300	
	Accounts Receivable		339,300
d.	Purchases	175,900	
	Accounts Payable		175,900
e.	Accounts Payable	7,430	
	Purchase Returns and Allowances		7,430
f.	Accounts Payable	194,400	
	Purchase Discounts		6,000
	Cash		188,400
g.	Freight In	9,300	
	Cash		9,300

Requirement 2

Jan King Distributing Company
Work Sheet
for the year ended December 31, 19X3

Account Title	Trial Balance Debit	Trial Balance Credit	Adjustments Debit	Adjustments Credit	Income Statement Debit	Income Statement Credit	Balance Sheet Debit	Balance Sheet Credit
Cash	5,670						5,670	
Accounts receivable	37,100						37,100	
Inventory	60,500		(g2) 65,800	(g1) 60,500			65,800	
Supplies	3,930			(a) 2,580			1,350	
Prepaid rent	6,000			(b) 5,000			1,000	
Furniture and fixtures	26,500						26,500	
Accumulated depreciation		21,200		(d) 2,650				23,850
Accounts payable		46,340						46,340
Salary payable				(e) 1,300				1,300
Interest payable				(f) 600				600
Unearned sales revenue		3,500	(c) 1,100					2,400
Note payable, long-term		35,000						35,000
Jan King, capital		23,680						23,680
Jan King, withdrawals	48,000						48,000	
Income summary			(g1) 60,500	(g2) 65,800	60,500	65,800		
Sales revenue		346,700		(c) 1,100		347,800		
Sales discounts	10,300				10,300			
Sales returns and allowances	8,200				8,200			
Purchases	175,900				175,900			
Purchase discounts		6,000				6,000		
Purchase returns and allowances		7,430				7,430		
Freight In	9,300				9,300			
Salary expense	82,750		(e) 1,300		84,050			
Rent expense	7,000		(b) 5,000		12,000			
Depreciation expense			(d) 2,650		2,650			
Utilities expense	5,800				5,800			
Supplies expense			(a) 2,580		2,580			
Interest expense	2,900		(f) 600		3,500			
	489,850	489,850	139,530	139,530	374,780	427,030	185,420	133,170
Net income					52,250			52,250
					427,030	427,030	185,420	185,420

Requirement 3

Adjusting entries

19X3

Dec. 31	Supplies Expense..	2,580	
	Supplies		2,580
31	Rent Expense..	5,000	
	Prepaid Rent..		5,000
31	Unearned Sales Revenue...................................	1,100	
	Sales Revenue		1,100
31	Depreciation Expense ($26,500/10)	2,650	
	Accumulated Depreciation		2,650
31	Salary Expense..	1,300	
	Salary Payable..		1,300
31	Interest Expense	600	
	Interest Payable		600
31	Income Summary	60,500	
	Inventory		60,500
31	Inventory	65,800	
	Income Summary		65,800

Closing entries

19X3

Dec. 31	Sales Revenue...	347,800	
	Purchase Discounts	6,000	
	Purchase Returns and Allowances................	7,430	
	Income Summary..		361,230
31	Income Summary..	314,280	
	Sales Discounts..		10,300
	Sales Returns and Allowances..................		8,200
	Purchases		175,900
	Freight In..		9,300
	Salary Expense		84,050
	Rent Expense		12,000
	Depreciation Expense....................................		2,650
	Utilities Expense		5,800
	Supplies Expense		2,580
	Interest Expense		3,500
31	Income Summary		
	($65,800 + $361,230 − $60,500 − $314,280)	52,250	
	Jan King, Capital..		52,250
31	Jan King, Capital...	48,000	
	Jan King, Withdrawals		48,000

Income Summary

Adj.	60,500	Adj.	65,800	
Clo.	314,280	Clo.	361,230	
Clo.	52,250	Bal.	52,250	

Turn back to p. 225 for the solution to requirement 4, which shows the financial statements for Jan King Distributing Company.

Comprehensive Problem for Part One

Completing a Merchandiser's Accounting Cycle

The end-of-month trial balance of Lansing Building Materials at January 31 of the current year follows:

Lansing Building Materials
Trial Balance
January 31, 19XX

Account Number	Account	Balance Debit	Balance Credit
11	Cash	$ 6,430	
12	Accounts receivable	19,090	
13	Inventory	65,400	
14	Supplies	2,700	
15	Building	195,000	
16	Accumulated depreciation — building		$ 36,000
17	Fixtures	45,600	
18	Accumulated depreciation — fixtures		5,800
21	Accounts payable		28,300
22	Salary payable		
23	Interest payable		
24	Unearned sales revenue		6,560
25	Note payable, long-term		87,000
31	Ed Lansing, capital		144,980
32	Ed Lansing, withdrawals	9,200	
41	Sales revenue		177,970
42	Sales discounts	7,300	
43	Sales returns and allowances	8,140	
51	Purchases	103,000	
52	Purchase discounts		4,230
53	Purchase returns and allowances		2,600
54	Selling expense	21,520	
55	General expense	10,060	
56	Interest expense		
	Total	$493,440	$493,440

Additional data at January 31, 19XX:

a. Supplies consumed during the month, $1,500. One half is selling expense, and the other half is general expense.

b. Depreciation for the month: building, $4,000; fixtures, $4,800. One fourth of depreciation is selling expense, and three fourths is general expense.

c. Unearned sales revenue still unearned, $1,200.

d. Accrued salaries, a general expense, $1,150.

e. Accrued interest expense, $780.

f. Inventory on hand, $60,720.

Required

1. Using T-accounts, open the accounts listed on the trial balance, inserting their unadjusted balances. Date the balances of the following accounts January 1: Inventory; Supplies; Building; Accumulated Depreciation — Building; Fixtures; Accumulated Depreciation — Fixtures; Unearned Sales Revenue; and Ed Lansing, Capital. Date the balance of Ed Lansing, Withdrawals, January 31.

2. Enter the trial balance on a work sheet, and complete the work sheet for the month ended January 31 of the current year. Lansing groups all operating expenses under two accounts, Selling Expense and General Expense. Leave two blank lines under Selling Expense and three blank lines under General Expense.

3. Prepare the company's multiple-step income statement and statement of owner's equity for the month ended January 31 of the current year. Also prepare the balance sheet at the date in report form.

4. Journalize the adjusting and closing entries at January 31, using page 3 of the journal.

5. Post the adjusting and closing entries, using dates and posting references.

6. Compute Lansing's current ratio and debt ratio at January 31, and compare these values with the industry averages of 1.9 for the current ratio and .57 for the debt ratio. Compute the gross margin percentage and the rate of inventory turnover for the month, and compare these ratio values with the industry averages of .26 for the gross margin percentage of .5 for inventory turnover. Does Lansing Building Materials appear to be stronger or weaker than the average company in the building materials industry?

Answers to Self-Study Questions

1. a	6. c
2. b ($440,000 – $210,000 = $230,000)	7. c
3. d	8. a
4. d	9. c
5. b	10. d

Chapter 6

Accounting Information Systems

"Diners Club was the first credit card company. It was started in 1952 as a club for frequent diners by a man who ran out of money at a restaurant....

Before 1984, [Diners Club sevice] representatives had to start a file for each card holder inquiry, keep track of the accumulating paperwork until it had all been received, make a decision, and then contract the card holder. All the files were kept on paper. The personal card group handles about 10,000 pieces of correspondence a month, so there was a lot of clerical effort maintaining the paper files.

With the image processing system [which can convert pictures, drawings, and written characters to machine-readable form], all correspondence to the personal card group is scanned at the mail room to digitize it. Each digitized image is stored on an optical storage system and given four indices for retrieval purposes — date received, date of credit card charge, account number, and amount. From there, only the electronic images are used; the paper is discarded."

As you read Chapter 6, consider how an efficient accounting information system enables a company to process thousands (or millions) of transactions daily, yet only requires an occasional (weekly or monthly) single jounal entry to the general ledger.

Source: *I/S Analyzer* (formerly *EDP Analyzer*), (May 1989), vol. 27, no. 5, p. 1

An **accounting information system** — often called, simply, an *information system* — is the combination of personnel, records and procedures that a business uses to meet its needs for financial data. Because each business has different information demands, each uses a different accounting information system. For example, a jewelry store earns revenue by selling inventory, so the store's management usually wants an up-to-the-minute, accurate record of the level of goods on hand for sale. A physician, however, earns revenue by providing service, and there is little or no inventory to control. The physician needs to keep track of the patient name and diagnosis plus any special work done. The jewelry store and the physician, then, need different information systems to answer the special sorts of questions that arise as they conduct their business. For maximum effectiveness, the information system is tailored to the business's specific needs.

A basic understanding of accounting systems is important for managing and evaluating a business. As a manager, you may be tempted to reply, "I can always hire an accountant to design the information system and do the accounting." Perhaps, but you will be better able to communicate with the members of your organization if you understand how the accounting system operates. The accounting system is the glue that holds the various parts of an organization together. It helps managers stay on top of their responsibilities. Indeed, a potential buyer of a business examines its accounting system to understand how the organization works.

Also, you do not want your employees to take advantage of you by manipulating your accounting system to cover theft. Business owners who are unfamiliar with accounting systems are victims of this practice to an alarming degree.

This chapter looks at accounting information system designs and how they are implemented. It also provides a basic model of information processing and discusses what makes an information system effective. The chapter then discusses computer data processing and illustrates special journals and ledgers that accountants use to streamline information systems.

Accounting System Design and Installation

System Design   An accounting information system begins with a design. The manager and the designer study the business's goals and organizational structure. They also identify management's information needs, then break down the required information-processing tasks. The designer must consider the personnel who will operate the system, the documents and reports to be produced, and the equipment to be used. Almost every information system uses a computer for at least some tasks. Some public accounting firms specialize in system design and install the accounting system for their clients.

System Installation   Installation includes selecting and training employees to operate the system, testing the system and modifying it as needed. For a large system, installation may take months or even years. Often installation is more difficult than planned. Even after careful consideration in the design phase, unforeseen difficulties may emerge. If the system is not debugged, the business will have a well-designed system that is not performing its intended tasks.

Basic Model of Information Processing

Processing information means collecting, organizing, and processing data and communicating the information to statement users. In addition, accounting data are used by managers. For example, accounts receivable might be analyzed to identify the biggest customers, who will receive special privileges. Exhibit 6-1 shows how the basic model of information processing relates to an accounting system.

1. The *source data* for the accounting system are the documents, such as invoices, statements, and canceled cheques that business transactions generate.
2. *Organizing and processing* data requires transaction analysis, journalizing, posting, and preparation of the work sheet.
3. The output is *information* — the *financial statements*.

Notice that the system converts data to reports, fulfilling accounting's role of providing information.

An Effective Information System

Each business's accounting information system follows the basic model of information processing shown in Exhibit 6-1. Besides following these steps, a well-designed information system offers control, compatibility, flexibility and an acceptable cost/benefit relationship.

Control

A good accounting information system gives management control over operations. **Internal controls** are the methods and procedures the management of a business

> **OBJECTIVE 1**
> Describe the features of an effective information system

EXHIBIT 6-1   *Information-Processing Model and the Accounting System*

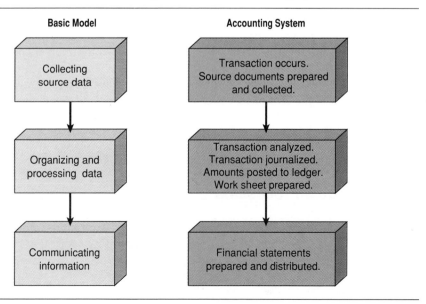

uses to safeguard its assets, to prevent and detect error and fraud, to optimize the use of resources (that is, to ensure as far as practical that reliable information is provided to determine business policies and to monitor the implementation of such policies), and to maintain reliable control systems (that is, to ensure that reliable and timely information is provided to manangement). For example, most companies exert tight controls over cash disbursement to avoid theft through unauthorized payments. Also, keeping accurate records of accounts receivable is the only way to ensure that customers are billed and collections are received on time. The internal controls control assets to different degrees. Usually control over cash is tighter than control over supplies and prepaid expenses, because cash is more open to theft. Chapter 7 details internal control procedures.

Compatibility

An information system meets the compatibility guideline when it works smoothly with the particular structure, personnel and special features of the business. For example, Eaton's needed to keep track of customer warranties, and so designed its warranty information system to keep track of customers and their warranties using the customer's phone number. One company may be organized by geographical region and another company by product line. The accounting system for the first company would accumulate revenues and expenses by region. The second company's system would group revenues and expenses by product. Any combination of data accumulation by region and by product is possible — whatever best suits the business. The compatibility guideline means designing the information system with the human factor in mind.

Flexibility

Organizations evolve. They develop new products, sell off unprofitable operations and adjust employee pay scales. Changes in the business often call for changes in the accounting system. A well-designed system meets the flexibility guideline if it can accommodate such changes without needing a complete overhaul. In most organizations, systems are rarely replaced in their entirety. For example, a system for control of cash might be installed one year and a system for controlling inventories a year later.

Acceptable Cost/Benefit Relationship

Control, compatibility and flexibility can be achieved in an accounting system, but they cost money. At some point, the cost of the system outweighs its benefits. Identifying that point is the job of the accountant as systems analyst and the manager as user of the information.

Consider the growing number of businesses that have bought computers. For many companies, the computer saves time and money and results in improved decisions. The benefits usually far exceed the cost of a simple computer system. In other cases, the savings are not sufficient to justify the cost of an increasingly elaborate system.

Computer Data Processing _____

Much data processing in business is done by computer. Computers offer significant advantages in accuracy and in the volume of accounting work that can be performed.

Components of a Computer System

The components of a computer data processing system are *hardware, software*, and *personnel*.

Hardware   Computer **hardware** is the equipment that makes up the system. A **mainframe system** is characterized by a single computer that can handle a large volume of transactions very quickly. It can be used locally or by employees at various locations. Employees enter data into the mainframe through remote terminals. In large systems, the employees may be scattered all over the world yet have access to the same computer. Smaller mainframe systems, called **minicomputers**, operate like large systems but on a smaller scale.

Exhibit 6-2 shows a microcomputer system, which is based on a different concept. In a **microcomputer** system, each work station has its own computer, often called a personal computer (PC). These small computers can be connected so that employees can work on the same project together. A group of microcomputers connected for common use is called a *network* or *local area network*; the network achieves many of the benefits of a mainframe system. Microcomputer systems are popular because they are more flexible and less expensive than large mainframes.

Software   Computer **software** is the set of programs, or instructions, that cause the computer to perform the work desired. In a computer system, transactions are not entered into the accounting records by writing entries in a journal. They are entered by typing data on a keyboard similar to that of a typewriter. The keyboard is wired to the computer, which converts the typed data into instructions the computer uses to process the data.

Mainframe software includes programs written in computer languages such as FORTRAN, COBOL, and PL/1. Microcomputers use software based on computer languages such as BASIC and PASCAL. Other micro software is designed to do specialized tasks. For example, LOTUS 1-2-3, Excel, Supercalc, and Quattro are spreadsheet packages that allow the storage and manipulation of large amounts of data. There

EXHIBIT 6-2   *Microcomputer System*

are financial accounting packages such as Simply Accounting, Abacus, ACCPAC, and NewViews that perform accounting activities such as journalizing and posting, and that can be used to prepare financial statements. For example, ACCPAC General Ledger and Financial Reporter program processes data and prints the balance sheet, income statement and subsidiary records of accounts receivable, accounts payable and payroll, among many other accounting tasks. Microcomputer software is popular because much of it is menu driven. This means by following instructions, the *menu*, you can do complex tasks with little or no computer training.

Personnel   Computer personnel in a mainframe system include systems analysts, programmers, and machine operators. The *systems analyst* designs the system, based on managers' information needs and the available accounting data. It is the analyst's job to design systems that convert data into useful information — at the lowest cost. The *programmer* writes the programs (instructions) that direct the computer's actions. The computer *operator* runs the machine.

In microcomputer systems, the distinction between the programmer and the operator becomes blurry, because an employee may handle both responsibilities. For example, a marketing manager may use a microcomputer to identify the territory needing an advertising campaign. The company treasurer may use a micro to analyze the effects of borrowing money at various interest rates. The controller may prepare the budget on a micro. These people may program the computer to meet their specific needs and also operate the machine.

Batch versus On-line Processing

Computers process data in two main ways: in batches and on-line. **Batch processing** handles similar transactions in a group or batch. Payroll accounting systems use batch processing. Suppose each employee fills out a weekly time sheet showing the number of hours worked. Stored in the computer are the employee's hourly pay and payroll deductions. The machine operator enters the hours worked, and the computer multiplies hours by hourly pay to determine each employee's gross pay. The computer subtracts deductions to compute net pay and prints payroll cheques for the net amount. It also prints the weekly payroll report and updates the ledger accounts — all in one batch operation.

On-line processing (also called **real-time processing**) handles transaction data continuously, often from various locations, rather than in batches at a single location. In retail stores like The Bay and Eaton's, the cash register does more than make change. It also doubles as a computer terminal. When you charge merchandise at an Eaton's store, the transaction is recorded at Eaton's dataprocessing center directly from the store cash register. For any one transaction the computer at the dataprocessing center may perform the following steps:

1. Accounts Receivable
   a. Compares your account number to the list of approved accounts.
      Assume your account is approved.
   b. Adds the amount of this transaction to your previous balance and determines whether the new balance, including this transaction amount, exceeds your credit limit.
      Assume it does not exceed your credit limit.
      Debits the Accounts Receivable account and updates your personal account balance to include the effect of this transaction.

2. Sales Revenue: Credits the Sales Revenue account.

3. Inventory
   a. Updates inventory records for the decrease due to this transaction.
   b. Prepares an order for replacement merchandise if the updated quantity on hand is below the reorder point.

The interactive nature of on-line processing — accounting for accounts receivable, sales and inventory simultaneously —requires a large share of the computer's capacity. On-line processing, therefore, is used more in mainframe systems than in micro systems.

Overview of an Accounting Information System

The purpose of an accounting information system is to produce the financial statements and other reports used by managers, creditors and interested people who evaluate the business. Companies use computers to meet specific needs. One company's accounting system may use a computer for accounts receivable and cash receipts and a manual system for the rest of its business. Another business may computerize payroll, accounts payable and cash disbursements, with the remainder accounted for manually. Many large companies have completely computerized accounting information systems, and many small businesses use mostly manual systems. Each entity designs its system to achieve the goals of control, compatibility, flexibility and an acceptable cost/benefit relationship. Exhibit 6-3 diagrams a typical accounting information system for a merchandising business.

Accounting procedures may be manual or computerized, mainframe or microcomputer, batch or on-line. The remainder of the chapter describes some of the more important aspects of the system described in Exhibit 6-3. Later chapters discuss the remaining system topics diagrammed in the exhibit.

Special Accounting Journals

The journal entries illustrated so far in this book have been made in the *general journal*. In practice, however, it is inefficient to record all transactions there.

Think of using the general journal to debit Accounts Receivable and credit Sales Revenue for each credit sale made in a department store on a busy Saturday! Assuming you survived that, consider posting each journal entry to the ledger. Not only would the work be tedious, but it would be time-consuming and expensive.

EXHIBIT 6-3   *Overview of an Accounting Information System*

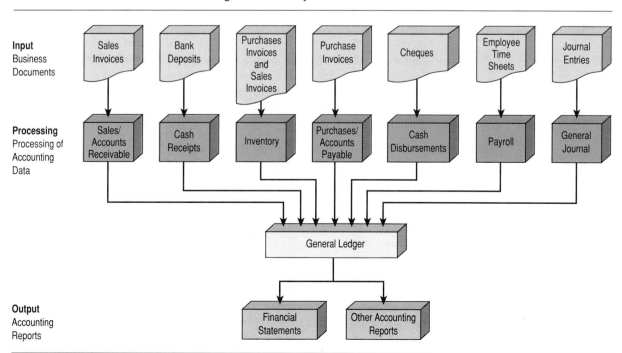

In fact, most of a business's transactions fall into one of four categories, so accountants use special journals to record these transactions. This system reduces the time and cost otherwise spent journalizing, as we will see. The four categories of transactions, the related special journal and the posting abbreviations follow:

Transaction	Special Journal	Posting Abbreviation
1. Sales on account	Sales journal	S.
2. Cash receipt	Cash receipts journal	CR.
3. Purchase on account	Purchases journal	P.
4. Cash disbursement	Cash disbursements journal	CD.

Businesses use the **general journal** for transactions that do not fit one of the special journals. For example, adjusting and closing entries are entered in the general journal. Its posting abbreviation is J.

Sales Journal

OBJECTIVE 2

Use the sales journal

Most merchandisers sell at least some of their inventory on account. These *credit sales* are recorded in the **sales journal**, also called the *credit sales journal*. Credit sales of assets other than inventory (for example, buildings) occur infrequently and are recorded in the general journal.

Exhibit 6-4 illustrates a sales journal (Panel A) and the related posting to the ledgers (Panel B) of Austin Sound, the stereo shop we introduced in Chapter 5.

The sales journal in Exhibit 6-4 (Panel A) has only one amount column, on the far right. Each entry in this column is a debit (Dr.) to Accounts Receivable and a Credit (Cr.) to Sales Revenue, as the heading above this column indicates. For each transaction, the accountant enters the date, invoice number and customer account, along with the transaction amount. This streamlined way of recording sales on account saves a vast amount of time that would be spent writing account titles and dollar amounts in the general journal.

In recording credit sales in the previous chapter, we did not keep a record of the names of credit sale customers. In practice the business must know the amount receivable from each customer. How else can the company keep track of who owes it money, and how much?

Consider the first transaction. On November 2, Austin Sound sold stereo equipment on account to Claudette Trudeau for $935. The invoice number is 422. All this information appears on a single line in the sales journal. Note that no explanation is necessary. The transaction's presence in the sales journal means that it is a credit sale, debited to Accounts Receivable — Claudette Trudeau and credited to Sales Revenue. To gain any additional information about the transaction, a person looks up the actual invoice.

Posting to the General Ledger   Note the term *general ledger*. The ledger we have used so far is the **general ledger**, which holds the accounts reported in the financial statements. However, we will soon introduce other ledgers.

Posting from the sales journal to the general ledger is done monthly. First, the amounts in the journal are summed. In Exhibit 6-4, the total credit sales for November are $3,319. Recall that this column has two headings, Accounts Receivable and Sales Revenue. When the $3,319 is posted to these accounts in the general ledger, the accountant enters their account numbers beneath the total in the sales journal. Note in Panel B of Exhibit 6-4 that the account number for Accounts Receivable is 12 and the account number for Sales Revenue is 41. These account numbers are written beneath the credit sales total in the sales journal to signify that the $3,319 has been posted to the two accounts. The $3,319 is a debit to Accounts Receivable and a credit to Sales Revenue, as the heading in the sales journal states.

EXHIBIT 6-4   *Sales Journal and Posting to Ledgers*

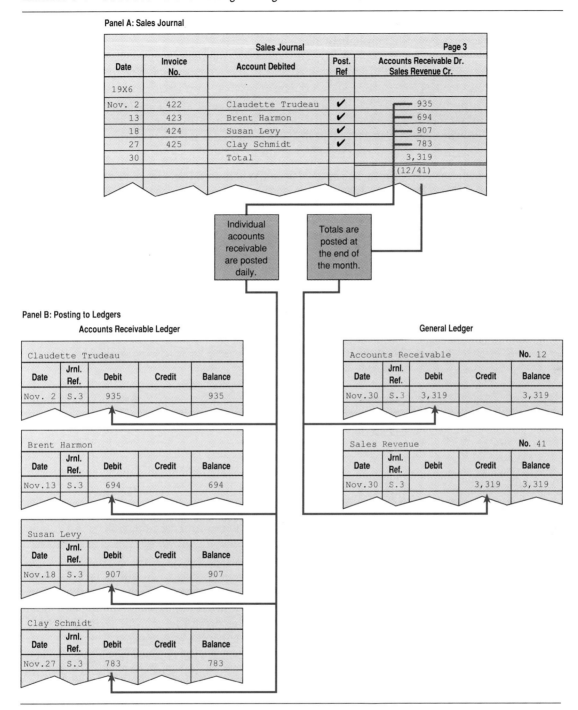

Panel A: Sales Journal

Sales Journal				Page 3
Date	Invoice No.	Account Debited	Post. Ref	Accounts Receivable Dr. Sales Revenue Cr.
19X6				
Nov. 2	422	Claudette Trudeau	✔	935
13	423	Brent Harmon	✔	694
18	424	Susan Levy	✔	907
27	425	Clay Schmidt	✔	783
30		Total		3,319
				(12/41)

Individual accounts receivable are posted daily.

Totals are posted at the end of the month.

Panel B: Posting to Ledgers

Accounts Receivable Ledger

Claudette Trudeau

Date	Jrnl. Ref.	Debit	Credit	Balance
Nov. 2	S.3	935		935

Brent Harmon

Date	Jrnl. Ref.	Debit	Credit	Balance
Nov.13	S.3	694		694

Susan Levy

Date	Jrnl. Ref.	Debit	Credit	Balance
Nov.18	S.3	907		907

Clay Schmidt

Date	Jrnl. Ref.	Debit	Credit	Balance
Nov.27	S.3	783		783

General Ledger

Accounts Receivable   No. 12

Date	Jrnl. Ref.	Debit	Credit	Balance
Nov.30	S.3	3,319		3,319

Sales Revenue   No. 41

Date	Jrnl. Ref.	Debit	Credit	Balance
Nov.30	S.3		3,319	3,319

The number of the account debited (12) appears on the left and the number of the account credited (41) on the right.

Posting to the Subsidiary Ledger   The $3,319 sum of the November debits does not identify the amount receivable from any specific customer. Most businesses would find keeping a separate accounts receivable account in the general ledger for each customer to be unmanageable. A business may have thousands of customers. Imagine how many pages thick the general ledger for Eaton's would be. Locating a specific customer's account among the other accounts (like Cash, Inventory, Salary Expense, and so on) would be frustrating and time-consuming. To streamline operations, businesses instead place the accounts of their individual

OBJECTIVE 3

Use control accounts and subsidiary ledgers

credit customers in a subsidiary ledger, called the Accounts Receivable ledger. A **subsidiary ledger** is a book or file of accounts that provides supporting details on individual balances, the total of which appears in the general ledger. The customer accounts are filed alphabetically.

Amounts in the sales journal are posted to the subsidiary ledger daily to keep a current record of the amount receivable from each customer. Note that the amounts are debits. Daily posting allows the business to answer customer inquiries promptly. Suppose Claudette Trudeau telephones Austin Sound on November 11 to ask how much money she owes. The subsidiary ledger readily provides that information.

When each transaction amount is posted to the subsidiary ledger, a check mark is written in the posting reference column of the sales journal.

Journal References in the Ledgers   When amounts are posted to the ledgers, the journal page number is written in the account to identify the source of the data. All transaction data in Exhibit 6-4 originated on page 3 of the sales journal so all posting references in the ledger accounts are S.3. The S. indicates sales journal.

Trace all the postings in Exhibit 6-4. The most effective way to learn about accounting systems and special journals is to study the flow of data. The arrows indicate the direction of the information.

The arrows show the links between the individual customer accounts in the subsidiary ledger and the Accounts Receivable account. These links are summarized as follows:

Accounts Receivable debit balance $3,319

Customer Accounts Receivable

Customer	Balance
Claudette Trudeau	$ 935
Brent Harmon..	694
Susan Levy...	907
Clay Schmidt	783
Total accounts receivable	$3,319

Accounts Receivable in the general ledger is a **control account**, which is an account whose balance equals the sum of the balances of a group of related accounts in a subsidiary ledger. In this simple illustration, Accounts Receivable's balance is the total amount of credit sales. The individual customer accounts are subsidiary accounts. They are "controlled" by the Accounts Receivable account in the general ledger.

Let us look at the advantages the sales journal offers. Each transaction is entered on a single line, and the account titles do not have to be written. The accountant, then, does not have to write as much in the sales journal as in the general journal. Also, the sales journal streamlines posting. That is, fewer postings to the general ledger are necessary. Suppose that Austin Sound had 400 credit sales for the month. How many postings to the general ledger would be made from the sales journal? There are only two: one to Accounts Receivable and one to Sales Revenue. How many postings would there be from the general journal? The total would be 800, that is, 400 debits to Accounts Receivable and 400 credits to Sales Revenue.

Additional data can be recorded in the sales journal. For example, a company may add a column to record sale terms, such as 2/10 n/30. The design of the journal depends on the business's needs for information.

OBJECTIVE 4
Use the cash receipts journal

Cash Receipts Journal

Cash transactions are common in most businesses because cash receipts from customers are the lifeblood of business. To streamline the recording of repetitive cash receipt transactions, accountants use the **cash receipts journal**.

EXHIBIT 6-5   *Cash Receipts Journal and Posting to Ledgers*

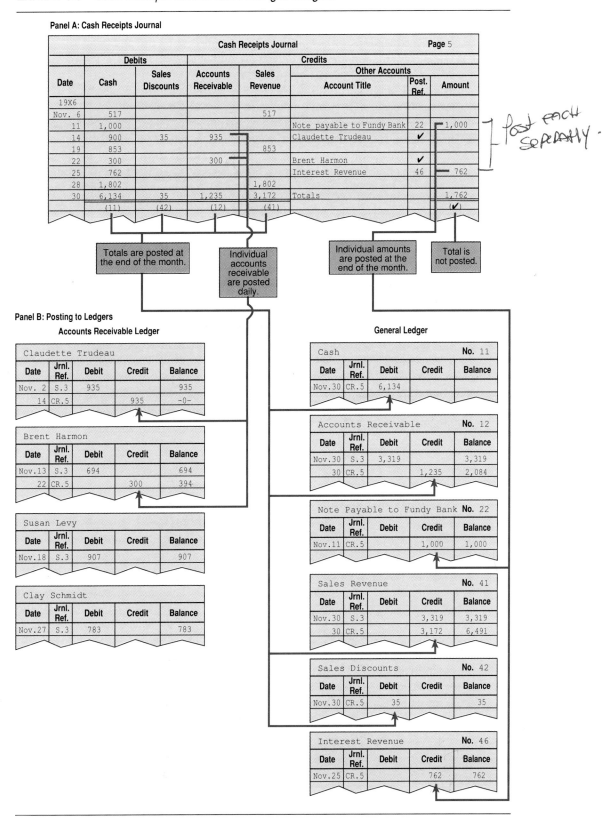

Panel A in Exhibit 6-5, illustrates the cash receipts journal. The related posting to ledgers is shown in Panel B. The exhibit illustrates November transactions for Austin Sound.

Every transaction recorded in this journal is a cash receipt, so the first column is for debits to the Cash account. The next column is for debits to Sales Discounts on collections from customers. In a typical merchandising business, the main sources of cash are collections on account and cash sales. Thus the cash receipts journal has credit columns for Accounts Receivable and Sales Revenue. The journal also has a credit column for Other Accounts, which lists sources of cash other than cash sales and collections on account. This Other Accounts column is also used to record the names of customers from whom cash is received on account.

In Exhibit 6-5, cash sales occurred on November 6, 19 and 28. Observe the debits to Cash and the credits to Sales Revenue ($517, $853 and $1,802).

On November 11, Austin Sound borrowed $1,000 from Fundy Bank. Cash is debited, and Note Payable to Fundy Bank is credited in the Other Accounts column because no specific credit column is set up to account for borrowings. For this transaction, it is necessary to write the account title, Note Payable to Fundy Bank, in the Other Accounts/Account Title column to record the source of cash.

On November 25, Austin Sound collected $762 of interest revenue. The account credited, Interest Revenue, must be written in the Other Accounts column. The November 11 and 25 transactions illustrate an important fact about business. Different entities have different types of transactions, and they design their special journals to meet their particular needs. In this case, the Other Accounts Credit column is the catch-all that is used to record all nonroutine cash receipt transactions.

On November 14, Austin Sound collected $900 from Claudette Trudeau. Referring back to Exhibit 6-4, we see that on November 2 Austin Sound sold merchandise for $935 to Ms. Trudeau. Assume that the terms of sale allowed a $35 discount for prompt payment and that she paid within the discount period. Austin's cash receipts is recorded by debiting Cash for $900 and Sales Discounts for $35 and by crediting Accounts Receivable for $935. Note that the customer's name appears in the Other Accounts/Account Title column. This enables the business to keep exact track of each customer's account in the subsidiary ledger.

On November 22, the business collected $300 on account from Brent Harmon, who was paying for part of the November 13 purchase. Assume no discount applied to this collection.

Total debits should equal total credits in the cash receipts journal. This equality holds for each transaction and for the monthly totals. For example, the first transaction has a $517 debit and an equal credit. For the month, total debits ($6,134 + $35 = $6,169) equal total credits ($1,235 + $3,172 + $1,762 = $6,169).

Posting to the General Ledger   The column totals are posted monthly. To indicate their posting, the account number is written below the column total in the cash receipts journal. Note the account number for Cash (11) below the column total $6,134, and trace the posting to Cash in the general ledger. Likewise, the Sales Discounts, Accounts Receivable, and Sales Revenue column totals also are posted to the general ledger.

The column total for Other Accounts is not posted. Instead, these credits are posted individually. In Exhibit 6-5, the November 11 transaction reads "Note Payable to Fundy Bank." This account's number (22) in the Post. Ref. column indicates that the transaction amount was posted individually. The check mark, instead of an account number, below the column total indicates that the column total was not posted. The November 25 collection of interest revenue is also posted individually. These amounts can be posted to the general ledger at the end of the month. However, they should be dated in the ledger accounts based on their actual date in the journal. This makes it easy to trace the amounts back to the journal.

Posting to the Subsidiary Ledger   Amounts from the cash receipts journal are posted to the subsidiary accounts receivable ledger daily to keep the individual balances up to date. The postings to the accounts receivable ledger are credits. Trace the $935 posting to Claudette Trudeau's account. It reduces the balance in her account to zero. The $300 receipt from Brent Harmon reduces his accounts receivable balance to $394.

After posting, the sum of the individual balances that remain in the accounts receivable ledger equals the general ledger balance in Accounts Receivable ($2,084). Austin Sound may prepare a November 30 list of account balances from the subsidiary ledger as a check of the accuracy of journalizing and posting:

Customer Accounts Receivable	
Customer	**Balance**
Brent Harmon..	$ 394
Susan Levy..	907
Clay Schmidt	783
Total accounts receivable	$2,084

Keeping good accounts receivable records reduces errors and helps customer relations.

The cash receipts journal offers the same advantages as the sales journal: streamlined journalizing of transactions and fewer postings to the ledgers.

Summary Problem for Your Review

A company completed the following selected transactions during March:

Mar. 4   Received $500 from a cash sale to a customer.
    6   Received $60 on account from Brady Lee. The full invoice amount was $65, but Lee paid within the discount period to gain the $5 discount.
    9   Received $1,080 on a note receivable from Beverly Mann. This amount includes the $1,000 note receivable plus $80 of interest revenue.
   15   Received $800 from a cash sale to a customer.
   24   Borrowed $2,200 by signing a note payable to the Bank of the Rockies.
   27   Received $1,200 on account from Lance Albert. Payment was received after the discount period lapsed.

The general ledger showed the following balances at February 28: Cash, debit balance of $1,117; Accounts Receivable, debit balance of $2,790; Note Receivable — Beverly Mann, debit balance of $1,000. The accounts receivable subsidiary ledger at February 28 contained debit balances as follows: Lance Albert, $1,840; Melinda Fultz, $885; Brady Lee, $65.

Required

1. Record the transactions in the cash receipts journal, page 7.

2. Compute column totals at March 31. Show that total debits equal total credits in the cash receipts journal.

3. Post to the general ledger and the accounts receivable subsidiary ledger. Use complete posting references, including the account numbers illustrated: Cash, 11; Accounts Receivable, 12; Note Receivable — Beverly Mann, 13; Note Payable — Bank of the Rockies, 22; Sales Revenue, 41; Sales Discounts, 42; Interest Revenue, 46. Insert a check mark (✔) in the posting reference column for each February 28 account balance.

4. Prove the accuracy of posting by showing that the total of the balances in the subsidiary ledger equals the general ledger balance in Accounts Receivable.

SOLUTION TO REVIEW PROBLEM

Requirements 1 and 2

	Cash Receipts Journal						Page 7

	Debits		Credits				
					Other Accounts		
Date	Cash	Sales Discounts	Accounts Receivable	Sales Revenue	Account Title	Post. Ref.	Amount
Mar. 4	500			500			
6	60	5	65		Brady Lee	✔	
9	1,080				Note Receivable — Beverly Mann	13	1,000
					Interest Revenue	46	80
15	800			800			
24	2,200				Note Payable — Bank of the Rockies	22	2,200
27	1,200		1,200		Lance Albert	✔	
31	5,840	5	1,265	1,300	Total		3,280
	(11)	(42)	(12)	(41)			(✔)

5,845   5,845

Requirement 3

Accounts Receivable Ledger
Lance Albert

Date	Jrnl. Ref.	Debit	Credit	Balance
Feb. 28	✔			1,840
Mar. 27	CR. 7		1,200	640

Melinda Fultz

Date	Jrnl. Ref.	Debit	Credit	Balance
Feb. 28	✔			885

Brady Lee

Date	Jrnl. Ref.	Debit	Credit	Balance
Feb. 28	✔			65
Mar. 6	CR.		65	—

General Ledger
Cash   No. 11

Date	Jrnl. Ref.	Debit	Credit	Balance
Feb. 28	✔			1,117
Mar. 31	CR. 7	5,840		6,957

Accounts Receivable   No. 12

Date	Jrnl. Ref.	Debit	Credit	Balance
Feb. 28	✔			2,790
Mar. 31	CR. 7		1,265	1,525

Note Receivable — Beverly Mann   No. 13

Date	Jrnl. Ref.	Debit	Credit	Balance
Feb. 28	✔			1,000
Mar. 9	CR. 7		1,000	—

Note Payable — Bank of the Rockies No. 22

Date	Jrnl. Ref.	Debit	Credit	Balance
Mar. 24	CR. 7		2,200	2,200

Sales Revenue   **No. 41**

Date	Jrnl. Ref.	Debit	Credit	Balance
Mar. 31	CR. 7		1,300	1,300

Sales Discount   **No. 42**

Date	Jrnl. Ref.	Debit	Credit	Balance
Mar. 31	CR. 7	5		5

Interest Revenue   **No. 46**

Date	Jrnl. Ref.	Debit	Credit	Balance
Mar. 9	CR. 7		80	80

Requirement 4

Lance Albert	$ 640
Melinda Fultz	885
Total accounts receivable	$1,525

This total agrees with the balance in Accounts Receivable.

Purchases Journal

> **OBJECTIVE 5**
> Use the purchases
> journal

A merchandising business purchases inventory and supplies frequently. Such purchases are usually made on account. The **purchases journal** is designed to account for all purchases of inventory, supplies and other assets *on account*. It can also be used to record expenses incurred on account. Cash purchases are recorded in the cash disbursements journal.

Exhibit 6-6 illustrates Austin Sound's purchases journal (Panel A) and posting to ledgers (Panel B).[1]

The purchases journal in Exhibit 6-6 has amount columns for credits to Accounts Payable and debits to Purchases, Supplies and Other Accounts. The Other Accounts columns accommodate purchases of assets other than inventory and supplies. These columns make the journal flexible enough to accommodate a wide variety of transactions. Each business designs its purchases journal to meet its own needs for information and efficiency. Accounts Payable is credited for all transactions recorded in the purchases journal. Inventory purchases are debited to Purchases. Purchases of supplies are debited to Supplies.

---

[1]This is the only special journal that we illustrate with the credit column placed to the left and the debit columns to the right. This arrangement of columns focuses on Accounts Payable, which is credited for each entry to this journal — and on the individual supplier to be paid.

EXHIBIT 6-6   *Purchases Journal and Posting to Ledgers*

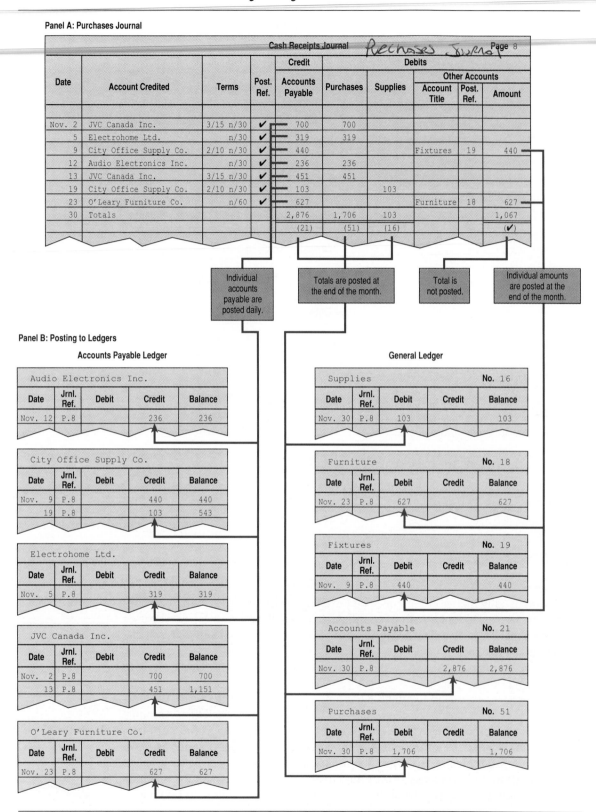

Panel A: Purchases Journal

Date	Account Credited	Terms	Post. Ref.	Credit Accounts Payable	Purchases	Supplies	Account Title	Post. Ref.	Amount
Nov. 2	JVC Canada Inc.	3/15 n/30	✔	700	700				
5	Electrohome Ltd.	n/30	✔	319	319				
9	City Office Supply Co.	2/10 n/30	✔	440			Fixtures	19	440
12	Audio Electronics Inc.	n/30	✔	236	236				
13	JVC Canada Inc.	3/15 n/30	✔	451	451				
19	City Office Supply Co.	2/10 n/30	✔	103		103			
23	O'Leary Furniture Co.	n/60	✔	627			Furniture	18	627
30	Totals			2,876	1,706	103			1,067
				(21)	(51)	(16)			(✔)

Individual accounts payable are posted daily.

Totals are posted at the end of the month.

Total is not posted.

Individual amounts are posted at the end of the month.

Panel B: Posting to Ledgers

Accounts Payable Ledger

Audio Electronics Inc.

Date	Jrnl. Ref.	Debit	Credit	Balance
Nov. 12	P.8		236	236

City Office Supply Co.

Date	Jrnl. Ref.	Debit	Credit	Balance
Nov. 9	P.8		440	440
19	P.8		103	543

Electrohome Ltd.

Date	Jrnl. Ref.	Debit	Credit	Balance
Nov. 5	P.8		319	319

JVC Canada Inc.

Date	Jrnl. Ref.	Debit	Credit	Balance
Nov. 2	P.8		700	700
13	P.8		451	1,151

O'Leary Furniture Co.

Date	Jrnl. Ref.	Debit	Credit	Balance
Nov. 23	P.8		627	627

General Ledger

Supplies   No. 16

Date	Jrnl. Ref.	Debit	Credit	Balance
Nov. 30	P.8	103		103

Furniture   No. 18

Date	Jrnl. Ref.	Debit	Credit	Balance
Nov. 23	P.8	627		627

Fixtures   No. 19

Date	Jrnl. Ref.	Debit	Credit	Balance
Nov. 9	P.8	440		440

Accounts Payable   No. 21

Date	Jrnl. Ref.	Debit	Credit	Balance
Nov. 30	P.8		2,876	2,876

Purchases   No. 51

Date	Jrnl. Ref.	Debit	Credit	Balance
Nov. 30	P.8	1,706		1,706

On November 2, Austin Sound Stereo Center purchased from JVC Canada Inc. stereo inventory costing $700. The creditor's name (JVC Canada Inc.) is entered in the Account Credited column. The purchase terms of 3/15 n/30 are also entered to help identify the due date and the discount available. Accounts Payable is credited and Purchases is debited for the transaction amount. On November 19, a credit purchase of supplies is entered as a debit to Supplies and a credit to Accounts Payable.

Note the November 9 purchase of fixtures from City Office Supply. Since the purchases journal contains no column for fixtures, the Other Accounts debit column is used. Because this was a credit purchase, the accountant enters the creditor name (City Office Supply) in the Account Credited column and writes "Fixtures" in the Other Accounts/Account Title column.

The total credits in the journal ($2,876) are compared to the total debits ($1,706 + $103 + $1,067 = $2,876) to prove the accuracy of the entries in the purchases journal.

To pay debts efficiently, a company must know how much it owes particular creditors. The Accounts Payable account in the general ledger shows only a single total, however, and therefore does not indicate the amount owed to each creditor. Companies keep an accounts payable subsidiary ledger. The accounts payable ledger lists the creditors in alphabetical order, along with the amounts owed to them. Exhibit 6-6 shows Austin Sound's accounts payable subsidiary ledger, which includes accounts for Audio Electronics, City Office Supply and others. After posting at the end of the period, the total of the individual balances in the subsidiary ledger equals the balance in the Accounts Payable control account in the general ledger. This system is much like the accounts receivable system discussed earlier in the chapter.

Posting from the Purchases Journal Posting from the purchases journal is similar to posting from the sales journal and the cash receipts journal. Exhibit 6-7, Panel B, illustrates the posting process.

Individual accounts payable in the *accounts payable subsidiary ledger* are posted daily, and column totals and other amounts are posted to the *general ledger* at the end of the month. In the ledger accounts, P. 8 indicates the source of the posted amounts, that is, page 8 of the purchases journal.

Use of the special purchases journal offers advantages over the general journal. Each transaction is *journalized* on one line, and the general ledger accounts do not have to be written. A written explanation of each transaction is unnecessary because each transaction is a purchase on account. Posting to the general ledger is streamlined with the special journal because monthly totals can be posted to the general ledger. Contrast the number of postings from the purchases journal in Exhibit 6-6 with the number that would be required if the general journal were used to record the same seven transactions. Use of the purchases journal requires only five general ledger postings — $2,876 to Accounts Payable, $1,706 to Purchases, $103 to Supplies, $440 to Fixtures and $627 to Furniture. Without the purchases journal, there would have been fourteen postings, two for each of the seven transactions.

Cash Disbursements Journal

Businesses make most cash disbursements by cheque. All payments by cheque are recorded in the **cash disbursements journal**. Other titles of this special journal are the *cheque register* and the *cash payments journal*. Like the other special journals, it has multiple columns for recording cash payments that occur frequently.

Exhibit 6-7, Panel A, illustrates the cash disbursements journal, and Panel B shows the postings to the ledgers of Austin Sound.

The cash disbursements journal in the exhibit has two debit columns —for Accounts Payable and Other Accounts — and two credit columns — for Cash and Purchase Discounts. It also has columns for the date and cheque number of each cash payment.

Suppose a business makes numerous cash purchases of inventory. What additional column would its cash disbursements journal need to be most useful? A column for Purchases, which would appear under the Debits heading, would streamline the accounting.

> **OBJECTIVE 6**
>
> Use the cash disbursements journal

EXHIBIT 6-7   *Cash Disbursements Journal and Posting to Ledgers*

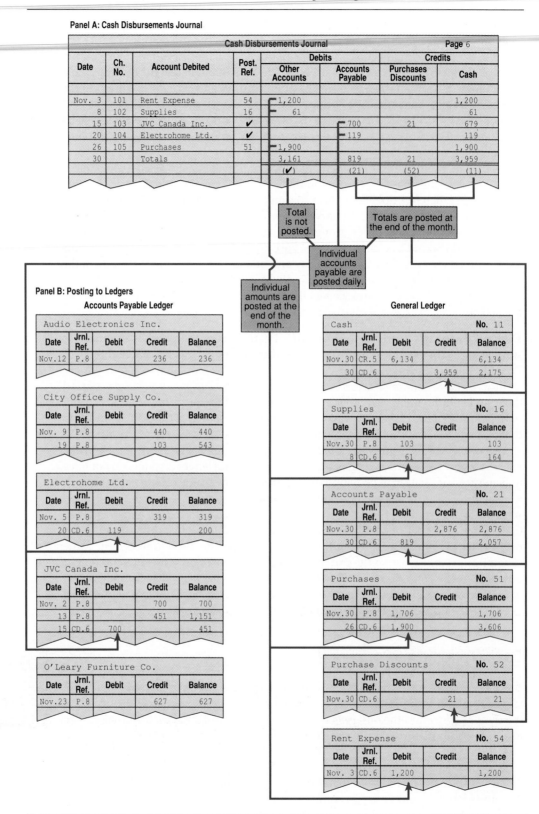

All entries in the cash disbursements journal include a credit to Cash. Payments on account are debits to Accounts Payable. On November 15, Austin Sound paid JVC Canada on account, with credit terms of 3/15 n/30 (for details, see the first transaction in Exhibit 6-6). Therefore, Austin took the 3 percent discount and paid $679 ($700 less the $21 discount).

The Other Accounts column is used to record debits to accounts for which no special column exists. For example, on November 3, Austin Sound paid rent expense of $1,200, and on November 8, the business purchased supplies for $61.

As with all other journals, the total debits ($3,161 + $819 = $3,980) should equal the total credits ($21 + $3,959 = $3,980).

Posting from the Cash Disbursements Journal   Posting from the cash disbursements journal is similar to posting from the cash receipts journal. Individual creditor amounts are posted daily, and column totals and Other Accounts are posted at the end of the month. Exhibit 6-7, Panel B, illustrates the posting process.

Observe the effect of posting to the Accounts Payable account in the general ledger. The first posted amount in the Accounts Payable account (credit $2,876) originated in the purchases journal, page 8 (P.8). The second posted amount (debit $819) came from the cash disbursements journal, page 6 (CD.6). The resulting credit balance in Accounts Payable is $2,057. Also, see the Cash account. After posting, its debit balance is $2,175.

Amounts in the Other Accounts column are posted individually (for example, Rent Expense — debit $1,200). When each Other Accounts amount is posted to the general ledger, the account number is written in the Post. Ref. column of the journal.

As a proof of accuracy, companies total the individual creditor balances in the accounts payable subsidiary ledger for comparison with the Accounts Payable balance in the general ledger.

Creditor Accounts Payable

Creditor	Balance
Audio Electronics	$ 236
City Office Supply	543
JVC Canada Inc.	451
O'Leary Furniture	627
Electrohome Ltd.	200
Total accounts payable	$2,057

This total, computed at the end of the period, agrees with the Accounts Payable balance in Exhibit 6-7. Agreement of the two amounts suggests that journalizing and posting have been performed correctly and that the resulting account balances are correct.

Use of the cash disbursements journal streamlines journalizing and posting in the same way as for the other special journals.

The Credit Memorandum: A Basic Business Document _____

OBJECTIVE 7

Journalize return and allowance transactions

Customers sometimes bring merchandise back to the seller, and sellers grant sales allowances to customers because of product defects and for other reasons. The effect of sales returns and sales allowances is the same — both decrease net sales in the same way a sales discount does. The document issued by the seller to indicate having credited the customer's Account Receivable is called a **credit memorandum** or **credit memo**, because the company gives a customer credit for the returned merchandise. When a company issues a credit memo, it records the transaction by debiting Sales Returns and Allowances and crediting Accounts Receivable.

Suppose Austin Sound sold two stereo speakers for $198 on account to Maria Schultz. Later she discovered a defect and returned the speakers. Austin Sound would issue to Ms. Schultz a credit memo like the one in Exhibit 6-8.

EXHIBIT 6-8   *Credit Memorandum*

Credit Memorandum   No. 27

Austin Sound Stereo Center   **Date**   November 6, 19X6
305 Robie Street
Halifax, Nova Scotia B3H 4K7

Customer Name   Maria Schultz

                     3007 Cobourg Road

                     Halifax, Nova Scotia B3H 2Y8

Reason for Credit   Defective merchandise returned

Description	Amount
2 Trailblazer JU170456 Speakers	$198

To record the *sales return*, Austin Sound would make the following entry in the general journal:

General Journal   Page 9

Date	Accounts	Post. Ref.	Debit	Credit
Nov. 6	Sales Returns and Allowances	43	198	
	Accounts Receivable — Maria Schultz	12/✔		198
	Credit memo no. 27.			

The debit side of the entry is posted to Sales Return and Allowances. Its account number (43) is written in the posting reference column when $198 is posted. The credit side of the entry requires two $198 postings: one to Accounts Receivable, the control account in the general ledger (account number 12), and the other to Maria Schultz's account in the accounts receivable subsidiary ledger. These credit postings explain why the document is called a credit memo.

Observe that the posting references of the credit include two notations. The account number (12) denotes the posting to Accounts Receivable in the general ledger. The check mark (✔) denotes the posting to Ms. Schultz's account in the subsidiary ledger. Why are two postings needed? Because this is the general journal. Without specially designed columns, it is necessary to write both posting references on the same line. Posting to the general ledger usually occurs monthly; and posting to the subsidiary ledger, daily.

Suppose Ms. Schultz had paid cash. Austin Sound would either give her a credit memo or refund her cash. Austin Sound would record the cash refund in the *cash disbursements journal* as follows:

Cash Disbursements Journal   Page 8

				Debits		Credits	
Date	Ch. No.	Account Debited	Post. Ref.	Other Accounts	Accounts Payable	Purchase Discounts	Cash
Nov. 6	106	Sales Returns and Allowances	43	198			198

A business with a high volume of sales returns, such as a department store chain, may find it efficient to use a specific journal for sales returns and allowances.

The Debit Memorandum: A Basic Business Document _____

Purchase Returns occur when a business returns goods to the seller. The procedures for handling purchase returns are similar to those dealing with sales returns. The purchaser gives the merchandise back to the seller and receives either a cash refund or replacement goods.

When a business returns merchandise to the seller, it may also send a business document known as a **debit memorandum** or **debit memo**. This document states that the buyer no longer owes the seller for the amount of the returned purchase. The buyer debits the Accounts Payable to the seller and credits Purchase Returns and Allowances. If the volume of purchase returns is high enough, the business may use a special journal for purchase returns.

Many businesses record their purchase returns in the general journal, not in a special journal. Austin Sound would record its return of defective speakers to JVC as follows:

Date	Accounts	Post. Ref.	Debit	Credit
Nov. 6	Accounts Payable — JVC Canada Inc. Purchase Returns and Allowances... Debit memo no. 16.	21/✔ 53	244	 244

General Journal — Page 9

Sales Tax _____

In Chapter 4, the federal Goods and Services Tax (GST) was discussed; recall that the GST is collected at each level of transaction right down to the consumer, the final level. The discussion that follows relates to consumption or sales taxes levied by all the provices except Alberta. The Yukon and the Northwest Territories also do not have a sales tax. Sellers must add the tax to the sale amount, then pay the tax to the provincial government. In most jurisdictions, sales tax is levied only on final consumers, so retail businesses usually do not pay sales tax on the goods they purchase for resale. For example, Gaber Stereo would not pay tax on a purchase of equipment from JVC Canada, a wholesaler. However, when retailers like Gaber Stereo make sales, they must collect sales tax from the consumer. In effect, retailers serve as collecting agents for the taxing authorities. The amount of tax depends on the total sales.

Retailers set up procedures to collect the tax, account for it and pay it on time. Invoices may be preprinted with a place for entering the sales tax amount, and the general ledger has an account entitled Sales Tax Payable. The sales journal may include a special column for sales tax, such as the one illustrated in Exhibit 6-9. The sales tax rate in the exhibit is 7 percent, the rate of sales tax in Saskatchewan and Manitoba.

Note that the amount debited to Accounts Receivable ($3,551.33) is the sum of the credits to Sales Tax Payable ($232.33) and Sales Revenue ($3,319.00). This is so because the customers' payments, the Accounts Receivable figures, are partly for the purchase of merchandise (Sales Revenue) and partly for tax created by the sale. Individual customer accounts are posted daily to the accounts receivable subsidiary ledger, and each column total is posted at the end of the month. The check marks in the Posting Reference column show that individual amounts have been posted

EXHIBIT 6-9   *Sales Journal Designed to Account for Sales Tax*

Sales Journal   Page 4

Date	Invoice No.	Account Debited	Post. Ref.	Accounts Receivable Dr.	Sales Tax Payable Cr.	Sales Revenue Cr.
19X6						
Nov. 2	422	Anne Fortin	✔	1,000.45	65.45	935.00
13	423	Brent Mooney	✔	742.58	48.58	694.00
18	424	Debby Levy	✔	970.49	63.49	907.00
27	425	Dan Girardi	✔	837.81	54.81	783.00
30		Totals		3,551.33	232.33	3,319.00

to the customer accounts. The absence of account numbers under the column totals shows that the total amounts have not yet been posted.

Most companies that use cash registers have them programmed to calculate separate totals, as sales are being rung in, of taxable items and nontaxable items; the register then calculates the relevant taxes — sales tax, if applicable, and GST — and computes the total owing. Due to the fact that the provincial sales tax and the federal GST are not applicable to all items (for example, food and prescription medicines are excluded from both; reading material is excluded from most sales taxes but not from the GST), most businesses calculate sales tax and GST at the time of sale.

A business, whose sales are all taxable, may use a simplified approach to account for sales tax as follows. The business enters a single amount, which is the sum of sales revenue and sales tax, in the Sales Revenue account. This amount is what the customer pays the retailer. At the end of the period, the business computes the tax collected and transfers that amount from Sales Revenue to Sales Tax Payable through a general journal entry. This procedure eliminates the need for a special multicolumn journal.

Suppose a retailer's Sales Revenue account shows a $11,100 balance at the end of the period. This retailer chooses to enter the full amount of each sale — the actual sales revenue and the sales tax — as Sales Revenue. How does the retailer divide the total amount into its two parts?

To compute the actual sales revenue, the Sales Revenue balance is divided by 1 plus the tax rate. Assume that sales tax is 11 percent, the sales tax rate in New Brunswick. Thus the retailer divides $11,100 by 1.11 (1 + .11), which yields $10,000. Subtracting the actual sales revenue, the $10,000, from the $11,100 total yields $1,100, the sales tax. The retailer makes the following entry in the general journal:

General Journal   Page 9

Date	Accounts	Post. Ref.	Debit	Credit
July 31	Sales Revenue...	41	1100	
	Sales Tax Payable................................	28		1100
	To transfer sales tax to the liability account			

Sales tax and GST are more fully discussed in Chapter 11.

Balancing the Ledgers

At the end of the period, after all postings, equality should exist among

1. Total debits and total credits in the general ledger. These amounts are used to prepare the trial balance that has been used throughout Chapters 3 to 5.
2. The balance of the Accounts Receivable control account in the general ledger and the sum of individual customer accounts in the accounts receivable subsidiary ledger.
3. The balance of the Accounts Payable control account in the general ledger and the sum of individual creditor accounts in the accounts payable subsidiary ledger.

This process is called **balancing the ledgers** or proving the ledgers. It is an important control procedure because it helps assure the accuracy of the accounting records. Equality between Accounts Receivable control and the accounts receivable subsidiary ledger was proved as shown in Exhibit 6-5 (p. 265). A simpler and less costly procedure is to total the individual customer balances on a calculator tape for comparison to Accounts Receivable control. Balancing the accounts payable ledger follows the same pattern as illustrated on p. 273.

Documents as Journals

Many small businesses streamline their accounting systems to save money by using the actual business documents as the journals. For example, Austin Sound could let its sales invoices serve as its sales journal and keep all invoices for credit sales in a looseleaf binder. At the end of the period, the accountant simply totals the sales on account and posts that amount to Accounts Receivable and Sales Revenue. Also, the accountant can post directly from invoices to customer accounts in the accounts receivable ledger. This "journal-less" system reduces accounting cost, because the accountant does not have to write in journals the information already in the business documents.

Computers and Special Journals

The manual accounting system we discuss in this chapter should help you understand the importance of computers for companies with large numbers of customers and suppliers and a high volume of transactions. Imagine entering manually the few transactions in this chapter — multiplied by a thousand or even ten thousand.

Computerizing special journals requires no drastic change in the accounting system's design. Systems designers create a special screen for each accounting application — credit sales, cash collections, credit purchases, and cash payments. The special screen for credit sales would ask the person at the computer keyboard, for example, a terminal at a cash register, to type in the following information: date, customer number, customer name, invoice number, and the dollar amount of the sale. These data can generate debits and credits to the subsidiary accounts receivable, debits to Cash, and monthly customer statements that show activity and ending balance. Also, additional computer files keep information on individual customers and vendors.

Ensuring that the general ledger Accounts Receivable balance or the Accounts Payable balance equals the sum of the balances in the subsidiary ledger is routine with a computerized system. Posting to subsidiary accounts is automatic. With daily sales stored electronically, computerized posting to the general ledger may occur daily.

Summary Problem for Your Review

Identify the journal in which each of the following transactions would be recorded. Use journal abbreviations: sales journal = S; cash receipts journal = CR; purchases journal = P; cash disbursements journal = CD; general journal = J.

Cash sale _____

Sale on account _____

Loaned cash on note receivable _____

Received cash on account _____

Purchase of building on long-term note payable ___

Paid cash on account _____

Cash purchase of inventory_____

Owner investment of cash in the business _____

Owner withdrawal of cash _____

Purchase of supplies on account _____

Receipt of cash on account _____

Adjusting entry for accrued salaries _____

Cash purchase of land _____

Credit purchase of inventory _____

Collection of interest revenue_____

Paid interest expense _____

Cash sale of equipment _____

Closing entries _____

Owner investment of land in the business _____

SOLUTION TO REVIEW PROBLEM

Cash sale _____ CR

Sale on account _____ S

Loaned cash on note receivable _____ CD

Received cash on account_____ CR

Purchase of building on long-term note payable __J

Paid cash on account _____ CD

Cash purchase of inventory_____ CD

Owner investment of cash in the business ____ CR

Owner withdrawal of cash _____ CD

Purchase of supplies on account _____ P

Receipt of cash on account_____ CR

Adjusting entry for accrued salaries _____ J

Cash purchase of land _____ CD

Credit purchase of inventory _____ P

Collection of interest revenue _____ CR

Paid interest expense _____ CD

Cash sale of equipment _____ CR

Closing entries_____ J

Owner investment of land in the business ___ J

Summary

An efficient accounting system combines *personnel*, *records*, and *procedures* to meet the information needs of a business. Processing accounting information means collecting data from source documents, organizing and recording the data, and communicating the information through the financial statements. Each business designs its accounting system to satisfy its particular information needs.

To be effective, the system must provide management with the information needed to *control* the organization. Also, the system must be *compatible* with the operations of the business. Further, businesses change, so the system must be *flexible* enough to handle new needs. Finally, the system must be *cost-beneficial*.

Computer data processing systems include *hardware*, *software*, and *personnel*. Hardware may consist of a mainframe computer or microcomputers. Computer operators use software to process data on-line or in batches.

Many businesses use special journals to account for repetitive transactions such as credit sales, cash receipts, credit purchases, and cash disbursements. Special journals cut down the amount of writing and number of postings required. Some businesses find it efficient to use source documents as journals. Computer systems can be programmed to possess all the special journal features described in this chapter. The major goal of system design is efficient, routine handling of high volumes of transactions. Special journals were originally created to meet that objective. Similarly, computer systems can store records of sales, cash receipts, purchases, and cash disbursements and print special journals as required.

Businesses use a subsidiary ledger to account for individual customer accounts receivable. The subsidiary ledger gives information on each customer's account. The total of the subsidiary ledger's individual account balances must match the balance in the Accounts Receivable control account in the general ledger. Companies may also keep a subsidiary ledger for accounts payable.

Self-Study Questions

Test your understanding of the chapter by marking the correct answer for each of the following questions:

1. Why does a jewelry store need a different kind of accounting system than that a physician uses? *(p. 256)*
   a. They have different kinds of employees.
   b. They have different kinds of journals and ledgers.
   c. They have different kinds of business transactions.
   d. They work different hours.

2. Which feature of an effective information system is most concerned with safeguarding assets? *(pp. 257–258)*
   a. Control   c. Flexibility
   b. Compatibility   d. Acceptable cost/benefit relationship

3. Which of the following components of a computerized accounting system is more likely to be developed in-house rather than by outsiders? Why? *(pp. 259–260)*
   a. Hardware, because of the desire for control
   b. Hardware, because of the desire for compatibility
   c. Software, because of the desire for control
   d. Software, because of the desire for compatibility

4. Special journals help most by *(pp. 261–262)*
   a. Limiting the number of transactions that have to be recorded
   b. Reducing the cost of operating the accounting system
   c. Improving accuracy in posting to subsidiary ledgers
   d. Easing the preparation of the financial statements

5. Galvan Company recorded 523 credit sale transactions in the sales journal. How many postings would be required if these transactions were recorded in the general journal? *(p. 266)*
   a. 523   c. 1,569
   b. 1,046   d. 2,092

6. Which two dollar-amount columns in the cash receipts journal will be used the most by a department store that makes half of its sales for cash and half on credit? *(p. 265)*
   a. Cash Debit and Sales Discounts Debit
   b. Cash Debit and Accounts Receivable Credit
   c. Cash Debit and Other Accounts Credit
   d. Accounts Receivable Debit and Sales Revenue Credit

7. Entries in the purchases journal are posted to the *(p. 270)*
   a. General ledger only
   b. General ledger and the Accounts payable ledger
   c. General ledger and the Accounts receivable ledger
   d. Accounts receivable ledger and the Accounts payable ledger

8. Every entry in the cash disbursements journal includes a *(p. 272)*
   a. Debit to Accounts Payable
   b. Debit to an Other Account
   c. Credit to Purchase Discounts
   d. Credit to Cash

9. Mazarotti Company has issued a debit memo. The related journal entry is *(p. 275)*

   a. Accounts Payable XXX
       Purchase Returns and Allowances XXX
   b. Purchase Returns and Allowances XXX
       Accounts Payable XXX
   c. Accounts Receivable XXX
       Sales Returns and Allowances XXX
   d. Sales Returns and Allowances XXX
       Accounts Receivable XXX

10. Balancing the ledgers at the end of the period is most closely related to *(p. 277)*
    a. Control
    b. Compatibility
    c. Flexibility
    d. Acceptable cost/benefit relationship

Answers to the self-Study Questions are at the end of the chapter.

Accounting Vocabulary

accounting information
  system *(p. 256)*
balancing the ledgers
  (p. 277)
batch processing *(p. 260)*
cash disbursements
  journal *(p. 271)*
cash receipts journal
  (p. 264)

control account *(p. 264)*
credit memo *(p. 273)*
debit memo *(p. 275)*
general journal *(p. 262)*
general ledger *(p. 262)*
hardware *(p. 259)*
internal controls *(p. 257)*
mainframe system
  (p. 259)

microcomputers *(p. 259)*
minicomputers *(p. 259)*
on-line processing
  (p. 260)
purchases journal *(p. 269)*
sales journal *(p. 262)*
software *(p. 259)*
subsidiary ledger *(p. 264)*

ASSIGNMENT MATERIAL _____

Questions

1. Briefly describe the two phases of implementing an accounting system.
2. Describe the basic information processing model of an accounting system.
3. What are the attributes of an effective information system? Briefly describe each attribute.
4. How does a mainframe computer system differ from a microcomputer system?
5. Identify three computer languages used with mainframes. Identify four software programs used with microcomputers.
6. Distinguish batch computer processing from on-line processing.
7. Describe an on-line computer processing operation for accounts receivable, sales, and inventory by a large retailer, such as Eaton's or The Bay.
8. Name four special journals used in accounting systems. For what type of transaction is each designed?
9. Describe the two advantages that special journals have over recording all transactions in the general journal.
10. What is a control account, and how is it related to a subsidiary ledger? Name two common control accounts.

11. Graff Company's sales journal has one amount column headed Accounts Receivable Dr. and Sales Revenue Cr. In this journal, 86 transactions are recorded. How many posting references appear in the journal? State what each posting reference represents.

12. Use S = Sales; CR = Cash Receipts; P = Purchases; CD = Cash Disbursements; and SRA = Sales Returns and Allowances to identify the special journal in which the following column headings appear. Some headings may appear in more than one journal.

Sales Revenue Cr._____   Invoice No. _____

Accounts Payable Dr. _____   Sales Discounts Dr. _____

Cash Dr._____   Other Accounts Cr. _____

Purchase Discounts Cr. _____   Purchases Dr. _____

Accounts Receivable Cr. _____   Cash Cr. _____

Cheque No._____   Credit Memo No._____

Other Accounts Dr. _____   Accounts Payable Cr. _____

Post. Ref. _____   Accounts Receivable Dr._____

13. Identify two ways a check mark (✔) is used as a posting reference in the cash receipts journal.

14. The accountant for Bannister Company posted all amounts correctly from the cash receipts journal to the general ledger. However, she failed to post three credits to customer accounts in the accounts receivable subsidiary ledger. How would this error be detected?

15. In posting from the cash receipts journal of Enfield Homebuilders, the accountant failed to post the amount of the sales revenue credit column. Identify two ways this error can be detected.

16. At what two times is posting done from a special journal? What items are posted at each time?

17. For what purposes are a credit memo and a debit memo issued? Who issues each document, the seller or the purchaser?

18. The following entry appears in the general journal:

Nov. 25   Sales Returns and Allowances........................   539

          Accounts Receivable — B. Goodwin..........   539

Prepare likely posting references.

19. Describe two ways to account for sales tax collected from customers.

20. What is the purpose of balancing the ledgers?

21. Posting from the journals of McKedrick Realty is complete. However, the total of the individual balances in the accounts payable subsidiary ledger does not equal the balance in the Accounts Payable control account in the general ledger. Does this necessarily indicate that the trial balance is out of balance? Give your reason.

22. Assume that posting is completed. The trial balance shows no errors, but the sum of the individual accounts payable does not equal the Accounts Payable control balance in the general ledger. What two errors could cause this problem?

23. Describe how some businesses use their documents as journals.

Exercises

Exercise 6-1   *Using the sales and cash receipts journals* **(L.O. 2, 4)**

The sales and cash receipts journals of CompuGraphics Company include the following entries:

Sales Journal

Date	Account Debited	Post. Ref.	Amount
Oct. 7	C. Carlson	✔	730
10	T. Muecke	✔	3,100
10	E. Lovell	✔	190
12	B. Goebel	✔	5,470
31	Total		9,490

Cash Receipts Journal

	Debits			Credits			
						Other Accounts	
Date	Cash	Sales Discounts	Accounts Receivable	Sales Revenue	Account Title	Post. Ref.	Amount
Oct. 16					C. Carlson	✔	
19					E. Lovell	✔	
24	100			100			
30					T. Muecke	✔	

CompuGraphics makes all sales on credit terms of 2/10 n/30. Complete the cash receipts journal for those transactions indicated. Also, total the journal and show that total debits equal total credits. Assume that each cash receipt was for the full amount of the receivable.

Exercise 6-2   *Classifying postings from the cash receipts journal* **(L.O. 3, 4)**

The cash receipts journal of Schwarzkopf, Inc. follows:

Cash Receipts Journal   Page 7

	Debits			Credits			
						Other Accounts	
Date	Cash	Sales Discounts	Accounts Receivable	Sales Revenue	Account Title	Post Ref.	Amount
Dec. 2	794	16	810		Swingline Co.	(a)	
9	1,291		1,291		Kamm, Inc.	(b)	
14	3,904			3,904		(c)	
19	4,480				Note Receivable	(d)	4,000
					Interest Revenue	(e)	480
30	314	7	321		L. M. Roose	(f)	
31	4,235			4,235		(g)	
31	15,018	23	2,422	8,139	Totals		4,480
	(h)	(i)	(j)	(k)			(l)

Required

Identify each posting reference (a) through (l) as (1) a posting to the general ledger as a column total, (2) a posting to the general ledger as an individual amount, (3) a posting to a subsidiary ledger account, or (4) an amount not posted.

Exercise 6-3   *Identifying transactions from postings to the accounts receivable ledger* **(L.O. 3)**

An account in the accounts receivable ledger of Tyler Pipe Company follows:

John Babcock

Date		Jrnl. Ref.	Dr.	Cr.	Balance	
May 1	....				703	(Dr)
10	....	S.5	1,180		1,883	(Dr)
15	....	J.8		191	1,692	(Dr)
21	....	CR.9		703	989	(Dr)

Required

Describe the three posted transactions.

Exercise 6-4   *Posting directly from sales invoices; balancing the ledgers* **(L.O. 3)**

Emery Printing Company uses its sales invoices as the sales journal and posts directly from them to the accounts receivable subsidiary ledger. During June, the company made the following sales on account:

Date	Invoice No.	Customer Name	Amount
June 6	256	Emily Jacques	$ 716
9	257	Forrest Ashworth	798
13	258	Paul Scott	550
16	259	Jan Childres	3,678
22	260	Emily Jacques	1,915
30	261	Jan Childres	800
		Total	$8,457

Required

1. Open general ledger accounts for Accounts Receivable and Sales Revenue and post to those accounts. Use dates and use June Sales as the journal reference in the ledger accounts.

2. Open customer accounts in the accounts receivable subsidiary ledger and post to those accounts. Use dates and use invoice numbers as journal references.

3. Balance the ledgers.

Exercise 6-5   *Recording purchase transactions in the general journal and purchases journal* **(L.O. 5)**

During April, Ippolito, Inc. completed the following credit purchase transactions:

April 4	Purchased inventory, $1,604, from McGraw Ltd.
7	Purchased supplies, $107, from Paine Corp.
19	Purchased equipment, $1,903, from Liston-Fry Co.
27	Purchased inventory, $2,210, from Milan, Inc.

Record these transactions first in the general journal — with explanations — and then in the purchases journal. Omit credit terms and posting references. Which procedure for recording transactions is quicker?

Exercise 6-6 *Posting from the purchases journal; balancing the ledgers* **(L.O. 3, 5)**

The purchases journal of Odegaard Company follows:

Purchases Journal Page 7

Date	Account Credited	Terms	Post. Ref.	Account Payable Cr.	Purchases Dr.	Supplies Dr.	Other Accounts Dr. Acct. Title	Post. Ref.	Amt. Dr.
Sept. 2	Schaeffer Company	n/30		1,100	1,100				
5	Rolf Office Supply	n/30		175		175			
13	Schaeffer Company	2/10 n/30		347	347				
26	Marks Equipment Company	n/30		916			Equipment		916
30	Totals			2,538	1,447	175			916

Required

1. Open general ledger accounts for Supplies, Equipment, Accounts Payable and Purchases. Post to these accounts from the purchases journal. Use dates and posting references in the ledger accounts.

2. Open accounts in the accounts payable subsidiary ledger for Schaeffer Company, Rolf Office Supply, and Marks Equipment Company. Post from the purchases journal. Use dates and journal references in the ledger accounts.

3. Balance the Accounts Payable control account in the general ledger with the total of the balances in the accounts payable subsidiary ledger.

Exercise 6-7 *Using the cash disbursements journal* **(L.O. 6)**

During July, Scott Paper had the following transactions:

July 3 Paid $792 on account to Hellenic Corp. net of an $8 discount.
6 Purchased inventory for cash, $817.
11 Paid $375 for supplies.
15 Purchased inventory on credit from Monroe Corporation, $774.
16 Paid $8,062 on account to LaGrange Associates; there was no discount.
21 Purchased furniture for cash, $960.
26 Paid $3,910 on account to Graff Software. The discount was $90.
31 Made a semiannual interest payment of $800 on a long-term note payable. The entire payment was for interest.

Required

1. Draw a cash disbursements journal similar to the one illustrated in this chapter. Omit the cheque number (Ch. No.) and posting reference (Post. Ref.) columns.

2. Record the transactions in the journal. Which transaction should not be recorded in the cash disbursements journal? In what journal does it belong?

3. Total the amount columns of the journal. Determine that the total debits equal the total credits.

Exercise 6-8   *Using business documents to record transactions* **(L.O. 6)**

The following documents describe two business transactions:

Invoice		
Date:	August 14, 19X0	
Sold to:	Zephyr Bicycle Shop	
Sold by:	Schwinn Company	
Terms:	2/10 n/30	

Items Purchased	Bicycles	
Quantity	**Price**	**Total**
4	$90	$360
2	70	140
5	60	300
Total		$800

Debit Memo		
Date:	August 20, 19X0	
Issued to:	Schwinn Company	
Issued by:	Zephyr Bicycle Shop	

Items Returneed	Bicycles	
Quantity	**Price**	**Total**
1	$90	$ 90
1	70	70
Total		$160

Reason:	Wrong sizes	

Use the general journal to record these transactions and Zephyr's cash payment on August 21. Record the transactions first on the books of Zephyr Bicycle Shop and, second, on the books of Schwinn Company, which makes and sells bicycles. Round to the nearest dollar. Explanations are not required. Set up your answer in the following format:

Date	Zephyr Journal Entries	Schwinn Journal Entries

Exercise 6-9   *Journalizing return and allowance transactions* **(L.O. 7)**

Medoff Company records returns and allowances in its general journal. During June, the company had the following transactions:

June 4	Issued credit memo to Fidelity, Inc., for inventory that Fidelity returned to us	$1,043
10	Received debit memo from B. R. Inman, who purchased merchandise from us on June 6. We shipped the wrong items, and Inman returned them to us	1,238
14	Issued debit memo for merchandise we purchased from Wyle Supply Company that was damaged in shipment. We returned the damaged inventory to Wyle	4,600
22	Received credit memo from Dietrich Distributing Co., from whom we purchased inventory on June 15. Dietrich discovered that they overcharged us	300

Required

Journalize the transactions in the general journal. Explanations are not required.

Exercise 6-10   *Detecting errors in the special journals* **(L.O. 2, 3, 4, 6)**

Financial MicroSystems uses special journals for credit sales, cash receipts, credit purchases and cash disbursements, and the subsidiary ledgers illustrated in this chapter. During March, the accountant made four errors. State the procedure that will detect each error described in the following:

a. Posted a $260 debit to Raoul Gortari's account in the accounts receivable subsidiary ledger as a $260 credit.

b. Added the Cash Credit column of the cash disbursements journal as $4,176 and posted this incorrect amount to the Cash account. The correct total was $4,026.

c. Recorded receipt of $500 on account from Eichler, Inc., as a credit to Accounts Receivable in the cash receipts journal. Failed to record "Eichler, Inc."

d. Failed to post the total of the Accounts Receivable Dr./Sales Revenue Cr. column of the sales journal.

Problems   (Group A)

Problem 6-1A   *Features of an effective information system* **(L.O. 1)**

Discuss the features of an effective information system. Write at least two sentences on each feature. Indicate which feature you believe is most important, and defend your position.

Problem 6-2A   *Using the sales, cash receipts and general journals* **(L.O. 2, 4, 7)**

The general ledger of Monterrey Telecommunications Company includes the following accounts:

Cash	111	Sales Revenue	411
Accounts Receivable	112	Sales Discounts	412
Notes Receivable	115	Sales Returns and Allowances	413
Equipment	141	Interest Revenue	417
Land	142	Gain on Sale of Land	418

All credit sales are on the company's standard terms of 2/10 n/30. Transactions in February that affected sales and cash receipts were as follows:

Feb. 1   Sold inventory on credit to G. M. Titcher, $900.
      5   As an accommodation to another company, sold new equipment for its cost of $770, receiving cash in this amount.
      6   Cash sales for the week totaled $2,107.
      8   Sold merchandise on account to McNair Co., $2,830.
      9   Sold land that cost $22,000 for cash of $40,000.
     11   Sold goods on account to Nickerson Builders, $6,099.
     11   Received cash from G. M. Titcher in full settlement of her account receivable from February 1.
     13   Cash sales for the week were $1,995.
     15   Sold inventory on credit to Montez and Montez, a partnership, $800.
     18   Issued credit memo to McNair Co. for $120 of merchandise returned to us by McNair. The goods we shipped were unsatisfactory.
     19   Sold merchandise on account to Nickerson Builders, $3,900.
     20   Cash sales for the week were $2,330.
     21   Received $1,200 cash from McNair Co. in partial settlement of its account receivable. There was no discount.
     22   Received cash from Montez and Montez for its account receivable from February 15.

Feb. 22 Sold goods on account to Diamond, Inc., $2,022.

25 Collected $4,200 on a note receivable, of which $200 was interest.

27 Cash sales for the week totaled $2,970.

27 Sold inventory on account to Littleton Corporation, $2,290.

28 Issued credit memo to Diamond, Inc. for $680 for damaged goods it returned to us.

28 Received $1,510 cash on account from McNair Co. There was no discount.

Required

1. Use the appropriate journal to record the above transactions in a single-column sales journal (omit the Invoice No. column), a cash receipts journal, and a general journal. Monterrey records sales returns and allowances in the general journal.

2. Total each column of the cash receipts journal. Determine that the total debits equal the total credits.

3. Show how postings would be made from the journals by writing the account numbers and check marks in the appropriate places in the journals.

Problem 6-3A *Correcting errors in the cash receipts journal* **(L.O. 4)**

The cash receipts journal below contains five entries. All five entries are for legitimate cash receipt transactions, but the journal contains some errors in recording the transactions. In fact, only one entry is correct, and each of the other four entries contains one error.

		Cash Receipts Journal			Page 5		
	Debits		**Credits**				
					Other Accounts		
Date	**Cash**	**Sales Discounts**	**Accounts Receivable**	**Sales Revenue**	**Account Title**	**P.R.**	**Amount**
7/5	611	34	645		Meg Davis	✔	
9			346	346	Carl Ryther	✔	
10	8,000			8,000	Land	19	
19	73						
31	1,060			1,133			
	9,744	34	991	9,479	Totals		
	(11)	(42)	(12)	(41)			(✔)

Total Dr. = $9,778   Total Cr. = $10,470

Required

1. Identify the correct entry.

2. Identify the error in each of the other four entries.

3. Using the following format, prepare a corrected cash receipts journal.

	Debits		**Credits**				
					Other Accounts		
Date	**Cash**	**Sales Discounts**	**Accounts Receivable**	**Sales Revenue**	**Account Title**	**P.R.**	**Amount**
7/5					Meg Davis	✔	
9					Carl Ryther	✔	
10					Land	19	
19							
31							
	10,090	34	991	1,133	Totals		8,000
	(11)	(42)	(12)	(41)			(✔)

Cash Receipts Journal   **Page 5**

Total Dr. = $10,124   Total Cr. = $10,124

Problem 6-4A   *Using the purchases, cash disbursements and general journals* **(L.O. 5, 6, 7)**

The general ledger of Greensboro Custom Frames includes the following accounts:

Cash	111	Purchases	511
Prepaid Insurance	116	Purchase Discounts	512
Supplies	117	Purchase Returns and Allowances	513
Equipment	149	Rent Expense	562
Accounts Payable	211	Utilities Expense	565

Transactions in March that affected purchases and cash disbursements were as follows:

Mar. 1   Paid monthly rent, debiting Rent Expense for $1,150.

3   Purchased inventory on credit from Broussard Ltd., $4,600. Terms were 2/15 n/45.

6   Purchased supplies on credit terms of 2/10 n/30 from Harmon Sales, $800.

7   Paid gas and water bills, $406.

10   Purchased equipment on account from Lancer Co., $1,050. Payment terms were 2/10 n/30.

11   Returned the equipment to Lancer Co. It was defective. We issued a debit memo for $1,050 and mailed a copy to Lancer.

12   Paid Broussard Ltd. the amount owed on the purchase of March 3.

12   Purchased inventory on account from Lancer Co., $1,100. Terms were 2/10 n/30.

14   Purchased inventory for cash, $1,585.

15   Paid an insurance premium, debiting Prepaid Insurance, $2,416.

16   Paid our account payable to Harmon Sales, less the discount, from March 6.

17   Paid electricity bill, $165.

20   Paid account payable to Lancer Co., less the discount, from March 12.

21   Purchased supplies on account from Master Supply, $754. Terms were net 30.

22   Purchased part of inventory on credit terms of 1/10 n/30 from Linz Brothers, $3,400.

26   Returned part of inventory purchased on March 22, to Linz Brothers, issuing a debit memo for $500.

31   Paid Linz Brothers the net amount owed from March 22, less the return on March 26.

Required

1. Use the appropriate journal to record the above transactions in a purchases journal, a cash disbursements journal (omit the Cheque No. column), and a general journal. Greensboro records purchase returns in the general journal.

2. Total each column of the special journals. Show that the total debits equal the total credits in each special journal.

3. Show how postings would be made from the journals by writing the account numbers and check marks in the appropriate places in the journals.

Problem 6-5A *Using the sales, cash receipts and general journals; posting and balancing the ledgers* **(L.O. 2, 3, 4, 7)**

During June, Boatright Custom Floors engaged in the following transactions:

June 1 Issued invoice no. 113 for credit sale to Aspen, Inc., $4,750. All credit sales are on the company's standard terms of 2/10 n/30.
    3 Collected cash of $882 from Leah Burnet in payment of her account receivable within the discount period.
    6 Cash sales for the week totaled $1,748.
    7 Collected note receivable, $3,500, plus 10 percent interest.
    9 Issued invoice no. 114 for sale on account to Wilder Co., $4,300.
    11 Received cash from Aspen Inc. in full settlement of its account receivable from the sale on June 1.
    13 Cash sales for the week were $2,964.
    14 Sold inventory on account to Goss Corp., issuing invoice no. 115 for $858.
    15 Issued credit memo to Goss Corp. for $154 of merchandise returned to us by Goss. Part of the goods we shipped were defective.
    19 Received cash from Wilder Co. in full settlement of its account receivable from June 9.
    20 Cash sales for the week were $2,175.
    22 Received cash of $2,904 from Goss Corp. on account from June 1.
    24 Sold supplies to an employee for cash of $106, which was Boatright's cost.
    27 Cash Sales for the week totaled $1,650.
    28 Issued invoice no. 116 to Thompson Co. for credit sale of inventory, $5,194.
    29 Sold goods on credit to Leah Burnett, issuing invoice no. 117 for $3,819.
    29 Issued credit memo to Leah Burnett for $1,397 of inventory she returned to us because it was unsatisfactory.

The general ledger of Boatright Custom Floors includes the following accounts and balances at June 1:

Account Number	Account Title	Balance	Account Number	Account Title	Balance
111	Cash	$4,217	411	Sales Revenue	
112	Accounts Receivable	3,804	412	Sales Discounts	
116	Supplies	1,290	413	Sales Returns and	
141	Notes Receivable	7,100		Allowances	
			418	Interest Revenue	

Boatright's accounts receivable subsidiary ledger includes the following accounts and balances at June 1: Aspen Inc., -0-; Leah Burnett, $900; Goss Corp., $2,904; Thompson Co., -0-; and Wilder Co., -0-.

Required

1. Open the general ledger and the accounts receivable subsidiary ledger accounts given, inserting their balances at June 1.

2. Record the above transactions on page 6 of a single-column sales journal, page 9 of a cash receipts journal and page 5 of a general journal, as appropriate. Boatright records sales returns and allowances in the general journal.

3. Post daily to the accounts receivable subsidiary ledger. On June 30 post to the general ledger.

4. Total each column of the special journals. Show that the total debits equal the total credits in each special journal.

5. Balance the total of the customer account balances in the accounts receivable subsidiary ledger against the Accounts Receivable balance in the general ledger.

Problem 6-6A *Using the purchases, cash disbursements and general journals; posting and balancing the ledgers* **(L.O. 3, 5, 6, 7)**

De Gortari Company's September transactions affecting purchases and cash disbursements were as follows:

Sept. 1 Issued cheque no. 406 to pay Canadair on account. De Gortari received a 2 percent discount for prompt payment.

1 Issued cheque no. 407 to pay quarterly rent, debiting Prepaid Rent for $2,100.

2 Issued cheque no. 408 to pay net amount owed to Lynn Co. De Gortari took a 3 percent discount.

5 Purchased supplies on credit terms of 2/10 n/30 from Westside Supply, $121.

7 Paid delivery expense, issuing cheque no. 409 for $739.

10 Purchased inventory on account from Hayden, Inc., $2,008. Payment terms were net 30.

11 Returned the inventory to Hayden, Inc., because it was defective. We issued a debit memo and mailed a copy to Hayden.

15 Issued cheque no. 410 for a cash purchase of inventory, $2,332.

15 Paid semimonthly payroll with cheque no. 411 for $1,224.

19 Issued cheque no. 412 to pay our account payable to Westside Supply from September 5.

21 Purchased inventory on credit terms of 2/10 n/30 from Lynn Co., $4,150.

24 Purchased machinery on credit terms of 2/10 n/30 from Canadair, $3,195.

26 Purchased supplies on account from Hayden, Inc., $467. Terms were net 30.

29 Issued cheque no. 413 to Lynn Co., paying the net amount owed from September 21.

30 Paid semimonthly payroll with cheque no. 414 for $1,224.

The general ledger of De Gortari Company includes the following accounts and balances at September 1:

Account Number	Account Title	Balance	Account Number	Account Title	Balance
111	Cash	$15,996	511	Purchases	
115	Prepaid Rent		512	Purchase Discounts	
116	Supplies	703	513	Purchase Returns	
151	Machinery	21,800		and Allowances	
211	Accounts Payable	2,700	521	Salary Expense	
			551	Delivery Expense	

De Gortari's accounts payable subsidiary ledger includes the following balances at September 1: Canadair, $1,200; Hayden, Inc., -0-; Lynn Co., $1,500; Westside Supply, -0-.

Required

1. Open the general ledger and the accounts payable subsidiary ledger accounts, inserting their balances at September 1.

2. Record the above transactions on page 10 of a purchases journal, page 5 of a cash disbursements journal, and page 8 of a general journal, as appropriate. De Gortari records purchase returns in the general journal.

3. Post daily to the accounts payable subsidiary ledger. On September 30 post to the general ledger.

4. Total each column of the special journals. Determine that the total debits equal the total credits in each special journal.

5. Balance the total of the creditor account balances in the accounts payable subsidiary ledger against the balance of the Accounts Payable control account in the general ledger.

Problem 6-7A   *Using all the journals, posting, and balancing the ledgers* **(L.O. 2, 3, 4, 5, 6, 7)**

Talbert Company completed the following transactions during July:

July 2 Issued invoice no. 913 for sale on account to N.J. Seiko, $4,100.
   3 Purchased inventory on credit terms of 3/10 n/60 from Chicosky Co., $2,467.
   5 Sold inventory for cash, $1,077.
   5 Issued cheque no. 532 to purchase furniture for cash, $2,185.
   8 Collected interest revenue of $1,775.
   9 Issued invoice no. 914 for sale on account to Bell Co., $5,550.
   10 Purchased inventory for cash, $1,143, issuing cheque no. 533.
   12 Received cash from N.J. Seiko in full settlement of her account receivable, net of a 2 percent discount, from the sale on July 2.
   13 Issued cheque no. 534 to pay Chicosky Co. the net amount owed from July 3.
   13 Purchased supplies on account from Manley, Inc., $441. Terms were net end-of-month.
   15 Sold inventory on account to M.O. Brown, issuing invoice no. 915 for $665.
   17 Issued credit memo to M.O. Brown for $665 for defective merchandise returned to us by Brown.
   18 Issued invoice no. 916 for credit sale to N.J. Seiko, $357.
   19 Received $5,439 from Bell Co. in full settlement of its account receivable, $5,550, from July 9.
   20 Purchased inventory on credit terms of net 30 from Sims Distributing, $2,047.
   22 Purchased furniture on credit terms of 3/10 n/60 from Chicosky Co., $645.
   22 Issued cheque no. 535 to pay for insurance coverage, debiting Prepaid Insurance for $1,000.
   24 Sold supplies to an employee for cash of $54, which was Talbert's cost.
   25 Issued cheque no. 536 to pay utilities, $453.
   28 Purchased inventory on credit terms of 2/10 n/30 from Manley, Inc., $675.
   29 Returned damaged inventory to Manley, Inc., issuing a debit memo for $675.

July 29 Sold goods on account to Bell Co., issuing invoice no. 917 for $496.
 30 Issued cheque no. 537 to pay Manley, Inc., the amount owed from July 13.
 31 Received $357 on account from N.J. Seiko on credit sale of July 18.
 31 Issued cheque no. 538 to pay monthly salaries, $3,619.

Required

1. Open the following general ledger accounts using the account numbers given:

Cash	111	Sales Returns and Allowances	413
Accounts Receivable	112	Interest Revenue	419
Supplies	116	Purchases	511
Prepaid Insurance	117	Purchase Discounts	512
Furniture	151	Purchase Returns	
Accounts Payable	211	and Allowances	513
Sales Revenue	411	Salary Expense	531
Sales Discounts	412	Utilities Expense	541

2. Open these accounts in the subsidiary ledgers:
 Accounts receivable subsidiary ledger: Bell Co., M.O. Brown, and N.J. Seiko.
 Accounts payable subsidiary ledger: Chicosky Co., Manley, Inc., and Sims Distributing.

3. Enter the transactions in a sales journal (page 7), a cash receipts journal (page 5), a purchases journal (page 10), a cash disbursements journal (page 8) and a general journal (page 6), as appropriate.

4. Post daily to the accounts receivable subsidiary ledger and the accounts payable subsidiary ledger. On July 31, post to the general ledger.

5. Total each column of the special journals. Show that the total debits equal the total credits in each special journal.

6. Balance the total of the customer account balances in the accounts receivable subsidiary ledger against Accounts Receivable in the general ledger. Do the same for the accounts payable subsidiary ledger and Accounts Payable in the general ledger.

(Group B)

Problem 6-1B *Components of a computer information system (L.O. 1)*

Discuss the interaction among the three components of a computer information system. Indicate which component is the most important in any information system — computer or manual — and defend your position.

Problem 6-2B *Using the sales, cash receipts and general journals (L.O. 2, 4, 7)*

The general ledger of Fuselier, Inc., includes the following accounts, among others:

Cash	11	Sales Revenue	41
Accounts Receivable	12	Sales Discounts	42
Notes Receivable	15	Sales Returns and Allowances	43
Supplies	16	Interest Revenue	47
Land	18		

All credit sales are on the company's standard terms of 2/10 n/30. Transactions in May that affected sales and cash receipts were as follows:

May 2   Sold inventory on credit to Dockery Co., $700.

   4   As an accommodation to a competitor, sold supplies at cost, $85, receiving cash.

   7   Cash sales for the week totaled $1,890.

   9   Sold merchandise on account to A. L. Prince, $7,320.

   10   Sold land that cost $10,000 for cash of $10,000.

   11   Sold goods on account to Sloan Electric, $5,104.

   12   Received cash from Dockery Co. in full settlement of its account receivable from May 2.

   14   Cash sales for the week were $2,106.

   15   Sold inventory on credit to the partnership of Wilkie & Blinn, $3,650.

   18   Issued credit memo to A. L. Prince for $600 of merchandise returned to us by Prince. The goods shipped were unsatisfactory.

   20   Sold merchandise on account to Sloan Electric, $629.

   21   Cash sales for the week were $990.

   22   Received $4,000 cash from A. L. Prince in partial settlement of his account receivable.

   25   Received cash from Wilkie & Blinn for its account receivable from May 15.

   25   Sold goods on account to Olsen, Inc., $720.

   27   Collected $5,125 on a note receivable, of which $125 was interest.

   28   Cash sales for the week totaled $3,774.

   29   Sold inventory on account to R. O. Bankston, $242.

   30   Issued credit memo to Olsen Inc., for $40 for inventory the company returned to us because it was damaged in shipment.

   31   Received $2,720 cash on account from A. L. Prince.

Required

1. Fuselier records sales returns and allowances in the general journal. Use the appropriate journal to record the above transactions in a single-column sales journal (omit the Invoice No. column), a cash receipts journal, and a general journal.

2. Total each column of the cash receipts journal. Show that the total debits equal the total credits.

3. Show how postings would be made from the journals by writing the account numbers and check marks in the appropriate places in the journals.

Problem 6-3B   *Correcting errors in the cash receipts journal (L.O. 4)*

The cash receipts journal below contains five entries. All five entries are for legitimate cash receipt transactions, but the journal contains some errors in recording the transactions. In fact, only one entry is correct, and each of the other four entries contains one error.

Required

1. Identify the correct entry.

2. Identify the error in each of the other four entries.

3. Using the following format, prepare a corrected cash receipts journal.

Cash Receipts Journal   Page 13

	Debits		Credits				
					Other Accounts		
Date	Cash	Sales Discounts	Accounts Receivable	Sales Revenue	Account Title	P.R.	Amount
5/6		500		500			
7	429	22			Mike Harrison	✔	451
12	2,160				Note Receivable	13	2000
					Interest Revenue	45	160
18				330			
24	1,100		770				
	3,689	522	770	830	Totals		2611
	(11)	(42)	(12)	(41)			(✔)

Total Dr. = $4,211   Total Cr. = $4,211

Cash Receipts Journal   Page 13

	Debits		Credits				
					Other Accounts		
Date	Cash	Sales Discounts	Accounts Receivable	Sales Revenue	Account Title	P.R.	Amount
5/6							
7					Mike Harrison	✔	
12					Note Receivable	13	
					Interest Revenue	45	
18							
24							
	4,189	22	1,221	830	Totals		2,160
	(11)	(42)	(12)	(41)			(✔)

Total Dr.=$4,211   Total Cr.=$4,211

Problem 6-4B   *Using the purchases, cash disbursements and general journals* (L.O. 5, 6, 7)

The general ledger of Schiffman, Inc., includes the following accounts:

Cash	11	Purchases		51
Prepaid Insurance	16	Purchase Discounts		52
Supplies	17	Purchase Returns and Allowances		53
Furniture	19	Rent Expense		56
Accounts Payable	21	Utilities Expense		58

Transactions in August that affected purchases and cash disbursements were as follows:

Aug. 1   Purchased inventory on credit from Wood Co., $3,400. Terms were 2/10 n/30.

Aug. 1   Paid monthly rent, debiting Rent Expense for $2,000.
      5   Purchased supplies on credit terms of 2/10 n/30 from Ross Supply, $450.
      8   Paid electricity bill, $588.
      9   Purchased furniture on account from A-1 Office Supply, $4,100. Payment terms were net 30.
     10   Returned the furniture to A-1 Office Supply. It was the wrong colour. Issued a debit memo for $4,100, and mailed a copy to A-1 Office Supply.
     11   Paid Wood Co. the amount owed on the purchase of August 1.
     12   Purchased furniture on account from Wynne, Inc., $4,400. Terms were 3/10 n/30.
     13   Purchased inventory for cash, $655.
     14   Paid a semiannual insurance premium, debiting Prepaid Insurance, $1,200.
     15   Paid our account payable to Ross Supply, from August 5.
     18   Paid gas and water bills, $196.
     21   Purchased inventory on credit terms of 1/10 n/45 from Software, Inc., $5,200.
     21   Paid account payable to Wynne, Inc. from August 12.
     22   Purchased supplies on account from Office Sales, Inc., $274. Terms were net 30.
     25   Returned part of the inventory purchased on August 21 to Software, Inc., issuing a debit memo for $1,200.
     31   Paid Software, Inc. the net amount owed from August 21, less the return, on August 25.

Required

1. Schiffman, Inc. records purchase returns in the general journal. Use the appropriate journal to record the above transactions in a purchases journal, a cash disbursements journal (omit the Cheque No. column), and a general journal.

2. Total each column of the special journals. Show that the total debits equal the total credits in each special journal.

3. Show how postings would be made from the journals by writing the account numbers and check marks in the appropriate places in the journals.

Problem 6-5B   *Using the sales, cash receipts and general journals; posting and balancing the ledgers (L.O. 2, 3, 4, 7)*

During April, Baldwin Wallace Co. had these transactions:

Apr. 2   Issued invoice no. 436 for credit sale to Vail Co., $5,200. All credit sales are made on the company's standard terms of 2/10 n/30.
      3   Collected cash from H.M. Burger in payment of his account receivable within the discount period.
      5   Cash sales for the week totaled $2,057.
      7   Collected note receivable, $2,000, plus interest of $210.
     10   Issued invoice no. 437 for sale on account to Van Allen Co., $1,850.
     11   Sold supplies to an employee for cash of $54, which was the cost.
     12   Received $5,096 cash from Vail Co. in full settlement of its account receivable from the sale of April 2.
     12   Cash sales for the week were $1,698.
     14   Sold inventory on account to Electro, Inc., issuing invoice no. 438 for $2,000.
     16   Issued credit memo to Electro, Inc., for $610 of merchandise returned to us by Electro. Part of the shipped goods were damaged.
     19   Cash sales for the week were $3,130.
     20   Received $1,813 from Van Allen Co. in full settlement of its account receivable, $1,850, from April 10.

Apr. 25   Received cash of $7,455 from Electro, Inc. on account.
     26   Cash sales for the week totaled $2,744.
     27   Issued invoice no. 439 to Clay Co. for credit sales of inventory, $3,640.
     28   Sold goods on credit to H.M. Burger, issuing invoice no. 440 for $2,689.
     30   Issued credit memo to H.M. Burger for $404 for inventory he returned
           to us because it was unsatisfactory.

The general ledger of Baldwin Wallace includes the following accounts and balances at April 1:

Account Number	Account Title	Balance	Account Number	Account Title	Balance
111	Cash............................	$ 3,579	411	Sales Revenue............	
112	Accounts Receivable	10,555	412	Sales Discounts..........	
116	Supplies.....................	1,756	413	Sales Returns and	
141	Notes Receivable......	5,000		Allowances	
			418	Interest Revenue	

Baldwin Wallace's accounts receivable subsidiary ledger includes the following accounts and balances at April 1: H.M. Burger, $3,100; Clay Co., -0-; Electro, Inc., $7,455; Vail Co., -0-; and Van Allen Co., -0-.

Required

1. Open the general ledger and the accounts receivable subsidiary ledger accounts given, inserting their balances at April 1.

2. Record the transactions on page 4 of a single-column sales journal, page 13 of a cash receipts journal, and page 7 of a general journal, as appropriate. Baldwin Wallace records sales returns and allowances in the general journal.

3. Post daily to the accounts receivable subsidiary ledger, and on April 30 post to the general ledger.

4. Show that the total debits equal the total credits in each special journal.

5. Balance the total of the customer account balances in the accounts receivable subsidiary ledger against the Accounts Receivable balance in the general ledger.

Problem 6-6B   *Using the purchases, cash disbursements and general journals; posting and balancing the ledgers (L.O. 3, 5, 6, 7)*

Noonan Company's November purchases and cash disbursement transactions are as follows:

Nov. 1   Issued cheque no. 346 to pay ENTEL Corp. in full on account. Noonan received a 2 percent discount for prompt payment.
      1   Issued cheque no. 347 to pay quarterly rent, debiting Prepaid Rent for $2,400.
      2   Issued cheque no. 348 to pay net amount owed to Arbor Machine Co., Noonan took a 2 percent discount.
      5   Purchased supplies on credit terms of 1/10 n/30 from Chin Music Co., $264.
      7   Paid delivery expense, issuing cheque no. 349 for $388.
     10   Purchased inventory on account from W. A. Mozart, Inc., $1,681. Payment terms were net 30.
     11   Returned the inventory to W. A. Mozart, Inc. It was defective. We issued a debit memo and mailed a copy to Mozart.
     15   Issued cheque no. 350 for a cash purchase of inventory, $2,889.

Nov. 15   Paid semimonthly payroll with cheque no. 351 for $1,595.

    19   Issued cheque no. 352 to pay our account payable to Chin Music Co. from November 5.

    21   Purchased inventory on credit terms of 2/10 n/30 from Arbor Machine Co., $3,250.

    24   Purchased machinery on credit terms of 2/10 n/30 from ENTEL Corp., $1,558.

    26   Purchased supplies on account from W. A. Mozart, Inc., $309. Terms were net 30.

    29   Issued cheque no. 353 to Arbor Machine Co., paying the net amount owed from November 21.

    30   Paid semimonthly payroll with cheque no. 354 for $1,595.

The general ledger of Noonan Company includes the following accounts and balances at November 1:

Account Number	Account Title	Balance	Account Number	Account Title	Balance
111	Cash	$17,674	511	Purchases	
115	Prepaid Rent	800	512	Purchase Discounts....	
116	Supplies	884	513	Purchase Returns	
151	Machinery	33,600		and Allowances......	
211	Accounts Payable...	3,750	521	Salary Expense	
			551	Delivery Expense	

Noonan's accounts payable subsidiary ledger includes the following balances at November 1: Arbor Machine Co., $650; Chin Music, Co., -0-; ENTEL Corp., $3,100; and W. A. Mozart, Inc., -0-.

Required

1. Open the general ledger and the accounts payable subsidiary ledger accounts given, inserting their balances at November 1.

2. Record the above transactions on page 3 of a purchases journal, page 8 of a cash disbursements journal, and page 12 of a general journal, as appropriate. Noonan records purchase returns in the general journal.

3. Post daily to the accounts payable subsidiary ledger. Post to the general ledger on November 30.

4. Total each column of the special journals. Show that the total debits equal the total credits in each special journal.

5. Balance the total of the creditor account balances in the accounts payable subsidiary ledger against the balance of the Accounts Payable control account in the general ledger.

Problem 6-7B   *Using all the journals, posting and balancing the ledgers   (L.O. 2, 3, 4, 5, 6, 7)*

Van Tright Sales Company had these transactions during January:

Jan. 2   Issued invoice no. 191 for sale on account to L. E. Wooten, $2,350.

    3   Purchased inventory on credit terms of 3/10 n/60 from Delwood Plaza, $1,900.

    4   Sold inventory for cash, $808.

    5   Issued cheque no. 473 to purchase furniture for cash, $1,087.

    8   Collected interest revenue of $440.

    9   Issued invoice no. 192 for sale on account to Krotez, Co., $6,250.

Jan. 10　Purchased inventory for cash, $776, issuing cheque no. 474.

12　Received cash from L. E. Wooten in full settlement of her account receivable, net of a 2 percent discount, from the sale of January 2.

13　Issued cheque no. 475 to pay Delwood Plaza net amount owed from January 3.

13　Purchased supplies on account from Havrilla Corp., $689. Terms were net end-of-month.

15　Sold inventory on account to J. R. Wakeland, issuing invoice no. 193 for $743.

17　Issued credit memo to J. R. Wakeland for $743 for defective merchandise returned to us by Wakeland.

18　Issued invoice no. 194 for credit sale to L. E. Wooten, $1,825.

19　Received cash from Krotez Co. in full settlement of its account receivable from January 9.

20　Purchased inventory on credit terms of net 30 from Jasper Sales, $2,150.

22　Purchased furniture on credit terms of 3/10 n/60 from Delwood Plaza, $775.

22　Issued cheque no. 476 to pay for insurance coverage, debiting Prepaid Insurance for $1,345.

24　Sold supplies to an employee for cash of $86, which was Van Tright's cost.

25　Issued cheque no. 477 to pay utilities, $388.

28　Purchased inventory on credit terms of 2/10 n/30 from Havrilla Corp., $421.

29　Returned damaged inventory to Havrilla Corp., issuing a debit memo for $421.

29　Sold goods on account to Krotez Co., issuing invoice no. 195 for $567.

30　Issued cheque no. 478 to pay Havrilla Corp. on account from January 13.

31　Received cash on account from L. E. Wooten on credit sale of January 18.

31　Issued cheque no. 479 to pay monthly salaries, $3,200.

Required

1. Open the following general ledger accounts using these account numbers:

Cash	111	Sales Returns and Allowances	413
Accounts Receivable	112	Interest Revenue	419
Supplies	116	Purchases	511
Prepaid Insurance	117	Purchase Discounts	512
Furniture	151	Purchase Returns	
Accounts Payable	211	and Allowances	513
Sales Revenue	411	Salary Expense	531
Sales Discounts	412	Utilities Expense	541

2. Open these accounts in the subsidiary ledgers. Accounts receivable subsidiary ledger: Krotez, Co., J. R. Wakeland, and L. E. Wooten. Accounts payable subsidiary ledger: Delwood Plaza, Havrilla Corp., and Jasper Sales.

3. Enter the transactions in a sales journal (page 8), a cash receipts journal (page 3), a purchases journal (page 6), a cash disbursements journal (page 9), and a general journal (page 4), as appropriate.

4. Post daily to the accounts receivable subsidiary ledger and to the accounts payable subsidiary ledger. On January 31, post to the general ledger.

5. Total each column of the special journals. Show that the total debits equal the total credits in each special journal.

6. Balance the total of the customer account balances in the accounts receivable subsidiary ledger against Accounts Receivable in the general ledger. Do the same for the accounts payable subsidiary ledger and Accounts Payable in the general ledger.

Extending Your Knowledge

Decision Problems

1. Reconstructing transactions from amounts posted to the accounts receivable ledger (L.O. 2, 3, 4)

A fire destroyed some accounting records of Roemer Company. The owner, Charles Roemer, asks for your help in reconstructing the records. He needs to know the beginning and ending balances of Accounts Receivable and the credit sales and cash receipts on account from customers during March. All Roemer Company sales are on credit, with payment terms of 2/10 n/30. All cash receipts on account reached Roemer within the 10-day discount period, except as noted. The only accounting record preserved from the fire is the accounts receivable subsidiary ledger, which follows:

Grant Adams

Date	Item	Jrnl. Ref.	Debit	Credit	Balance
Mar. 8		S6	2,178		2,178
16		S.6	903		3,081
18		CR.8		2,178	903
19		J.5		221	682
27		CR.8		682	-0-

Lou Gross

Date	Item	Jrnl. Ref.	Debit	Credit	Balance
Mar. 1	Balance				1,096
5		CR.8		1,096	-0-
11		S.6	396		396
21		CR.8		396	-0-
24		S.6	1,944		1,944

Norris Associates

Date	Item	Jrnl. Ref.	Debit	Credit	Balance
Mar. 1	Balance				883
15		S.6	2,635		3,518
29		CR.8		883*	2,635

---

* Cash receipt did not occur within the discount period.

Suzuki, Inc.

Date	Item	Ref. Jrnl.	Debit	Credit	Balance
Mar. 1	Balance				440
3		CR.8		440	-0-
25		S.6	3,655		3,655
29		S.6	1,123		4,778

2. Understanding an accounting system (L.O. 1, 3, 6)

The external auditor must ensure that the amounts shown on the balance sheet for Accounts Receivable represent actual amounts that customers owe the company. Each customer account in the accounts receivable subsidiary ledger must represent an actual credit sale to the person indicated, and the customer's balance must not have been collected. This auditing concept is called *validity,* or *validating* the accounts receivable.

The auditor must also ensure that all amounts that the company owes are included in Accounts Payable and other liability accounts. For example, all credit purchases of inventory made by the company (and not yet paid) should be included in the balance of the Accounts Payable account. This auditing concept is called *completeness.*

Required

Suggest how an auditor might test a customer's account receivable balance for validity. Indicate how the auditor might test the balance of the Accounts Payable account for completeness.

Ethical Issue

On a recent trip to Poland, Randolph Buchholz, sales manager of Microelectronic Devices, took his wife at company expense. Melanie Johnson, vice-president of sales and Buchholz's boss, thought his total travel and entertainment expenses of $10,000 seemed excessive. However, Johnson approved the reimbursement because she owed Buchholz a favor. Johnson, well aware that the company president routinely reviewed all expenses recorded in the cash disbursements journal, had the accountant record the expenses of Buchholz's wife in the general journal as follows:

Sales Promotion Expense..	3,500	
Cash		3,500

Required

1. Does recording the transaction in the general journal rather than in the cash disbursements journal affect the amounts of cash and total expenses reported in the financial statements?
2. Why did Ms. Johnson want this transaction recorded in the general journal?
3. What is the ethical issue in this situation? What role does accounting play?

Answers to Self-Study Questions

1. c
2. a
3. d
4. b
5. c [523 × 3 (one debit, one credit, and one to the accounts receivable ledger) = 1,569]

6. b
7. b
8. d
9. a
10. a

Chapter 7

Internal Control
and Cash Transactions

Canadian businesses lose an estimated $20 billion a year from internal theft. Don Holmes, a forensic accountant with Ernst and Young, Chartered Accountants, talks about some real frauds which have occurred in Canada recently.

"A purchasing agent for a large contractor managed to steal supplies from his employer before the employer even had them. The contractor had annual sales of $200 million and spent about half as much on construction materials, so there was lots of scope for the crook to operate. He would place orders for $12,000 worth of materials, which would be recorded as having been dropped off overnight at a job site. In fact, he had an arrangement with an associate through another contractor who would pick the stuff up and sell it on the black market. In some cases, the associate may have sold supplies to the purchasing agent's own employer, who thus had to pay for them a second time."

By the time the purchasing agent was caught, after sixteen months of operating the scam, he had bilked the company of more than $300,000.

As you read this chapter, consider whether this theft could have been prevented by some type of internal control, or whether businesses are forever vulnerable to dishonest employees.

Source: Daniel Stoffman, "How to Steal from the Company," *Canadian Business* (June 1991), pp. 56-58, 60.

LEARNING OBJECTIVES

After studying this chapter, you should be able to

1 Define internal control

2 Identify the characteristics of effective internal control

3 Prepare a bank reconciliation and related journal entries

4 Apply internal controls to cash receipts

5 Apply internal controls to cash disbursements

6 Account for petty cash transactions

7 Use the voucher system

OBJECTIVE 1

Define internal control

Among all the receivables, payables, inventory, and capital assets, it is easy to lose sight of the basics of running a business. Cash is the scarcest asset, and having enough of it to weather hard times and expand is the secret of success. How does a business protect its cash and other assets? With internal controls.

You learned in Chapter 6 that a well-designed accounting system helps managers control the business. Chapter 7 looks in more detail at internal control and accounting for cash. Section 5200.03 of the *CICA Handbook* states that **internal control** consists of the policies and procedures established and maintained by management to assist in achieving its objective of ensuring the orderly and efficient conduct of a company's business. Appendix C to Sections 5200–5220 indicates that management's internal control objectives are

1. Optimizing the use of resources.
2. Preventing and detecting error and fraud.
3. Safeguarding assets.
4. Maintaining reliable control systems.

A company's internal control consists of two elements: (1) the control environment, which in essence consists of the actions, policies, and procedures that reflect the attitudes of top management and the owners of a company about control and its importance to the entity; and (2) the control systems which can be divided into two components — the accounting system and the control procedures. The accounting system refers to the policies and procedures that pertain to the collection, recording and processing of data and reporting information, while the control procedures pertain to enhancing the reliability of the data and information.

This chapter focuses on internal controls that relate to the safeguarding of cash and the controls systems that promote the accuracy of records of cash transactions.

During the 1970s and 1980s, many illegal payments, embezzlements, and other criminal business practices came to light. Some very large and otherwise well run companies in Canada and the United States discovered that their internal control systems were flawed, permitting these illegal activities. Concerned citizens wanted to know why the companies' internal controls had failed to alert management that these crimes had been committed. Formerly, internal control was viewed as an auditing consideration. These days, management has become more concerned about internal control, and usually mentions it specifically in the management statement included in the annual report (Exhibit 7-1). In March, 1992, the sections of the *CICA Handbook* concerned with the external auditor's evaluation of and reliance on internal control were substantially revised to focus more closely on management's role and responsibilities.

Wise managers have always been interested in internal control, and many businesses have strong internal control as a result. However, the concerns of the 1970s

EXHIBIT 7-1 *Excerpts from Management Statements of TransCanada PipeLines Limited and Four Seasons Hotels Inc.*

Report of Management
TransCanada PipeLines Limited

The accompanying consolidated financial statements included in the Annual Report are the responsibility of management and have been approved by the Board of Directors of the Company. . . .

The Board of Directors has appointed an Audit Committee consisting solely of directors who are not officers of the Company to review with management and the independent auditors the annual consolidated financial statements of the Company prior to submission to the Board of Directors for final approval. The Audit Committee also meets periodically during the year with management and the internal and external auditors either individually or as a group.

Internal and external auditors have free access to the Audit Committee without obtaining prior management approval.

The independent auditors, Peat Marwick, have been appointed by the shareholders to express an opinion as to whether the consolidated financial statements present fairly the Company's financial position, operating results and changes in financial position in conformity with generally accepted accounting principles. . . .

Management's Responsibility for Financial Reporting
Four Seasons Hotels Inc.

The management of Four Seasons Hotels Inc. is responsible for the preparation and integrity of the financial statements and related financial information of the Company. The consolidated financial statements, notes and other financial information included in the Annual Report were prepared in accordance with accounting principles generally accepted in Canada. The statements also include estimated amounts based on informed judgement of current and future events. These estimates are made with appropriate consideration of the materiality of the amounts involved. The financial information presented elsewhere in the Annual Report is consistent with that in the financial statements.

Management maintains a system of internal controls and budgeting procedures which are designed to provide reasonable assurance that assets are safeguarded and transactions are executed and recorded in accordance with management's authorization. To augment the internal control system, the Company maintains a comprehensive program of internal audits covering significant aspects of the Company's operations.

The Company's Audit Committee is appointed by the Board of Directors annually. The Committee meets with management and with the independent auditors (who have free access to the Audit Committee) to satisfy itself that each group is properly discharging its responsibilities and to review the financial statements and the independent auditors' report. The Audit Committee reports its findings to the Board of Directors for their consideration in approving the financial statements for issuance to the shareholders.

Peat Marwick, the independent auditors appointed by the shareholders of the Company, have examined the financial statements in accordance with generally accepted auditing standards and their report follows.

Isadore Sharp,
Chairman and President

H. Roger Garland,
Executive Vice-President
Development, Finance and
Administration

and 1980s have further increased management's interest. Often, the audit committees[1] of the board of directors has responsibility for accepting reports on internal control from both the internal and external auditors. Note the statements to that effect in the management report from TransCanada PipeLines in Exhibit 7-1, and the discussion of the role of the audit committee in the financial statements of Schneider Corporation in Appendix C. If the auditors report problems with some or all of the internal controls to the audit committee, that body can suggest to the full board of directors that management be required to make necessary changes to the internal controls in question.

Exhibit 7-1 presents excerpts from two fairly typical reports from management by TransCanada PipeLines Limited and Four Seasons Hotels Inc. TransCanada PipeLines' report, taken from a recent annual report, indicates that management is responsible for the financial statements. It points out that the audit committee is independent, that is, none of its members are officers or part of management. The audit committee meets ". . . periodically with management and the internal and external auditors either independently or in a group." Note that the internal and external auditors report directly to the audit committee and do not need management approval to do so. The responsibilities of the external auditors, Peat Marwick, are described.

The management report issued by Four Seasons Hotels Inc. included in a recent annual report is signed by the chairman and president and by the executive vice-president. Note in the second paragraph the statement of management's responsibility for internal control and of how management discharges that responsibility. The relationship between the audit committee and the auditors is explained, as is the case with TransCanada PipeLines.

OBJECTIVE 2

Identify the characteristics of effective internal control

Effective Internal Control

Whether the business is Air Canada or a local department store, its internal control, if effective, has the following noteworthy characteristics.

Competent and Reliable Personnel

Employees should be *competent* and *reliable*. Paying top salaries to attract top-quality employees, training them to do their job well and supervising their work all help to build a competent staff. A business adds flexibility to its staffing by rotating employees through various jobs. If one employee is sick or on vacation, a second employee is already trained to step in and do the job.

Rotating employees through various jobs also promotes reliability. Employees are less likely to handle their jobs improperly if they know that their misconduct may come to light when a second employee takes over the job. This same reasoning leads businesses to require that employees take an annual vacation. A second employee, stepping in to handle the position, may uncover any wrongdoing.

Assignment of Responsibilities

In a business with effective internal control, no important duty is overlooked. A model of such assignment of responsibilities appears in the corporate organizational chart in Exhibit 7-2.

---

[1] An audit committee is a committee of the board of directors of a corporation. Incorporating acts such as the *Canada Business Corporations Act* require that a corporation has an audit committee, and that a majority of the members of the audit committee be independent of the company (that is, that they not be officers or employees of the company). In many companies, both the internal and external auditors report to the audit committee (see Exhibit 7-2).

EXHIBIT 7-2 *Organization Chart of a Corporation*

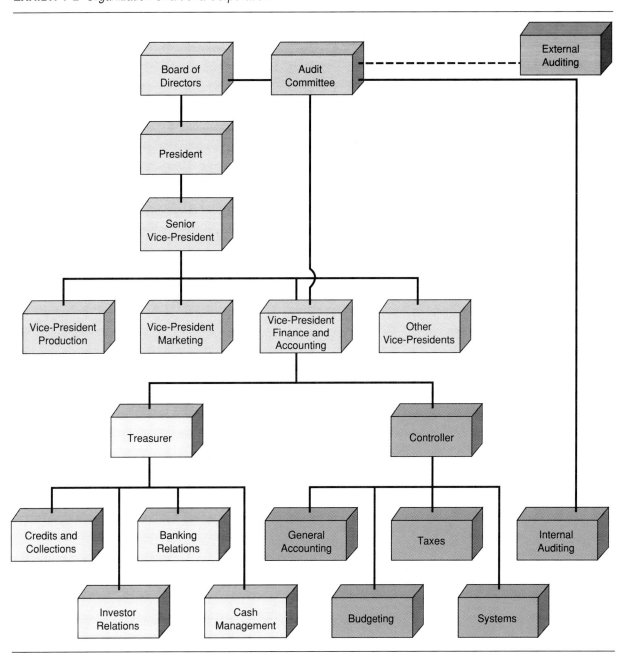

Notice that the corporation has a vice-president of finance and accounting. Two other officers, the treasurer and the controller, report to the vice-president. The treasurer is responsible for cash management. The controller performs accounting duties.

Within this organization, the controller may be responsible for approving invoices for payment and the treasurer may actually sign the cheques. Working under the controller, one accountant may be responsible for property taxes, a second for income taxes and a third for sales tax and the GST. In sum, all duties are clearly defined and assigned to individuals who bear responsibility for carrying them out.

Proper Authorization

An organization generally has a written set of rules that outlines approved procedures. Any deviation from standard policy requires *proper authorization*. For example, managers or assistant managers of retail stores must approve customer cheques for amounts above the store's usual limit. Likewise, deans or department chairpersons of colleges and universities must give the authorization for a first- or second-year student to enroll in courses otherwise restricted to upper-year students.

Separation of Duties

Smart management divides the responsibilities for transactions between two or more people or departments. Separation of duties limits chances for fraud and promotes the accuracy of accounting records. This crucial and often neglected component of internal control may be subdivided into four parts.

1. *Separation of operations from accounting.* The entire accounting function should be completely separate from operating departments so that objective records may be kept. For example, product inspectors, not machine operators, should count units produced by a manufacturing process. Accountants, not salespersons, should keep inventory records. Observe the separation of accounting from production and marketing in Exhibit 7-2.

2. *Separation of the custody of assets from accounting.* To reduce temptation and fraud, the accountant should not handle cash and the cashier should not have access to ledger accounts. If one employee had both cash-handling and accounting duties, this person would be able to steal cash and conceal the theft by making a bogus entry on the books. We see this component of internal control in the organization chart in Exhibit 7-2. Note that the treasurer has custody of cash and the controller accounts for cash. Neither person has both responsibilities.

Warehouse employees with no accounting duties should control inventory. If they were allowed to account for the inventory, they could steal it and write it off as obsolete. In a computerized accounting system, a person with custody of assets should not have access to the computer programs. Similarly, the programmer should not have access to tempting assets like cash.

3. *Separation of the authorization of transactions from the custody of related assets.* If possible, persons who authorize transactions should not handle the related asset. For example, the same individual should not authorize the payment of a supplier's invoice and also sign the cheque to pay the invoice. With both duties, the person can authorize payments to him- or herself and then sign the cheques. By separating these duties, only legitimate bills get paid.

For another example, an individual who handles cash receipts should not have the authority to write off accounts receivable. (Businesses that sell on credit declare certain of their accounts receivable as uncollectible, realizing that these receivables will never be collected. Chapter 8 looks at uncollectible accounts receivable in detail.) Suppose the company shown in Exhibit 7-2 employs V. Saucier. He works in credits and collections under the treasurer, and handles cash receipts from customers.

Among the business's accounts receivable in the subsidiary ledger is Gina Kowalski's $500 balance. Saucier could label Kowalski's account as uncollectible, and the business might cease trying to collect from her. When Kowalski mails a $500 cheque to pay off her balance, Saucier forges the endorsement and pockets the money. Kowalski, of course, has no reason to notify anyone else at the business that she has mailed a cheque so that Saucier's crime goes undetected. This theft would have been avoided by denying Saucier either the access to cash receipts or the authority to declare accounts uncollectible.

4. *Separation of duties within the accounting function.* Independent performance of various phases of accounting helps minimize errors and the opportunities for fraud.

For example, different accountants in a manual system keep the cash receipts and cash disbursements journals. In a computer system, the employees who enter data into the computer do not authorize accounts to be written off.

Internal and External Audits

It is not economically feasible for auditors to examine all the transactions during a period. They must rely to some degree on the accounting system to produce accurate accounting records. To gauge the reliability of the company's accounting system, auditors evaluate its internal control. Auditors also spot weaknesses in internal control and recommend corrections. Auditors offer objectivity in their reports, while managers, immersed in operations, may overlook the weaknesses.

Audits are internal or external. Exhibit 7-2 shows *internal auditors* as employees of the business reporting directly to the audit committee. Some organizations have internal auditors report directly to the vice-president. Throughout the year, they audit various segments of the organization. *External auditors* are not employees of the business. These people, employed by a public accounting firm, are hired by an entity as independent outsiders to audit the entity as a whole. The external auditors are and the internal auditors should be independent of the operations they examine. Sometimes external auditors and internal auditors examine the same parts of the organization, but often they are concerned with different aspects of it and/or their approaches may differ.

An auditor may find that an employee has both cash-handling and cash-accounting duties, or may learn that a cash shortage has resulted from lax efforts to collect accounts receivable. In such cases, the auditor suggests improvements. Auditors' recommendations assist the business in running smoothly and economically.

Documents and Records

Business *documents and records* vary considerably, from source documents like sales invoices and purchase orders to special journals and subsidiary ledgers. Specially designed records, for example, the special journals discussed in the last chapter, speed the flow of paper work and enhance efficiency.

Documents should be prenumbered and access to them controlled. A gap in the numbered sequence calls attention to a missing document.

Prenumbering cash sale receipts discourages theft by the cashier because the copy retained by the cashier, which lists the amount of sale, can be checked against the actual amount of cash received. If receipts are not prenumbered, the cashier can destroy the copy and pocket the cash sale amount. However, if receipts are prenumbered, the missing copy can easily be identified.

Limitations of Internal Control _____

Most internal control measures can be overcome. Systems designed to thwart an *individual* employee's fraud may be beaten by two or more employees working as a team — colluding — to defraud the firm. Consider a movie theatre. The ticket seller takes in the cash, and the ticket taker tears the tickets in half so that they cannot be reused, retaining the torn ticket stubs. But suppose they put a scheme together in which the ticket seller pockets the cash for ten tickets and the ticket taker pockets ten stubs. Who would catch them? The manager could take the additional control measure of counting the people in the theatre and matching that figure against the number of ticket stubs retained. But that takes time away from other duties. As you see, the stricter the internal control, the more expensive it becomes.

Internal control that is too complex may strangle people in red tape. Efficiency and control are hurt rather than helped. The more complicated the system, the more time and money it takes to maintain. Just how tight should internal control be? Managers must make sensible judgments. Investments in internal control must be judged in the light of costs and benefits.

The Bank Account as a Control Device

Keeping cash in a *bank account* is part of internal control because banks have established practices for safeguarding cash. Banks also provide depositors with detailed records of cash transactions. To take full advantage of these control features, the business should deposit all cash receipts in the bank account and make all cash payments through it (except petty cash disbursements, which we look at later). We now discuss banking records and documents.

For many businesses, cash is the most important asset. After all, cash is the most common means of exchange, and most transactions ultimately affect cash.

Cash is the most tempting asset for theft. Consequently, internal controls for cash are more elaborate than for most other assets. The rest of this chapter describes internal control over cash. We consider cash to be not just paper money and coins but also cheques, money orders and money kept in bank accounts. Cash does not include stamps because they are supplies, nor IOUs payable to the business because they are receivables.

Signature Card   Banks require each person authorized to transact business through an account in that bank to sign a *signature card*. The bank compares the signatures on documents against the signature card to protect the bank and the depositor against forgery.

Deposit Ticket   Banks supply standard forms as *deposit tickets* or *deposit slips*. The customer fills in the dollar amount and date of deposit. The customer retains either (1) a duplicate copy of the deposit ticket, or (2) a deposit receipt, depending on the bank's practice, as proof of transaction.

Cheque   To draw money from an account, the depositor writes a **cheque**, which is a document that instructs the bank to pay the designated person or business the specified amount of money. There are three parties to a cheque: the *maker*, who signs the cheque; the *payee*, to whose order the cheque is drawn; and the *bank* on which the cheque is drawn.

Most cheques are serially numbered and preprinted with the name and address of the depositor and the bank. The cheques have places for the date, the name of the payee, the signature of the maker, and the amount. The bank name and identification number and the depositor account number are usually imprinted in magnetic ink for machine processing.

Exhibit 7-3 shows a cheque drawn on the bank account of Business Research, Inc. The cheque has two parts: the cheque itself and the remittance advice. The remittance advice, an optional attachment, tells the payee the reason for payment. The maker (Business Research) retains a carbon copy of the cheque for its recording in the cheque register (cash disbursements journal). Note that internal controls at Business Research require two signatures on cheques.

Bank Statement   Most banks send monthly **bank statements** to their depositors. The statement shows the account's beginning and ending balance for the period and lists the month's transactions. Included with the statement are the maker's *cancelled cheques*, those cheques that have been paid by the bank on behalf of the depositor. The bank statement also lists any other deposits and changes in the account. Deposits appear in chronological order, and cheques also appear in chronological order cashed by the bank.

EXHIBIT 7-3 *Cheque with Remittance Advice*

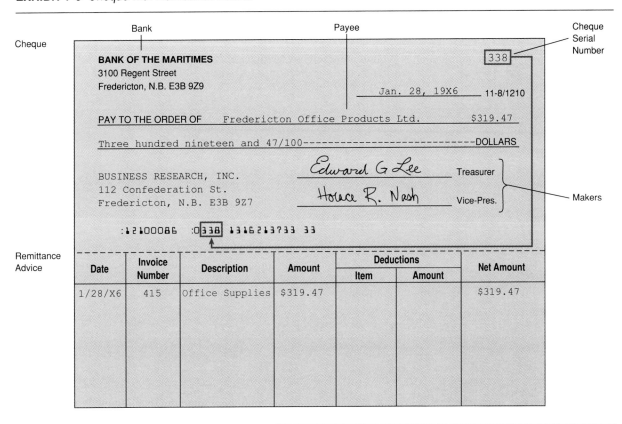

Exhibit 7-4 is the bank statement of Business Research, Inc. for the month ended January 31, 19X6. At many banks, some depositors receive their statements on the first of the month, some on the second, and so on. This spacing eliminates the clerical burden of supplying all the statements at one time. Most businesses, like Business Research, receive their bank statement for the calendar month.

Bank Reconciliation   There are two records of the business's cash: its Cash account in its own general ledger, and the bank statement which tells the actual amount of cash the business has in the bank. The balance in the business's Cash account rarely equals the balance shown on the bank statement.

The books and the bank statement may show different amounts but both are correct. The difference arises because of a time-lag in recording certain transactions. When a firm writes a cheque, it immediately credits its Cash account. The bank, however, will not subtract the amount of the cheque until the cheque reaches it for payment. This may take days, even weeks, if the payee waits to cash the cheque. Likewise, the business debits Cash for all cash receipts, and it may take a day or so for the bank to add this amount to the business's bank balance.

Good internal control means knowing where a company's money comes from, how it is spent, and what the current cash balance is. How else can the accountant keep the accurate records that management needs to make informed decisions? The accountant must report the correct cash amount on the balance sheet. To ensure accuracy, the accountant explains the reasons for the difference between the firm's records and bank statement figures on a certain date. This process is called the **bank reconciliation**. Properly done, the bank reconciliation assures that all cash transactions have been accounted for, and that bank and book records of cash are correct. Internal control is enhanced if an independent person reviews the reconciliation.

EXHIBIT 7-4 *Bank Statement*

THE TORONTO-DOMINION BANK
MONEY BUILDER ACCOUNT

SHOPPING CONCOURSE BRANCH
TORONTO DOMINION CENTRE
TORONTO, ONTARIO   M5K 1A2   **Tel:**

1024/ 0/ 5

MS TONI B   CROWN
27 SENECA ST
NORTH YORK, ON

M2P 1W9

For Current Interest Rates:	**Statement of Account**		**Statement From - To**
CALL TD GREEN INFOLINE 1-800-387-2092 QUEBEC 1-800-387-1500 TORONTO 982-7730	**Branch No.** **Account No.** 1024 0692-3103424		MAR 2/93 – MAR 31/93 **Page** 1 **of** 1

DESCRIPTION	W/F	WITHDRAWALS	DEPOSITS	DATE	BALANCE
BALANCE FORWARD				MAR02	.00
OPEN ACCOUNT			5,000.00	MAR02	
GREEN MACH DEPOSIT			500.00	MAR02	
GREEN MACH DEPOSIT			500.00	MAR02	
PAYROLL DEPOSIT E			500.00	MAR02	
PURCHASE	0.45	500.00		MAR02	
PURCHASE	0.45	500.00		MAR02	
CHQ #100 -30000507	0.60	1.00		MAR02	
CHQ #200 -30000407	0.60	2.00		MAR02	
GREEN MACH WITHDRAWL	0.45	500.00		MAR02	
GREEN MACH WITHDRAWL	0.45	500.00		MAR02	
INTERAC NETWORK WD	0.45	500.00		MAR02	
INTERAC NETWORK WD	0.45	500.00		MAR02	
INTERAC NETWORK WD	0.45	500.00		MAR02	2,997.00
GREEN MACH DEPOSIT			500.00	MAR04	
GREEN MACH DEPOSIT			500.00	MAR04	
PAYROLL DEPOSIT E			500.00	MAR04	
PURCHASE	0.45	500.00		MAR04	
PURCHASE	0.45	500.00		MAR04	
CHQ #100 -30000407	0.60	1.00		MAR04	
CHQ #200 -30000407	0.60	2.00		MAR04	
GREEN MACH WITHDRAWL	0.45	500.00		MAR04	
GREEN MACH WITHDRAWL	0.45	500.00		MAR04	
INTERAC NETWORK WD	0.45	500.00		MAR04	
INTERAC NETWORK WD	0.45	500.00		MAR04	
INTERAC NETWORK WD	0.45	500.00		MAR04	994.00
INTEREST CREDIT			.49	MAR31	
WITHDRAWAL FEES		1.80		MAR31	
INTERAC FEES 6X1.00		6.00		MAR31	986.69
		7,013.80	8,000.49		

Withdrawal Fees (definitions over)	**Calculations**	**No-charge levels**	**Waived items**	**Net W/F**
SELF-SERVICE BANKING	14 X .45= 6.30	$ 700.00	14	$0.00
CHEQUES	4 X .60= 2.40	$1000.00	1 FREE	$1.80
IN-BRANCH WITHDRAWALS	0 X .60= 0.00	$1000.00	0	$0.00

GROSS WITHDRAWAL FEES	$8.70	NET WITHDRAWAL FEES :	$1.80
MINIMUM BALANCE	$994.00		

YOU SAVED $6.90 IN WITHDRAWAL FEES THIS MONTH. GREEN MACHINE WITHDRAWALS ARE
30% CHEAPER THAN IN-BRANCH WITHDRAWALS. SO VISIT YOUR GREEN MACHINE TODAY!

DEST=014, PROD=MBA, ENGLISH
EASY DECISION. ASK YOUR BRANCH ABOUT THE
INVESTMENT OPPORTUNITIES AVAILABLE AT TD.

Common items that cause differences between the bank balance and the business are

1. Items recorded by the company but not yet recorded by the *bank*:
   a. **Deposits in transit** (outstanding deposits)   The company has recorded these deposits, but the bank has not.
   b. **Outstanding cheques**   These cheques have been issued by the company and recorded on its books but have not yet been paid by its bank.
2. Items recorded by the bank but not yet recorded by the *company*:
   a. **Bank collections**   The bank sometimes collects money on behalf of depositors. Some businesses have their customers pay directly to the company bank account. This practice, called a lock-box system, reduces the possibility of theft and places the business's cash in circulation faster than if the cash had to be collected and deposited by company personnel. An example is a bank's collecting cash on a note receivable and interest revenue for the depositor. The bank may notify the depositor of these bank collections on the bank statement.
   b. **Service charge**   This amount is the bank's fee for processing the depositor's transactions. Banks commonly base service charge on the balance in the account. The depositor learns the amount of service charge from the bank statement.
   c. *Interest revenue on chequing account*   Many banks pay interest to depositors who keep a large enough balance of cash in the account. This is generally the case with business chequing accounts. The bank notifies the depositor of this interest on the bank statement.
   d. **NSF (nonsufficient funds) cheques** received from customers. To understand how to handle NSF cheques, also called "hot cheques," you first need to know the route a cheque takes. The maker writes the cheque, credits Cash to record the payment on the books and gives the cheque to the payee. On receiving the cheque, the payee debits Cash on his or her books and deposits the cheque in the bank. The payee's bank immediately adds the receipt amount to the payee's bank balance on the assumption that the cheque is good. The cheque is returned to the maker's bank, which then deducts the cheque amount from the maker's bank balance. If the maker's bank balance is insufficient to pay the cheque, the maker's bank refuses to pay the cheque, reverses this deduction and sends an NSF notice back to the payee's bank. That bank subtracts the cheque amount from the payee's bank balance and notifies the payee of this action. This process may take from three to seven days. The company may learn of NSF cheques through the bank statement, which lists the NSF cheque as a charge (subtraction), as shown near the bottom of Exhibit 7-4.
   e. *Cheques collected, deposited and returned to the payee by the bank for reasons other than NSF*   Banks return cheques to the payee if (1) the maker's account has closed, (2) the date is stale, usually six months or more, before the cheque is deposited, (3) the signature is not authorized, (4) the cheque has been altered, or (5) the cheque form is improper. Accounting for all returned cheques is the same as for NSF cheques.
   f. *The cost of printed cheques*   This charge against the company's bank account balance is handled like a service charge.
3. Errors by either the company or the bank. For example, a bank may improperly charge (decrease) the bank balance of Business Research, Inc. for a cheque drawn by another company, perhaps Business Research Associates. Or a company may miscompute its bank balance on its own books. Computational errors are becoming less frequent with the widespread use of computers. Nevertheless, all errors must be corrected, and the corrections will be a part of the bank reconciliation.

Steps in Preparing the Bank Reconciliation

The steps in preparing the bank reconciliation are

1. Start with two figures, the balance shown on the bank statement (*balance per bank*) and the balance in the company's Cash account (*balance per books*) as in Panel B, Exhibit 7-5. These two amounts will probably disagree because of the timing differences discussed earlier.

2. Add to, or subtract from, the *bank* balance those items that appear on the books but not on the bank statement.
    a. Add *deposits in transit* to the bank balance. Deposits in transit are identified by comparing the deposits listed on the bank statement to the company list of cash receipts. They show up as cash receipts on the books but not as deposits on the bank statement. As a control measure, the accountant should also ensure that deposits in transit from the preceding month appear on the current month's bank statement. If they do not, the deposits may be lost.
    b. Subtract *outstanding cheques* from the bank balance. Outstanding cheques are identified by comparing the canceled cheques returned with the bank statement to the company list of cheques in the cash disbursements journal. They show up as cash payments on the books but not as paid cheques on the bank statement. This comparison also verifies that all cheques paid by the bank were valid company cheques and correctly recorded by the bank and by the company. Outstanding cheques are usually the most numerous item on a bank reconciliation.

3. Add to, or subtract from, the *book* balance those items that appear on the bank statement but not on the company books.
    a. Add to the book balance (1) *bank collections* and (2) any *interest revenue* earned on the money in the bank. These items are identified by comparing the deposits listed on the bank statement to the company list of cash receipts. They show up as cash receipts on the bank statement but not as cash payments on the books.
    b. Subtract from the book balance (1) *service charges*, (2) *cost of printed cheques*, and (3) *other bank charges* (for example, charges for NSF or stale dated cheques). These items are identified by comparing the other charges listed on the bank statement to the cash disbursements recorded on the company books. They show up as subtractions on the bank statement but not as cash payments on the books.

4. Compute the *adjusted bank balance* and *adjusted book balance*. The two adjusted balances should be equal.

5. Journalize each item in 3, that is, each item listed on the book portion of the bank reconciliation. These items must be recorded on the company books because they affect cash.

6. Correct all book errors, and notify the bank of any errors it has made.

OBJECTIVE 3

Prepare a bank reconciliation and related journal entries

Bank Reconciliation Illustrated

The bank statement in Exhibit 7-4 indicates that the January 31 bank balance of Business Research, Inc. is $5,388.48. However, the company's Cash account has a balance of $3,294.21. In following the steps outlined above, the accountant finds these reconciling items:

1. The January 30 deposit of $1,591.63 does not appear on the bank statement.
2. The bank erroneously charged a $100 cheque (number 656) written by Business Research Associates against the Business Research, Inc. account.

3. Five company cheques issued late in January and recorded in the cash disbursements journal have not been paid by the bank.

Cheque No.	Date	Amount
337	Jan. 27	$286.00
338	28	319.47
339	28	83.00
340	29	203.14
341	30	458.53

4. The bank collected on behalf of the company a note receivable, $2,114 (including interest revenue of $214). This cash receipt has not been recorded in the cash receipts journal.

5. The bank statement shows interest revenue of $28.01 that the bank has paid the company on its cash balance.

6. Cheque number 333 for $150 paid to Brown Company on account was recorded in the cash disbursements journal as a $510 amount, creating a $360 understatement of the Cash balance per books.

7. The bank service charge for the month was $14.25.

EXHIBIT 7-5 *Bank Reconciliation*

Panel A: Reconciling Items

1. Deposit in transit, $1,591.63.
2. Bank error; add $100 to bank balance.
3. Outstanding cheques: no. 337, $286.00; no. 338, $319.47; no. 339, $83.00; no. 340, $203.14; no. 341, $458.53.
4. Bank collection, $2,114, including interest revenue of $214.

5. Interest earned on bank balance, $28.01.
6. Book error; add $360 to book balance.
7. Bank service charge, $14.25.
8. NSF cheque from L. Ross, $52.

Panel B: Bank Reconciliation

Business Research, Inc.
Bank Reconciliation
January 31, 19X6

Bank			Books		
Balance, January 31		$5,388.48	Balance, January 31		$3,294.21
Add:			Add:		
1. Deposit of Janaury 30 in transit		1,591.63	4. Bank collection of note receivable, including interest revenue of $214		2,114.00
2. Correction of bank error — Business Research Associates cheque erroneously charged against company account		100.00	5. Interest revenue earned on bank balance		28.01
		$7,080.11	6. Correction of book error — Overstated amount of cheque no. 333		360.00
3. Less: outstanding cheques					5,796.22
No. 337	$286.00				
338	319.47		Less:		
339	83.00		7. Service charge	$14.25	
340	203.14		8. NSF cheque	52.00	(66.25)
341	458.53	(1,350.14)			
Adjusted bank balance		$5,729.97	Adjusted book balance		$5,729.97

8. The bank statement shows an NSF cheque for $52 that was received from customer L. Ross.

Exhibit 7-5 is the bank reconciliation based on the above data. Panel A lists the reconciling items, which are keyed by number to the actual reconciliation in Panel B. Note that after the reconciliation, the adjusted bank balance equals the adjusted book balance. This equality is the accuracy check for the reconciliation.

Recording Entries from the Reconciliation

The bank reconciliation does not directly affect the journals or ledgers. Like the work sheet, the reconciliation is an accountant's tool, separate from the company's books.

The bank reconciliation acts as a control device by signaling the company to record transactions listed as reconciling items in the Books section because the company has not yet done so. For example, the bank collected the note receivable on behalf of the company, but the company has not yet recorded this cash receipt. In fact, the company learned of the cash receipt only when it received the bank statement.

Why does the company *not* need to record the reconciling items on the Bank side of the reconciliation? Those items have already been recorded on the company books.

Based on the reconciliation in Exhibit 7-5, Business Research, Inc. makes these entries. They are dated January 31 to bring the Cash account to the correct balance on that date.

Jan.	31	Cash...	2,114.00	
		Notes Receivable..		1,900.00
		Interest Revenue		214.00
		Note receivable collected by bank.		
	31	Cash...	28.01	
		Interest Revenue		28.01
		Interest earned on bank balance.		
	31	Cash...	360.00	
		Accounts Payable — Brown Co.................		360.00
		Correction of Cheque Register, cheque no. 333.		
	31	Miscellaneous Expense.....................................	14.25	
		Cash		14.25
		Bank service charges.		
	31	Accounts Receivable — L. Ross......................	52.00	
		Cash		52.00
		NSF cheque returned by bank.		

Note: Miscellaneous Expense is debited for the bank service charge because the service charge pertains to no particular expense category.

These entries bring the business's books up to date.

The entry for the NSF cheque needs explanation. Upon learning that L. Ross's $52 cheque was no good, Business Research credits Cash to bring the Cash account up to date. Since Business Research still has a receivable from Ross, it debits Accounts Receivable — L. Ross and pursues collection from him.

Summary Problem for Your Review

1. The cash account of Kao Company at February 28, 19X3 follows:

Cash

Feb.	1	Balance	3,995	Feb.	3		400
	6		800		12		3,100
	15		1,800		19		1,100
	23		1,100		25		500
	28		2,400		27		900
	28	Balance	4,095				

2. Kao Company receives this bank statement on February 28, 19X3 (negative amounts appear in parentheses):

Bank Statement for February, 19X3

Beginning balance			$3,995
Deposits			
Feb. 7		$ 800	
15		1,800	
24		1,100	3,700
Cheques (total per day)			
Feb. 8		$ 400	
16		3,100	
23		1,100	(4,600)
Other items			
Service charge			(10)
NSF cheque from M. E. Crown			(700)
Bank collection of note receivable for the company..			1,000*
Interest on account balance			15
Ending balance			$3,400

*Includes interest of $119.

Additional data: Kao Company deposits all cash receipts in the bank and makes all cash disbursements by cheque.

Required

1. Prepare the bank reconciliation of Kao Company at February 28, 19X3.
2. Record the entries based on the bank reconciliation.

SOLUTION TO REVIEW PROBLEM

Requirement 1

Kao Company
Bank Reconciliation
February 28, 19X3

Bank

Balance, February 28, 19X3		$3,400
Add: Deposit of February 28 in transit		2,400
		5,800
Less: Outstanding cheques issued on Feb. 25		
($500) and Feb. 27 ($900)		(1,400)
Adjusted bank balance, February 28, 19X3		$4,400

Books

Balance, February 28, 19X3		$4,095
Add: Bank collection of note receivable,		
including interest of $119		1,000
Add: Interest earned on bank balance		15
		5,110
Less: Service charge	$ 10	
NSF cheque	700	(710)
Adjusted book balance, February 28, 19X3		$4,400

Requirement 2

Feb.	28	Cash	1,000	
		Note Receivable ($1,100 – $119)		881
		Interest Revenue		119
		Note receivable collected by bank.		
	28	Cash	15	
		Interest Revenue		15
		Interest earned on bank balance		
	28	Miscellaneous Expense	10	
		Cash		10
		Bank service charge.		
	28	Accounts Receivable — M. E. Crown	700	
		Cash		700
		NSF cheque returned by bank.		

Reporting of Cash

Cash is the first current asset listed on the balance sheet of most companies. Even small businesses have several bank accounts and one or more petty cash funds that are kept on hand for making small disbursements. However, companies usually combine all cash amounts into a single total for reporting on the balance sheet. They also include liquid assets like time deposits and certificates of deposit. These are interest-bearing accounts that can be withdrawn with no penalty after a short period of time. Although they are slightly less liquid than cash, they are sufficiently similar to be reported along with cash. For example, the balance sheet of National Trustco. Inc., Canada's third largest trust company with branches from Vancouver to Quebec City, recently reported (in thousands of dollars):

Assets

Cash and short-term investments................................		$ 1,609,058
Securities		907,367
Loans		
Mortgages	11,422,656	
Other	2,477,811	13,900,467
		$16,416,892

It is important to perform the bank reconciliation on the balance sheet date in order to be assured of reporting the correct amount of cash.

Internal Control over Cash Receipts

Internal control over cash receipts ensures that all cash receipts are deposited in the bank and the company's accounting records are correct. Many businesses receive cash over the counter and through the mail. Each source of cash receipts calls for *security measures*.

> **OBJECTIVE 4**
>
> Apply internal controls to cash receipts

The cash register offers management control over cash received in a store. First, the machine should be positioned so that customers can see the amounts the cashier enters into the register. No person willingly pays more than the marked price for an item, so the customer helps prevent the sales clerk from overcharging and pocketing the excess over actual prices. Also, customers should be encouraged to request a receipt to make sure each sale is recorded in the register.

Second, the register's cash drawer opens only when the sales clerk enters an amount on the keys. A roll of tape locked inside the machine records each amount entered. At the end of the day, a manager proves the cash by comparing the total amount in the cash drawer against the tape's total. This step helps prevent outright theft by the clerk. For security reasons, the clerk should not have access to the tape.

Third, pricing merchandise at "uneven" amounts, say, $3.95 instead of $4.00, means that the clerk generally must make change, which in turn means having to get into the cash drawer. This requires entering the amount of the sale on the keys and so onto the register tape.

At the end of the day, the cashier or other employee with cash-handling duties deposits the cash in the bank. The tape goes to the accounting department as the basis for an entry in the cash receipts journal. These security measures, coupled with periodic on-site inspection by a manager, discourage fraud.

All incoming mail should be opened by a mail-room employee. This person should compare the actual enclosed amount of cash or cheque with the attached remittance advice. If no advice was sent, the mail-room employee should prepare one and enter the amount of each receipt on a control tape. At the end of the day, this control tape is given to a responsible official, such as the controller, for verification. Cash receipts should be given to the cashier, who combines them with any cash received over the counter and prepares the bank deposit.

Having a mail-room employee to be the first to handle postal cash receipts is just another application of a good internal control procedure — in this case, separation of duties. If the accountants opened postal cash receipts, they could easily hide a theft.

The mail-room employee forwards the remittance advices to the accounting department. They provide the data for entries in the cash receipts journal and postings to customers' accounts in the accounts receivable ledger. As a final step, the controller compares the three records of the day's cash receipts: (1) the control tape total from the mail room, (2) the bank deposit amount from the cashier, and (3) the debit to Cash from the accounting department.

An added measure used to control cash receipts is a *fidelity bond*, which is an insurance policy that the business buys to guard against theft. The fidelity bond helps in two ways. First, the insurance company that issues the policy investigates the backgrounds of the workers whose activities will be covered, such as the mail-room employees who handle incoming cash and the employees who handle inventory. Second, if the company suffers a loss due to the misconduct of a covered employee, the insurance company reimburses the business.

Cash Short and Over A difference often exists between actual cash receipts and the day's record of cash received. Usually the difference is small and results from honest errors. Suppose the tapes from a cash register of a large department store indicate sales revenue of $25,000, but the cash received is $24,980. To record the day's sales for that register, the store would make this entry:

Cash	24,980	
Cash Short and Over	20	
Sales Revenue..		25,000

As the entry shows, Cash Short and Over is debited when sales revenue exceeds cash receipts. This account is credited when cash receipts exceed sales. A debit balance appears on the income statement as Miscellaneous Expense, a credit balance as Other Revenue.

This account's balance should be small. The debits and credits for Cash Short and Over collected over an accounting period tend to cancel each other out. A large balance signals the accountant to investigate. For example, too large a debit balance may mean an employee is stealing. Cash Short and Over, then, acts as an internal control device.

<table>
<tr><td>

OBJECTIVE 5

Apply internal controls
to cash disbursements

</td></tr>
</table>

Internal Control over Cash Disbursements

Payment by *cheque* is an important control over cash disbursements. First, the cheque acts as a source document. Second, to be valid the cheque must be signed by an authorized official, so that each payment by cheque draws the attention of management. Before signing the cheque, the manager should study the invoice, receiving report, purchase order and other supporting documents. (A discussion of these documents follows.) As further security and control over cash disbursements, many firms require two signatures on a cheque, as in Exhibit 7-3. To avoid document alteration, some firms also use machines that indelibly stamp the amount on the cheque.

In very small businesses, the proprietor or partners may control cash disbursements by reviewing the supporting documents themselves and personally writing all cheques. In larger businesses, however, this is impractical. Therefore the duties of approving invoices for payment and writing cheques are performed by authorized employees. Strong internal control is achieved through clear-cut assignment of responsibility, proper authorization and separation of duties.

Controlling the Cost of Inventory

Cost of goods sold is the major expense of most merchandising businesses. Therefore, it is important to control the cost of inventory purchases. Overall control is achieved by the same measures used to control all other cash disbursements — assignment of responsibility, authorization for payment, separation of duties, and so on.

A measure that is designed specifically to control the cost of inventory concerns the manner of recording purchases. There are two ways to record purchases: (1) at the *gross* cost, as illustrated thus far; and (2) at the *net* cost, which takes into account any discount on the purchase. For example, a $2,000 invoice subject to credit terms of 2/10 n/30 could be recorded at gross ($2,000) or net ($1,960). The discount terms of 2/10 n/30 (that is, a 2 percent discount for payment within 10 days, or the full $2,000 within 30 days) indicate a very high rate of interest when expressed as an annual rate. Paying after the discount period costs 2 percent for the extra 20 days of credit, an annual rate of 36.5 percent (.02x365 days/20 days = .365). For this reason, companies adopt the policy of taking all such discounts.

Recording the purchase at its net amount has a control advantage because it highlights the inefficiency of paying late. Recorded at net cost, the purchase entry is

Purchases ($2,000 – $40)................................	1,960	
Accounts Payable		1,960
Purchase on account.		

The actual cost of the inventory is $1,960 because this is the cash cost of the goods if they are paid for immediately. The gross cost of $2,000 includes a $40 charge for payment beyond the discount period. Therefore, the net cost method is preferable. To see the control advantage of the net cost approach, suppose the invoice is *not* paid within the discount period. This inefficiency costs an extra $40, debited to Purchase Discounts Lost as follows:

Accounts Payable...	1,960	
Purchase Discounts Lost................................	40	
Cash in Bank...		2,000
Payment after discount period.		

Purchase Discounts Lost is an expense account reported as Other Expense on the income statement.

Mathieu Company	
Income Statement	
year ended December 31, 19X8	

Sales revenue...	$700,000
Cost of goods sold	380,000
Gross margin..	320,000
Operating expenses...	230,000
Income from operations	90,000
Other revenue (expense)	
Purchase discounts lost	**(2,000)**
Net income	$ 88,000

Reporting Purchase Discounts Lost on the income statement draws attention to the inefficiency of losing the discounts. The net method thus captures the information needed to evaluate employee performance. Managers can then correct those actions that led to payment of the full amount. Contrast this accounting treatment with recording the purchases at gross cost. There is no record of the discount because the purchase and related payment are both recorded at $2,000. Managers lose the notification provided by the Purchase Discounts Lost account.

Petty Cash Disbursements

It would be uneconomical for a business to write a separate cheque for an executive's taxi fare, a box of pencils needed right away, or the delivery of a special message across town. Therefore, companies keep a small amount of cash on hand to pay for such minor amounts. This fund is called **petty cash**.

Even though the individual amounts paid through the petty cash fund may be small, such expenses occur so often that the total amount over an accounting period may grow quite large. Thus the business needs to set up these controls over petty cash: (1) designate an employee to administer the fund as its custodian, (2) keep a specific amount of cash on hand, (3) support all fund disbursements with a petty cash ticket or voucher, and (4) replenish the fund through normal cash disbursement procedures.

To open the petty cash fund, a payment is approved for a predetermined amount and a cheque for this amount is issued to Petty Cash. Assume that on February 28 the business decides to establish a petty cash fund of $200. The custodian cashes the cheque and places the currency and coin in the fund, which may be a cash box, safe, or other device. The petty cash custodian is assigned the responsibility for controlling the fund. Starting the fund is recorded as follows:

Feb. 28	Petty Cash...	200	
	Cash in Bank		200
	To open the petty cash fund.		

OBJECTIVE 6

Account for petty cash transactions

For each petty cash disbursement, the custodian prepares a *petty cash ticket* like the one illustrated in Exhibit 7-6.

Observe the signatures (or initials, for the custodian) that identify the recipient of petty cash and the fund custodian. Requiring both signatures reduces unauthorized cash disbursements. The custodian keeps all the petty cash tickets in the fund. The sum of the cash plus the total of the ticket amounts should equal the opening balance at all times, in this case, $200. Also, the Petty Cash account keeps its prescribed $200 balance at all times. Maintaining the Petty Cash account at this balance, supported by the fund (cash plus tickets totaling the fund amount) is a characteristic of an **imprest system**. The control feature of an imprest system is that it clearly identifies the amount of money that the fund custodian is responsible for.

Disbursements reduce the amount of cash in the fund, so that periodically the fund must be replenished. Suppose that on March 31 the fund has $118 in cash and $82 in tickets. A cheque for $82 is issued, made payable to Petty Cash. The fund custodian cashes this cheque for currency and coins, and puts the money in the fund to return its actual cash to $200. The petty cash tickets identify the accounts to be debited: Store Supplies for $23, Delivery Expense for $17 and Miscellaneous Selling Expense for $42. The entry to record replenishment of the fund is

Mar. 31	Store Supplies	23	
	Delivery Expense	17	
	Miscellaneous Selling Expense...........	42	
	Cash in Bank		82
	To replenish the petty cash fund.		

EXHIBIT 7-6 *Petty Cash Ticket*

PETTY CASH TICKET	
Date __Mar. 25, 19X4__	No. __45__
Amount __$23.00__	
For __Box of floppy diskettes__	
Debit __Office Supplies, Acct. No. 145__	
Received by __*Lewis Wright*__	Fund Custodian __WAR__

If this cash payment exceeds the sum of the tickets, that is, if the fund comes up short, Cash Short and Over is debited for the missing amount. If the sum of the tickets exceeds the payment, Cash Short and Over is credited. Note that replenishing the fund does *not* affect the Petty Cash account. Petty Cash keeps its $200 balance at all times.

Whenever petty cash runs low, the fund is replenished. It must be replenished on the balance sheet date. Otherwise, the reported balance for Petty Cash will be overstated by the amount of the tickets in the fund. The income statement will understate the expenses listed on these tickets.

Petty Cash is debited only when starting the fund (see the February 28 entry) or changing its amount. In our illustration, suppose the business decides to raise the fund amount from $200 to $250 because of increased demand for petty cash. This step would require a $50 debit to Petty Cash.

The Voucher System

> **OBJECTIVE 7**
> Use the voucher system

As we saw in Chapter 6, some businesses use the purchases journal and the cash disbursements journal to record cash payments. Other businesses use a voucher system. The **voucher system** of recording cash payments offers the business greater internal control by formalizing the process of approving and recording invoices for payment. We will examine the voucher system as it is used by a merchandising business.

The voucher system uses (1) vouchers, (2) a voucher register, (3) an unpaid voucher file, (4) a cheque register, and (5) a paid voucher file. The merchandising business we discuss has separate departments for purchasing goods, receiving goods, disbursing cash, and accounting.

Vouchers A **voucher** is a document authorizing a cash disbursement. The accounting department prepares vouchers. Exhibit 7-7 illustrates the voucher of Bliss Wholesale Company. In addition to places for writing in the *payee, due date, terms, description*, and *invoice amount*, the voucher includes a section for designated officers to sign their *approval* for payment. The back of the voucher has places for recording the *account debited, date paid*, and *cheque number*. You should locate these nine items in Exhibit 7-7.

To better understand the voucher system, let us take an in-depth look at the purchasing process. Exhibit 7-8 lists the various business documents used to ensure that the company receives the goods it ordered and pays only for the goods it has actually received.

The purchasing process starts when the sales department identifies the need for merchandise and prepares a *purchase request* (or requisition). A separate purchasing department specializes in locating the best buys, and mails a *purchase order* to the supplier, the outside company that sells the needed goods. When the supplier ships the goods to the requesting business, the supplier also mails the *invoice* (or bill), which is a notification of the need to pay. As the goods arrive, the receiving department checks them for any damage, and lists the merchandise received on a document called the *receiving report*. The accounting department prepares a *voucher* and attaches all the foregoing documents, checks them for accuracy and agreement, and forwards this voucher packet to designated officers for approval and payment. The voucher packet includes the voucher, invoice, receiving report, purchase order, and purchase request, as shown in Exhibit 7-9.

Before approving the voucher, the controller and the treasurer should examine a sample of vouchers to determine that the following control steps have been performed by the accounting department:

EXHIBIT 7-7 Voucher

Front of
Voucher

				Voucher No. 326

BLISS WHOLESALE COMPANY

Payee   John Forsyth Co.
Address   31 Young St.
              Kitchener, Ontario N2H 4Y7

Due Date March 7
Terms   2/10 n/30

Date	Invoice No.	Description	Amount
Mar. 1	6380	144 men's shirts stock no. X14	$1,800

Approved *Jane Trent*   **Approved** *Bob Kraft*
              Controller   **Treasurer**

Back of
Voucher

Voucher No. 326
Payee John Forsyth Co.

Invoice Amount   1,800

Discount   36

Net Amount $1,764

Due Date   Mar. 7

Date Paid   Mar. 6

Cheque No.   694

Account Distribution

Account Debited	Acct. No.	Amount
Purchases	501	1,800
Store Supplies	145	
Salary Expense	538	
Advertising Expense	542	
Utilities Expense	548	
Delivery Expense	544	
Total		1,800

EXHIBIT 7-8 Purchasing Process

Business Document	Prepared by	Sent to
Purchase request	Sales department	Purchasing department
Purchase order	Purchasing department	Outside company that sells the needed merchandise (supplier or vendor)
Invoice	Outside company that sells the needed merchandise (supplier or vendor)	Accounting department
Receiving report	Receiving department	Accounting department
Voucher	Accounting department	Officer who signs the cheque

EXHIBIT 7-9 *Voucher Packet*

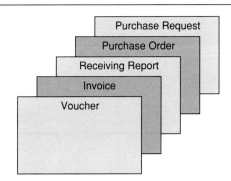

1. The invoice is compared to a copy of the purchase order and purchase request to ensure that the business pays cash only for the goods that it ordered.

2. The invoice is compared to the receiving report to ensure that cash is paid only for the goods that are actually received.

3. The mathematical accuracy of the invoice is proved.

Voucher Register   After approval by the designated officers, the voucher goes to the accounting department where it is recorded in the **voucher register**. This journal is similar to the purchases journal (discussed in Chapter 6), but the voucher register is more comprehensive. In a voucher system, *all* expenditures are recorded first in the voucher register. This is a fundamental control feature of the voucher system because it centralizes the initial recording of all expenditures in this one journal. That is, all cash payments must be vouchered and approved prior to payment. For each transaction, the debit is to the account for which payment is being made, and the credit is to Vouchers Payable, the account that replaces Accounts Payable if a voucher system is used. Exhibit 7-10 illustrates the voucher register of Bliss Wholesale Company.

The voucher register has columns to record payment date and cheque number, which are entered when the voucher is paid. The absence of a payment date and cheque number means that the voucher is unpaid. In Exhibit 7-10, for example, Bliss Wholesale has a $2,202 liability at March 31 for vouchers 330 ($369 payable to the *Daily Journal*), 348 ($1,638 payable to Carr Products), and 350 ($195 payable to Consumers Gas Company). If these were the company's only unpaid vouchers at March 31, the balance sheet would report:

> Current liabilities
>   Accounts payable* $2,202

*Usually reported as Accounts Payable, even by companies that use a voucher system.

Unpaid Voucher File   After recording a voucher in the voucher register, the accountant places the voucher packet in the unpaid voucher file, where it stays until the voucher is paid. The unpaid voucher file acts as the accounts payable subsidiary ledger because each voucher serves as an individual account payable. Thus no need exists for a separate accounts payable ledger.

The unpaid voucher file has 31 slots, one for each day of the month. Each voucher is filed according to its due date. For example, voucher no. 326 in Exhibit 7-7 was due March 7, so that it was filed in the slot marked 7.

Cheque Register   The **cheque register** is the journal in which are recorded all cheques issued in a voucher system. It replaces the cash disbursements journal. All entries in the cheque register debit Vouchers Payable and credit Cash (and Purchase Discounts, as appropriate).

EXHIBIT 7-10 *Voucher Register*

Voucher Register   Page 16

Date	Voucher No.	Payee	Payment Date	Cheque No.	Credit: Vouchers Payable	Debit: Purchases	Store Supplies	Salary Expense	Advertising Expense	Utilities Expense	Delivery Expense	Other Accounts Title	No.	Amount
Mar. 1	326	John Forsyth Co.	3/6	694	1,800	1,800								
1	327	Howell Properties	3/2	693	1,500							Rent Expense	547	1,500
4	328	Bell Telephone	3/10	696	128					128				
5	329	Schick Supplies	3/11	697	85		85							
8	330	Daily Journal			369				369					
9	331	Ace Delivery Service	3/9	695	37						37			
26	348	Carr Products			1,638	1,638								
28	349	Petty Cash	3/31	717	82		23				17	Miscellaneous Selling Expense	563	42
29	350	Consumers Gas Co.	3/31	718	195					195				
30	351	Foothills Bank	3/31	718	360							Interest Expense	546	360
31	352	Ralph Grant	3/31	719	864			864						
31		Totals			12,580	6,209	137	1,781	753	602	185			2,913
					(201)	(501)	(145)	(538)	(542)	(548)	(544)			(✓)

Account numbers in parentheses indicate the accounts to which these amounts have been posted.

EXHIBIT 7-11 *Cheque Register*

				Debit	Credit	
Date	Cheque No.	Payee	Voucher No.	Vouchers Payable	Purchase Discounts	Cash in Bank
Mar. 1	692	Trent Co.	322	600	18	582
2	693	Howell Properties	327	1,500		1,500
6	694	John Forsyth Co.	326	1,800	36	1,764
9	695	Ace Delivery Service	331	37		37
10	696	Bell Telephone	328	128		128
11	697	Schick Supplies	329	85		85
31	717	Petty Cash	349	82		82
31	718	Foothills Bank	351	360		360
31	719	Ralph Grant	352	864		864
31	720	Krasner Supply Co.	336	92		92
31		Totals		11,406	317	11,089
				(201)	(503)	(103)

Account numbers in parentheses indicate the accounts to which these amounts have been posted.

Exhibit 7-11 shows a cheque register. Notice that all transactions include a credit to the Cash in Bank account.

Account numbers in parentheses indicate the accounts to which these amounts have been posted.

On or before the due date, the accountant removes the voucher packet from the unpaid voucher file and sends it to the officers for signing. After the cheques are signed, the cheque number and payment date are entered on the back of the voucher, in the cheque register and in the voucher register.

Paid Voucher File   After payment, the voucher packet is cancelled to avoid paying the bill twice. Typically, a hole is punched through the voucher packet. It is then filed alphabetically by payee name. Most businesses also file a copy in numerical sequence by voucher number as a cross reference. With this dual filing system, a voucher can be located using either classification scheme.

In summary, the voucher system works as follows:

1. The accounting department prepares a *voucher* for each invoice to be paid.
2. Supporting documents (invoice, receiving report, purchase order, and purchase request) are compared in the accounting department for accuracy and attached to the voucher. These make up the *voucher packet*.
3. Designated officials examine the supporting documents and approve the voucher for payment.
4. The accounting department enters the voucher in the *voucher register*. The entry is a debit to the account of the item purchased (for example, Purchases) and a credit to Vouchers Payable. The voucher remains in the *unpaid voucher file* until payment.
5. Prior to the invoice due date, a cheque is issued to pay the voucher. The official

reviews the supporting document and signs the cheque.

6. The accounting department enters the cheque in the *cheque register,* and updates the voucher and voucher register to record payment. All cheques are debits to Vouchers Payable and credits to Cash.

7. Paid vouchers are canceled and filed by payee name and by voucher number.

To gain a complete understanding of the voucher system, trace voucher no. 326 from Exhibit 7-7 through the voucher register in Exhibit 7-10 to the cheque register in Exhibit 7-11. Also, trace the cheque register entries from Exhibit 7-11 back to Exhibit 7-10.

Computers, Internal Control, and Cash

Within a single company, each department may take steps to maintain control over its assets and accounting records. Consider a large company like Nothern Telecom Ltd., a manufacturer of a wide range of electronic equipment especially for the telecommunications industry. Computerized record keeping means that the raw data provided by one department leads to a whole array of *accurate* output — from journals to ledgers to cheques and so on — all consistent with the original information. Manually copying information, a time-consuming, error-prone process, is reduced or eliminated.

If Northern Telecom's system is well designed, each department can ensure that its transactions are processed correctly. The user department needs to maintain record counts or dollar control totals. For example, the accounts receivable department submits daily credit sales totals for processing by the computing department. The accounts receivable department expects a printout showing a total sales amount agreeing with the control total that was calculated *before* its documents went to the computer department. This amount is the control figure.

The accounts receivable department — and every other department — relies on the computing department to post correctly the thousands of customer accounts. To assure proper posting, customer account numbers may have been devised so that the last digit is a mathematical function of the previous digits, for example, 1,359, where $1 + 3 + 5 = 9$. Any miskeying of a customer account number would trigger an error message to the data entry clerk, and the computer would not accept that number.

Also the computer has brought about an important development in cash payments. **Electronic funds transfer** (EFT) is a system that relies on electronic impulses — not paper documents — to handle cash transactions. To manage payroll, an employer enters the employee's name, wages, and any other necessary data on a magnetic tape, which is transferred to a bank. The bank runs the tape, which automatically decreases the business's cash account and increases the employee's cash account. Some retailers use EFT to handle sales. Customers pay with a card that activates a computer. The computer automatically decreases the customer's bank account balance and increases the store's account balance.

EFT systems reduce the cost of processing cash transactions. However, this savings is achieved by reducing the documentary evidence of transactions. Traditional approaches to internal control have relied on documents, so that EFT and other computer systems pose a significant challenge to managers and accountants who design and enforce internal control systems. Computer systems also create problems in protecting private information. For example, a group of students gained access to highly confidential hospital patient data by computer! Such situations point to the need for computer security measures.

Summary Problem for Your Review

Grudnitski Ltd. established a $300 petty cash fund. James C. Brown is the fund custodian. At the end of the first week, the petty cash fund contains the following:

1. Cash: $171
2. Petty cash tickets

No.	Amount	Issued to	Signed by	Account Debited
44	$14	B. Jarvis	B. Jarvis and JCB	Office Supplies
45	9	S. Bell	S. Bell	Miscellaneous Expense
47	43	R. Tate	R. Tate and JCB	—
48	33	G. Ghiz	G. Ghiz and JCB	Travel Expense

Required

1. Identify the four internal control weaknesses revealed in the above data.
2. Prepare the general journal entries to record
   a. Establishment of the petty cash fund.
   b. Replenishment of the fund. Assume petty cash ticket no. 47 was issued for the purchase of office supplies.
3. What is the balance in the Petty Cash account immediately before replenishment? Immediately after replenishment?

SOLUTION TO REVIEW PROBLEM

Requirement 1

The four internal control weaknesses are

a. Petty cash ticket no. 46 is missing. Coupled with weakness b, this omission raises questions about the administration of the petty cash fund and about how the petty cash funds were used.

b. The $171 cash balance means that $129 has been disbursed ($300 − $171 = $129). However, the total amount of the petty cash tickets is only $99 ($14 + $9 + $43 + $33). The fund, then, is $30 short of cash ($129 − $99 = $30). Was petty cash ticket no. 46 issued for $30? The data in the problem offer no hint that helps answer this question. In a real-world setting, management would investigate the problem.

c. The petty cash custodian (JCB) did not sign petty cash ticket no. 45. This omission may have been an oversight on his part. However, it raises the question of whether he authorized the disbursement. Both the fund custodian and recipient of cash should sign the ticket.

d. Petty cash ticket no. 47 does not indicate which account to debit. What did Tate do with the money, and what account should be debited? At worst, the funds have been stolen. At best, asking the custodian to reconstruct the transaction from memory is haphazard. With no better choice available, debit Miscellaneous Expense.

Requirement 2

Petty cash journal entries

a. Entry to establish the petty cash fund

Petty Cash..	300	
Cash in Bank...		300

b. Entry to replenish the fund

Office Supplies...	14	
Miscellaneous Expense ($9 + $43)...............................	52	
Travel Expense..	33	
Cash Short and Over...	30	
Cash in Bank...		129

Requirement 3

The balance in Petty Cash is *always* its specified balance, in this case $300, as shown by posting the above entries to the account.

Petty Cash

(a) 300

Note that the entry to establish the fund (entry a) debits Petty Cash. The entry to replenish the fund (entry b) neither debits nor credits Petty Cash.

Summary

Internal controls should optimize the use of resources, prevent and detect error and fraud, safeguard assets, and maintain reliable control systems. Effective internal control includes these features: *reliable personnel, clear-cut assignment of responsibility, proper authorization,* and *separation of duties,* which is the primary element of internal control. Many businesses use security devices, audits, and specially designed documents and records in their internal control systems.

The *bank account* helps control and safeguard cash. Businesses use the *bank statement* and *bank reconciliation* to account for banking transactions. An *imprest system* is used to control petty cash disbursements. Many companies record purchases at *net cost* in order to highlight the inefficiency of paying invoices late and thus losing purchase discounts.

Businesses often control cash disbursements by using a *voucher system,* which features the voucher, unpaid voucher file, voucher register, and cheque register.

Businesses may handle their payroll by computer and through *electronic funds transfers.* Internal control for computerized accounting systems must meet the same basic standards that internal control for manual systems does.

Self-Study Questions

Test your understanding of the chapter by marking the correct answer for each of the following questions:

1. Which of the following is an objective of internal control? *(p. 302)*
   a. Safeguarding assets
   b. Maintaining reliable control systems
   c. Optimizing the use of resources
   d. Preventing and detecting fraud and error
   e. All the above are objectives of internal control.

2. Which of the characteristics of an effective system of internal control is violated by allowing the employee who handles inventory to also account for inventory? *(p. 306)*
   a. Competent and reliable personnel
   b. Assignment of responsibilities
   c. Proper authorization
   d. Separation of duties

3. What control function is performed by auditors? *(p. 307)*
   a. Objective opinion of the effectiveness of the internal control system
   b. Assurance that all transactions are accounted for correctly
   c. Communication of the results of the audit to regulatory agencies
   d. Guarantee that a proper separation of duties exists within the business

4. The bank account serves as a control device over *(pp. 308, 317–319)*
   a. Cash receipts
   b. Cash disbursements
   c. Both of the above
   d. None of the above

5. Which of the following items appears on the bank side of a bank reconciliation? *(pp. 313–314)*
   a. Book error
   b. Outstanding cheque
   c. NSF cheque
   d. Interest revenue earned on bank balance

6. Which of the following reconciling items requires a journal entry on the books of the company? *(pp. 313–314)*
   a. Book error
   b. Outstanding cheque
   c. NSF cheque
   d. Interest revenue earned on bank balance
   e. All of the above, except b
   f. None of the above

7. What is the major internal control measure over the cash receipts of a Zellers store? *(pp. 317–318)*
   a. Reporting the day's cash receipts to the controller
   b. Preparing a petty cash ticket for all disbursements from the fund
   c. Pricing merchandise at uneven amounts, coupled with use of a cash register
   d. Channeling all cash receipts through the mail room, whose employees have no cash-accounting responsibilities

8. What is the control advantage of the net method of accounting for inventory purchases? *(p. 319)*
   a. It highlights the inefficiency of losing purchase discounts.
   b. It guarantees that all purchase discounts will be taken.
   c. It automatically increases the business's cash balance.
   d. It results in a higher quality of inventory on hand for customers.

9. The internal control feature that is specific to petty cash is *(p. 320)*
   a. Separation of duties
   b. Assignment of responsibility
   c. Proper authorization
   d. The imprest system

10. The most fundamental control feature provided by a voucher system is *(p. 323)*
    a. Assuring that only approved invoices are paid
    b. Centralizing the recording of all expenditures in one place — the voucher register
    c. Using the cheque register along with the voucher register
    d. Placing all incoming invoices in the unpaid voucher file

Answers to the Self-Study Questions are at the end of the chapter.

Accounting Vocabulary

bank collections (p. 311)	electronic fund	outstanding cheque (p. 311)
bank reconciliation (p. 309)	transfer (EFT) (p. 326)	petty cash (p. 319)
bank statement (p. 308)	imprest system (p. 320)	service charge (p. 311)
cheque (p. 308)	internal control (p. 302)	voucher (p. 321)
cheque register (p. 323)	nonsufficient fund	voucher register (p. 323)
deposit in transit (p. 311)	(NSF) cheque (p. 311)	voucher system (p. 321)

ASSIGNMENT MATERIAL _____

Questions

1. Which of the features of effective internal control is the most fundamental? Why?

2. What is the role of the Audit Committee? Do the examples of the reports from management in the text support your answer? How?

3. Which company employees bear primary responsibility for a company's financial statements and for maintaining the company's system of internal control? How do these persons carry out this responsibility?

4. Identify features of an effective system of internal control.

5. Separation of duties may be divided into four parts. What are they?

6. How can internal control systems be circumvented?

7. Are internal control systems designed to be foolproof and perfect? What is a fundamental constraint in planning and maintaining systems?

8. Briefly state how each of the following serves as an internal control measure over cash: bank account, signature card, deposit ticket, and bank statement.

9. What is the remittance advice of a cheque? What use does it serve?

10. Each of the items in the following list must be accounted for in the bank reconciliation. Next to each item, enter the appropriate letter from the following possible treatments: (a) bank side of reconciliation — add the item; (b) bank side of reconciliation — subtract the item; (c) book side of reconciliation — add the item; and (d) book side of reconciliation — subtract the item.

    _____   Outstanding cheque
    _____   NSF cheque
    _____   Bank service charge
    _____   Cost of printed cheques
    _____   Bank error that decreased bank balance
    _____   Deposit in transit
    _____   Bank collection
    _____   Customer's cheque returned because of unauthorized signature
    _____   Book error that increased balance of Cash account

11. What purpose does a bank reconciliation serve?

12. Suppose a company has six bank accounts, two petty cash funds and three certificates of deposit that can be withdrawn on demand. How many cash amounts would this company likely report on its balance sheet?

13. What role does a cash register play in an internal control system?

14. Describe internal control procedures for cash received by mail.

15. Large businesses often have elaborate internal control systems that may be uneconomical for small businesses. Where does the internal control rest in small proprietorships, and how do they control cash disbursements?

16. What is the internal control advantage of recording purchases at net cost?

17. What balance does the Petty Cash account have at all times? Does this balance always equal the amount of cash in the fund? When are the two amounts equal? When are they unequal?

18. List the five elements of a voucher system and briefly describe the purpose of each.

19. Describe how a voucher system works.

20. What documents make up the voucher packet? Describe three procedures that use the voucher packet to ensure that each payment is appropriate.

21. Why should the same employee not write the computer programs for cash disbursements, sign cheques, and mail the cheques to payees?

Exercises

Exercise 7-1   *Identifying internal control strengths and weaknesses* **(L.O. 2)**

The following situations suggest either a strength or weakness in internal control. Identify each as strength or weakness and give the reason for your answer.

a. The vice-president who signs cheques assumes the accounting department has matched the invoice with other supporting documents and therefore does not examine the voucher packet.

b. Purchase invoices are recorded at net amount to highlight purchase discounts lost because of late payment.

c. The accounting department orders merchandise and approves vouchers for payment.

d. The operator of the computer has no other accounting or cash-handling duties.

e. Cash received over the counter is controlled by the sales clerk, who rings up the sale and places the cash in the register. The sales clerk has access to the control tape stored in the register.

f. Cash received by mail goes straight to the accountant, who debits Cash and credits Accounts Receivable from the customer.

Exercise 7-2   *Identifying internal controls* **(L.O. 2)**

Identify the missing internal control characteristic in the following situations:

a. Business is slow at the Freddy Wood Theater on Tuesday, Wednesday and Thursday nights. To reduce expenses the owner decides not to use a ticket taker on those nights. The ticket seller (cashier) is told to keep the tickets as a record of the number sold.

b. The manager of a discount store wants to speed the flow of customers through check-out. She decides to reduce the time spent by cashiers making change, so she prices merchandise at round dollar amounts — such as $8.00 and $15.00 — instead of the customary amounts — $7.95 and $14.95.

c. Grocery stores such as Save-on-Foods and Great Canadian Superstore purchase large quantities of their merchandise from a few suppliers. At another grocery store the manager decides to reduce paper work. He eliminates the requirement that a receiving department employee prepare a receiving report, which lists the quantities of items received from the supplier.

d. When business is brisk, Mac's Milk and many other retail stores deposit cash in the bank several times during the day. The manager at another convenience store wants to reduce the time spent by employees delivering cash to the bank, so he starts a new policy. Cash will build up over Saturdays and Sundays, and the total two-day amount will be deposited on Sunday evening.

e. In the course of auditing the records of a company, you find that the same employee orders merchandise and approves invoices for payment.

Exercise 7-3   *Classifying bank reconciliation items* **(L.O. 3)**

The following seven items may appear on a bank reconciliation:

a. Outstanding cheques.
b. Bank error: the bank charged our account for a cheque written by another customer.
c. Service charge.
d. Deposits in transit.
e. NSF cheque.
f. Bank collection of a note receivable on our behalf.
g. Book error: We debited Cash for $1,000. The correct debit was $100.

Classify each item as (1) an addition to the bank balance, (2) a subtraction from the bank balance, (3) an addition to the book balance, or (4) a subtraction from the book balance.

Exercise 7-4   *Bank reconciliation* **(L.O. 3)**

Betsy Willis's chequebook lists the following:

Date	Cheque No.	Item	Cheque	Deposit	Balance
9/1					$ 525
4	622	Apple Tree Gift Shop	$19		506
9		Dividends		$ 116	622
13	623	B.C. Telephone	43		579
14	624	Gulf Oil Co.	58		521
18	625	Cash	50		471
26	626	St. Alban's Anglican Church	25		446
28	627	Bent Tree Apartments	275		171
30		Paycheque		1,000	1,171

The September bank statement shows:

Balance		$525
Add: Deposits...		116
Deduct cheques: <u>No.</u>	<u>Amount</u>	
622	$19	
623	43	
624	68*	
625	50	(180)
Other charges		
Printed cheques	$ 8	
Service charge..	12	(20)
Balance		$441

* This is the correct amount of cheque number 624.

Required

Prepare Betsy's bank reconciliation at September 30.

Exercise 7-5 *Bank reconciliation (L.O. 3)*

Pierre Morris operates four Chevron stations. He has just received the monthly bank statement at October 31 from the Bank of Nova Scotia, and the statement shows an ending balance of $3,940. Listed on the statement are a service charge of $12, two NSF cheques totaling $74, and a $9 charge for printed cheques. In reviewing his cash records, Morris identifies outstanding cheques totaling $467 and an October 31 deposit of $788 which does not appear on the bank statement. During October, he recorded a $190 cheque for the salary of a part-time employee by debiting Salary Expense and crediting Cash for $19. Morris's cash account shows an October 31 cash balance of $4,527. Prepare the bank reconciliation at October 31.

Exercise 7-6 *Journal entries from a bank reconciliation (L.O. 3)*

Using the data from Exercise 7-5, record the entries that Morris should make in the general journal on October 31. Include an explanation for each of the entries.

Exercise 7-7 *Internal control over cash receipts (L.O. 4)*

A cash register is located in each department of Woodwyn's Discount Store. The register shows the amount of each sale, the cash received from the customer, and any change returned to the customer. The machine also produces a customer receipt but keeps no record of transactions. At the end of the day, the clerk counts the cash in the register and gives it to the cashier for deposit in the company bank account.

Required

Write a memo to convince the store manager that there is an internal control weakness over cash receipts. Identify the weakness that gives an employee the best opportunity to steal cash, and state how to prevent this theft.

Exercise 7-8 *Income statements with purchases at gross and at net (L.O. 5)*

Assume Bulova Company, the watch manufacturer, began July with inventory of $570,000, and ended the month with inventory of $510,000. During July, the company purchased $800,000 of inventory, and took the 2 percent discount on $700,000 of the purchases. The remaining $100,000 in inventory cost was paid after the discount period. Sales during July were $1,600,000, and operating expenses (including income tax) were $490,000.

Required

1. Prepare the company's income statement for July assuming Bulova records inventory purchases at gross cost.

2. Prepare the company's income statement for July assuming the company records inventory purchases at net cost.

3. Which method provides the internal control advantage? Describe how this internal control feature works.

Exercise 7-9   *Purchases at gross and at net (L.O. 5)*

Rolfe Office Supplies uses a voucher system. Prepare its general journal entries for the following transactions under two assumptions (explanations are not required):

Assumption 1 — Inventory purchases recorded at gross cost
Assumption 2 — Inventory purchases recorded at net cost

May   3   Purchased inventory costing $5,100 on account, subject to terms of 2/10 n/30.
    11   Paid the liability created on May 3.
    14   Purchased inventory costing $2,200 on account, subject to terms of 2/10 n/30.
    27   Paid the liability created on May 14.

Which method provides Rolfe Office Supplies with a measure of discounts lost? Describe how this internal control feature works.

Exercise 7-10   *Accounting for petty cash (L.O. 5, 6)*

United Way of Regina, Saskatchewan created a $100 imprest petty cash fund. During the first month of use, the fund custodian authorized and signed petty cash tickets as follows:

Ticket No.	Item	Account Debited	Amount
1	Delivery of pledge cards to donors	Delivery Expense	$22.19
2	Mail package	Postage Expense	2.80
3	Newsletter	Supplies Expense	4.14
4	Key to closet	Miscellaneous Expense	.85
5	Waste basket	Miscellaneous Expense	3.78
6	Staples	Supplies Expense	5.37

Required

1. Make general journal entries for creation of the petty cash fund and its replenishment. Include explanations.
2. Immediately prior to replenishment, describe the items in the fund.
3. Immediately after replenishment, describe the items in the fund.

Exercise 7-11   *Petty cash voucher system (L.O. 6, 7)*

Record the following selected transactions in general journal format (explanations are not required):

April 1   Issued voucher no. 637 to establish a petty cash fund with a $300 balance.
    1   Issued cheque no. 344 to pay voucher no. 637.
    2   Journalized the day's cash sales. Cash register tapes show a $2,859 total, but the cash in the register is only $2,853.
    10   The petty cash fund has $169 in cash and $131 in petty cash tickets issued to pay for Office Supplies ($61), Delivery Expense ($23) and Entertainment Expense ($47). Issued voucher no. 669 to replenish the fund.
    10   Issued cheque no. 402 to pay voucher no. 669.

Problems   *(Group A)*

Problem 7-1A   *Identifying the characteristics of an effective internal control system* **(L.O. 1)**

Nassar Real Estate Development Company prospered during the lengthy economic expansion of the 1980s. Business was so good that the company bothered with few internal controls. The recent decline in the local real estate market, however, has caused Nassar to experience a shortage of cash. Abraham Nassar, the company owner, is looking for ways to save money.

Required

As controller of the company, write a memorandum to convince Mr. Nassar of the company's need for a system of internal control. Be specific in telling him how an internal control system could possibly lead to saving money. Include the definition of internal control, and briefly discuss each characteristic beginning with competent and reliable personnel.

Problem 7-2A   *Identifying internal control weaknesses* **(L.O. 2, 4, 5)**

Each of the following situations has an internal control weakness:

a. Jack Kiger owns a firm that performs engineering services. His staff consists of twelve professional engineers, and he manages the office. Often his work requires him to travel to meet with clients. During the past six months, he has observed that when he returns from a business trip, the engineering jobs in the office have not progressed satisfactorily. He learns that when he is away several of his senior employees take over office management and neglect their engineering duties. One employee could manage the office.

b. Marta Frazier has been an employee of Griffith's Shoe Store for many years. Because the business is relatively small, Marta performs all accounting duties, including opening the mail, preparing the bank deposit, and preparing the bank reconciliation.

c. Most large companies have internal audit staffs that continuously evaluate the business's internal control. Part of the auditor's job is to evaluate how efficiently the company is running. For example, is the company purchasing inventory from the least expensive wholesaler? After a particularly bad year, Mason Tile Company eliminates its internal audit department to reduce expenses.

d. Public accounting firms, law firms, and other professional organizations use paraprofessional employees to do some of their routine tasks. For example, an accounting paraprofessional might examine documents to assist a public accountant in conducting an audit. In the public accounting firm of Grosso Howe, Lou Grosso, the senior partner, turns over a significant portion of his high-level audit work to his paraprofessional staff.

e. In evaluating the internal control over cash disbursements, an auditor learns that the purchasing agent is responsible for purchasing diamonds for use in the company's manufacturing process, approving the invoices for payment, and signing the cheques. No supervisor reviews the purchasing agent's work.

Required

1. Identify the missing internal control characteristic in each situation.
2. Identify the business's possible problem.
3. Propose a solution to the problem.

Problem 7-3A *Identifying internal control weakness* **(L.O. 2)**

Rocky Mountain Supply Co. makes all sales on credit. Cash receipts arrive by mail, usually within 30 days of the sale. Jan Sharp opens envelopes and separates the cheques from the accompanying remittance advices. Sharp forwards the cheques to another employee who makes the daily bank deposit but has no access to the accounting records. Sharp sends the remittance advices, which show the amount of cash received, to the accounting department for entry in the accounts. Sharp's only other duty is to grant sales allowances to customers. When she receives a customer cheque for less than the full amount of the invoice, she records the sales allowance and forwards the document to the accounting department.

Required

You are the outside auditor of Rocky Mountain Supply Co. Write a memo to the company president to identify the internal control weakness in this situation. State how to correct the weakness.

Problem 7-4A *Bank reconciliation and related journal entries* **(L.O. 3)**

The August 31 bank statement of Master Control, Inc. has just arrived from The Bank of Montreal. To prepare the Master Control bank reconciliation, you gather the following data:

a. Master Control's Cash account shows a balance of $5,616.14 on August 31.

b. The bank statement includes two charges for returned cheques from customers. One is a $395.00 cheque received from Shoreline Express and deposited on August 20, returned by Shoreline's bank with the imprint "Unauthorized Signature." The other is an NSF cheque in the amount of $146.67 received from Lipsey, Inc. This cheque had been deposited on August 17.

c. The following Master Control cheques are outstanding at August 31:

Cheque No.	Amount
237	$ 46.10
288	141.00
291	578.05
293	11.87
294	609.51
295	8.88
296	101.63

d. The bank statement includes a deposit of $1,191.17, collected by the bank on behalf of Master Control. Of the total, $1,011.81 is collection of a note receivable, and the remainder is interest revenue.

e. The bank statement shows that Master Control earned $38.19 in interest on its bank balance during August. This amount was added to Master Control's account by the bank.

f. The bank statement lists a $10.50 subtraction for the bank service charge.

g. On August 31, the Master Control treasurer deposited $306.15, but this deposit does not appear on the bank statement.

h. The bank statement includes a $300.00 deposit that Master Control did not make. The bank had erroneously credited the Master Control account for another bank customer's deposit.

i. The August 31 bank balance is $7,784.22.

Required

1. Prepare the bank reconciliation for Master Control, Inc. at August 31.

2. Record in general journal form the entries necessary to bring the book balance of Cash into agreement with the adjusted book balance on the reconciliation. Include an explanation for each entry.

Problem 7-5A *Bank reconciliation and related journal entries* **(L.O. 3)**

Assume selected columns of the cash receipts journal and the cheque register of Hard Rock Café appear as follows at April 30, 19X4:

Cash Receipts Journal (Posting reference is CR)			*Cheque Register* (Posting reference is CD)	
Date	Cash Debit		Cheque No.	Cash Credit
Apr. 2	$ 4,174		3113	$ 991
8	407		3114	147
10	559		3115	1,930
16	2,187		3116	664
22	1,854		3117	1,472
29	1,060		3118	1,000
30	337		3119	632
Total	$ 10,578		3120	1,675
			3121	100
			3122	2,413
			Total	$11,024

Assume the Cash account of Hard Rock Café shows the following information at April 30, 19X4:

Cash

Date	Item	Jrnl. Ref.	Debit	Credit	Balance
Apr. 1	Balance				7,911
30		CR. 6	10,578		18,489
30		CD. 11		11,024	7,465

Hard Rock Café received the following bank statement on April 30, 19X4:

Bank Statement for April 19X4

Beginning Balance..		$ 7,911
Deposits and other Credits		
Apr. 4	$ 4,174	
9	407	
12	559	
17	2,187	
22	1,368 BC	
23	1,854	10,549
Cheques and other Debits		
Apr. 7	$ 991	
13	1,390	
14	903 US	
15	147	

April 18		664	
26		1,472	
30		1,000	
30	20 SC	6,587	
Ending Balance			$11,873

BC = Bank Collection; US = Unauthorized Signature; SC = Service Charge

Additional data for the bank reconciliation include:

a. The unauthorized signature cheque was received from S.M. Holt.

b. The $1,368 bank collection of a note receivable on April 22 included $185 interest revenue.

c. The correct amount of cheque number 3115, a payment on account, is $1,390. (The Hard Rock Café accountant mistakenly recorded the cheque for $1,930.)

Required

1. Prepare the bank reconciliation of Hard Rock Café at April 30, 19X4.
2. Record the entries based on the bank reconciliation. Include explanations.

Problem 7-6A   *Recording and reporting purchases at gross and at net (L.O. 5)*

Dickens & Briscoe, a partnership, does not use a voucher system. On June 1 of the current year, the company had inventory of $71,300. On June 30, the company had inventory of $74,100. Net sales for June were $263,700, and operating expenses were $106,200. During June, Dickens & Briscoe completed the following transactions:

June   2   Purchased inventory costing $41,800 under terms of 2/10 n/30.
   8   Returned $5,800 of the inventory purchased on June 2.
   11   Purchased inventory costing $39,000 on credit terms of 2/10 n/45.
   11   Paid the amount owed from the June 2 invoice, net of the return on June 8.
   17   Purchased inventory costing $47,300 on credit terms of 2/10 n/30.
   20   Paid for the inventory purchased on June 11.
   30   Paid for the purchase on June 17.

Required

1. Assuming Dickens & Briscoe records inventory purchases at gross cost,
   a. Record the transactions in a general journal. Explanations are not required.
   b. Prepare the company's income statement for June of the current year.
2. Assuming Dickens & Briscoe records inventory purchases at net cost,
   a. Record the transactions in a general journal. Explanations are not required.
   b. Prepare the company's income statement for June of the current year.
3. Which method of recording purchases offers the internal control advantage? Give your reason.

Problem 7-7A   *Accounting for petty cash transactions (L.O. 5,6)*

Suppose that on June 1, Hitachi Electronics opens a district office in Gander, Newfoundland, and creates a petty cash fund with an imprest balance of $350. During June, Sharon Dietz, the fund custodian, signs the following petty cash tickets:

Ticket Number	Item	Amount
1	Postage for package received	$ 8.40
2	Decorations and refreshments for office party	13.19
3	Two boxes of floppy disks	16.82
4	Typewriter ribbons	27.13
5	Dinner money for sales manager entertaining a customer	50.00
6	Plane ticket for executive business trip to St. John's	69.00
7	Delivery of package across town	6.30

On June 30, prior to replenishment, the fund contains these tickets plus $147.51. The accounts affected by petty cash disbursements are Office Supplies Expense, Travel Expense, Delivery Expense, Entertainment Expense and Postage Expense.

Required

1. Explain the characteristics and the internal control features of an imprest fund.

2. Make the general journal entries to create the fund and to replenish it. Include explanations. Also, briefly describe what the custodian does on these dates.

3. Make the entry on July 1 to increase the fund balance to $500. Include an explanation and briefly describe what the custodian does.

Problem 7-8A   *Voucher system entries* *(L.O. 7)*

Assume a ComputerGraphics store in Chilliwack, B.C. uses a voucher system and records purchases at gross cost. Assume further that the store completed the following transactions during January:

Jan. 3 Issued voucher no. 135 payable to B.C. Telephone for telephone service of $1,007.

5 Issued voucher no. 136 payable to IBM for the purchase of inventory costing $15,500, with payment terms of 3/10 n/30.

6 Issued voucher no. 137 payable to City Supply Corp. for inventory costing $250, with payment terms of 2/10 n/45

7 Issued cheque no. 404 to pay voucher no. 136.

10 Issued cheque no. 405 to pay voucher no. 135.

14 Issued cheque no. 406 to pay voucher no. 137.

15 Issued voucher no. 138 payable to *The Chilliwack Progress* for advertising of $1,990.

17 Issued voucher no. 139 payable to replenish the petty cash fund. The payee is Petty Cash, and the petty cash tickets list Store Supplies ($16), Delivery Expense ($96) and Miscellaneous Expense ($64). Also issued cheque no. 407 to pay the voucher.

18 Issued voucher no. 140 payable to Apple Computer Company for inventory costing $27,600, with payment terms of 2/10 n/30.

24 Issued voucher no. 141 payable to city of Chilliwack for property tax of $4,235.

27 Issued voucher no. 142 payable to Western Bank for payment of a note payable ($10,000) and interest expense ($1,200).

30 Issued cheque no. 408 to pay voucher no. 140.

31 Issued voucher no. 143 to pay salesperson salary of $2,309 to Lester Gibbs. Also issued cheque no. 409 to pay the voucher.

Required

1. Record ComputerGraphics' transactions in a voucher register and a cheque register like those illustrated in the chapter. Posting references are unnecessary.

2. Open the Vouchers Payable account and post amounts to that account.

3. Prepare the list of unpaid vouchers at January 31 and show that the total matches the balance of Vouchers Payable.

Problem 7-9A *Voucher system; purchases at net* **(L.O. 7)**

Assume that the ComputerGraphics store in Problem 7-8A records its purchases of inventory at net cost.

Required

1. Record the transactions of Problem 7-8A in a voucher register and a cheque register. To account for purchase discounts lost, it is necessary to use a cheque register designed as follows:

				Debit		Credit
Date	Cheque No.	Payee	Voucher No.	Vouchers Payable	Purchase Discounts Lost	Cash in Bank

Cheque Register — Page 4

2. Post to the Vouchers Payable account.

3. Prepare the list of unpaid vouchers at January 31, and show that the total matches the balance of Vouchers Payable.

(Group B)

Problem 7-1B *Identifying the characteristics of an effective internal control system* **(L.O. 1)**

An employee of McNemar Aircraft Service Company recently stole thousands of dollars of the company's cash. The company has decided to install a new system of internal controls.

Required

As controller of McNemar Aircraft Service, write a memo to the president explaining how a separation of duties helps to safeguard assets.

Problem 7-2B *Identifying internal control weaknesses* **(L.O. 2, 4, 5)**

Each of the following situations has an internal control weakness:

a. Discount stores such as Saan and Biway receive a large portion of their sales revenue in cash, with the remainder in credit card sales. To reduce expenses, a store manager ceases purchasing fidelity bonds on the cashiers.

b. The office supply company from which Toland Sporting Goods purchases cash receipt forms recently notified Toland that the last shipped receipts were not prenumbered. Dick Toland, the owner, replied that he did not use the receipt numbers, so the omission is not important.

c. Lancer Computer Programs is a software company that specializes in computer programs with accounting applications. The company's most popular program prepares the general journal, cash receipts journal, voucher register, cheque register, accounts receivable subsidiary ledger and general ledger. In the company's early days, the owner and eight employees wrote the computer programs, lined up manufacturers to produce the diskettes, sold the products to stores such as ComputerLand and ComputerCraft, and performed the general management and accounting of the company. As the company has grown, the number of employees has increased dramatically. Recently, the development of a new software program stopped while the programmers redesigned Lancer's accounting system. Lancer's own accountants could have performed this task.

d. Myra Jones, a widow with no known sources of outside income, has been a trusted employee of Stone Products Company for 15 years. She performs all cash handling and accounting duties, including opening the mail, preparing the bank deposit, accounting for all aspects of cash and accounts receivable, and preparing the bank reconciliation. She has just purchased a new Cadillac and a new home in an expensive suburb. Lou Stone, the owner of the company, wonders how she can afford these luxuries on her salary.

e. Linda Cyert employs three professional interior designers in her design studio. She is located in an area with a lot of new construction, and her business is booming. Ordinarily, Linda does all the purchasing of furniture, draperies, carpets, fabrics, sewing services, and other materials and labor needed to complete jobs. During the summer she takes a long vacation, and in her absence she allows each designer to purchase materials and labor. At her return, Cyert reviews operations and notes that expenses are much higher and net income much lower than in the past.

Required

1. Identify the missing internal control characteristic in each situation.
2. Identify the business's possible problem.
3. Propose a solution to the problem.

Problem 7-3B   *Identifying internal control weakness* **(L.O. 2)**

Algonquin Dental Supply makes all sales on credit. Cash receipts arrive by mail, usually within 30 days of the sale. Brad Stokes opens envelopes and separates the cheques from the accompanying remittance advices. Stokes forwards the cheques to another employee who makes the daily bank deposit but has no access to the accounting records. Stokes sends the remittance advices, which show the amount of cash received, to the accounting department for entry in the accounts. Stokes's only other duty is to grant sales allowances to customers. When he receives a customer cheque for less than the full amount of the invoice, he records the sales allowance and forwards the document to the accounting department.

Required

You are the outside auditor of Algonquin Dental Supply. Write a memo to the company president to identify the internal control weakness in this situation. State how to correct the weakness.

Problem 7-4B   *Bank reconciliation and related journal entries* **(L.O. 3)**

The May 31 bank statement of Pressler Institute has just arrived from Central Bank. To prepare the Pressler bank reconciliation, you gather the following data:

a. The May 31 bank balance is $4,330.82.
b. The bank statement includes two charges for returned cheques from customers. One is an NSF cheque in the amount of $67.50 received from Harley Doherty, a customer, recorded on the books by a debit to Cash and deposited on May 19. The

other is a $195.03 cheque received from Maria Gucci and deposited on May 21. It was returned by Ms. Gucci's bank with the imprint "Unauthorized Signature."

c. The following Pressler cheques are outstanding at May 31:

Cheque No.	Amount
616	$403.00
802	74.25
806	36.60
809	161.38
810	229.05
811	48.91

d. The bank statement includes two special deposits: $899.14, which is the amount of dividend revenue the bank collected from Canadian General Electric on behalf of Pressler; and $16.86, the interest revenue Pressler earned on its bank balance during May.

e. The bank statement lists a $6.25 subtraction for the bank service charge.

f. On May 31, the Pressler treasurer deposited $381.14, but this deposit does not appear on the bank statement.

g. The bank statement includes a $410.00 deduction for a cheque drawn by Marimont Freight, Inc. Pressler promptly notified the bank of its error.

h. Pressler's Cash account shows a balance of $3,521.55 on May 31.

Required

1. Prepare the bank reconciliation for Pressler Institute at May 31.

2. Record in general journal form the entries necessary to bring the book balance of Cash into agreement with the adjusted book balance on the reconciliation. Include an explanation for each entry.

Problem 7-5B *Bank reconciliation and related journal entries* **(L.O. 3)**

Selected columns of the cash receipts journal and cheque register of Gulf Resources appear as follows at March 31, 19X5:

Cash Receipts Journal (Posting reference is CR)		Cheque Register (Posting reference is CD)	
Date	Cash Debit	Cheque No.	Cash Credit
Mar. 4	$2,716	1413	$ 1,465
9	544	1414	1,004
11	1,655	1415	450
14	896	1416	8
17	367	1417	775
25	890	1418	88
31	2,038	1419	4,126
Total	$9,106	1420	930
		1421	200
		1422	2,267
		Total	$11,313

Assume the Cash account of Gulf Resources shows the following information on March 31, 19X5:

Cash

Date	Item	Jrnl. Ref.	Debit	Credit	Balance
Mar. 1	Balance				14,188
31		CR. 10	9,106		23,294
31		CD. 16		11,313	11,981

Gulf Resources received the following bank statement on March 31, 19X5:

Bank Statement for March 19X5

Beginning Balance...		$14,634
Deposits and other Credits		
Mar. 5..	$2,716	
10...	544	
11...	1,655	
15...	896	
18...	367	
25...	890	
31...	1,000 BC	8,068
Cheques and other Debits		
Mar. 1..	441 NSF	
2..	446	
9..	1,465	
13...	1,004	
14...	450	
15...	8	
22...	775	
29...	88	
31...	4,216	
31...	25 SC	(8,918)
Ending Balance...		$13,784

BC = Bank Collection; NSF = Nonsufficient Fund Cheque; SC = Service Charge

Additional data for the bank reconciliation include:

a. The NSF cheque was received late in February from L.M. Arnett.

b. The $1,000 bank collection of a note receivable on March 31 included $122 interest revenue.

c. The correct amount of cheque no. 1419, a payment on account, is $4,216. (The Gulf Resources accountant mistakenly recorded the cheque for $4,126.)

d. The cheque that cleared the bank on March 2 was written during February.

Required

1. Prepare the bank reconciliation of Gulf Resources at March 31, 19X5.
2. Record the entries based on the bank reconciliation. Include explanations.

Problem 7-6B *Recording and reporting purchases at gross and at net (L.O. 5)*

Advanced Design, Inc. does not use a voucher system. On May 1, of the current year the company had inventory of $58,000. On May 31, the company had inventory of $53,700. Net sales for May were $212,800 and operating expenses were $65,100. During May, Advanced Design completed the following transactions:

May 3   Purchased inventory costing $38,500 under terms of 2/10 n/30.
      7   Returned $2,000 of the inventory purchased on May 3.
     10   Purchased inventory costing $28,500 on credit terms of 2/10 n/45.
     12   Paid the amount owed from the May 3 invoice, net of the return on May 7.
     18   Purchased inventory costing $34,000 on credit terms of 2/10 n/30.
     19   Paid for the inventory purchased on May 10.
     29   Paid for the purchase on May 18.

Required

1. Assuming Advanced Design records inventory purchases at gross cost,
   a. Record the transactions in a general journal. Explanations are not required.
   b. Prepare the company's income statement for May of the current year.

2. Assuming Advanced Design records inventory purchases at net cost,
   a. Record the transactions in a general journal. Explanations are not required.
   b. Prepare the company's income statement for May of the current year.

3. Which method of recording purchases offers the internal control advantage? Give your reason.

Problem 7-7B   *Accounting for petty cash transactions (L.O. 5, 6)*

Suppose that on April 1, Ontario Hydro opens a regional office in Orillia and creates a petty cash fund with an imprest balance of $200. During April, Eleanor McGillicuddy, the fund custodian, signs the following petty cash tickets:

Ticket Number	Item	Amount
101	Pencils	$ 6.89
102	Cab fare for executive	25.00
103	Delivery of package across town	7.75
104	Dinner money for executives entertaining a customer	80.00
105	Postage for package received	10.00
106	Refreshments for office party	8.22
107	Two boxes of floppy disks	14.37

On April 30, prior to replenishment, the fund contains these tickets plus $34.77. The accounts affected by petty cash disbursements are Office Supplies Expense, Travel Expense, Delivery Expense, Entertainment Expense, and Postage Expense.

Required

1. Explain the characteristics and internal control features of an imprest fund.

2. Make general journal entries to create the fund and to replenish it. Include explanations. Also, briefly describe what the custodian does on these dates.

3. Make the entry on May 1 to increase the fund balance to $300. Include an explanation and briefly describe what the custodian does.

Problem 7-8B   *Voucher system entries (L.O. 7)*

Assume Eaton's, the department-store chain, uses a voucher system and records purchases at *gross* cost. Assume further that an Eaton's store completed the following transactions during July:

July 2 Issued voucher no. 614 payable to Hathaway Shirt Company for the purchase of inventory costing $21,000, with payment terms of 2/10 n/30.

3 Issued voucher no. 615 payable to Edison Electric for electricity usage of $2,589.

5 Issued cheque no. 344 to pay voucher no. 614.

6 Issued voucher no. 616 payable to Baylor Supply Ltd. for inventory costing $850, with payment terms of 2/10 n/45.

7 Issued cheque no. 345 to pay voucher no. 615.

13 Issued voucher no. 617 payable to replenish the petty cash fund. The payee is Petty Cash, and the petty cash tickets list store supplies ($119), delivery expense ($48) and miscellaneous expense ($36). Also issued cheque no. 346 to pay the voucher.

14 Issued cheque no. 347 to pay voucher no. 616.

18 Issued voucher no. 618 payable to the London Free Press for advertising, $2,800.

19 Issued voucher no. 619 payable to Levi Strauss & Company for inventory costing $65,800, with payment terms of 3/10 n/30.

28 Issued voucher no. 620 payable to city of London for property tax of $9,165.

30 Issued cheque no. 348 to pay voucher no. 619.

31 Issued voucher no. 621 payable to Middlesex Bank for interest expense of $7,000.

31 Issued voucher no. 622 to pay executive salary of $4,644 to Sharon Kratzman. Also issued cheque no. 349 to pay the voucher.

Required

1. Record Eaton's transactions in a voucher register and a cheque register like those illustrated in the chapter. Posting references are unnecessary.

2. Open the Vouchers Payable account with a zero beginning balance and post amounts to that account.

3. Prepare the list of unpaid vouchers at July 31 and show that the total matches the balance of Vouchers Payable.

Problem 7-9B   *Voucher system; purchases at net* **(L.O. 7)**

Assume that the Eaton's store in Problem 7-8B records its purchases of inventory at net cost.

Required

1. Record the transactions of Problem 7-8B in a voucher register and a cheque register. To account for purchase discounts lost, it is necessary to use a cheque register designed as follows:

Cheque Register

				Debit		Credit
Date	Cheque No.	Payee	Voucher No.	Vouchers Payable	Purchase Discounts Lost	Cash in Bank

2. Post to the Vouchers Payable account.

3. Prepare the list of unpaid vouchers at July 31 and show that the total matches the balance of Vouchers Payable.

Extending Your Knowledge

Decision Problems

1. Using the bank reconciliation to detect a theft (L.O. 3)

Agricultural Equipment Company has poor internal control over its cash transactions. Recently Grace Goodrich, the owner, has suspected the cashier of stealing. Details of the business's cash position at September 30 follow:

1. The Cash account shows a balance of $19,502. This amount includes a September 30 deposit of $3,794 that does not appear on the September 30 bank statement.

2. The September 30 bank statement shows a balance of $16,424. The bank statement lists a $200 credit for a bank collection, an $8 debit for the service charge and a $36 debit for an NSF cheque. The Agricultural Equipment accountant has not recorded any of these items on the books.

3. At September 30 the following cheques are outstanding:

Cheque No.	Amount
154	$116
256	150
278	253
291	190
292	206
293	145

4. The cashier handles all incoming cash and makes bank deposits. He also reconciles the monthly bank statement. His September 30 reconciliation follows:

Balance per books, September 30		$19,502
Add: Outstanding cheques............................		560
Bank collection..		200
		20,262
Less: Deposits in transit	$3,794	
Service charge	8	
NSF cheque	36	3,838
Balance per bank, September 30		$16,424

Goodrich has requested that you determine whether the cashier has stolen cash from the business and, if so, how much. Goodrich also asks you to identify how the cashier has attempted to conceal the theft. To make this determination, you perform your own bank reconciliation using the format illustrated in the chapter. There are no bank or book errors. Goodrich also asks you to evaluate the internal controls and recommend any changes needed to improve them.

2. The role of internal control (L.O. 2)

The following questions are unrelated except that they all pertain to internal control:

1. Separation of duties is an important consideration if a system of internal control is to be effective. Why is this so?

2. Cash may be a relatively small item on the financial statements. Nevertheless, internal control over cash is very important. Why do you think this is true?

3. Archer Ltd. requires that all documents supporting a cheque be canceled by the person who signs the cheque. Why do you think this practice is required? What might happen if it were not required?

4. Many managers think that safeguarding assets is the most important objective of internal control systems. Auditors, on the other hand, emphasize reliable accounting data. Explain why auditors are more concerned about the quality of the accounting records.

Ethical Issue

Trevor Smith owns apartment buildings in British Columbia, Alberta, and Manitoba. Each property has a manager who collects rent, arranges for repairs, and runs advertisements in the local newspaper. The property managers transfer cash to Smith monthly and prepare their own bank reconciliations.

The manager in Alberta has been stealing large sums of money. To cover the theft, he understates the amount of outstanding cheques on the monthly bank reconciliation. As a result, each monthly bank reconciliation appears to balance. However, the balance sheet reports more cash than Smith actually has in the bank. In negotiating the sale of the Alberta property, Smith is showing the balance sheet to prospective investors.

Required

1. Identify two parties other than Smith who can be harmed by this theft. In what ways can they be harmed?

2. Discuss the role accounting plays in this situation.

Financial Statement Problems

1. Internal controls and cash (L.O. 1)

Study the manangement's report and the auditors' report on Schneider's financial statements, given in Appendix C. Answer the following questions about Schneider's internal controls and cash position:

1. What is the name of Schneider's outside auditing firm? What office of this firm signed the auditor's report? How long after Schneider's year end did the auditors issue their opinion?

2. Who bears primary responsibility for the financial statements? How can you tell?

3. Does it appear that the Schneider's internal controls are adequate? How can you tell?

4. What standard of auditing did the outside auditors use in examining the Schneider financial statements? By what accounting standards were the statements evaluated?

5. By how much did Schneider's cash position change during 1991? The statement of changes in financial position (discussed in detail in a later chapter) tells why this increase occurred. Which type of activity — operating, investing, or financing — contributed most to this increase?

2. Audit opinion, management responsibility, internal controls, and cash (L.O. 1)

Obtain the annual report of an actual company of your choosing. Study the auditor's report and the management statement of responsibility (if present) in conjunction with the financial statements. Answer these questions about the company:

1. What is the name of the company's outside auditing firm? What office of this firm signed the audit report? How long after the company's year end did the auditors issue their opinion?

2. Who bears primary responsibility for the financial statements? How can you tell?

3. Does it appear that the company's internal controls are adequate? Give your reason.

4. What standard of auditing did the outside auditors use in examining the company's financial statements? By what accounting standards were the statements evaluated?

5. By how much did the company's cash position (including cash equivalents) change during the current year? The statement of changes in financial position (discussed in a later chapter) tells why this increase occurred. Which type of activity — operating, investing, or financing — contributed most to the change in the cash balance?

6. Where is the balance of petty cash reported? Name the financial statement and the account, and identify the specific amount that includes petty cash.

Answers to Self-Study Questions

1.	e	6.	e
2.	d	7.	c
3.	a	8.	a
4.	c	9.	d
5.	b	10.	b

Comprehensive Problem for Part Two

Complete Accounting Cycle for a Merchandising Entity; Special Journals

J.T. McCord Sporting Goods closes its books and prepares financial statements at the end of each month. The company completed the following transactions during August:

Aug. 1 Issued cheque no. 682 for August office rent of $2,000. (Debit Rent Expense.)

2 Issued cheque no. 683 to pay salaries of $1,240, which includes salary payable of $930 from July 31. McCord does *not* use reversing entries.

2 Issued invoice no. 503 for sale on account to R.T. Loeb, $600.

3 Purchased inventory on credit terms of 1/15 n/60 from Grant Publishers, $1,400.

4 Received net amount of cash on account from Fullam Company, $2,156, within the discount period.

4 Sold inventory for cash, $330.

5 Issued credit memo no. 267 to Park-Hee, Inc. for merchandise returned to McCord, $550.

5 Issued cheque no. 684 to purchase supplies for cash, $780.

Aug. 6   Collected interest revenue of $1,100.

       7   Issued invoice no. 504 for sale on account to K.D. Skipper, $2,400.

       8   Issued cheque no. 685 to pay Federal Company $2,600 of the amount owed at July 31. This payment occurred after the end of the discount period.

     11   Issued cheque no. 686 to pay Grant Publishers the net amount owed from August 3.

     12   Received cash from R.T. Loeb in full settlement of her account receivable from August 2.

     16   Issued cheque no. 687 to pay salary expense of $1,240.

     19   Purchased inventory for cash, $850, issuing cheque no. 688.

     22   Purchased furniture on credit terms of 3/15 n/60 from Beaver Corporation, $510.

     23   Sold inventory on account to Fullam Company, issuing invoice no. 505 for $9,966.

     24   Received half of the July 31 amount receivable from K.D. Skipper — after the end of the discount period.

     25   Issued cheque no. 689 to pay utilities, $432.

     26   Purchased supplies on credit terms of 2/10 n/30 from Federal Company, $180.

     30   Returned damaged inventory to company from whom McCord made the cash purchase on August 19, receiving cash of $850.

     30   Granted a sales allowance of $175 to K.D. Skipper, issuing credit memo no. 268.

     31   Purchased inventory on credit terms of 1/10 n/30 from Suncrest Supply, $8,330.

     31   Issued cheque no. 690 to J.T. McCord, owner of the business, for personal withdrawal, $1,700.

Required

1. Open these accounts with their account numbers and July 31 balances in the various ledgers.

General Ledger

101	Cash	$ 4,490
102	Accounts Receivable	22,560
104	Interest Receivable	
105	Inventory	41,800
109	Supplies	1,340
117	Prepaid Insurance	2,200
140	Note Receivable, Long-term	11,000
160	Furniture	37,270
161	Accumulated Depreciation	10,550
201	Accounts Payable	12,600
204	Salary Payable	930
207	Interest Payable	320
208	Unearned Sales Revenue	
220	Note Payable, Long-term	42,000
301	J.T. McCord, Capital	54,260
302	J.T. McCord, Withdrawals	
400	Income Summary	
401	Sales Revenue	
402	Sales Discounts	
403	Sales Returns and Allowances	
410	Interest Revenue	
501	Purchases	

General Ledger

502	Purchase Discounts ....
503	Purchase Returns and Allowances....
510	Salary Expense ....
513	Rent Expense ....
514	Depreciation Expense ....
516	Insurance Expense...............................
517	Utilities Expense ....
519	Supplies Expense.................................
523	Interest Expense..................................

Accounts Receivable Subsidiary Ledger as at July 31   Fullam Company, $2,200; R.T. Loeb, $0; Park-Hee, Inc., $11,590; K.D. Skipper, $8,770.

Accounts Payable Subsidiary Ledger as at July 31   Beaver Corporation, $0; Federal Company, $12,600; Grant Publishers, $0; Suncrest Supply, $0.

2. Journalize the August transactions in a sales journal (page 4), a cash receipts journal (page 11), a purchases journal (page 8), a cash disbursements journal (page 5), and a general journal (page 9). Use the journals as illustrated in Chapter 6. McCord makes all credit sales on terms of 2/10 n/30.

3. Post daily to the accounts receivable subsidiary ledger and the accounts payable subsidiary ledger. On August 31, post to the general ledger.

4. Prepare a trial balance in the Trial Balance columns of a work sheet, and use the following information to complete the work sheet for the month ended August 31:
   a. Accrued interest revenue, $100.
   b. Supplies on hand, $990.
   c. Prepaid insurance expired, $550.
   d. Depreciation expense, $230.
   e. Accrued salary expense, $1,030.
   f. Accrued interest expense, $320.
   g. Unearned sales revenue, $450.*
   h. Inventory on hand, $47,700.

   * Sales revenue was credited when collected in advance. At August 31, $450 of unearned sales revenue needs to be recorded.

5. Prepare J.T. McCord's bank reconciliation at August 31. The bank statement shows a cash balance of $2,863, and lists all cash receipts for the month except the amount received on the 30th. Cheques 689 and 690 did not clear the bank during August. The bank statement also reveals a bank error. The bank mistakenly deducted $870 for cheque number 684. J.T. McCord keeps just enough money on deposit to avoid service charges but earns no interest on the bank balance.

6. Prepare McCord's multiple-step income statement and statement of owner's equity for August. Prepare the balance sheet at August 31.

7. Journalize and post the adjusting and closing entries.

8. Prepare a postclosing trial balance at August 31. Also, balance the total of the customer accounts in the accounts receivable subsidiary ledger against the Accounts Receivable balance in the general ledger. Do the same for the accounts payable subsidiary ledger and Accounts Payable in the general ledger.

Chapter 8

Accounts and Notes Receivable

Have you ever been out with a friend, to a movie or for a night on the town, who at some point remarks that he is out of money and asks if you could lend him $20.00 until payday? No problem, you say, and you advance the $20.00 fully expecting to be repaid in a week or two. A few weeks pass without mention of the $20.00, so you remind your friend of his obligation to you. He insists the money is coming, but his sister's birthday is just around the corner — could you wait a little longer? This conversation is repeated several times over the next few months, with a new excuse each time. After about three months you accept the fact that the $20.00 is gone forever. You are certain your friend does not even remember that he ever owed you anything. About six months after the outing, you mention the money to your friend for the last time.

This is a common experience between friends; businesses also lend money to customers and occasionally these amounts, too, are not repaid. Friends are unlikely to keep detailed accounting records, but when a company has thousands of customers, accounts receivable records are essential. One important accounts receivable question which must be addressed is, when should one record the bad debt expense for unpaid amounts due? For example, if you did record your friend's bad debt, would it be when you first accepted that your friend would not repay the amount (three months after the fact), or would it be when you stopped reminding him of the $20.00 (six months after the outing)?

As you read this chapter, consider what the appropriate accounting solution to this matter is, and how this solution affects the determination of a business's income.

LEARNING OBJECTIVES

After studying this chapter, you should be able to

1 Use the allowance method of accounting for uncollectibles

2 Estimate uncollectibles by the percentage of sales and the aging approaches

3 Use the direct write-off method of accounting for uncollectibles

4 Identify internal control weaknesses in accounts receivable

5 Account for notes receivable

6 Report receivables on the balance sheet

7 Use financial ratios to evaluate a company's position

From automobiles to houses to bicycles to dinners, people buy on credit every day. As high as annual credit sales for retailers are, credit sales are even higher for manufacturers and wholesalers. Clearly, credit sales lie at the heart of the Canadian economy, as they do in other developed countries.

Each credit transaction involves at least two parties: the **creditor**, who sells a service or merchandise, and the **debtor**, who makes the purchase and creates a payable. This chapter focuses on the creditor's accounting. The accounts that generally appear on a creditor's balance sheet are highlighted in Exhibit 8-1. We will discuss these accounts in our study of receivables.

EXHIBIT 8-1 *Balance Sheet*

Example Company
Balance Sheet
Date

Assets			Liabilities		
Current			Current		
Cash		$X,XXX	Accounts payable		$X,XXX
Accounts receivable	**X,XXX**		Notes payable, short-term		X,XXX
Less: Allowance for			Accrued current liabilities		X,XXX
uncollectible accounts	**(XXX)**	**X,XXX**	Total current liabilities		X,XXX
Notes receivable, short-term		**X,XXX**			
Inventories		X,XXX	Long-term		
Prepaid expenses		X,XXX	Notes payable, long-term		X,XXX
Total		X,XXX	Total liabilities		$X,XXX
Investments and long-term receivables			**Owner's Equity**		
Investments in other companies		X,XXX	Capital		X,XXX
Notes receivable, long-term		**X,XXX**	Total liabilities and owner's equity		$X,XXX
Other receivables		**X,XXX**			
Total		X,XXX			
Capital assets					
Property, plant and equipment		X,XXX			
Total assets		$X,XXX			

Different Types of Receivables_____

A receivable arises when a business (or person) sells goods or services to a second business (or person) on credit. A receivable is the seller's claim against the buyer for the amount of the transaction.

Receivables are monetary claims against businesses and individuals. They are acquired mainly by selling goods and services, and by lending money.

The two basic types of receivables are accounts receivable and notes receivable. A business's *accounts receivable* are the amounts that its customers owe it. These accounts receivables are sometimes called *trade receivables*. They are *current assets*.

Accounts receivable should be distinguished from accruals, notes, and other assets not arising from everyday sales because accounts receivable pertain to the main thrust of the business's operations. Moreover, amounts included as accounts receivable should be collectible according to the business's normal sale terms, such as net 30, or 2/10 n/30.

Notes receivable are more formal than accounts receivable. The debtor in a note receivable arrangement promises in writing to pay the creditor a definite sum at a definite future date. The terms of these notes usually extend for at least 60 days. A written document known as a *promissory note* serves as evidence of the receivable. A note may require the debtor to pledge *security* for the loan. This means that the borrower promises that the lender may claim certain assets if the borrower fails to pay the amount due at maturity.

Notes receivable due within one year or less are *current assets*. Those notes due beyond one year are *long-term receivables*. Some notes receivable are collected in periodic installments. The portion due within one year is a current asset, with the remaining amount a long-term asset. The Toronto-Dominion Bank may hold a $6,000 note receivable from you, but only the $1,500 you owe on it this year is a current asset to the Toronto-Dominion Bank.

Other receivables is a miscellaneous category that includes loans to employees and branch companies. Usually these are long-term assets, but they are current if receivable within one year or less. Long-term notes receivable and other receivables are often reported on the balance sheet after current assets and before plant assets as shown in Exhibit 8-1.

Each type of receivable is a separate account in the general ledger, and may be supported by a subsidiary ledger if needed.

The Credit Department _____

A customer who buys goods using a credit card is buying on account. This transaction creates a receivable for the store. Most companies with a high proportion of sales on account, for example, Canadian Tire, have a separate credit department. This department evaluates customers who apply for credit cards by using standard formulas, which include the applicant's income and credit history, among other factors, for deciding which customers the store will sell to on account. After approving a customer, the credit department monitors customer payment records. Customers with a history of paying on time may receive higher and higher credit limits. Those who fail to pay on time have their limits reduced or eliminated. The credit department also assists the accounting department in measuring collection losses on customers who do not pay.

Uncollectible Accounts (Bad Debts) _____

Selling on credit creates both a benefit and a cost. Customers unwilling or unable to pay cash immediately may make a purchase on credit. Revenue and profit rise as sales increase. The cost to the seller of extending credit arises when credit customers do not pay off their debts. Accountants label this cost **uncollectible account expense, doubtful account expense,** or **bad debt expense.**

The extent of uncollectible account expense varies from company to company. Uncollectible account expense depends on the credit risks that managers are willing to accept. Many small retail businesses accept a higher level of risk than large stores like The Bay. Why? Small businesses often have personal ties to customers, which increases the likelihood that customers will pay their accounts.

Measuring Uncollectible Accounts

OBJECTIVE 1

Use the allowance method of accounting for uncollectibles

For a firm that sells on credit, uncollectible account expense is as much a part of doing business as salary expense and depreciation expense. Uncollectible Account Expense, an operating expense, must be measured, recorded and reported. To do so, accountants use the allowance method or the direct write-off method.

Allowance Method   To present the most accurate financial statements possible, accountants in firms with large credit sales use the **allowance method** of measuring bad debts. This method records collection losses based on estimates instead of waiting to see which customers the business will not collect from.

Smart managers know that not every customer will pay in full. But at the time of sale, managers do not know which customers will not pay. Managers do not simply credit Accounts Receivable to write off a customer's account until the business has exhausted its collection effort.

Rather than try to guess which accounts will go bad, managers, based on collection experience, estimate the total bad debt expense for the period. The business debits Uncollectible Account Expense (or Doubtful Account Expense) for the estimated amount, and credits **Allowance for Uncollectible Accounts** (or **Allowance for Doubtful Accounts**), a contra account related to Accounts Receivable. This account holds the estimated amount of collection losses.

To properly match expense against revenue, the uncollectible account expense is estimated, based on past collection experience, and recorded as an adjusting entry during the same period in which the sales are made. This expense entry has two effects: (1) it decreases net income by debiting an expense account, and (2) it decreases *net* accounts receivable by crediting the allowance account. (Allowance for Uncollectible Accounts, the contra account, is subtracted from Accounts Receivable to measure *net* accounts receivable.)

Assume the company's sales for 19X1 are $240,000, and that past collection experience suggests estimated bad debts of $3,100 for the year. The 19X1 journal entries are as follows, with accounts receivable from customers Rolf and Anderson shown separately for emphasis:

19X1	Accounts Receivable — Rolf	1,300	
	Accounts Receivable — Anderson	1,700	
	Accounts Receivable — Various Customers	237,000	
	Sales Revenue		240,000
	To record credit sales.		
19X1	Uncollectible Account Expense	3,100	
	Allowance for Uncollectible Accounts		3,100
	To record estimated bad debt expense, based on past collection experience.		

The account balances at December 31, 19X1 are as follows:

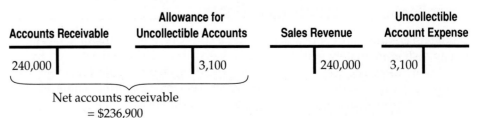

Accounts Receivable	Allowance for Uncollectible Accounts	Sales Revenue	Uncollectible Account Expense
240,000	3,100	240,000	3,100

Net accounts receivable
= $236,900

The 19X1 financial statements will report:

Income Statement	19X1
Revenue	
Sales revenue..	$240,000
Expense	
Uncollectible account expense..	3,100

Balance Sheet	December 31,19X1
Current assets	
Accounts receivable	$240,000
Less: Allowance for uncollectible accounts......................	3,100
Net accounts receivable..	$236,900

Writing off Uncollectible Accounts

During 19X2, the company collects on most of the accounts receivable. However, the credit department determines that customers Rolf and Anderson cannot pay the amounts they owe. The accountant writes off their receivables and makes the following entries:

19X2	Cash	235,000	
	Accounts Receivable —		
	Various Customers.....................................		235,000
	To record collections on account		
19X2	Allowance for Uncollectible Accounts..............	3,000	
	Accounts Receivable — Rolf		1,300
	Accounts Receivable — Anderson		1,700
	To write off uncollectible accounts.		

The write-off entry has no effect on net income because it includes no debit to an expense account. The entry also has no effect on net accounts receivable because both the Allowance account debited and the Accounts Receivable account credited are part of net accounts receivable. The account balances at December 31, 19X2 are as follows:

Accounts Receivable		Allowance for Uncollectible Accounts	
240,000	235,000	3,000	3,100
	1,300		100
	1,700		
2,000			

The financial statements for 19X1 and 19X2 will report the following. In order to highlight the matching of expense and revenue, we are assuming no sales are made in 19X2.

Income Statement	19X1	19X2
Revenue		
Sales revenue	$240,000	$ 0
Expense		
Uncollectible account expense	3,100	0

Balance Sheet	December 31,	
	19X1	19X2
Current assets		
Accounts receivable...	$240,000	$2,000
Less: Allowance for uncollectible accounts.............	3,100	100
Net accounts receivable..	$236,900	$1,900

Bad Debt Write-offs Rarely Equal Allowance for Uncollectibles

The amounts written off in bad debt write-offs of customer accounts are the actual amounts due from the customers, but the allowance amount is based on estimates. Write-offs equal the allowance only if the estimate of bad debts is perfect — a rare occurrence. Usually the difference between write-offs and the allowance is small, as shown in the preceding example. If the allowance is too large for one period, the estimate of bad debts for the next period can be cut back. If the allowance is too low, an adjusting entry debiting Uncollectible Account Expense and crediting Allowance for Uncollectible Accounts can be made at the end of the period. This credit brings the Allowance account to a realistic balance. Estimating uncollectibles will be discussed shortly.

Recoveries of Uncollectible Accounts

When an account receivable is written off as uncollectible, the customer still has an obligation to pay. However, the likelihood of receiving cash is so low that the company ceases its collection effort and writes off the account. Such accounts are filed for use in future credit decisions. Some companies turn them over to a lawyer for collection in the hope of recovering part of the receivable. To record a recovery, the accountant reverses the write-off and records the collection in the regular manner. The reversal of the write-off is needed to give the customer account receivable a debit balance.

Assume that the write-off of Rolf's account ($1,300) occurs in February 19X2. In August, Rolf pays the account in full. The journal entries for this situation follow:

Feb.	19X2	To write off Rolf's account as uncollectible (same as above):		
		Allowance for Uncollectible Accounts	1,300	
		Accounts Receivable — Rolf		1,300
Aug.	19X2	To reinstate Rolf's account:		
		Accounts Receivable — Rolf	1,300	
		Allowance for Uncollectible Accounts ..		1,300
		To record collection from Rolf:		
		Cash	1,300	
		Accounts Receivable — Rolf		1,300

Estimating Uncollectibles

The more accurate the estimate, the more reliable the information in the statements. How are bad debt estimates made?

The most logical way to estimate bad debts is to look at the business's past records. Both the *percentage of sales* method and the *aging of accounts receivable* method use the company's collection experience.

OBJECTIVE 2

Estimate uncollectibles by the percentage of sales and the aging approaches

Percentage-of-Sales   A popular method for estimating uncollectibles computes the expense as a percentage of total credit sales (or total sales). Uncollectible account expense is recorded as an adjusting entry at the end of the period.

Basing its decision on figures from the last four periods, a business estimates that bad debt expense will be 2.5 percent of credit sales. If credit sales for 19X3 total $500,000, the adjusting entry to record bad debt expense for the year is

Adjusting Entries

Dec. 31	Uncollectible Account Expense		
	($500,000 × .025)..	12,500	
	Allowance for Uncollectible Accounts......		12,500

Under the percentage of sales method, the amount of this entry ignores the prior balance in Allowance for Uncollectible Accounts.

A business may change the percentage rate from year to year, depending on its collection experience. Suppose collections of accounts receivable in 19X4 are greater, and write-offs are less, than expected. The credit balance in Allowance for Doubtful Accounts would be too large in relation to the debit balance of Accounts Receivable. How would the business change its bad debt percentage rate in this case? *Decreasing* the percentage rate would reduce the credit entry to the allowance account, and the allowance account balance would not grow too large.

New businesses, with no credit history on which to base their rates, may obtain estimated bad debt percentages from industry trade journals, government publications, and other sources of collection data.

Aging the Accounts   The second popular method of estimating bad debts is called **aging the accounts**. In this approach, individual accounts receivable are analyzed according to the length of time that they have been receivable from the customer. Performed manually, this is time-consuming. Computers greatly ease the burden. Schmidt Home Builders groups its accounts receivable into 30-day periods, as the accompanying table shows:

	Age of Account				
Customer Name	1-30 Days	31-60 Days	61-90 Days	Over 90 Days	Total Balance
Oxwall Tools Corp...............	$20,000				$ 20,000
Calgary Pneumatic Parts Ltd..........................	10,000				10,000
Red Deer Pipe Corp.............		$13,000	$10,000		23,000
Seal Coatings, Inc.................			3,000	$1,000	4,000
Other accounts*....................	39,000	12,000	2,000	2,000	55,000
Totals.....................................	$69,000	$25,000	$15,000	$3,000	$112,000
Estimated percentage uncollectible	0.1%	1%	5%	90%	
Allowance for Uncollectible Accounts	$69	$250	$750	$2,700	$3,769

* Each of the "Other accounts" would appear individually.

Schmidt bases the percentage figures on the company's collection experience. In the past, the business has collected all but 0.1 percent of accounts aged from 1 to 30 days, all but 1 percent of accounts aged 31 to 60 days, and so on.

The total amount receivable in each age group is multiplied by the appropriate percentage figure. For example, the $69,000 in accounts aged 1 to 30 days is multiplied by 0.1 percent (.001), which comes to $69.00. The total balance needed in the Allowance for Uncollectible Accounts, $3,769, is the sum of the amounts computed for the various groups ($69 + $250 + $750 + $2,700).

Suppose the Allowance account has a $2,100 *credit* balance from the previous period, that is, before any current-period adjustment:

Allowance for Uncollectible Accounts

	Unadjusted balance	2,100

Under the aging method, the adjusting entry is designed to adjust this account balance from $2,100 to $3,769, the needed amount. To bring the Allowance balance up to date, Schmidt makes this entry:

Adjusting Entries

Dec. 31	Uncollectible Account Expense	1,669	
	Allowance for Uncollectible Accounts		
	($3,769 – $2,100)		1,669

Observe that under the aging method, the adjusting entry takes into account the prior balance in Allowance for Uncollectibles. Now the Allowance account has the correct balance:

Allowance for Uncollectible Accounts

	Unadjusted balance	2,100
	Adjustment amount	1,669
	Adjusted balance	3,769

It is possible that the allowance account might have a *debit* balance at year end prior to the adjusting entry. How can this occur? Bad debit write-offs during the year could have exceeded the allowance amount. Suppose the unadjusted Allowance for Uncollectible Accounts balance is a *debit* amount of $1,500:

Allowance for Uncollectible Accounts

Unadjusted balance	1,500	

In this situation, the adjusting entry is

Adjusting Entries

Dec. 31	Uncollectible Account Expense	5,269	
	Allowance for Uncollectible Accounts		
	($3,769 + $1,500)...		5,269

After posting, the allowance account is up to date:

Allowance for Uncollectible Accounts

Unadjusted balance	1,500	Adjustment amount	5,269
		Adjusted balance	3,769

On the balance sheet, the $3,769 is subtracted from the Accounts Receivable figure, which is $112,000 in the table on p. 357, to report the expected realizable value of the accounts receivable — $108,231 ($112,000 – $3,769).

In addition to supplying the information needed for accurate financial reporting, the aging method directs management's attention to the accounts that should be pursued for payment.

Comparing the Percentage of Sales and the Aging Methods   In practice, many companies use both the percentage of sales and the aging of accounts methods. For interim statements, monthly or quarterly, companies use the percent of sales method because it is easier to apply. At the end of the year, some companies use the aging method to ensure that Accounts Receivable is reported at expected realizable value. For this reason, auditors usually require an aging of the accounts on the year-end date. The two methods work well together, because the percent of sales approach focuses on measuring bad debt expense on the income statement, whereas the aging approach is designed to measure net accounts receivable on the balance sheet.

Direct Write-off Method   Under the **direct write-off method** of accounting for bad debts, the company waits until the credit department decides that a customer's account receivable is uncollectible. Then the accountant debits Uncollectible Account Expense and credits the customer's account receivable to write off the account.

Assume it is 19X2 and most credit customers have paid for their 19X1 purchases. At this point, the credit department believes that two customers, Chou and Smith, will never pay. The department directs the accountant to write off Chou and Smith as bad debts.

The following entries show the business's accounting for 19X1 credit sales, and 19X2 collections and uncollectible accounts:

> **OBJECTIVE 3**
>
> Use the direct write-off method of accounting for uncollectibles

19X1	Accounts Receivable — Chou	800	
	Accounts Receivable — Smith	1,200	
	Accounts Receivable — Various		
	Customers	98,000	
	Sales Revenue		100,000
	To record credit sales of $100,000.		
19X2	Cash	97,000	
	Accounts Receivable — Various		
	Customers		97,000
	To record cash collections of $97,000.		
19X2	Uncollectible Account Expense	2,000	
	Accounts Receivable — Chou		800
	Accounts Receivable — Smith		1,200
	To write off uncollectible accounts and record bad debt expense of $2,000.		

Of course, this company would continue making credit sales as an important part of doing business. But what we want to know right now is how the direct write-off method affects financial statements. To see its impact most clearly, let us assume that the company stopped making credit sales altogether in 19X2. Consider the following partial financial statements for 19X1 and 19X2, based on the above journal entries:

Income Statement	**19X1**	**19X2**
Revenue		
Sales revenue	$100,000	$ 0
Expense		
Uncollectible account expense	0	2,000

Balance Sheet	**December 31,**	
	19X1	**19X2**
Accounts receivable	$100,000	$1,000

Let us ask two important questions about this approach to accounting for bad debts:

1.   How accurately does the direct write-off method measure income? As we have seen, following generally accepted accounting principles means matching an accounting period's expenses against its revenues. This provides the most accurate picture of operating income, which measures how well a business's operations are running. But the direct write-off method does not match a period's bad debt expense against the same period's sales revenues. In our example, the full amount of sales revenues appears for 19X1, but the expenses incurred to generate this revenue — the bad debts — appear in 19X2. This gives misleading income figures for both years, as would failing to report any other expense, such as salary, depreciation, and so on, in the correct period. The $2,000 bad debt expense should be matched against the $100,000 sales revenues.

2.   How accurately does the direct write-off method value accounts receivable? The 19X1 balance sheet shows accounts receivable at the full $100,000 figure. But any businessperson knows that bad debts are unavoidable when selling on credit. No intelligent manager expects to collect the entire amount. Is the $100,000 figure, then, the expected realizable value of the account? No, showing the full $100,000 in the balance sheet falsely implies that these accounts receivable are worth their face value.

The direct write-off method is simple to use, and it causes no great error if collection losses are insignificant in amount. However, you see that the resulting accounting records are not as accurate as they could be. The allowance method is the better way to account for uncollectible expense.

Credit Balances in Accounts Receivable

Occasionally, customers overpay their accounts or return merchandise for which they have already paid. The result is a credit balance in the customer's accounts receivable. Assume the company's subsidiary ledger contains 213 accounts, with balances as shown:

210	accounts with *debit* balances totaling	$185,000
3	accounts with *credit* balances totaling	2,800
	Net total of all balances	$182,200

The company should *not* report the asset Accounts Receivable at the net amount, $182,200. Why not? The credit balance ($2,800) is a liability. Like any other liability, customer credit balances are debts of the business. A balance sheet that did not indicate to management or to other financial statement users that the company had this liability amount would be misleading if the $2,800 is material in relation to net income or total current assets. Therefore, the company would report on its balance sheet:

Assets		**Liabilities**	
Current		Current	
Accounts receivable...	$185,000	Credit balances in	
		customer accounts	$2,800

Credit Card Sales

Credit card sales are common in retailing. American Express, Diners Club, en Route, Visa, and MasterCard are popular.

The customer presents the credit card as payment for a purchase. The seller prepares a sales invoice in triplicate. The customer and the seller keep copies as receipts. The third copy goes to the credit card company, which then pays the seller the transaction amount and bills the customer.

Credit cards offer consumers the convenience of buying without having to pay the cash immediately. Also, consumers receive a monthly statement from the credit card company, detailing each credit card transaction. They can write a single cheque to cover the entire month's credit card purchases.

Retailers also benefit from credit card sales. They do not have to check a customer's credit rating. The company that issues the card has already done so. Retailers do not have to keep an accounts receivable subsidiary ledger account for each customer, and they do not have to collect cash from customers. The copy of the sales invoice that retailers send to the credit card company signals the card issuer to pursue payment. Further, retailers receive cash more quickly from the credit card companies than they would from the customers themselves. Of course, these services to the seller do not come free.

The seller receives less than 100 percent of the face value of the invoice. The credit card company takes a discount[1] on the sale to cover its services. The seller's entry to record a $100 en Route sale is

Accounts Receivable — en Route	100	
Sales Revenue		100

On collection of the discounted value, assuming a rate of 5 percent, the seller records

Cash	95	
Credit Card Discount Expense	5	
Accounts Receivable — en Route		100

Internal Control over Collections of Accounts Receivable

OBJECTIVE 4

Identify internal control weaknesses in accounts receivable

Businesses that sell on credit receive most of their cash receipts by mail. Internal control over collections on account is an important part of overall internal control. Chapter 7 detailed control procedures over cash receipts, but a critical element of internal control deserves emphasis here: the separation of cash-handling and cash-accounting duties. Consider the following case.

Butler Supply Co. is a small, family-owned business that takes pride in the loyalty of its workers. Most company employees have been with the Butlers for at least five years. The company makes 90 percent of its sales on account.

The office staff consists of a bookkeeper and a supervisor. The bookkeeper maintains the general ledger and the accounts receivable subsidiary ledger. He also makes the daily bank deposit. The supervisor prepares monthly financial statements and any special reports the Butlers require. She also takes sales orders from customers and serves as office manager.

Can you identify the internal control weakness? The bookkeeper has access to the general ledger, accounts receivable subsidiary ledger, and cash. The bookkeeper could take a customer cheque and write off the customer's account as uncollectible.[2] Unless the supervisor or some other manager reviews the bookkeeper's work regularly, the theft may go undetected. In small businesses like Butler Supply Co., such a review may not be routinely performed.

---

[1] The rate varies among companies and over time.
[2] The bookkeeper would need to forge the endorsements of the cheques and deposit them in a bank account he controls.

How can this control weakness be corrected? The supervisor could open in-coming mail and make the daily bank deposit. The bookkeeper should not be al-lowed to handle cash. Only the remittance slips would be forwarded to the bookkeeper to indicate which customer accounts to credit. Removing cash-han-dling duties from the bookkeeper — and keeping the accounts receivable sub-sidiary ledger away from the supervisor — separates duties and strengthens internal control. It reduces an employee's opportunity to steal cash and then cover it up with a false credit to a customer account.

Another step should be taken. The bookkeeper should total the amount posted as credits to customer accounts receivable each day. The owner should then com-pare this total with the day's bank deposit slip. Agreement of the two records gives some assurance that the customer accounts were posted correctly and helps avoid accounting errors. Also, the owner should prepare the bank reconciliation.

Summary Problem for Your Review

Wolfville Lumber Ltd. is a chain of hardware and building supply stores concen-trated in the Maritimes. The company's year-end balance sheets for 19X3 and 19X2 reported:

	19X3	19X2
Receivables	$7,455,648	$8,803,342
Allowance for doubtful receivables	(224,458)	(164,360)

Required

1. How much did Wolfville Lumber Ltd. expect to collect from its accounts re-ceivable at the 19X3 year-end?

2. Suppose Wolfville Lumber estimated doubtful account (uncollectible account) ex-pense for 19X4 to be $267,360, and sales for 19X4 is $8,912,123.
   a. Prepare the journal entry using Wolfville Lumber's terminology (Doubtful Account Expense and Allowance for Doubtful Receivables).
   b. Did Wolfville Lumber change the percentage of sales used to calculate Doubtful Account Expense from 19X3 (when it was 2.7 percent) to 19X4?

3. Assume that during 19X4, Wolfville Lumber wrote off as uncollectible an ac-count receivable of $35,000 from Fundy Company. Journalize this transaction using Wolfville's terminology.

4. Which entry records a decrease in net income? Which entry records a decrease in net accounts receivable?

5. Assume that accounts receivable of $195,000 in addition to the write-off de-scribed in requirement 3 were written off in 19X4, and that Accounts Receivable totaled $7,987,965 at the 19X4 year-end.
   a. What would the Allowance for Doubtful Receivables be at the 19X4 year-end?
   b. What would net accounts receivable be at the 19X4 year-end?

SOLUTION TO REVIEW PROBLEM

1. Wolfville Lumber expected to collect $7,231,190.

2. a. Doubtful Account Expense 267,360
      Allowance for Doubtful Receivables 267,360

 b. The percentage used in 19X4 was 3 percent, an increase of .3 percent.

3. Allowance for Doubtful Receivables............................ 35,000

   Receivables — Fundy Company   35,000

4. Entry 2a. records both a decrease in net income and a decrease in net accounts receivable. The debit to Doubtful Account Expense indicates the decrease in net income. The credit to Allowance for Doubtful Receivables indicates the decrease in net accounts receivable. The Allowance account is a contra account to Receivables. Therefore, crediting the Allowance account increases its own balance and decreases net accounts receivable.

  Entry 3 has no effect on net accounts receivable. The $35,000 debit to the Allowance account records an increase in net accounts receivable, and the $35,000 credit to Receivables records a decrease in net accounts receivable. The debit and credit counterbalance.

5. a. The Allowance for Doubtful Receivables would be $261,818 ($224,458 − $230,000 × $35,000 + $195,000 + $267,360).

  b. Net accounts receivable would be $7,726,147 ($7,987,965 − $261,818).

Notes Receivable

As we pointed out earlier in this chapter, notes receivable are more formal arrangements than accounts receivable. Often the debtor signs a promissory note, which serves as evidence of the debt. Let us take a moment to define the special terms used to discuss notes receivable:

 Promissory note. A written promise to pay a specified sum of money at a particular future date.

 Maker of a note. The person or business that signs the note and promises to pay the amount required by the note agreement. The maker is the debtor.

 Payee of the note. The person or business to whom the maker promises future payment. The payee is the creditor.

 Principal amount or **principal**. The amount loaned out by the payee and borrowed by the maker of the note.

 Interest. The revenue to the payee for loaning out the principal and the expense to the maker for borrowing the principal.

 Interest period. The period of time during which interest is to be computed. It extends from the original date of the note to the maturity date. Also called the *note period* or *note term*.

 Interest rate. The percentage rate that is multiplied by the principal amount to compute the amount of interest on the note.

 Maturity date or *due date*. The date on which final payment of the note is due. Debts with a maturity date are permitted by law to be paid three days after their maturity or due date. These three days are called "days of grace."

 Maturity value. The sum of principal and interest due at the maturity date of a note.

 Exhibit 8-2 illustrates a promissory note. Study it carefully, and identify each of the above items for the note agreement.

Identifying the Maturity Date of a Note

Some notes specify the maturity date of a note, as shown in Exhibit 8-2. Other notes state the period of the note, in days or months. When the period is given in months,

EXHIBIT 8-2 *A Promissory Note*

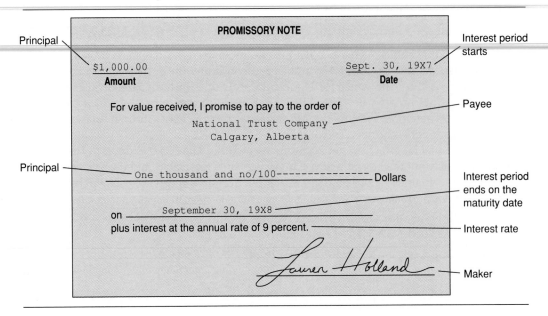

the note's maturity date falls on the same day of the month as the date the note was issued. For example, a 6-month note dated February 16 matures on August 16. With the days of grace taken into account, the note must be repaid by August 19.

When the period is given in days, the maturity date is determined by counting the days from date of issue. A 120-day note dated September 14, 19X2, matures on January 12, 19X3, as shown below:

Month		Number of Days	Cumulative Total
Sept.	19X2	16*	16
Oct.	19X2	31	47
Nov.	19X2	30	77
Dec.	19X2	31	108
Jan.	19X3	12	120

*30 – 14 = 16

The note would have to be repaid by January 15, 19X3.

Computing Interest on a Note

The formula for computing interest is

Principal × Rate × Time = Amount of Interest

Using the data in Exhibit 8-2, National Trust Company computes its interest revenue for 1 year on its note receivable as:

Principal		Rate		Time		Interest
$1,000	×	.09	×	1 (yr.)	=	$90

The *maturity value* of the note is $1,090 ($1,000 principal + $90 interest). Note that the time element is one (1) because interest is computed over a 1-year period.

When the interest period of a note is stated in months, we compute the interest based on the 12-month year. Interest on a $2,000 note at 15 percent for 3 months is computed as

Principal		Rate		Time		Interest
$2,000	×	.15	×	3/12	=	$75

When the interest period of a note is stated in days, we sometimes compute interest based on a 365-day year. The interest on a $5,000 note at 12 percent for 60 days is computed as

Principal		Rate		Time		Interest
$5,000	×	.12	×	60/365	=	$98.63

Recording Notes Receivable

Consider the loan agreement shown in Exhibit 8-2. After Holland signs the note and presents it to the trust company, National Trust gives her $1,000 cash. At maturity date, Holland pays the bank $1,090 ($1,000 principal + $90 interest). The trust company's entries are

> **OBJECTIVE 5**
> Account for notes receivable

Sept. 30, 19X7	Note Receivable — L. Holland................	1,000	
	Cash...		1,000
	To record the loan.		
Sept. 30, 19X8	Cash...	1,090	
	Note Receivable — L. Holland..........		1,000
	Interest Revenue ($1,000 × .09 × 1)....		90
	To record collection at maturity.		

Some companies sell merchandise in exchange for notes receivable. This arrangement occurs often when the payment term extends beyond the customary accounts receivable period, which generally ranges from 30 to 60 days.

Suppose that on October 20, 19X3, Canadian General Electric (CGE) sells equipment for $15,000 to Dorman Builders. Dorman signs a 90-day promissory note at 10 percent interest. CGE's entries to record the sale and collection from Dorman are

Oct. 20, 19X3	Note Receivable		
	— Dorman Builders.....................	15,000	
	Sales Revenue..........................		15,000
	To record sale.		
Jan. 18, 19X4	Cash...	15,370	
	Note Receivable		
	— Dorman Builders................		15,000
	Interest Revenue		
	($15,000 × .10 × 90/365).........		370
	To record collection at maturity.		

A company may accept a note receivable from a trade customer who fails to pay an account receivable within the customary 30 to 60 days. The customer signs a promissory note (that is, becomes the maker of the note) and gives it to the creditor (who becomes the payee).

Suppose Maison Fortin Inc. sees that it will not be able to pay off its account payable to Hoffman Supply, which is due in 15 days. Hoffman may accept a note receivable from Maison Fortin. Hoffman's entry is

May 3	Note Receivable — Maison Fortin Inc...................	2,400	
	Accounts Receivable —		
	Maison Fortin Inc.		2,400
	To receive a note on account from a customer.		

Hoffman later records interest and collection as illustrated in the preceding examples.

Why does a company accept a note receivable instead of pressing its demand for payment of the account receivable? The company may pursue payment but learn that its customer does not have the money. A note receivable gives the company written evidence of the maker's debt, which may aid any legal action for collection. Also, the note receivable may carry a pledge by the maker that gives the payee certain assets if cash is not received by the due date. The company's reward for its patience in collecting is the interest revenue that it earns on the note receivable.

Discounting a Note Receivable

A note receivable is a *negotiable instrument*, which means it is readily transferable from one business or person to another, and may be sold for cash. To get cash quickly, payees sometimes sell a note receivable to another party before the note matures. The payee endorses the note and hands it over to the note purchaser, often a bank, who collects the maturity value of the note at the maturity date.

Selling a note receivable before maturity is called **discounting a note receivable** because the payee of the note receives less than its maturity value. This lower price decreases the amount of interest revenue the original payee earns on the note. Giving up some of this interest is the price the payee pays for the convenience of receiving cash early.

Return to the preceding example with Canadian General Electric and Dorman. Recall that the maturity date of the Dorman note is January 18, 19X4. Let us assume CGE discounts the Dorman note at the National Bank on December 9, 19X3. The discount period, which is the number of days from the date of discounting to the date of maturity (the period the bank will hold the note), is 40 days: 22 days in December and 18 days in January. Assume the bank applies a 12 percent interest rate in computing the discounted value of the note. The bank will want to use a discount rate that is higher than the interest rate on the note in order to increase its earnings. CGE may be willing to accept this higher rate in order to get cash quickly. The discounted value, called the *proceeds*, is the amount that CGE receives from the bank. The proceeds are computed as follows:

	Principal amount	$15,000	
+	Interest ($15,000 × .10 × 90/365)	370	
=	Maturity value..	$15,370	$168 $168
−	Discount ($15,370 × .12 × 40/365)....................	(202)	
=	Proceeds	$15,168	

At maturity the bank collects $15,370 from the maker of the note, earning $202 of interest revenue.

Observe two points in the above computation: (1) the discount is computed on the *maturity value* of the note (principal + interest) rather than on the original principal amount; and (2) the discount period extends *backward* from the maturity date (January 18, 19X4) to the date of discounting (December 9, 19X3). Follow this diagram:

Oct. 20, 19X3		90 Days		Jan. 18, 19X4
Principal $15,000	+	Interest $370	=	Maturity $15,370
		Dec. 9, 19X3	40 Days	Jan. 18, 19X4
		Proceeds $15,168	= Discount $202	− Maturity $15,370

Canadian General Electric's entry to record discounting the note is

Dec. 9, 19X3	Cash	15,168	
	Note Receivable		
	— Dorman Builders...........................		15,000
	Interest Revenue		
	($15,168 – $15,000)		168
	To record discounting a note receivable.		

When the proceeds from discounting a note receivable are less than the principal amount of the note, the payee records a debit to Interest Expense for the amount of the difference. For example, CGE could discount the note receivable for cash proceeds of $14,980. The entry to record this transaction is

Dec. 9 19X3	Cash...	14,980	
	Interest Expense..	20	
	Note Receivable — Dorman Builders..		15,000

When Receive less (handwritten annotation)

The term *discount* has been used here to distinguish the interest earned by the payee of the note from the interest to be earned by the purchaser of the note. Fundamentally, the discount is interest.

Contingent Liabilities on Discounted Notes Receivable

Discounting a note receivable creates a **contingent** (that is, potential) **liability** for the endorser. The contingent liability is, if the maker of the note (Dorman, to continue our example) fails to pay the maturity value to the new payee (the bank), the original payee (Canadian General Electric, the note's endorser) legally must pay the bank the amount due.[3] Now we see why the liability is "potential." If Dorman pays the bank, CGE can forget the note. But if Dorman dishonors the note (fails to pay it), CGE has an actual liability.

This contingent liability exists from the time of endorsement to the maturity date of the note. In our example, the contingent liability exists from December 9, 19X3 when CGE endorsed the note to the January 18, 19X4 maturity date.

Contingent liabilities are not reported with actual liabilities on the balance sheet. After all, they are not real debts. However, financial-statement users should be alerted that the business has incurred *potential* debts. Generally accepted accounting principles require disclosure of material contingent liabilities; most businesses report contingent liabilities in a footnote to the financial statements. Canadian General Electric's end-of-period balance sheet might carry this note:

> As of December 31, 19X3, the Company is contingently liable on notes receivable discounted in the amount of $15,000.

Dishonored Notes Receivable

If the maker of a note does not pay a note receivable at maturity (plus the days of grace), the maker is said to **dishonor** or **default on** the note. Because the term of the note has expired, the note agreement is no longer in force, nor is it negotiable. However, the payee still has a claim against the maker of the note for payment, and usually transfers the claim from the note receivable account to Accounts Receivable. The payee records interest revenue earned on the note and debits Accounts Receivable for full maturity value of the note.

---

[3] The discounting agreement between the endorser and the purchaser may specify that the endorser has no liability if the note is dishonored at maturity.

Suppose Rubinstein Jewelers has a six-month, 10 percent note receivable for $1,200 from D. Hatachi. On the February 3 maturity date, Hatachi defaults. Rubinstein Jewelers would record the default as follows:

Feb. 3	Accounts Receivable — D. Hatachi	
	[$1,200 + ($1,200 × .10 × %₂)].............................. 1,260	
	Note Receivable — D. Hatachi.........................	1,200
	Interest Revenue ($1,200 × .10 × %₂)	60
	To record dishonor of note receivable.	

Rubinstein would pursue collection from Hatachi as a promissory note default. The company may treat accounts receivable such as this as a special category to highlight them for added collection efforts. If the account receivable later proves uncollectible, the account is written off against Allowance for Uncollectible Accounts in the manner previously discussed.

The maker may dishonor a note after it has been discounted by the original payee. For example, suppose Dorman Builders dishonors its note (maturity value, $15,370) to Canadian General Electric after CGE has discounted the note to the bank. On dishonor, the bank adds a *protest fee* to cover the cost of a statement about the facts of the dishonor and requests payment from CGE, which then becomes the holder of the dishonored note. Assume CGE pays the maturity value of the note, plus the $25 protest fee, to the bank. This creates an obligation for Dorman to CGE. CGE then presents the statement to Dorman and makes the following entry on the maturity date of the note:

Jan. 18, 19X4	Accounts Receivable — Dorman	
	Builders ($15,370 + $25) 15,395	
	Cash	15,395
	To record payment of dishonored note re-ceivable that has been discounted.	

CGE's collection of cash or write-off of the uncollected account receivable would be recorded in the normal manner, depending on the ultimate outcome. If CGE charges Dorman additional interest, CGE's collection entry debits Cash and credits Accounts Receivable and Interest Revenue.

Accruing Interest Revenue

Notes receivable may be outstanding at the end of the accounting period. The interest revenue that was accrued on the note up to that point should be recorded as part of that period's earnings. Recall that interest revenue is earned over time, not just when cash is received.

Suppose the Royal Bank receives a one-year, $1,000 note receivable, with 9 percent interest, on August 1, 19X7. The bank's accounting period ends October 31. How much of the total interest revenue does the Royal Bank earn in 19X7? How much in 19X8?

The bank will earn three months' interest in 19X7 for August, September, and October. In 19X8, the bank will earn nine months' interest for November, 19X7 through July. 19X8. Therefore, at October 31, 19X7, the Royal Bank will make the following adjusting entry to accrue interest revenue:

Oct. 31, 19X7	Interest Receivable ($1,000 × .09 × ³⁄₁₂)......... 22.50	
	Interest Revenue	22.50
	To accrue interest revenue earned in 19X7 but not yet received.	

Then, on the maturity date the Royal Bank may record collection of principal and interest as follows:

July 31, 19X8   Cash [$1,000 + ($1,000.09)].......................   1,090.00
              Note Receivable 1,000.00
              Interest Receivable
               ($1,000 $\times$ .09 $\times$ $\frac{3}{12}$)...........................   22.50
              Interest Revenue
               ($1,000 $\times$ .09 $\times$ $\frac{9}{12}$)...........................   67.50
              To record collection of note receiable
              on which interest has been previously
              accrued.

The entries to accrue interest revenue earned in 19X7 and record collection in 19X8 assign the correct amount of interest to each year.

Reporting Receivables and Allowances: Actual Reports

We will now look at how some companies report their receivables and allowances for uncollectibles in the financial statements. The terminology and setup vary, but you can understand these actual presentations based on what you have learned in this chapter.

Section 3020.01 in the *CICA Handbook* indicates that because "...it is... assumed that adequate allowance for doubtful accounts has been made... it is not considered necessary to refer to [the] allowance" in the financial statements. The 1991 edition of *Financial Reporting in Canada*, published by the CICA, indicates that 6 percent of the 300 companies surveyed made reference, on the balance sheet or in the notes, to the allowance in 1990.[4]

One Canadian company that did provide information was BCE. In their 1991 annual report, they reported (amounts in millions):

OBJECTIVE 6
Report receivables on the balance sheet

	1991	1990
Current assets		
Accounts receivable (note 8)	3,992	3,930

Notes to the Consolidated Financial Statements
8. Accounts receivable
   Provision for uncollectibles was $61 million (1990: $50 million).

Harsco Corporation, a diversified U.S. manufacturer with operations in Canada, reports in its 1991 financial statements (in thousands):

	1991	1990
Current assets		
Notes and accounts receivable, less allowance for uncollectible accounts ($13,489 and $13,578)	273,864	216,970

To figure the total accounts receivable amount, add the allowance to the net accounts receivable amount. For 1991, $273,864 + $13,489 = $287,353.

While some companies such as BCE and Harsco provide information about the allowance for doubtful accounts, as was suggested above, many companies in

[4] *Financial Reporting in Canada 1991*, 19th edition (Toronto: CICA, 1992) p. 76.

Canada such as Canadian General Electric tend to show only net accounts receivable. They do not show the allowance. For example, Canadian General Electric reports a single amount for its current receivables in the body of the balance sheet, and supplements it with a detailed note (amounts in thousands).

Current receivables (note 8)...	$340,182

Note 8:   Current receivables

Customer accounts	$294,790
Parent company	23,932
Advance to related company	1,086
Progress payments to suppliers..	3,888
Other receivables	16,486
Total	$340,182

CGE also has long-term receivables of $10,598,000. The balance is located between Current Assets and Plant and Equipment on the balance sheet.

MacLean Hunter, the publishing, broadcasting and cable television conglomerate, includes long-term receivables after fixed assets. The exact placement is less important than the fact that the long-term receivables are properly described and not included with current assets.

A manufacturer of machinery related to construction that was called Anthes Industries reported in a note to the financial statements that the company was contingently liable under sales contracts financed by others in the amount of $1,500,000. The note to the financial statements suggests that Anthes sold equipment on a finance contract, and then sold the contract to a financial institution. As the seller, Anthes was contingently liable if the purchaser did not pay the financial institution.

OBJECTIVE 7

Use financial ratios to evaluate a company's position

Use of Accounting Information in Decision-Making

The balance sheet lists assets in the order of relative liquidity. Cash, of course, comes first because it is the medium of exchange, and can be used to purchase any item or pay any bill. Current receivables are less liquid than cash because receivables must be collected. Merchandise inventory is less liquid than receivables because the goods must first be sold, which creates a receivable that can be collected. Exhibit 8-1 provides an example of a balance sheet showing these accounts.

In making decisions, owners and managers use some ratios based on the relative liquidity of assets. In Chapter 4, for example, we discussed the current ratio, which indicates the ability to pay current liabilities with current assets. A more stringent measure of the ability to pay current liabilities is the **acid-test** (or **quick**) ratio. The acid-test ratio assumes that all current liabilities are payable immediately, and that the debtor will convert the most liquid assets to cash. The three most liquid asset categories are cash, short-term investments, and current receivables. Short-term investments (covered in Chapter 17) are the second most liquid assets because they are readily convertible to cash at the will of the owner. All the owner must do to generate cash is sell these investments. The acid-test ratio is computed as follows:

$$\text{Acid-test ratio} = \frac{\text{Cash + Short-term investments +}\ \text{Net current receivables}}{\text{Total current liabilities}}$$

The higher the acid-test ratio, the better able the business is to pay its current liabilities. An increasing acid-test ratio over time usually indicates improving business operations.

Inventory is excluded from the acid-test ratio because it may not be easy to sell the goods. A company may have an acceptable current ratio and a poor acid-test ratio because of a large amount of inventory. Note that inventory is included in the computation of the current ratio but not of the acid-test ratio.

What is an acceptable acid-test ratio value? It depends on the industry. Automobile dealers can operate smoothly with an acid-test ratio of .20. The average acid-test ratio for women's dress manufacturers is .90. Most department stores' ratio values cluster about .80, and travel agencies average 1.10. In general, an acid-test ratio of 1.00 is considered safe.

After a business makes a credit sale, the next critical event in the business cycle is collection of the receivable. Several financial ratios center on receivables. **Days' sales in receivables**, also called the *collection period*, indicates how many days it takes to collect the average level of receivables. The shorter the collection period, the more quickly the organization can use cash for operations. The longer the collection period, the less cash is available to pay bills and expand. Days' sales in receivables can be computed in two steps, as follows:

1. One day's sales $= \dfrac{\text{Net sales}}{\text{365 days}}$

2. Days' sales in average accounts receivable $= \dfrac{\text{Average net accounts receivable}}{\text{One day's sales}} = \dfrac{(\text{Beginning net receivables} + \text{Ending net receivables})/2}{\text{One day's sales}}$

The length of the collection period depends on the credit terms of the company's sales. For example, sales on net 30 terms should be collected within approximately 30 days. When there is a discount, such as 2/10 net 30, the collection period may be shorter. Terms of net 45 or net 60 will result in longer collection periods. Companies watch their collection period closely. Whenever the collection period lengthens, the business must find other sources of financing, such as borrowing. During recessions, customers pay more slowly, and a longer collection period is unavoidable.

Computers and Accounts Receivable

Accounting for receivables for a company like McCain Foods Ltd. requires tens of thousands of postings to customer accounts each month for credit sales and cash collections. Manual accounting methods cannot keep up.

Accounts Receivable can be set up on a computer as a menu-driven module (a module is a part of a software program). The menu — so called because it presents the user with a number of choices, as a diner would have at a restaurant — allows the user to choose the appropriate action. The person at the keyboard could choose to set up the accounts receivable ledger, to modify the ledger, or to take whatever action is appropriate. The screen would then ask for information from the computer operator: customer number, product number of the items ordered, number of items ordered, discount terms, shipment terms, and so on.

The computer then creates a sales invoice. At the same time, the computer generates records that lead to the sales journal printout. The printout is checked and approved. Finally, computerized posting to the general ledger and the accounts receivable subledger occurs.

Computerized accounting packages prepare a report for aging accounts receivable. The computer accesses files of customer data, and sorts accounts by customer number and date of invoice.

Computers also discount notes. If the company deals with relatively few discounted notes, a spreadsheet may handle the accounting (if the accounting software package does not include a special function for discounting). The column heads would be date of note, principal amount, interest rate, maturity date, maturity value, date of discounting, and so on. Big-league spreadsheets calculate interest based on their internal calendar. The accountant need not even enter the number of days the note is outstanding.

Summary Problem for Your Review

Suppose Petro-Canada engaged in the following transactions:

19X4

Apr.	4	Loaned $8,000 to Bland Ltd., a service station operator. Received a one-year, 10 percent note.
June	4	Discounted the Bland note at the bank at a discount rate of 12 percent.
Nov.	30	Loaned $6,000 to Houle, Inc., a regional distributor of Petro-Canada products, on a three-month, 11 percent note.

19X5

Feb.	28	Collected the Houle note at maturity.

Petro-Canada's accounting period ends on December 31.

Required

Explanations are not needed.

1. Record the 19X4 transactions on April 4, June 4 and November 30 on Petro-Canada's books.
2. Make any adjusting entries needed on December 31, 19X4.
3. Record the February 28, 19X5 collection of the Houle note.
4. Which transaction creates a contingent liability for Petro-Canada? When does the contingency begin? When does it end?
5. Write a footnote that Petro-Canada could use in its 19X4 financial statements to report the contingent liability.

SOLUTION TO REVIEW PROBLEM

19X4

1. Apr.	4	Note Receivable — Bland Ltd.	8,000	
		Cash		8,000
	June 4	Cash..	7,920*	
		Interest Expense..	80	
		Note Receivable — Bland Ltd.............		8,000
	Nov. 30	Note Receivable — Houle, Inc...................	6,000	
		Cash		6,000

*Computation of proceeds

Principal	$8,000
+ Interest ($8,000 × .10 × $^{12}/_{12}$)...............	800
= Maturity value.................................	8,800
− Discount ($8,800 × .12 × $^{10}/_{12}$)............	880
= Proceeds	$7,920

2.   **Adjusting Entries**

19X4

	Dec. 31	Interest Receivable ($6,000 x .11 x ½).........	55	
		Interest Revenue		55

3.

19X5

Feb. 28

Cash [$6,000 + ($6,000 × .11 × ³/₁₂)]	6,165		
Note Receivable — Houle, Inc.............		6,000	
Interest Receivable................................		55	
Interest Revenue ($6,000 × .11 × ²/₁₂)		110	

4. Discounting the Bland note receivable creates a contingent liability for Petro-Canada. The contingency exists from the date of discounting the note receivable (June 4) to the maturity date of the note (April 4, 19X5).

5. Note XX — Contingent liabilities: At December 31, 19X4, the Company is contingently liable on notes receivable discounted in the amount of $8,000. (Note: In reality, the contingent liability is so small relative to Petro-Canada's assets that its existence would not be disclosed; the example is illustrative.)

Summary

Credit sales create receivables. Accounts receivable are usually current assets, and notes receivable may be current or long-term.

Uncollectible receivables are accounted for by the allowance method or the direct write-off method. The *allowance method* matches expenses to sales revenue, and also results in a more realistic measure of net accounts receivable. The *percentage of sales method* and the *aging of accounts receivable method* are the two main approaches to estimating bad debts under the allowance method. The *direct write-off method* is easy to apply, but it fails to match the uncollectible account expense to the corresponding sales revenue. Also, Accounts Receivable are reported at their full amount, which misleadingly suggests that the company expects to collect all its accounts receivable.

In *credit card* sales, the seller receives cash from the credit card company (Visa, for example), which bills the customer. For the convenience of receiving cash immediately, the seller pays a fee, which is a percentage of the sale.

Companies that sell on credit receive most customer collections in the mail. Good *internal control* over mailed-in cash receipts means separating cash-handling duties from cash-accounting duties.

Notes receivable are formal credit agreements. Interest earned by the creditor is computed by multiplying the note's principal amount by the interest rate times the length of the interest period. Remember, the law allows the maker three extra days after the maturity date, the *days of grace*, to repay the payee.

Because notes receivable are negotiable, they may be sold. Selling a note receivable, called *discounting a note*, creates a *contingent (possible) liability* for the note's payee.

Accounts receivable and notes receivable usually appear at their net amount in the balance sheet in Canada; the allowance for doubtful accounts may or may not be disclosed. Companies use various formats and terms to report these assets.

Self-Study Questions

Test your understanding of the chapter by marking the correct answer for each of the following questions:

1. The party that holds a receivable is called the *(p. 352)*
   - a. Creditor
   - b. Debtor
   - c. Maker
   - d. Security holder

2. The function of the credit department is to *(p. 353)*
   a. Collect accounts receivable from customers
   b. Report bad credit risks to other companies
   c. Evaluate customers who apply for credit
   d. Write off uncollectible accounts receivable

3. Longview, Inc. made the following entry related to uncollectibles:

   Uncollectible Account Expense 1,900
       Allowance for Uncollectible Accounts..............   1,900

   The purpose of this entry is to *(p. 354)*
   a. Write off uncollectibles   c. Age the accounts receivable
   b. Close the expense account   d. Record bad debt expense

4. Longview, Inc. also made this entry:

   Allowance for Uncollectible Accounts 2,110
       Accounts Receivable (detailed).........................   2,110

   The purpose of this entry is to *(p. 355)*
   a. Write off uncollectibles   c. Age the accounts receivable
   b. Close the expense account   d. Record bad debt expense

5. The credit balance in Allowance for Uncollectibles is $14,300 prior to the adjusting entries at the end of the period. The aging of accounts indicates that an allowance of $78,900 is needed. The amount of expense to record is *(p. 358)*
   a. $14,300   c. $78,900
   b. $64,600   d. $93,200

6. The most important internal control over cash receipts is *(p. 361)*
   a. Assigning an honest employee the responsibility for handling cash
   b. Separating the cash-handling and cash-accounting duties
   c. Ensuring that cash is deposited in the bank daily
   d. Centralizing the opening of incoming mail in a single location

7. A six-month, $30,000 note specifies interest of 9 percent. The full amount of interest on this note will be *(pp. 364–5)*
   a. $450   c. $1,350
   b. $900   d. $2,700

8. The note in the preceding question was issued on August 31, and the company's accounting year ends on December 31. The year-end balance sheet will report interest receivable of *(pp. 368–9)*
   a. $450   c. $1,350
   b. $900   d. $2,700

9. Discounting a note receivable is a way to *(p. 366)*
   a. Collect on a note   c. Both of the above
   b. Increase interest revenue   d. None of the above

10. Discounting a note receivable creates a (an) *(p. 367)*
    a. Cash disbursement   c. Protest fee
    b. Interest expense   d. Contingent liability

Answers to the Self-Study Questions are at the end of the chapter.

Accounting Vocabulary

acid-test ratio *(p. 370)*	allowance method	debtor *(p. 352)*
aging of accounts	*(p. 354)*	default on a note *(p. 367)*
receivable *(p. 357)*	bad debt expense *(p. 353)*	direct write-off method
allowance for doubtful	contingent liability	*(p. 359)*
accounts *(p. 354)*	*(p. 367)*	discounting a note
allowance for	creditor *(p. 352)*	receivable *(p. 366)*
uncollectible	day's sales in	dishonor of a note
accounts *(p. 354)*	receivables *(p. 371)*	*(p. 367)*

doubtful account
    expense *(p. 353)*
interest *(p. 363)*
interest period *(p. 363)*
interest rate *(p. 363)*
maker of a note *(p. 363)*

maturity date *(p. 363)*
maturity value *(p. 363)*
other receivables *(p. 352)*
payee of a note *(p. 363)*
principal amount *(p. 363)*
promissory note *(p. 363)*

quick ratio *(p. 370)*
receivable *(p. 352)*
uncollectible account
    expense *(p. 353)*

ASSIGNMENT MATERIAL _____

Questions

1. Name the two parties to a receivable/payable transaction. Which party has the receivable? Which party has the payable? Which party has the asset? Which party has the liability?

2. List three categories of receivables. State how each category is classified for reporting on the balance sheet.

3. Name the two methods of accounting for uncollectible receivables. Which method is easier to apply? Which method is consistent with generally accepted accounting principles?

4. Which of the two methods of accounting for uncollectible accounts is preferable? Why?

5. Identify the accounts debited and credited to account for uncollectibles under (a) the allowance method, and (b) the direct write-off method.

6. What is another term for Allowance for Uncollectible Accounts? What are two other terms for Uncollectible Account Expense?

7. Which entry decreases net income under the allowance method of accounting for uncollectibles: the entry to record uncollectible account expense, or the entry to write off an uncollectible account receivable?

8. May a customer pay his or her account receivable after it has been written off? If not, why not? If so, what entries are made to account for reinstating the customer's account and for collecting cash from the customer?

9. Identify and briefly describe the two ways to estimate bad debt expense and uncollectible accounts.

10. Briefly describe how a company may use both the percentage-of-sales method and aging method to account for uncollectibles.

11. How does a credit balance arise in a customer's account receivable? How does the company report this credit balance on its balance sheet?

12. Many businesses receive most of their cash on credit sales through the mail. Suppose you own a business so large that you must hire employees to handle cash receipts and perform the related accounting duties. What internal control feature should you use to ensure that cash received from customers is not taken by a dishonest employee?

13. Use the terms *maker, payee, principal amount, maturity date, promissory note,* and *interest* in an appropriate sentence or two.

14. For each of the following notes receivable, compute the amount of interest revenue earned during 19X6:

		Principal	Interest Rate	Interest Period	Maturity Date
a.	Note 1	$ 10,000	9%	90 days	11/30/19X6
b.	2	50,000	10	6 months	9/30/19X6
c.	3	100,000	8	5 years	12/31/19X7
d.	4	15,000	12	60 days	1/15/19X7

15. Name three situations in which a company might receive a note receivable. For each situation, show the account debited and the account credited to record receipt of the note.

16. Suppose you hold a 180-day, $5,000 note receivable that specifies 10 percent interest. After 60 days you discount the note at 12 percent. How much cash do you receive?

17. How does a contingent liability differ from an ordinary liability? How does discounting a note receivable create a contingent liability? When does the contingency cease to exist?

18. When the maker of a note dishonors the note at maturity, what accounts does the payee debit and credit?

19. Why does the payee of a note receivable usually need to make adjusting entries for interest at the end of the accounting period?

20. Recall the real-world disclosures of receivables the chapter presents. Show three ways to report Accounts Receivable of $100,000 and Allowance for Uncollectible Accounts of $2,800 on the balance sheet or in the related notes.

21. Why is the acid-test ratio a more stringent measure of the ability to pay current liabilities than is the current ratio?

22. Which measure of days' sales in receivables is preferable, 30 or 40? Give your reason.

Exercises

Exercise 8-1 *Using the allowance method for bad debts* **(L.O. 1)**

On September 30, Maxwell Ltd. had a $26,000 debit balance in Accounts Receivable. During October, the company had sales of $135,000, which included $88,000 in credit sales. October collections were $91,000 and write-offs of uncollectible receivables totaled $1,070. Other data include:

a. September 30 credit balance in Allowance for Uncollectible Accounts, $2,100.

b. Uncollectible account expense, estimated as 2 percent of credit sales.

Required

1. Prepare journal entries to record sales, collections, uncollectible account expense by the allowance method, and write-offs of uncollectibles during October.

2. Show the ending balances in Accounts Receivable, Allowance for Uncollectible Accounts, and Net Accounts Receivable at October 31. Does Maxwell expect to collect the net amount of the receivable?

Exercise 8-2 *Recording bad debts by the allowance method* **(L.O. 1)**

Prepare general journal entries to record the following transactions under the allowance method of accounting for uncollectibles:

Apr. 2   Sold merchandise for $3,700 on credit terms of 2/10 n/30 to McBee Sales Company.

May 28   Received legal notification that McBee Sales Company was bankrupt. Wrote off McBee's accounts receivable balance.

Aug. 11   Received $2,000 from McBee Sales Company, together with a letter indicating that the company intended to pay its account within the next month.

     30   Received the remaining amount due from McBee.

Exercise 8-3   *Using the aging approach to estimate bad debts* **(L.O. 1, 2)**

At December 31, 19X7, the accounts receivable balance of Granite Shoals, Inc. is $266,000. The allowance for doubtful accounts has a $3,910 credit balance. Accountants for Granite Shoals prepare the following aging schedule for its accounts receivable:

Total Balance	Age of Accounts			
	1–30 Days	*31–60 Days*	*61–90 Days*	*Over 90 Days*
$266,000	$104,000	$78,000	$69,000	$15,000
Estimated percentage uncollectible	0.3%	1.2%	6.0%	50%

Journalize the adjusting entry for doubtful accounts based on the aging schedule. Show the T-account for the allowance.

Exercise 8-4   *Using the direct write-off method for bad debts* **(L.O. 3)**

Refer to the situation of Exercise 8-1.

Required

1. Record uncollectible account expense for October by the direct write-off method.
2. What amount of net accounts receivable would Maxwell Ltd. report on its October 31 balance sheet under the direct write-off method? Does Maxwell expect to collect this much of the receivable? Give your reason.

Exercise 8-5   *Controlling cash receipts from customers* **(L.O. 4)**

As a recent college graduate, you land your first job in the customer collections department of Coffey & Schwayze, a partnership. Lela Coffey, the president, has asked you to propose a system to ensure that cash received by mail from customers is properly handled. Draft a short memorandum identifying the essential element in your proposed plan, and state why this element is important. Refer to Chapter 7 if necessary.

Exercise 8-6   *Recording a note receivable and accruing interest revenue* **(L.O. 5)**

Record the following transactions in the general journal.

Nov.	1	Loaned $30,000 cash to E. Tremblay on a 1-year, 9 percent note.
Dec.	3	Sold goods to Lofland, Inc., receiving a 90-day, 12 percent note for $3,750.
	16	Received a $2,000, 6-month, 12 percent note on account from J. Baker.
	31	Accrued interest revenue on all notes receivable.

Exercise 8.7   *Recording a note receivable and accruing interest revenue* **(L.O. 5)**

Record the following transactions in the general journal:

Apr. 1, 19X2	Loaned $6,000 to Linda Rutishauser on a 1-year, 9 percent note.
Dec. 31, 19X2	Accrued interest revenue on the Rutishauser note.
	Closed the interest revenue account.
Apr. 1, 19X3	Received the maturity value of the note from Linda Rutishauser.

Exercise 8-8   *Accounting for a dishonored note receivable (L.0. 5)*

Record the following transactions in the general journal, assuming the company uses the allowance method to account for uncollectibles:

May 18   Sold goods to Computer Specialties, receiving a 120-day, 12 percent note for $2,700.
Sept. 15   The note is dishonored.
Nov. 30   After pursuing collection from Computer Specialties, wrote off their account as uncollectible.

Exercise 8-9   *Recording notes receivable, discounting a note, and reporting the contingent liability in a footnote (L.0. 5, 6)*

Prepare general journal entries to record the following transactions:

Aug. 14   Sold goods on account to Bert Lewis, $2,900.
Dec.   2   Received a $2,900, 180-day, 10 percent note from Bert Lewis in satisfaction of his past-due account receivable.
      30   Sold the Lewis note by discounting it to a bank at 15 percent. (Use a 360-day year, and round amounts to the nearest dollar.)

Write the footnote to disclose the contingent liability at December 31.

Exercise 8-10   *Recording bad debts by the allowance method (L.0. 1, 2, 6)*

At December 31, 19X5, Knudsen Ltd. has an accounts receivable balance of $129,000. Sales revenue for 19X5 is $950,000, including credit sales of $600,000. For each of the following situations, prepare the year-end adjusting entry to record doubtful account expense. Show how the accounts receivable and the allowance for doubtful accounts are reported on the balance sheet.

a. Allowance for Doubtful Accounts has a credit balance before adjustment of $1,600. Knudsen Ltd. estimates that doubtful account expense for the year is ½ of 1 percent of credit sales.

b. Allowance for Doubtful Accounts has a debit balance before adjustment of $1,100. Knudsen Ltd. estimates that $4,600 of the accounts receivable will prove uncollectible.

Exercise 8-11   *Reporting receivables with credit balances (L.0. 6)*

The accounts receivable subsidiary ledger includes the following summarized data:

83 accounts with debit balances totaling........................	$113,650
9 accounts with credit balances totaling.......................	3,980
Net total of balances...	$109,670

The company accountant proposes to report only the net total of $109,670. Show how these data sould be reported on the balance sheet.

Exercise 8-12   *Evaluating ratio data (L.0. 7)*

Stedman's, a department store, reported the following amounts in its 19X8 financial statements. The 19X7 figures are given for comparison.

	19X8		19X7	
Current assets				
Cash..		$ 12,000		$ 8,000
Short-term investments..........		13,000		11,000
Accounts receivable	$ 80,000		$74,000	
Less: Allowance for				
uncollectibles	7,000	73,000	6,000	68,000
Inventory		191,000		187,000
Prepaid insurance.....................		2,000		2,000
Total current assets..............		291,000		276,000
Total current liabilities..................		114,000		107,000
Net sales...		813,000		762,000

Required

1. Determine whether the acid-test ratio improved or deteriorated from 19X7 to 19X8. How does Stedman's acid-test ratio compare with the industry average of .80?

2. Compare the days' sales in receivables measure for 19X8 with the company's credit terms of net 30.

Problems   (Group A)

Problem 8-1A *Accounting for uncollectibles by the direct write-off and allowance methods (L.0. 1, 2, 3, 6)*

On May 31, Gallerie Lafleur had a $216,000 debit balance in Accounts Receivable. During June, the gallery had sales revenue of $788,000, which included $640,000 in credit sales. Other data for June include:

a. Collections on account receivable, $599,400.
b. Write-offs of uncollectible receivables, $8,700.

Required

1. Record uncollectible account expense for June by the direct write-off method. Show all June activity in Accounts Receivable and Uncollectible Account Expense.

2. Record uncollectible account expense and write-offs of customer accounts for June by the allowance method. Show all June activity in Accounts Receivable, Allowance for Uncollectible Accounts, and Uncollectible Account Expense. The May 31 unadjusted balance in Allowance for Uncollectible Accounts was $2,200 (credit). Uncollectible Account Expense was estimated at 2 percent of credit sales.

3. What amount of uncollectible account expense would Gallerie Lafleur report on its June income statement under the two methods? Which amount better matches expense with revenue? Give your reason.

4. What amount of net accounts receivable would Gallerie Lafleur report on its June 30 balance sheet under the two methods? Which amount is more realistic? Give your reason.

Problem 8-2A *Uncollectibles, notes receivable, discounting notes, dishonored notes, and accrued interest revenue* **(L.O. 2, 5)**

Assume Canada Packers, manufacturer of meat products, completed the following selected transactions:

19X5

Nov.	1	Sold goods to Eckerd Grocery Co., receiving a $22,000, 3-month, 12 percent note.
Dec.	31	Made an adjusting entry to accrue interest on the Eckerd Grocery note.
	31	Made an adjusting entry to record doubtful account expense based on an aging of accounts receivable. The aging analysis indicates that $197,400 of accounts receivable will not be collected. Prior to this adjustment, the credit balance in Allowance for Doubtful Accounts is $189,900.

19X6

Feb.	1	Collected the maturity value of the Eckerd Grocery note.
	23	Received a 90-day, 15 percent, $4,000 note from Bliss, Inc. on account. (February has 28 days this year.)
Mar.	31	Discounted the Bliss, Inc. note to Bytown Bank at 20 percent.
Apr.	23	Sold merchandise to K Lynn Ltd., receiving a 60-day, 10 percent note for $6,000.
June	22	K Lynn Ltd. dishonored its note at maturity; converted the maturity value of the note to an account receivable.
July	15	Loaned $8,500 cash to McNeil, Inc., receiving a 30-day, 12 percent note.
	17	Sold merchandise to Grant Corp., receiving a 3-month, 10 percent, $8,000 note.
Aug.	5	Collected $6,100 on account from K Lynn Ltd.
	14	Collected the maturity value of the McNeil, Inc. note.
	17	Discounted the Grant Corp. note to Bytown Bank at 15 percent.
Oct.	17	Grant Corp. dishonored its note at maturity; paid Bytown Bank the maturity value of the note plus a protest fee of $50, and debited an account receivable from Grant Corp.
Dec.	15	Wrote off as uncollectible the account receivable from Grant Corp.

Required

Record the transactions in the general journal. Explanations are not required.

Problem 8-3A   *Using the percent of sales and aging approaches for uncollectibles* **(L.O. 2, 6)**

Reynaldo Ltd. completed the following selected transactions during 19X1 and 19X2:

19X1

Dec.	31	Estimated that uncollectible account expense for the year was ½ of 1 percent on credit sales of $450,000 and recorded that amount as expense.
	31	Made the appropriate closing entry.

19X2

Feb.	4	Sold inventory to Gary Carter, $1,521, on credit terms of 2/10 n/30.
July	1	Wrote off Gary Carter's account as uncollectible after repeated efforts to collect from him.
Oct.	19	Received $521 from Gary Carter, along with a letter stating his intention to pay his debt in full within 30 days. Reinstated his account in full.
Nov.	15	Received the balance due from Gary Carter.
Dec.	31	Made a compound entry to write off the following accounts as uncollectible: Kris Moore, $899; Marie Mandue, $530; and Grant Frycer, $672.

31   Estimated that uncollectible account expense for the year was ½ of 1
     percent on credit sales of $540,000 and recorded the expense.

31   Made the appropriate closing entry.

Required

1. Open general ledger accounts for Allowance for Uncollectible Accounts and
   Uncollectible Account Expense. Keep running balances.

2. Record the transactions in the general journal and post to the two ledger accounts.

3. The December 31, 19X2 balance of Accounts Receivable is $158,300. Show how
   Accounts Receivable would be reported at that date.

4. Assume that Reynaldo Ltd. begins aging its accounts receivable on December 31,
   19X2. The balance in Accounts Receivable is $158,300; the credit balance in
   Allowance for Uncollectible Accounts is $149; and the company estimates that
   $3,245 of its accounts receivable will prove uncollectible.

   a. Make the adjusting entry for uncollectibles.

   b. Show how Accounts Receivable will be reported on the December 31, 19X2 bal-
      ance sheet.

Problem 8-4A   *Using the percent of sales and aging approaches for uncollectibles* **(L.O. 2, 6)**

The December 31, 19X4 balance sheet of Bonini Limited reports the following:

Accounts Receivable	$141,000
Allowance for Doubtful Accounts (credit balance)	3,200

At the end of each quarter, Bonini estimates doubtful account expense to be 1½
percent of credit sales. At the end of the year, the company ages its accounts receivable and adjusts the balance in Allowance for Doubtful Accounts to correspond to the aging schedule. During 19X5, Bonini completes the following selected
transactions:

Jan. 16   Wrote off as uncollectible the $403 account receivable from Platt Ltd.
           and the $1,719 account receivable from Wise Corp.

Mar. 31   Recorded doubtful account expense based on credit sales of $100,000.

Apr. 15   Received $300 from Wise Corp. after prolonged negotiations with Wise's
           lawyer. Bonini has no hope of collecting the remainder.

May 13   Wrote off as uncollectible the $2,980 account receivable from M. E. Cate.

June 30   Recorded doubtful account expense based on credit sales of $114,000.

Aug. 9   Made a compound entry to write off the following uncollectible ac-
           counts: Clifford Ltd. $235; Matz, Inc., $188; and Lew Norris, $1,006.

Sept. 30   Recorded doubtful account expense based on credit sales of $130,000.

Oct. 18   Wrote off as uncollectible the $767 account receivable from Bliss, Inc.
           and the $430 account receivable from Micro Data.

Dec. 31   Recorded doubtful account expense based on the following summary of
           the aging of accounts receivable.

Total Balance	Age of Accounts			
	1–30 Days	**31–60 Days**	**61–90 Days**	**Over 90 Days**
$127,400	$74,600	$31,100	$12,000	$9,700
Estimated percentage uncollectible	0.1%	0.4%	5.0%	30.0%

Dec. 31   Made the closing entry for Doubtful Account Expense for the entire year.

Required

1. Record the transactions in the general journal.
2. Open the Allowance for Doubtful Accounts and post entries affecting that account. Keep a running balance.
3. Most companies report two-year comparative financial statements. If Bonini's Accounts Receivable balance is $127,400 at December 31, 19X5, show how the company would report its accounts receivable on a comparative balance sheet for 19X5 and 19X4, as follows:

	19X5	19X4
Accounts receivable		
Less: Allowance for doubtful accounts		
Net accounts receivable..........................		

Problem 8-5A   *Controlling cash receipts from customers* (L.O. 4)

Medical Laboratory Service provides laboratory testing for samples that veterinarians send in. All work is performed on account, with regular monthly billing to participating veterinarians. Ajit Singh, accountant for Medical Laboratory Service, receives and opens the mail. Company procedure requires him to separate customer cheques from the remittance slips, which list the amounts he posts as credits to customer accounts receivable. Singh deposits the cheques in the bank. He computes each day's total amount posted to customer accounts and agrees this total to the bank deposit slip. This is intended to ensure that all receipts are deposited in the bank.

Required

As the auditor of Medical Laboratory Service, write a memo to management to evaluate the company's internal controls over cash receipts from customers. If the system is effective, identify its strong features. If the system has flaws, propose a way to strengthen the controls.

Problem 8-6A   *Accounting for notes receivable, including discounting notes and accruing interest revenue* (L.O. 5)

A company received the following notes during 19X5. Notes 1, 2, and 3 were discounted on the dates and at the rates indicated.

Note	Date	Principal Amount	Interest Rate	Term	Date Discounted	Discount Rate
1	July 15	$ 6,000	8%	6 months	Oct. 15	12%
2	Aug. 19	11,000	12	90 days	Aug. 30	15
3	Sept. 1	16,000	15	120 days	Nov. 2	20
4	Oct. 30	7,000	12	3 months	—	—
5	Nov. 19	15,000	10	60 days	—	—
6	Dec. 1	12,000	9	1 year	—	—

Required

As necessary in requirements 1 through 5, identify each note by number, compute interest using a 365-day year for those notes with terms specified in days or years, round all interest amounts to the nearest dollar, and present entries in general journal form. Explanations are not required.

1. Determine the due date and maturity value of each note.

2. For each discounted note, determine the discount and proceeds from sale of the note.

3. Journalize the discounting of notes 1 and 2.

4. Journalize a single adjusting entry at December 31, 19X5 to record interest revenue on notes 4, 5, and 6.

5. Journalize the collection of principal and interest on note 4.

Problem 8-7A   *Notes receivable, discounted notes, dishonored notes, and accrued interest revenue (L.O. 2, 5)*

Record the following selected transactions in the general journal. Explanations are not required.

19X2

Dec. 21   Received a $10,800, 30-day, 10 percent note on account from Myron Blake.

31   Made an adjusting entry to accrue interest on the Blake note.

31   Made an adjusting entry to record doubtful account expense in the amount of ⅔ of 1 percent on credit sales of $604,800.

31   Made a compound closing entry for the appropriate accounts.

19X3

Jan. 20   Collected the maturity value of the Blake note.

Apr. 19   Sold merchandise to city of Lethbridge, receiving $500 cash, and a 120-day, 12 percent note for $5,000.

May 1   Discounted the city of Lethbridge note to Prairie Bank at 15 percent.

Sept. 14   Loaned $6,000 cash to Banff Investors, receiving a 3-month, 13 percent note.

30   Received a $1,675, 60-day, 16 percent note from Matt Kurtz on his past-due account receivable.

Nov. 29   Matt Kurtz dishonoured his note at maturity; accrued no interest revenue and wrote off the note as uncollectible, debiting Allowance for Doubtful Accounts.

Dec. 14   Collected the maturity value of the Banff Investors note.

31   Wrote off as uncollectible the accounts receivable of Ty Larson, $330, and Terry Gee, $460.

Problem 8-8A   *Using ratio data to evaluate a company's position (L.O. 7)*

The comparative financial statements of Timber Mills Corp. for 19X6, 19X5, and 19X4 included the following selected data:

	Millions		
	19X6	19X5	19X4
Balance Sheet...			
Current assets			
Cash	$ 49	$ 66	$ 51
Short-term investments.............................	131	174	122
Receivables, net of allowance for			
doubtful accounts of $6, $6, and $5......	237	265	218
Inventories	389	341	302
Prepaid expenses	61	27	46

Total current assets	867	873	739
Total current liabilities	482	528	403
Income statement			
Sales revenue	$5,189	$4,995	$4,206
Cost of sales	2,834	2,636	2,418

Required

1. For 19X6 and 19X5 compute these ratios:
   a. Current ratio
   b. Acid-test ratio
   c. Inventory turnover
   d. Days' sales in average receivables
2. Explain for top management which ratio values showed improvement from 19X5 to 19X6, and which ratio values showed deterioration. Which item in the financial statements caused some ratio values to improve and others to deteriorate?

(Group B)

Problem 8-1B   *Accounting for uncollectibles by the direct write-off and allowance methods* **(L.O. 1, 2, 3, 6)**

On February 28, Courtney Fashions had a $72,000 debit balance in Accounts Receivable. During March, the business had sales revenue of $509,000, which included $443,000 in credit sales. Other data for March include

a. Collections on account receivable, $451,600.

b. Write-offs of uncollectible receivables, $3,300.

Required

1. Record uncollectible account expense for March by the direct write-off method. Show all March activity in Accounts Receivable and Uncollectible Account Expense.

2. Record uncollectible account expense and write-offs of customer accounts for March by the allowance method. Show all March activity in Accounts Receivable, Allowance for Uncollectible Accounts, and Uncollectible Account Expense. The February 28 unadjusted balance in Allowance for Uncollectible Accounts was $800 (debit). Uncollectible Account Expense was estimated at 2 percent of credit sales.

3. What amount of uncollectible account expense would Courtney Fashions report on its March income statement under the two methods? Which amount best matches expense with revenue? Give your reason.

4. What amount of net accounts receivable would Courtney Fashions report on its March 31 balance sheet under the two methods? Which amount is more realistic? Give your reason.

Problem 8-2B   *Uncollectibles, notes receivable, discounting notes, dishonored notes and accrued interest revenue* **(L.O. 2, 5)**

Assume Chandler Dairy, producer of dairy products, completed the following selected transactions:

19X4
Dec.   1   Sold goods to Assaf Grocery Co., receiving a $15,000, 3-month, 10 percent note.

31   Made an adjusting entry to accrue interest on the Assaf Grocery note.

31   Made an adjusting entry to record doubtful account expense based on an aging of accounts receivable. The aging analysis indicates that $355,800 of accounts receivable will not be collected. Prior to this adjustment, the credit balance in Allowance for Doubtful Accounts is $346,100.

19X5

Feb. 18   Received a 90-day, 10 percent, $5,000 note from Ecstasy, Inc. on account. (February has 28 days this year.)

Mar. 1   Collected the maturity value of the Assaf Grocery note.

8   Discounted the Ecstasy, Inc. note to Breton Bank at 16 percent.

Apr. 21   Sold merchandise to K Chen Ltd., receiving a 60-day, 9 percent note for $4,000.

June 20   K Chen Ltd. dishonored its note at maturity and converted the maturity value of the note to an account receivable.

July 12   Loaned $60,000 cash to McNeice, Inc., receiving a 90-day, 13 percent note.

13   Sold merchandise to Grubb Corp., receiving a 4-month, 12 percent, $2,500 note.

Aug. 2   Collected $4,060 on account from K Chen Ltd.

Sep. 13   Discounted the Grubb Corp. note to Breton Bank at 18 percent.

Oct. 10   Collected the maturity value of the McNeice Inc. note.

Nov. 13   Grubb Corp. dishonored its note at maturity; paid Breton Bank the maturity value of the note plus a protest fee of $35, and debited an account receivable from Grubb Corp.

Dec. 31   Wrote off as uncollectible the account receivable from Grubb Corp.

Required

Record the transactions in the general journal. Explanations are not required.

Problem 8-3B   *Using the percent of sales and aging approaches for uncollectibles (L.O. 2, 6)*

Alomar Ltd. completed the following transactions during 19X1 and 19X2:

19X1

Dec. 31   Estimated that uncollectible account expense for the year was ¾ of 1 percent on credit sales of $300,000 and recorded that amount as expense.

31   Made the appropriate closing entry.

19X2

Jan. 17   Sold inventory to Joe Carter, $652, on credit terms of 2/10 n/30.

June 29   Wrote off Joe Carter's account as uncollectible after repeated efforts to collect from him.

Aug. 6   Received $250 from Joe Carter, along with a letter stating his intention to pay his debt in full within 30 days. Reinstated his account in full.

Sept. 4   Received the balance due from Joe Carter.

Dec. 31   Made a compound entry to write off the following accounts as uncollectible: Kris Masse, $737; Bud Mandy, $348; and Chuck Prince, $622.

31   Estimated that uncollectible account expense for the year was ⅔ of 1 percent on credit sales of $420,000 and recorded that amount as expense.

31   Made the appropriate closing entry.

Required

1. Open general ledger accounts for Allowance for Uncollectible Accounts and Uncollectible Account Expense. Keep running balances.

2. Record the transactions in the general journal and post to the two ledger accounts.

3. The December 31, 19X2, balance of Accounts Receivable is $123,000. Show how Accounts Receivable would be reported at that date.

4. Assume that Alomar Ltd. begins aging accounts receivable on December 31, 19X2. The balance in Accounts Receivable is $123,000; the credit balance in Allowance for Uncollectible Accounts is $543, and the company estimates that $2,600 of its accounts receivable will prove uncollectible.
   a. Make the adjusting entry for uncollectibles.
   b. Show how Accounts Receivable will be reported on the December 31, 19X2, balance sheet.

Problem 8-4B *Using the percent-of-sales and aging approaches for uncollectibles* **(L.O. 2, 6)**

The December 31, 19X6 balance sheet of Gemini Limited reports the following:

Accounts Receivable...	$256,000
Allowance for Doubtful Accounts (credit balance)	7,100

At the end of each quarter, Gemini estimates doubtful account expense to be 2 percent of credit sales. At the end of the year, the company ages its accounts receivable and adjusts the balance in Allowance for Doubtful Accounts to correspond to the aging schedule. During 19X7, Gemini completes the following selected transactions:

Jan. 31   Wrote off as uncollectible the $855 account receivable from Smart Co. and the $3,287 account receivable from Wisdom Corp.

Mar. 31   Recorded doubtful account expense based on credit sales of $120,000.

May 2   Received $1,000 from Wisdom Corp. after prolonged negotiations with Wisdom's lawyer. Gemini has no hope of collecting the remainder.

June 15   Wrote off as uncollectible the $1,120 account receivable from M. E. Cat.

June 30   Recorded doubtful account expense based on credit sales of $166,000.

July 14   Made a compound entry to write off the following uncollectible accounts: Caldwell Ltd. $766; Fred, Inc., $2,413; and Les Pay, $134.

Sept. 30   Recorded doubtful account expense based on credit sales of $141,400.

Nov. 22   Wrote off the following accounts receivable as uncollectible: Bliss, Inc., $1,345; Micro Data, $2,109; and Queen Street Plaza, $755.

Dec. 31   Recorded doubtful account expense based on the following summary of the aging of accounts receivable:

Total Balance	Age of Accounts			
	1–30 Days	**31–60 Days**	**61–90 Days**	**Over 90 Days**
$294,600	$161,500	$86,000	$32,000	$15,100
Estimated percentage uncollectible	*3 23*	*430*	*1200*	*7580*
	0.2%	0.5%	4.0%	50.0%

9583

Dec. 31   Made the closing entry for Doubtful Account Expense for the entire year.

Required

1. Record the transactions in the general journal.

2. Open the Allowance for Doubtful Accounts and post entries affecting that account. Keep a running balance.

3. Most companies report two-year comparative financial statements. If Gemini's Accounts Receivable balance is $294,600 at December 31, 19X7, show how the

company would report its accounts receivable in a comparative balance sheet for 19X7 and 19X6, as follows:

	19X7	19X6
Accounts receivable		
Less: Allowance for doubtful accounts		
Net accounts receivable..........................		

Problem 8-5B   *Controlling cash receipts from customers (L.0. 4)*

Mountain Sporting Goods distributes merchandise to sporting goods stores. All sales are on credit, so virtually all cash receipts arrive in the mail. Amy Ing, the company president, has just returned from a trade association meeting with new ideas for the business. Among other things, Ing plans to institute stronger internal controls over cash receipts from customers.

Required

Outline a set of procedures to ensure that all cash receipts are deposited in the bank, and that the total amounts of each day's cash receipts are posted as credits to customer accounts receivable.

Problem 8-6B   *Accounting for notes receivable, including discounting notes and accruing interest revenue (L.0. 5)*

A company received the following notes during 19X3. Notes 1, 2, and 3 were discounted on the dates and at the rates indicated:

Note	Date	Principal Amount	Interest Rate	Term	Date Discounted	Discount Rate
1	July 12	$12,000	10%	3 months	Aug. 12	15%
2	Sept. 4	6,000	11	90 days	Sept. 30	13
3	Oct. 21	5,000	15	60 days	Nov. 3	18
4	Nov. 30	12,000	12	6 months	—	—
5	Dec. 7	9,000	10	30 days	—	—
6	Dec. 23	15,000	9	1 year	—	—

Required

As necessary in requirements 1 through 5, identify each note by number, compute interest using a 365-day year for those notes with terms specified in days or years, round all interest amounts to the nearest dollar, and present entries in general journal form. Explanations are not required.

1. Determine the due date and maturity value of each note.
2. For each discounted note, determine the discount and proceeds from sale of the note.
3. Journalize the discounting of notes 1 and 2.
4. Journalize a single adjusting entry at December 31, 19X3 to record accrued interest revenue on notes 4, 5, and 6.
5. Journalize the collection of principal and interest on note 5.

Problem 8-7B   *Notes receivable, discounted notes, dishonored notes, and accrued interest evenue* **(L.O. 2, 5)**

Record the following selected transactions in the general journal. Explanations are not required.

19X6

Dec. 19   Received a $5,000, 60-day, 12 percent note on account from Claude Bernard.
    31   Made an adjusting entry to accrue interest on the Bernard note.
    31   Made an adjusting entry to record doubtful account expense in the amount of $\%_0$ of 1 percent of credit sales of $474,500.
    31   Made a compound closing entry for the appropriate accounts.

19X7

Feb. 17   Collected the maturity value of the Bernard note.
Mar. 22   Sold merchandise to Kamloops Power Company, receiving $1,400 cash, and a 90-day, 10 percent note for $6,000.
May   3   Discounted the Kamloops Power Company note to the Bank of the Rockies at 15 percent.
June 1   Loaned $10,000 cash to Linz Brothers, receiving a 6-month, 11 percent note.
Oct. 31   Received a $1,500, 60-day, 12 percent note from Ned Pierce on his past-due account receivable.
Dec. 1   Collected the maturity value of the Linz Brothers note.
    30   Ned Pierce dishonored his note at maturity; accrued no interest revenue and wrote off the note receivable as uncollectible.
    31   Wrote off as uncollectible the accounts receivable of Al Bynum, $435 and Ray Sharp, $276.

Problem 8-8B   *Using ratio data to evaluate a company's position* **(L.O. 7)**

The comparative financial statements of Domingo Catalogue Merchants for 19X4, 19X3, and 19X2 included the following selected data:

	Millions		
	19X4	19X3	19X2
Balance Sheet			
Current assets			
Cash	$ 17	$ 28	$ 22
Short-term investments	73	101	69
Receivables, net of allowance for doubtful accounts of $7, $6, and $4	136	154	127
Inventories	428	373	341
Prepaid expenses	42	31	25
Total current assets	696	687	584
Total current liabilities	430	446	388
Income Statement			
Sales revenue	$2,671	$2,505	$1,944
Cost of sales	1,180	1,160	963

Required

1. For 19X4 and 19X3 compute these ratios:
    a. Current ratio
    b. Acid-test ratio
    c. Inventory turnover
    d. Days' sales in average receivables

2. Explain for top management which ratio values showed improvement from 19X3 to 19X4, and which ratio values showed deterioration. Which item in the financial statements caused some ratio values to improve and others to deteriorate?

Extending Your Knowledge

Decision Problems

1. *Uncollectible accounts and evaluating a business (L.O. 1, 2, 3, 5, 6)*

Bentwood Appliances sells its products either for cash or on notes receivable that earn interest. The business uses the direct write-off method to account for bad debts. Mark Moore, the owner, has prepared Bentwood's financial statements. The most recent comparative income statements, for 19X3 and 19X2, are as follows:

	19X3	19X2
Total revenue	$210,000	$195,000
Total expenses	157,000	153,000
Net income	$ 53,000	$ 42,000

Based on the increase in net income, Moore seeks to expand his operations. He asks you to invest $50,000 in the business. You and Moore have several meetings, at which you learn that notes receivable from customers were $200,000 at the end of 19X1, and $400,000 at the end of 19X2. Also, total revenues for 19X3 and 19X2 include interest at 15 percent on the year's beginning notes receivable balance. Total expenses include doubtful account expense of $2,000 each year, based on the direct write-off basis. Moore estimates that doubtful account expense would be 2 percent of sales revenue if the allowance method were used.

Required

1. Prepare for the Bentwood Appliances a comparative single-step income statement that identifies sales revenue, interest revenue, doubtful account expense, and other expenses, all computed in accordance with generally accepted accounting principles.
2. Is Bentwood's future as promising as Moore's income statement makes it appear? Give the reason for your answer.

2. *Estimating the collectibility of accounts receivable (L.O. 1, 6, 7)*

Assume you work in the corporate loan department of Brunswick Bank. Maria Presti, owner of MP Manufacturing Inc., a manufacturer of wooden furniture, has come to you seeking a loan of $350,000 to buy new manufacturing equipment to expand her operations. She proposes to use her accounts receivable as collateral for the loan, and has provided you with the following information from her most recent audited financial statements:

	19X9	19X8	19X7
Sales	$1,475	$1,589	$1,502
Cost of goods sold..	876	947	905
Gross profit	599	642	597
Other expenses	518	487	453
Net profit before taxes....................................	$ 81	$ 155	$ 144
Accounts receivable...	458	387	374
Allowance for doubtful accounts	23	31	29

Required

1. What analysis would you perform on the information Presti has provided? Would you grant the loan based on this information? Give your reason.
2. What additional information would you request from Presti? Give your reason.
3. Assume Presti provided you with the information requested in requirement 2. What would make you change the decision you made in requirement 1?

Ethical Issue

Goodwill Finance Ltd. is in the consumer loan business. It borrows from banks, and loans out the money at higher interest rates. Goodwill's bank requires Goodwill to submit quarterly financial statements in order to keep its line of credit. Goodwill's main asset is Notes Receivable. Therefore, Uncollectible Account Expense and Allowance for Uncollectible Accounts are important accounts.

Goodwill's owner, Jacob Featherstone, likes net income to increase in a smooth pattern rather than to increase in some periods and decrease in other periods. To report smoothly increasing net income, Featherstone underestimates Uncollectible Account Expense in some periods. In other periods, Featherstone overestimates the expense. He reasons that the income overstatements roughly offset the income understatements over time.

Required

Is Goodwill's practice of smoothing income ethical? Give your reasons.

Financial Statement Problems

1. Accounts receivable and related uncollectibles (L.O. 1)

Use data from the Schneider balance sheet and the related titled Accounts Receivable in Appendix C to answer these questions.

1. How much did Schneider's customers owe the company at October 27, 1990? (Assume an allowance for doubtful accounts of $1,550,000.)
2. Journalize the following for the year ended October 26, 1991, using Schneider's actual account titles. Explanations are not required.
   a. Net sales revenue of $630,966,000. Give one entry for the year's total, assuming all net sales revenue is earned on account.
   b. Doubtful account expense, estimated to equal .5 percent of net sales.
   c. Cash collections on account, $623,988,170.
   d. Write-offs of uncollectibles totaling $3,254,830.
3. Post to Accounts Receivable and Allowance for Doubtful Accounts, inserting these accounts' October 27, 1990 balances.

4. After posting, compare your account balances to those at October 26, 1991 in the Accounts Receivable. Your figures should agree with the Schneider actual amounts.

5. How much did Schneider's customers owe the company at October 26, 1991? How much of this total did Schneider expect to collect? Describe in words the amount reported for Accounts Receivable on Schneider's October 26, 1991 balance sheet.

2. *Accounts receivable, uncollectibles, and notes receivable (L.O. 1, 5)*

Obtain the annual report of an actual company of your choosing.

Required

1. How much did customers owe the company at the end of the current year? Of this amount how much did the company expect to collect? How much did the company expect not to collect?

2. Assume during the current year that the company recorded doubtful account expense equal to 1 percent of net sales. Starting with the beginning balance, analyze the Allowance for Doubtful Accounts to determine the amount of the receivable write-offs during the current year. If the company does not provide information on the allowance for doubtful accounts, assume it is 3 percent of accounts receivable.

3. If the company does not have notes receivable, you may skip this requirement. If notes receivable are present at the end of the current year, assume their interest rate is 9 percent. Also assume that no new notes receivable arose during the following year. Journalize these transactions that took place during the following year:
   a. Received cash for 75 percent of the interest revenue earned during the year.
   b. Accrued the remaining portion of the interest revenue earned during the year.
   c. At year end collected one half of the notes receivable.

4. Suppose the company discounted a $500,000 note receivable. Under what heading in the annual report would the company report the discounting of a note receivable? Show how the company would disclose this fact.

Answers to Self-Study Questions

1. a		6. b	
2. c		7. c ($30,000 × .09 × $\frac{6}{12}$ = $1,350)	
3. d		8. b ($30,000 × .09 × $\frac{4}{12}$ = $900)	
4. a		9. a	
5. b ($78,900 − $14,300 = $64,600)		10. d	

Chapter 9

Merchandise Inventory

Zachary Wholesale Plumbing Supplies Limited is a supplier of bathroom and kitchen fixtures. At any point in time the inventory will include about four different product lines of kitchen or bathroom sinks, shower enclosures, and bathtubs. For each product line, Zachary carries about ten of the items in inventory. In addition, the store carries the supplies to install these fixtures.

Auditors are completing the audit for the business's first year-end of December 31, 1993. They have just left for the day, and Zachary Quigley, the owner, is confused by, and somewhat concerned with, some of their findings. Everyone is in agreement on the quantities for the various items on hand at the year-end, but the auditors have suggested three different valuations for this inventory. These values and the resulting net income are:

Costing Method	Value of Ending Inventory	Net Income (Loss) before Income Taxes*
Weighted-average cost	$167,567	$ 9,821
FIFO	183,435	25,689
LIFO	145,512	(12,234)

Zachary knows for sure that he has about $12,000 in cash in the business's bank account, and that he has not paid any money for income taxes which will result from the 1993 income. Furthermore, when the bank extended a loan to the business, it insisted that the inventory must be at least $150,000, as it was used as security for the loan. If the value of the inventory went below $150,000, the loan of $50,000 would have to be paid immediately.

Who is right? Are all the amounts right? Should Zachary go back to his old job where he was earning $30,000 a year? How can the business keep the cash in the bank, as it needs it for other purposes besides paying taxes? As you read Chapter 9, you will gain insight into this accounting dilemma, and be able to come up with your own answer to Zachary's problem.

---

* Income tax rate will be about 25 percent.

LEARNING OBJECTIVES

After studying this chapter, you should be able to

1 Apply four inventory costing methods

2 Describe the income effects of the inventory costing methods

3 Apply the lower-of-cost-or-market rule to inventory

4 Explain why inventory errors counterbalance

5 Estimate inventory by two methods

6 Account for inventory by the periodic and perpetual systems

Merchandise inventory is the largest *current asset* on the balance sheet of most businesses that manufacture or buy inventory for resale. John Labatt, in 1991, reported inventories of $444 million, compared to receivables of $409 million. Inventories are important to merchandisers of all sizes. Buying and selling inventory is the heart of wholesaling and retailing, whether the business is Eaton's, Loblaws, or the corner hardware store.

If inventory is the major current asset of most merchandisers, what is their major expense? It is *cost of sales* or *cost of goods sold*. Cost of goods sold is the total cost of inventory sold during the period. It includes all costs relating to the inventory sold: the cost of manufacturing or purchasing the inventory, and such acquisition costs as freight and insurance. Selling costs including shipping are normally excluded. For many other companies, cost of goods sold is greater than all other expenses combined. For the year ended December 31, 1991, BCE Inc. reported its cost of sales for telecommunications equipment manufacturing at $5,420 million, compared to other operating expenses for that segment of $2,962 million.

Exhibit 9-1 traces the flow of inventory costs during the accounting period. The model presented in Exhibit 9-1 is fundamental to accounting for inventory.

The business starts each period with **beginning inventory**, the goods that are left over from the preceding period. During the period, the business purchases additional goods for resale. Together, beginning inventory and net purchases make up **goods available for sale**. Over the course of the period, the business sells some of the available goods. The cost of the inventory sold to customers is called the **cost of goods sold**. This cost is an expense because the inventory is no longer of use to the company. The goods still on hand at the end of the period are called **ending inventory**. Its cost is an asset because these goods are still available for sale.

EXHIBIT 9-1 *Flow of Inventory Costs*

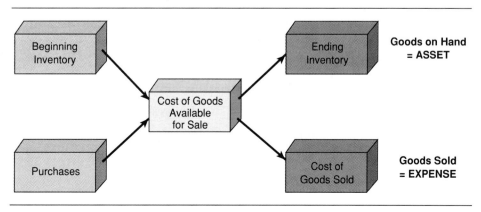

EXHIBIT 9-2 *Inventory and Cost of Goods Sold for Gillespie Hardware Ltd.*

		(amounts in thousands)
	Beginning inventory	$ 276
+	Purchases	1,348
=	Cost of goods available for sale	1,624
−	Ending inventory	317
=	Cost of goods sold	$1,307

Exhibit 9-2 uses data from the financial statements of Gillespie Hardware Ltd., a chain of hardware stores, to present the flow of inventory costs in a different format. Notice that ending inventory is subtracted from cost of goods available for sale to figure the cost of goods sold. Throughout this chapter, we ignore Goods and Services Tax (GST) on inventory purchases and freight-in to avoid clutter. GST is covered in Chapter 11.

The rest of this chapter fills in the details of our inventory cost flow model.

Figuring the Cost of Inventory

A necessary step in accounting for inventory is determining the cost of *ending inventory*. At the end of each period the *quantity* of inventory is multiplied by the *unit cost* of inventory to compute the cost of ending inventory.

Determining the Quantity of Inventory   Most businesses physically count their inventory at least once each year, often on the last day of the fiscal year. Inventory, an asset, must be reported accurately on the balance sheet.

You may have worked at a grocery store, fast-food outlet, or some other type of retail business. If so, you will recall the process of "taking the inventory." Some entities shut the business down to get a good count of inventory on hand. Others count the goods on a weekend. Still others inventory the merchandise while business is being conducted. How is it done in a large organization?

Assume Gillespie Hardware takes a complete physical inventory on its year-end date. Teams of counters in the company's approximately 17 stores record the quantities of each inventory item on hand. Each store forwards its total count to corporate headquarters, where home office employees determine the inventory grand total.

Complications may arise in determining the inventory quantity. Suppose the business has purchased some goods that are in transit when the inventory is counted. Even though these items are not physically present, they should be included in the inventory count if title to the goods has passed to the purchaser, Gillespie Hardware. When title passes from seller to purchaser, the purchaser becomes the legal owner of the goods.

The FOB (free on board) terms of the transaction govern when title passes from the seller to the purchaser. **FOB shipping point** indicates that title passes when the goods leave the seller's place of business. **FOB destination** means that title passes when the goods arrive at the purchaser's location. Therefore, goods in transit that are purchased FOB shipping point should be included in the purchaser's inventory. Goods in transit that are bought FOB destination should not be included.

Usually, the business has a purchase invoice, which lists the quantity of goods in transit and shows the FOB terms. Similarly, the business may have sold inventory that has not yet been shipped to the customer. If title has passed, these goods should be excluded from the seller's inventory, even though they may still be at the seller's place of business.

Another complication in counting inventory arises from consigned goods. In a **consignment** arrangement, the owner of the inventory (the consignor) transfers the goods to another business (the consignee). For a fee, the consignee sells the inventory on the owner's behalf. The consignee does *not* take title to the consigned goods and, therefore, should not include them in its own inventory. Consignments are common in retailing. Suppose Gillespie Hardware is the consignee for some Stanley tools in its stores. Should Gillespie include this consigned merchandise in its inventory count? No, because Gillespie does not own the goods. Instead, the Stanley wholesaler (the consignor) includes the consigned goods in his or her inventory. A rule of thumb is to include in inventory only what the business owns.

Determining the Unit Cost of Inventory   Inventories are normally accounted for at historical cost, as the *cost principle* requires. **Inventory cost** is the price the business pays to acquire the inventory — not the selling price of the goods. Suppose a business purchases inventory for $10 and offers it for sale at $15. The inventory cost is reported at $10, not $15. Inventory cost includes its invoice price, less any purchase discount, plus tariffs, transportation charges, insurance while in transit, and all other costs incurred to make the goods ready for sale.

While the retailer paid GST on the purchase, the amount paid is recoverable as a deduction from the GST collected when the retailer sells the inventory. For example, Gillespie would pay $63 GST ($900 × .07 percent, the GST rate) on a purchase of a $900 home air-conditioner from the manufacturer. When Gillespie Hardware sells the air-conditioner the following month for $1,400, they would charge the purchaser GST of $98 ($1,400 × .07). Later Gillespie Hardware would remit $35 ($98 – $63) to Revenue Canada in connection with the purchase and sale.

The inventory quantity multiplied by the unit cost equals the cost of inventory. Thirty tape recorders at a cost to the retailer of $100 each results in an inventory cost of $3,000.

Inventory Costing Methods

Determining the unit cost of inventory is easy when the unit cost remains constant during the period. However, the unit cost often changes. For example, during times of inflation, prices rise. The tape recorder model that cost the retailer $100 in January may cost $115 in June and $122 in October. Suppose the retailer sells 15 tape recorders in November. How many of them cost $100, $115 and $122? To compute the cost of goods sold and ending inventory amounts, the accountant must have some means of assigning the business's cost to each item sold. The four costing methods that GAAP allows are

> **OBJECTIVE 1**
>
> Apply four inventory costing methods

1. Specific unit cost
2. Average cost
3. First-in, first-out (FIFO) cost
4. Last-in, first-out (LIFO) cost

A company may use any of these methods. Many companies use several methods — different methods for different categories of inventory.

Specific Unit Cost

Some businesses deal in inventory items that may be identified individually, like automobiles, jewels and real estate. These businesses usually cost their inventory at the specific cost of the particular unit. For instance, a Chevrolet dealer may have two vehicles in the showroom, a "stripped-down" model that cost $16,000 and a "loaded" model that cost $21,000. If the dealer sells the loaded model for $23,700, cost of goods sold is $21,000, the cost of the specific unit. The gross margin on this sale is $2,700 ($23,700 – $21,000). If the stripped-down auto is the only unit left in inventory at the end of the period, ending inventory is $16,000, the cost to the retailer of the specific unit on hand.

The **specific unit cost method** is also called the *specific identification* method. This method is not practical for inventory items that do not have unique characteristics, such as bushels of wheat, gallons of paint or boxes of laundry detergent.

Weighted-Average Cost, FIFO Cost and LIFO Cost

The weighted-average cost, first-in, first-out (FIFO), and last-in, first-out (LIFO) methods are fundamentally different from the specific unit cost method. These methods do not assign to inventory the specific cost of particular units. Instead, they assume different flows of costs into and out of inventory.

Weighted-Average Cost The **weighted-average cost method**, often called the **average cost method,** is based on the weighted-average cost of inventory during the period. Average cost is determined by dividing the cost of goods available for sale (beginning inventory plus purchases) by the number of units available. Ending inventory and cost of goods sold are computed by multiplying the number of units by the weighted-average cost per unit. Assume that cost of goods available for sale is $90, and 60 units are available. Weighted-average cost is $1.50 per unit ($90/60 = $1.50). Ending inventory of 20 units has an average cost of $30 (20 × $1.50 = $30). Cost of goods sold (40 units) is $60 (40 × $1.50). Panel A of Exhibit 9-3 gives the data in more detail. Panel B of the exhibit shows the weighted-average cost computations.

First-in, First-out (FIFO) Cost Under the **first-in, first-out (FIFO) method**, the company must keep a record of the cost of each inventory unit purchased. The unit costs used in computing the ending inventory may be different from the unit costs used in computing the cost of goods sold. Under FIFO, the first costs into inventory are the first costs out to cost of goods sold, hence the name *first-in, first-out*. Ending inventory is based on the costs of the most recent purchases. In our example, the FIFO cost of ending inventory is $36. Cost of goods sold is $54. Panel A of Exhibit 9-3 gives the data, and Panel B shows the FIFO computations.

Last-in, First-out (LIFO) Cost The **last-in, first-out (LIFO) method** also depends on the costs of particular inventory purchases. LIFO is the opposite of FIFO. Under LIFO, the last costs into inventory are the first costs out to cost of goods sold. This leaves the oldest costs (those of beginning inventory and the earliest purchases of the period) in ending inventory. In our example, the LIFO cost of ending inventory is $24. Cost of goods sold is $66. Panel A of Exhibit 9-3 gives the data, and Panel B shows the LIFO computations.

Income Effects of FIFO, LIFO, and Average Cost _____

OBJECTIVE 2

Describe the income effects of the inventory costing methods

In our discussion and examples, the cost of inventory rose over the accounting period. When prices change, different costing methods produce different cost of goods sold and ending inventory figures, as Exhibit 9-3 shows. When prices are increasing, FIFO ending inventory is *highest* because it is priced at the most recent costs, which are the highest. LIFO ending inventory is *lowest* because it is priced at the oldest costs, which are the lowest. *Weighted-average* cost avoids the extremes of FIFO and LIFO. When inventory costs are decreasing, FIFO ending inventory is lowest, and LIFO is highest.

Exhibit 9-4 summarizes the income effects of the three inventory methods using the data from Exhibit 9-3. Study the exhibit carefully, focusing on ending inventory, cost of goods sold and gross margin.

EXHIBIT 9-3 *Inventory and Cost of Goods Sold under Average, FIFO, and LIFO Inventory Costing Methods*

Panel A: Illustrative Data

Beginning inventory (10 units @ $1 per unit)		$ 10
Purchases		
No. 1 (25 units @ $1.40 per unit).....................................	$ 35	
No. 2 (25 units @ $1.80 per unit).....................................	45	
Total..		80
Cost of goods available for sale (60 units)...........................		$ 90
Ending inventory (20 units @ $? per unit)..........................		?
Cost of goods sold (40 units @ $? per unit)		$?

Panel B: Ending Inventory and Cost of Goods Sold

Weighted-Average Cost Method

Cost of goods available for sale — see Panel A		
(60 units @ average cost of $1.50* per unit)		$ 90
Ending inventory (20 units @ $1.50 per unit).......................................		$ 30
Cost of goods sold (40 units @ $1.50 per unit)		$ 60

*Cost of goods available for sale	$ 90
Number of units available for sale..	÷ 60
Average cost per unit	$1.50

FIFO Cost Method

Cost of goods available for sale (60 units — see Panel A)		$ 90
Ending inventory (cost of the *last* 20 units available)		
20 units @ $1.80 per unit (from purchase no. 2)		36
Cost of goods sold (cost of the *first* 40 units available)		
10 units @ $1.00 per unit (all of beginning inventory)	$ 10	
25 units @ $1.40 per unit (all of purchase no. 1)	35	
5 units @ $1.80 per unit (from purchase no. 2)	9	
Total		$ 54

LIFO Cost Method

Cost of goods available for sale (60 units — see Panel A)		$90
Ending inventory (cost of the *first* 20 units available)		
10 units @ $1.00 per unit (all of beginning inventory)	$ 10	
10 units @ $1.40 per unit (from purchase no. 1).........	14	
Total..		24
Cost of goods sold (cost of the last 40 units available)		
25 units @ $1.80 per unit (all of purchase no. 2)	$ 45	
15 units @ $1.40 per unit (from purchase no. 1).........	21	
Total..		$66

Generally Accepted Accounting Principles: A Comparison of the Inventory Methods _____

We may ask two questions to judge the inventory costing methods. (1) How well does each method match inventory expense (the cost of goods sold) to sales revenue on the income statement? (2) Which method reports the most up-to-date inventory

EXHIBIT 9-4 *Income Effects of FIFO, LIFO, and Average Cost Inventory Methods*

	FIFO		LIFO		Weighted-Average	
Sales revenue (assumed)		$100,000		$100,000		$100,000
Cost of goods sold						
Goods available for sale (assumed)....	$ 90,000		$ 90,000		$ 90,000	
Ending inventory	**36,000**		**24,000**		**30,000**	
Cost of goods sold..............................		54,000		66,000		60,000
Gross margin..		**$46,000**		**$34,000**		**$40,000**

Summary of Income Effects: When Inventory Costs Are Increasing

FIFO —	Highest ending inventory	LIFO —	Lowest ending inventory	Weighted-average —	Results fall
	Lowest cost of goods sold		Highest cost of goods sold		between the
	Highest gross margin		Lowest gross margin		extremes of
					FIFO and
					LIFO

amount on the balance sheet? The weighted-average cost method produces amounts between the extremes of LIFO and FIFO.

LIFO better matches the current value of cost of goods sold with current revenue by assigning to this expense the most recent inventory costs. By contrast, FIFO matches the oldest inventory costs against the period's revenue — a poor matching of current expense with current revenue.

FIFO reports the most current inventory costs on the balance sheet. LIFO can result in absurd balance sheet valuations of inventories because the oldest prices are left in ending inventory.

FIFO is criticized because it overstates income by so-called inventory profit during periods of inflation. Briefly, **inventory profit** is the difference between gross margin figured on the FIFO basis and gross margin figured on the LIFO basis. Exhibit 9-4 illustrates inventory profit. The $12,000 difference between FIFO and LIFO gross margins ($46,000 – $34,000 = $12,000) results from the difference in cost of goods sold and in ending inventory. This $12,000 amount is called *FIFO inventory profit, phantom profit,* or *illusory profit.* Why? Because to stay in business, the company must replace the inventory it has sold. The replacement cost of the merchandise is essentially the same as the cost of goods sold under LIFO ($66,000), not the FIFO amount ($54,000).

LIFO is criticized because it allows managers to manipulate net income. Assume inventory prices are rising rapidly, and a company wants to show less income for the year. Managers can buy a large amount of inventory near the end of the year. Under LIFO these high inventory costs immediately become expense — as cost of goods sold. As a result, the income statement reports a lower net income. Conversely, if the business is having a bad year, management may wish to increase reported income. To do so, managers can delay a large purchase of high-cost inventory until the next period. This inventory is not expensed as cost of goods sold in the current year. Thus management avoids decreasing the current year's reported income.

LIFO is very popular in the United States where its use is permitted for tax purposes. As you can see in Exhibit 9-4, in a period of rising prices (such as we have had since World War II), LIFO leads to the lowest income of the three methods and, in the United States, to the lowest taxes.

LIFO is not allowed for income tax purposes in Canada, but a company can use it for accounting purposes. That is probably why in Canada very few companies use LIFO (2 percent); here the largest percentage uses FIFO (40 percent), while the next largest number uses average cost (32 percent).[1]

---

[1] *Financial Reporting in Canada, 1991,* 19th edition, Toronto: CICA, 1992, p. 78.

A company may want to report the highest income, and FIFO meets this need when prices are rising. When prices are falling, LIFO reports the highest income.

Which inventory method is best? There is no single answer to this question. Different companies have different motives for the inventory method they choose. Emco Limited and Nova Corporation of Alberta use FIFO. Haley Industries Limited uses average cost for finished goods and work in process, specific cost for patterns, and FIFO for raw materials and supplies. Lake Ontario Cement uses average cost for all inventory. Celanese Canada is one of the few companies that uses LIFO. The companies disclose the method used under the heading "Significant Accounting Policies" or "Summary of Significant Accounting Policies" in the notes to the financial statements. Edmonton Telephones Corporation's specific disclosure is:

> **(c) Inventory:**
> Inventories are valued at the lower of cost and moving average cost and net realizable value. ...

Ivaco Inc.'s disclosure is

> **Inventories**
> Inventories are stated at the lower of cost (determined substantially on the first-in, first-out method) and net realizable value. ...

Consistency Principle

The **consistency principle** states that businesses must use the same accounting methods and procedures from period to period. Consistency makes it possible to compare a company's financial statements from one period to the next.

Suppose you are analyzing a company's net income pattern. The company has switched from LIFO to FIFO. Its net income has increased dramatically, but only as a result of the change in inventory method. If you did not know of the change, you might believe that the company's increased income arose from improved operations, which is not the case.

The consistency principle does not require that all companies within an industry use the same accounting method. Nor does it mean that a company may never change its own accounting method. However, a company making an accounting change must disclose the effect of the change on net income in the notes to the financial statements.

Summary Problem for Your Review

Suppose a Northern Telecom division that handles telephone components has these inventory records for January 19X6:

Date		Item	Quantity	Unit Cost	Sale Price
Jan.	1	Beginning inventory	100 units	$ 8	
	6	Purchase	60	9	
	13	Sale	70		$ 20
	21	Purchase	150	9	
	24	Sale	210		22
	27	Purchase	90	10	
	30	Sale	30		25

Company accounting records reveal that related operating expense for January was $1,900.

Required

1. Prepare the January income statement, using the following format. (Round figures to whole dollar amounts.)

Northern Telecom (telephone components division) Partial Income Statement for the month ended January 31, 19X6			
	LIFO	FIFO	Weighted-Average
Sales revenue	—	—	—
Cost of goods sold..			
Beginning inventory.................................	—	—	—
Purchases	—	—	—
Cost of goods available for sale	—	—	—
Ending inventory......................................	—	—	—
Cost of goods sold	—	—	—
Gross margin	—	—	—
Operating expenses	—	—	—
Operating income	—	—	—

2. Suppose you are the financial vice-president of Northern Telecom. Which inventory method would you use if your motive is to
   a. Minimize income taxes?
   b. Report the highest operating income?
   c. Report operating income between the extremes of FIFO and LIFO?
   d. Report inventory at the most current cost?
   e. Attain the best matching of current expense with current revenue?

   State the reason for each of your answers.

SOLUTION TO REVIEW PROBLEM

Requirement 1

Northern Telecom (telephone components division) Partial Income Statement for the month ended January 31, 19X6						
	LIFO		FIFO		Weighted-Average	
Sales revenue.............................		$6,770		$6,770		$6,770
Cost of goods sold						
Beginning inventory	$800		$800		$800	
Purchases..............................	2,790		2,790		2,790	
Cost of goods available for sale	3,590		3,590		3,590	
Ending inventory..................	720		900		808	
Cost of goods sold		2,870		2,690		2,782
Gross margin.............................		3,900		4,080		3,988
Operating expenses..................		1,900		1,900		1,900
Operating income.....................		$2,000		$2,180		$2,088

Computations

Sales revenue	(70 × $20)	+ (210 × $22) + (30 × $25) = $6,770
Beginning inventory	100 × $8	= $800
Purchases	(60 × $9)	+ (150 × $9) + (90 × $10) = $2,790
Ending inventory: LIFO	90* × $8	= $720
FIFO	90 × $10	= $900
Weighted-average	90 × $8.75**	= $808 (rounded from $807.75)

---

*Number of units in ending inventory = 100 + 60 – 70 + 150 – 210 + 90 – 30 = 90
**$3,590/400 units = $8.975 per unit
Number of units available = 100+ 60 + 150 + 90 = 400

Requirement 2

a. Use average cost to minimize income taxes. Operating income under LIFO is lowest when inventory unit costs are increasing, as they are in this case (from $8 to $10). Remember, LIFO cannot be used for income tax purposes in Canada. Average cost produces the next lowest income and, since it can be used for tax purposes, the lowest income taxes.

b. Use FIFO to report the highest operating income. Income under FIFO is highest when inventory unit costs are increasing, as in this situation.

c. Use weighted-average cost to report an operating income amount between the LIFO and FIFO extremes. This is true in this problem situation and in others whether inventory unit costs are increasing or decreasing.

d. Use FIFO to report inventory at the most current cost. The oldest inventory costs are expensed as cost of goods sold, leaving in ending inventory the most recent (most current) costs of the period.

e. Use LIFO to attain the best matching of current expense with current revenue. The most recent (most current) inventory costs are expensed as cost of goods sold.

Accounting Conservatism _____

Conservatism in accounting means to report items in the financial statements at amounts that lead to the gloomiest immediate financial results. Conservatism comes into play when there are alternative ways to account for an item. What advantage does conservatism give a business? Management often looks on the brighter side of operations, and may overstate a company's income and asset values. Many accountants regard conservatism as a counterbalance to management's optimistic tendencies. The goal is for financial statements to present realistic figures.

Conservatism appears in accounting guidelines like "anticipate no gains, but provide for all probable losses," and "if in doubt, record an asset at the lowest reasonable amount and a liability at the highest reasonable amount."

Accountants generally regard the historical cost of acquiring an asset as its maximum value. Even if the current market value of the asset increases above its cost, businesses do not write up (that is, increase) the asset's accounting value. Assume that a company purchased land for $100,000, and its value increased to $300,000. Accounting conservatism dictates that the historical cost $100,000 be maintained as the accounting value of the land.

Conservatism also directs accountants to decrease the accounting value of an asset if it appears unrealistically high, even if no transaction occurs. Assume that a company paid $35,000 for inventory that has become obsolete, and its current value is only $12,000. Conservatism dictates that the inventory be written down (that is, decreased) to $12,000.

Lower-of-Cost-or-Market Rule

The **lower-of-cost-or-market rule** (abbreviated as LCM) shows accounting conservatism in action. LCM requires that an asset be reported in the financial statements at the lower of its historical cost or its market value. Applied to inventories, market value may mean *current replacement cost* (that is, how much the business would have to pay in the market on that day to purchase the same amount of inventory on hand), or it may mean *net realizable value* (that is, the gross amount the business could get if it sold the inventory less the costs of selling it). If the replacement cost or net realizable value of inventory falls below its historical cost, the business must write down the value of its goods. The business reports ending inventory at its LCM value on the balance sheet. If a company has a warehouse full of obsolete inventory, this inventory must be written down to market value. How is the write-down accomplished?

Suppose a business paid $3,000 for inventory on September 26. By December 31, its value has fallen. The inventory can now be replaced for $2,200. Market value, defined in this instance as current replacement cost, is below cost, and the December 31 balance sheet reports this inventory at its LCM value of $2,200. Usually, the market value of inventory is higher than historical cost, so that inventory's LCM value is cost for most companies. Exhibit 9-5 presents the effects of LCM on the income statement and the balance sheet. The point of the exhibit is to show that the lower of (1) cost or (2) market value (replacement cost) is the relevant amount for valuing inventory on the income statement and the balance sheet. Companies are not required to show both cost and market value amounts. However, they may report the higher amount in parentheses, as shown on the balance sheet in the exhibit.

LCM states that of the $3,000 cost of ending inventory in Exhibit 9-5, $800 is considered to have expired even though the inventory was not sold during the period. Its replacement cost is only $2,200, and that amount is carried forward to the

---

OBJECTIVE 3

Apply the lower-of-cost-or-market rule to inventory

EXHIBIT 9-5 *Lower-of-Cost-or-Market (LCM) Effects*

Income Statement

Sales revenue		$20,000
Cost of goods sold		
Beginning inventory (LCM = Cost)	$ 2,800	
Net purchases	11,000	
Cost of goods available for sale	13,800	
Ending inventory —		
Cost = $3,000		
Replacement cost (market value) = $2,200		
LCM = Market	2,200	
Cost of goods sold		11,600
Gross margin		$ 8,400

Balance Sheet

Current assets		
Cash	$ XXX	
Short-term investments	XXX	
Accounts reveivable	XXX	
Inventories, at LCM (Cost, $3,000)	2,200	
Prepaid investments	XXX	
Total current assets	$X,XXX	

next period as the cost of beginning inventory. Suppose during the next period, the replacement cost of this inventory increases to $2,500. Accounting conservatism states that it would not be appropriate to write up the book value of inventory. The market value of inventory ($2,200 in this case) is used as its cost in future LCM determinations.

Examine the income statement effect of LCM in Exhibit 9-5. What expense absorbs the impact of the $800 inventory write down? Cost of goods sold is increased by $800 because ending inventory is $800 less at market ($2,200) than it would have been at cost ($3,000).

	Ending Inventory at		
	Cost	**LCM**	
Cost of goods available for sale	$13,800	$13,800	
Ending inventory			
Cost	3,000		} $800 Lower
Replacement cost (market value)		2,200	} at LCM
Cost of goods sold	$10,800	$11,600	} $800 Higher at LCM

Exhibit 9-5 also reports the application of LCM for inventories in the body of the balance sheet. Companies often disclose LCM in notes to their financial statements, as shown below for Spar Aerospace Limited:

> FROM NOTE 1
> **(c) Inventories**
> Inventories of raw materials and finished goods are valued at the lower of cost . . . and market value determined as the lesser of replacement cost or net realizable value.

Federal Pioneer Limited, a manufacturing company, states the following in the notes to the financial statements:

> FROM NOTE 2 — SIGNIFICANT ACCOUNTING POLICIES
> **Inventories**
> Raw material inventories are valued at lower of cost and replacement cost while work in process and finished goods are valued at the lower of cost and net realizable value....

Effect of Inventory Errors _____

Businesses determine inventory amounts at the end of the period. In the process of counting the items, applying unit costs and computing amounts, errors may arise. As the period 1 segment of Exhibit 9-6 shows, an error in the ending inventory amount creates errors in the cost of goods sold and gross margin amounts. Compare period 1, when ending inventory is overstated, and cost of goods sold is understated, each by $5,000, with period 3, which is correct. Period 1 should look exactly like period 3.

Recall that one period's ending inventory is the next period's beginning inventory. Thus the error in ending inventory carries over into the next period. Note the highlighted amounts in Exhibit 9-6.

Because the same ending inventory figure that is *subtracted* in computing cost of goods sold in one period is *added* as beginning inventory to compute cost of goods sold in the next period, the error's effect cancels out at the end of the second period. The overstatement of cost of goods sold in period 2 counterbalances the under-

OBJECTIVE 4

Explain why inventory errors counterbalance

EXHIBIT 9-6 *Effects of Inventory Errors*

	Period 1		Period 2		Period 3	
	Ending Inventory Overstated by $5,000		Beginning Inventory Overstated by $5,000		Correct	
Sales revenue		$100,000		$100,000		$100,000
Cost of goods sold						
Beginning inventory	$10,000		**$15,000**		$10,000	
Net purchases	50,000		50,000		50,000	
Cost of goods available for sale	60,000		65,000		60,000	
Ending inventory	**15,000**		10,000		10,000	
Cost of goods sold...........................		45,000		55,000		50,000
Gross margin...		**$55,000**		**$45,000**		$50,000
			$100,000			

The authors thank Carl High for this example.

statement in cost of goods sold in period 1. Thus the total gross margin amount for the two periods is the correct $100,000 figure, whether or not an error entered into the computation.

However, inventory errors cannot be ignored simply because they counterbalance. Suppose you are analyzing trends in the business's operations. Exhibit 9-6 shows a drop in gross margin from period 1 to period 2, followed by an increase in period 3. But that picture of operations is untrue because of the accounting error. Correct gross margin is $50,000 each period. To provide accurate information for decision-making, all inventory errors should be corrected.

Methods of Estimating Inventory

OBJECTIVE 5

Estimate inventory by two methods

Often a business must *estimate* the value of its inventory. Because of cost and inconvenience, few companies physically count their inventories at the end of each month, Yet they may need monthly financial statements. A fire or a flood may destroy inventory, and to file an insurance claim, the business must estimate the value of its loss. In both cases, the business needs to know the value of ending inventory without being able to count it. Two methods for estimating ending inventory are the *gross margin method* (or *gross profit method*) and the *retail method*. These methods are widely used in practice.

Gross Margin (Gross Profit) Method

The **gross margin method** is a way of estimating inventory based on the familiar cost of goods sold model:

$$\begin{array}{rl} & \textbf{Beginning inventory} \\ + & \textbf{Net purchases} \\ \hline = & \textbf{Cost of goods available for sale} \\ - & \textbf{Ending inventory} \\ \hline = & \textbf{Cost of goods sold} \end{array}$$

EXHIBIT 9-7 *Gross Margin Method of Estimating Inventory (amounts assumed)*

Beginning inventory..		$14,000
Net purchases..		66,000
Cost of goods available for sale.....................................		80,000
Cost of goods sold		
Net sales revenue..	$100,000	
Less estimated gross margin of 40%.........................	40,000	
Estimated cost of goods sold		60,000
Estimated cost of *ending inventory*................................		$20,000

Rearranging *ending inventory* and *cost of goods sold*, the model becomes useful for estimating ending inventory:

> **Beginning inventory**
> **+ Net purchases**
> _____
> **= Cost of goods available for sale**
> **– Cost of goods sold**
> _____
> **= Ending inventory**

Suppose a fire destroys your business's inventory. To collect insurance, you must estimate the cost of the ending inventory. If the fire did not also destroy your accounting records, beginning inventory and net purchases amounts may be taken directly from the accounting records. The Sales Revenue, Sales Returns, and Sales Discounts accounts indicate net sales up to the date of the fire. Using the entity's normal *gross margin rate* (that is, gross margin divided by net sales revenue), you can estimate cost of goods sold. The last step is to subtract cost of goods sold from goods available to estimate ending inventory. Exhibit 9-7 illustrates the gross margin method.

Accountants, managers and auditors use the gross margin method to test the overall reasonableness of an ending inventory amount that has been determined by a physical count for all types of businesses. This method helps detect large errors.

Retail Method

Retail establishments (department stores, drug stores, hardware stores, and so on) use the **retail method** to estimate their inventory cost. The retail method, like the gross margin method, is based on the cost of goods sold model. However, the retail method requires that the business record inventory purchases both at *cost*, as shown in the purchase records, and at *retail* (selling) price, as shown on the price tags. This is not a burden because price tags show the retail price of inventory, and most retailers set their retail prices by adding standard markups to their cost. For example, a department store may pay $6 for a man's belt, mark it up $4, and price the belt at $10 retail. In the retail method, the seller's inventory cost is determined by working backward from its retail value. Exhibit 9-8 illustrates the process.

In Exhibit 9-8 the accounting records show the goods available for sale at cost ($168,000) and at retail ($280,000). The cost ratio is .60 ($168,000/$280,000). For simplicity, we round all such percentages to two decimal places in this chapter. Subtracting *net sales revenue* (a retail amount) from *goods available for sale at retail* yields *ending inventory at retail* ($50,000). The business multiplies *ending inventory at retail* by the cost ratio to figure *ending inventory at cost* ($30,000).

Suppose the retailer has four categories of inventory, each with a different cost ratio. How would the business use the retail method to estimate the overall cost of

EXHIBIT 9-8 *Retail Method of Estimating Inventory (amounts assumed)*

	Cost	Retail
Beginning inventory..	$ 24,000	$ 40,000
Net purchases..	144,000	240,000
Goods available for sale...	$168,000	$280,000
Cost ratio: $168,000/$280,000 =.60		
Less: Net sales revenue (which is stated at retail).......		(230,000)
Ending inventory, at retail..		$ 50,000
Ending inventory, at cost ($50,000 × .60)	$ 30,000	

the ending inventory? Apply the retail method separately to each category of inventory, using its specific cost ratio; then add the costs of the four categories to determine the overall cost of inventory.

Even though the retail method is an estimation technique, some retailers use it to compute inventory value for their financial statements. They make physical counts of inventory at times other than the end of the year. For example, Silcorp Limited, whose operations include several convenience store chains, reports in the notes to the financial statements that "Cost is determined by the retail method . . . for convenience stores' inventories. . . . " Slightly more than 4 percent of the 300 companies included in the CICA survey of financial reporting report that they use the retail method.[2]

Periodic and Perpetual Inventory Systems

OBJECTIVE 6

Account for inventory by the periodic and perpetual systems

Different businesses have different inventory information needs. We now look at the two inventory systems: the *periodic system* and the *perpetual system*.

Periodic Inventory System

In the **periodic inventory system**, the business does not keep a continuous record of the inventory on hand. Instead, at the end of the period, the business makes a physical count of the on-hand inventory and applies the appropriate unit costs to determine the cost of ending inventory. The business makes the standard end-of-period inventory entries, as discussed in Chapter 5 and shown in the example that follows. This system is also called the *physical system* because it relies on the actual physical count of inventory. The periodic system is used to account for inventory items that have a low unit cost. Low-cost items may not be valuable enough to warrant the cost of keeping a running record of the inventory on hand.

Entries under the Periodic System In the periodic system, the business records purchases of inventory in the Purchases account (an expense account). At the end of the period, the business removes the beginning balance from the Inventory account and enters the ending balance, as determined by the physical count; Purchases is closed to the income summary. Assume the following data for a Zellers store's January transactions:

Beginning inventory	$ 80,000
Ending inventory...	102,000
Credit purchases (net of discounts and returns)...................................	600,000
Credit and cash sales (net of discounts and returns)	900,000

---

[2] *Financial Reporting in Canada, 1991*, 19th edition, Toronto: CICA, 1992, p. 78.

Summary entries for April

To record credit purchases

Purchases..	600,000	
Accounts Payable...		600,000

To record sales

Accounts Receivable/Cash...	900,000	
Sales Revenue		900,000

Inventory entries at the end of the period

Income Summary	80,000	
Inventory (beginning balance)		80,000
Inventory (ending balance)...	102,000	
Income Summary		102,000

Reporting on the financial statements

Balance sheet at January 31

Inventory	$102,000

Income statement for January

Sales revenue		$900,000
Cost of goods sold		
Begining inventory	$ 80,000	
Net Purchases	600,000	
Cost of goods available	680,000	
Ending inventory	102,000	
Cost of goods sold..............................		$578,000
Gross margin...		$322,000

Perpetual Inventory System

In the **perpetual inventory system**, the business keeps a continuous record for each inventory item. The records thus show the inventory on hand at all times. Perpetual records are useful in preparing monthly, quarterly, or other interim financial statements. The business can determine the cost of ending inventory, and the cost of goods sold directly from the accounts without having to physically count the merchandise.

The perpetual system offers a higher degree of control over inventory than the periodic system does because information is always up to date. Consequently, businesses use the perpetual system for high-unit-cost inventories such as gemstones and automobiles. Nevertheless, companies physically count their inventory at least once each year to check the accuracy of their perpetual records.

Perpetual inventory records can be computer listings of inventory items or inventory cards like the Infotech World record shown in Exhibit 9-9. The accountant adds information to the computer list or the card on a daily basis. A running balance conveniently shows the latest inventory value. The perpetual record serves as a subsidiary record to the inventory account in the general ledger.

The perpetual inventory record indicates that the business uses the FIFO basis, as shown by the November 30 sale. The cost of the first unit sold is the oldest unit cost on hand. Perpetual records may also be kept on the LIFO basis or the weighted-average basis. However, most companies that use the weighted-average or LIFO basis keep their perpetual records on either a FIFO or stated-in-units basis. This is much easier to compute and minimizes bookkeeping costs. At the end of the period, these companies convert ending inventory and cost of goods sold to LIFO or weighted-average cost basis for the financial statements. Perpetual inventory records provide information such as the following:

1. When customers inquire about how soon they can get a home computer, the salesperson can answer the question after referring to the perpetual inventory

EXHIBIT 9-9 *Perpetual Inventory Card — FIFO Basis*

Item: Home Computer Model RK-42

Date	Received Unit Qty.	Cost	Total	Sold Unit Qty.	Cost	Total	Balance Unit Qty.	Cost	Total
Nov. 1							14	$300	$4,200
5				4	$300	$1,200	10	300	3,000
7				9	300	2,700	1	300	300
12	5	$320	$1,600				1	300	300
							5	320	1,600
26	7	$330	2,310				1	300	300
							5	320	1,600
							7	330	2,310
30				1	300	300	1	320	320
	4	320	1,280	7	330	2,310			
Totals	12	—	$3,910	18	—	$5,480	8	—	$2,630

record. On November 8, the salesperson would reply that the company's stock is low, and the customer may have to wait a few days. On November 27, the salesperson could offer immediate delivery.

2. The perpetual records alert the business to reorder when inventory becomes low. On November 8, the company would be wise to purchase inventory. Sales might be lost if the business could not promise immediate delivery.

3. At November 30, the company prepares monthly financial statements. The perpetual inventory records show the company's ending inventory of home computers at $2,630, and its cost of goods sold for this product at $5,480. No physical count is necessary at this time. However, a physical inventory is needed once a year to verify the accuracy of the records.

Perpetual inventory records are becoming increasingly sophisticated. It was reported in the business press that Hostess Frito-Lay's decision support system allows management to track weekly sales of each route salesperson. Management can respond to problems in order to correct them much more quickly than under the old periodic system where information might take months to reach management.

Entries under the Perpetual System   In the perpetual system, the business records purchases of inventory by debiting the Inventory account. When the business makes a sale, two entries are necessary. The company records the sale in the usual manner — debits Cash or Accounts Receivable and credits Sales Revenue. The company also debits Cost of Goods Sold and credits Inventory for cost. The debit to Inventory (for purchases) and the credit to Inventory (for sales) serve to keep an up-to-date record of inventory on hand. Therefore, no end-of-period adjusting entries are needed. The Inventory account already carries the correct ending balance.

In the perpetual system, Cost of Goods Sold is an account in the general ledger. By contrast, in the periodic system, cost of goods sold is simply a total on the income statement.

To illustrate the entries under the perpetual system, let us apply the same data from the Zellers store we used in discussing the periodic system, which follow:

Ending inventory..	$102,000
Credit purchases (net of discounts and returns)..................................	600,000
Credit and cash sales (net of discounts and returns)	900,000
Cost of goods sold..	578,000

Summary entries for January

To record credit purchases

Inventory	600,000	
Accounts Payable		600,000

To record sales

Accounts Receivable/Cash...	900,000	
Sales revenue...		900,000
Cost of Goods Sold..	578,000	
Inventory		578,000

Reporting on the financial statements

Balance sheet at January 31

Inventory..	$102,000

Income statement for January

Sales revenue...	$900,000
Cost of goods sold	578,000
Gross margin	$322,000

You should compare the entries and financial statement presentations under the *periodic* and *perpetual* systems. Note that the entries to record purchases and sales differ under the two systems, but that the financial statement amounts are the same.

Internal Control over Inventory

Internal control over inventory is important because inventory is the lifeblood of a merchandiser. Successful companies take great care to protect their inventory. Elements of good internal control over inventory include

1. Physically counting inventory at least once each year no matter which system is used.
2. Maintaining efficient purchasing, receiving, and shipping procedures.
3. Storing inventory to protect it against theft, damage and decay.
4. Limiting access to inventory to personnel who do *not* have access to the accounting records.
5. Keeping perpetual inventory records for high-unit-cost merchandise.
6. Purchasing inventory in economical quantities.
7. Keeping enough inventory on hand to prevent shortages which lead to lost sales.
8. Not keeping too large an inventory stockpiled, thus avoiding the expense of tying up money in unneeded items.

The annual physical count of inventory (item 1) is necessary because the only way to be certain of the amount of inventory on hand is to count it. Errors arise in the best accounting systems, and the count is needed to establish the correct value of the inventory. When an error is detected, the records are brought into agreement with the physical count.

Keeping inventory handlers away from the accounting records (item 4) is an essential separation of duties, discussed in Chapter 7. An employee with access to inventory and the accounting records can steal the goods and make an entry to conceal the theft. For example, he or she could increase the amount of an inventory write-down to make it appear that goods decreased in value when in fact they were stolen.

Computerized Inventory Records

Computer systems have revolutionized accounting for inventory. Perpetual inventory systems are rapidly replacing periodic methods. Computerized systems can provide up-to-the-minute inventory data useful for managing the business. They help cut accounting cost by processing large numbers of transactions without computational error. Computer systems also enhance internal control. Computerized inventory systems also increase efficiency because managers always know the quantity and cost of inventory on hand. Managers can make better decisions about quantities to buy, prices to pay for the inventory, prices to charge customers, and sale terms to offer. Knowing the quantity on hand helps safeguard the inventory.

Computer inventory systems vary considerably. At one extreme are complex systems used by huge retailers like Eaton's, Woodward's, and Canadian Tire. Purchases of inventory are recorded in perpetual records stored in a central computer. The inventory tags are coded electronically for updating the perpetual records when a sale is recorded on the cash register. Have you noticed sales clerks passing the inventory ticket over a particular area of the checkout counter? A sensing device in the counter decodes the stock number, quantity, cost and sale price of the item sold. In other systems, the sales clerk passes an electronic device over the inventory tag. The computer records the sale and updates the inventory records. In effect, a journal entry is recorded for each sale, a procedure that is not economical without a computer.

Small companies also use minicomputers and microcomputers to keep perpetual inventory records. These systems may be similar to the systems used by large companies. In less sophisticated systems, a company may have sales clerks write inventory stock numbers on sales slips. The stock number identifies the particular item of inventory such as men's shirts or children's shoes. The business may accumulate all sales slips for the week. If the company has its own computer system, an employee may type the sales information into the computer and store the perpetual records on a magnetic disk. To learn the quantity, cost or other characteristic of a particular item of inventory, a manager can view the inventory record on the computer monitor. For broader-based decisions affecting the entire inventory, managers use printouts of all items in stock. Many small businesses hire outside computer service centers to do much of the accounting for inventory. Regardless of the arrangement, managers get periodic printouts showing inventory data needed for managing the business. Manual reporting of this information is more time-consuming and expensive.

Summary Problems for Your Review

Problem 1

Centronics Data Computer Ltd. reported a net loss for the year. In its financial statements, the company noted:

Balance Sheet

Current assets

Inventories (notes 1C and 2)....................................... $48,051,000

Note 1C: Inventories are stated at the lower of cost or market. Cost is determined on a first-in, first-out (FIFO) basis.

Note 2: Declining . . . market conditions during [the] fiscal [year] adversely affected anticipated sales of the Company's older printer products; . . . Accordingly, the statement of loss . . . includes a [debit] of $9,600,000.

Required

1. At which amount did Centronics report its inventory, cost or market value? How can you tell?
2. If the reported inventory of $48,051,000 represents market value, what was the cost of the inventory?

Problem 2

Beaver Building Supply Limited reported using the FIFO inventory method. Its inventory amount was $176 million.

Required

1. Suppose that during the period covered by this report, the company made an error that understated its inventory by $15 million. What effect would this error have on *cost of goods sold* and *gross margin* of the period? On *cost of goods sold* and *gross margin* of the following period? On *total gross margin* of both periods combined?
2. When Beaver Building Supply reported the above amount for inventory, prices were rising. Would FIFO or LIFO have shown a higher gross margin? Why?

SOLUTIONS TO REVIEW PROBLEMS

Problem 1

1. Centronics reported its inventory at *market value,* as indicated by (a) their valuing inventories at LCM, and (b) the declining market conditions that caused the company to "include a [debit] of $9,600,000" in "the statement of loss." The company debited the $9,600,000 to a loss account or to cost of goods sold. The credit side of the entry was to Inventory — for a write-down to market value.
2. The cost of inventory before the write-down was $57,651,000 ($48,051,000 + $9,600,000). The $48,051,000 market value is what is left of the original cost. Thus the amount to be carried forward to future periods is $48,051,000.

Problem 2

1. Understating ending inventory by $15 million has the following effects on *cost of goods sold* and *gross margin*:

	Cost of Goods Sold	Gross Margin
Period during which error was made	OVERSTATED by $15 million	UNDERSTATED by $15 million
Following period	UNDERSTATED by $15 million	OVERSTATED by $15 million
Combined total	CORRECTLY STATED	CORRECTLY STATED

2. When prices are rising, FIFO results in higher gross margin than LIFO. FIFO matches against sales revenue the lower inventory costs of beginning inventory and purchases made during the early part of the period.

Summary

Accounting for inventory plays an important part in merchandisers' accounting systems because selling inventory is the heart of their business. Inventory is generally the largest current asset on their balance sheet, and inventory expense, called *cost of goods sold*, is usually the largest expense on the income statement.

Businesses multiply the quantity of inventory items by their unit cost to determine inventory cost. Inventory costing methods are *specific unit cost; weighted-average cost; first-in, first-out (FIFO) cost*; and *last-in, first-out (LIFO) cost*. Only businesses that sell unique items like automobiles and jewels use the specific unit cost method. Most other companies use the other methods.

FIFO reports ending inventory at the most current cost. LIFO reports cost of goods sold at the most current cost. When inventory costs increase, LIFO produces the highest cost of goods sold and the lowest income. FIFO results in the highest income. The weighted-average cost method avoids the extremes of FIFO and LIFO.

The *consistency principle* demands that a business stick with the inventory method it chooses. If a change in inventory method is warranted, the company should apply the change retroactively, if possible, and disclose the effect of the change on income in the notes to the financial statements. The *lower-of-cost-or-market rule*, an example of accounting *conservatism*, requires that businesses report inventory on the balance sheet at the lower of its cost or market, which may be the current replacement value or net realizable value.

The *gross profit method* and the *retail method* are two techniques for estimating the cost of inventory. These methods come in handy for preparing interim financial statements, and for estimating the cost of inventory destroyed by fire and other casualties.

Merchandisers with high-price-tag items generally use the *perpetual inventory system*, which features a running inventory balance. In the past, merchandisers handling low-price-tag items used the *periodic system*. Recent advances in information technology have led to the replacement of periodic inventory systems with perpetual systems. A physical count of inventory is needed in both systems for control purposes.

Self-Study Questions

Test your understanding of the chapter by marking the correct answer to each of the following questions:

1. Which of the following items is the greatest in dollar amount? *(p. 394)*
   a. Beginning inventory   d. Ending inventory
   b. Purchases   e. Cost of goods sold
   c. Cost of goods available for sale

2. Sound Warehouse counts 15,000 compact discs, including 1,000 CDs held on consignment, in its Halifax store. The business has purchased an additional 2,000 CDs on FOB destination terms. These goods are still in transit. Each CD costs $3.40. The cost of the inventory to report on the balance sheet is *(p. 395)*
   a. $47,600   c. $54,400
   b. $51,000   d. $57,800

3. The inventory costing method that best matches current expense with current revenues is *(pp. 397–98)*
   a. Specific unit cost
   b. Average cost
   c. FIFO
   d. LIFO
   e. FIFO or LIFO, depending on whether inventory costs are increasing or decreasing

4. The consistency principle has the most direct impact on *(p. 399)*
   a. Whether to include or exclude an item in inventory
   b. Whether to change from one inventory method or another
   c. Whether to write inventory down to a market value below cost
   d. Whether to use the periodic or the perpetual inventory system

5. Application of the lower-of-cost-or-market rule often results in *(p. 402)*
   a. Higher ending inventory
   b. Lower ending inventory
   c. A counterbalancing error
   d. A change from one inventory method to another

6. An error understated ending inventory of 19X7. This error will *(p. 403)*
   a. Overstate 19X7 cost of sales
   b. Understate 19X8 cost of sales
   c. Not affect owner's equity at the end of 19X8
   d. All of the above

7. Beginning inventory was $35,000, purchases were $146,000 and sales totaled $240,000. With a normal gross margin rate of 35 percent, how much is ending inventory? *(p. 404)*
   a. $25,000
   b. $35,000
   c. $97,000
   d. $181,000

8. Beginning inventory was $20,000 at cost and $40,000 at retail. Purchases were $120,000 at cost and $210,000 at retail. Sales were $200,000. How much is ending inventory at cost? *(p. 405)*
   a. $22,000
   b. $26,000
   c. $28,000
   d. $50,000

9. The year-end entry to close beginning inventory in a perpetual inventory system is *(p. 409)*
   a. Income Summary XXX
        Inventory XXX
   b. Inventory XXX
        Income Summary XXX
   c. Either of the above, depending on whether inventory increased or decreased during the period
   d. Not needed

10. Which of the following statements is true? *(pp. 409–10)*
    a. Separation of duties is not an important element of internal control for inventories.
    b. The perpetual system is used primarily for low-unit-cost inventory.
    c. An annual physical count of inventory is needed regardless of the type of inventory system used.
    d. All the above are true.

Answers to the Self-Study Questions are at the end of the chapter.

Accounting Vocabulary

average cost method *(p. 396)*

beginning inventory *(p. 393)*

conservatism *(p. 401)*

consignment *(p. 395)*

consistency principle *(p. 399)*

cost of goods sold *(p. 393)*

ending inventory *(p. 393)*

first-in, first-out (FIFO) method *(p. 396)*

FOB destination *(p. 394)*

FOB shipping point *(p. 394)*

goods available for sale
(p. 393)

gross margin (gross
profit) method (p. 404)

inventory cost (p. 395)

last-in, first-out (LIFO)
method (p. 396)

lower-of-cost-or-market
(LCM) rule (p. 402)

periodic inventory
system (p. 406)

perpetual inventory
system (p. 407)

retail method (p. 405)

specific unit cost method
(p. 396)

weighted-average
cost method (p. 396)

ASSIGNMENT MATERIAL

Questions

1. Why is merchandise inventory so important to a retailer or wholesaler?

2. If beginning inventory is $10,000, purchases total $85,000 and ending inventory is $12,700, how much is cost of goods sold?

3. If beginning inventory is $32,000, purchases total $119,000 and cost of goods sold is $127,000, how much is ending inventory?

4. What role does the cost principle play in accounting for inventory?

5. What two items determine the cost of ending inventory?

6. Briefly describe the four generally accepted inventory cost methods. During a period of rising prices, which method produces the highest reported income? Which produces the lowest reported income?

7. Which inventory costing method produces the ending inventory valued at the most current cost? Which method produces the cost-of-goods-sold amount valued at the most current cost?

8. Why is LIFO the most popular method in the United States? Why is it so little used in Canada? Do these reasons accord with the notion that the inventory costing method should produce the most accurate data on the income statement?

9. Which inventory costing method produces the most accurate data on the balance sheet? Why?

10. What is inventory profit? Which method produces it?

11. How does the consistency principle affect accounting for inventory?

12. Briefly describe the influence that the concept of conservatism has on accounting for inventory.

13. Manley Ltd.'s inventory has a cost of $48,000 at the end of the year, and the current replacement cost of the inventory is $51,000. At which amount should the company report the inventory on its balance sheet? Suppose the current replacement cost of the inventory is $45,000 instead of $51,000. At which amount should Manley report the inventory? What rule governs your answers to these questions?

14. Gabriel Ltd. accidentally overstated its ending inventory by $10,000 at the end of period 1. Is gross margin of period 1 overstated or understated? Is gross margin of period 2 overstated, understated, or unaffected by the period 1 error? Is total gross margin for the two periods overstated, understated, or correct? Give the reason for your answer.

15. The market referred to in the lower-of-cost-or-market rule may have two meanings. Describe each of them.

16. Identify two methods of estimating inventory amounts. What familiar model underlies both estimation methods?

17. A fire destroyed the inventory of Olivera Company, but the accounting records were saved. The beginning inventory was $22,000, purchases for the period were $71,000, and sales were $140,000. Olivera's customary gross margin is 45 percent of sales. Use the gross margin method to estimate the cost of the inventory destroyed by the fire.

18. Suppose your company deals in expensive jewelry. Which inventory system should you use to achieve good internal control over the inventory? If your business is a hardware store that sells low-cost goods, which inventory system would you be likely to use? Why would you choose this system?

19. Identify the accounts debited and credited in the standard purchase and sale entries under (a) the periodic inventory system, and (b) the perpetual inventory system.

20. What is the role of the physical count of inventory in (a) the periodic inventory system, and (b) the perpetual inventory system?

21. True or false? A company that sells inventory of low unit cost needs no internal controls over the goods. Any inventory loss would probably be small.

Exercises

Exercise 9-1 *Computing ending inventory by four methods* **(L.O. 1)**

Malzone Precision Instruments' inventory records for industrial switches indicate the following at October 31:

Oct.	1	Beginning inventory	10 units @ $130
	8	Purchase	4 units @ 140
	15	Purchase	11 units @ 150
	26	Purchase	5 units @ 156

The physical count of inventory at October 31 indicates that eight units are on hand, and the company owns them. Compute ending inventory and cost of goods sold using each of the following methods:

1. Specific unit cost, assuming five $150 units and three $130 units are on hand
2. Weighted-average cost
3. First in, first out
4. Last in, first out

Exercise 9-2 *Recording periodic inventory transactions* **(L.O. 1)**

Use the data in Exercise 9-1 and the periodic inventory system to journalize:

1. Total October purchases in one summary entry. All purchases were on credit.
2. Total October sales in one summary entry. Assume the selling price was $300 per unit, and all sales were on credit.
3. October 31 entries for inventory. Malzone Precision Instruments uses FIFO.

Exercise 9-3 *Converting LIFO financial statements to the FIFO basis* **(L.O. 1,2)**

Hennig Nursery reported:

Balance sheet	19X5	19X4
Inventories — note 4	$ 65,800	$ 59,300
Income statement		
Net purchases	404,100	372,700
Cost of goods sold	397,600	381,400

Note 4: The company determines inventory cost by the last-in, first-out method. If the first-in, first-out method were used, ending inventories would be $5,200 higher at year end 19X5 and $3,500 higher at year end 19X4.

Required

Show the cost-of-goods-sold computations for 19X5 under LIFO and FIFO. Which method would result in higher reported income? Show the amount of the difference.

Exercise 9-4   *Note disclosure of a change in inventory method (L.O. 2)*

A company has used the first-in, first-out inventory method for many years. At the start of the current year the company switched to the last-in, first-out method. This change decreased net income by $263,000. Write the note to disclose this accounting change in the company's financial statements.

Exercise 9-5   *The effect of lower-of-cost-or-market on the income statement (L.O. 3)*

From the following inventory records of DeGaulle Corporation for 19X7, prepare the company's income statement through gross margin. Apply the lower-of-cost-or-market rule.

Beginning inventory (average cost)	300 @ $41.33	=	$ 12,399
(replacement cost)........	300 @ 41.91	=	12,573
Purchases during the year	2,600 @ 45.50	=	118,300
Ending inventory (average cost)	400 @ 45.07	=	18,028
(replacement cost)	400 @ 42.10	=	16,840
Sales during the year	2,500 @ 80.00*	=	200,000

*Selling price per unit.

Exercise 9-6   *Applying the lower-of-cost-or-market rule (L.O. 3)*

Imhoff Ltd.'s income statement for March reported the following data:

Income Statement

Sales revenue		$88,000
Cost of goods sold		
Beginning inventory	$17,200	
Net purchases	51,700	
Cost of goods available for sale	68,900	
Ending inventory	22,800	
Cost of goods sold..		46,100
Gross margin..		$41,900

Prior to releasing the financial statements, it was discovered that the current replacement cost of ending inventory was $20,400. Correct the above data to include the lower-of-cost-or-market value of ending inventory. Also, show how inventory would be reported on the balance sheet.

Exercise 9-7   *Correcting an inventory error (L.O. 4)*

Robinette Auto Supply reported the following comparative income statement for the years ended September 30, 19X5 and 19X4:

Robinette Auto Supply
Income Statements
For the Year ended September 30,

	19X5		19X4	
Sales revenue		$132,300		$121,700
Cost of goods sold				
Beginning inventory............	$14,000		$12,800	
Net purchases.......................	72,000		66,000	
Cost of goods available........	86,000		78,800	
Ending inventory	16,600		14,000	
Cost of goods sold................		69,400		64,800
Gross margin.............................		62,900		56,900
Operating expenses		30,300		26,100
Net income.................................		$ 32,600		$ 30,800

During 19X5, accountants for the company discovered that ending 19X4 inventory was understated by $1,500. Prepare the corrected comparative income statement for the two-year period. What was the effect of the error on net income for the two years combined? Explain your answer.

Exercise 9-8   *Estimating inventory by the gross margin method* **(L.O. 5)**

Jansen Unpainted Furniture began April with inventory of $41,000. The business made net purchases of $37,600 and had net sales of $55,000 before a fire destroyed the company's inventory. For the past several years, Jansen's gross margin on sales has been 40 percent. Estimate the cost of the inventory destroyed by the fire.

Exercise 9-9   *Estimating inventory by the retail method* **(L.O. 5)**

Assume the inventory records of A & B Sound, a regional chain of stereo shops, revealed the following:

	At Cost	At Retail
Beginning inventory	$ 30,400	$ 48,000
Net purchases...	113,000	191,000
Net sales...		201,000

Use the retail inventory method to estimate the ending inventory of the business.

Exercise 9-10   *Recording perpetual inventory transactions* **(L.O. 6)**

Jerrel Bolton Chevrolet Ltd. keeps perpetual inventory records for its automobile parts inventory. During May, the company made credit purchases of inventory parts costing $93,300. Cash sales came to $63,100, credit sales on notes receivable totaled $85,400, and cost of goods sold reached $119,550. Record these summary transactions in the general journal.

Exercise 9-11   *Computing the ending amount of a perpetual inventory* **(L.O. 6)**

Piazza String World Music Center carries a large inventory of guitars, keyboards, and other musical instruments. Because each item is expensive, Piazza uses a perpetual inventory system. Company records indicate the following for a particular line of Casio keyboards:

Date	Item	Quantity	Unit Cost
May 1	Balance	5	$80
6	Sale	3	
8	Purchase	11	85
17	Sale	4	
30	Sale	3	

Compute ending inventory and cost of goods sold for keyboards by the FIFO method. Also show the computation of cost of goods sold by the standard formula: Beginning inventory + Purchases – Ending inventory = Cost of goods sold.

Problems   (Group A)

Problem 9-1A   *Computing inventory by three methods (L.O. 1)*

Emerson Electric Co. began the year with 73 units of inventory that cost $26 each. During the year Emerson made the following purchases:

Mar. 11	113 @ $27
May 2	81 @ 29
July 19	167 @ 32
Nov. 18	44 @ 36

The company uses the periodic inventory system, and the physical count at December 31 indicates that ending inventory consists of 91 units.

Required

Compute the ending inventory and cost of goods sold amounts under (1) weighted-average cost, (2) FIFO cost, and (3) LIFO cost. Round weighted-average cost per unit to the nearest cent, and round all other amounts to the nearest dollar.

Problem 9-2A   *Computing inventory, cost of goods sold, and FIFO inventory profit (L.O. 1,2)*

Irene's Beverage Distributors specializes in soft drinks. The business began operations on January 1, 19X1, with an inventory of 500 cases of drinks that cost $2.01 per case. During the first month of operations, the store purchased inventory as follows:

Purchase no. 1	60 @ $2.10
Purchase no. 2	120 @ 2.35
Purchase no. 3	600 @ 2.50
Purchase no. 4	40 @ 2.75

The ending inventory consists of 500 cases of drinks.

Required

1. Complete the following tabulation, rounding weighted-average cost to the nearest cent and all other amounts to the nearest dollar:

	Ending Inventory	Cost of Goods Sold
a. Weighted-average cost	_____	_____
b. FIFO cost	_____	_____
c. LIFO cost	_____	_____

2. Compute the amount of inventory profit under FIFO.
3. Which method produces the most current ending inventory cost? Which method produces the most current cost-of-goods-sold amount? Give the reason for your answers.

Problem 9-3A   *Preparing an income statement directly from the accounts* **(L.O. 1,2)**

The records of Upjohn Healthcare Products include the following accounts for one of its products at December 31 of the current year:

Inventory

Jan.	1	Balance	{700 units @ $7.00}	4,900

Purchases

Jan.	6	300 units @ $7.05	2,115
Mar.	19	1,100 units @ 7.35	8,085
June	22	8,400 units @ 7.50	63,000
Oct.	4	500 units @ 8.80	4,400
Dec.	31	Balance	77,600

Sales Revenue

Feb.	5	1,000 units @ $12.00	12,000
Apr.	10	700 units @ 12.10	8,470
July	31	1,800 units @ 13.25	23,850
Sept.	4	3,500 units @ 13.50	47,250
Nov.	27	3,100 units @ 15.00	46,500
Dec.	31	Balance	138,070

Required

1. Compute the quantities of goods in (a) ending inventory, and (b) cost of goods sold during the year.
2. Prepare a partial income statement through gross margin under the weighted-average cost, FIFO cost, and LIFO cost methods.

Problem 9-4A   *Converting an actual company's reported income from the LIFO basis to the FIFO basis* **(L.O. 2)**

Colgate-Palmolive Company uses the LIFO method for inventories. In a recent annual report, Colgate-Palmolive reported these amounts on the balance sheet (in millions):

	December 31,	
	19X9	19X8
Inventories	$591	$630

A note to the financial statements indicated that if current cost (assume FIFO) had been used, inventories would have been higher by $25 million at the end of 19X9 and higher by $21 million at the end of 19X8. The income statement reported sales revenue of $5,039 million and cost of goods sold of $2,843 million for 19X9.

Required

1. Show the computation of Colgate-Palmolive's cost of goods sold and gross margin for 19X9 by the LIFO method as actually reported.

2. Compute Colgate-Palmolive's cost of goods sold and gross margin for 19X9 by the FIFO method.

3. Which method makes the company look better in 19X9? Give your reason. What is the amount of inventory profit for 19X9?

Problem 9-5A   *Applying the lower-of-cost-or-market rule   (L.O. 3)*

The financial statements of Dubrovnik Business Systems were prepared on the cost basis without considering whether the market value of ending inventory was less than cost. Following are selected data from those statements:

From the income statement

Sales revenue..		$278,000
Cost of goods sold		
Beginning inventory	$ 60,000	
Net purchases	122,000	
Cost of goods available for sale.................................	182,000	
Ending inventory...	53,000	
Cost of goods sold		129,000
Gross margin..		$149,000

From the balance sheet

Current assets	
Inventory	$ 53,000

The replacement costs were $68,000 for beginning inventory and $51,000 for ending inventory.

Required

1. Revise the data to include the appropriate lower-of-cost-or-market value of inventory.

2. How is the lower-of-cost-or-market rule conservative? How is conservatism shown in Dubrovnik's situation?

Problem 9-6A   *Correcting inventory errors over a three-year period   (L.O. 4)*

The Elm Mott Custom Window Frames books show these data (in millions):

	19X6		19X5		19X4	
Net sales revenue		$350		$280		$240
Cost of goods sold						
Beginning inventory	$ 65		$ 55		$ 70	
Net purchases	195		135		130	
Cost of goods available.........	260		190		200	
Less ending inventory	70		65		55	
Cost of goods sold		190		125		145
Gross margin..............................		160		155		95
Operating expenses...................		113		109		76
Net income		$ 47		$ 46		$ 19

In early 19X7, a team of internal auditors discovered that the ending inventory of 19X4 had been overstated by $12 million. Also, the ending inventory for 19X6 had been understated by $8 million. The ending inventory at December 31, 19X5 was correct.

Required

1. Prepare corrected income statements for the three years.
2. State whether each year's net income and owner's equity amounts are understated or overstated. For each incorrect figure, indicate the amount of the understatement or overstatement.

Problem 9-7A   *Estimating inventory by the gross margin method; preparing a multiple-step income statement* **(L.O. 5)**

Assume Baldwin Piano Company estimates its inventory by the gross margin method when preparing monthly financial statements. For the past two years, the gross margin has averaged 40 percent of net sales. Assume further that the company's inventory records for stores in Southwestern Ontario reveal the following data:

Inventory, July 1..	$ 267,000
Transactions during July	
Purchases...	3,689,000
Purchase discounts...	26,000
Purchase returns..	12,000
Sales..	6,230,000
Sales returns	22,000

Required

1. Estimate the July 31 inventory using the gross margin method.
2. Prepare the July income statement through gross margin for the Baldwin Piano stores in Southwestern Ontario. Use the multiple-step format.

Problem 9-8A   *Estimating inventory by the retail method; recording periodic inventory transactions* **(L.O. 5)**

The fiscal year of K-Mart Canada ends on January 31. Assume the following inventory data for the hardware department of a K-Mart store:

	Cost	Retail
Inventory, Jan. 31, 19X3	$ 31,200	$ 63,300
Transactions during the year ended January 31, 19X4		
Purchases...	154,732	301,190
Purchase returns..	5,800	11,290
Sales..		314,600
Sales returns		18,190

Required

1. Use the retail method to estimate the cost of the store's ending inventory of hardware at January 31, 19X4.
2. Assuming K-Mart uses the periodic inventory system, prepare general journal entries to record:
   a. Inventory purchases and sales during fiscal year 19X4. Assume all purchases and one half of company sales were on credit. All other sales were for cash.
   b. Inventory entries at January 31, 19X4. Closing entries for Purchases and Purchase Returns are not required.

Problem 9-9A *Using the perpetual inventory system; applying the lower-of-cost-or-market rule (L.O. 3,6)*

Midas is a popular brand of automobile mufflers. Assume the following data for a particular muffler at Midas Muffler store:

	Purchased	Sold	Balance
Dec. 31, 19X3			120 @ $6 = $720
Mar. 15, 19X4	50 @ $7 = $350		
Apr. 10		80	
May 29	100 @ 8 = 800		
Aug. 3		130	
Nov. 16	90 @ 9 = 810		
Dec. 12		70	

Required

1. Prepare a perpetual inventory card for Midas, using the FIFO method.

2. Assume Midas sold the 130 units on August 3 on account for $22 each. Record the sale and related cost of goods sold in the general journal under the FIFO method.

3. Suppose the current replacement cost of the ending inventory of this Midas store is $750 at December 31, 19X4. Use the answer to requirement 1 to compute the lower-of-cost-or-market (LCM) value of the ending inventory.

Problem 9-10A *Recording periodic and perpetual inventory transactions (L.O. 6)*

Klassen Sales Ltd. records reveal the following at December 31 of the current year:

Inventory

Jan.	1	Balance	{900 units @ $7.00}	6,300	

Purchases

Feb.	4	300 units @ $7.05	2,115	
Apr.	11	1,100 units @ 7.35	8,085	
June	22	8,400 units @ 7.50	63,000	
Aug.	19	500 units @ 8.80	4,400	
Dec.	31	Balance		77,600

Sales Revenue

Mar.	8	1,000 units @ $12.00	12,000
May	24	700 units @ 12.10	8,470
Aug.	19	1,800 units @ 13.25	23,850
Oct.	4	3,500 units @ 13.50	47,250
Nov.	14	3,100 units @ 15.00	46,500
Dec.	31	Balance	138,070

Required

Make summary journal entries to record:

1. Purchases, sales, and end-of-period inventory entries, assuming Klassen uses the periodic inventory system and the FIFO cost method. All purchases are on credit. Cash sales are $20,000, with the remaining sales on account.

2. Purchases, sales, and cost of goods sold, assuming Klassen uses the perpetual inventory system and the FIFO cost method. All purchases are on credit. Cash sales are $20,000, with the remaining sales on account.

(Group B)

Problem 9-1B *Computing inventory by three methods (L.O. 1)*

Swirl Vision Center began the year with 140 units of inventory that cost $80 each. During the year, Swirl made the following purchases:

Feb.	3	217 @	$ 81
Apr.	12	95 @	82
Aug.	8	210 @	84
Oct.	24	248 @	88

The company uses the periodic inventory system, and the physical count at December 31 indicates that ending inventory consists of 229 units.

Required

Compute the ending inventory and cost of goods sold, amounts under (1) weighted-average cost, (2) FIFO cost and (3) LIFO cost. Round weighted-average cost per unit to the nearest cent, and round all other amounts to the nearest dollar.

Problem 9-2B *Computing inventory, cost of goods sold, and FIFO inventory profits (L.O. 1,2)*

Shellenberger's specializes in men's shirts. The store began operations on January 1, 19X1, with an inventory of 200 shirts that cost $13 each. During the year, the store purchased inventory as follows:

Purchase no. 1	110 @	$ 14
Purchase no. 2	80 @	15
Purchase no. 3	320 @	15
Purchase no. 4	100 @	18

The ending inventory consists of 150 shirts.

Required

1. Complete the following tabulation, rounding average cost to the nearest cent and all other amounts to the nearest dollar:

	Ending Inventory	Cost of Goods Sold
a. Weighted-average cost	_____	_____
b. FIFO cost	_____	_____
c. LIFO cost	_____	_____

2. Compute the amount of inventory profit under FIFO.
3. Which method produces the most current ending inventory cost? Which method produces the most current cost-of-goods-sold amount? Give the reason for your answers.

Problem 9-3B *Preparing an income statement directly from the accounts* **(L.O. 1,2)**

The periodic inventory records of The Kitchen Cupboard include the following accounts for one of its products at December 31 of the current year:

Inventory

Jan.	1	Balance	300 units @ $ 3.00	1,210	
			100 units @ 3.10		

Purchases

Feb.	6	800 units @ $ 3.15	2,520	
May	19	600 units @ 3.35	2,010	
Aug.	12	460 units @ 3.50	1,610	
Oct.	4	800 units @ 3.75	3,000	
Dec.	31	Balance	9,140	

Sales Revenue

		Mar.	12	500 units @ $ 4.00	2,000
		June	9	1,100 units @ 4.20	4,620
		Aug.	21	300 units @ 4.50	1,350
		Nov.	2	600 units @ 4.50	2,700
		Dec.	18	100 units @ 4.75	475
		Dec.	31	Balance	11,145

Required

1. Compute the quantities of goods in (a) ending inventory, and (b) cost of goods sold during the year.

2. Prepare a partial income statement through gross margin under the weighted-average cost, FIFO cost, and LIFO cost methods. Round weighted-average cost to the nearest cent and all other amounts to the nearest dollar.

Problem 9-4B *Converting a company's reported income from the LIFO basis to the FIFO basis* **(L.O. 2)**

Shopper's Canada uses the LIFO method for inventories. In a recent annual report, Shopper's reported these amounts on the balance sheet (in millions):

	End of Fiscal Year	
	19X6	19X5
Merchandise inventories...	$2,168	$2,298

A note to the financial statements indicated that if another method (assume FIFO) had been used, inventories would have been higher by $10 million at the end of fiscal year 19X6 and higher by $16 million at the end of 19X5. The income statement reported sales revenue of $14,740 million and cost of goods sold of $9,786 million for 19X6.

Required

1. Show the computation of Shopper's cost of goods sold and gross margin for fiscal year 19X6 by the LIFO method as actually reported.

2. Compute Shopper's cost of goods sold and gross margin for 19X6 by the FIFO method.

3. Which method makes the company look better? Were inventory costs increasing or decreasing during 19X6? How can you tell?

Problem 9-5B   *Applying the lower-of-cost-or-market rule (L.O. 3)*

Assume that accountants prepared the financial statements of Takamoto TV and Appliance on the cost basis without considering whether the replacement value of ending inventory was less than cost. Following are selected data from those statements:

From the income statement

Sales revenue		$832,000
Cost of goods sold		
Beginning inventory...	$104,000	
Net purchases..	493,000	
Cost of goods available for sale	597,000	
Ending inventory	143,000	
Cost of goods sold..		454,000
Gross margin...		$378,000

From the balance sheet

Current assets	
Inventory...	$143,000

The replacement costs were $107,000 for beginning inventory and $135,000 for ending inventory.

Required

1. Revise the data to include the appropriate lower-of-cost-or-market value of inventory.
2. How is the lower-of-cost-or-market rule conservative? How does Takamoto's situation display conservatism?

Problem 9-6B   *Correcting inventory errors over a three-year period (L.O. 4)*

The accounting records of the Tanglewood Farms Restaurant chain show these data (in millions):

	19X3		19X2		19X1	
Net sales revenue...................		$200		$160		$175
Cost of goods sold						
Beginning inventory.........	$ 15		$ 25		$ 40	
Net purchases....................	135		100		90	
Cost of goods available....	150		125		130	
Less ending inventory......	30		15		25	
Cost of goods sold		120		110		105
Gross margin		80		50		70
Operating expenses...............		74		38		46
Net income.............................		$ 6		$ 12		$ 24

In early 19X4, a team of internal auditors discovered that the ending inventory of 19X1 had been understated by $8 million. Also, the ending inventory for 19X3 had been overstated by $5 million. The ending inventory at December 31, 19X2 was correct.

Required

1. Prepare corrected income statements for the three years.

2. State whether each year's net income as reported here and the related owner's equity amounts are understated or overstated. For each incorrect figure, indicate the amount of the understatement or overstatement.

Problem 9-7B   *Estimating inventory by the gross margin method; preparing a multiple-step income statement (L.O. 5)*

Assume Taco Time estimates its inventory by the gross margin method when preparing monthly financial statements. For the past two years, gross margin has averaged 25 percent of net sales. Assume further that the company's inventory records for stores in Alberta reveal the following data:

Inventory, March 1	$ 398,000
Transactions during March	
Purchases	6,585,000
Purchase discounts	149,000
Purchase returns	8,000
Sales	8,667,000
Sales returns	17,000

Required

1. Estimate the March 31 inventory using the gross margin method.

2. Prepare the March income statement through gross margin for the Taco Time stores in Alberta. Use the multiple-step format.

Problem 9-8B   *Estimating inventory by the retail method; recording periodic inventory transactions (L.O. 5)*

The fiscal year of Woodward's Ltd. (and many other retailers) ends on January 31. Assume the following inventory data for the housewares department of a Woodward's store:

	Cost	Retail
Inventory, Jan. 31, 19X5	$ 84,500	$153,636
Transactions during the year ended January 31, 19X6		
Purchases	419,220	762,500
Purchase returns	18,090	33,172
Sales		690,300
Sales returns		15,140

Required

1. Use the retail method to estimate the cost of the store's ending inventory of housewares at January 31, 19X6. Round off the ratio to two decimal places.

2. Assuming Woodward uses the periodic inventory system, prepare general journal entries to record:
   a. Inventory purchases and sales during fiscal year 19X6. Assume all purchases and 10 percent of company sales were on credit. All other sales were for cash.
   b. Inventory entries at January 31, 19X6. Closing entries for Purchases and Purchase Returns are not required.

Problem 9-9B   *Using the perpetual inventory system; applying the lower-of-cost-or-market rule* **(L.O. 3,6)**

Northern Telecom manufactures high-technology products used in the communications and other industries. Assume the following data for Northern Telecom's product SR450:

	Purchased	Sold	Balance
Dec. 31, 19X1			110 @ $5 = $550
Feb. 10, 19X2	80 @ $6 = $480		
Apr. 7		160	
May 29	110 @ 7 = 770		
July 13		120	
Oct. 4	100 @ 8 = 800		
Nov. 22		80	

Required

1. Prepare a perpetual inventory record for product SR450, using the FIFO method.

2. Assume Northern Telecom sold the 160 units on April 7 on account for $13 each. Record the sale and related cost of goods sold in the general journal under the FIFO method.

3. Suppose the current replacement cost of the ending inventory of product SR450 is $305 at December 31, 19X2. Use the answer to requirement 1 to compute the lower-of-cost-or-market (LCM) value of the ending inventory.

Problem 9-10B   *Recording periodic and perpetual inventory transactions* **(L.O. 6)**

Diego Associates records reveal the following at December 31 of the current year:

Inventory

Jan. 1 Balance	{ 400 units @ $3.00 } 1,510
	{ 100 units @ 3.10 }

Purchases

Jan. 22	800 units @ $3.15	2,520
Apr 8	600 units @ 3.35	2,010
July 12	460 units @ 3.50	1,610
Sep. 11	800 units @ 3.75	3,000
Dec. 31 Balance		9,140

Sales Revenue

Feb. 8	500 units @ $4.00	2,000
Apr. 22	1,100 units @ 4.20	4,620
July 21	300 units @ 4.50	1,350
Oct. 14	600 units @ 4.50	2,700
Nov. 27	100 units @ 4.75	475
Dec. 31 Balance		11,145

Required

Make summary journal entries to record:

1. Purchases, sales and end-of-period inventory entries, assuming Diego Associates uses the periodic inventory system and the FIFO method. All purchases are on credit. Cash sales are $4,000, with the remaining sales on account.

2. Purchases, sales and cost of goods sold, assuming Diego Associates uses the perpetual inventory system and the FIFO method. All purchases are on credit. Cash sales total $4,000, with the remainder on account.

Extending Your Knowledge

Decision Problems

1. Assessing the impact of a year-end purchase of inventory (L.O. 2)

Tailwind Cycling Center is nearing the end of its first year of operations. The company made the following inventory purchases:

January	1,000	$100	$100,000
March	1,000	100	100,000
May	1,000	110	110,000
July	1,000	130	130,000
September	1,000	140	140,000
November	1,000	150	150,000
Totals	6,000		$730,000

Sales for the year will be 5,000 units for $1,200,000 revenue. Expenses other than cost of goods sold and income taxes will be $200,000. The president of the company is undecided about whether to adopt FIFO or LIFO.

The company has storage capacity for 5,000 additional units of inventory. Inventory prices are expected to stay at $150 per unit for the next few months. The president is considering purchasing 4,000 additional units of inventory at $150 each before the end of the year. He wishes to know how the purchase would affect net income before taxes under both FIFO and LIFO.

Required

1. To help the company decide, prepare income statements under FIFO and under LIFO, both without and with the year-end purchase of 4,000 units of inventory at $150 per unit.

2. Compare net income before taxes under FIFO without and with the year-end purchase. Make the same comparison under LIFO. Under which method does the year-end purchase have the greater effect on net income before taxes?

3. Under which method can a year-end purchase be made in order to manipulate net income before taxes?

2. Assessing the impact of the inventory costing method on the financial statements (L.O. 2,3)

The inventory costing method chosen by a company can affect the financial statements and thus the decisions of the users of those statements.

Required

1. A leading accounting researcher stated that one inventory costing method reports the most recent costs in the income statement, while another method reports the most recent costs in the balance sheet. In this person's opinion, this results in one or the other of the statements being "inaccurate" when prices are rising. What did the researcher mean?

2. Conservatism is an accepted accounting concept. Would you want management to be conservative in accounting for inventory if you were (a) a shareholder, and (b) a prospective shareholder? Give your reason.

3. Beechwood Ltd. follows conservative accounting and writes the value of its inventory of bicycles down to market, which has declined below cost. The following year, an unexpected cycling craze results in a demand for bicycles that far exceeds supply, and the market price increases well above the previous cost. What effect will conservatism have on the income of Beechwood over the two years?

Ethical Issue

During 19X6, Crocker-Hinds Company changed to the LIFO method of accounting for inventory. Suppose that during 19X7, Crocker-Hinds changes back to the FIFO method, and in the following year switches back to LIFO again.

Required

1. What would you think of a company's ethics if it changed accounting methods every year?

2. What accounting principle would changing methods every year violate?

3. Who can be harmed when a company changes its accounting methods too often? How?

Financial Statement Problems

1. Inventories (L.O. 1, 2)

The notes are an important part of a company's financial statements, giving valuable details that would clutter the tabular data presented in the statements. This problem will help you learn to use a company's inventory notes. Refer to the Schneider Corporation statements and the related notes in Appendix C. Answer the following questions:

1. How much were Schneider Corporation's total inventories at October 26, 1991?

2. How does Schneider Corporation value its inventories? Which cost methods does the company use?

3. By rearranging the cost-of-goods-sold formula, you can solve for net purchases and costs of production, which are not disclosed in Schneider Corporation's statements. Show how to compute Schneider Corporation's net purchases and costs of production for 1990 and 1991. Inventory on October 28, 1989 was $50,524,000.

2. Inventories (L.O. 1,2)

Obtain the annual report of an actual company that includes inventories among its current assets. Answer these questions about the company.

1. How much were the company's total inventories at the end of the current year? At the end of the preceding year?

2. How does the company value its inventories? Which cost method or methods does the company use?

3. Depending on the nature of the company's business, would you expect the company to use a periodic inventory system or a perpetual system? Give your reason.

4. By rearranging the cost-of-goods-sold formula, you can solve for net purchases, which are not disclosed. Show how to compute the company's net purchases during the current year. You should examine the company's note titled Inventories, Merchandise inventories, or by a similar term. If the company discloses several categories of inventories, including a title similar to Finished Goods, use the beginning and ending balances of Finished Goods for the computation of net purchases. If only one category of Inventories is disclosed, use these beginning and ending balances.

Answers to Self-Study Questions

1. c
2. a $(15,000 - 1,000) \times \$3.40 = \$47,600$
3. d
4. b
5. b
6. d
7. a $\$35,000 + \$146,000 = \$181,000$
   $\$240,000 - (.35 \times \$240,000) = \$156,000$
   $\$181,000 - \$156,000 = \$25,000$

	Cost	Retail	
8. c Beginning inventory	$ 20,000	$ 40,000	
Purchases	120,000	210,000	**Cost Ratio**
Goods available	140,000 ÷	250,000	= .56
Sales		200,000	
Ending inventory — at retail		$ 50,000	
at cost ($50,000 × .56)	$ 28,000		

9. d
10. c

Chapter 10

Capital Assets, Intangibles, and Related Expenses

Capital assets and intangibles represent the largest group of assets on the financial statements of most non-retailing companies. Of the largest 200 Canadian corporations, most report several hundred million dollars worth of such assets. What is frequently forgotten by users when they review these financial statements is that the costs reported are not what the assets are worth today, but rather what they cost when they were purchased, net of the depreciation recorded since this date.

Capital assets are valued at their historical cost. Consider what this means for Tamarac Properties Limited, a typical real estate and property management company. It bought several high rise apartment buildings in Vancouver in the mid-1960s for about $8 million. Currently, these properties are reported on their financial statements at a net book value of about $3.5 million. However, the current market value of these assets exceeds $30 million.

So what does this imply about the shareholders' equity on these financial statements? Simply that if the properties are undervalued, then, dollar for dollar, equity is also understated.

The Hudson's Bay Corporation is over 300 years old, Molson Breweries is over 200, and Seagram Distillers and the Bank of Montreal are over 150. Each has substantial land holdings bought long ago. Next time you see one of these corporations' properties, imagine how little was actually paid for it, and the large, unrecognized appreciation in the value of this asset, which their financial statements do not report.

As you read Chapter 10, consider how the basis of valuation of capital assets for accounting purposes differs from the notion of value we use in our day-to-day activities.

Source: "Canada's Largest 500 Corporations," *The Financial Post*, 1992.

LEARNING OBJECTIVES

After studying this chapter, you should be able to

1 Identify the elements of property, plant and equipment's cost

2 Explain the concept of amortization (depreciation)

3 Account for depreciation by three methods

4 Identify the best depreciation method for income tax purposes

5 Account for disposal of property, plant and equipment

6 Account for wasting assets and amortization (depletion)

7 Account for intangible assets and amortization

8 Distinguish betterments from repairs

Long-lived assets used in the operation of the business and not held for sale as investments are termed **capital assets**. They can be divided into property, plant and equipment, wasting assets (for example, **natural resources** such as mining properties, and oil and gas properties), and intangibles. *Property, plant and equipment* and **wasting assets** are those long-lived assets that are tangible. Their usefulness lies in their physical form, for instance, land, buildings and equipment, and coal and other minerals. Of the capital assets, land is unique. Its cost is not amortized — expensed over time — because its value does not decrease like that of other assets.

Intangible assets are useful not because of their physical characteristics, but because of the special rights they carry. Patents, copyrights, and trademarks are intangible assets. The Dolby noise-reduction process is an example of a famous patent. Accounting for intangibles is similar to accounting for property, plant and equipment.

This area has its own terminology. The *CICA Handbook* uses the term **amortization** to describe the allocating of the **cost of a capital asset** over its useful life; companies in Canada more commonly use the terms shown in Exhibit 10-1 to describe amortization expenses with respect to the various capital assets listed.

The first half of the chapter discusses and illustrates how to identify the cost of property, plant and equipment and how to expense its cost. The second half considers disposing of property, plant and equipment and how to account for natural resources and intangible assets. Unless stated otherwise, we describe accounting in accordance with generally accepted accounting principles, as distinguished from reporting to Revenue Canada for income tax purposes.

EXHIBIT 10-1 *Terminology Used in Accounting for Property, Plant and Equipment, Wasting Assets, and Intangible Assets*

Asset Account on Balance Sheet	Related Expense Account on Income Statement
Land	None
Buildings, Machinery and Equipment, Furniture and Fixtures	Depreciation
Wasting Assets (Natural Resources)	Depletion
Intangibles	Amortization

The Cost of Property, Plant and Equipment_____

The cost principle directs a business to carry an asset on the balance sheet at the amount paid for it. The cost of *property, plant and equipment* is the purchase price, taxes, purchase commissions, and all other amounts paid to acquire the asset and to ready it for its intended use. As the types of cost differ for various categories of property, plant and equipment, we discuss the major groups individually.

Land

The cost of land includes its purchase price (cash plus any note payable given), brokerage commission, survey fees, legal fees, and any back property taxes that the purchaser pays. Land cost also includes any expenditures for grading and clearing the land, and for demolishing or removing any unwanted buildings.

The cost of land does *not* include the cost of fencing, paving, sprinkler systems, and lighting. These separate capital assets, called *land improvements*, are subject to amortization.

Suppose you are a real estate developer, and you sign a $300,000 note payable to purchase 100 hectares of land for subdivision into 5-hectare lots. You also pay $10,000 in brokerage commission, $8,000 in transfer taxes, $5,000 for removal of an old building, a $1,000 survey fee, and $26,000 for the construction of fences, all in cash. What is the cost of this land?

> **OBJECTIVE 1**
> Identify the elements of property, plant and equipment's cost

Purchase price of land		$300,000
Add related costs costs:		
Brokerage commission	$10,000	
Transfer taxes..	8,000	
Removal of building	5,000	
Survey fee...	1,000	
Total incidental costs		24,000
Total cost of land		$324,000

Notice that all the costs except the cost of the fences is included in the cost of the land. The entry to record purchase of the land is

Land	324,000	
Note Payable...		300,000
Cash..		24,000

Buildings

The cost of constructing a building includes architectural fees, building permits, contractors' charges, and payments for materials, labor, and overhead. When an existing building (new or old) is purchased, its cost includes the purchase price, brokerage commission, sales and other taxes, and cash or credit expenditures for repairing and renovating the building for its intended purpose. The properties mentioned in the chapter-opening vignette would be classifed as buildings; the land they stand on would be classified separately.

Machinery and Equipment

The cost of machinery and equipment includes its purchase price (less any discounts), transportation charges, insurance while in transit, sales and other taxes, purchase commission, installation costs, and any expenditures to test the asset before placing it in service. Transport vehicles are also equipment. Companies may carry a Ships account for ocean-going vessels and ships that ply the Great Lakes.

Land Improvements

In the above example, the cost of the fences ($26,000) is not part of the cost of the land. Instead, the $26,000 would be recorded in a separate account entitled Land Improvements. This account includes cost for such other items as roads, driveways, parking lots and sprinkler systems. Although these assets are located on the land, they are subject to decay. Therefore their cost should be amortized, as we discuss later in this chapter. Also, the cost of a new building constructed on the land is a debit to the asset account Building.

Group (or Basket) Purchases of Assets

Businesses often purchase several assets (as a group or in a "basket") for a single amount. For example, a company may pay one price for land and an office building. The company must identify the cost of each asset. The total cost is divided between the assets according to their relative sales (or market) values. This allocation technique is called the **relative-sales-value method**.

Suppose Magna International Inc. purchases land and a building in Saint John for a Maritime plant. The building sits on 2 hectares of land and the combined purchase price of land and building is $2,800,000. An appraisal indicates that the land's market (sales) value is $300,000 and the building's market (sales) value is $2,700,000.

An accountant first figures the ratio of each asset's market price to the total market price. Total appraised value is $3,000,000. Thus land, valued at $300,000, is 10 percent of the total market value. Building's appraised value is 90 percent of the total.

Asset	Market (Sales) Value		Total Market Value		Percentage
Land	$ 300,000	÷	$3,000,000	=	10%
Building	2,700,000	÷	$3,000,000	=	90
Total	$3,000,000				100%

The percentage for each asset is multiplied by the total purchase price to give its cost in the purchase.

Asset	Total Purchase Price		Percentage		Allocated Cost
Land	$2,800,000	×	.10	=	$ 280,000
Building	$2,800,000	×	.90	=	2,520,000
Total			1.00		$2,800,000

Assuming Magna pays cash, the entry to record the purchase of the land and building is

Land	280,000	
Building	2,520,000	
Cash		2,800,000

Amortization of Capital Assets _____

The process of allocating a capital asset's cost to expense is called *amortization* in Section 3060 of the *CICA Handbook*. The more common term used to describe the allocation of the cost when referring to capital assets such as property, plant and equipment is *depreciation*, and that is the term we will use in this book. Depreciation is designed to match the expense of an asset against the revenue generated over that asset's life as the matching principle directs. The primary purpose of depreciation accounting is therefore to measure income. Of less importance is the need to account for the asset's decline in usefulness.

Suppose a company buys a computer. The business believes the computer offers four years of service after which obsolescence will make it worthless. Using straight-line depreciation (which we discuss later in this chapter), the business expenses one quarter of the asset's cost in each of its four years of use.

Let us contrast what depreciation accounting *is* with what it is *not*. (1) *Depreciation is not a process of valuation.* Businesses do not record depreciation based on appraisals of their capital assets made at the end of each period. Instead, businesses allocate the asset's cost to the periods of its useful life based on a specific depreciation method. (We discuss these methods in this chapter.) (2) *Depreciation does not mean that the business sets aside cash to replace assets as they become fully depreciated.* Establishing such a cash fund is a decision entirely separate from depreciation. *Accumulated depreciation* is that portion of the capital asset's cost that has already been recorded as an expense. Accumulated depreciation does not represent a growing amount of cash.

Determining the Useful Life of Property, Plant and Equipment

No asset (other than land) offers an unlimited useful life. For some property, plant and equipment physical *wear and tear* from operations and the elements may be the important cause of depreciation. For example, physical deterioration takes its toll on the usefulness of trucks and furniture.

Assets such as computers, other electronic equipment, and airplanes may become *obsolete* before they physically deteriorate. An asset is obsolete when another asset can do the job better or more efficiently. Thus an asset's useful life may be much shorter than its physical life. Accountants usually depreciate computers over a short period, perhaps four years, even though they know the computers will remain in working condition much longer. Whether wear and tear or obsolescence causes depreciation, the asset's cost is depreciated over its expected useful life.

Measuring Depreciation

To measure depreciation for property, plant and equipment, we must know its *cost*, *estimated useful life*, and *estimated residual value*.

Cost is the purchase price of the asset. We discussed cost under the heading The Cost of Property, Plant and Equipment at the beginning of this chapter.

Estimated useful life is the length of the service the business expects to get from the asset. Useful life may be expressed in years (as we have seen so far), units of output, kilometres, or other measures. For example, the useful life of a building is stated in years. The useful life of a bookbinding machine may be stated as the number of books the machine is expected to bind, that is, its expected units of output. A reasonable measure of a delivery truck's useful life is the total number of kilometres the truck is expected to travel. Companies base such estimates on past experience and information from industry trade magazines and government publications.

Estimated residual value is the expected net realizable or cash value of the asset at the end of its *useful* life; *salvage value* or *scrap value* is the residual value of the asset at the end of its life and is usually negligible. For example, a business may believe that a machine's useful life will be seven years. After that time, the company expects to sell the machine as scrap metal. The amount the business believes it can get for the machine is the estimated residual value and, in this case, is also the salvage value. In computing depreciation, estimated residual value is *not* depreciated, because the business expects to receive this amount from disposing of the asset. The full cost of property, plant and equipment is depreciated if it is expected to have no residual value. The asset's cost minus its estimated residual value is called the **depreciable cost**.

Of the factors entering the computation of depreciation, only one factor is known — cost. The other two factors, residual value and useful life, must be estimated. Depreciation, then, is an estimated amount.

Depreciation Methods

OBJECTIVE 3 Account for depreciation by three methods	Three methods for computing depreciation will be discussed in this text: straight-line, units-of-production, and declining-balance. These three methods allocate different amounts of depreciation expense to different periods. However, they all result in the same total amount of depreciation, the asset's depreciable cost over the life of the asset. Exhibit 10-2 presents the data used to illustrate depreciation computations by the three methods.

EXHIBIT 10-2 *Data for Depreciation Computations*

Data Item	Amount
Cost of limousine	$55,000
Estimated residual value	9,000
Depreciable cost	$46,000
Estimated useful life	
Years	5 years
Units of production.......................................	400,000 units

Straight-Line (SL) Method

In the **straight-line (SL) method**, an equal amount of depreciation expense is assigned to each year (or period) of asset use. Depreciable cost is divided by useful life in years to determine the annual depreciation expense. The equation for SL depreciation, applied to the limo data from Exhibit 10-2, is

$$\text{Straight-line depreciation per year} = \frac{\text{Cost-Residual value}}{\text{Useful life in years}}$$

$$= \frac{\$55,000 - \$9,000}{5}$$

$$= \$9,200$$

Assume that the limo was purchased on January 1, 19X1, and the business's fiscal year ends on December 31. A *straight-line depreciation schedule* is presented in Exhibit 10-3.

The final column of Exhibit 10-3 shows the asset's *book value*, which is its cost less accumulated depreciation. Book value is also called carrying value.

As an asset is used, accumulated depreciation increases and the book value decreases. (Note the Accumulated Depreciation column and the Book Value column.) An asset's final book value is its *residual value* ($9,000 in Exhibit 10-3). At the end of its useful life, the asset is said to be fully depreciated.

Units-of-Production (UOP) Method

In the **units-of-production (UOP)** method, a fixed amount of depreciation is assigned to each unit of output produced by the capital asset. Depreciable cost is

EXHIBIT 10-3 *Straight-Line Depreciation Schedule*

Date	Asset Cost	Depreciation Rate		Depreciable Cost		Depreciation Amount	Accumulated Depreciation	Asset Book Value
1-1-X1	$55,000							$55,000
12-31-X1		.20	×	$46,000	=	$9,200	$ 9,200	45,800
12-31-X2		.20	×	46,000	=	9,200	18,400	36,600
12-31-X3		.20	×	46,000	=	9,200	27,600	27,400
12-31-X4		.20	×	46,000	=	9,200	36,800	18,200
12-31-X5		.20	×	46,000	=	9,200	46,000	9,000

divided by useful life in units to determine this amount. This per-unit depreciation expense is multiplied by the number of units produced each period to compute depreciation for the period. The UOP depreciation equation for the limo data in Exhibit 10-2 is

$$\text{Units-of-production depreciation per unit of output} = \frac{\text{Cost-Residual}}{\text{Useful life in units}}$$

$$= \frac{\$55,000 - \$9,000}{400,000 \text{ kilometres}}$$

$$= \$.115$$

Assume the limo was driven 90,000 kilometres (*kilometres* are the *units* in our example) during the first year, 120,000 during the second, 100,000 during the third, 60,000 during the fourth, and 30,000 during the fifth. The UOP depreciation schedule for this asset is shown in Exhibit 10-4.

The amount of UOP depreciation per period varies with the number of units the asset produces. Note that the total number of units produced is 400,000 — the measure of this asset's useful life. Therefore, UOP depreciation does not depend directly on time as the other methods do.

EXHIBIT 10-4 *Units-of-Production Depreciation Schedule*

Date	Asset Cost	Depreciation Per Unit		Number of Units		Depreciation Amount	Accumulated Depreciation	Asset Book Value
1-1-19X1	$55,000							$55,000
12-31-19X1		$.115	×	90,000	=	$10,350	$10,350	44,650
12-31-19X2		.115	×	120,000	=	13,800	24,150	30,850
12-31-19X3		.115	×	100,000	=	11,500	35,650	19,350
12-31-19X4		.115	×	60,000	=	6,900	42,550	12,450
12-31-19X5		.115	×	30,000	=	3,450	46,000	9,000

Declining-Balance (DB) Method

The **declining-balance method (DB)** is one of the accelerated-depreciation methods; the other is sum-of-years-digits, which is not widely used in Canada and so will not be discussed in this text. An *accelerated-depreciation* method writes off a relatively larger amount of the asset's cost nearer the start of its useful life than does straight-line. There are two methods in common use in Canada for computing DB depreciation; each is discussed in turn below.

Depreciation Based on Revenue Canada Rates Revenue Canada publishes the maximum depreciation rates for various capital assets that it will allow taxpayers to use to compute deductions from income for income tax purposes. Depreciation allowed for income tax purposes is called **capital cost allowance**; and the rates allowed are called *capital cost allowance rates*.

Some typical Revenue Canada rates are

Automobiles	30%
Brick, concrete or stone buildings	5
Computer software..	100
Office furniture and fixtures...	20
Video games, coin-operated	40

Thus, since the capital cost allowance rate allowed for automobiles is 30 percent, a company choosing to use the Revenue Canada rates would use a depreciation rate of 30 percent. Many companies, who use accelerated depreciation for accounting purposes, use the rates allowed by Revenue Canada for convenience. We now discuss the issue of depreciation and income taxes.

When a company uses the Revenue Canada rates, the annual depreciation is computed as follows:

First, the rate, which is obtained from Revenue Canada's *Income Tax Regulations*, is multiplied by the period's beginning asset book value (cost less accumulated depreciation).[1] The residual value of the asset is ignored in computing depreciation by the DB method except during the last year.

Second, the final year's depreciation amount is used to reduce the asset's book value to its residual value. In Exhibit 10-5, the fifth and final year's depreciation is $4,205.

EXHIBIT 10-5 *Revenue Canada Rate Depreciation Schedule*

		Depreciation for the Year				
Date	Asset Cost	Depreciation Rate	Depreciable Cost	Depreciation Amount	Accumulated Depreciation	Asset Book Value
1-1-19X1	$55,000					$55,000
12-31-19X1		.30 ×	$55,000 =	$16,500	$16,500	38,500
12-31-19X2		.30 ×	38,500 =	11,550	28,050	26,950
12-31-19X3		.30 ×	26,950 =	8,085	36,135	18,865
12-31-19X4		.30 ×	18,865 =	5,660	41,795	13,205
12-31-19X5				4,205*	46,000	9,000

* Last-year depreciation is the amount needed to reduce asset book value to the residual value ($13,205 − $9,000 = $4,205).

[1] At the time of writing, Revenue Canada permits the taxpayer to use only 50 percent of the normal capital cost allowance in the first year and the full amount thereafter; for ease of computation in this chapter, we will claim full capital cost allowance every year it is claimed.

Double-Declining Balance (DDB)   This method involves computing annual depreciation by multiplying the asset's book value by a constant percentage, which is two times the straight-line depreciation rate. DDB rates are computed as follows:

First, the straight-line depreciation rate per year is computed. For example, a 5-year limousine has a straight-line depreciation rate of ⅕ or 20 percent. A 10-year asset has a straight-line rate of ¹⁄₁₀ or 10 percent, and so on.

Second, the straight-line rate is multiplied by 2 to compute the DDB rate. The DDB rate for a 5-year asset is 40 percent (20% × 2 = 40%). For a 10-year asset the DDB rate is 20 percent (10% × 2 = 20%).

Third, the DDB rate is multiplied by the period's beginning asset book value (cost less accumulated depreciation). Residual value of the asset is ignored in computing depreciation by the DDB method, except during the last year.

The DDB rate for the limousine in Exhibit 10-2 is

$$\textbf{DDB rate per year} = \left(\frac{1}{\textbf{Useful life in years}} \times 2 \right) = \left(\frac{1}{\textbf{5 years}} \times 2 \right)$$

$$= (20\% \times 2) = 40\%$$

The DDB depreciation schedule for the asset is illustrated in Exhibit 10-6.

Fourth, the final year's depreciation amount is the amount needed to reduce the asset's book value to its residual value. In Exhibit 10-6, the fourth and second-last year's depreciation is $2,880 (the $11,880 book value less the $9,000 residual value). DDB can produce this result if the estimated residual value is much larger than 10 percent of the original cost.

EXHIBIT 10-6 *Double-Declining Balance Depreciation Schedule*

			Depreciation for the Year					Asset Book Value
Date	Asset Cost	DDB Rate		Asset Book Value		Depreciation Amount	Accumulated Depreciation	
1-1-19X1	$55,000							$55,000
12-31-19X1		.40	×	$55,000	=	$22,000	$22,000	33,000
12-31-19X2		.40	×	33,000	=	13,200	35,200	19,800
12-31-19X3		.40	×	19,800	=	7,920	43,120	11,880
12-31-19X4						2,880*	46,000	9,000
12-31-19X5 **								

* Depreciation in year 19X4 is the amount needed to reduce asset book value to the residual value ($11,880 − $9,000 = $2,880).
**Because of the relatively high residual value, there would be no depreciation expense in the final year.

Summary

The DB method differs from the other methods in two ways: (1) the asset's residual value is ignored initially, and (2) the final year's calculation is changed in order to bring the asset's book value to the residual value.

Most companies that use the DB method do not calculate depreciation on each capital asset separately, but rather they add the cost of each asset to a pool of similar assets and calculate depreciation on the undepreciated balance in the pool. This method is not as accurate as performing the individual calculations as illustrated in Exhibits 10-5 and 10-6, but it is much simpler and the degree of inaccuracy is small.

Comparison of the Depreciation Methods

Compare the three methods in terms of the yearly amount of depreciation:

			Amount of Depreciation Per Year	
			Declining Balance	
Year	Straight-Line	Units-of-Production	Double-Declining-Balance	Revenue Canada Rates
1	$ 9,200	$ 11,350	$22,000	$16,500
2	9,200	13,800	13,200	11,550
3	9,200	11,500	7,920	8,085
4	9,200	6,900	2,880	5,660
5	9,200	3,450	—	4,205
Total	$46,000	$46,000	$46,000	$46,000

The yearly amount of depreciation varies by method, but the total $46,000 depreciable cost systematically becomes expense under all three methods.

Generally accepted accounting principles (GAAP) direct a business to match the expense of an asset to the revenue that the asset produces. For a capital asset that generates revenue fairly evenly over time, the straight-line method best meets the matching principle.

The units-of-production method best fits those assets that wear out because of physical use, not obsolescence. Depreciation is recorded only when the asset is used, and the more units the asset generates in a given year, the greater the depreciation expense.

The accelerated method applies best to those assets that generate greater revenue earlier in their useful lives. The greater expense recorded under the accelerated method in the early periods matches best against those periods' greater revenue.

Exhibit 10-7 graphs the relationship between annual depreciation amounts for straight-line, units-of-production, and the declining-balance methods.

The graph of straight-line depreciation is flat because annual depreciation is the same amount in each period. Units-of-production depreciation follows no particular pattern because annual depreciation depends on the use of the asset. The greater the use, the greater is the amount of depreciation. Accelerated depreciation is greatest in the asset's first year and less in the later years.

A recent survey indicated that over 87 percent of companies use the straight-line method, approximately 30 percent use an accelerated method, and approximately

EXHIBIT 10-7 *Depreciation Patterns*

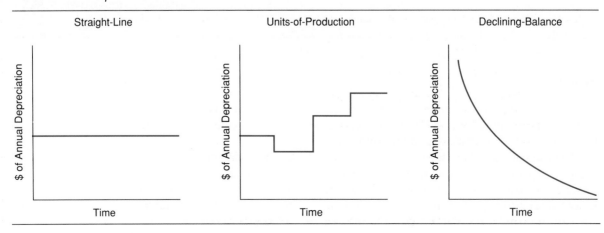

23 percent use the units-of-production method. (Some companies use more than one method for different kinds of capital assets, so the total exceeds 100 percent.)[2] For example, John Labatt uses straight-line, while George Weston uses straight-line and units-of-production. Maclean Hunter uses straight-line for most fixed assets and declining-balance for some buildings, some equipment, and all vehicles.

Summary Problem for Your Review

Hubbard Company purchased office furniture on January 1, 19X5 for $44,000. The expected life of the equipment is 10 years and its residual value is $4,000. Under two depreciation methods, the annual depreciation expense and the balance of accumulated depreciation at the end of 19X5 and 19X6 are

	Method A		Method B	
Year	Annual Depreciation Expense	Accumulated Depreciation	Annual Depreciation Expense	Accumulated Depreciation
19X5	$4,000	$4,000	$8,800	$ 8,800
19X6	4,000	8,000	7,040	15,840

Required

1. Identify the depreciation method used in each instance, and show the equation and computation for each. (Round off to the nearest dollar.)

2. Assume continued use of the same method through year 19X7. Determine the annual depreciation expense, accumulated depreciation, and book value of the equipment for 19X5 through 19X7 under each method.

SOLUTION TO REVIEW PROBLEM

Requirement 1

Method A: Straight-line

> **Depreciable cost = $40,000 ($44,000 – $4,000)**
>
> **Each year: $40,000/10 years = $4,000**

Method B: Declining-balance (Revenue Canada rate)

> **Rate = 20%**
>
> **19X5: .20 × $44,000 = $8,800**
>
> **19X6: .20 × ($44,000 – $8,800) = $7,040**

[2] *Financial Reporting in Canada, 1991*, 19th edition, Toronto: CICA, 1992, p. 151.

Requirement 2

| | Method A | | | Method B | | |
| | Straight-Line | | | Declining-Balance (Revenue Canada) | | |
Year	Annual Depreciation Expense	Accumulated Depreciation	Book Value	Annual Depreciation Expense	Accumulated Depreciation	Book Value
Start			$44,000			$44,000
19X5	$4,000	$ 4,000	40,000	$8,800	$ 8,800	35,200
19X6	4,000	8,000	36,000	7,040	15,840	28,160
19X7	4,000	12,000	32,000	5,632	21,472	22,528

Computations for 19X7

Straight-line:	**$40,000/10 years = $4,000**
Declining-balance (Revenue Canada):	**.20 × $28,160 = $5,632**

Depreciation and Income Taxes

The majority of companies use the straight-line method for reporting to their shareholders and creditors on their financial statements. They keep a separate set of records of the capital cost allowance they claim on their tax return. The capital cost allowance rates published by Revenue Canada are maximums. A company may claim from zero to the maximum capital cost allowance allowed in a year. Most companies claim the maximum capital cost allowance using the declining-balance method.

Suppose you are a business manager. Revenue Canada will allow you to use any one of the three methods we have discussed as long as the amount you are claiming does not exceed their maximum. Which method would you choose? You will probably choose Revenue Canada's capital cost allowance rate because it is the maximum allowed. It provides the largest deduction from income as quickly as possible, thus decreasing your immediate tax payments. The cash you save may be applied to best fit your business needs. This is the strategy most businesses follow. For example, Irwin Toy Limited reports in its summary of accounting policies that the company uses the straight-line method and the declining-balance method to depreciate property, plant and equipment for financial statement purposes, and that the rates used for tax purposes are in excess of those used for financial statement purposes.

To understand the relationships among cash flow (cash provided by operations), depreciation, and capital cost allowance and income tax, consider the following example. Straight-line depreciation is $9,200 while the maximum capital cost allowance allowed is $16,500. Assume the business has $400,000 in cash sales and $300,000 in operating expenses during the asset's first year, and the income tax rate is 40 percent. The cash flow analysis appears in Exhibit 10-8.

Exhibit 10-8 highlights several important business relationships. Compare the amount of cash provided by operations before income tax. Both columns show $100,000. If there were no income taxes, the total cash provided by operations would be the same regardless of the depreciation method used. Depreciation is a noncash expense and so does not affect cash from operations.

EXHIBIT 10-8 *Cash Flow Advantage of Declining-Balance (Revenue Canada — RC) Depreciation over Straight-Line (SL) Depreciation for Income Tax Purposes*

	Income Tax Rate 40 Percent	
	SL	RC
Revenues	$400,000	$400,000
Cash operating expense	300,000	300,000
Cash provided by operations before income tax	100,000	100,000
Capital cost allowance		
(Depreciation — a noncash expense)	9,200	16,500
Income before income tax	90,800	83,500
Income tax expense (40%)	36,320	33,400
Net income	$ 54,480	$ 50,100
Supplementary cash flow analysis		
Cash provided by operations		
before income tax	$100,000	$100,000
Income tax expense	36,320	33,400
Cash provided by operations	$ 63,680	$ 66,600
Extra cash available for investment		
if RC is used ($66,600 – $63,680)		$ 2,920
Assumed earnings rate		
on investment of extra cash		× .10
Cash advantage of using RC over SL		$ 292

However, capital cost allowance is a tax-deductible expense. The higher the capital cost allowance, the lower the income before tax, and thus the lower the income tax payment. Therefore, using the maximum capital cost allowance available, the Revenue Canada rate helps conserve cash for use in the business. Exhibit 10-8 indicates that the business will have $2,920 more cash at the end of the first year if it uses RC depreciation instead of SL ($66,600 against $63,680). Suppose the company invests this money to earn a return of 10 percent during the second year. Then the company will be better off by $292 ($2,920 × 10%=$292). The cash advantage of using the RC method is the $292 of additional revenue.

Special Issues in Depreciation Accounting

Two special issues in depreciation accounting are (1) depreciation for partial years, and (2) change in the useful life of a depreciable asset.

Depreciation for Partial Years

Companies purchase capital assets as needed. They do not wait until the beginning of a year or a month. Therefore, companies must develop policies to compute depreciation for partial years. Suppose a company purchases a building on April 1 for $500,000. The building's estimated life is 20 years and its estimated residual value is $80,000. The company's fiscal year ends on December 31. Consider how the company computes depreciation for the year ended December 31.

Many companies compute partial-year depreciation by first computing a full year's depreciation. They then multiply this amount by the fraction of the year they held the asset. Assuming the straight-line method, the year's depreciation is $15,750, computed as follows:

$$\frac{(\$500,000 - \$80,000)}{20} = \$21,000 \text{ per year} \times \frac{9}{12} = \$15,750$$

What if the company bought the asset on April 18? A widely used policy suggests businesses record no depreciation on assets purchased after the fifteenth of the month and record a full month's depreciation on an asset bought on or before the fifteenth. Thus the company would record no depreciation for April on an April 18 purchase. In this case, the year's depreciation would be $14,000 ($21,000 × 8/12).

How is partial-year depreciation computed under the other depreciation methods? Suppose this building is acquired on October 4, and the company uses the declining-balance (Revenue Canada) method. For brick buildings, the RC rate is 5 percent. First-year depreciation using the Revenue Canada rates would be $25,000 ($500,000 × .05), and the depreciation amount for October, November, and December is $6,250 ($25,000 × 3/12). Depreciation in year 2 would be 5 percent of the undepreciated balance of $493,750 ($500,000 − $ 6,250), or $24,688 (.05 × $493,750).

No special computation is needed for partial-year depreciation under the units-of-production method. Simply use the number of units produced, regardless of the time period the asset is held.

Change in the Useful Life of a Depreciable Asset

As previously discussed, a business must estimate the useful life of a capital asset to compute depreciation. This prediction is the most difficult part of accounting for depreciation. After the asset is put into use, the business is able to refine its estimate based on experience and new information. Such a change is called a change in accounting estimate. In an actual example, Electrohome Ltd. included the following note in a recent financial statement:

> **4. Changes in accounting estimates**
> ...The depreciation rate for broadcasting equipment was reviewed, and to represent more fairly the expected life of that equipment the rate was changed during the year from 25% to 20%. This change in accounting estimate has not been applied retroactively and has the effect of reducing depreciation expense for the current year by $108,000.

Such accounting changes are common because no business has perfect foresight. Generally accepted accounting principles require the business to report the nature, reason and effect of the change on net income, as the Electrohome example shows. To *record* a change in accounting estimate, the remaining book value of the asset is spread over its adjusted remaining useful life. The adjusted useful life may be longer or shorter than the original useful life.

Assume that a Regsask Inc. machine cost $40,000, and the company originally believed the asset had an 8-year useful life with no residual value. Using the straight-line method, the company would record $5,000 depreciation each year ($40,000/8 years = $5,000). Suppose Regsask used the asset for 2 years. Accumulated depreciation reached $10,000, leaving a book value of $30,000 ($40,000 − $10,000). From its experience with the asset during the first 2 years, management believes the asset will remain useful for an additional 10 years. The company would compute a revised annual depreciation amount and record it as follows:

Asset's Remaining Book Value		(New) Estimated Useful Life Remaining		(New) Annual Depreciation Amount
$30,000	÷	10 years	=	$3,000

Yearly depreciation entry based on new estimated useful life is

Depreciation Expense — Machine	3,000	
Accumulated Depreciation — Machine		3,000

Using Fully Depreciated Assets

A fully depreciated asset is one that has reached the end of its estimated useful life. No more depreciation is recorded for the asset. If the asset is no longer suitable for its purpose, the asset is disposed of, as discussed in the next section. However, the company may be in a cash bind and unable to replace the asset. Or the asset's useful life may have been underestimated at the outset. In any event, companies sometimes continue using fully depreciated assets. The asset account and its related accumulated depreciation account remain in the ledger, even though no additional depreciation is recorded for the asset.

Disposal of Property, Plant and Equipment

Eventually, a capital asset ceases to serve a company's needs. The asset may have become worn out, obsolete, or for some other reason, no longer useful to the business. Generally, a company disposes of the asset by selling or exchanging it. If the asset cannot be sold or exchanged, then disposal takes the form of junking the asset. Whatever the method of disposal, the business should bring depreciation up to date to measure the asset's final book value properly.

OBJECTIVE 5
Account for disposal of property, plant and equipment

To account for disposal, credit the asset account and debit its related accumulated depreciation account. Suppose the final year's depreciation expense has just been recorded for a machine that cost $6,000 and was estimated to have zero residual value. The machine's accumulated depreciation thus totals $6,000. Assuming this asset cannot be sold or exchanged, the entry to record its disposal is

Accumulated Depreciation — Machinery...........................	6,000	
Machinery		6,000
To dispose of a fully depreciated machine.		

If assets are junked prior to being fully depreciated, the company records a loss equal to the asset's book value. Suppose store fixtures that cost $4,000 are disposed of in this manner. Accumulated depreciation is $3,000 and book value is therefore $1,000. Disposal of these store fixtures is recorded as follows:

Accumulated Depreciation — Store Fixtures......................	3,000	
Loss on Disposal of Store Fixtures.......................................	1,000	
Store Fixtures		4,000
To dispose of store fixtures.		

Loss accounts such as Loss on Disposal of Store Fixtures decrease net income. Losses are reported on the income statement and are closed to Income Summary along with expenses.

Selling a Capital Asset

Suppose the business sells furniture on September 30, 19X4 for $5,000 cash. The furniture cost $10,000 when purchased on January 1, 19X1 and has been depreciated on a straight-line basis. The business estimated a 10-year useful life and no residual value. Prior to recording the sale of the furniture, accountants must update depreciation. Since the business uses the calendar year as its accounting period, partial depreciation must be recorded for the asset's expense from January 1, 19X4 to the sale date. The straight-line depreciation entry at September 30, 19X4 is

Sept. 30	Depreciation Expense ($10,000/10 years × ½)	750	
	Accumulated Depreciation — Furniture		750
	To update depreciation.		

After this entry is posted, the Furniture and the Accumulated Depreciation — Furniture accounts appear as follows. The furniture book value is $6,250 ($10,000 – $3,750).

Furniture		Accumulated Depreciation — Furniture	
Jan. 1, 19X1 10,000			Dec. 31, 19X1 1,000
			Dec. 31, 19X2 1,000
			Dec. 31, 19X3 1,000
			Sept. 30, 19X4 750
			Balance 3,750

The entry to record sale of the furniture for $5,000 cash is

Sept. 30	Cash	5,000	
	Loss on Sale of Furniture	1,250	
	Accumulated Depreciation — Furniture	3,750	
	Furniture		10,000
	To sell furniture.		

When recording the sale of a capital asset, the business must remove the balances in the asset account (Furniture, in this case) and its related accumulated depreciation account, and also record a gain or a loss if the amount of cash received differs from the asset's book value. In our example, cash of $5,000 is less than the book value of the furniture, $6,250. The result is a loss of $1,250.

Suppose the sale price had been $7,000. The business would have had a gain of $750 (Cash, $7,000 – asset book value, $6,250). The entry to record this transaction would be

Sept. 30	Cash	7,000	
	Accumulated Depreciation — Furniture	3,750	
	Furniture		10,000
	Gain on Sale of Furniture		750
	To sell furniture		

A gain is recorded when an asset is sold for a price greater than the asset's book value. A loss is recorded when the sale price is less than book value. Gains increase net income, as revenues do. They are reported on the income statement and closed to Income Summary along with the revenues.

Exchanging a Capital Asset

Businesses often exchange (trade in) their old capital assets for similar assets that are newer and more efficient. For example, a pizzeria may decide to trade in its 5-year-old delivery car for a new model. To record the exchange, the business must remove from the books the balances for the asset being exchanged and its related accumulated depreciation account.

Assume that the pizzeria's old delivery car cost $9,000 and has accumulated depreciation totaling $8,000. The book value, then, is $1,000. The new delivery car, say, a Ford Escort, costs $13,200, and the auto dealer offers a $1,000 trade-in allowance. The pizzeria pays cash for the remaining $12,200. The trade-in is recorded with this entry:

Delivery Auto (new)..	13,200	
Accumulated Depreciation (old)	8,000	
Delivery Auto (old)...		9,000
Cash ($13,200 – $1,000)...		12,200

In this example, the book value and the trade-in allowance are both $1,000, and so no gain or loss occurs on the exchange. Usually, however, an exchange results in a gain or a loss. If the trade-in allowance received is greater than the book value of the asset being given, the business has a gain. If the trade-in allowance received is less than the book value of the asset given, the business has a loss. However, generally accepted accounting principles do not allow losses and gains to be recognized on the exchange of *similar* assets; the cost of the new asset is adjusted to reflect the loss or gain. Gains or losses are allowed on the exchange of *dissimilar* assets. We now turn to the entries exchanges, continuing our delivery-car example and its data.[3]

Situation 1   Loss on Asset Exchange

Assume that the new Escort has a cash price of $13,200, and the dealer gives a trade-in allowance of $600 on the old vehicle. The pizzeria pays the balance, $12,600 in cash. The loss on the exchange is $400 (book value of old asset given, $1,000, minus trade-in allowance received, $600). The acquisition price of the new automobile is udjusted to reflect the loss, and is $13,600 ($13,200 + 400). The entry to record this exchange is

Delivery Auto (new)..	13,600	
Accumulated Depreciation — Delivery Auto (old)	8,000	
Delivery Auto (old)		9,000
Cash		12,600

Situation 2   Gain on Asset Exchange

Assume that the new Escort's cash price is $13,200, and the dealer gives a $1,300 trade-in allowance. The pizzeria pays the balance in cash. The gain is $300 (trade-in allowance received, $1,300, minus book value of old asset given, $1,000). The acquisition price of the new automobile is $12,900 ($13,200 – $300). The entry to record this exchange is

Delivery Auto (new)..	12,900	
Accumulated Depreciation — Delivery Auto...................	8,000	
Delivery Auto (old)		9,000
Cash		11,900

Control of Capital Assets

Control of capital assets includes safeguarding them and having an adequate accounting system. To see the need for controlling capital assets, consider the following actual situation. The home office and top managers of the company are in Calgary. The company manufactures gas pumps in Michigan, which are sold in Europe. Top managers and owners of the company rarely see the manufacturing plant and therefore cannot control capital assets by on-the-spot management. What features does their internal control need?

Safeguarding capital assets includes:

1. Assigning responsibility for custody of the assets.

---

[3] GAAP rules for exchanges may differ from income tax rules. In this discussion, we are concerned with the accounting rules.

EXHIBIT 10-9 *Capital Asset Ledger Card*

| Asset | Clothing racks | | Location | Ladies better dresses |
| Employee responsible for the asset | Department manager |

Cost	$190,000		Purchased From	Boone Supply Co.
Depreciation Method	SL
Useful Life	10 years		Resale Value	$10,000
General Ledger Account	Store fixtures

| Date | Explanation | Asset | | | Accumulated Depreciation | | |
		Dr	Cr	Bal	Dr	Cr	Bal
July 3, 19X4	Purchase	190,000		190,000			
Dec. 31, 19X4	Deprec.					9,000	9,000
Dec. 31, 19X5	Deprec.					18,000	27,000
Dec. 31, 19X6	Deprec.					18,000	45,000

2. Separating custody of assets from accounting for the assets. (This is a cornerstone of internal control in almost every area.)

3. Setting up security measures, for instance, guards and restricted access to capital assets, to prevent theft.

4. Protecting them from the elements (rain, snow, and so on).

5. Having adequate insurance against fire, storm, and other casualty losses.

6. Training operating personnel in the proper use of the asset.

7. Keeping a regular maintenance schedule.

Capital assets are controlled in much the same way that high-priced inventory is controlled — with the help of subsidiary records. For capital assets, companies use a capital asset ledger. Each capital asset is represented by a card describing the asset, and listing its location and the employee responsible for it. These details aid in safeguarding the asset. The ledger card also shows the asset's cost, useful life, and other accounting data. Exhibit 10-9 is an example.

The ledger card provides the data for computing depreciation on the asset. It serves as a subsidiary record of accumulated depreciation. The asset balance ($190,000) and accumulated depreciation amount ($45,000) agree with the balances in the respective general ledger accounts (Store Fixtures and Accumulated Depreciation — Store Fixtures).

OBJECTIVE 6
Account for wasting assets and amortization (depletion)

Accounting for Wasting Assets and Depletion

Wasting assets or *natural resources* such as iron ore, coal, oil, gas, and timber are capital assets of a special type. An investment in natural resources could be described as an investment in inventories in the ground (coal) or on top of the ground (timber). As capital assets (such as machines) are expensed or amortized through depreciation, natural resource assets are expensed through depletion. **Depletion expense** is that portion of the cost of natural resources that is used up in a particular period. Depletion expense is computed in the same way as *units-of-production* depreciation.

An oil well may cost $100,000 and contain an estimated 10,000 barrels of oil. The depletion rate would be $10 per barrel ($100,000/10,000 barrels). If 3,000 barrels are extracted during the first year, depletion expense is $30,000 (3,000 barrels × $10 per barrel). The depletion entry for the year is

| Depletion Expense (3,000 barrels × $10) | 30,000 | |
| Accumulated Depletion — Oil | | 30,000 |

If 4,500 barrels are removed the second year, that period's depletion is $45,000 (4,500 barrels × $10 per barrel). Accumulated Depletion is a contra account similar to Accumulated Depreciation.

Natural resource assets can be reported as follows:

Capital Assets		
Property, Plant and Equipment		
Land		$120,000
Buildings	$800,000	
Equipment...	160,000	
	960,000	
Less: Accumulated Depreciation	410,000	
Total Property, Plant and Equipment......................		550,000
Oil and Gas Properties		
Oil...	$340,000	
Less: Accumulated Depletion	90,000	
Total Oil and Gas Properties....................................		250,000
Total Capital Assets		$920,000

Future Removal and Site Restoration Costs   There is increasing concern by individuals and governments about the environment. Often, in the past, a company exploiting natural resources, such as a mining company, would simply abandon the site once the ore body was played out. Now, there is legislation in most jurisdictions requiring a natural resource company to remove buildings, equipment and waste, and to restore the site once a location is to be dismantled and abandoned.

The costs of future removal and site restoration at a property are a charge against all revenues earned from that property; matching suggests that such costs should be accumulated over the economic life of the location. The *CICA Handbook* in Section 3060 requires a natural resource company to accrue future removal and site restoration costs net of expected recoveries by charging income "in a rational and systematic manner." The accrual should be shown as a liability on the balance sheet. When the costs cannot be reasonably determined, a contingent liability should be disclosed in the notes to the financial statements.

Accounting for Intangible Assets and Amortization _____

Intangible assets are a class of capital assets that are not physical in nature. Instead, these assets consist of special rights to current and expected future benefits from patents, copyrights, trademarks, franchises, leaseholds, and goodwill.

The acquisition cost of an intangible asset is debited to an asset account. The intangible is expensed through **amortization**, the systematic reduction of a lump-sum amount. Amortization applies to intangible assets in the same way depreciation applies to property, plant and equipment, and depletion applies to wasting assets.

Amortization is generally computed on a straight-line basis over the asset's estimated useful life — up to a maximum of 40 years, according to convention and thus to GAAP. However, obsolescence often makes an intangible asset's useful life shorter than its legal life. Amortization expense for intangibles is written off directly against the intangible asset account rather than held in an accumulated amortization account. The residual value of most intangible assets is zero.

Assume that a business purchases a patent on a special manufacturing process. Legally, the patent may run for 17 years. However, the business realizes that new technologies will limit the patented process's life to 4 years. If the patent cost $80,000, each year's amortization expense is $20,000 ($80,000/4). The balance sheet reports the patent at its acquisition cost less amortization expense to date. After 1

> **OBJECTIVE 7**
> Account for intangible assets and amortization

year, the patent has a $60,000 balance ($80,000 – $20,000), after 2 years a $40,000 balance, and so on.

Patents are federal government grants giving a holder the exclusive right for 17 years to produce and sell an invention. Patented products include Bombardier Skidoos and the Spar Aerospace "Arm" used on the NASA space shuttle flights which you probably have seen on television. Like any other asset, a patent may be purchased. Suppose a company pays $170,000 to acquire a patent, and the business believes the expected useful life of the patent is only 5 years. Amortization expense is $34,000 per year ($170,000/5 years). The company's acquisition and amortization entries for this patent are

Jan.	1	Patent...	170,000	
		Cash		170,000
		To acquire a patent.		
Dec.	31	Amortization Expense		
		— Patents ($170,000/5)................................	34,000	
		Patent...		34,000
		To amortize the cost of a patent.		

Copyrights are exclusive rights to reproduce and sell a book, musical composition, film, or other work of art. Issued by the federal government, copyrights extend 50 years beyond the author's, composer's, or artist's life. The cost of obtaining a copyright from the government is low, but a company may pay a large sum to purchase an existing copyright from the owner. For example, a publisher may pay the author of a popular novel $1 million or more for the book's copyright. The useful life of a copyright for a popular book may be usually no longer than 2 or 3 years, so that each period's amortization amount is a considerable portion of the copyright's cost; on the other hand, some copyrights, especially of musical compositions, such as works by the Beatles, or *American Pie* by Don McLean, seem to be popular over several decades.

Trademarks and **trade names** are distinctive identifications of products or services. For example, The Sports Network has its distinct logo of the yellow letters TSN on a black background shaped like a television screen; Apple Computer has the multi-coloured apple with the bite out of it; and the Edmonton Oilers and Toronto Blue Jays have insignia that identify their respective teams. Molson Export, Swiss Chalet chicken, Petro-Canada, and Roots are everyday trade names. Advertising slogans such as Speedy Muffler's "At Speedy you're a somebody," Japan Camera Center's "Where memories develop... right before your eyes", or Shoppers Drug Mart's "Everything you want in a drugstore" are also legally protected.

The cost of a trademark or trade name is amortized over its useful life, not to exceed 40 years. The cost of advertising and promotions that use the trademark or trade name is not a part of the asset's cost but a debit to the advertising expense account.

Franchises and **licenses** are privileges granted by a private business or a government to sell a product or service in accordance with specified conditions. The Calgary Flames hockey organization is a franchise granted to its owners by the National Hockey League. IGA Food Markets and Re/Max Ltd. are well-known franchises. Union Gas holds a franchise to provide gas to residents and businesses in certain parts of the country. The acquisition costs of franchises and licenses are amortized over their useful lives rather than over legal lives, subject to the 40-year maximum.

A **leasehold** is a prepayment that a lessee (renter) makes to secure the use of an asset from a lessor (landlord). Often leases require the lessee to make this prepayment in addition to monthly rental payments. The lessee debits the monthly lease payments to the Rent Expense account. The prepayment, however, is a debit to an intangible asset account entitled Leaseholds. This amount is amortized over the life of the lease by debiting Rent Expense and crediting Leaseholds. Some leases stipulate that the last year's rent must be paid in advance when the lease is signed. This prepayment is debited to Leaseholds and transferred to Rent Expense during the last year of the lease.

Sometimes lessees modify or improve the leased asset. For example, a lessee may construct a fence on leased land. The lessee debits the cost of the fence to a separate intangible asset account, Leasehold Improvements, and amortizes its cost over the term of the lease.

Goodwill in accounting is a more limited term than in everyday use, as in "goodwill among men." In accounting, *goodwill* is defined as the excess of the cost of an acquired company over the sum of the market values of its net assets (assets minus liabilities). Suppose Company A acquires Company B at a cost of $10 million. The market value of Company B's assets is $9 million, and its liabilities total $1 million. In this case, Company A paid $2 million for goodwill, computed as follows:

Purchase price paid for Company B.............................		$10 million
Sum of the market value of Company B's assets.........	$9 million	
Less: Company B's liabilities	1 million	
Market value of Company B's net assets.....................		8 million
Excess is called *goodwill*		$ 2 million

Company A's entry to record the acquisition of Company B, including its goodwill, would be

Assets (Cash, Receivables, Inventories,		
Capital Assets, all at market value)	9,000,000	
Goodwill	2,000,000	
Liabilities..		1,000,000
Cash		10,000,000

Goodwill has the following special features:

1. Goodwill is recorded, at its cost, only when it is purchased in the acquisition of another company. Even though a favorable location, a superior product, or an outstanding reputation may create goodwill for a company, it is never recorded by that entity. Instead, goodwill is recorded only by another company that purchases the entity with goodwill. A purchase transaction provides objective evidence of the value of the goodwill.

2. According to generally accepted accounting principles, goodwill is amortized on a straight-line basis over a period of not less than two years and not to exceed 40 years. In reality, the goodwill of many entities increases in value.

Computers and Amortization

A computer is invaluable in helping keep track of all capital asset transactions. The general ledger account machinery may have hundreds of subsidiary accounts each with its own Accumulated Depreciation account.

Complications in tax law have resulted in complex depreciation calculations. As was mentioned above, many companies use one depreciation rate for accounting purposes and another for tax purposes, and must keep track of accumulated depreciation under both methods. Computers greatly ease the accounting burden.

Companies of all sizes may use depreciation modules included with their computerized accounting packages. The computer performs its functions accurately, but an accountant with a solid knowledge of tax law and amortization must ensure that the calculations are reasonable. Auditors use their own computer packages to perform independent recalculations of amortization.

Betterments versus Repairs

When a company makes a capital asset expenditure, it must decide whether to debit an asset account or an expense account. In this context, *expenditure* refers either to a cash or a credit purchase of goods or of services related to the asset. Examples of these expenditures range from replacing the windshield wipers on an automobile to adding a wing to a building.

Expenditures that increase the capacity or efficiency of the asset or extend its useful life are called **betterments**. For example, the cost of a major overhaul that extends a taxi's useful life is a betterment. The amount of the **capital expenditure**, said to be *capitalized*, for a betterment is a debit to an asset account. For the cost of a betterment on the taxi, we would debit the asset account Automobile.

Other expenditures do not extend the asset's capacity or efficiency. Expenditures that merely maintain the asset in its existing condition or restore the asset to good working order are called **repairs**; they are expenses and are matched against revenue. Examples include the costs of repainting a taxi, repairing a dented fender, and replacing tires. The work that creates the repair, said to be *expensed*, is a debit to an expense account. For the ordinary repairs on the taxi, we would debit Repair Expense.

The distinction between betterments and repairs is often a matter of opinion. Does the work extend the life of the asset, or does it only maintain the asset in good order? When doubt exists as to whether to debit an asset or an expense, companies tend to debit an expense, for two reasons. First, many expenditures are minor in amount, and most companies have a policy of debiting expense for all expenditures below a specified minimum, such as $1,000. Second, the income tax motive favors debiting all borderline expenditures to expense in order to create an immediate tax deduction. Betterments are not immediate tax deductions.

Exhibit 10-10 illustrates the distinction between betterments and repairs (expense) for several delivery truck expenditures.

Treating a betterment as a repair, or vice versa, creates errors in the financial statements. Suppose a company incurs the cost of a betterment to enhance the service potential of equipment and erroneously expenses this cost. It is a capital expenditure that should have been debited to an asset account. This accounting error overstates expenses and understates net income on the income statement. On the balance sheet, the equipment account is understated, and so is owner's equity. Capitalizing the cost of an ordinary repair creates the opposite error. Expenses are understated and net income is overstated on the income statement. The balance sheet reports overstated amounts for assets and owners' equity.

EXHIBIT 10-10 *Delivery Truck Expenditures*

Debit an Asset Account for Betterments	Debit Repair and Maintenance Expense for Repairs

Betterment
  Major engine overhaul
Modification of body for new
  use of truck
Addition to storage capacity
  of truck
	Repairs
	  Repair of transmission or other
	    mechanism
	  Oil change, lubrication, and
	    so on
	  Replacement tires, windshield,
	    and the like
	  Paint job

Summary Problems for Your Review

Problem 1

The figures that follow appear in requirement 2, Solution to Review Problem, on p. 442.

Year	Method A Straight-Line			Method B Declining-Balance (Revenue Canada)		
	Annual Depreciation Expense	Accumulated Depreciation	Book Value	Annual Depreciation Expense	Accumulated Depreciation	Book Value
Start			$44,000			$44,000
19X5	$4,000	$ 4,000	40,000	$8,800	$ 8,800	35,200
19X6	4,000	8,000	36,000	7,040	15,840	28,160
19X7	4,000	12,000	32,000	5,632	21,472	22,528

Required

Suppose Revenue Canada permitted a choice between these two depreciation methods. Which depreciation method would you select for income tax purposes? Why?

Problem 2

A corporation purchased a building at a cost of $500,000 on January 1, 19X3. Management has depreciated the building by using the straight-line method, a 35-year life, and a residual value of $150,000. On July 1, 19X7, the company sold the building for $575,000 cash. The fiscal year of the corporation ends on December 31.

Required

Record depreciation for 19X7 and record the sale of the building on July 1, 19X7.

SOLUTIONS TO REVIEW PROBLEMS

Problem 1

For tax purposes, most companies select the maximum amount allowed by Revenue Canada, which results in accelerated depreciation of the equipment. Accelerated depreciation minimizes taxable income and income tax payments in the early years of the asset's life, thereby maximizing the business's cash at the earliest possible time. Straight-line spreads depreciation evenly over the life of the asset which would *not* minimize income tax in the same way.

Problem 2

19X7
July 1   Depreciation Expense — Building
         [($500,000 – $150,000)/(35 years × ½ year)]   5,000
            Accumulated Depreciation — Building   5,000
         To update depreciation.

July 1	Cash..	575,000	
	Accumulated Depreciation — Building		
	[($500,000 – $150,000)/(35 years × 4½ years)] .	45,000	
	Building..		500,000
	Gain on Sale of Building................................		120,000
	To record sale of building.		

Summary

Capital assets are long-lived assets that the business uses in its operation. These assets are not held for sale as inventory. The term used to describe the expensing of capital assets is *amortization*; depreciation and depletion are used to describe amortization of certain assets.

One category of capital assets is *property, plant and equipment*. The term commonly used to describe the expensing of property, plant and equipment is *depreciation*. Land, however, is not depreciated.

A second category of capital assets is natural resources, also known as *wasting assets*. Amortization of wasting assets is more commonly called *depletion*.

A third category of capital assets, *intangibles*, refers to rights, which have no physical form. The cost of intangibles is expensed through amortization, the same term that is used for capital assets generally.

Businesses usually compute the depreciation of property, plant and equipment by three methods: *straight-line, units-of-production*, and the *declining balance* (accelerated) methods — using either *double-declining-balance* or *Revenue Canada* rates. Most companies use the straight-line method for financial reporting purposes, and almost all companies use the Revenue Canada rates for income tax purposes. Revenue Canada rates are the maximum allowed, and result in greater tax deductions early in the asset's life. These deductions decrease income tax payments, and conserve cash that the company can use in its business.

Before disposing of a capital asset, the business updates the asset's depreciation. Disposal is recorded by removing the book balances from both the asset account and its related accumulated depreciation account. Disposal may result in a gain or a loss.

Depletion of natural resources is computed on a units-of-production basis. *Amortization* of intangibles is computed on a straight-line basis over a maximum of 40 years. However, the useful lives of most intangibles are shorter than their legal lives.

Betterments increase the capacity or efficiency of an asset, or extend its useful life. Accordingly, they are debited to an asset account. *Repairs*, on the other hand, merely maintain the asset's usefulness, and are debited to an expense account.

Self-Study Questions

Test your understanding of the chapter by marking the correct answer for each of the following questions:

1. Which of the following payments is not included in the cost of land? *(p. 433)*
    a. Removal of old building
    b. Legal fees
    c. Back property taxes paid at acquisition
    d. Cost of fencing and lighting

2. A business paid $120,000 for two machines valued at $90,000 and $60,000. The business will record these machines at *(p. 434)*
   a. $90,000 and $60,000
   b. $60,000 each
   c. $72,000 and $48,000
   d. $70,000 and $50,000

3. Which of the following definitions fits depreciation? *(pp. 434–35)*
   a. Allocation of the asset's market value to expense over its useful life
   b. Allocation of the asset's cost to expense over its useful life
   c. Decreases in the asset's market value over its useful life
   d. Increases in the fund set aside to replace the asset when it is worn out

4. Which depreciation method's amounts are not computed based on time? *(p. 439)*
   a. Straight-line
   b. Units-of-production
   c. Declining-balance

5. Which depreciation method gives the largest amount of expense in the early years of using the asset and therefore is best for income tax purposes? *(p. 442)*
   a. Straight-line
   b. Units-of-production
   c. Declining-balance
   d. All are equal

6. A company paid $450,000 for a building and was depreciating it by the straight-line method over a 40-year life with estimated residual value of $50,000. After 10 years, it became evident that the building's remaining useful life would be 40 years. Depreciation for the eleventh year is *(pp. 444–45)*
   a. $7,500
   b. $8,750
   c. $10,000
   d. $12,500

7. Labrador, Inc. scrapped an automobile that cost $14,000 and had book value of $1,100. The entry to record this disposal is *(p. 445)*

   a. Loss on Disposal of Automobile............................ 1,100
         Automobile 1,100
   b. Accumulated Depreciation..................................... 14,000
         Automobile 14,000
   c. Accumulated Depreciation..................................... 12,900
         Automobile 12,900
   d. Accumulated Depreciation..................................... 12,900
         Loss of Disposal of Automobile............................ 1,100
         Automobile 14,000

8. Depletion is computed in the same manner as which depreciation method? *(p. 448)*
   a. Straight-line
   b. Units-of-production
   c. Declining balance

9. Lacy Corporation paid $550,000 to acquire Gentsch, Inc. Gentsch's assets had a market value of $900,000 and its liabilities were $400,000. In recording the acquisition, Lacy will record goodwill of *(p. 451)*
   a. $50,000
   b. $100,000
   c. $550,000
   d. $0

10. Which of the following items is a repair? *(p. 452)*
    a. New brakes for delivery truck
    b. Repaving of a company parking lot
    c. Cost of a new engine for a truck
    d. Building permit paid to construct an addition to an existing building

Answers to the Self-Study Questions are at the end of the chapter.

Accounting Vocabulary

amortization *(p. 432, 449)*
betterments *(p. 452)*
capital assets *(p. 432)*
capital cost allowance
    (p. 438)
copyright *(p. 450)*
cost of capital asset
    (p. 432)
depletion expense
    (p. 448)
declining-balance (DB)
    method *(p. 438)*
depreciable cost *(p. 435)*

double-declining-
    balance (DDB) *(p. 439)*
estimated residual value
    (p. 435)
estimated useful life
    (p. 435)
franchises and licenses
    (p. 450)
goodwill *(p. 451)*
intangible assets *(p. 432)*
leaseholds *(p. 450)*
natural resources *(p. 432)*
patents *(p. 450)*

relative-sales-value
    method *(p. 434)*
repair *(p. 452)*
Revenue Canada (RC)
    rates *(p. 438)*
straight-line (SL) method
    (p. 436)
trademarks and trade
    names *(p. 450)*
units-of-production
    (UOP) method *(p. 436)*
wasting assets *(p. 432)*

ASSIGNMENT MATERIAL _____

Questions

1. To what types of long-lived assets do the following expenses apply: depreciation, depletion, and amortization?

2. Describe how to measure the cost of a capital asset. Would an ordinary cost of repairing the asset after it is placed in service be included in the asset's cost?

3. Suppose land is purchased for $100,000. How do you account for the $8,000 cost of removing an unwanted building?

4. When assets are purchased as a group for a single price and no individual asset cost is given, how is each asset's cost determined?

5. Define depreciation. Present the common misconceptions about depreciation.

6. Which depreciation method does each of the following graphs characterize: straight-line, units-of-production, or declining-balance?

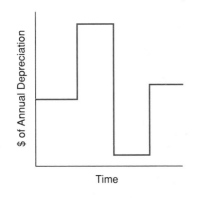
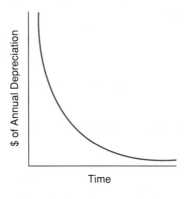
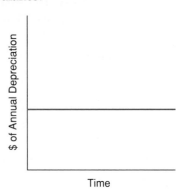

7. Which of the three depreciation methods results in the most depreciation in the first year of the asset's life?

8. Explain the concept of declining-balance depreciation. Which other depreciation method is used in the definition of declining-balance depreciation?

9. The level of business activity fluctuates widely for Harwood Delivery Service, reaching its peak around Christmas each year. At other times, business is slow. What depreciation method is most appropriate for the company's fleet of Chevy Luv trucks?

10. Oswalt Computer Service Center uses the most advanced computers available to keep a competitive edge over other service centres. To maintain this advantage, Oswalt usually replaces its computers before they are worn out. Describe the major factors affecting the useful life of a plant asset and indicate which seems more relevant to Oswalt's computers.

11. Estimated residual value is not considered in computing depreciation during the early years of the asset's life by one of the methods. Which method is it?

12. Which depreciation method is best from an income tax standpoint? Why?

13. How does depreciation affect income taxes? How does depreciation affect cash provided by operations?

14. Describe how to compute depreciation for less than a full year, and how to account for depreciation for less than a full month.

15. Ragland Company paid $10,000 for office furniture. The company expected it to remain in service for 6 years and to have a $1,000 residual value. After 2 years' use, company accountants believe the furniture will last an additional 6 years. How much depreciation will Ragland record for each of these last 6 years, assuming straight-line depreciation and no change in the estimated residual value?

16. When a company sells a capital asset before the year's end, what must it record before accounting for the sale?

17. Describe how to determine whether a company experiences a gain or a loss when an old capital asset is exchanged for a new one. Does generally accepted accounting favor the recognition of gains or losses?

18. Identify seven elements of internal control designed to safeguard capital assets.

19. What expense applies to natural resources? By which amortization method is this expense computed?

20. How do intangible assets differ from most other assets? Why are they assets at all? What expense applies to intangible assets?

21. Why is the cost of patents and other intangible assets often expensed over a shorter period than the legal life of the asset?

22. Your company has just purchased another company for $400,000. The market value of the other company's net assets is $325,000. What is the $75,000 excess called? What type of asset is it? What is the maximum period over which its cost is amortized under generally accepted accounting principles?

23. Northern Telecom is recognized as a world leader in the manufacture and sale of telephone equipment. The company's success has created vast amounts of business goodwill. Would you expect to see this goodwill reported on Northern Telecom's financial statements? Why, or why not?

24. Distinguish a betterment from a repair. Why are they treated differently for accounting purposes?

Exercises

Exercise 10-1 *Identifying the elements of a capital asset's cost* *(L.O. 1)*

A company purchased land, paying $56,000 cash as a down payment and signing a $120,000 note payable for the balance. In addition, the company paid delinquent property tax of $2,000, a legal fee of $500, and a $3,400 charge for leveling the land and removing an unwanted building. The company constructed an office building on the land at a cost of $410,000. It also paid $12,000 for a fence around the boundary of the property, $2,400 for the company sign near the entrance to the property, and $6,000 for special lighting of the grounds. Determine the cost of the company's land, land improvements, and building.

Exercise 10-2   *Allocating cost to assets acquired in a basket purchase (L.O. 1)*

Dartmouth Research Center bought three used machines in a $20,000 purchase. An independent appraisal of the machines produced the following figures:

Machine No.	Appraised Value
1	$ 4,000
2	12,000
3	8,000

Assuming Dartmouth paid cash for the machines, record the purchase in the general journal, identifying each machine's individual cost in a separate Machine account.

Exercise 10-3   *Explaining the concept of amortization (L.O. 2)*

Brian Marling has just slept through the class in which Professor Spyros explained the concept of amortization. Because the next test is scheduled for Wednesday, Brian telephones Michelle White to get her notes from the lecture. Michelle's notes are concise: "Amortization — Sounds like Greek to me." Brian next tries Desirée Mare, who says she thinks amortization is what happens when an asset wears out. Orry Skrypec is confident that amortization is the process of building up a cash fund to replace an asset at the end of its useful life. Explain the concept of amortization for Brian. Evaluate the explanations of Desirée and Orry. Be specific.

Exercise 10-4   *Computing depreciation by four methods (L.O. 3)*

A company delivery truck was acquired on January 2, 19X1 for $12,000. The truck was expected to remain in service for 4 years and last 88,000 kilometres. At the end of its useful life, company officials estimated that the truck's residual value would be $1,000. The truck traveled 24,000 kilometres in the first year, 28,000 in the second year, 21,000 in the third year, and 15,000 in the fourth year. Prepare a schedule of depreciation expense per year for the truck using straight-line, units-of-production, and the two declining-balance methods (double-declining-balance and Revenue Canada rates). Assume full depreciation can be charged in the first year under the Revenue Canada method. The Revenue Canada rate is 30 percent. Show your computations.

Exercise 10-5   *Recording partial-year depreciation computed by two methods (L.O. 3)*

Situation 1   Hunt Corporation purchased office furniture on June 3, 19X4 for $2,600 cash. Donna Hunt expects it to remain useful for 8 years and to have a residual value of $200. Hunt uses the straight-line depreciation method. Record Hunt's depreciation on the furniture for the year ended December 31, 19X4.

Situation 2   Chen Company purchased equipment on October 19, 19X2 for $19,500, signing a note payable for that amount. Chen estimated that this equipment will be useful for 3 years and have a residual value of $1,500. Assuming Chen uses double-declining-balance depreciation, record Chen's depreciation on the machine for the year ended December 31, 19X2.

Exercise 10-6   *Journalizing a change in a capital asset's useful life (L.O. 3)*

A company purchased a building for $680,000 and depreciated it on a straight-line basis over a 30-year period. The estimated residual value was $80,000. After using the building for 15 years, the company realized that wear and tear on the building would force the company to replace it before 30 years. Starting with the 16th year, the company began depreciating the building over a revised total life of 20 years, retaining the $80,000 estimated residual value. Record depreciation expense on the building for years 15 and 16.

Exercise 10-7 *Preparing a property, plant and equipment ledger card; units-of-production depreciation (L.O. 3)*

McBee Delivery Service uses ledger cards to account for its delivery vehicles, which are located at the company's service garage. The fleet of vehicles cost $96,000 when purchased from Ericksen Ford Company on September 1, 19X2. This cost is the debit balance in the Delivery Vehicles account in the general ledger. McBee uses the units-of-production depreciation method, and estimates a useful life of 480,000 kilometres and a $6,000 residual value for the trucks. The garage supervisor is responsible for the vehicles. The company's fiscal year ends on December 31. Kilometres traveled were 30,000 in 19X2; 105,000 in 19X3; and 98,000 in 19X4. Complete a ledger card for these vehicles through December 31, 19X4, using a format similar to Exhibit 10-9.

Exercise 10-8 *Identifying depreciation methods for income tax and financial reporting purposes (L.O. 4)*

Identify the depreciation method that would be most advantageous from an income tax perspective. Which depreciation method do most companies use for reporting to their shareholders and creditors on their financial statements?

Exercise 10-9 *Recording the sale of a capital asset (L.O. 5)*

On January 2, 19X1, Oakwood Sales Ltd. purchased store fixtures for $7,700 cash, expecting the fixtures to remain in service for 10 years. Oakwood has depreciated the fixtures by the Revenue Canada rate of 20 percent, assuming no estimated residual value and that full depreciation can be deducted in the first year. On October 30, 19X8, Oakwood sold the fixtures for $850 cash. Record depreciation expense on the fixtures for the 10 months ended October 30, 19X8, and also record the sale of the fixtures. Oakwood's year end is December 31.

Exercise 10-10 *Exchanging capital assets (L.O. 5)*

A machine cost $10,000. At the end of 4 years, its accumulated depreciation was $4,500. For each of the following situations, record the trade-in of this old machine for a new, similar machine.

Situation 1 The new machine had a cash price of $12,400; the dealer allowed a trade-in allowance of $4,000 on the old machine; and you paid the $8,400 balance in cash.

Situation 2 The new machine had a cash price of $13,000; the dealer allowed a trade-in allowance of $5,900 on the old machine; and you signed a note payable for the $7,100 balance.

Exercise 10-11 *Recording wasting assets and depletion (L.O. 6)*

Sasquatch Mining Company Ltd. paid $198,500 for the right to extract ore from a 200,000-tonne mineral deposit. In addition to the purchase price, Sasquatch also paid a $500 filing fee and a $1,000 license fee to the province of British Columbia. Because Sasquatch purchased the rights to the minerals only, the company expected the asset to have zero residual value when fully depleted. During the first year of production, Sasquatch removed 35,000 tonnes of ore. Make general journal entries to record (1) purchase of the mineral rights (debit Mineral Asset), (2) payment of fees, and (3) depletion for first-year production.

Exercise 10-12   *Recording intangibles, amortization, and a change in the asset's useful life (L.O. 7)*

Part 1   Lutz Corporation manufactures high-speed printers and has recently purchased for $3.52 million a patent for the design for a new laser printer. Although it gives legal protection for 17 years, the patent is expected to provide Lutz with a competitive advantage for only 8 years. Assuming the straight-line method of amortization, use general journal entries to record (1) the purchase of the patent, and (2) amortization for 1 year.

Part 2   After using the patent for 4 years, Lutz learns at an industry trade show that another company is designing a more efficient printer. Based on this new information, Lutz decides, starting with year 5, to amortize the remaining cost of the patent over 2 additional years, giving the patent a total useful life of 6 years. Record amortization for year 5.

Exercise 10-13   *Computing and recording goodwill (L.O. 7)*

Company P purchased Company S, paying $1 million cash. The market value of Company S assets was $1.7 million, and Company S had liabilities of $1.1 million.

1. Compute the cost of the goodwill purchased by Company P.
2. Record the purchase by Company P.
3. Record amortization of goodwill for 1 year, assuming the straight-line method and a useful life of 10 years.

Exercise 10-14   *Distinguishing betterments from repairs (L.O. 8)*

Classify each of the following expenditures as a betterment or a repair (expense) related to machinery: (a) purchase price; (b) sales tax paid on the purchase price; (c) transportation and insurance while machinery is in transport from seller to buyer; (d) installation; (e) training of personnel for initial operation of the machinery; (f) special reinforcement to the machinery platform; (g) income tax paid on income earned from the sale of products manufactured by the machinery; (h) major overhaul to extend useful life by three years; (i) ordinary recurring repairs to keep the machinery in good working order; (j) lubrication of the machinery before it is placed in service; and (k) periodic lubrication after the machinery is placed in service.

Problems   (Group A)

Problem 10-1A   *Identifying the elements of a capital asset's cost (L.O. 1)*

Anotelli, Inc. incurred the following costs in acquiring land, making land improvements, and constructing and furnishing an office building.

a. Purchase price of 4 hectares of land, including an old building that will be used for storage (land market value is $380,000; building market value is $20,000)	$316,000
b. Landscaping (additional dirt and earth moving)	8,100
c. Fence around the boundary of the land	17,650
d. Legal fee for title search on the land	600
e. Delinquent real estate taxes on the land to be paid by Anotelli	5,900
f. Company signs at front of the company property	1,800
g. Building permit for the office building	350

h. Architect fee for the design of the office building........................... 19,800

i. Masonry, carpentry, roofing, and other labor to construct
    office building 509,000

j. Concrete, wood, steel girders, and other materials used in the
    construction of the office building 214,000

k. Renovation of the storage building.. 41,800

l. Repair of storm damage to storage building during
    construction 2,200

m. Landscaping (trees and shrubs)... 6,400

n. Parking lot and concrete walks on the property 19,750

o. Lights for the parking lot, walkways, and company signs 7,300

p. Supervisory salary of construction supervisor (85 percent to
    office building, 9 percent to fencing, parking lot and concrete
    walks, and 6 percent to storage building renovation).................... 40,000

q. Office furniture for the office building 107,100

r. Transportation and installation of furniture................................... 1,100

Anotelli depreciates buildings over 40 years, land improvements over 20 years, and furniture over 8 years, all on a straight-line basis with zero residual value.

Required

1. Using the following format, account for each cost by listing it as a debit to Land, Land Improvements, Office Building, Storage Building, or Furniture:

Item	Land	Land Improvements	Office Building	Storage Building	Furniture
a	$	$	$	$	$
:					
r					
Totals	$	$	$	$	$

2. Assuming that all construction was complete and the assets were placed in service on May 4, record depreciation for the year ended December 31. Round off figures to the nearest dollar.

Problem 10-2A   *Explaining the concept of depreciation (L.O. 2)*

The board of directors of Parksville Parking Lot Limited is reviewing the 19X8 annual report. A new board member, a consulting psychologist with little business experience, questions the company accountant about the depreciation amounts. The psychologist wonders why depreciation expense has decreased from $20,000 in 19X6, to $18,400 in 19X7, and to $17,200 in 19X8. She states that she could understand the decreasing annual amounts if the company had been disposing of properties each year, but that has not occurred. Further, she notes that growth in the city is increasing the values of company properties. Why is the company recording depreciation when the property values are increasing?

Required

Write a paragraph or two to explain the concept of depreciation to the psychologist and to answer her questions.

Problem 10-3A   *Computing depreciation by four methods and the cash flow advantage of declining-balance depreciation for tax purposes (L.O. 3, 4)*

On January 9, 19X1, Morse, Inc. paid $92,000 for equipment used in manufacturing automotive supplies. In addition to the basic purchase price, the company paid $700 transportation charges, $100 insurance for the goods in transit, $4,100 sales tax, and $3,100 for a special platform on which to place the equipment in the plant. Morse management estimates that the equipment will remain in service for 5 years and have a residual value of $10,000. The equipment will produce 50,000 units in the first year, with annual production decreasing by 5,000 units during each of the next 4 years (that is, 45,000 units in year 2, 40,000 units in year 3, and so on). In trying to decide which depreciation method to use, Ted Morse has requested a depreciation schedule for each of the four generally accepted depreciation methods: straight-line, units-of-production, and the two declining-balance methods: double-declining-balanceand declining-balance using the Revenue Canada rate of 30 percent.

Required

1. For each of the four generally accepted depreciation methods, prepare a depreciation schedule showing asset cost, depreciation expense, accumulated depreciation, and asset book value. Use the format of Exhibits 10-3 through 10-6. Assume full depreciation can be deducted in the first year under the Revenue Canada rate method.

2. Morse reports to shareholders and creditors in the financial statements using the depreciation method that maximizes reported income in the early years of asset use. For income tax purposes, however, the company uses the depreciation method that minimizes income tax payments in those early years. Consider the first year Morse uses the equipment. Identify the depreciation methods that meet Morse's objectives.

3. Assume cash provided by operations before income tax is $120,000 for the equipment's first year. The income tax rate is 30 percent. For the two depreciation methods identified in requirement 2, compare the net income and cash provided by operations (cash flow). Use the format of Exhibit 10-8 for your answer. Show which method gives the net-income advantage, and which method gives the cash-flow advantage. Ignore the earnings rate in the cash-flow analysis.

Problem 10-4A   *Journalizing and posting capital asset transactions; betterments versus repairs (L.O. 1, 3, 5, 8)*

Assume that a Shoppers Drug Mart store completed the following transactions:

19X2
Jan.   6   Paid $9,000 cash for a used delivery truck.
    7   Paid $800 to have the truck engine overhauled.
    8   Paid $200 to have the truck modified for business use.
Aug. 21   Paid $156 for a minor tuneup.
Dec. 31   Recorded depreciation on the truck by the double-declining-balance method. (Assume a 4-year life.)
    31   Closed the appropriate accounts.
19X3
Feb.   8   Traded in the delivery truck for a new truck costing $13,000. The dealer granted a $4,000 allowance on the old truck, and the store paid the balance in cash. Recorded 19X3 depreciation for the year to date and then recorded the exchange of trucks.
July   8   Repaired the new truck's damaged fender for $625 cash.
Dec. 31   Recorded depreciation on the new truck by the double-declining-balance method. (Assume a 4-year life.)
    31   Closed the appropriate accounts.

Required

1. Open the following accounts in the general ledger: Delivery Trucks; Accumulated Depreciation — Delivery Trucks; Truck Repair Expense; and Depreciation Expense — Delivery Trucks.

2. Record the transactions in the general journal and post to the ledger accounts opened.

Problem 10-5A *Recording capital asset transactions; exchanges; changes in useful life* **(L.O. 1, 3, 5, 8)**

Laidlaw Transportation Ltd. provides nationwide general freight service. The company's balance sheet includes the following assets under Property, Plant and Equipment: Land, Buildings, Motor Carrier Equipment, and Leasehold Improvements. Assume the company has a separate accumulated depreciation account for each of these assets except land and leasehold improvements. Amortization on leasehold improvements is credited directly to the Leasehold Improvements account rather than to Accumulated Amortization — Leasehold Improvements.

Assume that Laidlaw completed the following transactions at one of its branches:

Jan. 5 Traded in motor-carrier equipment with book value of $47,000 (cost of $130,000) for similar new equipment with a cash cost of $176,000. Laidlaw received a trade-in allowance of $50,000 on the old equipment and paid the remainder in cash.

Feb. 22 Purchased motor-carrier equipment for $136,000 plus 5 percent sales tax and a $200 registration fee. The company gave a 60-day, 12 percent note in payment.

Apr. 23 Paid the equipment note and related interest.

July 9 Sold a building that had cost $550,000 and had accumulated depreciation of $247,500 through December 31 of the preceding year. Depreciation is computed on a straight-line basis. The building has a 30-year useful life and a residual value of $55,000. Laidlaw received $100,000 cash and a $600,000 note receivable.

Aug. 16 Paid cash for leasehold improvements at a cost of $10,200.

Oct. 26 Purchased land and a building for a single price of $300,000. An independent appraisal valued the land at $115,000, and the building at $230,000.

Dec. 31 Recorded depreciation as follows:

Motor-carrier equipment has an expected useful life of 5 years and an estimated residual value of 5 percent of cost. Depreciation is computed by the Revenue Canada rate method using a rate of 30 percent. Make separate depreciation entries for equipment acquired on January 5 and February 22.

Amortization on leasehold improvements is computed on a straight-line basis over the life of the lease, which is 10 years, with zero residual value.

Depreciation on buildings is computed by the straight-line method. The company had assigned to its older buildings, which cost $2,000,000, an estimated useful life of 30 years with a residual value equal to 10 percent of the asset cost. However, management has come to believe that the buildings will remain useful for a total of 40 years. Residual value remains unchanged. The company has used all its buildings, except for the one purchased on October 26, for 10 years. The new building carries a 40-year useful life and a residual value equal to 10 percent of its cost. Make separate entries for depreciation on the building acquired on October 26 and the other buildings purchased in earlier years.

Required

Record the transactions in the general journal.

Problem 10-6A *Distinguishing betterments from repairs; preparing a property, plant and equipment ledger card* **(L.O. 3, 5, 8)**

Suppose Pacific Tire Supply Company uses ledger cards to control its service trucks, purchased from Paproski Motors Ltd. The supervisor is responsible for the trucks, which are located at the company's service garage. The following transactions were completed during 19X3 and 19X4:

19X3

Jan.	6	Paid $10,420 cash for a used service truck (truck no. 501).
	7	Paid $2,500 to have the truck engine overhauled.
	8	Paid $180 to have the truck modified for business use.
Nov.	5	Paid $107 for replacement of one tire.
Dec.	31	Recorded depreciation on the truck by the double-declining-balance method, based on a 4-year useful life and a $1,100 residual value.

19X4

Jul.	16	Repaired a damaged fender on truck no. 501 at a cash cost of $877.
Sept.	6	Traded in service truck no. 501 for a new one (truck no. 633) with a cash cost of $18,000. The dealer granted a $4,500 allowance on the old truck, and Pacific Tire paid the balance in cash. Recorded 19X4 depreciation for year to date and then recorded exchange of the trucks.
Dec.	31	Recorded depreciation on truck no. 633 by the double-declining-balance method, based on a 4-year life and a $1,500 residual value.

Required

1. Identify the betterments and the repairs in the transactions. Which expenditures are debited to an asset account? Which expenditures are debited to an expense account?

2. Prepare a separate ledger card for each of the trucks.

Problem 10-7A *Recording intangibles, wasting assets, and the related expenses* **(L.O. 6, 7)**

Part 1 Canadian Pacific Ltd. is one of Canada's largest holding companies. The company's balance sheet includes the assets Natural Gas, Oil, and Coal.

Suppose Canadian Pacific paid $1.5 million cash for a lease giving the firm the right to work a mine that contained an estimated 125,000 tonnes of coal. Assume that the company paid $10,000 to remove unwanted buildings from the land and $45,000 to prepare the surface for mining. Further assume that Canadian Pacific signed a $20,000 note payable to a landscaping company to return the land surface to its original condition after the lease ends. During the first year, Canadian Pacific removed 35,000 tonnes of coal, which it sold on account for $17 per tonne.

Required

Make general journal entries to record all transactions related to the coal, including depletion and sale of the first-year production.

Part 2 Scott's Hospitality Inc., among its other businesses, operates Kentucky Fried Chicken franchised restaurants. The company's balance sheet reports the asset Cost in Excess of Net Assets of Purchased Businesses. Assume that Scott purchased this asset as part of the acquisition of another company, which carried these figures:

Book value of assets	$2.4 million
Market value of assets	3.1 million
Liabilities	2.2 million

Required

1. What is another title for the asset Cost in Excess of Net Assets of Purchased Businesses?

2. Make the general journal entry to record Scott's purchase of the other company for $1.3 million cash.

3. Assuming Scott's amortizes Cost in Excess of Net Assets of Purchased Businesses over 20 years, record the straight-line amortization for one year.

Part 3.   Suppose Scott's Hospitality purchased a Kentucky Fried Chicken franchise license for $240,000. In addition to the basic purchase price, Scott's also paid a lawyer $8,000 for assistance with the negotiations. Management believes the appropriate amortization period for its cost of the franchise license is 8 years.

Required

Make general journal entries to record the franchise transactions, including straight-line amortization for one year.

(Group B)

Problem 10-1B   *Identifying the elements of a capital asset's cost (L.O. 1)*

Mazzoti Ltd. incurred the following costs in acquiring land and a garage, making land improvements, and constructing and furnishing a home office building.

a. Purchase price of 3½ hectares of land, including an old building that will be used as a garage for company vehicles (land market value is $600,000; building market value is $60,000)	$550,000
b. Delinquent real estate taxes on the land to be paid by Mazzoti	3,700
c. Landscaping (additional dirt and earth moving)	3,550
d. Legal fees on the land acquisition	1,000
e. Fence around the boundary of the land	14,100
f. Building permit for the home office building	200
g. Architect fee for the design of the home office building	25,000
h. Company signs near front and rear approaches to the company property	23,550
i. Renovation of the garage	23,800
j. Concrete, wood, steel girders, and other materials used in the construction of the home office building	514,000
k. Masonry, carpentry, roofing, and other labor to construct home office building	734,000
l. Repair of vandalism damage to home office building during construction	4,100
m. Parking lots and concrete walks on the property	17,450
n. Lights for the parking lot, walkways, and company signs	8,900
o. Supervisory salary of construction supervisor (90 percent to home office building, 6 percent to fencing, parking lot and concrete walks, and 4 percent to garage renovation)	55,000

p. Office furniture for the home office building 123,500

q. Transportation of furniture from seller to the home office
building 700

r. Landscaping (trees and shrubs)... 9,100

Mazzoti depreciates buildings over 40 years, land improvements over 20 years and furniture over 8 years, all on a straight-line basis with zero residual value.

Required

1. Using the following format, account for each cost by listing it as a debit to Land, Land Improvements, Home Office Building, Garage or Furniture:

Item	Land	Land Improvements	Home Office Building	Garage	Furniture
a	$	$	$	$	$
:					
r					
Totals	$	$	$	$	$

2. Assuming that all construction was complete and the assets were placed in service on March 19, record depreciation for the year ended December 31. (Round figures to the nearest dollar.)

Problem 10-2B   *Explaining the concept of depreciation (L.O. 2)*

The board of directors of Nanaimo Construction, Inc. is having its regular quarterly meeting. Accounting policies are on the agenda, and depreciation is being discussed. A new board member, a physician, has some strong opinions about two aspects of depreciation policy. Dr. Quan argues that depreciation must be coupled with a fund to replace company assets. Otherwise, he argues, there is no substance to depreciation. He also challenges the 5-year estimated life over which Nanaimo is depreciating company computers. He notes that the computers will last much longer and should be depreciated over at least 10 years.

Required

Write a paragraph or two to explain the concept of depreciation to Dr. Quan and to answer his arguments.

Problem 10-3B   *Computing depreciation by three methods and the cash flow advantage of accelerated depreciation for tax purposes (L.O. 3, 4)*

On January 2, 19X1, Miske, Inc. purchased 3 used delivery trucks at a total cost of $53,000. Before placing the trucks in service, the company spent $1,200 painting them, $1,800 replacing their tires, and $4,000 overhauling their engines and reconditioning their bodies. Miske management estimates that the trucks will remain in service for 6 years and have a residual value of $6,000. The trucks' combined annual usage is expected to be 16,000 kilometres in each of the first 4 years and 18,000 kilometres in each of the next 2 years. In trying to decide which depreciation method to use, Lynn Miske, the general manager, requests a depreciation schedule for each of the following generally accepted depreciation methods: straight-line, units-of-production, and declining-balance using the Revenue Canada rate of 30 percent.

Required

1. Assuming Miske depreciates its delivery trucks as a unit, prepare a depreciation schedule for each of the three generally accepted depreciation methods, showing asset cost, depreciation expense, accumulated depreciation and asset book value. Use the formats of Exhibits 10-3 through 10-5.

2. Miske reports to shareholders and creditors in the financial statements using the depreciation method that maximizes reported income in the early years of asset use. For income tax purposes, however, the company uses the depreciation method that minimizes income tax payments in those early years. Consider the first year that Miske uses the delivery trucks. Identify the depreciation methods that meet the general manager's objectives. Assume Miske can deduct full depreciation in the first year for income tax purposes.

3. Assume cash provided by operations before income tax is $80,000 for the delivery truck's first year. The income tax rate is 30 percent. For the two depreciation methods identified in requirement 2, compare the net income and cash provided by operations (cash flow). Use the format of Exhibit 10-8 for your answer. Show which method gives the net-income advantage, and which method gives the cash-flow advantage.

Problem 10-4B   *Journalizing and posting capital asset transactions; betterments versus repairs (L.O. 1, 3, 5, 8)*

Saskatchewan Power Corporation provides electrical power to Saskatchewan. Assume that the company completed the following transactions:

19X4

Jan.	3	Paid $22,000 cash for a used service truck.
	5	Paid $1,200 to have the truck engine overhauled.
	7	Paid $300 to have the truck modified for business use.
Oct.	3	Paid $930 for transmission repair and oil change.
Dec.	31	Used the double-declining-balance method to record depreciation on the truck. (Assume a 4-year life.)
	31	Closed the appropriate accounts.

19X5

Mar.	13	Replaced the truck's broken windshield for $275 cash.
June	26	Traded in the service truck for a new truck costing $27,000. The dealer granted an $8,000 allowance on the old truck, and Saskatchewan Power paid the balance in cash. Recorded 19X5 depreciation for the year to date and then recorded the exchange of trucks.
Dec.	31	Used the double-declining-balance method to record depreciation on the new truck. (Assume a 4-year life.)
	31	Closed the appropriate accounts.

Required

1. Open the following accounts in the general ledger: Service Trucks; Accumulated Depreciation — Service Trucks; Truck Repair Expense; and Depreciation Expense — Service Trucks.

2. Record the transactions in the general journal and post to the ledger accounts opened.

Problem 10-5B   *Recording capital asset transactions; exchanges; changes in useful life (L.O. 1, 3, 5, 8)*

A. C. Nielsen Company of Canada Ltd. surveys Canadian viewing trends. Nielsen's balance sheet reports the following assets under Property and Equipment: Land,

Buildings, Office Furniture, Communication Equipment, Televideo Equipment, and Leasehold Improvements. The company has a separate accumulated depreciation account for each of these assets except land and leasehold improvements. Amortization on leasehold improvements is credited directly to the Leasehold Improvements account rather than to Accumulated Depreciation — Leasehold Improvements.

Assume that Nielsen completed the following transactions:

Jan. 4 Traded in communication equipment with book value of $31,000 (cost of $66,000) for similar new equipment with a cash cost of $78,000. The seller gave Nielsen a trade-in allowance of $20,000 on the old equipment, and Nielsen paid the remainder in cash.

19 Purchased office furniture for $45,000 plus 6 percent sales tax and $300 shipping charge. The company gave a 90-day, 10 percent note in payment.

Apr. 19 Paid the furniture note and related interest.

Aug. 29 Sold a building that had cost $475,000 and had accumulated depreciation of $353,500 through December 31 of the preceding year. Depreciation is computed on a straight-line basis. The building has a 30-year useful life and a residual value of $47,500. Nielsen received $250,000 cash and a $750,000 note receivable.

Sept. 6 Paid cash for leasehold improvements at a cost of $26,000.

Nov. 10 Purchased used communication and televideo equipment from the Decima Research polling organization. Total cost was $90,000 paid in cash. An independent appraisal valued the communication equipment at $65,000 and the televideo equipment at $35,000.

Dec. 31 Recorded depreciation as follows:

Equipment is depreciated by the double-declining-balance method over a 5-year life. Record depreciation on the equipment purchased on January 4 and on November 10 separately.

Office furniture has an expected useful life of 8 years with an estimated residual value of $5,000. Depreciation is computed using the Revenue Canada rate (20 percent).

Amortization on leasehold improvements is computed on a straight-line basis over the life of the lease, which is 6 years, with zero residual value.

Depreciation on buildings is computed by the straight-line method. The company had assigned buildings an estimated useful life of 30 years and a residual value that is 10 percent of cost. After using the buildings for 20 years, the company has come to believe that their total useful life will be 35 years. Residual value remains unchanged. The buildings cost $16,000,000.

Required

Record the transactions in the general journal.

Problem 10-6B *Distinguishing betterments from repairs; preparing property, plant, and equipment ledger cards* **(L.O. 3, 5, 8)**

Suppose Nova Scotia Boat Repair Co. uses ledger cards to control its service trucks, purchased from Wallen Motor Company. The supervisor is responsible for the trucks, which are located at the company's service garage. The following transactions were completed during 19X6 and 19X7:

19X6

Jan. 10 Paid $14,000 cash for a used service truck (truck no. 214).

11 Paid $1,500 to have the truck engine overhauled.

	12	Paid $250 to have the truck modified for business use.
Aug.	3	Paid $603 for transmission repair and oil change.
Dec.	31	Recorded depreciation on the truck by the double-declining-balance method, based on a 5-year life and a $1,500 residual value.

19X7

Mar.	13	Replaced a damaged bumper on truck no. 214 at a cash cost of $295.
May	12	Traded in service truck no. 214 for a new one (truck no. 267) with a cash cost of $23,500. The dealer granted a $9,000 allowance on the old truck, and Nova Scotia Boat Repair Co. paid the balance in cash. Recorded 19X7 depreciation for year to date and then recorded exchange of the trucks.
Dec.	31	Recorded depreciation on truck no. 267 by the double-declining-balance method, based on a 5-year life and a $2,000 residual value.

Required

1. Identify the betterments and the repairs in the transactions. Which expenditures are debited to an asset account? Which expenditures are debited to an expense account?

2. Prepare a separate ledger card for each of the trucks.

Problem 10-7B   *Recording intangibles, wasting assets, and the related expenses* **(L.O. 6, 7)**

Part 1   TransCanada PipeLines Ltd. owns gas transmission facilities and other energy related assets. The company's balance sheet includes the asset Oil Properties.

Suppose TransCanada paid $6 million cash for an oil lease that contained an estimated reserve of 725,000 barrels of oil. Assume that the company paid $350,000 for additional geological tests of the property and $110,000 to prepare the surface for drilling. Prior to production, the company signed a $65,000 note payable to have a building constructed on the property. Because the building provides on-site headquarters for the drilling effort and will be abandoned when the oil is depleted, its cost is debited to the Oil Properties account and included in depletion charges. During the first year of production, TransCanada removed 82,000 barrels of oil, which it sold on credit for $19 per barrel.

Required

Make general journal entries to record all transactions related to the oil and gas property, including depletion and sale of the first-year production.

Part 2   Newfoundland Telephone provides telephone service to most of Newfoundland and Labrador. The company's balance sheet reports the asset Cost of Acquisitions in Excess of the Fair Market Value of the Net Assets of Subsidiaries. Assume that Newfoundland Telephone purchased this asset as part of the acquisition of another company, which carried these figures:

Book value of assets	$640,000
Market value of assets	920,000
Liabilities	405,000

Required

1. What is another title for the asset Cost of Acquisitions in Excess of the Fair Market Value of the Net Assets of Subsidiaries?

2. Make the general journal entry to record Newfoundland Telephone's purchase of the other company for $600,000 cash.

3. Assuming Newfoundland Telephone amortizes Cost of Acquisitions in Excess of the Fair Market Value of the Net Assets of Subsidiaries over 20 years, record the straight-line amortization for one year.

Part 3 Suppose Northern Telecom purchased a patent for $190,000. Before using the patent, Northern Telecom incurred an additional cost of $25,000 for a lawsuit to defend the company's right to purchase it. Even though the patent gives Northern Telecom legal protection for 17 years, company management has decided to amortize its cost over a 5-year period because of the industry's fast-changing technologies.

Required

Make general journal entries to record the patent transactions, including straight-line amortization for one year.

Extending Your Knowledge

Decision Problems

1. Measuring profitability based on different inventory and depreciation methods (L.O. 3)

Suppose you are considering investing in two businesses, Frycer, Inc. and Bergdahl Ltd. The two companies are virtually identical, and both began operations at the beginning of the current year. During the year, each company purchased inventory as follows:

Jan.	4	12,000	units at $4	=	$ 48,000
Apr.	6	5,000	5	=	25,000
Aug.	9	7,000	6	=	42,000
Nov.	27	10,000	7	=	70,000
Totals		34,000			$185,000

Over the first year, both companies sold 25,000 units of inventory.

In early January, both companies purchased equipment costing $200,000 that had a 10-year estimated useful life and a $20,000 residual value. Frycer, Inc. uses the first-in, first-out (FIFO) method for its inventory and straight-line depreciation for its equipment. Bergdahl Ltd. uses last-in, first-out (LIFO) and double-declining-balance depreciation. Both companies' trial balances at December 31 included the following:

Sales revenue	$300,000
Purchases	185,000
Operating expenses	80,000

Required

1. Prepare both companies' income statements, disregarding income taxes.

2. Prepare a schedule that shows why one company appears to be more profitable than the other. Explain the schedule and amounts in your own words. What accounts for the different amounts?

3. Is one company more profitable than the other? Give your reason.

2. *Plant and equipment and intangible assets (L.O. 7, 8)*

The following questions are unrelated except that they apply to fixed assets and intangible assets:

1. The manager of Meadowlake Ltd. regularly buys plant and equipment and debits the cost to Repairs and Maintenance Expense. Why would he do that, since he knows this action violates GAAP?

2. The manager of Spruce Lake Limited regularly debits the cost of repairs and maintenance of plant and equipment to Plant and Equipment. Why would she do that, since she knows she is violating GAAP?

3. It has been suggested that, since many intangible assets have no value except to the company that owns them, they should be valued at $1.00 or zero on the balance sheet. Many accountants disagree with this view. Which view do you support? Why?

Ethical Issue

Champion Air Filters purchased land and a building for a lump sum of $3 million. To get the maximum tax deduction, Champion managers allocated 90 percent of the purchase price to the building and only 10 percent to the land. A more realistic allocation would have been 75 percent to the building and 25 percent to the land.

Required

1. Explain the tax advantage of allocating too much to the building and too little to the land.

2. Was Champion's allocation ethical? If so, state why. If not, why not? Identify who was harmed.

Financial Statement Problems

1. *Property, plant and equipment and intangible assets (L.O. 4, 5, 8)*

Refer to the Schneider Corporation's financial statements in Appendix C and answer the following questions.

1. Which depreciation method does Schneider use for the purposes of reporting to shareholders and creditors in the financial statements? What type of depreciation method does the company use for income tax purposes? Why is this method preferable for income tax purposes?

2. What was the amount of depreciation and amortization expense for 1991? Assume that 80 percent of the depreciation and amortization expense relates to depreciation of plant and equipment (with the balance of this expense relating to the amortization of Other Assets). Record depreciation expense for 1991.

3. The statement of changes in financial position reports purchases of property, plant and equipment and the proceeds (sale prices) received on disposal of equipment. How much were Schneider's additions to property, plant and equipment during 1991? Journalize Schneider's acquisition of these assets. Consider acquisitions only.

4. The statement of changes in financial position notes that Schneider received $168,000 on the sale of plant equipment during 1991. This statement also notes on the bottom portion that a loss on sale of equipment was $387,000. Assume the equipment that was sold had a cost of $955,000. What was the accumulated depreciation of the equipment that was sold? Record the sale of these assets.

2. Capital assets (L.O. 3, 5, 7)

Obtain the annual report of an actual company of your choosing.

Answer these questions about the company. Concentrate on the current year in the annual report you select.

1. Which depreciation method or methods does the company use for reporting to shareholders and creditors in the financial statements? Does the company disclose the estimated useful lives of capital assets for depreciation purposes? If so, identify the useful lives.

2. Depreciation and amortization expenses are often combined since they are similar. Many income statements embed depreciation and amortization in other expense amounts. To learn the amounts of these expenses, it often becomes necessary to examine the Statement of Changes in Financial Position cash flows. Where does your company report depreciation and amortization? What were these expenses for the current year? (Note: The company you selected may have only depreciation — no amortization.)

3. How much did the company spend to acquire capital assets during the current year? Journalize the acquisitions in a single entry.

4. How much did the company receive on the sale of capital assets? Assume a particular cost and accumulated depreciation of the capital assets sold. Journalize the sale of the capital assets, assuming the sale resulted in a $700,000 loss.

5. What categories of intangible assets does the company report? What is their reported amount?

Answers to Self-Study Questions

1. d
2. c [$90,000/($90,000 + $60,000)$120,000 = $72,000;
   $60,000/($90,000 + $60,000)$120,000 = $48,000]
3. b
4. b
5. c
6. a Depreciable cost = $450,000 − $50,000 = $400,000
   $400,000/40 years = $10,000 per year
   $400,000 − ($10,000 10 years) = $300,000/40 years = $7,500 per year
7. d
8. b
9. a $550,000 − ($900,000 − $400,000) = $50,000
10. a

Chapter 11

Current Liabilities and Payroll Accounting

Imagine being a director of a large public corporation, the shares of which are actively traded on the Toronto Stock Exchange, and which is being sued by local residents in one of the communities where it has a factory. The plaintiffs allege that the factory is discharging toxic fumes that have serious short- and long-term health effects. They want over $100 million in damages.

The directors are addressing the issue of how this matter should be disclosed in the annual financial statements. The company recently became aware of the health risk and immediately took steps to reduce the toxic emission. It has confidentially received the advice of experts in the area of toxic wastes who agree with the allegations of the residents with respect to the health effects of emissions. Finally, it knows that if the matter goes to court, damages of at least $25 million will be awarded even if it uses the best legal counsel.

The discussion in the meeting focuses on the effect of reporting this issue on the price of the company's share and how it will be used in court by the plaintiffs. As the litigation has already been widely reported, they agree that the majority of the effect on share price has already occurred (the share price fell by 20 percent immediately after the press reported the suit being initiated). They agree therefore to disclose in the notes to the financial statements the general details of the plaintiff's allegations. The more difficult issue is whether any amount should be charged against the current period's income. Recording any amount in the financial statements will be taken by the plaintiffs as an admission of guilt and will thereby undermine part of the defense. If the full $25 million is recorded, the plaintiffs will argue first that the company is admitting guilt, and second that the $25 million is the least they should receive. Whatever the company does will affect its bargaining position in these proceedings; this is a loss/loss situation.

What would you do?

LEARNING OBJECTIVES

After studying this chapter, you should be able to

1 Account for current liabilities	*4* Make basic payroll entries
2 Account for contingent liabilities	*5* Use a payroll-accounting system
3 Compute payroll amounts	*6* Report current liabilities

A *liability* is an obligation to transfer assets or to provide services in the future. The obligation may arise from a transaction with an outside party. For example, a business incurs a liability when it issues a note payable to buy equipment or to borrow money. Also, the obligation may arise in the absence of individual transactions. For example, interest expense accrues with the passage of time. Until this interest is paid it is a liability. Income tax, a liability of corporations, accrues as income is earned. Proper accounting for liabilities is as important as proper accounting for assets. The failure to record an accrued liability causes the balance sheet to understate the related expense and thus overstate owner's equity. An overly positive view of the business is the result.

> **OBJECTIVE 1**
>
> Account for current liabilities

Current liabilities are obligations due within one year or within the company's operating cycle if it is longer than one year. Obligations due beyond this period of time are classified as long-term liabilities. We discuss long-term liabilities in Chapter 16. We now turn to accounting for current liabilities, including those arising from payroll expenses.

Current Liabilities of Known Amount

Current liabilities fall into one of two categories: those of a known amount and those whose amount must be estimated. We look first at current liabilities of known amount.

Trade Accounts Payable

Amounts owed to suppliers for products or services that are purchased on open account are accounts payable. We have seen many accounts payable examples in previous chapters. For example, a business may purchase inventories and office supplies on an account payable.

Short-Term Notes Payable

Short-term notes payable, a common form of financing, are notes payable that are due within one year. Companies often issue short-term notes payable to borrow cash or to purchase inventory or capital assets. In addition to recording the note payable and its eventual payment, the business must also accrue interest expense and interest payable at the end of the period. The following entries are typical of this liability:

19X1			
Sept. 30	Purchases..	8,000	
	Note Payable, Short-Term		8,000
	Purchase of inventory by issuing a one-year 10 percent note payable.		

Dec. 31   Interest Expense ($8,000 × .10 × ³⁄₁₂)..................   200
     Interest Payable..   200
     Adjusting entry to accrue interest expense
     at year end.

The balance sheet at December 31, 19X1, will report the Note Payable of $8,000 and the related Interest Payable of $200 as current liabilities. The 19X1 income statement will report interest expense of $200.
    The following entry records the note's payment:

19X2
Sept. 30   Note Payable, Short-Term................................   8,000
     Interest Payable...   200
     Interest Expense ($8,000 × .10 × ⁹⁄₁₂)..................   600
      Cash [$8,000 + ($8,000 × .10)]......................   8,800
     Payment of a note payable and interest at
     maturity.

The cash payment entry must split the total interest on the note between the portion accrued at the end of the previous period ($200) and the period's expense ($600).

Short-Term Notes Payable Issued at a Discount

In another common borrowing arrangement, a company may **discount a note payable** at the bank. Discounting means that the bank subtracts the interest amount from the note's face value. The borrower receives the net amount. In effect, the borrower prepays the interest, which is computed on the principal of the note.
    Suppose Inco Ltd. discounts a $100,000, 60-day note payable to their bank at 12 percent. The company will receive $98,027, that is, the $100,000 face value less interest of $1,973 ($100,000 × .12 × ⁶⁰⁄₃₆₅). Assume this transaction occurs on November 25, 19X1. Inco's entries to record discounting the note would be

19X1
Nov. 25   Cash ($100,000 – $1973)...............................   98,027
     Discount on Note Payable ($100,000 × .12 × ⁶⁰⁄₃₆₅).....   1,973
      Note Payable, Short-Term.....................................   100,000
     Discounted a $100,000, 60-day, 12-percent note
     payable to borrow cash.

Discount on Note Payable is a contra account to the liability Note Payable, Short-Term. A balance sheet prepared immediately after this transaction would report the note payable at its net amount of $98,027, as follows:

Current liabilities
    Note payable, short-term............................. $100,000
      Less: Discount on note payable ....   (1,973)
    Note payable, short-term, net.................... $ 98,027

The accrued interest at year end must still be recorded, as it would for any note payable. The adjusting entry at December 31 records interest for 36 days as follows:

19X1
Dec. 31   Interest Expense ($100,000 × .12 × ³⁶⁄₃₆₅)   1,184
     Discount on Note Payable.....................................   1,184
     Adjusting entry to accrue interest expense at year
     end.

This entry credits the Discount account instead of Interest Payable. Why? Because the Discount balance represents future interest expense, and the accrual of interest records the current-period portion of the expense. Furthermore, crediting the Discount reduces this contra account's balance and increases the net amount of the Note Payable. After the adjusting entry, only $789 of the Discount remains, and the carrying value of the Note Payable increases to $99,211, as follows:

Current liabilities		
Note payable, short-term..	$100,000	
Less: Discount on note payable		
($1,973 – $1,184)...	(789)	
Note payable, short-term, net	$ 99,211	

Finally, the business records the note's payment:

19X2			
Jan. 24	Interest Expense ($100,000 × .12 × $^{24}/_{365}$)	789	
	Discount on Note Payable		789
	To record interest expense.		
	Note Payable, Short-Term..	100,000	
	Cash..		100,000
	To pay note payable at maturity.		

After these entries, the balances in the note payable account and the discount account are zero. Each period's income statement reports the appropriate amount of interest expense.

Goods and Services Tax and Sales Tax Payable

There are two basic consumption taxes levied on purchases in Canada that will be visible to the consumer: the goods and services tax (GST) levied by the federal government and provincial sales taxes (PST) levied by all the provinces except Alberta; there are, at present, no sales taxes in the Yukon or the Northwest Territories. There are also excise or luxury taxes, sometimes called "sin taxes," which are a form of sales tax levied by the federal and provincial governments on products such as cigarettes, jewelery and alcoholic beverages; these taxes are hidden in that they are collected by the manufacturer. The focus of discussion in this section will be on the consumption or visible taxes; the goods and services tax and provincial sales taxes will be discussed in turn below. In order to simplify the discussion, the material concerning calculation and payment of the GST will exclude the PST and the material concerning calculation and payment of the PST will generally exclude the GST.

Goods and Services Tax

In 1991, the federal government passed legislation eliminating existing taxes imposed on manufactured and imported goods. At the same time, it implemented a goods and services tax (GST) that is collected from the ultimate consumer and includes most goods and services consumed in Canada. The tax and its application is covered in an introductory tax course and is beyond the scope of this text; the ensuing discussion deals primarily with basic facts about the tax and how to account for it.

There are three categories of goods and services with respect to the GST:

1. Zero-rated supplies such as basic groceries, prescription drugs, and medical devices;
2. Exempt supplies such as educational services, health care services, and financial services; and
3. Taxable supplies, which basically includes everything that is not zero-rated or exempt.

The GST rate is 7 percent. The tax is collected by the individual or entity (called the *registrant*) supplying the taxable good or service (called *taxable supplies*) to the final consumer and remitted to the Receiver General. Suppliers of taxable goods and services have to pay tax on their purchases, but are able to deduct the amount of GST paid (called an *input tax credit*) from the GST they have collected from their sales of goods and services in calculating the amount due the government. The GST Return and the net tax must be remitted to the Receiver General quarterly for most registrants and monthly for larger registrants.

For example, Mary Janicek purchases a power lawn mower with a view to earning money by cutting grass during the summer.[1] The lawn mower cost $250; the GST would be $17.50. Because Mary is planning to use the mower exclusively to cut grass for a fee, she could recover the $17.50. However, she would have to charge all her customers the 7 percent GST on sales of her lawn-mowing services and remit it to the government. During the three-month first quarter, Mary earned revenue of $2,000.00 and thus collected $2,140.00. She spent $107.00; $100.00 plus GST of $7.00 on gasoline for the mower. Her input tax credit of $24.50 included the $17.50 GST on the lawn mower and $7.00 GST on gasoline for the mower. The entries to record these transactions would be

Equipment	267.50	
Cash		267.50
To record purchase of power mower.		
Supplies Expense	107.00	
Cash		107.00
To record purchase of gasoline for power mower.		
Cash	2,140.00	
Lawn-mowing Revenue		2,000.00
GST Payable		140.00
To record revenue earned from mowing lawns.		

Mary would be required to remit $115.50 ($140.00 – $24.50) as her first quarterly payment. Since Mary would be recovering the GST paid on the purchase of the mower and gasoline, she would credit the recovery to the fixed asset account, Equipment, and the expense account, Supplies Expense. The entry would be as follows:

GST Payable	140.00	
Cash		115.50
Equipment		17.50
Supplies Expense		7.00
To record payment of GST payable net of input tax credits.		

Because they collect the GST for the federal Government, the registrants owe the Receiver General the net tax collected; the account Goods and Services Tax Payable is a current liability. For example, Maclean Hunter Limited reports a current liability in its December 31, 1991, financial statements: "Income and other taxes payable $24.1 (millions)." Earlier in the same annual report, Maclean Hunter, as part of Management Discussion and Analysis, indicates that "Sales taxes collected on goods and services, including net Canadian GST" amounted to $64 million in 1991.

Provincial Sales Tax

As was mentioned above, all the provinces, except Alberta, the Yukon and the Northwest Territories, levy a sales tax on sales to the final consumers of products;

---

[1] In reality, Mary Janicek's business would be below the threshold of $30,000, so Mary is unlikely to be a registrant. The scenario is illustrative.

they are not levied on sales to wholesalers or retailers. The final sellers charge their customers the sales tax in addition to the price of the item sold. At the time of this writing, four provinces charge PST on the sum of the price of the good or service purchased plus the GST; three provinces calculate PST and GST separately; and two provinces have harmonized the GST and PST. For example, Nova Scotia charges PST on GST; a taxable sale of $100.00 would have GST of $7.00 (.07 × $100.00) and PST of $10.70 (.10 × ($100.00 + $7.00)). Ontario charges PST and GST separately; a taxable sale of $100.00 would have GST of $7.00 (.07 × $100.00) and PST of $8.00 (.08 × $100.00). Quebec has harmonized the PST and the GST; a taxable sale of $100.00 would have PST and GST of $15.00 [(.08 × $100.00) + (.07 × $100.00)].

Consider Super Stereo Products Inc., an electronics superstore located in Ottawa. Super Stereo does not pay sales tax on its purchase of a TV set from Electrohome but you would have to pay the Province of Ontario's 8 percent provincial sales tax to Super Stereo when you buy an Electrohome set from the store. Super Stereo pays the sales tax to the provincial government. Electrohome would not have a sales tax liability at its year end, but Super Stereo probably would.

Suppose one Saturday's sales at the Super Stereo Store totaled $20,000. The business would have collected an additional 8 percent in sales tax, which would equal $1,600 ($20,000 × .08). The business would record that day's sales as follows:

Cash ($20,000 × 1.08)...	21,600	
Sales Revenue..		20,000
Sales Tax Payable ($20,000 × .08)		1,600
To record cash sales of $20,000 subject to 8 percent sales tax.		

Because the retailers owe the province the sales tax collected, the account Sales Tax Payable is a current liability. For example, Imasco Limited reports a current liability in its December 31, 1991, financial statements — "Income, Excise and Other Taxes" of $139.7 million; it is reasonable to assume that provincial sales taxes would be part of that liability.

Companies forward the collected sales tax to the taxing authority at regular intervals, at which time they debit Sales Tax Payable and credit Cash. Observe that Sales Tax Payable does not correspond to any sales tax expense that the business is incurring. Nor does this liability arise from the purchase of any asset. Rather, it is the cash that the business is collecting for the government.

Many companies consider it inefficient to credit Sales Tax Payable when recording sales. They record the sale in an amount that includes the tax. Then prior to paying tax to the province, they make a single entry for the entire period's transactions to bring Sales Revenue and Sales Tax Payable to their correct balances.

Suppose a company located in Vancouver had sales in July of $100,000, subject to the B.C. retail sales tax of 6 percent. Its summary entry to record the month's sales could be

July 31	Cash ($100,000 × 1.06)..	106,000	
	Sales Revenue...		106,000
	To record sales for the month.		

The entry to adjust Sales Revenue and Sales Tax Payable to their correct balances is

July 31	Sales Revenue [$106,000 – ($106,000 ÷ 1.06)]	6,000	
	Sales Tax Payable		6,000
	To record sales tax.		

Companies that follow this procedure need to make an adjusting entry at the end of the period in order to report the correct amounts of revenue and liability on their financial statements.

Current Portion of Long-Term Debt

Some long-term notes payable and long-term bonds payable must be paid in installments. The **current portion of long-term debt**, or *current maturity*, is the amount of the principal that is due within one year. This amount does not include the interest due. Of course, any liability for accrued interest payable must also be reported but a separate account, Interest Payable, is used for that purpose.

Edmonton Telephones Corporation owed almost $209.5 million on long-term debt at December 31, 1991, the end of its fiscal year. Slightly more than $19.3 million was a current liability because it was due within one year. The remaining $190.2 million was a long-term liability. Edmonton Telephones December 31, 1991, balance sheet reported:

Current Liabilities (in part)	(000s)
Interest payable (Included in Accounts payable)......	$ 7,859
Current portion of debentures payable	19,274

Long-Term Debt and Other Liabilities (in part)	
Long-term debentures payable	$190,192

Accrued Expenses

As shown in the Edmonton Telephones presentation, accrued expenses, such as interest expense, create current liabilities because the interest is due within the year. Therefore, the interest payable (accrued interest) is reported as a current liability. Other important liabilities for accrued expenses are payroll and the related payroll withholdings, which we discuss in the second part of this chapter.

Unearned Revenues   *Ch. 3*

Unearned revenues are also called *deferred revenues, revenues collected in advance* and *customer prepayments*. Each account title indicates that the business has received cash from its customers before earning the revenue. The company has an obligation to provide goods or services to the customer.

The Financial Post may be purchased daily or by means of a subscription. When subscribers pay in advance to have *The Financial Post* delivered to their home or business, Financial Post Publications incurs a liability to provide future service. The liability account is called Unearned Subscription Revenue (which could also be titled Unearned Subscription Income or Deferred Subscription Income).

Assume that Financial Post Publications charges $585 for Mary Bish's three-year subscription to *The Financial Post*. Financial Post Publications' entries would be

19X1
Jan. 1   Cash 585
        Unearned Subscription Revenue 585
        To record receipt of cash at start of a three-year
        subscription.

19X1, 19X2, 19X3
Dec. 31   Unearned Subscription Revenue 195
        Subscription Revenue ($585/3).............................. 195
        To record subscription revenue earned at the end of
        each of three years.

Financial Post Corporation's financial statements would report this sequence:

		December 31	
Balance Sheet	Year 1	Year 2	Year 3
Current liabilities			
Unearned subscription revenue......................................	$390	$195	$-0-

Income Statement	Year 1	Year 2	Year 3
Revenues			
Subscription revenue..	$195	$195	$195

Customer Deposits Payable

Some companies require cash deposits from customers as security on borrowed assets. These amounts are called Customer Deposits Payable because the company must refund the cash to the customer under certain conditions.

For example, telephone companies may demand a cash deposit from a customer before installing a telephone. Utility companies and businesses that lend tools and appliances commonly demand a deposit as protection against damage and theft. When the customer ends the service or returns the borrowed asset, the company refunds the cash deposit — if the customer has paid all the bills and has not damaged the company's property. Because the company generally must return the deposit, that cash is a liability. The uncertainty of when the deposits will be refunded and their relatively small amounts cause many companies to classify Customer Deposits Payable as current liabilities. This is consistent with the concept of conservatism.

Certain manufacturers of products sold through individual dealers, such as Avon or Mary Kay, require deposits from the dealers who sell their products; the deposit is usually equal to the cost of the sample kit provided to the merchandiser. Companies, whose products are sold in returnable containers, collect deposits on those containers. The most common example is the deposit on soda pop bottles. In both cases the deposits are shown as current liabilities by the manufacturers. The amounts are relatively small and so are included with accounts payable and accrued charges.

Current Liabilities That Must Be Estimated

A business may know that a liability exists but not know the amount. The liability may not simply be ignored. The unknown amount of a liability must be estimated for reporting on the balance sheet.

Estimated current liabilities vary among companies. As an example, let us look at Estimated Warranty Payable, a liability account common among merchandisers.

Estimated Warranty Payable

Many manufacturers and some merchandising companies guarantee their products against defects under *warranty* agreements. The warranty period may extend for any length of time. Ninety-day warranties and one-year warranties are common.

Whatever the warranty's lifetime, the matching principle demands that the company record the *warranty expense* in the same period that the business recognizes sales revenue. After all, offering the warranty (and incurring any possible expense through the warranty agreement) is a part of generating revenue through sales. At the time of the sale, however, the company does not know which products are defective. The exact amount of warranty expense cannot be known with certainty, so the business must estimate its warranty expense and open the related liability account — Estimated Warranty Payable (also called *Accrued Warranty Costs* and *Product Warranty Liability*). Even though the warranty liability is a contingency, it is accounted for as an actual liability because the obligation for warranty expense has occurred and its amount can be estimated.

Companies may make a reliable estimate of their warranty expense based on their experience. Assume a company made sales of $200,000, subject to product warranties. Company management, noting that in past years between 2 percent and 4 percent of products proved defective, estimates that 3 percent of the products will require repair or replacement during the one-year warranty period. The company records warranty expense of $6,000 ($200,000 × .03) for the period:

Warranty Expense	6,000	
Estimated Warranty Payable.......................................		6,000
To accrue warranty expense.		

Assume that defective merchandise totals $5,800. The company may either repair or replace it. Corresponding entries follow.

Estimated Warranty Payable	5,800	
Cash		5,800
To repair defective products sold under warranty.		
Estimated Warranty Payable	5,800	
Inventory..		5,800
To replace defective products sold under warranty.		

Note that the expense is $6,000 on the income statement no matter what the cash payment or the cost of the replacement inventory. In future periods, the company may come to debit the liability Estimated Warranty Payable for the remaining $200. However, *when* the company repairs or replaces defective merchandise has no bearing on when the company records warranty expense. The business records warranty expense in the same period as the sale.

Other Estimated Current Liabilities

Estimated Vacation Pay Liability   Most companies grant paid vacations to their employees. The employees receive this benefit during the time they take their vacation, but they earn the compensation by working the other days of the year. The law requires most employers to provide a minimum of two weeks holiday per year, although some employers provide longer holidays to employees who have worked for the company for ten or more years. To match expense with revenue properly, the company accrues the vacation pay expense and liability for each of the 50 workweeks of the year. Then, the company records payment during the two-week vacation period. Employee turnover, terminations, and ineligibility force companies to estimate the vacation pay liability.

Suppose a company's January payroll is $100,000 and vacation pay adds 4 percent (two weeks of annual vacation divided by 50 workweeks each year). Experience indicates that only 80 percent of the vacations owed will be taken, so the January vacation pay estimate is $3,200 ($100,000 × .04 × .80). In Janaury, the company records the vacation pay accrual as follows:

Jan. 31	Vacation Pay Expense	3,200	
	Estimated Vacation Pay Liability		3,200

Each month thereafter, the company makes a similar entry for 4 percent of the payroll.

If an employee takes a vacation in August, his or her $2,000 monthly salary is recorded as follows:

Aug. 31	Estimated Vacation Pay Liability	2,000
	Various Witholding Accounts and	
	Wages Payable[2]	2,000

Estimated Frequent Flyer Liability of an Airline Company   In a typical frequent flyer plan arrangement, a passenger who travels a certain number of kilometres can take a free trip or rent a car or hotel room. The operating expense of providing this free service creates a liability for the airline. When should the expense and estimated frequent flyer liability be recorded? As the airline earns revenue from its paying customers. Under the matching principle, a company should record expense when it earns the related revenue. Because the ultimate cost of providing the free transportation is uncertain, the airline must estimate this expense and the related liability. Suppose Air Canada records revenue of $240,000,000 in February. Further, assume Air Canada estimates this revenue-producing travel will give its Aeroplan frequent flyer customers free trips that are estimated to cost Air Canada 3 percent of the revenue. Air Canada would record Aeroplan expense and liability as follows:

Feb. 28	Aeroplan Expense ($240,000,000 × .03)	7,200,000
	Estimated Aeroplan Liability	7,200,000

In July, when an Areoplan member takes a free trip costing the airline $150, Air Canada could record the transaction as follows:

July 8	Estimated Aeroplan Liability	150
	Various operating expenses	150

The credit side of this entry would depend on the airline's particular situation. The expenses incurred would relate to the cash cost the services provided to the Aeroplan passenger such as ticket and baggage handling, and inflight meals and beverages.

Contingent Liabilities   *Co - Sign , law Suit*

> **OBJECTIVE 2**
>
> Account for contingent liabilities

MUSt DiSClose
to Share Holders

A *contingent liability* is not an actual liability. Instead, it is a potential liability that depends on a *future* event arising out of a past transaction. For example, a town government may sue the company that installed new street lights, claiming that the electrical wiring is faulty. The past transaction is the street-light installation. The future event is the court case that will decide the suit. The lighting company thus faces a contingent liability, which may or may not become an actual obligation.

It would be unethical for the company to withhold knowledge of the lawsuit from its creditors or from anyone considering investing in the business. A person or business could be misled into thinking the company is stronger financially than it really is. The disclosure principle of accounting requires a company to report any information deemed relevant to outsiders of the business. The goal is to arm people with relevant, reliable information for decision-making.

---

[2] The various payroll accounts are discussed later in the chapter.

Sometimes the contingent liability has a definite amount. From Chapter 8 recall that the payee of a discounted note has a contingent liability. If the maker of the note pays at maturity, the contingent liability ceases to exist. However, if the maker defaults, the payee, who sold the note, must pay its maturity value to the purchaser. In this case, the payee knows the note's maturity value, which is the amount of the contingent liability.

Another contingent liability of known amount arises from guaranteeing that a second company will pay a note payable that it owes a third party. This practice, called *cosigning a note*, obligates the guarantor to pay the note and interest if, and only if, the primary debtor fails to pay. Thus the guarantor has a contingent liability until the note becomes due. If the primary debtor pays off, the contingent liability ceases to exist. If the primary debtor fails to pay, the guarantor's liability becomes actual.

Sometimes the amount that will have to be paid, if the contingent liability becomes an actual liability, is not known at the balance sheet date. For example, companies face lawsuits, which may cause possible future obligations of amounts to be determined by the courts. Revenue Canada may have indicated to the entity that a reassessment of its income and taxes has been made or is forthcoming but the company may not know the amount of its liability at the time the financial statements are prepared.

Contingent liabilities are normally disclosed in the notes to the financial statements unless both the confirming future event is likely and the amount of the loss can be reasonably estimated, in which case the amount of the loss should be accrued in the financial statements. When the loss is both likely and estimable, then it is less a contingent loss than a real loss; that is why the loss is accrued or put through the books as of the statement date. For example, suppose Revenue Canada had reassessed a company prior to its year end at December 31, 19X7 disallowing expenses claimed by the company on its 19X5 tax return. If the company decided to accept the reassessment (in which case the confirming future event is likely and the amount known), it should accrue the additional tax payable. If, on the other hand, the company had decided to appeal the reassessment (that is, neither condition is met), the reassessment should be treated as a contingency and shown in the notes.

A few companies draw attention to the footnote describing the contingent liability by making reference to it on the balance sheet. The most common locations for the reference are between liabilities and owners' equity and after owners' equity.

Dreco Energy Services Ltd., an Edmonton based company that designs, manufactures and sells or rents equipment and supplies related to the oil- and gas-drilling and well-servicing business reports the following in the notes to the financial statements under the heading "Contingencies":

(a)   Incidental to the business of the Company, the Company and one or more of its subsidiaries are parties to various lawsuits which allege negligence and liability for product failure or non-performance and claim damages arising therefrom. In management's opinion, to the extent the claims represented by any of these lawsuits are valid, they are either not material or are covered by insurance.

(b)   At August 31, 1991, $5,037,000 ($5,416,000 in 1990) in letters of credit had been issued by the Company in connection with certain contracts and obligations. These letters of credit are released upon performance of the Company's contractual obligations under letters of credit. Should the company default in such performance, the Company will become liable for all or a portion of the outstanding letters of credit.

Summary Problem for Your Review

This problem consists of three independent parts:

1. Suppose a Harvey's hamburger restaurant in Nova Scotia made cash sales of $4,000 subject to the 7 percent GST and 10 percent provincial sales tax. Record the sales and the related consumption taxes (Nova Scotia charges PST on GST). Also record payment of the sales tax to the provincial government and the GST to the Receiver General (assume input tax credits amount to $129.00).

2. Suppose at June 30, 19X2, McCain Foods Ltd. reported a 9 percent long-term debt as follows:

Current Liabilities (in part)	millions
Portion of long-term debt due within one year	$ 3.0
Interest payable ($20.5 \times .09 \times \frac{3}{12}$)...	.46

Long-Term Debt and Other Liabilities (in part)	
Long-term debt	$17.5

Assume the company pays interest on its long-term debt on March 31.
Show how McCain would report its liabilities on the year-end balance sheet at June 30, 19X3. Assume the current maturity of its long-term debt is $4 million and the long-term portion is $18 million.

3. What distinguishes a contingent liability from an actual liability?

SOLUTION TO REVIEW PROBLEM

1.

Cash [($4,000 \times 1.07) \times 1.10$]..	4,708	
Sales Revenue		4,000
GST Payable ($4,000 \times .07$)		280
Sales Tax Payable ($4,280 \times .10$)..		428

To record cash sales and related GST and provincial sales tax.

GST Payable ($280 – $129)...	151	
Sales Tax Payable	428	
Cash...		450
Various accounts to be credited for the input tax credit		129

To pay GST to the Receiver General, net of the input tax credit, and sales tax to the provincial government.

2. McCain Foods Ltd.'s balance sheet at June 30, 19X3 would be as follows:

Current Liabilities (in part)	millions
Portion of long-term debt due within one year..............	$4.0
Interest payable ($22 \times .09 \times \frac{3}{12}$)...	.50

Long-Term Debt and Other Liabilities (in part)	
Long-term debt...	$18.0

3. A contingent liability is a potential liability, which may or may not become an actual liability. It arises out of a past transaction and depends on a future event to determine if it will become an actual liability.

Next class

Accounting for Payroll

OBJECTIVE 3

Compute payroll amounts

Payroll, also called *employee compensation*, is a major expense of many businesses. For service organizations, such as public accounting firms, real estate brokers and travel agents, payroll is the major expense of conducting business. Service organizations sell their employees' service, so employment compensation is their primary cost of doing business, just as cost of goods sold is the largest expense in merchandising.

Employment compensation takes different forms. Some employees collect a **salary**, which is income stated at a yearly, monthly or weekly rate. Other employees work for **wages**, which is employee pay stated at an hourly figure. Sales employees often receive a **commission**, which is a percentage of the sales the employee has made. Some companies reward excellent performance with a **bonus**, an amount over and above regular compensation.

Businesses often pay employees at a base rate for a set number of hours called straight time. For working any additional hours — called *overtime* — the employee receives a higher rate.

Assume that Lucy Childres is an accountant for an electronics company. Lucy earns $600 per week straight time. The company work week runs 40 hours, so Lucy's hourly wage is $15 ($600/40). Her company pays her **time and a half** for overtime. The rate is 150 percent (1.5 times) the straight-time rate. Thus Lucy earns $22.50 for each hour of overtime she works ($15.00 × 1.5 = $22.50). For working 42 hours during a week, she earns $645, computed as follows:

Straight-time pay for 40 hours.................................	$600
Overtime pay for 2 overtime hours (2 × $22.50)......	45
Total pay...	$645

Gross Pay and Net Pay

Many years ago,[3] employees brought home all that they had earned. For example, Lucy Childres would have taken home the full $645 total that she made. Payroll accounting was straightforward. Those days are long past.

The federal government and most provincial governments demand that employers act as collection agents for employee taxes, which are deducted from employee cheques. Insurance companies, labor unions, charitable organizations such as the United Way, and other organizations may also take pieces of employees' pay. Amounts withheld from an employee's cheque are called deductions.

Gross pay is the total amount of salary, wages, commissions, or any other employee compensation before taxes and other deductions are taken out. **Net pay** is the amount that the employee actually takes home.

In addition to employee taxes that employers must withhold from pay, employers themselves must pay some payroll expenses. Many companies also pay employee **fringe benefits**, such as health and life insurance and retirement pay. Payroll accounting has become quite complex. Let us turn now to a discussion of payroll deductions.

---

[3] Income taxes were first imposed by the federal government in Canada in 1917 as a temporary measure to provide funds for the conduct of Canada's efforts in World War I.

Payroll Deductions

Payroll deductions that are *withheld* from employees' pay fall into two categories: (1) *required deductions*, which include employee income tax, unemployment insurance, and Canada Pension or Quebec Pension Plan deductions; and (2) *optional deductions*, which include union dues, insurance premiums, charitable contributions, and other amounts that are withheld at the employee's request. After they are withheld, payroll deductions become the liability of the employer, who assumes responsibility for paying the outside party. For example, the employer pays the government the employee income tax withheld and pays the union the employee union dues withheld.

Required Payroll Deductions

Employee Withheld Income Tax Payable   The law requires most employers to withhold income tax from their employees' salaries and wages. The amount of income tax deducted from gross pay is called **withheld income tax**. For many employees, this deduction is the largest. The amount withheld depends on the employee's gross pay and on the number of withholding allowances the employee claims.

Each employee files a Form TD1 with the employer. Exhibit 11-1 is an example of Form TD1 it has been completed by Roberta C. Dean who has a spouse Pierre, who is an author with an estimated income of $3,000, and two children under the age of 18. Roberta claims $6,456 for herself, $2,918 for Pierre and $417 for each of the children for a total claim of $10,208.[4] Roberta selects a net claim code of 3. Roberta's employer will use the net claim code number to compute the amount of income tax that should be withheld from Roberta's monthly salary.

Revenue Canada provides tax tables each year that the employer uses with the TD1s to calculate the amount of income tax to be withheld each pay period.

The employer sends its employees' withheld income tax to the government. The amount of the income tax withheld determines how often the employer submits tax payments. Most employers must remit the taxes to the government at least monthly; larger employers must remit two or four times a month, depending on the total amounts withheld. Every business must account for payroll taxes on a calendar-year basis regardless of its fiscal year.

The employer accumulates taxes in the Employees' Withheld Income Tax Payable account. The word *payable* indicates that the account is a liability to the employer, even though the employees are the people taxed.

Employee Withheld Canada (or Quebec) Pension Plan Contributions Payable   The **Canada** (or **Quebec**) **Pension Plan** (CPP or QPP) provides retirement, disability and death benefits to employees who are covered by it. Employers are required to deduct premiums from each employee required to make a contribution (basically all employees between 18 and 70 years of age). The maximum pensionable earnings for CPP are $32,200 and the basic exemption is $3,200. The premium is 2.4 percent of wages in excess of the basic exemption of $3,200, up to a maximum contribution in a year of $696.00 [($32,200 – $3,200) × .024]. If CPP is being calculated for weekly wages, the premium would be calculated as 2.4 percent times wages in excess of the weekly exemption of $61.54 ($3,200/52); similarly, CPP would be calculated for employees paid monthly on wages in excess of the monthly exemption of $266.67. For example, if Martine Violette earned $500.00 in the week ending May 5, 19X2, and if her total CPP withholdings for 19X2 were less than $696.00, her employer would withhold $10.52 [($500.00 – $61.54) × 2.4] for CPP in calculating her net pay.

---

[4] Family Allowance was eliminated in 1993. For purposes of discussion, we will use a claim code of 3; an employee may use the code indicated or a lower number.

Revenue Canada provides tables that the employer uses to calculate how much to deduct from each employee's pay each pay period; the tables take into account the basic exemption of $3,200 of income but also assume that the employee will be working for twelve months. For example, if your total employment income was earned when you worked for two months during the summer and earned $2,500 per month, the withholding would be $53.60 each month ($107.20), the normal deduction for an employee earning $2,500 per month. However, based on your total income of $5,000 (2 × $2,500) and the basic exemption of $3,200, the government will require you to pay $43.20 [($5,000 − $3,200) × 2.4)] and will refund your overpayment of $64.00.

Once the employee reaches the maximum contribution of $696.00, the employer stops deducting for that year. Some employees may have had more than one employer in a year; for example, you may have had a job for the summer and now have a part-time job while you are back at school. Canada requires each employer to deduct Canada Pension Plan contributions; however, you recover the overpayment when you file your income tax return for the year.

The employer must remit the Canada Pension Plan contributions withheld and the employer's share, discussed below, every month to Revenue Canada. Larger employers must remit two or four times a month, depending on the amounts withheld.

Employee Withheld Unemployment Insurance Premiums Payable   The

Unemployment Insurance Act requires employers to deduct unemployment insurance premiums from each employee each time that employee is paid. The purpose of the Unemployment Insurance Fund is to provide assistance to contributors to the fund who cannot work for a variety of reasons. The most common reason is that the employee has been laid off; another reason is maternity leave.

Revenue Canada provides tables for calculating withholdings for a range of pay periods. Employees who work less than 15 hours a week or whose projected annual income will not exceed $7,384 are not required to pay unemployment insurance and thus do not have it deducted from their pay. For example, an employee whose monthly income is $500 would not pay unemployment insurance premiums since the gross pay is less than the minimum of $615.33 ($7,384.00/12). The employee premium is 3.0 percent of earnings to a maximum contribution of $1,107.60 (3.0 percent of maximum insurable earnings of $36,920.00). The premium is calulated by taking the amount earned per pay period and multiplying it by 3.0 percent. For example, an employee earning $2,000 per month would pay a premium of $60.00 ($2,000 × 3.0).

As with the Canada Pension Plan, Revenue Canada requires every employer to deduct Unemployment Insurance premiums from every eligible employee. Overpayments may be recovered when the employee files his or her income tax return. The tables attempt to spread the withholding over the year for the employee and to ensure that the maximum yearly withholding is not exceeded. As the section at the base of Panel C of Exhibit 11-2 demonstrates, a maximum withholding per pay period is specified; an employee who is paid monthly will have a maximum wiholding of $92.30.

The employer must remit the Unemployment Insurance premiums withheld and the employer's share, discussed below, to Revenue Canada every month. Larger employers must remit two or four times a month depending on the amounts withheld.

Optional Payroll Deductions

As a convenience to their employees, many companies make payroll deductions and disburse cash according to employee instructions. Union dues, insurance payments, payroll savings plans and gifts to charities such as the United Way are examples. The account Employees' Union Dues Payable holds employee deductions for union membership.

EXHIBIT 11-1 *1992 Personal Tax Credit Return (Form TDI)*

Revenue Canada   Revenu Canada
Taxation   Impôt

page 1

TD1 (E)
Rev.92

1992 Personal Tax Credit Return

Family name (Please print)	Usual first name and initials	Employee number
Dean	Roberta C.	3637

Address	**For non-residents only** Country of permanent residence	Social insurance number
3817 29th Avenue		767 676 767

Owen Sound, Ontario	Postal code: N4K 2x9	Date of Birth: Day 07 Month 02 Year 39

Instructions

Please fill out this form so your employer or payer will know how much tax to deduct regularly from your pay. Otherwise, you will be allowed **only** the basic personal amount of $6,456. Regular deductions will help you avoid having to pay when you file your income tax return.

You must complete this form if you receive   salary, wages, commissions or any other remuneration; superannuation or pension benefits including an annuity payment made under a superannuation or pension fund or plan; Unemployment Insurance benefits including training allowances.

You may also complete this form if you receive payments under registered retirement income funds and/or registered retirement savings plans.

Give the completed form to your employer or payer. If you are a pensioner who receives Canada Pension Plan benefits, Old Age Security or Guaranteed Income Supplements, please send the completed form to the Regional Office of Health and Welfare Canada.

Need help? If you need help to complete this form, ask your employer or payer, or call the Source Deductions section of your Revenue Canada district taxation office. Before you do this, see the additional information on page 2 under "Notes to employees and payees."

1. **Are you a non-resident of Canada?** (See note 1 on page 2.) If so, and you'll be including **less than** 90% of your 1992 total world income when calculating your taxable income earned in Canada, enter claim code 0 in the box on line 17, and sign the form. If you are a resident of Canada, go to item 2.

2. **Basic personal amount.** (Everyone may claim $6,456.) ▶ $6,456.   2.

3. (a) **Are you married and supporting your spouse?** (See notes 4 and 5 on page 2.)
   or
   (b) **Are you single, divorced, separated or widowed and supporting a relative who lives with you who is either your parent or grandparent, OR who is under 19 at the end of 1992, OR 19 or older and infirm?** (See notes 2, 3 and 4 on page 2.)

   Note: A spouse or dependant claimed here cannot be claimed again on lines 4 or 5.

   If you answered yes to either (a) or (b) and your spouse's or dependant's 1992 net income will be:

	$5,918 (c)
under $538, CLAIM $5,380	**Minus:** Spouse's or dependant's net income 3,000 (d)
between $538 and $5,918, CLAIM (e) ⟶	Claim (c minus d) 2,918 (e)
over $5,918, CLAIM $0	

   ▶ 2,918   3.

4. **Do you have any dependants who will be under 19 at the end of 1992?** (See notes 2 and 4 on page 2.) If so, and your 1992 net income will be **higher** than your spouse's, calculate the amount to claim for **each** dependant. If you are not married, please see notes 2, 3 and 4 on page 2.

   Note: If you have three or more dependants who will be under 19 at the end of the year, you do not have to claim them in the order they were born. You may claim them in the **most beneficial** order. For example, if your youngest dependant has a net income of $4,000, and your other two dependants have no income, you could claim your youngest dependant as the first dependant (claim 0). Then you would claim the other two as second and third dependants.

   First and second dependant
   If your dependant's 1992 net income will be:

	$3,107 (c)		Dependants
under $2,690, CLAIM $417	**Minus:**	1st	417
between $2,690 and $3,107, CLAIM (e) ⟶	Dependant's net income 736 (d)	2nd	417
over $3,107, CLAIM $0	Claim (c minus d) 2,471 (e)	3rd	
		4th	

   Third and each additional dependant
   If your dependant's 1992 net income will be:

	$3,524 (c)		5th
under $2,690, CLAIM $834	**Minus:**		6th
between $2,690 and $3,524, CLAIM (e) ⟶	Dependant's net income ____ (d)		
over $3,524, CLAIM $0.	Claim (c minus d) ____ (e)	Total	▶ 834 4.

5. **Do you have any infirm dependants who will be 19 or older at the end of 1992?** (See notes 2 and 4 on page 2.) If so, and your dependant's net income will be:

	$4,273 (c)		Dependants
	Minus:	1st	
under $2,690, CLAIM $1,583	Dependant's net income ____ (d)	2nd	
between $2,690 and $4,273, CLAIM (e) ⟶	Claim (c minus d) ____ (e)	3rd	
over $4,273, CLAIM $0		Total	▶ Nil 5.

6. **Do you receive eligible pension income?** (See note 6 on page 2.) If so, claim your pension income amount or $1,000, whichever is less. ▶ ____   6.

7. **Will you be 65 or older at the end of 1992?** If so, claim $3,482. ▶ ____   7.

8. **Are you disabled?** (See note 7 on page 2.) If so, claim $4,233. ▶ ____   8.

9. **Are you a student?** If so, claim:

   Tuition fees paid for courses you take in 1992 to attend either a university, college or a certified educational institution. If you receive any scholarships, fellowships or bursaries in 1992, subtract the amount over $500 from your tuition fees before you claim them. ____

   $60 for each month in 1992 that you will be enrolled full-time in a qualifying educational program at either a university, college or a school offering job retraining courses or correspondence courses. ____   Total ____ ▶ ____   9.

10.   Total (Add 2 to 9 - Please enter this amount on line 11 on page 2.) 10,208   10.

(See reverse)

Source: Revenue Canada Taxation. Reproduced with permission of the Minister of Supply and Services Canada.

EXHIBIT 11-1   *(continued)*

page 2

11.	Total (from line 10 on page 1) 10,208	11.

12. Are you claiming any transfers of unused pension income, age, disability, tuition fees and education amounts from your spouse and/or dependants? (See note 10 below.)

If your **spouse receives eligible pension income,** you can claim any unused balance to a maximum of $1,000. (See note 6 below.)

If your **spouse will be 65 or older** in 1992, you can claim any unused balance to a maximum of $3,482.

If your **spouse and/or dependants are disabled,** you can claim any unused balance to a maximum of $4,233 for each. (See note 7 below.)

If you are supporting a **spouse and/or dependants who are attending either a university, college or a certified educational institution,** you can claim the unused balance to a maximum of $3,529 for each. (See item 9 on page 1.)

Total ▶ _____ 12.

13. Total claim amount - Add lines 11 and 12. ▶ 10,208 13.

14. Will you or your spouse receive Family Allowance (baby bonus) payments in 1992? If so, your 1992 net income will be **higher** than your spouse's, enter the amount of Family Allowance payments you will receive in 1992. If you are not married, see note 3 below. $(12 \times 44.7) + (12 \times 50.10)$ ▶ 1,129 14.

Voluntary: If your 1992 taxable income will be **more than $29,590,** and you'll be reporting **Family Allowance income,** your employer will not be withholding enough tax. If you wish to have this additional tax withheld, use the following table to calculate the amount and enter the result on line 18. If you already have additional tax withheld, show the total of both amounts on line 18.

Pay period		Number of children		Enter this amount on line 18
Weekly	$1 X	_____	=	$ _____
Biweekly or semimonthly	$2 X	_____	=	$ _____
Monthly	$5 X	_____	=	$ _____

15. Net claim amount - Line 13 minus line 14. ▶ 9,079 15.

16. Is your estimated total income for 1992 (excluding Family Allowance payments) less than your net claim amount on line 15? If so, enter E in the box on line 17, and tax will **not** be deducted from your pay. Otherwise, go to line 17.

17. Net claim code - Match your net claim amount from line 15 with the table below to determine your net claim code, and enter this code in the box. If you already have a code in the box, go to line 18.   [3] 17.

18. Do you want to increase the amount of tax to be deducted from your salary or from other amounts paid to you such as pensions, commissions etc.? (See note 8 below.) If so, state the amount of additional tax you wish to have deducted from each payment. ▶ _____ 18.

19. Will you be living in the Yukon, Northwest Territories or another designated area for more than six months in a row beginning or ending in 1992? If so, claim $7.50 for each day that you live in a designated area, **or** if you maintain a "self-contained domestic establishment" in a designated area, and you are the only person within that establishment claiming this deduction, claim $15 for each day. You **cannot claim** more than 20% of your net income for 1992. (See note 9 below.) ▶ _____ 19.

I CERTIFY that the information given in this return is correct and complete.

Signature   Date

If your status changes, complete a new return within seven days. It's an offence to make a false return.

Notes to employees and payees

1. If you're in doubt about your **non-resident** status, please contact the Source Deductions section of your district office. If you are a non-resident, and you will be including 90% or more of your 1992 total world income when determining your taxable income earned in Canada, you can claim certain personal amounts. Again for more information, contact your district office.

2. A **dependant** is an individual who is dependent on you for support and is either under 19 at the end of 1992, OR 19 or older and physically or mentally infirm. This includes a child, grandchild, parent, grandparent, brother, sister, aunt, uncle, niece or nephew (including in-laws). Except in the case of a child or grandchild, this individual must also be living in Canada.

3. Except for married individuals, the person who receives the **Family Allowance** must report the benefits and claim the amount for dependent children. Whoever claims the dependant for an equivalent-to-married amount must report the Family Allowance for that dependant, regardless of who receives the Family Allowance benefits.

4. Your spouse's or dependant's **net income,** for tax withholding purposes, is the total annual income from all sources including salary, pensions, Old Age Security, UI benefits, Workers' Compensation and social assistance (welfare) payments minus annual deductions for registered pension plan and registered retirement savings plan contributions.

5. If you **marry** during the year, your spouse's net income includes the income earned before and during marriage.

6. **Eligible pension income** includes pension payments received from a pension plan or fund as a life annuity, and foreign pension payments. It does not include payments from Canada or Quebec Pension plans, Old Age Security, guaranteed income supplement and lump-sum withdrawals from a pension fund.

7. To claim a **disability amount,** an individual must be severely impaired (mentally or physically) in 1992 and have a Disability Tax Credit Certificate. Such an impairment must markedly restrict the individual's daily living activites. The impairment must have lasted or be expected to last for a continuous period of at least 12 months.

8. You may find it convenient to deduct additional tax on line 18 for other income you receive that has little or no tax deducted from it. For example, UI benefits, Old Age Security, investment or rental income.

9. **"Self-contained domestic establishment"** means the dwelling house, apartment or similar place where you sleep and eat. It does not include a bunkhouse, dormitory, hotel room or rooms in a boarding house. For more information, including a list of the designated areas, see the *Northern Residents Deductions Tax Guide,* available at any district office.

10. Your spouse and/or dependants must first use any applicable pension income, age, disability, tuition fees and education amounts to reduce their federal tax to zero before they can **transfer** any **unused balance** of these amounts to you.

1992 Net claim codes	
Net claim amount Over - Not over	Claim code
No claim amount	0
$ 0 - $6,456	1
6,456 - 8,037	2
8,037 - 9,619	3
9,619 - 11,202	4
11,202 - 12,783	5
12,783 - 14,364	6
14,364 - 15,946	7
15,946 - 17,527	8
17,527 - 19,109	9
19,109 - 20,693	10
20,693 and over	X
No tax withholding required	E

Cette formule est disponible en français.

Form authorized by the Minister of National Revenue

Employer Payroll Costs

Employers bear expenses for at least three payroll costs: (1) Canada Pension Plan contributions, (2) Unemployment Insurance Plan premiums and (3) Workers' Compensation Plan premiums. In addition, Manitoba and Newfoundland levy a health and post-secondary education tax on employers while Ontario and Quebec levy a health tax on employers in those provinces. As mentioned above, most employers must remit both employee and employer shares monthly. Larger employers must remit twice or four times monthly depending on the size of their payroll. Workers' Compensation payments are remitted quarterly.

Employer Canada Pension Plan Contributions In addition to being responsible for deducting and remitting the employee contribution to the Canada Pension plan, the employer must also pay into the program. The employer must match the employee's contribution of 2.4 percent of gross pay in excess of $3,200 to a maximum payment of $696.00. Every employer must do so whether or not the employee also contributes elsewhere. Unlike the employee, the employer may not obtain a refund for overpayment.

Employer Unemployment Insurance Premiums The employer calculates the employee's premium and remits it together with the employer's share, which is generally 1.4 times the employee's premium, to Revenue Canada. The dollar amount of the employer's contribution would be 1.4 times the maximum employee's contribution of $1,107.60 or $1,550.64. Almost all employers and employees are covered by this program.

Workers' Compensation Premiums Unlike the previous two programs, which are administered by the federal government, the **Workers' Compensation** plan is provincially administered. The purpose of the program is to provide financial support for workers injured on the job. The cost of the coverage is borne by the employer; the employee does not pay a premium to the fund.

In Manitoba, almost all employees are covered by the program. There are over 70 different categories that the Workers' Compensation Board uses to ascertain the cost of coverage. The category a group of workers is assigned to is based on the risk of injury to workers in that group based on that group's and like groups' experience. The employer pays a premium equal to the rate assessed times the employer's gross payroll. Thus, in February 19X2, the employer estimates gross payroll for 19X2 and sends that information plus any premium owing from 19X1 to the provincial government. Premiums, based on that estimated payroll, are remitted quarterly in most cases. In February 19X3, the employer estimates gross payroll for 19X3, calculates any premium owing for 19X2 based on the excess of actual wages over estimated wages for 19X2, and sends the estimate and premium owing to the provincial government.

Provincial Payroll Taxes As was mentioned earlier, certain provinces levy taxes on employers to pay for provincial health care while others levy a combined health care and post-secondary education tax to pay for provincial health care and post-secondary education. Quebec and Newfoundland have fixed rates of tax while the other two provinces vary the rate employers are taxed. In Ontario, the rate of tax increases with the annual payroll amount, while it decreases in Manitoba.

Payroll Withholding Tables

We have discussed the tables that employers use in calculating the withholdings that must be made from employees' wages for income taxes, Canada (or Quebec) Pension contributions and Unemployment Insurance premiums. Exhibit 11-2 provides illustrations of all three tables for a resident of Ontario for 1992. Roberta Dean is paid a salary of $2,000 twice a month (semi-monthly). From Panel A, you can see

EXHIBIT 11-2   *Payroll Withholding Tables*

Panel A
Table 3
Ontario
Semi-Monthly Income Tax Deductions
Basis: 24 Pay Periods Per Year

Semi-Monthly Pay Use appropriate bracket	If the employee's Net Claim Code on Form TD1 Is										
	0	1	2	3	4	5	6	7	8	9	10
From Less than	Deduct from each pay										
1926 – 1952	601.05	528.80	519.95	502.25	484.55	466.85	449.15	431.45	413.75	396.05	378.30
1952 – 1978	611.70	539.45	530.60	512.90	495.20	477.50	459.80	442.10	424.40	406.70	389.00
1978 – 2004	622.40	550.15	541.30	523.60	505.90	488.20	470.50	452.80	435.10	417.40	399.70
2004 – 2030	633.10	560.85	552.00	534.30	516.55	498.85	481.15	463.45	445.75	428.10	410.35
2030 – 2056	643.75	571.50	562.65	544.95	527.25	509.55	491.85	474.15	456.45	438.75	421.05

Panel B
Canada Pension Plan Contributions

Semi-Monthly Pay Period

Remuneration From To	C.P.P.	Remuneration From To	C.P.P.	Remuneration From To	C.P.P.	Remuneration From To	C.P.P.
1336.88 – 1337.28	28.89	1941.88 – 1951.87	43.53	2661.88 – 2671.87	60.81	3381.88 – 3391.87	78.09
1337.29 – 1337.70	28.90	1951.88 – 1961.87	43.77	2671.88 – 2681.87	61.05	3391.88 – 3401.87	78.33
1337.71 – 1338.12	28.91	1961.88 – 1971.87	44.01	2681.88 – 2691.87	61.29	3401.88 – 3411.87	78.57
1338.13 – 1338.53	28.92	1971.88 – 1981.87	44.25	2691.88 – 2701.87	61.53	3411.88 – 3421.87	78.81
1338.54 – 1338.95	28.93	1981.88 – 1991.87	44.49	2701.88 – 2711.87	61.77	3421.88 – 3431.87	79.05
1338.96 – 1339.37	28.94	1991.88 – 2001.87	44.73	2711.88 – 2721.87	62.01	3431.88 – 3441.87	79.29
1339.38 – 1339.78	28.95	2001.88 – 2011.87	44.97	2721.88 – 2731.87	62.25	3441.88 – 3451.87	79.53
1339.79 – 1340.20	28.96	2011.88 – 2021.87	45.21	2731.88 – 2741.87	62.49	3451.88 – 3461.87	79.77
1340.21 – 1340.62	28.97	2021.86 – 2031.87	45.45	2741.88 – 2751.87	62.73	3461.88 – 3471.87	80.01

Panel C
Unemployment Insurance Premiums

For the maximum premium deduction for various pay periods see bottom of this page.

Remuneration From To	U.I. Premium	Remuneration From To	U.I. Premium	Remuneration From To	U.I. Premium	Remuneration From To	U.I. Premium
1926.17 – 1926.49	57.79	1950.17 – 1950.49	58.51	1974.17 – 1974.49	59.23	1998.17 – 1998.49	59.95
1926.50 – 1926.83	57.80	1950.50 – 1950.83	58.52	1974.50 – 1974.83	59.24	1998.50 – 1998.83	59.96
1926.84 – 1927.16	57.81	1950.84 – 1951.16	58.53	1974.84 – 1975.16	59.25	1998.84 – 1999.16	59.97
1927.17 – 1927.49	57.82	1951.17 – 1951.49	58.54	1975.17 – 1975.49	59.26	1999.17 – 1999.49	59.98
1927.50 – 1927.83	57.83	1951.50 – 1951.83	58.55	1975.50 – 1975.83	59.27	1999.50 – 1999.83	59.99
1928.17 – 1928.49	57.85	1952.17 – 1952.49	58.57	1976.17 – 1976.49	59.29	2000.17 – 2000.49	60.01
1928.50 – 1928.83	57.86	1952.50 – 1952.83	58.58	1976.50 – 1976.83	59.30	2000.50 – 2000.83	60.02
1928.84 – 1929.16	57.87	1952.84 – 1953.16	58.59	1976.84 – 1977.16	59.31	2000.84 – 2001.16	60.03

Maximum Premium Deduction for a Pay Period of the stated frequency.	Weekly:	21.30	10 pp per year :	110.76
	Bi-Weekly:	42.60	13 pp per year :	85.20
	Semi-Monthly:	46.15	22 pp per year :	50.35
	Monthly:	92.30		

EXHIBIT 11-3   *Typical Disbursement of Payroll Costs by an Employer Company (Ontario)*

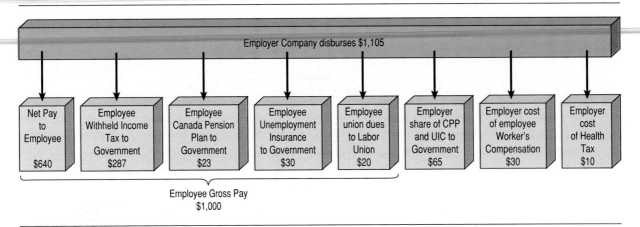

that, based on her net claim code of 3, she would have income tax of $523.60 withheld. Her Canada Pension deduction, Panel B, would be $44.73 and her Unemployment Insurance premium, Panel C, would be $46.15. The Unemployment Insurance table reads $60.00 but remember the maximum premium is $1,107.60; the box at the bottom of the table states that the maximum deduction for an employee paid twice monthly would be $46.15. The employer's share would be $44.73 for Canada Pension (matches employee's share), while the employer's share for Unemployment Insurance would be $64.61 (1.4 times employee share).

Exhibit 11-3 shows a typical disbursement of payroll costs by an employer company for a single employee.

Payroll Entries

Exhibit 11-4 summarizes an employer's entries to record a monthly payroll of $10,000 (all amounts are assumed for illustration only).

Entry A in Exhibit 11-3 records the employer's salary expense, which is the gross salary of all employees ($10,000) for a month. From this amount the employer collects for the federal government income tax, Canada Pension (except in Quebec where it is Quebec Pension) and Unemployment Insurance. Union dues are also collected from this amount by the employer on behalf of the union that represents the employees. The remaining amount is the employees' net (take-home) pay of $7,964. In this payroll transaction the employer acts as a collection agent for Revenue Canada (income tax and Canada Pension), the Unemployment Insurance Commission and the union, withholding the employees' contributions from their gross pay.

Entry B represents the employer's share of Canada Pension and Unemployment Insurance. Remember, the employer's share is 1.0 times and 1.4 times the employee's share respectively for these two deductions.

Entry C records employee benefits paid by the employer. This employer is located in Newfoundland and must pay that province's Health and Post-Secondary Tax. In provinces where there is no provincial health insurance tax, some employers pay employee provincial health insurance premiums as a benefit to the employee and other employers do not. Since provincial health insurance premiums must be paid by law, if the employer did not pay them, they would be deducted from the employees' pay in Entry A. This company also has a life insurance plan for its employees for which it pays the premiums.

In the exhibit, the total payroll expense for the month is made up of base salary ($10,000) plus the employer's share of Canada Pension and Unemployment Insurance ($799) plus fringe benefits ($618 + $182) for a total of $11,599. There

EXHIBIT 11-4   *Payroll Accounting by the Employer*

A.   Salary Expense (or Wage or Commission Expense) 10,000
          Employee Withheld Income Tax Payable 1,200
          Canada Pension Plan Payable 387
          Unemployment Insurance Payable 294
          Employee Union Dues Payable 155
          Salaries Payable to Employees (net pay) 7,964
     To record salary expense and employee withholdings.

B.   Canada Pension and Unemployment Insurance Expense   799
          Canada Pension Plan Payable (1.0 × $387) 387
          Unemployment Insurance Payable (1.4 × $294) 412
     To record employer's share of Canada Pension and
     Unemployment Insurance.

C.   Provincial Employer's Health and Post-Secondary
          Insurance Tax 618
     Employee Life Insurance Expense 182
          Employee Benefits Payable 800
     To record employee benefits payable by employer.

would also be Workers' Compensation, which, you will recall, is paid completely by the employer.

A company's payments to people who are not employees (outsiders called *independent contractors*) are not company payroll expenses. Consider two CAs, Fermi and Scott. Fermi is the corporation's chief financial officer. Scott is the corporation's outside auditor. Fermi is an employee, and his compensation is a debit to Salary Expense. Scott, on the other hand, performs auditing service for many clients, and her payments are debits to Auditing Expense. Any payment for services performed by a person outside the company is a debit to an expense account other than payroll. The account to debit depends on the type of work the independent contractor performs for the business.

The Payroll System

Good business means paying employees all that they have earned — and paying them on time. Also, companies face the legal responsibility of remitting amounts withheld from employees, as we have seen. These demands require companies to process a great deal of payroll data. Efficient accounting is important. To make payroll accounting accurate and effective, accountants have developed the payroll system.

The components of the payroll system are a *payroll register*, a *special payroll bank account*, *payroll cheques*, and an *earnings record* for each employee.

Payroll Register

Each pay period, the company organizes the payroll data in a special journal called the *payroll register* or *payroll journal*. This register lists each employee and the figures the business needs to record payroll amounts. The payroll register, which resembles the cash disbursement register, or cheque register, also serves as a cheque register by providing a column for recording each payroll cheque number.

The payroll register in Exhibit 11-5 includes sections for recording Gross Pay, Deductions, Net Pay, and Account Debited. *Gross Pay* has columns for straight-time

EXHIBIT 11-5 Payroll Register

Week ended December 27, 19X3		a	b	c	d	e	f	g	h	i	j	k	l
		Gross Pay			Deductions					Net Pay		Account Debited	
Employee Name	Hours	Straight-time	Overtime	Total	Federal Income Tax	Canada Pension Plan	Unemploy-ment Insurance	Winnipeg United Way	Total	(c-h) Amount	Cheque No.	Office Salary Expense	Sales Salary Expense
Chen, W.L.	40	500.00		500.00	82.10	10.52	15.00	2.00	109.62	390.38	1621	500.00	
Drago, C.L.	46	400.00	90.00	490.00	71.90	10.28	14.70	2.00	98.88	391.12	1622		490.00
Ellis, M.	41	560.00	21.00	581.00	116.40	10.74	17.43		144.57	463.43	1623	581.00	
Trimble, E.A	40	1,360.00		1,360.00	426.20	31.28	21.30	15.00	493.78	866.22	1641		1,360.00
Total		12,940.00	714.00	13,654.00	3,167.76	327.70	385.12	155.00	4,035.58	9,618.42		4,464.00	9,190.00

pay, overtime pay, and total gross pay for each employee. Columns under the *Deductions* heading vary from company to company. Of course the employer <u>must</u> deduct federal income tax, Canada Pension contributions and Unemployment Insurance premiums. Additional column headings depend on which optional deductions the business handles. In the exhibit, the employer deducts employee withholdings and gifts to United Way and then sends the amounts to the proper parties. The business may add deduction columns as needed. The Net Pay section lists each employee's net (take-home) pay and the number of the cheque issued to him or her. The last two columns indicate the Account Debited for the employee's gross pay. (The company has office workers and sales people.)

In the exhibit, W.L. Chen earned gross pay of $500. His net pay was $390.38, paid with cheque number 1621. Chen is an office worker, so his salary is debited to Office Salaries Expense.

The payroll register in Exhibit 11-5 gives the employer the information needed to record salary expense for the pay period. Using the total amounts for columns d through l, the employer records total salary expense as follows:

Dec. 27	Office Salaries Expense....................................	4,464.00	
	Sales Salaries Expense......................................	9,190.00	
	Employee Withheld Income Tax Payable.		3,167.76
	Employee Withheld Canada Pension		
	Plan Payable		327.70
	Employee Withheld Unemployment		
	Insurance Payable...................................		385.12
	Employee Gifts to United Way Payable ...		155.00
	Salaries Payable to Employees...................		9,618.42

Payroll Bank Account

Once the payroll has been recorded, the company books include a credit balance in Salaries Payable to Employees for net pay of $9,618.42. (See column i in Exhibit 11-5). How the business pays this liability depends on its payroll system. Many companies disburse paycheques to employees from a special payroll bank account. The employer draws a cheque for net pay ($9,618.42 in our illustration) on its regular bank account and deposits this in the special payroll bank account called an *imprest* payroll account. Then the company writes paycheques to employees out of the payroll account. When all the paycheques clear the bank, the payroll account has a zero balance, ready for the activity of the next pay period. Disbursing paycheques from a separate bank account isolates net pay for analysis and control, as discussed later in the chapter.

Other payroll disbursements, for withholdings, union dues, and so on, are neither as numerous nor as frequent as weekly or monthly paycheques. The employer pays taxes, union dues and charities from its regular bank account.

Payroll Cheques

Most companies pay employees by cheque. A *payroll cheque* is like any other cheque except that its perforated attachment lists the employee's gross pay, payroll deductions, and net pay. These amounts are taken from the payroll register. Exhibit 11-6 shows payroll cheque number 1622, issued to C.L. Drago for net pay of $391.12 earned during the week ended December 27, 19X3. To check your ability to use payroll data, trace all amounts on the cheque attachment to the payroll register in Exhibit 11-5.

EXHIBIT 11-6   *Payroll Cheque*

Blumenthal's								1622	
Payroll Account									
Winnipeg, Manitoba					12-27 19 X3				

Pay to the Order of _____ C.L. Drago _____ $ | 391.12

Three hundred and ninety-one & 12/100------------------------ Dollars

Toronto-Dominion Bank
Winnipeg,
Manitoba R2W 3Y1

Anna Figaro
Treasurer

•⑆⑆⑆⑈⑆⑆⑆⑆⑆ 0787⑉ 5000045⑊⑉

Pay			Deductions					Net Pay	Cheque No.
Straight-time	Over-time	Gross	Income Tax	C.P.P.	Unemploy-ment Ins.	United Way	Total		
400.00	90.00	490.00	71.90	10.28	14.70	2.00	98.88	391.12	1622

Recording Cash Disbursements for Payroll _____

Most employers must make at least three entries to record payroll cash disbursements: payments of earnings to employees, payments of payroll withholdings to the government and payments to third parties for employee fringe benefits.

Cash Payments to Employees   When the employer issues payroll cheques to employees, the company debits Salaries Payable to Employees and credits Cash.

Using the data in Exhibit 11-5, the company would make the following entry to record the cash payment (column i) for the December 27 weekly payroll:

Dec. 27	Salaries Payable to Employees.......................	9,618.42	
	Cash...		9,618.42

Sending Payroll Withholdings to the Government and Other Organizations   The employer must send income taxes withheld from employees, pay and the employee deductions and employer's share of Canada (or Quebec) Pension Plan contributions and Unemployment Insurance premiums to Revenue Canada; the payment for a given month is due on or before the 15th day of the following month. In addition, the employer has to remit any withholdings for union dues, charitable gifts, etc.; the payment would probably be made in the following month. Assume federal income tax of $9,880.00, Canada Pension Plan contributions of $953.90, Unemployment Insurance premiums of $1,109.80, and United Way contributions of $465.00 were deducted in calculating the net pay for the employees of Blumenthal's for the three weeks ended December 6, 13 and 20, 19X3. Based on those amounts and columns d through j in Exhibit 11-5, the business would record payments to Revenue Canada for $4,553.58 and Winnipeg United Way for $155.00 as follows:

Jan. 7	Employee Withheld Income Tax	
	Payable ($9,880.00 + $3,167.76).................	13,047.76
	Employee Withheld Canada Pension	
	Plan Payable ($953.90 + $327.70)..............	1,281.60
	Employee Withheld Unemployment	
	Insurance Payable ($1,109.80 + $385.12)..	1,494.92

Jan. 7   Canada Pension Plan Expense (1 × $1,281.60)   1,281.60
          Unemployment Insurance Expense
            (1.4 × $1,494.92) 2,092.88
              Cash..   19,198.76

Jan. 18   Employee Gifts to United Way Payable
            ($465.00 + $155.00)..   620.00
              Cash..   620.00

Recall that Manitoba is one of the provinces that levies a tax on payroll to pay for health and post-secondary education in the province. The tax is payable on or before the 15th of the following month. There is no tax on the first $600,000 of payroll, 4.5 percent on the next $600,000, and 2.25 percent on payroll over $1,200,000. Assume that Blumenthal's payroll passed $600,000 with the November 15, 19X3 payroll and that the payroll and benefits totaled $42,000 for the weeks of December 6, 13, and 20, 19X3. Based on those amounts and the total payroll of December 27, 19X3 from Exhibit 11-5, the journal entry to record payment to the Province of Manitoba follows:

Jan. 10   Health and Post-Secondary Tax Levy Expense
            [($42,000.00 + $13,654.00) × .045] 2,504.43
              Cash 2,504.43

Payments to Third Parties for Fringe Benefits   The employer sometimes pays for employees' dental insurance coverage and for a company pension plan. Assuming the total cash payment for these benefits is $1,927.14, this entry would be

Jan. 10   Employee Benefits Payable............................. 1,927.14
              Cash..   1,927.14

Earnings Record

The employer must file Summary of Remuneration Paid returns with Revenue Canada and must provide the employee with a statement of Remuneration Paid, Form T4, at the end of the year. Therefore, employers maintain an earnings record for each employee. Exhibit 11-7 is a five-week excerpt from the earnings record of employee C.L. Drago.

The employee earnings record is not a journal or a ledger, and it is not required by law. It is an accounting tool, like the work sheet, that the employer uses to prepare payroll tax reports. The information provided on the earnings record with respect to year-to-date earnings also indicates when an employee has earned $29,000, the point at which employer can stop withholding Canada Pension Plan contributions. There is no maximum income tax deduction and recall from Panel C in Exhibit 11-2 that the Unemployment Insurance premium tables indicate the maximum premium deduction for the various pay periods so that the employer will not deduct more than the maximum.

Exhibit 11-8 is the Statement of Remuneration paid, Form T4 Supplementary, for employee C. L. Drago. The employer prepares this form for each employee and a form called a T4 Summary, which summarizes the information on the T4 Supplementaries issued by the employer for that year. The employer sends the T4 Summary and one copy of each T4 Supplementary to Revenue Canada by February 28 each year. Revenue Canada uses the documents to ensure that the employer has correctly paid to the government all amounts withheld on its behalf from employees together with the employer's share. The employee gets two copies of the T4 Supplementary; one copy must be filed with the employee's income tax return while the second copy is for the employee's records. Revenue Canada matches the

Justan Accounting fees

EXHIBIT 11-7 *Employee Earnings Record for 19X3*

Employee Name and Address:

Drago, C.L.
1400 Wellington Crescent
Winnipeg, Manitoba R3P 1E5

Social Insurance No.: 987-010-789
Marital Status: Married
Net Claims Code: 4
Pay Rate: $400 per week
Job Title: Salesperson

Week Ended	Gross Pay					Deductions					Net Pay	
	Hours	Straight-time	Overtime	Total	To Date	Federal Income Tax	Canada Pension Plan	Unemployment Insurance	Winnipeg United Way	Total	Amount	Cheque No.
Nov. 29	40	400.00		400.00	21,340.00	48.00	8.12	12.00	2.00	70.12	329.88	1525
Dec. 6	40	400.00		400.00	21,740.00	48.00	8.12	12.00	2.00	70.12	329.88	1548
Dec. 13	44	400.00	60.00	460.00	22,200.00	63.75	9.56	13.80	2.00	89.11	370.89	1574
Dec. 20	48	400.00	120.00	520.00	22,720.00	78.00	11.00	15.60	2.00	106.60	413.40	1598
Dec. 27	46	400.00	90.00	490.00	23,210.00	71.90	10.28	14.70	2.00	98.88	391.12	1622
Total		20,800.00	2,410.00	23,210.00		2,809.30	480.24	696.30	104.00	4,089.84	19,120.16	

EXHIBIT 11-8 *Employee Statement of Remuneration Paid (Form T4)*

Revenue Canada Revenu Canada
Taxation Impôt

T4 - 1991
Supplementary
Supplémentaire

STATEMENT OF REMUNERATION PAID
ÉTAT DE LA RÉMUNÉRATION PAYÉE

9160631

14 EMPLOYMENT INCOME BEFORE DEDUCTIONS REVENUS D'EMPLOI AVANT RETENUES	16 EMPLOYEE'S PENSION CONTRIBUTIONS CANADA PLAN QUÉBEC PLAN DU CANADA COTISATIONS DE PENSIONS (EMPLOYÉ) DU QUÉBEC	18 EMPLOYEE'S UI PREMIUMS COTISATIONS DE L'EMPLOYÉ À	20 REGISTERED PENSION PLAN CONTRIBUTIONS COTISATIONS À UN RÉGIME DE PENSIONS AGRÉÉ	22 INCOME TAX DEDUCTED IMPÔT SUR LE REVENU RETENU	24 UI INSURABLE EARNINGS GAINS ASSURABLES D'A-C	26 CPP PENSIONABLE EARNINGS GAINS DONNANT DROIT À PENSION - RPC	28 EXEMPT CPP/QPP UI RPC/RR A-C EXEMPTION
23,810,00	480,24	696,30		2,809,30	23,210,00	20,010,00	

BOX 14 AMOUNT ALREADY INCLUDES ANY AMOUNT IN BOXES 30, 32, 34, 36, 38, 40 AND 42 LE MONTANT DE LA CASE 14 COMPREND DÉJÀ TOUS LES MONTANTS DES CASES 30, 92	TAXABLE ALLOWANCES AND BENEFITS ALLOCATIONS ET AVANTAGES IMPOSABLES	32 TRAVEL IN A PRESCRIBED AREA VOYAGE DANS UNE RÉGION VISÉE PAR RÈGLEMENT	34 PERSONAL USE OF EMPLOYER'S AUTO USAGE PERSONNEL DE L'AUTO DE L'EMPLOYEUR	36 INTEREST-FREE AND LOW-INTEREST LOANS PRÊTS SANS INTÉRÊT OU À FAIBLE INTÉRÊT	38 STOCK OPTION BENEFITS OPTION D'ACHAT	40 OTHER TAXABLE ALLOWANCES AND BENEFITS AVANTAGES	42 EMPLOYMENT COMMISSIONS COMMISSIONS D'EMPLOI

30 HOUSING BOARD AND LODGING LOGEMENT PENSION ET LOGEMENT		50 PENSION PLAN OR DPSP REGISTRATION NUMBER NUMÉRO D'ENREGISTREMENT D'UN	52 PENSION ADJUSTMENT FACTEUR D'ÉQUIVALENCE	10 PROVINCE OF EMPLOYMENT PROVINCE	12 SOCIAL INSURANCE NUMBER * NUMÉRO D'ASSURANCE SOCIALE *
				Manitoba	978 010 789

* IF YOUR SOCIAL INSURANCE NUMBER IS NOT SHOWN IN THIS BOX, SEE THE BACK OF THIS FORM.
* SI VOTRE NUMÉRO D'ASSURANCE SOCIALE NE FIGURE PAS DANS

44 UNION DUES COTISATIONS SYNDICALES	46 CHARITABLE DONATIONS DONS DE CHARITÉ	48 PAYMENTS TO DPSP PAIEMENTS À UN RPDB
	104,00	

FOOTNOTES;
NOTES;

INITIALS
INITIALES

EMPLOYEE'S NAME AND ADDRESS - NOM ET ADRESSE DE L'EMPLOYÉ

SURNAME (IN CAPITAL LETTERS) FIRST NAME
NOM DE FAMILLE (EN CAPITALES) PRÉNOM

Drago, C.L.
1400 Wellington Crescent
Winnipeg, Manitoba
R3P 1E5

54 ACCOUNT NUMBER
NUMÉRO DE COMPTE
387 - 035

EMPLOYER'S NAME
NOM DE L'EMPLOYEUR

Blumenthal's

56 EMPLOYEE NUMBER
NUMÉRO DE L'EMPLOYÉ

RETURN WITH T4 SUMMARY
À RETOURNER AVEC LA T4 SOMMAIRE 1

Source: Revenue Canada Taxation. Reproduced with permission of the Minister of Supply and Services Canada.

income on the T4 supplementary filed by the employer against the income reported on the employee's income tax return, filed by the employee, to ensure that the employee properly reported his or her income from employment.

Internal Control over Payroll

The internal controls over cash disbursements discussed in Chapter 7 apply to payroll. In addition, companies adopt special controls in payroll accounting. The large number of transactions and the many different parties involved increase the risk of a control failure. Accounting systems feature two types of special controls over payroll: controls for efficiency and controls for safeguarding cash.

Controls for Efficiency

For companies with many employees, reconciling the bank account can be time consuming owing to the large number of outstanding payroll cheques. For example, a March 30 payroll cheque would probably not have time to clear the bank before a bank statement on March 31. This cheque and others in a March 30 payroll would be outstanding. Identifying a large number of outstanding cheques for the bank reconciliation increases accounting expense. To limit the number of outstanding cheques, many companies use two payroll bank accounts. They make payroll disbursements from one payroll account one month and from the other payroll account the next month. By reconciling each account every other month, a March 30 paycheque has until April 30 to clear the bank before the account is reconciled. This essentially eliminates outstanding cheques, cuts down the time it takes to prepare the bank reconciliation, and decreases accounting expense. Also, many companies' cheques become void if not cashed within a certain period of time. This too limits the number of outstanding cheques.

Other payroll controls for efficiency include following established policies for hiring and firing employees and complying with government regulations. Hiring and firing policies provide guidelines for keeping a qualified, diligent work force dedicated to achieving the business's goals. Complying with government regulations helps companies avoid paying fines and penalties.

Controls for Safeguarding of Cash

Owners and managers of small businesses can monitor their payroll disbursements by personal contact with their employees. Large corporations cannot do so. These businesses must establish controls to assure that payroll disbursements are made only to legitimate employees and for the correct amounts. A particular danger is that payroll cheques may be written to a fictitious employee and cashed by a dishonest employee. To guard against this crime and other possible breakdowns in internal control, large businesses adopt strict internal control policies.

The duties of hiring and firing employees should be separated from the duties of distributing paycheques. Otherwise, a dishonest supervisor, for example, could add a fictitious employee to the payroll. When paycheques are issued, the supervisor could simply pocket the nonexistent person's paycheque for his or her own use.

Requiring an identification badge bearing an employee's photograph helps internal control. Issuing paycheques only to employees with badges ensures only actual employees receive pay.

On occasion management should instruct an employee from the home office, perhaps an internal auditor, to distribute cheques in the branch office personally rather than have the payroll department mail the cheques. No one will claim a paycheque that has been issued to a fictitious employee. Any cheque left over after distribution may signal that payroll fraud has been attempted. Management should pursue an investigation.

A time-keeping system helps ensure that employees have actually worked the number of hours claimed. Having employees punch time cards at the start and end of the work day proves their attendance, as long as management makes sure that no employee punches in and out for others, too. Some companies have their workers fill in weekly or monthly time sheets.

Again we see that the key to good internal control is separation of duties. The responsibilities of the personnel department, payroll department, accounting department, time-card management, and paycheque distribution should be kept separate.

Reporting Payroll Expense and Liabilities

At the end of its fiscal year, the company reports the amount of *payroll liability* owed to all parties: employees, Revenue Canada, provincial governments, unions, and so forth. Payroll liability is *not* the payroll expense for the year. The liability at year end is the amount that is still unpaid. Payroll expense appears on the income statement, payroll liability on the balance sheet.

Inco Limited reported reported accrued payrolls and benefits of approximately $167 million (Inco reports in U.S. funds in its financial statements) as a current liability on its December 31, 1991, balance sheet (Exhibit 11-9). However, Inco's payroll expense for the year far exceeded $167 million; total operating expenses exceeded $2.5 billion. Exhibit 11-9 also presents the other current liabilities that we have discussed in this chapter.

EXHIBIT 11-9   *Partial Inco Limited Balance Sheet*

OBJECTIVE 6
Report current liabilities

Current Liabilities	(U.S. $ in thousands)
Notes payable	$ 74,363
Long-term debt due within one year	205,281
Accounts payable	186,296
Accrued payrolls and benefits	167,004
Accrued interest	46,095
Other accrued liabilities	182,897
Income and mining taxes payable	62,340
Total current liabilities	$924,276

Exhibit 11-10 summarizes all the current liabilities that we have discussed in this chapter.

Computer Accounting Systems for Current Liabilities

Current liabilities arising from a high volume of similar transactions are well suited to computerized accounting. One of the most common transactions of a merchandiser is the credit purchase of inventory. It is efficient to integrate the accounts payable and perpetual inventory systems. When merchandise dips below a predetermined level, the system automatically prepares a purchase request. After the order is placed and the goods are received, inventory and accounts payable data are entered into the computer's memory. The computer reads the memory, then debits Inventory and credits Accounts Payable to account for the purchase. For payments, the computer debits Accounts Payable and credits Cash. The program may also update account balances and print journals, ledger accounts, and the financial statements.

EXHIBIT 11-10   *Categories of Current Liabilities*

Amount of liability known when recorded	Amount of liability that must be estimated when recorded
Trade accounts payable	Warranties payable
Short-term notes payable	Income tax payable
Sales tax payable	Vacation pay liability
Current portion of long-term debt	
Accrued expenses payable:	
Interest payable	
Payroll liabilities (salaries payable, wages payable and commissions payable)	
Payroll withholdings payable (employee and employer)	
Unearned revenues (revenues collected in advance of being earned)	
Customer deposits payable	
Customer prepayments	

The face amount of notes payable and their interest rates and payment dates can be stored for electronic data processing. Computer programs calculate interest, print the interest cheques, journalize the transactions and update account balances.

Payroll transactions are also ideally suited to computer processing. Employee pay rates and withholding data are stored in the computer's memory. Each payroll period, computer operators enter the number of hours worked by each employee. The machine performs the calculations, prints the payroll register and paycheques, and updates the employee earnings records. The program also computes and prepares semi-monthly, monthly, quarterly or annual reports as required by government agencies such as Revenue Canada. Expense and liability accounts are automatically updated for the payroll transactions.

Summary Problem for Your Review

Beth Denius Ltd., a clothing store, employs one salesperson, Alan Kingsley. His straight-time pay is $420 per week. He earns time and a half for hours worked in excess of 35 per week. For Kingsley's wage rate and "net claim code" on his TD1, the income tax withholding rate is approximately 15 percent. Canada Pension is 2.4 percent on income in excess of $61.54 per week while Unemployment Insurance premiums are 3.0 percent. In addition, Denius pays Kingsley's Blue Cross supplemental health insurance premiums of $31.42 a month and dental insurance premiums of $18.50 a month.

During the week ended February 28, 19X3, Kingsley worked 48 hours.

Required

1. Compute Kingsley's gross pay and net pay for the week.
2. Record the following payroll entries that Denius would make:
   a. Expense for Kingsley's wages including overtime pay
   b. Cost of employer's share of Kingsley's withholdings
   c. Expense for fringe benefits

d. Payment of cash to Kingsley
e. Payment Denius must make to Revenue Canada
f. Payment of fringe benefits

3. How much total payroll expense did Denius incur for the week? How much cash did the business spend on its payroll?

SOLUTION TO REVIEW PROBLEM

Requirement 1

Gross pay:

Straight-time for 35 hours..		$420.00
Overtime pay		
Rate per hour ($420/35 × 1.5)	$18.00	
Hours (48 – 35)...	× 13	234.00
Total gross pay..		$654.00

Deductions:

Gross pay		$654.00
Less: Withheld income tax ($654 × .15)...............................	$71.94	
Withheld Canada Pension [($654 – 61.54) × .024]...............	14.21	
Withheld Unemployment Insurance ($654 × .03)..............	19.62	105.77
Net pay..		548.23

Requirement 2

a. Sales Salary Expense..	654.00	
Employee Withheld Income Tax Payable		71.94
Employee Canada Pension Payable		14.21
Employee Unemployment Insurance Payable.................		19.62
Wages payable to employee..		548.23
b. Canada Pension Plan Expense ($14.21 × 1)	14.21	
Unemployment Insurance Expense ($19.62 × 1.4)...............	27.46	
Employer Canada Pension Plan Payable.........................		14.21
Employer Unemployment Insurance Payable		27.46
c. Medical and Dental Expense ($31.42 + $18.50).....................	49.92	
Employee Benefits Payable...		49.92
d. Wages Payable to Employee..	548.23	
Cash..		548.23
e. Employee Withheld Income Tax Payable	71.94	
Employee Canada Pension Payable	14.21	
Employee Unemployment Insurance Payable	19.62	
Employer Canada Pension Plan Payable.............................	14.21	
Employer Unemployment Insurance Payable.....................	27.46	
Cash..		147.44
f. Employee Benefits Payable...	49.92	
Cash..		49.92

Requirement 3

Denius incurred *total payroll expense* of $731.59 (gross salary of $640.00 + employer's cost re Canada Pension of $14.21 + employer's cost re Unemployment Insurance of $27.46 + fringe benefits of $49.92). See entries a to c.

Denius paid cash of $745.59 on payroll (Kingsley's net pay of $548.23 + payment to Revenue Canada of $147.44 + fringe benefits of $49.92). See entries d to f.

Summary

Current liabilities may be divided into those of *known amount* and those that must be *estimated.* Trade accounts payable, short-term notes payable, and the related liability for accrued expenses are among current liabilities of known amount. Current liabilities that must be estimated are warranties payable and a corporation's income tax payable.

Contingent liabilities are not actual liabilities but potential liabilities that may arise in the future. Contingent liabilities, like current liabilities, may be of known amount or an indefinite amount. A business that faces a lawsuit not yet decided in court has a contingent liability of indefinite amount.

Payroll accounting handles the expenses and liabilities arising from compensating employees. Employers must withhold income taxes, Canada (or Quebec) Pension Plan contributions and Unemployment Insurance premiums from employees' pay and send these three *withholdings* together with the employer's share of the latter two to the government. In addition, many employers allow their employees to pay for insurance and union dues and to make gifts to charities through payroll deductions. An employee's net pay is the gross pay less all withholdings and optional deductions.

An *employer's* payroll expenses include the employer's share of Canada (or Quebec) Pension contributions and Unemployment Insurance premiums; employers also pay provincial health and post-secondary taxes in those provinces which levy them and Workers' Compensation. Also, employers may provide their employees with benefits, like payment of the employee's provincial health insurance, life insurance coverage and retirement pensions.

A *payroll system* consists of a payroll register, a payroll bank account, payroll cheques and an earnings record for each employee. Good *internal controls* over payroll disbursements help the business to conduct payroll accounting efficiently and to safeguard the company's cash. The cornerstone of internal controls is the separation of duties.

Current liabilities arising from a high volume of repetitive transactions are well suited to computer processing. Trade accounts payable, notes payable and the related interest, and payroll are three examples.

Self-Study Questions

Test your understanding of the chapter by marking the correct answer for each of the following questions:

1. A $10,000, 9 percent, one-year note payable was issued on July 31. The balance sheet at December 31 will report interest payable of *(p. 474–75)*
   a. $0 because the interest is not due yet
   b. $300
   c. $375
   d. $900

2. If the note payable in the preceding question had been discounted, the cash proceeds from issuance would have been *(p. 475)*

   a. $9,100   c. $9,700
   b. $9,625   d. $10,000

3. Which of the following liabilities creates no expense for the company? *(p. 478)*
   a. Interest   c. Unemployment Insurance
   b. Sales tax   d. Warranty

4. Suppose Canadian Tire estimates that warranty costs will equal 1 percent of tire sales. Assume that November sales totaled $900,000, and the company's outlay

in tires and cash to satisfy warranty claims was $7,400. How much warranty expense should the November income statement report? *(p. 480)*

   a. $1,600   c. $9,000

   b. $7,400   d. $16,400

5. XYZ Company is a defendant in a lawsuit that claims damages of $55,000. On the balance sheet date, it appears unlikely that the court will render a judgment against the company. How should XYZ report this event in its financial statements? *(pp. 482–83)*

   a. Omit mention because no judgment has been rendered

   b. Disclose the contingent liability in a note

   c. Report the loss on the income statement and the liability on the balance sheet

   d. Both b and c

6. Emilie Frontenac's weekly pay for 40 hours is $320, plus time and half for overtime. The tax rate, based on her income level and deductions, is 16 percent, the Quebec Pension Plan rate is 2.4 percent on her weekly earnings in excess of $61.54, and the Unemployment Insurance rate is 3.0 percent on her weekly earnings in excess of $142.00. What is Emilie's take-home pay for a week in which she works 50 hours? *(pp. 485–92)*

   a. $351.58   c. $347.32

   b. $350.01   d. $345.84

7. Which of the following represents a cost to the employer? *(p. 490)*

   a. Withheld income tax   c. Unemployment Insurance

   b. Canada Pension   d. Both b and c

8. The main reason for using a separate payroll bank account is to *(p. 495)*

   a. Safeguard cash by preventing the writing of payroll cheques to fictitious employees

   b. Safeguard cash by limiting paycheques to amounts based on time cards

   c. Increase efficiency by isolating payroll disbursements for analysis and control

   d. All of the above

9. The key to good internal controls in the payroll area is *(p. 500)*

   a. Using a payroll bank account   c. Using a payroll register

   b. Separating payroll duties   d. Using time cards

10. Which of the following items is reported as current liability on the balance sheet? *(p. 501)*

   a. Short-term notes payable   c. Accrued payroll withholdings

   b. Estimated warranties   d. All of the above

Answers to the Self-Study Questions are at the end of the chapter.

Accounting Vocabulary

bonus *(p. 485)*	fringe benefits *(p. 485)*	Unemployment
Canada (or Quebec)	gross pay *(p. 485)*	Insurance *(p. 485)*
Pension Plan *(p. 486)*	net pay *(p. 485)*	wages *(p. 485)*
commission *(p. 485)*	payroll *(p. 485)*	withheld income tax
current portion of	salary *(p. 485)*	*(p. 486)*
long-term debt *(p. 479)*	short-term note payable	Workers' Compensation
discounting a note	*(p. 474)*	*(p. 490)*
payable *(p. 475)*	time and a half *(p. 485)*	

ASSIGNMENT MATERIAL ————————————————

Questions

1. Give a more descriptive account title for each of the following current liabilities: Accrued Interest, Accrued Salaries, Accrued Income Tax.

2. What distinguishes a current liability from a long-term liability? What distinguishes a contingent liability from an actual liability?

3. A company purchases a machine by signing a $21,000, 10 percent, one-year note payable on July 31. Interest is to be paid at maturity. What two current liabilities related to this purchase does the company report on its December 31 balance sheet? What is the amount of each liability?

4. A company borrowed cash by discounting a $15,000, 8 percent, six-month note payable to the bank, receiving cash of $14,400. (a) Show how the amount of cash was computed. Also, identify (b) the total amount of interest expense to be recognized on this note and (c) the amount of the borrower's cash payment at maturity.

5. Explain how GST that is paid by consumers is a liability of the store that sold the merchandise. To whom is it paid?

6. What is meant by the term *current portion of long-term debt*, and how is this item reported in the financial statements?

7. At the beginning of the school term, what type of account is the tuition that your college or university collects from students? What type of account is the tuition at the end of the school term?

8. Why is a customer deposit a liability? Give an example.

9. Patton Company warrants its products against defects for three years from date of sale. During the current year, the company made sales of $300,000. Store management estimated warranty costs on those sales would total $18,000 over the three-year warranty period. Ultimately, the company paid $22,000 cash on warranties. What is the company's warranty expense for the year? What accounting principle governs this answer?

10. Identify two contingent liabilities of a definite amount and two contingent liabilities of an indefinite amount.

11. Describe two ways to report contingent liabilities.

12. Why is payroll expense relatively more important to a service business such as a CA firm than it is to a merchandising company?

13. Two persons are studying Allen Company's manufacturing process. One person is Allen's factory supervisor, and the other person is an outside consultant who is an expert in the industry. Which person's salary is the payroll expense of Allen Company? Identify the expense account that Allen would debit to record the pay of each person.

14. What are two elements of an employee's payroll expense in addition to salaries, wages, commissions, and overtime pay?

15. What determines the amount of income tax that is withheld from employee paycheques?

16. What is the Canada Pension Plan? Who pays it? What are the funds used for?

17. Identify two required deductions and four optional deductions from employee paycheques.

18. Identify three employee benefit expenses an employer pays.

19. Who pays Unemployment Insurance premiums? What are these funds used for?

20. Briefly describe a payroll accounting system's components and their functions.

21. How much Unemployment Insurance has been withheld from the pay of an employee who has earned $52,288 during the current year? How much must the employer pay for this employee?

22. Briefly describe the two principal categories of internal controls over payroll.

23. Why do some companies use two special payroll bank accounts?

24. Identify three internal controls designed to safeguard payroll cash.

Exercises

Exercise 11-1 *Recording sales tax and GST* **(L.O. 1)**

Make general journal entries to record the following transactions of Ransom Distributors, Inc. for a two-month period. Explanations are not required.

Mar. 31 Recorded cash sales of $83,600 for the month, plus provincial sales tax of 8 percent collected on behalf of the province of Saskatchewan and goods and services tax of 7 percent. Record the two taxes in separate accounts.

Apr. 6 Sent March provincial and goods and services taxes to appropriate authorities. Assume no GST input tax credits.

Exercise 11-2 *Accounting for warranty expense and the related liability* **(L.O. 1)**

The accounting records of Shotwell, Inc. included the following balances at the end of the period:

Estimated Warranty Payable	Sales Revenue	Warranty Expense
Beg. bal. 4,100	141,000	

In the past, Shotwell's warranty expense has been 7 percent of sales. During the current period, Shotwell paid $9,430 to satisfy the warranty claims of customers.

Required

1. Record Shotwell's warranty expense for the period and the company's cash payments during the period to satisfy warranty claims. Explanations are not required.
2. What ending balance of Estimated Warranty Payable will Shotwell report on its balance sheet?

Exercise 11-3 *Recording note payable transactions* **(L.O. 1)**

Record the following note payable transactions of McBee Company in the company's general journal. Explanations are not required.

19X2
May 1 Purchased equipment costing $6,000 by issuing a one-year, 10 percent note payable.
Dec. 31 Accrued interest on the note payable.
19X3
May 1 Paid the note payable at maturity.

Exercise 11-4 *Discounting a note payable* **(L.O. 1)**

On November 1, 19X4, Maxwell Company discounted a six-month, $12,000 note payable to the bank at 10 percent.

Required

1. Prepare general journal entries to record (a) issuance of the note, (b) accrual of interest at December 31, and (c) payment of the note at maturity in 19X5.
2. Show how Maxwell would report the note on the December 31, 19X4, balance sheet.

Exercise 11-5 *Reporting a contingent liability* **(L.O. 2)**

Falcon Lamp Corp. is a defendant in lawsuits brought against the marketing and distribution of its products. Damages of $1.8 million are claimed against Falcon, but the company denies the charges and is vigorously defending itself. In a recent talk-show interview, the president of the company stated that he could not predict the outcome of the lawsuits. Nevertheless, he said, management does not believe that any actual liabilities resulting from the lawsuits will significantly affect the company's financial position.

Required

Describe what, if any, disclosure Falcon Lamp should provide of this contingent liability. Total liabilities are $4.7 million. If you believe note disclosure is required, write the note to describe the contingency.

Exercise 11-6 *Accruing a contingency* **(L.O. 2)**

Refer to the Falcon Lamp Corp. situation in the preceding exercise. Suppose that Falcon Lamp's lawyers advise that a preliminary judgment of $500,000 has been rendered against the company.

Required

Describe how to report this situation in the Falcon Lamp Corp. financial statements. Journalize any entry required under GAAP. Explanations are not required.

Exercise 11-7 *Computing net pay* **(L.O. 3)**

Chil Pilsbury is a salesclerk in the men's department of The Bay in Calgary. He earns a base monthly salary of $600 plus a 9 percent commission on his sales. Through payroll deductions, Chil donates $5 per month to a charitable organization and pays dental insurance premiums of $38.25. Compute Chil's gross pay and net pay for December, assuming his sales for the month are $61,300. The income tax rate on his earnings is 20 percent, the Canada Pension Plan contribution is 2.4 percent (subject to the basic deduction of $3,200 and the maximum contribution of $696.00), and the Unemployment Insurance Plan premium rate is 3 percent (subject to the maximum premium of $1,107.60). During the first 11 months of the year, Chil earned $57,140.

Exercise 11-8 *Computing and recording gross pay and net pay* **(L.O. 3, 4)**

Rosemarie Libbus works for a Quik Trip convenience store for straight-time earnings of $8 per hour, with time and a half for hours in excess of 40 per week. Rosemarie's payroll deductions include income tax of 7 percent, Canada Pension is 2.4 percent on earnings in excess of $61 per week, and Unemployment Insurance is 3.0 percent on earnings. In addition, Rosemarie contributes $5 per week to the United Way. Assuming Rosemarie worked 43 hours during the week, (1) compute her gross pay and net pay for the week, and (2) make a general journal entry to record the store's wage expense for Rosemarie's work, including her payroll deductions. Round all amounts to the nearest cent.

Exercise 11-9 *Computing and recording gross pay and net pay* **(L.O. 3, 4)**

Lorna Quigley works as a supervisor for Books Incorporated in Toronto, Ontario. Her semi-monthly pay is $1,951. Her net claim code as per Form TD1 is 1. Lorna does not have any deductions from her pay other than the normal deductions.

Required

Using the tables on Exhibit 11-2, compute Lorna's net pay for the semi-monthly pay period ending February 15, 19X5. Also, prepare the necessary journal entry that Books Incorporated would make in its accounts to record this payment. No explanation is required.

Exercise 11-10 *Recording a payroll (L.O. 3, 4)*

Emilio's Department Store incurred salary expense of $42,000 for December. The store's payroll expense includes Canada Pension of 2.4 percent (ignore the basic exemption for this question) and Unemployment Insurance of 1.4 times the employee rate of 3.0 percent. Also the store provides the following fringe benefits for employees: dental insurance (cost to the store $1,134.68); life insurance (cost to the store $351.07); and pension benefits through a private plan (cost to the store $707.60). Record Emilio's payroll expenses for Canada Pension and Unemployment Insurance and employee fringe benefits.

Exercise 11-11 *Reporting current and long-term liabilities (L.O. 6)*

Suppose Woodward's borrowed $500,000 on December 31, 19X0, by issuing 9 percent long-term debt that must be paid in annual installments of $100,000 plus interest each January 2. By inserting appropriate amounts in the following excerpts from the company's partial balance sheet, show how Woodward's would report its long-term debt.

| | December 31, | | | | |
	19X1	19X2	19X3	19X4	19X5
Current liabilities					
Current portion of long-term debt.........	$ _____	$ _____	$ _____	$ _____	$ _____
Interest payable	$ _____	$ _____	$ _____	$ _____	$ _____
Long-term liabilities					
Long-term debt...	$ _____	$ _____	$ _____	$ _____	$ _____

Excercise 11-12 *Reporting current and long-term liabilities (L.O. 6)*

Assume Wilson Sporting Goods completed these selected transactions during December 19X6:

1. Sport Spectrum, a chain of sporting goods stores, ordered $60,000 worth of baseball and golf equipment. With its order, Sport Spectrum sent a cheque for $60,000. Wilson will ship the goods on January 3, 19X7.

2. The December payroll of $295,000 is subject to employee withheld income tax of 20 percent, Canada Pension Plan expenses of 4.8 percent (employee and employer), Unemployment Insurance deductions of 3.0 percent for the employee and 1.4 time the employee rate of 3.0 percent for the employer. On December 31, Wilson pays employees but accrues all tax amounts.

3. Sales of $2,000,000 are subject to estimated warranty cost of 1.4 percent.

4. On December 2, Wilson signed a $100,000 note payable that requires annual payments of $20,000 plus 9 percent interest on the unpaid balance each December 2.

Required

Report these items on Wilson's balance sheet at December 31, 19X6.

Problems   (Group A)

Problem 11-1A   *Journalizing liability-related transactions* (L.O. 1)

The following transactions of Lancaster Company occurred during 19X2 and 19X3. Record the transactions in the company's general journal. Explanations are not required.

19X2

Feb.   3   Purchased a machine for $4,200, signing a six-month, 11 percent note payable.

28   Recorded the week's sales of $27,000, one third for cash, and two thirds on credit. All sales amounts are subject to a 5 percent provincial sales tax plus 7 percent Goods and Services tax.

Mar. 7   Sent the last week's provincial and Goods and Services taxes to the appropriate authorities.

Apr. 30   Borrowed $100,000 on a 9 percent note payable that calls for annual installment payments of $25,000 principal plus interest.

May 10   Received $1,125 in security deposits from customers. Lancaster refunds most deposits within three months.

Aug.   3   Paid the six-month, 11 percent note at maturity.

10   Refunded security deposits of $1,125 to customers.

Sept. 14   Discounted a $6,000, 12 percent, 60-day note payable to the bank, receiving cash for the net amount after interest was deducted from the note's maturity value.

Nov. 13   Recognized interest on the 12 percent discounted note and paid off the note at maturity.

30   Purchased inventory at a cost of $7,200, signing a 10 percent, three-month note payable for that amount.

Dec. 31   Accrued warranty expense, which is estimated at 3 percent of sales of $145,000.

31   Accrued interest on all outstanding notes payable. Make a separate interest accrual entry for each note payable.

19X3

Feb. 28   Paid off the 10 percent inventory note, plus interest, at maturity.

Apr. 30   Paid the first installment and interest for one year on the long-term note payable.

Problem 11-2A   *Identifying contingent liabilities* (L.O. 2)

Hunting Horn Farm provides riding lessons for girls ages 8 through 15. Most students are beginners, and none of the girls owns her own horse. Janet Christie, the owner of Hunting Horn, uses horses stabled at her farm and owned by the Averys. Most of the horses are for sale, but the economy has been bad for several years and horse sales have been slow. The Averys are happy that Janet uses their horses in exchange for rooming and boarding them. Because of a recent financial setback, Janet cannot afford insurance. She seeks your advice about her business exposure to liabilities.

Required

Write a memorandum to inform Janet of specific contingent liabilities that could arise from the business. It will be necessary to define a contingent liability because she is a professional horse trainer, not a businessperson. Propose a way for Janet to limit her exposure to these possible liabilities.

Problem 11-3A *Computing and reporting payroll amounts* **(L.O. 3, 4)**

The partial monthly records of Friedrich Company show the following figures:

Employee Earnings

(1) Straight-time earnings......	?
(2) Overtime pay......................	$ 5,109
(3) Total employee earnings..	?

Deductions and Net Pay

(4) Withheld income tax.........	9,293
(5) Canada Pension.................	1,852
(6) Unemployment Insurance	2,685

Accounts Debited

(7) Dental and drug insurance.....................	$ 1,373
(8) Total deductions..................	?
(9) Net pay	58,813
(10) Salary Expense.....................	31,278
(11) Wage Expense......................	?
(12) Sales Commission Expense	27,931

Required

1. Determine the missing amounts on lines (1), (3), (8), and (11).

2. Prepare the general journal entry to record Friedrich's payroll for the month. Credit Payrolls Payable for net pay. No explanation is required.

Problem 11-4A *Computing and recording payroll amounts* **(L.O. 3, 4)**

Assume that Greta Gunderson is a commercial lender in Northwest Bank's mortgage department in Dawson Creek. During 19X2, she worked for the bank all year at a $4,500 monthly salary. She also earned a year-end bonus equal to 12 percent of her salary.

Gunderson's monthly income tax withholding for 19X2 was $1,225.90. Also, she paid a one-time withholding tax of $2,316.00 on her bonus cheque. She paid $101.60 per month towards the Canada Pension Plan until the maximum had been withheld. In addition, Gunderson's employer deducted $92.30 per month for unemployment insurance until the maximum had been withheld. Gunderson authorized the following deductions: 1 percent per month of her monthly pay to the Northwest Bank's charitable donation fund and $28.00 per month for life insurance.

Northwest Bank incurred Canada Pension expense equal to the amount deducted from Gunderson's pay. Unemployment Insurance cost the bank 1.4 times the amount deducted from Gunderson's pay. In addition, the bank provided Gunderson with the following fringe benefits: dental and drug insurance at a cost of $52 per month, and pension benefits to be paid to Gunderson upon retirement. The pension contribution is based on her income and was $4,114.00 in 19X2.

Required

1. Compute Gunderson's gross pay, payroll deductions and net pay for the full year 19X2. Round all amounts to the nearest dollar.

2. Compute Northwest Bank's total 19X2 payroll cost for Gunderson.

3. Prepare Northwest Bank's summary general journal entries to record its expense for

   a. Gunderson's total earnings for the year, her payroll deductions and her net pay. Debit Salary Expense and Executive Bonus Compensation as appropriate. Credit liability accounts for the payroll deductions and Cash for net pay.

   b. Employer payroll expenses for Gunderson. Credit liability accounts.

   c. Fringe benefits provided to Gunderson. Credit a liability account.

Problem 11-5A   *Selecting the correct data to record a payroll* **(L.O. 4)**

Assume the following payroll information appeared in the records of a small plant operated by Ford Motor Co. of Canada:

	Payroll for week ended Friday, July 31, 19X4	Payroll for month of July 19X4
Salaries		
Supervisor salaries...	$42,375	$162,639
Office salaries	9,088	37,261
Deductions		
Employee withheld income tax.........................	12,960	50,182
Employee withheld Canada Pension Plan		
contributions	1,266	5,092
Employee Unemployment Insurance..............	1,522	5,980
Employee union dues	708	2,903
Employee Canada Savings Bonds...................	665	2,727
Net Pay...	34,342	133,016
Employer Payroll Costs		
Canada Pension Plan..	1,266	5,092
Unemployment Insurance.................................	2,131	8,372
Worker's Compensation	314	1,599
Employer Cost of Fringe Benefits for Employees		
Dental insurance...	2,034	7,904
Life insurance..	1,053	4,096
Pension	1,667	6,835

Note: One challenge of this problem is to use only the relevant data. Not all the information given is necessary for making the required journal entries.

Required

1. Prepare the general journal entries to record the payroll for the week ended July 31, including all payroll withholdings and expenses.

2. Prepare the general journal entry to record the payment of the week's salaries to employees on July 31.

3. Assume that Ford pays all its liabilities to the federal government once a month while payments to the Worker's Compensation Board are made quarterly. Prepare the general journal entry to record the August 19X9 payment to Revenue Canada. (Liabilities to Revenue Canada include income tax withheld and the employee's share and employer's share of Canada Pension and Unemployment Insurance.)

4. Assume Ford pays all other payroll liabilities (except Worker's Compensation) shortly after the end of the month. Prepare a single general journal entry to record the August 3 payment for these July liabilities.

Problem 11-6A   *Journalizing, posting and reporting liabilities* **(L.O. 1, 2, 4, 6)**

The Loflin Company general ledger at September 30, 19X7, the end of the company's fiscal year, includes the following account balances before adjusting entries. Parentheses indicate a debit balance.

Notes Payable, Short-Term ..	$29,000	Employer Payroll Costs		
Discount on Notes Payable..	(2,100)	Payable.............................		_____
Accounts Payable	88,240	Employee Benefits Payable		_____
Current Portion of Long-......		Estimated Vacation Pay		
Term Debt Payable	_____	Liability.............................		_____
Interest Payable	_____	Sales Tax Payable	$	372
Salary Payable.......................	_____	Property Tax Payable...........		1,433
Employee Withholdings		Unearned Rent Revenue.....		3,900
Payable...............................	_____	Long-Term Debt Payable		220,000

The additional data needed to develop the adjusting entries at September 30 are as follows:

a. The $29,000 balance in Notes Payable, Short-Term consists of two notes. The first note, with a principal amount of $21,000, was issued on August 31, matures one year from date of issuance, and was discounted at 10 percent. The second note, with a principal amount of $8,000, was issued on September 2 for a term of 90 days and bears interest at 9 percent. It was not discounted.

b. The long-term debt is payable in annual installments of $55,000, with the next installment due on January 31, 19X8. On that date, Loflin will also pay one year's interest at 10.5 percent. Interest was last paid on January 31, 19X7. To shift the current installment of the long-term debt to a current liability, debit Long-Term Debt Payable and credit Current Portion of Long-Term Debt Payable.

c. Gross salaries for the last payroll of the fiscal year were $4,319. Of this amount, employee withholdings were $958, and salary payable was $3,361.

d. Employer payroll costs were $755, and Loflin's liability for employee life insurance was $1,004.

e. Loflin estimates that vacation pay is 4 percent of gross salaries of $52,625 for the year.

f. On August 1, the company collected six months' rent of $3,900 in advance.

g. At June 30 ,Loflin is the defendant in a $200,000 lawsuit, which the company expects to win. However, the outcome is uncertain.

Required

1. Open the listed accounts, inserting their unadjusted September 30 balances.

2. Journalize and post the September 30 adjusting entries to the accounts opened. Key adjusting entries by letter.

3. Prepare the liability section of Loflin's balance sheet at September 30.

Problem 11-7A   *Using a payroll register; recording a payroll* **(L.O. 5)**

Assume that payroll records of a district sales office of Purolator Courier provided the following information for the weekly pay period ended December 18, 19X3:

Employee	Hours Worked	Weekly Earnings Rate	Income Tax	Canada Pension	Unemployment Insurance	Earnings through Previous Week
Tina Fortin	43	$400	$ 80.75	$ 9.61	$11.01	$17,060
Leroy Dixon	46	480	109.50	12.82	14.23	22,365
Karol Stastny	41	800	200.00	—	16.00	39,247
David Trent	40	240	32.30	5.10	6.40	3,413

Tina Fortin and David Trent work in the office, and Leroy Dixon and Karol Stastny work in sales. All employees are paid time and a half for hours worked in excess of 40 per week. For convenience, round all amounts to the nearest dollar. Show computations.

Required

1. Enter the appropriate information in a payroll register similar to Exhibit 11-5.
2. Record the payroll information in the general journal.
3. Assume that the first payroll cheque is number 178, paid to Tina Fortin. Record the cheque numbers in the payroll register. Also, prepare the general journal entry to record payment of net pay to the employees.
4. The employer's payroll costs derive from matching the employee's Canada Pension Plan contribution and paying 1.4 times the employee's Unemployment Insurance premium. Record the employer's payroll costs in the general journal.
5. Why is no Canada Pension deducted for Stastny?

Problem 11-8A   *Computing and recording payroll amounts and using a payroll register (L.O. 3, 4, 5)*

The following data pertains to the three salaried employees who work for Layne Ltd., retailer of high fashion clothing in Hamilton, Ontario for the semi-monthly pay period ending June 15, 19X5.

Employee	Gross Pay	Gross pay to May 31 (5 months)	TD1 Net Claim Code	Department
Robbins, M.	$1,951	$19,260	3	Sales
Jennings, P.	1,975	19,780	2	Office
Nelson, W.	2,000	20,000	0	Sales

Layne Ltd. is not obliged to pay Workers' Compensation premiums for these workers. The company pays full premiums on medical/dental coverage for the employees and their families. These semi-monthly premium payments are $65 per employee. Pam Jennings' gross pay to May 31 includes a $5,000 bonus received in April.

Required

1. Determine the net pay which each of these employees will receive on June 15. Use the tables on Exhibit 11-2 to calculate these amounts.
2. Prepare the payroll register for these three employees.
3. Prepare the general journal entry to record payments to the employees of the semi-monthly payroll on June 15, 19X5.

Problem 11-9A   *Reporting current liabilities (L.O. 6)*

Following are six pertinent facts about events during the year at Chevalier Products:

1. On August 31, Chevalier signed a six-month, 12 percent note payable to purchase a machine costing $31,000. The note requires payment of principal and interest at maturity.
2. On October 31, Chevalier received rent of $2,000 in advance for a lease on a building. This rent will be earned evenly over four months.
3. On November 30, Chevalier discounted a $10,000 note payable to St. Lawrence Bank. The interest rate on the one-year note is 12 percent.

4. December sales totaled $104,000 and Chevalier collected provincial sales tax of 5 percent plus Goods and Services tax of 7 percent. This amount will be sent to the appropriate authorities early in January.

5. Chevalier owes $75,000 on a long-term note payable. At December 31, $25,000 of this principal plus $900 of accrued interest are payable within one year.

6. Sales of $909,000 were covered by Chevalier's product warranty. At January 1, estimated warranty payable was $11,300. During the year Chevalier recorded warranty expense of $27,900 and paid warranty claims of $30,100.

Required

For each item, indicate the account and the related amount to be reported as a current liability on Chevalier's December 31 balance sheet.

(Group B)

Problem 11-1B   *Journalizing liability-related transactions (L.O. 1)*

The following transactions of Munoz, Inc., occurred during 19X4 and 19X5. Record the transactions in the company's general journal. Explanations are not required.

19X4

Jan. 9   Purchased a machine at a cost of $5,000, signing a 12 percent, six-month note payable for that amount.

29   Recorded the week's sales of $22,200, three fourths on credit and one fourth for cash. Sales amounts are subject to an additional 6 percent provincial sales tax plus 7 percent GST.

Feb. 5   Sent the last week's provincial and GST tax to the appropriate authorities.

28   Borrowed $300,000 on a 10 percent note payble that calls for annual installment payments of $50,000 principal plus interest.

Apr. 8   Received $778 in deposits from distributors of company products. Munoz refunds the deposits after six months.

July 9   Paid the six-month, 12 percent note at maturity.

Oct. 8   Refunded security deposits of $778 to distributors.

22   Discounted a $5,000, 10 percent, 90-day note payable to the bank, receiving cash for the net amount after interest was deducted from the note's maturity value.

Nov.30   Purchased inventory for $3,100, signing a six-month, 8 percent note payable.

Dec. 31   Accrued warranty expense, which is estimated at 2½ percent of sales of $650,000.

31   Accured interest on all outstanding notes payable. Make a separate interest accrual entry for each note payable.

19X5

Jan.20   Paid off the 10 percent discounted note payable. Made a separate entry for the interest.

Feb. 28   Paid the first installment and interest for one year on the long-term note payble.

May 31   Paid off the 8 percent note plus interest at maturity.

Problem 11-2B   *Identifying contingent liabilities (L.O. 2)*

Covert Buick Company is the only Buick dealer in Nanaimo, British Columbia, and one of the largest Buick dealers on Vancouver Island. The dealership sells new and used cars and operates a body shop and a service department. Duke Covert, the general manager, is considering changing insurance companies because of a disagreement with Doug Stillwell, Nanaimo agent for the Travelers Insurance Company. Travelers is doubling Covert's liability insurance cost for the next year. In discussing insurance coverage with you, a trusted business associate, Stillwell brings up the subject of contingent liabilities.

Required

Write a memorandum to inform Covert Buick Company of specific contingent liabilities arising from the business. In your discussion, define a contingent liability.

Problem 11-3B *Computing and recording payroll amounts (L.O. 3, 4)*

The partial monthly records of The Art Center show the following figures:

Employee Earnings			****		
(1) Straight-time employee earnings	$16,431		(6) Unemployment Insurance....	$	680
			(7) Medical insurance		668
(2) Overtime pay	?		(8) Total deductions		3,409
(3) Total employee earnings	?		(9) Net pay		15,936
Deductions and Net Pay			**Accounts Debited**		
			(10) Salary Expense		?
(4) Withheld income tax	1,403		(11) Wage Expense		4,573
(5) Canada Pension	?		(12) Sales Commission Expense..		5,077

Required

1. Determine the missing amounts on lines (2), (3), (5), and (10).

2. Prepare the general journal entry to record The Art Center's payroll for the month. Credit Payrolls Payable for net pay. No explanation is required.

Problem 11-4B *Computing and recording payroll amounts (L.O. 3, 4)*

Assume that Seth Reichlin is Vice-President of the Bank of Prince Edward Island's (BPEI) leasing operations in Charlottetown. During 19X6 he worked for the company all year at a $3,625 monthly salary. He also earned a year-end bonus equal to 10 percent of his salary.

Reichlin's federal income tax withheld during 19X6 was $985.40 per month. Also, there was a one-time federal withholding tax of $712.50 on his bonus cheque. He paid $85.12 per month into the Canada Pension Plan until he had paid the maximum. In addition, Reichlin paid $92.30 per month to the Unemployment Insurance Commission through his employer until the maximum had been reached. He had authorized the BPEI to make the following payroll deductions: life insurance of $19 per month; United Way of Charlottetown of $35 per month.

The Bank of Prince Edward Island incurred Canada Pension expense equal to the amount deducted from Reichlin's pay and Unemployment Insurance expense equal to 1.4 times the amount Reichlin paid. In addition, the bank paid dental and drug insurance of $32.00 per month and pension benefits of 8 percent of his base salary.

Required

1. Compute Reichlin's gross pay, payroll deductions, and net pay for the full year 19X6. Round all amounts to the nearest dollar.

2. Compute Bank of Prince Edward Island's total 19X6 payroll cost for Reichlin.

3. Prepare BPEI's summary general journal entries to record its expense for
   a. Reichlin's total earnings for the year, his payroll deductions, and his net pay. Debit Salary Expense and Executive Bonus Compensation as appropriate. Credit liability accounts for the payroll deductions and Cash for net pay.

b. Employer payroll expenses on Reichlin. Credit liability accounts.
c. Fringe benefits provided to Reichlin. Credit a liability account.

Problem 11-5B   *Selecting the correct data to record a payroll* **(L.O. 4)**

Assume these payroll data are in the records of *Car and Driver* magazine:

	Payroll for week ended Friday, March 31, 19X9	Payroll for month of March 19X9
Salaries		
Editorial salaries	$6,811	$28,278
Warehousing salaries	3,118	13,128
Deductions		
Employee withheld income tax	2,219	9,773
Employee Canada Pension Plan contributions	192	806
Employee Unemployment Insurance	240	947
Employee contributions to United Way	367	1,545
Employee Canada Savings Bonds	288	1,213
Net pay	6,623	27,122
Employer Payroll Expense		
Canada Pension Plan	192	806
Unemployment Insurance	336	1,326
Worker's Compensation	77	320
Employer Cost of Fringe Benefits for Employees		
Dental insurance	663	2,791
Life insurance	324	1,368
Pensions	451	1,899

Note: One challenge of this problem is to use only the relevant data. Not all the information given is necessary for making the required journal entries.

Required

1. Prepare the general journal entries to record the payroll for the week ended March 31, including all payroll withholdings and expenses.

2. Prepare the general journal entry to record the payment of the week's salaries to employees on March 31.

3. Assume that *Car and Driver* pays all its liabilities to the federal government in a single monthly amount while payments to the Worker's Compensation Board are made quarterly. Prepare the general journal entry to record the April 19X9 payment to Revenue Canada. (Liabilities to Revenue Canada include income tax withheld and the employee's share and employer's share of Canada Pension and Unemployment Insurance.)

4. Assume *Car and Driver* pays all other payroll liabilities (except Worker's Compensation) shortly after the end of the month. Prepare a single general journal entry to record the April 4 payment for these March liabilities.

Problem 11-6B   *Journalizing, posting and reporting liabilities* **(L.O. 1, 2, 4, 6)**

The general ledger of Tea Rose, Inc., at June 30, 19X3, end of the company's fiscal year, includes the following account balances before adjusting entries. Parentheses indicate a debit balance.

Notes Payable, Short-Term.	$ 25,000	Employee Benefits		
Discount on Notes Payable.	(900)	Payable............................		_____
Accounts Payable.................	105,520	Estimated Vacation Pay		
Current Portion of Long-		Liability............................		_____
Term Debt Payable..........	_____	Sales Tax Payable	$	738
Interest Payable	_____	Customer Deposits		
Salary Payable	_____	Payable...........................		6,950
Employee Payroll		Unearned Rent Revenue...		4,800
Withholdings Payable.....	_____	Long-Term Debt Payable ..		120,000
Employer Payroll				
Expense Payable..............	_____			

The additional data needed to develop the adjusting entries at June 30 are as follows:

a. The $25,000 balance in Notes Payable, Short-Term consists of two notes. The first note, with a principal amount of $15,000, was issued on January 31. It matures six months from date of issuance and was discounted at 12 percent. The second note, with a principal amount of $10,000, was issued on April 22 for a term of 90 days. It bears interest at 10 percent. It was not discounted. Interest on this note will be paid at maturity.

b. The long-term debt is payable in annual installments of $40,000 with the next installment due on July 31. On that date, Tea Rose will also pay one year's interest at 9 percent. Interest was last paid on July 31 of the preceding year. To shift the current installment of the long-term debt to a current liability, debit Long-Term Debt Payable and credit Current Portion of Long-Term Debt Payable.

c. Gross salaries for the last payroll of the fiscal year were $5,044. Of this amount, employee payroll withholdings payable were $1,088, and salary payable was $3,956.

d. Employer payroll expense payable was $876, and Tea Rose's liability for employee health insurance was $1,046.

e. Tea Rose estimates that vacation pay expense is 4 percent of gross salaries of $190,500 for the year.

f. On February 1, the company collected one year's rent of $4,800 in advance.

g. At June 30, Tea Rose is the defendant in a $500,000 lawsuit, which the company expects to win. However, the outcome is uncertain.

Required

1. Open the listed accounts, inserting their unadjusted June 30 balances.
2. Journalize and post the June 30 adjusting entries to the accounts opened. Key adjusting entries by letter.
3. Prepare the liability section of the balance sheet at June 30.

Problem 11-7B   *Using payroll register; recording a payroll* **(L.O. 5)**

Assume that the payroll records of a district sales office of Regina Freight Corporation provided the following information for the weekly pay period ended December 21, 19X5:

Employee	Hours Worked	Hourly Earnings Rate	Income Tax	Canada Pension	Unemployment Insurance	Earnings through Previous Week
Maria Kokoros	42	$18	$185.80	$ 0	$ 0	$42,474
James English	47	8	55.90	8.70	11.09	23,154
Louise French	40	11	80.75	9.50	11.90	4,880
Robert LaFlair	41	16	139.80	0	0	39,600

James English and Louise French work in the office, and Maria Kokoros and Robert LaFlair work in sales. All employees are paid time and a half for hours worked in excess of 40 per week. For convenience, round all amounts to the nearest dollar. Show computations.

Required

1. Enter the appropriate information in a payroll register similar to Exhibit 11-5.
2. Record the payroll information in the general journal.
3. Assume that the first payroll cheque is number 319, paid to Maria Kokoros. Record the cheque numbers in the payroll register. Also, prepare the general journal entry to record payment of net pay to the employees.
4. The employer's payroll costs include matching the employee's Canada Pension Plan contribution and paying 1.4 times the employee's Unemployment Insurance premium. Record the employer's payroll costs in the general journal.
5. Why was no Canada Pension or Unemployment Insurance deducted for Kokoros and LaFlair?

Problem 11-8B   *Computing and recording payroll amounts and using a payroll register* **(L.O. 3, 4, 5)**

The following data pertains to three salaried employees who work for Cal Van Auto Ltd., a retailer of automobile parts in Smith Falls, Ontario, for the semi-monthly pay period ending August 15, 19X5.

Employee	Gross Pay	Gross pay to July 31 (7 months)	TD1 Net Claim Code	Department
Wood, D.	$1,944	$ 9,720	1	Sales
Smith, P.	2,025	28,350	2	Office
Peters, S.	2,010	22,550	0	Sales

Cal Van is not obliged to pay Workers' Compensation premiums for these workers. The company pays half of the premiums on medical/dental coverage for their employees and families,with the employee paying the other half through payroll deductions. The total semi-monthly premium payments are $75 per employee.

Required

1. Determine the net pay which each of these employees would receive on August 15. Use the tables on Exhibit 11-2 to calculate these amounts.
2. Prepare the payroll register for these three employees.
3. Prepare the general journal entry to record payment of the semi-monthly payroll on August 15, 19X5.

Problem 11-9B   *Reporting current liabilities* **(L.O. 6)**

Following are six pertinent facts about events during the current year at Woodhaven Sales:

1. On September 30, Woodhaven signed a six-month, 9 percent note payable to purchase inventory costing $30,000. The note requires payment of principal and interest at maturity.
2. On October 31, Woodhaven discounted a $50,000 note payable to the Bank of Newfoundland. The interest rate on the one-year note is 10 percent.
3. On November 30, Woodhaven received rent of $4,200 in advance for a lease on a building. This rent will be earned evenly over three months.

4. December sales totaled $38,000 and Woodhaven Sales collected provincial sales tax of 8 percent plus Goods and Services tax of 7 percent. This amount will be sent to the appropriate authorities early in January.

5. Woodhaven owes $100,000 on a long-term note payable. At December 31, $20,000 of this principal plus $2,100 of accrued interest are payable within one year.

6. Sales of $430,000 were covered by Woodhaven's product warranty. At January 1, estimated warranty payable was $8,100. During the year Woodhaven recorded warranty expense of $22,300 and paid warranty claims of $23,600.

Required

For each item, indicate the account and the related amount to be reported as a current liability on Woodhaven's December 31 balance sheet.

Extending Your Knowledge

Decision Problems

1. Identifying internal control weaknesses and their solution (L.O. 5)

Hall Custom Homes is a large home-building business in Edmonton, Alberta. The owner and manager is Lawrence Hall, who oversees all company operations. He employs 15 work crews, each made up of 6 to 10 members. Construction supervisors, who report directly to Hall, lead the crews. Most supervisors are long-time employees, so Hall trusts them greatly. Hall's office staff consists of an accountant and an office manager.

Because employee turnover is rapid in the construction industry, supervisors hire and terminate their own crew members. Supervisors notify the office of all personnel changes. Also, supervisors forward to the office the employee TD1 forms, which the crew members fill out to claim tax-withholding exemptions. Each Thursday the supervisors submit weekly time sheets for their crews, and the accountant prepares the payroll. At noon on Friday the supervisors come to the office to get paycheques for distribution to the workers at 5 p.m.

Hall's accountant prepares the payroll, including the payroll cheques, which are written on a single payroll bank account. Hall signs all payroll cheques after matching the employee name to the time sheets submitted by the supervisor. Often the construction workers wait several days to cash their paycheques. To verify that each construction worker is a bona fide employee, the accountant matches the employee's endorsement signature on the back of the canceled payroll cheque with the signature on that employee's TD1 form.

Required

1. List one efficiency weakness in Hall's payroll accounting system. How can Hall correct this weakness?

2. Identify one way that a supervisor can defraud Hall under the present system.

3. Discuss a control feature Hall can use to safeguard against the fraud you identified in requirement 2.

2.   Questions about liabilities (L.O. 1, 2)

The following questions are not related.

a. A friend comments that he thought that liabilities represented amounts owed by a company and asks why unearned revenues are shown as a current liability. How would you respond?

b. A warranty is like a contingent liability in that the amount to be paid is not known at year end. Why are warranties payable shown as a current liability while contingent liabilities are reported in the notes to the financial statements?

c. Auditors have procedures for determining whether they have discovered all of a company's contingent liabilities. These procedures differ from the procedures used for determining that accounts payable are correctly stated. If you were an auditor, how would you go about identifying a client's contingent liabilities?

Ethical Issue

IBM is the defendant in numerous lawsuits claiming unfair trade practices. IBM has strong incentives not to disclose these contingent liabilities. However, generally accepted accounting principles require companies to report their contingent liabilities.

Required

1. State why a company would prefer not to disclose its contingent liabilities.

2. Describe how a bank could be harmed if a company seeking a loan did not disclose its contingent liabilities.

3. What is the ethical tightrope that a company must walk in reporting its contingent liabilities?

Financial Statement Problems

1.   Current and contingent liabilities (L.O. 1, 2, 6)

Details about a company's current and contingent liabilities appear in a number of places in the annual report. Use the Schneider financial statements in Appendix C to answer these questions.

1. What is the balance of Schneider's accounts payable at October 26, 1991? What do you think the major components of the accounts payable and accrued liabilities are?

2. How much were the current maturities of Schneider's long-term debt at October 26, 1991? Are any debt issues due to mature in the fiscal year ended October 31, 1992? If there are, describe the issue (Hint: See note 6).

3. Does Schneider have any contingent liabilities at October 26, 1991?

4. Schneider has a number of operating leases outstanding at October 26, 1991. The payments on those leases are not a liability at October 26, 1991, but a specified amount is due in the fiscal year ended October 31, 1992. What is that amount? Why do you think it is reported in the financial statements?

2.   Current and contingent liabilities and payroll (L.O. 1, 2, 6)

Obtain the annual report of an actual company of your choosing. Details about the company's current and contingent liabilities and payroll costs may appear in a number of places in the annual report. Use the statements of the company you select to answer these questions. Concentrate on the current year in the annual report.

1. Give the breakdown of the company's current liabilities at the end of the current year. Journalize the payment in the following year of Accounts Payable reported on the balance sheet.

2. How much of the company's long-term debt at the end of the current year was reported as a current liability? Do the notes to the financial statements identify the specific items of long-term debt coming due within the next year? If so, identify the specific liabilities.

3. Identify the payroll-related current liability at the end of the current year. Give its amount, and record its payment in the next year.

4. Does the company report any unearned revenue? If so, identify the item and give its amount.

5. Where does the company report contingent liabilities — on the face of the balance sheet or in a note? Give important details about the company's contingent liabilities at the end of the current year.

Comprehensive Problem for Part Three

Comparing Two Businesses

At age 25, you invented a mechanical pencil that is now being sold worldwide. After laboring diligently for several years, you have recently sold the business to a large company. Now you are ready to invest in a small resort property located where the golf is great and your family and friends will enjoy visiting. Several locations fit this description: Jekyll Island, Nova Scotia; Long Beach, Vancouver Island; and Kingsmere, Quebec. Each place has its appeal, but Jekyll Island finally wins out. The main allure is that prices there are low, so a dollar will stretch further. Two small resorts are available, both with access to a golf course designed by Jack Nicklaus. The property owners provide the following data:

	Jekyll Island Resort	Kingsmere Resort
Cash	$ 44,100	$ 63,800
Accounts receivable	20,500	18,300
Inventory	74,200	68,400
Land	270,600	269,200
Buildings	1,880,000	1,960,000
Accumulated depreciation	(350,000)	(822,600)
Furniture and fixtures	740,000	933,000
Accumulated depreciation	(207,000)	(416,300)
Total assets	$2,472,400	$2,073,800
Total liabilities	$1,124,300	$1,008,500
Owner equity	1,348,100	1,065,300
Total liabilities and owner equity	$2,472,400	$2,073,800

Income statements for the last three years report total net income before taxes of $441,000 for Jekyll Island Resort and $283,000 for Kingsmere Resort.

Inventories   Jekyll Island uses the FIFO inventory method, and Kingsmere uses the LIFO method. If Jekyll Island had used LIFO, its reported inventory would have been $7,000 lower. If Kingsmere had used FIFO, its reported inventory would have been $6,000 higher. Three years ago there was little difference between LIFO and FIFO amounts for either company.

Capital Assets   Jekyll Island uses the straight-line depreciation method and an estimated useful life of 40 years for buildings and 10 years for furniture and fixtures. Estimated residual values are $480,000 for buildings and $50,000 for furniture and fixtures. Jekyll Island's buildings are 10 years old, and the furniture and fixtures have been used for 3 years.

Kingsmere uses the double-declining-balance method and depreciates buildings over 30 years with an estimated residual value of $460,000. The furniture and fixtures, now 3 years old, are being depreciated over 10 years with an estimated residual value of $85,000.

Accounts Receivable   Jekyll Island uses the direct write-off method for uncollectibles. Kingsmere uses the allowance method. The Jekyll Island owner estimates that $2,000 of Jekyll Island's receivables are doubtful. Prior to the current year, uncollectibles were insignificant. Kingsmere's receivables are already reported at net realizable value.

Required

1. Puzzled at first by how to compare the two resorts, you decide to convert Jekyll Island's balance sheet to the accounting methods and the estimated useful lives used by Kingsmere. Round all depreciation amounts to the nearest $100. The necessary revisions will not affect Jekyll Island's total liabilities.

2. Convert Jekyll Island's total net income for the last three years to reflect the accounting methods used by Kingsmere. Round all depreciation amounts to the nearest $100.

3. Compare the pictures of the two resorts after revising Jekyll Island's figures with the pictures of the two resorts beforehand. Which resort looked better at the outset? Which resort looks better when they are placed on equal footing?

Answers to Self-Study Questions

1. c $10,000 \times .09 \times ^5\!/_{12} = $375
2. a $10,000 - ($10,000 \times .09) = $9,100
3. b
4. c $900,000 \times .01 = $9,000
5. b
6. a Overtime pay: $320/40 = $8 \times 1.5 = $12 per hour $\times$ 10 hours = $120
   Gross pay = $320 + $120 = $440
   Deductions = ($440 \times .16) + [($440 - $61.54) \times .024] + [($440 - $142) \times .03]
   $= $70.40 + 9.08 + 8.94 = $88.42
   Take-home pay = $440.00 - 88.42 = $351.58

7. d
8. c
9. b
10. d

Chapter 12

The Foundation for Generally Accepted Accounting Principles

In 1986, Conrad Black and his flagship company, Hollinger Inc., completed the purchase of 83 percent of The Daily Telegraph PLC (the publisher of one of Britian's most prestigious newspapers) for $259 million. This acquisition put Black in a league with other Canadians such as Lord Beaverbrook and Lord Thompson, owners of some of the largest newspaper and magazine publishing empires in the world.

Several items in the GAAP-prepared, external financial statements of The Daily Telegraph PLC appeared to understate the value of the company. The building that the newspaper owned was recorded at its historical net book value, which was less than its then current fair market value. Black proceeded to sell the building for upwards of $80 million. Further, the financial statements showed unearned revenue for subscription fees — money that had been paid to the company, but for which the newspapers had not yet been delivered in return. Implied in this liability was an asset that was not on the financial statements — a strong and loyal readership that would continue to subscribe

to the newspaper in the future. Finally, the newspaper was poorly managed and used outdated printing technology. Black knew that with a new, decisive, hard-nosed management team, effective use of assets to generate positive cash flows, and a little bit of luck, he could turn Hollinger's investment into one of the more successful business transactions of the 1980s. The jury is still out, but every indication is that Black was right.

What Black and other informed users of financial statements understand is that GAAP financial statements are useful for making business decisions, but often these statements do not tell the whole story. As you read Chapter 12, consider why we continue to use historical costs rather than current costs, why some assets, such as future readership or a skilled work force, are not on the balance sheet, and what the implied challenge is to the accounting profession, maintaining and enhancing the usefulness of external financial statements for making decisions.

Source: W. Michael Fletcher, "The Presses are Rolling," *CGA Magazine* (July 1991), pp. 36-41; and Alexander Ross, "Black Ink," *Canadian Business* (November 1991), pp. 24-29, 32, 34, 36.

LEARNING OBJECTIVES

After studying this chapter, you should be able to

1 Identify the basic objective of financial reporting

2 Identify and apply the underlying concepts of accounting

3 Identify and apply the principles of accounting

4 Allocate revenue to the appropriate period by four methods

5 Report information that satisfies the disclosure principle

6 Apply two constraints to accounting

Throughout the first eleven chapters, we have introduced key concepts and principles as they have applied to the topics under discussion. For example, Chapter 1 introduced the entity concept so that we could account for the transactions of a particular business. In Chapter 2, we discussed the revenue and matching principles as the guidelines for measuring income. Now that you have an overview of the accounting process, we consider the full range of accounting concepts and principles. Collectively, they form the foundation for accounting practice — GAAP.

Every technical field seems to have professional associations and regulatory bodies that govern its practice. Accounting is no exception. In Canada, the Canadian Institute of Chartered Accountants (CICA) has had the responsibility for issuing accounting standards that form the basis of generally accepted accounting principles or GAAP. Initially, from 1946, when the first accounting standard was issued by the CICA's Accounting and Auditing Research Committee, until 1972, the CICA assumed for itself the responsibility for issuing accounting standards.[1]

Then in 1972, the Canadian Securities Administrators, a body composed of officials appointed by the provincial governments with securities exchanges to set securities law, issued National Policy Statement 27 (NP 27) designating the *CICA Handbook* as generally accepted accounting principles (GAAP). In 1975, the *Canada Business Corporations Act* did likewise. The *Ontario Securities Act* in 1978 also designated the *CICA Handbook* as GAAP (Exhibit 12-1). In these ways, the CICA became the official promulgator of generally accepted accounting principles. Exhibit 12-1 illustrates how the authority for setting GAAP is delegated to the CICA by the federal and provincial governments and the Securities Administrators.

From the date of the first accounting standard in 1946 until 1968, some 26 "bulletins" were issued by the Accounting and Auditing Research Committee. In 1968, the CICA changed the format of pronouncements; from that date they became *Recommendations* and were the italicized portions of a looseleaf binder entitled the *CICA Handbook*. Sections 1000 to 4999 (Volume I) of the *Handbook* are concerned with accounting, while Sections 5000 to 9200 (Volume II) are concerned with auditing. The Recommendations are standards or regulations that must be followed, except in those rare cases where a particular Recommendation or Recommendations would not lead to fair presentation. In those cases, the accountant should, using professional judgment, select the appropriate accounting principle. An accountant who determines that the *Handbook* is not appropriate and selects some other basis of accounting must be prepared to defend that decision. The *Handbook* also includes *Accounting Guidelines* and *Auditing Guidelines*. They do not have the force of Recommendations and are issued simply to suggest methods for dealing with issues that are not covered by Recommendations. Frequently, they become replaced eventually by Recommendations on the issues.

---

[1] This material is from George J. Murphy, "A Chronology of the Development of Corporate Financial Reporting in Canada: 1850 to 1983." *The Accounting Historians Journal*, Spring, 1986.

EXHIBIT 12-1 *Flow of Authority for Developing GAAP*

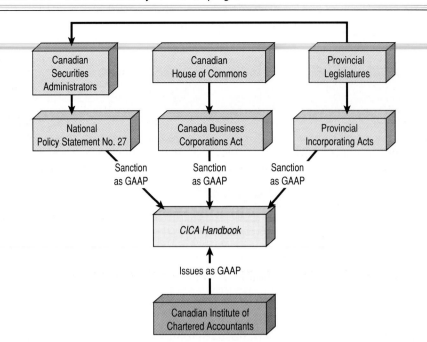

In 1972, the Accounting and Auditing Research Committee was split into two committees — the Accounting Research Committee (ARC), renamed in 1982, the Accounting Standards Committee (AcSC) and the Auditing Standards Committee (AuSC). In 1992, the two committees were renamed the Accounting Standards Board and the Auditing Standards Board respectively. The former has the responsibility for establishing accounting standards, while the latter has the responsibility for establishing auditing standards. The CICA established another standards committee in 1981, the Public Sector Accounting and Auditing Standards Committee (PSAAC), and a new handbook to contain the standards promulgated by that body. The PSAAC issues standards dealing with accounting by and auditing of public sector entities, such as Transport Canada, provincial liquor commissions, municipalities, hospitals and school boards. The Recommendations issued by PSAAC have the same force as standards issued by the Accounting Standards Board and the Auditing Standards Board except that they apply only to public sector entities.

Each new accounting Recommendation issued by the Accounting Standards Board becomes part of GAAP, the "accounting law of the land." In the same way that our laws draw authority from their acceptance by the people, GAAP depends on the general acceptance by the business community. Throughout this book, we refer to GAAP as the proper way to do accounting.

Setting accounting standards is a complex process. The **Accounting Standards Board** does research on a particular issue, for example, the proper accounting for a lease. A document called an exposure draft is issued; it is a draft of the proposed new *Handbook* material. It is distributed by the Accounting Standards Board to all interested parties who are asked to make comments by a specified date. The Accounting Standards Board considers the responses to the exposure draft and issues a new Recommendation, which becomes part of the *Handbook*. Occasionally, the proposed *Handbook* section is redrafted and re-exposed as a re-exposure draft to get additional comments before it is incorporated into the *Handbook*.

The concern had been expressed for some time that the process described in the preceding paragraph was too long and drawn out; that is, the period between the time when a new accounting issue surfaced and the time a Recommendation setting out the proper accounting procedure for the issue was promulgated was too lengthy. The *Report of the Commission to Study the Public's Expectations of Audits* (Macdonald Commission)[2] suggested that the CICA should set up a procedure for dealing with new or emerging issues more expeditiously.

In 1988, the CICA set up the **Emerging Issues Committee** (EIC) to develop appropriate accounting standards for emerging accounting issues on a timely basis. The abstracts of issues published by the EIC are considered to be an authoritative source of GAAP in the absence of an accounting Recommendation. At the time of this writing, 37 abstracts of issues had been published by the EIC.

Individuals and companies often exert pressure on the Accounting Standards Board in their efforts to shape accounting decisions to their advantage. Occasionally governmental bodies have exerted pressure when they perceived that a proposed standard was not in harmony with government policy. Accountants also try to influence accounting decisions.

We have seen that GAAP guides companies in their financial statement preparation. Independent auditing firms of public accountants hold the responsibility for making sure companies do indeed follow GAAP.

Sources of Generally Accepted Accounting Principles

While the primary source of GAAP is the Recommendations in the *CICA Handbook*, they cannot possibly cover all the situations that accountants encounter. When situations not covered by the Recommendations in the *CICA Handbook* arise, Section 1000.60 of the *Handbook* suggests that the accountant should use other accounting principles that are either

1. Generally accepted by virtue of being general practice (accounting principles that have general acceptance even though they are not codified); or of being industry practice (some industries, such as the Canadian Institute of Public Real Estate Companies, or CIPREC, have developed and enunciated principles for their industry); or

2. In the professional judgment of the accountant, consistent with the Recommendations in the *Handbook,* and developed through consultation with or reference to one or more of the following sources:
   a. Other parts of the *Handbook*
   b. General practice
   c. Accounting Guidelines. The Accounting Standards Board issues Guidelines which are that body's interpretations of Recommendations or opinions on issues that are not yet codified as Recommendations
   d. Abstracts of Issues by the Emerging Issues Committee (discussed earlier)
   e. International Accounting Standards. The Canadian Institute of Chartered Accountants, along with the Certified General Accountants Association of Canada and the Society of Management Accountants of Canada, are charter members of the International Federation of Accountants. This body, which includes as members professional accounting organizations in more than 75 countries, is attempting through the International Accounting Standards Committee to harmonize GAAP in those countries by issuing *international accounting standards* (IASs). Other members include the United Kingdom, the

---

[2] The CICA set up an eight-person commission to study the public's expectations of audits; the commission, named for its chairperson, William A. Macdonald, reported in 1988. For a discussion of the Macdonald Commission's findings, see either the *Report of the Commission to Study the Public's Expectations of Audits* published by the CICA, or the July, 1988 issue of *CAmagazine*.

   The commission considered the accounting and auditing standard-setting process as part of its mandate; 6 of the 50 recommendations made by the commission dealt with accounting standards.

United States, the member countries of the European Community, Japan and Australia. Section 1501 of the *Handbook* lists the 30 international accounting standards that have been issued to date. IASs do not override Canadian GAAP as set forth in the *Handbook*, which has precedence as local regulation. The Accounting Standards Board is attempting, where possible, to harmonize the Recommendations in the *CICA Handbook* with the IASs

f. Authoritative pronouncements from other jurisdictions. The Financial Accounting Standards Board (FASB), the body responsible for setting accounting standards in the United States, has issued a number of accounting standards in areas where there may not be a pronouncement from the CICA

g. CICA research studies. The CICA has issued a number of research studies, such as Financial Statements for Pension Plan Participants, that provide guidance to accountants. In addition, the Certified General Accountants Association of Canada and the Society of Management Accountants of Canada publish research studies dealing with accounting issues

h. Accounting texts and professional journals such as *CA magazine* and the *Journal of Accountancy* (published in the U.S. by the AICPA).

If confronted with an accounting issue that is not dealt with by the *CICA Handbook*, you should consider these sources and select the most appropriate treatment, that is, the one that provides the most informative disclosure.

Overview of Generally Accepted Accounting Principles

In December 1988, the then Accounting Standards Committee issued *CICA Handbook* Section 1000, "Financial Statement Concepts." The new section's purpose is to " . . . describe the concepts underlying the development and use of accounting principles in the general purpose financial statements . . . of profit oriented enterprises." The Accouting Standards Committee expected the section to be used by accountants in guiding their professional judgment in the preparation and audit of financial statements.

Accounting principles differ from natural laws like the law of gravity. Accounting principles draw their authority from their acceptance in the business community rather than from their ability to explain physical phenomena. Thus they really are generally accepted by those people and organizations who need guidelines in accounting for their financial undertakings. Exhibit 12-2 diagrams how we move from the objectives of financial reporting to the financial statements.

EXHIBIT 12-2   *Overview of Generally Accepted Accounting Principles*

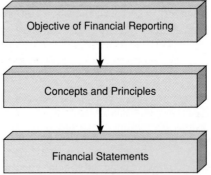

We now look at the objective of financial reporting. This objective tells what financial accounting is intended to accomplish. Thus it provides the goal for accounting information. Next, we examine particular accounting concepts and principles used to implement the objective. What is the difference between a concept and a principle? The concepts are broader in their application, and the principles are more specific. Last, we discuss the financial statements, the end product of financial accounting, and their elements — assets, liabilities, owner's equity revenues, expenses, and so on.

Objective of Financial Reporting

The basic objective of financial reporting is to provide information that is useful in making investment and lending decisions. To be useful in decision-making, the *CICA Handbook*, in Section 1000, states that information in financial statements should be *understandable, relevant, reliable* and *comparable*.

> **OBJECTIVE 1**
> Identify the basic objective of financial reporting

The information must be understandable to users if they are to be able to use it. Relevant information is useful for making predictions and for evaluating past performance. Reliable information is free from error and the bias of a particular viewpoint; it is in agreement with the underlying events and transactions. Comparable information can be compared from period to period to help investors and creditors track the business's progress through time. These characteristics combine to shape the concepts and principles that make up GAAP. Exhibit 12-3 summarizes the qualities that increase the value of accounting information.

EXHIBIT 12-3 *Qualities that Increase the Value of Information for Decision-making*

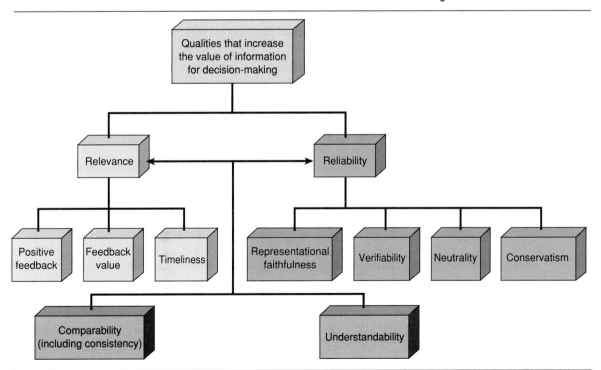

Underlying Concepts

Entity Concept

The **entity concept** is the most basic concept in accounting because it draws a boundary around the organization being accounted for. That is, the transactions of each entity are accounted for separately from transactions of all other organizations and persons, including the owners of the entity. This separation allows us to measure the performance and the financial position of each entity independent of all other entities.

A business entity may be a sole proprietorship (owned and operated by a single individual), a partnership or a large corporation like Petro-Canada. The entity concept applies with equal force to all types and sizes of organizations. The proprietor of a travel agency, for example, accounts for his or her personal transactions separately from those of the business. This division allows the proprietor to evaluate the success or failure of the travel agency. If he or she were to mix personal and business accounting records, it would mean losing sight of of the information needed to evaluate the business alone.

At the other end of the spectrum, Petro-Canada is a giant company with oil exploration, oil-refining, and retail gasoline sales operations. Petro-Canada accounts for each of these divisions separately in order to know which part of the business is earning a profit, which needs to borrow money, and so on. The entity concept also provides the basis for consolidating subentities into a single set of financial statements. Petro-Canada reports a single set of financial statements to the public.

The entity concept also applies to nonprofit organizations such as churches, synagogues and government agencies. A hospital, for example, may have an emergency room, a pediatrics unit and a surgery unit. The accounting system of the hospital should account for each separately to allow the managers to evaluate the progress of each unit.

Going-Concern Concept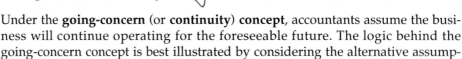

Under the **going-concern** (or **continuity**) **concept**, accountants assume the business will continue operating for the foreseeable future. The logic behind the going-concern concept is best illustrated by considering the alternative assumption: going out of business.

When a business stops, it sells its assets, converting them to cash. This process is called *liquidation*. With the cash, the business pays off its liabilities, and the owners keep any remaining cash. In liquidation, the amount of cash for which the assets are sold measures their current value. Likewise, the liabilities are paid off at their current value. However, if the business does not halt operations — if it remains a going concern — how are its assets and liabilities reported on the balance sheet?

For a going concern, the business reports assets and liabilities based on historical cost. To consider what an asset may be worth on the current market requires making an estimate. This may or may not be objective. Under the going-concern concept, it is assumed the entity will continue long enough for it to recover the costs of its assets.

The going-concern concept allows for the reporting of assets and liabilities as current or long-term, a distinction that investors and creditors find useful in evaluating a company. For example, a creditor wants to know the portion of a company's liabilities that are scheduled to come due within the next year and the portion payable beyond the year. The assumption is that the entity will continue in business and honour its commitment.

Time-Period Concept

The **time-period concept** ensures that accounting information is reported at regular intervals. This timely presentation of accounting data aids the comparison of business operations over time; from year to year, quarter to quarter, and so on. Managers, owners, lenders and other people and businesses need regular reports to assess the business's success — or failure. These persons are making decisions daily.

Although the ultimate success of a company cannot be known for sure until the business liquidates, decision-makers cannot wait until liquidation to learn whether operations yielded a profit.

Nearly all companies use the year as their basic time period. *Annual* reports are common in business. Companies also prepare quarterly and monthly reports (called *interim reports*) to meet managers', investors' and creditors' need for timely information.

The time-period concept underlies the use of accruals. Suppose the business's accounting year ends at December 31 and the business has accrued (but will not pay until the next accounting period) $900 in salary expense. To tie this expense to the appropriate period, the accountant enters this adjusting entry, as we have seen:

Dec. 31   Salary Expense..   900
                    Salary Payable...   900

Accrual entries assign revenue and expense amounts to the correct accounting period and thus help produce meaningful financial statements.

Approximately 66 percent of all companies report their financial statements on a calendar-year basis, January through December; the remaining 34 percent's year ends are spread evenly over the other eleven months.

Stable-Monetary-Unit Concept

Accounting information is expressed primarily in monetary terms. The monetary unit is the prime means of measuring assets. This measure is not surprising given that money is the common denominator in business transactions. In Canada, the monetary unit is the dollar; in Great Britain, the pound sterling; and in Japan, the yen. The stable-monetary-unit concept provides an orderly basis for handling account balances to produce the financial statements.

Unlike a litre, a metre and many other measurements, the value of the monetary unit may change over time. Most of us are familiar with inflation. Groceries that cost $50 three years ago may cost $55 today. The value of the dollar changes. In view of the fact that the dollar does not maintain a constant value, how does a business measure the worth of assets and liabilities acquired over a long span of time? The business records all assets and liabilities at cost. Each asset and each liability on the balance sheet is the sum of all the individual dollar amounts added over time. For example, if a company bought 40 hectares of land in 1975 for $60,000 and another 40 hectares of land in 1985 for $300,000, the asset Land on the balance sheet carries a $360,000 balance, and the change in the purchasing power of the dollar is ignored. The **stable-monetary-unit concept** is the accountant's basis for ignoring the effect of inflation and making no adjustments for the changing value of the dollar. Let us look at the shortcomings of this concept.

Suppose another company paid $600,000 for the same 80 hectares of land in 1993. Its land would be the same as the preceding company's land, but its balance sheet would show a much higher amount for the land. How do we compare the two companies' balance sheets? The comparison based on the stable-monetary-unit concept may not be valid because mixing dollar values at different times is like mixing apples and oranges.

Some businesspeople and academics believe that accounting information must be restated for changes in the dollar's purchasing power. *CICA Handbook*, Section 4510, "Reporting the Effects of Changing Prices," was part of the *Handbook* from its insertion in December, 1982, until its withdrawal in March, 1992. In Section 4510, the CICA encouraged large companies to present supplementary, inflation-adjusted information in their financial reports. Generally, however, accounting is based on historical costs.

Accounting Principles

Reliability (Objectivity) Principle

OBJECTIVE 3

Identify and apply the principles of accounting

The **reliability principle** requires that accounting information be dependable — free from significant error and bias. Users of accounting information may rely on its truthfulness. To be reliable, information must be verifiable by people outside the business. Financial statement users may consider information reliable if independent experts agree that the information is based on objective and honest measurement.

Consider the error from a company's failure to accrue interest revenue at the end of an accounting period. This error results in understated interest revenue and understated net income. Clearly, this company's accounting information is unreliable.

Biased information, data prepared from a particular viewpoint and not based on objective facts, is also unreliable. Suppose a company purchased inventory for $25,000. At the end of the accounting period, the inventory has declined in value and can be replaced for $20,000. Under the lower-of-cost-or-market rule, the company must record a $5,000 loss for the decrease in the inventory's value. Company management may believe that the appropriate value for the inventory is $22,000, but that amount is only an opinion. If management reports the $22,000 figure, total assets and owner's equity will be overstated on the balance sheet. Income will be overstated on the income statement.

To establish a *reliable* figure for the inventory's value, management could get a current price list from the inventory supplier or call in an outside professional appraiser to revalue the inventory. Evidence obtained from outside the company usually leads to reliable, verifiable information. The reliability principle applies to all financial accounting information, from assets to owner's equity on the balance sheet and from revenue to net income on the income statement.

Comparability Principle

The **comparability principle** has two requirements. First, accounting information must be comparable from business to business. Second, a single business's financial statements from one period must be comparable to those from the next period. The CICA encourages comparability in order to make possible useful analysis from business to business, from period to period.

Standard formats for financial statements promote comparability among companies. Using the same terms to describe the statement elements (assets, liabilities, revenues, and so on) aids the comparison process.

Even among companies that adhere to standard formats and standard terms, comparability may be less than perfect. Comparisons of companies that use different inventory methods (LIFO and FIFO, for example) are difficult. When GAAP allows a choice among acceptable accounting methods in inventory, depreciation and other areas, comparability may be hard to achieve.

Recall that the comparability principle directs each individual company to produce accounting information that is comparable over time. To achieve this quality, which accountants call *consistency*, companies must follow the same accounting practices from period to period. The business that uses FIFO for inventory and straight-line for depreciation in one period ought to use those same methods in the next period. Otherwise, a financial statement user could not tell whether changes in income and asset values result from operations or from the way the business accounts for operations.

Companies may change accounting methods, however, in response to a change in business operations. A company may open up a new product line that calls for a different inventory method. GAAP allows the company to make a change in accounting method, but the business must include a description of the change and indicate the effect of the change on net income in the notes to the financial statements.

Section 1506, "Accounting Changes," suggests that a change in accounting policy should be applied retroactively and that prior period's financial statements should be restated. The fact of restatement and the effect of the restatement should be disclosed in the notes. If the change is applied retroactively without restatement, that fact should be disclosed. If the change is not applied retroactively, that fact should be disclosed.

Cost Principle

The **cost principle** states that assets and services are recorded at their purchase cost and that the accounting record of the asset continues to be based on cost rather than current market value. By specifying that assets be recorded at cost, this principle also governs the recording of liabilities and owner's equity. Suppose that a land developer purchased 20 hectares of land for $50,000 plus a real estate commission of $2,000. Additional costs included fees paid to the municipality ($1,500), utility hookups ($8,000) and landscaping ($20,000), for a total cost of $81,500. The Land account carries this balance because it is the cost of bringing the land to its intended use. Assume that the developer holds the land for one year, then offers it for sale at a price of $200,000. The cost principle requires the accounting value of the land to remain at $81,500.

The developer may wish to lure buyers by showing them a balance sheet that reports the land at $200,000. However, this would be inappropriate under GAAP because $200,000 is merely the developer's opinion of what the land is worth.

The underlying basis for the cost principle is the reliability principle. Cost is a reliable value for assets and services, because cost is supported by completed transactions between parties with opposing interests. Buyers try to pay the lowest price possible and sellers try to sell for the highest price. The actual cost of an asset or service is objective evidence of its value.

Revenue Principle

The **revenue principle** provides guidance on the *timing* of the recording of revenue and the *amount* of revenue to record. The general rule is that revenue should be recorded when it is earned and not before.

Some revenues, such as interest and rent, accrue with the passage of time. Their timing and amount are easy to figure. The accountant records the amount of revenue earned over each period of time.

Other revenues are earned by selling goods or rendering services. Identifying *when* these revenues are earned depends on more factors than the passage of time. Under the revenue principle, three conditions must be met before revenue is recorded: (1) the seller has done everything necessary to expect to collect from the buyer; (2) the amount of revenue can be objectively measured; and (3) collectibility is reasonably assured. In most cases, these conditions are met at the point of sale or when services are performed.

The *amount* of revenue to record is the value of the assets received, usually cash or a receivable. However, situations may arise in which the amount of revenue or the timing of earning the revenue is not easily determined. We turn now to four methods that guide the accountant in applying the revenue principle in different circumstances.

Sales Method   Under the **sales method**, revenue is recorded at the point of sale. Consider a retail sale in a hardware store. At the point of sale, the customer pays the store and takes the merchandise. The store records the sale by debiting Cash and crediting Sales Revenue. In other situations, the point of sale occurs when the seller ships the goods to the buyer. Suppose a mining company sells iron ore to Dofasco. By shipping the ore to Dofasco, the mining company has completed its duty and

OBJECTIVE 4

Allocate revenue to the appropriate period by four methods

may expect to collect cash for the revenue earned. If the amount of revenue can be objectively measured and collection is reasonably certain, the mining company can then record revenue. The sale entry is a debit to Accounts Receivable and a credit to Sales Revenue. The sales method is used for most sales of goods and services.

Collection Method   The **collection method** is used only if the receipt of cash is uncertain. Under this method, the seller waits until cash is received to record the sale. This method is a form of cash-basis accounting and, as such, its use is discouraged by Revenue Canada; it is not widely used. Companies that use the collection method do so because they often find it difficult to collect their receivables. They may not reasonably assume that they can collect the revenue, so they wait until the cash is actually received before recording it. The collection method is conservative because revenue is not recorded in advance of its receipt.

Installment Method   The **installment method** is a type of collection method that is used for installment sales. In a typical installment sale, the buyer makes a down payment when the contract is signed and pays the remainder in installments. Department stores (such as Eaton's and Zellers), auto dealers and appliance stores sell on the installment plan. This method is also used for income tax purposes. Under the installment method, gross profit (sales revenue minus cost of goods sold) is recorded as cash is collected.

Suppose Canadian Tire sells a snowblower for a down payment of $280 plus twelve monthly installments of $25 and 24 monthly installments of $20.00, (a total of $1,060). Canadian Tire's cost of the snowblower is $636, so the gross profit is $424, computed as follows:

Installment sale...	$1,060
Cost of the snowblower sold	636
Gross profit...	$ 424

To determine the gross profit associated with each collection under the installment method, we must compute the gross profit percentage as follows:

$$\text{Gross profit percentage} = \frac{\text{Gross profit}}{\text{Installment sale}} = \frac{\$424}{\$1,060} = 40\%$$

Gross profit of $112 (.40 × $280) would be recorded upon receipt of the down payment. We next apply the gross profit percentage to each year's collections. The result is the amount of gross profit recorded as revenue at the time of cash receipt.

Year	Collections	×	Gross Profit Percentage	=	Gross Profit
1	$300	×	40%	=	$120
2	240	×	40	=	96
3	240	×	40	=	96
Total	780	×	40%	=	312

Accountants would record gross profit of $120 in year 1, $96 in year 2, and year 3. The total gross profit ($312) is the same as under the sales method. However, under the sales method, the full $312 of gross profit would be recorded at the beginning of the contract.

Of course, companies make installment sales year after year. If the company's sales mix changed from year to year, each year's sales may have a different gross profit percentage. In the preceding example, year 1 installment sales earned gross profit of 40 percent. Suppose year 2 sales earn gross profit of 45 percent, year 3 sales earn 42 percent, and year 4 sales earn 35 percent. The total gross profit for a year is the sum of all the gross profit amounts recorded on cash collections made that year.

Using assumed cash receipts on installment sales made in years 2, 3 and 4, the gross profit computations for years 1 through 4 follow. All year 1 amounts are taken from our computations above.

	Year 1 Sales	Year 2 Sales	Year 3 Sales	Year 4 Sales
Gross profit percentage	40%	45%	42%	35%

Gross profit by year

	Year 1	Year 2	Year 3	Year 4
Year 1 sales	$80,000 × .40 = $32,000	$120,000 × .40 = $48,000	$140,000 × .40 = $56,000	$160,000 × .40 = $64,000
Year 2 sales		90,000 × .45 = 40,500	100,000 × .45 = 45,000	20,000 × .45 = 9,000
Year 3 sales			75,000 × .42 = 31,500	65,000 × .42 = 27,300
Year 4 sales				30,000 × .35 = 10,500
Total gross profit	$32,000	$88,500	$132,500	$110,800

The installment method is attractive for income tax purposes, because it postpones the recording of revenue and thus the payment of taxes. Under generally accepted accounting principles, this method is permissible only when collection of the outstanding balance is not certain. Some companies use the installment method for tax purposes and sales method for their financial statements.

Percentage-of-Completion Method   Construction of office buildings, bridges, dams and other large assets often extends over several years. The accounting issue for the construction company is when to record the revenue. The most conservative approach is to record all the revenue earned on the project in the period when the project is completed. This procedure, called the **completed-contract method**, is acceptable under GAAP in limited circumstances.

Under the preferred method, called the **percentage-of-completion method**, the construction company recognizes revenue as work is performed. Each year the company estimates the percentage of project completion as construction progresses. One way to make this estimate is to compare the cost incurred for the year to the total estimated project cost. This percentage is then multiplied by the total project revenue to compute the construction revenue for the year. Construction income for the year is revenue minus cost.

Assume Mannix Construction Company receives a contract to build a power plant for a price of $42 million. Mannix estimates total costs of $36 million over the three-year construction period: $6 million in year 1, $18 million in year 2, and $12 million in year 3. Construction revenue and income during the three years are as follows (amounts in millions):

Year	Cost for Year	Total Project Cost	Percentage of Project Completion for Year	Total Project Revenue	Construction Revenue for Year	Construction Income for Year
1	$ 6	$36	$ 6/$36 = $\frac{1}{6}$	$42	$42 × $\frac{1}{6}$ = $ 7	$ 7 − $ 6 = $1
2	18	36	18/ 36 = $\frac{1}{2}$	42	42 × $\frac{1}{2}$ = 21	21 − 18 = 3
3	12	36	12/ 36 = $\frac{1}{3}$	42	42 × $\frac{1}{3}$ = 14	14 − 12 = 2
	$36				$42	$42 $36 $6

The percentage-of-completion method is appropriate when the company can estimate the degree of completion during the construction period, which most construction companies can do. When estimates are not possible, the completed-contract method is required. If Mannix Construction had used the completed-contract method, its income statement for year 3 would report total project revenue of $42 million, total project expenses of $36 million, and income of $6 million. The income statements of years 1 and 2 would report nothing concerning this project. Most accountants believe the results under the percentage-of-completion method are more realistic.

Matching Principle

The **matching principle** governs the recording and reporting of expenses. This principle goes hand in hand with the revenue principle to govern income recognition in accounting. Recall that income is revenue minus expense. During any period, the company first measures its revenues by the revenue principle. The company then identifies and measures all the expenses it incurred during the period to earn the revenues. To *match* the expenses against the revenues means to subtract the expenses from the revenues. The result is the income for the period.

Some expenses are easy to match against particular revenues. For example, cost of goods sold relates directly to sales revenue because without the sales, there would be no cost of goods sold. Commissions and fees paid for selling the goods, delivery expense and sales supplies expense relate to sales revenue for the same reason.

Other expenses are not so easily linked to particular sales because they occur whether or not any revenues arise. Depreciation, salaries and all types of home-office expense are in this category. Accountants usually match these expenses against revenue on a time basis. For example, the company's home-office building may be used for general management, manufacturing and marketing. Straight-line depreciation of a 40-year-old building assigns one fortieth of the building's cost to expense each year, whatever the level of revenue. The annual salary expense for an employee is the person's total salary for the year, regardless of revenue.

Losses, like expenses, are matched against revenue on a time basis. For example, if an asset like inventory loses value, the loss is recorded when it occurs, without regard for the revenues earned during the period.

Disclosure Principle

The **disclosure principle** holds that a company's financial statements should report enough information for outsiders to make knowledgeable decisions about the company. In short, the company should report sufficient *understandable, relevant, reliable* and *comparable* information about its economic affairs. This section of the chapter discusses and illustrates nine types of disclosures.

Summary of Significant Accounting Policies   To evaluate a company, investors and creditors need to know how its financial statements were prepared. This consideration is especially important when the company can choose from several acceptable methods. Companies summarize their accounting policies in the

OBJECTIVE 5

Report information that satisfies the disclosure principle

first note to their financial statements. The note may include both monetary amounts and written descriptions. Companies commonly disclose how they have applied accounting principles. For example, the depreciation method, consolidation basis, inventory valuation, fixed assets, and foreign currency translation are five items commonly disclosed.[3]

John Labatt Limited reported the following in its notes to its April 30, 1991 financial statements:

Notes to the Consolidated Financial statements

1. Summary of Significant Accounting Policies [in part]
The financial statements have been prepared in accordance with accounting principles generally accepted in Canada and conform in all material respects with International Accounting Standards. Significant accounting policies observed in their preparation are summarized below.

Principles of consolidation
The consolidated financial statements include the accounts of all subsidiary companies. The results of operations of subsidiaries acquired or sold during the year are included from or to their respective dates of acquisition or sale.

Inventories
Inventories, other than returnable containers, are valued at the lower of cost and net realizable value, cost being determined on a first-in, first-out basis. Returnable containers are valued at redemption price or at amortized cost not exceeding replacement cost.

Property, plant and equipment
Property, plant and equipment are recorded at cost. Depreciation is provided on a straight-line basis over the estimated useful lives of the assets, generally at rates of 2½% for buildings, 10% for machinery and equipment, and 20% for vehicles.

The Company capitalizes interest costs on major construction projects when the period of construction exceeds one year. Capitalization of interest ceases once operations commence at the facility. Interest capitalized at April 30, 1991 and 1990 was not material.

Long-term investments
Investments in companies and partnerships over which the Company has significant influence ("partly owned businesses") are accounted for using the equity method. At April 30, 1991, the unamortized balance of goodwill arising from the acquisition of partly owned businesses amounted to $28 million ($29 million in 1990).

Investments in other companies are carried at the lower of cost and net realizable value. Income from these investments is recognized when dividends are received.

Contingent Liabilities   Companies are usually eager to disclose good news. The disclosure principle requires them to report bad news as well. For example, a company may be a defendant in a lawsuit with an uncertain outcome. Will the contingency — the possibility of a negative outcome — result in an actual loss to the company? Will it endanger the company's ability to continue as a going concern? Investors, lenders and other interested parties need the full financial picture. A bank may decide not to loan additional money because of the contingency. A labor union may note the contingency and lower its demand for an increase in employee

---

[3] *Financial Reporting in Canada, 1991,* 19th edition (Toronto: CICA, 1992), p. 20.

wages. The disclosure principle requires the company to report whether the lawsuit is likely to result in a liability and, if so, the expected amount.

As discussed in Chapter 11, most companies disclose their contingent liabilities in notes to the financial statements. An example is the following note excerpted from the December 31, 1991 financial statements of Canadian National Railways. CN reported that its contingent liabilities arose from outstanding and possible lawsuits against the company.

> c) Contingencies
> In the normal course of its operations, the Company becomes involved in various legal actions, including claims relating to injuries, damage to property and environmental matters. While the final outcome with respect to actions outstanding or pending at December 31, 1991 cannot be predicted with certainty, it is the opinion of management that their resolution will not have a material adverse effect on the System's financial position.

Probable Losses   The disclosure principle directs a business to record and report a probable loss before it occurs if the loss is likely and its amount can be estimated. Ivaco Inc. reported such a loss in its 1991 financial statements. Observe that the disposal of assets has not occurred yet, but the company does expect the disposal to result in a loss.

> 12. Gain (loss) from Discontinued Operations
> During 1991, additional operations of Sivaco Wire Group were discontinued. The results of these operations and the provision for their respective shut down costs aggregate to a loss of $11,566,000. This loss, after deducting applicable income taxes of $4,323,000 has been shown as Gain (loss) from discontinued operations.

Accounting Changes   Consistent use of accounting methods and procedures is important, as we saw in discussing comparability. When a company does change from one accounting method or procedure to another, it must include a description of the change and indicate the effect of the change on net income in the notes to the financial statements. Two common accounting changes are *changes in accounting principles* and *changes in accounting estimates*.

A **change in accounting principle** is a change in accounting method. A switch from the FIFO method to the LIFO method for inventories and a switch from the accelerated depreciation method to the straight-line method are examples of accounting changes. Special rules that apply to changes in accounting principles are discussed in later accounting courses. Whatever the change in principle, the notes to the financial statements must inform the reader that the change has occurred.

Maclean Hunter Limited disclosed the following accounting change in its December 31, 1991 financial statements, after the company had changed its policy pertaining to the amotization of intangible assets:

> **2. Change in Accounting Policy**
> Effective Jaunuary 1, 1991, the Company changed its accounting policy pertaining to the amortization of intangible assets, which include broadcast licenses, cable television franchises, circulation bases, subscriber lists and radio paging frequencies, to comply with the [Recommendations] of the Canadian Institute of Chartered Accountants [*Handbook*] Section 3060. Previously, if the life of the intangible asset was considered to be indefinite, the asset was not amortized. Under the new accounting policy, intangible assets are amortized on a straight-line basis over their estimated economic life up to a maximum of 40 years, except

> for cable television franchises which are amortized using the sinking fund method with an interest rate of 40% over periods not exceeding 40 years.
>
> The effect of this change in accounting policy has been to reduce net income in 1991 by $6.0 million (4¢ per share) and to reduce net income in 1990 by $5.4 million (3¢ per share). The new requirements have been applied retroactively, so the results for 1990 have been restated and retained earnings at January 31, 1990 have been reduced by $7.7 million.

A **change in accounting estimate** occurs in the course of business as the company alters earlier expectations. A company may record uncollectible accounts expense based on the estimate that bad debts will equal 2 percent of sales. If actual collections exceed this estimate, the company may lower its estimated expense to 1½ percent of sales in the future.

A company may originally estimate that a new Ford Econoline delivery van will provide four years' service. After two years of using the truck, the company sees that the truck's full useful life will stretch to six years. The company must recompute depreciation based on this new information at the start of the truck's third year of service. Assume that this truck cost $16,000, has an estimated residual value of $2,000 and is depreciated by the straight-line method.

Annual depreciation for each of the first two years of the asset's life is $3,500, computed as follows:

$$\text{Depreciation per year} = \frac{\$16,000 - \$2,000}{4 \text{ years}} = \$3,500$$

Changes in estimate are accounted for by spreading the asset's remaining book value over its remaining life. Annual depreciation after the change in accounting estimate is $1,750, computed in the following manner:

$$\text{Depreciation per year} = \frac{\text{Remaining depreciable book value}}{\text{Remaining life}}$$

$$= \frac{\$16,000 - \$2,000 - (3,500 \times 2)}{6 \text{ total years} - 2 \text{ years used}}$$

$$= \frac{\$7,000}{4 \text{ years}}$$

$$= \$1,750$$

This revised amount of depreciation is recorded in the usual manner.

ATCO Ltd. disclosed a similar change in accounting estimate in its financial statements for the year ended December 31, 1990. Observe that Harding reported the nature of the change, the reason for making the change, and its effect on income:

> **9. PROPERTY, PLANT AND EQUIPMENT**
>
> Effective January 1, 1990 the Corporation revised the estimated useful life of its space rental assets from ten to fifteen years. The effect of this change has been applied prospectively and increased earnings in 1990 by $3,025,000 ($.10 per share).

Subsequent Events   A company usually takes several weeks after the end of the year to close its books and to publish its financial statements. Occasionally, events occur during this period that affect the interpretation of the information in those financial statements. Such an occurrence is called a **subsequent event** and should be disclosed in the prior period's statements. The most common examples of subsequent events are borrowing money, paying debts, making investments, selling assets and becoming a defendant in a lawsuit.

Doman Industries Limited, a major producer of forest products located in British Columbia, reported the following subsequent event in its financial statements for the year ended December 31, 1991. Note that the company makes refernce to a pro forma balance sheet presented with the financial statements as suggested by Section 3820.13 of the *CICA Handbook* to show the effect of the subsequent event on the company's financial position.

15. SUBSEQUENT EVENTS (in part)

The pro forma balance sheet has been presented to show the effect of the following transactions as if they had been completed on December 31, 1991:

(a) On March 12, 1992, the Company issued 4,000,000 special warrants (the "Special Warrants") which are exchangeable into Class B non-voting shares, series 2 on a one-for-one basis without any additional payment. The gross proceeds from this issue of $26,500,000 are presently being held in escrow, subject to the issuance of a receipt for a prospectus by the regulatory authorities in certain of the provinces of Canada. The Company expects that the special warrants will be exchanged for the shares shortly thereafter.

The expenses, including commissions to the Dealers, of issuing the Special Warrants, currently estimated to be $1,560,000, will be charged, net of deferred taxes of approximately $684,000, to retained earnings. The net proceeds from the issue will be used temporarily to reduce short-term bank indebtedness and ultimately to fund capital expenditures.

Business Segments   Most large companies operate in more than one area. Each area is called a *business segment*. Lord Kenneth Thomson not only controls Thomson newspapers through a holding company but also The Bay, Simpsons, Zellers, an oil company and other differing businesses. Canadian Pacific owns hotels, mining companies, steamships, trucking companies, oil companies, paper companies as well as real estate interests. Diversification like this is not limited to large international companies. A realtor may also own a restaurant. A farmer may sell farm implements. An automobile dealer may also own a furniture store.

Suppose you are considering investing in a company that is active in the footwear industry but also owns a meat packer and several leisure resorts. Assume the Canadian footwear industry is in retreat because of intense foreign competition. With income and asset data broken down by business segments, you can determine how much of the company's assets are committed to each segment and which lines of business are most (and least) profitable. Companies disclose segment data in notes to their financial statements.

The following note in the John Labatt Limited April 30, 1991 financial statement meets the GAAP requirement for adequate disclosure of segmented information:

20. SEGMENTED FINANCIAL INFORMATION
Information by class of business
The classes of business are as follows:

The Brewing segment comprises the brewing activities in Canada, the United States and Italy, the sale in other countries of beers brewed in Canada, the United States and Italy, and the marketing in the United Kingdom of lager produced and distributed under agreements with United Kingdom brewers.

The Food segment comprises the production and sale of dairy products, food products and fruit juices primarily in Canada and the United States.

Wholly and majority-owned Entertainment operations and relevant corporate expenses are allocated to the two business segments. Partly owned businesses are not allocated.

The following is a summary of key financial information by business segment for the years ended April 30, 1991 and 1990:

(in millions)	1991		1990	
	Gross sales		**Gross sales**	
Brewing	$2,045		$1,920	
Food	3,327		3,354	
	$5,370		$5,274	

	Depreciation & amortization	**Earnings before interest & tax**	**Depreciation & amortization**	**Earnings before interest & tax**
Brewing	$60	$109	$52	$174
Food	90	90	82	90
	$150	$199	$134	$264
Interest expense		(41)		(33)
Earnings before income taxes		$158		$231

	Fixed asset additions, net	**Net assets employed**	**Fixed asset additions, net**	**Net assets employed**
Brewing	$104	$ 727	$ 98	$ 717
Food	87	1,319	108	1,233
	$191	2,046	$206	1,950
Short-term investments		300		300
Investments in partly owned businesses		123		113
Current liabilities other than bank advances and short-term notes		669		583
Total assets per consolidated balance sheets		$3,138		$2,946

Information by geographic segment

The Company operates principally in the geographic areas of Canada and the United States. Geographic segmentation is determined on the basis of the business location where the sale originates.

Operations in the United Kingdom and Italy did not constitute reportable geographic segments and are included in the Canadian segments below. Corporate expenses are allocated to the two geographic segments. Partly owned businesses are not allocated.

The following is a summary of key financial information by geographic segment for the years ended April 30, 1991 and 1990:

(in millions)	1991	1990
	Gross sales	Gross sales
Canada	$3,585	$3,372
United States	1,785	1,902
	$5,370	$5,274

	Depreciation & amortization	Earnings before interest & tax	Depreciation & amortization	Earnings before interest & tax
Canada	$ 97	$188	$ 86	$240
United States	53	11	48	24
	$150	$199	$134	$264
Interest expense		(41)		(33)
Earnings before income taxes		$158		$231

	Fixed asset additions, net	Net assets employed	Fixed asset additions, net	Net assets employed
Canada	$158	$1,291	$158	$1,092
United States	33	755	48	858
	$191	2,046	$206	1,950
Short-term investments		300		300
Investments in partly owned businesses		123		113
Current liabilities other than bank advances and short-term notes		669		583
Total assets per consolidated balance sheets		$3,138		$2,946

To satisfy the disclosure principle, John Labatt discloses gross sales, income before taxes and net assets employed two ways: by business segments and by geographic area. GAAP also requires companies to disclose capital asset additions and depreciation and amortization by business segment.

Long-term Commitments   Many companies make **long-term commitments** that involve making payments that may be unequal in amount over a series of years. Users of the company's financial statements will have an incomplete picture of the company's future cash flows unless information about the future committed payments is disclosed in the notes. An example of such a future commitment of payments is a capital lease, such as the lease Air Canada enters into when it acquires a plane for its fleet. Capital leases are studied in later financial accounting courses; all you need to know at this point is that the company, Air Canada, acquires an asset, a plane, and a liability, a series of payments over a number of years. So a reader of Air Canada's financial statements is aware of these future payments and when they are to be made, GAAP requires the year-by-year payments to be disclosed.

Air Canada discloses information about commitments to purchase aircraft and spare parts and operating lease payments in the following note from its December 31, 1991 financial statements:

12. Commitments

The Corporation has commitments to purchase aircraft and spare engines for U.S. $888 [million] and CDN $18 [million] which are payable as follows:

	US	CDN
1992	$434	$18
1993	402	—
1994	52	—
1995	—	—

Excluded from the aircraft commitments is an amount of U.S. $224 for the purchase of six Airbus A320 aircraft which have been forward sold to a third party. Other commitments for property, ground equipment, and spare parts, amount to approximately CDN $55 [million].

Future minimum lease payments under operating leases of aircraft and other property total $1,772 [million] and are payable as follows:

	Operating Leases of Aircraft	Operating Leases of Other Property
1992	$ 150	$ 49
1993	129	39
1994	116	35
1995	99	28
1996	94	23
Remaining years	778	232
	$1,366	$406

Related Party Transactions   A basic assumption underlying the financial statements is that the transactions underlying the numbers in the financial statements were made at arm's length. The usual definition of an arm's length transaction is a transaction between a buyer and a seller who are independent of each other or unrelated; as such, each can and will work to obtain the most favorable terms for the transaction. Most, and perhaps even all, of a company's transactions will be with unrelated parties. However, some transactions may be between the company and a party related to it. For example, Loblaws stores, owned through Loblaw Companies by George Weston Limited, buy baked goods from Weston Bakeries, owned through Weston Foods by George Weston Limited. Because the two companies have the same parent, they are considered to be related parties.

While most related party or non-arm's length transactions are conducted at fair prices (the same prices that arm's length transactions would be), there is a possibility that the buyer or seller obtained a financial advantage that would not have otherwise been possible. For that reason, GAAP requires that related party transactions be disclosed. In its December 31, 1991 financial statements Saskatchewan Water Corporation disclosed information about transactions with various Saskatchewan Crown controlled departments, agencies and corporations to which Saskatchewan Water is related:

16. RELATED PARTY TRANSACTIONS

Included in these financial statements are income and expense amounts resulting from routine operating transactions conducted at prevailing market prices with various Saskatchewan Crown controlled departments, agencies and corporations with which the corporation is related. Account balances resulting from these transactions are included in the statement of financial position and are settled on normal trade terms.

Other amounts due to and from related parties and the terms of settlement are described separately in the financial statements and the notes thereto.

As an example of a related party transaction, the Statement of Operations shows a line item "Grants from Province of Saskatchewan."

Economic Dependence   Some companies become dependent on other companies as either suppliers or customers. For example, a small manufacturer of furniture may sell all or most of its output to one customer, a department store chain. A small brewer may buy all its bottles from one large glassmaking company. The small manufacturer and the small brewer are said to be economically dependent.

If the department store chain stops buying from the manufacturer, the manufacturer may go out of business before it can develop a new customer base. If the glassmaker stops selling bottles to the brewer, the brewer may get into financial difficulty unless a new supplier can be found quickly. It is important that users of financial statements be aware of economic dependence and so GAAP requires that companies that are economically dependent disclose that fact.

TransCanada Pipelines provides the following information on its principal customers in the notes to its December 31, 1987 financial statements. Total natural gas sales for the period were $3,057,100,000.

(C) PRINCIPAL CUSTOMERS

The following table sets forth the Company's revenues generated by the Pipeline segment from natural gas sales under long-term contracts and transportation services to its five principal customers:

Year Ended December 31 (millions of dollars)	1987	1986	1985
The Consumers' Gas Company Ltd	943.01	195.01	206.2
Union Gas Limited	598.9	885.7	958.8
Gaz Metropolitain, Inc.	373.8	482.1	506.7
ICG (Ontario) Ltd.	302.3	391.3	438.9
Great Lakes Gas Transmission Company	168.0	214.1	245.2

Constraints on Accounting

OBJECTIVE 6

Apply two constraints to accounting

Do financial statements report every detail, no matter how small, to meet the need for understandable, relevant, reliable and comparable information? If they did, the result would be an avalanche of data. To address this problem, accountants use the *materiality concept*. Also, a company's top managers are responsible for its financial statements. To add balance to managers' optimism, which could bias the statements and present too favorable a picture of company operations, accountants follow the *conservatism concept*. This section discusses these constraints on accounting information.

Materiality Concept

The **materiality concept** states that a company must perform strictly proper accounting only for items and transactions that are significant to the business's financial statements. Information is significant (accountants call it *material*) when its inclusion and correct presentation in the financial statement would cause a statement user to change a decision because of that information. Immaterial (insignificant) items justify less than perfect accounting. The inclusion and proper presentation of *immaterial* items would not affect a statement user's decision. The materiality concept frees accountants from having to compute and report every last item in strict accordance with GAAP. Thus the materiality concept reduces the cost of accounting.

How does a business decide where to draw the line between what is material and what is immaterial? This decision rests to a great degree on how large the business is. Canadian Tire, for example, holds more than $2.2 billion in assets. Management would likely treat as immaterial a $100 purchase of wastebaskets. These wastebaskets may well remain useful for ten years. Strictly speaking, Canadian Tire should capitalize their cost and depreciate the wastebaskets. However, this treatment is not practical. The accounting cost of computing, recording and properly reporting this asset outweighs the information provided. No statement user (a potential investor or lender) would change a decision based on so insignificant (immaterial) an amount. The cost of accounting in this case outweighs the benefit of the resulting information.

Large companies may draw the materiality line at as high a figure as $10,000 and expense any smaller amount. Smaller firms may choose to expense only those items less than $50. Materiality varies from company to company. An amount that is material to the local service station may not be material to Loblaws.

The materiality concept does not free a business from having to account for every item. Canadian Tire, for example, must still account for the wastebaskets. They would credit Cash (or Accounts Payable) to record their purchase, of course, but what account would they debit? Because the amount is immaterial, management may decide to debit Supplies Expense. No matter what account receives the debit, no statement user's decision would be changed by the information.

Conservatism Concept

Business managers are often optimists. Asked how well the company is doing, its president will likely answer, "Great, we're having our best year ever." Without constraints this optimism could find its way into the company's reported assets and profits. Managers may try to present too favorable a view of the company. For example, they may pressure accountants to capitalize costs associated with fixed assets that should be expensed. This would result in less immediate expense and higher current income on the income statement. The balance sheet would report unduly high fixed asset values and owner's equity. The overall result would be that the managers' performance would appear to be better than it actually was. Traditionally, accountants have been conservative to counter management's optimism.

Conservatism has been interpreted as "Anticipate no profits, but anticipate all losses." A clear-cut example is the lower-of-cost-or-market (LCM) method for inventories. Under LCM, inventory is reported at the lower of its cost or market value, which results in higher cost of goods sold and lower net income. Thus profits and assets are reported at their lowest reasonable amount. Other conservative accounting practices include the LIFO method for inventories when inventory costs are increasing, accelerated depreciation and the completed-contract method for construction revenues. These methods result in earlier recording of expenses or later recording of revenues. Both effects postpone the reporting of net income and therefore are conservative.

In recent years, conservatism's effect on accounting has decreased. Conservatism should not mean deliberate understatement of assets, profits and owner's equity. However, if two different values can be used for an asset or a liability, the concept suggests using the less optimistic value. Conservatism is a secondary consideration in accounting. Understandable, relevant, reliable and comparable information is the goal, and conservatism is a factor only after these primary goals are met.

You should recognize that conservatism for the company may not be in every users' best interest; conservatism has a down side. If a company follows the cost principle for all its assets, real estate will appear on the balance sheet at cost. If a company located in Vancouver bought land on West Georgia St. 60 years ago, the land would appear on the balance sheet at the cost at that time. Since then, inflation and the strong economic growth that has occured in Vancouver and British Columbia has increased the value of the land many times. A shareholder of the Vancouver company might sell his or her shares based on the value of the land that is shown on the balance sheet and not on its much higher market value. On the other hand, a new purchaser of the Vancouver company's shares would benefit if the company sold the land and distributed part of the proceeds to existing share-holders. In short, conservatism has much to recommend it — the benefits outweigh the costs — but there are costs.

Financial Statements and Their Elements

We have examined the concepts and principles that guide businesses in shaping ac-counting practice. The CICA aims for financial statements that best meet user needs for business information.

This accounting information appears in four statements: the balance sheet, the in-come statement, the statement of owner's equity and the statement of changes in financial position (which we cover in Chapter 18). The CICA provides definitions for the elements that make up these statements. Financial information presenta-tion, to be most useful to the greatest number of financial statement users, must be presented in a standard format with well-defined terms, as we learned in our dis-cussion of the comparability concept.

The Canadian Institute of Chartered Accountants in "Financial Statement Concepts," Section 1000 of the *CICA Handbook,* provides authoritative definitions of the elements of financial statements.

Balance Sheet Elements

Assets are economic resources controlled by an entity as a result of past transac-tions or events from which future economic benefits may be obtained.

Liabilities are obligations of an entity arising from past transactions or events, the set-tlement of which may result in the transfer or use of assets, provision of services or other yielding of economic benefits in the future.

Equity (Owner's Equity), also *net assets,* is the ownership interest in the assets of a profit-oriented entity after deducting its liabilities. Net assets or equity of a non-profit organization is the residual interest after deducting the organization's liabilities.

Income Statement Elements

Revenues are increases in economic resources, either by way of inflows or en-hancements of assets or reductions of liabilities, resulting from the ordinary activ-ities of an entity, normally from the sale of goods, the rendering of services or the use by others of entity resources yielding rent, interest, royalties or dividends.

Expenses are decreases in economic resources, either by way of outflows or reduc-tions of assets or incurrences of liabilities, resulting from the ordinary revenue gen-erating or service delivery activities of an entity.

EXHIBIT 12-4   *Reporting Revenues, Expenses, Gains and Losses*

Multiple-Step Income Statement			Single-Step Income Statement		
Sales revenue		$XXX	Revenues and gains		
Cost of goods sold		XXX	Sales revenue		XXX
Gross profit		XXX	Gain on sale of land		XXX
Operating expenses		XXX	Total revenues and gains		XXX
Income from operations		XXX	Expenses and losses		
Other items			Cost of goods sold	$XXX	
Gain on sale of land	$XXX		Operating expenses	XXX	
Loss due to fire	XXX	XXX	Loss due to fire	XXX	
			Total expenses and losses		XXX
Net income		XXX	Net income		$XXX

Gains are increases in equity from peripheral or incidental transactions and events affecting an entity and from all other transactions, events and circumstances affecting the entity except those that result from revenues or equity contributions.

Losses are decreases in equity from peripheral or incidental transactions and events affecting an entity and from all other transactions, events and circumstances affecting the entity except those that result from expenses or distributions of equity.

Note that *revenues* and *expenses* arise from the business's ongoing central operations, but *gains* and *losses* do not. Sales and interest earned are revenues because most companies make sales and earn interest as part of their central operations. Selling cars and trucks lies at the heart of an automobile dealership. To this business, a gain on the sale of a truck is revenue and a loss on the sale is expense. However, a gain on the sale of a truck is not revenue for a trucking company because that entity buys trucks for use rather than for sale. Selling a truck is not a part of central operations. Exhibit 12-4 shows how to report revenues, expenses, gains and losses on a multiple-step and a single-step income statement.

Statement of Owner's Equity Elements   *Investments by owners* are increases in owner's equity that result from the owner's transferring to the entity something of value. The most common investment is cash, but owners sometimes invest land, buildings, legal services or other assets. In some cases, an owner's investment in the business may consist of paying off its liabilities. *Distributions to owners* are decreases in owner's equity that result from the owner's transferring assets or services from the business to himself or herself, or from the business taking on the owner's liabilities. When the business is a corporation, owner withdrawals are called *dividends*. The most commonly distributed asset is cash, but businesses sometimes distribute other assets, such as stock investments they hold in other companies, to their owners.

Accounting Standards Throughout the World _____

We have focused on the principles of accounting that are generally accepted in Canada. Most of the methods of accounting are consistent throughout the world. Double-entry bookkeeping, the accrual accounting system, and basic accounting statements are used worldwide. Differences, however, do exist among countries; recall the discussion on p. 527 that listed the sources of GAAP and the discussion about Section 1501, "International Accounting Standards."

In discussing depreciation in Chapter 10, we emphasized that in Canada the methods used for reporting to Revenue Canada often differ from the methods used for reporting to shareholders. In contrast, tax reporting and shareholder reporting are identical in many countries. For example, France has a *Plan compatible* that specifies a National Uniform Chart of Accounts used for both tax returns and reporting to shareholders. German financial reporting is also determined primarily by tax laws. If accounting records are not kept according to strict tax laws, the tax authorities can reject the records as a basis for taxation.

In some countries, tax laws have a major influence on shareholder reporting even if tax and shareholder reports are not required to be identical. In Japan, for example, certain principles are allowed for tax purposes only if they are also used for shareholder reporting.

A significant difference among countries is the extent to which financial statements account for inflation. Earlier in this chapter (p. 531), Section 4510, "Reporting the Effects of Changing Prices" was discussed; recall that it was part of the *CICA Handbook* from 1982 to March, 1992, when it was withdrawn. Even when it was part of the *Handbook*, compliance was voluntary. In contrast, some countries have full or partial adjustment for inflation as part of their reporting to both investors and tax authorities. For example, Argentina and Brazil, which have experienced very high inflation rates, require all statements to be adjusted for changes in the general price level.

The globalization of business enterprises and capital markets is creating much interest in establishing common, worldwide accounting standards. There are probably too many cultural, social, and political differences to expect complete worldwide standardization of financial reporting in the near future. However, the number of differences is decreasing. Cooperation among accountants has been fostered by the International Federation of Accountants (IFAC) through the standards (IASs) formulated and published by its standard-setting body, the International Accounting Standards Committee (IASC).

Summary Problem for Your Review

This chapter has discussed the following principles and concepts:

Entity concept	Cost principle
Going-concern concept	Revenue principle
Time-period concept	Matching principle
Reliability principle	Disclosure principle
Comparability principle	Materiality concept

Required

Indicate which of these concepts is being violated in each of the following situations:

1. A construction company signs a two-year contract to build a bridge for the province of Nova Scotia. The president of the company immediately records the full contract price as revenue.

2. Competition has taken away much of the business of a small airline. The airline is unwilling to report its plans to sell half its fleet of planes.

3. After starting the business in February 19X2, a coal-mining company keeps no accounting records for 19X2, 19X3 and 19X4. The owner is waiting until the mine is exhausted to determine the success or failure of the business.

4. Assets recorded at cost by a drug store chain are written up to their fair market value at the end of each year.

5. The accountant for a manufacturing company keeps detailed depreciation records on every asset no matter how small its value.

6. A physician mixes her personal accounting records with those of the medical practice.

7. Expenses are reported whenever the bookkeeper records them rather than when related revenues are earned.

8. The damaged inventory of a discount store is being written down. The store manager bases the write-down entry on his own subjective opinion in order to minimize income taxes.

9. A quick-copy center changes accounting methods every year in order to report the maximum amount of net income possible under generally accepted accounting principles.

10. The owners of a private nursing home base its accounting records on the assumption that the nursing home might have to close at any time. The nursing home has a long record of service to the community.

SOLUTION TO REVIEW PROBLEM

1. Revenue principle
2. Disclosure principle
3. Time-period concept
4. Cost principle
5. Materiality concept

6. Entity concept
7. Matching principle
8. Reliability principle
9. Comparability principle
10. Going-concern concept

Summary

The Canadian Institute of Chartered Accountants (CICA) formulates generally accepted accounting principles (GAAP) to provide understandable, relevant, reliable and comparable accounting information. Information must be *understandable* by users if it is to be used. *Relevant* information allows users to make business predictions and to evaluate past decisions. *Reliable* data are free from error and bias. Accounting information is also intended to be *comparable* from company to company and from period to period.

Four concepts underlie accounting. The most basic, the *entity concept*, draws clear boundaries around the accounting unit or entity. The entity, based on the *going-concern concept*, is assumed to remain in business for the foreseeable future. The *time-period concept* holds that accounting information is reported for particular time periods such as months, quarters and years. Under the *stable-monetary-unit concept*, no adjustment is made for the changing value of the dollar.

Accounting principles provide detailed guidelines for recording transactions and preparing the financial statements. The *reliability* and *comparability* principles require that accounting information be based on objective data and be useful for comparing companies across different time periods. The *cost principle* governs accounting for assets and liabilities, and the *revenue principle* governs accounting for revenues. *Matching* is the basis for recording expenses. The *disclosure* principle requires companies to report their accounting policies, contingent liabilities, probable future losses, accounting changes, subsequent events, business-segment data, long-term commitments, related party transactions and economic dependence. They use different disclosure techniques.

Two constraints on accounting are materiality and conservatism. The *materiality concept* allows companies to avoid the cost of accounting for immaterial items. *Conservatism* constrains the optimism of managers by anticipating no profits, but anticipating all losses.

Financial statements and their elements include:

1. *Balance sheet: assets, liabilities,* and *equity (owner's equity)*
2. *Income statement: revenues, expenses, gains,* and *losses*
3. *Statement of owner's equity: investments by owners,* and *distributions to owners.*

The fourth statement is the *statement of changes in financial position.*

Self-Study Questions

Test your understanding of the chapter by marking the correct answer for each of the following questions:

1. The organization that issues accounting pronouncements that make up GAAP is the *(p. 525)*
   a. Government of Canada
   b. National Securities Administrators
   c. Accounting Standards Board
   d. Ontario Securities Commission

2. Which of the following characteristics of accounting information does the objective of financial reporting omit? *(p. 529)*
   a. Timeliness
   b. Relevance
   c. Reliability
   d. Comparability

3. A new business is starting. The president wishes to wait until significant contracts have been fulfilled before reporting the results of the business's operations. Which underlying concept serves as the basis for preparing financial statements at regular intervals? *(pp. 530–31)*
   a. Entity
   b. Going-concern
   c. Time-period
   d. Stable-monetary-unit

4. Which of these revenue methods is the most conservative? *(p. 545)*
   a. Sales method
   b. Collection method
   c. Percentage-of-completion method
   d. All the above are equally conservative

5. Suppose a Woodwards store sells $10,000 worth of kitchen appliances on the installment plan and collects a down payment of $1,500. Woodwards' cost of the appliances is $7,000. How much gross profit will the company report on the down payment under the installment revenue method? *(pp. 534–35)*
   a. $450
   b. $1,500
   c. $3,000
   d. $10,000

6. A construction company spent $180,000 during the current year on a building with a contract price of $900,000. The company estimated total construction cost at $720,000. How much construction income will the company report under the percentage-of-completion method? *(pp. 535–36)*
   a. $45,000
   b. $144,000
   c. $180,000
   d. $225,000

7. Which of the following items should be disclosed to satisfy the adequate disclosure principle? *(pp. 536–44)*
   a. Contingent liabilities
   b. Probable losses
   c. Accounting changes
   d. All of the above

8. Important subsequent events should be disclosed because they *(pp. 539–40)*
   a. Occur immediately after the current period
   b. Describe changes in accounting methods
   c. Reveal losses that have a high probability of occurring in the future
   d. May affect the interpretation of the current-period financial statements

9. Which of the following statements is most in keeping with the materiality concept? *(p. 545)*
   a. Accountants record material losses but are reluctant to record material gains.
   b. Different companies have different materiality limits, depending on their size.
   c. Business-segment data are disclosed to fulfill the materiality concept.
   d. Companies report all the information needed to communicate a material view of the entity.

10. Gains and losses are most similar to *(p. 547)*
    a. Assets and liabilities
    b. Revenues and expenses
    c. Investments by owners and distributions to owners

Answers to the Self-Study Questions are at the end of the chapter.

Accounting Vocabulary

Accounting Standards Board *(p. 526)*

change in accounting estimate *(p. 539)*

change in accounting principle *(p. 538)*

collection method *(p. 534)*

comparability principle *(p. 532)*

completed-contract method *(p. 535)*

cost principle *(p. 533)*

disclosure principle *(p. 536)*

economic dependence *(p. 544)*

Emerging Issues Committee *(p. 527)*

entity concept *(p. 529)*

gains *(p. 547)*

going-concern concept *(p. 530)*

installment method *(p. 534)*

long-term commitments *(p. 542)*

losses *(p. 547)*

matching principle *(p. 536)*

materiality concept *(p. 545)*

percentage-of-completion method *(p. 535)*

reliability principle *(p. 532)*

revenue principle *(p. 533)*

sales method *(p. 533)*

stable-monetary-unit concept *(p. 531)*

subsequent event *(p. 539)*

time-period concept *(p. 530)*

ASSIGNMENT MATERIAL _____

Questions

1. How do accounting principles differ from natural laws?
2. State the basic objective of financial reporting.
3. What three characteristics make accounting information useful for decision making? Briefly discuss each characteristic.
4. What is the entity concept?
5. How does the going-concern concept affect accounting? What is liquidation?
6. Identify two practical results of the time-period concept.
7. What is the shortcoming of the stable-monetary-unit concept?
8. What are the two requirements of the comparability principle?
9. Why is consistency important in accounting?
10. Discuss the relationship between the cost principle and the reliability principle.
11. What three conditions must be met before revenue is recorded? What determines the amount of the revenue?

12. Which revenue recognition method is more conservative, the sales method or the collection method? Give your reason.

13. Suppose Eaton's sold land for $200,000 on an installment basis, receiving a down payment of $50,000 to be followed by 12 installments of $12,500 each. If Eaton's cost of the land was $120,000, how much gross profit would Eaton's record under the installment method (a) when the down payment is received, and (b) when each installment is received?

14. Briefly discuss two methods of recognizing revenue on long-term construction contracts.

15. Give two examples of expenses that are easy to relate to sales revenue and two examples of expenses that are not so easy to relate to particular sales. On what basis are the latter expenses matched against revenue?

16. ABC Limited agreed on November 22, 19X7 to sell an unprofitable manufacturing plant. ABC estimates on December 31 that the company is likely to incur a $4 million loss on the sale when it is finalized in 19X8. In which year should ABC report the loss? What accounting principle governs this situation?

17. Identify three items commonly disclosed in a company's summary of significant accounting policies.

18. What is a subsequent event? Why should companies disclose important subsequent events in their financial statements?

19. How does information on business segments help an investor?

20. Classify each of the following as a change in accounting principle or a change in accounting estimate:
    a. Change from straight-line to double-declining-balance depreciation.
    b. Change in the uncollectibility of accounts receivable.
    c. Change from LIFO to FIFO for inventory.
    d. Change from the percentage-of-completion method to the completed-contract method for revenue on long-term construction contracts.
    e. Change from an 8-year life to a 10-year life for a machine.
    f. Change in estimated warranty expense rate stated as a percent of sales.

21. Sloan Sales Inc. expenses the cost of plant assets below $500 at the time of purchase. What accounting concept allows this departure from strictly proper accounting? Why would Sloan Sales follow such a policy?

22. Give three examples of conservative accounting methods, stating why the methods are conservative.

23. Identify two balance sheet elements that are defined independently and give the definition of the third balance sheet element.

24. Briefrly define each of the following terms and explain why information about each is important to users of financial statements:
    a. Related party transactions
    b. Economic dependence

25. The four income statement elements may be divided into two pairs of similar elements. What elements make up these two pairs?

Exercises

Exercise 12-1 *Identifying the objective of financial reporting* **(L.O. 1)**

As a financial analyst with Midland Walwyn, your job is to follow the aerospace industry. Specifically, you compare companies in this industry so that you may recommend to Midland Walwyn clients which companies to invest in. What is the basic objective of financial reporting? Briefly discuss some of the predictions and related evaluations of past performance that an investment analyst would make.

Also state why the analyst feels more comfortable using information that has been audited by an independent CA.

Exercise 12-2   *Applying accounting concepts* **(L.O. 2)**

The Granville Straight is a newspaper devoted to cultural affairs in Vancouver and surrounding areas in British Columbia. Its owner, Marla Griffis, is better attuned to cultural affairs than to the business aspects of running a newspaper. Readership is at an all-time high, but the financial position of the business has suffered. For each of the following items indicate the accounting action needed at December 31, the end of the accounting year. Also identify the underlying accounting concept most directly applicable to your answer.

a. On March 31, *The Granville Straight* had to borrow $200,000 to pay bills. The interest rate of this one-year loan is 11 percent, payable March 31.

b. Griffis intermingles her personal assets with those of the business. In applying for the $200,000 loan, she wanted to include on the company books her Lincoln automobile, which was worth $24,000. Her reasoning was that the business is a proprietorship and that her personal assets are available to the newspaper if needed.

c. Its financial position is so dismal that *The Granville Straight* is in danger of failure. Assets measured at historical cost total $1.3 million, but their current market value is only $900,000, which barely exceeds liabilities of $850,000. For now it appears that the newspaper will remain in business.

Exercise 12-3   *Reporting assets as a going concern and as a liquidating entity* **(L.O. 2, 3)**

Robarts Limited has the following assets:

Cash, $9,000.
Accounts Receivable, $25,600; allowance for uncollectible accounts, $4,300.
Office supplies, cost $280; scrap value $70.
Office machinery, cost $72,000; accumulated depreciation $14,000; current sales value, $47,400.
Land, cost $85,000; current sales value $135,000.

Required

1. Assume Robarts continues as a going concern. Compute the amount of its assets for reporting on the balance sheet.

2. Assume Robarts is going out of business by liquidating its assets. Compute the amount of its assets at liquidation value.

Exercise 12-4   *Reporting assets under GAAP* **(L.O. 3)**

Identify the amount at which each of the following assets should be reported in the financial statements of Gravel Limited. Cite the concept, principle, or constraint that is most applicable to each answer.

a. Gravel purchased a machine for $25,000, less a $1,300 cash discount. To ship the machine to the office, Gravel paid transportation charges of $500 and insurance of $200 while in transit. After using the machine for one month, Gravel purchases lubricating oil costing $150 for use in operating the machine.

b. Inventory has a cost of $72,000, but its current market value is $69,400.

c. Gravel purchased land for $175,000 and paid $2,500 to have the land surveyed, $15,400 to have old buildings removed, and $40,300 for grading land. Gravel is offering the land for sale at $225,000 and has received a $200,000 offer.

Exercise 12-5   *Reporting income under GAAP* **(L.O. 3)**

Lotus Management Inc. failed to record the following items at December 31, 19X4, the end of its fiscal year:

Accrued salary expense, $1,300.
Prepaid insurance, $700.
Accrued interest expense, $600.
Depreciation expense, $500.

Instead of recording the accrued expenses at December 31, 19X4, Lotus recorded the expenses when it paid them in 19X5. The company recorded the insurance as expense when it was prepaid for one year, early in 19X4. Depreciation expense for 19X5 was correctly recorded.

Lotus incorrectly reported net income of $10,000 in 19X4 and $7,400 in 19X5 because of the above errors.

Required

Compute Lotus's correct net income for 19X4 and 19X5. Compare the corrected trend in net income with the originally reported trend.

Exercise 12-6   *Reporting revenues under GAAP* **(L.O. 4)**

For each of the following situations, indicate the amount of revenue to report for the current year ended December 31 and for the following year:

a. Sold merchandise for $4,400, receiving a down payment of $1,100 and the customer's receivable for the balance. The company accounts for these sales by the sales method.

b. On April 1, loaned $35,000 at 12 percent on a three-year note.

c. Performed $900 of services for a high-risk customer on August 18, accounting for the revenue by the collection method. At December 31, the company had received $200 of the total; $550 was received the following year.

d. On September 1, collected one year's rent of $12,000 in advance on a building leased to another company.

e. Sold gift certificates, collecting $4,000 in advance. At December 31, $2,200 of the gifts have been claimed. The remainder were claimed during the next year.

Exercise 12-7   *Computing gross profit under the sales method and the installment method* **(L.O. 4)**

Allied Appliance Store sells on the installment plan. The store's installment sales figures for 19X7 follow:

Sales	$390,000
Down payments received on the sales	80,000
Collections on installments	170,000
Inventory at beginning of 19X7	60,000
Inventory at end of 19X7	42,000
Purchases	216,000

Required

Compute the store's gross profit if it uses (a) the sales method of revenue recognition, and (b) the installment method.

Exercise 12-8 *Computing construction revenue under the completed-contract method and the percentage-of-completion method (L.O. 4)*

McMinn Construction Corp. builds bridges for the province of Alberta. The construction period typically extends for several years. During 19X5, McMinn completed a small bridge with a contract price of $500,000. McMinn's $320,000 cost of the bridge was incurred as follows: $20,000 in 19X3; $180,000 in 19X4; and $120,000 in 19X5. Compute McMinn's revenue for each year 19X3 through 19X5 if the company uses (a) the completed-contract method, and (b) the percentage-of-completion method. Which method better matches expense with revenue?

Exercise 12-9 *Changing the useful life of a depreciable asset (L.O. 5)*

McMinn Construction Corp. uses a crane on its construction projects. The company purchased the crane early in January 19X3 for $400,000. For 19X3 and 19X4 depreciation was taken by the straight-line method based on an eight-year life and an estimated residual value of $80,000. In early 19X5, it became evident that the crane would be useful beyond the original life of eight years. Therefore, beginning in 19X5, McMinn changed the depreciable life of the crane to a total life of ten years. The company retained the straight-line method and did not alter the residual value.

Required

Prepare McMinn's depreciation entries for 19X4 and 19X5. Identify the accounting principles most important in this situation.

Exercise 12-10 *Identifying subsequent events for the financial statements (L.O. 5)*

Champlain Inc. experienced the following events after May 31, 19X8, the end of the company's fiscal year, but before publication of its financial statements on July 12:

a. Increased demand for Champlain products suggests that the next fiscal year will be the best in the company's history.

b. On July 6, Champlain is sued for $3 million. Loss of the lawsuit could lead to Champlain's bankruptcy.

c. Champlain collected $126,000 of the $480,000 accounts receivable reported on the May 31 balance sheet. Champlain expects to collect the remainder in the course of business during the next fiscal year.

d. A major customer, who owed Champlain $220,000 at May 31, declared bankruptcy on June 21.

e. Champlain sales personnel received a contract to supply Bronson Inc. with laser equipment.

Required

Identify the subsequent events that Champlain should disclose in its May 31, 19X8 financial statements.

Exercise 12-11 *Using accounting concepts and principles (L.O. 2, 6)*

Identify the accounting concept or principle, if any, that is violated in each of the following situations. You may choose from among disclosure, conservatism, cost, entity and matching.

a. The inventory of a clothing store has a current market value of $62,000. The store reports the inventory at its cost of $106,000.

b. The owner of a court reporting service used the business bank account to pay her family's household expenses, making no note that the expenses were personal.

c. A manufacturing company changed from the FIFO inventory method to the LIFO method and failed to disclose the accounting change in the financial statements.

d. A paper company that purchased 1,000 hectares of timberland at $300 per hectare in 1973 reports the land at its current market value of $3,000 per hectare.

e. A railroad records depreciation during years when net income is high but fails to record depreciation when net income is low. Revenues are relatively constant.

Exercise 12-12   *Using accounting concepts and principles* (L.O. 2, 6)

Indicate the accounting concept or principle that applies to the following situations. Choose among comparability, materiality, reliability, revenue and time period.

a. Lim Ting Restaurant was recently sued for $200,000, but the plaintiff has indicated a willingness to settle for less than that amount. Lim Ting hopes to settle for $50,000, but their lawyers believe the settlement will be between $90,000 and $100,000. Lim Ting's auditor reports the settlement as a real liability on the balance sheet. The only remaining issue is whether to report the liability at $50,000 or at $95,000.

b. Northern Lights Limited is considering publishing quarterly financial statements to provide more current information about its affairs.

c. POA, Inc. is negotiating the sale of $500,000 of inventory. POA has been in financial difficulty and desperately needs to report this sale on its income statement of the current year. At December 31, the end of the company's accounting year, the sale has not been closed.

d. New Wave Distributors expenses the cost of plant assets that cost less than $300.

e. Although Bracken Corp. could increase its reported income by changing depreciation methods, Bracken management has decided not to make the change.

Problems   (Group A)

Problem 12-1A   *Disclosing a change in accounting method* (L.O. 1, 5)

Your company's board of directors is debating a change from the FIFO inventory method to the weighted-average method. The main points of contention are the effects of the accounting change on net income and cash flow. Two members of the board favor keeping the FIFO method because of its effect on net income during periods of rising prices. Recently, however, prices have risen so fast that other members of the board think the company is wasting money by paying too high taxes. These board members are willing to have the company report lower income in order to save precious cash. All members of the board agree that if the company changes inventory methods, it would be best not to disclose the change in the annual report.

Required

Assume the board of directors has decided to change accounting methods. Draft a memorandum to convince the board members of the need to disclose the relevant aspects of the accounting change. Explain to the board in your memorandum the basic objective of financial reporting. Also draft the disclosure note to report the accounting change in the financial statements, using your own made-up figures to disclose relevant information about the change. Discuss how the information in your proposed disclosure note meets the objective of financial reporting. Refer to two accounting principles directly applicable to this situation.

Problem 12-2A   *Identifying the basis for good accounting practices* **(L.O. 2, 3, 6)**

The following accounting practices are in accord with generally accepted accounting principles. Identify all the accounting concepts and principles that form the basis for each accounting practice. More than one concept or principle may apply.

a. A theater company accrues employee salaries at year end even though the salaries will be paid during the first few days of the new year.

b. Assets are reported at liquidation value on the financial statements of a company that is going out of business.

c. The cost of machinery is being depreciated over a 5-year life because independent engineers believe the machinery will become obsolete after that time. (The company had hoped to depreciate the machinery over 10 years to report lower depreciation and higher net income in the early years of the asset's life.)

d. A manufacturing firm built some specialized equipment for its own use. The equipment would have cost $110,000 if purchased from an outside company, but the cost of constructing the equipment was only $89,000. The firm recorded the equipment at cost of $89,000.

e. Depreciation of the home-office building is difficult to relate to particular sales. Therefore, the company records depreciation expense on a time basis.

f. A company wishes to change its method of accounting for revenue. However, the company does not switch because it wants to use the same accounting method that other companies in the industry use.

g. Because it is often difficult to collect installment receivables, a retailer uses the installment method of revenue recognition rather than the sales method.

h. The cost of office equipment such as staplers and wastebaskets is not capitalized and depreciated because of their relative insignificance.

i. A fire destroyed the company garage after December 31, 19X7 and before the financial statements were published in early February 19X8. Although the fire loss is insured, reconstruction of the garage will disrupt the company's operations. This subsequent event will be reported in the 19X7 financial statements.

j. A paint company accounts for its operations by dividing the business into four separate units. This division enables the company to evaluate each unit apart from the others.

Problem 12-3A   *Identifying the concepts and principles violated by bad accounting*
practices **(L.O. 2, 3, 6)**

The following accounting practices are not in accord with generally accepted accounting principles. A few of the practices violate more than one concept or principle. Identify all the accounting concepts and principles not followed in each situation.

a. All amounts on the balance sheet and income statement of Business Products Inc. have been adjusted for changes in the value of the dollar during the period.

b. Rizzuto Grain Ltd. records one half of the depreciation of its grain silos when it purchases them and the other half over their estimated useful lives.

c. Day's Boutique sells high-fashion clothing to customers on credit. Thus far, collection losses on receivables have been very small. Nevertheless, Bonnie Day, the owner, uses the collection method to recognize revenue. The entity's revenue is understated because credit sales are not accounted for properly.

d. Alvarez Importers changed from the FIFO method to the LIFO method for inventory but did not report the accounting change in the financial statements.

e. Quebec Ironworks, Inc. applied the lower-of-cost-or-market method to account for its inventory. Quebec Ironworks used an estimate of the inventory value developed by its management. This estimate differed widely from estimates supplied by two independent appraisers. The estimates of the two appraisers were close together.

f. Butler Manufacturing does not report a lawsuit in which it is the defendant. Alvin Butler, the president, argues that the outcome of the case is uncertain and that to report the lawsuit would introduce subjective data into the financial statements.

g. Todd Department Store records cost of goods sold in a predetermined amount each month regardless of the level of sales.

h. Tim Ihnacek is having difficulty evaluating the success of his advertising firm because he fails to separate business assets from personal assets.

i. Tapes Unlimited is continuing in business, but its owner accounts for assets as though the store were liquidating.

j. Major Construction Corporation recognizes all revenue on long-term construction projects at the start of construction.

Problem 12-4A   *Using the installment-revenue method* **(L.O. 4)**

Meridian Electrical makes all sales on the installment basis but uses the sales method to record revenue. The company's income statements for the most recent three years are as follows:

	Year 1	Year 2	Year 3
Sales	$380,000	$404,000	$370,000
Cost of goods sold	190,000	181,800	199,800
Gross profit	190,000	222,200	170,200
Operating expenses	110,600	130,700	125,100
Net income	$ 79,400	$ 91,500	$ 45,100
Collections from sales of year 1	$140,000	$151,000	$ 72,000
2		143,000	209,000
3			163,000

Required

Compute the amount of net income Meridian would have reported if the company had used the installment method for revenue. Ignore the effect of uncollectible accounts and present your answer in the following format:

Installment-method net income	Year 1	Year 2	Year 3
Gross profit	$	$	$
Operating expenses	110,600	130,700	125,100
Net income	$	$	$

Problem 12-5A   *Using the installment-revenue method* **(L.O. 4)**

Bayview Resorts sells land on the installment plan. Collections of installment receivables have deteriorated. The company's accountants are considering the different methods of recording revenues. Revenue, expense, and collection data for the current year are as follows:

	19X3
Installment sales	$2,400,000
Cost of land sold...	1,320,000
Collections of installment receivables from sales of 19X2...................	760,000
19X3...................	520,000

The gross profit percentage of 19X2 installment sales was 46 percent.

Required

1. Which method should be used to account for revenues if collections are extremely doubtful? If collections are reasonably assured? Which method is more advantageous for income tax purposes? Why?
2. Compute gross profit for 19X3 under the sales method, the collection method, and the installment method.

Problem 12-6A *Accounting for construction income* **(L.O. 4)**

Diamond Bridge Inc. constructs bridges under long-term contracts. During 19X5, Diamond began three projects that progressed according to the following schedule during 19X5, 19X6 and 19X7:

Project	Contract Price	Total Project Cost	19X5 Cost for Year	19X5 % Completed during Year	19X6 Cost for Year	19X6 % Completed during Year	19X7 Cost for Year	19X7 % Completed during Year
1	$2,400,000	$1,800,000	$1,800,000	100%	—	—	—	—
2	3,100,000	2,200,000	484,000	22	$1,716,000	78%	—	—
3	1,900,000	1,400,000	280,000	20	840,000	60	$280,000	20%

Required

1. Assume Diamond uses the completed-contract method for construction revenue. Compute the company's construction revenue and income to be reported in 19X5, 19X6, and 19X7.
2. Compute Diamond's construction revenue and income to be reported in the three years if the company uses the percentage-of-completion method.

Problem 12-7A *Accounting for revenues and expenses according to GAAP* **(L.O. 2, 3, 4)**

Roberta Katz established Katz Home Furnishings in January 19X7. During 19X7, 19X8, and most of 19X9, Katz kept the company's books and prepared its financial statements, although she had no training or experience in accounting. As a result, the accounts and statements contain numerous errors. For example, Katz recorded only cash receipts from customers as revenue. The sales method is appropriate for the business. She recorded inventory purchases as the cost of goods sold. When the current market value of her company's equipment increased by $6,200 in 19X7 and by $1,700 in 19X9, Katz debited the Equipment account and credited Revenue. She recorded no depreciation during 19X7, 19X8 and 19X9.

Late in 19X9, Katz employed an accountant, who determined that depreciable assets of the firm cost $150,000 on June 30, 19X7, had an expected residual value of $10,000, and a total useful life of eight years. The accountant believes the straight-line depreciation method is appropriate for Katz's plant assets. The company's fiscal year ends December 31. At the end of 19X9 the company's records reveal the following amounts in the accompanying table.

	19X7	19X8	19X9
Reported net income (net loss)	$ 24,300	$ (6,200)	$ 62,900
Sales	131,800	164,700	226,100
Cash collections from customers	106,500	151,300	239,600
Purchases of inventory	100,600	136,000	191,700
Ending inventory	20,800	47,400	83,700
Accrued expenses not recorded at year end; these expenses were recorded during the next year, when paid	3,800	2,700	6,800
Depreciation expense recorded	-0-	-0-	-0-
Revenue recorded for increase in the value of equipment	6,200		1,700

Required

Apply the concepts and principles of GAAP to compute the correct net income of Katz Home Furnishings for 19X7, 19X8, and 19X9.

Problem 12-8A   *Recording and reporting transactions according to GAAP (L.O. 2, 3, 4, 5, 6)*

The accounting records of Mortensen Publishing Inc. reveal the following information prior to closing the books at April 30, the end of the current fiscal year:

a. Accounts receivable include $12,600 from Miller Bookstore, which has declared bankruptcy. Mortensen, which uses the allowance method to account for bad debts, expects to receive only one-fourth of the amount receivable from Miller.

b. No interest has been accrued on a $35,000, 12 percent, 90-day note payable issued on March 31.

c. The merchandise inventory, with a cost of $54,000, has a current market value of only $51,700. Mortensen uses a periodic inventory system and has not made the April 30 entry to record ending inventory.

d. Property tax is due each April 30, and Mortensen has received the city property tax bill of $4,960. However, the company has not recorded property tax at April 30 because Mortensen plans to record the tax when it is paid in May.

e. The company's office building was recently valued by independent appraisers at $750,000. This valuation is $150,000 more than Mortensen paid for the building and is $410,000 more than its cost less accumulated depreciation.

f. Three years ago on May 1, Mortensen paid $440,000 for its printing equipment. The company has depreciated the equipment by the straight-line method over an expected useful life of 10 years using a residual value of $40,000. Having used the equipment for 2 years, Mortensen determined at the beginning of the current year that it will remain in service for a total of only 8 years. The company will continue to use the straight-line method and $40,000 residual value for accounting purposes.

g. On May 13, before Mortensen issued its financial statements for the year ended April 30, the company's principal customer, Mears, Rareback and Co., declared its intention to cease doing business with Mortensen. This event is significant because for the past 10 years Mears has accounted for approximately 65 percent of Mortensen's sales. Consequently, Mortensen's ability to sustain its recent level of sales in future years is seriously in doubt.

Required

Make all journal entries needed at April 30 to record this information. Explanations are not required. Identify those items not requiring a journal entry, giving the reason why an entry is not needed. If a note to the financial statements is needed, write the note.

(Group B)

Problem 12-1B *Disclosing significant accounting policies* **(L.O. 1, 5)**

BPI Systems, a company that constructs large office buildings, is approaching the end of its first year of operations. Three projects are under way and scheduled for completion during the next year. The board of directors is considering the adoption of certain accounting policies. After a lengthy discussion, the board decides to use the percentage-of-completion method for long-term construction contracts. The board further decides to use the weighted-average method for inventory and to apply the straight-line depreciation method for capital assets. Estimated useful lives of capital assets range from 5 years for tools to 10 years for equipment and to 20 years for buildings. Disclosure of the accounting policies used by BPI Systems is a point of contention because two influential board members believe that it will enable competitors to gain an undue advantage.

Required

Draft a memorandum to convince the board members of the need to disclose significant accounting policies. In this memo, explain the basic objective of financial reporting. Also draft the note to disclose the company's accounting methods. Relate the information in your proposed disclosure note to the objective of financial accounting.

Problem 12-2B *Identifying the basis for good accounting practices* **(L.O. 2, 3, 6)**

The following accounting practices are in accord with generally accepted accounting principles. Identify all the accounting concepts and principles that form the basis for each accounting practice. More than one concept or principle may apply.

a. TGI Friday's, a restaurant, makes such small payments for fire insurance that the company expenses them and makes no year-end adjustment for prepaid insurance.

b. The inventory of a personal computer store declined substantially in value because of changing technology, and the store wrote its computer inventory down to the lower of cost or market.

c. A construction company changed from the completed-contract method to the percentage-of-completion method of recording revenue on its long-term construction contracts. The company disclosed this accounting change in the notes to its financial statements.

d. A mining company recorded an intangible asset at the cost of the mineral lease and all other costs necessary to bring the mine to the point of production. After the mine was in operation, the company amortized the asset's cost as expense in proportion to the revenues from sale of the minerals.

e. Because of a downturn in the economy, a jeweler increased his business's allowance for doubtful accounts.

f. The personal residence of the owner of a freight company is not disclosed in the financial statements of the business.

g. A manufacturing company's capital assets are carried on the books at cost under the assumption that the company will remain in operation for the foreseeable future.

h. A clothing store discloses in notes to its financial statements that it uses the FIFO inventory method.

i. A real estate developer paid $1.3 million for land and held it for three years before selling it for $2 million. There was significant inflation during this period, but the developer reports the $.7 million gain on sale with no adjustment for the change in the value of the dollar.

j. Liabilities are reported in two categories, current and long-term.

Problem 12-3B   *Identifying the concepts and principles violated by bad accounting practices* **(L.O. 2, 3, 6)**

The following accounting practices are not in accord with generally accepted accounting principles. Identify the single accounting concept or principle that is most clearly violated by each accounting practice.

a. The balance sheet of Rhonda Green's dental practice includes significant receivables that she will probably never collect. Nevertheless, Green's accountant refuses to use the collection method to account for revenue.

b. The current market value of Miska Electronics' inventory is $119,000, but the company reports its inventory at cost of $134,000. The decline in value is permanent.

c. The liabilities of Waco Jet Corporation exceed the company's assets. To get a loan from the bank, Waco Jet's owner, Slade McQueen, includes his personal investments as assets on the balance sheet of the business.

d. Singh Corporation increases the carrying value of its land based on recent sales of adjacent property.

e. Mission Ford Sales records expenses on an irregular basis without regard to the pattern of the company's revenues.

f. Waterloo Software Ltd. omits the significant accounting policies note from its financial statements because the company uses the same accounting methods that its competitors use.

g. Royal Iron Works regularly changes accounting methods in order to report a target amount of net income each year.

h. Alberta Land Inc. reports land at its market value of $820,000, which is greater than the cost of $400,000.

i. A flood on July 2 caused $150,000 in damage to Yukon Construction property. The company did not report the flood as a subsequent event in the June 30 financial statements.

j. Victoria, Inc. overstates depreciation expense in order to report low amounts of net income.

Problem 12-4B   *Using the installment-revenue method* **(L.O. 4)**

Pine Valley Appliance Store makes all sales on the installment basis but uses the sales method to record revenue. The company's income statements for the most recent three years follow:

	Year 1	Year 2	Year 3
Sales...	$240,000	$210,000	$290,000
Cost of goods sold.................................	144,000	121,800	179,800
Gross profit...	96,000	88,200	110,200
Operating expenses................................	51,400	49,300	61,300
Net income...	$ 44,600	$ 38,900	$ 48,900
Collections from sales of year 1.............	$100,000	$ 75,000	$ 60,000
2.............		68,000	120,000
3.............			145,000

Required

Compute the amount of net income Pine Valley would have reported if the company had used the installment method for revenue. Ignore the effect of uncollectible accounts and present your answer in the following format:

Installment-method net income	Year 1	Year 2	Year 3
Gross profit..	$	$	$
Operating expenses...............................	51,400	49,300	61,300
Net income (net loss)	$	$	$

Problem 12-5B *Using the installment revenue method* **(L.O. 4)**

Nickel City Appliances sells on the installment plan. Collections of installment receivables have deteriorated. The store's accountants are considering the different methods of recording revenues. Revenue, expense, and collection data for the current year are as follows:

	19X6
Installment sales	$120,000
Cost of goods sold	72,000
Collections of installment receivables from sales of 19X5.............................	40,000
19X6.............................	24,000

The gross profit percentage on 19X5 installment sales was 42 percent.

Required

1. Which method should be used to account for revenues if collections are reasonably assured? If collections are extremely doubtful? Which method is more advantageous for income tax purposes? Why?
2. Compute gross profit for 19X6 under the sales method, the collection method, and the installment method.

Problem 12-6B *Accounting for construction income* **(L.O. 4)**

B.C. Shipbuilding Corporation participates in the construction of small ships under long-term contracts. During 19X7, B.C. began three projects that progressed according to the following schedule during 19X7, 19X8, and 19X9:

			19X5		19X6		19X7	
Project	Contract Price	Total Project Cost	Cost for Year	% Completed during Year	Cost for Year	% Completed during Year	Cost for Year	% Completed during Year
1	$2,100,000	$1,200,000	$ 400,000	$33\frac{1}{3}$%	$ 800,000	$66\frac{2}{3}$%	—	—
2	1,200,000	880,000	880,000	100	—	—	—	—
3	7,400,000	6,300,000	1,260,000	20	2,205,000	35	$2,835,000	45%

Required

1. Assume B.C. Shipbuilding uses the completed-contract method for construction revenue. Compute the company's construction revenue and income to be reported in 19X7, 19X8, and 19X9.
2. Compute B.C.'s construction revenue and income to be reported in the three years if the company uses the percentage-of-completion method.

Problem 12-7B *Accounting for revenues and expenses according to GAAP* **(L.O. 2, 3, 4)**

Nathan Nielsen established Nielsen Furniture Importers in January 19X4 to import furniture from Denmark. During 19X4 and 19X5 Nielsen kept the company's books and prepared the financial statements, although he had no training or experience in accounting. As a result, the accounts contain numerous errors. Nielsen recorded revenue from sales on the collection method, which is not appropriate for the company. Nielsen should have been using the sales method for revenues. He also recorded inventory purchases as the cost of goods sold.

When the value of the company warehouse increased by $50,000 in 19X6, Nielsen recorded an increase in the Building account and credited Revenue. On January 2, 19X4, he borrowed $30,000 on a 9 percent, three-year note. He intended to wait until 19X7, when the note was due, to record the full amount of interest expense for three years. The company's records reveal the following amounts:

	19X4	19X5	19X6
Reported net income (net loss)	$(15,200)	$ 31,600	$ 64,100
Sales	256,700	303,500	366,800
Cash collections from customers	210,400	309,000	317,800
Purchases of inventory	141,000	187,400	202,300
Ending inventory	35,800	59,900	73,400
Accrued expenses not recorded at year end; these expenses were recorded during the next year, when paid	13,500	22,600	30,100
Interest expense recorded	-0-	-0-	-0-
Revenue recorded for increase in the value of the store building			50,000

Required

In early 19X7 Nielsen employed you as an accountant. Apply the concepts and principles of GAAP to compute the correct net income of Nielsen Furniture Importers for 19X4, 19X5, and 19X6.

Problem 12-8B   *Recording and reporting transactions according to GAAP (L.O. 2, 3, 4, 5, 6)*

The accounting records of P.E.I. Wholesale Distributors reveal the following information prior to closing the books at September 30, the end of the current fiscal year:

a. Accounts receivable include $63,000 from Glenwood Drug Corporation, which has declared bankruptcy. P.E.I., which uses the allowance method to account for bad debts, expects to receive one third of the amount receivable from Glenwood.

b. No interest has been accrued on a $25,000, 12 percent, six-month note receivable that was received on May 31.

c. The merchandise inventory, with a cost of $69,000, has a current market value of only $58,000. P.E.I. uses a periodic inventory system and has not made the September 30 entry to record ending inventory.

d. Accrued salaries of $12,100 have been earned by P.E.I. employees but have not been recorded at September 30 because the company plans to record the salaries when it pays them in October.

e. The company's office building has been valued recently by independent appraisers at $400,000. This valuation is $180,000 more than P.E.I. paid for the building and is $270,000 more than its cost less accumulated depreciation.

f. Two years ago on October 1, P.E.I. paid $120,000 for its delivery trucks. During the prior year the company has depreciated the trucks by the straight-line method over an expected useful life of 4 years, using a residual value of $10,000. After using the trucks for the first year, P.E.I. decided at the beginning of the current year that the trucks will remain in service for a total of 5 years. The company will continue to use the straight-line method and the $10,000 residual value for accounting purposes.

g. On October 19, before P.E.I. issued its financial statements for the year ended September 30, a competitor sued the company for damages of $500,000. Lawyers for P.E.I. believe P.E.I. will win the case. However, a $500,000 loss would make it difficult for the company to continue in business.

Required

Make all journal entries needed at September 30 to record this information. Explanations are not required. Identify those items not requiring a journal entry, giving the reason why an entry is not needed. If a note to the financial statements is needed, write the note.

Extending Your Knowledge

Decision Problems

1. Measuring income according to GAAP (L.O. 2, 3, 4)

O'Hara Furniture Limited was founded in January 19X5 by Bernard and Virginia O'Hara, who share the management of the business. Virginia does the purchasing and manages the sales staff. Bernard keeps the books and handles financial matters. The O'Haras believe the store has prospered, but they are uncertain about precisely how well it has done. It is now December 31, 19X5, and they are trying to decide whether to borrow a substantial sum in order to expand the business.

They have asked your help because of your accounting knowledge. You learn that the O'Haras opened the store with an initial investment of $51,000 cash and a building valued at $100,000. The cash receipts totaled $180,000, which included collections, $15,000 invested by the O'Haras, $50,000 borrowed from the bank in the name of the furniture store, and $7,500 of earnings from a family inheritance. The store made credit sales of $105,000 that have not been collected at December 31. The O'Haras purchased furniture inventory on credit for $160,000, and inventory at December 31, 19X5 was $75,000. The store paid $90,000 on account.

The 19X5 cash expenses were $92,000. Additional miscellaneous expenses totaled $2,700 at year's end. These expenses included the O'Haras' household costs of $10,000 and interest on the business debt. The $5,000 of depreciation on the store building was omitted.

Bernard and Virginia have decided to proceed with the expansion plan only if net income for the first year was $40,000 or more. Bernard's analysis of the cash account leads him to believe that net income was $49,000, so he is ready to expand. You are less certain than Bernard of the wisdom of this decision primarily because the O'Haras have mixed personal and business assets.

Required

1. Use a Cash T-account to show how Bernard arrived at the $49,000 amount for net income.

2. Prepare the income statement of the furniture store of 19X5.

3. Should the O'Haras borrow to expand their business?

4. Which accounting concept or principle is most fundamental to this problem situation?

2. Examining the disclosure principle (L.O. 3, 5)

1. It has been suggested that the disclosure principle is perhaps one of the most important concepts and principles underlying financial reporting. Why is it so important?

2. "Disclosure of Accounting Policies," Section 1505 of the *CICA Handbook*, was added to the *Handbook* in October, 1974. Discuss the probable impact the addition of Section 1505 had on users of financial statements. Consider users before and after its introduction.

3. Accounting researchers are studying the understandability of financial statements. Why are they doing this? What contribution might their research make?

4. The text suggests that subsequent events and long-term commitments should be disclosed in the notes to the financial statements. What about these two items makes their disclosure so important to users?

5. *Financial Reporting in Canada*[2] reported that about one in three of the companies surveyed for its 1991 edition reported the revenue principle or revenue recognition method used in preparing their financial statements. Why do you think these companies reported that information? What might we assume about the other 209 companies in the survey with respect to revenue recognition?

Ethical Issue

Some real estate companies sell land under terms that permit low down payments by purchasers and stretch payments over many years. In many cases in the past, the land had not yet been subdivided into the individual lots that would be sold. Also, the land often had not been landscaped. Estimating the cost of preparing the land for eventual use was difficult. Under accounting practices widespread in the 1960s and 1970s, real estate companies could record the full amount of the revenue in the year of the sale. These companies were thus able to report unusually high net incomes even though their cash collections were quite low.

Required

1. What three conditions must a company meet in order to record revenue on a sale? Which conditions did the real estate companies meet? Which conditions did they not meet?

2. Which revenue method were companies using during the 1960s and 1970s? In your opinion, was it ethical for these companies to use this method? Give your reason.

3. Which collection method is well suited for this situation? Give your reason.

Financial Statement Problems

1. Disclosure in action (L.O. 5)

The notes to the financial statements are an integral part of the financial statements. Examine Schneider Corporation's financial statements in Appendix C, and answer these questions:

1. Note 1, "Significant accounting policies," is perhaps the most important of the notes; it describes the accounting policies followed in preparing the financial statements. Schneider, as a producer of meat, poultry, cheese and baked goods products, carries significant quantities of inventory. How is this inventory valued? Why is it important to disclose the basis of valuation of inventory for Schneider'?

---

[2] *Financial Reporting in Canada*, 19th edition (Toronto: CICA, 1991), p. 20.

2. Note 1(c) and note 4 describe how interest costs are capitalized on major projects during the period of construction. Why is it reasonable to include these interest costs as part of the cost of the constructed asset? Do you see any problems with this accounting policy?

3. Note 4 indicates that the Board of Directors of the Schneider Corporation has approved capital expenditures of over $5 million. Note 6 presents principal payments on debentures and loans over the next five years. Finally, note 11 lists operating lease payments, which the corporation is committed to as at October 26, 1991. Why is this information disclosed in the financial statements? How would users of the financial statements incorporate this data into their evaluation of the company?

4. Note 9 describes the accounting treatment of a trade commission ruling during fiscal year 1991. Why is this event treated as a prior year's adjustment? How would treating this event as part of fiscal year 1991 affect your assessment of this year's results?

5. Included in the notes to the financial statements is a short reference to the amount of Schneider's sales to foreign customers (see note 12). What percentage of sales are to customers outside of Canada for 1991 and for 1990? Are foreign sales a significant part of Schneider's sales?

6. Explain how the concept of materiality is evident in the financial statements.

2. Disclosure in action (L.O. 5)

Obtain the annual report of an actual company of your choosing. Use the company's financial statements and related notes to answer these questions illustrating the disclosure principle. Concentrate on the current year in the annual report you select.

1. Identify any unusual items, discontinued operations, effects of accounting changes, or extraordinary items reported on the income statements. Examine any notes that give additional details about these special items of income or loss. Identify their individual amounts and state whether each item increased or decreased net income.

2. What are the company's business segments? These may be reported by geographical area, by product line, or in both ways. Identify each segment's revenues and operating income or net income for the current year.

3. Examine the company's multi-year financial summary. Compute the percentage increase or decrease in total revenues over this entire period. Compute the percentage increase or decrease in net income over the same period. Which increased faster, total revenues or net income?

Answers to Self-Study Questions

1. c
2. a
3. c
4. b
5. a ($10,000 – $7,000)/$10,000 = .30 × $1,500 = $450
6. a $180,000/$720,000 = .25 × $900,000 = $225,000;
   $225,00 – $180,000 = $45,000

7. d
8. d
9. b
10. b

Chapter 13

Accounting for Partnerships

"That rotten [so-and-so]! After all I've done for him over the last 20 years, and that's the way he treats me? Well, he ought to think again. My lawyer's got a nice little surprise waiting for him!"

Sound familiar? The cries of an angry wife railing against her husband during a stormy divorce? A good guess, but wrong. This was a man recently overheard in a [Montreal] restaurant. He was talking about his business partner.

It reminded us of how much the business partnerships we've seen over the years look like marriages. They begin with heady dreams. They bristle with excitement through a start-up period that's much like a honeymoon. After a while, they settle into a "reality" phase when the bloom leaves the rose. Then, sadly, many of them sink into a prolonged period of disenchantment. Cracks widen into crevasses between the partners. Then one day a partner wakes up and says, "I can't take this any longer." And a painful separation and "divorce" unfold.

Source: Peter Wylie and Mardy Grothe, "Breaking Up Is Hard to Do," *Nation's Business* (July 1988), p. 24.

LEARNING OBJECTIVES

After studying this chapter, you should be able to

1 Identify the characteristics, including advantages and disadvantages, of a partnership

2 Account for partners' initial investments in a partnership

3 Use different methods to allocate profits and losses to the partners

4 Account for the admission of a new partner to the business

5 Account for the withdrawal of a partner from the business

6 Account for the liquidation of a partnership

7 Prepare partnership financial statements

Forming a partnership is easy. It requires no permission from government authorities and involves no legal procedures, with the exception that most provinces require most partnerships to register information such as the name of the partners and the name under which the business will be carried on.[1] When two persons decide to go into business together, a partnership is automatically formed.

A **partnership** is an association of two or more persons who co-own a business for profit. This definition is common to the various provincial partnership acts which tend to prescribe similar rules with respect to the organization and operation of partnerships in their jurisdiction.

A partnership brings together the capital, talents, and experience of the partners. Business opportunities closed to an individual may open up to a partnership. Suppose neither Pedigo nor Yu has enough capital individually to buy a $300,000 parcel of land. They may be able to afford it together in a partnership. Or Van Allen, a tax accountant, and Kahn, an investment counselor, may pool their talents and know-how. Their partnership may offer a fuller range of money management services than either person could offer alone. Combining their experience may increase income for each of them.

Partnerships come in all sizes. Many partnerships have fewer than ten partners. Some physicians may have ten or more partners while some of the largest law firms in Canada have more than 120 partners.[2] The largest CA firms in Canada have from more than 300 to more than 650 partners.[3]

Characteristics of a Partnership

Starting a partnership is voluntary. A person cannot be forced to join a partnership, and partners cannot be forced to accept another person as a partner. Although the partnership agreement may be oral, a written agreement between the partners reduces the chance of a misunderstanding. Several features are unique to the partnership form of business. The following characteristics distinguish partnerships from sole proprietorships and from corporations, which we examine in later chapters.

OBJECTIVE 1

Identify the characteristics, including advantages and disadvantages, of a partnership

---

[1] Smyth, J.E., D.A. Soberman, and A.J. Easson, *The Law and Business Administration in Canada*, 6th edition. (Scarborough: Prentice Hall Canada Inc., 1991), p. 756.

[2] *The Financial Post 500, 1992* (Toronto: The Financial Post Company, 1992), p. 164.

[3] *The Financial Post 500, 1992* (Toronto: The Financial Post Company, 1992), p. 166.

The Written Partnership Agreement

A business partnership is like a marriage. To be successful, the partners must co-operate. However, business partners do not vow to remain together for life. Business partnerships come and go. To make certain that each partner fully understands how a particular partnership operates and to lower the chances that any partner might misunderstand how the business is run, partners may draw up a **partnership agreement**. This agreement is a contract between the partners, so transactions involving the agreement are governed by contract law. The provincial legislatures in Canada have passed their respective versions of a partnership act, the terms of which apply in the absence of a partnership agreement or in the absence of particular matters in the partnership agreement.[4]

The partnership agreement should make the following points clear:

1. Name, location, and nature of the business
2. Name, capital investment, and duties of each partner
3. Method of sharing profits and losses by the partners
4. Withdrawals allowed to the partners
5. Procedures for settling disputes between the partners
6. Procedures for admitting new partners
7. Procedures for settling up with a partner who withdraws from the business
8. Procedures for liquidating the partnership: selling the assets, paying the liabilities, and disbursing any remaining cash to the partners

As partners enter and leave the business, the old partnership is dissolved and a new partnership is formed. Drawing up a new agreement for each new partnership may be expensive and time-consuming.

Limited Life

A partnership has a life limited by the length of time that all partners continue to own the business. When a partner withdraws from the business, that partnership ceases to exist. A new partnership may emerge to continue the same business, but the old partnership has been *dissolved*. **Dissolution** is the ending of a partnership. Likewise, the addition of a new partner dissolves the old partnership and creates a new partnership. Partnerships are sometimes formed for a particular business venture, like a mining operation or a real estate investment. When the mine is depleted or the real estate is sold, the partnership may be dissolved.

Mutual Agency

Mutual agency in a partnership means that every partner can bind the business to a contract within the scope of the partnership's regular business operations. If an individual partner in a public accounting firm enters into a contract with a person or another business to provide accounting service, then the firm (not the individual who signs the contract) is bound to provide that service. However, if that same public accounting firm signs a contract to purchase home lawn services for the summer months, the partnership would not be bound to pay. Contracting for lawn services does not fall within the partnership's regular business operations.

---

[4] Smyth, J.E., D.A. Soberman, and A.J. Easson, *The Law and Business Administration in Canada*, 6th edition. (Scarborough: Prentice Hall Canada Inc., 1991), pp. 744–56.

Unlimited Liability

Each partner has an **unlimited personal liability** for the debts of the partnership. When a partnership cannot pay its debts with business assets, the partners must use their personal assets to meet the debt.

Arcand and Davis are the two partners in AD Company. The business has had an unsuccessful year, and the partnership's liabilities exceed its assets by $120,000. Arcand and Davis must pay this amount with their personal assets.

Recall that each partner has *unlimited liability*. If a partner is unable to pay his or her part of the debt, the other partner (or partners) must make payment. If Davis can pay only $50,000 of the liability, Arcand must pay $70,000. Arcand would then seek the extra $10,000 she had to pay from Davis in a separate action.

Unlimited liability and mutual agency are closely related. A dishonest partner or a partner with poor judgment may commit the partnership to a contract under which the business loses money. In turn, creditors may force all the partners to pay the debt from their personal assets. Hence, a business partner should be chosen with great care.

Partners can avoid unlimited personal liability for partnership obligations by forming a limited partnership. In this form of business organization, one or more of the general partners assumes the unlimited liability for business debts. In addition, there is another class of owners — limited partners. The limited partners can lose only as much as their investment in the business. In this sense, limited partners have limited liability similar to the limited liability that shareholders in a corporation have.

Co-ownership of Property

Any asset (cash, inventory, machinery, and so on) that a partner invests into the partnership becomes the joint property of all the partners. Also, each partner has a claim to the business's profits.

No Partnership Income Taxes

A partnership pays no income tax on its business income. Instead, the net income of the partnership is divided, and becomes the taxable income of the partners. Suppose AD Company earned net income of $80,000, shared equally by partners Arcand and Davis. AD Company would pay no income tax *as a business entity*. However, Arcand and Davis would pay income tax as individuals on their $40,000 shares of partnership income.

Accounting for a partnership is much like accounting for a proprietorship. We record buying and selling, collecting, and paying in a partnership just as we do for a business with only one owner. However, because a partnership has more than one owner, the partnership must have more than one owner's equity account. Every partner in the business, whether the firm has two or two hundred partners, has an individual owner's equity account. Often these accounts carry the name of the particular partner and the word *capital*. For example, the owner's equity account for Larry Insdorf would read "Insdorf, Capital"or "Larry Insdorf, Capital." Similarly, each partner has a withdrawal account. If the number of partners is large, the general ledger may contain the single account Partners' Capital or Owners' Equity. A subsidiary ledger can be used for individual partner accounts.

Let us see how to account for the multiple owners' equity accounts, and learn how they appear on the balance sheet, by taking a look at how to account for starting up a partnership.

Initial Investments by Partners

Partners in a new partnership may invest assets and liabilities in the business. These contributions are entered in the books in the same way that a proprietor's assets and liabilities are recorded. Subtracting each person's liabilities from his or her assets yields the amount to be credited to the owner's equity account for that person. The partners may hire an independent firm to appraise their assets and liabilities at current market value at the time a partnership is formed. This outside evaluation assures an objective valuation for what each partner brings into the business.

> **OBJECTIVE 2**
>
> Account for partners' initial investments in a partnership

Assume Benz and Hanna form a partnership to manufacture and sell computer software. Benz brings to the partnership cash of $10,000, accounts receivable of $30,000, inventory of $70,000, computer equipment with a cost of $600,000 and accumulated depreciation of $120,000, and accounts payable of $85,000. Hanna contributes cash of $5,000 and a software program. The development of this program cost Hanna $18,000, but its current market value is much greater. Suppose the partners agree on the following values based on an independent appraisal:

Benz's contributions

Cash, $10,000; inventory, $70,000; and accounts payable, $85,000 (the appraiser believes the current market values for these items equal Benz's values)

Accounts receivable, $30,000, less allowance for doubtful accounts of $5,000

Computer equipment, $450,000

Hanna's contributions

Cash, $5,000

Computer software, $100,000

Note that current market value differs only slightly from book value for Benz's computer equipment. However, the appraiser valued Hanna's $18,000 computer software at the much higher $100,000 figure. The partners record their initial investments at the current market values. The title of each owner's equity account includes the owner's name and Capital.

Benz's investment

June	1	Cash	10,000	
		Accounts Receivable...	30,000	
		Inventory...	70,000	
		Computer Equipment	450,000	
		Allowance for Doubtful Accounts.............		5,000
		Accounts Payable		85,000
		Benz, Capital		470,000
		To record Benz's investment in the partnership.		

Hanna's investment

June	1	Cash	5,000	
		Computer Software	100,000	
		Hanna, Capital..		105,000
		To record Hanna's investment in the partnership.		

The initial partnership balance sheet reports these amounts as follows:

Benz and Hanna
Balance Sheet
June 1, 19X5

Assets			Liabilities		
Cash..............................		$ 15,000	Accounts payable....................		$ 85,000
Accounts receivable.....	$30,000				
Less: Allowance for					
doubtful accounts....	5,000	25,000	**Capital**		
Inventory......................		70,000	Benz, capital..............................		470,000
Computer equipment .		450,000	Hanna, capital..........................		105,000
Computer software		100,000	Total liabilities		
Total assets...................		$660,000	and capital...........................		$660,000

Each owner's capital account appears under the heading Capital. Having more than one capital account distinguishes a partnership balance sheet from a proprietorship balance sheet.

Sharing Partnership Profits and Losses

How to allocate profits and losses among partners is one of the most challenging aspects of managing a partnership. If the partners have not drawn up an agreement, or if the agreement does not state how the partners will divide profits and losses, then, according to law, the partners must share profits and losses equally. If the agreement specifies a method for sharing profits but not losses, then losses are shared in the same proportion as profits. For example, a partner receiving 75 percent of the profits would likewise absorb 75 percent of any losses.

In some cases, an equal division is not fair. One partner may perform more work for the business than the other partner, or one partner may make a larger capital contribution. In the preceding example, Hanna might agree to work longer hours for the partnership than Benz in order to earn a greater share of profits. Benz could argue that she should receive more of the profits because she contributed more net assets ($470,000) than Hanna did ($105,000). Hanna might contend that his computer software program is the partnership's most important asset, and that his share of the profits should be greater than Benz's share. Arriving at fair sharing of profits and losses in a partnership may be difficult. We now discuss the options available in determining partners' shares.

Sharing Based on a Stated Fraction

Partners may agree to any profit-and-loss-sharing method they desire. Suppose the partnership agreement of Cagle and Elias allocates two thirds of the business profits and losses to Cagle and one third to Elias. If net income for the year is $90,000, and all revenue and expense accounts have been closed, the Income Summary account has a credit balance of $90,000 as follows:

> **OBJECTIVE 3**
> Use different methods to allocate profits and losses to the partners

Income Summary	
	Bal. 90,000

The entry to close this account and allocate the profit to the partners' capital accounts is

Dec. 31	Income Summary..	90,000	
	Cagle, Capital ($90,000 × ⅔)		60,000
	Elias, Capital ($90,000 × ⅓).........................		30,000
	To allocate net income to partners.		

Consider the effect of this entry. Does Cagle get cash of $60,000 and Elias cash of $30,000? No. The increase in the capital accounts of the partners cannot be linked to any particular asset, including cash. Instead, the entry indicates that Cagle's ownership in all the assets of the business increased by $60,000 and Elias's by $30,000.

If the year's operations resulted in a net loss of $66,000, the Income Summary account would have a debit balance of $66,000. In that case, the closing entry to allocate the loss to the partners' capital accounts would be

Dec. 31	Cagle, Capital ($66,000 × ⅔)	44,000	
	Elias, Capital ($66,000 × ⅓)	22,000	
	Income Summary		66,000
	To allocate net loss to partners.		

Sharing Based on Partners' Capital Contributions

Profits and losses are often allocated in proportion to the partners' capital contributions in the business. Suppose Antoine, Barber, and Culomovic are partners in ABC Company. Their capital accounts have the following balances at the end of the year, before the closing entries:

Antoine, Capital	$ 40,000
Barber, Capital	60,000
Culomovic, Capital	50,000
Total capital balances	$150,000

Assume that the partnership earned a profit of $120,000 for the year. To allocate this amount based on capital contributions, each partner's percentage share of the partnership's total capital balance must be computed. We simply divide each partner's contribution by the total capital amount. These figures, multiplied by the $120,000 profit amount, yield each partner's share of the year's profits:

Antoine:	$40,000/$150,000 × $120,000	=	$ 32,000
Barber:	$60,000/$150,000 × $120,000	=	48,000
Culomovic:	$50,000/$150,000 × $120,000	=	40,000
	Net income allocated to partners	=	$120,000

The closing entry to allocate the profit to the partners' capital accounts is

Dec. 31	Income Summary	120,000	
	Antoine, Capital		32,000
	Barber, Capital		48,000
	Culomovic, Capital		40,000
	To allocate net income to partners.		

After this closing entry, the partners' capital balances are

Antoine, Capital ($40,000 + $32,000)	$ 72,000
Barber, Capital ($60,000 + $48,000)	108,000
Culomovic, Capital ($50,000 + $40,000)	90,000
Total capital balances after allocation of net income	$270,000

Sharing Based on Capital Contributions and Service to the Partnership

One partner, regardless of his or her capital contribution, may put more work into the business than the other partners. Even among partners who log equal service time, one person's superior experience and knowledge may command a greater share of income. To reward the harder-working or more valuable person, the profit-and-loss-sharing method may be based on a combination of contributed capital *and* service to the business.

Assume Randolph and Scott formed a partnership in which Randolph invested $60,000 and Scott invested $40,000, a total of $100,000. Scott devotes more time to the partnership and earns the larger salary. Accordingly, the two partners have agreed to share profits as follows:

1. The first $50,000 of partnership profits is to be allocated based on partners' capital contributions to the business.
2. The next $60,000 of profits is to be allocated based on service, with Randolph receiving $24,000 and Scott receiving $36,000.
3. Any remaining amount is allocated equally.

If net income for the first year is $125,000, the partners' shares of this profit are computed as follows:

	Randolph	Scott	Total
Total net income..			$125,000
Sharing of first $50,000 of net income,			
based on capital contributions:			
Randolph ($60,000/$100,000 × $50,000)................	$30,000		
Scott ($40,000/$100,000 × $50,000).........................		$20,000	
Total..			50,000
Net income remaining for allocation..........................			75,000
Sharing of next $60,000, based on service:			
Randolph	24,000		
Scott...		36,000	
Total..			60,000
Net income left for allocation			15,000
Remainder shared equally:			
Randolph ($15,000 × ½)..	7,500		
Scott ($15,000 × ½)...		7,500	
Total..			15,000
Net income left for allocation			$ -0-
Net income allocated to the partners.........................	$61,500	$63,500	$125,000

Based on this allocation, the closing entry is

Dec. 31	Income Summary	125,000	
	Randolph, Capital......................................		61,500
	Scott, Capital		63,500
	To allocate net income to partners.		

Sharing Based on Salaries and Interest

Partners may be rewarded for their service and their capital contributions to the business in other ways. In one sharing plan, the partners are allocated salaries plus interest on their capital balances. Assume Massey and Vanier form an oil-exploration partnership. At the beginning of the year, their capital balances are $80,000 and $100,000 respectively. The partnership agreement allocates annual salary of $43,000 to Massey and $35,000 to Vanier. After salaries are allocated, each partner earns 8 percent interest on his beginning capital balance. Any remaining net income is divided equally. Partnership profit of $96,000 would be allocated as follows:

	Massey	Vanier	Total
Total net income...			$96,000
First, salaries:			
Massey	$43,000		
Vanier		$35,000	
Total			78,000
Net income remaining for allocation			18,000
Second, interest on beginning capital balances:			
Massey ($80,000 × .08)...	6,400		
Vanier ($100,000 × .08)		8,000	
Total			14,400
Net income remaining for allocation			3,600
Third, remainder shared equally:			
Massey ($3,600 × ½)	1,800		
Vanier ($3,600 × ½)		1,800	
Total			3,600
Net income remaining for allocation			$ -0-
Net income allocated to the partners......................	$51,200	$44,800	$96,000

Based on this allocation, the closing entry is

Dec. 31	Income Summary	96,000	
	Massey, Capital..		51,200
	Vanier, Capital...		44,800
	To allocate net income to partners.		

These salaries and interest amounts are *not* business expenses in the usual sense. Partners do not work for their own business to earn a salary, as an employee does. They do not loan money to their own business to earn interest. Their goal is for the partnership to earn a profit. Therefore, salaries and interest in partnership agreements are simply ways of expressing the allocation of profits and losses to the partners. For example, the salary component of partner income rewards service to the partnership. The interest component rewards a partner's investment of cash or other assets in the business.

In the preceding illustration, net income exceeded the sum of salary and interest. If the partnership profit is less than the allocated sum of salary and interest, a negative remainder will occur at some stage in the allocation process. Even so, the partners use the same method for allocation purposes. For example, assume that Massey and Vanier Partnership earned only $82,000.

	Massey	Vanier	Total
Total net income...			$82,000
First, salaries:			
Massey	$43,000		
Vanier		$35,000	
Total			78,000
Net income remaining for allocation			4,000
Second, interest on beginning capital balances:			
Massey ($80,000 × .08)...	6,400		
Vanier ($100,000 × .08)		8,000	
Total			14,400
Net income remaining for allocation			(10,400)
Third, remainder shared equally:			
Massey ($10,400 × ½)	(5,200)		

Vanier ($10,400 × ½)			(5,200)
Total			(10,400)
Net income remaining for allocation			$ -0-
Net income allocated to the partners	$44,200	$37,800	$82,000

A net loss would be allocated to Massey and Vanier in the same manner outlined for net income. The sharing procedure would begin with the net loss, and then allocate salary, interest, and any other specified amounts to the partners.

We see that partners may allocate profits and losses based on a stated fraction, contributed capital, service, interest on capital, or any combination of these factors. Each partnership shapes its profit-and-loss-sharing ratio to fit its own needs.

Partner Drawings

Partners, like anyone else, need cash for personal living expenses. Partnership agreements usually allow partners to withdraw cash or other assets from the business. Drawings from a partnership are recorded exactly as illustrated in previous chapters for drawings from a proprietorship. Assume Massey and Vanier are each allowed a monthly withdrawal of $3,500. The partnership records the March withdrawal with this entry:

Mar. 31	Massey, Drawing	3,500	
	Vanier, Drawing	3,500	
	Cash		7,000
	Monthly partner withdrawals.		

During the year, each partner's drawing account accumulates 12 such amounts, a total of $42,000 ($3,500 × 12). At the end of the period, the general ledger shows the following account balances immediately after net income has been closed to the partners' capital accounts. Assume these beginning balances for Massey and Vanier at the start of the year, and that $82,000 of profit has been allocated based on the preceding illustration.

Massey, Capital			**Vanier, Capital**	
	Jan. 1 Bal. 80,000			Jan. 1 Bal. 100,000
	Dec. 31 Net inc. 44,200			Dec. 31 Net inc. 37,800

Massey, Drawing			**Vanier, Drawing**	
Dec. 31 Bal. 42,000			Dec. 31 Bal. 42,000	

The withdrawal accounts must be closed at the end of the period. The final closing entries transfer their balances to the partner's capital account as follows:

Dec. 31	Massey, Capital	42,000	
	Massey, Drawing		42,000
	Vanier, Capital	42,000	
	Vanier, Drawing		42,000
	To close partner drawing accounts.		

After closing, the accounts appear as follows:

Massey, Capital			
→Dec. 31 Clo.	42,000	Jan. 1 Bal.	80,000
		Dec. 31 Net inc.	44,200
		Dec. 31 Bal.	82,200

Vanier, Capital			
→Dec. 31 Clo.	42,000	Jan. 1 Bal.	100,000
		Dec. 31 Net inc.	37,800
		Dec. 31 Bal.	95,800

Massey, Drawing			
Dec. 31 Bal.	42,000	Dec. 31 Clo.	42,000

Vanier, Drawing			
Dec. 31 Clo.	42,000	Dec. 31 Clo.	42,000

In this case, Massey withdrew less than his share of the partnership net income. Consequently, his capital account grew during the period. Vanier, however, withdrew more than his share of net income. His capital account decreased.

Partnerships, as we have mentioned, do not last forever. We turn now to a discussion of how partnerships dissolve — and how new partnerships arise.

Dissolution of a Partnership

A partnership lasts only as long as its partners remain in the business. The addition of a new member or the withdrawal of an existing member dissolves the partnership.

Often a new partnership is formed to carry on the former partnership's business. In fact, the new partnership may choose to retain the dissolved partnership's name. KPMG Peat Marwick Thorne, for example, is an accounting firm from which partners retire, and which admits new partners during the year. Thus the former partnership dissolves and a new partnership begins many times. The business, however, retains the name and continues operations. Other partnerships may dissolve and then reform under a new name. Let us look now at the ways that a new member may gain admission into an existing partnership.

Admission by Purchasing a Partner's Interest

A person may become a member of a partnership by gaining the approval of the other partner (or partners) for entrance into the firm, *and* by purchasing a present partner's interest in the business. Let us assume that Fisher and Levesque have a partnership that has the following balance sheet:

Cash	$ 40,000	Total liabilities	$120,000
Other assets	360,000	Fisher, capital	110,000
		Levesque, capital	170,000
		Total liabilities	
Total assets	$400,000	and capital	$400,000

Business is going so well that Fisher receives an offer from Dynak, an outside party, to buy her $110,000 interest in the business for $150,000. Fisher agrees to sell out to Dynak, and Levesque approves Dynak as a new partner. The firm records the transfer of capital interest in the business with this entry:

OBJECTIVE 4

Account for the admission of a new partner to the business

Apr. 16	Fisher, Capital	110,000	
	Dynak, Capital		110,000
	To transfer Fisher's equity in the business to Dynak.		

The debit side of the entry closes Fisher's capital account because she is no longer a partner in the firm. The credit side opens Dynak's capital account because Fisher's equity has been transferred to Dynak. Notice that the entry amount is Fisher's capital balance ($110,000) and not the $150,000 price that Dynak paid Fisher to buy into the business. The full $150,000 goes to Fisher. In this example, the partnership receives no cash because the transaction was between Dynak and Fisher, not between Dynak and the partnership. Suppose Dynak pays Fisher less than Fisher's capital balance. That does not affect the entry on the partnership books. Fisher's equity is transferred to Dynak at book value ($110,000).

The old partnership has dissolved. Levesque and Dynak draw up a new partnership agreement, with a new profit-and-loss-sharing ratio, and continue business operations. If Levesque does not accept Dynak as a partner, the Fisher and Levesque partnership would be dissolved, and Dynak would be precluded from buying Fisher's interest.

Admission by Investing in the Partnership

A person may also be admitted as a partner by investing directly in the partnership rather than by purchasing an existing partner's interest. The new partner contributes assets (for example, cash, inventory, or equipment) to the business. Assume that the partnership of Ingel and Jay has the following assets, liabilities, and capital:

Cash..................................	$ 20,000	Total liabilities....................	$100,000
Other assets	240,000	Ingel, capital.......................	70,000
		Jay, capital..........................	90,000
		Total liabilities	
Total assets....................	$260,000	and capital.....................	$260,000

Kahn offers to invest equipment and land (Other assets) with a market value of $80,000 to persuade the existing partners to take her into the business. Ingel and Jay agree to dissolve the existing partnership and to start up a new business, giving Kahn one-third interest in exchange for the contributed assets. The entry to record Kahn's investment is

July 18	Other Assets	80,000	
	Kahn, Capital..		80,000
	To admit L. Kahn as a partner with a		
	one-third interest in the business.		

After this entry, the partnership books show:

Cash..................................	$ 20,000	Total liabilities	$100,000
Other assets		Ingel, capital	70,000
($240,000 + $80,000)......	320,000	Jay, capital	90,000
		Kahn, capital.......................	80,000
		Total liabilities	
Total assets....................	$340,000	and capital	$340,000

Kahn's one-third interest in the partnership [$80,000/($70,000 + $90,000 + $80,000) = ⅓] does not necessarily entitle her to one third of the profits. The sharing of profits and losses is a separate consideration in the partnership agreement.

In the previous example, Dynak paid an individual member (Fisher), not the partnership. Note that Kahn's payment (the other assets) goes into the partnership.

Admission by Investing in the Partnership — Bonus to the Old Partners
The more successful a partnership, the higher the payment the partners may demand

from a person entering the business. Partners in a business that is doing quite well might require an incoming person to pay them a bonus. The bonus increases the current partners' capital accounts.

Suppose that Nagasawa and Schwende's partnership has earned above-average profits for ten years. The two partners share profits and losses equally. The balance sheet carries these figures:

Cash	$ 40,000	Total liabilities...................	$100,000
Other assets........................	210,000	Nagasawa, capital	70,000
		Schwende, capital.............	80,000
		Total liabilities	
Total assets	$250,000	and capital	$250,000

The partners agree to admit Parker to a one-fourth interest with his cash investment of $90,000. Parker's capital balance on the partnership books is $60,000, computed as follows:

Partnership capital before Parker is admitted ($70,000 + $80,000)	$150,000
Parker's investment in the partnership	90,000
Partnership capital after Parker is admitted	$240,000
Parker's capital in the partnership ($240,000 × ¼)	$ 60,000

The entry on the partnership books to record Parker's investment is

Mar.	1	Cash...	90,000	
		Parker, Capital..		60,000
		Nagasawa, Capital ($30,000 x ½)...........		15,000
		Schwende, Capital ($30,000 x ½)		15,000
		To admit G. Parker as a partner with a		
		one-fourth interest in the business.		

Parker's capital account is credited for his one-fourth interest in the partnership. The other partners share the $30,000 difference between Parker's investment ($90,000) and his equity in the business ($60,000). This difference is accounted for as income to the old partners and is, therefore, allocated to them based on their profit-and-loss ratio.

The new partnership's balance sheet reports these amounts:

Cash ($40,000 + $90,000) ..	$130,000	Total liabilities...................	$100,000
Other assets........................	210,000	Nagasawa, capital	
		($70,000 + $15,000).......	85,000
		Schwende, capital	
		($80,000 + $15,000).......	95,000
		Parker, capital....................	60,000
		Total liabilities	
Total assets	$340,000	and capital	$340,000

Admission by Investing in the Partnership — Bonus to the New Partner

A potential new partner may be so important that the existing partners offer him or her a partnership share that includes a bonus. A law firm may strongly desire a former premier, cabinet minister, or other official as a partner because of the person's reputation. A restaurant owner may want to go into partnership with a famous sports personality like Lanny MacDonald or Elizabeth Manley.

Suppose Page and Osuka is a law partnership. The firm's balance sheet appears as follows:

Cash	$140,000	Total liabilities	$120,000
Other assets	360,000	Page, capital	230,000
		Osuka, capital	150,000
		Total liabilities	
Total assets	$500,000	and capital	$500,000

The partners admit Schiller, a former attorney general, as a partner with a one-third interest in exchange for his cash investment of $100,000. At the time of Schiller's admission, the firm's capital is $380,000 (Page, $230,000 and Osuka, $150,000). Page and Osuka share profits and losses in the ratio of two thirds to Page and one third to Osuka. The computation of Schiller's equity in the partnership is

Partnership capital before Schiller is admitted ($230,000 + $150,000)	$380,000
Schiller's investment in the partnership	100,000
Partnership capital after Schiller is admitted	$480,000
Schiller's capital in the partnership ($480,000 × ⅓)	$160,000

The capital accounts of Page and Osuka are debited for the $60,000 difference between the new partner's equity ($160,000) and his investment ($100,000). The existing partners share this decrease in capital, which is accounted for as though it were a loss, based on their profit-and-loss ratio.

The entry to record Schiller's investment is

Aug. 24	Cash	100,000	
	Page, Capital ($60,000 × ⅔)	40,000	
	Osuka, Capital ($60,000 × ⅓)	20,000	
	Schiller, Capital		160,000
	To admit M. Schiller as a partner with a one-third interest in the business.		

The new partnership's balance sheet reports these amounts:

Cash		Total liabilities	$120,000
($140,000 + $100,000)	$240,000	Page, capital	
Other assets	360,000	($230,000 – $40,000)	190,000
		Osuka, capital	
		($150,000 – $20,000)	130,000
		Schiller, capital	160,000
		Total liabilities	
Total assets	$600,000	and capital	$600,000

Summary Problem for Your Review

The partnership of Taylor and Uvalde is considering admitting Vaughn as a partner on January 1, 19X8. The partnership general ledger includes the following balances on that date:

Cash	$ 9,000	Total liabilities...................	$ 50,000
Other assets........................	110,000	Taylor, capital.....................	45,000
		Uvalde, capital...................	24,000
		Total liabilities	
Total assets....................	$119,000	and capital.....................	$119,000

Taylor's share of profits and losses is 60 percent and Uvalde's share is 40 percent.

Required
Items 1 and 2 are independent.

1. Suppose Vaughn pays Uvalde $31,000 to acquire Uvalde's interest in the business after Uvalde obtains Taylor's approval of Vaughn as a partner.
   a. Record the transfer of owner's equity on the partnership books.
   b. Prepare the partnership balance sheet immediately after Vaughn is admitted as a partner.
2. Suppose Vaughn becomes a partner by investing $31,000 cash to acquire a one-fourth interest in the business.
   a. Compute Vaughn's capital balance.
   b. Prepare the partnership balance sheet immediately after Vaughn is admitted as a partner. Include the heading.
3. Which way of admitting Vaughn to the partnership increases its total assets? Give your reason.

SOLUTION TO REVIEW PROBLEM

Requirement 1

a.
Jan.	1	Uvalde, Capital...	24,000	
		Vaughn, Capital..		24,000
		To transfer Uvalde's equity in the partnership to Vaughn.		

b. The balance sheet for the partnership of Taylor and Vaughn is identical to the balance sheet given for Taylor and Uvalde in the problem, except for Vaughn's name replaces Uvalde's name in the title and in the listing of capital accounts.

Requirement 2

a. Computation of Vaughn's capital balance:

Partnership capital before Vaughn is admitted ($45,000 + $24,000)	$ 69,000
Vaughn's investment in the partnership	31,000
Partnership capital after Vaughn is admitted	$100,000
Vaughn's capital in the partnership ($100,000 × ¼)	$ 25,000

Jan.	1	Cash	31,000	
		Vaughn, Capital		25,000
		Taylor, Capital		
		[($31,000 – $25,000) × .60].................		3,600
		Uvalde, Capital		
		[($31,000 – $25,000) × .40].................		2,400
		To admit Vaughn as a partner with a one-fourth interest in the business.		

b.

Taylor, Uvalde and Vaughn
Balance Sheet
January 1, 19X8

Cash		Total liabilities	$ 50,000
($9,000 + $31,000)................	$ 40,000	Taylor, capital	
Other assets	110,000	($45,000 + $3,600)..............	48,600
		Uvalde, capital	
		($24,000 + $2,400)..............	26,400
		Vaughn, capital	25,000
		Total liabilities	
Total assets..........................	$150,000	and capital	$150,000

Requirement 3

Vaughn's investment in the partnership increases its total assets by the amount of his contribution. Total assets of the business are $150,000 after his investment, compared to $119,000 before. By contrast, Vaughn's purchase of Uvalde's interest in the business is a personal transaction between the two individuals. It does not affect the assets of the partnership regardless of the amount Vaughn pays Uvalde.

Withdrawal of a Partner _____

A partner may withdraw from the business for many reasons, including retirement or a dispute with the other partners. The partnership agreement should contain a provision to govern how to settle with a withdrawing partner. In the simplest case, as illustrated on p. 578, a partner may withdraw and sell his or her interest to another partner in a personal transaction. The only entry needed to record this transfer of equity debits the withdrawing partner's capital account and credits the purchaser's capital account. The dollar amount of the entry is the capital balance of the withdrawing partner, regardless of the price paid by the purchaser. The accounting when one current partner buys a second partner's interest is the same as when an outside party buys a current partner's interest.

> **OBJECTIVE 5**
> Account for the withdrawal of a partner from the business

If the partner withdraws in the middle of the accounting period, the partnership books should be updated to determine the withdrawing partner's capital balance. The business must measure net income or net loss for the fraction of the year up to the withdrawal date, and allocate profit or loss according to the existing ratio. After closing the books, the business then accounts for the change in partnership capital.

The withdrawing partner may receive his or her share of the business in partnership assets other than cash. The question then arises of what value to assign the partnership assets: book value or current market value. The settlement procedure may specify that an independent appraisal of the assets to determine their current market value. If market values have changed, the appraisal will result in a revaluing of the partnership assets. Thus the partners share in any market value changes that their efforts caused.

Suppose Isaac is retiring in midyear from the partnership of Green, Maslowski, and Isaac. After the books have been adjusted for partial-period income but before the asset appraisal, revaluation, and closing entries, the balance sheet reports:

Cash............................	$ 39,000	Total liabilities......................	$ 80,000
Inventory..................................	44,000	Green, capital..........................	54,000
Land	55,000	Maslowski, capital	43,000
Building.................... $95,000		Isaac, capital............................	21,000
Less: Accumulated			
depreciation 35,000	60,000	Total liabilities	
Total assets	$198,000	and capital..........................	$198,000

Assume an independent appraiser revalues the inventory at $38,000 (down from $44,000), and the land at $101,000 (up from $55,000). The partners share the differences between these assets' market values and their prior book values based on their profit-and-loss ratio. The partnership agreement has allocated one fourth of the profits to Green, one half to Maslowski, and one fourth to Isaac. (This ratio may be written 1:2:1 for one part to Green, two parts to Maslowski and one part to Isaac.) For each share that Green or Isaac has, Maslowski has two. The entries to record the revaluation of the inventory and land are

July 31	Green, Capital ($6,000 × ¼)..................................	1,500	
	Maslowski, Capital ($6,000 × ½)	3,000	
	Isaac, Capital ($6,000 × ¼)...................................	1,500	
	Inventory ($44,000 – $38,000)		6,000
	To revalue the inventory and allocate the loss in value to the partners.		
31	Land ($101,000 – $55,000)	46,000	
	Green, Capital ($46,000 × ¼)........................		11,500
	Maslowski, Capital ($46,000 × ½)		23,000
	Isaac, Capital ($46,000 × ¼).........................		11,500
	To revalue the land and allocate the gain in value to the partners.		

After the revaluations, the partnership balance sheet reports:

Cash	$ 39,000	Total liabilities.........................	$ 80,000
Inventory.................................	38,000	Green, capital ($54,000 –	
Land	101,000	$1,500 + $11,500)	64,000
Building.................... $95,000		Maslowski, capital ($43,000 –	
Less: Accumulated		$3,000 + $23,000)	63,000
depreciation... 35,000	60,000	Isaac, capital ($21,000 –	
		$1,500 + $11,500)	31,000
		Total liabilities	
Total assets....................	$238,000	and capital	$238,000

The books now carry the assets at current market value, which becomes the new book value; the capital accounts have been adjusted accordingly. Isaac has a claim to $31,000 in partnership assets. How is her withdrawal from the business accounted for?

Withdrawal at Book Value

If Isaac withdraws by taking cash equal to the book value of her owner's equity, the entry would be

July 31	Isaac, Capital..	31,000	
	Cash...		31,000
	To record withdrawal of Karen Isaac from the partnership.		

This entry records the payment of partnership cash to Isaac and the closing of her capital account upon withdrawal from the business.

Withdrawal at Less Than Book Value

Sometimes withdrawing partners may be so eager to leave the business that they are willing to take less than their equity. This situation has occurred in real estate and oil-drilling partnerships. Assume Isaac withdraws from the business, and agrees to take partnership cash of $10,000 and the new partnership's note for $15,000. This $25,000 settlement is $6,000 less than Isaac's $31,000 equity in the business. The remaining partners share this $6,000 difference, which is a gain to them, according to their profit-and-loss ratio. However, since Isaac has withdrawn from the partnership, a new agreement — and a new profit-and-loss ratio — must be drawn up. Maslowski and Green, in forming a new partnership, may decide on any ratio that they see fit. Let us assume they agree that Maslowski will earn two thirds of partnership profits and losses, and Green one third. The entry to record Isaac's withdrawal at less than book value is

July	31	Isaac, Capital	31,000	
		Cash		10,000
		Note Payable to Karen Isaac		15,000
		Green, Capital ($6,000 × 1/3)		2,000
		Maslowski, Capital ($6,000 × 2/3)		4,000
		To record withdrawal of Karen Isaac from the partnership.		

Isaac's account is closed, and Maslowski and Green may or may not continue the business.

Withdrawal at More Than Book Value

The settlement with a withdrawing partner may allow the partner to take assets of greater value than the book value of his or her capital. Also, the remaining partners may be so eager for the withdrawing partner to leave the firm that they pay the partner a bonus to withdraw from the business. In either case, the partner's withdrawal causes a decrease in the book equity of the remaining partners. This decrease is allocated to the partners based on their profit-and-loss ratio.

Assume Chang, Daley and Evans share profits in a ratio of 3:2:1. Their partnership accounts include the following balances:

Cash	$50,000	Total liabilities	$110,000
Other assets	220,000	Chang, capital	80,000
		Daley, capital	50,000
		Evans, capital	30,000
		Total liabilities	
Total assets	$270,000	and capital	$270,000

Assume Evans withdraws, taking $15,000 in cash and the new partnership's note for $25,000. This $40,000 settlement exceeds Evans's capital balance by $10,000. Chang and Daley share this loss in equity according to their profit-and-loss ratio (3 : 2). The withdrawal entry is

Nov.	30	Evans, Capital	30,000	
		Chang, Capital ($10,000 × 3/5)	6,000	
		Daley, Capital ($10,000 × 2/5)	4,000	
		Cash		15,000
		Note Payable to R. Evans		25,000
		To record withdrawal of R. Evans from the partnership.		

The withdrawal entry closes Evans's capital account and updates those of Chang and Daley.

Death of a Partner

The death of a partner, like any other form of partnership withdrawal, dissolves a partnership. The partnership accounts are adjusted to measure net income or loss for the fraction of the year up to the date of death, then closed to determine the partners' capital balances on that date. Settlement with the deceased partner's estate is based on the partnership agreement. The estate commonly receives partnership assets equal to the partner's capital balance. The partnership closes the deceased partner's capital account with a debit. This entry credits a payable to the estate.

Alternatively, a remaining partner may purchase the deceased partner's equity. The deceased partner's equity is debited and the purchaser's equity is credited. The amount of this entry is the ending credit balance in the deceased partner's capital account.

Liquidation of a Partnership

OBJECTIVE 6

Account for the liquidation of a partnership

Admission of a new partner or withdrawal or death of an existing partner dissolves the partnership. However, the business may continue operating with no apparent change to outsiders such as customers and creditors.

Business **liquidation**, however, is the process of going out of business by selling the entity's assets and paying its liabilities. The final step in liquidation of a business is the *distribution of the remaining cash to the owners*. Before liquidating the business, the books should be adjusted and closed. After closing, only asset, liability and partners' capital accounts remain open.

Liquidation of a partnership includes three basic steps:

1. Sell the assets. Allocate the gain or loss to the partners' capital accounts based on the profit-and-loss ratio.
2. Pay the partnership liabilities.
3. Disburse the remaining cash to the partners based on their capital balances.

In actual practice, the liquidation of a business can stretch over weeks or months. Selling every asset and paying every liability of the entity takes time. To avoid excessive detail in our illustrations, we include only two asset categories, Cash and Noncash Assets, and a single liability category, Liabilities. Our examples also assume that the business sells the noncash assets in a single transaction and pays the liabilities in a single transaction.

Assume that Aviron, Bloch, and Zhang have shared profits and losses in the ratio of 3:1:1. (This ratio is equal to ⅗, ⅕, ⅕, or a 60-percent, 20-percent, 20-percent sharing ratio.) They decide to liquidate their partnership. After the books are adjusted and closed, the general ledger contains the following balances:

Cash	$ 10,000	Liabilities	$ 30,000
Noncash assets	90,000	Aviron, capital	40,000
		Bloch, capital	20,000
		Zhang, capital	10,000
		Total liabilities	
Total assets	$100,000	and capital	$100,000

We will use the Aviron, Bloch, and Zhang partnership data to illustrate accounting for liquidation in three different situations.

Sale of Noncash Assets at a Gain

Assume the partnership sells its noncash assets (shown on the balance sheet at $90,000) for cash of $150,000. The partnership realizes a gain of $60,000, which is allocated to the partners based on their profit-and-loss-sharing ratio. The entry to record this sale and allocation of the gain is

Oct. 31	Cash..	150,000	
	Noncash Asset..		90,000
	Aviron, Capital ($60,000 × .60)		36,000
	Bloch, Capital ($60,000 × .20)		12,000
	Zhang, Capital ($60,000 × .20)..............		12,000
	To sell noncash assets in liquidation and allocate gain to partners.		

The partnership must next pay off its liabilities:

Oct. 31	Liabilities..	30,000	
	Cash..		30,000
	To pay liabilities in liquidation.		

In the final liquidation transaction, the remaining cash is disbursed to the partners. The partners share in the cash according to their capital balances. (By contrast, *gains* and *losses* on the sale of assets are shared by the partners based on their profit-and-loss-sharing ratio.) The amount of cash left in the partnership is $130,000 — the $10,000 beginning balance plus the $150,000 cash sale of assets minus the $30,000 cash payment of liabilities. The partners divide the remaining cash according to their capital balances.

Oct. 31	Aviron, Capital ($40,000 + $36,000)...........	76,000	
	Bloch, Capital ($20,000 + $12,000).............	32,000	
	Zhang, Capital ($10,000 + $12,000)	22,000	
	Cash		130,000
	To disburse cash to partners in liquidation.		

A convenient way to summarize the transactions in a partnership liquidation is given in Exhibit 13-1.

EXHIBIT 13-1 *Partnership Liquidation: Sale of Assets at a Gain*

					Capital		
	Cash	+ Noncash Assets	= Liabilities	+	Aviron (60%) +	Bloch (20%) +	Zhang (20%)
Balances before sale of assets..............................	$ 10,000	$ 90,000	$ 30,000		$ 40,000	$ 20,000	$ 10,000
Sale of assets and sharing of gain..............	150,000	(90,000)			36,000	12,000	12,000
Balances	160,000	-0-	30,000		76,000	32,000	22,000
Payment of liabilities	(30,000)		(30,000)				
Balances	130,000	-0-	-0-		76,000	32,000	22,000
Disbursement of cash to partners.....................	(130,000)				(76,000)	(32,000)	(22,000)
Balances	$ -0-	$ -0-	$ -0-		$ -0-	$ -0-	$ -0-

After the disbursement of cash to the partners, the business has no assets, liabilities or owners' equity. The balances are all zero. At all times, partnership assets must equal partnership liabilities plus partnership capital, according to the accounting equation:

	Total Assets	=	Total Liabilities	+	Total Capital
Before liquidation	$100,000	=	$30,000	+	$ 70,000
After sale of assets	160,000	=	30,000	+	130,000
After payment of liabilities	130,000	=	0	+	130,000
After final disbursement to the partners	0	=	0	+	0

Sale of Noncash Assets at a Loss

Assume that Aviron, Bloch, and Zhang sell the noncash assets for $75,000, realizing a loss of $15,000. The summary of transactions appears in Exhibit 13-2.

EXHIBIT 13-2 *Partnership Liquidation: Sale of Assets at a Loss*

	Cash	+ Noncash Assets	= Liabilities	+	Aviron Capital (60%)	+	Bloch Capital (20%)	+	Zhang Capital (20%)
Balances before sale of assets	$10,000	$90,000	$30,000		$ 40,000		$20,000		$10,000
Sale of assets and sharing of loss	75,000	(90,000)			(9,000)		(3,000)		(3,000)
Balances	85,000	-0-	30,000		31,000		17,000		7,000
Payment of liabilities	(30,000)		(30,000)						
Balances	55,000	-0-	-0-		31,000		17,000		7,000
Disbursement of cash to partners	(55,000)				(31,000)		(17,000)		(7,000)
Balances	$ -0-	$ -0-	$ -0-		$ -0-		$ -0-		$ -0-

The journal entries to record the liquidation transactions are

Oct.	31	Cash	75,000	
		Aviron, Capital ($15,000 × .60)	9,000	
		Bloch, Capital ($15,000 × .20)	3,000	
		Zhang, Capital ($15,000 × .20)	3,000	
		Noncash Assets		90,000
		To sell noncash assets in liquidation and allocate loss to partners.		
	31	Liabilities	30,000	
		Cash		30,000
		To pay liabilities in liquidation.		
	31	Aviron, Capital ($40,000 – $9,000)	31,000	
		Bloch, Capital ($20,000 – $3,000)	17,000	
		Zhang, Capital ($10,000 – $3,000)	7,000	
		Cash		55,000
		To disburse cash to partners in liquidation.		

Sale of Noncash Assets at a Loss — Deficiency in a Partner's Capital

Account The sale of noncash assets at a loss may result in a debit balance in a partner's capital account. This situation is called a **capital deficiency** because the partner's capital balance is insufficient to cover his or her share of the partnership's loss. The unlimited liability of partners forces the other partners to absorb this deficiency through debits to their own capital accounts if the deficient partner does not erase his or her deficiency. The deficiency is a loss to the other partners, and they share it based on their profit-and-loss ratio.

Deficient Partner Unable To Erase Deficiency Assume that Aviron, Bloch, and Zhang's partnership has had losses for several years. The market value of the noncash assets of the business is far less than book value ($90,000). In liquidation, the partnership sells these assets for $30,000, realizing a loss of $60,000. Zhang's 20 percent share of this loss is $12,000. Because the loss exceeds his $10,000 capital balance, Zhang's account has a $2,000 deficit. Zhang is obligated to contribute personal funds to the business in order to meet this debt. Assume that Zhang cannot erase the deficiency by contributing personal assets. Because of mutual agency, the other partners must absorb the deficiency before the final distribution of cash.

Because Aviron and Bloch share losses in the ratio of 3:1, Aviron absorbs three fourths of the deficiency [3/(3 + 1)= ¾], and Bloch absorbs one fourth [1/(3 + 1) = ¼]. Aviron's share of Zhang's $2,000 deficiency is $1,500 ($2,000 × ¾), and Bloch's share is $500 ($2,000 × ¼).

The journal entries to record the foregoing liquidation transactions are

Oct.	31	Cash...	30,000	
		Aviron, Capital ($60,000 × .60)......................	36,000	
		Bloch, Capital ($60,000 × .20).........................	12,000	
		Zhang, Capital ($60,000 × .20)........................	12,000	
		Noncash Assets..		90,000
		To sell noncash assets in liquidation and allocate loss to partners.		
	31	Liabilities..	30,000	
		Cash..		30,000
		To pay liabilities in liquidation.		
	31	Aviron, Capital ($2,000 × ¾)..............................	1,500	
		Bloch, Capital ($2,000 × ¼)...............................	500	
		Zhang, Capital...		2,000
		To allocate Zhang's capital deficiency to the other partners.		
	31	Aviron, Capital ($40,000 – $36,000 – $1,500)...	2,500	
		Bloch, Capital ($20,000 – $12,000 – $500).........	7,500	
		Cash...		10,000
		To disburse cash to partners in liquidation.		

The summary of transactions in Exhibit 13-3 includes a separate transaction (highlighted) to allocate Zhang's deficiency to Aviron and Bloch.

Deficient Partner Erases Deficiency A partner may erase his or her deficiency by contributing cash or other assets to the partnership. Such contributions are credited to the deficient partner's account and then distributed to the other partners. Suppose Zhang erases his deficiency by investing $2,000 cash in the partnership.

The journal entries to record Zhang's contribution and the disbursement of cash to the partners are

EXHIBIT 13-3 *Deficient Partner Unable to Erase a Capital Deficiency*

	Cash	+ Noncash Assets	= Liabilities	+ Aviron (60%)	+ Bloch (20%)	+ Zhang (20%)
					Capital	
Balances before sale of assets	$10,000	$90,000	$30,000	$40,000	$20,000	$10,000
Sale of assets and sharing of loss	30,000	(90,000)		(36,000)	(12,000)	(12,000)
Balances	40,000	-0-	30,000	4,000	8,000	(2,000)
Payment of liabilities	(30,000)		(30,000)			
Balances	10,000	-0-	-0-	4,000	8,000	(2,000)
Sharing of Zhang's deficiency by Aviron and Bloch				(1,500)	(500)	2,000
Balances	10,000	-0-	-0-	2,500	7,500	-0-
Disbursement of cash to partners	(10,000)			(2,500)	(7,500)	
Balances	$ -0-	$ -0-	$ -0-	$ -0-	$ -0-	$ -0-

Oct. 31	Cash	2,000	
	Zhang, Capital		2,000
	Zhang's contribution to erase his capital deficiency in liquidation.		
Oct. 31	Aviron, Capital	4,000	
	Bloch, Capital	8,000	
	Cash		12,000
	To disburse cash to partners in liquidation.		

In this case, the summary of transactions, beginning with the balances after payment of the liabilities, appears in Exhibit 13-4.

EXHIBIT 13-4 *Partnership Liquidation: Partner Erases Capital Deficiency*

	Cash	+ Noncash Assets	= Liabilities	+ Aviron (60%)	+ Bloch (20%)	+ Zhang (20%)
					Capital	
Balances after payment of liabilities	$ 10,000	$ -0-	$ -0-	$ 4,000	$ 8,000	$(2,000)
Zhang's contribution to erase his deficiency	2,000	-0-	-0-			2,000
Balances	12,000	-0-	-0-	4,000	8,000	-0-
Disbursement of cash to partners	(12,000)			(4,000)	(8,000)	
Balances	$ -0-	$ -0-	$ -0-	$ -0-	$ -0-	$ -0-

Partnership Financial Statements

Partnership financial statements are much like those of a proprietorship. However, a partnership income statement includes a section showing the division of net income to the partners. For example, the partnership of Gray and Hayward might report its income statement for the year ended June 30, 19X6 as follows:

Gray and Hayward Income Statement for the year ended June 30, 19X6	
Sales revenue	$381,000
Net income	$79,000
Allocation of net income	
M. Gray	$36,600
L. Hayward	42,400
Total	$79,000

Large partnerships may not find it feasible to report the net income of every partner. Instead, the firm may report the allocation of net income to active and retired partners and average earnings per partner. For example, the public accounting firm of Main, Price & Anders reported the following:

Main, Price & Anders Combined Statement of Earnings for the year ended August 31, 19X0	
Fees for Professional Services	$9,144,920
Earnings for the year	$2,978,800
Allocation of earnings	
To partners active during the year —	
Resigned, retired, and deceased partners	$ 199,010
Partners active at year end	2,532,700
To retired and deceased partners —	
Retirement and death benefits	83,100
Not allocated to partners —	
Retained for specific partnership purposes	163,990
	$2,978,800
Average earnings per partner at year end	
(28 partners)	$ 106,400

Exhibit 13-5 summarizes the financial statements of a proprietorship and a partnership.

EXHIBIT 13-5 *Financial Statements of a Proprietorship and a Partnership*

Income Statements
for the year ended December 31, 19X1

Proprietorship		Partnership		
Revenues......................	$460	Revenues..		$460
Expenses	(270)	Expenses		(270)
Net income	$190	Net income		$190
		Allocation of net income		
		To Smith	$114	
		To Jones	76	$190

Statements of Owner's Equity
for the year ended December 31, 19X1

Proprietorship		Partnership		
			Smith	Jones
Capital, December 31, 19X0...........................	$ 90	Capital, December 31, 19X0	$ 50	$ 40
Additional investments..............	10	Additional investments	10	—
Net income	190	Net income	114	76
Subtotal	290	Subtotal	174	116
Drawings.......................	(120)	Drawings	(72)	(48)
Capital, December 31, 19X1...........................	$ 170	Capital, December 31, 19X1	$102	$ 68

Balance Sheets
December 31, 19X1

Proprietorship		Partnership		
Assets		**Assets**		
Cash and other assets	$170	Cash and other assets		$170
		Owners' Equity		
		Smith, capital		$102
Owner's Equity		Jones, capital		68
Smith, capital	$170	Total capital		$170

Summary Problem for Your Review

The partnership of Prolux, Roberts and Satulsky is liquidating. Its accounts have the following balances after closing:

Cash..	$ 22,000	Liabilities	$ 77,000
Noncash assets......................	104,000	Prolux, capital.......................	23,000
		Roberts, capital	10,000
		Satulsky, capital	16,000
		Total liabilities	
Total assets.......................	$126,000	and capital.......................	$126,000

The partnership agreement allocates profits to Prolux, Roberts, and Satulsky in the ratio of 3 : 4 : 3. In liquidation, the noncash assets were sold in a single transaction for $64,000 on May 31, 19X7. The partnership paid the liabilities the same day.

Required

1. Journalize the liquidation transactions. The partnership books remain open until June 7 to allow Roberts to make an additional $4,000 contribution to the business in view of her capital deficiency. This cash is immediately disbursed to the other partners. Use T-accounts if necessary.

2. Prepare a summary of the liquidation transactions, as illustrated in the chapter. Roberts invests cash of $4,000 in the partnership in partial settlement of her capital deficiency. The other partners absorb the remainder of Roberts's capital deficiency.

SOLUTION TO REVIEW PROBLEM

Requirement 1
Liquidation journal entries

May 31	Cash	64,000	
	Prolux, Capital		
	[($104,000 – $64,000) × .30].........................	12,000	
	Roberts, Capital		
	[($104,000 – $64,000) × .40].........................	16,000	
	Satulsky, Capital		
	[($104,000 – $64,000) × .30].........................	12,000	
	Noncash Assets		104,000
	To sell noncash assets in liquidation and distribute loss to partners.		
May 31	Liabilities...	77,000	
	Cash		77,000
	To pay liabilities in liquidation.		
June 7	Cash	4,000	
	Roberts, Capital..		4,000
	Roberts's contribution to erase part of her capital deficiency in liquidation.		

After posting the entries, Roberts's capital account still has a $2,000 deficiency, indicated by its debit balance:

Roberts, Capital

Loss on sale	16,000		Bal.	10,000
			Investment	4,000
Bal.	2,000			

Prolux and Satulsky must make up Roberts's remaining $2,000 deficiency. Since Prolux and Satulsky had equal shares in the partnership profit-and-loss ratio (30 percent each), they divide Roberts's deficiency equally.

June 7	Prolux, Capital ($2,000 × ½)...............................	1,000	
	Satulsky, Capital ($2,000 × ½)............................	1,000	
	Roberts, Capital...		2,000
	To allocate Roberts's capital deficiency to the other partners.		

At this point, the capital accounts of Prolux and Satulsky appear as follows:

Prolux, Capital				Satulsky, Capital			
Loss on sale	12,000	Bal.	23,000	Loss on sale	12,000	Bal.	16,000
Loss on Roberts	1,000			Loss on Roberts	1,000		
		Bal.	10,000			Bal.	3,000

The final disbursement entry is

June	7	Prolux, Capital	10,000	
		Satulsky, Capital	3,000	
		Cash...		13,000
		To disburse cash to partners in liquidation.		

Activity in the Cash account appears as follows:

Cash			
Bal.	22,000	Payment of liabilities	77,000
Sale of assets	64,000		
Roberts's contribution	4,000		
Bal.	13,000	Final distribution	13,000

Requirement 2
Summary of liquidation transactions

					Capital		
	Cash +	Noncash Assets	= Liabilities +		Prolux (30%) +	Roberts (40%) +	Satulsky (30%)
Balances before sale of assets	$22,000	$104,000	$77,000		$23,000	$10,000	$16,000
Sale of assets and sharing of loss...	64,000	(104,000)			(12,000)	(16,000)	(12,000)
Balances	86,000	-0-	77,000		11,000	(6,000)	4,000
Payment of liabilities....................	(77,000)		(77,000)				
Balances	9,000	-0-	-0-		11,000	(6,000)	4,000
Roberts's investment of cash to erase part of her deficiency	4,000					4,000	
Balances	13,000	-0-	-0-		11,000	(2,000)	4,000
Sharing of Roberts's deficiency by Prolux and Satulsky............					(1,000)	2,000	(1,000)
Balances	13,000	-0-	-0-		10,000	-0-	3,000
Disbursement of cash to partners	(13,000)				(10,000)		(3,000)
Balances	$ -0-	$ -0-	$ -0-		$ -0-	$ -0-	$ -0-

Summary

A *partnership* is a business co-owned by two or more persons for profit. The characteristics of this form of business organization are its *ease of formation, limited life, mutual agency, unlimited liability,* and *no partnership income taxes.*

A written *partnership agreement* establishes procedures for admission of a new partner, withdrawals of a partner, and the sharing of profits and losses among the partners.

When a new partner is admitted to the firm or an existing partner withdraws, the old partnership is *dissolved* or ceases to exist. A new partnership may or may not emerge to continue the business.

Accounting for a partnership is similar to accounting for a proprietorship. However, a partnership has more than one owner. Each partner has an individual capital account and a withdrawal account.

Partners share net income or loss in any manner they choose. Common sharing agreements base the *profit-and-loss ratio* on a stated fraction, partners' capital contributions, and/or their service to the partnership. Some partnerships call the cash withdrawals of partners *salaries* and *interest*, but these amounts are not expenses of the business. Instead, they are merely ways of allocating partnership net income to the partners.

An outside person may become a partner by purchasing a current partner's interest or by investing in the partnership. In some cases the new partner must pay the current partners a bonus to join. In other situations the new partner may receive a bonus to join.

When a partner withdraws, partnership assets may be reappraised. Partners share any gain or loss on the asset revaluation based on their profit-and-loss ratio. The withdrawing partner may receive payment equal to, greater than, or less than his or her capital book value, depending on the agreement with the other partners.

In *liquidation*, a partnership goes out of business by selling the assets, paying the liabilities and disbursing any remaining cash to the partners. Any partner's capital deficiency, which may result from sale of assets at a loss, must be absorbed before remaining cash is distributed.

Partnership *financial statements* are similar to those of a proprietorship. However, the partnership income statement commonly reports the allocation of net income to the partners.

Self-Study Questions

Test your understanding of the chapter by marking the correct answer for each of the following questions:

1. Which of these characteristics does not apply to a partnership? *(pp. 570–71)*
   a. Unlimited life
   b. Mutual agency
   c. Unlimited liability
   d. No business income tax

2. A partnership records a partner's investment of assets in the business at *(p. 572)*
   a. The partner's book value of the assets invested
   b. The market value of the assets invested
   c. A special value set by the partners
   d. Any of the above, depending upon the partnership agreement

3. The partnership of Lane, Murdock, and Nu divides profits in the ratio of 4:5:3. During 19X6, the business earned $40,000. Nu's share of this income is *(p. 573)*
   a. $10,000
   b. $13,333
   c. $16,000
   d. $16,667

4. Suppose the partnership of Lane, Murdock, and Nu in the preceding question lost $40,000 during 19X6. Murdock's share of this loss is *(p. 573)*
   a. Not determinable because the ratio applies only to profits
   b. $13,333
   c. $16,000
   d. $16,667

5. Placido, Quinn, and Rolfe share profits and losses ⅕, ⅙ and ¹⁹⁄₃₀. During 19X3, the first year of their partnership, the business earned $120,000, and each partner withdrew $50,000 for personal use. What is the balance in Rolfe's capital account after all closing entries? *(p. 577)*
   a. Not determinable because Rolfe's beginning capital balance is not given
   b. Minus $10,000
   c. $26,000
   d. $70,000

6. Fuller buys into the partnership of Graff and Harrell by purchasing a one-third interest for $55,000. Prior to Fuller's entry, Graff's capital balance was $46,000, and Harrell's balance was $52,000. The entry to record Fuller's buying into the business is *(p. 579)*

   a. Cash........................ 55,000
         Fuller, Capital...   55,000

   b. Graff, Capital 27,500
         Harrell, Capital.... 27,500
         Fuller, Capital...   55,000

   c. Cash............................ 55,000
         Fuller, Capital   51,000
         Graff, Capital   2,000
         Harrell, Capital....   2,000

   d. Cash............................ 51,000
         Graff, Capital............. 2,000
         Harrell, Capital 2,000
         Fuller, Capital   55,000

7. Thomas, Valik and Wollenberg share profits and losses equally. Their capital balances are $40,000, $50,000, and $60,000 respectively, when Wollenberg sells her interest in the partnership to Valik for $90,000. Thomas and Valik continue the business. Immediately after Wollenberg's retirement, the total assets of the partnership are *(p. 583)*
   a. Increased by $30,000
   b. Increased by $90,000
   c. Decreased by $60,000
   d. The same as before Wollenberg sold her interest to Valik

8. Prior to Hogg's withdrawal from the partnership of Hogg, Hamm and Bacon, the partners' capital balances were $140,000, $110,000 and $250,000 respectively. The partners share profits and losses ⅓, ¼ and ⁵⁄₁₂. The appraisal indicates that assets should be written down by $36,000. Hamm's share of the write-down is *(pp. 584–85)*
   a. $7,920   c. $12,000
   b. $9,000   d. $18,000

9. Closing the business, selling the assets, paying the liabilities and disbursing remaining cash to the owners is called *(p. 586)*
   a. Dissolution   c. Withdrawal
   b. Forming a new partnership d. Liquidation

10. A and B have shared profits and losses equally. Immediately prior to the final cash disbursement in a liquidation of their partnership, the books show:

Cash		Liabilities		A,Capital		B,Capital
$100,000	=	$-0-	+	$60,000	+	$40,000

   How much cash should A receive? *(p. 588)*
   a. $40,000   c. $60,000
   b. $50,000   d. None of the above

Answers to the Self-Study Questions are at the end of the chapter.

Accounting Vocabulary

capital deficiency *(p. 589)*   partnership *(p. 569)*   unlimited personal
dissolution *(p. 570)*   partnership agreement   liability *(p. 571)*
liquidation *(p. 586)*   *(p. 570)*
mutual agency *(p. 570)*

ASSIGNMENT MATERIAL ―――――――――――――――

Questions

1. What is another name for a partnership agreement? List eight items that the agreement should specify.

2. Montgomery, who is a partner in M&N Associates, commits the firm to a contract for a job within the scope of its regular business operations. What term describes Montgomery's ability to obligate the partnership?

3. If a partnership cannot pay a debt, who must make payment? What term describes this obligation of the partners?

4. How is partnership income taxed?

5. Identify the advantages and disadvantages of the partnership form of business organization.

6. Randall and Smith's partnership agreement states that Randall gets 60 percent of profits and Smith gets 40 percent. If the agreement does not discuss the treatment of losses, how are losses shared? How do the partners share profits and losses if the agreement specifies no profit-and-loss-sharing ratio?

7. Are salary and interest allocated to partners' expenses of the business? Why or why not?

8. What determines the amount of the credit to a partner's capital account when the partner contributes assets other than cash to the business?

9. Do partner withdrawals of cash for personal use affect the sharing of profits and losses by the partner? If so, explain how. If not, explain why not.

10. Name two events that can cause the dissolution of a partnership?

11. Briefly describe how to account for the purchase of an existing partner's interest in the business.

12. Malcolm purchases Brown's interest in the Brown & Kareem partnership. What right does Malcolm obtain from the purchase? What is required for Malcolm to become Kareem's partner?

13. Assissi and Carter each have capital of $75,000 in their business and share profits in the ratio of 55 : 45. Denman acquires a one-fifth share in the partnership by investing cash of $50,000. What are the capital balances of the three partners immediately after Denman is admitted?

14. When a partner resigns from the partnership and receives assets greater than her capital balance, how is the excess shared by the other partners?

15. Why are the assets of a partnership often revalued when a partner is about to withdraw from the firm?

16. Distinguish between dissolution and liquidation of a partnership.

17. Name the three steps in liquidating a partnership.

18. Why does the cash of a partnership equal the sum of its partner capital balances after the business sells its noncash assets and pays its liabilities?

19. The partnership of Ralls and Sauls is in the process of liquidation. How do the partners share (a) gains and losses on the sale of noncash assets, and (b) the final cash disbursement?

20. Fernandez, Chretien, and Ghiz are partners, sharing profits and losses in the ratio of 3 : 2 : 1. In liquidation, Ghiz's share of losses on the sale of assets exceeds his capital balance. What becomes of Ghiz's capital deficiency if Ghiz cannot make it up?

21. Compare and contrast the financial statements of a proprietorship and a partnership.

22. Summarize the situations in which partnership allocations are based on (a) the profit-and-loss ratio, and (b) the partners' capital balances.

Exercises

Exercise 13-1 *Organizing a business as a partnership (L.O. 1)*

Alan Bowden, a friend from college, approaches you about forming a partnership to export software. Since graduation, Alan has worked for the Export-Import Bank, developing important contacts among government officials and business leaders in Poland and Hungary. Eager to upgrade their data-processing capabilities, Eastern Europeans are looking for ways to obtain American computers. Alan believes he is in a unique position to capitalize on this opportunity. With your expertise in finance, you would have responsibility for accounting and finance in the partnership.

Required

Discuss the advantages and disadvantages of organizing the export business as a partnership rather than a proprietorship. Comment on the way partnership income is taxed.

Exercise 13-2 *Recording a partner's investment (L.O. 2)*

Ann Clinton has operated an apartment-locater service as a proprietorship. She and Amanda Doss have decided to reorganize the business as a partnership. Ann's investment in the partnership consists of cash, $3,700; accounts receivable, $10,600 less allowance for uncollectibles, $800; office furniture, $2,700 less accumulated depreciation, $1,100; a small building, $55,000 less accumulated depreciation, $27,500; accounts payable, $3,300; and a note payable to the bank, $10,000.

To determine Ann's equity in the partnership, she and Amanda hire an independent appraiser. This outside party provides the following market values of the assets and liabilities that Ann is contributing to the business: cash, accounts receivable, office furniture, accounts payable, and note payable — the same as Ann's book value; allowance for uncollectible accounts, $2,900; building, $35,000; and accrued expenses payable (including interest on the note payable), $1,200.

Required

Make the entry on the partnership books to record Ann's investment.

Exercise 13-3 *Computing partners' shares of net income and net loss (L.O. 3)*

Roy Dean and Joe Edwards form a partnership, investing $30,000 and $60,000 respectively. Determine their shares of net income or net loss for each of the following situations:

a. Net loss is $31,000, and the partners have no written partnership agreement.

b. Net income is $102,000 and the partnership agreement states that the partners share profits and losses based on their capital contributions.

c. Net loss is $78,000, and the partnership agreement states that the partners share profits based on their capital contributions.

d. Net income is $125,000. The first $60,000 is shared based on the partner capital contributions. The next $45,000 is based on partner service, with Dean receiving 30 percent and Edwards receiving 70 percent. The remainder is shared equally.

Exercise 13-4   *Computing partners' capital balances* **(L.O. 3)**

Roy Dean withdrew cash of $62,000 for personal use, and Joe Edwards withdrew cash of $50,000 during the year. Using the data from situation d in Exercise 13-3, journalize the entries to close the (a) income summary account, and (b) the partners' drawing accounts. Explanations are not required.

Indicate the amount of increase or decrease in each partner's capital balance. What was the overall effect on partnership capital?

Exercise 13-5   *Admitting a new partner* **(L.O. 4)**

Jack Phillips is admitted to a partnership. Prior to the admission of Phillips, the partnership books show Susan Recker's capital balance at $100,000 and Lewis Schmitz's capital balance at $50,000. Compute the amount of each partner's equity on the books of the new partnership under each of the following plans:

a. Phillips pays $50,000 for Schmitz's equity. Phillips's payment is not an investment in the partnership but instead goes directly to Schmitz.

b. Phillips invests $50,000 to acquire a one-fourth interest in the partnership.

c. Phillips invests $70,000 to acquire a one-fourth interest in the partnership.

Exercise 13-6   *Recording the admission of a new partner* **(L.O. 4)**

Make the partnership journal entry to record the admission of Phillips under plans a, b, and c in Exercise 13-5. Explanations are not required.

Exercise 13-7   *Withdrawal of a partner* **(L.O. 5)**

After closing the books, T&W's partnership balance sheet reports owner's equity of $50,000 for T. and $70,000 for W. Partner T. is withdrawing from the firm. T. and W. agree to write down partnership assets by $40,000. They have shared profits and losses in the ratio of one third to T. and two thirds to W. If the partnership agreement states that a withdrawing partner will receive assets equal to the book value of his owner's equity, how much will T. receive?

W. will continue to operate the business as a proprietorship. What is W.'s beginning capital on the proprietorship books?

Exercise 13-8   *Withdrawal of a partner* **(L.O. 5)**

Lana Brown is retiring from the partnership of Brown, Green, and White on May 31. After the books are closed on that date, the partner capital balances are Brown, $36,000; Green, $51,000; and White, $22,000. The partners agree to have the partnership assets revalued to current market values. The independent appraiser reports that the book value of the inventory should be decreased by $3,000, and the book value of the building should be increased by $35,000. The partners agree to these revaluations. The profit-and-loss ratio has been 5 : 3 : 2 for Brown, Green, and White respectively. In retiring from the firm, Brown receives $30,000 cash and a $25,000 note from the partnership. Journalize (a) the asset revaluations, and (b) Brown's withdrawal from the firm.

Exercise 13-9   *Liquidation of a partnership* **(L.O. 6)**

Marsh, Ng, and Orsulak are liquidating their partnership. Before selling the noncash assets and paying the liabilities, the capital balances are Marsh, $23,000; Ng, $14,000; and Orsulak, $11,000. The partnership agreement divides profits and losses equally.

a. After selling the noncash assets and paying the liabilities, the partnership has cash of $48,000. How much cash will each partner receive in final liquidation?

b. After selling the noncash assets and paying the liabilities, the partnership has cash of $39,000. How much cash will each partner receive in final liquidation?

Exercise 13-10   *Liquidation of a partnership* **(L.O. 6)**

Prior to liquidation, the accounting records of Pratt, Qualls, and Ramirez included the following balances and profit-and-loss-sharing percentages:

		Noncash				Capital		
	Cash	+	Assets	= Liabilities	+	Pratt (40%)	Qualls (30%)	Ramirez (30%)
Balances before sale of assets	$8,000		$57,000	$19,000		$20,000	$15,000	$11,000

The partnership sold the noncash assets for $63,000, paid the liabilities, and disbursed the remaining cash to the partners. Complete the summary of transactions in the liquidation of the partnership. Use the format illustrated in the chapter.

Exercise 13-11   *Preparing a partnership balance sheet* **(L.O. 7)**

On October 31, 19X9, Alpha and Beta agree to combine their proprietorships as a partnership. Their balance sheets on October 31 are as follows:

Assets	Alpha's Business Book Value	Alpha's Business Current Market Value	Beta's Business Book Value	Beta's Business Current Market Value
Cash	$ 8,000	$ 8,000	$ 3,700	$ 3,700
Accounts receivable (net)	8,000	6,300	22,000	20,200
Inventory	34,000	35,100	51,000	46,000
Capital assets (net)	53,500	57,400	121,800	123,500
Total assets	$103,500	$106,800	$198,500	$193,400

Liabilities and Capital				
Accounts payable	$ 9,100	$ 9,100	$ 23,600	$ 23,600
Accrued expenses payable	1,400	1,400	2,200	2,200
Notes payable			75,000	75,000
Alpha, capital	93,000	96,300		
Beta, capital			97,700	92,600
Total liabilities and capital	$103,500	$106,800	$198,500	$193,400

Required

Prepare the partnership balance sheet at October 31, 19X9.

Problems   (Group A)

Problem 13-1A *Writing a partnership agreement* (L.O. 1)

John Haggai and Jody Magliolo are discussing the formation of a partnership to manufacture trapper-keeper ring binders used by schoolchildren. John is especially artistic, and he is convinced that his designs will draw large sales volumes. Jody is an excellent salesperson, and she has already lined up several large stores to sell the merchandise.

Required

Write a partnership agreement to cover all elements essential for the business to operate smoothly. Make up names, amounts, profit-and-loss sharing percentages, and so on as needed.

Problem 13-2A *Investments by partners* (L.O. 2, 7)

On June 30, McMinn and Pellerin formed a partnership. The partners agreed to invest equal amounts of capital. McMinn invested her proprietorship's assets and liabilities (credit balances in parentheses).

On June 30, Pellerin invested cash in an amount equal to the current market value of McMinn's partnership capital. The partners decided that McMinn would earn two thirds of partnership profits because she would manage the business. Pellerin agreed to accept one third of profits. During the remainder of the year, the partnership earned $60,000. McMinn's drawings were $35,200, and Pellerin's drawings were $23,000.

	McMinn's Book Value	Current Market Value
Accounts receivable	$16,300	$16,300
Allowance for doubtful accounts	(-0-)	(1,050)
Inventory	22,340	24,100
Prepaid expenses	1,700	1,700
Office equipment	45,900	27,600
Accumulated depreciation	(15,300)	(-0-)
Accounts payable	(19,100)	(19,100)

Required

1. Journalize the partners' initial investments.
2. Prepare the partnership balance sheet immediately after its formation on June 30.
3. Journalize the December 31 entries to close the Income Summary account and the partner drawing accounts.

Problem 13-3A *Computing partners' shares of net income and net loss* (L.O. 3, 7)

D. Hogan, E. Stanford, and S. Reichlin have formed a partnership. Hogan invested $15,000, Stanford $18,000, and Reichlin $27,000. Hogan will manage the store, Stanford will work in the store half time, and Reichlin will not work in the business.

Required

1. Compute the partners' shares of profits and losses under each of the following plans:
   a. Net loss is $63,900, and the partnership agreement does not specify how profits and losses are shared.

b. Net loss is $70,000, and the partnership agreement allocates 40 percent of profits to Hogan, 25 percent to Stanford, and 35 percent to Reichlin. The agreement does not discuss the sharing of losses.

c. Net income is $92,000. The first $40,000 is allocated based on salaries, with Hogan receiving $28,000 and Stanford receiving $12,000. The remainder is allocated based on partner capital contributions.

d. Net income for the year ended January 31, 19X8 is $162,000. The first $75,000 is allocated based on partner capital contributions. The next $36,000 is based on service, with Hogan receiving $28,000 and Stanford receiving $8,000. Any remainder is shared equally.

2. Revenues for the year ended January 31, 19X8 were $872,000 and expenses were $710,000. Under plan d, prepare the partnership income statement for the year.

Problem 13-4A   *Recording changes in partnership capital* **(L.O. 4, 5)**

Englewood Consulting Associates is a partnership, and its owners are considering admitting Hilda Newton as a new partner. On March 31 of the current year, the capital accounts of the three existing partners and their shares of profits and losses are as follows:

	Capital	Profit-and-Loss Percent
Jim Zook	$ 50,000	15%
Richard Land	125,000	30
Jennifer Lim	200,000	55

Required

Journalize the admission of Newton as a partner on March 31 for each of the following independent situations:

1. Land gives his partnership share to H. Newton, who is his daughter.
2. Newton pays Lim $145,000 cash to purchase half of Lim's interest in the partnership.
3. Newton invests $75,000 in the partnership, acquiring a one-sixth interest in the business.
4. Newton invests $75,000 in the partnership, acquiring a one-fifth interest in the business.
5. Newton invests $50,000 in the partnership, acquiring a 10 percent interest in the business.

Problem 13-5A   *Recording changes in partnership capital* **(L.O. 4, 5)**

Pediatric Associates is a partnership owned by three individuals. The partners share profits and losses in the ratio of 31 percent to Turman, 38 percent to Herron and 31 percent to Tyler. At December 31, 19X7, the firm has the following balance sheet:

Cash		$ 31,000	Total liabilities		$ 94,000
Accounts receivable	$22,000				
Less: Allowance					
for uncollectibles	4,000	18,000	Turman, capital		84,000
Building	$310,000		Herron, capital		49,000
Less: Accumulated			Tyler, capital		62,000
depreciation	70,000	240,000	Total liabilities		
Total assets		$289,000	and capital		$289,000

Herron withdraws from the partnership on December 31, 19X7 to establish her own consulting practice.

Required

Record Herron's withdrawal from the partnership under the following plans:

1. Herron gives her interest in the business to Zagat, her niece.

2. In personal transactions, Herron sells her equity in the partnership to Grimes and Hirsh, who each pay Herron $50,000 for one half of her interest. Turman and Tyler agree to accept Grimes and Hirsh as partners.

3. The partnership pays Herron cash of $15,000, and gives her a note payable for the remainder of her book equity in settlement of her partnership interest.

4. Herron receives cash of $10,000 and a note for $70,000 from the partnership.

5. The partners agree that the building is worth only $280,000, and that its accumulated depreciation should remain at $70,000. After the revaluation, the partnership settles with Herron by giving her cash of $10,600 and a note payable for the remainder of her book equity.

Problem 13-6A   *Liquidation of a partnership* (L.O. 6)

The partnership of Monet, Dixon, and Palma has experienced operating losses for three consecutive years. The partners, who have shared profits and losses in the ratio of Monet 10 percent, Dixon 30 percent, and Palma 60 percent, are considering the liquidation of the business. They ask you to analyze the effects of liquidation under various possibilities about the sale of the noncash assets. They present the following condensed partnership balance sheet at December 31, end of the current year:

Cash..............................	$ 27,000	Liabilities......................................	$131,000
Noncash assets..............	202,000	Monet, capital.............................	13,000
		Dixon, capital	39,000
		Palma, capital.............................	46,000
Total assets	$229,000	Total liabilities and capital....	$229,000

Required

1. Prepare a summary of liquidation transactions (as illustrated in the chapter) for each of the following situations:
   a. The noncash assets are sold for $212,000.
   b. The noncash assets are sold for $182,000.
   c. The noncash assets are sold for $122,000, and the partner with a capital deficiency pays cash to the partnership to erase the deficiency.
   d. The noncash assets are sold for $112,000, and the partner with a capital deficiency is personally bankrupt.

2. Make the journal entries to record the liquidation transactions in requirement 1d.

Problem 13-7A   *Liquidation of a partnership* (L.O. 6)

BP&O is a partnership owned by Bell, Pastena, and O'Donnell, who share profits and losses in the ratio of 5 : 3 : 2. The adjusted trial balance of the partnership (in condensed form) at September 30, end of the current fiscal year, follows:

BP&O
Adjusted Trial Balance
September 30, 19XX

Cash	$ 15,000	
Noncash assets	177,000	
Liabilities		$138,000
Bell, capital		57,000
Pastena, capital		53,000
O'Donnell, capital		14,000
Bell, drawing	45,000	
Pastena, drawing	37,000	
O'Donnell, drawing	18,000	
Revenues		211,000
Expenses	181,000	
Totals	$473,000	$473,000

Required

1. Prepare the September 30 entries to close the revenue, expense, income summary, and drawing accounts.

2. Insert the opening capital balances in the partner capital accounts, post the closing entries to the capital accounts, and determine each partner's ending capital balance.

3. The partnership liquidates on September 30 by selling the noncash assets for $142,000. Using the ending balances of the partner capital accounts, prepare a summary of liquidation transactions (as illustrated in the chapter). Any partner with a capital deficiency is unable to contribute assets to erase the deficiency.

(Group B)

Problem 13-1B   *Writing a partnership agreement* **(L.O. 1)**

Cindy Marable and Sara Gish are discussing the formation of a partnership to import fabric from Guatemala. Cindy is especially artistic, so she will travel to Central America to buy merchandise. Sara is an excellent salesperson, and has already lined up several large stores to sell the fabric.

Required

Write a partnership agreement to cover all elements essential for the business to operate smoothly. Make up names, amounts, profit-and-loss sharing percentages, and so on as needed.

Problem 13-2B   *Investments by partners* **(L.O. 2, 7)**

Papineau and Hutton formed a partnership on March 15. The partners agreed to invest equal amounts of capital. Hutton invested her proprietorship's assets and liabilities (credit balances in parentheses):

	Hutton's Book Value	Current Market Value
Accounts receivable	$ 12,000	$12,000
Allowance for doubtful accounts	(740)	(1,360)
Inventory	43,850	51,220
Prepaid expenses	2,400	2,400
Store equipment	36,700	26,600
Accumulated depreciation	(9,200)	(-0-)
Accounts payable	(22,300)	(22,300)

On March 15, Papineau invested cash in an amount equal to the current market value of Hutton's partnership capital. The partners decided that Hutton would earn 70 percent of partnership profits because she would manage the business. Papineau agreed to accept 30 percent of profits. During the period ended December 31, the partnership earned $70,000. Papineau's drawings were $32,000 and Hutton's drawings were $36,000.

Required

1. Journalize the partners' initial investments.
2. Prepare the partnership balance sheet immediately after its formation on March 15.
3. Journalize the December 31 entries to close the Income Summary account and the partner drawing accounts.

Problem 13-3B *Computing partners' shares of net income and net loss* **(L.O. 3, 7)**

J. Warner, S. Deitmer, and R. Mullaney have formed a partnership. Warner invested $20,000, Deitmer $40,000, and Mullaney $60,000. Warner will manage the store, Deitmer will work in the store three quarters of the time, and Mullaney will not work in the business.

Required

1. Compute the partners' shares of profits and losses under each of the following plans:
   a. Net income is $36,000, and the partnership agreement does not specify how profits and losses are shared.
   b. Net loss is $47,000, and the partnership agreement allocates 45 percent of profits to Warner, 35 percent to Deitmer, and 20 percent to Mullaney. The agreement does not discuss the sharing of losses.
   c. Net income is $104,000. The first $50,000 is allocated based on salaries of $34,000 for Warner and $16,000 for Deitmer. The remainder is allocated based on partner capital contributions.
   d. Net income for the year ended September 30, 19X4 is $91,000. The first $30,000 is allocated based on partner capital contributions. The next $30,000 is based on service, with $20,000 going to Warner and $10,000 going to Deitmer. Any remainder is shared equally.
2. Revenues for the year ended September 30, 19X4 were $572,000 and expenses were $481,000. Under plan d, prepare the partnership income statement for the year.

Problem 13-4B *Recording changes in partnership capital* **(L.O. 4, 5)**

Red River Resort is a partnership, and its owners are considering admitting Greg Lake as a new partner. On July 31 of the current year the capital accounts of the three existing partners and their shares of profits and losses are as follows:

	Capital	Profit-and-Loss Ratio
Ellen Urlang	$44,000	⅙
Amy Sharp	70,000	⅓
Bob Hayes	86,000	½

Required

Journalize the admission of Lake as a partner on July 31 for each of the following independent situations:

1. Urlang gives her partnership share to Lake, who is her nephew.
2. Lake pays Hayes $50,000 cash to purchase one half of Hayes's interest.
3. Lake invests $50,000 in the partnership, acquiring a one-fifth interest in the business.
4. Lake invests $50,000 in the partnership, acquiring a 15 percent interest in the business.
5. Lake invests $25,000 in the partnership, acquiring a 15 percent interest in the business.

Problem 13-5B   *Recording changes in partnership capital* **(L.O. 4, 5)**

Boat Town is a partnership owned by three individuals. The partners share profits and losses in the ratio of 30 percent to Golden, 40 percent to Ramos, and 30 percent to Miller. At December 31, 19X6, the firm has the following balance sheet:

Cash		$ 25,000	Total liabilities		$103,000
Accounts receivable.....	$ 16,000				
Less: Allowance					
for uncollectibles..	1,000	15,000			
Inventory		92,000	Golden, capital		34,000
Equipment	130,000		Miller, capital		53,000
Less: Accumulated			Ramos, capital		42,000
depreciation	30,000	100,000	Total liabilities		
Total assets		$232,000	and capital		$232,000

Golden withdraws from the partnership on this date.

Required

Record Golden's withdrawal from the partnership under the following plans:

1. Golden gives his interest in the business to Kamanga, his son-in-law.
2. In personal transactions, Golden sells his equity in the partnership to Meyers and Shankar, who each pay Golden $15,000 for one half of his interest. Miller and Ramos agree to accept Meyers and Shankar as partners.
3. The partnership pays Golden cash of $5,000, and gives him a note payable for the remainder of his book equity in settlement of his partnership interest.
4. Golden receives cash of $20,000 and a note for $20,000 from the partnership.
5. The partners agree that the equipment is worth $150,000, and that accumulated depreciation should remain at $30,000. After the revaluation, the partnership settles with Golden by giving him cash of $10,000 and inventory for the remainder of his book equity.

Problem 13-6B   *Liquidation of a partnership* **(L.O. 6)**

The partnership of Yagoda, Kelly, and Dobbs has experienced operating losses for three consecutive years. The partners, who have shared profits and losses in the ratio of Yagoda 15 percent, Kelly 60 percent, and Dobbs 25 percent, are considering the liquidation of the business. They ask you to analyze the effects of liquidation under various assumptions about the sale of the noncash assets. They present the following condensed partnership balance sheet at December 31, end of the current year:

Cash	$ 7,000	Liabilities	$ 63,000
Noncash assets	163,000	Yagoda, capital	19,000
		Kelly, capital	66,000
		Dobbs, capital	22,000
		Total liabilities	
Total assets	$170,000	and capital	$170,000

Required

1. Prepare a summary of liquidation transactions (as illustrated in the chapter) for each of the following situations:
   a. The noncash assets are sold for $175,000.
   b. The noncash assets are sold for $141,000.
   c. The noncash assets are sold for $63,000, and the partner with a capital deficiency is personally bankrupt.
   d. The noncash assets are sold for $56,000, and the partner with a capital deficiency pays cash of $3,000 to the partnership to erase part of the deficiency.
2. Make the journal entries to record the liquidation transactions in requirement 1d.

Problem 13-7B   *Liquidation of a partnership (L.O. 6)*

Triad Company is a partnership owned by Ryan, St. Laurent, and Goldberg, who share profits and losses in the ratio of 1 : 3 : 4. The adjusted trial balance of the partnership (in condensed form) at June 30, end of the current fiscal year, follows:

Triad Company
Adjusted Trial Balance
June 30, 19XX

Cash	$ 21,000	
Noncash assets	126,000	
Liabilities		$107,000
Ryan, capital		22,000
St. Laurent, capital		41,000
Goldberg, capital		62,000
Ryan, drawing	24,000	
St. Laurent, drawing	35,000	
Goldberg, drawing	54,000	
Revenues		118,000
Expenses	90,000	
Totals	$350,000	$350,000

Required

1. Prepare the June 30 entries to close the revenue, expense, income summary, and drawing accounts.
2. Insert the opening capital balances in the partner capital accounts, post the closing entries to the capital accounts, and determine each partner's ending capital balance.
3. The partnership liquidates on June 30 by selling the noncash assets for $102,000. Using the ending balances of the partner capital accounts, prepare a summary of liquidation transactions (as illustrated in the chapter). Any partner with a capital deficiency is unable to contribute assets to erase the deficiency.

Extending Your Knowledge

Decision Problems

1. Disagreements among partners (L.O. 3)

Clay Grant invested $30,000 and Elaine Marsh invested $10,000 in a public relations firm that has operated for ten years. Neither partner has made an additional investment. They have shared profits and losses in the ratio of 3 : 1, which is the ratio of their investments in the business. Grant manages the office, supervises the 16 employees and does the accounting. Marsh, the moderator of a television talk show, is responsible for marketing. Her high profile generates important revenue for the business. During the year ended December 19X4, the partnership earned net income of $87,000, shared in the 3 : 1 ratio. On December 31, 19X4, Grant's capital balance was $150,000 and Marsh's capital balance was $100,000.

Required

Respond to each of the following situations:

1. What explains the difference between the ratio of partner capital balances at December 31, 19X4, and the 3 : 1 ratio of partner investments and profit sharing?
2. Marsh believes the profit-and-loss-sharing ratio is unfair. She proposes a change, but Grant insists on keeping the 3 : 1 ratio. What two factors may underlie Marsh's unhappiness?
3. During January 19X5, Grant learned that revenues of $16,000 were omitted from the reported 19X4 income. He brings this to Marsh's attention, pointing out that his share of this added income is three fourths, or $12,000, and Marsh's share is one fourth, or $4,000. Marsh believes they should share this added income based on their capital balances: 60 percent (or $9,600) to Grant, and 40 percent (or $6,400) to Marsh. Which partner is correct? Why?
4. Assume that an account payable of $10,000 for an operating expense in 19X4 was omitted from 19X4 reported income. How would the partners share this amount?

2. Questions about partnerships (L.O. 1, 5)

1. The text suggests that a written partnership agreement may be drawn up between the partners in a partnership. One benefit of an agreement is that it provides a mechanism for resolving disputes between the partners. List five areas of dispute that might be resolved by a partnership agreement.
2. The statement has been made that "If you must take on a partner, make sure the partner is richer than you are." Why is this statement valid?
3. Zalinski, Waller, and Gunz is a partnership of CGAs. Gunz is planning to move to Australia. What are the options open to her to convert her share of the partnership assets to cash?

Ethical Issue

Paula Eagle and Edward Stone operate Noteworthy, a gift shop in The Empress Hotel on Vancouver Island, British Columbia. The partners split profits and losses equally, and each takes an annual salary of $30,000. To even out the work load,

Edward does the buying and Paula serves as the accountant. From time to time, they use small amounts of store merchandise for personal use. In preparing for a large private party, Paula took engraved invitations, napkins, place mats, and other goods that cost $800. She recorded the transaction as follows:

           Cost of Goods Sold   800
                Inventory   800

Required

1. How should Paula have recorded this transaction?
2. Discuss the ethical dimension of Paula's action.

Answers to Self-Study Questions

1. a
2. b
3. a ($40,000 × 3/12 = $10,000)
4. d ($40,000 × 5/12 = $16,667)
5. a
6. c [($46,000 + $52,000 + $55,000) × 1/3 = $51,000; $55,000 − $51,000 = $4,000; $4,000 ÷ 2 = $2,000 each to Graff and Harrell]
7. d
8. b ($36,000 × 1/4 = $9,000)
9. d
10. c

Chapter 14

Corporations: Organization, Capital Stock, and the Balance Sheet

"When former banker Allen Lambert began receiving invitations to sit on corporate boards in the 1950s, he soon discovered that some of his fellow outside directors shared two attributes — a lack of curiosity and a healthy appetite. These directors remained silent throughout most of the proceedings. 'On some boards,' recalls Lambert, retired chairman and president of the Toronto-Dominion Bank, 'the chairman and president almost felt you were challenging them if you asked questions.' Instead, most outside directors held their tongues and looked forward to having their lunch. 'It was a very good lunch, and you got your fee,' he says. 'The fees are better now, and the lunch is shorter.'

These small changes are part of a revolution that is transforming corporate boardrooms in Canada. Not only are outside directors expected to speak up, but they are also required to ask tough questions. Failure to do so can be downright dangerous — negligent directors face lawsuits from minority shareholders and prosecution under stringent environment laws."

As you read Chapter 14, you will note that one of the fundamental rights of each common share is the right to one vote for a director on the Board of Directors. The board in turn sets the direction and strategy of the company, and employs management personnel to implement this plan. As fierce global competition and multinational corporations become the rule for business in the 1990s, this voting power of the common share is becoming one of the keys to survival. An ineffective board often translates into a stagnant corporation, which in time either goes bankrupt or is bought out by a dynamic company with an effective Board of Directors.

Source: Arthur Johnson, "Directors: New Breed in a Hot Seat," *Canadian Business* (June 1991), pp. 74-78, 81, 83. Arthur Johnson is Executive Editor of *Canadian Business Magazine*.

LEARNING OBJECTIVES

After studying this chapter, you should be able to

1 Identify the characteristics of a corporation

2 Record the issuance of stock

3 Prepare the shareholders' equity section of a corporation balance sheet

4 Account for the incorporation of a going business

5 Allocate dividends to preferred and common stock

6 Compute two standard profitability measures

7 Distinguish among various stock "values"

The corporation is the dominant form of business organization in Canada. Although proprietorships and partnerships are more numerous, corporations transact more business and are larger in terms of total assets, sales revenue, and number of employees. Most well-known companies, such as Canadian Pacific Ltd., Noranda Inc., and Moore Corp., are corporations. Their full names include Limited, Incorporated, or Corporation (abbreviated Ltd., Inc., and Corp.) to indicate they are corporations. This and the next three chapters discuss corporations.

> **OBJECTIVE 1**
>
> Identify the characteristics of a corporation

Characteristics of a Corporation

Why is the corporation form of business so attractive? We now look at the features that distinguish corporations from proprietorships and partnerships.

Separate Legal Entity

A **corporation** is a business entity formed under federal or provincial law. The federal or provincial government grants **articles of incorporation**, which consist of a document that gives the governing body's permission to form a corporation.

A corporation is a distinct entity from a legal perspective. We may consider the corporation as an artificial person that exists apart from its owners, who are called **shareholders**. The corporation has many of the rights that a person has. For example, a corporation may buy, own, and sell property. Assets and liabilities in the business belong to the corporation. The corporation may enter into contracts, sue, and be sued.

The owners' equity of a corporation is divided into shares of **stock**. A person becomes a shareholder by purchasing the stock of the corporation. The articles of incorporation specify how much stock the corporation can issue (sell) and lists the other details of its relationships with the federal or provincial government under whose laws it is incorporated. The articles specify the maximum stock the corporation can issue — the maximum is described as the **authorized** stock; the stock the corporation sells to outsiders is the **issued** (or *issued and outstanding*) **stock**.

Continuous Life and Transferability of Ownership

Most corporations have continuous lives regardless of changes in the ownership of their stock. Shareholders may transfer stock as they wish. They may sell or trade the stock to another person, give it away, bequeath it in a will, or dispose of it in any other way they desire. The transfer of the stock does not affect the continuity of the corporation. Proprietorships and partnerships, on the other hand, terminate when their ownership changes.

No Mutual Agency

Mutual agency of the owners is not present in a corporation. The shareholder of a corporation cannot commit the corporation to a contract (unless he or she is also an officer in the business). For this reason, a shareholder need not exercise the care that partners must in selecting co-owners of the business.

Limited Liability of Shareholders

A shareholder has **limited liability** for corporation debts. He or she has no personal obligation for corporation liabilities. The most that a shareholder can lose on an investment in a corporation's stock is the cost of the investment. Recall that proprietors and partners are personally liable for the debts of their businesses.

The combination of limited liability and no mutual agency means that persons can invest limited amounts in a corporation, without fear of losing all their personal wealth because of a business failure. This feature enables a corporation to raise more capital from a wider group of investors than proprietorships and partnerships.

Separation of Ownership and Management

Shareholders own the business, but a board of directors elected by the shareholders, such as that mentioned in the chapter-opening vignette, appoints corporate officers to manage the business. Thus shareholders may invest $100 or $1 million in the corporation without having to manage the business or disrupt their personal affairs.

However, this separation between owners (shareholders) and management may create problems. Corporate officers may decide to run the business for their own benefit and not to the shareholders' advantage. Shareholders may find it difficult to lodge an effective protest against management policy because of the distance between them and management.

Corporate Taxation

Corporations are separate taxable entities. They pay a variety of taxes not borne by proprietorships or partnerships, such as federal and provincial income taxes. Corporate earnings are subject to **double taxation**. First, corporations pay their own income taxes on corporate income. Then, the shareholders pay personal income tax on the cash dividends that they receive from corporations, although the tax rate is usually lower than for regular income. This is different from proprietorships and partnerships, which pay no business income tax. Instead, the tax falls solely on the owners who are taxed on their share of the proprietorship or partnership income.

Government Regulation

Strong government regulation is an important disadvantage to the corporation. Because shareholders have only limited liability for corporation debts, outsiders doing business with the corporation can look no further than the corporation itself for any claims that may arise against the business. To protect persons who loan money to a corporation or who invest in its stock, the federal and provincial governments monitor the affairs of corporations. This government regulation consists mainly of ensuring that corporations disclose the business information that investors and creditors need to make informed decisions. For many corporations, adhering to this government regulation is expensive.

Organization of a Corporation

Creation of a corporation begins when its organizers, called the **incorporators**, obtain articles of incorporation from the federal or provincial government. The articles of incorporation include the authorization for the corporation to issue a certain number of shares of stock, which are shares of ownership in the corporation. The incorporators pay fees and file the required documents with the incorporating jurisdiction. Then the corporation comes into existence. The incorporators agree to a set of **bylaws**, which act as the constitution for governing the corporation.

The ultimate control of the corporation rests with the shareholders, who receive one vote for each share of voting stock they own. The shareholders elect the members of the **board of directors**, which sets policy for the corporation and appoints the officers. The board elects a **chairperson**, who usually is the most powerful person in the corporation. The board also designates the **president**, who is the chief operating officer in charge of managing day-to-day operations. Most corporations also have vice-presidents in charge of sales, manufacturing, accounting and finance, and other key areas. Often the president and one or more vice-presidents are also elected to the board of directors. Exhibit 14-1 shows the authority structure in a corporation.

All corporations have an annual meeting at which the shareholders elect directors and make other shareholder decisions such as appointing the external auditors. Shareholders unable to attend this annual meeting may vote on corporation matters by use of a **proxy**, which is a legal document that expresses the shareholder's preference and appoints another person to cast the vote.

The structure of proprietorships, partnerships, and corporations is similar in that all three types of business have owners, managers, and employees. In proprietorships and partnerships, policy decisions are usually made by the owners — the proprietor or the partners. In a corporation, however, the managers who set policy

EXHIBIT 14-1 *Authority Structure in a Corporation*

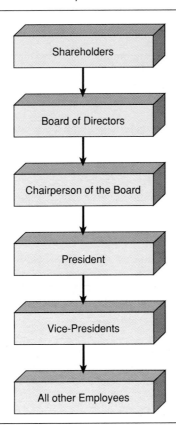

are appointed by the board of directors, and may or may not be owners (shareholders).

A corporation keeps a subsidiary record of its shareholders. The business must notify the shareholders of the annual shareholder meeting, send them financial statements, usually in the form of an annual report, and mail them dividend payments (which we discuss later in this chapter). Large companies use a registrar to maintain the shareholder list and a transfer agent to issue stock certificates. Banks or trust companies provide these registration and transfer services. The transfer agent handles the change in stock ownership from one shareholder to another.

Capital Stock

A corporation issues stock certificates to its owners in exchange for their investments in the business. The basic unit of capital stock is called a *share*. A corporation may issue a share certificate for any number of shares it wishes — one share, 100 shares, or any other number. Exhibit 14-2 depicts an actual share certificate for 50 shares of The National Victoria and Grey Trustco Limited stock. The certificate shows the company name, shareholder name, and number of shares.

Stock in the hands of a shareholder is said to be **outstanding**. The total number of shares of stock outstanding at any time represents 100 percent ownership of the corporation. Because stock represents the corporation's capital, it is often called capital stock.

Shareholders' Equity

The balance sheet of a corporation reports assets and liabilities in the same way as a proprietorship or a partnership. However, owners' equity of a corporation, called **shareholders' equity**, is reported differently. Incorporating acts require corporations to report the sources of their capital. The two most basic sources of capital are

EXHIBIT 14-2 *Share Certificate*

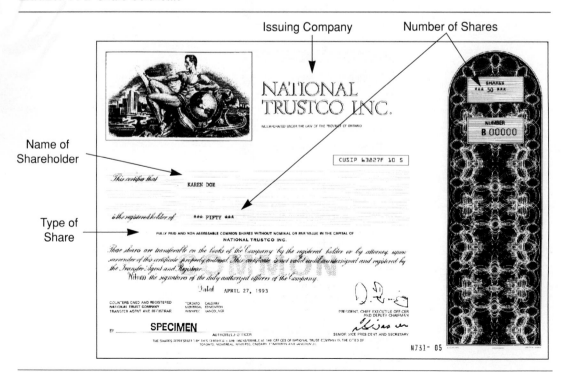

EXHIBIT 14-3 *Simplified Corporation Balance Sheet*

Assets...............................	$600,000	Liabilities	$240,000
		Shareholders' Equity	
		Capital stock.................	**200,000**
		Retained earnings	**160,000**
		Total shareholders'	
		equity..............................	**360,000**
		Total liabilities and	
Total assets..........................	$600,000	shareholders' equity	$600,000

investments by the shareholders, called **capital stock** or **share capital**, and the capital earned through the profitable operations of the business, called **retained earnings**. While the *Canada Business Corporations Act* and several of the provincial incorporating acts use the term **stated capital** to describe capital stock, this text will use the more common term, capital stock. Exhibit 14-3 outlines a simplified corporation balance sheet to show how to report these categories of shareholders' equity.

An investment of cash or any other asset in a corporation increases its assets and shareholders' equity. The corporation's entry for receipt of a $20,000 shareholder investment in the business is

Oct.	20	Cash	20,000	
		Capital Stock..		20,000
		Investment by shareholder.		

Capital stock is regarded as the permanent capital of the business because it is not subject to withdrawal by the shareholders.

Profitable operations produce income, which increases shareholders' equity through an account called Retained Earnings. At the end of the year, the balance of the Income Summary account is closed to Retained Earnings. For example, if net income is $95,000, Income Summary will have a $95,000 credit balance. The closing entry will debit Income Summary to transfer net income to Retained Earnings as follows:

Dec.	31	Income Summary..	95,000	
		Retained Earnings.......................................		95,000
		To close Income Summary by transferring		
		net *income* to Retained Earnings.		

If operations produce a net loss rather than net income, the Income Summary account will have a debit balance. Income Summary must be credited to close it. With a $60,000 loss, the closing entry is

Dec.	31	Retained Earnings..	60,000	
		Income Summary..		60,000
		To close Income Summary by transferring		
		net *loss* to Retained Earnings.		

A large loss may cause a debit balance in the Retained Earnings account. This condition, called a Retained Earnings **deficit** or accumulated deficit, is reported on the balance sheet as a negative amount in shareholders' equity. Assume a $50,000 deficit:

Shareholders' Equity

Capital stock..	$200,000
Deficit...	(50,000)
Total shareholders' equity..............................	$150,000

If the corporation has been profitable and has sufficient cash, a distribution of cash may be made to the shareholders. Such distributions, called **dividends**, decrease both the assets and the retained earnings of the business. The balance of the Retained Earnings account at any time is the sum of earnings accumulated since incorporation, minus any losses, and minus all dividends distributed to shareholders. Retained Earnings is entirely separate from the capital stock invested in the business by the shareholders.

Some people think of Retained Earnings as a fund of cash. It is not, because Retained Earnings is an element of shareholders' equity, representing a claim against all assets resulting from cumulative earnings minus cumulative dividends since the corporation's beginning.

Shareholder Rights

The owner of a share of stock has certain rights that are set out in the corporation's articles of incorporation; these vary from company to company, and even between classes of stock within a company. In addition, the shareholder may have other rights granted by the legislation under which the corporation receives its articles. While those rights outlined in the articles of incorporation are specific to an individual company, those set forth by legislation are shared by shareholders of all companies incorporated under that legislation. The articles of incorporation, for example, may specify that the shareholder of a Class A common share is entitled to one vote at shareholders' meetings, while the shareholder of a Class B common share is not entitled to vote. An example of a shared right is that under the *Canada Business Corporations Act*, shareholders may require the directors of the company to call a meeting of the shareholders.

Some of the rights normally attached to common shares [1] are:

1. The right to sell the shares.
2. The right to vote at shareholders' meetings.
3. The right to a proportionate share of any dividends declared by the directors for that class of shares.
4. The right to receive a proportionate share of any assets, on the winding-up of the company, after the creditors and any classes of shares that rank above that class have been paid.

Classes of Stock

Corporations issue different types of stock to appeal to a wide variety of investors. The stock of a corporation may be either common or preferred.

Common and Preferred Stock

Every corporation issues **common stock**, the most basic form of capital stock. Unless designated otherwise, the word *stock* is understood to mean "common stock." Companies may issue different classes of common stock. For example, some companies issue Class A common stock, which usually carries the right to vote,

---

[1] The rights enumerated are basic rights common to incorporating legislation generally. For a more complete listing, the interested reader is referred to: *Canada Business Corporations Act with Regulations, 1991*, 18th edition, Don Mills, Ontario: CCH Canadian Limited, 1991; *Canada Business Corporations Act* in *The Revised Statutes of Canada*; and Alan D. Stickler, *Canada Business Corporations Act*, 3rd edition, revised by Christina S. R. Drummond, Toronto: Butterworths, 1987.

and Class B common stock, which may be nonvoting. (Classes of common stock may also be designated Series A, Series B, and so on, with each series having certain unique features such as a fixed dividend or a redemption feature.) The general ledger has a separate account for each class of common stock. In describing a corporation, we would say the common shareholders are the owners of the business.

Some corporations issue **preferred stock**. Often the right to vote is withheld from preferred shareholders. Preferred stock usually gives its owners certain advantages over common shareholders. These benefits frequently include the priority to receive dividends before the common shareholders, and the priority to receive assets before the common shareholders if the corporation liquidates. Because of the priorities that preferred shareholders often have, we see that common stock represents the residual ownership in the corporation's assets after subtracting the liabilities and the claims of preferred shareholders. Preferred shares usually indicate the annual dividend. Lefarge Corporation, the cement and building materials company, has $1.88 convertible preferred shares and $2.44 convertible preferred shares; $1.88 and $2.44 are the annual dividend rates. Companies may issue different classes of preferred stock. (Class A and Class B or Series A and Series B, for example). Each class is recorded in a separate account in the general ledger.

The 1991 annual report of Doman Industries Limited indicates that the company has the right to issue, that is, the articles of incorporation have authorized,

> 5,000,000 Class A preferred shares
> 100,000 Class B preferred shares
>
> 29,000,000 Class A common shares
> 60,000,000 Class B common shares

and that Doman had issued at December 31, 1991,

> 573,553 Class A preferred, series 2
> 6,390,511 Class A common
> 12,994,704 Class B nonvoting, series 2 [common]

Par Value and No-Par Stock

Par value is an arbitrary amount assigned to a share of stock in the articles of incorporation by the company issuing it. For example, National Trust, through a predecessor company, used to issue common shares with a $2.00 par value. When a common share was sold, $2.00 would be allocated to Common Stock and any consideration received in excess of $2.00 would be recorded as a premium on (that) common stock. Par value shares are gradually being eliminated by the various jurisdictions in Canada and exist today only in a very few of those jurisdictions. The discussion of par value stock is included for completeness, and because it remains a popular class in the United States.

No-par shares are shares of stock that do not have a value assigned to them by the articles of incorporation. The board of directors assigns a value to the shares when they are issued; this value is known as the *stated value*. For example, Dajol Inc. has authorization to issue 100,000 shares of common stock, having no-par value assigned to them by the articles of incorporation. Dajol needs $50,000 at incorporation, and might issue 10,000 shares for $5.00 per share, 2,000 shares at $25.00 per share, or 1,000 shares at $50.00 per share, and so on. The point is that Dajol can assign whatever value to the shares the board of directors wishes. Normally, the stated value would be credited to Common Stock when the stock is issued.

The value of a corporation's capital stock or stated capital is the sum of the shares issued times the stated values of those shares at the time of issue. For example, if YDR Ltd. issued 1,000 common shares at a stated value of $8.00 per share, 2,000 shares at $12.00 per share, and 500 shares at $15.00 per share, its capital stock or stated capital would be $39,500 [(1,000 × $8) + (2,000 × $12) + (500 × $15)].

The *Canada Business Corporations Act* and most provincial incorporating acts now require common and preferred shares to be issued without nominal or par value. The full value of the proceeds from the sale of stock by a company must be allocated to the capital account for that stock. For example, if National Trust were to issue 100 shares of common stock for $2,500 (that is, at a stated value of $25.00 per share), $2,500 would be credited to Common Stock.

Issuing Stock

Large corporations such as BCE Inc., TransCanada PipeLines Ltd., and John Labatt Ltd. need huge quatities of money to operate. They cannot expect to finance all their operations through borrowing. They need capital that they can raise by issuing stock. The articles of incorporation that the incorporators receive from the federal or provincial government includes an authorization for the business to issue (that is, to sell) a certain number of shares of stock. Corporations may sell the stock directly to the shareholders, or they may use the service of an underwriter, such as the brokerage firms RBC Dominion Securities and Richardson Greenshields. The agreement between a corporation and its underwriter will vary, but typically the underwriter will commit to placing all of the share issue it can with its customers, and to buying any unsold shares for its own account. In another form of contract, the underwriter agrees to do its best to sell all the share issue but makes no guarantees. The underwriter makes its money by selling the shares for a higher price than it pays to the corporation issuing the shares.

The corporation need not issue all the stock that the articles allow — authorized stock can, and often does, exceed issued stock. Management may hold some stock back and issue it later if the need for additional capital arises. The stock that the corporation does issue to shareholders is called *issued stock*. Only by issuing stock (not by receiving authorization) does the corporation increase the asset and owner's equity amounts on its balance sheet.

The price that the shareholder pays to acquire stock from the corporation is called the *issue price*. A combination of market factors — including the company's comparative earnings record, financial position, prospects for success, and general business conditions — determines issue price. Investors will not pay more than market value for the stock. The following sections show how to account for the issuance of stock.

Issuing Common Stock

OBJECTIVE 2

Record the issuance of stock

Issuing Common Stock at a Stated Value   Suppose Medina Corporation issues 500 shares of its common stock for cash, and the directors determine that the shares will be issued with a stated value of $10 per share. The stock issuance entry is

Jan.	8	Cash (500 × $10)..	5,000	
		Common Stock		5,000
		To issue common stock at $10 per share.		

The amount invested in the corporation, $5,000 in this case, is called capital stock. The credit to Common Stock records an increase in the capital stock of the corporation.

The following example illustrates the shareholders' equity section of Medina Corporation after it had issued the 500 shares. Assume that the articles of incorporation granted to Medina authorize it to issue 5,000 common shares, that 1,500 shares had been issued for a stated value of $6.00 per share prior to January, and that the company had $3,000 in retained earnings. The corporation would report shareholders' equity as follows:

Shareholders' Equity

Capital stock	
Common stock, 5,000 shares authorized,	
2,000 shares issued...	$14,000
Retained earnings	3,000
Total shareholders' equity	$17,000

The authorized common stock reports the maximum number of shares the company may issue under its articles of incorporation.

Issuing Common Stock for Assets Other Than Cash   When a corporation issues stock in exchange for assets other than cash, it debits the assets received for their current market value and credits the capital accounts accordingly. The assets' prior book value does not matter because the shareholder will demand stock equal to the market value of the asset given. Assume Kahn Corporation issues 15,000 shares of its common stock for equipment worth $15,000 and a building worth $120,000. The entry is

Nov. 12	Equipment...	15,000	
	Building	120,000	
	Common Stock		135,000
	To issue 15,000 shares of common stock in		
	exchange for equipment and a building.		

Common stock increases by the amount of the assets' current market value, $135,000 in this case; the stated value or value assigned to the shares would be $9.00 ($135,000/15,000) per share.

Issuing Common Stock through Subscriptions   Established companies usually issue stock and receive the full price in a single transaction. New corporations, to gauge their ability to raise capital, may take subscriptions for their stock. A **stock subscription** is a contract that obligates an investor to purchase the corporation's stock at a later date. Because a contract exists between the two parties, the corporation acquires an asset, Subscription Receivable, when it receives the subscription. The investor gains an equity in the corporation by promising to pay the subscription amount. Depending on the subscription agreement, the subscriber may pay the subscription in a lump sum or in installments.

The *Canada Business Corporations Act* and several of the provincial incorporating acts do not permit a corporation to issue shares until the full subscription price has been paid. It should be noted that some authorities believe amounts received should be shown as a liability and not as part of capital stock.

Assume Medina Corporation receives a subscription on May 31 for 1,000 shares of common stock. The subscription price is $22 per share. The subscriber makes a down payment of $6,000, and agrees to pay the $16,000 balance in two monthly installments of $8,000 each. Medina Corporation will issue the shares when the subscriber pays in full. The entry to record receipt of the subscription is

May 31	Cash...	6,000	
	Subscription Receivable — Common		
	($22,000 – $6,000)...	16,000	
	Common Stock Subscribed (1,000 × $22)..		22,000
	To receive common stock subscription at		
	$22 per share.		

Subscription Receivable — Common is a current asset if collection is expected within one year. Otherwise it is long-term and is reported in the Other Assets category on the balance sheet. Common Stock Subscribed is an element of shareholders' equity, reported immediately beneath Common Stock on the balance sheet. The "Subscribed" label will be eliminated when the subscription is paid off and the stock is issued. The entries to record receipt of the two installments and issuance of the stock are

June	30	Cash ($16,000 × ½)	8,000	
		Subscription Receivable — Common		8,000
		To collect first installment on common stock subscription.		
July	31	Cash ($16,000 × ½)	8,000	
		Subscription Receivable — Common		8,000
		To collect second installment on common stock subscription.		
	31	Common Stock Subscribed	22,000	
		Common Stock		22,000
		To issue common stock under subscription agreement.		

The last entry is needed to transfer the value of the stock from the Subscribed account to Common Stock.

Because the subscription is a legally binding contract, subscribers are obliged to pay their subscriptions in full. If a subscriber does not, the company may cancel the subscription and claim the amount already paid, cancel the subscription and refund the amount already paid, or issue shares with a value of the amount already paid (that is, issue fewer shares than were subscribed for).

Issuing Par Value Common Stock at a Premium   A corporation in a province that permits par value stock usually issues its common stock for a price above par value. The excess amount above par is called a *premium*. Assume Olde Corp. issues 100 shares of $10 par value common stock for a price of $25; the total proceeds would be $2,500 (100 × $25). The $15 per share difference is a premium. This sale of stock increases the corporation's capital stock by $2,500, the total issue price of the stock. Both the par value of the stock and the premium are part of capital stock. A premium on the sale of stock is not gain, income, or profit to the corporation, because the entity is dealing with its own shareholders. This illustrates one of the fundamentals of accounting: a company cannot earn a profit or incur a loss when it sells its stock to or buys its stock from its own shareholders.

The entry to record the issue of 100 $10 par value shares at $25 by Olde Corp. would be

Jan.	23	Cash (100 × $25)	2,500	
		Common Stock (100 × $10).........................		1,000
		Contributed Surplus (100 × $15)		1,500
		To issue common stock at a premium.		

Since both par value and premium amounts increase the corporation's capital, they appear in the shareholders' equity section of the balance sheet. At the end of the first year, Olde Corp. would report shareholders' equity on its balance sheet as follows, assuming the articles of incorporation authorize 20,000 shares of common stock, 1,000 shares were previously issued at par, and retained earnings is $8,500:

Shareholders' Equity

Capital stock	
Common stock, $10 par, 20,000 shares	
authorized, 1,100 shares issued	$11,000
Contributed Surplus	1,500
Total capital stock	12,500
Retained earnings	8,500
Total shareholders' equity	$21,000

We determine the dollar amount reported for common stock by multiplying the total number of shares issued (1,000 issued previously + 100) by the par value per share.

Issuing Preferred Stock

While not all corporations issue preferred stock, recent editions of *Financial Reporting in Canada* published by the Canadian Institute of Chartered Accountants report that slightly more than two thirds of the 300 companies reporting mentioned preferred shares in the shareholders' equity section of their balance sheets. Accounting for preferred shares follows the pattern illustrated for common stock.

Assume the Medina Corporation articles of incorporation authorize issuance of 5,000 preferred shares with an annual dividend of $11.00 per share. On July 31, the company issues 400 shares at a stated price of $110.00 per share. The issuance entry is

July	31	Cash (400 × $110)	44,000	
		Preferred Stock		44,000
		To issue preferred stock.		

Summary

Let us review the first half of this chapter by showing the shareholders' equity section of Medina Corporation's balance sheet at May 31. (Assume that all figures, which are arbitrary, are correct.) Note the two sections of shareholders' equity: capital stock and retained earnings. Also observe the order of the equity accounts: preferred stock, common stock, and common stock subscribed. If Medina had a Preferred Stock Subscribed account, it would appear after Preferred Stock (corresponding to the order illustrated for the common stock accounts).

> **OBJECTIVE 3**
>
> Prepare the shareholders' equity section of a corporation balance sheet

Shareholders' Equity

Capital stock	
Preferred stock, $11.00, 5,000 shares authorized,	
400 shares issued	$44,000
Common stock, 5,000 shares authorized,	
2,000 shares issued	14,000
Common stock subscribed, 1,000 shares	22,000
Total capital stock	80,000
Retained earnings	3,000
Total shareholders' equity	$83,000

Summary Problem for Your Review

1. Test your understanding of the first half of this chapter by answering whether each of the following statements is true or false:

   _____   a. A shareholder may bind the corporation to a contract.

   _____   b. The policy-making body in a corporation is called the board of directors.

   _____   c. The owner of 100 shares of preferred stock has greater voting rights than the owner of 100 shares of common stock.

   _____   d. A company incorporated under the *Canada Business Corporations Act* must assign the proceeds of a stock issue to the capital account for that stock.

   _____   e. All shares of common stock issued and outstanding have voting rights.

   _____   f. Issuance of 1,000 common shares at $12 increases owners' equity by $12,000.

   _____   g. The stated value of a stock is the value assigned to the stock by the company issuing it at the date issued or subscribed.

   _____   h. A corporation issues its preferred stock in exchange for land and a building with a combined market value of $200,000. This transaction increases the corporation's owners' equity by $200,000 regardless of the assets' prior book value.

   _____   i. Receipt of a subscription contract does not increase the shareholders' equity of the corporation unless the subscriber makes a down payment.

   _____   j. Common Stock Subscribed is a part of shareholders' equity.

2. Tundra Co. Ltd., incorporated under the *Canada Business Corporations Act*, had three transactions during the year involving its common shares. On January 15, 10,000 shares were issued with a stated value of $7.80 per share. On February 28, subscriptions were received for 4,000 shares with a stated value of $8.50 per share; $4.50 was received on each share subscribed. On August 8, 6,000 shares were issued in exchange for land with a market value of $52,000. Tundra's articles of incorporation state that 50,000 common shares are authorized.

   Required

   1. Prepare the journal entry to record the transaction of January 15.
   2. Prepare the journal entry to record the transaction of February 28.
   3. Prepare the journal entry to record the transaction of August 8.
   4. Set up the shareholders' equity section for Tundra Co. Ltd. after the three transactions have taken place.
   5. What is the total capital stock of the company?

SOLUTIONS TO SUMMARY PROBLEM

1. Answers to true-false statements:

a. False	b. True	c. False	d. True	e. False
f. True	g. True	h. True	i. False	j. True

2. a.   Jan.   15   Cash (10,000 × $7.80)   78,000
                      Common Stock.......................................   78,000
                      To issue common stock at $7.80 per share.

   b.   Feb.   28   Cash (4,000 × $4.50)   18,000
                    Subscriptions Receivable.............................   16,000
                      Common Stock Subscribed
                        (4,000 × $8.50)   34,000
                      To receive common stock subscription
                      at $8.50 per share.

   c.   Aug.   8   Land   52,000
                      Common Stock.......................................   52,000
                      To issue 6,000 shares of common stock in
                      exchange for land.

   d.   Shareholders' Equity
                      Capital stock
                        Common stock, 50,000 shares
                        authorized, 16,000 shares issued.... $130,000
                        Common stock subscribed but
                        not issued..   34,000
                                                                                 $164,000

   e.   Capital stock is $164,000.

Donated Capital

Corporations occasionally receive gifts or donations. For example, a city council may offer a company free land to encourage it to locate in their city. The free land is called a donation. Also, a shareholder may make a donation to the corporation in the form of cash, land or other assets, or stock that the corporation can resell.

A donation is a gift that increases the assets of the corporation. However, the donor (giver) receives no ownership interest in the company in return. A transaction to receive a donation does not increase the corporation's revenue, and thus it does not affect income. Instead, the donation creates a special category of shareholders' equity called **donated capital**. The corporation records a donation by debiting the asset received at its current market value, and by crediting Donated Capital, a shareholders' equity account.

Suppose Burlington Ltd. receives 100 hectares of land as a donation from the city of Lethbridge, Alberta. The current market value of the land is $150,000. Burlington records receipt of the donation as follows:

   Apr.   18   Land   150,000
                Donated Capital   150,000
                To receive land as a donation from the city.

Donated capital is reported on the balance sheet after the stock accounts in the capital stock section of shareholders' equity.

Incorporation of a Going Business

You may dream of having your own business someday, or you may currently be a business proprietor or partner. Businesses that begin as a proprietorship or a partnership often incorporate at a later date. By incorporating a going business, the proprietor or partner avoid the unlimited liability for business debts. And as we discussed earlier, incorporating also makes it easier to raise capital.

OBJECTIVE 4

Account for the incorporation of a going business

To account for the incorporation of a going business, we close the owner equity accounts of the prior entity and set up the shareholder equity accounts of the corporation. Suppose B. C. Coast Travel Associates is a partnership owned by Joe Suzuki and Monica Lee. The partnership balance sheet, after all adjustments and closing entries, reports Joe Suzuki, Capital, of $50,000, and Monica Lee, Capital, of $70,000. They incorporate the travel agency as B. C. Coast Travel Company, Inc. with an authorization to issue 200,000 shares of common stock. Joe and Monica agree to receive common stock equal in stated value to their partnership owner equity balances. The entry to record the incorporation of the business is

Feb.	1	Joe Suzuki, Capital	50,000	
		Monica Lee, Capital...	70,000	
		Common Stock...		120,000
		To incorporate the business, close the capital accounts of the partnership and issue common stock to the incorporators.		

Organization Cost

The costs of organizing a corporation include legal fees for preparing documents and advising on procedures, fees and taxes paid to the incorporating jurisdiction, and charges by promoters for selling the company's stock. These costs are grouped in an account titled Organization Cost, which is an asset because these costs contribute to a business's start-up. Suppose Mary's Good Wings and Ribs Ltd. pays legal fees and incorporation fees of $15,500 to organize the corporation under the *Canada Business Corporations Act* in Newfoundland. In addition, an investment dealer charges a fee of $12,000 for selling 20,000 shares of Mary's Good Wings and Ribs Ltd. common stock for $160,000 and receives 2,000 common shares as payment. Mary's Good Wings and Ribs Ltd.'s journal entries to record these organization costs are

Mar.	31	Organization Cost	15,500	
		Cash...		15,500
		Legal fees and incorporation fees to organize the corporation.		
Apr.	3	Cash	160,000	
		Organization Cost..	12,000	
		Common Stock		172,000
		To record receipt of funds from sale of common stock and issue of shares to investment dealer for selling stock in organization.		

Organization Cost is an *intangible asset*, reported on the balance sheet along with patents, trademarks, goodwill, and any other intangibles. We know that an intangible asset should be amortized over its useful life, and organization costs will benefit the corporation for as long as the corporation operates. But how long will that be? We cannot know in advance. Revenue Canada allows corporations to write organization expenses off against taxable income. While the *CICA Handbook* does not require organization costs to be amortized, most companies write organization costs off quickly because of their relatively small size. As is true with other intangibles, amortization expense for the year should be disclosed.

Dividend Dates

A corporation must declare a dividend before paying it. The board of directors alone has the authority to declare a dividend. The corporation has no obligation to pay a dividend until the board declares one, but once declared, the dividend becomes a legal liability of the corporation. Three relevant dates for dividends are

1. *Declaration date*   On the declaration date, the board of directors announces the intention to pay the dividend. The declaration creates a liability for the corporation. Declaration is recorded by debiting Retained Earnings and crediting Dividends Payable.

2. *Date of record*   The people who own the stock on the date of record receive the dividend. The corporation announces the record date, which follows the declaration date by a few weeks, as part of the declaration. The corporation makes no journal entry on the date of record because no transaction occurs. Nevertheless, much work takes place behind the scenes to identify the shareholders of record on this date properly, because the stock is being traded continuously.

3. *Payment date*   Payment of the dividend usually follows the record date by two to four weeks. Payment is recorded by debiting Dividends Payable and crediting Cash.

Dividends on Preferred and Common Stock _____

Declaration of a cash dividend is recorded by debiting Retained Earnings and crediting Dividends Payable as follows:

June 19	Retained Earnings	XXX	
	Dividends Payable		XXX
	To declare a cash dividend.		

Payment of the dividend occurs, as was noted above, on the payment date, and is recorded:

July 2	Dividends Payable	XXX	
	Cash...		XXX
	To pay a cash dividend.		

Dividends Payable is a current liability. When a company has issued both preferred and common stock, the preferred shareholders receive their dividends first. The common shareholders receive dividends only if the total declared dividend is large enough to pay the preferred shareholders first.

Pine Industries, Inc., in addition to its common stock, has 9,000 shares of preferred stock outstanding. Preferred dividends are paid at the annual rate of $1.75 per share. Assume Pine declares an annual dividend of $150,000. The allocation to preferred and common shareholders is

	Total Dividend of $150,000
Preferred dividend (9,000 shares x $1.75 per share).........................	$ 15,750
Common dividend (remainder: $150,000 – $15,750).........................	134,250
Total dividend...	$150,000

OBJECTIVE 5

Allocate dividends to preferred and common stock

If Pine declares only a $20,000 dividend, preferred shareholders receive $15,750 and the common shareholders receive $4,250 ($20,000 – $15,750).

This example illustrates an important relationship between preferred stock and common stock. To an investor, the preferred stock is safer because it receives dividends first (as well as ranking ahead of common shares on dissolution). For example, if Pine Industries earns only enough net income to pay the preferred shareholders' dividends, the owners of common stock receive no dividends at all. However, the earnings potential from an investment in common stock is much greater than from an investment in preferred stock. Preferred dividends are usually limited to the specified amount, but there is no upper limit on the amount of common dividends.

We have noted that preferred shareholders enjoy the advantage of priority over common shareholders in receiving dividends. The dividend preference is normally stated as a dollar amount. (In those rare cases where the preferred shares have a par value, the dividend preference may be stated as a percentage of the par value rate.) For example, the preferred stock may be "$3 preferred," meaning that the shareholders receive an annual dividend of $3 per share.

Cumulative Preferred Stock

The allocation of dividends may be complex if the preferred stock is *cumulative*. Corporations sometimes fail to pay a dividend to their preferred shareholders. The passed dividends are said to be **in arrears**. The owners of **cumulative preferred stock** must receive all dividends in arrears before the corporation pays dividends to the common shareholders. The cumulative feature is not automatic to preferred shares but must be assigned to the preferred shares in the articles of incorporation.

The preferred stock of Pine Industries is cumulative. Suppose the company passed the 19X4 preferred dividend of $15,750. Before paying dividends to its common shareholders in 19X5, the company must first pay preferred dividends of $15,750 for both 19X4 and 19X5, a total of $31,500.

Assume that Pine Industries passes its 19X4 preferred dividend. In 19X5, the company declares a $50,000 dividend. The entry to record the declaration is

Sept. 6	Retained Earnings	50,000	
	Dividends Payable, Preferred		
	($15,750 × 2)...		31,500
	Dividends Payable, Common		
	($50,000 – $31,500)...................................		18,500
	To declare a cash dividend.		

If the preferred stock is not designated as cumulative, the corporation is not obligated to pay dividends in arrears. Suppose that the Pine Industries preferred stock was not cumulative, and the company passed the 19X4 preferred dividend of $15,750. The preferred shareholders would lose the 19X4 dividend forever. Of course, the common shareholders would not receive a 19X4 dividend either. Before paying any common dividends in 19X5, the company would have to pay the 19X5 preferred dividend of $15,750.

Having dividends in arrears on cumulative preferred stock is not a liability to the corporation. (A liability for dividends arises only after the board of directors declares the dividend.) Nevertheless, a corporation must report cumulative preferred dividends in arrears in the notes to the financial statements. This information alerts common shareholders to how much in cumulative preferred dividends must be paid before any dividends will be paid on the common stock. This gives the common shareholders an idea about the likelihood of receiving dividends and satisfies the disclosure principle.

Note disclosure of cumulative preferred dividends might take the following form. Observe the two references to note 3 in this section of the balance sheet. The "$3.00" after "Preferred stock" is the dividend rate.

Preferred stock, $3.00, 10,000 shares authorized, 2,000 shares issued (note 3)	$100,000
Retained earnings (note 3)...	414,000

Note 3: Cumulative preferred dividends in arrears. At December 31, 19X2, dividends on the company's $3.00 preferred stock were in arrears for 19X1 and 19X2, in the amount of $12,000 ($3.00 × 2,000 × 2 years).

Participating Preferred Stock

The allocation of dividends may be complex if the preferred stock is *participating*. The owners of **participating preferred stock** may receive (that is, *participate in*) dividends beyond the stated amount. Assume that the corporation declares a dividend. First, the preferred shareholders receive their dividends. If the corporation has declared a large enough dividend, then the common shareholders receive their dividends. If an additional dividend amount remains to be distributed, common shareholders and participating preferred shareholders share it. For example, the owners of a $4 preferred stock must receive the specified annual dividend of $4 per share before the common shareholders receive any dividends. Then a $4 dividend is paid on each common share. The participation feature takes effect only after the preferred and common shareholders have received the specified $4 rate. Payment of an extra *common* dividend of, say, $1.50 is accompanied by a $1.50 dividend on each participating preferred share.

Participating preferred stock is rare. In fact, preferred stock is nonparticipating unless it is specifically described as participating in the articles of incorporation. Therefore, if the preferred stock in our example is not participating (the usual case), the largest annual dividend that a preferred shareholder will receive in our illustration is $4.

Convertible Preferred Stock _____

Convertible preferred stock may be exchanged by the preferred shareholders, if they choose, for another specified class of stock in the corporation. For example, the preferred stock of Rainy River Lumber Ltd. is convertible into the company's common stock. A note to Rainy River's balance sheet describes the conversion terms as follows:

> The . . . preferred stock is convertible at the rate of 6.51 shares of common stock for each share of preferred stock outstanding.

If you owned 100 shares of Rainy River's convertible preferred stock, you could convert it into 651 (100 × 6.51) shares of Rainy River Lumber common stock. Under what condition would you exercise the conversion privilege? You would do so if the market value of the common stock that you could receive from conversion exceeded the market value of the preferred stock that you presently held. This way, you as an investor could increase your personal wealth.

Rainy River Lumber convertible preferred stock was issued at $100 per share, and the common stock at $1. The company would record the conversion at the value of the 100 preferred shares on the Rainy River Lumber books, or $10,000 (100 × $100). The conversion of the 100 shares of preferred stock into 651 shares of common stock would be recorded as follows:

Mar.	7	Preferred Stock (100 × $100)	10,000	
		Common Stock (651 shares)		10,000
		Conversion of preferred stock into common.		

Summary

Preferred stock, as we see, offers alternative features not available to common stock. Preferred stock may be cumulative or not cumulative, participating or not participating, and convertible or not convertible. In addition, preferred stock is usually preferred when dividends are distributed, and when the assets are distributed to shareholders upon liquidation of the company.

Rate of Return on Total Assets and Rate of Return on Shareholders' Equity _____

Investors and creditors are constantly evaluating the ability of managers to earn profits. Investors search for companies whose stocks are likely to incease in value. Creditors are interested in profitable companies that can pay their debts. Investment and credit decisions often include a comparison of companies. But a comparison of Northern Telecom's net income to the net income of a new company in the electronics industry simply is not meaningful. Northern Telecom's profits run into hundreds of millions of dollars, which likely exceed the new company's total sales. Does that automatically make Northern Telecom a better investment? Not necessarily. To make relevant comparisons between companies different in size, scope of operations, or any other measure, investors, creditors, and managers use some standard profitability measures, including rate of return on total assets and rate of return on shareholders' equity.

The **rate of return on total assets,** or simply **return on assets,** measures a company's success in using its assets to earn income for the persons who are financing the business. Creditors have loaned money to the corporation and earn interest. Shareholders have invested in the corporation's stock and expect the company to earn net income. The sum of interest expense and net income is the return to the two groups that have financed the corporation's activities, and this is the numerator of the return on assets ratio. The denominator is average total assets. Return on assets is computed as follows, using the actual data from the 1991 annual report of Québec-Téléphone (amounts in thousands of dollars):

OBJECTIVE 6
Compute two standard profitability measures

$$\frac{\text{Rate of}}{\text{return}} \atop \text{on total} \atop \text{assets} = \frac{\text{Net income} + \text{Interest expense}}{\text{Average total assets}} = \frac{\$26,716 + \$17,952}{(\$449,430 + \$442,148)/2} = \frac{\$44,668}{\$445,789} = .10$$

Net income and interest expense are taken from the income statement. Average total assets are computed from the beginning and ending balance sheets. How is this profitability measure used in decision-making? To compare companies. By relating the sum of net income and interest expense to average total assets, we have a standard measure that describes the profitability of of all types of companies. Investment dealers like Richardson Greenshields and Nesbitt Thomson Corp. often single out particular industries as good investments. For example, brokerage analysts may believe that the publishing and printing industry is in a growth phase. These analysts would identify specific publishing and printing companies whose profitabilities are likely to lead the industry and are therefore sound investments. Return on assets is one measure of profitability.

What is a good rate of return on total assets? There is no single answer to this question because rates of return vary widely by industry. For example, consumer products companies earn much higher returns than do utilities or grocery store chains.

Rate of return on shareholders' equity, often called **return on equity**, shows the relationship between net income and average common shareholders' equity. The numerator is net income minus preferred dividends, information taken from the income statement and statement of retained earnings. The denominator is average common shareholders' equity — total shareholders' equity minus preferred equity. Québec-Téléphone's rate of return on common shareholders' equity for 1991 is computed as follows (amounts in thousands):

$$\begin{matrix} \text{Rate of} \\ \text{return} \\ \text{on common} \\ \text{share-} \\ \text{holders'} \\ \text{equity} \end{matrix} = \frac{\begin{matrix} \text{Net income} - \\ \text{Preferred} \\ \text{dividends} \end{matrix}}{\begin{matrix} \text{Average} \\ \text{common} \\ \text{shareholders'} \\ \text{equity} \end{matrix}} = \frac{\$26,716 - \$561}{(\$188,432 + \$178,431)/2} = \frac{\$26,155}{\$183,432} = .143$$

Observe that the return on equity (14 percent) is higher than the return on assets (10 percent). This difference results from the interest expense component of return on assets. Companies such as Québec-Téléphone borrow at one rate, say, 9 percent, and invest the funds to earn a higher rate, say, 11 percent. The company's creditors are guaranteed a fixed rate of return on their loans. The shareholders, conversely, have no guarantee that the corporation will earn net income, so their investments are riskier. Consequently, shareholders demand a higher rate of return than do creditors, and this explains why return on equity should exceed return on assets. If return on assets is higher, the company is in trouble.

Investors and creditors use return on common shareholders' equity in much the same way as they use return on total assets — to compare companies. The higher the rate of return, the more successful the company. An 18 percent return on common shareholders' equity is considered quite good in most industries. Investors also compare a company's return on shareholders' equity to interest rates available in the market. If interest rates are almost as high as return on equity, many investors will lend their money to earn interest rather than invest in common shares. They choose to forego the extra risk of investing in stock when the rate of return on equity is too low.

Different Values of Stock

The business community refers to several different *stock values*. These values include market value, redemption value, liquidation value, and book value.

Market Value

A stock's **market value** is the price for which a person could buy or sell a share of the stock. The issuing corporation's net income, financial position, its future prospects, and the general economic conditions determine market value, also called market price. Daily newspapers report the market price of many stocks. Corporate annual reports generally provide quarterly market price data for the past five or ten years. In almost all cases, shareholders are more concerned about the market value of a stock than any of the other values discussed below. A stock *listed at* (an alternative term is *quoted at*) 29¼ sells for, or may be bought for, $29.25 per share. The purchase of 100 shares of this stock would cost $2,925 ($29.25 × 100), plus a commission. If you were selling 100 shares of this stock, you would receive cash of $2,925 less a commission. The commission is the fee an investor pays to a stockbroker for buying or selling the stock.

Redemption Value

Preferred stock's fixed dividend rate makes it somewhat like debt. However, companies do not get a tax deduction for preferred dividend payments. Thus they may wish to buy back (or redeem) their preferred stock to avoid paying the dividends.

OBJECTIVE 7

Distinguish among various stock "values"

Preferred stock that provides for redemption at a set price is called redeemable preferred stock. In some cases, the company has the *option* of redeeming its preferred stock at a set price. In other cases, the company is *obligated* to redeem the preferred stock. The price the corporation agrees to pay for the stock, which is set when the stock is issued, is called **redemption value**.

For example, the redeemable preferred stock of Piney Point Industries, Inc. is "redeemable at the option of the Company at $25 per share." Beginning in 19X2, Piney Point is "required to redeem annually 6,765 shares of the preferred stock ($169,125 annually)." Piney Point's annual redemption payment to the preferred shareholders will include this redemption value plus any dividends in arrears.

Liquidation Value

The **liquidation value** of a share of company stock is equal to the net realizable value of the assets less the cash required to pay the liabilities divided by the number of shares outstanding. Liquidation value is rarely equal to either market value or book value.

For example, Douglas Ltd. has 10,000 common shares outstanding. The shares are trading on the stock market at $29.50; that is, they have a market value of $29.50 per share. The company's assets have a net realizable value of $336,000, while liabilities amount to $62,000; the liquidation value per share is $27.40 ($336,000 − $62,000) divided by 10,000 shares.

Occasionally, you will read in a business newspaper like *The Financial Post* that a company's break-up value (liquidation value) per share is greater than its market value per share. That means that the total market value of the company's individual assets, minus its liabilities, exceeds the total market value of the company's shares.

Book Value

The **book value** of a stock is the amount of owners' equity on the company's books for each share of its stock. Corporations often report this amount in their annual reports. If the company has only common stock outstanding, its book value is computed by dividing total shareholders' equity by the number of shares outstanding. A company with shareholders' equity of $180,000 and 5,000 shares of common stock outstanding has book value of $36 per share ($180,000/5,000 shares).

If the company has both preferred and common stock outstanding, the preferred shareholders usually have the first claim to owners' equity. Ordinarily, preferred stock has a specified liquidation or redemption value. The book value of preferred is its redemption value plus any cumulative dividends in arrears on the stock. Its book value *per share* equals the sum of the redemption value and any cumulative dividends in arrears divided by the number of preferred shares outstanding. After the corporation figures the preferred shares' book value, it computes the common stock book value per share. The corporation divides the common equity (total shareholders' equity minus preferred equity) by the number of common shares outstanding.

Assume that the company balance sheet reports the following amounts:

Shareholders' Equity

Capital stock	
Preferred stock, $6.00, 5,000 shares authorized,	
400 shares issued	$ 44,000
Common stock, 20,000 shares authorized,	
4,500 shares issued	117,000
Common stock subscribed, 1,000 shares	10,000
Total capital stock	171,000
Retained earnings	85,000
Total shareholders' equity	$256,000

Suppose that four years (including the current year) of cumulative preferred dividends are in arrears and preferred stock has a redemption value of $130 per share. Book value computations do not treat subscribed stock as though it were issued stock; the 1,000 shares and the $10,000 are excluded from the calculation.

The book value per share computations for this corporation follow:

Preferred

Redemption value (400 shares × $130)	$ 52,000
Cumulative dividends (400 × $6.00 × 4).......................................	9,600
Shareholders' equity allocated to preferred	$ 61,600
Book value per share ($61,600/400 shares)	$ 154.00

Common

Total shareholders' equity..	$256,000
Less: Shareholders' equity allocated to preferred................................	61,600
	$194,400
Less: Common stock subscribed	10,000
Shareholders' equity available	
for common shareholders	$184,400
Book value per share ($184,400/4,500 shares)	$40.98

How is book value per share used in decision-making? Companies negotiating the purchase of a corporation may wish to know the book value of its stock, especially if the stock is not publicly traded. The book value of shareholders' equity may figure into the negotiated purchase price. Corporations, especially those whose shares are not publicly traded, may buy out a retiring executive, agreeing to pay the book value of the person's stock in the company. In general, however, book value is not directly related to the market value of stock and is, at best, a weak substitute for market value.

Summary Problems for Your Review

1. Use the following accounts and related balances to prepare the classified balance sheet of Whitehall, Inc. at September 30, 19X4. Use the account format of the balance sheet.

Common stock,		Inventory	$ 85,000
50,000 shares authorized,		Property, plant and	
20,000 shares issued........	$135,000	equipment, net..................	225,000
Dividends payable	4,000	Donated capital	18,000
Cash....................................	9,000	Accounts receivable, net.....	23,000
Accounts payable	28,000	Preferred stock, $3.75,	
Stock subscription		10,000 shares authorized,	
receivable — common....	2,000	2,000 shares issued	24,000
Retained earnings..............	38,000	Common stock subscribed,	
Organization cost, net.......	1,000	3,000 shares	21,000
Long-term note payable ...	74,000	Accrued liabilities	3,000

2. The balance sheet of Trendline Corporation reported the following at March 31, 19X6, end of its fiscal year.

Shareholders' Equity

Preferred stock, $4.00, cumulative 1,000 shares authorized and issued..	$110,000
Common stock, 100,000 shares authorized, 50,000 shares issued......	464,000
Common stock subscribed (1,700 shares)...	17,500
Donated capital...	55,000
Retained earnings..	330,000
Total shareholders' equity...	$976,500

Required

a. Is the preferred stock cumulative or noncumulative? Is it participating or non-participating? How can you tell?

b. What is the total amount of the annual preferred dividend?

c. Assume the common shares were all issued at the same time. What was the selling price per share?

d. What is the subscription price per share of the common stock?

e. What was the market value of the assets donated to the corporation?

f. Compute the book value per share of the preferred stock and the common stock. The preferred stock has no specified redemption value. No prior year preferred dividends are in arrears, but Trendline has not declared the current-year dividend.

SOLUTIONS TO REVIEW PROBLEMS

1.

Whitehall, Inc.
Balance Sheet
September 30, 19X4

Assets			Liabilities		
Current			**Current**		
Cash	$ 9,000		Accounts payable		$ 28,000
Accounts receivable, net....................	23,000		Dividends payable		4,000
Stock subscription receivable			Accrued liabilities..		3,000
— common.....................................	2,000		Total current liabilities		35,000
Inventory	85,000		Long-term note payable		74,000
Total current assets........................	119,000		Total liabilities.......................................		109,000
Property, plant and equipment, net.......	225,000		**Shareholders' Equity**		
Intangible assets			Capital stock		
Organization cost, net.........................	1,000		Preferred stock, $3.75, 10,000 shares authorized, 2,000 shares issued.................	$ 24,000	
			Common stock, 50,000 shares authorized, 20,000 shares issued...............	135,000	
			Common stock subscribed, 3,000 shares.............................	21,000	
			Donated capital............................	18,000	
			Total capital stock	198,000	
			Retained earnings	38,000	
			Total shareholders' equity		236,000
			Total liabilities and		
Total assets...	$345,000		shareholders' equity..............		$345,000

2. Answers to Trendline Corporation questions:

   a. The preferred stock is cumulative as is noted in its description; it is nonpart-
      icipating because it is not specifically labeled otherwise.
   b. Total annual preferred dividend: $4,000 (1,000 × $4.00)
   c. Price per share: $9.28 ($464,000/50,000 shares issued)
   d. Subscription price: $10.29 ($17,500/1,700)
   e. Market value of donated assets: $55,000
   f. Book values per share of preferred and common stock:

   Preferred
Book value..	$110,000
Cumulative dividend for current year (1,000 x $4.00).....	4,000
Shareholders' equity allocated to preferred.......................	$114,000
Book value per share ($114,000/1,000 shares)..................	$ 114.00

   Common
Total shareholders' equity...	$976,500
Less: Shareholders' equity allocated to preferred	114,000
	$862,500
Less: Common stock subscribed...	17,500
Shareholders' equity available	
for common shareholders...	$845,000
Book value per share	
($845,000/50,000 shares)...	$ 16.90

Summary

A corporation is a separate legal and business entity. *Continuous life,* the *ease of raising large amounts of capital* and *transferring ownership,* and *limited liability* are among
the advantages of the corporate form of organization. An important disadvantage
is *double taxation.* Corporations pay *income taxes,* and shareholders pay tax on dividends. *Shareholders* are the owners of corporations. They elect a *board of directors,*
which elects a chairperson and appoints the officers to manage the business.

Corporations may issue different classes of stock: *common* and *preferred.*
Corporations may also issue stock under a *subscription* agreement. The balance
sheet carries the capital raised through stock issuance under the heading Capital
Stock or Share Capital in the shareholders' equity section.

Corporations may receive *donations* from outsiders or from shareholders. Donated
Capital is a shareholders' equity account.

Only when the board of directors declares a *dividend* does the corporation incur
the liability to pay dividends. Preferred stock usually has priority over common
stock in the distribution of dividends, which are normally stated as a dollar amount
per share. In addition, preferred stock has a claim to dividends in arrears if it is
cumulative and a claim to further dividends if it is *participating. Convertible* preferred stock may be exchanged for other specified classes of the corporation's shares
and are normally exchanged for common stock.

Return on assets and *return on shareholders' equity* are two standard measures of
profitability. A healthy company's return on equity should exceed its return on
assets.

A stock's *market value* is the price for which a share may be bought or sold.
Redemption value, liquidation value, and *book value* — the amount of owners' equity
per share of company stock — are other values that may apply to stock.

Self-Study Questions

Test your understanding of the chapter by marking the best answer for each of the following questions:

1. Which of the following is a disadvantage of the corporate form of business organization? *(p. 612)*
   a. Limited liability of shareholders
   b. Double taxation
   c. No mutual agency
   d. Transferability of ownership

2. The person with the most power in a corporation is the *(p. 613)*
   a. Incorporator
   b. Chairperson of the board
   c. President
   d. Vice-president

3. The dollar amount of the shareholder investments in a corporation is called *(pp. 614–15)*
   a. Outstanding stock
   b. Total shareholders' equity
   c. Capital stock
   d. Retained earnings

4. The arbitrary value assigned to a share of stock by the board of directors is called *(p. 617)*
   a. Market value
   b. Liquidation value
   c. Book value
   d. Stated value

5. Stock issued by a corporation incorporated under the *Canada Business Corporations Act* normally has *(pp. 617–18)*
   a. No par value
   b. A par value set by management
   c. A par value set by the government
   d. A par value of $10.00

6. Mangum Corporation receives a subscription for 1,000 shares of preferred stock at $104 per share. This transaction increases Mangum's capital stock by *(p. 621)*
   a. $0 because the corporation received no cash
   b. $4,000
   c. $100,000
   d. $104,000

7. Organization cost is classified as a (an) *(p. 624)*
   a. Operating expense
   b. Current asset
   c. Contra item in shareholders' equity
   d. None of the above

8. Trade Days, Inc. has 10,000 shares of $3.50 cumulative preferred stock, and 100,000 of common stock outstanding. Two years' preferred dividends are in arrears. Trade Days declares a cash dividend large enough to pay the preferred dividends in arrears, the preferred dividend for the current period, and a $1.50 dividend to common. What is the total amount of the dividend? *(p. 626)*
   a. $255,000   b. $220,000   c. $150,000   d. $105,000

9. The preferred stock of Trade Days, Inc. in the preceding question was issued at $55 per share. Each preferred share can be converted into 10 common shares. The entry to record the conversion of this preferred stock into common is *(p. 627)*

   a. Cash 550,000
       Preferred Stock 500,000
       Common Stock 50,000

   b. Preferred Stock 500,000
       Capital Stock in Excess of Par — Preferred Stock   50,000
       Common Stock 550,000

   c. Preferred Stock 550,000
       Common Stock 550,000

d. Preferred Stock   550,000
  Common Stock   400,000
  Capital Stock in Excess of Par
    — Common Stock   150,000

10. When an investor is buying stock as an investment, the value of most direct concern is *(p. 629–30)*
  a. Par value   b. Market value   c. Liquidation value   d. Book value

Answers to the Self-Study Questions are at the end of the chapter.

Accounting Vocabulary

articles of incorporation
  (p. 611)
authorized stock *(p. 611)*
board of directors *(p. 613)*
book value of stock
  (p. 630)
bylaws *(p. 613)*
capital stock *(p. 615)*
chairperson of the board
  (p. 613)
common stock *(p. 616)*
convertible preferred
  stock *(p. 627)*
corporation *(p. 611)*
cumulative preferred
  stock *(p. 626)*
deficit *(p. 615)*
dividends *(p. 616)*

dividends in arrears
  (p. 626)
donated capital *(p. 623)*
double taxation *(p. 612)*
incorporator *(p. 613)*
issued stock *(p. 611)*
limited liability *(p. 612)*
liquidation value of
  stock *(p. 630)*
market value of stock
  (p. 629)
no-par stock *(p. 617)*
organization cost *(p. 624)*
outstanding stock
  (p. 614)
participating preferred
  stock *(p. 627)*
preferred stock *(p. 617)*

president *(p. 613)*
proxy *(p. 613)*
rate of return on total
  assets *(p. 628)*
rate of return on share-
  holders' equity *(p. 628)*
redemption value of
  stock *(p. 630)*
retained earnings *(p. 615)*
return on assets *(p. 628)*
return on equity *(p. 628)*
share capital *(p. 615)*
shareholder *(p. 611)*
shareholders' equity
  (p. 614)
stated capital *(p. 615)*
stock *(p. 611)*
stock subscription *(p. 619)*

ASSIGNMENT MATERIAL _____

Questions

1. Why is a corporation called a creature of the government?

2. Identify the characteristics of a corporation.

3. Explain why owners of shares in corporations face a tax disadvantage.

4. Briefly outline the steps in the organization of a corporation.

5. How are the structures of a partnership and a corporation similar and different?

6. Name the four rights of a shareholder. Are preferred shares automatically non-voting? Explain how a right may be withheld from a shareholder.

7. Which event increases the assets of the corporation: authorization of shares or issuance of shares? Explain.

8. Suppose Watgold Ltd. issued 1,000 shares of its $3.65 preferred shares for $120. How much would this transaction increase the company's capital stock? How much would it increase retained earnings? How much would it increase annual cash dividend payments?

9. Woodstock Ltd. issued 100 shares of common stock for $15.00 per share and 200 shares for $16.00 per share. What would the journal entry to record the combined issue be?

10. How does issuance of 1,000 shares of common stock for land and a building, together worth $150,000, affect capital stock?

11. Why does receipt of a stock subscription increase the corporation's assets and owner's equity?

12. Give an example of a transaction that creates donated capital for a corporation.

13. Journalize the incorporation of the Barnes & Connally partnership.

14. Rank the following accounts in the order they would appear on the balance sheet: Common Stock, Organization Cost, Donated Capital, Preferred Stock, Common Stock Subscribed, Stock Subscription Receivable (due within six months), Retained Earnings, Dividends Payable. Also, give each account's balance sheet classification.

15. What type of account is Organization Cost? Briefly describe how to account for organization cost.

16. Briefly discuss the three important dates for a dividend.

17. Mancini Inc. has 3,000 shares of its $2.50 preferred stock outstanding. Dividends for 19X1 and 19X2 are in arrears, and the company has declared no dividends on preferred stock for the current year, 19X3. Assume that Mancini declares total dividends of $35,000 at the end of 19X3. Show how to allocate the dividends to preferred and common (a) if preferred is cumulative, and (b) if preferred is noncumulative.

18. As a preferred shareholder, would you rather own cumulative or noncumulative preferred? If all other factors are the same, would the corporation rather the preferred stock be cumulative or noncumulative? Give your reason.

19. How are cumulative preferred dividends in arrears reported in the financial statements? When do dividends become a liability of the corporation?

20. Distinguish between the market value of stock and the book value of stock. Which is more important to investors?

21. How is book value per share of common stock computed when the company has both preferred stock and common stock outstanding?

22. Why should a healthy company's rate of return on shareholders' equity exceed its rate of return on total assets?

Exercises

Exercise 14-1   *Organizing a corporation (L.O. 1)*

Matt Stamp and Chip Spowart-Brown are opening a limousine service to be named S&S Transportation Limited. They need outside capital, so they plan to organize the business as a corporation. Because your office is in the same building, they come to you for advice. Write a memorandum informing them of the steps in forming a corporation. Identify specific documents used in this process, and name the different parties involved in the ownership and management of a corporation.

Exercise 14-2   *Issuing stock (L.O. 2)*

Journalize the following stock issuance transactions of Souris Corporation. Explanations are not required.

Feb. 19   Issued 1,000 shares of common stock for cash of $12.50 per share.
Mar. 3   Sold 300 shares of $4.50 Class A preferred stock for $12,000 cash.
      11   Received inventory valued at $25,000 and equipment with market value of $16,000 for 3,300 shares of common stock.
      15   Issued 1,000 shares of $2.50, no-par Class B preferred stock with stated value of $60 per share.

Exercise 14-3   *Stock subscriptions* **(L.O. 2)**

Durham Ltd. has just been organized and is selling its stock through stock subscriptions. Record the following selected transactions that occurred during June 19X6.

June   3   Received a subscription to 500 shares of common stock at the subscription price of $20 per share. The subscriber paid one fourth of the subscription amount as a down payment. The corporation will issue the stock when it is fully paid.

     18   Collected one half of the amount receivable from the subscriber.

July   3   Collected the remainder from the subscriber and issued the stock.

Exercise 14-4   *Recording issuance of stock* **(L.O. 2)**

The actual balance sheet of Gulf Resources & Chemical Corporation, as adapted, reported the following shareholders' equity. Note that Gulf has two separate classes of preferred stock, labeled as Series A and Series B. All dollar amounts, except for per-share amounts, are given in thousands.

Shareholders' Investment
(same as shareholders' equity)

Preferred stock, authorized 4,000,000 shares (note 7)	
Series A..	$ 174
Series B..	7,520
Common stock, authorized 20,000,000, [issued and]	
outstanding 9,130,000 shares	69,195

Note 7: Preferred Stock: **Shares [Issued and]**
                             Outstanding

             Series A......................... 58,000
             Series B......................... 376,000

Required

Assume that the Series A preferred stock was issued for $3 cash per share, the Series B preferred was issued for $20 cash per share, and the common was issued for cash of $69,195,000. Make the summary journal entries to record issuance of all the Gulf Resources stock. Explanations are not required.

Exercise 14-5   *Shareholders' equity section of a balance sheet* **(L.O. 3)**

The articles of incorporation for Dartmouth Corporation authorizes the issuance of 5,000 shares of Class A preferred stock, 1,000 shares of Class B preferred stock, and 10,000 shares of common stock. During a two-month period, Dartmouth completed these stock-issuance transactions:

June 23   Issued 1,000 shares of common stock for cash of $12.50 per share.

July   2   Sold 300 shares of $4.50 Class A preferred stock for $20,000 cash.

    12   Received inventory valued at $25,000 and equipment with market value of $16,000 for 3,300 shares of common stock.

    17   Issued 1,000 shares of $2.50 Class B preferred stock. The issue price was cash of $60 per share.

Prepare the shareholders' equity section of the Dartmouth balance sheet for the transactions given in this exercise. Retained Earnings has a balance of $63,000.

Exercise 14-6   *Capital stock for a corporation   (L.O. 2)*

Errico Inc. has recently organized. The company issued common stock to a lawyer who gave Errico legal services of $6,200 to help in organizing the corporation. It issued common stock to another person in exchange for his patent with a market value of $40,000. In addition, Errico received cash both for 2,000 shares of its preferred stock at $110 per share and for 26,000 shares of its common stock at $15 per share. The city of North Bay donated 50 hectares of land to the company as a plant site. The market value of the land was $300,000. Without making journal entries, determine the total capital stock created by these transactions.

Exercise 14-7   *Shareholders' equity section of a balance sheet   (L.O. 3)*

China Palace Corporation has the following selected account balances at June 30, 19X7. Prepare the shareholders' equity section of the company's balance sheet.

Common stock,		Inventory............................	$112,000
500,000 shares authorized,		Machinery and equipment	109,000
120,000 shares issued..........	$600,000	Preferred stock	
Donated capital	103,000	subscription receivable	8,000
Accumulated depreciation —		Preferred stock, $1.00,	
machinery and equipment.	62,000	20,000 shares authorized,	
Retained earnings.....................	119,000	10,000 shares issued	288,000
Preferred stock subscribed,		Organization cost, net	3,000
1,000 shares	20,000		

Exercise 14-8   *Incorporating a partnership   (L.O. 4)*

The Kingston Jaybirds are a semiprofessional baseball team that has been operated as a partnership by D. Robertson and G. Childres. In addition to their management responsibilities, Robertson also plays second base and Childres sells hot dogs. Journalize the following transactions in the first month of operation as a corporation:

May 14   The incorporators paid legal fees of $990 and other fees of $500 to obtain articles of incorporation.

  14   Issued 2,500 shares of common stock to Robertson and 1,000 shares to Childres. Robertson's capital balance on the partnership books was $20,000, and Childres's capital balance was $8,000.

  18   The city of Kingston donated 20 hectares of land to the corporation for a stadium site. The land's market value was $40,000.

Exercise 14-9   *Computing dividends on preferred and common stock   (L.O. 5)*

The following elements of shareholders' equity are adapted from the balance sheet of Whirland Chemical Corporation. All dollar amounts, except the dividends per share, are given in thousands.

Shareholders' Equity

Preferred stock, cumulative and nonparticipating (note 7)	
Series A, 80,000 shares authorized, 58,000 shares issued	$ 58
Series B, 600,000 shares authorized, 376,000 shares issued	376
Common stock, 1,000,000 shares authorized, 91,300 shares issued.........	913

Note 7: Preferred stock:

	Designated Annual Cash Dividend Per Share
Series A	$ .20
Series B	1.30

Assume that the Series A preferred has preference over Series B preferred, and the company has paid all dividends through 19X4.

Required

Compute the dividends to both series of preferred and to common for 19X5 and 19X6 if total dividends are $0 in 19X5 and $1,200,000 in 19X6. Round to the nearest dollar.

Exercise 14-10 *Book value per share of preferred and common stock* **(L.O. 6)**

The balance sheet of International Graphics Corporation reported the following:

Redeemable preferred stock; redemption value $5,103	$ 4,860
Common shareholders' equity 8,120 shares issued	
and outstanding	216,788
Total shareholders' equity	$221,648

Assume that International has paid preferred dividends for the current year and all prior years (no dividends in arrears), and the company has 100 shares of preferred stock outstanding. Retained earnings, included in common shareholders' equity, was $135,588. Compute the book value per share of the preferred stock and the common stock.

Exercise 14-11 *Book value per share of preferred and common stock; preferred dividends in arrears* **(L.O. 5, 6)**

Refer to Exercise 14-10. Compute the book value per share of the preferred stock and the common stock, assuming that three years' preferred dividends (including dividends for the current year) are in arrears. Assume the preferred stock is cumulative and its dividend rate is $3.00 per share.

Exercise 14-12 *Evaluating profitability* **(L.O. 7)**

PEI Services, Inc., reported these figures for 19X7 and 19X6:

	19X7	19X6
Income statement		
Interest Expense	$ 7,400	$ 7,100
Net Income...	24,000	21,700
Balance sheet		
Total assets	351,000	317,000
Preferred stock, $1.30, 100 shares issued and outstanding	2,500	2,500
Common shareholders' equity...	164,000	151,000
Total shareholders' equity	166,500	153,500

Compute rate of return on total assets and rate of return on common shareholders' equity for 19X7. Do these rates of return suggest strength or weakness? Give your reason.

Problems   (Group A)

Problem 14-1A *Organizing a corporation* **(L.O. 1)**

Marla Fredricks and Allison LaChapelle are opening a Grand & Toy office supply store in a shopping center in Kinistino, Saskatchewan. The area is growing, and no competitors are located in the immediate vicinity. Their most fundamental decision is how to organize the business. Marla thinks the partnership form is best. Allison favors the corporate form of organization. They seek your advice.

Required

Discuss the advantages and disadvantages of organizing the business as a corporation.

Problem 14-2A   *Journalizing corporation transactions and preparing the shareholders' equity section of the balance sheet (L.O. 2, 3)*

Multipurpose Corporation received articles of incorporation from the Government of Canada. The company is authorized to issue 20,000 shares of $2.50 preferred stock and 300,000 shares of common stock. During its start-up phase, the company completed the following transactions:

Oct.	2	Paid fees of $4,000 and incorporation taxes of $3,000 to the Government of Canada to obtain the articles of incorporation.
	4	Issued 900 shares of common stock to the promoters who organized the corporation. Their fee was $45,000.
	5	Accepted subscriptions for 1,000 shares of common stock at $50 per share and received a down payment of one fourth of the subscription amount.
	9	Issued 2,000 shares of common stock in exchange for equipment valued at $100,000.
	14	Issued 600 shares of preferred stock for cash of $54 per share.
	30	Collected one third of the stock subscription receivable.
	31	Earned a small profit for October and closed the $12,600 credit balance of Income Summary into Retained Earnings.

Required

1. Record the transactions in the general journal.
2. Prepare the shareholders' equity section of the Multipurpose balance sheet at October 31.

Problem 14-3A   *Journalizing corporation transactions and preparing the shareholders' equity section of the balance sheet (L.O. 2, 3)*

The partners who owned Wolfson & Stauffer wished to avoid the unlimited personal liability of the partnership form of business, so they incorporated the partnership as Financial Consultants, Inc. The articles of incorporation from the federal government authorizes the corporation to issue 10,000 shares of $6.00 preferred stock and 250,000 shares of common stock. In its first month, Financial Consultants completed the following transactions:

Dec.	1	Paid incorporation taxes of $1,500 and paid legal fees of $2,000 to organize as a corporation.
	3	Issued 750 shares of common stock to the promoter for assistance with issuance of the common stock. The promotion fee was $7,500.
	3	Issued 5,100 shares of common stock to Wolfson and 3,800 shares to Stauffer in return for the net assets of the partnership. Wolfson's capital balance on the partnership books was $51,000, and Stauffer's capital balance was $38,000.
	5	Accepted subscriptions for 5,000 shares of common stock at $10 per share and received a down payment of 25 percent of the subscription

7   Received a small parcel of land valued at $84,000 as a donation from the city of Moose Jaw.

12 Issued 1,000 shares of preferred stock to acquire a patent with a market value of $110,000.

22 Issued 1,500 shares of common stock for $10 cash per share.

28 Collected 20 percent of the stock subscription receivable.

Required

1. Record the transactions in the general journal.

2. Prepare the shareholders' equity section of the Financial Consultants balance sheet at December 31. Retained Earnings balance is $91,300.

Problem 14-4A *Shareholders' equity section of the balance sheet* **(L.O. 3)**

Shareholders' equity information is given for Baker Corporation and Wang, Inc. The two companies are independent.

Baker Corporation   Baker Corporation is authorized to issue 50,000 shares of common stock. All the stock was issued at $8 per share. The company incurred a net loss of $12,000 in 19X1. It earned net income of $60,000 in 19X2 and $130,000 in 19X3. The company declared no dividends during the three-year period.

Wang, Inc. Wang's articles of incorporation authorizes the company to issue 10,000 shares of $2.50 preferred stock and 120,000 shares of common stock. Wang issued 1,000 shares of the preferred stock at $110 per share. It issued 40,000 shares of the common stock for a total of $320,000. The company's retained earnings balance at the beginning of 19X3 was $72,000 and net income for the year was $90,000. During 19X3, the company declared the specified dividend on preferred and a $.50 per share dividend on common. Preferred dividends for 19X2 were in arrears.

Required

For each company, prepare the shareholders' equity section of its balance sheet at December 31, 19X3. Show the computation of all amounts. Entries are not required.

Problem 14-5A *Analyzing the shareholders' equity of an actual corporation* **(L.O. 3, 5)**

The purpose of this problem is to familiarize you with the financial statement information of a real company, U and I Corp. U and I, which makes food products and livestock feeds, included the following shareholders' equity on its year-end balance sheet at February 28:

Shareholders' Equity	($ thousands)
Voting Preferred Stock, $1.25 cumulative;	
authorized 100,000 shares in each class:	
Class A — issued 75,473 shares	$ 1,736
Class B — issued 92,172 shares	2,120
Common stock: authorized 5,000,000 shares; issued 2,870,950 shares	14,355
Retained earnings	8,336
	$26,547

Required

1. Identify the different issues of stock U and I has outstanding.

2. Is the preferred stock participating or nonparticipating? How can you tell?

3. Give the summary entries to record issuance of all the U and I stock. Assume that all the stock was issued for cash. Explanations are not required.

4. Suppose U and I passed its preferred dividends for one year. Would the company have to pay these dividends in arrears before paying dividends to the common shareholders? Give your reason.

5. What amount of preferred dividends must U and I declare and pay each year to avoid having preferred dividends in arrears?

6. Assume preferred dividends are in arrears for 19X8.
   a. Write note 5 of the February 28, 19X8 financial statements to disclose the dividends in arrears.
   b. Record the declaration of a $500,000 dividend in the year ended February 28, 19X9. An explanation is not required.

Problem 14-6A   *Preparing a corporation balance sheet* **(L.O. 3, 7)**

The following accounts and related balances of Superior Coal and Iron, Inc. are arranged in no particular order. Use them to prepare the company's classified balance sheet in the account format at June 30, 19X2. Also compute rate of return on total assets and rate of return on common shareholders' equity for the year ended June 30, 19X2. Do these rates of return suggest strength or weakness? Give your reason.

Trademark, net..................	$ 9,000	Net income........................	$ 31,000
Organization cost, net......	14,000	Total assets, June 30,	
Preferred stock, $ .20,		19X1	504,000
10,000 shares		Interest expense...............	6,100
authorized and issued	27,000	Property, plant and	
Stock subscription		equipment, net	267,000
receivable — common	12,000	Common stock, 500,000	
Cash.....................................	19,000	shares authorized	
Accounts receivable, net..	34,000	214,000 shares	
Accrued liabilities.............	26,000	issued...........................	233,000
Long-term note payable..	72,000	Prepaid expenses	10,000
Inventory	148,000	Common stock	
Dividends payable	9,000	subscribed 22,000	
Retained earnings	?	shares...........................	22,000
Accounts payable	31,000	Donated capital...............	6,000
Common shareholders'			
equity, June 30, 19X1 ...	322,000		

Problem 14-7A   *Computing dividends on preferred and common stock* **(L.O. 5)**

Continental Corporation has 10,000 shares of $3.50 preferred stock and 50,000 shares of common stock outstanding. Continental declared and paid the following dividends during a three-year period: 19X1, $20,000; 19X2, $90,000; and 19X3, $265,000.

Required

1. Compute the total dividends to preferred stock and common stock for each of the three years if
   a. Preferred is noncumulative and nonparticipating.
   b. Preferred is cumulative and nonparticipating.

2. For requirement 1b, record the declaration of the 19X3 dividends on December 28, 19X3 and the payment of the dividends on January 17, 19X4.

Problem 14-8A   *Analyzing the shareholders' equity of an actual corporation* **(L.O. 5, 6)**

The balance sheet of Fort Murray Drilling Company Limited reported the following:

Shareholders' Investment
(same as shareholders' equity)

Redeemable non-voting preferred stock, $2.60, authorized 10,000 shares; issued 8,000 shares (Redemption value $358,000)...	$320,000
Common stock, authorized 75,000 shares; issued 36,000 shares	285,000
Retained earnings	119,000
Total shareholders' investment..	$724,000

Preferred dividends have not been paid for three years, including the current year. On the balance sheet date, the market value of the Fort Murray common stock was $7.50 per share.

Required

1. Is the preferred stock cumulative or noncumulative, participating or nonparticipating? How can you tell?
2. What is the amount of the annual preferred dividend?
3. Which class of shareholders controls the company? Give your reason.
4. What is the total capital stock of the company?
5. What was the total market value of the common stock?
6. Compute the book value per share of the preferred stock and the common stock.

(Group B)

Problem 14-1B   *Organizing a corporation* **(L.O. 1)**

Patrick Ledoux and Michael Suttle are opening a restaurant in a growing section of St. Vincent's, Newfoundland. There are no competing family restaurants in the immediate vicinity. Their most fundamental decision is how to organize the business. Patrick thinks the partnership form is best. Michael favors the corporate form of organization. They seek your advice.

Required

Discuss the advantages and disadvantages of organizing the business as a corporation.

Problem 14-2B   *Journalizing corporation transactions and preparing the shareholders' equity section of the balance sheet* **(L.O. 2, 3)**

Greenlawn Inc. was organized under the laws of the province of Nova Scotia. The articles of incorporation authorize Greenlawn to issue 100,000 shares of $3 preferred stock and 500,000 shares of common stock. During its start-up phase, the company completed the following transactions:

July   5   Paid fees of $12,000 to the province of Nova Scotia to obtain the articles of incorporation and file the required documents for incorporation.

6   Issued 500 shares of common stock to the promoters who organized the corporation. Their fee was $20,000.

7   Accepted subscriptions for 1,000 shares of common stock at $30 per share and received a down payment of one third of the subscription amount.

12   Issued 300 shares of preferred stock for cash of $20,000.

14   Issued 800 shares of common stock in exchange for land valued at $24,000.

31   Collected one half of the stock subscription receivable.

31   Earned a small profit for July and closed the $21,000 credit balance of Income Summary into the Retained Earnings account.

Required

1. Record the transactions in the general journal.

2. Prepare the shareholders' equity section of the Greenlawn balance sheet at July 31.

Problem 14-3B   *Journalizing corporation transactions and preparing the shareholders' equity section of the balance sheet* **(L.O. 2, 3)**

The partnership of Starr & Wagner needed additional capital to expand into new markets, so the business incorporated as Micro Devices, Inc. The articles of incorporation from the Government of Canada authorizes Micro Devices to issue 50,000 shares of $6.00 preferred stock and 100,000 shares of common stock. In its first month, Micro Devices completed the following transactions:

Dec.   1   Paid incorporation fees of $500 and taxes of $2,100 to the Government of Canada and paid legal fees of $1,000 to organize as a corporation.

2   Issued 300 shares of common stock to the promoter for assistance with issuance of the common stock. The promotional fee was $1,800.

2   Issued 9,000 shares of common stock to Starr and 12,000 shares to Wagner in return for the net assets of the partnership. Starr's capital balance on the partnership books was $54,000, and Wagner's capital balance was $72,000.

4   Accepted subscriptions for 4,000 shares of common stock at $6 per share and received a down payment of 20 percent of the subscription amount.

8   Received a small parcel of land valued at $80,000 as a donation from the city of Brandon.

10   Issued 400 shares of preferred stock to acquire a patent with a market value of $50,000.

16   Issued 600 shares of common stock for cash of $3,600.

30   Collected one third of the stock subscription receivable.

Required

1. Record the transactions in the general journal.

2. Prepare the shareholders' equity section of the Micro Devices balance sheet at December 31. Retained Earnings' balance is $42,100.

Problem 14-4B   *Shareholders' equity section of the balance sheet* **(L.O. 3)**

The following summaries for Beliveau, Inc. and Monroe Corporation provide the information needed to prepare the shareholders' equity section of the company balance sheet. The two companies are independent.

Beliveau, Inc.   Beliveau, Inc. is authorized to issue 50,000 shares of common stock. All the stock was issued at $6 per share. The company incurred net losses of

$30,000 in 19X1 and $14,000 in 19X2. It earned net incomes of $23,000 in 19X3 and $52,000 in 19X4. The company declared no dividends during the four-year period.

Monroe Corporation   Monroe's articles of incorporation authorizes the company to issue 5,000 shares of $5.00 cumulative preferred stock and 500,000 shares of common stock. Monroe issued 1,000 shares of the preferred stock at $105 per share. It issued 100,000 shares of the common stock for $150,000. The company's retained earnings balance at the beginning of 19X4 was $120,000. Net income for 19X4 was $80,000, and the company declared a $5.00 preferred share dividend for 19X4. Preferred share dividends for 19X3 were in arrears.

Required

For each company, prepare the shareholders' equity section of its balance sheet at December 31, 19X4. Show the computation of all amounts. Entries are not required.

Problem 14-5B   *Analyzing the shareholders' equity of a corporation (L.O. 3, 5)*

The purpose of this problem is to familiarize you with the financial statement information of a real company. Hamilton Steel Corporation is a large steel company. Hamilton included the following in its shareholders' equity on its balance sheet:

Shareholders' Equity	($ millions)
Preferred Stock	
Authorized 20,000,000 shares in each class; issued:	
$5.00 Cumulative Convertible Preferred Stock, 2,500,000 shares	$ 125
$2.50 Cumulative Convertible Preferred Stock, 4,000,000 shares	100
Common stock	
Authorized 80,000,000 shares; issued 48,308,516 shares	621
Retained earnings...	529
	$1,375

Required

1. Identify the different issues of stock Hamilton has outstanding.
2. Is the preferred stock participating or nonparticipating? How can you tell?
3. Suppose Hamilton passed its preferred dividends for one year. Would the company have to pay these dividends in arrears before paying dividends to the common shareholders? Give your reason.
4. What amount of preferred dividends must Hamilton declare and pay each year to avoid having preferred dividends in arrears?
5. Assume preferred dividends are in arrears for 19X5.
   a. Write note 6 of the December 31, 19X5 financial statements to disclose the dividends in arrears.
   b. Journalize the declaration of a $60 million dividend for 19X6. An explanation is not required.

Problem 14-6B   *Preparing a corporation balance sheet; measuring profitability (L.O. 3, 7)*

The following accounts and related balances of Maritimes Ltd. are arranged in no particular order. Use them to prepare the company's classified balance sheet in the account format at November 30, 19X7. Also compute rate of return on total assets and rate of return on common shareholders' equity for the year ended November 30, 19X7. Do these rates of return suggest strength or weakness? Give your reason.

Accounts payable..............	$ 31,000	Long-term note payable ..	$104,000
Stock subscription		Accounts receivable, net..	101,000
receivable, preferred....	1,000	Preferred stock, $.40	
Retained earnings	?	25,000 shares	
Common stock,		authorized, 3,000	
100,000 shares		shares issued	30,000
authorized, 42,000		Cash.....................................	41,000
shares issued..................	295,000	Inventory	226,000
Dividends payable............	3,000	Property, plant and	
Total assets, Nov. 30, 19X6	781,000	equipment, net.............	378,000
Net income.........................	36,200	Organization cost, net......	6,000
Common shareholders'		Prepaid expenses..............	13,000
equity, Nov. 30, 19X6 ...	483,000	Preferred stock	
Interest expense.................	12,800	subscribed 700 shares..	7,000
Donated capital	109,000	Patent, net.........................	31,000
Accrued liabilities	17,000		

Problem 14-7B   *Computing dividends on preferred and common stock* **(L.O. 5)**

Ayr Ltd. has 5,000 shares of $.50 preferred stock and 100,000 shares of common stock outstanding. During a three-year period, Ayr declared and paid cash dividends as follows: 19X1, $0; 19X2, $10,000; and 19X3, $27,000.

Required

1. Compute the total dividends to preferred stock and common stock for each of the three years if
   a. Preferred is noncumulative and nonparticipating.
   b. Preferred is cumulative and nonparticipating.
2. For requirement 1b, record the declaration of the 19X3 dividends on December 22, 19X3 and the payment of the dividends on January 14, 19X4.

Problem 14-8B   *Analyzing the shareholders' equity of an actual corporation* **(L.O. 5, 6)**

The balance sheet of Oak Manufacturing, Inc. reported the following:

Shareholders' Investment (same as shareholders' equity)	($ Thousands)
Cumulative convertible preferred stock, $.16;	
authorized 20,000; issued 9,000	$ 45
Common stock, authorized 40,000 shares;	
issued 16,000 shares	192
Deficit...	(77)
Total shareholders' investment	$160

The preferred stock has a redemption value of $6 per share, and preferred dividends are in arrears for two years, including the current year. On the balance sheet date, the market value of the Oak Manufacturing common stock was $7.50 per share.

Required

1. Is the preferred stock cumulative or noncumulative, participating, or nonparticipating? How can you tell?
2. What is the amount of the annual preferred dividend?
3. What is the total capital stock of the company?

4. What was the total market value of the common stock?

5. Compute the book value per share of the preferred stock and the common stock.

Extending Your Knowledge

Decision Problems

1. Evaluating alternative ways of raising capital (L.O. 2, 3)

J. McDade and M. Fineberg have written a computer program for a video game that they believe will rival Nintendo. They need additional capital to market the product, and they plan to incorporate their partnership. They are considering alternative capital structures for the corporation. Their primary goal is to raise as much capital as possible without giving up control of the business. The partners plan to receive 170,000 shares of the corporation's common stock in return for the net assets of the partnership. After the partnership books are closed and the assets adjusted to current market value, McDade's capital balance is $90,000 and Fineberg's balance is $80,000.

The corporation's plans for the articles of incorporation include an authorization to issue 5,000 shares of preferred stock and 500,000 shares of common stock. McDade and Fineberg are uncertain about the most desirable features for the preferred stock. Prior to incorporating, the partners have discussed their plans with two investment groups. The corporation can obtain capital from outside investors under either of the following plans:

Plan 1   Group 1 will invest $105,000 to acquire 1,000 shares of $5.00, preferred stock and $130,000 to acquire 130,000 shares of common stock. Each preferred share receives 50 votes on matters that come before the shareholders. The investors in Group 1 would attempt to control the corporation if they have the majority of the corporate votes.

Plan 2   Group 2 will invest $220,000 to acquire 2,000 shares of $6.00 nonvoting, noncumulative, participating preferred stock.

Required

Assume the corporation receives its articles of incorporation.

1. Journalize the issuance of common stock to McDade and Fineberg.
2. Journalize the issuance of stock to the outsiders under both plans.
3. Assume net income for the first year is $130,000 and total dividends of $19,800 are properly subtracted from retained earnings. Prepare the shareholders' equity section of the corporation balance sheet under both plans.
4. Recommend one of the plans to McDade and Fineberg. Give your reasons.

2. Questions about corporations (L.O. 2, 6)

1. Why do you think capital stock and retained earnings are shown separately in the shareholders' equity section?
2. Mary Reznick, major shareholder of M-R Inc., proposes to sell some land she owns to the company for common shares in M-R. What problem does M-R, Inc. face in recording the transaction?

3. Preferred shares generally are preferred with respect to dividends and on liquidation. Why would investors buy common shares when preferred shares are available?

4. What does it mean if the liquidation value of a company's preferred stock is greater than its market value.

5. If you owned 100 shares of stock in Magna Corporation and someone offered to buy the stock for its book value, would you accept their offer? Why or why not?

Ethical Issue

George Campbell paid $50,000 for a franchise that entitled him to market Success Associates software programs in the countries of the European Common Market. Campbell intended to sell individual franchises for the major language groups of western Europe — German, French, English, Spanish, and Italian. Naturally, investors considering buying a franchise from Campbell asked to see the financial statements of his business.

Believing the value of the franchise to be greater than $50,000, Campbell sought to capitalize his own franchise at $500,000. The law firm of McDonald and LaDue helped Campbell form a corporation authorized to issue 500,000 common shares. Lawyers suggested the following chain of transactions:

1. A third party borrows $500,000 and purchases the franchise from Campbell.

2. Campbell pays the corporation $500,000 to acquire all its stock.

3. The corporation buys the franchise from the third party, who repays the loan.

In the final analysis, the third party is debt-free and out of the picture. Campbell owns all the corporation's stock, and the corporation owns the franchise. The corporation balance sheet lists a franchise acquired at a cost of $500,000. This balance sheet is Campbell's most valuable marketing tool.

Required

1. What is unethical about this situation?

2. Who can be harmed? How can they be harmed? What role does accounting play?

Financial Statement Problems

1. Shareholders' equity (L.O. 2)

The Schneider Corporation financial statements appear in Appendix C. Answer these questions about the company's capital stock. Information on the capital stock is found in note 7 of the financial statements.

1. What classes of stock does the balance sheet report? How many shares are authorized? How many shares were outstanding at October 26, 1991?

2. For issuances of stock, Schneider obviously credited the Capital Stock account for a specific amount per share. What was the average issue price per share?

3. Like most other corporations, Schneider allows its employees to purchase the company's stock through stock purchase plans. Record Schneider's issuance of shares under these plans during 1991.

4. During the year Schneider issued Class A shares for a purpose other than that described in 3. Describe the transaction.

2. Shareholders' equity (L.O. 2, 6)

Obtain the annual report of an actual company of your choosing. Annual reports are available in various forms including the original document in hard copy, micro-fiche, and computerized data bases.

Answer these questions about the company. Concentrate on the current year in the annual report you select.

1. What classes of stock does the company have outstanding? How many shares are authorized? How many shares were outstanding on the most current balance sheet date?
2. Under what title does the company report additional capital stock?
3. How much is total shareholders' equity? If the total is not labeled, compute total shareholders' equity.
4. Using the company's terminology, journalize the issuance of 100,000 shares of the company's common stock at $55 per share. Recompute all account balances to include the effect of this transaction.
5. Compute the average amount paid in per share of the company's common stock. Then examine the recent market prices of the company's stock in the multiyear summary of financial data. Compare the average amount paid in per share with recent market prices to determine whether the bulk of the company's stock was issued within the recent past. Give the reason for your answer.

Answers to Self-Study Questions

1. b
2. b
3. c
4. d
5. a
6. d (1,000 shares × $104 = $104,000)
7. d Intangible asset
8. a [(10,000 × $3.50 × 3 = $105,000) + (100,000 × $1.50 = $150,000) = $255,000]
9. c
10. b

Chapter 15

Corporations: Retained Earnings, Dividends, and the Income Statement

North Canadian Oils Ltd. (NCO), an oil and gas exploration company based in Calgary, recently announced that it would continue to pay annual dividends of $7 million to its preferred shareholders and a further $7 million to its common shareholders. On the surface, nothing seems out of the ordinary. But NCO only expects to have a net income of $4 million for 1992!

Norm Gish, president and chief executive officer for NCO, when asked about the dividend policy, stated, "We're taking the long-term view. We're secure in the company's financial strength. Just because we have one down year is no reason to punish the common shareholders."

If Norm is right, and 1992 was an exceptionally poor year, then 1993's net income should be sufficient to restore retained earnings to their 1991 level, or greater. That is, net income should be greater than $24 million for 1993. But what if he is wrong?

Chapter 15 discusses how dividends are the distribution of a company's earnings to its shareholders, and retained earnings are its cumulative earnings since its incorporation less those amounts distributed to shareholders; that is, the earnings retained by the company. Sound financial policy suggests that a company should not distribute all its annual earnings, but retain some to finance future growth. If Norm is wrong, and 1993's net income is not greater than $24 million, then NCO's 1992 payment of dividends in excess of net income is not sustainable. The 1992 common share dividends would be in fact a return *of* capital, not a return *on* capital!

Source: Tamsin Carlisle, "North Canadian to Pay Dividends Despite Red Ink," *The Financial Post* (May 15, 1992), p. 17.

LEARNING OBJECTIVES

After studying this chapter, you should be able to

1 Account for stock dividends

2 Distinguish stock splits from stock dividends

3 Account for repurchased capital stock

4 Report restrictions of retained earnings

5 Identify the elements of a corporation income statement

6 Account for prior period adjustments

Chapter 14 introduced the corporate form of business. Chapter 15 continues our discussion of corporation retained earnings and cash dividends, and also considers stock dividends, purchases by the corporation of its own shares, and the corporate income statement.

Retained Earnings and Dividends

We have seen that the equity section on the corporation balance sheet is called shareholders' equity. The capital stock accounts and retained earnings make up the shareholders' equity section.

Retained Earnings is the corporation account that carries the balance of the business's net income less its net losses from operations and less any declared dividends accumulated over the corporation's lifetime. *Retained* means "held on to." Retained Earnings is income accumulated to cover dividends and any future losses. Because Retained Earnings is an owners' equity account, it normally has a credit balance. A survey of 300 Canadian corporations indicates that the term "Retained Earnings" is used by 80 percent of those reporting; 14 percent used the term "Deficit" while the remaining 6 percent used a variety of terms.[1]

A debit balance in Retained Earnings, which arises when a corporation's accumulated net losses and any declared dividends exceed its accumulated net income, is called a *deficit*. This amount is subtracted from the sum of the credit balances in the other owners' equity accounts on the balance sheet to determine total shareholders' equity. As was noted above, in 1990, 14 percent of 300 companies surveyed had a retained earnings deficit.

At the end of each accounting period, the Income Summary account, which carries the balance of net income for the period, is closed to the Retained Earnings account. Assume the following amounts are drawn from a corporation's temporary accounts:

Income Summary

Dec. 31, 19X1	Expenses	750,000	Dec. 31, 19X1	Revenues	850,000
			Dec. 31, 19X1	Bal.	100,000

This final closing entry transfers net income from Income Summary to Retained Earnings:

19X1				
Dec. 31	Income Summary	100,000	
	Retained Earnings		100,000
	To close net income to Retained Earnings.		

---

[1] *Financial Reporting in Canada, 1991*, 19th edition (Toronto: CICA, 1992), p.144.

If 19X1 was the corporation's first year of operations, the Retained Earnings account now has an ending balance of $100,000:

Retained Earnings

Jan. 1, 19X1	Bal.	-0-
Dec. 31, 19X1	Net income	100,000
Dec. 31, 19X1	Bal.	100,000

If expenses exceeded revenues by $60,000 for the year, there would be a net loss, which would produce this debit balance in Income Summary:

Income Summary

Dec. 31, 19X1	Expenses	470,000	Dec. 31, 19X1	Revenues	410,000
Dec. 31, 19X1	Bal.	60,000			

To close a $60,000 loss, we would credit Income Summary and debit Retained Earnings, as follows:

19X1			
Dec. 31	Retained Earnings	60,000	
	Income Summary		60,000
	To close net loss to Retained Earnings.		

After posting, Income Summary's balance is zero, and the Retained Earnings balance is decreased by $60,000.

Remember that the account title includes the word *earnings.* Credits to the Retained Earnings account arise only from net income. When we examine a corporation's financial statements and want to learn how much net income the corporation has earned and retained in the business, we turn to Retained Earnings.

After the corporation has earned net income, its board of directors may declare and pay a cash dividend to the shareholders. The entry on January 15, 19X2 to record the declaration of a $35,000 dividend is

19X2			
Jan. 15	Retained Earnings	35,000	
	Dividends Payable		35,000
	To declare a cash dividend.		

After the dividend declaration is posted, the Retained Earnings account has a $65,000 credit balance:

Retained Earnings

Jan. 15, 19X2	Dividend	35,000	Jan. 1, 19X2	Bal.	100,000
			Jan. 15, 19X2	Bal.	65,000

The Retained Earnings account is not a reservoir of cash waiting for the board of directors to pay dividends to the shareholders. Instead, Retained Earnings is an owners' equity account representing a claim on all assets in general and not on any asset in particular. Its balance is the cumulative, lifetime earnings of the company less its cumulative losses and dividends. In fact, the corporation may have a large balance in Retained Earnings but not have the cash to pay a dividend. Why? One reason could be that the company purchased a building. The company may have abundant cash from borrowing but very little retained earnings. To declare a dividend, the company must have an adequate balance in Retained Earnings. To pay the dividend, it must have the cash. Cash and Retained Earnings are two entirely separate accounts sharing no necessary relationship.

Stock Dividends

A **stock dividend** is a proportional distribution by a corporation of its own stock to its shareholders. Stock dividends are fundamentally different from cash dividends because stock dividends do not transfer the assets of the corporation to the shareholders. Cash dividends are distributions of the asset cash, but stock dividends cause changes *only* in the shareholders' equity of the corporation. The effect of a stock dividend is an increase in the stock account and a decrease in Retained Earnings. Because both of these accounts are elements of shareholders' equity, total shareholders' equity is unchanged. There is merely a transfer from one shareholders' equity account to another, and no asset or liability is affected by a stock dividend.

The corporation distributes stock dividends to shareholders in proportion to the number of shares they already own. For example, suppose you owned 300 shares of Canadian Pacific Ltd. common stock. If Canadian Pacific distributed a 10 percent common stock dividend, you would receive 30 (300 × .10) additional shares. You would now own 330 shares of the stock. All other Canadian Pacific shareholders would receive additional shares equal to 10 percent of their prior holdings. You would all be in the same relative position after the dividend as you were before.

In distributing a stock dividend, the corporation gives up no assets. Why, then, do companies issue stock dividends?

Reasons for Stock Dividends

The principal reason a corporation may choose to distribute stock dividends is to continue dividends but conserve cash. A company may want to keep cash in the business in order to expand, buy inventory, pay off debts, and so on. Yet the company may wish to continue dividends in some form. To do so, the corporation may distribute a stock dividend. Shareholders pay tax on cash dividends but not on stock dividends.

A second, and less compelling reason, is to reduce the market price per share of its stock. Many companies pay low cash dividends and grow by reinvesting their earnings in operations. As they grow, the company's stock price increases. If the price gets high enough, eventually some potential investors may be prevented from purchasing the stock. If the stock dividend is large enough (for example, more than 25 percent of common stock issued and outstanding), its distribution may cause the market price of a share of the company's stock to decrease because of the increased supply of the stock.

Suppose the market price of a share of stock is $50. If the corporation doubles the number of shares of its stock outstanding by issuing a stock dividend, the market price of the stock is likely to drop by approximately one half, to $25 per share. The objective of such a large stock dividend is to make the stock less expensive and thus attractive to a wider range of investors.

Entries for Stock Dividends

The board of directors announces stock dividends on the declaration date. The date of record and the distribution date follow. (This is the same sequence of dates used for a cash dividend.) The declaration of a stock dividend does *not* create a liability because the corporation is not obligated to pay assets. (Recall that a liability is a claim on *assets*.) Instead, the corporation has declared its intention to distribute

OBJECTIVE 1

Account for stock dividends

its stock. Assume General Lumber Corporation has the following shareholders' equity prior to the dividend:

Shareholders' Equity

Capital stock	
Common stock, 50,000 shares authorized, 20,000 shares issued...........	$270,000
Total capital stock...	270,000
Retained earnings...	85,000
Total shareholders' equity..	$355,000

Of concern about stock dividends is how to determine the amount to transfer from retained earnings to the capital stock account. The *Canada Business Corporations Act* suggests that the market value of the shares issued is the appropriate amount to transfer, while other incorporating acts allow the directors to set a value on the shares. If market value were to be used, it would be the market value on the date the dividend is declared. If any other value were to be used, it would be determined by the directors at the time of declaration. This issue is not dealt with in the *CICA Handbook*. The market value of the shares issued would seem to be an appropriate valuation in any event and will be used in this text.

Assume General Lumber Corporation declares a 10 percent common stock dividend on November 17. The company will distribute 2,000 (20,000 × .10) shares in the dividend. On November 17 the market value of its common stock is $16 per share. Using the market value approach, Retained Earnings is debited for the market value of the 2,000 dividend shares and Common Stock Dividend Distributable is credited. General Lumber makes the following entry on the declaration date.

Nov. 17	Retained earnings (20,000 × .10 × $16)............	32,000	
	Common Stock Dividend Distributable...		32,000
	To declare a 10 percent common stock dividend.		

On the distribution (payment) date, the company records issuance of the dividend shares as follows:

Dec. 12	Common Stock Dividend Distributable.........	32,000	
	Common Stock..		32,000
	To issue common stock in a stock dividend.		

Common Stock Dividend Distributable is an owner's equity account. (It is *not* a liability because the corporation has no obligation to pay assets.) If the company prepares financial statements after the declaration of the stock dividend but before issuing it, Common Stock Dividend Distributable is reported in the shareholders' equity section of the balance sheet immediately after Common Stock and Common Stock Subscribed. However, this account holds the value of the dividend shares only from the declaration date to the date of distribution.

The following tabulation shows the changes in shareholders' equity caused by the stock dividend:

Shareholders' Equity	Before the Dividend	After the Dividend	Change
Capital stock			
Common stock, 50,000 shares authorized, 20,000 shares issued......	$270,000		
22,000 shares issued		$302,000	**Up by $32,000**
Total capital stock	270,000	302,000	**Up by $32,000**
Retained earnings	85,000	53,000	**Down by $32,000**
Total shareholders' equity	$355,000	$355,000	**Unchanged**

Compare shareholders' equity before and after the stock dividend. Observe the increase in the balance of Common Stock and the decrease in Retained Earnings. Also observe that total shareholders' equity is unchanged from $355,000.

Amount of Retained Earnings Transferred in a Stock Dividend Stock dividends are said to be *capitalized retained earnings* because they transfer an amount from retained earnings to capital stock. The capital stock accounts are more permanent than retained earnings because they are not subject to dividends. As we saw in the preceding illustration, the amount transferred from Retained Earnings in a stock dividend is the market value of the dividend shares. Therefore, many shareholders view stock dividends as distributions little different from cash dividends.

Stock Splits

As was already noted, a large stock dividend may decrease the market price of the stock. The stock then becomes attractive to more people. A stock split also decreases the market price of stock — with the intention of making the stock more attractive. A **stock split** is an increase in the number of outstanding shares of stock coupled with a proportionate reduction in the book value per share of the stock. For example, if the company splits its stock 2 for 1, the number of outstanding shares is doubled and each share's book value is halved. Many large companies in Canada, Dofasco, Toronto-Dominion Bank, St. Lawrence Cement, National Trust, and others, have split their stock.

A second reason for a stock split is that conventional wisdom suggests that the investors in the stock market believe that companies use a stock split to signal an increase in dividends and so will bid up the price of the shares in anticipation of that increase.

Assume that the market price of a share of Star Ltd. common stock is $120 and that the company wishes to decrease the market price to approximately $30. Star Ltd. decides to split the common stock 4 for 1 in the expectation that the stock's market price would fall from $120 to $30. A 4-for-1 stock split means that the company would have four times as many shares of stock outstanding after the split as it had before and that each share's book value would be quartered. Assume Star had 12,000 shares of common stock issued and outstanding before the split.

Shareholders' Equity	($ thousands)
Capital stock	
Common stock, 90,000 shares authorized, **12,000 shares issued**........	$ 950
Total capital stock..	950
Retained earnings	2,000
Total shareholders' equity	$2,950

After the 4-for-1 split, Star would have 48,000 shares (12,000 shares × 4) of common stock outstanding. Total shareholders' equity would be exactly as before the stock split. Indeed, the balance in the Common Stock account does not even change. Only the number of shares issued and the book value per share change. Compare the highlighted figures in the two shareholders' equity presentations.

Shareholders' Equity	($ thousands)
Capital stock	
Common stock, 360,000 shares authorized, **48,000 shares issued**......	$ 950
Total capital stock..	950
Retained earnings	2,000
Total shareholders' equity	$2,950

EXHIBIT 15-1   *Effects of Dividends and Stock Splits on Total Shareholders' Equity*

	Declaration	Payment of Cash or Distribution of Stock
Cash dividend..	Decrease	None
Stock dividend...	None	None
Stock split..	None	None

Source: Adapted from Beverly Terry.

Because the stock split affects no account balances, no formal journal entry is necessary. Instead, the split is recorded in a memorandum entry such as the following:

Aug. 19   Distributed three additional shares of common stock for each old share previously outstanding.

A company may engage in a reverse split to decrease the number of shares of stock outstanding. For example, Star could split its stock 1 for 4 which would reduce the number of shares issued and outstanding from 12,000 to 3,000. Reverse splits are rare.

Stock Dividends and Stock Splits

OBJECTIVE 2

Distinguish stock splits from stock dividends

A stock dividend and a stock split both increase the number of shares of stock owned per shareholder. Also, neither a stock dividend nor a stock split changes the investor's total cost of the stock owned. For example, assume you paid $3,000 to acquire 150 shares of Potash Corporation of Saskatchewan common stock. If Potash Corporation distributes a 100 percent stock dividend, your 150 shares increase to 300, but your total cost is still $3,000. Likewise, if Potash Corporation distributes a 2-for-1 stock split, your shares increase in number to 300, but your total cost is unchanged. Neither type of stock action is taxable income to the investor.

Both a stock dividend and a stock split increase the corporation's number of shares outstanding. For example, a 100 percent stock dividend and a 2-for-1 stock split both double the outstanding shares and are likely to cut the stock's market price per share in half. They differ in that a stock *dividend* shifts an amount from retained earnings to capital stock, leaving book value per share unchanged. A stock *split* affects no account balances whatsoever but instead changes the book value of the stock.

Exhibit 15-1 summarizes the effects of dividends and stock splits on total shareholders' equity.

Repurchase of Capital Stock

Corporations may **repurchase stock** from their shareholders for several reasons: (1) the company may have issued all its authorized stock and need the stock for distributions to officers and employees under bonus plans or stock purchase plans; (2) the purchase may help support the stock's current market price by decreasing the supply of stock available to the public; and (3) management may gather in the stock to avoid a takeover by an outside party.

The *Canada Business Corporations Act* requires a corporation that purchases its own stock to cancel the shares bought; it may do so by treating the purchased shares as authorized but unissued, and issue them in the normal way at a later date or it may cancel them outright. Several of the provincial incorporating acts also require that the shares be treated this way, while other incorporating acts permit the corporation to hold the shares as treasury stock (in effect, the corporation holds the stock in its treasury) and resell them.

Shares that are canceled outright may not be re-issued. The effect of purchasing an outstanding share is to reduce the number of shares issued; the effect of canceling a share outright is to reduce the number of shares authorized.

For practical purposes, treasury stock is like unissued stock: neither category of stock is outstanding in the hands of shareholders. The company does not receive cash dividends on its treasury stock, and treasury stock does not entitle the company to vote or to receive assets in liquidation. The difference between unissued stock and treasury stock is that treasury stock has been issued and bought back.

The repurchase of its own stock by a company decreases the company's assets and its shareholders' equity. The size of the company literally decreases, as shown on the balance sheet. The *Canada Business Corporations Act* and most of the provincial incorporating acts do not permit a corporation to acquire its own shares if such reacquisition would result in the corporation being unable to pay its liabilities as they become due.

For companies incorporated under the *Canada Business Corporations Act* and in jurisdictions where repurchased stock must be canceled or treated as unissued, the Common Stock account is debited. In those jurisdictions where treasury stock is permitted, the entry to record a purchase of treasury stock would include a debit to Treasury Stock and a credit to Cash. The Treasury Stock account has a debit balance, which is the opposite of the other owners' equity accounts. Therefore, Treasury Stock is a contra shareholders' equity account; it is deducted from the total of capital stock and Retained Earnings to compute total shareholders' equity.

Repurchase of Capital Stock

The *CICA Handbook* requires a company that purchases its own shares at a price equal to or greater than the issue price to debit Common Stock (or Preferred Stock as the case may be) for the issue price; any excess should be debited to Retained Earnings. When the shares are purchased at a price less than the issue price, the excess of the issue price over the purchase price should be credited to Contributed Surplus. In situations where the shares are issued at different prices, the average issue price should be used. (In jurisdictions where par value stock is permitted, the excess of the price paid over par would be debited to Contributed Surplus.)

Suppose Farwest Drilling Inc. had the following shareholders' equity before purchasing 1,000 of its own shares; its 8,000 shares were issued at the same price, as follows:

Shareholders' Equity

Capital stock	
Common stock, 10,000 shares authorized, 8,000 shares issued..............	$20,000
Total capital stock...	20,000
Retained earnings..	14,600
Total shareholders' equity..	$34,600

> **OBJECTIVE 3**
> Account for repurchased capital stock

On November 22, Farwest purchases 1,000 shares of its common stock, paying cash of $7.50 per share; the shares had been issued at $2.50 ($20,000/8,000). The shares are to be canceled. Farwest records the purchase as follows:

(cancelled)

Nov. 22	Common Stock...		2,500	
	Retained Earnings...		5,000	
	Cash			7,500
	Purchased 1,000 shares of stock at $7.50 per share.			

The shareholders' equity section of Farwest's balance sheet would appear as follows after the transaction:

Shareholders' Equity

Capital stock

Common stock, 9,000 shares authorized, 7,000 shares issued	$17,500
Total capital stock	17,500
Retained earnings	9,600
Total shareholders' equity	$27,100

Observe that the purchase of the stock decreased the number of shares authorized and decreased the number of shares issued and outstanding. Only outstanding shares have a vote, receive cash dividends, and share in assets if the corporation liquidates. Notice that the dollar amount shown for Capital Stock and Retained Earnings decreased by $2,500 and $5,000 respectively.

The articles of incorporation for Eastern Exploration Ltd., issued under the *Canada Business Corporations Act,* authorized it to issue 100,000 shares of common stock. By February 28 of this year, Eastern had issued 40,000 shares at an average price of $20.00 per share. Common Stock on the balance sheet amounted to $800,000. Retained Earnings was $187,396.

On March 20, Eastern purchases 2,000 shares at $15.00 per share and records the transaction as follows:

March	20	Common Stock (2,000 × $20).......................	40,000	
		Contributed Surplus [2,000 × ($20 – 15)]..		10,000
		Cash (2,000 × $15)		30,000
		Purchased 2,000 shares of stock at $15		
		per share.		

The shareholders' equity section of Eastern Exploration's balance sheet would appear as follows after the transaction:

Shareholders' Equity

Capital stock

Common stock, 100,000 shares authorized, 38,000 shares issued	$760,000
Contributed Surplus (note 6)	10,000
Total capital stock	$770,000
Retained earnings	187,396
Total shareholders' equity	$957,396

Note 6: During the year, the company acquired 2,000 shares of common stock at a price of $15.00 per share; the shares had been issued at $20.00 per share.

Sale of Repurchased Capital Stock

A company incorporated under the *Canada Business Corporations Act* may re-issue the shares that it previously had repurchased. The sale would be treated like a normal sale of authorized but unissued stock. As with accounting for the purchase of its own stock, accounting for the re-sale of the stock is different for companies in those jurisdictions that do not require such shares to be canceled as the *Canada Business Corporations Act* does.

No Gain or Loss from Repurchased Capital Stock Transactions

The repurchase and sale of its own stock do not affect net income. Sale of repurchased stock above cost is an increase in capital stock, not income. Likewise, sale of repurchased stock below cost is a decrease in capital stock, not a loss. Repurchased stock transactions take place between the business and its owner's, the shareholders. If the company is able to issue the shares at a price in excess of the price paid for them, the company would earn a "profit" on the transaction. However, the profit is not a real profit; it does not appear on the income statement. Instead, it would be reflected in the Common Stock account, since the proceeds of the sale of shares is credited in total to the Common Stock account. Similarly, if the company issued the shares at a price that was less than the price paid for them, the "loss" would be reflected in the Common Stock account.

Suppose Farwest Drilling sold 500 shares of common stock at $10.00 per share shortly after the purchase of 1,000 shares described above. Farwest records the sale as follows:

Dec.	5	Cash...	5,000	
		Common Stock		5,000
		To sell 500 shares of stock at $10.00 per share.		

If Farwest had sold the 500 shares for $2.00 per share, the sale would be recorded as follows:

Dec.	5	Cash	1,000	
		Common Stock...		1,000
		To sell 500 shares of stock at $2.00 per share.		

Does this mean that a company cannot increase its net assets by repurchasing stock low and selling it high? Not at all. Management may repurchase stock because it believes the market price of its stock is too low. For example, a company may buy 500 shares of its stock at $10 per share. Suppose it holds the stock as the market price rises and resells the stock at $14 per share. The net assets of the company increase by $2,000 [500 shares × ($14 − $10 = $4 difference per share)]. This increase is reported as capital stock and not as income.

IF market price
↑ Company can
sell & make $ on
Assets.

Summary Problem for Your Review

Pierre Caron, Inc. reported the following shareholders' equity:

Shareholders' Equity

Preferred stock, $1.00	
Authorized: 10,000 shares	
Issued: None..	$ —
Common stock	
Authorized: 30,000 shares	
Issued: 13,733 shares	49,266
Earnings retained in business	89,320
	$138,586

Required

1. What was the average issue price per share of the common stock?
2. How many shares of Caron's common stock are outstanding?
3. Journalize the issuance of 1,200 shares of common stock at $4 per share. Use Caron's account titles.
4. How many shares of common stock would be outstanding after Caron splits its common stock (computed in requirement 3) 3 for 1?
5. Using Caron account titles, journalize the declaration of a stock dividend when the market price of Caron common stock is $3 per share. Consider each of the following stock dividends independently:
   a. Caron declares a 10 percent common stock dividend on the shares outstanding, computed in requirement 2.
   b. Caron declares a 50 percent common stock dividend on the shares outstanding, computed in requirement 2.
6. Journalize the following repurchase and sale of its stock transactions by Caron, assuming they occur in the order given:
   a. Caron purchases 500 shares at $8 per share.
   b. Caron purchases 500 shares at $3 per share.
   c. Caron sells 100 shares for $9 per share.
7. How many shares of Caron's common stock would be outstanding after the transactions in requirement 6 take place. Ignore the transactions in requirements 4 and 5.

SOLUTION TO SUMMARY PROBLEM

1. Average issue price of the common stock was $3.59 per share ($49,266/13,733 shares = $3.59).
2. Shares outstanding = 13,733.
3. Cash (1,200 × $4) 4,800
       Common Stock.. 4,800
   To issue common stock.
4. Shares outstanding after a 3-for-1 stock split = 41,199, (13,733 shares outstanding × 3).
5. a. Earnings Retained in Business
       (13,733 × .10 × $3) 4,120
         Common Stock Dividend Distributable 4,120
       To declare a 10 percent common stock dividend.
   b. Earnings Retained in Business
       (13,733 × .50 × $3) 20,600
         Common Stock Dividend Distributable 20,600
       To declare a 50 percent common stock dividend.
6. a. Common Stock (500 × $3.59) 1,795
       Retained Earnings [500 × ($8.00 – $3.59)] 2,205
         Cash 4,000
       To purchase 500 shares at $8.00 per share.
   b. Common Stock (500 × $3.59) 1,795
         Contributed Surplus [500 × ($3.59 – $3.00)] 295
         Cash 1,500
       To purchase 500 shares at $3.00 per share.
   c. Cash (100 × $9.00) 900
         Common Stock 900
       To sell 100 shares at $9.00 per share.
7. Shares outstanding = 12,833 (13,733 – 500 – 500 + 100)

Restrictions on Retained Earnings ————————————

Dividends and repurchases of capital stock require payments by the corporation to its shareholders. In fact, repurchases of capital stock are returns of capital stock to the shareholders. These outlays decrease the corporation's assets, so fewer assets are available to pay liabilities. Therefore, its creditors may seek to restrict a corporation's dividend payments and capital stock repurchases. For example, a bank may agree to loan $500,000 only if the borrowing corporation limits dividend payments and repurchases of its stock.

To ensure that corporations maintain a minimum level of shareholders' equity for the protection of creditors, as was noted above, incorporating acts restrict the amount of its own stock that a corporation may repurchase. The maximum amount a corporation can pay its shareholders without decreasing capital stock is its balance of retained earnings. Therefore, restrictions on dividends and stock repurchases focus on the balance of retained earnings.

Companies usually report their retained earnings restrictions in notes to the financial statements. The following actual disclosure in the 1988 financial statements by Mitel Corporation is typical:

Note 10 — Capital Stock (in part)
F. Dividend Restriction on Common Shares

The Company may not pay cash dividends on its common shares until it has made certain investments in equipment in Canada, according to the terms of an agreement made with the Canadian Government for microelectronics development. In addition, the Company may not declare cash dividends on common shares or shares ranking junior to the R&D Preferred Shares unless dividends on the R&D Preferred Shares or Series A Preferred Shares have been declared and paid, or set aside for payment.

> **OBJECTIVE 4**
> Report restrictions of retained earnings

Appropriations of Retained Earnings

Appropriations are restrictions of Retained Earnings that are recorded by formal journal entries. A corporation may appropriate (segregate in a separate account) a portion of Retained Earnings for a specific use. For example, the board of directors may appropriate part of Retained Earnings for building a new manufacturing plant, for meeting possible future liabilities or other reasons. A debit to Retained Earnings and a credit to a separate account — Retained Earnings Restricted for Plant Expansion — records the appropriation.

An appropriation does *not* decrease total retained earnings. Any appropriated amount is simply a portion of retained earnings that is earmarked for a particular purpose. When the need for the appropriation no longer exists, an entry debits the Retained Earnings Appropriated account and credits Retained Earnings. This entry closes the Appropriation account and returns its amount back to the regular Retained Earnings account.

Retained earnings appropriations are rare. Corporations generally disclose any retained earnings restrictions in the notes to the financial statements as illustrated in the preceding section. The notes give the corporation more room to describe the nature and amounts of any restrictions. Thus corporations satisfy the requirement for adequate disclosure.

Disclosing any restriction on retained earnings is important to shareholders and possible investors because the restricted amounts may not be used for dividends. A corporation with a $100,000 balance in Retained Earnings and a $60,000 restriction may declare a maximum dividend of $40,000, if the cash is available and the board of directors so decides.

Variations in Reporting Shareholders' Equity _____

Real-world accounting and business practices may use terminology and formats in reporting shareholders' equity that differ from our general examples. We use a more detailed format in this book to help you learn from the components of the shareholders' equity section. Companies assume that readers of their statements already understand the omitted details.

One of the most important skills you will learn in this course is the ability to understand the financial statements of actual companies. Thus we present in Exhibit 15-2 a side-by-side comparison of our general teaching format and the format of the Bank of Montreal taken from its 1991 annual report. Note the following points with respect to the real-world format illustrated in Exhibit 15-2 and also with regard to actual financial statements:

1. The Bank of Montreal uses the heading Share Capital rather than Capital Stock.
2. Some companies combine all classes of capital stock into a single line item and provide specifics in the notes. The Bank of Montreal has combined the two classes of preferred stock in a single line item but does show preferred and common separately.
3. The preferred and common shares are described fully in the notes with respect to shares authorized and issued; the information in the balance sheet is limited to a description of the class and total amount for which the two classes of shares were issued.
4. Restrictions on and appropriations of retained earnings are shown in the notes by most actual companies.
5. Often total shareholders' equity is not specifically labeled.
6. A difference you will often note between the owners' equity in the general teaching format and the real-world format is the combining of contributed capital and donated capital in the latter.

Corporation Income Statement _____

A corporation's net income receives more attention than any other item in the financial statements. Net income measures the business's ability to earn a profit and answers the question of how successfully the company has managed its operations. To shareholders, the larger the corporation's profit, the greater the likelihood of dividends will be. To creditors, the larger the corporation's profit, the better able it is to pay its debts. Net income builds up a company's assets and owners' equity. It also helps to attract capital from new investors who hope to receive dividends from future successful operations.

Suppose you are considering investing in the stock of two manufacturing companies. In reading their annual reports and examining their past records, you learn that the companies showed the same net income figure for last year and that each company has increased its net income by 15 percent annually over the last five years. You observe, however, that the two companies have generated income in different ways.

Company A's income has resulted from the successful management of its central operations (manufacturing). Company B's manufacturing operations have been flat for two years. Its growth in net income has resulted from selling off segments of its business at a profit. Which company would you invest in?

Company A holds the promise of better future earnings. This corporation earns profits from continuing operations. We may reasonably expect the business to match its past earnings in the future. Company B shows no growth from operations. Its net income results from one-time transactions, the selling off of its operating assets. Sooner or later, Company B will have sold off the last of its assets used

EXHIBIT 15-2   *Formats for Reporting Shareholders' Equity**

General Teaching Format		Real-World Format	
Shareholders' Equity **($ amounts in thousands)**		**Shareholders' Equity** **($ amounts in thousands)**	
Capital Stock		Share capital (note 13)	
50,000,000 Class A Preferred		Preferred shares	$ 717,591
shares authorized,		Common shares	2,416,303
18,703,625 issued	$ 467,591		
12,500,000 Class B Preferred			
shares authorized,			
10,000,000 issued	250,000		
Unlimited number of			
common shares authorized			
(Proceeds not to exceed			
$5.5 billion),			
119,385,179 issued	2,416,303		
Retained earnings...........................	1,416,215	Retained earnings................................	1,416,215
Total shareholders' equity	$ 4,550,109	Total shareholders' equity..................	$4,550,109

Note 13: Share Capital

Authorized

50,000,000   Class A Preferred Shares without par value, issuable in series. The aggregate consideration for all Class A Preferred Shares shall not exceed $1 billion.

12,500,000   Class B Preferred Shares without part value, issuable in series. The aggregate consideration for all Class B Preferred Shares shall not exceed $250 million. These shares may be issued in foreign currencies.

Unlimited number of Common Shares without par value. The aggregate consideration for all common shares shall not exceed $5.5 billion

Outstanding 1991

	Number of shares	Amount ($ in thousands)
Preferred Shares		
Class A: Series 3 a	10,703,625	$ 267,591
: Series 4 b	8,000,000	200,000
Class B: Series 1 c	10,000,000	250,000
Common Shares d & e	119,385,179	2,416,303
Total Outstanding Share Capital		**$3,133,894**

a   The Class A Preferred Shares Series 3 have a cumulative minimum quarterly dividend equal to the greater of $0.53125 per share or one quarter of 75% of the Bank's average prime rate (as defined) times $25.00. These shares are redeemable, at the Bank's option, from February, 1, 1991 to January 31, 1992 at $25.60 per share, and thereafter at declining premiums. Redemption is subject to the prior approval of the Superintendent of Financial Institutions.

In August, 1991, the Bank, having received regulatory approval, announced its intention to repurchase, through to December 31, 1991, up to 50% of the 11,000,000 outstanding Series 3 Shares for cancellation. As at October 31, 1991, 296,375 shares had been repurchased for cancellation.

b   The Class A Preferred Shares Series 4 have a minimum quarterly noncumulative dividend equal to the greater of $0.5625 per share or 56.60% of the cash dividend paid on common shares of the Bank. These shares are redeemable from September 20, 1999, at the Bank's option, for either (1) cash at $25.00 per share, or (2) common shares of the Bank. By terms of the issue, the exchange ratio is set

at 95% of the average trading price (as defined) of the Bank's common shares. Redemption is subject to the prior approval of the Superintendent of Financial Institutions.

c   During the year, 10,000,000 Class B Preferred Shares Series 1 were issued for cash of $250 million. The shares have a quarterly noncumulative dividend of $0.5625 per share. These shares are redeemable from February 25, 2001, at the Bank's option, for either (1) cash at $25.00 per share, or (2) common shares of the Bank. By terms of the issue, the exchange ratio is set at the greater of $2.50 and 95% of the average trading price (as defined) of the Bank's common shares. Redemption is subject to the prior approval of the Superintendent of Financial Institutions.

d   During the year 4,390,649 (1990 — 4,234,445) common shares were issued under the Shareholder Dividend Reinvestment and Share Purchase Plan for a total value of $140.5 million (1990 — $113.5 million).

e   As at October 31, 1991, 4,039,610 common shares were reserved for possible issuance in respect of the Shareholder Dividend Reinvestment and Share Purchase Plan.

* GAAP suggests the presentation of comparative data; in order to simplify the illustration, data are presented for 1991 only.

in operations. When that occurs, the business will have no means of generating income. Based on this reasoning, your decision is to invest in the stock of Company A.

This example points to two important investment considerations: the *trend* of a company's earnings and the *makeup* of its net income. More intelligent investment decisions are likely if the income statement separates the results of central, continuing operations from special, one-time gains and losses. We now discuss the components of the corporation income statement. We will see how the income statement reports the results of operations in a manner that allows statement users to get a good look at the business's operations. Exhibit 15-3 will be used throughout these discussions. The items of primary interest are highlighted for emphasis.

Continuing Operations

We have seen that income from a business's **continuing operations** helps financial statement users make predictions about the business's future earnings. In the income statement of Exhibit 15-3, the topmost section reports income from continuing operations. This part of the business is expected to continue from period to period. We may use this information to predict that Electronics Corporation will earn income of approximately $54,000 next year.

EXHIBIT 15-3 *Corporation Income Statement*

OBJECTIVE 5

Identify the elements of a corporation income statement

Electronics Corporation
Income Statement
for the year ended December 31, 19X5

Sales revenue		$500,000
Cost of goods sold		240,000
Gross margin		260,000
Operating expenses (detailed)		181,000
Operating income		79,000
Other gains (losses)		
Gain on sale of machinery		11,000
Income from continuing operations before income tax		90,000
Income tax expense		36,000
Income before discontinued operations		
and extraordinary items		54,000
Discontinued operations		
Operating income, $30,000, less		
income tax of $12,000	$18,000	
Gain on disposal, $5,000, less		
income tax of $2,000	3,000	21,000
Income before extraordinary items		75,000
Extraordinary tornado loss	(10,000)	
Less income tax saving	4,000	(6,000)
Net income		$ 69,000
Earnings per share of common stock		
(30,000 shares outstanding)		
Income before discontinued operations and		
extraordinary items		$ 1.80
Income from discontinued operations		.70
Income before extraordinary items		2.50
Extraordinary loss		(.20)
Net income		$ 2.30

Note that income tax expense has been deducted in arriving at income from continuing operations. The tax that corporations pay on their income is a significant expense. The combined federal and provincial income tax rates for corporations varies from time to time, for type and size of company, and from province to province; the current rates range from 17 percent to a maximum rate of 46 percent. For computational ease, let us use an income tax rate of 40 percent in our illustrations. This is a reasonable estimate of combined federal and provincial income taxes. The $36,000 income tax expense in Exhibit 15-3 equals the pretax income from continuing operations multiplied by the tax rate ($90,000 × .40 = $36,000).

Discontinued Operations

Most large corporations engage in several lines of business. For example, Canadian Pacific Ltd. is best known for transportation, but it also has subsidiaries in mining, forestry products, real estate, hotels, securities and insurance; several years ago it sold off CP Air. Bombardier Inc., best known for its Skidoos and Seadoos, also owns Short Bros, a airplane-builder in Ireland, and manufactures subways cars for a world market. We call each significant part of a company a **segment of the business**.

A company may sell a segment of its business. Such a sale is not a regular source of income because a company cannot keep on selling its segments indefinitely. The sale of a business segment is viewed as a one-time transaction. The *CICA Handbook*, in Section 3475, "Discontinued Operations," requires that the income statement carry information on the segment that has been disposed of, under the heading **Discontinued Operations**. This section of the income statement is divided into two components: (1) operating income or (loss) on the segment that is disposed of and (2) and gain (or loss) on the disposal. Income and gain are taxed at the 40 percent rate and reported as follows:

Discontinued operations
Operating income, $30,000, less income tax, $12,000............................ $18,000
Gain on disposal, $5,000, less income tax, $2,000................................... <u>3,000</u>
$21,000

Trace this presentation to Exhibit 15-3.

It is necessary to separate discontinued operations into these two components because the company may operate the discontinued segment for part of the year. This is the operating income (or loss) component; it should include the results of operations of the segment from the beginning of the period to the disposal date. There is usually also a gain (or loss) on disposal. The transaction may not have been completed at the company's year end and so the gain (or loss) may have to be estimated. Following the conservatism concept, the estimated loss should be recorded in the accounts at year end while an estimated gain would not be recognized until it was realized.

It is important that the assets, liabilities, and operations of the segment can be clearly identified as separate from those of other operations of the company. The notes to the financial statements should disclose fully the nature of the discontinued operations and other relevant information about the discontinued operations, such as revenue to the date of discontinuance.

Discontinued operations are common in business. Recent examples include the sale, mentioned above, by Canadian Pacific of CP Air to PWA Corp. (Pacific Western Airways) and the sale by Imasco Limited of Peoples Drug Stores Incorporated, a U.S. drug store chain.

Extraordinary Gains and Losses

Extraordinary gains and losses, also called **extraordinary items**, must meet three criteria to be classed as extraordinary. They must have all of these characteristics (*CICA Handbook*, Section 3480):

1. An item is extraordinary only if it is not expected to occur frequently. For example, a company that had property on a flood plain that was covered with water every four or five years could not treat losses from flood waters as extraordinary.

2. An item is extraordinary only if it is not typical of the normal business activities of the company. For example, inventory losses or gains, or losses from the sale of property would not be considered extraordinary, since a company that owned either one might normally expect to suffer a loss as a result of that ownership.

3. A gain or loss is extraordinary only if it does not depend on decisions or determinations made by management. For example, the gain on the sale of property held for expansion would not be an extraordinary gain whereas the gain on the expropriation of land by a municipality would normally be considered extraordinary.

In short, to be classed as extraordinary, a transaction must be infrequent, unusual and its result determined externally.

Extraordinary items are reported along with their income tax effect. Assume Electronics Corporation lost $10,000 of inventory in a tornado. This loss, which reduces income, also reduces the company's income tax. The tax effect of the loss is computed by multiplying the amount of the loss by the tax rate. The tax effect decreases the net amount of the loss in the same way that the tax effect of income reduces the amount of net income. An extraordinary loss is reported along with its tax effect as follows:

Extraordinary tornado loss...	$(10,000)	
Less income tax saving	4,000	$(6,000)

Trace this item to the income statement in Exhibit 15-3. An extraordinary gain is reported the same way, net of the income tax on the gain.

Gains and losses from unusual or infrequent transactions, such as gains or losses from fixed asset disposals or losses resulting from employee strikes, would be separately disclosed on the income statement as part of income before discontinued operations and extraordinary items. An example is the gain on the sale of machinery in Exhibit 15-3.

Earnings Per Share (EPS)

The final segment of a corporation income statement presents the company's earnings per share, abbreviated as EPS. In fact, GAAP requires that corporations disclose EPS figures on the income statement or in a note to the financial statements.

Earnings per share is the amount of a company's net income per share of its outstanding common stock. EPS is a key measure of a business's success. Consider a corporation with net income of $200,000 and 100,000 shares of common stock outstanding. Its EPS is $2 ($200,000/100,000). A second corporation may also have net income of $200,000 but only 50,000 shares of common stock outstanding. Its EPS is $4 ($200,000/50,000).

Just as the corporation lists separately its different sources of income from continuing operations, discontinued operations, and so on, it must list separately the EPS figure for income before discontinued operations and extraordinary items and net income for the period. The *CICA Handbook*, in Section 3500.11, suggests that "it may also be desirable to show the per share figure for discontinued operations and extraordinary items to emphasize their significance to the overall results."

Consider the income statement of Electronics Corporation shown in Exhibit 15-3; in 19X5, it had 30,000 common shares outstanding. Income before discontinued operations and extraordinary items was $54,000, income from discontinued operations net of tax was $21,000, and there was an extraordinary loss, net of tax saving, of $6,000. Adhering to the *CICA Handbook,* it also presents the following disclosures:

Disclosure required
  Income per share before discontinued operations and
    extraordinary items ($54,000/30,000) $1.80
  Net income per share [($54,000 + $21,000 − $6,000)/30,000].............. 2.30
Disclosure not required, but suggested for clarity
  Income per share from discontinued operations ($21,000/30,000)... .70
  Loss per share from extraordinary items ($6,000/30,000) .... (.20)

Remember that the disclosure required by the *CICA Handbook* is a minimum. It is often in the user's interest to exceed that minimum as was done in Exhibit 15-3. The income statement user can better understand the sources of the business's EPS amounts when presented in this detail.

Weighted Average Number of Shares of Common Stock Outstanding
Computing EPS is straightforward if the number of common shares outstanding does not change over the entire accounting period. For many corporations, however, this figure varies over the course of the year. Consider a corporation that had 100,000 shares outstanding from January through November, then purchased 60,000 of its own shares for cancellation. This company's EPS would be misleadingly high if computed using 40,000 (100,000 − 60,000) shares. To make EPS as meaningful as possible, corporations use the weighted average number of common shares outstanding during the period.

Let us assume the following figures for Diskette Demo Corporation. From January through May, the company had 240,000 shares of common stock outstanding; from June through August, 200,000 shares; and from September through December, 210,000 shares. We compute the weighted average by considering the outstanding shares per month as a fraction of the year:

Number of Common Shares Outstanding		Fraction of Year			Weighted Average Number of Common Shares Outstanding
240,000	×	5/12	(January through May)	=	100,000
200,000	×	3/12	(June through August)	=	50,000
210,000	×	4/12	(September through December)	=	70,000
			Weighted average number of common shares outstanding during the year	=	220,000

The 220,000 weighted average would be divided into net income to compute the corporation's EPS.

Preferred Dividends
Throughout the EPS discussion we have used only the number of shares of common stock outstanding. Holders of preferred stock have no claim to the business's income beyond the stated preferred dividend (unless the preferred stock is participating preferred, but such stock is rare and will be ignored for purposes of this discussion). Even though preferred stock has no claims, preferred dividends do affect the EPS figure. Recall, the EPS is earnings per share of common stock. Also recall that dividends on preferred stock are paid first. Therefore, preferred dividends must be subtracted from income subtotals (income before discontinued operations and extraordinary items and net income) in the computation of EPS.

If Electronics Corporation had 10,000 shares of preferred stock outstanding, each with a $1.50 dividend, the annual preferred dividend would be $15,000 (10,000 ×

$1.50). The $15,000 would be subtracted from the two income subtotals resulting in the following EPS computations:

Income before discontinued operations and extraordinary
items [($54,000 − $15,000)/30,000] $1.30
Net income [($69,000 − $15,000)/30,000] 1.80

Dilution   Some corporations make their bonds or preferred stock more attractive to investors by offering conversion privileges, which permit the holder to convert the bond or preferred stock into some specified number of shares of common stock. Holders of convertible bonds or convertible preferred stock may exchange their securities for common shares. If in fact the bonds or preferred shares are converted into common stock, then the EPS will be diluted (reduced) because more common shares are divided into net income. Because convertible bonds or convertible preferred shares can be traded in for common stock, the common shareholders want to know the amount of the decrease in EPS that would occur if conversion took place. To provide this information, corporations, with convertible bonds or preferred shares outstanding, present two sets of EPS amounts: EPS based on outstanding common shares (*basic EPS*), and EPS based on outstanding common shares plus the number of additional common shares that would arise from conversion of the convertible bonds and convertible preferred shares into common (*fully diluted EPS*). The topic of dilution can be very complex and is covered more fully in intermediate accounting texts.

EPS is the most widely used accounting figure. Many income statement users place top priority on EPS. Also, a stock's market price is related to a company's EPS. By dividing the market price of a company's stock by its EPS, we compute a statistic called the *price-to-earnings* or *price-earnings ratio*. *The Financial Post* reports the price-earnings ratios (listed as P/E) daily for hundreds of companies listed on the Toronto, Montreal, and New York Stock Exchanges.

Statement of Retained Earnings

Retained earnings may be a significant portion of a corporation's owner's equity. The year's income increases the retained earnings balance, and dividends decrease it. Retained earnings are so important that corporations prepare a financial statement outlining the major changes in this equity account, much as the statement of owner's equity presents information on changes in the equity of a proprietorship. The statement of retained earnings for Electronics Corporation appears in Exhibit 15-4.

Some companies report income and retained earnings on a single statement. Exhibit 15-5 illustrates how Electronics would combine its income statement and its statement of retained earnings.

EXHIBIT 15-4   *Statement of Retained Earnings*

Electronics Corporation
Statement of Retained Earnings
for the year ended December 31, 19X5

Retained earnings balance, December 31, 19X4....................................	$ 130,000
Net income for 19X5..	69,000
	199,000
Dividends for 19X5	(21,000)
Retained earnings balance, December 31, 19X5....................................	$178,000

EXHIBIT 15-5 *Statement of Income and Retained Earnings*

Electronics Corporation
Statememt of Income and Retained Earnings
for the year ended December 31, 19X5

Sales revenue	$500,000
Cost of goods sold	240,000
Net income for 19X5	69,000
Retained earnings, December 31, 19X4	130,000
	199,000
Dividends for 19X5	(21,000)
Retained earnings, December 31, 19X5	$178,000

Earnings per share of common stock (30,000 shares outstanding)

Income before discontinued operations and extraordinary items	$1.80
Income from discontinued operations	.70
Income before extraordinary items	2.50
Extraordinary loss	(.20)
Net income	$2.30

Prior Period Adjustments

OBJECTIVE 6
Account for prior period adjustments

What happens when a company makes an error in recording revenues or expenses? Detecting the error in the period in which it occurs allows the company to make a correction before preparing that period's financial statements. But failure to detect the error until a later period means that the business will have reported an incorrect amount of income on its income statement. After closing the revenue and expense accounts, the Retained Earnings account will absorb the effect of the error, and its balance will be wrong until the error is corrected.

Corrections to the beginning balance of Retained Earnings for errors of an earlier period are called **prior period adjustments**. The correcting entry includes a debit or credit to Retained Earnings for the error amount and a debit or credit to the asset or liability account that was misstated. The prior period adjustment appears on the corporation's statement of retained earnings to indicate to readers the amount and the nature of the change in the Retained Earnings balance.

Assume that Paquette Corporation recorded income tax expense for 19X4 as $30,000. The correct amount was $40,000. This error resulted in understating 19X4 expenses by $10,000 and overstating net income by $10,000. A re-assessment from Revenue Canada in 19X5 for the additional $10,000 in taxes alerts the Paquette management to the mistake. The entry to record this prior period adjustment in 19X5 is

19X5			
June 19	Retained Earnings	10,000	
	Income Tax Payable		10,000
	Prior period adjustment to correct error in recording income tax expense of 19X4.		

The debit to Retained Earnings excludes the error correction from the income statement of 19X5. Recall the matching principle. If Income Tax Expense is debited when the prior period adjustment is recorded in 19X5, then this $10,000 in taxes would appear on the 19X5 income statement. This would not be proper since the expense arose from 19X4 operations.

This prior period adjustment would appear on the statement of retained earnings, as follows:

Paquette Corporation
Statement of Retained Earnings
for the year ended December 31, 19X5

Retained earnings balance, December 31, 19X4,	
as originally reported	$390,000
Prior period adjustment — debit to correct error	
in recording income tax expense of 19X4	(10,000)
Retained earnings balance, December 31, 19X4,	
as adjusted	380,000
Net income for 19X5	114,000
	494,000
Dividends for 19X5	(41,000)
Retained earnings balance, December 31, 19X5	$453,000

Our example shows a prior period adjustment for additional expense. To make a prior period adjustment for additional income, retained earnings is credited and the misstated asset or liability is debited.

Summary Problem for Your Review

The following information was taken from the ledger of Ansong Corporation:

Loss on sale of discontinued		Selling expenses	$ 78,000
operations	$20,000	Common stock,	
Prior period adjustment		40,000 shares issued	155,000
— credit to Retained		Sales revenue	620,000
Earnings	5,000	Interest expense	30,000
Gain on sale of capital assets..	21,000	Extraordinary gain	26,000
Cost of goods sold	380,000	Operating income,	
Income tax expense (saving)		discontinued operations	30,000
Continuing operations	32,000	Loss due to lawsuit	11,000
Discontinued operations		General expenses	62,000
Operating income	12,000	Preferred stock, $8.00,	
Loss on sale	(8,000)	500 shares issued	57,000
Extraordinary gain	10,000	Retained earnings,	
Dividends	16,000	beginning as originally	
		reported	103,000

Required

Prepare a single-step income statement and a statement of retained earnings for Ansong Corporation for the current year ended December 31. Include the earnings per share presentation and show computations. Assume no changes in the stock accounts during the year.

Ansong Corporation
Income Statement
for the year ended December 31, 19XX

Revenue and gains			
Sales revenue..			$620,000
Gain on sale of capital assets............................			21,000
Total revenues and gains............................			641,000
Expenses and losses			
Cost of goods sold		$380,000	
Selling expenses..		78,000	
General expenses...		62,000	
Interest expense		30,000	
Loss due to lawsuit...		11,000	
Income tax expense		32,000	
Total expenses and losses			593,000
Income before discontinued operations and			
extraordinary items..			48,000
Discontinued operations			
Operating income...	$30,000		
Less income tax...	12,000	18,000	
Loss on sale of discontinued operations	(20,000)		
Less income tax saving	8,000	(12,000)	6,000
Income before extraordinary items.....................			54,000
Extraordinary gain		26,000	
Less income tax...		10,000	16,000
Net income			$ 70,000

Earnings per share	
Income before discontinued operations and	
extraordinary item [($48,000 – $4,000)/40,000 shares].........................	$1.10*
Income from discontinued operations ($6,000/40,000 shares)	.15
Income before extraordinary items [($54,000 – $4,000)/40,000 shares].......	1.25
Extraordinary gain ($16,000/40,000 shares)	.40
Net income [($70,000 – $4,000)/40,000 shares]...	$1.65*

Computations

$$\text{EPS} = \frac{\text{Income} - \text{Preferred dividends}}{\text{Common shares outstanding}}$$

Preferred dividends: $500 \times \$8.00 = \$4,000$

---

* These calculations are required; the other EPS calculations are included to make the statements more informative for users.

Ansong Corporation
Statement of Retained Earnings
for the year ended December 31, 19XX

Retained earnings balance, beginning, as originally reported	$ 103,000
Prior period adjustment — credit	5,000
Retained earnings balance, beginning, as adjusted.................................	108,000
Net income for current year...	70,000
....	178,000
Dividends for current year..	(16,000)
Retained earnings balance, ending...	$ 162,000

Summary

Retained Earnings carries the balance of the business's net income accumulated over its lifetime, less its declared dividends and any net losses. *Cash dividends* are distributions of corporate assets made possible by earnings. *Stock dividends* are distributions of the corporation's own stock to its shareholders. Stock dividends and *stock splits* increase the number of shares outstanding and generally lower the market price per share of stock.

A corporation may repurchase its own stock that has been issued and is outstanding. The corporation then may issue repurchased stock in the normal way but more often cancels the repurchased shares. Some jurisdictions allow a corporation to hold repurchased shares as *treasury stock.*

Retained earnings may be *restricted* by law or contract or by the corporation itself. An *appropriation* is a restriction of retained earnings that is recorded by formal journal entries.

The corporate *income statement* lists separately the various sources of income — *income before discontinued operations and extraordinary items*, which includes other gains and losses, *discontinued operations*, and *extraordinary gains and losses*. The bottom line of the income statement reports *net income* or *net loss* for the period. *Income tax expense* and *earnings-per-share* figures also appear on the income statement, likewise divided into different categories based on the nature of income. The *statement of retained earnings* reports the causes for changes in the Retained Earnings account. This statement may be combined with the income statement.

Self-Study Questions

Test your understanding of the chapter by marking the best answer for each of the following questions:

1. If the closing entry to the Income Summary account is a credit, this implies *(p. 651)*
   a. The company experienced a net loss during the period.
   b. The company earned net income during the period.
   c. The company declared a dividend during the period.
   d. This amount is a prior period adjustment.

2. Hall Limited issued 100,000 common shares on January 1, 19X1 for $6.00 per share. On May 31, 19X4, Hall repurchased and retired 10,000 common shares for $8.00 per share. The journal entry on May 31, 19X4 would be *(p. 657)*

    a. Common Stock.. 80,000
        Cash.. 80,000
    b. Common Stock.. 60,000
        Cash.. 60,000
    c. Common Stock.. 60,000
        Retained earnings... 20,000
        Cash.. 80,000
    d. Common Stock.. 60,000
        Contributed Surplus 20,000
        Cash.. 80,000

3. Meyer's Thrifty Acres Ltd. has 10,000 shares of common stock outstanding; the stock was issued at $20.00 per share. The stock's market value is $37 per share. Meyer's board of directors declares and distributes a common stock dividend of one share for every ten held. Which of the following entries shows the full effect of declaring and distributing the dividend? *(p. 654)*

    a. Retained Earnings 37,000
        Common Stock Dividend Distributable 20,000
        Contributed Surplus — Common.................... 17,000

    b. Retained Earnings 20,000
        Common Stock... 20,000

    c. Retained Earnings 17,000
        Contributed Surplus — Common.................... 17,000

    d. Retained Earnings 37,000
        Common Stock... 37,000

4. Lang Real Estate Investment Corporation declared and distributed a 50 percent stock dividend. Which of the following stock splits would have the same effect on the number of Lang shares outstanding? *(pp. 655–56)*

    a. 2 for 1   c. 4 for 3
    b. 3 for 2   d. 5 for 4

5. A company purchased 10,000 shares of its common stock that had been issued at $1.50 a share paying $6 per share. This transaction *(pp. 656–57)*

    a. Has no effect on company assets
    b. Has no effect on owners' equity
    c. Decreases owners' equity by $15,000
    d. Decreases owners' equity by $60,000

6. A restriction of retained earnings *(p. 661)*

    a. Has no effect on total retained earnings
    b. Reduces retained earnings available for the declaration of dividends
    c. Is usually reported by a note
    d. All of the above

7. Which of the following items is not reported on the income statement? *(p. 664)*

    a. Issue price of stock   c. Income tax expense
    b. Extraordinary gains and losses   d. Earnings per share

8. The income statement item that is likely to be most useful for predicting income from year to year is *(pp. 664–65)*

    a. Extraordinary items   c. Income from continuing operations
    b. Discontinued operations   d. Net income

9. In computing earnings per share (EPS), dividends on preferred stock are *(p. 667)*
   a. Added because they represent earnings to the preferred shareholders
   b. Subtracted because they represent earnings to the preferred shareholders
   c. Ignored because they do not pertain to the common stock
   d. Reported separately on the income statement

10. A corporation accidentally overlooked an accrual of property tax expense at December 31, 19X4. Accountants for the company detect the error early in 19X5 before the expense is paid. The entry to record this prior period adjustment is *(p. 634)*

   a. Retained Earnings...   XXX   c. Retained Earnings   XXX
         Property Tax   Property Tax
            Expense   XXX   Payable..............   XXX

   b. Property Tax   d. Property Tax
         Expense.....................   XXX   Payable...................   XXX
         Property Tax   Property Tax
            Payable   XXX   Expense.............   XXX

Answers to the Self-Study Questions are at the end of the chapter.

Accounting Vocabulary

appropriation of retained earnings *(p. 661)*
continuing operations *(p. 664)*
discontinued operations *(p. 665)*

earnings per share (EPS) *(p. 666)*
extraordinary item *(p. 665)*
prior period adjustment *(p. 669)*

repurchase (of own) stock *(p. 656)*
segment of a business *(p. 665)*
stock dividend *(p. 653)*
stock split *(p. 655)*

ASSIGNMENT MATERIAL _____

Questions

1. Identify the two main parts of shareholders' equity.

2. Identify the account debited and the account credited from the last closing entry a corporation makes each year. What is the purpose of this entry?

3. Ametek, Inc. reported a cash balance of $73 million and a retained earnings balance of $162.5 million. Explain how Ametek can have so much more retained earnings than cash. In your answer, identify the nature of retained earnings and state how it ties to cash.

4. A friend of yours receives a stock dividend on an investment. He believes stock dividends are the same as cash dividends. Explain why this is not true.

5. Give two reasons for a corporation to distribute a stock dividend.

6. A corporation declares a stock dividend on December 21 and reports Stock Dividend Payable as a liability on the December 31 balance sheet. Is this correct? Give your reason.

7. What value is normally assigned to shares issued as a stock dividend?

8. To an investor, a stock split and a stock dividend have essentially the same effect. Explain the similarity and difference to the corporation between a 100 percent stock dividend and a 2-for-1 stock split.

9. Give three reasons why a corporation may repurchase its own shares.

10. What effect does the repurchase of capital stock have on the (a) assets, and (b) issued and outstanding stock of the corporation?

11. What effect does the repurchase and cancellation of common stock have on the (a) assets, (b) authorized stock, and (c) issued and outstanding stock of the corporation?

12. What does the *Canada Business Corporations Act* (CBCA) require a company to do when it repurchases its own stock?

13. Are there any exceptions to the requirement of the CBCA mentioned in question 12? If so, what are they?

14. Incorporating legislation frequently has a prohibition on a corporation purchasing its own stock in certain circumstances. What are those circumstances? Why does the prohibition exist?

15. Why do creditors wish to restrict a corporation's payment of cash dividends and repurchases of the corporation's stock?

16. What are two ways to report a retained earnings restriction? Which way is more common?

17. Identify three items on the income statement that generate income tax expense. What is an income tax saving, and how does it arise?

18. Why is it important for a corporation to report income from continuing operations separately from discontinued operations and extraordinary items?

19. Give two examples of extraordinary gains and losses and four examples of gains and loses that are not extraordinary.

20. What is the most widely used of all accounting statistics? What is the price-earnings ratio? Compute the price-earnings ratio for a company with EPS of $2 and a market price of $12 per share of common stock.

21. What is the earnings per share of a company with net income of $5,500 and issued common stock of 12,000 shares?

22. What account do all prior period adjustments affect? On what financial statement are prior period adjustments reported?

Exercises

Exercise 15-1   *Journalizing dividends and reporting shareholders' equity* **(L.O. 1)**

Eatmore Hamburger System, Inc. is authorized to issue 100,000 shares of common stock. The company issued 50,000 shares at $6 per share, and all 50,000 shares are outstanding. When the retained earnings balance was $300,000, Eatmore declared and distributed a 50 percent stock dividend, using the market value of $1.00 per share. Later, Eatmore declared and paid a $.20 per share cash dividend.

Required

1. Journalize the declaration and distribution of the stock dividend.
2. Journalize the declaration and payment of the cash dividend.
3. Prepare the shareholders' equity section of the balance sheet after both dividends.

Exercise 15-2   *Journalizing a stock dividend and reporting shareholders' equity* **(L.O. 1)**

The shareholders' equity for Tick Tock Jewelry Ltd. on September 30, 19X4 (end of the company's fiscal year) follows:

Shareholders' Equity

Common stock, 100,000 shares authorized,	
50,000 shares issued..	$550,000
Retained earnings...	280,000
Total shareholders' equity	$830,000

On November 16, the market price of Tick Tock's common stock was $12 per share and the company declared a 10 percent stock dividend. Tick Tock issued the dividend shares on November 30.

Required

1. Journalize the declaration and distribution of the stock dividend.
2. Prepare the shareholders' equity section of the balance sheet after the stock dividend.

Exercise 15-3 *Reporting shareholders' equity after a stock split* **(L.O. 2)**

McMillan Enterprises had the following shareholders' equity at May 31:

Common stock, 200,000 shares authorized, 50,000 shares issued	$680,000
Retained earnings...	210,000
Total shareholders' equity...	$890,000

On June 7, McMillan split its common stock 4 for 1. Make the memorandum entry to record the stock split, and prepare the shareholders' equity section of the balance sheet immediately after the split.

Exercise 15-4 *Journalizing repurchase of company stock and reporting shareholders' equity* **(L.O. 3)**

Northwest Distributing Ltd. had the following shareholders' equity on November 30:

Shareholders' Equity

Common stock, 500,000 shares authorized, 50,000	
shares issued..	$400,000
Retained earnings...	220,000
Total shareholders' equity	$620,000

On December 19, the company repurchased and retired 2,000 shares of common stock at $7 per share. Journalize this transaction and prepare the shareholders' equity section of the balance sheet at December 31.

Exercise 15-5 *Reporting a retained earnings restriction* **(L.O. 4)**

The agreement under which Brookview Sales, Inc. issued its long-term debt requires the restriction of $250,000 of the company's retained earnings balance. Total retained earnings is $470,000, and total capital stock is $820,000.

Required

Show how to report shareholders' equity (including retained earnings) on Brookview's balance sheet, assuming:

1. Brookview discloses the restriction in a note. Write the note.
2. Brookview appropriates retained earnings in the amount of the restriction and includes no note in its statements.

Exercise 15-6   *Preparing a multiple-step income statement* **(L.O. 5)**

The ledger of a corporation contains the following information for 19X7 operations:

Cost of goods sold....................	$45,000	Income tax saving — loss on	
Loss on discontinued		discontinued operations...	$20,000
operations............................	50,000	Extraordinary gain.................	12,000
Income tax expense —		Sales revenue	130,000
extraordinary gain...............	4,800	Operating expenses	
		(including income tax)......	60,000

Required

Prepare a multiple-step income statement for 19X7. Omit earnings per share. Was 19X7 a good year or a bad year for this corporation? Explain your answer in terms of the outlook for 19X8.

Exercise 15-7   *Computing earnings per share* **(L.O. 5)**

Benavides Inc. earned net income of $56,000 for the second quarter of 19X6. The ledger reveals the following figures:

Preferred stock, $1.75 per year, 1,600 shares issued and outstanding....... $ 70,000
Common stock, 42,000 shares issued 420,000

Required

Compute EPS for the quarter, assuming no changes in the stock accounts during the quarter.

Exercise 15-8   *Computing earnings per share* **(L.O. 5)**

Greenlawn Supply Ltd. had 40,000 shares of common stock and 10,000 shares of $.50 preferred stock outstanding on December 31, 19X8. On April 30, 19X9, the company issued 12,000 additional common shares and ended 19X9 with 52,000 shares of common stock outstanding. Income from continuing operations of 19X9 was $115,400, and loss on discontinued operations (net of income tax) was $8,280. The company had an extraordinary gain (net of tax) of $55,200.

Required

Compute Greenlawn's EPS amounts for 19X9, starting with income before discontinued operations and extraordinary items.

Exercise 15-9   *Preparing a statement of retained earnings with a prior period adjustment* **(L.O. 6)**

Posen Inc., a soft-drink company, reported a prior period adjustment in 19X9. An accounting error caused net income of prior years to be overstated by $5.2 million. Retained earnings at January 1, 19X9, as previously reported, stood at $412.3 million. Net income for 19X9 was $92.1 million, and dividends were $39.8 million. Prepare the company's statement of retained earnings for the year ended December 31, 19X9.

Exercise 15-10   *Preparing a combined statement of income and retained earnings (L.O. 5, 6)*

Dutch Boy Ltd. had retained earnings of $812.6 million at the beginning of 19X7. The company showed these figures at December 31, 19X7:

	($ millions)
Increases in retained earnings	
Net income	$135.1
Decreases in retained earnings	
Cash dividends — preferred..	2.3
common	85.2
Debit to retained earnings due to purchase of preferred stock	9.7

Required

Beginning with net income, prepare a combined statement of income and retained earnings for Dutch Boy for 19X7. The debit to Retained Earnings was caused by Dutch Boy's paying $9.7 million more to retire its preferred stock than the original issue price of the stock.

Problems   (Group A)

Problem 15-1A   *Journalizing shareholders' equity transactions (L.O. 1, 3, 6)*

Trail Corporation completed the following selected transactions during 19X6:

Jan. 13   Discovered that income tax expense of 19X5 was understated by $9,000. Record a prior period adjustment to correct the error.

21   Split common stock 3 for 1 by calling in the 10,000 shares of old common and issuing 30,000 shares of new common.

Feb.   6   Declared a cash dividend on the 4,000 shares of $2.25 preferred stock. Declared a $.20 per share dividend on the common stock outstanding. The date of record was February 27, and the payment date was March 20.

Mar. 20   Paid the cash dividends.

Apr. 18   Declared a 50 percent stock dividend on the common stock to holders of record April 30, with distribution set for May 30. The market value of the common stock was $8 per share.

May 30   Issued the stock dividend shares.

June 18   Purchased 2,000 shares of the company's own common stock at $12 per share; average issue price was $8 per share.

Nov. 14   Issued 800 shares of common stock for $10 per share.

Required

Record the transactions in the general journal.

Problem 15-2A   *Journalizing dividend and repurchase of stock transactions and reporting shareholders' equity (L.O. 1, 2, 3)*

The balance sheet of Carmel Service Inc. at December 31, 19X7 reported 10,000 shares of $.50 cumulative preferred stock authorized and outstanding. The preferred was issued in 19X1 at $8 per share. Carmel also had 500,000 shares of common stock authorized with 100,000 shares issued at an average price of $4.00 each. Retained Earnings had a balance of $58,000, and the preferred dividend for 19X7 was in arrears. During the two-year period ended December 31, 19X9, the company completed the following selected transactions:

19X8

Feb.   15   Purchased 5,000 shares of the company's own common stock at $6 per share.

Apr.   2   Declared the cash dividend on the preferred stock in arrears for 19X7 and the current cash dividend on preferred. The date of record was April 16, and the payment date was May 1.

May   1   Paid the cash dividends.

May   2   Purchased and retired all the preferred stock at $7.50 per share.

Dec.   31   Earned net income of $55,000 for the year.

19X9

Mar.   8   Issued 2,000 shares of common stock for $7 per share.

Sept. 28   Declared a 10 percent stock dividend on the outstanding common stock to holders of record October 15, with distribution set for October 31. The market value of Carmel common stock was $5 per share.

Oct.   31   Issued the stock dividend shares.

Nov.   5   Split the common stock 2 for 1.

Dec.   31   Earned net income of $73,000 during the year.

Required

1. Record the transactions in the general journal. Explanations are not required.
2. Prepare the shareholders' equity section of the balance sheet at two dates: December 31, 19X8 and December 31, 19X9.

Problem 15-3A   *Using actual-company data to record transactions and report earnings per share (L.O. 1, 3, 5)*

The following four items were taken from actual financial statements that reported amounts in millions, rounded to the nearest $100,000.

Hampton Industries, Inc. declared and paid cash dividends of $.1 million to preferred shareholders and also declared and issued a 10 percent stock dividend on its 2.0 million common shares outstanding. The issue price of Hampton's common stock was $1.00 per share, and the market value of the stock at the time of the stock dividend was $6.50 per share.

Required

1. Journalize the declaration and payment of the cash dividend.
2. Journalize the declaration and issuance of the stock dividend.

Crown Cork & Seal Corp., purchased and retired 800,000 shares of its common stock at a cost of $40 per share. Assume that the common stock was issued for $9 per share.

Required

3. Journalize the purchase and retirement of the common stock.

G.C. Murphy Limited reported a $1.3 million extraordinary gain on expropriation of land by the city of Halifax; the land had cost of $300,000. The tax on the gain was $400,000. Murphy's income before extraordinary item was $17.0 million, and the company had 4.1 million shares of common stock outstanding.

Required

4. Journalize the transaction.
5. Show how Murphy reported earnings per share for the year.

Problem 15-4A   *Repurchasing stock to fight off a takeover of the corporation* **(L.O. 3)**

Inuik Corporation is positioned ideally in its industry. Located in the Northwest Territories, Inuik is the only company with reliable sources for its imported gifts. The company does a brisk business with specialty stores. Inuik's recent success has made the company a prime target for a takeover. An investment group from the Yukon is attempting to buy 51 percent of Inuik's outstanding stock against the wishes of Inuik's board of directors. Board members are convinced that the Yukon investors would sell off the most desirable pieces of the business and leave little of value.

At the most recent board meeting, several suggestions were advanced to fight off the hostile takeover bid. The suggestion with the most promise is to purchase and retire a huge quantity of stock. Inuik has the cash to carry out this plan.

Required

1. As a significant shareholder of Inuik, write a memorandum to explain for the board how the repurchase and retirement of stock would make it more difficult for the Yukon group to take over Inuik. Include in your memo a discussion of the effect that repurchasing stock would have on stock outstanding and on the size of the corporation.

2. Suppose Inuik management is successful in fighting off the takeover bid and later issues shares at prices greater than the purchase price. Explain what effect these sales will have on assets, shareholders' equity, and net income.

Problem 15-5A   *Journalizing prior period adjustments and dividend and repurchase of stock transactions; reporting retained earnings and shareholders' equity* **(L.O. 1, 3, 6)**

The balance sheet of Camrose Corporation at December 31, 19X3 presented the following shareholder's equity:

Capital stock
Common stock, 250,000 shares authorized, 50,000 shares issued.........	$ 400,000
Total capital stock...	400,000
Retained earnings..	110,000
Total shareholders' equity...	$510,000

During 19X4, Camrose completed the following selected transactions:

Jan. 7 Discovered that income tax expense of 19X3 was understated by $4,000. Recorded a prior period adjustment to correct the error.

Mar. 29 Declared a 10 percent stock dividend on the common stock. The market value of Camrose common stock was $7 per share. The record date was April 19, with distribution set for May 19.

May 19 Issued the stock dividend shares.

July 13 Purchased 2,000 shares of the company's own common stock at $6 per share.

Oct. 4 Sold 600 shares of common stock for $8 per share.

Dec. 27 Declared a $.20 per share dividend on the common stock outstanding. The date of record was January 17, 19X5, and the payment date was January 31.

     31 Closed the $62,000 credit balance of Income Summary to Retained Earnings.

Required

1. Record the transactions in the general journal.

2. Prepare the retained earnings statement at December 31, 19X4.

3. Prepare the shareholders' equity section of the balance sheet at December 31, 19X4.

Problem 15-6A *Preparing a single-step income statement and a statement of retained earnings and reporting shareholders' equity on the balance sheet* **(L.O. 5, 6)**

The following information was taken from the ledger and other records of Mancini Corporation at June 30, 19X5:

Interest expense	$ 23,000	Dividends on common	
Gain on settlement of		stock	$ 12,000
lawsuit.................................	8,000	Sales revenue	589,000
Sales returns	15,000	Retained earnings	
Contributed surplus from		beginning, as	
retirement of preferred		originally reported	63,000
stock.....................................	16,000	Selling expenses....................	87,000
Interest revenue	5,000	Common stock,	
General expenses	71,000	20,000 shares authorized	
Loss on sale of		and issued	322,000
discontinued segment.......	8,000	Sales discounts......................	7,000
Prior period		Extraordinary gain...............	34,000
adjustment-debit to		Operating loss, discontinued	
Retained Earnings	4,000	segment..............................	9,000
Cost of goods sold	319,000	Loss on sale of capital	
Income tax expense (saving):		assets	10,000
Continuing operations......	28,000	Dividends on preferred	
Discontinued segment:		stock	?
Operating loss	(3,600)	Preferred stock, $1.50,	
Loss on sale....................	(3,200)	20,000 shares authorized	
Extraordinary gain	13,800	4,000 shares issued	100,000

Required

1. Prepare a single-step income statement, including earnings per share, for Mancini Corporation for the fiscal year ended June 30, 19X5. Evaluate income for the year ended June 30, 19X5 in terms of the outlook for 19X6. Assume 19X5 was a typical year and that Mancini managers hoped to earn income from continuing operations equal to 8 percent of net sales.

2. Prepare the statement of retained earnings for the year ended June 30, 19X5.

3. Prepare the shareholders' equity section of the balance sheet at that date.

Problem 15-7A *Preparing a corrected combined statement of income and retained earnings* **(L.O. 5, 6)**

Leslie Gose, accountant for Stinnett Catering Limited, was injured in a sailing accident. Another employee prepared the following income statement for the fiscal year ended June 30, 19X4:

Stinnett Catering Limited
Income Statement
June 30, 19X4

Revenues and gains		
Sales		$533,000
Gain on retirement of preferred stock		
(issued for $70,000; purchased for $59,000)		11,000
Total revenues and gains..		644,000
Expenses and losses		
Cost of goods sold..	$233,000	
Selling expenses	103,000	
General expenses	74,000	
Sales returns..	22,000	
Prior period adjustment — debit...............................	4,000	
Dividends...	15,000	
Sales discounts..	10,000	
Income tax expense...	32,000	
Total expenses and losses...		493,000
Income from operations		151,000
Other gains and losses		
Extraordinary gain...	30,000	
Operating income on discontinued segment..............	25,000	
Loss on sale of discontinued operations.....................	(40,000)	
Total other gains		15,000
Net income		$166,000
Earnings per share...		$ 6.92

The individual amounts listed on the income statement are correct. However, some accounts are reported incorrectly, and others do not belong on the income statement at all. Also, income tax (40 percent) has not been applied to all appropriate figures. Stinnett issued 20,000 shares of common stock in 19X1. The retained earnings balance, as originally reported at June 30, 19X3, was $63,000.

Required

Prepare a corrected combined statement of income and retained earnings for fiscal year 19X4. Prepare the income statement in single-step format.

Problem 15-8A   *Computing earnings per share and reporting a retained earnings*
restriction (L.O. 4, 5, 6)

Tradewinds Travel Ltd.'s capital structure at December 31, 19X2, included 5,000 shares of $2.50 preferred stock and 130,000 shares of common stock. Common shares outstanding during 19X3 were 130,000 January through February; 119,000 during March; 121,000 April through October; and 128,000 during November and December. Income from continuing operations during 19X3 was $371,885. The company discontinued a segment of the business at a gain of $69,160, and an extraordinary item generated a loss of $49,510. The board of directors of Tradewinds has restricted $300,000 of retained earnings for expansion of the company's office facilities.

Required

1. Compute Tradewinds' earnings per share. Start with income from continuing operations. Income and loss amounts are net of income tax.

2. Show two ways of reporting Tradewinds' retained earnings restriction. Retained earnings at December 31, 19X2 was $439,800, and total capital stock at December 31, 19X3 is $947,610. Tradewinds declared no dividends during 19X3.

(Group B)

Problem 15-1B   *Journalizing shareholders' equity transactions* **(L.O. 1, 3)**

Yukon Corporation completed the following selected transactions during the current year:

Jan.	9	Discovered that income tax expense of the preceding year was understated by $5,000. Recorded a prior period adjustment to correct the error.
Feb.	10	Split the company's 20,000 shares of common stock 2 for 1.
Mar.	18	Declared a cash dividend on the $5.00 preferred stock (1,000 shares outstanding). Declared at $.20 per share dividend on the common stock outstanding. The date of record was April 2, and the payment date was April 23.
Apr.	23	Paid the cash dividends.
July	30	Declared a 10 percent stock dividend on the common stock to holders of record August 21, with distribution set for September 11. The market value of the common stock was $15 per share.
Sept.	11	Issued the stock dividend shares.
	26	Repurchased 2,000 shares of the company's own common stock at $16 per share. The stock had an avergae cost of $6 per share.
Nov.	8	Sold 1,000 shares of common stock for $20 per share.
Dec.	13	Sold 500 shares of common stock for $14 per share.

Required

Record the transactions in the general journal.

Problem 15-2B   *Journalizing dividend and repurchase of stock transactions and reporting shareholders' equity* **(L.O. 1, 2)**

The balance sheet of Summerside Sales Ltd. at December 31, 19X5 reported 100,000 shares of common stock authorized, with 30,000 shares issued and a Common Stock balance of $180,000. Summerside Sales also had 5,000 shares of $.60 preferred stock authorized and outstanding. The preferred stock was issued in 19X1 at $10.00 per share. Retained Earnings had a credit balance of $104,000. During the two-year period ended December 31, 19X7, the company completed the following selected transactions:

19X6		
Mar.	15	Repurchased 1,000 shares of the company's own common stock at $5 per share.
July	2	Declared the annual $.60 cash dividend on the preferred stock and a $.75-per-share cash dividend on the common stock. The date of record was July 16, and the payment date was July 31.
July	31	Paid the cash dividends.
Nov.	30	Declared a 20 percent stock dividend on the outstanding common stock to holders of record December 21, with distribution set for January 11, 19X7. The market value of Summerside Sales common stock was $10 per share.
Dec.	31	Earned net income of $70,000 for the year.

19X7

Jan.	11	Issued the stock dividend shares.
June	30	Declared the annual $.60 cash dividend on the preferred stock. The date of record was July 14, and the payment date was July 29.
July	29	Paid the cash dividends.
Aug.	2	Purchased and retired all the preferred stock at $14 per share.
Oct.	8	Sold 800 shares of common stock for $12 per share.
Dec.	19	Split the common stock 2 for 1 by issuing two new shares for each old share previously issued. Prior to the split, the corporation had issued 35,800 shares.
	31	Earned net income of $81,000 during the year.

Required

1. Record the transactions in the general journal. Explanations are not required.
2. Prepare the shareholders' equity section of the balance sheet at two dates: December 31, 19X6 and December 31, 19X7.

Problem 15-3B   *Using actual-company data to record transactions and report earnings per share (L.O. 1, 3, 5)*

The following three items were taken from the financial statements of actual companies that showed amounts in millions and rounded to the nearest $100,000:

General Tire & Rubber Limited declared and paid cash dividends of $35.2 million to its common shareholders, and also declared and issued a 2 percent stock dividend on its 23.6 million common shares outstanding. The market value of General's common stock at the time of the stock dividend was $60 per share.

Required

1. Journalize the declaration and payment of the cash dividend.
2. Journalize declaration and issuance of the stock dividend.

Chesapeake Corporation reported a $4.0 million extraordinary loss that resulted from expropriation of capital assets (with a cost of $10 million and accumulated depreciation of $6 million) in a foreign country. The tax saving was $1.6 million. Chesapeake's income before the extraordinary item was $8.5 million, and the company had 6.4 million shares of common stock outstanding.

Required

3. Journalize the transaction.
4. Show how Chesapeake reported earnings per share for the year.

Problem 15-4B   *Increasing dividends to fight off a takeover of the corporation (L.O. 1)*

Albert Song Corporation is positioned ideally in the clothing business. Located in Toronto, Ontario, Song is the only company with a highly developed distribution network. The company does a brisk business with high fashion stores. Song's success has made the company a prime target for a takeover. Against the wishes of Song's board of directors, an investment group from Vancouver is attempting to buy 51 percent of Song's outstanding stock. Board members are convinced that the Vancouver investors would sell off the most desirable pieces of the business and leave little of value.

At the most recent board meeting, several suggestions were advanced to fight off the hostile takeover bid. One suggestion is to increase the stock outstanding by distributing a 100 percent stock dividend.

Required

As a significant shareholder of Song, write a short memo to explain to the board whether distributing the stock dividend would make it more difficult for the investor group to take over Albert Song Corporation. Include in your memo a discussion of the effect that the stock dividend would have on assets, liabilities, and total shareholders' equity, that is, the dividend's effect on the size of the corporation.

Problem 15-5B *Journalizing prior period adjustments and dividend and repurchase of stock transactions; reporting retained earnings and shareholders' equity* **(L.O. 1, 3, 6)**

The balance sheet of Flin Flon Inc. at December 31, 19X1 reported the following shareholders' equity:

Capital Stock	
Common stock, 100,000 shares authorized, 20,000 shares issued	$500,000
Total capital stock	500,000
Retained earnings	190,000
Total shareholders' equity	$690,000

During 19X2, Flin Flon completed the following selected transactions:

Jan.	11	Discovered that income tax expense of 19X1 was overstated by $19,000. Recorded a prior period adjustment to correct the error.
Apr.	30	Declared a 10 percent stock dividend on the common stock. The market value of Flin Flon common stock was $24 per share. The record date was May 21, with distribution set for June 5.
June	5	Issued the stock dividend shares.
July	29	Purchased 2,000 shares of the company's own common stock at $21 per share; avergae issue price is $25.00.
Nov.	13	Sold 1,000 shares of common stock for $22 per share.
Nov.	27	Declared a $.30 per share dividend on the common stock outstanding. The date of record was December 17, and the payment date was January 7, 19X3.
Dec.	31	Closed the $80,000 credit balance of Income Summary to Retained Earnings.

Required

1. Record the transactions in the general journal.
2. Prepare a retained earnings statement at December 31, 19X2.
3. Prepare the shareholders' equity section of the balance sheet at December 31, 19X2.

Problem 15-6B *Preparing a single-step income statement and a statement of retained earnings: reporting shareholders' equity on the balance sheet* **(L.O. 5, 6)**

The following information was taken from the ledger and other records of Rivera Corp. at September 30, 19X6:

Gain on sale of		Sales revenue.........................	$860,000
discontinued segment.......	$ 20,000	Dividends	35,000
Prior period		Interest revenue	4,000
adjustment — credit to		Extraordinary loss	33,000
Retained Earnings..............	6,000	Operating loss,	
Sales discounts	18,000	discontinued segment....	15,000
Interest expense......................	11,000	Loss on insurance	
Cost of goods sold..................	364,000	settlement	12,000
Loss on sale of capital		General expenses.................	113,000
assets....................................	8,000	Preferred stock, $3,	
Sales returns............................	9,000	10,000 shares authorized	
Income tax expense (saving):		5,000 shares issued	200,000
Continuing operations	72,000	Retained earnings,	
Discontinued segment:		beginning, as	
Operating loss	(6,000)	originally reported	88,000
Gain on sale	8,000	Selling expenses..................	136,000
Extraordinary loss..............	(13,000)	Common stock, no-par,	
		24,000 shares	
		authorized and issued ...	$266,000

Required

1. Prepare a single-step income statement, including earnings per share, for Rivera Corp., for the fiscal year ended September 30, 19X6. Evaluate income for the year ended September 30, 19X6 in terms of the outlook for 19X7. Assume 19X6 was a typical year and that Rivera managers hoped to earn income from continuing operations equal to 14 percent of net sales.

2. Prepare the statement of retained earnings for the year ended September 30, 19X6.

3. Prepare the shareholders' equity section of the balance sheet at that date.

Problem 15-7B   *Preparing a corrected combined statement of income and retained earnings* **(L.O. 5, 6)**

Monica Hearn, accountant for International Food Incorporated, was injured in a skiing accident. Another employee prepared the accompanying income statement for the fiscal year ended December 31, 19X3.

The individual amounts listed on the income statement are correct. However, some accounts are reported incorrectly, and others do not belong on the income statement at all. Also, income tax (40 percent) has not been applied to all appropriate figures. International issued 50,000 shares of common stock in 19X1. The retained earnings balance, as originally reported at December 31, 19X2, was $111,000.

Required

Prepare a corrected combined statement of income and retained earnings for 19X3. Prepare the income statement in single-step format.

International Foods Incorporated
Income Statement
19X3

Revenue and gains	
Sales	$362,000
Prior period adjustment — credit	14,000
Gain on retirement of preferred stock	
(issued for $81,000; purchased for $71,000)	10,000
Total revenues and gains...	466,000

Expenses and losses

Cost of goods sold	$145,000	
Selling expenses	76,000	
General expenses	61,000	
Sales returns	11,000	
Dividends	7,000	
Sales discounts	6,000	
Income tax expense	20,000	
Total expenses and losses		326,000
Income from operations		140,000
Other gains and losses		
Gain on sale of discontinued operations	10,000	
Extraordinary flood loss	(20,000)	
Operating loss on discontinued segment	(15,000)	
Total other losses		(25,000)
Net income		$115,000
Earnings per share		$ 2.21

Problem 15-8B *Computing earnings per share and reporting a retained earnings restriction* **(L.O. 4, 5, 6)**

The capital structure of Montpelier Gardens Inc. at December 31, 19X6, included 20,000 shares of $1.25 preferred stock and 44,000 shares of common stock. The 20,000 preferred shares were issued in 19X3. Common shares outstanding during 19X7 were 44,000 January through May; 50,000 June through August; and 60,500 September through December. Income from continuing operations during 19X7 was $81,100. The company discontinued a segment of the business at a loss of $6,630, and an extraordinary item generated a gain of $33,660. Montpelier's board of directors restricts $135,000 of retained earnings for contingencies.

Required

1. Compute Montpelier's earnings per share. Start with income from continuing operations. Income and loss amounts are net of income tax.

2. Show two ways of reporting Montpelier's retained earnings restriction. Retained earnings at December 31, 19X6 was $190,000, and total capital stock at December 31, 19X7 is $230,000. Montpelier declared no dividends in 19X7.

Extending Your Knowledge

Decision Problems

1. Analyzing cash dividends and stock dividends (L.O. 1)

Pacific Coast Ltd. had the following shareholders' equity on June 30 of the current year, 19X4:

Common stock, 100,000 shares issued	$ 750,000
Retained earnings	830,000
Total shareholders' equity	$1,580,000

In the past, Pacific Coast has paid an annual cash dividend of $1.50 per share. Despite the large retained earnings balance, the board of directors wished to conserve cash for expansion. In 19X3, the board delayed the payment of cash dividends by one month and in the meantime distributed a 20 percent stock dividend. During the following year, 19X4, the company's cash position improved. The board declared and paid a cash dividend of $1.25 per share.

Suppose you own 4,000 shares of Pacific Coast common stock, acquired three years ago. The market price of the stock was $30 per share before any of the above dividends.

Required

1. How did the stock dividend affect your proportionate ownership in the company? Explain.
2. What amount of cash dividends did you receive in 19X2? What amount of cash dividends will you receive after the above dividend action?
3. Immediately after the stock dividend was distributed, the market value of Pacific Coast stock decreased from $30 per share to $25 per share. Does this represent a loss to you? Explain.
4. Suppose Pacific Coast announced at the time of the stock dividend that the company will continue to pay the annual $1.50 cash dividend per share, even after the stock dividend. Would you expect the market price of the stock to decrease to $25 per share as in requirement 3 above? Explain.

2. Earnings and dividends (L.O. 1, 3, 5)

a. An investor noted that the market price of stocks seemed to decline after the date of record. Why do you think that would be the case?
b. The treasurer of Miske Brewing Corp. wanted to disclose a large loss as an extraordinary item because Miske produced too much product just prior to a very cool summer. Why do you think the treasurer wanted to use that particular disclosure? Would such disclosure be acceptable?
c. Corporations sometimes purchase their own stock. When asked why they do so, management often respond that they feel the stock is undervalued. What advantage would the company gain by buying and selling its own stock under these circumstances?
d. Carter Inc. earned a significant profit in the year ended November 30, 19X2 because land it held was expropriated for a new highway. The company proposes to treat the sale of land to the government as other revenue. Why do you think Carter is proposing such treatment? Is this disclosure appropriate?

Ethical Issue

Oklatex Corporation is an independent oil producer in Alberta. In February, company geologists discovered a pool of oil that tripled the company's proven reserves. Prior to disclosing the new oil to the public, top managers of the company quietly bought most of Oklatex stock for themselves personally. After the discovery announcement, Oklatex stock price increased from $13 to $40.

Required

1. Did Oklatex managers behave ethically? Explain your answer.
2. Identify the accounting principle relevant to this situation.
3. Who was helped and who was harmed by management's action?

Financial Statement Problems

1. Retained earnings and earnings per share (L.O. 3, 5)

Use the Schneider Corporation financial statements in Appendix C to answer these questions:

1. Schneider reports stock outstanding on the balance sheet and gives details in the notes to the financial statements. At October 26, 1991, how many shares of Schneider common stock were outstanding? How many Class A shares were authorized but not issued? How many Class A shares did Schneider issue during the current fiscal year?
2. Prepare a T-account for Retained Earnings to show the beginning and ending balances and all activity in the account during 1991.
3. Show how to compute earnings per share for 1991.

2. Common stock, retained earnings, and earnings per share (L.O. 3, 5, 6)

Obtain the annual report of an actual company of your choosing. Answer these questions about the company. Concentrate on the current year in the annual report you select.

1. How many shares of common stock did the company have outstanding at the end of the current year? How many shares had the company issued at the date of the previous balance sheet?
2. Compute average cost per share of common stock.
3. Prepare a T-account for Retained Earnings to show the beginning and ending balances and all activity in the account during the current year.
4. Did the company have any prior period adjustments during any year reported in the annual report? How can you tell?
5. Show how to compute all earnings (losses) *per share* amounts for the current year.

Answers to Self-Study Questions

1. a	6. d
2. c	7. a
3. d	8. c
4. b	9. b
5. d	10. c

Chapter 16

Corporations:
Long-Term Liabilities

Type	Name	Interest Rate %	Maturity Date	Bid $	Yield %
Prov.	Alberta	10.250	Aug. 22, 2001	108.45	8.88
Prov.	Ontario	10.500	Dec. 12, 2001	108.75	9.10
Corp.	B.C. Tel.	10.250	Oct. 15, 2001	104.50	9.50
Corp.	Bank of Nova Scotia	10.750	Mar. 26, 2001	107.25	9.50
Corp.	Hudson Bay Acceptance	13.750	Feb. 1, 2001	111.00	11.68
Fed.	Canada	15.750	Feb. 1, 2001	140.50	8.91
Fed.	Canada	9.500	Oct. 1, 2001	105.90	8.55
Fed.	Canada	9.750	Dec. 1, 2001	107.85	8.52

This bond information was published in *The Financial Post** on June 8, 1992, p. 35, for bonds as at June 5, 1992.

How do you read it? The first and second columns identify the type of bond — whether it was issued by a provincial government (prov.), the federal government (fed.), or a corporation (corp.); and the name of the issuer. The third column lists the stated interest rate on the bond; the fourth, the date the principal amount is due; the fifth, the price buyers were paying for the bond exclusive of accrued interest on June 5, 1992; and the last column, the actual rate of return a holder would experience if the bond were held to maturity, receiving the stated interest rate and bought at the bid price.

Notice the difference in the bid price, from a low of $104.50 to a high of $140.50. The yields vary from 8.52 percent to 11.68 percent. The interest rates go from 9.50 percent to 15.750 percent.

Why the differences between these long-term liabilities, which all mature in about eight to nine years from the date of this information, that is, in 2001? What determines the price of a bond? As you read Chapter 16, consider how risk, the stated interest rate, the current prevailing interest rates, and the term to maturity all influence bond price. Why not look up the price of these bonds in today's newspapers — almost certainly they will be different from the price on June 5, 1992.

* As provided by Securities Valuation Company.

Corporations may finance (that is, raise money for) their operations in different ways. They may issue stock to their owners, and they may reinvest assets earned by profitable operations, as we have seen. This chapter discusses the third way of financing operations, *long-term liabilities*.

Two common long-term liabilities are notes payable and bonds payable. A note payable, which we studied in Chapter 11, is a promissory note issued by the company to borrow money from a single lender, like a bank or a supplier. **Bonds payable** are groups of notes payable issued to multiple lenders, called bondholders. This chapter also discusses accounting for lease liabilities and pension liabilities.

The Nature of Bonds

A company needing millions of dollars may be unable to borrow so large an amount from a single lender. To gain access to more investors, the company may issue bonds. Each bond is, in effect, a long-term note payable that bears interest. Bonds are debts to the company for the amounts borrowed from the investors.

Purchasers of bonds receive a bond certificate, which carries the issuing company's name. The certificate also states the *principal*, which is the amount that the company has borrowed from the bondholder. This figure, typically stated in units of $1,000, is also called the bond's face value, maturity value or par value. The bond obligates the issuing company to pay the holder the principal amount at a specific future date, called the maturity date, which also appears on the certificate.

Bondholders loan their money to companies for a price: interest on the principal. The bond certificate states the interest rate that the issuer will pay the holder and the dates that the interest payments are due (generally twice a year). Some bond certificates name the bondholder (the investor). When the company pays back the principal, the holder returns the certificate, which the company retires (or cancels). Exhibit 16-1 shows an actual bond certificate, with the various features highlighted.

The board of directors may authorize a bond issue. In some companies the shareholders — as owners — may also have to vote their approval.

Issuing bonds usually requires the services of a securities firm, like Richardson Greenshields, to act as the *underwriter* of the bond issue. The **underwriter** purchases the bonds from the issuing company and resells them to its clients, or it may sell the bonds for a commission from the issuer, agreeing to buy all unsold bonds.

Types of Bonds

Bonds may be *registered* bonds or *coupon* bonds. The owner of a **registered bond** receives interest cheques from the issuing company, which keeps a listing of the

EXHIBIT 16-1 *Bond (Note) Certificate*

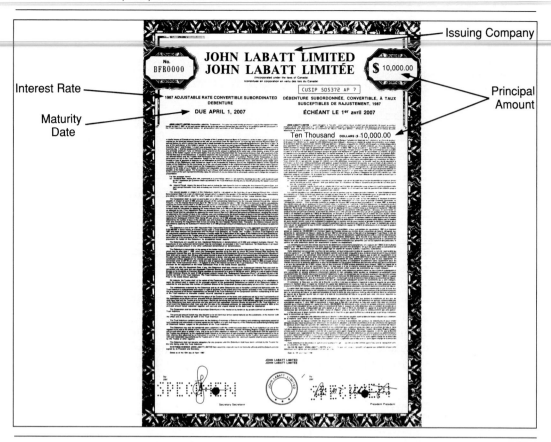

names and addresses of the bondholders. Owners of **coupon bonds** receive interest by detaching a perforated coupon (which states the interest due and the date of payment) from the bond and depositing it in a bank for collection. A company with coupon bonds needs no registry of bondholders. The responsibility for cashing coupons rests with the bondholders. Most bonds issued today are registered.

All the bonds in a particular issue may mature at the same time (**term bonds**), or they may mature in installments over a period (**serial bonds**). By issuing serial bonds, the company spreads its principal payments over time and avoids paying the entire principal at one time. Serial bonds are like installment notes payable.

Secured or *mortgage* bonds give the bondholder the right to take specified assets of the issuer if the company *defaults*, that is, fails to pay interest or principal. Unsecured bonds, called **debentures**, are backed only by the good faith of the borrower.

A secured bond is not necessarily more attractive to an investor than is a debenture. The primary motive of a person investing in bonds is to receive the interest amounts and the bonds' maturity value on time. Thus a debenture from a business with an excellent record in meeting obligations may be more attractive to an investor than is a secured bond from a business that has just been started or that has a bad credit record.

Bond Prices

Investors may transfer ownership through bond markets. The bond market in Canada is called the over the counter (OTC) market. It is a network of investment dealers who trade bonds issued by the Government of Canada and Crown corporations, the provinces, municipalities and regions, and corporations. Bond prices are

EXHIBIT 16-2   *Bond Price Information*

Bonds	Int. Rate %	Maturity Date	Bid $	Yield %
BC Telephone	10.25	Oct. 15/01	104.50	9.50

quoted at a percentage of their maturity value using $100 as a base. For example, a $1,000 bond quoted at 100 is bought or sold for $1,000, which is 100 percent of its maturity value. The same bond quoted at 101½ has a market price of $1,015 (101½ percent of its maturity value, or $1,000 × 1.015).

Exhibit 16-2 contains actual price information for bonds of BC Telephone, taken from the opening vignette.

On June 5, 1992, BC Telephone's 10.25 percent $1,000 par value bonds, maturing October 15, 2001 (indicated by 01), had a bid price of $104.50, or $1,045.00 which provided a yield of 9.50 percent (the yield rate is based on the market rate and time to maturity). Five months later, *The Financial Post* showed a bid price for the same bonds of $105.87; the yield was 8.40 percent.

The factors that affect the market price of a bond include the length of time left until the bond matures. The sooner the maturity date, the closer the bond will be to its maturity value. Also, the bonds issued by a company with a proven ability to meet all payments commands a higher price than an issue from a company with a poor record. Bond price hinges, too, on the rates of other available investment plans. Is a 12 percent bond the best way to invest $1,000, or does another investment strategy pay a higher rate? Of course, the higher the percentage rate, the higher the market price will be. Buying a 13 percent bond will cost you more than buying an 8 percent bond, given that both issues have the same maturity date and have been issued by equally sound businesses.

A bond issued at a price above its maturity value is said to be issued at a **premium**, and a bond issued at a price below maturity value has a **discount**. As a bond nears maturity, its market price moves toward its maturity value. On the maturity date, the market value of a bond equals exactly its maturity value because the company that issued the bond pays that amount to retire the bond.

Present Value[1]

A dollar received today is worth more than a dollar received in the future. You may invest today's dollar and earn income from it. Likewise, deferring any payment gives your money a period to grow. Money earns income over time, a fact called the *time value of money.* Let us examine how the time value of money affects the pricing of bonds.

Assume a bond with a face value of $1,000 reaches maturity three years from today and carries no interest. Would you pay $1,000 to purchase the bond? No, because the payment of $1,000 today to receive the same amount in the future provides you with no income on the investment. You would not be taking advantage of the time value of money. Just how much would you pay today in order to receive $1,000 at the end of three years? The answer is some amount less than $1,000. Let us suppose that you feel $750 is a good price. By investing $750 now to receive $1,000 later, you earn $250 interest revenue over the three years. The issuing company sees the transaction this way: It pays you $250 interest expense for the use of your $750 for three years.

---

[1] The chapter appendix covers present value in more detail.

The amount that a person would invest *at the present time* to receive a greater amount at a future date is called the **present value** of a future amount. In our example, $750 is the present value of the $1,000 amount to be received three years later.

Our $750 bond price is a reasonable estimate. The exact present value of any future amount depends on (1) the amount of the future payment (or receipt), (2) the length of time from the investment to the date when the future amount is to be received (or paid), and (3) the interest rate during the period. Present value is always less than the future amount. We discuss the method of computing present value in the appendix that follows this chapter. We need to be aware of the present-value concept, however, in the discussion of bond prices that follows. Therefore, please study the appendix now.

Bond Interest Rates

Bonds are sold at market price, which is the amount that investors are willing to pay. Market price is the bond's present value, which equals the present value of the principal payment plus the present value of the cash interest payments (which are made quarterly, semiannually, or annually over the term of the bond).

Two interest rates work to set the price of a bond. The **contract interest rate** or **stated rate** is the interest rate that determines the amount of cash interest the borrower pays — and the investor receives — each year. For example, the Toronto-Dominion Bank's 8 percent bonds have a contract interest rate of 8 percent. Thus Toronto-Dominion pays $8,000 of interest annually on each $100,000 bond. Each semiannual interest payment is $4,000 ($100,000 × .08 × ½).

The **market interest rate** or **effective rate** is the rate that investors demand for loaning their money. The market rate varies, sometimes daily. A company often issues bonds with a contract interest rate that differs from the prevailing market interest rate. This is so because the market rate changes between the date on which the company decides to borrow the money and orders the bonds to be printed and the date when the bonds are actually put up for sale.

Toronto-Dominion may issue its 8 percent bonds when the market rate has risen to 9 percent. Will the Toronto-Dominion bonds attract investors in this market? No, because investors can earn 9 percent on other bonds. Therefore, investors will purchase Toronto-Dominion bonds only at a price less than the face or maturity value. The difference between the lower price and face value is a *discount*. Conversely, if the market interest rate is 7 percent, Toronto-Dominion's 8 percent bonds will be so attractive that investors will pay more than face value for them. The difference between the higher price and face value is a *premium*.

Issuing Bonds Payable _____

Suppose the Toronto-Dominion Bank has $50 million in 8 percent bonds that mature in 10 years. Assume that Toronto-Dominion issues these bonds at par on January 1, 1993. The issuance entry is

1993				
Jan.	1	Cash	50,000,000	
		Bonds Payable..................................		50,000,000
		To issue 8%, 10-year bonds at par.		

The corporation that is borrowing money makes a one-time entry similar to this to record the receipt of cash and the issuance of bonds. Afterward, investors buy and sell the bonds through the bond markets. The buy-and-sell transactions between investors do not involve the corporation that issued the bonds. It keeps no records of these transactions, except for the names and addresses of the bondholders. This information is needed for mailing the interest and principal payments.

Interest payments for these bonds occur each January 1 and July 1. Toronto-Dominion's entry to record the first semiannual interest payment is

```
1993
July    1    Interest Expense
                  ($50,000,000 × .08 × ½) .....................    2,000,000
                  Cash.................................................                    2,000,000
             To pay semiannual interest on bonds
             payable.
```

At maturity, Toronto-Dominion will record payment of the bonds as follows:

```
2003
Jan.    1    Bonds Payable......................................    50,000,000
                  Cash.................................................                    50,000,000
             To pay bonds payable at maturity.
```

Issuing Bonds Payable between Interest Dates

The foregoing entries to record Toronto-Dominion's bond transactions are straightforward because the company issued the bonds on an interest payment date (January 1). However, corporations often issue bonds between interest dates.

Suppose Nova Scotia Power issues $75 million of 12 percent debentures due June 15, 2003. These bonds are dated June 15, 1993, and carry the price "100 plus accrued interest from date of original issue." An investor purchasing the bonds after the bond date must pay market value *plus accrued interest*. The issuing company will pay the full semiannual interest amount to the bondholder at the next interest payment date. Companies do not split semiannual interest payments among two or more investors who happen to hold the bonds during a six-month interest period.

Assume that Nova Scotia Power sells $100,000 of its bonds on July 15, 1993, one month after the date of original issue on June 15. Also assume that the market price of the bonds on July 15 is the face value. The company receives one month's accrued interest in addition to the bond's face value. Nova Scotia Power's entry to record issuance of the bonds payable is

```
1993
July   15    Cash.............................................    101,000
                  Bonds Payable ......................................                    100,000
                  Interest Payable ($100,000 × .12 × ½) .......                      1,000
             To issue 12%, 10-year bonds at par, one
             month after the original issue date.
```

Nova Scotia Power's entry to record the first semiannual interest payment is

```
1993
Dec.   15    Interest Expense ($100,000 × .12 × 5⁄12).......    5,000
             Interest Payable..........................................    1,000
                  Cash ($100,000 × .12 × ½).....................                      6,000
             To pay semiannual interest on bonds
             payable.
```

The debit to Interest Payable eliminates the credit balance in that account from July 15. Nova Scotia Power has now paid off that liability.

Note that Nova Scotia Power pays a full six months' interest on December 15. After subtracting the one month's accrued interest received at the time of issuing the bond, Nova Scotia Power has recorded interest expense for five months ($5,000). This interest expense is the correct amount for the five months that the bonds have been outstanding.

Selling bonds between interest dates at market value plus accrued interest simplifies the borrower's bookkeeping. The business pays the same amount of interest on each bond regardless of the length of time the person has held the bond. The business need not compute each bondholder's interest payment on an individual basis. Imagine the paperwork necessary to keep track of the interest due hundreds of bondholders who each bought bonds on a different date.

When an investor sells bonds to another investor, the price is always "plus accrued interest." Suppose you hold bonds as an investment for two months of a semiannual interest period and sell the bonds to another investor before receiving your interest. The person who buys the bonds will receive your two months of interest plus his or her own four months of interest on the next specified interest date. Business practice dictates that you must collect your share of the interest when you sell the bonds. For this reason, all bond transactions are "plus accrued interest."

Issuing Bonds Payable at a Discount

We know that market conditions may force the issuing corporation to accept a discount price for its bonds. Suppose BCE issues $100,000 of its 8 percent, 10-year bonds when the market interest rate is slightly above 8 percent. The market price of the bonds drops to 98, which means 98 percent of face or par value. BCE receives $98,000 ($100,000 × .98) at issuance. The entry is

```
1994
Jan.  1   Cash ($100,000 × .98) ...................................   98,000
          Discount on Bonds Payable .......................    2,000
             Bonds Payable .........................................             100,000
          To issue 8%, 10-year bonds at a discount.
```

After posting, the bond accounts have the following balances:

Bonds Payable	Discount on Bonds Payable
100,000	2,000

BCE's balance sheet immediately after issuance of the bonds reports:

Long-term liabilities
    Bonds payable, 8%, due 2001 .... $100,000
    Less: Discount on bonds payable 2,000 $98,000

Discount on Bonds Payable is a contra account to Bonds Payable. Subtracting its balance from Bonds Payable yields the book value, or carrying value, of the bonds. The relationship between Bonds Payable and the Discount account is similar to the relationships between Equipment and Accumulated Depreciation and between Accounts Receivable and Allowance for Uncollectible Accounts. Thus BCE's liability is $98,000, which is the amount the company borrowed. If BCE were to pay off the bonds immediately (an unlikely occurrence), BCE's required outlay would be $98,000 because the market price of the bonds is $98,000.

Interest Expense on Bonds Issued at a Discount   Earlier, we discussed the difference between the contract interest rate and the market interest rate. Suppose the market rate is 8¼ percent when BCE issues its 8 percent bonds. The ¼ percent interest rate difference creates the $2,000 discount on the bonds. BCE borrows $98,000 cash but must pay $100,000 cash when the bonds mature 10 years later. What happens to the $2,000 balance of the discount account over the life of the bond issue?

The $2,000 is in reality an additional interest expense to the issuing company. That amount is a cost (beyond the stated interest rate) that the business pays for borrowing the investors' money.

The discount amount is an interest expense not paid until the bond matures. However, the borrower (the bond issuer) benefits from the use of the investors' money each accounting period over the full term of the bond issue. The matching principle directs the business to match expense against its revenues on a period-by-period basis. The discount is allocated to interest expense through amortization each accounting period over the life of the bonds.

Straight-line Amortization of Account   We may amortize bond discount by dividing it into equal amounts for each interest period. This method is called *straight-line amortization*. In our example, the beginning discount is $2,000, and there are 20 semiannual interest periods during the bonds' 10-year life. Therefore, ½₀ of the $2,000 ($100) of bond discount is amortized each interest period. BCE's semiannual interest entry on July 1, 1994 is

<table>
<tr><td colspan="2">1994</td><td></td><td></td><td></td></tr>
<tr><td>July</td><td>1</td><td>Interest Expense..</td><td>4,100</td><td></td></tr>
<tr><td></td><td></td><td>Cash ($100,000 × .08 × ½₂).........................</td><td></td><td>4,000</td></tr>
<tr><td></td><td></td><td>Discount on Bonds Payable</td><td></td><td></td></tr>
<tr><td></td><td></td><td>($2,000/20)..</td><td></td><td>100</td></tr>
<tr><td></td><td></td><td>To pay semiannual interest and amortize</td><td></td><td></td></tr>
<tr><td></td><td></td><td>discount on bonds payable.</td><td></td><td></td></tr>
</table>

Interest expense of $4,100 is the sum of the contract interest ($4,000, which is paid in cash) plus the amount of discount amortized ($100). Discount on Bonds Payable is credited to amortize (reduce) the account's debit balance. Because Discount on Bonds Payable is a contra account, each reduction in its balance increases the book value of Bonds Payable. Twenty amortization entries will decrease the discount balance to zero, which means that Bonds Payable will have increased by $2,000 up to its face value of $100,000. The entry to pay off the bonds at maturity is

<table>
<tr><td colspan="2">2004</td><td></td><td></td><td></td></tr>
<tr><td>Jan.</td><td>1</td><td>Bonds Payable ....</td><td>100,000</td><td></td></tr>
<tr><td></td><td></td><td>Cash..</td><td></td><td>100,000</td></tr>
<tr><td></td><td></td><td>To pay bonds payable at maturity.</td><td></td><td></td></tr>
</table>

Issuing Bonds Payable at a Premium

To illustrate issuing bonds at a premium, let us change the BCE Inc. example. Assume that the market interest rate is 7½ percent when the company issues its 8 percent, 10-year bonds. Because 8 percent bonds are attractive in this market, investors pay a premium price to acquire them. If the bonds are priced at 103½ (103.5 percent of par value) BCE receives $103,500 cash upon issuance. The entry is

<table>
<tr><td colspan="2">1994</td><td></td><td></td><td></td></tr>
<tr><td>Jan.</td><td>1</td><td>Cash ($100,000 × 1.035)..............................</td><td>103,500</td><td></td></tr>
<tr><td></td><td></td><td>Bonds Payable ....</td><td></td><td>100,000</td></tr>
<tr><td></td><td></td><td>Premium on Bonds Payable ....</td><td></td><td>3,500</td></tr>
<tr><td></td><td></td><td>To issue 8%, 10-year bonds at a premium.</td><td></td><td></td></tr>
</table>

After posting, the bond accounts have the following balances:

<table>
<tr><td colspan="2" align="center">**Bonds Payable**</td><td colspan="2" align="center">**Premium on Bonds Payable**</td></tr>
<tr><td></td><td>100,000</td><td></td><td>3,500</td></tr>
</table>

> ### OBJECTIVE 1
> Account for basic bonds payable transactions using the straight-line amortization method

BCE's balance sheet immediately after issuance of the bonds reports:

Long-term liabilities
Bonds payable, 8%, due 2004................................ $100,000
Premium on bonds payable 3,500 $103,500

Premium on Bonds Payable is added to Bonds Payable to show the book value, or carrying value, of the bonds. BCE's liability is $103,500, which is the amount that the company borrowed. Immediate payment of the bonds would require an outlay of $103,500 because the market price of the bonds at issuance is $103,500. The investors would be unwilling to give up bonds for less than their market value.

Interest Expense on Bonds Issued at a Premium The ½ percent difference between the 8 percent contract rate on the bonds and the 7½ percent market interest rate creates the $3,500 premium. BCE borrows $103,500 cash but must pay only $100,000 cash at maturity. We treat the premium as a savings of interest expense to BCE. The premium cuts BCE's cost of borrowing the money. We account for the premium much as we handled the discount. We amortize the bond premium as a decrease in interest expense over the life of the bonds.

Straight-line Amortization of Premium In our example, the beginning premium is $3,500, and there are 20 semiannual interest periods during the bonds' 10-year life. Therefore, ¹⁄₂₀ of the $3,500 ($175) of bond premium is amortized each interest period. BCE's semiannual interest entry on July 1, 1991 is

1994
July 1 Interest Expense.. 3,825
   Premium on Bonds Payable
    ($3,500/20)... 175
    Cash ($100,000 × .08 × ½)..........................   4,000
   To pay semiannual interest and amortize
   premium on bonds payable.

Interest expense of $3,825 is the remainder of the contract cash interest ($4,000) less the amount of premium amortized ($175). The debit to Premium on Bonds Payable reduces its credit balance.

Reporting Bonds Payable

Bonds payable are reported on the balance sheet at their maturity amount plus any unamortized premium or minus any unamortized discount. For example, BCE in the preceding example would have amortized Premium on Bonds Payable for two semiannual periods ($175 × 2 = $350). The BCE balance sheet would show these bonds payable as follows:

Long-term liabilities
Bonds Payable, 8% due 2004................................ $100,000
Premium on bonds payable
[$3,500 – (2 × $175)]... 3,150 $103,150

Over the life of the bonds, twenty amortization entries will decrease the premium balance to zero. The payment at maturity will debit Bonds Payable and credit Cash for $100,000.

Adjusting Entries for Interest Expense _____

Companies issue bonds when they need cash. The interest payments seldom occur on the end of the company's fiscal year. Nevertheless, interest expense must be accrued at the end of the period to measure income accurately. The accrual entry may often be complicated by the need to amortize a discount or a premium for only a partial interest period.

Suppose Nova Corp. issues $100,000 of its 8 percent, 10-year bonds at a $2,000 discount on October 1, 1993. Assume that interest payments occur on March 31 and September 30 each year. On December 31, Nova records interest for the three-month period (October, November and December) as follows:

```
1993
Dec. 31   Interest Expense.............................................   2,050
              Interest Payable ($100,000 × .08 × 3/12)......              2,000
              Discount on Bonds Payable
                 ($2,000/10 x 3/12).....................................               50
          To accrue three months' interest and amor-
          tize discount on bonds payable for three
          months.
```

Interest Payable is credited for the three months of cash interest that have accrued since September 30. Discount on Bonds Payable is credited for three months of amortization.

The balance sheet at December 31, 1993 reports Interest Payable of $2,000 as a current liability. Bonds Payable appears as a long-term liability, presented as follows:

```
Long-term liabilities
   Bonds payable, 8%, due 2003 ...............................   $100,000
   Less: Discount on bonds payable ($2,000 – $50).          1,950      $98,050
```

Observe that the balance of Discount on Bonds Payable decreases by $50. The bonds' carrying value increases by the same amount. The bonds' carrying value continues to increase over its 10-year life, reaching $100,000 at maturity when the discount will be fully amortized.

The next semiannual interest payment occurs on March 31, 1994 as follows:

```
1994
Mar. 31   Interest Expense .............................................   2,050
          Interest Payable .............................................   2,000
              Cash ($100,000 × .08 × 6/12) ........................              4,000
              Discount on Bonds Payable
                 ($2,000/10 × 3/12) .....................................               50
          To pay semiannual interest, part of which
          was accrued, and amortize three months'
          discount on bonds payable.
```

Amortization of a premium over a partial interest period is similar except that Premium on Bonds Payable is debited.

Summary Problem for Your Review

Assume that Hydro-Québec has outstanding an issue of 9 percent bonds that mature on May 1, 2014. Further, assume that the bonds are dated May 1, 1994 and Hydro-Québec pays interest each April 30 and October 31.

Required

1. Will the bonds be issued at par, at a premium, or at a discount if the market interest rate is 8 percent at date of issuance? What if the market interest rate is 10 percent?

2. Assume Hydro-Québec issued $1,000,000 of the bonds at 104 on May 1, 1994
   a. Record issuance of the bonds.
   b. Record the interest payment and amortization of premium or discount on October 31, 1994.
   c. Accrue interest and amortize premium or discount on December 31, 1994.
   d. Show how the company would report the bonds on the balance sheet at December 31, 1994.
   e. Record the interest payment on April 30, 1995.

SOLUTION TO REVIEW PROBLEM

Requirement 1

If the market interest rate is 8 percent, 9 percent bonds will be issued at a *premium*. If the market rate is 10 percent, the 9 percent bonds will be issued at a *discount*.

Requirement 2

1994			
a. May 1	Cash ($1,000,000 × 1.04)............................	1,040,000	
	Bonds Payable		1,000,000
	Premium on Bonds Payable		40,000
	To issue 9%, 20-year bonds at a premium.		
b. Oct. 31	Interest Expense	44,000	
	Premium on Bonds Payable		
	($40,000/40)	1,000	
	Cash ($1,000,000 × .09 × ½)		45,000
	To pay semiannual interest and amortize premium on bonds payable.		
c. Dec. 31	Interest Expense	14,667	
	Premium on Bonds Payable		
	($40,000/40 × ⅔)...................................	333	
	Interest Payable		
	($1,000,000 × .09 × ⅔)		15,000
	To accrue interest and amortize bond premium for two months.		
d. Long-term liabilities			
	Bonds payable, 9%, due 2010.................	1,000,000	
	Premium on bonds payable		
	($40,000 − $1,000 − $333)	38,667	1,038,667
1995			
e. Apr. 30	Interest Expense	29,333	
	Interest Payable	15,000	
	Premium on Bonds Payable		
	($40,000/40 × ⅔)...................................	667	
	Cash ($1,000,000 × .09 × ½)		45,000
	To pay semiannual interest, part of which was accrued, and amortize four months' premium on bonds payable.		

SUPPLEMENT TO SUMMARY PROBLEM SOLUTION

Bond problems include many details. You may find it helpful to check your work. We verify the answers to the Summary Problem in this supplement.

On April 30, 1995, the bonds have been outstanding for one year. After the entries have been recorded, the account balances should show the results of one year's cash interest payments and one year's bond premium amortization.

Fact 1	Cash interest payments should be $90,000 ($1,000,000 × .09).
Accuracy check	Two credits to Cash of $45,000 each = $90,000. Cash payments are correct.
Fact 2	Premium amortization should be $2,000 ($40,000/40 semiannual periods × 2 semiannual periods in 1 year).
Accuracy check	Three debits to Premium on Bonds Payable ($1,000 + $333 + $667) = $2,000. Premium amortization is correct.
Fact 3	Also we can check the accuracy of interest expense recorded during the year ended December 31, 1994.

The bonds in this problem will be outstanding for a total of 20 years, or 240 (that is, 20 × 12) months. During 1994, the bonds are outstanding for 8 months (May through December).

Interest expense for 8 months *equals* payment of cash interest for 8 months minus premium amortization for 8 months.

Interest expense should therefore be ($1,000,000 × .09 × $\frac{8}{12}$ = $60,000) minus [($40,000/240) × 8 = $1,333] or ($60,000 − $1,333 = $58,667).

Accuracy check: Two debits to Interest Expense ($44,000 + $14,667) = $58,667. Interest expense for 1994 is correct.

Effective-Interest Method of Amortization

The straight-line amortization method has a theoretical weakness. Each period's amortization amount for a premium or discount is the same dollar amount over the life of the bonds. However, over that time the bonds' carrying value continues to increase (with a discount) or decrease (with a premium). Thus the fixed dollar amount of amortization changes as a percentage of the bonds' carrying value, making it appear that the bond issuer's interest rate changes over time. This appearance is misleading because in fact the issuer locked in a fixed interest rate when the bonds were issued. The interest rate on the bonds does not change.

We will see how the effective-interest method keeps each interest expense amount at the same percentage of the bonds' carrying value for every interest payment over the bonds' life. The total amount amortized over the life of the bonds is the same under both methods. GAAP does not specify which method should be used. U.S. GAAP favors the effective-interest method because it does a better job of matching. However, the straight-line method is popular because of its simplicity.

Effective-Interest Method of Amortizing Discount

Assume that Dofasco Inc. issues $100,000 of its 9 percent bonds at a time when the market rate of interest is 10 percent. Also assume that these bonds mature in five years and pay interest semiannually, so there are 10 semiannual interest payments. The issue price of the bonds is $96,149.[2] The discount on these bonds is $3,851 ($100,000 − $96,149).

OBJECTIVE 2

Amortize bond discount and premium by the effective-interest method

---

[2] We compute this present value using the tables that appear in the appendix to this chapter.

EXHIBIT 16-3 *Effective-Interest Method of Amortizing Bond Discount*

Panel A: Bond Data

Maturity value, $100,000
Contract interest rate, 9%
Interest paid, 4½% semiannually, $4,500 ($100,000 × .045)
Market interest rate at time of issue, 10% annually, 5% semiannually
Issue price, $96,149

Panel B: Amortization Table

	A	B	C	D	E
Semiannual Interest Period	Interest Payment (4½% of Maturity Value)	Interest Expense (5% of Preceding Bond Carrying Amount)	Discount Amortization (B – A)	Discount Account Balance (D – C)	Bond Carrying Amount ($100,000 – D)
Issue Date				$3,851	$ 96,149
1	$4,500	$4,807	$307	3,544	96,456
2	4,500	4,823	323	3,221	96,779
3	4,500	4,839	339	2,882	97,118
4	4,500	4,856	356	2,526	97,474
5	4,500	4,874	374	2,152	97,848
6	4,500	4,892	392	1,760	98,240
7	4,500	4,912	412	1,348	98,652
8	4,500	4,933	433	915	99,085
9	4,500	4,954	454	461	99,539
10	4,500	4,961*	461	-0-	100,000

*Adjusted for effect of rounding.

Exhibit 16-3 illustrates amortization of the discount by the effective-interest method. The exhibit reveals the following important facts about effective-interest-method amortization of bond discount:

Column A   The semiannual interest payments are constant because they are governed by the contract interest rate and the bonds' maturity value.

Column B   The interest expense each period is computed by multiplying the preceding bond carrying value by the market interest rate (5 percent semiannually). This rate is the effective-interest rate because its effect determines the interest expense each period. The amount of interest each period increases as the effective-interest rate, a constant, is applied to the increasing bond carrying value (column E).

Column C   The excess of each interest expense amount (column B) over each interest payment amount (column A) is the discount amortization for the period.

Column D   The discount balance decreases by the amount of amortization for the period (column C). The discount decreases from $3,851 at the bonds' issue date to zero at their maturity. The balance of the discount plus the bonds' carrying value equal the bonds' maturity value.

Column E   The bonds' carrying value increases from $96,149 at issuance to $100,000 at maturity.

Recall that we want to present interest expense amounts over the full life of the bonds at a fixed percentage of the bonds' carrying value. The 5 percent rate (the effective-interest rate) *is* that percentage. We have figured the cost of the money borrowed by the bond issuer, the interest expense, as a constant percentage of the carrying value of the bonds. The dollar *amount* of interest expense varies from period to period but not the interest percentage *rate*.

The accounts debited and credited under the effective-interest amortization method and the straight-line method are the same. Only the amounts differ. We may take the amortization amounts directly from the table in the exhibit. We assume that the first interest payment occurs on July 1 and use the appropriate amounts from Exhibit 16-3, reading across the line for the first interest payment date:

July	1	Interest Expense (column B)	4,807	
		Discount on Bonds Payable (column C)..		307
		Cash (column A)		4,500
		To pay semiannual interest and amortize discount on bonds payable.		

Effective-Interest Method of Amortizing Premium

Let us modify the Dofasco example to illustrate the effective-interest method of amortizing bond premium. Assume that Dofasco issues $100,000 of five-year, 9 percent bonds that pay interest semiannually. If the bonds are issued when the market interest rate is 8 percent, their issue price is $104,100.[3] The premium on these bonds is $4,100, and Exhibit 16-4 illustrates amortization of the premium by the interest method.

EXHIBIT 16-4   *Effective-Interest Method of Amortizing Bond Premium*

Panel A: Bond Data

Maturity value, $100,000
Contract interest rate, 9%
Interest paid, 4½% semiannually, $4,500 ($100,000 × .045)
Market interest rate at time of issue, 8% annually, 4% semiannually
Issue price, $104,100

Panel B: Amortization Table

Semiannual Interest Period	A Interest Payment (4½% of Maturity Value)	B Interest Expense (4% of Preceding Bond Carrying Amount)	C Premium Amortization (A – B)	D Premium Account Balance (D – C)	E Bond Carrying Amount ($100,000 + D)
Issue Date				$4,100	$104,100
1	$4,500	$4,164	$336	3,764	103,764
2	4,500	4,151	349	3,415	103,415
3	4,500	4,137	363	3,052	103,052
4	4,500	4,122	378	2,674	102,674
5	4,500	4,107	393	2,281	102,281
6	4,500	4,091	409	1,872	101,872
7	4,500	4,075	425	1,447	101,447
8	4,500	4,058	442	1,005	101,005
9	4,500	4,040	460	545	100,545
10	4,500	3,955*	545	-0-	100,000

*Adjusted for effect of rounding.

---

[3] We compute the present value of the bonds using the tables in this chapter's appendix.

Exhibit 16-4 reveals the following important facts about the effective-interest method of amortizing bond premium:

Column A   The semiannual interest payments are a constant amount fixed by the contract interest rate and the bonds' maturity value.

Column B   The interest expense each period is computed by multiplying the preceding bond carrying value by the effective-interest rate (4 percent semiannually). Observe that the amount of interest decreases each period as the bond carrying value decreases.

Column C   The excess of each interest payment (column A) over the period's interest expense (column B) is the premium amortization for the period.

Column D   The premium balance decreases by the amount of amortization for the period (column C) from $4,100 at issuance to zero at maturity. The bonds' carrying value plus the premium balance equal the bonds' maturity value.

Column E   The bonds' carrying value decreases from $104,100 at issuance to $100,000 at maturity.

Assuming that the first interest payment occurs on October 31, we read across the line for the first interest payment date and pick up the appropriate amounts.

Oct. 31	Interest Expense (column B)............................	4,164	
	Premium on Bonds Payable (column C)......	336	
	Cash (column A)...		4,500
	To pay semiannual interest and amortize discount on bonds payable.		

At year end it is necessary to make an adjusting entry for accrued interest and amortization of the bond premium for a partial period. In our example, the last interest payment occurred on October 31. The adjustment for November and December must cover two months, or one third of a semiannual period. The entry, with amounts drawn from line 2 in Exhibit 16-4 is

Dec. 31	Interest Expense ($4,151 × ⅓)............................	1,384	
	Premium on Bonds Payable ($349 × ⅓).........	116	
	Interest Payable ($4,500 × ⅓)......................		1,500
	To accrue two months' interest and amortize premium on bonds payable for two months.		

The second interest payment occurs on April 30 of the following year. The payment of $4,500 includes interest expense for four months (January through April), the interest payable at December 31, and premium amortization for four months. The payment entry is

Apr. 30	Interest Expense ($4,151 × ⅔)............................	2,767	
	Interest Payable	1,500	
	Premium on Bonds Payable ($349 × ⅔).........	233	
	Cash...		4,500
	To pay semiannual interest, some of which was accrued, and amortize premium on bonds payable for four months.		

If these bonds had been issued at a discount, procedures for these interest entries would be the same, except that Discount on Bonds Payable would be credited.

Bond Sinking Fund

Bond indentures, the contracts under which bonds are issued, often require the borrower to make regular periodic payments to a *bond sinking fund*. A fund is a group of assets that are segregated for a particular purpose. A **bond sinking fund** is used to retire bonds payable at maturity. A trustee manages this fund for the issuer, investing the company's payments in income-earning assets. The company's payments into the fund and the interest revenue — which the trustee reinvests in the fund — accumulate. The target amount of the sinking fund is the face value of the bond issue at maturity. When the bonds come due, the trustee sells the sinking-fund assets and uses the cash proceeds to pay off the bonds. The bond sinking fund provides security of payment to investors in unsecured bonds.

Most companies report sinking funds under the heading Investments, a separate asset category between current assets and capital assets on the balance sheet. A bond sinking fund is not a current asset because it may not be used to pay current liabilities. Accounting for the interest, dividends, and other earnings on the bond sinking fund requires use of the accounts Sinking Fund and Sinking Fund Revenue.

Sobey's Stores Limited has outstanding $9.25 million of 13 percent sinking fund debentures. The company must make annual sinking-fund payments. The entry to deposit $500,000 with the trustee is

Jan.	5	Sinking Fund..	500,000	
		Cash...		500,000
		To make annual sinking fund deposit.		

If the trustee invests the cash and reports annual sinking fund revenue of $50,000, the fund grows by this amount, and Sobey's makes the following entry at year end:

Dec.	31	Sinking Fund..	50,000	
		Sinking Fund Revenue		50,000
		To record sinking fund earnings.		

Assume that Sobey's has made the required sinking fund payments over a period of years and that these payments plus the fund earnings have accumulated a cash balance of $9.45 million at maturity. The trustee pays off the bonds and returns the excess cash to Sobey's, which makes the following entry:

Jan.	4	Cash..	200,000	
		Bonds Payable...	9,250,000	
		Sinking Fund.......................................		9,450,000
		To record payment of bonds payable and receipt of excess sinking fund cash at maturity.		

If the fund balance is less than the bonds' maturity value, the entry is similar to the foregoing entry. However, the company pays the extra amount and credits Cash.

Retirement of Bonds Payable

Normally companies wait until maturity to pay off, or retire, their bonds payable. All bond discount or premium has been amortized, and the retirement entry debits Bonds Payable and credits Cash for the bonds' maturity value.

Companies sometimes retire their bonds payable prior to maturity. The main reason for retiring bonds early is to relieve the pressure of making interest payments. Interest rates fluctuate. The company may be able to borrow at a lower

OBJECTIVE 3

Account for retirement of bonds payable

interest rate and use the proceeds from new bonds to pay off the old bonds, which bear a higher rate.

Some bonds are **callable**, which means that the issuer may call or pay off the bonds at a specified price whenever the issuer wants. The call price is usually a few percent above the face value or par, perhaps 104 or 105. Callable bonds give the issuer the benefit of being able to take advantage of low interest rates by paying off the bonds at the most favorable time. As an alternative to calling the bonds the issuer may purchase them in the open market at their current market price. Whether the bonds are called or purchased in the open market, the journal entry is the same.

Air Products Canada Ltd. has $7,000,000 of debentures outstanding with unamortized discount of $35,000. Lower interest rates in the market may convince management to pay off these bonds now. Assume that the bonds are callable at 103. If the market price of the bonds is 99¼, will Air Products call the bonds or purchase them in the open market? The market price is lower than the call price, so market price is the better choice, as shown in the following tabulation:

Face value of bonds being retired............................	$7,000,000
Unamortized discount	35,000
Book value	6,965,000
Market price ($7,000,000 × .9925).............................	6,947,500
Gain on retirement...	$ 17,500

The entry to record retirement of the bonds, immediately after an interest date, is

June 30	Bonds Payable..	7,000,000	
	Discount on Bonds Payable...............		35,000
	Cash ($7,000,000 × .9925)		6,947,500
	Gain on Retirement of		
	Bonds Payable		17,500
	To retire bonds payable before maturity.		

The entry removes the bonds payable and the related discount from the accounts and records a gain on retirement. Of course, any existing premium would be removed with a debit. If Air Products Canada had retired only half of these bonds, the accountant would remove half of the discount or premium. Likewise, if the price paid to retire the bonds exceeds their carrying value, the retirement entry would record a loss with a debit to the account Loss on Retirement of Bonds. GAAP requires that gains and losses on early retirement of debt, that are both abnormal in size and unusual, be classified as unusual and be reported separately as a line item on the income statement before discontinued operations and extraordinary items.

Convertible Bonds and Notes

Many corporate bonds and notes payable have the feature of being convertible into a specified number of shares of the common stock of the issuing company at the option of the investor. These bonds and notes, called **convertible bonds** (or **notes**), combine the safety of assured receipts of principal and interest on the bonds with the opportunity for large gains on the stock. The conversion feature is so attractive that investors usually accept a lower contract, or stated, interest rate than they would on nonconvertible bonds. The lower interest rate benefits the issuer. Convertible bonds are recorded like any other debt at issuance.

If the market price of the issuing company's stock gets high enough, the bondholders will convert the bonds into stock. The corporation records conversion by debiting the bond accounts and crediting the shareholders' equity accounts. The carrying value of the bonds becomes the book value of the newly issued stock. No gain or loss is recorded.

Maclean Hunter Limited has 8¼ percent convertible debentures outstanding with a carrying value of $52.3 million; the debentures are due May 1, 2004. They are convertible into common shares up to May 1, 1994, at a conversion price of $5.0625 per common share. Assume that $2 million of debentures were converted into 395,062 ($2,000,000/$5.0625) common shares on May 1, 1993. Maclean Hunter's entry to record conversion is

1993			
May 1	Debentures Outstanding........................	2,000,000	
	Share Capital		2,000,000
	To record conversion of $2,000,000 debentures outstanding into 395,062 common shares.		

Observe that the carrying value of the debentures becomes the amount of increase in shareholders' equity.

Current Portion of Long-Term Debt

Serial bonds and serial notes are payable in serials, or installments. The portion payable within one year is a current liability, and the remaining debt is long-term. At December 31, 1993, Mapco, Inc. had $70 million of 8.7 percent notes payable. The notes are due in $8 million annual installments through 2001 with a final installment of $6 million due in 2002. Therefore, $8 million is a current liability at December 31, 1993, and $62 million is a long-term liability. Mapco reported this installment note payable among its liabilities as follows:

	$ millions
Current liabilities	
Current portion of long-term debt..	$ 8
Long-term debt, excluding amounts payable within one year	62

Mortgage Notes Payable

You have probably heard of mortgage payments. Many notes payable are mortgage notes, which actually contain two agreements. The *note* is the borrower's promise to pay the lender the amount of the debt. The **mortgage**, a security agreement related to the note, is the borrower's promise to transfer the legal title to certain assets to the lender if the debt is not paid on schedule. The borrower is said to pledge these assets as security for the note. Often the asset that is pledged was acquired with the borrowed money. For example, most homeowners sign mortgage notes to purchase their residences, pledging that property as security for the loan. Businesses sign mortgage notes to acquire buildings, equipment, and other long-term assets. Mortgage notes are usually serial notes that require monthly or quarterly payments.

Advantage of Financing Operations with Debt versus Stock

Businesses acquire assets in different ways. Management may decide to purchase or to lease equipment. The money to finance the asset may come from the business's retained earnings, a note payable, a stock issue, or a bond issue. Each financing strategy has its advantages and disadvantages. Let us examine how issuing stock compares with issuing bonds.

OBJECTIVE 5

Explain the advantages and disadvantages of borrowing

Bonds differ from stocks in important ways. Stock shares give the holder part ownership of the corporation and a voice in management. Bonds merely give the holder a creditor's claim to the debtor's assets. Bond certificates carry dates for maturity and interest payments, unlike stock, which does not come due at any specific time. Companies are not obligated to declare dividends on stock.

Issuing stock raises capital without incurring the liabilities and interest expense that accompany bonds. However, by issuing stock the business spreads the ownership, control, and income of the corporation among more shares. Management may wish to avoid this dilution of its ownership. Borrowing money through bonds raises liabilities and interest expense, which the corporation must pay whether or not it earns a profit. But borrowing does not affect shareholder control: bondholders are creditors with no voice in management. Borrowing also provides a tax advantage in that interest expense is tax deductible. Dividends paid to shareholders are not tax deductible because they are not an expense.

Exhibit 16-5 illustrates the earnings-per-share (EPS) advantage of borrowing. Suppose a corporation with 100,000 shares of common stock outstanding needs $500,000 for expansion. Management is considering two financing plans. Plan 1 is to issue $500,000 of 10-percent bonds payable, and Plan 2 is to issue 50,000 shares of common stock for $500,000. Management believes the new cash can be invested in operations to earn income of $200,000 before interest and taxes.

The earnings-per-share amount is higher if the company borrows. The business earns more on the investment ($90,000) than the interest it pays on the bonds ($50,000). Earning more income than the borrowed amount increases the earnings for common shareholders, and is called **trading on the equity**. It is widely used in business to increase earnings per share of common stock.

Dividend payments to the new shareholders under Plan 2 would also make borrowing more attractive than issuing stock. Assume that net income is entirely an increase in cash. If under Plan 2 the company were to pay dividends of $50,000 (the same as the interest expense under Plan 1), its net cash inflow would be $70,000 ($120,000 – $50,000), compared to $90,000 under Plan 1.

Borrowing, however, has its disadvantages. Interest expense may be high enough to eliminate net income and lead to a cash crisis and even bankruptcy. Also, borrowing creates liabilities that accrue during bad years as well as during good years. In contrast, a company that issues stock can omit its dividends during a bad year.

Recently in Canada we have seen several situations in which a company's interest payments caused financial distress to the organization. The two better-known corporations who have had this problem are Campeau Corporation and Olympia & York.

EXHIBIT 16-5 Earnings-per-Share Advantage of Borrowing

	Plan 1 Borrow $500,000 at 10%	Plan 2 Issue $500,000 of Common Stock
Income before interest and income tax	$200,000	$200,000
Less: interest expense ($500,000 × .10)............	50,000	-0-
Income before income tax	150,000	200,000
Less: income tax expense (40%)	60,000	80,000
Net income	$ 90,000	$120,000
Earnings per share on new project		
Plan 1 ($90,000/100,000 shares)	$ .90	
Plan 2 ($120,000/150,000 shares)		$ .80

Lease Liabilities

A **lease** is a rental agreement in which the tenant (**lessee**) agrees to make rent payments to the property owner (**lessor**) in exchange for the use of the asset. Leasing allows the lessee to acquire the use of a needed asset without having to make the large initial cash down payment that purchase agreements require. Accountants divide leases into two types when considering the lease from the lessee's perspective: operating and capital. The lessor divides capital leases into two kinds: *sales-type leases*, in which the lessor is usually a manufacturer or dealer, and *direct financing leases*, in which the lessor is usually not a manufacturer or dealer but provides financing. This text will consider the broader term, *capital lease*, and not the kinds of capital lease.

<table><tr><td>**OBJECTIVE 6**
Account for lease transactions and pension liabilities</td></tr></table>

Operating Leases

Operating leases are usually short-term or cancelable. Many apartment leases and most car-rental agreements extend a year or less. These operating leases give the lessee the right to use the asset, but provide the lessee with no continuing rights to the asset. The lessor retains the usual risks and rewards of owning the leased asset. To account for an operating lease, the lessee debits Rent Expense (or Lease Expense) and credits Cash for the amount of the lease payment. The lessee's books do not report the leased asset or any lease liability (except perhaps a prepaid rent amount or a rent accrual at the end of the period).

Capital Leases

More and more businesses nationwide are turning to capital leasing to finance the acquisition of assets. A **capital lease** is long-term and noncancelable. Accounting for a capital lease is much like accounting for a purchase. The lessor removes the asset from his or her books. The lessee enters the asset into his or her accounts and records a lease liability at the beginning of the lease term.

Many companies lease some of their capital assets rather than buy them. A recent survey of 300 companies indicates that while almost 90 percent (266) have long-term debt, one third (102) have capital leases.[4]

Finning Ltd., the heavy equipment company, has its head office in Vancouver. Suppose Finning leases a building, agreeing to pay $10,000 annually for a 20-year period, with the first payment due immediately. This arrangement is similar to purchasing the building on an installment plan. In an installment purchase, Finning would debit Building and credit Cash and Installment Note Payable. The company would then pay interest and principal on the note payable and record depreciation on the building. Accounting for a capital lease follows this pattern.

Finning records the building at cost, which is the sum of the $10,000 initial payment plus the present value of the 19 future lease payments of $10,000 each. The company credits Cash for the initial payment and credits Lease Liability for the present value of the future lease payments. Assume the interest rate on Finning's lease is 10 percent and the present value (PV) of the future lease payments is $83,650.[5] At the beginning of the lease term, Finning makes the following entry:

---

[4] *Financial Reporting in Canada, 1991*, 19th edition (Toronto: CICA, 1992) pp. 102 and 120.

[5] This computation appears in the chapter appendix.

```
19X1
May   1   Leased Building ($10,000 + $83,650) ..........   93,650
                Cash ........................................................              10,000
                Lease Liability (PV of future
                    lease payments) ......................................              83,650
                To lease a building and make the first an-
                nual lease payment on the capital lease.
```

Because Finning has capitalized the building, the company records depreciation. Assume the building has an expected life of 25 years. It is depreciated over the
lease term of 20 years because the lessee has the use of the building only for that period. No residual value enters into the depreciation computation because the lessee
will have no residual asset when the building is returned to the lessor at the expi-
ration of the lease. Therefore, the annual depreciation entry is

```
19X2
Apr.  30   Depreciation Expense ($93,650/20) ...........   4,683
                Accumulated Depreciation
                    — Leased Building ...............................              4,683
                To record depreciation on leased building.
```

At year end, Finning must also accrue interest on the lease liability. Interest expense is computed by multiplying the lease liability by the interest rate on the
lease. The following entry credits Lease Liability (not Interest Payable) for this interest accrual:

```
19X2
Apr.  30   Interest Expense ($83,650 × .10) ..................   8,365
                Lease Liability ..........................................              8,365
                To accrue interest on the lease liability.
```

The balance sheet at December 31, 19X1 reports:

Assets

Capital assets		
Building under lease	$93,650	
Less: Accumulated depreciation	4,683	$88,967

Liabilities

Current liabilities	
Lease liability (next payment due on May 1, 19X2)	$10,000
Long-term liabilities	
Lease liability [beginning balance ($83,650) + interest accrual	
($8,365) – current portion ($10,000)]	82,015

In addition, the lessee must report the minimum capital lease payments for the
next five years in the notes to the financial statements.

The lease liability is split into current and long-term portions because the next
payment ($10,000) is a current liability and the remainder is long-term. The May 1,
19X2 lease payment is recorded as follows:

```
May   1   Lease Liability .............................................   10,000
                Cash ........................................................              10,000
                To make second annual lease payment on
                building.
```

Distinguishing a Capital Lease from an Operating Lease   Generally accountants consider whether a lease meets the conditions outlined below, which would make it a capital lease. If the lease does not, it is considered to be an operating lease.

The *CICA Handbook* in Section 3065.04 to .13 suggests that a lease is a capital lease from the perspective of the lessee if one or more of the following conditions are present at the beginning of the lease:

1. There is reasonable assurance that the lessee will obtain ownership of the leased asset at the end of the lease term.

2. The lease term is of such a length that the lessee will obtain almost all of the benefits from the use of the leased asset.

3. The lessor would both recover the original investment and earn a return on that investment from the lease.

A lease which does not meet any of the above conditions is probably an operating lease and should be accounted for as such.

A lease is a capital lease from the perspective of the lessor if any one of the three conditions outlined above is present and *both* the following are present:

1. The credit risk associated with the lease is normal.

2. The amounts of any unreimbursable costs to the lessor are estimable.

Off-Balance-Sheet Financing

An important part of business is obtaining the funds needed to acquire assets. To finance operations, a company may issue stock, borrow money, or retain earnings in the business. Notice that all three of these financing plans affect the right-hand side of the balance sheet. Issuing stock affects preferred or common stock. Borrowing creates notes or bonds payable. Internal funds come from retained earnings.

Off-balance-sheet financing is the acquisition of assets or services whose resulting debt is not reported on the balance sheet. A prime example is an operating lease. The lessee has the use of the leased asset, but neither the asset nor any lease liability is reported on the balance sheet. In the past, most leases were accounted for by the operating method. However, the *CICA Handbook* in Section 3065 has required businesses to account for an increasing number of leases by the capital lease method. Also, Section 3065 has brought about detailed reporting of operating lease payments in the notes to the financial statements; minimum operating lease payments for the next five years must be reported. The inclusion of more lease information, be they capital or operating leases, makes the accounting information for decision-making more complete.

Pension Liabilities

Most companies have a pension plan for their employees. A **pension** is employee compensation that is received during retirement. Employees earn the pensions by their service, so the company records pension expense while employees work for the company. While employees may also contribute to a company pension plan, the following discussion relates to employer contributions to a pension plan for employees.

The *CICA Handbook* in Section 3460 gives the rules for measuring pension expense. To record the company's payment into a pension plan, the company debits Pension Expense and credits Cash. Trustees such as trust companies and pension trusts manage pension plans. They receive the employer payments and any employee contributions, then invest these amounts for the future benefit of the employees. The goal is to have the funds available to meet any obligations to retirees, much as a bond sinking fund is designed to retire bonds payable at maturity.

While employees are perhaps those most interested in the status of their employer's pension plan, others such as creditors are also interested because pension plan assets and obligations can be large in proportion to a company's financial position. A company with a large underfunded pension liability could find itself in financial difficulties that would affect all creditors. For example, the financial statements of Maclean Hunter Limited recently reported that while the company's total assets were $1,753.6 million, the assets in the company's pension plans were $284 million (the accrued liabilities under the plan were estimated at $254 million).

Section 3460 defines two types of pension plan: a *defined benefit plan*, in which the benefits to be paid to the employee upon retirement are specified and the company must ensure that adequate funds will be available to make the specified payments, and a *defined contribution plan*, in which the contribution is defined and the benefits depend on what is available when the employee retires. Each will be discussed in turn.

A **defined benefit plan** must have an actuarial evaluation at least every three years to ensure that there will be sufficient funds available to make the required payments to each member of the plan on his or her retirement. In conducting the valuation, the plan actuaries will determine the actuarial present value of the plan benefits, compare that to the plan assets and determine whether the plan has a surplus or deficit. Section 3460 requires that the actuarial present value of plan benefits for employee services to the reporting date and the value of pension plan assets be disclosed in the financial statements. A recent annual report issued by National Trustco Inc. includes the following note to the financial statements:

> 11. PENSION PLAN (in thousands of dollars)
> The Company maintains a contributory defined benefit plan covering substantially all employees. The plan provides pensions based on length of service and career earnings with periodic upgrades.
>   Actuarial reports prepared during the year indicate that the present value of the accrued pension benefits and net assets, at market value, available to provide for these benefits as at October 31 are as follows:
>
> | | 1991 | 1990 |
> |--------------------------|-----------|-----------|
> | Accrued pension benefits | $107,630 | $ 98,817 |
> | Pension fund assets | 143,430 | 115,732 |

The accounting for defined benefits pension plans is complex and is demonstrated in subsequent accounting courses.

A **defined contribution plan** is an accumulation of the employer and employee contributions. The required disclosure is the present value of required future contributions by the company for employee services to the reporting date. For example, the disclosure for Elora Ltd. could be as follows:

> NOTES TO THE FINANCIAL STATEMENTS
> 8. The company has a defined contribution pension plan which covers all the company's employees. The present value of required future contributions in respect of past service by employees of the company was $759,256 at the year end.

Section 3460 of the *CICA Handbook* required companies to disclose pension assets and liabilities for defined benefit plans and unfunded obligations for past service for defined contribution plans, starting in 1990. Before that date, pensions were another example of off-balance-sheet financing. Companies received the benefit of their employees' service but could avoid reporting pension liabilities on the balance sheet.

Computers and Corporate Financial Planning ─────────

Corporations, large and small, deal with complex financial planning issues. A large corporation such as McCain Foods Ltd. might consider how to finance a new project. Suppose McCain wants to build a new potato processing and packaging plant, and expects total costs of $25,000,000. How does McCain find the best way to raise the needed funds? Financial-modeling techniques on microcomputers can help answer these questions, thanks to spreadsheet capabilities.

The company may consider the financing alternatives: issue common stock, preferred stock, bonds, or some combination of them; or build the plant, sell it to a second company, and lease the plant back from the second company — such a transaction is called a *sale-and-leaseback*. The assessment of the alternatives by McCain is often called "what-if" analysis, that is, "what if" we finance with common stock, "what if" we finance with new bonds, and so on.

The answers to these "what if" questions appear on a spreadsheet template that projects the company's financial statements for, say, the next five years, A preferred stock issue would probably mean higher annual dividend payments than would a common stock issue. The financial statements would show this higher payment. Likewise, long-term borrowing would involve interest expense, but these charges are tax-deductible, unlike dividend payments to shareholders. The spreadsheet could show the consequences of financing through stock and through bonds, with a summary such as Exhibit 16-5. By studying the projected financial statements, management can select the most favorable path.

Nonmonetary considerations cannot be modeled so easily on a spreadsheet. For example, is the company willing to dilute the control of present shareholders by issuing more stock? If the company borrows the needed funds, will the rating (by a bond rating service such as Dominion Bond Rating Service) of its existing bonds suffer? Computers are not as well-suited to answering qualitative questions such as these.

Summary Problem for Your Review

Québecor Inc. has outstanding an issue of 8 percent convertible bonds that mature in 2012. Suppose the bonds were dated October 1, 1992, and pay interest each April 1 and October 1.

Required

1. Complete the following effective-interest amortization table through October 1, 1994.

   Bond data:

   Maturity value, $100,000
   Contract interest rate, 8%
   Interest paid, 4% semiannually, $4,000 ($100,000 × .04)

   Market interest rate at time of issue, 9% annually, 4½% semiannually
   Issue price, 90¾

Amortization table:

Semiannual Interest Period	A Interest Payment (4% of Maturity Value)	B Interest Expense (4 ½% of Preceding Bond Carrying Amount)	C Discount Amortization (B – A)	D Discount Account Balance (D – C)	E Bond Carrying Amount ($100,000 – D)
10-1-92					
4-1-93					
10-1-93					
4-1-94					
10-1-94					

2. Using the amortization table, record the following transactions:
   a. Issuance of the bonds on October 1, 1992.
   b. Accrual of interest and amortization of discount on December 31, 1992.
   c. Payment of interest and amortization of discount on April 1, 1993.
   d. Conversion of one third of the bonds payable into common stock on October 2, 1994.
   e. Retirement of two thirds of the bonds payable on October 2, 1994. Purchase price of the bonds was 102.

SOLUTION TO REVIEW PROBLEM

Requirement 1 Amortization Table

Semiannual Interest Period	A Interest Payment (4% of Maturity Value)	B Interest Expense (4 ½% of Preceding Bond Carrying Amount)	C Discount Amortization (B – A)	D Discount Account Balance (D – C)	E Bond Carrying Amount ($100,000 – D)
10-1-92				$9,250	$90,750
4-1-93	$4,000	$4,084	$84	9,166	90,834
10-1-93	4,000	4,088	88	9,070	90,922
4-1-94	4,000	4,091	91	8,987	91,013
10-1-94	4,000	4,096	96	8,891	91,109

Requirement 2

1992
a. Oct. 1   Cash ($100,000 × .9075) 90,750
              Discount on Bonds Payable 9,250
                  Bonds Payable 100,000
              To issue 8%, 20-year bonds at a discount.

b. Dec.31   Interest Expense ($4,084 × ⅜)....................... 2,042
                  Discount on Bonds Payable ($84 × ⅜) 42
                  Interest Payable ($4,000 × ⅜).................... 2,000
              To accrue interest and amortize bond dis-
              count for three months.

1993
c. Apr. 1   Interest Expense... 2,042
              Interest Payable 2,000
                  Discount on Bonds Payable ($84 × ⅜) 42
                  Cash 4,000
              To pay semiannual interest, part of which
              was accrued, and amortize three months'
              discount on bonds payble.

1994

d. Oct. 2 Bonds Payable ($100,000 × ⅓)....................... 33,333
                Discount on Bonds Payable
                    ($8,891 × ⅓)... 2,964
                Common Stock ($91,109 × ⅓)................... 30,369
                To record conversion of bonds payable.

e. Oct. 2 Bonds Payable ($100,000 × ⅔)....................... 66,667
                Loss on Retirement of Bonds....................... 7,260
                Discount on Bonds Payable
                    ($8,891 × ⅔)... 5,927
                Cash ($100,000 × ⅔ × 1.02)...................... 68,000
                To retire bonds payable before maturity.

Summary

A corporation may borrow money by issuing bonds and long-term notes payable. A bond contract, called an *indenture*, specifies the maturity value of the bonds, the contract interest rate, and the dates for paying interest and principal. The owner of *registered* bonds receives an interest cheque from the company. The owner of *coupon* bonds receives interest by depositing an interest coupon in the bank. Bonds may be secured (*mortgage* bonds) or unsecured (*debenture* bonds).

Bonds are traded through organized markets, such as the Over-the-Counter market. Bonds are typically divided into $1,000 units. Their prices are quoted at a percentage of face value.

Market interest rates fluctuate and may differ from the contract rate on a bond. If a bond's contract rate exceeds the market rate, the bond sells at a *premium*. A bond with a contract rate below the market rate sells at a *discount*.

Money earns income over time, a fact that gives rise to the present value concept. An investor will pay a price for a bond equal to the present value of the bond principal plus the present value of the bond interest.

Straight-line amortization allocates an equal amount of premium or discount to each interest period. In the *effective-interest method* of amortization, the market rate at the time of issuance is multiplied by the bonds' carrying value to determine the interest expense each period and to compute the amount of discount or premium amortization.

A *bond sinking fund* accumulates the money to pay the bonds' face value at maturity. Companies may retire their bonds payable before maturity. *Callable* bonds give the borrower the right to pay off the bonds at a specified call price, or the company may purchase the bonds in the open market. Any gain or loss on an early extinguishment of debt is classified as an unusual item.

Convertible bonds and notes give the investor the privilege of trading the bonds for stock of the issuing corporation. The carrying value of the bonds becomes the book value of the newly issued stock.

A lease is a rental agreement between the *lessee* and the *lessor*. In an *operating lease*, the lessor retains the usual risks and rights of owning the asset. The lessee debits Rent Expense and credits Cash when making lease payments. A *capital lease* is long-term, noncancelable, and similar to an installment purchase of the leased asset. In a capital lease, the lessee capitalizes the leased asset and reports a lease liability.

In the case of *defined benefit pension plans*, companies report *accrued pension benefits* and *pension assets* in the financial statements; in the case of *defined contribution pension plans*, companies report *unfunded obligations* for past service.

Self-Study Questions

Test your understanding of the chapter by marking the best answer for each of the following questions:

1. An unsecured bond is called a *(p. 692)*
   a. Serial bond
   b. Registered bond
   c. Debenture bond
   d. Mortgage bond

2. How much will an investor pay for a $100,000 bond priced at 101⅞, plus a brokerage commission of $1,100? *(pp. 692–93)*
   a. $100,000
   b. $101,000
   c. $101,875
   d. $102,975

3. A bond with a stated interest rate of 9½ percent is issued when the market interest rate is 9¾ percent. This bond will sell at *(p. 694)*
   a. Par value
   b. A discount
   c. A premium
   d. A price minus accrued interest

4. Ten-year, 11 percent bonds payable of $500,000 were issued for $532,000. Assume the straight-line amortization method is appropriate. The total annual interest expense on these bonds is *(p. 698)*
   a. $51,800
   b. $55,000
   c. $58,200
   d. A different amount each year because the bonds' book value decreases as the premium is amortized

5. Use the facts in the preceding question but assume the effective-interest method of amortization is used. Total annual interest expense on the bonds is *(pp. 703–04)*
   a. $51,800
   b. $55,000
   c. $58,200
   d. A decreasing amount each year because the bonds' book value decreases as the premium is amortized

6. Bonds payable with face value of $300,000 and carrying value of $288,000 are retired before their scheduled maturity with a cash outlay of $292,000. Which of the following entries correctly records this bond retirement? *(pp. 705–06)*

   a. Bonds Payable 300,000
      Discount on Bonds Payable...................................... 12,000
         Cash.. 292,000
         Gain on Retirement of Bonds Payable 20,000

   b. Bonds Payable 300,000
      Loss on Retirement of Bonds Payable.................... 4,000
         Discount on Bonds Payable................................ 12,000
         Cash.. 292,000

   c. Bonds Payable 300,000
         Discount on Bonds Payable................................ 6,000
         Cash.. 292,000
         Gain on Retirement of Bonds Payable 2,000

   d. Bonds Payable 288,000
      Discount on Bonds Payable...................................... 12,000
         Gain on Retirement of Bonds Payable 8,000
         Cash.. 292,000

7. In a capital lease, the lessee records *(pp. 707–11)*
   a. A leased asset and a lease liability
   b. Depreciation on the leased asset
   c. Interest on the lease liability
   d. All of the above

8. Which of the following is an example of off-balance-sheet financing? *(p. 711)*
   a. Operating lease
   b. Current portion of long-term debt
   c. Debenture bonds
   d. Convertible bonds

9. An advantage of financing operations with debt versus stock is *(p. 707–08)*
   a. The tax deductibility of interest expense on debt
   b. The legal requirement to pay interest and principal
   c. Lower interest payments compared to dividend payments
   d. All of the above

Answers to the Self-Study Questions are at the end of the chapter.

Accounting Vocabulary

bond discount *(p. 693)*
bond indenture *(p. 705)*
bond premium *(p. 693)*
bond sinking fund *(p. 705)*
bonds payable *(p. 691)*
callable bonds *(p. 705)*
capital lease *(p. 709)*
contract interest rate
   (p. 694)
convertible bonds *(p. 706)*
coupon bonds *(p. 692)*
debentures *(p. 692)*

defined benefit pension
   plan *(p. 712)*
defined contribution
   pension plan *(p. 712)*
effective-interest rate
   (p. 694)
lease *(p. 709)*
lessee *(p. 709)*
lessor *(p. 709)*
market interest rate
   (p. 694)
mortgage *(p. 707)*

off-balance-sheet
   financing *(p. 711)*
operating lease *(p. 709)*
pension *(p. 711)*
present value *(p. 694)*
registered bonds *(p. 691)*
serial bonds *(p. 692)*
stated interest rate *(p. 694)*
term bonds *(p. 692)*
trading on the equity
   (p. 708)
underwriter *(p. 691)*

ASSIGNMENT MATERIAL _____

Questions

1. Identify three ways to finance the operations of a corporation.
2. How do bonds payable differ from a note payable?
3. How does an underwriter assist with the issuance of bonds?
4. Why would an investor require the borrower to set up a sinking fund?
5. Compute the price to the nearest dollar for the following bonds with a face value of $10,000:
   a. 93   b. 88¾   c. 101⅜   d. 122½   e. 100
6. In which of the following situations will bonds sell at par? at a premium? at a discount?
   a.   9% bonds sold when the market rate is 9%.
   b.   9% bonds sold when the market rate is 10%.
   c.   9% bonds sold when the market rate is 8%.
7. Identify the accounts to debit and credit for transactions (a) to issue bonds at par, (b) to pay interest, (c) to accrue interest at year end, and (d) to pay off bonds at maturity.
8. Identify the accounts to debit and credit for transactions (a) to issue bonds at a discount, (b) to pay interest, (c) to accrue interest at year end, and (d) to pay off bonds at maturity.
9. Identify the accounts to debit and credit for transactions (a) to issue bonds at a premium, (b) to pay interest, (c) to accrue interest at year end, and (d) to pay off bonds at maturity.
10. Why are bonds sold for a price "plus accrued interest"? What happens to accrued interest when bonds are sold by an individual?

11. How does the straight-line method of amortizing bond discount (or premium) differ from the effective-interest method?

12. A company retires ten-year bonds payable of $100,000 after five years. The business issued the bonds at 104 and called them at 103. Compute the amount of gain or loss on retirement. How is this gain or loss reported on the income statement?

13. Bonds payable with a maturity value of $100,000 are callable at 102½. Their market price is 101¼. If you are the issuer of these bonds, how much will you pay to retire them before maturity?

14. Why are convertible bonds attractive to investors? Why are they popular with borrowers?

15. Describe how to report serial bonds payable on the balance sheet.

16. Contrast the effects on a company of issuing bonds versus issuing stock.

17. Identify the accounts a lessee debits and credits when making operating lease payments.

18. What characteristics distinguish a capital lease from an operating lease?

19. A business signs a capital lease for the use of a building. What accounts are debited and credited (a) to begin the lease term and make the first lease payment, (b) to record depreciation, (c) to accrue interest on the lease liability, and (d) to make the second lease payment?

20. Show how a lessee reports on the balance sheet any leased equipment and the related lease liability under a capital lease.

21. What is off-balance-sheet financing? Give two examples.

22. Distinguish a defined benefit pension plan from a defined contribution pension plan. What must be reported for each in the financial statements?

Exercises

Exercise 16-1 *Issuing bonds payable and paying interest* **(L.O. 1)**

Electronix, Inc. issues $300,000 of 10 percent, semiannual, 20-year bonds payable that are dated April 30. Record (a) issuance of bonds at par on May 31, and (b) the next semiannual interest payment on October 31.

Exercise 16-2 *Issuing bonds payable, paying and accruing interest, and amortizing discount by the straight-line method* **(L.O. 1)**

On February 1, MiniCalc Ltd. issues 20-year, 10 percent bonds payable with a face value of $1,000,000. The bonds sell at 98 and pay interest on January 31 and July 31. MiniCalc amortizes bond discount by the straight-line method. Record (a) issuance of the bonds on February 1, (b) the semiannual interest payment on July 31, and (c) the interest accrual on December 31.

Exercise 16-3 *Issuing bonds payable, paying and accruing interest, and amortizing premium by the straight-line method* **(L.O. 1)**

XIT Transportation Inc. issues 30-year, 8 percent bonds payable with a face value of $5,000,000 on March 31. The bonds sell at 101½ and pay interest on March 31 and September 30. Assume XIT amortizes bond premium by the straight-line method. Record (a) issuance of the bonds on March 31, (b) payment of interest on September 30, and (c) accrual of interest on December 31.

Exercise 16-4   *Preparing an effective-interest amortization table; recording interest payments and the related discount amortization (L.O. 2)*

Optic Devices Incorporated is authorized to issue $500,000 of 11 percent, 10-year bonds payable. On January 2, when the market interest rate is 12 percent, the company issues $400,000 of the bonds and receives cash of $377,060. Optic Devices amortizes bond discount by the effective-interest method.

Required

1. Prepare an amortization table for the first four semiannual interest periods. Follow the format of Panel B in Exhibit 16-3.
2. Record the first semiannual interest payment on June 30 and the second payment on December 31.

Exercise 16-5   *Preparing an effective-interest amortization table; recording interest accrual and payment and the related premium amortization (L.O. 2)*

On September 30, 1993, the market interest rate is 11 percent. Lancer Limited issues $300,000 of 12 percent, 20-year sinking-fund bonds at 108. The bonds pay interest on March 31 and September 30. Lancer amortizes bond premium by the effective-interest method.

Required

1. Prepare an amortization table for the first four semiannual interest periods. Follow the format of Panel B in Exhibit 16-4.
2. Record issuance of the bonds on September 30, 1993, the accrual of interest at December 31, 1993, and the semiannual interest payment on March 31, 1994.

Exercise 16-6   *Journalizing sinking-fund transactions (L.O. 2)*

Lancer established a sinking fund for the bond issue in Exercise 16-5. Record payment of $8,000 into the sinking fund on March 31, 1994. Also record sinking-fund revenue of $900 on December 31, 1994, and the payment of the bonds at maturity on September 30, 2013. At maturity date the sinking-fund balance was $296,000.

Exercise 16-7   *Recording retirement of bonds payable (L.O. 3)*

Alliance Corp. issued $500,000 of 9 percent bonds payable at 97 on October 1, 19X0. These bonds mature on October 1, 19X8, and are callable at 101. Allied pays interest each April 1 and October 1. On October 1, 19X5, when the bonds' market price is 104, Allied retires the bonds in the most economical way available. Record the payment of interest and amortization of bond discount at October 1, 19X5, and the retirement of the bonds on that date. Alliance uses the straight-line amortization method.

Exercise 16-8   *Recording conversion of bonds payable (L.O. 4)*

Mending Tape Limited issued $400,000 of 8½ percent bonds payable on July 1, 19X4, at a price of 101½. After 5 years, the bonds may be converted into the company's common stock. Each $1,000 face amount of bonds is convertible into 40 shares of common stock. The bonds' term to maturity is 15 years. On December 31, 19X9, bondholders exercised their right to convert the bonds into common stock.

Required

1. What would cause the bondholders to convert their bonds into common stock?

2. Without making journal entries, compute the carrying amount of the bonds payable at December 31, 19X9. Mending Tape Limited uses the straight-line method to amortize bond premium and discount.

3. All amortization has been recorded properly. Journalize the conversion transaction at December 31, 19X9.

Exercise 16-9   *Recording early retirement and conversion of bonds payable* **(L.O. 3, 4)**

High Value Hardware Corp. reported the following at September 30:

Long-term liabilities		
Convertible bonds payable, 9%,		
8 years to maturity	$200,000	
Discount on bonds payable	6,000	$194,000

Required

1. Record retirement of one half of the bonds on October 1 at the call price of 101.
2. Record conversion of one fourth of the bonds into 4,000 shares of High Value's common stock on October 1.

Exercise 16-10   *Reporting long-term debt and pension liability on the balance sheet* **(L.O. 5)**

a. A note to the financial statements of Mapco, Inc. reported (in thousands):

Note 5: Long-Term Debt	
Total	$537,888
Less: Current portion	22,085
Less: Unamortized discount	1,391
Long-term debt	$514,412

Assume that none of the unamortized discount relates to the current portion of long-term debt. Show how Mapco's balance sheet would report these liabilities.

b. El Campo Incorporated's pension plan has assets with a market value of $720,000. The plan's accumulated benefit obligation is $840,000. What should El Campo report in the notes to the financial statements and on its balance sheet?

Exercise 16-11   *Analyzing alternative plans for raising money* **(L.O. 5)**

MJ-R Corporation is considering two plans for raising $1,000,000 to expand operations. Plan A is to borrow at 10 percent, and Plan B is to issue 200,000 shares of common stock. Before any new financing, MJ-R has 200,000 shares of common stock outstanding. Management believes the company can use the new funds to earn income of $600,000 per year before interest and taxes. The income tax rate is 40 percent.

Required

Prepare an analysis like Exhibit 16-5 to determine which plan will result in higher earnings per share.

Exercise 16-12   *Journalizing capital lease and operating lease transactions* **(L.O. 6)**

A capital lease agreement for equipment requires 10 annual payments of $8,000, with the first payment due on January 2, 19X5, the date of the inception of the lease. The present value of the 9 future lease payments at 12 percent is $42,624.

a. Journalize the following lessee transactions:

19X5

Jan. 2 Beginning of lease term and first annual payment.
Dec. 31 Depreciation of equipment.
     31 Interest expense on lease liability.

19X6

Jan. 2 Second annual lease payment.

b. Journalize the January 2, 19X5 lease payment if this is an operating lease.

Problems   *(Group A)*

Problem 16-1A *Journalizing bond transactions (at par) and reporting bonds payable on the balance sheet* **(L.O. 1)**

The board of directors of Alberta Stampede Ltd. authorizes the issue of $2 million of 8 percent, 20-year bonds payable. The semiannual dates are February 28 and August 31. The bonds are issued through an underwriter on April 30, 19X7 at par plus accrued interest.

Required

1. Journalize the following transactions:
   a. Issuance of the bonds on April 30, 19X7.
   b. Payment of interest on August 31, 19X7.
   c. Accrual of interest on December 31, 19X7.
   d. Payment of interest on February 28, 19X8.
2. Check your recorded interest expense for 19X7, using as a model the supplement to the summary problem on p. 701.
3. Report interest payable and bonds payable as they would appear on the Alberta Stampede Ltd. balance sheet at December 31, 19X7.

Problem 16-2A *Issuing notes at a premium, amortizing by the straight-line method, and reporting notes payable on the balance sheet* **(L.O. 1)**

On March 1, 19X6, Crown Center Corporation issues 9¼ percent, 10-year notes payable with a face value of $300,000. The notes pay interest on February 28 and August 31, and Crown Center amortizes premium and discount by the straight-line method.

Required

1. If the market interest rate is 10½ percent when Crown Center issues its notes, will the notes be priced at par, at a premium, or at a discount? Explain.
2. If the market interest rate is 8⅝ percent when Crown Center issues its notes, will the notes be priced at par, at a premium, or at a discount? Explain.
3. Assume the issue price of the notes is 103. Journalize the following note payable transactions:
   a. Issuance of the notes on March 1, 19X6.
   b. Payment of interest and amortization of premium on August 31, 19X6.
   c. Accrual of interest and amortization of premium on December 31, 19X6.
   d. Payment of interest and amortization of premium on February 28, 19X7.
4. Check your recorded interest expense for the year ended February 28, 19X7, using as a model the supplement to the summary problem on p. 701.
5. Report interest payable and notes payable as they would appear on the Crown Center balance sheet at December 31, 19X6.

Problem 16-3A *Analyzing a company's long-term debt, journalizing its transactions, and reporting the long-term debt on the balance sheet* **(L.O. 2)**

Assume that the notes to Park Lane Towers Ltd.'s financial statements reported the following data on September 30, year 1 (the end of the fiscal year):

NOTE E: LONG-TERM DEBT	
7% debentures due year 20, net of unamortized discount	
of $71,645 (effective-interest rate of 11%)..............................	$159,855
Notes payable, interest of 8.67%, due in annual amounts	
of $22,840 in years 5 through 16...	274,080

Assume Park Lane amortizes discount by the effective-interest method.

Required

1. Answer the following questions about Park Lane's long-term liabilities:
   a. What is the maturity value of the 7 percent debenture bonds?
   b. What are Park Lane's annual cash interest payments on the 7 percent debenture bonds?
   c. What is the carrying amount of the 7 percent debenture bonds at September 30, year 1?

2. Prepare an amortization table through September 30, year 4 for the 7 percent debenture bonds. Round all amounts to the nearestd dollar and assume Park Lane pays interest annually on September 30. Use the following format for the amortization table:

End of Annual Interest Period	A Interest Payment (7% of Maturity Value)	B Interest Expense (11% of Preceding Bond Carrying Amount)	C Discount Amortization (B – A)	D Discount Account Balance (D – C)	E Bond Carrying Amount ($231,500 – D)
Sept. 30, yr. 1					
Sept. 30, yr. 2					
Sept. 30, yr. 3					
Sept. 30, yr. 4					

3. Record the September 30, year 3 and year 4 interest payments on the 7 percent debenture bonds.

4. There is no premium or discount on the notes payable. Assuming annual interest is paid on September 30 each year, record Park Lane's September 30, year 2 interest payment on the notes payable. Round interest to the nearest thousand dollars.

5. Show how Park Lane would report the debenture bonds payable and notes payable at September 30, year 4.

Problem 16-4A *Issuing convertible bonds at a discount, amortizing by the effective-interest method, retiring bonds early, converting bonds, and reporting the bonds payable on the balance sheet* **(L.O. 2, 3, 4)**

On December 31, 19X1, Youth Development Institute Inc. issues 11 percent, 10-year convertible bonds with a maturity value of $500,000. The semiannual interest dates are June 30 and December 31. The market interest rate is 13 percent, and the issue price of the bonds is 89. The Institute amortizes bond premium and discount by the effective-interest method.

Required

1. Prepare an effective-interest method amortization table like Exhibit 16-3 for the first four semiannual interest periods.

2. Journalize the following transactions:
   a. Issuance of the bonds on December 31, 19X1. Credit Convertible Bonds Payable.
   b. Payment of interest on June 30, 19X2.
   c. Payment of interest on December 31, 19X2.
   d. Retirement of bonds with face value of $100,000 on July 1, 19X3. The Institute purchases the bonds at 94 in the open market.
   e. Conversion by the bondholders on July 1, 19X3 of bonds with face value of $200,000 into 50,000 shares of Youth Development common stock.

3. Prepare the balance sheet presentation of the bonds payable that are outstanding at December 31, 19X3.

Problem 16-5A   *Journalizing bonds payable and capital lease transactions (L.O. 1, 6)*

Journalize the following transactions of Oriental Rug Corporation:

1994

Jan. 1 Issued $2,000,000 of 9 percent, 10-year bonds payable at 97.
      1 Signed a 5-year capital lease on machinery. The agreement requires annual lease payments of $16,000, with the first payment due immediately. At 12 percent, the present value of the four future lease payments is $48,590.

July 1 Paid semiannual interest and amortized discount by the straight-line method on our 9 percent bonds payable.
      1 Made the $100,000 sinking-fund payment required by the indenture on our 9 percent bonds payable.

Dec. 31 Accrued semiannual interest expense and amortized discount by the straight-line method on our 9 percent bonds payable.
     31 Recorded depreciation on leased machinery.
     31 Accrued interest expense on the lease liability.
     31 Recorded bond sinking-fund earnings of $5,500.

2004

Jan. 1 Paid the 9 percent bonds at maturity from the sinking fund ($1,993,000) and the remainder from the company cash.

Problem 16-6A   *Financing operations with debt or with stock (L.O. 5)*

Marketing studies have shown that consumers prefer upscale stores, and recent trends in industry sales have supported the research. To capitalize on this trend, Modern Views, Inc. is embarking on a massive expansion. Plans call for opening 10 new stores within the next 18 months. Each store is scheduled to be 50 percent larger than the company's existing stores, furnished more elaborately, and stocked with more expensive merchandise. Management estimates that company operations will provide $8 million of the cash needed for expansion. Modern Views must raise the remaining $5.5 million from outsiders. The board of directors is considering obtaining the $5.5 million either through borrowing or by issuing common stock.

Required

Discuss for company management the advantages and disadvantages of borrowing and of issuing common stock to raise the needed cash. Which method of raising the funds would you recommend?

Problem 16-7A *Reporting liabilities on the balance sheet (L.O. 6)*

The Silverstein Corporation records include the following items:

Bonds payable, current		Mortgage note payable,	
portion	$ 75,000	long-term	$ 82,000
Capital lease liability,		Accumulated depreciation,	
long-term	81,000	equipment	46,000
Discount on bonds		Bond sinking fund	119,000
payable	7,000	Capital lease liability,	
Interest revenue	5,000	current.............................	18,000
Equipment acquired		Mortgage note payable,	
under capital lease	113,000	current.............................	23,000
Interest payable	13,000	Bonds payable, long-term ..	400,000
Interest expense	57,000		

Required

Show how these items would be reported on the Silverstein balance sheet, including headings for current liabilities, long-term liabilities, and so on. Note disclosures are not required.

(Group B)

Problem 16-1B *Journalizing bond transactions (at par) and reporting bonds payable on the balance sheet (L.O. 1)*

The board of directors of Duck Lake Ltd. authorizes the issue of $3 million of 9 percent, 10-year bonds payable. The semiannual interest dates are May 31 and November 30. The bonds are issued through an underwriter on June 30, 19X5 at par plus accrued interest.

Required

1. Journalize the following transactions:
   a. Issuance of the bonds on June 30, 19X5.
   b. Payment of interest on November 30, 19X5.
   c. Accrual of interest on December 31, 19X5.
   d. Payment of interest on May 31, 19X6.

2. Check your recorded interest expense for 19X5, using as a model the supplement to the summary problem on p. 701.

3. Report interest payable and bonds payable as they would appear on the Duck Lake Ltd. balance sheet at December 31, 19X5.

Problem 16-2B *Issuing bonds at a discount, amortizing by the straight-line method, and reporting bonds payable on the balance sheet (L.O. 1)*

On March 1, 19X4, Daigle, Inc. issues 10½ percent, 20-year bonds payable with a face value of $500,000. The bonds pay interest on February 28 and August 31. Daigle amortizes premium and discount by the straight-line method.

Required

1. If the market interest rate is 9⅜ percent when Daigle issues its bonds, will the bonds be priced at par, at a premium, or at a discount? Explain.

2. If the market interest rate is 10⅞ percent when Daigle issues its bonds, will the bonds be priced at par, at a premium, or at a discount? Explain.

3. Assume the issue price of the bonds is 96. Journalize the following bond transactions:
   a. Issuance of the bonds on March 1, 19X4.
   b. Payment of interest and amortization of discount on August 31, 19X4.
   c. Accrual of interest and amortization of discount on December 31, 19X4.
   d. Payment of interest and amortization of discount on February 28, 19X5.
4. Check your recorded interest expense for the year ended February 28, 19X5, using as a model the supplement to the summary problem on p. 701.
5. Report interest payable and bonds payable as they would appear on the Daigle balance sheet at December 31, 19X4.

Problem 16-3B   *Analyzing an actual company's long-term debt, journalizing its transactions, and reporting the long-term debt on the balance sheet* **(L.O. 2)**

The notes to Baker International's financial statements recently reported the following data on September 30, year 1 (the end of the fiscal year):

> NOTE 4: INDEBTEDNESS
> Long-term debt at September 30, year 1 included the following:
>
> 6.00% debentures due year 20 with an effective interest
>   rate of 14.66%, net of unamortized discount of
> $123,152,000.. $101,848,000
> Other indebtedness with an interest rate of 10.30%, due
> $12,108,000 in year 5 and $19,257,000 in year 6...............   31,365,000

Assume Baker amortizes discount by the effective-interest method.

Required

1. Answer the following questions about Baker's long-term liabilities:
   a. What is the maturity value of the 6 percent debenture bonds?
   b. What are Baker's annual cash interest payments on the 6 percent debenture bonds?
   c. What is the carrying amount of the 6 percent debenture bonds at September 30, year 1?
2. Prepare an amortization table through September 30, year 4 for the 6 percent debenture bonds. Round all amounts to the nearest thousand dollars, and assume Baker pays interest annually on September 30. Use the following format for the amortization table:

End of Annual Interest Period	A Interest Payment (6% of Maturity Value)	B Interest Expense (14.66% of Preceding Bond Carrying Amount)	C Discount Amortization (B – A)	D Discount Account Balance (D – C)	E Bond Carrying Amount ($225,000 – D)
Sept. 30, yr. 1					
Sept. 30, yr. 2					
Sept. 30, yr. 3					
Sept. 30, yr. 4					

3. Record the September 30, year 3 and year 4 interest payments on the 6 percent debenture bonds.
4. There is no premium or discount on the other indebtedness. Assuming annual interest is paid on September 30 each year, record Baker's September 30, year 2 interest payment on the other indebtedness. Round interest to the nearest thousand dollars.

5. Show how Baker would report the debenture bonds payable and other indebtedness of September 30, year 4.

Problem 16-4B *Issuing convertible bonds at a premium, amortizing by the effective-interest method, retiring bonds early, converting bonds, and reporting the bonds payable on the balance sheet* **(L.O. 2, 3, 4)**

On December 31, 19X1, Don Ami Inc. issues 12 percent, 10-year convertible bonds with a maturity value of $300,000. The semiannual interest dates are June 30 and December 31. The market interest rate is 11 percent, and the issue price of the bonds is 106. Don Ami amortizes bond premium and discount by the effective-interest method.

Required

1. Prepare an effective-interest method amortization table like Exhibit 16-4 for the first four semiannual interest periods.

2. Journalize the following transactions:
   a. Issuance of the bonds on December 31, 19X1. Credit Convertible Bonds Payable.
   b. Payment of interest on June 30, 19X2.
   c. Payment of interest on December 31, 19X2.
   d. Retirement of bonds with face value of $100,000 on July 1, 19X3. Don Ami pays the call price of 102.
   e. Conversion by the bondholders on July 1, 19X3 of bonds with face value of $150,000 into 10,000 shares of Don Ami common stock.

3. Prepare the balance sheet presentation of the bonds payable that are outstanding at December 31, 19X3.

Problem 16-5B *Journalizing bonds payable and capital lease transactions* **(L.O. 1, 6)**

Journalize the following transactions of Gundersen Corporation:

1994
Jan. 1 Issued $500,000 of 8 percent, 10-year bonds payable at 93.
      1 Signed a 5-year capital lease on equipment. The agreement requires annual lease payments of $20,000, with the first payment due immediately. At 12 percent, the present value of the four future lease payments is $60,750.
July 1 Paid semiannual interest and amortized discount by the straight-line method on our 8 percent bonds payable.
      1 Made the $25,000 sinking-fund payment required by the indenture on our 8 percent bonds payable.
Dec. 31 Accrued semiannual interest expense, and amortized discount by the straight-line method on our 8 percent bonds payable.
     31 Recorded depreciation on leased equipment.
     31 Accrued interest expense on the lease liability.
     31 Recorded bond sinking-fund earnings of $1,000.
2004
Jan. 1 Paid the 8 percent bonds at maturity from the sinking fund and received excess cash of $7,800.

Problem 16-6B *Financing operations with debt instead of with stock* **(L.O. 5)**

Two businesses must consider how to raise $10 million.

Truro Corporation is in the midst of its most successful period since it began operations in 1960. For each of the past 10 years, net income and earnings per share have increased by 15 percent per annum. The outlook for the future is equally bright, with new markets opening up and competitors unable to manufacture products of Truro's quality. Truro Corporation is planning a large-scale expansion.

Nova Scotia Limited has fallen on hard times. Net income has remained flat for five of the last six years, even falling by 10 percent from last year's level of profits. Top management has experienced unusual turnover, and the company lacks strong leadership. To become competitive again, Nova Scotia Limited desperately needs $10 million for expansion.

Required

Propose a plan for each company to raise the needed cash. Which company should borrow? Which company should issue stock? Consider the advantages and disadvantages of raising money by borrowing and by issuing stock, and discuss them in your answer.

Problem 16-7B *Reporting liabilities on the balance sheet* (L.O. 6)

The accounting records of Musberger, Inc. include the following items:

Bond sinking fund................	$ 80,000	Mortgage note payable,	
Bonds payable, long-term ...	180,000	long-term.........................	$ 67,000
Premium on bonds		Building acquired under	
payable............................	13,000	capital lease....................	190,000
Interest payable....................	9,200	Interest expense..................	47,000
Interest revenue	5,300	Bonds payable,	
Capital lease liability,		current portion	60,000
long-term	73,000	Accumulated depreciation,	
		building	108,000

Required

Show how these items would be reported on the Musberger balance sheet, including headings for current liabilities, long-term liabilities, and so on. Note disclosures are not required.

Extending Your Knowledge

Decision Problems

1. Analyzing alternative ways of raising $5 million (L.O. 6)

Business is going well for BPI Systems, Inc. The board of directors of this family-owned company believes that BPI could earn an additional $2,000,000 in income before interest and taxes by expanding into new markets. However, the $5,000,000 that the business needs for growth cannot be raised within the family. The directors, who strongly wish to retain family control of BPI, must consider issuing securities to outsiders. They are considering three financing plans.

Plan A is to borrow at 9 percent. Plan B is to issue 200,000 shares of common stock. Plan C is to issue 100,000 shares of nonvoting, $3.75 cumulative preferred stock. BPI presently has 500,000 shares of common stock outstanding. The income tax rate is 40 percent.

Required

1. Prepare an analysis similar to Exhibit 16-5 to determine which plan will result in the highest earnings per share of common stock.

2. Recommend one plan to the board of directors. Give your reasons.

2. Questions about long-term debt (L.O. 6 and Appendix)

The following questions are not related.

a. Why do you think corporations prefer operating leases over capital leases? How do you think a shareholder would view an operating lease?

b. Companies like to borrow for longer terms when interest rates are low, and for shorter terms when interest rates are high? Why is this statement true?

c. If you were to win $2,000,000 from Lotto 649, you would receive the $2,000,000, whereas if you were to win $2,000,000 in one of the big U.S. lotteries, you would receive 20 annual payments of $100,000. Are the prizes equivalent? If not, why not?

Ethical Issue

Ling-Temco-Vought, Inc. (LTV), manufacturer of aircraft and related electronic devices, borrowed heavily during the 1960s to exploit the advantage of financing operations with debt. At first, LTV was able to earn operating income much higher than its interest expense and was therefore quite profitable. However, when the business cycle turned down, LTV's debt burden pushed the company to the brink of bankruptcy. Operating income was less than interest expense.

Required

Is it unethical for managers to saddle a company with a high level of debt? Or is it just risky? Who could be hurt by a company's taking on too much debt? Discuss.

Financial Statement Problems

1. Long-term debt (L.O. 2, 3)

Schneider Corporation's consolidated balance sheet, consolidated statements of changes in financial position, and note 6 to the financial statements (all given in Appendix C) provide details about the company's long-term debt.

1. How much long-term debt did Schneider pay off during 1991? How much new long-term debt did the company incur during 1991? Journalize these transactions using Schneider's actual account titles and data from the Statement of Changes in Financial Position.

2. Prepare a T-account for Debentures and Loans to show the beginning and ending balances and all activity in the account during 1991 based on note 6 to the consolidated financial statements. (Note: You must take into account the changes in debentures and loans due within one year.)

3. Journalize, in a single entry, Schneider's interest expense for 1991.

4. What are the amounts of the principal that must be repaid within the next five years? Why would users of the financial statements find this information useful to know?

5. What restrictions have debenture and loan holders imposed on Schneider? Why would they place these restrictions on the corporation?

2. Long-term debt (L.O. 1, 2, 3)

Obtain the annual report of an actual company of your choosing. Answer these questions about the company. Concentrate on the current year in the annual report you select.

1. Examine the statement of changes in financial position. How much long-term debt did the company pay off during the current year? How much new long-term debt did the company incur during the year? Journalize these transactions using the company's actual account balances.

2. Prepare a T-account for the Long-Term Debt account to show the beginning and ending balances and all activity in the account during the year. If there is a discrepancy, insert this amount in the appropriate place. Note: Even the authors cannot explain some details in actual financial statements!

3. Study the notes to the financial statements. Is any of the company's retained earnings balance restricted as a result of borrowings? If so, indicate the amount of the retained earnings balance that is restricted and the amount that is unrestricted. How will the restriction affect the company's dividend payments in the future?

Appendix

Present Value

After studying this appendix, you should be able to

1. Compute the market value of a note or a bond.
2. Determine the cost of an asset acquired through a capital lease.

Present value (PV) has many applications in accounting. For example, a company may issue 10 percent bonds payable when the market interest rate is 11 percent. The company needs to know how much cash it will receive from issuing the bonds. The investors must determine how much to pay for the bonds. Both parties must compute the present value of the bonds. Another example is the acquisition of an asset through a capital lease. The lessee must know the cost of the asset. The concept of time value of money requires us to evaluate bonds, leases, and investments in terms of present value.

Suppose an investment promises to pay you $5,000 at the *end* of one year. How much would you pay *now* to acquire this investment? You would be willing to pay the present value of the $5,000, which is a future amount.

Present value depends on three factors: (1) the amount of payment (or receipt), (2) the length of time between investment and future receipt (or payment), and (3) the interest rate. The process of computing a present value is called *discounting* because the present value is *less* than the future value.

In our investment example, the future receipt is $5,000. The investment period is one year. Assume that you demand an annual interest rate of 10 percent on your investment. With all three factors specified, you can compute the present value of $5,000 at 10 percent for one year. The computation is

$$\frac{\text{Future value}}{(1 + \text{Interest rate})} = \frac{\$5,000}{1.10} = \$4,545$$

(Throughout this discussion we round off to the nearest dollar.) By turning the problem around, we verify the present value computation:

Amount invested (present value)	$4,545
Expected earnings ($4,545 × .10)	455
Amount to be received one year from now (future value)	$5,000

The $455 income amount is interest revenue, also called the return on the investment.

If the $5,000 is to be received two years from now, you would pay only $4,132 for the investment, computed as follows:

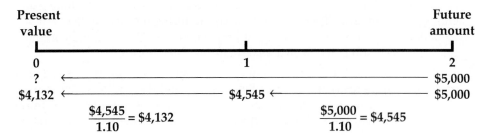

By turning the problem around, we verify that $4,132 accumulates to $5,000 at 10 percent for two years.

Amount invested (present value)	$4,132
Expected earnings for first year ($4,132 × .10)	413
Amount invested after one year...	4,545
Expected earnings for second year ($4,545 × .10)	455
Amount to be received two years from now (future value)	$5,000

You would pay $4,132 (the present value of $5,000) to receive the $5,000 future amount at the end of two years at 10 percent per year. The $868 difference between the amount invested ($4,132) and the amount to be received ($5,000) is the return on the investment, the sum of the two interest receipts: $413 + $455 = $868.

Present-Value Tables

We can compute present value by using the formula

$$\text{Present value} = \frac{\text{Future value}}{(1 + \text{interest rate})}$$

as we have shown. However, figuring present value "by hand" for investments spanning many years becomes drawn out. The "number crunching" presents too many opportunities for arithmetical errors. Present-value tables ease our work. Let us re-examine our examples of present value by using Table 16-1.

For the 10 percent investment for one year, we find the junction under 10% and across from 1 in the period column. The table figure of 0.909 is computed as follows: $\frac{1}{1.10}$ = 0.909. This work has been done for us, and only the present values are given in the table. Note that the table heading states $1. To figure present value for $5,000, we multiply 0.909 by $5,000. The result is $4,545, which matches the result we obtained by hand.

For the two-year investment, we read down from 10 percent and across from the period 2 row. We multiply 0.826 (which is computed as follows: $\frac{.909}{1.10}$ = 0.826) by $5,000 and get $4,130, which confirms our earlier computation of $4,132 (the difference is due to rounding in the present-value table). We can compute the present value of any single future amount using the table.

Present Value of an Annuity

The investment in the preceding example provided the investor with only a single future receipt ($5,000 at the end of two years). Some investments, called annuities, provide multiple receipts of an equal amount at fixed intervals over the investment's duration.

Table 16-1   *Present Value of $1*

Periods	4%	5%	6%	7%	Present Value 8%	10%	12%	14%	16%
1	0.962	0.952	0.943	0.935	0.926	0.909	0.893	0.877	0.862
2	0.925	0.907	0.890	0.873	0.857	0.826	0.797	0.769	0.743
3	0.889	0.864	0.840	0.816	0.794	0.751	0.712	0.675	0.641
4	0.855	0.823	0.792	0.763	0.735	0.683	0.636	0.592	0.552
5	0.822	0.784	0.747	0.713	0.681	0.621	0.567	0.519	0.476
6	0.790	0.746	0.705	0.666	0.630	0.564	0.507	0.456	0.410
7	0.760	0.711	0.665	0.623	0.583	0.513	0.452	0.400	0.354
8	0.731	0.677	0.627	0.582	0.540	0.467	0.404	0.351	0.305
9	0.703	0.645	0.592	0.544	0.500	0.424	0.361	0.308	0.263
10	0.676	0.614	0.558	0.508	0.463	0.386	0.322	0.270	0.227
11	0.650	0.585	0.527	0.475	0.429	0.350	0.287	0.237	0.195
12	0.625	0.557	0.497	0.444	0.397	0.319	0.257	0.208	0.168
13	0.601	0.530	0.469	0.415	0.368	0.290	0.229	0.182	0.145
14	0.577	0.505	0.442	0.388	0.340	0.263	0.205	0.160	0.125
15	0.555	0.481	0.417	0.362	0.315	0.239	0.183	0.140	0.108
16	0.534	0.458	0.394	0.339	0.292	0.218	0.163	0.123	0.093
17	0.513	0.436	0.371	0.317	0.270	0.198	0.146	0.108	0.080
18	0.494	0.416	0.350	0.296	0.250	0.180	0.130	0.095	0.069
19	0.475	0.396	0.331	0.277	0.232	0.164	0.116	0.083	0.060
20	0.456	0.377	0.312	0.258	0.215	0.149	0.104	0.073	0.051

Consider an investment that promises *annual* cash receipts of $10,000 to be received at the end of each of three years. Assume that you demand a 12 percent return on your investment. What is the investment's present value? What would you pay today to acquire the investment? The investment spans three periods, and you would pay the sum of three present values. The computation is

Year	Annual Cash Receipt	Present Value of $1 at 12% (Table 1)	Present Value of Annual Cash Receipt
1	$10,000	0.893	$ 8,930
2	10,000	0.797	7,970
3	10,000	0.712	7,120
Total present value of investment...............................			$24,020

The present value of this annuity is $24,020. By paying this amount today, you would receive $10,000 at the end of each of three years while earning 12 percent on your investment.

The example illustrates repetitive computations of the three future amounts, a time-consuming process. One way to ease the computational burden is to add the three present values of $1 (0.893 + 0.797 + 0.712) and multiply their sum (2.402) by the annual cash receipt ($10,000) to obtain the present value of the annuity ($10,000 × 2.402 = $24,020).

An easier approach is to use a present value of an annuity table. Table 16-2 shows the present value of $1 to be received periodically for a given number of periods.[1]

---

[1] Appendix B provides a more extensive table for the present value of an annuity of $1. It also gives the amounts for the future value of an annuity of $1. (The future-value amounts are presented for completeness and are not required for the present-value analysis.)

Table 16-2 *Present Value of Annuity of $1*

					Present Value				
Periods	4%	5%	6%	7%	8%	10%	12%	14%	16%
1	0.962	0.952	0.943	0.935	0.926	0.909	0.893	0.877	0.862
2	1.886	1.859	1.833	1.808	1.783	1.736	1.690	1.647	1.605
3	2.775	2.723	2.673	2.624	2.577	2.487	2.402	2.322	2.246
4	3.630	3.546	3.465	3.387	3.312	3.170	3.037	2.914	2.798
5	4.452	4.329	4.212	4.100	3.993	3.791	3.605	3.433	3.274
6	5.242	5.076	4.917	4.767	4.623	4.355	4.111	3.889	3.685
7	6.002	5.786	5.582	5.389	5.206	4.868	4.564	4.288	4.039
8	6.733	6.463	6.210	5.971	5.747	5.335	4.968	4.639	4.344
9	7.435	7.108	6.802	6.515	6.247	5.759	5.328	4.946	4.607
10	8.111	7.722	7.360	7.024	6.710	6.145	5.650	5.216	4.833
11	8.760	8.306	7.887	7.499	7.139	6.495	5.938	5.453	5.029
12	9.385	8.863	8.384	7.943	7.536	6.814	6.194	5.660	5.197
13	9.986	9.394	8.853	8.358	7.904	7.103	6.424	5.842	5.342
14	10.563	9.899	9.295	8.745	8.244	7.367	6.628	6.002	5.468
15	11.118	10.380	9.712	9.108	8.559	7.606	6.811	6.142	5.575
16	11.652	10.838	10.106	9.447	8.851	7.824	6.974	6.265	5.669
17	12.166	11.274	10.477	9.763	9.122	8.022	7.120	6.373	5.749
18	12.659	11.690	10.828	10.059	9.372	8.201	7.250	6.467	5.818
19	13.134	12.085	11.158	10.336	9.604	8.365	7.366	6.550	5.877
20	13.590	12.462	11.470	10.594	9.818	8.514	7.469	6.623	5.929

The present value of a three-period annuity at 12 percent is 2.402. Thus $10,000 received annually at the end of each of three years, discounted at 12 percent, is $24,020 ($10,000 × 2.402), which is the present value.

Present Value of Bonds Payable

The present value of a bond (its market price) is the present value of the future principal amount at maturity plus the present value of the future contract interest payments. The principal is a single amount to be paid at maturity. The interest is an annuity because it occurs periodically.

Let us compute the present value of the 9 percent, five-year bonds of John Labatt. The face value of the bonds is $100,000, and they pay 4½ percent contract (cash) interest semiannually. At issuance the market interest rate is 10 percent, but it is computed at 5 percent semiannually. Therefore, the effective-interest rate for each of the 10 semiannual periods is 5 percent. We use 5 percent in computing the present value of the maturity and of the interest. The market price of these bonds is $96,149, as follows:

	Effective annual interest rate ÷ 2		Number of semiannual interest payments	
	↓		↓	
PV of principal				
$100,000 × PV of single amount at 5%		for	10 periods	
($100,000 × .614 — Table 16–1)..........		....	....	$61,400
PV of interest				
($100,000 × .045) × PV of annuity at 5%		for	10 periods	
($4,500 × 7.722 — Table 16–2)...				34,749
PV (market price) of bonds...				$96,149

The market price of the John Labatt bonds shows a discount because the contract interest rate on the bonds (9 percent) is less than the market interest rate (10 percent). We discuss these bonds in more detail on pp. 701–703.

Let us consider a premium price for the John Labatt bonds. Assume that the market interest rate is 8 percent at issuance. The effective-interest rate is 4 percent for each of the 10 semiannual periods.

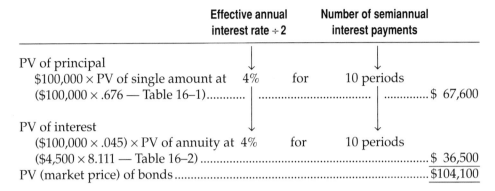

	Effective annual interest rate ÷ 2	Number of semiannual interest payments	
PV of principal			
$100,000 × PV of single amount at 4%	for	10 periods	
($100,000 × .676 — Table 16–1)............	....	....	$ 67,600
PV of interest			
($100,000 × .045) × PV of annuity at 4%	for	10 periods	
($4,500 × 8.111 — Table 16–2)		....	$ 36,500
PV (market price) of bonds...		....	$104,100

We discuss accounting for these bonds on pp. 703–704.

Capital Leases

How does a lessee compute the cost of an asset acquired through a capital lease? Consider that the lessee gets the use of the asset but does not pay for the leased asset in full at the beginning of the lease. Therefore, the lessee must record the leased asset at the present value of the lease liability. The time value of money must be weighed.

The cost of the asset to the lessee is the sum of any payment made at the beginning of the lease period plus the present value of the future lease payments. The lease payments are equal amounts occurring at regular intervals, that is, they are annuity payments.

Consider a 20-year building lease of Finning Ltd., the heavy equipment company. The lease requires 20 annual payments of $10,000 each, with the first payment due immediately. The interest rate in the lease is 10 percent, and the present value of the 19 future payments is $83,650 ($10,000 × PV of annuity at 10 percent for 19 periods, or 8.365 from Table 16–2). Finning's cost of the building is $93,650 (the sum of the initial payment, $10,000, plus the present value of the future payments, $83,650). The entries for a capital lease are illustrated on pp. 709–711.

APPENDIX ASSIGNMENT MATERIAL

Problem 16A-1   *Computing the present values of notes and bonds*

Determine the present value of the following notes and bonds:

a. $40,000, five-year note payable with contract interest rate of 11 percent, paid annually. The market interest rate at issuance is 12 percent.

b. Ten-year bonds payable with maturity value of $100,000 and contract interest rate of 12 percent, paid semiannually. The market rate of interest is 10 percent at issuance.

c. Same bonds payable as in question b, but the market interest rate is 8 percent.

d. Same bonds payable as in question b, but the market interest rate is 12 percent.

Problem 16A-2   *Computing a bond's present value; recording its issuance at a discount and interest payments*

On December 31, 19X1, when the market interest rate is 8 percent, Unitrode Corporation issues $300,000 of 10-year, 7.25 percent bonds payable. The bonds pay interest semiannually.

Required

1. Determine the present value of the bonds at issuance.
2. Assume that the bonds are issued at the price computed in requirement 1. Prepare an effective-interest method amortization table for the first two semiannual interest periods.
3. Using the amortization table prepared in requirement 2, journalize issuance of the bonds and the first two interest payments.

Problem 16A-3   *Computing a bond's present value; recording its issuance at a premium and interest payments*

On December 31, 19X1, when the market interest rate is 10 percent, RTE Ltd. issues $2,000,000 of 10-year, 12.5 percent bonds payable. The bonds pay interest semiannually.

Required

1. Determine the present value of the bonds at issuance.
2. Assuming the bonds were issued at the price computed in requirement 1, prepare an effective-interest method amortization table for the first two semiannual interest periods.
3. Using the amortization table in requirement 2, journalize issuance of the bonds on December 31, 19X1 and the first two interest payments on June 30 and December 31, 19X2.

Problem 16A-4   *Computing the cost of equipment acquired under a capital lease, and recording the lease transactions*

Montgomery Limited acquired equipment under a capital lease that requires six annual lease payments of $10,000. The first payment is due when the lease begins, on January 1, 19X6. Future payments are due on January 1 of each year of the lease term. The interest rate in the lease is 16 percent.

Required

1. Compute Montgomery's cost of the equipment.
2. Journalize the (a) acquisition of the equipment, (b) depreciation for 19X6, (c) accrued interest at December 31, 19X6, and (d) second lease payment on January 1, 19X7.

Answers to Self-Study Questions

1. c
2. d   [($100,000 × 1.01875) + $1,100 = $102,975]
3. b
4. a   [($500,000 × .11) − ($32,000/10) = $51,800]
5. d
6. b
7. d
8. a

Chapter 17

Corporations: Investments and Accounting for International Operations

Imagine operating a company with eighteen factories in Europe and a sales force in sixteen different European countries, with revenues of about $1.2 billion from this territory (which is about half of the total sales of the company). Add to this an equally large North American division. What do you have? McCain Foods Ltd. of Florenceville, New Brunswick, one of the world's largest producers of frozen french fries.

Consider the challenges of running such a company: dealing with a multitude of different foreign currencies, acknowledging and appreciating the unique cultural and business heritages of the different countries and regions, facilitating communications between managers who may speak any of at least six different languages, keeping abreast of what each country's autonomous operations are up to, identifying operations that are in need of assistance or doing exceptionally well, and preparing monthly consolidated financial statements for the president (either Harrison or Wallace McCain) and other executives to review.

How does McCain do it? Each month every business unit in the world files a thick report to head office in Florenceville, containing statistics ranging from gross sales to the fat content in each batch of french fries. Head office analyzes the data and, where results are significantly different from what was expected, follows up on opportunities and problems that the information suggests. Harrison and Wallace McCain set broad targets and strategies for the company, but it is up to the managing directors in each country to implement them. A big percentage of the company's income is based on how well each country meets these targets.

As you read Chapter 17, consider how essential reliable accounting information is to success in world markets, where competition does not necessarily respect borders. Accurate consolidated financial statements like McCain's are a vital part of staying ahead of the competition.

Source: Peggy Berkowitz, "You Say Potato, They Say McCain," *Canadian Business* (December 1991), pp. 44-46, 48.

LEARNING OBJECTIVES

After studying this chapter, you should be able to

1 Account for stock investments by the cost (LCM) method

2 Use the equity method for stock investments

3 Consolidate parent and subsidiary balance sheets

4 Eliminate intercompany items from a consolidated balance sheet

5 Account for investments in bonds

6 Account for transactions stated in a foreign currency

In this chapter, we discuss how to account for investments in stocks — including consolidation accounting — and bonds. We also consider the challenging area of accounting for international operations.

Accounting for Investments

Stock Prices

Investors buy more stocks in transactions among themselves than in purchases directly from the issuing company. Each share of stock is issued only once, but it may be traded among investors many times thereafter. People and businesses buy and sell stocks from each other in markets, such as the Toronto, Montreal, Vancouver and Alberta Stock Exchanges. Recall that stock ownership is transferable. Investors trade millions of stock shares each day. Brokers like RBC Dominion Securities and Richardson Greenshields handle stock transactions for a commission.

A broker may "quote you a stock price," which means state the current market price per share. The financial community quotes stock prices in dollars and one-eighth fractions. A stock selling at 32⅛ costs $32.125 per share. A stock listed at 55¾ sells at $55.75. Financial publications and many newspapers carry daily information on the stock issues of thousands of corporations. These one-line summaries carry information as of the close of trading the previous day.

Exhibit 17-1 presents information for the common stock of John Labatt, a brewer and food and beverage company, just as it appears in *The Financial Post*.[1]

During the previous 52 weeks, Labatt common stock reached a high of $30.125 and a low of $24.125. The annual cash dividend is $.80 per share. *The Financial Post* comes out in the morning so the information relates to the previous day; the high

EXHIBIT 17-1   *Stock Price Information*

| 52 Weeks | | | Div | | | Cls or | Net | Vol | Yeild | P/E |
High	Low	Stock	Rate	High	Low	Latest	Chge	100s	%	Ratio
$30⅛	24⅛	Labatt, John	0.80	$29⅛	29	29	$-⅛$	98	2.8	27.9

---

[1] *The Financial Post*, September 9, 1992, p. 18.

and low prices were $29.125 and $29.00 while the closing price was $29.00 (if there had been no trading on the previous day, the latest, or most recent price, would be given). The closing price on the previous day was down $.125 from the closing price of one trading day earlier. During the previous day, 9,800 (98 × 100) shares of John Labatt stock were traded. The yield (dividend per share divided by price per share) is 2.8 percent while the P/E ratio (ratio of earnings per share to the share price) is 27.9/1.

What causes a change in a stock's price? The company's net income trend, the development of new products, court rulings, new legislation, business success and upward market trends drive a stock's price up, and business failures and bad economic news pull it down. The market sets the price at which a stock changes hands.

Investments in Stock

To begin the discussion of investments in stock, we need to define two key terms. The person or company that owns stock in a corporation is the *investor*. The corporation that issued the stock is the *investee*. If you own shares of Labatt common stock, you are an investor and Labatt is the investee.

A business may purchase another corporation's stock simply to put extra cash to work in the hope of earning dividends and gains on the sale of the stock. Alternatively, the business may make the investment to gain a degree of control over the investee's operation. After all, stock is ownership. An investor holding 25 percent of the outstanding stock of the investee owns one fourth of the business. This one-quarter voice in electing the directors of the corporation is likely to give the investor a lot of say in how the investee conducts its business. An investor holding more than 50 percent of the outstanding shares controls the investee.

Let us consider why one corporation might want to gain a say in another corporation's business. The investor may want to exert some control over the level of dividends paid by the investee. Or perhaps the investor regards the investee as a good investment opportunity. The investee might have a line of products closely linked to the investor's own sales items. By influencing the investee's business, the investor may be able to exert some control on product distribution, control over critical raw materials or supplies, product-line improvements, pricing strategies and other important business considerations. A swimming-pool manufacturer might want to purchase stock in a diving-board company, a landscape company, a swimsuit maker or some other corporation with related business.

Why doesn't the investor simply diversify its own operations, expanding into diving boards, landscaping, swimsuits and other related products? The cost may be too great. Also, the investor may not have experience with these other products. Why challenge a successful business in the marketplace when the investor can "buy into" a successful corporation's existing operations? The reasons for investing in a corporation in order to affect its operations to some degree make corporate investments attractive to many businesses.

Investments are not without risk. To offset the ill effects of a sudden downturn in the operations of any one investee, smart investors diversify by holding a portfolio of stocks. The portfolio holds investments in different companies. By diversifying its holdings, the investor gains protection from losing too much if any one investee runs into problems and its stock price plummets.

Classifying Stock Investments

Investments in stock are assets to the investor. The investments may be short-term or long-term. Short-term investments are typically decribed on the balance sheet as **temporary investments, marketable securities** or **short-term investments** and are classified as current assets. To be listed on the balance sheet as current assets,

EXHIBIT 17-2   *Reporting Investments on the Balance Sheet*

Current Assets		
Cash..	$X	
Short-term investments..	**X**	
Accounts receivable	X	
Inventories..	X	
Prepaid expenses...	X	
Total current assets...		$X
Long-term investments (or simply, **Investments**)...............................		**X**
Property, plant and equipment		X
Intangible assets		X
Other assets		X

investments must be liquid (readily convertible to cash). Also, the investor's intent is important; the investor must intend either to convert the investments to cash within one year or to use them to pay a current liability. Investments not meeting these two requirements are classified on the balance sheet as **long-term investments**.

Short-term investments include treasury bills, certificates of deposit, and stocks and bonds of other companies. Long-term investments include bond sinking funds, and stocks, bonds and other assets that the investor expects to hold longer than one year or that are not readily marketable, for instance, real estate not used in the operations of the business. Exhibit 17-2 shows the positions of short-term and long-term investments on the balance sheet.

Observe that we report assets in the order of their liquidity. Cash is the most liquid asset, followed by Short-Term Investments, Accounts Receivable, and so on. Long-Term Investments are less liquid than Current Assets but more liquid than Property, Plant and Equipment.

Accounting for Stock Investments

Accounting for stock investments varies with the nature and extent of the investment. The specific accounting method that GAAP directs us to follow depends first on whether the investment is short-term or long-term and second on the percentage of the investee's voting stock that the investor holds.

Short-term Investments: The Cost Method (with LCM)

The **cost method** (with lower of cost or market) is used to account for short-term investments in stock. Cost is used as the initial amount for recording investments and as the basis for measuring gains and losses on their sale. These investments are reported on the balance sheet at the *lower of their cost or market value*. Therefore, we refer to the overall method as cost (with lower of cost or market or LCM).

All investments, including short-term investments, are recorded initially at cost. Cost is the price paid for the stock plus the brokerage commission. Accountants have no separate account for the brokerage commission paid. Suppose that Athabasca Ltd. purchases 1,000 shares of Noranda Inc. common stock at the market price of 36¼ and pays a $500 commission. Athabasca intends to sell this investment within one year or less and, therefore, classifies it as short-term. Athabasca's entry to record the investment is

Aug. 22	Short-term Investment in Noranda Common	
	Stock [(1,000 × $36.25) + $500].....................	36,750

Cash.. 36,750
Purchased 1,000 shares of Noranda common
stock at $36.25 plus commission of $500.

Assume Athabasca receives a $.22 per share cash dividend on the Noranda stock. Athabasca's entry to record receipt of the dividends is

Oct. 14   Cash (1,000 × $.22) 220
                Dividend Revenue...................................... 220
          Received $.22 per share cash dividend on
          Noranda common stock.

OBJECTIVE 1

Account for stock investments by the cost (LCM) method

Dividends do not accrue with the passage of time (as interest does). The investee has no liability for dividends until the dividends are declared. An investor makes no accrual entry for dividend revenue at year end in anticipation of a dividend declaration.

However, if a dividend declaration *does* occur before year end, say, on December 28, the investor *may* debit Dividend Receivable and credit Dividend Revenue on that date. The investor would then report this receivable and the revenue in the December 31 financial statements. Receipt of the cash dividend in January would be recorded by a debit to Cash and a credit to Dividend Receivable. The more common practice, however, is to record the dividend as income when it is received.

Receipt of a *stock* dividend is not income to the investor, and no formal journal entry is needed. As we have seen, a stock dividend increases the number of shares held by the investor but does not affect the total cost of the investment. The *cost per share* of the stock investment therefore decreases. The investor usually makes a memorandum entry of the number of dividend shares received and the new cost per share. Assume that Athabasca Ltd. receives a 10 percent stock dividend on its 1,000-share investment in Noranda, which cost $36,750. Athabasca would make a memorandum entry along this line:

Nov. 22   Received 100 shares of Noranda common stock in
          10 percent stock dividend. New cost per share is $33.41
          ($36,750/1,100 shares).

Any gain or loss on the sale of the investment is the difference between the sale proceeds and the cost of the investment. Assume that Athabasca sells 400 shares of Noranda stock for $35 per share, less a $280 commission. The entry to record the sale is

Dec. 18   Cash [(400 × $35) – $280] 13,720
                Short-Term Investment in Noranda
                Common Stock (400 × $33.41) 13,364
                Gain on Sale of Investment.................. 356
          Sold 400 shares of investment in Noranda
          common stock.

Observe that the cost per share of the investment ($33.41) is based on the total number of shares held, including those received as a dividend.

Reporting Short-Term Investments at Lower of Cost or Market (LCM)

Because of accounting conservatism, short-term investments are reported at the lower of their cost or market (LCM or LOCAM) value. Canadian practice, in the absence of standards in the *CICA Handbook,* is to calculate market value on an investment-by-investment basis or on the portfolio as a whole. In either event, the basis of valuation for cost and market values should be disclosed. Assume a company owns three short-term investments with the following costs and market values:

Short-term Investment Portfolio

Stock	Cost	Current Market Value
Dofasco Inc.	$155,625	$126,275
Toronto-Dominion Bank	67,000	86,200
George Weston Limited	186,000	174,500
Total	$408,625	$386,975

The investor owning the portfolio has two choices when determining the value of the portfolio for balance sheet purposes. The first considers the portfolio on a security-by-security basis. The investor would write the book value of the two stocks (Dofasco and Weston) whose market price has dropped below the price paid for them, down to their market values of $126,275 and $174,500 respectively. The market price of Toronto-Dominion is greater than cost, so no adjustment would be made to its book value. The journal entry to record the write down would be as follows:

Loss of Marketable Securities	40,850	
Marketable Securities...		40,850

To write down investment in Dofasco ($155,625 – $126,275 = $29,350) and George Weston ($186,000 – $174,500 = $11,500) to market.

The investor's balance sheet would report short-term investments as follows:

Current Assets

Cash	$	XXX
Short-term investments, at lower of cost or market value (note 4)		367,775
Accounts receivable, net of allowance of $XXX		XXX

Note 4. Short-Term Investments
Short-term investments are reported at the lower of their cost or market value. At December 31, 19XX, market value was $386,975.

Under this option, the investor would write down the book value of individual stocks to their market values, where cost was greater than market, irrespective of whether or not the total market value of the portfolio was greater than or less than cost.

The investor's other option would be to apply the LCM rule to the entire portfolio and write it down to market. The journal entry to record the write down would be

Loss on Marketable Securities	21,650	
Marketable Securities...		21,650

To write down investment portfolio to market.

The investor's balance sheet would report short-term investments as follows:

Current Assets

Cash...	$	XXX
Short-term investments, at market value (note 4)		386,975
Accounts receivable, net of allowance of $XXX.............................		XXX

Note 4. Short-term Investments
Short-term investments are reported at the lower of their cost or market value. At December 31,
19XX, cost was $408,625.

Under the second option, if the portfolio cost is lower than market value, the investor reports short-term investments at cost and discloses market value in the note.

Conservatism requires that an investor write the book value of stocks or portfolios down to market when cost exceeds market, but does not permit the investor to write up the book value of those same stocks or portfolios when their market value subsequently rises above the written down book values.

Long-Term Investments

An investor may own numerous investments, some short-term and others long-term. For accounting purposes, the two investment portfolios are not mixed. They are reported separately on the balance sheet, as shown in Exhibit 17-2. *Long-term* is not often used in the account title. An investment is understood to be long-term unless specifically labeled as short-term and included with current assets.

Long-term investments may be of several different types depending on the purpose of the investment and thus the percentage of voting interest acquired. Each of the three types is introduced in the following paragraphs and discussed more fully in turn below.

An investor may make a *portfolio investment* where the purpose is similar to that of short-term investing; the investor will hold the investment to earn dividends or interest but has no long-term interest in the investee. In such a situation, the investor will generally hold less than 20 percent of the voting interest of the investee. Such an investor would normally account for the investment using the *cost method*.

An investor may also make an investment in the investee of such magnitude that the investor exerts a significant influence on the investee. An investor holding more than 20 percent of the voting interest of the investee generally, but not always, is considered to exert significant influence. Such an investor would normally account for the investment using the *equity method*.

The investor may make an investment in the investee that exceeds 50 percent of the voting interest and thus is able to control the operations and activities of the investee. Such investees are called subsidiaries; subsidiaries's financial statements are normally consolidated with those of the parent.

Long-Term Investments Accounted for by the Cost Method

Accounting for portfolio investments follows the procedures outlined for short-term investments, that is, the **cost method**. The beginning accounting value is cost, which is debited to an Investments account at the date of purchase. Dividends are treated as income. Gains and losses are recorded on sales. Long-term investments are normally reported on the balance sheet at cost. Section 3050.20 states that if the market price of one of the stocks in the portfolio drops below cost, and the decline is thought to be other than temporary, the stock's book value would be written down to market and carried at that value in the future. The determination of whether or not the decline is temporary is management's.

Long-Term Investments Accounted for by the Equity Method

The cost method of accounting for long-term investments applies when an investor holds less than 20 percent of the investee's voting stock. Such an investor usually plays no important role in the investee's operations. However, an investee with a larger stock holding (normally thought of as being between 20 percent and 50 percent of the investee's voting stock) may significantly influence how the investee operates the business. Such an investor can likely affect the investee's decisions on dividend policy, product lines, sources of supply and other important matters. Since the investor has a voice in shaping business policy and operations, accountants believe that some measure of the business's success and failure should be included in accounting for the investment. We use the equity method to account for investments in which the investor can significantly influence the decision of the investee.

Investments accounted for by the **equity method** are recorded initially at cost. Suppose Nova Corp. pays $400,000 for 30 percent of the common stock of White Rock Corporation. Nova's entry to record the purchase of this investment is

Jan. 6	Investment in White Rock Common Stock .	400,000	
	Cash..		400,000
	To purchase 30% investment in White Rock		
	common stock.		

Under the equity method, Nova, as the investor, applies its percentage of ownership, 30 percent in our example, in recording its share of the investee's net income and dividends. If White Rock reports net income of $125,000 for the year, Nova records 30 percent of this amount as an increase in the investment account and as equity-method investment revenue, as follows:

OBJECTIVE 2

Use the equity method for stock investments

Dec. 31	Investment in White Rock Common		
	Stock ($125,000 × .30)	37,500	
	Equity-Method Investment Revenue		37,500
	To record 30% of White Rock net income.		

The Investment Revenue account carries the Equity-Method label to identify its source. This labeling is similar to distinguishing Sales Revenue from Service Revenue.

The investor increases the Investment account and records Investment Revenue when the investee reports income because of the close relationship between the two companies. As the investee's owner equity increases, so does the Investment account on the books of the investor.

Nova records its proportionate part of cash dividends received from White Rock. Assuming White Rock declares and pays a cash dividend of $50,000, Nova receives 30 percent of this dividend, recording it as follows:

Jan. 17	Cash ($50,000 × .30)	15,000	
	Investment in White Rock Common Stock		15,000
	To record receipt of 30% of White Rock		
	cash dividend.		

Observe that the Investment account is credited for the receipt of a dividend on an equity-method investment. Why? It is because the dividend decreases the investee's owner's equity and so it also reduces the investor's investment. In effect, the investor received cash for this portion of the investment.

After the above entries are posted, Nova's Investment account reflects its equity in the net assets of White Rock:

Investment in White Rock Common Stock

19X1			19X2		
Jan. 6	Purchase	400,000	Jan.17	Dividends	15,000
Dec. 31	Net income	37,500			
19X2					
Jan. 17	Balance	422,500			

Gain or loss on the sale of an equity-method investment is measured as the difference between the sale proceeds and the carrying value of the investment. For example, sale of one tenth of the White Rock common stock for $41,000 would be recorded as follows:

Feb. 13	Cash	41,000	
	Loss on Sale of Investment...............................	1,250	
	Investment in White Rock Common Stock		
	($422,500 × 1⁄10)		42,250
	Sold one-tenth of investment in White Rock		
	common stock.		

Companies with investments accounted for by the equity method often refer to the investee as an affiliated company. The account title Investments in Affiliated Companies refers to investments that are accounted for by the equity method.

Long-Term Investments Accounted for by the Consolidation Method

Most large corporations own controlling interests in other corporations. A **controlling** (or **majority**) **interest** is normally the ownership of more than 50 percent of the investee's voting stock. Such an investment enables the investor to elect a majority of the investee's board of directors and so control the investee. The investor is called the **parent** company, and the investee company, as mentioned earlier, is called the **subsidiary**. For example, Loblaw Companies Limited, the grocery store chain, is 70 percent owned by George Weston Ltd. Galen Weston and the other shareholders of George Weston Ltd. control that company and, because George Weston Ltd. owns Loblaw, they also control Loblaw.

Why have subsidiaries? Why not have the corporation take the form of a single legal entity? Subsidiaries may limit the parent's liabilities in a risky venture, and may ease expansion into foreign countries. For example, Chieftain International, Inc., the natural gas and oil exploration and production company located in Edmonton, has a U.S. subsidiary, Chieftain International (U.S.) Inc., and two U.K. subsidiaries, Chieftain Exploration (U.K.) Limited and Chieftan International North Sea Limited. Those companies conduct operations for Chieftain in those two countries respectively.

Consolidation accounting is a method of combining the financial statements of two or more companies that are controlled by the same owners. This method implements the entity concept by reporting a single set of financial statements for the consolidated entity, which carries the name of the parent company.

Consolidated statements combine the balance sheets, income statements, and other financial statements of the parent company with those of the subsidiaries into an overall set as if the parents and its subsidiaries were a single entity. The goal is to provide a better perspective on operations than could be obtained by examining the separate reports of each of the individual companies. The assets, liabilities, revenues and expenses of each subsidiary are added to the parent's accounts. The consolidated financial statements (balance sheet, income statement, and so on) present the combined account balances. For example, the balance in the Cash account of Loblaw Companies is added to the balance in the George Weston Ltd. Cash account, and the sum of the two amounts is presented as a single amount in the consolidated balance sheet of George Weston Ltd. Each account balance of a subsidiary loses its identity in the consolidated statements. George Weston Ltd. financial statements are entitled "George Weston Ltd. and Consolidated Subsidiaries." Loblaw Companies and the names of all other George Weston Ltd. subsidiaries do not appear in the statement titles. But the names of the subsidiary companies are listed in the parent company's annual report. A reader of corporate annual reports

Exhibit 17-3   *Parent Company with Consolidated Subsidiaries and an Equity Method Investment*

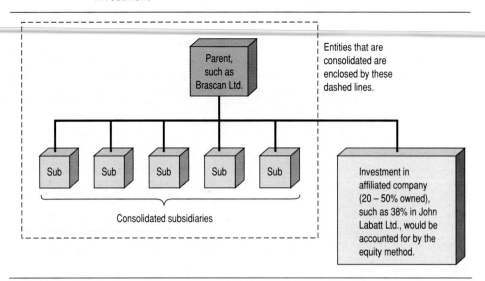

cannot hope to understand them without knowing how consolidated statements are prepared. Exhibit 17-3 diagrams a corporate structure whose parent corporation owns controlling interests in five subsidiary companies and an equity-method investment in another investee company.

<table>
<tr><td>

OBJECTIVE 3

Consolidate parent and subsidiary balance sheets

</td><td>

Consolidated Balance Sheet: Parent Owns All of Subsidiary's Stock   Suppose that Parent Corporation purchased all the outstanding common stock of Subsidiary Corporation at its book value of $150,000. In addition, Parent Corporation loaned Subsidiary Corporation $80,000. Note that the $150,000 is paid to the former owners of Susidiary Corporation as private investors. The $150,000 is not an addition to the existing assets and shareholder's equity of Subsidiary Corporation. That is, the books of Subsidiary Corporation are completely unaffected by Parent Corporation's initial investment and Parent's subsequent acccounting for that investment. Subsidiary Corporation is not dissolved. It lives on as a separate legal entity but with a new owner, Parent Corporation.

</td></tr>
</table>

Parent Books[2]		**Subsidiary Books**	
Investment in Subsidiary			
Corporation	150,000	No entry	
Cash		150,000	Cash	80,000
Note receivable from			Note Payable	
Subsidiary	80,000	to Parent		80,000
Cash		80,000		

Each legal entity has its individual set of books. The consolidated entity does not keep a separate set of books. Instead a work sheet is used to prepare the consolidated statements. A major concern in consolidation accounting is this: *Do not double-count.*

Companies may prepare a consolidated balance sheet immediately after acquisition. The consolidated balance sheet shows all the assets and liabilities of the parent and the subsidiary. The Investment in Subsidiary account on the parent's books

---

[2] The parent company may use either the cost method or the equity method for work sheet entries to the Investment account. Regardless of the method used, the consolidated statements are the same. Advanced accounting courses deal with this topic.

represents all the assets and liabilities of the subsidiary. The consolidated statements cannot show both the investment account plus the amounts for the subsidiaries assets and liabilities. That would count the same resources twice. In fact, the intercompany accounts — those that appear in both the parent's books and the subsidiary's books — should not be included in the consolidated statements at all. To avoid this double-counting we eliminate (a) the $150,000 Investment in Subsidiary on the parent's books, and the $150,000 shareholder's equity on the subsidiary's books (which consists of $100,000 Common Stock and $50,000 Retained Earnings) and (b) the intercompany $80,000 note.

Explanation of Elimination   Entry (a). Exhibit 17-4 shows the work sheet for consolidating the balance sheet. Consider the elimination entry for the parent-subsidiary ownership accounts, which are intercompany accounts. Entry (a) credits the parent Investment account to eliminate its debit balance. It also eliminates the subsidiary's shareholder's equity accounts by debiting Common Stock for $110,000 and Retained Earnings for $50,000. The resulting consolidated balance sheet reports no Investment in Subsidiary account, and the Common Stock and Retained Earnings are those of the parent Corporation only. The consolidated balance sheet amounts are in the final column of the consolidation work sheet.

> **OBJECTIVE 4**
>
> Eliminate intercompany items from a consolidated balance sheet

In summary, if the intercompany accounts were not eliminated, there would be double-counting in the consolidated statement. The following chart summarizes the parent-subsidiary relationship:

Entity	Types of Records
Parent Corporation	Parent books
+ Subsidiary Corporation	Subsidiary books
= Preliminary consolidated balance sheet	No separate books, but periodically Parent and Subsidiary assets and liabilities are added together in a work sheet.
– Eliminating entries	Intercompany accounts are offset against each other to eliminate double-counting.
= Consolidated balance sheet to outside investors	The report of the overall economic entity.

EXHIBIT 17-4   *Work Sheet for Consolidated Balance Sheet: Parent Corporation Owns All of Subsidiary Corporation's Stock*

Assets	Parent Corporation	Subsidiary Corporation	Eliminations Debit	Eliminations Credit	Consolidated Amounts
Cash	12,000	18,000			30,000
Notes receivable from Subsidiary	80,000	—		(b) 80,000	—
Inventory	104,000	91,000			195,000
Investment in Subsidiary	150,000	—		(a) 150,000	—
Other assets	218,000	138,000			356,000
Total	564,000	247,000			581,000
Liabilities and Shareholders' Equity					
Accounts payable	43,000	17,000			60,000
Notes payable	190,000	80,000	(b) 80,000		190,000
Common stock	176,000	100,000	(a) 100,000		176,000
Retained earnings	155,000	50,000	(a) 50,000		155,000
Total	564,000	247,000	230,000	230,000	581,000

Explanation of Elimination   Entry (b). Parent Corporation loaned $80,000 to Subsidiary Corporation, and Subsidiary signed a note payable to Parent. Therefore, Parent's balance sheet includes an $80,000 note receivable and Subsidiary's balance sheet reports a note payable for this amount. This loan was entirely within the consolidated entity and so must be eliminated. Entry (b) accomplishes this. The $80,000 credit in the elimination column of the work sheet offsets Parent's debit balance in Notes Receivable from Subsidiary. After this work sheet entry, the consolidated amount for notes receivable is zero. The $80,000 debit in the elimination column offsets the credit balance of Subsidiary's notes payable, and the resulting consolidated amount for notes payable is the amount owed to those outside the consolidated entity.

Parent Company Buys Subsidiary's Stock at a Price above Book Value[3]   A company may acquire a controlling interest in a subsidiary by paying a price above the book value of the subsidiary's owners' equity, which we assume is equal to the fair value of the subsidiary's net assets (assets minus liabilities). The excess of the price paid over book value is *goodwill*. What drives a company's market value up? The company may create goodwill through its superior products, service, or location. Goodwill was discussed in Chapter 10.

The subsidiary does not record goodwill. Doing so would violate the reliability principle. Goodwill is recorded only when a company purchases it as part of the acquisition of another company, that is, when a parent company purchases a subsidiary. The goodwill is recorded in the process of consolidating the parent and subsidiary financial statements.

Suppose Parent Corporation paid $450,000 to acquire 100 percent of the common stock of Subsidiary Corporation, which had Common Stock of $200,000 and Retained Earnings of $180,000. Parent's payment included $70,000 for goodwill ($450,000 − $200,000 − $180,000 = $70,000). The entry to eliminate Parent's Investment account against Subsidiary's equity accounts is

Common Stock, Subsidiary	200,000	
Retained Earnings, Subsidiary	180,000	
Goodwill	70,000	
Investment in Subsidiary		450,000

To eliminate cost of investment in subsidiary against Subsidiary's equity balances and to recognize Subsidiary's unrecorded goodwill.

In actual practice, this entry would be made only on the consolidation work sheet. Here we show it in general journal form for instructional purposes.

The asset goodwill is reported on the consolidated balance sheet among the intangible assets, after capital assets. Goodwill is amortized to expense over its useful life, not to exceed 40 years.

Consolidated Balance Sheet: Parent Owns Less Than 100 Percent of Subsidiary's Stock   When a parent company owns more than 50 percent (a majority) of the subsidiary's stock but less than 100 percent of it, a new category of owners' equity, called minority interest, must appear on the consolidated balance sheet. Suppose Parent buys 75 percent of Subsidiary's common stock. The minority interest is the remaining 25 percent of Subsidiary's equity. Thus **minority interest** is the subsidiary's equity that is held by shareholders other than the parent company. While the *CICA Handbook* is silent on where minority interest should be disclosed on the balance sheet, accepted practice is to disclose it between liabilities and owner's equity.

---

[3] For simplicity, we are assuming that the fair market value of the subsidiary's net assets (assets minus liabilities) equals the book value of the company's owners' equity. Advanced courses consider other situations.

EXHIBIT 17-5 *Work Sheet for Consolidated Balance Sheet: Parent (P Ltd.) Owns Less Than 100 Percent of Subsidiary's (S Ltd.) Stock*

Assets	P Ltd.	S Ltd.	Eliminations Debit	Eliminations Credit	Consolidated Amounts
Cash...	33,000	18,000			51,000
Notes receivable from P......................	—	50,000		(b) 50,000	—
Accounts receivable, net.....................	54,000	39,000			93,000
Inventory	92,000	66,000			158,000
Investment in S	120,000	—		(a) 120,000	—
Plant and equipment, net....................	230,000	123,000			353,000
Total...	529,000	296,000			655,000
Liabilities and Shareholders' Equity					
Accounts payable...............................	141,000	94,000			235,000
Notes payable....................................	50,000	42,000	(b) 50,000		42,000
Common stock	170,000	100,000	(a) 100,000		170,000
Retained earnings	168,000	60,000	(a) 60,000		168,000
Minority interest	—	—		(a) 40,000	40,000
Total...	529,000	296,000	210,000	210,000	655,000

Assume P Ltd. buys 75 percent of S Ltd.'s common stock. Also, P owes S $50,000 on a note payable to S. Exhibit 17-5 is the consolidation work sheet. Again, focus on the Eliminations columns and the Consolidated Amounts.

Entry (a) eliminates P Ltd.'s Investment balance of $120,000 against the $160,000 owner's equity of S Ltd. Observe that all of S's equity is eliminated even though P holds only 75 percent of S's stock. The remaining 25 percent interest in S's equity is credited to Minority Interest ($160,000 × .25 = $40,000). Thus Entry (a) reclassifies 25 percent of S Ltd.'s equity as minority interest.

Entry (b) in Exhibit 17-5 eliminates S Ltd.'s $50,000 note receivable against P's note payable of the same amount. The consolidated amount of notes payable ($42,000) is the amount that S Ltd. owes to outsiders.

The consolidated balance sheet of P Ltd., based on the work sheet of Exhibit 17-5, is

P Ltd. and Consolidated Subsidiary
Consolidated Balance Sheet
December 31, 19XX

Assets

Cash...	$ 51,000
Accounts receivable, net..	93,000
Inventory...	158,000
Plant and equipment, net	353,000
Total assets...	$655,000

Liabilities and Shareholders' Equity

Accounts payable	$235,000
Notes payable...	42,000
Minority interest	40,000
Common stock	170,000
Retained earnings..	168,000
Total liabilities and shareholders' equity	$655,000

The consolidated balance sheet reveals that ownership of P Ltd. and its consolidated subsidiary is divided between P's shareholders (common stock and retained earnings totaling $338,000) and the minority shareholders of S Ltd. ($40,000).

Income of a Consolidated Entity   The income of a consolidated entity is the net income of the parent plus the parent's proportion of the subsidiaries' net income. Suppose Parent Inc. owns all the stock of Subsidiary S-1 Inc. and 60 percent of the stock of Subsidiary S-2 Inc. During the year just ended, Parent earned net income of $330,000, S-1 earned $150,000 and S-2 had a net loss of $100,000. Parent would report net income of $420,000, computed as follows:

	Net Income (Net Loss)	Parent Shareholders' Ownership	Parent Net Income (Net Loss)
Parent Inc............................	$330,000	100%	$330,000
Subsidiary S-1	150,000	100	150,000
Subsidiary S-2	(100,000)	60	(60,000)
Consolidated net income ...			$420,000

The parent's net income is the same amount that would be recorded under the equity method. However, the equity method stops short of reporting the investee's assets and liabilities on the parent balance sheet because with an investment in the range of 20 – 50 percent, the investor owns less than a controlling interest in the investee company.

The procedures for preparation of a consolidated income statement parallel those outlined above for the balance sheet. The consolidated income statement is discussed in an advanced course.

Investments in Bonds and Notes _____

Industrial and commercial companies invest far more in stock than they do in bonds. The major investors in bonds are financial institutions, such as pension plans, trust companies and insurance companies. For every issuer of bonds payable, at least one investor owns the bonds. The relationship between the issuer and the investor may be diagrammed as follows:

OBJECTIVE 5

Account for
investments in bonds

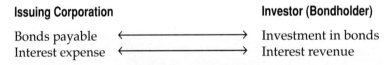

Issuing Corporation		Investor (Bondholder)
Bonds payable	⟷	Investment in bonds
Interest expense	⟷	Interest revenue

The dollar amount of a bond transaction is the same for issuer and investor, but the accounts debited and credited differ. However, the accounts are parallel. For example, the issuer's interest expense is the investor's interest revenue.

An investment in bonds is classified either as short-term (a current asset) or as long-term. An investment is a current asset if (1) the investment is liquid (can readily be sold for cash, such as a Government of Canada bond) and (2) the owner intends to convert it to cash within one year or to use it to pay a current liability. An investment that is intended to be held longer than a year is classified as long-term.

Bond investments are recorded at cost, which includes the purchase price and any brokerage fees. Amortization of bond premium or discount is *not* recorded on short-term investments because the investor plans to hold the bonds for so short a period that any amortization would be immaterial. On the other hand, investors hold long-term investments for a significant period and therefore amortize any premium or discount on the bonds.

Let us look at accounting for a *short-term* bond investment. Suppose that an investor purchases $10,000 of bonds on August 1, 19X2, paying 93 plus accrued interest and a brokerage commission of $250. The annual contract or stated interest rate is 12 percent, paid semiannually on April 1 and October 1. The cost of the bonds is $9,550 [($10,000 × .93) + $250]. In addition, the investor pays accrued interest for the four months (April through July) since the last interest payment. The investor records the purchase on August 1 as follows:

Aug. 1	Short-Term Investment in Bonds		
	[($10,000 × .93) + $250].................................	9,550	
	Interest Receivable ($10,000 × .12 × $^{4}/_{12}$)	400	
	Cash...		9,950
	To purchase short-term bond investment.		

Accrued interest is *not* included in the cost of the investment but is debited to Interest Receivable.

The investor's entry for receipt of the first semiannual interest amount on October 1 is

Oct. 1	Cash ($10,000 × .12 × $^{6}/_{12}$)	600	
	Interest Receivable		400
	Interest Revenue ($10,000 × .12 × $^{2}/_{12}$)		200
	To receive semiannual interest, part of which		
	was accrued.		

At October 1, the investor has held the bonds for two months. The entry correctly credits Interest Revenue for two months' interest. This entry does not include discount amortization on the bonds because the investment is short-term.

At December 31, the investor accrues interest revenue for three months (October, November and December), debiting Interest Receivable and crediting Interest Revenue for $300 ($10,000 × .12 × $^{3}/_{12}$). The investor's December 31 balance sheet reports the following information (we assume that the market price of the bonds is 96):

Current assets
Short-term investment in bonds (note 4)...................................... $9,550
Interest receivable 300

Note 4: Short-term investments
At December 31, the current market value of short-term investments in bonds was $9,600.

Observe that the investment is reported at cost, with the current market value disclosed in a note. The market value may also be reported parenthetically.

Current assets
Short-term investment in bonds
(Current market value, $9,600)... $9,550
Interest receivable... 300

The investor measures any gain or loss on sale as the difference between the sale price (less any broker's commission) and the cost of the investment. For example, sale of the bonds for $9,700 will result in a gain of $150. This gain is reported as Other Revenue on a multiple-step income statement or beneath Sales Revenue among the revenues and gains on a single-step statement. A loss would be reported as Other Expense on a multiple-step statement or among the expenses on a single-step statement.

Accounting for *long-term* investments in bonds follows the general pattern illustrated for short-term investments. For long-term investments, however, discount or premium is amortized to account more precisely for interest revenue. This additional step is needed because the bond investment will be held for longer than a year and, therefore, the amortization amount is likely to be material. The amortization of discount or premium on a bond investment affects Interest Revenue in the same way that the amortization affects Interest Expense for the company that issued the bonds.

The accountant records amortization on the cash interest dates and at year end, along with the accrual of interest receivable. Accountants rarely use separate discount and premium accounts for investments. Amortization of a discount is recorded by directly debiting the Long-Term Investment in Bonds account and crediting Interest Revenue. Amortization of a premium is credited directly to the Long-Term Investment account. This entry debits Interest Revenue. These entries bring the investment balance to the bonds' face value on the maturity date and record the correct amount of interest revenue each period.

Suppose the $10,000 of 12 percent bonds in the preceding illustration were purchased on August 1, 19X2, as a long-term investment. Interest dates are April 1 and October 1. These bonds mature on October 1, 19X6, so they will be outstanding for 50 months. Assume amortization of the discount by the straight-line method. The following entries for a long-term investment highlight the differences between accounting for a short-term bond investment and for a long-term bond investment:

Aug. 1	**Long-Term Investment in Bonds**			
	[($10,000 × .93) + $250]		9,550	
	Interest Receivable ($10,000 × .12 × $^4/_{12}$)		400	
	Cash			9,950
	To purchase long-term bond investment.			
Oct. 1	Cash ($10,000 × .12 × $^6/_{12}$)		600	
	Interest Receivable			400
	Interest Revenue ($10,000 × .12 × $^2/_{12}$)			200
	To receive semiannual interest, part of which was accrued.			
Oct. 1	**Long-Term Investment in Bonds**			
	[($10,000 − $9,550)/50 × 2]		**18**	
	Interest Revenue			**18**
	To amortize discount on bond investment for two months.			
Dec. 31	Interest Receivable ($10,000 × .12 × $^3/_{12}$)		300	
	Interest Revenue			300
	To accrue interest revenue for three months.			
Dec. 31	**Long-term Investment in Bonds**			
	[($10,000 − $9,550)/50 × 3]		**27**	
	Interest Revenue			**27**
	To amortize discount on bond investment for three months.			

The financial statements at December 31, 19X2 report the following effects of this long-term investment in bonds (assume the bonds' market price is 102):

Balance sheet at December 31, 19X2:
  Current assets
    Interest receivable .... $ 300
    Total current assets .... X,XXX

  Long-term investments in bonds ($9,550 + $18 + $27) — note 6 9,595

  Note 6: Long-term investments.
  At December 31, 19X1, the current market value of long-term investments in bonds was $10,200.

Income statement (multiple-step) for the year ended December 31, 19X2:
  Other revenues
    Interest revenue ($200 + $18 + $300 + $27) $545

EXHIBIT 17-6 *Accounting Methods for Investments*

Type of Investments	Accounting Method
Short-term investment in stock..	Cost (lower of cost or market)
Long-term investment in stock	
Investor owns less than 20 percent of investee stock.........	Cost (lower of cost or market if decline in market is not temporary)
Investor owns 20 – 50 percent of investee stock.................	Equity
Investor owns greater than 50 percent of investee stock ...	Consolidation
Short-term investment in bonds..	Cost (lower of cost or market)
Long-term investment in bonds	Amortized cost

In particular, note that the long-term bonds are reported by the *amortized cost* method.

The amortization entry for a premium debits Interest Revenue and credits Long-Term Investment in Bonds. Where discount or premium is amortized by the straight-line method, accounting for long-term investments follows the pattern illustrated above. Effective-interest amortization amounts are computed as shown for bonds payable in Chapter 16.

Exhibit 17-6 summarizes the accounting methods for investments.

Summary Problem for Your Review

This problem consists of four independent items.

1. Identify the appropriate accounting method for each of the following situations:

   a. Investment in 25 percent of investee's stock and investor plans to hold

   b. Investor intends to sell three months after year end

   c. Investment in more than 50 percent of investee's stock

2. At what amount should the following long-term investment portfolio be reported on the Decmber 31 balance sheet? All the investments are less than 5 percent of the investee's stock. Journalize any adjusting entry required by these data.

Stock	Investment Cost	Current Market Value
Dreco Energy Services	$10,750	$17,750
Loblaw Companies	5,000	9,125
National Trust	26,250	18,750

3. Investor Ltd. paid $67,900 to acquire a 40 percent equity-method investment in the common stock of Investee Ltd. At the end of the first year, Investee's net

income was $80,000, and Investee declared and paid cash dividends of $55,000. Journalize Investor's (a) purchase of the investment, (b) share of Investee's net income, (c) receipt of dividends from Investee, and (d) sale of Investee stock for $80,100.

4. Parent Corp. paid $100,000 for all the common stock of Subsidiary Corp., and Parent owes Subsidiary $20,000 on a note payable. Assume the fair value of Subsidiary's net assets is equal to book value. Complete the following consolidation work sheet:

Assets	Parent Corp.	Subsidiary Corp.	Eliminations Debit	Credit	Consolidated Amounts
Cash	7,000	4,000			
Note receivable from Parent	—	20,000			
Investment in Subsidiary	100,000	—			
Goodwill	—	—			
Other assets	108,000	99,000			
Total	215,000	123,000			
Liabilities and Shareholders' Equity					
Accounts payable	15,000	8,000			
Notes payable	20,000	30,000			
Common stock	135,000	60,000			
Retained earnings	45,000	25,000			
Total	215,000	123,000			

SOLUTION TO SUMMARY PROBLEM

1. a. Equity   b. Cost (LCM)   c. Consolidation
2. There are two possible solutions to this problem:

   a. Report the investments at cost, $45,625, because total cost is less than total market. No journal entry required.

Stock	Investment Cost	Current Market Value
Dreco Energy Services	$10,750	$17,750
Loblaw Companies	5,000	9,125
National Trust	26,250	18,750
Totals	$42,250	$45,625

   b. Report the investments at the lower of cost or market on an investment-by-investment basis because the market value for one or more of the investments (National Trust) is less than cost.

Stock (Note)	Lower of Investment Cost and Current Market Value
Dreco Energy Services	$10,750
Loblaw Companies	5,000
National Trust	18,750
Total	$34,500

Note: Market value is $45,625.

Adjusting entry:
Unrealized Loss on Long-Term Investments
($26,250 – $18,750) 7,500
Long-Term Investments.................................. 7,500
To write investments down to market value.

3.   a. Investment in Investee Common Stock 67,900
Cash 67,900
To purchase 40 percent investment in Investee
common stock.

b. Investment in Investee Common Stock
($80,000 × .40) 32,000
Equity-Method Investment Revenue................. 32,000
To record 40 percent of Investee net income.

c. Cash ($55,000 × .40) 22,000
Investment in Investee Common Stock............. 22,000
To record receipt of 40 percent of Investee cash
dividend.

d. Cash 80,100
Investment in Investee Common Stock
($67,900 + $32,000 – $22,000) 77,900
Gain on Sale of Investment 2,200
Sold investment in Investee common stock.

4.   Consolidation work sheet:

Assets	Parent Corp.	Subsidiary Corp.	Eliminations Debit	Eliminations Credit	Consolidated Amounts
Cash...	7,000	4,000			11,000
Note receivable from Parent	—	20,000		(a) 20,000	—
Investment in Subsidiary	100,000	—		(b) 100,000	—
Goodwill	—	—	(b) 15,000		15,000
Other assets	108,000	99,000			207,000
Total	215,000	123,000			233,000
Liabilities and Shareholders' Equity					
Accounts payable	15,000	8,000			23,000
Notes payable..	20,000	30,000	(a) 20,000		30,000
Common stock...	135,000	60,000	(b) 60,000		135,000
Retained earnings...................................	45,000	25,000	(b) 25,000		45,000
Total	215,000	123,000	120,000	120,000	233,000

Accounting for International Operations

Did you know that Inco and Bombardier earn more than half their revenues outside
of Canada? It is common for Canadian companies to do a large part of their business abroad. John Labatt, Molson, Northern Telecom, Alcan Aluminium, and McCain
Foods (as noted in the vignette), among others, are very active in other countries.

Accounting for business activities across national boundaries makes up the field
of *international accounting*. As communications and transportation improve and
trade barriers fall, global integration makes international accounting more important.

Economic Structures and Their Impact on International Accounting

The business environment varies widely across the globe. Toronto, Montreal and Vancouver reflect the diversity of the market-driven economy of Canada. Japan's economy is similar to ours, although Japanese business activity focuses more on imports and exports. The central government has controlled the economy of Hungary and other Eastern-bloc countries, so private business decisions are only beginning to take root there. In Brazil, extremely high rates of inflation have made historical-cost amounts meaningless. Accountants must continually adjust the price levels because of the rapid change in the value of the cruzeiro, Brazil's monetary unit. International accounting deals with these and other differences in economic structures.

Foreign Currencies and Foreign-Currency Exchange Rates

Each country uses its own national currency. Assume Spar Aerospace, sells a "space arm" to the U.S. NASA for use on a space shuttle. Will Spar receive Canadian dollars or U.S. dollars? If the transaction takes place in Canadian dollars, NASA must exchange its U.S. dollars for Canadian dollars in order to pay Spar Aerospace in Canadian currency. If the transaction takes place in U.S. dollars, Spar will receive U.S. dollars which it must exchange for Canadian dollars. In either case, a step has been added to the transaction: one company must convert domestic currency into foreign currency, or the other company must convert foreign currency into domestic currency.

The price of one nation's currency may be stated in terms of another country's monetary unit. This measure of one currency against another currency is called the **foreign-currency exchange rate**. In Exhibit 17-7, the dollar value of a French franc is $.41. This means that one French franc could be bought for forty-one cents. Other currencies, such as the pound and the yen (also listed in Exhibit 17-7), are similarly bought and sold.

We use the exchange rate to convert the cost of an item given in one currency to its cost in a second currency. We call this conversion a *translation*. Suppose an item costs two hundred French francs. To compute its cost in dollars, we multiply the amount in francs by the conversion rate: 200 French francs × $.41 = $82.

To aid the flow of international business, a market exists for foreign currencies. Traders buy and sell Canadian dollars, U.S. dollars, French francs, and other currencies in the same way that they buy and sell other commodities like beef, cotton, and automobiles. And just as supply and demand cause the prices of these other commodities to shift, so supply and demand for a particular currency cause exchange rates to fluctuate daily. When the demand for a nation's currency

Exhibit 17-7   *Foreign-Currency Exchange Rates*

Country	Monetary Unit	Dollar Value	Country	Monetary Unit	Dollar Value
United States	Dollar	$1.25	Great Britain	Pound	$2.02
European Common Market	European Currency Unit	1.62	Italy	Lira	.001
France	Franc	.41	Japan	Yen	.010
Germany	Mark	1.20	Mexico	Peso	.0004

Source: *The Financial Post*, October 20, 1992, p. 49.

exceeds the supply of that currency, its exchange rate rises. When supply exceeds demand, the currency's exchange rate falls.

Two main factors determine the supply and demand for a particular currency: (1) the ratio of a country's imports to its exports, and (2) the rate of return available in the country's capital markets.

The Import/Export Ratio   Japanese exports far surpass Japan's imports. Customers of Japanese companies must buy yen (the Japanese unit of currency) in the international currency market to pay for their purchases. This strong demand drives up the price—the foreign exchange rate—of the yen. France, on the other hand, imports more goods than it exports. French businesses must sell francs in order to buy the foreign currencies needed to acquire the foreign goods. This increases the supply of the French franc and so decreases its price.

The Rate of Return   The rate of return available in a country's capital markets affects the amount of investment funds flowing into the country. When rates of return are high in a politically stable country such as Canada, international investors buy stocks, bonds, and real estate in that country. This increases the demand for the nation's currency and drives up its exchange rate.

Currencies are often described in the financial press as "strong" or "weak." What do these terms mean? The exchange rate of a **strong currency** is rising relative to other nations' currencies. The exchange rate of a **weak currency** is falling relative to other currencies.

Suppose on October 5 *The Financial Post* listed the exchange rate for the British pound as $2.01. On January 6 the rate has changed to $1.99. We would say that the dollar has risen against the British pound—the dollar is stronger than the pound—because the pound has become less expensive, and so the dollar now buys more pounds. A stronger dollar would make travel to England more attractive to Canadians.

Assume that *The Financial Post* reports a rise in the exchange rate of the Japanese yen from $.010 to $.011. This indicates that the yen is stronger than the dollar. Japanese automobiles, cameras, and electronic products are more expensive because each dollar buys fewer yen.

In our example situation—in which the pound has dropped relative to the dollar and the yen has risen relative to the dollar—we would describe the yen as the strongest currency, the pound as the weakest currency, and the dollar as somewhere between the other two currencies.

Accounting for International Transactions _____

When a Canadian company transacts business with a foreign company, the transaction price can be stated either in dollars or in the national currency of the other company. If the price is stated in dollars, the Canadian company has no special accounting difficulties. The transaction is recorded and reported in dollars exactly as though the other company were also Canadian.

> **OBJECTIVE 6**
> Account for transactions stated in a foreign currency

Purchases on Account

If the transaction price is stated in units of the foreign currency, the Canadian company encounters two accounting steps. First, the transaction price must be translated into dollars for recording in the accounting records. Second, credit transactions (the most common international transaction) usually cause the Canadian company to experience a **foreign-currency transaction gain** or **loss**. This type of gain or loss occurs when the exchange rate changes between the date of the purchase on account and the date of the subsequent payment of cash.

The credit purchase creates an Account Payable that is recorded at the prevailing exchange rate. Later, when the buyer pays cash, the exchange rate has almost certainly changed. Accounts Payable is debited for the amount recorded earlier, and Cash is credited for the amount paid at the current exchange rate. A debit difference is a loss, and a credit difference is a gain.

Suppose on November 1, Eaton's Department Store imports Shalimar perfume from a French supplier at a price of 200,000 francs. The exchange rate is $.41 per French franc. Eaton's records this credit purchase as follows:

April. 1	Purchases...	82,000	
	Accounts Payable (200,000 × $.41)..............		82,000

Eaton's translates the French franc price of the merchandise (200,000 Fr) into dollars ($82,000) for recording the purchase and the related account payable.

If Eaton's were to pay this account immediately (which is unlikely in international commerce) Eaton's would debit Accounts Payable and credit Cash for $82,000. Suppose, however, that the credit terms specify payment within 60 days. On May 20, when Eaton's pays this debt, the exchange rate has fallen to $.40 per French franc. Eaton's payment entry is

May 20	Accounts Payable...	82,000	
	Cash (200,000 × $.40).......................................		80,000
	Foreign-Currency Transaction Gain...........		2,000

Eaton's has a gain because the company has settled the debt with fewer dollars than the amount of the original account payable. If on the payment date the exchange rate of the French franc had exceeded $.41, Eaton's would have paid more dollars than the original $82,000. The company would have recorded a loss on the transaction as a debit to Foreign-Currency Transaction Loss.

Sales on Account

International sales on account also may be measured in foreign currency. Suppose Bombardier sells some Ski Doos to the German government on December 9. The price of the Ski Doos is 140,000 German marks, and the exchange rate is $1.18 per German mark. Bombardier's sale entry is

Dec. 9	Accounts Receivable (140,000 × $1.18)	165,200	
	Sales revenue		165,200

Assume Bombardier collects from Germany on December 30, when the exchange rate has fallen to $1.15 per German mark. Bombardier receives fewer dollars than the recorded amount of the receivable and so experiences a foreign-currency transaction loss. The collection entry is

Dec. 30	Cash (140,000 × $1.15).......................................	161,000	
	Foreign-Currency Transaction Loss................	4,200	
	Accounts Receivable.....................................		165,200

Foreign-Currency Transaction Gains and Losses are combined for each accounting period. The net amount of gain or loss can be reported as Other Revenue and Expense on the income statement.

Unrealized Foreign-Currency Transaction Gains and Losses   Foreign-currency transactions gains and losses are *realized* when cash is paid or received. In the illustrations thus far, cash receipts and cash payments occurred in the same period as the related sale or purchase. This will not always be the case. For example, in the preceding example, suppose Bombardier collects from the German government during February. At January 31, the German mark is worth only $1.17.

This is $.01 less than the exchange rate at which Bombardier recorded the receivable. In this case Bombardier will record a foreign-currency transaction loss for the decrease in the dollar value of the account receivable. The adjusting entry is

Jan. 31	Foreign-Currency Transaction Loss		
	[140,000 × ($1.18 − $1.17)]...........................	1,400	
	Accounts Receivable..................................		1,400

This loss is *unrealized* in the sense that Bombardier has not yet received cash from the customer. Suppose Bombardier collects on February 7, when the exchange rate is $1.14 per mark. The cash receipt entry records a further loss as follows:

Jan. 9	Cash (140,000 × $1.14).....................................	159,600	
	Foreign-Currency Transaction Loss		
	[140,000 × ($1.17 − $1.14)]...........................	4,200	
	Accounts Receivable (165,200 − $1,400)...		163,800

Bombardier would have recorded a foreign-currency transaction gain on February 7 if the exchange rate had exceeded $1.17 per German mark. In that case the cash collection would have been greater than the carrying amount of Accounts Receivable.

Hedging: A Strategy to Avoid Foreign-Currency Transaction Losses

One approach to avoiding foreign-currency transaction losses is to insist that international transactions be settled in dollars, which puts the burden of currency translation on the foreign party. However, that strategy may alienate customers and result in lost sales, or it may cause suppliers to demand unreasonable credit terms. Another way for a company to insulate itself from the effects of fluctuating foreign-currency exchange rates is called hedging.

Hedging means to protect oneself from losing by engaging in a counterbalancing transaction. A Canadian company selling goods measured in Mexican pesos expects to receive a fixed number of pesos in the future. If the peso is weak, the Canadian company would expect the pesos to be worth fewer dollars than the amount of the receivable — an expected loss situation.

The Canadian company may have accumulated payables stated in Mexican pesos. Losses on the receipt of pesos would be approximately offset by gains on the payment of pesos to Mexican suppliers. Most companies do not have equal amounts of receivables and payables in the same foreign currency. However, buying futures contracts in the foreign currency to sell the foreign currency at a future date effectively creates a payable to offset a receivable and vice versa. Many companies that do business internationally use hedging techniques.

Consolidation of Foreign Subsidiaries

A Canadian company with a foreign subsidiary must consolidate the subsidiary's financial statements into its own statements for reporting to the public. The consolidation of a foreign subsidiary poses two special challenges. Many countries outside Canada specify accounting treatments that differ from Canadian accounting principles. For the purpose of reporting to the Canadian public, accountants for the parent company must first bring the subsidiary's statements into conformity with Canadian GAAP.

The second challenge arises when the subsidiary statements are expressed in a foreign currency. A preliminary step in the consolidation process is to translate the subsidiary statements into dollars. The *CICA Handbook* in Section 1650, "Foreign

Currency Translation," details two kinds of foreign operation, each of which embraces a different translation process. Further discussion of the translation process is the subject of an advanced financial accounting course and will not be covered in this text.

The process of translating a foreign subsidiary's financial statements into dollars may create a *foreign-currency translation adjustment*. This item appears in the financial statements of most multinational companies and is reported as part of shareholder's equity on the consolidated balance sheet.

For example, the shareholder's equity section of the April 30, 1992, balance sheet of John Labatt Limited includes the following:

	($ millions)
Share capital (note 13)	
Preferred shares	300
Common shares	337
Retained earnings	844
Cumulative translation adjustment	12

International Accounting Standards

The subject of International Accounting Standards was introduced in Chapter 12 as part of the discussion of the foundation of generally accepted accounting principles.

For the most part, accounting principles are similar from country to country. However, some important differences exist. For example, some countries, such as Italy, require financial statements to conform closely to income tax laws. In other countries, such as Brazil and Argentina, high inflation rates dictate that companies make price-level adjustments to report amounts in units of common purchasing power. Neither practice is followed as closely in Canada.

Several organizations are working to achieve worldwide harmony of accounting standards. Chief among these is the International Accounting Standards Committee (IASC). Headquartered in London, the IASC operates much as the CICA's Accounting Standards Board in Canada. It has the support of the accounting professions in Canada, the United States, most of the British Commonwealth countries, Japan, France, Germany, the Netherlands, and Mexico. However, the IASC has no authority to require compliance with its accounting standards. It must rely on cooperation by the various national accounting professions. Since its creation in 1973, the IASC has succeeded in narrowing some differences in international accounting standards.

Chapter 12 discussed the membership of three accounting bodies in Canada, CICA, CGAAC, and SMAC in the IASC. There was a brief discussion of the relationship between International Accounting Standards (IASs) issued by the IASC and the *CICA Handbook*. The CICA is attempting to harmonize the *Handbook* with the IASs.

Computers and Consolidations

Consider a large consolidated entity like Thompson Corp., a company with widely diversified operations and a large number of subsidiary firms included in its consolidated financial statements. Accountants performing Thompson's consolidations face several problems. One, all the subsidiaries may not all use the same accounting system and classifications. Two, finding intercompany receivables and payables may be difficult. A computer search for each of the many subsidiaries may be necessary to bring to light all intercompany items.

Large consolidated firms may custom design their own software to prepare consolidated financial statements. Alternatively, or in connection with custom-designed software, these businesses may use linked electronic spreadsheets (also called linked spreadsheets). With a linked spreadsheet, a value entered on one company's spreadsheet is automatically transmitted to other companies' spreadsheets as appropriate, a decision the computer makes based on account classification. Eliminations too can be entered on the linked spreadsheets. The amounts for the consolidated financial statements are drawn from this spreadsheet.

Windows® offers computer users access to multiple spreadsheets, or parts of spreadsheets, on screen at the same time. Consider the benefit of entering a change in the spreadsheet of a subsidiary and seeing immediately on screen its effect on the parent company.

Summary Problem for Your Review

Journalize the following transactions of Canada Corp.:

19X5

Nov. 16 Purchased equipment on account for 40,000 Swiss francs when the exchange rate was $1.075 per Swiss franc.

27 Sold merchandise on account to a Belgian company for 700,000 Belgian francs. Each franc is worth $.0407.

Dec. 22 Paid the Swiss company when the franc's exchange rate was $1.070.

31 Adjusted for the change in the exchange rate of the Belgian franc. Its current exchange rate is $.0402.

19X6

Jan. 4 Collected from the Belgian company. The exchange rate is $.0409.

SOLUTION TO REVIEW PROBLEM

1. Entries for transactions stated in foreign currencies:

19X5			
Nov. 16	Equipment (40,000 × $1.075)	43,000	
	Accounts Payable		43,000
27	Accounts Receivable (700,000 × $.0407)	28,490	
	Sales Revenue		28,490
Dec. 22	Accounts Payable	43,000	
	Cash (40,000 × $1.070)		42,800
	Foreign-Currency Transaction Gain		200
31	Foreign-Currency Transaction Loss		
	[700,000 × (.0407 – $.0402)]	350	
	Accounts Receivable		350
19X6			
Jan. 4	Cash (700,000 × .0409)	28, 630	
	Accounts Receivable		
	($28,490 – $350)		28, 140
	Foreign-Currency Transaction Gain		
	[700,000 × (.0409 – .0402)]		490

Summary

Investments are classified as short-term or long-term. *Short-term investments* are liquid, and the investor intends to convert them to cash within one year or less, or to use them to pay a current liability. All other investments are *long-term*.

Different methods are used to account for stock investments, depending on the investor's degree of influence over the investee. All investments are recorded initially at *cost*. Short-term investments are accounted for by the cost method (with lower-of-cost-or-market) and are reported on the balance sheet at the lower of their cost or current market (LCM) value. Dividends received are recorded as income.

Long-term investments of less than 20 percent of the investee's stock are also accounted for using the cost method. The *equity* method is used to account for investments of between 20 and 50 percent of the investee company's stock. Such an investment enables the investor to significantly influence the investee's activities. Investee income is recorded by the investor by debiting the Investment account and crediting an account entitled Equity-Method Investment Revenue. The investor records receipt of dividends from the investee by crediting the Investment account.

Ownership of more than 50 percent of the voting stock creates a parent-subsidiary relationship, and the *consolidation* method must be used. Because the parent has control over the subsidiary, the subsidiary's financial statements are included in the consolidated statements of the parent company. Two features of consolidation accounting are (1) addition of the parent and subsidiary accounts to prepare the parent's consolidated statements, and (2) elimination of intercompany items. When a parent owns less than 100 percent of the subsidiary's stock, the portion owned by outside investors is called *minority interest*. Purchase of a controlling interest at a cost greater than the fair value of the subsidiary's net assets creates an intangible asset called *goodwill*. A consolidation work sheet is used to prepare the consolidated financial statements.

International accounting deals with accounting for business activities across national boundaries. A key issue is the translation of foreign-currency accounts into dollars, accomplished through a *foreign-currency exchange rate*. Changes in exchange rates cause companies to experience *foreign-currency transaction gains and losses* on credit transactions.

Consolidation of a foreign subsidiary's financial statements with the Canadian parent must be done using Canadian accounting principles and requires adjusting the subsidiary statements into dollars. The translation process creates a *translation adjustment* that is reported in shareholders' equity. The International Accounting Standards Committee is working to harmonize accounting principles worldwide.

Self-Study Questions

Test your understanding of the chapter by marking the best answer for each of the following questions:

1. Short-term investments are reported on the balance sheet *(p. 738)*
   a. Immediately after cash
   b. Immediately after accounts receivable
   c. Immediately after inventory
   d. Immediately after current assets

2. Byforth, Inc. distributes a 10 percent stock dividend. An investor who owns Byforth stock should *(p. 739)*
   a. Debit Investment and credit Dividend Revenue for the book value of the stock received in the dividend distribution
   b. Debit Investment and credit Dividend Revenue for the market value of the stock received in the dividend distribution

    c. Debit Cash and credit Investment for the market value of the stock received in the dividend distribution

    d. Make a memorandum entry to record the new cost per share of Byforth stock held

3. Short-term investments are reported at the *(pp. 739–41)*

    a. Total cost of the portfolio

    b. Total market value of the portfolio

    c. Lower of total cost or total market value of the portfolio or lower of cost or market value on an investment-by-investment basis

    d. Total equity value of the portfolio

4. Putsch Corporation owns 30 percent of the voting stock of Mazelli, Inc. Mazelli reports net income of $100,000 and declares and pays cash dividends of $40,000. Which method should Putsch use to account for this investment? *(p. 741)*

    a. Cost   c. Equity

    b. Market value   d. Consolidation

5. Refer to the facts of the preceding question. What effect do Mazelli's income and dividends have on Putsch's net income? *(pp. 741–43)*

    a. Increase of $12,000   c. Increase of $30,000

    b. Increase of $18,000   d. Increase of $42,000

6. In applying the consolidation method, elimination entries are *(p. 745)*

    a. Necessary

    b. Required only when the parent has a receivable from or a payable to the subsidiary

    c. Required only when there is a minority interest

    d. Required only for the preparation of the consolidated balance sheet

7. Parent Corp. has separate net income of $155,000. Subsidiary A, which Parent owns 90 percent of, reports net income of $60,000, and Subsidiary B, which Parent owns 60 percent of, reports net income of $80,000. What is Parent Corp.'s consolidated net income? *(p. 748)*

    a. $155,000   c. $263,000

    b. $257,000   d. $295,000

8. On May 16, the exchange rate of the German mark was $1.25. On May 20, the exchange rate is $1.24. Which of the following statements is true? *(p. 754)*

    a. The dollar has risen against the mark.

    b. The dollar has fallen against the mark.

    c. The dollar is weaker than the mark.

    d. The dollar and the mark are equally strong.

9. A strong dollar encourages *(p. 755)*

    a. Travel to Canada by foreigners

    b. Purchase of Canadian goods by foreigners

    c. Canadians to travel abroad

    d. Canadians to save dollars

10. Ford Motor Company purchased auto accessories from an English supplier at a price of 500,000 British pounds. On the date of the credit purchase, the exchange rate of the British pound was $2.05. On the payment date, the exchange rate of the pound is $2.10. If payment is in pounds, Ford experiences *(p. 755)*

    a. A foreign-currency transaction gain of $25,000

    b. A foreign-currency transaction loss of $25,000

    c. Neither a transaction gain nor loss because the debt is paid in dollars

    d. None of the above

Answers to the Self-Study Questions are at the end of the chapter.

Accounting Vocabulary

consolidated statements *(p. 743)*	foreign-currency transaction gain or loss *(p. 755)*	parent company *(p. 743)* short-term investments *(p. 737)*
consolidation accounting *(p. 743)*	hedging *(p. 757)*	strong currency *(p. 755)*
controlling (majority) interest *(p. 743)*	long-term investments *(p. 738)*	subsidiary *(p. 743)* temporary
cost method *(p. 741)*	marketable	investments *(p. 737)*
equity method *(p. 742)*	securities *(p. 737)*	weak currency *(p. 755)*
foreign-currency exchange rate *(p. 754)*	minority interest *(p. 746)*	

ASSIGNMENT MATERIAL _____

Questions

1. How are stock prices quoted in the securities market? What is the investor's cost of 1,000 shares of BC Telephone $4.50 preferred stock at 55¾, with a brokerage commission of $1,350?

2. What distinguishes a short-term investment from a long-term investment?

3. Show the positions of short-term investments and long-term investments on the balance sheet.

4. Outline the accounting methods for the different types of stock investment.

5. How does an investor record the receipt of a cash dividend on an investment accounted for by the cost method? How does this investor record receipt of a stock dividend?

6. An investor paid $11,000 for 1,000 shares of stock and later received a 10 percent stock dividend. Compute the gain or loss on sale of 300 shares of the stock for $2,600.

7. At what amount are short-term investments reported on the balance sheet? Are the short-term and long-term investment portfolios mixed, or are they kept separate?

8. When is an investment accounted for by the equity method? Outline how to apply the equity method. Include in your answer how to record the purchase of the investment, the investor's proportion of the investee's net income, and receipt of a cash dividend from the investee. Describe how to measure gain or loss on sale of this investment.

9. Identify three transactions that cause debits or credits to an equity-method investment account.

10. What are two special features of the consolidation method for investments?

11. Why are intercompany items eliminated from consolidated financial statements? Name two intercompany items that are eliminated.

12. Name the account that expresses the excess of cost of an investment over the fair market value of the subsidiary's owner equity (net assets). What type of account is this, and where in the financial statements is it reported?

13. When a parent company buys less than 100 percent of a subsidiary's stock, a certain type of equity is created. What is it called and how do most companies report it?

14. How would you measure the net income of a parent company with three subsidiaries? Assume that two subsidiaries are wholly (100 percent) owned and that the parent owns 60 percent of the third subsidiary.

15. What is the difference between accounting for a short-term bond investment and a long-term bond investment?

16. Which situation results in a foreign-currency transaction gain for a Canadian business? Which situation results in a loss?
    a. Credit purchase denominated in pesos, followed by weakness in the peso
    b. Credit purchase denominated in pesos, followed by weakness in the dollar
    c. Credit sale denominated in pesos, followed by weakness in the peso
    d. Credit sale denominated in pesos, followed by weakness in the dollar

17. Explain the concept of hedging against foreign-currency transaction losses.

18. What is the difference between a realized foreign-currency transaction gain and an unrealized foreign-currency transaction gain?

Exercises

Exercise 17-1   *Journalizing transactions under the cost method (L.O. 1)*

Journalize the following investment transactions of Chateau Rose, Inc.:

a. Purchased 400 shares (8 percent) of Madison Corporation common stock at $44 per share, with brokerage commission of $300.
b. Received cash dividend of $1 per share on the Madison investment.
c. Received 200 shares of Madison common stock in a 50 percent stock dividend.
d. Sold 200 shares of Madison stock for $29 per share, less brokerage commission of $270.

Exercise 17-2   *Reporting investments at the lower of cost or market (L.O. 1)*

CP Rail recently reported the following information (not including the question mark) on its balance sheet:

Current Assets	(dollars in millions)
Cash and cash equivalents...	$398
Marketable securities [short-term investments], at lower of cost or market	?

Assume that the cost of CP Rail's short-term investments is $130 million and that current market value is $126 million.

Required

Apply the lower-of-cost-or-market method to CP Rail's short-term investments by inserting the appropriate amount in place of the question mark. Write a note to identify the method used to report short-term investments and to disclose cost and market value. Journalize any needed adjustment, assuming the marketable securities were purchased during the current year.

Exercise 17-3   *Journalizing transactions under the equity method (L.O. 2)*

Canadian National Railway System (CN) owns equity-method investments in several companies. Suppose CN paid $200,000 to acquire a 30 percent investment in XYZ Corp. Further, assume XYZ reported net income of $140,000 for the first year and declared and paid cash dividends of $70,000. Record the following in CN's general journal: (a) purchase of the investment, (b) CN's proportion of XYZ's net income, and (c) receipt of the cash dividends.

Exercise 17-4   *Recording equity-method transactions directly in the accounts (L.O. 2)*

Without making journal entries, record the transactions of Exercise 17-3 directly in the Investment in XYZ Common Stock account. Assume that after all the above transactions took place, CN sold its entire investment in XYZ common stock for cash of $270,000. Journalize the sale of the investment.

Exercise 17-5   *Comparing the cost and equity methods (L.O. 1, 2)*

Electrix Corporation paid $160,000 for a 30 percent investment in the common stock of Bluebonnet, Inc. For the first year, Bluebonnet reported net income of $84,000 and at year end declared and paid cash dividends of $16,000. On the balance sheet date the market value of Electrix's investment in Bluebonnet stock was $153,000.

Required

1. On Electrix's books, journalize the purchase of the investment, recognition of Electrix's portion of Bluebonnet's net income, and receipt of dividends from Bluebonnet under the equity method, which is appropriate for these circumstances.
2. Repeat requirement 1 but follow the cost method for comparison purposes only.
3. Show the amount that Electrix would report for the investment on its year-end balance sheet under the two methods.

Exercise 17-6   *Completing a consolidation work sheet with minority interest (L.O. 3, 4)*

Maxim Ltd., owns an 80 percent interest in Ultra Corporation. Complete the following consolidation work sheet:

Assets	Maxim Ltd.	Ultra Corporation
Cash	19,000	14,000
Accounts receivable, net	82,000	53,000
Note receivable from Maxim	—	12,000
Inventory	114,000	77,000
Investment in Ultra	80,000	—
Capital assets, net	186,000	129,000
Other assets	22,000	8,000
Total	503,000	293,000
Liabilities and Shareholders' Equity		
Accounts payable	44,000	26,000
Notes payable	47,000	36,000
Other liabilities	52,000	131,000
Minority interest	—	—
Common stock	200,000	80,000
Retained earnings	160,000	20,000
Total	503,000	293,000

Exercise 17-7   *Elimination entries under the consolidation method (L.O. 4)*

Assume on December 31 that Walker Financial Consultants Ltd., a 100 percent owned subsidiary of Northern Express Corp., had the following owner's equity:

Common Stock	$200,000
Retained Earnings	250,000

Assume further that Northern Express's cost of its investment in Walker was $450,000 and that Walker owed Northern Express $55,000 on a note.

Required

Give the work-sheet entry to eliminate (a) the investment of Northern Express and the shareholders' equity of Walker and (b) the note receivable of Northern Express and note payable of Walker.

Exercise 17-8 *Recording short-term bond investment transactions (L.O. 5)*

On June 30, Statistical Research, Inc. paid $92¼ for 8 percent bonds of Erdman Limited as a short-term investment. The maturity value of the bonds is $20,000, and they pay interest on March 31 and September 30. Record Statistical Research's purchase of the bond investment, the receipt of semiannual interest on September 30, and the accrual of interest revenue on December 31.

Exercise 17-9 *Recording long-term bond investment transactions (L.O. 5)*

Assume the Erdman Limited bonds in the preceding exercise are purchased as a long-term investment on June 30, 19X3. The bonds mature on September 30, 19X7.

Required

1. Using the straight-line method of amortizing the discount, journalize all transactions on the bonds for 19X3.

2. How much more interest revenue would the investor record in 19X3 for a long-term investment than for a short-term investment in these bonds? What accounts for this difference?

Exercise 17-10 *Journalizing foreign-currency transactions (L.O. 6)*

Journalize the following foreign-currency transactions:

Nov. 17   Purchased goods on account from a Japanese company. The price was 200,000 yen, and the exchange rate of the yen was $.010.

Dec. 16   Paid the Japanese supplier when the exchange rate was $.011.

    19   Sold merchandise on account to a French company at a price of 60,000 French francs. The exchange rate was $.41.

    31   Adjusted for the decrease in the value of the franc, which had an exchange rate of $.40.

Jan. 14   Collected from the French company. The exchange rate was $.42.

Problems   (Group A)

Problem 17-1A *Journalizing transactions under the cost and equity methods (L.O. 1,2)*

ConAgra, Inc. owns numerous investments in the stock of other companies. Assume ConAgra completed the following investment transactions:

19X6

Jan.   2   Purchased 24,000 shares (total issued and outstanding common shares, 100,000) of the common stock of Agribusiness, Inc. at total cost of $810,000.

Mar. 16   Purchased 1,000 shares of Apex Corp. common stock as a short-term investment, paying $43 per share plus brokerage commission of $900.

July   1   Purchased 8,000 additional shares of Agribusiness common stock at cost of $300,000.

Aug.   9   Received annual cash dividend of $.90 per share (total of $28,800) on the Agribusiness investment.

      30   Received semiannual cash dividend of $.70 per share on the Apex investment.

Sept. 14   Received 250 shares of Apex common stock in a 25 percent stock dividend.

Oct. 22   Sold 400 shares of Apex stock for $30¼ per share, less brokerage commission of $450.

Dec. 31   Received annual report from Agribusiness, Inc. Net income for the year was $700,000. Of this amount, ConAgra's proportion is 32 percent.

      19X7

Jan. 14   Sold 4,000 shares of Agribusiness stock for net cash of $157,000.

Required

Record the transactions in the general journal of ConAgra, Inc.

Problem 17-2A   *Applying the cost method (with LCM) and the equity method* (L.O. 1, 2)

The beginning balance sheet of Ranco Limited recently included:

Investments in Affiliates.................... $10,984,000

Investments in Affiliates refers to investments accounted for by the equity method. Ranco included its short-term investments among the current assets. Assume the company completed the following investment transactions during the year:

Jan.   2   Purchased 2,000 shares of common stock as a short-term investment, paying 12¼ per share plus brokerage commission of $1,000.

       5   Purchased new long-term investment in affiliate at cost of $540,000. Debit Investments in Affiliates.

Apr. 21   Received semiannual cash dividend of $.75 per share on the short-term investment purchased January 2.

May   17   Received cash dividend of $57,000 from affiliated company.

July 16   Sold 1,600 shares of the short-term investment (purchased on January 2) for $11 per share less brokerage commission of $720.

Sept. 8   Sold other short-term investments for $136,000, less brokerage commission of $5,100. Cost of these investments was $140,000.

Nov. 17   Received cash dividend of $49,000 from affiliated company.

Dec. 31   Received annual reports from affiliated companies. Their total net income for the year was $600,000. Of this amount, Ranco's proportion is 25 percent.

Required

1. Record the transactions in the general journal of Ranco Limited.

2. Post entries to the Investments in Affiliates T-account and determine its balance at December 31.

3. Assume the beginning balance of Short-Term Investments was cost of $293,600. Post entries to the Short-Term Investments T-account and determine its balance at December 31.

4. Assuming the market value of the short-term investment portfolio is $190,300 at December 31, show how Ranco would report short-term investments and investments in affiliates on the ending balance sheet. Ranco compares total portfolio cost to total portfolio market value in determining the lower of cost or market. Use the following format:

Cash...	$XXX
Short-term investments, at lower of cost or market (__?__ ,$__)	
Accounts receivable...	XXX
Total current assets	XXX
Investments in affiliates..	

Problem 17-3A   *Preparing a consolidated balance sheet; no minority interest* **(L.O. 3, 4)**

Lethbridge Ltd. paid $166,000 to acquire all the common stock of Calgary Corporation, and Calgary owes Lethbridge $81,000 on a note payable. Immediately after the purchase on June 30, 19X3, the two companies' balance sheets were as follows:

	Lethbridge Ltd.	Calgary Corporation
Assets		
Cash...	$ 21,000	$ 20,000
Accounts receivable, net........................	91,000	42,000
Note receivable from Calgary..............	81,000	—
Inventory	145,000	114,000
Investment in Calgary	166,000	—
Capital assets, net................................	178,000	219,000
Total...	$682,000	$395,000
Liabilities and Shareholders' Equity		
Accounts payable	$ 54,000	$ 49,000
Notes payable	177,000	149,000
Other liabilities	29,000	31,000
Common stock......................................	274,000	68,000
Retained earnings................................	148,000	98,000
Total...	$682,000	$395,000

Required

1. Prepare a consolidation work sheet.
2. Prepare the consolidated balance sheet on June 30, 19X3. Show total assets, total liabilities and total shareholders' equity. It is not necessary to classify assets and liabilities as current and long-term.

Problem 17-4A   *Preparing a consolidated balance sheet with minority interest* **(L.O. 3, 4)**

On March 22, 19X4, Abbott Corporation paid $180,000 to purchase 80 percent of the common stock of Zeta Inc., and Zeta owes Abbott $67,000 on a note payable. Immediately after the purchase, the two companies' balance sheets were as follows:

	Abbott Corporation	Zeta Inc.
Assets		
Cash	$ 41,000	$ 43,000
Accounts receivable, net	86,000	75,000
Note receivable from Zeta	67,000	—
Inventory...	128,000	81,000
Investment in Zeta	180,000	—
Capital assets, net................................	277,000	168,000
Total..	$779,000	$367,000

Liabilities and Shareholders' Equity

Accounts payable..................................	$ 72,000	$ 65,000
Notes payable......................................	301,000	67,000
Other liabilities....................................	11,000	10,000
Minority interest	—	—
Common stock......................................	141,000	60,000
Retained earnings	254,000	165,000
Total..	$779,000	$367,000

Required

1. Prepare a consolidation work sheet.
2. Prepare the consolidated balance sheet on March 22, 19X4. Show total assets, total liabilities and total shareholders' equity. It is not necessary to classify assets and liabilities as current and long-term.

Problem 17-5A   *Accounting for a long-term bond investment purchased at a premium (L.O. 5)*

Financial institutions such as insurance companies and pension plans hold large quantities of bond investments. Suppose Southwestern Mutual Life purchases $600,000 of 9 percent bonds of BC Tel Corporation for 101 on July 1, 19X1. These bonds pay interest on March 1 and September 1 each year. They mature on March 1, 19X8.

Required

1. Journalize Southwestern Mutual's purchase of the bonds as a long-term investment on July 1, 19X1, receipt of cash interest and amortization of premium on September 1, 19X1, and accrual of interest revenue and amortization of premium at December 31, 19X1. Assume the straight-line method is appropriate for amortizing premium.
2. Show all financial statement effects of this long-term bond investment at December 31, 19X1. Assume a multiple-step income statement.
3. Repeat requirement 2 under the assumption that Southwestern Mutual purchased these bonds as a short-term investment. Assume market value was 102.

Problem 17-6A   *Computing the cost of a bond investment and journalizing its transactions (L.O. 5)*

On December 31, 19X1, when the market interest rate is 12 percent, an investor purchases $500,000 of Advanced Systems 6-year, 11.4 percent bonds at issuance. Determine the cost (present value) of this long-term bond investment. Journalize the purchase on December 31, 19X1, the first semiannual interest receipt on June 30, 19X2, and the year-end interest receipt on December 31, 19X2. The investor uses the effective-interest amortization method. Prepare a schedule for amortizing the discount on bond investment through December 31, 19X2. If necessary, refer to Chapter 16 and its appendix.

Note: Problem 17-6A is based on the present-value appendix in Chapter 16.

Problem 17-7A   *Journalizing foreign-currency transactions and reporting the transaction gain or loss (L.O. 6)*

Suppose Pepsi-Cola Ltd. completed the following transactions:

Dec. 4   Sold soft drink syrup on account to a Mexican company for $36,000. The exchange rate of the Mexican peso is $.0004, and the customer agrees to pay in Canadian dollars.

  13   Purchased inventory on account from a U.S. company at a price of U.S. $100,000. The exchange rate of the American dollar is $1.25, and

payment will be in American dollars.

20   Sold goods on account to an English firm for 70,000 British pounds. Payment will be in pounds, and the exchange rate of the pound is $2.00.

27   Collected from the Mexican company. Exchange rate unchanged from December 4.

31   Adjusted the accounts for changes in foreign-currency exchange rates. Current rates: U.S. dollar, $1.23; British pound, $1.98.

Jan. 21   Paid the American company. The exchange rate of the U.S. dollar is $1.28.

Feb. 17   Collected from the English firm. The exchange rate of the British pound is $1.97.

Record these transactions in Pepsi-Cola's general journal, and show how to report the transaction gain or loss on the income statement.

(Group B)

Problem 17-1B   *Journalizing transactions under the cost and equity methods (L.O. 1, 2)*

Imasco Limited, the conglomerate, owns numerous investments in the stock of other companies. Assume Imasco completed the following investment transactions:

19X4

Mar. 19   Purchased 1,000 shares of ROX Corporation common stock as a short-term investment, paying $24 per share plus brokerage commission of $700.

Apr.   1   Purchased 8,000 shares (total issued and outstanding common shares, 38,400) of the common stock of MIC Limited at total cost of $800,000.

July   1   Purchased 1,600 additional shares of MIC Limited common stock at cost of $140,000.

Aug. 14   Received semiannual cash dividend of $.80 per share on the ROX investment.

Sept. 15   Received semiannual cash dividend of $1.50 per share on the MIC investment.

Oct. 12   Received ROX common stock in a 20 percent stock dividend. Round the new cost per share to the nearest cent.

Nov.   9   Sold 200 shares of ROX stock for $29 per share, less brokerage commission of $175.

Dec. 31   Received annual report from MIC Company. Net income for the year was $500,000. Of this amount, Imasco's proportion is 25 percent.

19X5

Feb.   6   Sold 1,920 shares of MIC stock for net cash of $205,000.

Required

Record the transactions in the general journal of Imasco Limited.

Problem 17-2B   *Applying the cost method (with LCM) and the equity method (L.O. 1, 2)*

The beginning balance sheet of Nova Corp. of Alberta recently included:

Investments in Affiliates $84,057,000

Investments in Affiliates refers to long-term investments accounted for by the equity method. Nova included its short-term investments among the current assets.

Assume the company completed the following investment transactions during the year:

Jan. 3 Purchased 6,000 shares of common stock as a short-term investment, paying $9¼ per share plus brokerage commission of $1,350.

4 Purchased new long-term investment in affiliate at cost of $450,000. Debit Investments in Affiliates.

May 14 Received semiannual cash dividend of $.82 per share on the short-term investment purchased January 3.

June 15 Received cash dividend of $27,000 from affiliated company.

Aug. 28 Sold 1,000 shares of the short-term investment (purchased on January 3) for $10½ per share, less brokerage commission of $750.

Oct. 24 Sold other short-term investments for $226,000, less brokerage commission of $11,400. Cost of these investments was $243,100.

Dec. 15 Received cash dividend of $29,000 from affiliated company.

31 Received annual reports from affiliated companies. Their total net income for the year was $620,000. Of this amount, Nova's proportion is 30 percent.

Required

1. Record the transactions in the general journal of Nova Corp.

2. Post entries to the Investments in Affiliates T-account, and determine its balance at December 31.

3. Assume the beginning balance of Short-Term Investments was cost of $356,400. Post entries to the Short-Term Investments T-account and determine its balance at December 31.

4. Assuming the market value of the short-term investment portfolio is $142,600 at December 31, show how Nova Corp. would report short-term investments and investments in affiliates on the ending balance sheet. Nova compares total portfolio cost to total portfolio market value in determining the lower of cost or market. Use the following format:

Cash .... $XXX
Short-term investments, at lower of cost or market (__?__ ,$___).........
Accounts receivable.. XXX

⌇ ⌇

Total current assets XXX
Investments in affiliates...

Problem 17-3B *Preparing a consolidated balance sheet; no minority interest (L.O. 3, 4)*

Prent Co. Ltd. paid $179,000 to acquire all the common stock of Stratford Corporation, and Stratford owes Prent $55,000 on a note payable. Immediately after the purchase on May 31, 19X7, the two companies' balance sheets were as follows:

	Prent Co. Ltd.	Stratford Corporation
Assets		
Cash...	$ 18,000	$ 32,000
Accounts receivable, net.......................	64,000	43,000
Note receivable from Stratford............	55,000	—
Inventory	171,000	153,000

Investment in Stratford..........................	179,000	—
Capital assets, net.................................	205,000	138,000
Total...	$692,000	$366,000

Liabilities and Shareholders' Equity		
Accounts payable	$ 76,000	$ 37,000
Notes payable	196,000	123,000
Other liabilities	44,000	27,000
Common stock.......................................	282,000	79,000
Retained earnings.................................	94,000	100,000
Total...	$692,000	$366,000

Required

1. Prepare a consolidation work sheet.
2. Prepare the consolidated balance sheet on May 31, 19X7. Show total assets, total liabilities, and total shareholders' equity. It is not necessary to classify assets and liabilities as current and long-term.

Problem 17-4B   *Preparing a consolidated balance sheet with goodwill (L.O. 3, 4)*

On August 17, 19X8, Marble Corporation paid $229,000 to purchase all the common stock of Granite Inc., and Granite owes Marble $42,000 on a note payable. All historical cost amounts are equal to their fair market value on August 17, 19X8. Immediately after the purchase, the two companies' balance sheets were as follows:

	Marble Corporation	Granite Inc.
Assets		
Cash	$ 23,000	$ 37,000
Accounts receivable, net	104,000	54,000
Note receivable from Granite..............	42,000	—
Inventory...	213,000	170,000
Investment in Granite	229,000	—
Capital assets, net	197,000	175,000
Goodwill	—	—
Total	$808,000	$436,000
Liabilities and Shareholders' Equity		
Accounts payable...................................	$119,000	$ 77,000
Notes payable..	223,000	71,000
Other liabilities.....................................	33,000	88,000
Common stock	219,000	90,000
Retained earnings	214,000	110,000
Total	$808,000	$436,000

Required

1. Prepare a consolidation work sheet.
2. Prepare the consolidated balance sheet on August 17, 19X8. Show total assets, total liabilities and total shareholders' equity. It is not necessary to classify assets and liabilities as current and long-term.

Problem 17-5B   *Accounting for a long-term bond investment purchased at a discount (L.O. 5)*

Financial institutions such as insurance companies and pension plans hold large quantities of bond investments. Suppose Aetna Life Insurance Company of Alberta purchases $500,000 of 8 percent bonds of General Motors of Canada for 97 on March 31, 19X0. These bonds pay interest on January 31 and July 31 each year. They mature on July 31, 19X8.

Required

1. Journalize Aetna's purchase of the bonds as a long-term investment on March 31, 19X0, receipt of cash interest and amortization of discount on July 31, 19X0, and accrual of interest revenue and amortization of discount at December 31, 19X0. Assume the straight-line method is appropriate for amortizing discount.

2. Show all financial statement effects of this long-term bond investment at December 31, 19X0. Assume a multiple-step income statement.

3. Repeat requirement 2 under the assumption that Aetna purchased these bonds as a short-term investment. Assume market value is $490,000.

Problem 17-6B   *Computing the cost of a bond investment and journalizing its transactions (L.O. 5)*

On December 31, 19X1, when the market interest rate is 10 percent, an investor purchases $400,000 of Jax Corp. 10-year, 12.5 percent bonds at issuance. Determine the cost (present value) of the bond investment. Assume that the investment is long-term. Journalize the purchase on December 31, 19X1, the first semiannual interest receipt on June 30, 19X2, and the year-end interest receipt on December 31, 19X2. The investor uses the effective-interest amortization method. Prepare a schedule for amortizing the premium on the bond investment through December 31, 19X2. If necessary, refer to Chapter 16 and its appendix.

Note: Problem 17-6B is based on the present-value appendix in Chapter 16.

Problem 17-7B   *Journalizing foreign-currency transactions and reporting the transaction gain or loss (L.O. 6)*

Suppose Xerox of Canada Ltd. completed the following transactions:

Dec.	1	Sold a photocopy machine on account to Pirelli Tire Company for $70,000. The exchange rate of the Italian lira is $.0007, and Pirelli agrees to pay in Canadian dollars.
	10	Purchased supplies on account from a U.S. company at a price of U.S. $50,000. The exchange rate of the U.S. dollar is $1.22, and payment will be in U.S. dollars.
	17	Sold a photocopy machine on account to an English firm for 100,000 British pounds. Payment will be in pounds, and the exchange rate of the pound is $1.95.
	22	Collected from Pirelli. The exchange rate of the lira has not changed since December 1.
	31	Adjusted the accounts for changes in foreign-currency exchange rates. Current rates: U.S. dollar, $1.21; British pound, $1.92.
Jan.	18	Paid the U.S. company. The exchange rate of the U.S. dollar is $1.23.
	24	Collected from the English firm. The exchange rate of the British pound is $1.94.

Record these transactions in Xerox's general journal, and show how to report the transaction gain or loss on the income statement.

Extending Your Knowledge

Decision Problems

1. Understanding the cost and equity methods of accounting for investments (L.O. 1, 2)

Bruce Joyce is the accountant for Dunrobin Inc., whose year end is December 31. The company made two investments during the first week of January, 19X7. Both investments are to be held for at least the next five years as investments. Information about each of the investments follows:

a. Dunrobin purchased 40 percent of the common stock of Lonesome Dove Ltd. for its book value of $200,000. During the year ended December 31, 19X7, Lonesome Dove earned $85,000 and paid a total dividend of $30,000.

b. Ten percent of the common stock of M-J Western Music Inc. was purchased for its book value of $50,000. During the year ended December 31, 19X7, M-J paid Dunrobin a dividend of $3,000. M-J earned a profit of $85,000 for that period.

Bruce has come to you as his auditor to ask you how to account for the investments. Dunrobin has never had such investments before. You attempt to explain the proper accounting to him by indicating that different accounting methods apply to different situations.

Required

Help Bruce understand by

1. Describing the methods of accounting applicable to these investments.
2. Identifying which method should be used to account for the investments in Lonesome Dove and M-J Western Music.

2. Understanding the consolidation method for investments (L.O. 3, 4)

Indira Agarwal inherited some investments, and she has received the annual reports of the companies in which the funds are invested. The financial statements of the companies are puzzling to Indira, and she asks you the following questions:

1. The companies label their financial statements as consolidated balance sheet, consolidated income statement, and so on. What are consolidated financial statements?
2. Notes to the statements indicate that "certain intercompany transactions, loans, and other accounts have been eliminated in preparing the consolidated financial statements." Why does a company eliminate transactions, loans, and accounts? Indira states that she thought a transaction was a transaction and that a loan obligated a company to pay real money. She wonders if the company is juggling the books to defraud Revenue Canada.
3. The balance sheet lists the asset Goodwill. What is Goodwill? Does this mean that the company's stock has increased in value?

Required

Respond to each of Indira's questions.

Ethical Issue

Montpelier Limited owns 18 percent of the voting stock of Nashua Corporation. The remainder of the Nashua stock is held by numerous investors with small holdings. Ralph Knox, president of Montpelier and a member of Nashua's Board of Directors, heavily influences Nashua's policies.

Under the cost method of accounting for investments, Montpelier's net income increases as it received dividends from Nashua. Montpelier pays President Knox a bonus computed as a percentage of Montpelier's net income. Therefore, Knox can control his personal bonus to a certain extent by influencing Nashua's dividends.

A recession occurs in 19X0, and corporate income is low. Knox uses his power to have Nashua Corporation pay a large cash dividend. This action requires Nashua to borrow so heavily that it may lead to financial difficulty.

Required

1. In getting Nashua to pay the large cash dividend, is Knox acting within his authority as a member of the Nashua Board of Directors? Are Knox's actions ethical? Whom can his actions harm?

2. Discuss how using the equity method of accounting for investments would decrease Knox's potential for manipulating his bonus.

Financial Statement Problems

1. Investments in stock (L.O. 1, 2, 3)

The Schneider financial statements and related notes in Appendix C describe some of the company's investment activity. Note 2 reveals that Schneider engaged in a number of acquisitions during the year.

Required

1. Can you tell from the financial statements and notes the method used to account for these companies?

2. Journalize the following transactions of fiscal 1991. Use the Schneider account titles and the information provided in Note 2. Assume for this problem that the financial data refers to a single acquisition where Schneider acquired 94.9 percent of a new subsidiary for total consideration of $11,918,000 and the assigned values provided are historical cost values from the subsidiary's books. Note, as all amounts in Note 2 are rounded to $1,000, use the same rounding in your answer.
   a. Record the journal entry Schneider would make for acquisition in its nonconsolidated accounting records
   b. Prepare the eliminating journal entry which Schneider would record to prepare its consolidated financial statements. Common stock of the subsidiary was $3,000,000, and total retained earnings was $7,830,000 as at the date of acquisition.

3. What is the only word that appears in the title of all of Schneider's financial statements? What does this word indicate? Name two companies that Schneider purchased 50 percent of the voting stock of in the year ended October 26, 1991. Of what company did Schneider buy 100 percent of the voting stock?

2. Investments in stock (L.O. 1, 2, 3)

Obtain the annual report of an actual company of your choosing. Answer these questions about the company. Concentrate on the current year in the annual report you select.

1. Many companies refer to other companies in which they own equity-method investments as affiliated companies. This signifies the close relationship between the two entities even though the investor does not own a controlling interest. Does the company have equity-method investments? Cite the evidence. If present, what were the balances in the investment account at the beginning and the end of the current year? If the company had no equity-method investments, skip the next question, and go to question 3.

2. Scan the income statement. If equity-method investments are present, what amount of revenue (or income) did the company earn on the investments during the current year? Scan the statement of changes in financial position. What amount of dividends did the company receive during the current year from companies in which it held equity-method investments? Note: The amount of dividends received may not be disclosed. If not, you can still compute the amount of dividends received — from the following T-account.

Investments, at Equity

Beg. bal. (from balance sheet)	W		
Equity-method revenue (from income statement)	X	**Dividends received (unknown; must compute)**	**Y**
End. bal. (from balance sheet)	Z		

3. The company probably owns some consolidated subsidiaries. You should be able to tell whether the parent company owns 100 percent or less of the subsidiaries. Examine the income statement and the balance sheet to determine whether there are any minority interests. If so, what does that fact indicate?

Comprehensive Problem for Part Five

Accounting for Corporate Transactions

North American Industries Ltd.'s articles of incorporation authorizes the company to issue 500,000 shares of common stock and 100,000 shares of $.50 preferred stock. During the first quarter of operations, North American completed the following selected transactions:

Oct. 1 Issued 75,000 shares of common stock for cash of $6 per share.
     2 Signed a capital lease for equipment. The lease requires a down payment of $50,000, plus 20 quarterly lease payments of $10,000. Present value of the future least payments is $135,900 at an annual interest rate of 16 percent.
     5 Issued 2,000 shares of preferred stock to lawyers who helped organize the corporation. Their bill listed legal services of $22,000.
    22 Received land from the province as an incentive for locating in New Brunswick. Fair market value of the land was $150,000.
    30 Purchased 5,000 shares (25 percent) of the outstanding common stock of Newbold Corporation as a long-term investment, $85,000.
Nov. 1 Issued $200,000 of 9 percent, 10-year bonds payable at 94.

14   Purchased short-term investments in the common stocks of Bombardier, $22,000, and ATCO Ltd., $31,000.

19   Experienced an extraordinary tornado loss of inventory that cost $21,000. Cash received from the insurance company was $8,000.

20   Repurchased 2,000 shares of the company's common stock at $5.00 per share.

Dec.   1   Received cash dividends of $1,100 on the Bombardier investment.

16   Sold 1,000 shares of the company's stock for cash of $6.25 per share.

29   Received a report from Newbold Corporation indicating the net income for November and December was $70,000.

30   Sold merchandise on account, $716,000. Cost of the goods was $439,000. Operating expenses totaled $174,000, with $166,000 of this amount paid in cash. North American uses a perpetual inventory system.

31   Accrued interest and amortized discount (straight-line method) on the bonds payable.

31   Accrued interest on the capital lease liability.

31   Depreciated the equipment acquired by the capital lease. The company uses the double-declining-balance method.

31   Market values of short-term investments: Pepsi-Cola stock, $24,000, and the Bridgestone stock, $30,000.

31   Accrued income tax expense of $20,000.

31   Closed all revenues, expenses, and losses to Retained Earnings in a single closing entry.

31   Declared a quarterly cash dividend of $.125 per share on the preferred stock. Record date is January 11, with payment scheduled for January 19.

Required

1. Record these transactions in the general journal. Explanations are not required.

2. Prepare a single-step income statement for the quarter ended December 31, including earnings per share. Income tax expense of $20,000 should be reported as follows: Income tax expense of $24,000 is used in arriving at income before extraordinary items. The tax effect of the extraordinary loss is an income tax saving of $4,000.

3. Report the liabilities and the shareholder's equity as they would appear on the balance sheet at December 31.

Answers to Self-Study Questions

1. a
2. d
3. c
4. c
5. c ($100,000 × .30 = $30,000; dividends have no effect on investor net income under the equity method)
6. a
7. b [$155,000 + ($60,000 × .90) + ($80,000 × .60) = $257,000]
8. a
9. c
10. b [500,000 × ($2.10 − $2.05) = $25,000]

Chapter 18

Statement of Changes in Financial Position

In October of 1991, *Canadian Business* magazine ran a cover story on Olympia and York Developments Ltd. (O&Y). The Toronto-based O&Y, a private company controlled by the Reichmann brothers, is one of the world's largest real estate development companies. The article focused on the company's ability to meet principal and interest payments on its outstanding debt.

> A recent [September 1991] rumor that O&Y had defaulted on a loan to Citibank sent shivers through U.S. financial markets, putting further downward pressure on already jittery bank bonds. An O&Y spokesman described the rumor as "malicious and groundless." A representative of Citibank dubbed it "patently ridiculous."

The article noted that O&Y needed to raise 600 million pounds for its debt on the Canary Wharf project in London, England.

The article also mentioned that in June, 1991, *Forbes* magazine had listed the Reichmanns as the seventh wealthiest family in the world with a net worth of U.S. $7 billion. In September, *Fortune* magazine listed them fourth with U.S. $12 billion.

However, by May 14, 1992, O&Y was having difficulty meeting required payments on some of its $14.3 billion debt.

The following observation was made toward the end of the article:

> For an ongoing business such as O&Y, the important figure is not net worth, but its cash flow over its debt service; that is, the stream of income from its assets set against the cash outflow of interest payments on borrowing against them. Businesses run into trouble not through lack of assets, but lack of cash.

The author is stressing the importance of cash flow in assessing a company's operations. As you read Chapter 18, consider why the Statement of Changes in Financial Position is for many companies the most important financial statement accountants prepare.

Sources: Peter Foster, "How Deep are Their Pockets," *Canadian Business*, (October 1991), pp. 38-40, 42, 44, 46-48, 50; and Susan Gittins, "Reichmanns File for Protection," The *Financial Post* (May 15, 1992), p. 1.

Income statements and balance sheets are anchored to the accrual basis of accounting for measuring performance and financial position. Another major statement, the statement of changes in financial position (SCFP), is required to provide a more extensive picture of performance and position.

Consider some common questions asked by managers, investors and creditors. What were the company's sources of cash during the period? Did operations — buying and selling the company's major products — generate the bulk of its cash receipts, or did the business have to sell off capital assets to keep the cash balance at an acceptable level? Did the company have to borrow heavily during the period? How did the entity spend its cash? Was it busy paying off debts, or were cash disbursements devoted to expanding the business? This chapter discusses the statement of changes in financial position. As its title implies, the SCFP helps explain a company's performance in generating cash.

The *CICA Handbook* in Section 1540 "Statement of Changes in Financial Position" "...focuses on the liquid financial resources readily available to the enterprise", which it defines as **cash and cash equivalents**; the enterprise's cash, net of short-term borrowings; and temporary investments. References in this chapter to cash will include cash and cash equivalents. **Cash flows** are cash receipts (increases in cash) and cash payments (disbursements or decreases in cash). The **Statement of Changes in Financial Position** reports cash receipts and cash disbursements classified according to the entity's major activities: operating, financing, and investing. The statement reports a net cash inflow or net cash outflow for each activity and for the overall business.

While the most common title of the statement is "Statement of Changes in Financial Position," some Canadian companies use the title "Statement of Cash Flow" or "Statement of Cash Flows." Section 1540 does not specify a particular title.

Purposes of the Statement of Changes in Financial Position

The statement of changes in financial position is designed to fulfill the following purposes:

1. *To predict future cash flows.* Cash, not reported accounting income, pays the bills. In many cases, a business's sources and uses of cash do not change dramatically from year to year. If so, past cash receipts and disbursements are a reasonably good predictor of future cash receipts and disbursements.

2. *To evaluate management decisions.* If managers make wise investment decisions, their businesses prosper. If they make unwise decisions, the businesses suffer. The

statement of changes in financial position reports the company's investment in plant and equipment and thus gives investors and creditors cash-flow information for evaluating managers' decisions.

3. *To determine the ability to pay dividends to shareholders and interest and principal to creditors.* Shareholders are interested in receiving dividends on their investments in the company's stock. Creditors want to receive their interest and principal amounts on time. The statement of changes in financial position helps investors and creditors predict whether the business can make these payments.

4. *To show the relationship of net income to changes in the business's cash.* Usually, cash and net income move together. High levels of income tend to lead to increases in cash, and vice versa. However, a company's cash balance can decrease when net income is high, and cash can increase when income is low. The failures of companies which were earning net income but had insufficient cash have pointed to the need for cash flow information.

Basic Concept of the Statement of Changes in Financial Position

The balance sheet reports the cash balance at the end of the period. By examining two consecutive balance sheets, you can tell whether cash increased or decreased during the period. However, the balance sheet does not indicate *why* the cash balance changed. The income statement reports revenues, expenses, and net income — clues about the sources and uses of cash — but still does not tell *why* cash increased or decreased.

The SCFP reports the entity's cash receipts and cash payments during the period (where cash came from and how it was spent). It explains the *causes* for the change in the cash balance. This information cannot be learned solely from the other financial statements.

The balance sheet is the only financial statement that is dated as of the end of the period. The income statement and the statement of retained earnings cover the period from beginning to end. The SCFP also covers the entire period and therefore is dated "For the Year Ended XXX" or "For the Month Ended XXX." Its timing and its position among the statements is shown in this diagram:

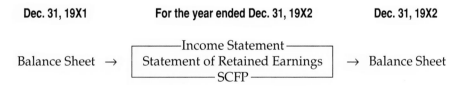

Dec. 31, 19X1	For the year ended Dec. 31, 19X2	Dec. 31, 19X2

Balance Sheet → [Income Statement / Statement of Retained Earnings / SCFP] → Balance Sheet

Operating, Financing and Investing Activities

A good way to evaluate a business is based on the three basic types of business activities undertaken. After the business is up and running, operations are the most important activity, followed by financing and investing activities. The statement of changes in financial position in Exhibit 18-1 shows how cash receipts and disbursements are divided into operating activities, financing activities, and investing activities. As Exhibit 18-1 illustrates, each set of activities (operating, financing, and investing) includes both cash inflows (receipts) and cash outflows (payments). Outflows are shown in parentheses to indicate that payments must be subtracted. Each section of the statement reports a net cash inflow or a net cash outflow.

Operating activities create revenues and expenses in the entity's major line of business. Therefore, operating activities affect the income statement, which reports the accrual-basis effects of operating activities. The statement of changes in financial

OBJECTIVE 2

Distinguish among operating, financing and investing activities

EXHIBIT 18-1   Statement of Changes in Financial Position

Anchor Ltd.
Statement of Changes in Financial Position
for the year ended December 31, 19X2
(amounts in thousands)

Cash flows from operating activities		
Receipts		
Collections from customers	$ 271	
Interest received on notes receivable	10	
Dividends received on investments in stock	9	
Total cash receipts		290
Payments		
To suppliers	$(133)	
To employees	(58)	
For interest	(16)	
For income tax	(15)	
Total cash payments		(222)
Net cash inflow from operating activities		68
Cash flows from financing activities		
Proceeds from issuance of common stock	$ 101	
Proceeds from issuance of long-term debt	94	
Payment of long-term debt	(11)	
Payment of dividends	(17)	
Net cash inflow from financing activities		167
Cash flows from investing activities		
Acquisition of capital assets	$(306)	
Loan to another company	(11)	
Proceeds from sale of capital assets	62	
Net cash outflow from investing activities		(255)
Net decrease in cash		**$(20)**
Cash balance, December 31, 19X1		42
Cash balance, December 31, 19X2		$ 22

position reports their impact on cash. The largest cash inflow from operations is collection of cash from customers. Less important inflows are receipts of interest on loans and dividends on stock investments. The operating cash flows include payments to suppliers and to employees and payments for interest and taxes. Anchor's net cash inflow from operating activities is $68,000. A large positive operating cash flow is a good sign about a company. In the long run, operations must be the main source of a business's cash.

Financing activities obtain the funds from investors and creditors needed to launch and sustain the business. Financing activities include issuing stock, borrowing money by issuing notes and bonds payable, and making payments to the shareholders — dividends and repurchases of the company's stock. Payments to the creditors include principal payments only. The payment of interest is an operating activity. Financing activities brought in net cash to Anchor of $167,000. One thing to watch among financing activities is whether the business is borrowing heavily. Excessive borrowing has been the downfall of many companies.

Investing activities increase and decrease the assets that the business has to work with. A purchase or sale of a capital asset like land, a building or equipment is an investing activity, as is the purchase or sale of an investment in stock or bonds of another company. On the statement of changes in financial position, investing

EXHIBIT 18-2   *Cash Receipts and Disbursements Reported on the Statement of Changes in Financial Position*

Operating Activities

Cash Receipts	Cash Disbursements
Collections from customers	Payments to suppliers
Receipts of interest and dividends on investments	Payments to employees
	Payments of interest and income tax
Other operating receipts	Other operating disbursements

Financing Activities

Cash Receipts	Cash Disbursements
Issuing stock	Repurchase of own shares
Borrowing money	Payment of dividends
	Paying principal amounts of debts

Investing Activities

Cash Receipts	Cash Disbursements
Sale of capital assets	Acquisition of capital assets
Sale of investments that are not cash equivalents	Acquisition of investments that are not cash equivalents
Cash receipts on loans receivable	Making loans

activities include more than the buying and selling of assets that are classified as investments on the balance sheet. Making a loan (an investing activity because the loan creates a receivable for the lender) and collecting on the loan are also reported as investing activities on the statement of changes in financial position. The acquisition of capital assets dominates the company's investing activities, which produce a net cash outflow of $255,000.

Investments in capital assets lay the foundation for future operations. A company that invests in plant and equipment appears stronger than one that is selling off its capital assets. Why? The latter company may have to sell income-producing assets in order to pay the bills. Its outlook is bleak.

Overall, Anchor's cash decreased by $20,000 during 19X2. The company began the year with cash of $42,000 and ended with $22,000.

Each of these categories of activities includes both cash receipts and cash disbursements, as shown in Exhibit 18-2. The exhibit lists the more common cash receipts and cash disbursements that appear on the statement of changes in financial position.

Discontinued Operations and Extraordinary Items

Just as discontinued operations and extraordinary items are to be shown separately on the income statement, so are they to be shown separately on the statement of changes in financial position. The cash inflow or outflow resulting from discontinued operations or from an extraordinary item should be shown as part of operating, financing or investing activities. For example, recent financial statements of Imasco Limited included a loss from discontinued operations as a reduction of cash from operating activities and as an outflow from investing activities. Intermetco Ltd.'s financial statements show an extraordinary item among operating activities, while those of Provigo Inc. and Selkirk Communications Ltd. include extraordinary items with investing activities.

Interest and Dividends

You may be puzzled by the listing of receipts of interest and dividends as operating activities. After all, these cash receipts result from investing activities. Interest comes from investment in loans, and dividends come from investments in stock. Equally puzzling is the listing of the payment of interest as part of operations. Interest expense results from borrowing money — a financing activity. Interest and dividends are included as operating activities because they affect the computation of net income. Interest revenue and dividend revenue increase net income, and interest expense decreases income. Therefore, cash receipts of interest and dividends and cash payments of interest are reported as operating activities on the SCFP.

In contrast, note that dividend payments are reported as a financing activity. This is so because they do not enter into the computation of net income but rather are payments to the entity's owners, who finance the business by holding its shares.

Preparing the Statement of Changes in Financial Position: The Direct Method

OBJECTIVE 3

Prepare a statement of changes in financial position using the direct method

There are two basic ways to present the statement of changes in financial position. Both methods arrive at the same subtotals for operating activities, financing activities, and investing activities, and the net change in cash for the period. They differ only in the manner of showing the cash flows from operating activities. The **direct method** lists the major categories of operating cash receipts and cash disbursements as shown in Exhibit 18-1. We discuss the indirect method later in the chapter.

Section 1540 of the *CICA Handbook* does not specify any particular format for the statement of changes in financial position except to require that activities generating or requiring cash or cash equivalents be classified as operating, financing or investing. This text orders the activities, operating, financing, and investing, in the order suggested in Section 1540. However, many Canadian companies follow the order suggested by U.S. standards of operating, investing, and financing. While either order is acceptable, it is appropriate to begin the statement with operating activities.

Illustrative Problem

Let us see how to prepare the statement of changes in financial position by the direct method in Exhibit 18-1. Suppose Anchor Ltd.'s accountants have assembled the following summary of 19X2 transactions. Those transactions with cash effects are denoted by an asterisk.

Summary of 19X2 Transactions

Operating Activities

  1. Sales on credit, $284,000.

*2. Collections from customers, $271,000.

  3. Interest revenue on notes receivable, $12,000.

*4. Collection of interest receivable, $10,000.

*5. Cash receipt of dividend revenue on investments in stock, $9,000.

  6. Cost of goods sold, $150,000.

  7. Purchases of inventory on credit, $147,000.

*8. Payments to suppliers, $133,000.

  9. Salary and wage expense, $56,000.

*10. Payments of salaries and wages, $58,000.

11. Depreciation expense, $18,000.

12. Other operating expense, $17,000.

*13. Interest expense and payments, $16,000.

*14. Income tax expense and payments, $15,000.

Financing Activities

*15. Proceeds from issuance of common stock, $101,000.

*16. Proceeds from issuance of long-term debt, $94,000.

*17. Payment of long-term debt, $11,000.

*18. Declaration and payment of cash dividends, $17,000.

Investing Activities

*19. Cash payments to acquire capital assets, $306,000.

*20. Loan to another company, $11,000.

*21. Proceeds from sale of capital assets, $62,000, including $8,000 gain.

These summary transactions give the data for both the income statement and the SCFP. Some transactions affect one statement, some the other. Sales, for example, are reported on the income statement, but cash collections appear on the SCFP. Other transactions, such as the cash receipt of dividend revenue, affect both statements. The statement of changes in financial position reports only those transactions with cash effects.

Preparation of the SCFP follows these steps: (1) identify the activities that increased cash and decreased cash — those items with asterisks in the Summary of 19X2 Transactions above; (2) classify each cash increase and each cash decrease as an operating activity, a financing activity or an investing activity; and (3) identify the cash effect of each transaction. Preparing the statement is discussed in the next section.

Cash Flows from Operating Activities   Operating cash flows are listed first because they are the largest and most important source of cash for most businesses. The failure of a company's operations to generate the bulk of its cash inflows for an extended period may signal trouble. This is not true of Anchor Ltd. in Exhibit 18-1. Its operating activities were the largest source of cash receipts, $290,000.

Cash Collections from Customers   Cash sales bring in cash immediately. Credit sales, however, increase Accounts Receivable but not Cash. Receipts of cash on account are a separate transaction, and only cash receipts are reported on the SCFP. "Collections from customers" on the statement includes both cash sales and collections of accounts receivable from credit sales. Collections from customers are Anchor's major operating source of cash, $271,000 in Exhibit 18-1.

Cash Receipts of Interest   Interest revenue is earned on notes receivable. The income statement reports interest revenue. As the clock ticks, interest accrues, but cash interest is received only on specified dates. Only the cash receipts of interest appear on the statement of changes in financial position, $10,000 in Exhibit 18-1.

Cash Receipts of Dividends   Dividends are earned on investments in stock. Dividend revenue is ordinarily recorded as an income item when cash is received. This cash receipt is reported on the SCFP, $9,000 in Exhibit 18-1. (Recall that dividends *received* are part of operating activities, but dividends *paid* are a financing activity.)

Payments to Suppliers   Payments to suppliers include all cash disbursements for inventory and operating expenses except employee compensation, interest and income taxes. Suppliers are those entities that provide the business with its inventory and essential services. For example, a clothing store's payments to John Forsythe, Dylex and Far West Mountain Wear are listed as payments to suppliers. A grocery store chain makes payments to suppliers like BC Sugar, Canada Packers and National Sea Products. Other suppliers provide advertising, utility, and other services that are classified as operating expenses. This category *excludes* payments to employees, payments for interest, and payments for income taxes because there are separate categories of operating cash payments. In Exhibit 18-1, Anchor Ltd. reports payments to suppliers of $133,000.

Payments to Employees   This category includes disbursements for salaries, wages, commissions, and other forms of employee compensation. Accrued amounts are excluded because they have not yet been paid. The income statement reports the expense, including accrued amounts. The statement of changes in financial position reports only the payments ($58,000) in Exhibit 18-1.

Payments for Interest Expense and Income Tax Expense   These cash payments are reported separately from the other expenses. Interest payments show the cash cost of borrowing money. Because excessive borrowing can lead to financial trouble, a large amount of interest payments may signal managers to examine this aspect of operations. Olympia & York, the real estate and resource conglomerate mentioned in the chapter-opening vignette, is an example of an enterprise that got into difficulty because of a large debt load. Income tax payments also deserve emphasis because of their significant amount. In the Anchor Ltd. illustration, these expenses equal the cash payments. Therefore, the same amount appears on the income statement and the statement of changes in financial position. In actual practice, this is rarely the case. Year-end accruals and other transactions usually cause the expense and cash payment amounts to differ. The SCFP reports the cash payments for interest ($16,000) and income tax ($15,000).

Depreciation, Depletion and Amortization Expenses   These expenses are *not* listed on the statement of changes in financial position in Exhibit 18-1 because they do not affect cash. For example, depreciation is recorded by debiting the expense and crediting Accumulated Depreciation. No debit or credit to the Cash account occurs.

Cash Flows from Financing Activities   Cash flows from financing include the following:

Proceeds from Issuance of Stock and Debt   Readers of the financial statements want to know how the entity obtains its financing. Issuing stock (preferred and common) and debt are two common ways to finance operations. In Exhibit 18-1, Anchor Ltd. issued common stock of $101,000 and long-term debt of $94,000.

Payment of Debt and Repurchases of the Company's Own Stock   The payment of debt decreases Cash, which is the opposite of borrowing money. Anchor Ltd. reports debt payments of $11,000. Other transactions in this category are repurchases of the company's stock.

Payment of Cash Dividends   The payment of cash dividends decreases Cash and is therefore reported as a cash payment, as illustrated by Anchor's $17,000 payment in Exhibit 18-1. A dividend in another form (a stock dividend, for example) has no effect on Cash and is *not* reported on the statement of changes in financial position.

Cash Flows from Investing Activities   Many analysts regard investing as a critical activity because a company's investments determine its future course. Large

purchases of capital assets signal expansion, which is usually a good sign about the company. Low levels of investing activities over a lengthy period mean the business is not replenishing its capital assets. Knowing these cash flows helps investors and creditors evaluate the direction that managers are charting for the business.

Cash Payments to Acquire Capital Assets and Investments, and Loans to Other Companies   These cash payments are similar because they acquire a noncash asset. The first transaction purchases capital assets, such as land, buildings and equipment ($306,000) in Exhibit 18-1. In the second transaction, Anchor Ltd. makes an $11,000 loan and obtains a note receivable. These are investing activities because the company is investing in assets for use in the business rather than for resale. These transactions have no effect on revenues or expenses and thus are not reported on the income statement. Another transaction in this category, not shown in Exhibit 18-1, is a purchase of an investment in stocks or bonds.

Proceeds from the Sale of Capital Assets and Investments, and Collections of Loans   These transactions are the opposites of acquisitions of capital assets and investments, and making loans. They are cash receipts from investment transactions.

The sale of the capital assets needs explanation. The statement of changes in financial position reports that Anchor Ltd. received $62,000 cash on the sale of capital assets. The income statement shows an $8,000 gain on this transaction. What is the appropriate amount to show on the statement of changes in financial position? It is $62,000, the cash proceeds from the sale. Assuming Anchor sold equipment that cost $64,000 and had accumulated depreciation of $10,000, the journal entry to record this sale is

Cash	62,000	
Accumulated Depreciation...	10,000	
Equipment		64,000
Gain on Sale of Capital Assets		
(from income statement)...		8,000

The analysis indicates that the book value of the equipment was $54,000 ($64,000 – $10,000). However, the book value of the asset sold is not reported on the SCFP. Only the cash proceeds of $62,000 are reported on the statement. For the income statement, only the gain is reported. Since a gain occurred, you may wonder why this cash receipt is not reported as part of operations. Operations consist of buying and selling merchandise or rendering services to earn revenue. Investing activities are the acquisition and disposition of assets used in operations. Therefore, the sale of capital assets and the sale of investments should be viewed as cash inflows from investing activities.

Investors and creditors are often critical of a company that sells large amounts of its capital assets. Such sales may signal an emergency. In other situations, selling off fixed assets may be good news about the company if it is getting rid of an unprofitable division. Whether sales of capital assets are good news or bad news should be evaluated in light of a company's operating and financing characteristics.

Focus of the Statement of Changes in Financial Position _____

The statement of changes in financial position focuses on the increase or decrease in cash during the period (highlighted in Exhibit 18-1 for emphasis). This check figure is taken from the comparative balance sheet that shows the beginning and ending balances. The SCFP, which adds up to the change in cash, shows the reasons why cash changed.

EXHIBIT 18-3   *Income Statement*

Anchor Ltd. Income Statement for the year ended December 31, 19X2 (amounts in thousands)		
Revenues and gains		
Sales revenue	$284	
Interest revenue	12	
Dividend revenue	9	
Gain on sale of capital assets	8	
Total revenues and gains		$313
Expenses		
Cost of goods sold	$150	
Salary and wage expense	56	
Depreciation expense	18	
Other operating expense	17	
Interest expense	16	
Income tax expense	15	
Total expenses		272
Net income		$ 41

Exhibit 18-1 illustrates how the cash-balance information may be shown at the bottom of an SCFP, a common format. Another common practice places the beginning cash balance at the top of the statement and the ending balance at the bottom. However, the *CICA Handbook* in Section 1540 does not require that the beginning and ending cash balances appear on the statement. Because the balance sheet reports these amounts, it is sufficient to show on the SCFP only the change that occurred during the period.

In our example, cash decreased by $20,000. Readers of the annual report might wonder why cash decreased during a good year. After all, Exhibit 18-3, Anchor Ltd.'s income statement, reports net income of $41,000. When a business is expanding, its cash often declines. Why? It is because cash is invested in capital assets such as land, buildings and equipment, as reported in the statement of changes in financial position. Conversely, cash may increase in a year when income is low, if the company borrows heavily. The statement of changes in financial position gives its readers a direct picture of where cash came from (cash inflows) and how cash was spent (cash outflows).

Summary Problem for Your Review

Acadia Corporation accounting records include the following information for the year ended June 30, 19X8:

1. Salary expense, $104,000.
2. Interest revenue, $8,000.
3. Proceeds from issuance of common stock, $31,000.
4. Declaration and payment of cash dividends, $22,000.
5. Collection of interest receivable, $7,000.

6. Payments of salaries, $110,000.

7. Credit sales, $358,000.

8. Loan to another company, $42,000.

9. Proceeds from sale of capital assets, $18,000, including $1,000 loss.

10. Collections from customers, $369,000.

11. Cash receipt of dividend revenue on stock investments, $3,000.

12. Payments to suppliers, $319,000.

13. Cash sales, $92,000.

14. Depreciation expense, $32,000.

15. Proceeds from issuance of short-term debt, $38,000.

16. Payments of long-term debt, $57,000.

17. Interest expense and payments, $11,000.

18. Loan collections, $51,000.

19. Proceeds from sale of investments, $22,000, including $13,000 gain.

20. Amortization expense, $5,000.

21. Purchases of inventory on credit, $297,000.

22. Income tax expense and payments, $16,000.

23. Cash payments to acquire capital assets, $83,000.

24. Cost of goods sold, $284,000.

25. Cash balance: June 30, 19X7 — $83,000

                  June 30, 19X8 — $54,000

Required

Prepare Acadia Corporation's statement of changes in financial position and income statement for the year ended June 30, 19X8. Follow the formats of Exhibits 18-1 and 18-3.

SOLUTION TO REVIEW PROBLEM

Acadia Corporation
Statement of Changes in Financial Position
for the year ended June 30, 19X8
(amounts in thousands)

Item No. (Reference Only)			
	Cash flows from operating activities		
	Receipts		
10, 13	Collections from customers ($369 + $92).........	$ 461	
5	Interest received on notes receivable...............	7	
11	Dividends received on investments in stock..	3	
	Total cash receipts..		471
	Payments		
12	To suppliers	$(319)	
6	To employees..	(110)	
17	For interest...	(11)	
22	For income tax...	(16)	
	Total cash payments.......................................		(456)
	Net cash inflow from operating activities..		15
	Cash flows from financing activities		
15	Proceeds from issuance of short-term debt.....	$ 38	

3	Proceeds from issuance of common stock	31	
16	Payments of long-term debt................................	(57)	
4	Dividends declared and paid.............................	(22)	
	Net cash outflow from financing activities..		(10)
	Cash flows from investing activities		
23	Acquisition of capital assets................................	$ (83)	
8	Loan to another company	(42)	
19	Proceeds from sale of investments.....................	22	
9	Proceeds from sale of capital assets	18	
18	Collection of loans	51	
	Net cash outflow from investing activities..		(34)
	Net decrease in cash		$(29)
25	Cash balance, June 30, 19X7		83
25	Cash balance, June 30, 19X8		$ 54

Acadia Corporation
Income Statement
for the year ended June 30, 19X8
(amounts in thousands)

Revenue and gains		
Sales revenue ($358 + $92)	$450	
Gain on sale of investments...	13	
Interest revenue	8	
Dividend revenue..	3	
Total revenues and gains..		474
Expenses and losses		
Cost of goods sold...	$284	
Salary expense	104	
Depreciation expense..	32	
Income tax expense..	16	
Interest expense	11	
Amortization expense..	5	
Loss on sale of capital assets..	1	
Total expenses...		453
Net income		$ 21

Computing Individual Amounts for the Statement of Changes in Financial Position

OBJECTIVE 4

Use the financial statements to compute the cash effects of a wide variety of business transactions

How do accountants compute the amounts for the statement of changes in financial position? Many accountants prepare the SCFP using the income statement amounts and *changes* in the related balance sheet accounts. Accountants label this the T-account approach.[1] Learning to analyze T-accounts in this manner is one of the most useful skills you will acquire from accounting. It will enable you to identify the cash effects of a wide variety of transactions. The following discussions use Anchor Ltd.'s comparative balance sheet in Exhibit 18-4 and income statement in Exhibit 18-3. For continuity, trace the cash amounts on the balance sheet in Exhibit 18-4 to the bottom part of the SCFP in Exhibit 18-1, p. 780.

---

[1] The chapter appendix covers the work sheet approach to preparation of the statement of changes in financial position.

EXHIBIT 18-4   *Comparative Balance Sheet*

Anchor Ltd.
Comparative Balance Sheet
December 31, 19X2 and 19X1
(amounts in thousands)

Assets	19X2	19X1	Increase (Decrease)
Current			
Cash	$ 22	$ 42	$(20)
Accounts receivable	93	80	13
Interest receivable...	3	1	2
Inventory	135	138	(3)
Prepaid expenses..	8	7	1
Long-term receivable from another company	11	—	11
Capital assets, net..	453	219	234
Total	$725	$487	$238
Liabilities			
Current			
Accounts payable	$ 91	$ 57	$ 34
Salary and wage payable	4	6	(2)
Accrued liabilities..	1	3	(2)
Long-term debt...	160	77	83
Shareholders' Equity			
Common stock...	359	258	101
Retained earnings...	110	86	24
Total	$725	$487	$238

Computing the Cash Amounts of Operating Activities

Computing Cash Collections from Customers   Collections can be computed by converting sales revenue (an accrual-basis amount) to the cash basis. A decrease in the balance of Accounts Receivable during the period indicates that cash collections exceeded sales revenue. Therefore, we add the decrease to sales revenue to compute collections. An increase in Accounts Receivable means that sales exceeded cash receipts. This amount is subtracted from sales to compute collections. These relationships suggest the following computation for collections from customers:

$$\begin{matrix} \textbf{Collections} \\ \textbf{from} \\ \textbf{customers} \end{matrix} = \textbf{Sales Revenue} \begin{cases} \textbf{+ Decrease in Accounts Receivable} \\ \textbf{or} \\ \textbf{- Increase in Accounts Receivable} \end{cases}$$

Anchor Ltd.'s income statement (Exhibit 18-3, p. 786) reports sales of $284,000. Exhibit 18-4 shows that Accounts Receivable increased from $80,000 at the beginning of the year to $93,000 at year end, a $13,000 increase. Based on these amounts, Collections equal $271,000: Sales Revenue, $284,000 minus the $13,000 increase in Accounts Receivable. Posting these amounts directly to Accounts Receivable highlights the collections amount, $271,000.

Accounts Receivable

Beginning balance....................	80,000		
Sales...	284,000	**Collections**	**271,000**
Ending balance..........................	93,000		

We see that this computation required the income statement account Sales Revenue and the *change* in the related balance sheet account, Accounts Receivable. The amount of cash collections from customers is derived from these accounts. Cash collections — and the other amounts reported on the SCFP — are *not* the balances of separate ledger accounts. Instead, the cash flow amounts must be computed by analysis of related income statement and balance sheet accounts, as illustrated in this section.

All collections of receivables can be computed in the same way. For example, the illustrative problem indicates that Anchor Ltd. received cash interest. To compute this operating cash receipt, note that the income statement, Exhibit 18-3, p. 786, reports interest revenue of $12,000. Interest Receivable's balance in Exhibit 18-4 increased by $2,000. Cash receipts of interest must be $10,000 ($12,000 – $2,000).

Computing Payments to Suppliers   This computation includes two parts, payments for inventory and payments for expenses other than interest and income tax.

Payments for inventory are computed by converting cost of goods sold to the cash basis. We accomplish this by analyzing Cost of Goods Sold and Accounts Payable. The computation of cash payments for inventory is

$$
\begin{matrix}
\text{Payments} \\
\text{for} \\
\text{inventory}
\end{matrix}
=
\begin{matrix}
\text{Cost of} \\
\text{Goods Sold}
\end{matrix}
\left\{
\begin{matrix}
+\ \text{Increase in} \\
\text{Inventory} \\
\text{or} \\
-\ \text{Decrease in} \\
\text{Inventory}
\end{matrix}
\right.
\text{and}
\left\{
\begin{matrix}
+\ \text{Decrease in} \\
\text{Accounts Payable*} \\
\text{or} \\
-\ \text{Increase in} \\
\text{Accounts Payable*}
\end{matrix}
\right.
$$

* + Decrease (or – Increase) in Short-Term Notes Payable for inventory purchases

The logic behind this computation is that an increase in inventory leads to an increase in accounts payable that finds its way into a cash payment. A decrease in accounts payable can occur only if cash was paid. By contrast, an increase in accounts payable indicates that cash was *not* paid. A detailed analysis will show the validity of this computation.

Anchor Ltd. reports cost of goods sold of $150,000. The balance sheet shows that Inventory decreased by $3,000. Accounts Payable increased by $34,000. These amounts combine to compute payments for inventory of $113,000: Cost of Goods Sold, $150,000, minus the decrease in Inventory, $3,000, minus the increase in Accounts Payable, $34,000 — a total of $113,000.

The T-account analysis also indicates payments of $113,000 (with Purchases inserted for completeness):

Cost of Goods Sold

Beginning inventory	138,000	Ending inventory	135,000
Purchases.................................	147,000		
Cost of goods sold..................	150,000		

Accounts Payable

		Beginning balance....................	57,000
Payments for inventory........	**113,000**	Purchases	147,000
		Ending balance..........................	91,000

Payments to suppliers ($133,000 in Exhibit 18-1) equal the sum of payments for inventory ($113,000) plus payments for operating expenses ($20,000), as explained next.

Computing Payments for Operating Expenses   Payments for operating expenses other than interest and income tax can be computed by analyzing Prepaid Expenses and Other Accrued Liabilities, as follows:

$$
\begin{array}{c}
\text{Payments} \\
\text{for operating} \\
\text{expenses}
\end{array}
=
\begin{array}{c}
\text{Operating} \\
\text{expenses other} \\
\text{than salaries,} \\
\text{wages, and} \\
\text{depreciation}
\end{array}
+
\left\{
\begin{array}{c}
\text{Increase in} \\
\text{Prepaid Expenses} \\
\text{or} \\
\text{Decrease in} \\
\text{Prepaid Expenses}
\end{array}
\right.
+ \text{and}
\left\{
\begin{array}{c}
\text{Decrease in} \\
\text{Accrued Liabilities} \\
\text{or} \\
\text{Increase in} \\
\text{Accrued Liabilities}
\end{array}
\right.
$$

Increases in prepaid expenses require cash payments, and decreases indicate that payments were less than expenses. Decreases in accrued liabilities can occur only from cash payments, and increases mean that cash was *not* paid.

Anchor's income statement reports operating expenses, other than salaries, wages and depreciation, of $17,000. The balance sheet shows that prepaid expenses increased by $1,000, and accrued liabilities decreased by $2,000. Based on these data, payments for operating expenses total $20,000 ($17,000 + $1,000 + $2,000).

This result is confirmed by the T-account analysis, as follows:

Prepaid Expenses

Beginning balance	7,000	Expiration of prepaid expense..	7,000 ←
Payments	**8,000**		
Ending balance	8,000		

Accrued Liabilities

Payment of beginning		Beginning balance	3,000
balance	**3,000**	Accrual of expense	
		at year end	1,000 ←
		Ending balance	1,000

Operating Expenses (other than Salaries, Wages and Depreciation)

→ Expiration of prepaid			
expense	7,000		
→ Accrual of expense at year end..	1,000		
Payments	**9,000**		
Ending balance	17,000		

Total payments = $20,000 ($8,000 + $3,000 + $9,000)

Computing Payments to Employees   The company may have separate accounts for salaries, wages and other forms of cash compensation to employees. To compute payments to employees, it is convenient to combine them into one account. Anchor's calculation begins with Salary and Wage Expense (an income statement account) and adjusts for the change in Salary and Wage Payable (a balance sheet account). The computation follows:

$$
\begin{array}{c}
\text{Payments} \\
\text{to} \\
\text{employees}
\end{array}
=
\begin{array}{c}
\text{Salary} \\
\text{and Wage} \\
\text{Expense}
\end{array}
\left\{
\begin{array}{c}
\textbf{+ Decrease in Salary and Wage Payable} \\
\textbf{or} \\
\textbf{– Increase in Salary and Wage Payable}
\end{array}
\right.
$$

A decrease in the liability is added because it requires a cash payment. An increase in the liability indicates that the expense exceeds cash payments, so the increase is subtracted. Anchor's salary and wage expense is $56,000. The balance sheet in Exhibit 18-4 reports a $2,000 decrease in the liability. Thus cash payments to employees are $58,000 ($56,000 + $2,000). This is confirmed by analysis of the Salary and Wage Payable account.

Salary and Wage Payable

		Beginning balance	6,000
Payments	58,000	Salary and wage expense	56,000
		Ending balance	4,000

Computing Payments of Interest and Income Taxes In our illustrative problem, the expense and payment amount is the same for each of these expenses. Therefore, no analysis is required to determine the payment amount. If the expense and the payment differ, the payment can be computed by analyzing the related liability account. The payment computation follows the pattern illustrated for payments to employees.

Computing the Cash Amounts of Financing Activities

Financing activities affect liability and shareholders' equity accounts, such as Notes Payable, Bonds Payable, Long-Term Debt, Common Stock and Retained Earnings. The cash amounts of financing activities can be computed by analyzing these accounts.

Computing Issuances and Payments of Long-Term Debt The beginning and ending balances of Long-Term Debt, Notes Payable or Bonds Payable are taken from the balance sheet. If either the amount of new issuances or the amount of the payments is known, the other amount can be computed. New debt issuances total $94,000. The computation of debt payments follows, using balances from Exhibit 18-4:

$$\begin{array}{ccccccc} \textbf{Beginning} & & \textbf{Issuance of} & & & & \textbf{Ending} \\ \textbf{Long-Term Debt} & + & \textbf{new debt} & - & \textbf{Payments} & = & \textbf{Long-term Debt} \\ \textbf{balance} & & & & & & \textbf{balance} \end{array}$$

$$\$77{,}000 \quad + \quad \$94{,}000 \quad - \quad \text{Payments} \quad = \quad \$160{,}000$$

Rearranging this equation results in the following:

$$- \textbf{Payments} = \$160{,}000 - \$77{,}000 - \$94{,}000$$
$$\textbf{Payments} = \$11{,}0000$$

This computation arises from analysis of the Long-term Debt account:

Long-term Debt

		Beginning balance	77,000
Payments	11,000	Issuance of new debt	94,000
		Ending balance	160,000

Computing Issuances and Repurchases of Stock The cash effects of these financing activities can be determined by analyzing the various stock accounts. It is convenient to work with a single summary account for stock as we do for capital assets below. Using Exhibit 18-4 data, we have:

Beginning Stock balance	+	Issuance of new stock	– Retirements	=	Ending Stock balance
$258,000	+	New Stock	– $0	=	$359,000

Isolating new stock gives the final equation:

Issuance of new stock = $359,000 – $258,000 = $101,000

The Common Stock T-account shows these amounts:

Common Stock

	Beginning balance	258,000
Retirements of stock............................ 0	**Issuance of new stock**...........	**101,000**
	Ending balance........................	359,000

Computing Dividend Payments   If the amount of the dividends is not given elsewhere (for example, in a statement of retained earnings), it can be computed by analyzing the Retained Earnings account. Beginning and ending amounts come from the balance sheet, and the income statement reports net income. Dividend declarations can be computed as shown here, using net income from Exhibit 18-3 and Retained Earnings balances from Exhibit 18-4. We assume Anchor Ltd. had no stock dividends or other transactions that affected Retained Earnings during the year. If, for example, a stock dividend and a cash dividend occurred during the year, total dividends must be separated into stock dividends and cash dividends because stock dividends do not affect cash.

Beginning Retained Earnings balance	+ Net income –	Dividend declarations	= Ending Retained Earnings balance
$86,000	+ $41,000 –	Dividends	= $110,000

Keeping dividends on the left-hand side produces the following equation:

$$- \text{Dividends} = \$110{,}000 - \$86{,}000 - \$41{,}000$$
$$\text{Dividends} = -\$110{,}000 + \$86{,}000 + \$41{,}000$$
$$\text{Dividends} = \$17{,}000$$

Analysis of the Retained Earnings T-account illustrates the equation approach:

Retained Earnings

	Beginning balance....................	86,000
Dividend declaration **17,000**	Net income...............................	41,000
	Ending balance........................	110,000

A change in the Dividends Payable account means that dividend payments differ from the amount declared. In this case, dividend payments are determined by first computing dividends declared as shown here. Then add the amount of any decrease in the balance of Dividends Payable or subtract the amount of any increase in that account balance. The result is the dividend payments figure. The Dividends Payable account illustrates the analysis:

Dividends Payable

		Beginning balance...................	XXX
Dividend payments.....................	XXX	Dividend declarations...........	XXX
		Ending balance.......................	XXX

Computing the Cash Amounts of Investing Activities

Investing activities affect asset accounts, such as Capital Assets, Investments and Notes Receivable. The cash amounts of investing activities can be identified by analyzing these accounts. Most data for the computations are taken directly from the income statement and beginning and ending balance sheets. Other amounts come from the analysis of accounts in the ledger.

Computing Acquisitions and Sales of Capital Assets   Most companies have separate accounts for Land, Buildings, Equipment, and other capital assets. It is helpful to combine these accounts into a single summary for computing the cash flows from acquisitions and sales of these assets. Also, we subtract accumulated depreciation from the assets' cost and work with a net figure for capital assets. This allows us to work with a single capital asset account as opposed to a large number of capital asset and related accumulated amortization accounts.

To illustrate, observe that Anchor Ltd.'s balance sheet (Exhibit 18-4) reports beginning capital assets, net of depreciation, of $219,000 and an ending net amount of $453,000. The income statement shows depreciation of $18,000 and a $8,000 gain on sale of capital assets. Further, the acquisitions total $306,000. How much are the proceeds from the sale of capital assets? First, we must determine their book value, computed as follows:

$$
\begin{matrix}
\textbf{Beginning} & & & & \textbf{Book value} & \textbf{Ending} \\
\textbf{Capital Asset} + \textbf{Acquisitions} - \textbf{Depreciation} - & \textbf{of capital} & = & \textbf{Capital Asset} \\
\textbf{balance (net)} & & & & \textbf{assets sold} & \textbf{balance (net)}
\end{matrix}
$$

$$
\$219,000 \ + \ \$306,000 \ - \ \$18,000 \ - \ \frac{\textbf{Book value}}{\textbf{sold}} = \ \$453,000
$$

Isolating book value sold on the left-hand side rearranges the equation as follows:

$$
- \textbf{Book value sold} = \$453,000 - \$219,000 - \$306,000 + \$18,000
$$
$$
\textbf{Book value sold} = \$54,000
$$

Now we can compute the sale proceeds as follows:

$$
\textbf{Sale proceeds} = \textbf{Book value sold, } \$54,000 + \textbf{Gain, } \$8,000 - \textbf{Loss, } \$0
$$
$$
= \$62,000
$$

Trace the sale proceeds of $62,000 to the statement of changes in financial position in Exhibit 18-1. If the sale resulted in a loss of $3,000, the sale proceeds would be $51,000 ($54,000 – $3,000), and the SCFP would report $51,000 as a cash receipt from this investing activity.

The book value of capital assets sold can also be computed by analysis of the Capital Assets T-account:

Capital Assets (net)

Beginning balance....................	219,000	Depreciation	18,000
Acquisitions	306,000	**Book value of assets sold**	**54,000**
Ending balance	453,000		

Computing Acquisitions and Sales of Assets Classified as Investments, and Loans and Their Collections Accountants use a separate category of assets for investments in stocks, bonds and other types of assets. The cash amounts of transactions involving these assets can be computed in the manner illustrated for capital assets. Investments are easier to analyze, however, because there is no depreciation to account for, as shown by the following T-account:

Investments

Beginning balance...........................	XXX		
Purchases......................................	XXX	Cost of investments sold..........	**XXX**
Ending balance..............................	XXX		

Loan transactions follow the pattern illustrated on pp. 789 – 790 for collections from customers. New loans cause a debit to a receivable and an outflow of cash. Collections increase cash and cause a credit to the receivable, as this T-account illustrates:

Loans and Notes Receivable

Beginning balance...........................	XXX		
New loans made............................	XXX	Collections	**XXX**
Ending balance..............................	XXX		

Noncash Financing and Investing Activities _____

Companies make investments that do not require cash. They also obtain financing other than cash. Our illustrative problem included none of these transactions.

Suppose Anchor Ltd. issued common stock with a stated value of $320,000 to acquire a warehouse. Anchor would journalize this transaction as follows:

Warehouse	320,000	
Common Stock..		320,000

Despite the fact that this transaction has no net effect on the statement of changes in financial position, Section 1540.20 of the *CICA Handbook* requires that noncash financing and investing activities be disclosed on the statement and that both sides of the transaction be disclosed separately (that is, it is inappropriate to disclose only the net effect of the transaction). In this case, the proceeds from the issue of the common stock will be included with investing activities, while the purchase of the building will be included with financing activities. The SCFP should indicate that the two transactions are related. The appropriate disclosure is illustrated in the solution to the review problem (Robins Corporation) on p. 801.

As was noted above, the transaction must be shown in its entirety; it is not appropriate to show only the net effects of the transaction. For example, if the purchase had been for common stock of $300,000 and for cash of $20,000, it would not be appropriate to show only the net effect on cash of $20,000. The SCFP would show a financing inflow of $300,000 for the common stock and an investing outflow of $320,000 for the building.

Preparing the Statement of Changes in Financial Position: The Indirect Method _____

An alternative way to compute cash flows from operating activities is the **indirect method**. This method, also called the **reconciliation method**, starts with net

EXHIBIT 18-5   *Statement of Changes in Financial Position*

Anchor Ltd.		
Statement of Changes in Financial Position: Indirect Method for Operating Activities		
for the year ended December 31, 19X2		
(amounts in thousands)		
Cash flows from operating activities		
Net income..		$ 41
Add (subtract) items that affect		
net income and cash flow differently:		
Depreciation...	$ 18	
Gain on sale of capital assets.....................................	(8)	
Increase in accounts receivable	(13)	
Increase in interest receivable....................................	(2)	
Decrease in inventory	3	
Increase in prepaid expenses.....................................	(1)	
Increase in accounts payable	34	
Decrease in salary and wage payable	(2)	
Decrease in accrued liabilities	(2)	27
Net cash inflow from operating activities		68
Cash flows from financing activities		
Proceeds from issuance of common stock....................	$ 101	
Proceeds from issuance of long-term debt...................	94	
Payment of long-term debt..	(11)	
Payment of dividends..	(17)	
Net cash inflow from financing activities...........		167
Cash flows from investing activities		
Acquisition of capital assets	$(306)	
Loan to another company...	(11)	
Proceeds from sale of capital assets	62	
Net cash outflow from investing activities..............		(255)
Net decrease in cash		$ (20)
Cash balance, December 31, 19X1		42
Cash balance, December 31, 19X2		$ 22

OBJECTIVE 5

Prepare a statement of changes in financial position using the indirect method

income and shows the reconciliation from net income to operating cash flows. It shows the link between net income and cash flow from operations better than the direct method. The main drawback of the indirect method is that it does not report the detailed operating cash flows: collections from customers and other cash receipts, payments to suppliers, payments to employees, and payments for interest and taxes.

The indirect method and the direct method are both used in Canada. These methods of preparing the statement of changes in financial position affect only the operating activities section of the statement. No difference exists in the reporting of financing activities and investing activities.

Exhibit 18-5 is Anchor Ltd.'s statement prepared by the indirect method. You will see that only the operating section of the statement differs from the direct method format in Exhibit 18-1 on p. 780.

Logic behind the Indirect Method

The operating section of the SCFP begins with net income, taken directly from the income statement. A series of additions and subtractions follows. These are labeled

"Add (subtract) items that affect net income and cash flow differently." In this section, we discuss those items.

Depreciation, Depletion and Amortization Expenses

These expenses are added back in going from net income to cash flow from operations. Let us see why. Depreciation is recorded as follows:

Depreciation Expense	18,000	
Accumulated Depreciation		18,000

This entry contains no debit or credit to Cash, so depreciation expense has no cash effect. However, depreciation is deducted from revenues in the computation of income. Therefore, in going from net income to cash flow from operations, we add depreciation back to net income. The addback simply cancels the earlier deduction. The following example should help. Suppose a company had two transactions during the period, a $1,000 cash sale and depreciation expense of $300. Net income is $700 ($1,000 – $300). Cash flow from operations is $1,000. To go from net income ($700) to cash flow ($1,000), we must add back the depreciation amount of $300.

All expenses with no cash effects are added back to net income on the statement of changes in financial position. Depletion and amortization are two other examples. Likewise, revenues that do not provide cash are subtracted from net income. An example is the equity-method investment revenue discussed in Chapter 17.

Gains and Losses on the Sale of Assets

Sales of capital assets are investing activities on the SCFP. A gain or loss on the sale is an adjustment to income. Exhibit 18-5 includes an adjustment for a gain. Recall that equipment with a book value of $54,000 was sold for $62,000, producing a gain of $8,000. The way to learn how to treat an item on the statement of changes in financial position is to examine the journal entry that recorded it, as discussed on p. 785.

The $8,000 gain is reported on the income statement and, therefore, is included in net income. However, the cash receipt from the sale is $62,000, which includes the gain. To avoid counting the gain twice, we need to remove its effect from income and report the cash receipt of $62,000 in the investing-activities section of the statement. Starting with net income, we subtract the gain. This deduction removes the gain's earlier effect on income. The sale of capital assets is reported as a $62,000 cash receipt from an investing activity, as shown in Exhibits 18-1 and 18-5.

A loss on the sale of capital assets is also an adjustment to net income on the SCFP. However, a loss is added back to income to compute cash flow from operations. The sale proceeds are reported under investing activities.

Changes in the Current Asset and Current Liability Accounts

Most current assets and current liabilities result from operating activities. Accounts receivable result from sales, inventory generates revenues, and prepaid expenses are used up in operations. On the liability side, accounts payable and short-term notes payable are incurred to buy inventory, and accrued liabilities relate to salaries, utilities and other expenses. Changes in these current accounts are reported as adjustments to net income on the statement of changes in financial position. The following rules apply:

1. An *increase* in a current asset other than cash (or cash equivalents) is subtracted from net income to compute cash flow from operations. Suppose a company makes a sale. Income is increased by the sale amount. However, collection of less than the full amount leaves Accounts Receivable with an increase. To compute the impact of revenue on the cash flow amount, it is necessary to subtract the $13,000 increase in Accounts Receivable from net income in Exhibit 18-5. The same logic applies to the other current assets. If they increase during the period, subtract the increase from net income.

2. A *decrease* in a current asset other than cash is added to net income. For example, suppose Accounts Receivable's balance decreased by $4,000 during the period.

Exhibit 18–6   *Relationship between Net Income and Net Cash Flow from Operating Activities: Indirect Method*

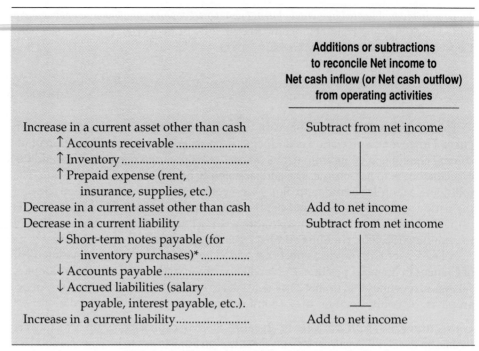

	Additions or subtractions to reconcile Net income to Net cash inflow (or Net cash outflow) from operating activities
Increase in a current asset other than cash 　↑ Accounts receivable .... 　↑ Inventory .... 　↑ Prepaid expense (rent, 　　　insurance, supplies, etc.)	Subtract from net income
Decrease in a current asset other than cash	Add to net income
Decrease in a current liability 　↓ Short-term notes payable (for 　　　inventory purchases)* .... 　↓ Accounts payable .... 　↓ Accrued liabilities (salary 　　　payable, interest payable, etc.).	Subtract from net income
Increase in a current liability.......................	Add to net income

*Short- term notes payable for general borrowing relate to financing, not operating, activities.

Author's Note: We thank Jean Marie Hudson for suggesting this exhibit

Cash receipts cause the Accounts Receivable balance to decrease, so decreases in Accounts Receivable and the other current assets are added to net income.

3. A *decrease* in a current liability is subtracted from net income. The payment of a current liability causes it to decrease, so decreases in current liabilities are subtracted from net income. For example, in Exhibit 18-5, the $2,000 decrease in Accrued Liabilities is subtracted from net income to compute net cash inflow from operating activities.

4. An *increase* in a current liability is added to net income. Suppose Accrued Liabilities increased during the year. This can occur only if cash is not spent to pay this liability, which means that cash payments are less than the related expense. Thus increases in current liabilities are added to net income.

Exhibit 18-6 summarizes these adjustments to convert net income to net cash inflow (or net cash outflow) from operating activities.

The computation of net cash inflow or net cash outflow from *operating* activities by the indirect method takes a path that is very different from the computation by the direct method. However, the two methods arrive at the same amount of net cash flow. This is shown in Exhibits 18-1 and 18-5, which report a net cash inflow of $68,000.

An Actual Statement of Changes in Financial Position

Exhibit 18-7 is an example of a statement of changes in financial position for an actual company, Armeno Resources Inc., a mining company located in British Columbia, with operations in North and South America and Africa.

Exhibit 18-7, similar to Exhibit 18-5, illustrates the indirect method. Many companies use it because it allows users to reconcile the statement of changes in

EXHIBIT 18-7   *Statement of Changes in Financial Position*

Armeno Resources Inc. Statement of Changes in Financial Position year ended October 31, 1991	
Cash provided from (used for)	
Operating activities	
Loss before other items..	$(1,936,901)
Items not affecting cash	
Depreciation and depletion..	25,250
Equity loss in joint venture...	13,854
	(1,897,797)
Changes in noncash working capital	472,876
Financing activities	
Issue of shares (net of issue costs)...	2,602,860
Loan and interest payable...	9,209
	2,612,069
Investing activities	
Advances from related companies..	59,121
Investment in joint venture corporation	(235,000)
Proceeds on the disposition of mineral claims....................	11,250
Purchase of fixed assets	(1,661)
Purchase of mineral properties...	(22,000)
Deferred exploration...	(93,373)
Investment in securities..	(92,982)
Other...	9,321
	(365,324)
Increase (decrease) in cash and cash equivalents	821,824
Cash and cash equivalents, beginning of year..........................	3,062
Cash and cash equivalents, end of year.....................................	$ 824,886

Note: The balance sheet of Armeno Resources shows balances for cash and cash equivalents of
$824,886 and $3,062 at October 31, 1991 and 1990 respectively.

financial position more easily to the income statement. There are, however, several differences between Exhibits 18-5 and 18-7. First, the company had a loss on operations so the income statement items not affecting cash are subtracted rather than added back as in Exhibit 18-5. Second, the company had an equity loss in a joint venture; as a noncash expense, an adjustment must be made for it. Third, the changes in noncash working capital accounts such as Accounts Receivable, Inventory and Accounts Payable are combined into a single number, $472,876, instead of being listed as they are in Exhibit 18-5.

Computers and the Statement of Changes in Financial Position

When the statement of changes in financial position became a required financial statement, computerized accounting systems were changed so that they could generate this statement as easily as they do the balance sheet and income statement. Consider the direct method for preparing the SCFP (see Exhibit 18-2). To get the amounts for the operating section, cash inflows and outflows (grouped by the related revenue and expense category) can be drawn from the posted files generated from cash receipts and cash payment records. Specifically, the cash receipts postings to Accounts Receivable provide the information necessary to show Cash Receipts from Customers. The computer adds the monthly postings to reach the yearly total. All other cash flows for operating activities, as well as cash flows for financing and investing activities, are handled similarly.

The computer can generate the SCFP using the indirect method with equal ease. The only additional information needed, noncash income statement flows and changes in noncash current assets and current liabilities, come from computer general ledger files.

Do not be misled into believing that the statement of changes in financial position created from a computer's general ledger files is automatically correct from the point of view of generally accepted accounting principles. For example, noncash financing and investing activities of a large organization, such as Bombardier Inc., might be incorrectly combined with the company's cash flows. The computerized system must be sophisticated enough to distinguish among various categories of cash activities. Most important, accountants must ensure that the computer software used for accounting purposes by their company produces output that adheres to generally accepted accounting principles. They must keep in mind that revisions to such software are relatively easy and may be made without their knowledge.

Summary Problem for Your Review

Prepare the 19X3 statement of changes in financial position for Robins Corporation, using the indirect method to report cash flows from operating activities.

| | December 31, | |
	19X3	19X2
Current assets		
Cash and cash equivalents	$ 19,000	$ 3,000
Accounts receivable	22,000	23,000
Inventories	34,000	31,000
Prepaid expenses	1,000	3,000
Current liabilities		
Notes payable (for inventory purchases)	$ 11,000	$ 7,000
Accounts payable	24,000	19,000
Accrued liabilities	7,000	9,000
Income and other taxes payable	10,000	10,000

Transaction data for 19X3

Purchase of equipment	$98,000	Depreciation expense		$ 7,000
Payment of cash dividends	18,000	Issuance of long-term note		
Net income	26,000	payable to borrow cash		7,000
Issuance of common stock		Issuance of common stock		
to retire bonds payable	13,000	for cash		19,000
Purchase of long-term		Sale of building		74,000
investment	8,000	Amortization expense		3,000
Issuance of long-term note		Repurchase of own shares		5,000
payable to purchase		Loss on sale of building		2,000
patent	37,000			

SOLUTION TO REVIEW PROBLEM

Robins Corporation
Statement of Changes in Financial Position
for the year ended December 31, 19X3

Cash flows from operating activities		
Net income..		$26,000
Add (subtract) items that affect net income and		
cash flow differently:		
Depreciation..	$ 7,000	
Amortization..	3,000	
Loss on sale of building...	2,000	
Decrease in accounts receivable...............................	1,000	
Increase in inventories..	(3,000)	
Decrease in prepaid expenses	2,000	
Increase in notes payable, short-term	4,000	
Increase in accounts payable....................................	5,000	
Decrease in accrued liabilities	(2,000)	19,000
Net cash inflow from operating activities		45,000
Cash flows from financing activities		
Issuance of long-term notes payable*............................	$ 44,000	
Issuance of common stock**..	32,000	
Payment of cash dividends	(18,000)	
Retirement of bonds payable**	(13,000)	
Repurchase of Robins Corporation shares.....................	(5,000)	
Net cash inflow from financing activities..................		40,000
Cash flows from investing activities		
Purchase of equipment..	$(98,000)	
Sale of building...	74,000	
Purchase of patent*..	(37,000)	
Purchase of long-term investment	(8,000)	
Net cash outflow from investing activities.................		(69,000)
Net increase in cash...		$16,000

---

* During the year, the company issued a long-term note payable in the amount of $37,000 and
used the proceeds to purchase a patent; notes were also issued for $7,000 cash.

** During the year, the company issued common stock in the amount of $13,000 and used the pro-
ceeds to retire bonds payable in the same amount; stock was also issued for $19,000 cash.

Summary

The *statement of changes in financial position* reports a business's cash receipts, cash
disbursements and net change in cash for the accounting period. It shows *why* cash
increased or decreased during the period. A required financial statement, it gives
a different view of the business from the accrual-basis statements. The statement of
changes in financial position helps financial statement users predict the future cash
flows of the entity. Cash includes cash on hand, cash in bank and *cash equivalents* such
as liquid, short-term investments.

The statement is divided into *operating activities, financing activities,* and *investing
activities.* Operating activities create revenues and expenses; financing activities
obtain the funds needed to launch and sustain the business; and investing activities

affect long-term assets. Each section of the statement includes cash receipts and cash payments and concludes with a net cash increase or decrease. In addition, *non-cash investing activities and financing activities* are also included in the SCFP.

Two formats are used to report operating activities. The *direct method* lists the major sources of cash receipts and disbursements, for example, cash collections from customers and cash payments to suppliers and to employees. The *indirect method* shows the reconciliation from net income to cash flow from operations.

Self-Study Questions

Test your understanding of the chapter by marking the best answer for each of the following questions:

1. The income statement and the balance sheet *(p. 778)*
   a. Report the cash effects of transactions
   b. Fail to report why cash changed during the period
   c. Report the sources and uses of cash during the period
   d. Are divided into operating, financing, and investing activities

2. The purpose of the statement of changes in financial position is to *(p. 779)*
   a. Predict future cash flows
   b. Evaluate management decisions
   c. Determine the ability to pay dividends and interest
   d. All of the above

3. A successful company's major source of cash should be *(pp. 779, 783)*
   a. Operating activities   c. Financing activities
   b. Investing activities   d. A combination of the above

4. Dividends paid to shareholders are usually reported on the statement of changes in financial position as a (an) *(pp. 783–84)*
   a. Operating activity   c. Financing activity
   b. Investing activity   d. Combination of the above

5. Which of the following items appears on a statement of changes in financial position prepared by the direct method? *(p. 780)*
   a. Depreciation expense   c. Loss on sale of capital assets
   b. Decrease in accounts receivable d. Cash payments to suppliers

6. Interest Receivable's beginning balance is $18,000, and its ending amount is $14,000. Interest revenue earned during the year is $43,000. How much cash interest was received? *(pp. 788–90)*
   a. $39,000   c. $45,000
   b. $43,000   d. $47,000

7. McGrath Ltd. sold an investment at a gain of $22,000. The Investment account reports a beginning balance of $104,000 and an ending balance of $91,000. During the year, McGrath purchased new investments costing $31,000. What were the proceeds from the sale of investments? *(p. 794)*
   a. $22,000   c. $66,000
   b. $44,000   d. $186,000

8. Noncash financing and investing activities *(p. 795)*
   a. Are reported in the main body of the SCFP
   b. Are reported in a separate schedule that accompanies the SCFP
   c. Are reported on the income statement
   d. Are not reported in the financial statements

9. The indirect method does a better job than the direct method at *(pp. 795–97)*
   a. Reporting the cash effects of financing activities
   b. Reporting why the cash balance changed
   c. Showing the link between net income and cash flow from operations
   d. Reporting the separate components of operating cash flows such as collections from customers and payments to suppliers and employees

10. Net income is $17,000, depreciation is $9,000, and amortization is $3,000. In addition, the sale of a capital asset generated a $4,000 gain. Current assets other than cash increased by $6,000, and current liabilities increased by $8,000. What was the amount of cash flow from operations? *(p. 798)*
    a. $23,000
    b. $27,000
    c. $31,000
    d. $35,000

Answers to the Self-Study Questions are at the end of the chapter.

Accounting Vocabulary

cash and cash equivalents *(p. 778)*
cash flows *(p. 778)*
direct method *(p. 782)*
financing activities *(p. 780)*

indirect method *(p. 795)*
investing activities *(p. 780)*
operating activities *(p. 779)*

reconciliation method *(p. 795)*
statement of changes in financial position *(p. 778)*

ASSIGNMENT MATERIAL

Questions

1. What information does the SCFP report that is not shown on the balance sheet, the income statement, or the statement of retained earnings?
2. Identify four purposes of the SCFP.
3. Identify and briefly describe the three types of activities that are reported on the SCFP.
4. How is the SCFP dated and why?
5. What is the check figure for the SCFP, where is it obtained, and how is it used?
6. What is the most important source of cash for most successful companies?
7. How can cash decrease during a year when income is high? How can cash increase during a year when income is low? How can investors and creditors learn these facts about the company?
8. DeBerg, Inc. prepares its SCFP using the *direct* method for operating activities. Identify the section of DeBerg's SCFP where each of the following transactions will appear. If the transaction does not appear on the SCFP, give the reason.

a. Cash	14,000	
Note Payable, Long-Term		14,000
b. Salary Expense	7,300	
Cash		7,300
c. Cash	28,400	
Sales Revenue		28,400
d. Amortization Expense	6,500	
Goodwill		6,500
e. Accounts Payable	1,400	
Cash		1,400

9. Why are depreciation, depletion and amortization expenses not reported on an SCFP that reports operating activities by the direct method? Why and how are these expenses reported on a statement prepared by the indirect method?
10. Mainline Distributing Inc. collected cash of $92,000 from customers and $6,000 interest on notes receivable. Cash payments included $24,000 to employees, $13,000 to suppliers, $6,000 as dividends to shareholders and $5,000 as a loan

to another company. How much was Mainline's net cash inflow from operating activities?

11. Summarize the major cash receipts and cash disbursements in the three categories of activities that appear on the SCFP.

12. Kirchner, Inc. recorded salary expense of $51,000 during a year when the balance of Salary Payable decreased from $10,000 to $2,000. How much cash did Kirchner pay to employees during the year? Where on the SCFP should Kirchner report this item?

13. Marshall Corporation's beginning capital asset balance, net of accumulated depreciation, was $193,000, and the ending amount was $176,000. Marshall recorded depreciation of $37,000 and sold capital assets with a book value of $9,000. How much cash did Marshall pay to purchase capital assets during the period? Where on the SCFP should Marshall report this item?

14. How should issuance of a note payable to purchase land be reported in the statement of changes in financial position? Identify three other transactions that fall in this same category.

15. Which format of the SCFP gives a clearer description of the individual cash flows from operating activities? Which format better shows the relationship between net income and operating cash flow?

16. An investment that cost $65,000 was sold for $80,000, resulting in a $15,000 gain. Show how to report this transaction on a SCFP prepared by the indirect method.

17. Identify the cash effects of increases and decreases in current assets other than cash. What are the cash effects of increases and decreases in current liabilities?

18. Milano Corporation earned net income of $38,000 and had depreciation expense of $22,000. Also, noncash current assets decreased $13,000, and current liabilities decreased $9,000. What was Milano's net cash flow from operating activities?

19. What is the difference between the direct method and the indirect method of reporting financing activities and investing activities?

20. Milgrom Company reports operating activities by the direct method. Does this method show the relationship between net income and cash flow from operations? If so, state how. If not, how can Milgrom satisfy this purpose of the SCFP?

Exercises

Exercise 18-1   *Identifying the purposes of the SCFP (L.O. 1)*

Monterrey Western, a real estate partnership, has experienced an unbroken string of ten years of growth in net income. Nevertheless, the business is facing bankruptcy! Creditors are calling all of Monterrey Western's outstanding loans for immediate payment, and the cash is simply not available. In trying to explain where Monterrey Western went wrong, it becomes clear that managers placed undue emphasis on net income and gave too little attention to cash flows.

Required

Write a brief memo, in your own words, to explain for Monterrey Western managers the purposes of the SCFP.

Exercise 18-2   *Identifying activities for the statement of changes in financial position (L.O. 2)*

Identify each of the following transactions as an operating activity (O), financing activity (F), an investing activity (I), a noncash financing and investing activity (NFI), or a transaction that is not reported on the statement of changes in financial position (N). Assume the direct method is used to report cash flows from operating activities.

_____ a. Purchase of long-term investment
_____ b. Payment of wages to employees
_____ c. Collection of cash interest
_____ d. Cash sale of land
_____ e. Distribution of stock dividend
_____ f. Acquisition of equipment by issuance of note payable
_____ g. Payment of long-term debt
_____ h. Acquisition of building by issuance of common stock
_____ i. Accrual of salary expense
_____ j. Payment of account payable
_____ k. Issuance of preferred stock for cash
_____ l. Payment of cash dividend
_____ m. Sale of long-term investment
_____ n. Amortization of bond discount
_____ o. Collection of account receivable
_____ p. Issuance of long-term note payable to borrow cash
_____ q. Depreciation of equipment
_____ r. Repurchase of common stock
_____ s. Issuance of common stock for cash

Exercise 18-3 *Classifying transactions for the statement of changes in financial position* **(L.O. 2)**

Indicate where, if at all, each of the following transactions would be reported on a SCFP prepared by the direct method, and the accompanying schedule of noncash financing and investing activities.

a. Accounts Payable	8,300	
Cash		8,300
b. Cash	81,000	
Common Stock		81,000
c. Common Stock	13,000	
Cash		13,000
d. Retained Earning	36,000	
Common Stock		36,000
e. Cash	2,000	
Interest Revenue		2,000
f. Land	87,700	
Cash		87,700
g. Salary Expense	4,300	
Cash		4,300
h. Equipment	18,000	
Cash		18,000
i. Cash	7,200	
Long-Term Investment		7,200
j. Bonds Payable	45,000	
Cash		45,000
k. Building	164,000	
Note Payable, Long-Term		164,000
l. Cash	1,400	
Accounts Receivable		1,400
m. Dividends Payable	16,500	
Cash		16,500
n. Furniture and Fixtures	22,100	
Note Payable, Short-Term		22,100

Exercise 18-4 *Computing cash flows from operating activities: direct method* **(L.O. 3)**

Analysis of the accounting records of Gibson Transfer Ltd. reveals:

Collection of dividend revenue	$ 7,000	Depreciation	$12,000
Payment of interest	16,000	Decrease in current liabilities	20,000
Cash sales	12,000	Increase in current assets other than cash	17,000
Loss on sale of land	5,000		
Acquisition of land	37,000	Payment of dividends	7,000
Payment of accounts payable	45,000	Collection of accounts receivable	93,000
Net income	24,000	Payment of salaries and wages	34,000
Payment of income tax	13,000		

Compute cash flows from operating activities by the direct method. Use the format of the operating activities section of Exhibit 18-1.

Exercise 18-5 *Identifying items for the statement of changes in financial position: direct method* **(L.O. 3)**

Selected accounts of Bismark, Inc. show:

Interest Receivable

Beginning balance	16,000	Cash receipts of interest	40,000
Interest revenue	40,000		
Ending balance	16,000		

Investments in Stock

Beginning balance	0	Cost of investments sold	9,000
Acquisitions	27,000		
Ending balance	18,000		

Long-Term Debt

Payments	69,000	Beginning balance	134,000
		Issuance of debt for cash	83,000
		Ending balance	148,000

For each account, identify the item or items that should appear on a SCFP prepared by the direct method. State where to report the item.

Exercise 18-6 *Preparing the statement of changes in financial position: direct method* **(L.O. 3)**

The income statement and additional data of Hillcrest Electric Company Ltd. follow:

Hillcrest Electric Company Ltd.
Income Statement
year ended September 30, 19X2

Revenues		
Sales revenue	$339,000	
Dividend revenue	8,000	$347,000

Expenses

Cost of goods sold	163,000	
Salary expense	85,000	
Depreciation expense	29,000	
Advertising expense	19,000	
Interest expense	2,000	
Income tax expense	9,000	307,000
Net income		$ 40,000

Additional data:

a. Collections from customers are $7,000 more than sales.

b. Payments to suppliers are $9,000 less than the sum of cost of goods sold plus advertising expense.

c. Payments to employees are $1,000 more than salary expense.

d. Dividend revenue, interest expense, and income tax expense equal their cash amounts.

e. Acquisition of capital assets is $116,000. Of this amount, $91,000 is paid in cash, $25,000 by signing a note payable.

f. Proceeds from sale of land, $19,000.

g. Proceeds from issuance of common stock, $30,000.

h. Payment of long-term note payable, $15,000.

i. Payment of dividends, $11,000.

j. Increase in cash balance, $?

Prepare Hillcrest Electric Company's SCFP. Report operating activities by the direct method.

Exercise 18-7   *Computing amounts for the SCFP* **(L.O. 4)**

Compute the following items for the SCFP:

a. Beginning and ending Accounts Receivable are $26,000 and $22,000, respectively. Credit sales for the period total $81,000. How much are cash collections?

b. Cost of goods sold is $71,000. Beginning Inventory balance is $25,000 and ending Inventory balance is $21,000. Beginning and ending Accounts Payable are $11,000 and $8,000 respectively. How much are cash payments for inventory?

Exercise 18-8   *Computing amounts for the statement of changes in financial position* **(L.O. 4)**

Compute the following items for the SCFP:

a. Beginning and ending Capital Assets, net, are $103,000 and $107,000 respectively. Depreciation for the period is $16,000, and acquisitions of net capital assets are $27,000. Capital assets were sold at a $1,000 loss. What were the cash proceeds of the sale?

b. Beginning and ending Retained Earnings are $45,000 and $73,000 respectively. Net income for the period is $62,000, and stock dividends are $12,000. How much are cash dividend payments?

Exercise 18-9   *Computing cash flows from operating activities: indirect method (L.O. 5)*

The accounting records of Mountain Coop Ltd. reveal the following:

Collection of dividend		Depreciation..............................	$21,000
revenue.................................	$ 7,000	Decrease in current	
Payment of interest.................	16,000	liabilities	20,000
Cash sales...............................	12,000	Increase in current assets	
Gain on sale of land................	5,000	other than cash	17,000
Acquisition of land	37,000	Payment of dividends............	7,000
Payment of accounts		Collection of accounts	
payable	45,000	receivable	97,000
Net income.............................	24,000	Payment of salaries and	
Payment of income tax............	13,000	wages	34,000

Compute cash flows from operating activities by the indirect method. Use the format of the operating section of Exhibit 18-5.

Exercise 18-10   *Classifying transactions for the statement of changes in financial position (L.O. 3, 5)*

Two transactions of Ferrari's Restaurant are recorded as follows:

a. Cash	9,000	
Accumulated Depreciation	83,000	
Loss on Sale of Equipment..	43,000	
Equipment		135,000
b. Land..	230,000	
Cash		130,000
Note Payable		100,000

Required

1. Indicate where, how, and in what amount to report these transactions on the SCFP. Ferrari reports cash flows from operating activities by the direct method.

2. Repeat requirement 1, assuming Ferrari reports cash flows from operating activities by the indirect method.

Exercise 18-11   *Preparing the SCFP by the indirect method (L.O. 5)*

Use the income statement of Hillcrest Electric Company in Exercise 18-6, plus these additional data:

a. Collections from customers are $7,000 more than sales.

b. Payments to suppliers are $9,000 less than the sum of cost of goods sold plus advertising expense.

c. Payments to employees are $1,000 more than salary expense.

d. Dividend revenue, interest expense, and income tax expense equal their cash amounts.

e. Acquisition of capital assets is $116,000. Of this amount, $91,000 is paid in cash, $25,000 by signing a note payable.

f. Proceeds from sale of land, $19,000.

g. Proceeds from issuance of common stock, $30,000.

h. Payment of long-term note payable, $15,000.

i. Payment of dividends, $11,000.

j. Increase in cash balance, $?

k. From the balance sheet:

| | September 30, | |
	19X2	19X1
Current Assets		
Accounts receivable	$51,000	$58,000
Inventory	83,000	77,000
Prepaid expenses	9,000	8,000
Current Liabilities		
Notes payable (for inventory purchases)	$20,000	$20,000
Accounts payable	35,000	22,000
Accrued liabilities	23,000	21,000

Prepare Hillcrest's SCFP for the year ended September 30, 19X2, using the indirect method.

Problems   *(Group A)*

Problem 18-1A   *Using cash-flow information to evaluate performance (L.O. 1)*

Top managers of Quest Programs Inc. are reviewing company performance for 19X7. The income statement reports a 20 percent increase in net income over 19X6. However, most of the increase resulted from an extraordinary gain on insurance proceeds covering fire damage to the manufacturing plant. The balance sheet shows large increases in receivables and inventory. The SCFP, in summarized form, reports the following:

Net cash outflow from operating activities	$(80,000)
Net cash inflow from financing activities	50,000
Net cash inflow from investing activities	40,000
Increase in cash during 19X7	$ 10,000

Required

Write a memo to give Quest managers your assessment of 19X7 operations and your outlook for the future. Focus on the information content of the cash flow data.

Problem 18-2A   *Preparing the statement of changes in financial position: direct method (L.O. 2, 3)*

Chilliwack Corporation accountants have developed the following data from the company's accounting records for the year ended April 30, 19X5:

1. Cash payments to acquire capital assets, $59,400.
2. Cost of goods sold, $382,600.
3. Proceeds from issuance of common stock, $8,000.
4. Payment of cash dividends, $48,400.
5. Collection of interest, $4,400.
6. Acquisition of equipment by issuing short-term note payable, $16,400.
7. Payments of salaries, $93,600.
8. Credit sales, $583,900.
9. Loan to another company, $12,500.
10. Proceeds from sale of capital assets, $22,400, including $6,800 loss.
11. Collections on accounts receivable, $562,600.

12. Interest revenue, $3,800.

13. Cash receipt of dividend revenue on stock investments, $4,100.

14. Payments to suppliers, $478,500.

15. Cash sales, $171,900.

16. Depreciation expense, $59,900.

17. Proceeds from issuance of short-term debt, $19,600.

18. Payments of long-term debt, $50,000.

19. Interest expense and payments, $13,300.

20. Salary expense, $95,300.

21. Loan collections, $12,800.

22. Proceeds from sale of investments, $9,100, including $2,000 gain.

23. Payment of short-term note payable by issuing common stock, $31,000.

24. Amortization expense, $2,900.

25. Income tax expense and payments, $37,900.

26. Cash balance: April 30, 19X4 — $39,300
               April 30, 19X5 — $?

Required

Prepare Chilliwack Corporation's SCFP for the year ended April 30, 19X5. Follow the format of Exhibit 18-1. Evaluate 19X5 from a cash-flow standpoint. Give your reasons.

Problem 18-3A   *Preparing the statement of changes in financial position: direct method (L.O. 2, 3, 4)*

The 19X5 comparative balance sheet and income statement of Casa Loma, Inc. follow:

Comparative Balance Sheet

	19X5	19X4	Increase (Decrease)
Current assets			
Cash and cash equivalents	$ 15,400	$ 5,300	$ 10,100
Accounts receivable	28,600	26,900	1,700
Interest receivable	1,900	700	1,200
Inventories	83,600	87,200	(3,600)
Prepaid expenses	2,500	1,900	600
Capital assets			
Land	89,000	60,000	29,000
Equipment, net	53,500	49,400	4,100
Total assets	$274,500	$231,400	$ 43,100
Current liabilities			
Accounts payable	$ 31,400	$ 28,800	$ 2,600
Interest payable	4,400	4,900	(500)
Salary payable	3,100	6,600	(3,500)
Other accrued liabilities	13,700	16,000	(2,300)
Income tax payable	8,900	7,700	1,200
Long-term liabilities			
Notes payable	75,000	100,000	(25,000)
Shareholders' equity			
Common stock	88,300	64,700	23,600
Retained earnings	49,700	2,700	47,000
Total liabilities and shareholders' equity	$274,500	$231,400	$ 43,100

Income Statement for 19X5

Revenues		
Sales revenue		$243,000
Interest revenue		8,600
Total revenues		251,600
Expenses		
Cost of goods sold	$92,400	
Salary expense	27,800	
Depreciation expense	4,000	
Other operating expense	10,500	
Interest expense	11,600	
Income tax expense	29,100	
Total expenses		175,400
Net income		$ 76,200

Casa Loma had no noncash financing and investing transactions during 19X5. During the year, there were no sales of land or equipment, no issuances of notes payable and no issuance or retirement of common stock.

Required

Prepare the 19X5 statement of changes in financial position, formatting operating activities by the direct method.

Problem 18-4A *Preparing the statement of changes in financial position: indirect method* **(L.O. 2, 5)**

Required

Using the Casa Loma data from the preceding problem, prepare the 19X5 SCFP by the indirect method. If your instructor also assigned problem 18-3A, prepare only the operating activities section of the statement.

Problem 18-5A *Preparing the statement of changes in financial position: indirect method* **(L.O. 2, 5)**

McAlister Overhead Door Systems, Inc. accountants have assembled the following data for the year ended December 31, 19X7:

	December 31,	
	19X7	**19X6**
Current accounts (all result from operations)		
Current assets		
Cash and cash equivalents	$85,700	$22,700
Accounts receivable	59,700	64,200
Inventories	88,600	83,000
Prepaid expenses	5,300	4,100
Current liabilities		
Notes payable (for inventory purchases)	$22,600	$18,300
Accounts payable	52,900	55,800
Income tax payable	18,600	16,700
Accrued liabilities	25,500	27,200

Transaction data for 19X7:

Acquisition of long-term		Sale of equipment	$ 58,000
investment	$ 31,600	Amortization expense	5,300

Acquisition of land by		Purchase and retirement	
issuing long-term note		of common stock	14,300
payable	113,000	Loss on sale of equipment	11,700
Stock dividends........................	31,800	Payment of cash dividends	18,300
Collection of loan	8,700	Issuance of long-term note	
Depreciation expense	26,800	payable to borrow cash	34,400
Acquisition of building	125,300	Net income...............................	67,100
Retirement of bonds payable		Issuance of common stock	
by issuing common stock ..	65,000	for cash	41,200

Required

Prepare McAlister's SCFP, using the indirect method to report operating activities.

Problem 18-6A *Preparing the statement of changes in financial position: indirect method* **(L.O. 2, 5)**

The comparative balance sheet of Westwood Sales Inc. at March 31, 19X7 reported the following:

	March 31,	
	19X7	**19X6**
Current Assets		
Cash and cash equivalents...........................	$ 9,100	$ 4,000
Accounts receivable	19,400	21,700
Inventories...	63,200	60,600
Prepaid expenses..	1,900	1,700
Current liabilities		
Notes payable (for inventory purchases)..	$ 4,000	$ 4,000
Accounts payable	30,300	27,600
Accrued liabilities..	10,700	11,100
Income tax payable	8,000	4,700

Westwood's transactions during the year ended March 31, 19X7 included the following:

Payment of cash dividend	$30,000	Cash acquisition of building .	$47,000
Cash acquisition of equipment	78,700	Net income...............................	70,000
Issuance of long-term note		Issuance of common stock	
payable to borrow cash	50,000	for cash	11,000
Acquisition of land by issuing		Stock dividend.........................	18,000
note payable.........................	62,000	Sale of long-term investment	13,700
Amortization expense	2,000	Depreciation expense	9,000

Required

Prepare Westwood Sales's SCFP for the year ended March 31, 19X7, using the indirect method to report cash flows from operating activities. All current account balances resulted from operating transactions.

Problem 18-7A *Preparing the statement of changes in financial position: direct and indirect methods* **(L.O. 3, 5)**

To prepare the SCFP, accountants for Fanshawe Corporation have summarized 19X3 activity in two accounts as follows:

Cash

Beginning balance.................	53,600	Payments on accounts payable	399,100
Collection of loan....................	13,000	Payments of dividends...........	27,200
Sale of investment..................	8,200	Payments of salaries	
Receipts of interest.................	12,600	and wages	143,800
Collections from customers...	706,700	Payments of interest	26,900
Issuance of common stock.....	19,300	Purchase of equipment..........	57,800
Receipts of dividends.............	4,500	Payments of operating	
		expenses	34,300
		Payment of long-term debt....	41,300
		Payment of income tax...........	18,900
Ending balance	68,600		

Common Stock

		Beginning balance...................	84,400
		Issuance for cash	19,300
		Issuance to acquire land.........	80,100
		Issuance to retire long-term	
		debt	19,000
		Ending balance.......................	202,800

Required

1. Prepare Fanshawe Corporations's SCFP for the year ended December 31, 19X3, using the direct method to report operating activities.

Fanshawe's 19X3 income statement and selected balance sheet data follow:

Fanshawe Corporation
Income Statement
for the year ended December 31, 19X3

Revenues		
Sales revenue...		$734,300
Interest revenue		12,600
Dividend revenue.......................................		4,500
Total revenues.....................................		$751,400
Expenses and losses		
Cost of goods sold....................................	$402,600	
Salary and wage expense	150,800	
Depreciation expense...............................	24,300	
Other operating expense	44,100	
Interest expense	28,800	
Income tax expense..................................	16,200	
Loss on sale of investments	1,100	
Total expenses......................................		667,900
Net income		$ 83,500

	Fanshawe Corporation Balance Sheet Data	Increase (Decrease)
Current assets		
Cash and cash equivalents		$?
Accounts receivable		27,600
Inventories		(11,800)
Prepaid expenses		600
Current liabilities		
Accounts payable		$(8,300)
Interest payable		1,900
Salary payable		7,000
Other accrued liabilities		10,400
Income tax payable		(2,700)

2. Use these data to prepare a supplementary schedule showing cash flows from operating activities by the indirect method. All activity in the current accounts results from operations.

Problem 18-8A   *Preparing the statement of changes in financial position: indirect and direct methods* **(L.O. 3, 4, 5)**

Karen Corporation's comparative balance sheet at June 30, 19X7 included the following balances:

Karen Corporation
Partial Balance Sheet
June 30, 19X7 and 19X6

	19X7	19X6	Increase (Decrease)
Current assets			
Cash	$21,300	$ 8,600	$12,700
Accounts receivable	45,900	48,300	(2,400)
Interest receivable	2,900	3,600	(700)
Inventories	68,600	60,200	8,400
Prepaid expenses	3,700	2,800	900
Current liabilities			
Notes payable, short-term			
(for general borrowing)	$13,400	$18,100	$(4,700)
Accounts payable	42,400	40,300	2,100
Income tax payable	13,800	14,500	(700)
Accrued liabilities	8,200	9,700	(1,500)
Interest payable	3,700	2,900	800
Salary payable	900	2,600	(1,700)

Transaction data for the year ended June 30, 19X7:

a. Net income, $56,200.

b. Depreciation expense on equipment, $10,200.

c. Purchased long-term investment, $4,900.

d. Sold land for $46,900, including $6,700 loss.

e. Acquired equipment by issuing long-term note payable, $14,300.

f. Paid long-term note payable, $61,000.

g. Received cash for issuance of common stock, $3,900.

h. Paid cash dividends, $38,100.

i. Paid short-term note payable by issuing common stock, $4,700.

Required

1. Prepare Karen's SCFP for the year ended June 30, 19X7, using the indirect method to report operating activities. All current accounts except short-term notes payable result from operating transactions.

2. Prepare a supplementary schedule showing cash flows from operations by the direct method. The income statement reports the following: sales, $237,300; interest revenue, $10,600; cost of goods sold, $82,800; salary expense, $38,800; other operating expenses, $37,200; depreciation expense, $10,200; income tax expense, $9,900; loss on sale of land, $6,700; interest expense, $6,100.

Problem 18-9A   *Comprehensive problem in preparing a statement of changes in financial position, direct and indirect methods, missing certain data* **(L.O. 3, 4, 5)**

Pandora Production Ltd.'s balance sheet as at December 31, 19X3 and 19X4 and income statement for the year ended December 31, 19X4 are as follows:

Pandora Productions Ltd.
Balance Sheet
December 31, 19X4 and 19X3

	19X4	19X3
Current assets		
Cash..	$ 21,500	$ 17,500
Accounts receivable...	175,000	143,700
Interest receivable	8,500	5,800
Inventory..	84,000	91,000
Prepaid advertising..	5,000	6,000
	294,000	264,000
Capital assets		
Land	200,000	100,000
Building...	600,000	700,000
Accumulated depreciation — building	(192,000)	(275,000)
Machinery	250,000	250,000
Accumulated depreciation — machinery..................	(129,500)	(115,000)
Total assets	$1,022,550	$924,000
Current liabilities		
Accounts payable..	$ 67,200	$75,000
Income taxes payable	21,800	25,000
Salary payable	6,900	8,000
Interest payable	9,000	8,500
	104,900	116,500
Long-term liabilities		
Notes payable...	75,000	150,000
Total liabilities...	179,900	266,500
Shareholders' equity		
Common stock..	500,000	400,000
Retained earnings	342,600	257,500
	842,600	657,500
Total liabilities and shareholders' equity..................	$1,022,500	$924,000

Pandora Productions Ltd.
Income Statement
for the year ended December 31, 19X4

Revenues and gain		
Sales revenue		$ 855,600
Interest revenue		102,400
Gain on disposal of building		45,000
Total revenues		$1,003,000
Expenses and losses		
Cost of goods sold	$412,300	
Salary expense	168,000	
Depreciation expense — building	67,000	
Depreciation expense — machinery	32,000	
Interest expense	12,900	
Advertising expense	23,100	
Loss on disposal of machinery	12,500	
Income tax expense	110,100	
Total expenses		837,900
Net income		$ 165,100

Additional information:

a. During the year, Pandora sold a building with an original cost of $500,000 and accumulated depreciation of $150,000.

b. During the year, a machine purchased in 19X1 for $75,000 was sold for cash proceeds of $45,000.

c. All accounts payable relate to purchases of inventory items.

d. Land was acquired in exchange of 10,000 common shares.

e. Neither the gain nor the loss on disposal of capital assets was considered extraordinary as an item.

Required

1. Prepare a statement of changes in financial position for the year ended December 31, 19X4 using the direct method. Funds are defined as cash.

2. Prepare a statement of changes in financial position for the year ended December 31, 19X4 using the indirect method. Funds are defined as cash.

(Group B)

Problem 18-1B   *Using cash-flow information to evaluate performance* **(L.O. 1)**

Top managers of Leadership Dynamics, Inc., are reviewing company performance for 19X4. The income statement reports a 12 percent increase in net income, for the fifth consecutive year with an income increase above 10 percent. The income statement includes a nonrecurring loss without which net income would have increased by 16 percent. The balance sheet shows modest increases in assets, liabilities, and shareholders' equity. The asset posting the largest increases is plant and equipment because the company is halfway through a five-year expansion program. No other assets and no liabilities are increasing dramatically. A summarized version of the SCFP reports the following:

Net cash inflow from operating activities..............	$120,000
Net cash inflow from financing activities..............	10,000
Net cash outflow from investing activities............	(90,000)
Increase in cash during 19X4	$ 40,000

Required

Write a memo to give top managers of Leadership Dynamics your assessment of 19X4 and your outlook for the future. Focus on the information content of the cash flow data.

Problem 18-2B   *Preparing the statement of changes in financial position: direct method* **(L.O. 1, 3)**

Athabasca Corporation accountants have developed the following data from the company's accounting records for the year ended July 31, 19X9:

1. Proceeds from issuance of short-term debt, $44,100.
2. Payments of long-term debt, $18,800.
3. Proceeds from sale of capital assets, $49,700, including $10,600 gain.
4. Interest revenue, $12,100.
5. Cash receipt of dividend revenue on stock investments, $5,700.
6. Payments to suppliers, $683,300.
7. Interest expense and payments, $37,800.
8. Salary expense, $105,300.
9. Cash payments to purchase capital assets, $181,000.
10. Cost of goods sold, $481,100.
11. Collection of interest revenue, $11,700.
12. Acquisition of equipment by issuing short-term note payable, $35,500.
13. Payments of salaries, $104,000.
14. Credit sales, $608,100.
15. Loan to another company, $35,000.
16. Income tax expense and payments, $56,400.
17. Depreciation expense, $27,700.
18. Collections on accounts receivable, $673,100.
19. Loan collections, $74,400.
20. Proceeds from sale of investments, $34,700, including $3,800 loss.
21. Payment of long-term debt by issuing preferred stock, $107,300.
22. Amortization expense, $23,900.
23. Cash sales, $146,000.
24. Proceeds from issuance of common stock, $116,900.
25. Payment of cash dividends, $50,500.
26. Cash balance: July 31, 19X8 — $53,800
    July 31, 19X9 — $?

Required

Prepare Athabasca Corporation's SCFP for the year ended July 31, 19X9. Follow the format of Exhibit 18-1, but do not show amounts in thousands. Evaluate 19X9 from a cash-flow standpoint. Give your reasons.

Problem 18-3B *Computing amounts for the statement of changes in financial position:*
direct method **(L.O. 2, 3, 4)**

The 19X3 comparative balance sheet and income statement of Custom Trailers, Inc.
follow:

Comparative Balance Sheet

	19X3	19X2	Increase (Decrease)
Current assets			
Cash and cash equivalents...........................	$ 37,500	$ 15,600	$ 21,900
Accounts receivable	41,500	43,100	(1,600)
Interest receivable	600	900	(300)
Inventories...	94,300	89,900	4,400
Prepaid expenses...	1,700	2,200	(500)
Capital assets			
Land	35,100	10,000	25,100
Equipment, net	100,900	93,700	7,200
Total assets...	$311,600	$255,400	$ 56,200
Current liabilities			
Accounts payable	$ 16,400	$ 17,900	$ (1,500)
Interest payable	6,300	6,700	(400)
Salary payable..	2,100	1,400	700
Other accrued liabilities	18,100	18,700	(600)
Income tax payable	6,300	3,800	2,500
Long-term liabilities			
Notes payable	55,000	65,000	(10,000)
Shareholders' equity			
Common stock..	131,100	122,300	8,800
Retained earnings..	76,300	19,600	56,700
Total liabilities and shareholders' equity.......	$311,600	$255,400	$ 56,200

Income Statement for 19X3

Revenues		
Sales revenue...		$461,800
Interest revenue		11,700
Total revenues...		473,500
Expenses		
Cost of goods sold	$205,200	
Salary expense	76,400	
Depreciation expense..................................	15,300	
Other operating expense	49,700	
Interest expense	24,600	
Income tax expense	16,900	
Total expenses...		388,100
Net income		$ 85,400

Custom Trailers had no noncash financing and investing transactions during 19X3.
During the year, there were no sales of land or equipment, no issuances of notes
payable, and no issue or repurchase of common stock.

Required

Prepare the 19X3 SCFP, formatting operating activities by the direct method.

Problem 18-4B   *Preparing the statement of changes in financial position: indirect method*
  (L.O. 2, 3, 5)

Required

Using the Custom Trailers data from the preceding problem, prepare the 19X3
SCFP by the indirect method. If your instructor also assigned Problem 18-3B, prepare only the operating activities section.

Problem 18-5B   *Preparing the statement of changes in financial position: indirect method* **(L.O. 2, 5)**

Accountants for LaDue Fashions Inc. have assembled the following data for the
year ended December 31, 19X4:

	December 31, 19X4	December 31, 19X3
Current accounts (all result from operations)		
Current assets		
Cash and cash equivalents	$30,600	$34,800
Accounts receivable	70,100	73,700
Inventories	90,600	96,500
Prepaid expenses	3,200	2,100
Current liabilities		
Notes payable (for inventory purchases)	$36,300	$36,800
Accounts payable	72,100	67,500
Income tax payable	5,900	6,800
Accrued liabilities	28,300	23,200

Transaction data for 19X4:

Acquisition of long-term investment	$ 44,800	Sale of long-term investment	$12,200
Acquisition of building by issuing long-term note payable	162,000	Amortization expense	1,100
		Payment of long-term debt....	47,800
Stock dividends	12,600	Gain on sale of investment....	3,500
Collection of loan	10,300	Payment of cash dividends ...	48,300
Depreciation expense	19,200	Issuance of long-term debt to borrow cash	21,000
Acquisition of equipment	69,000		
Payment of long-term debt by issuing common stock	89,400	Net income	92,500
		Issuance of preferred stock for cash	36,200

Required

Prepare LaDue Fashion's SCFP, using the indirect method to report operating activities.

Problem 18-6B   *Preparing the statement of changes in financial position: indirect method* **(L.O. 2, 5)**

The comparative balance sheet of Highland Recreation, Inc. at December 31, 19X5
reported the following:

| | December 31, | |
	19X5	19X4
Current Assets		
Cash and cash equivalents.........................	$10,600	$ 2,500
Accounts receivable	28,600	29,300
Inventories	51,600	53,000
Prepaid expenses...	4,200	3,700
Current liabilities		
Notes payable (for inventory purchases)..	$ 9,200	$ -0-
Accounts payable...	21,900	28,000
Accrued liabilities	14,300	16,800
Income tax payable	11,000	14,300

Highland's transactions during 19X5 included the following:

Retirement of bonds payable by issuing common stock.......................	$40,000	Sale of long-term investment............................	$ 6,000
		Depreciation expense	15,000
Amortization expense	5,000	Cash acquisition of	
Payment of cash dividends ...	17,000	building	104,000
Cash acquisition of		Net income...............................	21,600
equipment............................	55,000	Issuance of common stock	
Issuance of long-term note		for cash	105,600
payable to borrow cash	32,000	Stock dividend.........................	13,000

Required

Prepare Highland Recreation's SCFP for the year ended December 31, 19X5. Use the indirect method to report cash flows from operating activities. All current account balances result from operating transactions.

Problem 18-7B   *Preparing the statement of changes in financial position: direct and indirect methods (L.O. 3, 5)*

To prepare the SCFP, accountants for Cartier Corporation have summarized 19X8 activity in two accounts as follows:

Cash

Beginning balance...................	87,100	Payments of operating expenses..................................	46,100
Issuance of common stock.....	34,600		
Receipts of dividends.............	1,900	Payment of long-term debt	78,900
Collection of loan	18,500	Payment of income tax	8,000
Sale of investments................	9,900	Payments on accounts	
Receipts of interest.................	12,200	payable...................................	101,600
Collections from customers...	268,100	Payments of dividends............	12,200
Issuance of long-term debt	26,200	Payments of salaries	
		and wages..............................	67,500
		Payments of interest................	21,800
		Purchase of equipment............	79,900
Ending balance........................	42,500		

Common Stock

Beginning balance..................	103,500
Issuance for cash	34,600
Issuance to acquire land.........	62,100
Issuance to retire long-term	
debt	21,100
Ending balance.......................	221,300

Required

1. Prepare Cartier Corporation's SCFP for the year ended December 31, 19X8, using the direct method to report operating activities. Also prepare the accompanying schedule of noncash investing and financing activities.

Cartier's 19X8 income statement and selected balance sheet data follow:

Cartier Corporation
Income Statement
for the year ended December 31, 19X8

Revenues and gains		
Sales revenue		$251,800
Interest revenue...		12,200
Dividend revenue		1,900
Gain on sale of investments.....................		700
Total revenues and gains		266,600
Expenses		
Cost of goods sold......................................	$103,600	
Salary and wage expense..........................	66,800	
Depreciation expense	10,900	
Other operating expense...........................	44,700	
Interest expense...	24,100	
Income tax expense....................................	2,600	
Total expenses......................................		252,700
Net income..		$ 13,900

Cartier Corporation
Balance Sheet Data

	Increase (Decrease)
Current assets	
Cash and cash equivalents	$?
Accounts receivable..	(16,300)
Inventories	5,700
Prepaid expenses	(1,900)
Current liabilities	
Accounts payable...	$ 7,700
Interest payable..	2,300
Salary payable	(700)
Other accrued liabilities..	(3,300)
Income tax payable...	(5,400)

2. Use these data to prepare a supplementary schedule showing cash flows from operating activities by the indirect method. All activity in the current accounts results from operations.

Problem 18-8B   *Preparing the statement of changes in financial position: indirect and direct methods* **(L.O. 3, 4, 5)**

Henke-Ward Corporation's comparative balance sheet at September 30, 19X4 included the following balances:

Henke-Ward Corporation
Partial Balance Sheet
September 30, 19X4 and 19X3

	19X4	19X3	Increase (Decrease)
Current assets			
Cash..	$ 69,700	$ 17,600	$ 52,100
Accounts receivable	41,900	44,000	(2,100)
Interest receivable................................	4,100	2,800	1,300
Inventories...	121,700	116,900	4,800
Prepaid expenses..................................	8,600	9,300	(700)
Current liabilities			
Notes payable, short-term....................	$ 22,000	$ -0-	$ 22,000
Accounts payable	61,800	70,300	(8,500)
Income tax payable	21,800	24,600	(2,800)
Accrued liabilities.................................	17,900	29,100	(11,200)
Interest payable	4,500	3,200	1,300
Salary payable.......................................	1,500	1,100	400

Transaction data for the year ended September 30, 19X4:

a. Net income, $114,900.

b. Depreciation expense on equipment, $8,500.

c. Acquired long-term investments, $37,300.

d. Sold land for $38,100, including $10,900 gain.

e. Acquired equipment by issuing long-term note payable, $26,300.

f. Paid long-term note payable, $24,700.

g. Received cash of $51,900 for issuance of common stock.

h. Paid cash dividends, $64,300.

i. Acquired equipment by issuing short-term note payable, $22,000.

Required

1. Prepare Henke-Ward's SCFP for the year ended September 30, 19X4, using the indirect method to report operating activities. All current accounts except short-term notes payable result from operating transactions.

2. Prepare a supplementary schedule showing cash flows from operations by the direct method. The income statement reports the following: sales, $391,600; gain on sale of land, $10,900; interest revenue $7,300; cost of goods sold, $161,500; salary expense, $63,400; other operating expenses, $29,600; income tax expense, $18,400; interest expense, $13,500; depreciation expense, $8,500.

Problem 18-9B *Comprehensive problem in preparing a statement of changes in financial position, direct and indirect methods, missing certain data* **(L.O. 3, 4, 5)**

Eureka Wholesale Ltd.'s balance sheet as at December 31, 19X7 and 19X6 and income statement for the year ended December 31, 19X7 are as follows:

Eureka Wholesale Ltd.
Balance Sheet
December 31, 19X7 and 19X6

	19X7	19X6
Current assets		
Cash	$ 15,500	$ 21,500
Accounts receivable	125,000	151,000
Interest receivable	4,300	3,200
Dividends receivable	1,900	2,100
Inventory	125,000	111,000
Short-term investments	80,000	95,000
Prepeaid rent	15,000	20,000
	366,700	403,800
Capital assets		
Land	200,000	150,000
Building	650,000	650,000
Accumulated depreciation — building	(124,000)	(295,000)
Machinery	250,000	200,000
Accumulated depreciation — machinery	(92,500)	(75,000)
Total assets	$1,250,200	$1,033,800
Current liabilities		
Accounts payable	$ 79,400	$ 62,000
Income taxes payable	17,000	14,000
Salary payable	4,100	3,200
Interest payable	1,500	900
	102,000	80,100
Long-term liabilities		
Notes payable	175,000	125,000
Total liabilities	277,000	205,100
Shareholders' equity		
Common stock	225,000	175,000
Retained earnings	748,200	653,700
	973,200	828,700
Total liabilities and shareholders' equity	$1,250,200	$1,033,800

Eureka Wholesale Ltd.
Income Statement
for the year ended December 31, 19X7

Revenues and gain	
Sales revenue	$825,100
Interest revenue	31,900
Dividend income	17,200
Gain on disposal of short-term investments	15,000
Total revenues	$889,200

Expenses and losses

Cost of goods sold...	$382,000	
Salary expense	115,000	
Depreciation expense — building	42,500	
Depreciation expense — machinery............................	17,500	
Interest expense...	11,200	
Rent expense...	60,000	
Loss on disposal of building...	11,500	
Income tax expense...	100,000	
Total expenses..		739,700
Net income		$149,500

Additional information:

a. During the year, Eureka sold a building with an original cost of $400,000. Proceeds on disposal were $175,000.

b. During the year, short-term investments with a cost of $25,000 were sold for proceeds of $45,000.

c. All accounts payable relate to purchases of inventory items.

d. Machinery was acquired in exchange for 5,000 common shares.

Required

1. Prepare a statement of changes in financial position for the year ended December 31, 19X7 using the direct method. Funds are defined as cash.

2. Prepare a statement of changes in financial position for the year ended December 31, 19X7 using the indirect method. Funds are defined as cash.

Extending Your Knowledge

Decision Problems

1. Using the statement of changes in financial position to evaluate a company's operations (L.O. 1)

The statement of changes in financial position, in the not-too-distant past, included information in only two categories: sources of funds and uses of funds. Funds were usually defined as working capital (current assets minus current liabilities). The present-day statement provides information about cash flows from operating activities, financing activities, and investing activities. The earlier statement permitted the information to be about changes in working capital or in cash, while today's SCFP deals specifically with information about flows in cash and cash equivalents.

Required

1. Explain why you think the present day SCFP, with its disclosure of the three different kinds of activities, is or is not an improvement over the earlier model.

2. Is information about cash flows more informative to users than information about working capital flows?

3. Briefly explain why comparative balance sheets and a SCFP are more informative than just comparative balance sheets.

2. *Preparing and using the statement of changes in financial position to evaluate operations (L.O. 4, 5)*

The 19X6 comparative income statement and the 19X6 comparative balance sheet of Gruber Inc. have just been distributed at a meeting of the company's board of directors.

Gruber, Inc.
Comparative Income Statement
years ended December 31, 19X6 and 19X5
(amounts in thousands)

	19X6	19X5
Revenues and gains		
Sales revenue	$484	$310
Gain on sale of equipment (sale price, $33)	—	18
Totals	$484	$328
Expenses and losses		
Cost of goods sold	$221	$162
Salary expense	48	28
Depreciation expense	46	22
Interest expense	13	20
Amortization expense on patent	11	11
Loss on sale of land (sale price, $61)	—	35
Totals	339	278
Net income	$145	$ 50

Gruber, Inc.
Comparative Balance Sheet
December 31, 19X6 and 19X5
(amounts in thousands)

Assets	19X6	19X5
Cash	$ 23	$ 63
Accounts receivable, net	72	61
Inventories	194	181
Long-term investment	31	-0-
Property, plant and equipment	401	259
Accumulated depreciation	(244)	(198)
Patents	177	188
Totals	$654	$554

Liabilities and Owner's Equity		
Notes payable, short-term (for general borrowing)	$ 32	$101
Accounts payable	63	56
Accrued liabilities	12	17
Notes payable, long-term	147	163
Common stock	139	61
Retained earnings	261	156
Totals	$654	$554

In discussing the company's results of operations and year-end financial position, the members of the board of directors raise a fundamental question: Why is the cash balance so low? This question is especially troublesome to the board members because 19X6 showed record profits. As the controller of the company, you must answer the question.

Required

1. Prepare a SCFP for 19X6 in the format that best shows the relationship between net income and operating cash flow. The company sold no capital assets or long-term investments and issued no notes payable during 19X6. The changes in all current accounts except short-term notes payable arose from operations. There were no noncash financing and investing transactions during the year. Show all amounts in thousands.

2. Answer the board members' question: Why is the cash balance so low? In explaining the business's cash flows, identify two significant cash receipts that occurred during 19X5 but not in 19X6. Also point out the two largest cash disbursements during 19X6.

3. Considering net income and the company's cash flows during 19X6, was it a good year or a bad year? Give your reasons.

Ethical Issue

The *CICA Handbook* requires that all external financial statements include a statement of changes in financial position. The *Handbook* does not state a preference for either the direct or indirect method.

In the United States, *Statement No. 95* states the FASB's preference for the direct method of reporting cash flows from operating activities. In public hearings, however, companies have argued that it would be expensive to assemble the data required by the direct method. Therefore, *FASB Statement No. 95* permits the indirect method. Most companies follow the indirect-method format.

Required

1. Which method of reporting cash flows from operating activities is easier for you to understand — the direct method (p. 782) or the indirect method (p. 795)? Give your reason.

2. Consider the computations of operating cash flows outlined on pp. 788–792. Do the direct-method computations require many new data? Do the computations appear to be as expensive as companies have claimed?

3. Why do you think companies have resisted reporting operating cash flows by the direct method? Is this resistance in any way unethical? Give your reasons.

Financial Statement Problems

1. Using the statement of changes in financial position (L.O. 1, 2, 3, 4)

The Schneider Corporation's statement of changes in financial position appears in Appendix C. Use this statement along with the company's other financial statements to answer the following questions.

1. By which method does Schneider report net cash flows from *operating* activities? How can you tell?

2. Suppose Schneider reported net cash flows from operating activities by the direct method. Compute these amounts for 1991:
   a. Collections from customers.
   b. Payments for products sold. Assume that three quarters of the accounts payable and accrued liabilities relate to amounts owing to suppliers of goods held for re-sale.

3. Evaluate 1991 in terms of net income, cash flows, balance sheet position, and overall results. Be specific.

2. *Computing cash flow amounts and using cash flow data for analysis (L.O. 1, 2, 3, 4, 5)*

Obtain the annual report of an actual company of your choosing.

Answer these questions about the company. Concentrate on the current year in the annual report you select:

1. By which method does the company report net cash flows from *operating* activities? How can you tell?

2. Suppose the company reported net cash flows from operating activities by the direct method. Compute these amounts for the current year:
   a. Collections from customers.
   b. Payments to employees. Assume that the sum of Salary Expense, Wage Expense, and other payroll expenses for the current year make up 60 percent of Selling, General, and Administrative Expenses (or expense of similar title).
   c. Payments for income tax.

3. Evaluate the current year in terms of net income (or net loss), cash flows, balance sheet position, and overall results. Be specific.

Appendix

The Work Sheet Approach to Preparing the Statement of Changes in Financial Position

The main body of the chapter discusses the use of the SCFP in decision-making and shows how to prepare the statement using T-accounts. The T-account approach works well as a learning device, especially for simple situations. In actual practice, however, most companies face complex situations. In these cases, a work sheet can help accountants prepare the SCFP. This appendix shows how to prepare the SCFP using a specially designed work sheet.

The basic task in preparing the statement of changes in financial position is to account for all the cash effects of transactions that took the business from its beginning financial position to its ending financial position. Like the T-account approach, the work sheet approach helps the accountant identify the cash effects of all transactions of the period. The work sheet starts with the beginning balance sheet and concludes with the ending balance sheet. Two middle columns — one for debit amounts and the other for credit amounts — complete the work sheet. These columns, labeled Transaction Analysis, contain the data for the SCFP. Exhibit 18A-1 presents the basic framework of the work sheet. Accountants can prepare the statement directly from the lower part of the worksheet (Panel B in Exhibit 18A-1). The advantage of the work sheet approach is that it organizes in one place all relevant data for the statement's preparation. Exhibit 18A-1 and the other exhibits in this appendix are based on the Anchor Ltd. data in the chapter.

The work sheet can be used with either the direct method or the indirect method for operating activities. As with the T-account approach, cash flows from financing activities and cash flows from investing activities are unaffected by the method used for operating activities.

Exhibit 18A-1

Anchor Ltd.
Work Sheet for Statement of Changes in Financial Position
for the year ended December 31, 19X2

	Balances Dec. 31, 19X1	Transaction Analysis		Balances Dec. 31, 19X2
		Debit	Credit	
Panel A: Account Titles				
Cash................................				
Accounts receivable.......				
$\approx$				
Retained earnings				
Panel B: Statement of Changes in Financial Position				
Cash flows from operating activities......				
Cash flows from financing activities.......				
Cash flows from investing activities.......				
Net increase (decrease) in cash...........................				

Preparing the Work Sheet: Direct Method for Operating Activities

The direct method separates operating activities into cash receipts and cash payments. Exhibit 18A-2 is the work sheet for preparing the statement of changes in financial position by the direct method. The work sheet can be prepared by following these steps:

Step 1.   In Panel A, insert the beginning and ending balances for Cash, Accounts Receivable, and all other balance sheet accounts through Retained Earnings. The amounts are taken directly from the beginning and ending balance sheets in Exhibit 18-4, p. 789.

Step 2.   In Panel B, lay out the framework of the statement of changes in financial position as shown in Exhibit 18A-1, that is, enter the headings for cash flows from operating activities, financing activities, and investing activities. Exhibit 18A-2 is based on the direct method and splits operating activities into Receipts and Payments.

Step 3.   At the bottom of the work sheet, write Net Increase in Cash or Net Decrease in Cash, as the case may be. This final amount on the work sheet is the difference between ending cash and beginning cash, as reported on the balance sheet. Fundamentally, the SCFP is designed to explain *why* this change in cash occurred during the period.

Step 4.   Analyze the period's transactions in the middle columns of the work sheet. Transaction analysis is the most challenging part of preparing the work sheet. The remainder of this appendix explains this crucial step.

Step 5.   Prepare the SCFP directly from Panel B of the work sheet.

Transaction Analysis on the Work Sheet

For your convenience, we repeat the Anchor Ltd. transaction data from pp. 782–783 of the text. Transactions with cash effects are denoted by an asterisk.

Operating Activities
  a. Sales on credit, $284,000.
*b. Collections from customers, $271,000.
  c. Interest revenue earned, $12,000.
*d. Collection of interest receivable, $10,000.
*e. Cash receipt of dividend revenue, $9,000.
  f. Cost of goods sold, $150,000.
  g. Purchases of inventory on credit, $147,000.
*h. Payments to suppliers, $133,000.
  i. Salary and wage expense, $56,000.
*j. Payments of salaries and wages, $58,000.
  k. Depreciation expense, $18,000.
  l. Other operating expense, $17,000.
*m. Interest expense and payments, $16,000.
*n. Income tax expense and payments, $15,000.

Financing Activities
*o. Proceeds from issuance of common stock, $101,000.
*p. Proceeds from issuance of long-term debt, $94,000.
*q. Payments of long-term debt, $11,000.
*r. Declaration and payment of cash dividends, $17,000.

Investing Activities
*s. Cash payments to acquire capital assets, $306,000.
*t. Loan to another company, $11,000.
*u. Proceeds from sale of capital assets, $62,000, including $8,000 gain.

Operating Activities   The transaction analysis on the work sheet appears in the form of journal entries. Observe that only balance sheet accounts appear on the work sheet. There are no income statement accounts. Therefore, revenue transactions are entered on the work sheet as credits to Retained Earnings. For example, in transaction a, sales on account are entered on the work sheet by debiting Accounts Receivable and crediting Retained Earnings. Cash is neither debited nor credited because credit sales do not affect cash. Nevertheless, this transaction and all other transactions should be entered on the work sheet in order to identify all the cash effects of the period's transactions. In transaction c, the earning of interest revenue is entered by debiting Interest Receivable and crediting Retained Earnings.

The revenue transactions that generate cash are also recorded by crediting Retained Earnings. For example, transaction e is a cash receipt of dividend revenue. The work sheet entry credits Retained Earnings and debits Dividends Received as a cash receipt from operating activities. Transaction d is a collection of interest receivable. The work sheet entry debits Interest Received (a cash receipt from operating activities) and credits Interest Receivable.

Expense transactions are entered on the work sheet as debits to Retained Earnings. In transaction f, cost of goods sold is entered by debiting Retained Earnings and crediting Inventory. Transaction i for salary and wage expense is entered by debiting Retained Earnings and crediting Salary and Wage Payable. In transaction k, depreciation is entered by debiting Retained Earnings and crediting Capital Assets, Net (this work sheet uses no Accumulated Depreciation account). In transaction l, other operating expense is entered by debiting Retained Earnings and crediting Accrued Liabilities. These transactions should be entered on the work sheet even though they have no direct effect on cash.

Transaction m is a cash payment of interest expense. The work sheet entry debits Retained Earnings and credits Payments for Interest under operating activities. Transaction n is a cash payment for income tax.

Transaction h deserves special emphasis. The Payment to Suppliers of $133,000 includes three individual amounts: payments of accounts payable, $113,000; payments of accrued liabilities, $19,000; and payments of prepaid expenses, $1,000. How were these three amounts computed? These amounts are the differences needed to reconcile each account's beginning balance to its ending balance. For example, Prepaid Expenses increased from a beginning balance of $7,000 to an ending amount of $8,000. This increase must occur through a cash payment of $1,000 (transaction h3). Payments of prepaid expenses are labeled as Payments to Suppliers on the SCFP when operating activities are reported by the direct method. The $113,000 debit to Accounts Payable (transaction h1) is computed as the amount needed to complete the reconciliation from the beginning balance ($57,000) to the ending amount ($91,000), taking into consideration the $147,000 credit purchase of inventory in transaction g ($57,000 + $147,000 − $91,000 = $113,000). The $19,000 debit to Accrued Liabilities (transaction h2) is the amount needed to reconcile the beginning balance to the ending balance after considering the $17,000 credit amount in transaction l.

Financing Activities   The issuance of common stock for $101,000 cash (transaction o) is entered on the work sheet by debiting Proceeds from Issuance of Common Stock under financing activities and crediting Common Stock. The $94,000 issuance of long-term debt (transaction p) is entered in a similar manner but with a credit to Long-term Debt. The payment of long-term debt (transaction q) debits Long-term Debt and credits Payment of Long-term Debt under financing activities. The payment of dividends (transaction r) debits Retained Earnings and credits Payment of Dividends as a financing cash payment.

Investing Activities   The first investing activity listed in Panel B of the work sheet is transaction s, the $306,000 cash payment to acquire capital assets. This transaction is entered on the work sheet by debiting Capital Assets, Net and crediting Acquisition of Capital Assets under cash flows from operating activities. Transaction u is a cash receipt from an investing activity. The cash proceeds of $62,000 from sale of capital assets are entered as a cash receipt under investing activities. The $8,000 gain is credited to Retained Earnings, with the remaining $54,000 (the asset's book value) credited to Capital Assets, Net. Investing transaction t is a loan to another company, entered on the work sheet by debiting Long-term Receivable from Another Company and crediting Loan to Another Company under investing activities.

Net Increase (Decrease) in Cash   The net increase or net decrease in cash for the period is the balancing amount needed to equate the total debits and total credits ($567,000) on the SCFP. In Exhibit 18A-2, Anchor Ltd. experienced a $20,000 decrease in cash. This amount is entered as a credit to Cash (transaction v) at the top of the work sheet and a debit to Net Decrease in Cash at the bottom. Totaling the columns completes the work sheet.

Preparing the Statement of Changes in Financial Position from the Work Sheet

To prepare the SCFP, which appears as Exhibit 18-1, p. 780 of the text, the accountant has only to rewrite Panel B of the work sheet and add subtotals for the three categories of activities. In Exhibit 18A-2, net cash *inflows* from operating activities total $68,000 [receipts of $290,000 ($271,000 + $10,000 + $9,000) minus payments

Exhibit 18A-2

Anchor Ltd.
Work Sheet for Statement of Changes in Financial Position (Direct Method)
for the year ended December 31, 19X2

Panel A: Account Titles	Balances Dec. 31, 19X1	Transaction Analysis (amounts in thousands) Debit		Transaction Analysis (amounts in thousands) Credit		Balances Dec. 31, 19X2
Cash	42			(v)	20	22
Accounts receivable	80	(a)	284	(b)	271	93
Interest receivable	1	(c)	12	(d)	10	3
Inventory	138	(g)	147	(f)	150	135
Prepaid expenses	7	(h3)	1			8
Long-term receivable from another company	—	(t)	11			11
Capital assets, net	219	(s)	306	(k)	18	
				(u)	54	453
Totals	487					725
Accounts payable	57	(h1)	113	(g)	147	91
Salary and wage payable	6	(j)	58	(i)	56	4
Accrued liabilities	3	(h2)	19	(l)	17	1
Long-term debt	77	(q)	11	(p)	94	160
Common stock	258			(o)	101	359
Retained earnings	86	(f)	150	(a)	284	110
		(l)	17	(c)	12	
		(i)	56	(e)	9	
		(k)	18	(u)	8	
		(m)	16			
		(n)	15			
		(r)	17			
Totals	487		1,251		1,251	725
Panel B: Statement of Changes in Financial Position						
Cash flows from operating activities						
Receipts:						
Collections from customers		(b)	271			
Interest received		(d)	10			
Dividends received		(e)	9			
Payments:						
To suppliers				(h1)	113	
				(h2)	19	
				(h3)	1	
To employees				(j)	58	
For interest				(m)	16	
For income tax				(n)	15	
Cash flows from financing activities						
Proceeds from issuance of common stock		(o)	101			
Proceeds from issuance of long-term debt		(p)	94			
Payment of long-term debt				(q)	11	
Payment of dividends				(r)	17	
Cash flows from investing activities						
Acquisition of capital assets				(s)	306	
Proceeds from sale of capital assets		(u)	62			
Loan to another company				(t)	11	
			547		567	
Net decrease in cash		(v)	20			
Totals			567		567	

of $222,000 ($113,000 + $19,000 + $1,000 + $58,000 + $16,000 + $15,000)]. Net cash *inflows* from financing activities are $167,000 ($101,000 + $94,000 – $11,000 – $17,000). Net cash *outflows* from investing activities equal $255,000 ($306,000 + $11,000 – $62,000). Altogether, these three subtotals explain why cash decreased by $20,000 ($68,000 + $167,000 – $255,000 = –$20,000).

Preparing the Work Sheet: Indirect Method for Operating Activities _____

The indirect method shows the reconciliation from net income to net cash inflow (or net cash outflow) from operating activities. Exhibit 18A-3 is the work sheet for preparing the statement of changes in financial position by the indirect method.

The steps in completing the work sheet using the indirect method are the same as those taken using the direct method. However, the data for the operating cash flows come from different sources. Net income, depreciation, depletion and amortization, and gains and losses on disposals of capital assets come from the income statement. The changes in noncash current asset accounts (Receivables, Inventory, and Prepaid Expenses for Anchor Ltd.) and the current liability accounts (Accounts Payable, Salary and Wage Payable, and Accrued Liabilities) are taken directly from the comparative balance sheet.

The analysis of financing activities and investing activities uses the information presented on p. 783 and given on p. 829 of this appendix. As mentioned previously, there is no difference for financing activities or investing activities between the direct-method work sheet and the indirect-method work sheet. Therefore, the analysis that follows focuses on cash flows from operating activities. The Anchor Ltd. data come from the income statement (Exhibit 18-3, p. 786) and the comparative balance sheet (Exhibit 18-4, p. 789).

Transaction Analysis under the Indirect Method

Net income (transaction a) is the first operating cash inflow. Net income is entered on the work sheet as a debit to Net Income under cash flows from operating activities and a credit to Retained Earnings. Next come the additions to, and subtractions from, net income, starting with depreciation (transaction b), which is debited to Depreciation on the work sheet and credited to Capital Assets, Net. Transaction c is the sale of capital assets. The $8,000 gain on the sale is entered as a credit to Gain on Sale of Capital Assets under operating cash flows — a subtraction from net income. This credit removes the $8,000 amount of the gain from cash flow from operations because the cash proceeds from the sale were not $8,000. The cash proceeds were $62,000, so this amount is entered on the work sheet as a debit under investing activities. To complete entry c, the capital assets' book value of $54,000 ($62,000 – $8,000) is credited to the Capital Assets, Net account.

Entries d through j reconcile net income to cash flows from operations for increases and decreases in the current assets other than Cash and for increases and decreases in the current liabilities. Entry d debits Accounts Receivable for its $13,000 increase during the year. This decrease in cash flows is credited to Increase in Accounts Receivable under operating cash flows. Entries e and g are similar for Interest Receivable and Prepaid Expenses.

During the year, Inventory decreased by $3,000. This increase in cash is credited to Inventory in work sheet entry f, with the debit to Decrease in Inventory under operating activities.

Entry h records the $34,000 increase in Accounts Payable by crediting this account. The resulting increase in cash is debited to Increase in Accounts Payable under operating cash flows. Entry i debits Salary and Wage Payable for its $2,000 decrease, with the offsetting credit to Decrease in Salary and Wage Payable. Entry j for Accrued Liabilities is similar.

Exhibit 18A-3

Anchor Ltd.
Work Sheet for Statement of Changes in Financial Position (Indirect Method)
for the year ended December 31, 19X2

Panel A: Account Titles	Balances Dec. 31, 19X1	Transaction Analysis (Amounts in thousands) Debit		Transaction Analysis (Amounts in thousands) Credit		Balances Dec. 31, 19X2
Cash	42			(q)	20	22
Accounts receivable	80	(d)	13			93
Interest receivable	1	(e)	2			3
Inventory	138			(f)	3	135
Prepaid expenses	7	(g)	1			8
Long-term receivable from another company	—	(p)	11			11
Capital assets, net	219	(o)	306	(b)	18	
				(c)	54	453
Totals	487					725
Accounts payable	57			(h)	34	91
Salary and wage payable	6	(i)	2			4
Accrued liabilities	3	(j)	2			1
Long-term debt	77	(m)	11	(l)	94	160
Common stock	258			(k)	101	359
Retained earnings	86	(n)	17	(a)	41	110
Totals	487		365		365	725

Panel B: Statement of Changes in Financial Position						
Cash flows from operating activities						
Net income		(a)	41			
Add (subtract) items that affect net income						
and cash flow differently:						
Depreciation		(b)	18			
Gain on sale of capital assets				(c)	8	
Increase in accounts receivable				(d)	13	
Increase in interest receivable				(e)	2	
Decrease in inventory		(f)	3			
Increase in prepaid expenses				(g)	1	
Increase in accounts payable		(h)	34			
Decrease in salary and wage payable				(i)	2	
Decrease in accrued liabilities				(j)	2	
Cash flows from financing activities						
Proceeds from issuance of common stock		(k)	101			
Proceeds from issuance of long-term debt		(l)	94			
Payment of long-term debt				(m)	11	
Payment of dividends				(p)	17	
Cash flows from investing activities						
Acquisition of capital assets				(o)	306	
Proceeds from sale of capital assets		(c)	62			
Loan to another company				(p)	11	
			353		373	
Net decrease in cash		(q)	20			
Totals			373		373	

Exhibit 18A-4   *Noncash Financing and Investing Activities on the Work Sheet*

Crown Ltd.
Work Sheet for Statement of Changes in Financial Position
for the year ended December 31, 19X2

	Balances Dec. 31, 19X1	Transaction Analysis Debit	Transaction Analysis Credit	Balances Dec. 31, 19X2
Panel A: Account Titles				
Cash				
Accounts receivable.......................				
Building..	650,000	(t1) 320,000		970,000
Common Stock.............................	890,000		(t2) 320,000	1,210,000
Retained earnings				
Panel B: Statement of Changes **in Financial Position**				
Cash flows from operating activities				
Net increase (decrease) in cash....				
Noncash financing and investing transactions				
Purchase of building by issuance of common stock		(t2) 320,000	(t1) 320,000	

Do not be confused by the different keying of financing transactions and investing transactions in Exhibits 18A-2 and 18A-3. Except for the letters used to key transactions, the entries are identical. For example, the $306,000 acquisition of capital assets is transaction s in Exhibit 18A-2 and transaction o in Exhibit 18A-3. In each exhibit, we maintain a continuous listing of transactions starting with the letter a. The two exhibits simply have different keyed letters because of the number of transactions.

The final item in Exhibit 18A-3 is the Net Decrease in Cash — transaction q on the work sheet — a credit to Cash and a debit to Net Decrease in Cash, exactly as in Exhibit 18A-2.

To prepare the statement of changes in financial position from the work sheet, the accountant merely rewrites Panel B of the statement, adding subtotals for the three categories of activities. In Exhibit 18A-3, net cash inflow from operating activities is $68,000 ($41,000 + $18,000 + $3,000 + $34,000 − $8,000 − $13,000 − $2,000 − $1,000 − $2,000 − $2,000). Of course, this is the same amount of net cash inflow from operating activities computed under the direct method from Exhibit 18A-2. The indirect-method statement of changes in financial position appears in Exhibit 18-6, p. 798.

Noncash Financing and Investing Activities on the Work Sheet   Noncash financing and investing activities can also be analyzed on the work sheet. Because this type of transaction includes both a financing activity and an investing activity, it requires two work sheet entries. For example, suppose Crown Ltd. purchased a building by issuing common stock of $320,000. Exhibit 18A-4 illustrates the transaction analysis of this noncash financing and investing activity. Observe that Cash is unaffected.

Work sheet entry t1 records the purchase of the building, and entry t2 records the issuance of the stock. The order of these entries is unimportant.

APPENDIX ASSIGNMENT MATERIAL

Problem 18A-1   *Preparing the work sheet for the statement of changes in financial position: direct method*

The 19X3 comparative balance sheet and income statement of Gold Imari, Inc., follow:

Comparative Balance Sheet

	19X3	19X2	Increase (Decrease)
Current asset			
Cash and cash equivalents..............................	$ 37,500	$ 15,600	$21,900
Accounts receivable	41,500	43,100	(1,600)
Interest receivable..	600	900	(300)
Inventories..	94,300	89,900	4,400
Prepaid expenses..	1,700	2,200	(500)
Capital assets			
Land	35,100	10,000	25,100
Equipment, net	100,900	93,700	7,200
Total assets..	$311,600	$255,400	$56,200
Current liabilities			
Accounts payable	$ 16,400	$ 17,900	$ (1,500)
Interest payable	6,300	6,700	(400)
Salary payable...	2,100	1,400	700
Other accrued liabilities	18,100	18,700	(600)
Income tax payable	6,300	3,800	2,500
Long-term liabilities			
Notes payable	55,000	65,000	(10,000)
Shareholders' equity			
Common stock...	131,100	122,300	8,800
Retained earnings...	76,300	19,600	56,700
Total liabilities and shareholders' equity	$311,600	$255,400	$56,200

Income Statement for 19X3

Revenues		
Sales revenue		$461,800
Interest revenue...		11,700
Total revenues.....................................		473,500
Expenses		
Cost of goods sold......................................	$205,200	
Salary expense	76,400	
Depreciation expense	15,300	
Other operating expense..........................	49,700	
Interest expense...	24,600	
Income tax expense...................................	16,900	
Total expenses.....................................		388,100
Net income		$ 85,400

Gold Imari had no noncash financing and investing transactions during 19X3.

Required

Prepare the work sheet for the 19X3 statement of changes in financial position. Format cash flows from operating activities by the direct method.

Problem 18A-2 *Preparing the work sheet for the statement of changes in financial position:*
indirect method

Using the Gold Imari, Inc. data from the preceding problem, prepare the work sheet for the 19X3 statement of changes in financial position. Format cash flows from operating activities by the indirect method.

Problem 18A-3 *Preparing the work sheet for the statement of changes in financial position:*
indirect method

Longenecker-Scott Corporation's comparative balance sheet at September 30, 19X4 follows:

Longenecker-Scott Corporation			
Comparative Balance Sheet			
September 30, 19X4 and 19X3			
	19X4	**19X3**	**Increase (Decrease)**
Current assets			
Cash..	$ 69,700	$ 17,600	$ 52,100
Accounts receivable	41,900	44,000	(2,100)
Interest receivable..	4,100	2,800	1,300
Inventories...	121,700	116,900	4,800
Prepaid expenses..	8,600	9,300	(700)
Long-term investments	55,400	18,100	37,300
Capital assets			
Land	65,800	93,000	(27,200)
Equipment, net	89,500	49,700	39,800
Total assets..	$456,700	$351,400	$105,300
Current liabilities			
Notes payable, short-term...............................	$ 22,000	$ -0-	$ 22,000
Accounts payable..	61,800	70,300	(8,500)
Income tax payable	21,800	24,600	(2,800)
Accrued liabilities..	17,900	29,100	(11,200)
Interest payable	4,500	3,200	1,300
Salary payable...	1,500	1,100	400
Note payable, long-term	62,900	61,300	1,600
Shareholders' equity			
Common stock...	142,100	90,200	51,900
Retained earnings...	122,200	71,600	50,600
Total liabilities and shareholders' equity............	$456,700	$351,400	$105,300

Transaction data for the year ended September 30, 19X4:

a. Net income, $114,900.

b. Depreciation expense on equipment, $8,500.

c. Acquired long-term investments, $37,300.

d. Sold land for $38,100, including $10,900 gain.

e. Acquired equipment by issuing long-term note payable, $26,300.

f. Paid long-term note payable, $24,700.

g. Received cash of $51,900 for issuance of common stock.

h. Paid cash dividends, $64,300.

i. Acquired equipment by issuing short-term note payable, $22,000.

j. Inventory purchased on account, $166,300.

Required

Prepare Longenecker-Scott's work sheet for the statement of changes in financial position for the year ended September 30, 19X4, using the indirect method to report operating activities. Include on the work sheet the noncash financing and investing activities.

Problem 18A-4   *Preparing the work sheet for the statement of changes in financial position: direct method*

Refer to the data of Problem 18A-3.

Required

Prepare Longenecker-Scott's work sheet for the statement of changes in financial position for the year ended September 30, 19X4, using the direct method for operating activities. The income statement reports the following: sales, $391,600; gain on sale of land, $10,900; interest revenue, $7,300; cost of goods sold, $161,500; salary expense, $63,400; other operating expenses, $29,600; income tax expense, $18,400; interest expense, $13,500; depreciation expense, $8,500. Include on the work sheet the noncash financing and investing activities.

Answers to Self-Study Questions

1. b
2. d
3. a
4. c
5. d
6. d ($43,000 + $4,000 decrease in Interest Receivable = $47,000)
7. c ($104,000 + $31,000 − cost of investment sold = $91,000; Cost = $44,000; Proceeds = Cost, $44,000 + Gain, $22,000 = $66,000)
8. a
9. c
10. b ($17,000 + $9,000 + $3,000 − $4,000 − $6,000 + $8,000 = $27,000)

Chapter 19

Using Accounting Information to Make Business Decisions

Once debits equal credits, once net income is properly closed out to retained earnings, and once the SCFP reconciles with the change in cash position, your financial statements have value, right? Well, almost. These are necessary but not sufficient conditions for business success. The real value of financial statements lies in the ability of business people to use them to make informed decisions.

Vickie Kerr (inventor of a "better" potato chip), Chips Klein (inventor of a unique three-way mirror), Colleen McDonald (inventor of a portable highchair), and Leslie Dolman (inventor of a data-inputting device for disabled workers) have several things in common. Each has fundamental entrepreneurial skills, each has an invention that meets a need in the marketplace, and each has a willingness to take risks. Each of these women also has an understanding of how to use financial statements to monitor her business.

A careful analysis of measures of profitability enables them to minimize expenses. Reviewing balance sheet relationships helps them to monitor cash flow, inventory, and accounts receivable.

Clearly, their creative skills give them the competitive edge, but without the ability to analyze and interpret financial statements, their expertise would be wasted.

This chapter concludes the discussion of financial accounting. It was noted in Chapter 1 that accounting information plays a major role in decision-making. Chapter 19 consolidates the skills you have acquired by returning to this initial observation. As you read, consider whether any business person could conduct business without reliable financial accounting informaiton.

Source: Rachelle Beauchamp and Judith Potts, "Inventive Women," *Candian Banker* (January-February 1992), pp. 52–56.

LEARNING OBJECTIVES

After studying this chapter, you should be able to

1 Perform a horizontal analysis of comparative financial statements

2 Perform a vertical analysis of financial statements

3 Prepare common-size financial statements

4 Use the statement of changes in financial position in decision-making

5 Compute the standard financial ratios used for decision-making

6 Use ratios in decision-making

As this vignette illustrates, business people rely on accounting information to make business decisions. The balance sheet, the income statement, and the statement of changes in financial position provide a large part of the information that is used for making these decisions. In Chapters 1 through 18, we have described the process of accounting and the preparation of the financial statements. We have tried to relate each topic to the real world of business by showing the relevance of the accounting data. In this chapter, we discuss in more detail how to use the information that appears in these statements. (Appendix C features the financial statements of Schneiders Corporation. You may apply the analytical skills you learn in this chapter to those real-world data.)

Financial Statement Analysis

Financial statement analysis focuses on techniques used by analysts external to the organization, although managers use many of the same methods. These analysts rely on information available to the public. A major source of such information is the annual report. As you have learned in previous chapters, the financial statements include:

1. The basic financial statements: balance sheet, income statement, statement of retained earnings, and statement of changes in financial position;
2. The notes to the financial statements, including a statement of significant accounting policies;
3. Comparative financial information for at least the prior year;
4. The auditor's report.

In addition, the annual report will usually include: (1) management discussion and analysis of the company's past results and future prospects; (2) a management report; and (3) other financial information about the company.

Management's discussion and analysis (MD&A) is a relatively new development in financial reporting. While some companies have been providing a commentary on their past operations and expectations, it is only recently that such disclosure has become required and then only by larger companies registered with the various securities regulators in Canada, such as the Ontario Securities Commission (OSC). The description of MD&A in the OSC's Statement 5.10 is helpful in providing an understanding of the concept:

> MD&A is supplemental analysis and explanation which accompanies but does not form part of the financial statements. MD&A provides management with the opportunity to explain in narrative form its current financial situation and future prospects. MD&A is intended to give the investor the ability to look at the [company issuing the financial

statements] through the eyes of management by providing a historical and prospective analysis of the business of the [issuer]. MD&A requirements ask management to discuss the dynamics of the business and to analyze the financial statements. Coupled with the financial statements this information should allow investors to assess [the issuing company's] performance and future prospects.[1]

An example of MD&A is that provided in the 1992 annual report of Mark's Work Wearhouse. The report begins with a very thorough discussion of the company's operations over the year including detailed information with respect to the company's own stores and franchise operations. Operations by region are then discussed with information provided on per-square-foot sales and sales per resident of the six regions. Next, the MD&A examines franchise operations and then human resources; in the latter case, information is provided about sales per employee and sales per dollar of salary. Mark's Work Wearhouse's financial objectives are clearly stated so users will later be able to assess whether or not they were acheived. The next section provides an examination of the company's "Strategic Direction" — where management sees the company is heading with respect to how and where the company will market its products. Management then provides a detailed discussion and analysis of the financial results as presented in the financial statements. The MD&A concludes with a candid assessment of the risks and uncertainties facing the company.

Mark's Work Wearhouse is frequently cited by analysts and accounting professionals as providing one of the most informative and "user-friendly" annual reports. The consensus is that management makes a genuine attempt to provide honest information to users no matter how unpleasant, to the company, that information may be.

The MD&A from any company, together with the accounting information in the financial statements of that company helps investors and creditors interpret the financial statements. The balance sheet, income statement, and statement of changes in financial position are based on historical data; they state *what* has happened but rarely provide insights into *why* it has happened. MD&A offers top management's glimpses into the future. Investors and creditors are also interested in where the company is headed.

As a final note, while larger companies registered with the various securities commissions in Canada are required to provide MD&A with their annual filing, it is to be hoped that more companies will begin to provide such useful information to the users of their financial statements.

Objectives of Financial Statement Analysis

Investors purchase capital stock expecting to receive dividends and an increase in the value of their stock. Creditors make loans with the expectation of receiving interest and principal. Both groups risk not receiving their expected returns. They use financial statement analysis to (1) predict the amount of expected returns and (2) assess the risks associated with those returns.

Because creditors generally expect to receive specific fixed amounts and have first claim on the assets, they are most concerned with assessing short-term liquidity and long-term solvency. **Short-term liquidity** is an organization's ability to meet current payments as they become due. **Long-term solvency** is the ability to generate enough cash to pay long-term debts as they mature.

In contrast, investors are more concerned with profitability, dividends, and future security prices. Why? Because dividend payments depend on profitable

---

[1] The authors wish to thank Brenda Eprile, CA, Chief Accountant to the Ontario Securities Commission, for her assistance in providing the authors with a copy of OSC Statement 5.10.

operations, and stock price appreciation depends on the market's assessment of the company's prospects. Creditors also assess profitability because profitable operations are the prime source of cash to repay loans.

We divide the tools and techniques that the business community uses in evaluating financial statement information into three broad categories: horizontal analysis, vertical analysis and ratio analysis.

Horizontal Analysis

Many business decisions hinge on whether the numbers in sales, income, expenses, and so on, are increasing or decreasing over time. Has the sales figure risen from last year? From two years ago? By how many dollars? We may find that the net sales figure has risen by $20,000. This may be interesting, but considered alone it is not very useful for decision-making. An analysis of the *percentage change* in the net sales figure over time improves our ability to use the dollar amounts. It is more useful to know that sales have increased by 20 percent than to know that the increase in sales is $20,000.

The study of percentage changes in comparative statements is called **horizontal analysis**. Computing a percentage change in comparative statements requires two steps: (1) Compute the dollar amount of the change from the earlier (base) period to the later period, and (2) divide the dollar amount of change by the base period amount. Horizontal analysis is illustrated as follows:

	Year 3	Year 2	Year 1	Increase (Decrease) During Year 3 Amount	%	Increase (Decrease) During Year 2 Amount	%
Sales	$120,000	$100,000	$80,000	$20,000	20%	$20,000	25%
Net income	12,000	8,000	10,000	4,000	50%	(2,000)	(20%)

The increase in sales is $20,000 in both year 3 and year 2. However, the percentage increase in sales differs from year to year because of the change in the base amount. To compute the percentage change for year 2, we divide the amount of increase ($20,000) by the base period amount ($80,000), an increase of 25 percent. For year 3, the dollar amount increases again by $20,000. However, the base period amount for figuring this percentage change is $100,000. Dividing $20,000 by $100,000 computes a percentage increase of only 20 percent during year 3. Observe that net income *decreases* by 20 percent during year 2 and *increases* by 50 percent during year 3.

Detailed horizontal analyses of a comparative income statement and a comparative balance sheet are shown in the two right-hand columns of Exhibits 19-1 and 19-2. McColpin, Inc. is a small retailer of office furniture.

The comparative income statement in Exhibit 19-1 reveals that net sales increased by 6.8 percent during 19X7 and that the cost of goods sold grew by much less. As a result, gross profit rose by 17.3 percent. Note that general expenses actually decreased, and so the company significantly increased income from operations and net income during 19X7. Our analysis shows that 19X7 was a much better year than 19X6. We see that the growth in income resulted more from slowing the increase in expenses than from boosting sales revenue.

No percentage increase is computed for interest revenue because dividing the $4,000 increase by a zero amount would produce a meaningless percentage. Also, we compute no percentage change when a base-year amount is negative. For example, when a company goes from a net loss one year to a profit the next year, we would be dividing a positive number by a negative amount. Throughout this chapter, we discuss only some of the elements of the various statements that we

OBJECTIVE 1

Perform a horizontal
analysis of comparative
financial statements

EXHIBIT 19-1   Comparative Income Statement: Horizontal Analysis

McColpin, Inc.
Comparative Income Statement
years ended December 31, 19X7 and 19X6

	19X7	19X6	Increase (Decrease) Amount	Percent
Net sales	$858,000	$803,000	$55,000	6.8%
Cost of goods sold..............................	513,000	509,000	4,000	0.8
Gross profit	345,000	294,000	51,000	17.3
Operating expenses:				
Selling expenses............................	126,000	114,000	12,000	10.5
General expenses	118,000	123,000	(5,000)	(4.1)
Total operating expenses..................	244,000	237,000	7,000	3.0
Income from operations	101,000	57,000	44,000	77.2
Interest revenue.................................	4,000	—	4,000	—
Interest expense.................................	24,000	14,000	10,000	71.4
Income before income taxes	81,000	43,000	38,000	88.4
Income tax expense...........................	33,000	17,000	16,000	94.1
Net income..	$ 48,000	$ 26,000	$22,000	84.6

EXHIBIT 19-2   Comparative Balance Sheet: Horizontal Analysis

McColpin, Inc.
Comparative Balance Sheet
December 31, 19X7 and 19X6

	19X7	19X6	Increase (Decrease) Amount	Percent
Assets				
Currents assets				
Cash	$ 29,000	$ 32,000	$ (3,000)	(9.4%)
Accounts receivable, net..............	114,000	85,000	29,000	34.1
Inventories	113,000	111,000	2,000	1.8
Prepaid expenses..........................	6,000	8,000	(2,000)	(25.0)
Total current assets	262,000	236,000	26,000	11.0
Long-term investments......................	18,000	9,000	9,000	100.0
Property, plant and equipment,				
net..	507,000	399,000	108,000	27.1
Total assets..............................	$787,000	$644,000	$143,000	22.2
Liabilities				
Current liabilities				
Notes payable...............................	$ 42,000	$ 27,000	$ 15,000	55.6
Accounts payable	73,000	68,000	5,000	7.4
Accrued liabilities	27,000	31,000	(4,000)	(12.9)
Total current liabilities	142,000	126,000	16,000	12.7
Long-term debt...................................	289,000	198,000	91,000	46.0
Total liabilities	431,000	324,000	107,000	33.0
Shareholders' Equity				
Common stock....................................	186,000	186,000	—	0.0
Retained earnings..............................	170,000	134,000	36,000	26.9
Total shareholders' equity	356,000	320,000	36,000	11.3
Total liabilities and				
shareholders' equity...........	$787,000	$644,000	$143,000	22.2

present. For example, we mention McColpin's cost of goods sold but not its selling expenses. Understand, however, that the manager of the sales staff (and likely top management also) would examine the selling expenses in conducting a full analysis of the company's operations.

The comparative balance sheet in Exhibit 19-2 shows that 19X7 was a year of expansion for the company. Property, plant, and equipment, net of depreciation, increased by 27.1 percent. To help finance this expansion, McColpin borrowed heavily, increasing short-term notes payable by 55.6 percent and long-term debt by 46 percent. The increase in assets was also financed in part by profitable operations, as shown by the 26.9 percent increase in retained earnings.

The sharpest percentage increase on the balance sheet is in long-term investments (100 percent). However, the dollar amounts are small compared to the other balance sheet figures. Note this key point of financial analysis: percentage changes must be evaluated in terms of the item's relative importance to the company as a whole. In this instance, the large percentage increase in long-term investments means little because the company holds such a small amount. The 27.1 percent increase in property, plant and equipment is more important because their cost represents the largest asset and their use is intended to generate profits for years to come.

Trend Percentages

Trend percentages are a form of horizontal analysis. Trends are important indicators of the direction a business is taking. How have sales changed over a five-year period? What trend does gross profit show? These questions can be answered by an analysis of trend percentages over a representative period, such as the most recent five years or the most recent ten years. To gain a realistic view of the company, it is often necessary to examine more than just a two- or three-year period.

Trend percentages are computed by selecting a base year, with each amount during that year set equal to 100 percent. The amounts of each following year are expressed as a percent of the base amount. To compute trend percentages, divide each item for years after the base year by the corresponding amount during the base year. Suppose McColpin, Inc. showed sales, cost of goods sold and gross profit for the past six years as follows:

| | **(amounts in thousands)** | | | | | |
	19X7	**19X6**	**19X5**	**19X4**	**19X3**	**19X2**
Net sales	$858	$803	$781	$744	$719	$737
Cost of goods sold	513	509	490	464	450	471
Gross profit	$345	$294	$291	$280	$269	$266

Assume we want trend percentages for a five-year period starting with 19X3. We use 19X2 as the base year. Trend percentages for net sales are computed by dividing each net sales amount by the 19X2 amount of $737,000. Likewise, dividing each year's cost-of-goods-sold amount by the base-year amount ($471,000) yields the trend percentages for cost of goods sold. Gross-profit trend percentages are computed similarly. The resulting trend percentages follow (19X2, the base year = 100%):

	19X7	**19X6**	**19X5**	**19X4**	**19X3**	**19X2**
Net sales	116%	109%	106%	101%	98%	100%
Cost of goods sold	109	108	104	99	96	100
Gross profit	130	111	109	105	101	100

McColpin's sales and cost of goods sold have trended upward since a downturn in 19X3. Gross profit has increased steadily, with the most dramatic growth coming during 19X7. What signal about the company does this information provide? It suggests that operations are becoming increasingly more successful. A similar analysis can be performed for any related set of items in the financial statements. For example, an increase in inventory and accounts receivable, coupled with a decrease in sales, may reveal difficulty in making sales and collecting receivables.

Vertical Analysis

Horizontal analysis highlights changes in an item over time. However, no single technique provides a complete picture of a business. Another way to analyze a company is called vertical analysis.

Vertical analysis of a financial statement reveals the relationship of each statement item to the total, which is the 100 percent figure. For example, when an income statement is subjected to vertical analysis, new sales is usually the base. Suppose under normal conditions a company's gross profit is 50 percent of net sales. A drop in gross profit to 40 percent may cause the company to report a net loss on the income statement. Management, investors and creditors view a large decline in gross profit with alarm. Exhibit 19-3 shows the vertical analysis of McColpin, Inc.'s income statement as a percentage of net sales. Exhibit 19-4 shows the vertical analysis of the balance sheet amounts as a percentage of total assets.

The 19X7 comparative income statement (Exhibit 19-3) reports that cost of goods sold dropped to 59.8 percent of net sales from 63.4 percent in 19X6. This explains why the gross profit percentage arose in 19X7. The gross profit percentage is one of the most important pieces of information in financial analysis because it shows the relationship between net sales and cost of goods sold. All other things equal, a company that can steadily increase its gross profit percentage over a long period is more likely to succeed than a business whose gross profit percentage is steadily declining. The net income percentage almost doubled in 19X7, mostly because of the decrease in the cost-of-goods-sold percentage.

OBJECTIVE 2

Perform a vertical analysis of financial statements

EXHIBIT 19-3   *Comparative Income Statement: Vertical Analysis*

McColpin, Inc.
Comparative Income Statement
years ended December 31, 19X7 and 19X6

	19X7		19X6	
	Amount	Percent	Amount	Percent
Net sales	$858,000	100.0%	$803,000	100.0%
Cost of goods sold	513,000	59.8	509,000	63.4
Gross profit	345,000	40.2	294,000	36.6
Selling expenses	126,000	14.7	114,000	14.2
General expenses	118,000	13.7	123,000	15.3
Total operating expenses	244,000	28.4	237,000	29.5
Income from operations	101,000	11.8	57,000	7.1
Interest revenue	4,000	0.4	—	—
Interest expense	24,000	2.8	14,000	1.8
Income before income tax	81,000	9.4	43,000	5.3
Income tax expense	33,000	3.8	17,000	2.1
Net income	$ 48,000	5.6%	$ 26,000	3.2%

EXHIBIT 19-4   *Comparative Balance Sheet: Vertical Analysis*

McColpin, Inc.
Comparative Balance Sheet
December 31, 19X7 and 19X6

	19X7		19X6	
	Amount	Percent	Amount	Percent
Assets				
Current assets				
Cash	$ 29,000	3.7%	$ 32,000	5.0%
Accounts receivable, net	114,000	14.5	85,000	13.2
Inventories..................................	113,000	14.3	111,000	17.2
Prepaid expenses	6,000	0.8	8,000	1.2
Total current assets	262,000	33.3	236,000	36.6
Long-term investments..................	18,000	2.3	9,000	1.4
Property, plant and equipment, net	507,000	64.4	399,000	62.0
Total assets.............................	$787,000	100.0%	$644,000	100.0%
Liabilities				
Current liabilities				
Notes payable..............................	$ 42,000	5.3%	$ 27,000	4.2%
Accounts payable........................	73,000	9.3	68,000	10.6
Accrued liabilities.......................	27,000	3.4	31,000	4.8
Total current liabilities	142,000	18.0	126,000	19.6
Long-term debt	289,000	36.7	198,000	30.7
Total liabilities	431,000	54.7	324,000	50.3
Shareholders' Equity				
Common stock	186,000	23.7	186,000	28.9
Retained earnings	170,000	21.6	134,000	20.8
Total shareholders' equity	356,000	45.3	320,000	49.7
Total liabilities and				
shareholders' equity.........	$787,000	100.0%	$644,000	100.0%

Vertical analysis gives a view of the income statement that is different from the view provided by horizontal analysis. Decision-makers use these two forms of analysis together. For example, Exhibit 19-1 reports that gross profit increased by 17.3 percent, and net income increased by 84.6 percent from 19X6 to 19X7. Exhibit 19-3 indicates that gross profit grew from 36.6 percent of sales in 19X6 to 40.2 percent of sales in 19X7 and that net income has increased from 3.2 percent of sales to 5.6 percent of sales. Together, vertical analysis and horizontal analysis show a favorable improvement in McColpin's operations.

We can apply trend analysis to the balance sheet of McColpin, Inc., as Exhibit 19-4 shows. For example, among the changes during 19X7, we note that current assets have become a smaller percentage of total assets. A decrease in current assets may signal difficulty paying bills. However, this does not present a problem for McColpin, Inc. because current liabilities also decreased as a percentage of total assets during 19X7.

Common-Size Statements

The percentages in Exhibits 19-3 and 19-4 can be presented as a separate statement that reports only percentages (no dollar amounts). Such a statement, called a **common-size statement**, is a type of vertical analysis.

EXHIBIT 19-5   *Common-Size Analysis of Current Assets*

McColpin, Inc. Common-Size Analysis of Current Assets December 31, 19X7 and 19X6		
	Percent of Total Assets	
	19X7	19X6
Current assets		
Cash..	3.7%	5.0%
Accounts receivable, net..	14.5	13.2
Inventories..	14.3	17.2
Prepaid expenses..	8	1.2
Total current assets...	33.3%	36.6%

On a common-size income statement, each item is expressed as a percentage of the net sales amount. Net sales is the "common size" to which we relate the statement's other amounts. In the balance sheet, the "common size" is the total on each side of the accounting equation (total assets *or* the sum of total liabilities and shareholders' equity). A common-size statement eases the comparison of different companies because their amounts are stated in percentages.

Common-size statements may identify the need for corrective action. Exhibit 19-5 is the common-size analysis of current assets taken from Exhibit 19-4.

Exhibit 19-5 shows cash as a smaller percentage of total assets at December 31, 19X7 than at the previous year end. Accounts receivable, on the other hand, is a larger percentage of total assets. What could cause a decrease in cash and an increase in accounts receivable as percentages of total assets? McColpin may have been lax in collecting accounts receivable, which may explain a cash shortage and reveal that the company needs to pursue collection more vigorously. Or the company may have sold to less creditworthy customers. In any event, the company should monitor its cash position and collection of accounts receivable to avoid a cash shortage. Common-size statements provide information useful for this purpose.

Industry Comparisons

We study the records of a company in order to understand past results and predict future performance. Still, the knowledge that we can develop from a single company's records is limited to that one company. We may learn that gross profit has decreased and net income has increased steadily for the last ten years. While this information is helpful, it does not consider how businesses in the same industry have fared over this time. Have other companies in the same line of business increased their sales? Is there an industrywide decline in gross profit? Has cost of goods sold risen steeply for other businesses that sell the same products? Managers, investors, creditors and other interested parties need to know how one company compares to other companies in the same line of business.

Exhibit 19-6 gives the common-size income statement of McColpin, Inc. compared to the average for the retail furniture industry. This analysis compares McColpin to all other companies in its line of business. The industry averages are available from a variety of sources including industry trade journals.

Analysts specialize in a particular industry and make such comparisons in deciding which companies' stocks to buy or sell. For example, financial-service com-

EXHIBIT 19-6 *Common-Size Income Statement Compared to the Industry Average*

McColpin, Inc.
Common-Size Income Statement for Comparison with Industry Average
year ended December 31, 19X7

	McColpin, Inc.	Industry Average
Net sales	100.0%	100.0%
Cost of goods sold	59.8	61.8
Gross profit	**40.2**	**38.2**
Operating expenses		
Selling expenses	14.7	15.7
General expenses	13.7	12.9
Total operating expenses	28.4	28.6
Income from operations	**11.8**	**9.6**
Other revenue (expense)	(2.4)	(3.5)
Income before income tax	9.4	6.1
Income tax expense	3.8	2.4
Net income	**5.6%**	**3.7%**

panies like Richardson Greenshields have paper and forest products industry specialists, merchandising industry specialists, and so on. Boards of directors evaluate top managers based on how well the company compares with other companies in the industry. Exhibit 19-6 shows that McColpin compares favorably with competing furniture retailers. Its gross profit percentage is virtually identical to the industry average. The company does a good job of controlling expenses, and as a result, its percentage of income from operations and its net income percentage are significantly higher than the industry average.

Another use of common-size statements is to aid in the comparison of different-sized companies. Suppose you are considering an investment in the stock of a brewer, and you are choosing between John Labatt and the Brick Brewing Co. John Labatt is so much larger than the Brick that a direct comparison of their financial statements in dollar amounts is not meaningful. However, you can convert the two companies' income statements to common size and compare the percentages. You may find that one company has a higher percentage of its assets in inventory and the other company has a higher percentage of its liabilities in long-term debt.

Information Sources

Financial analysts draw their information from various sources. Annual and quarterly reports offer readers a good look at an individual business's operations. Publicly held companies must, in addition, submit annual reports that are more detailed to the provincial securities commission in each province where they are listed on a stock exchange (for example, the Alberta Securities Commission for the Alberta Stock Exchange). Business publications such as the daily and weekend *Financial Post* and the daily *Globe and Mail Report on Business* carry information about individual companies and Canadian industries. InfoGlobe and The Financial Post Information Service provide data to subscribers on public companies and industries in Canada, too. Credit agencies like Dun and Bradstreet Canada Limited, for example, and investment companies like Moodys, offer industry averages as part of their financial service.

The Statement of Changes in Financial Position in Decision-Making

The chapter so far has centered on the income statement and balance sheet. We may also perform horizontal and vertical analysis on the statement of changes in financial position. In the preceding chapter, we discussed how to prepare the statement. To discuss its role in decision-making, let us use Exhibit 19-7.

Some analysts use cash flow analysis to identify danger signals about a company's financial situation. For example, the statement in Exhibit 19-7 reveals what may be a weakness in DeMaris Corporation.

First, operations provided a net cash inflow of $52,000, which is much less than the $91,000 generated by the sale of fixed assets. An important question arises: Can the company remain in business by generating the majority of its cash by selling its capital assets? No, because these assets will be needed to manufacture the company's products in the future. Note also that borrowing by issuing bonds payable brought in $72,000. No company can long survive living on borrowed funds. DeMaris must eventually pay off the bonds. Indeed, the company paid $170,000 on older debt. Also, interest expense must be incurred as the price of borrowing. Successful companies like John Labatt, St. Lawrence Cement, and Canadian Pacific generate the greatest percentage of their cash from operations, not from selling their capital assets or from borrowing money. These conditions may be only temporary for DeMaris Corporation, but they are worth investigating.

The most important information that the statement of changes in financial position provides is a summary of the company's use of cash. How a company spends its cash today determines its sources of cash in the future. The company may wisely use its cash to purchase assets that will generate income in the years ahead. However, if a company invests unwisely, cash will eventually run short. DeMaris's statement of changes in financial position reveals problems. The exhibit information indicates that DeMaris invested in no fixed assets to replace those that it sold. The company

OBJECTIVE 4

Use the statement of changes in financial position in decision-making

EXHIBIT 19-7   *Statement of Changes in Financial Position*

DeMaris Corporation Statement of Changes in Financial Position for the current year		
Operating activities		
Income from operations..		$ 35,000
Add (subtract) noncash items:		
Depreciation...	$ 14,000	
Net increase in current assets other than cash	(5,000)	
Net increase in current liabilities....................	8,000	17,000
Net cash inflow from operating activities...........		52,000
Financing activities		
Issuance of bond payable...	$ 72,000	
Payment of long-term debt.......................................	(170,000)	
Payment of short-term debt......................................	(9,000)	
Payment of dividends...	(33,000)	
Net cash outflow from financing activities.........		(140,000)
Investing activities		
Sale of property, plant and equipment....................	$ 91,000	
Net cash inflow from investing activities...........		91,000
Increase in cash..		$ 3,000

may in fact be going out of business. Furthermore, DeMaris paid dividends of $33,000, an amount that is very close to its net income. Is the company retaining enough of its income to finance future operations without excessive borrowing? Analysts seek answers to questions such as this. They analyze the information from the statement of changes in financial position along with the information from the balance sheet and the income statement to form a well-rounded complete picture of the business.

Summary Problem for Your Review

Perform a horizontal analysis and a vertical analysis of the comparative income statement of TRE Corporation. State whether 19X3 was a good year or a bad year and give your reasons.

TRE Corporation
Comparative Income Statement
years ended December 31, 19X3 and 19X2

	19X3	19X2
Total revenues	$275,000	$225,000
Expenses		
Cost of products sold	$194,000	$165,000
Engineering, selling and administrative expenses	54,000	48,000
Interest expense	5,000	5,000
Income tax expense	9,000	3,000
Other expense (income)	1,000	(1,000)
Total expenses	263,000	220,000
Net earnings	$ 12,000	$ 5,000

SOLUTION TO REVIEW PROBLEM

TRE Corporation
Horizontal Analysis of Comparative Income Statement
years ended December 31, 19X3 and 19X2

	19X3	19X2	Increase (Decrease) Amount	Percent
Total revenues	$275,000	$225,000	$50,000	22.2%
Expenses				
Cost of products sold	$194,000	$165,000	$29,000	17.6
Engineering, selling and administrative expenses	54,000	48,000	6,000	12.5
Interest expense	5,000	5,000	—	—
Income tax expense	9,000	3,000	6,000	200.0
Other expense (income)	1,000	(1,000)	2,000	—
Total expenses	263,000	220,000	43,000	19.5
Net earnings	$ 12,000	$ 5,000	$ 7,000	140.0

TRE Corporation
Vertical Analysis of Comparative Income Statement
years ended December 31, 19X3 and 19X2

| | 19X3 | | 19X2 | |
	Amount	Percent	Amount	Percent
Total revenue..................................	$275,000	100.0%	$225,000	100.0%
Expenses:				
Cost of products sold...............	$194,000	70.5	$165,000	73.3
Engineering, selling and				
administrative expenses.....	54,000	19.6	48,000	21.3
Interest expense........................	5,000	1.8	5,000	2.2
Income tax expense..................	9,000	3.3	3,000	1.4
Other expense (income)	1,000	0.4	(1,000)	(0.4)
Total expenses...............................	263,000	95.6	220,000	97.8
Net earnings...................................	$ 12,000	4.4%	$ 5,000	2.2%

The horizontal analysis shows that total revenues increased 22.2 percent. This percentage increase was greater than the 19.5 percent increase in total expenses, resulting in a 140 percent increase in net earnings.

The vertical analysis shows decreases in the percentages of net sales consumed by the cost of products sold (from 73.3 percent to 70.5 percent) and the engineering, selling, and administrative expenses (from 21.3 percent to 19.6 percent). These two items are TRE's largest dollar expenses, so their percentage decreases are quite important. The relative reduction in expenses raised 19X3 net earnings to 4.4 percent of sales, compared to 2.2 percent the preceding year. The overall analysis indicates that 19X3 was significantly better than 19X2.

Using Ratios to Make Business Decisions _____

The preceding analyses were based on each financial statement considered alone. Another set of decision tools develops relationships among items taken from throughout the statements.

Ratios, introduced in Chapters 4, 5, 8, and 14, are important tools for financial analysis. A ratio expresses the relationship of one number to another number. For example, if the balance sheet shows current assets of $100,000 and current liabilities of $25,000, the ratio of current assets to current liabilities is $100,000 to $25,000. We simplify this numerical expression to the ratio of 4 to 1, which may also be written 4:1 and 4/1. Other acceptable ways of expressing this ratio include (1) "current assets are 400 percent of current liabilities" and (2) "the business has four dollars in current assets for every one dollar in current liabilities."

We often reduce the ratio fraction by writing the ratio as one figure over the other, for example, 4/1, and then dividing the numerator by the denominator. In this way, the ratio 4/1 may be expressed simply as 4. The 1 that represents the denominator of the fraction is understood, not written. Consider the ratio $175,000 : $165,000. After dividing the first figure by the second, we come to 1.06 : 1, which we state as 1.06. The second part of the ratio, the 1, again is understood. Ratios provide a convenient and useful way of expressing a relationship between numbers. For example, the ratio of current assets to current liabilities gives information about a company's ability to pay its current debts with existing current assets.

A manager, lender or financial analyst may use any ratio that is relevant to a particular decision. We discuss the more important ratios used in credit and investment analysis and in managing a business. Many companies include these ratios in a special section of their annual financial reports. Investment services, such as Moody's, Standard & Poor's, Robert Morris Associates, and others report these ratios for companies and industries. They are widely used in all aspects of business, such as finance, management, and marketing, as well as accounting.

Measuring the Ability to Pay Current Liabilities _____

Working capital is defined as current assets minus current liabilities. Working capital is widely used to measure a business's ability to meet its short-term obligations with its current assets. The larger the working capital, the better able the business is to pay its debts. Recall that capital (or owners' equity) is total assets minus total liabilities. Working capital is like a "current" version of total capital. The working capital amount considered alone, however, does not give a complete picture of the entity's working capital position. Consider two companies with equal working capital.

	Company A	Company B
Current assets..........................	$100,000	$200,000
Current liabilities....................	50,000	150,000
Working capital.......................	$ 50,000	$ 50,000

Both companies have working capital of $50,000, but Company A's working capital is as large as its current liabilities. Company B's working capital, on the other hand, is only one third as large as its current liabilities. Which business has a better working capital position? Company A, because its working capital is a higher percentage of current assets and current liabilities. To use working capital data in decision-making, it is helpful to develop ratios. Two decision tools based on working capital data are the *current ratio* and the *acid-test ratio*.

Current Ratio

The most common ratio using current asset and current liability data is the **current ratio** (see also Chapter 4), which is current assets divided by current liabilities. Recall the makeup of current assets and current liabilities. Inventory is converted to receivables through sales, the receivables are collected in cash, and the cash is used to buy inventory and pay current liabilities. A company's current assets and current liabilities represent the core of its day-to-day operations.

The current ratios of McColpin, Inc. at December 31, 19X7 and 19X6, follow (data from Exhibit 19-2):

> **OBJECTIVE 5**
> Compute the standard financial ratios used for decision-making

		Current Ratio of McColpin, Inc.	
Formula		**19X7**	**19X6**
Current ratio = $\dfrac{\text{Current assets}}{\text{Current liabilities}}$		$\dfrac{\$262,000}{\$142,000} = 1.85$	$\dfrac{\$236,000}{\$126,000} = 1.87$

The current ratio decreased slightly during 19X7. The average current ratio for furniture retailers is 1.80. Lenders, shareholders, and managers closely monitor changes in a company's current ratio. In general, a higher current ratio indicates a stronger financial position. A high current ratio suggests that the business has sufficient liquid assets to maintain normal business operations. Compare McColpin's current ratio with the current ratios of some actual companies.

Company	Current Ratio
Maclean Hunter Limited (Communications)	1.34
Loblaw Companies Limited (Merchandising)	1.33
Air Canada (Transportation)	1.15
Doman Industries Limited (Forest products)	1.53
Dreco Energy Services Ltd. (Energy)	3.67
Irwin Toy Limited (Toys and leisure products)	2.23

What is an acceptable current ratio? The answer to this question depends on the nature of the business. The current ratio will generally exceed 1.0. The companies listed above are typical of their industries; note that they range from 1.15 to 3.67.

Acid-Test Ratio

The **acid-test** (or **quick**) **ratio** (see also Chapter 8) tells us whether the entity could pay all its current liabilities if they came due immediately. That is, could the company pass this *acid test*? The company would convert its most liquid assets to cash. To compute the acid-test ratio, we add cash, short-term investments and net current receivables (accounts and notes receivable, net of allowances) and divide by current liabilities. Inventory and prepaid expenses are the two (usually) *significant* current assets not included in the acid-test computations. These accounts are omitted because they are the least liquid of the current assets. A business may not be able to convert them to cash immediately to pay current liabilities. The acid-test ratio measures liquidity using a narrower asset base than the current ratio does.

McColpin's acid-test ratios for 19X7 and 19X6 follow (data from Exhibit 19-2):

		Acid-Test Ratio of McColpin, Inc.	
	Formula	19X7	19X6
Acid-test = ratio	Cash + short-term investments + net current receivables / Current liabilities	$\dfrac{\$29,000 + \$0 + \$114,000}{\$142,000} = 1.01$	$\dfrac{\$32,000 + \$0 + \$85,000}{\$126,000} = .93$

The company's acid-test ratio improved considerably during 19X7. Its ratio of 1.01 is between those of Dreco Energy Resources (2.67) and Irwin Toy (1.15) and those of Maclean Hunter (.957), Air Canada (.89), Loblaw Companies (.53), and Doman Industries (.493).

Measuring the Ability to Sell Inventory and Collect Receivables

The ability to sell inventory and collect receivables is fundamental to business success. Recall the operating cycle of a merchandiser: cash to inventory to receivables and back to cash. This section discusses three ratios that measure the ability to sell inventory and collect receivables.

Inventory Turnover

Companies generally seek to achieve the quickest possible return on their investments. A return on an investment in inventory (usually a substantial amount) is no exception. The faster inventory sells, the sooner the business creates accounts receivable, and the sooner it collects cash.

Inventory turnover (see also Chapter 5) is a measure of the number of times a company sells its average level of inventory during a year. A high rate of turnover indicates relative ease in selling inventory, whereas a low turnover indicates difficulty in selling. Generally, companies prefer a high inventory turnover. A value of 6 means that the company's average level of inventory has been sold 6 times during the year. In most cases this is better than a turnover of 3 or 4. However, a high value can mean that the business is not keeping enough inventory on hand, and this can result in lost sales if the company cannot fill a customer's order. Therefore, a business strives for the most profitable rate of inventory turnover, not necessarily the highest.

To compute the inventory turnover ratio we divide cost of goods sold by the average inventory for the period. We use the cost of goods sold (not sales) in the computation because both cost of goods sold and inventory are stated *at cost*. Sales is stated at the sales value of inventory and therefore is not comparable to inventory cost.

McColpin's inventory turnover for 19X7 is

Formula	Inventory Turnover of McColpin, Inc.
$\text{Inventory turnover} = \dfrac{\text{Cost of goods sold}}{\text{Average inventory}}$	$\dfrac{\$513,000}{\$112,000} = 4.58$

Cost of goods sold appears in the income statement (Exhibit 19-1). Average inventory is figured by averaging the beginning inventory ($111,000) and ending inventory ($113,000). (See the balance sheet, Exhibit 19-2). If inventory levels vary greatly from month to month, compute the average by adding the 12 monthly balances and dividing this sum by 12.

Inventory turnover varies widely with the nature of the business. For example, most manufacturers of farm machinery have an inventory turnover close to 3 times a year. By contrast, companies that remove natural gas from the ground hold their inventory for a very short period of time and have an average turnover of 30. McColpin's turnover of 4.58 times a year is high for its industry, which has an average turnover of 2.70.

To evaluate fully a company's inventory turnover, compare the ratio over time. A sudden sharp decline or a steady decline over a long period suggests the need for corrective action. Analysts also compare a company's inventory turnover to other companies in the same industry and to the industry average.

Accounts Receivable Turnover

Accounts receivable turnover measures a company's ability to collect cash from credit customers. Generally, the higher the ratio, the more successfully the business collects cash, and the better off its operations are. However, too high a receivable turnover may indicate that credit is too tight, causing the loss of sales to good customers. To compute the accounts receivable turnover we divide net credit sales by average net accounts receivable. The resulting ratio indicates how many times during the year the average level of receivables was turned into cash.

McColpin's accounts receivable turnover ratio for 19X7 is computed as follows, assuming that all sales were on credit:

Formula	Accounts Receivable Turnover of McColpin, Inc.
$\text{Accounts receivable turnover} = \dfrac{\text{Net credit sales}}{\text{Average net accounts receivable}}$	$\dfrac{\$858,000}{\$99,500} = 8.62$

The sales figure comes from the income statement (Exhibit 19-1). McColpin makes all sales on credit. If the company makes both cash and credit sales, this ratio is best computed using only net credit sales. Average net accounts receivable is figured using the beginning accounts receivable balance ($85,000) and the ending balance ($114,000). (See the balance sheet in Exhibit 19-2.) If accounts receivable balances exhibit a seasonal pattern, compute the average using the 12 monthly balances.

Receivable turnover ratios vary little from company to company. Most companies' ratios range between 7.0 and 10.0. McColpin's receivable turnover of 8.62 falls within this range.

Days' Sales in Receivables

Businesses must convert accounts receivable to cash. The lower the Accounts Receivable balance, the more successful the business has been in converting receivables into cash, and the better off the business.

The **days'-sales-in-receivables** ratio (see also Chapter 8) tells us how many days' sales remain in Accounts Receivable. We express the money amount in terms of an average day's sales. This relation becomes clearer as we compute the ratio, a two-step process. First, divide net sales by 365 days to figure the average sales amount for one day. Second, divide this average day's sales amount into the average net accounts receivable.

The data to compute this ratio for McColpin, Inc. for 19X7 are taken from the income statement and the balance sheet.

Formula	Days' Sales in Accounts Receivable of McColpin, Inc.

Days' Sales in AVERAGE Accounts Receivable:

1. One day's sales $= \dfrac{\text{Net sales}}{\text{365 days}}$ $\dfrac{\$858,000}{\text{365 days}} = \$2,351$

2. Days' sales in average accounts receivable $= \dfrac{\text{Average net accounts receivable}}{\text{One day's sales}}$ $\dfrac{\$99,500}{\$2,351} = 42 \text{ days}$

The computation in two steps is designed to increase your understanding of the meaning of the ratio. We may compute days' sales in average receivables in one step: $\$99,500/(\$858,000/365 \text{ days}) = 42$ days.

McColpin's ratio tell us that 42 average days' sales remain in accounts receivable at the year end and need to be collected. The company will increase its cash inflow if it can decrease this ratio. To detect any changes over time in McColpin's ability to collect its receivables, let us compute the days' sales in receivables ratio at the beginning and the end of 19X7.

Days' Sales in ENDING 19X6 Accounts Receivable:

$$\text{One day's sales} = \frac{\$803,000}{\text{365 days}} = \$2,200$$

$$\text{Days' sales in ending 19X6 accounts receivable} = \frac{\$85,000}{\$2,200} = 39 \text{ days at beginning of 19X7}$$

Days' Sales in ENDING 19X7 Accounts Receivable:

$$\text{One day's sales} = \frac{\$858,000}{\text{365 days}} = \$2,351$$

$$\text{Days' sales in ending 19X7 accounts receivable} = \frac{\$114,000}{\$2,351} = 48 \text{ days at end of 19X7}$$

This analysis shows a drop in McColpin's collection of receivables: days' sales in accounts receivable has increased from 39 at the beginning of the year to 48 at year end. The credit and collection department should strengthen its collection efforts. Otherwise, the company may experience a cash shortage in 19X8 and beyond.

Measuring the Ability to Pay Long-Term Debt _____

The ratios discussed so far give us insight into current assets and current liabilities. They help us measure a business's ability to sell inventory, collect receivables and to pay current liabilities. Most businesses also have long-term debts. Bondholders and banks that loan money on long-term notes payable and bonds payable take special interest in a business's ability to meet long-term obligations. Two key indicators of a business's ability to pay long-term liabilities are the *debt ratio* and *times-interest-earned ratio*.

Debt Ratio

Suppose you are a loan officer at a bank and you are evaluating loan applications from two companies with equal sales revenue and total assets. Sales and total assets are the two most common measures of firm size. Both companies have asked to borrow $500,000, and each has agreed to repay the loan over a ten-year period. The first customer already owes $600,000 to another bank. The second owes only $250,000. Other things equal, which company is likely to get the loan at the lower interest rate? Why?

Company Two is more likely to get the loan. The bank faces less risk by loaning to Company Two because that company owes less to creditors than Company One owes.

This relationship between total liabilities and total assets, called the **debt ratio** (see also Chapter 4), tells us the proportion of the company's assets that it has financed with debt. If the debt ratio is 1, then debt has been used to finance all the assets. A debt ratio of .50 means that the company has used debt to finance half its assets. The owners of the business have financed the other half. The higher the debt ratio, the higher the strain of paying interest each year and the principal amount at maturity. The lower the ratio, the less the business's future obligations. Creditors view a high debt ratio with caution. If a business seeking financing already has many liabilities, then additional debt payments may be too much for the business to handle. Creditors, to help protect themselves, generally charge higher interest rates on new borrowing to companies with an already high debt ratio.

McColpin's debt ratio at the end of 19X7 and 19X6 follow (data from Exhibit 19-2):

	Debt Ratio of McColpin, Inc.	
Formula	**19X7**	**19X6**
Debt ratio = $\dfrac{\text{Total liabilities}}{\text{Total assets}}$	$\dfrac{\$431,000}{\$787,000} = .55$	$\dfrac{\$324,000}{\$644,000} = .50$

Recall from our vertical and horizontal analyses that McColpin, Inc. expanded operations by financing the purchase of property, plant and equipment through borrowing, which is common.

Even after the increase in 19X7, McColpin's debt is not very high. The average debt ratio for most companies ranges around .57 to .67, with relatively little variation from company to company. McColpin's .55 debt ratio indicates a fairly low-risk debt position.

Times-Interest-Earned Ratio

The debt ratio measures the effect of debt on the company's *financial position* (balance sheet) but says nothing about its ability to pay interest expense. Analysts use a second ratio, the **times-interest-earned ratio**, to relate income to interest expense. To compute this ratio, we divide income from operations by interest expense. This ratio measures the number of times that operating income can cover interest expense. For this reason, the ratio is also called the **interest-coverage ratio**. A high ratio indicates ease in paying interest expense; a low value suggests difficulty.

McColpin's times-interest-earned ratios follow (data from Exhibit 19-1):

		Times-Interest-Earned Ratio of McColpin, Inc.	
	Formula	19X7	19X6
Times-interest-earned = ratio	$\dfrac{\text{Income from operations}}{\text{Interest expense}}$	$\dfrac{\$101,000}{\$24,000} = 4.21$	$\dfrac{\$57,000}{\$14,000} = 4.07$

McColpin's interest-coverage ratio increased in 19X7. This is a favorable sign about the company, especially since the company's short-term notes payable and long-term debt rose substantially during the year. (See the horizontal analysis of Exhibit 19-2). McColpin's new capital assets, we conclude, have earned more in operating income than they have cost the business in interest expense. The company's coverage ratio of around 4 is significantly better than the 2.60 average for furniture retailers. The norm for business, as reported by Robert Morris Associates, falls in the range of 2.0 to 3.0 for most companies.

Based on its debt ratio and times-interest-earned ratio, McColpin appears to have little difficulty paying its liabilities, also called *servicing its debt*.

Measuring Profitability

The fundamental goal of business is to earn a profit. Ratios that measure profitability play a large role in decision-making. These ratios are reported in the business press, by investment services, and in the annual financial reports of companies.

Rate of Return on Net Sales

In business, the term *return* is used broadly and loosely as an evaluation of profitability. For example, consider a percentage called the **rate of return on net sales** or, simply **return on sales**. (The word *net* is usually omitted for convenience, even though the net sales figure is used to compute the ratio.) McColpin's rate of return on sales ratios follow:

		Rate of Return on Sales of McColpin, Inc.	
	Formula	19X7	19X6
Rate of return on = sales	$\dfrac{\text{Net income}}{\text{Net sales}}$	$\dfrac{\$48,000}{\$858,000} = .056$	$\dfrac{\$26,000}{\$803,000} = .032$

You will recognize this ratio from the vertical analysis of the income statement in Exhibit 19-3. The increase in McColpin's return on sales is significant and identifies McColpin as a leader in its industry. Companies strive for a high rate of return.

The higher the rate of return, the more net sales dollars are providing income to the business and the fewer net sales dollars are absorbed by expenses. The 5.6 percent rate is less than Telesat Canada (1991: 8.9 percent) and Edmonton Telephones (1991: 7.2 percent), and more than Nova Scotia Power (1991: 3.8 percent), Bombardier (1991: 3.5 percent), Maclean Hunter (1991: 3.3 percent), Inco (1991: 2.8 percent), and Loblaw Companies (1991: 1.2 percent). As these rates of return on sales indicate, this ratio varies widely from industry to industry.

One strategy for increasing the rate of return on sales is to develop a product that commands a premium price such as Bombardier's Ski-doo, Laura Secord chocolates, and certain brands of clothing, such as Far West and Mountain Equipment Co-op. Another strategy is to control costs. If successful, either strategy converts a higher proportion of sales into net income and increases the rate of return on net sales.

A return measure can be computed on any revenue and sales amount. Return on net sales, as we have seen, is net income divided by net sales. Return on total revenues is net income divided by total revenues. A company can compute a return on other specific portions of revenue as its information needs dictate.

Rate of Return on Total Assets

The **rate of return on total assets** or, simply, **return on assets** measures the success a company has in using its assets to earn a profit (see also Chapter 14). Creditors have loaned money to the company, and the interest they receive is the return on their investment. Shareholders have invested in the company's stock, and net income is their return. The sum of interest expense and net income is the return to the two groups that have financed the company's operations, and this amount is the numerator of the return on assets ratio. Average total assets is the denominator. McColpin's return on assets ratio follows:

		Rate of Return on Total Assets of McColpin, Inc.
	Formula	**19X7**

$$\text{Rate of return on assets} = \frac{\text{Net Income} + \text{interest expense}}{\text{Average total assets}} \qquad \frac{\$48,000 + \$24,000}{\$715,500} = .101$$

Net income and interest expense are taken from the income statement. To compute average total assets, we use beginning and ending total assets from the comparative balance sheet. McColpin's 10.1 percent return on assets is higher than the 4.9 percent average return on assets in the retail furniture industry and compares favorably with Québec Téléphone (1991: 8.5 percent), John Labatt (1992: 3.9 percent) and Triton Canada Resources (1990: 3.6 percent). Alberta Heritage Savings (1991: 10.95) and B.C. Bancorp (1991: 10.25 percent) earned somewhat higher returns.

Rate of Return on Common Shareholders' Equity

A popular measure of profitability is **rate of return on common shareholders' equity** (see also Chapter 14). This ratio shows the relationship between net income and common shareholders' investment in the company. To compute this ratio, we first subtract preferred dividends from net income. This leaves only net income available to the common shareholders, which is needed to compute the ratio. We then divide net income available to common shareholders by the average shareholders' equity during the year. Common shareholders' equity is total shareholders' equity minus preferred equity. McColpin's rate of return on common shareholders' equity follows, (data from Exhibits 19-1 and 19-2):

Rate of Return on Common
Shareholders' Equity of
McColpin, Inc.

Formula	19X7

$$\text{Rate of return on common shareholders' equity} = \frac{\text{Net income} - \text{preferred dividends}}{\text{Average common shareholders' equity}} \quad \frac{\$48,000 - \$0}{\$338,000} = .142$$

We compute average equity using the beginning and ending balances [($356,000 + $320,000)/2 = $338,000]. Observe that common shareholders' equity includes Retained Earnings.

McColpin's 14.2 percent return on common equity compares favorably with returns of companies in most industries, which average around 10 percent. However, some leading companies show higher ratios: Franco-Nevada Mining Corp. (1992: 19.5 percent), Scott's Hospitality (1991: 18.5 percent) and Royal Bank of Canada (1991: 15.4 percent).

Observe that return on equity (14.2 percent) is higher than return on assets (10.1 percent). This 4.1 percent difference results from borrowing at one rate, say, 8 percent, and investing the funds to earn a higher rate, such as McColpin's 14.2 percent return on shareholders' equity. This practice is called *trading on the equity*, or the use of **leverage**. It is directly related to the debt ratio. The higher the debt ratio, the higher the leverage. Companies that finance operations with debt are said to *lever* their positions. Leverage increases the risk to common shareholders. For McColpin, Inc. and many other companies, leverage increases profitability. That is not always the case, however. Leverage can also have a negative impact on profitability. If revenues drop, debt and interest expense still must be paid. Therefore, leverage is a double-edged sword, increasing profits during good times but compounding losses during bad times.

Earnings per Share of Common Stock

Earnings per share of common stock or, simply, **earnings per share (EPS)** is perhaps the most widely quoted of all financial statistics (see also Chapter 15). EPS is the only ratio that must appear on the face of the income statement. EPS is the amount of net income per share of the company's *common* stock. Earnings per share is computed by dividing net income available to common shareholders by the number of common shares outstanding during the year. Preferred dividends are subtracted from net income because the preferred shareholders have a prior claim to their dividends. McColpin has no preferred stock outstanding and so has no preferred dividends. McColpin's EPS for 19X7 and 19X6 follow. (Data are from Exhibits 19-1 and 19-2; the company had 10,000 shares of common stock outstanding throughout 19X6 and 19X7).

Earnings Per Share
of McColpin, Inc.

Formula	19X7	19X6

$$\text{Earnings per share of common stock (EPS)} = \frac{\text{Net income} - \text{preferred dividends}}{\text{Number of shares of common stock outstanding}} \quad \frac{\$48,000 - \$0}{10,000} = \$4.80 \quad \frac{\$26,000 - \$0}{10,000} = \$2.60$$

McColpin's EPS rose from $2.60 to $4.80, an increase of 85 percent. McColpin's shareholders should not expect such a significant boost in EPS every year. However, most companies strive to increase EPS by 10 to 15 percent annually, and the more successful companies do so. However, even the most dramatic upward trends include an occasional bad year or years, as did the late 1980s.

Analyzing Stock as an Investment

Investors purchase stock to earn a return on their investment. This return consists of two parts: (1) gains (or losses) from selling the stock at a price that is different from the investors' purchase price, and (2) dividends, the periodic distributions to shareholders. The ratios we examine in this section help analysts evaluate stock in terms of market price or dividend payments.

Price/Earnings Ratio

The **price/earnings ratio** is the ratio of the market price of a share of common stock to the company's earnings per share. This ratio, abbreviated P/E, appears in *The Financial Post* stock listings (p. 736). P/E plays an important part in evaluating decisions to buy, hold, and sell stocks.

The price/earnings ratios of McColpin, Inc. follow. The market price of its common stock was $50 at the end of 19X7 and $35 at the end of 19X6. These prices can be obtained from such sources as financial publications, a stockbroker, or an on-line database.

	Formula	Price/Earnings Ratio of McColpin, Inc.	
		19X7	19X6
Price/ earnings ratio =	Market price per share of common stock / Earnings per share	$\dfrac{\$50.00}{\$4.80} = 10.4$	$\dfrac{\$35.00}{\$2.60} = 13.5$

Given McColpin's 19X7 price/earnings ratio of 10.4, we would say that the company's stock is selling at 10.4 times earnings. The decline from the 19X6 P/E ratio of 13.5 is not a cause for alarm because the numerator (market price of the stock) is not under McColpin's control. The denominator (net income) is more controllable, and it increased during 19X7. Like most other ratios, P/E ratios vary from industry to industry, ranging in 1988 from 8 to 10 for electric utilities to 35 to 60 for companies that mine precious metals such as gold (like American Barrick and Hemlo Gold). Some more glamorous companies (like Toronto Sun Publishing) had P/E ratios over 80.

Dividend Yield

Dividend yield is the ratio of dividends per share of stock to the stock's market price per share. This ratio measures the percentage of a stock's market value that is returned annually as dividends, an important concern of shareholders. Preferred shareholders, who invest primarily to receive dividends, pay special attention to this ratio.

McColpin paid annual cash dividends of $1.20 per share in 19X7 and $1.00 in 19X6 and market prices of the company's common stock were $50 in 19X7 and $35.00 in 19X6. McColpin's dividend yields follow:

	Formula	Dividend Yield on Common Stock of McColpin, Inc.	
		19X7	19X6
Dividend yield on common stock =	Dividend per share of common stock / Market price per share of common stock	$\dfrac{\$1.20}{\$50.00} = .024$	$\dfrac{\$1.00}{\$35.00} = .029$

Investors who buy their McColpin common stock for $50 can expect to receive almost 2½ percent of their investment annually in the form of cash dividends. Dividend yields vary widely, from 5 to 8 percent for older established firms (like BCE Inc. and the Royal Bank) down to a range of 0 to 3 percent for growth-oriented companies (like Rogers Communications and Magna). McColpin's dividend yield places the company in the second group.

Book Value per Share of Common Stock

Book value per share of common stock (see also Chapter 14) is simply common shareholders' equity divided by the number of shares of common stock outstanding. Common shareholders' equity equals total shareholders' equity less preferred equity. McColpin has no preferred stock outstanding. Its book value per share of common stock ratios follow. Recall that 10,000 shares of common stock were outstanding at the end of years 19X7 and 19X6.

	Formula	Book Value per Share of the Common Stock of McColpin, Inc.	
		19X7	**19X6**
Book value per share of common stock	$=$ $\dfrac{\text{Total shareholder's equity} - \text{preferred equity}}{\text{Number of shares of common stock outstanding}}$	$\dfrac{\$356,000 - \$0}{10,000} = \$35.60$	$\dfrac{\$320,000 - \$0}{10,000} = \$32.00$

The market price of a company's stock usually exceeds its book value. Some investors buy a stock when its market value approaches book value. Suppose you decided to buy McColpin stock at the end of 19X6, when its market price of $35 was close to book value of $32. That investment would have proved wise. The stock's price increased to $50 in 19X7. Of course, when you bought the stock in 19X6, there was no guarantee the stock price would increase.

The Complexity of Business Decisions

OBJECTIVE 6

Use ratios in decision-making

Business decisions are made in a world of uncertainty. Legislation, international affairs, competition, scandals and many other factors can turn profits into losses, and vice versa. To be most useful, ratios should be analyzed over a period of years to take into account a representative group of these factors. Any one year, or even any two years, may not be representative of the company's performance over the long term.

For example, a business's acid-test ratio may show a substantial increase over a ten-year period. However, a two-year period during the early part of that decade might show a slight downturn. An evaluation based on the two-year analysis might lead to an unwise decision. To make the best use of ratios, we must consider them within a broad time frame.

As useful as ratios may be, they do have limitations. We may liken their use in decision-making to a physician's use of a thermometer. A reading of 39°C indicates that something is wrong with the patient, but the temperature alone does not indicate what the problem is or how to cure it.

In financial analysis, a sudden drop in a company's current ratio signals that *something* is wrong, but this change does not identify the problem or show how to correct it. The business manager must analyze the figures that go into the ratio to determine whether current assets have decreased, current liabilities have increased, or both. If current assets have dropped, is the problem a cash shortage? Are accounts receivable down? Are inventories too low? Only by analyzing the individual items that make up the ratio can the manager determine how to solve the problem. The manager must evaluate data on all ratios in the light of other information about the company and about its particular line of business, such as increased competition or a slowdown in the economy.

Uncertainty clouds business decisions. A decision-maker can never be sure how a course of action will turn out. For example, a careful analysis of ratios and other accounting information may suggest to management that the business should invest its excess cash in the stock of a microcomputer company. This industry may hold the prospect for the fastest return on an investment. A competing microcomputer company may come out with a new computer that sweeps the market, leaving the first company's stock worthless and the investing company with a loss. Ratio analysis cannot predict the future, but knowledge gained by a study of ratios and related information can help the analyst to make informed decisions.

Efficient Markets, Management Action, and Investor Decisions

Much research about accounting and finance has focused on whether the stock markets are "efficient." An **efficient capital market** is one in which the market prices fully reflect all information available to the public. Stocks are priced in full recognition of all publicly accessible data.

That a market is efficient has implications for management action and for investor decisions. It means that managers cannot fool the market with accounting gimmicks. As long as sufficient information is available, the market as a whole can translate accounting data into a "fair" price for the company's stock.

Suppose you are the president of Company A. Reported earnings per share are $4 and the stock price is $40 (a price-earnings ratio of 10). You believe the corporation's stock is underpriced in comparison with other companies in the same industry. To correct this situation you are considering changing your method of depreciation from accelerated to straight-line. The accounting change will increase earnings per share to $5. Will the stock then rise to $50? Probably not. The company's stock price will likely remain at $40 because the market can understand the accounting change. After all, the company merely changed its method of computing depreciation. There is no effect on the company's cash flows, and its economic position is unchanged.

In an efficient market, the search for "underpriced" stock is fruitless unless the investor has relevant private information. Moreover, it is unlawful to invest based on inside information, which is available only to corporate management. For outside investors in an efficient market, an appropriate investment strategy seeks to manage risk, to diversify, and to minimize transactions costs. The role of financial statement analysis consists mainly of identifying the risks of various stocks in order to manage the risk of the overall investment portfolio.

Computers and Financial Statement Analysis

How much can a computer help in analyzing financial statements for investment purposes? Time yourself as you perform one of the financial ratio problems in this chapter. Multiply your efforts by, say, 100 companies that you are comparing in terms of this ratio. Now consider ranking these 100 companies on the basis of four or five additional ratios.

Professional investment consultants may bring an impressive array of computer hardware and software into their analysis, but even individual investors can take advantage of the computer in determining their investments — rather than merely "playing a hunch." Individual investors may arm themselves with a microcomputer, a spreadsheet software package, a modem (which transports data from a centralized storage area into your computer across telephone lines), and a subscription to any one of several on-line financial databases. These on-line services offer quarterly financial figures for hundreds of public corporations going back as many as ten years.

Assume you wanted to perform an analysis to compare companies' recent earnings histories. You might have the computer compare hundreds of companies on the basis of price/earnings ratio and rates of return on shareholder's equity and total assets. The computer could then give you the names of 20 (or however many) companies that appear most favorable in terms of these ratios. Alternatively, you could have the computer download financial statement data to your spreadsheet (that is, place the data in the appropriate cells in your spreadsheet) and then "crunch" the numbers yourself.

Accountants use computerized financial analysis a great deal. Public accountants such as CAs, CGAs, or CMAs focus on the individual client. They want to know how the client is doing compared to the previous year and compared to other firms in the industry. Auditors also want to detect any emerging trends in the company's ratios and compare the results of actual operations with expected results. To do so, an auditor can download monthly financial statistics onto a spreadsheet and compute the financial ratios to gain insight into the client's situation.

Summary Problem for Your Review

This problem is based on the following financial data adapted from the financial statements of Big Bear Ltd., which operates approximately 100 family restaurants across Canada.

Big Bear Ltd.
Balance Sheets
19X3 and 19X2

	19X3	19X2
	(thousands of dollars)	
Assets		
Current assets		
Cash	$ 4,123	$ 6,453
Marketable securities (same as short-term investments)	4,236	—
Receivables, net..	6,331	7,739
Inventories...	5,840	4,069
Prepaid expenses and others	3,830	2,708
Total current assets	24,360	20,969
Net property, plant and equipment	35,330	28,821
Net property under capital leases	23,346	20,886
Intangibles and other assets..	10,493	11,349
Total assets	$93,529	$82,025
Liabilities and Shareholders' Equity		
Current liabilities		
Notes payable	$ 1,244	$ 785
Current installments of long-term debt and		
capital lease obligations..	5,220	6,654
Accounts payable — trade...	8,631	8,791
Accrued liabilities...	5,822	5,983
Total current liabilities	20,917	22,213

Long-term debt, less current installments....................................	22,195	15,549
Capital lease obligations, less current portion............................	24,296	22,350
Deferred income and deferred income taxes.............................	2,211	1,522
Total common shareholders' equity (shares outstanding		
3,017,381 at year end 19X3 and 2,729,274 at year end 19X2)	23,910	20,391
Total liabilities and shareholders' equity	$93,529	$82,025

Big Bear Ltd.
Statements of Earnings
years 19X3 and 19X2

	19X3	19X2
	(thousands of dollars)	
Total revenue..	$148,889	$140,539
Costs and expenses		
Cost of products sold	$114,335	$111,188
Selling, administrative and general expenses.......................	23,475	20,816
	137,810	132,004
Earnings from operations..	11,079	8,535
Interest expense	5,771	5,902
Earnings before income taxes...	5,308	2,633
Income taxes..	1,713	932
Net earnings..	$ 3,595	$ 1,701

Required

Compute the following ratios for Big Bear for 19X3:

1. Current ratio
2. Acid-test ratio
3. Inventory turnover
4. Days' sales (total revenue) in average receivables
5. Debt ratio
6. Times-interest-earned ratio
7. Rate of return on sales (total revenue)
8. Rate of return on total assets
9. Rate of return on common shareholders' equity
10. Price/earnings ratio, assuming the market price of common stock is $15.50 and earnings per share is $1.19.
11. Book value per share of common stock

SOLUTION TO REVIEW PROBLEM

1. $\text{Current Ratio} = \dfrac{\text{Current Assets}}{\text{Current Liabilities}} = \dfrac{\$24,360}{\$20,917} = 1.16$

2. $\dfrac{\text{Acid-Test Ratio}}{} = \dfrac{\text{Cash + Short-Term Investments + Net Current Receivables}}{\text{Current Liabilities}} = \dfrac{\$4,123 + \$4,236 + \$6,331}{\$20,917} = .70$

3. $\text{Inventory Turnover} = \dfrac{\text{Cost of Goods Sold}}{\text{Average Inventory}} = \dfrac{\$114,335}{(\$5,840 + \$4,069)/2} = 23.08$

4. Days' Sales (Total Revenue) in Average Receivables:

a. One day's sales $= \dfrac{\text{Net Sales}}{365 \text{ Days}} = \dfrac{\$148,889}{365} = \$407.92$

b. $\dfrac{\text{Days' sales in average accounts receivable}}{} = \dfrac{\text{Average Accounts Receivables}}{\text{One Day's Sales}} = \dfrac{(\$6,331 + \$7,739)/2}{\$407.92} = 17 \text{days}$

5. Debt Ratio $= \dfrac{\text{Total Liabilities}}{\text{Total Assets}} = \dfrac{\$20,917 + \$22,195 + \$24,296 + \$2,211}{\$93,529} = .74$

6. $\dfrac{\text{Times-Interest-Earned Ratio}}{} = \dfrac{\text{Income from Operations}}{\text{Interest Expense}} = \dfrac{\$11,079}{\$5,771} = 1.92$

7. $\dfrac{\text{Rate of Return on Sales (Total Revenue)}}{} = \dfrac{\text{Net Income}}{\text{Total Revenue}} = \dfrac{\$3,595}{\$148,889} = .024$

8. $\dfrac{\text{Rate of Return on Total Assets}}{} = \dfrac{\text{Net Income} + \text{Interest Expense}}{\text{Average Total Assets}} = \dfrac{\$3,595 + \$5,771}{(\$93,529 + \$82,025)/2} = .107$

9. $\dfrac{\text{Rate of Return on Common Shareholders' Equity}}{} = \dfrac{\text{Net Income} - \text{Preferred Dividends}}{\text{Average Common Shareholders' Equity}} = \dfrac{\$3,595 - \$0}{(\$23,910 + \$20,391)/2} = .162$

10. $\dfrac{\text{Price/ Earnings Ratio}}{} = \dfrac{\text{Market Price per Share of Common Stock}}{\text{Earnings per Share}} = \dfrac{\$15.50^*}{\$1.19^*} = 13.0$

11. $\dfrac{\text{Book Value per Share of of Common Stock}}{} = \dfrac{\text{Total Shareholders' Equity} - \text{Preferred Equity}}{\text{Number of Shares of Common Stock Outstanding}} = \dfrac{\$23,910,000^* - 0^*}{3,017,381^*} = \$7.92$

* All dollar amounts are expressed in thousands except those denoted by *.

Summary

Accounting provides information for decision-making. Banks loan money, investors buy stocks, and managers run businesses based on the analysis of accounting information.

Horizontal analysis shows the dollar amount and the percentage change in each financial statement item from one period to the next. *Vertical analysis* shows the relationship of each item in a financial statement to its total: total assets on the balance sheet and net sales on the income statement.

Common-size statements (a form of vertical analysis) show the component percentages of the items in a statement. Investment advisory services report common-size statements for various industries, and analysts use them to compare a company to its competitors and to the industry averages.

The *statement of changes in financial position* shows the net cash inflow or outflow caused by a company's operating, financing, and investing activities. By analyzing the inflows and outflows of cash listed on this statement, an analyst can see where a business's cash comes from and how it is being spent.

Ratios play an important part in business decision-making because they show relationships between financial statement items. Analysis of ratios over a period of time is an important way to track a company's progress. The accompanying list presents the ratios discussed in this chapter:

Ratio	Computation	Information Provided

Measuring the ability to pay current liabilities

1. Current ratio

$$\frac{\text{Current assets}}{\text{Current liabilities}}$$

Measures ability to pay liabilities from current assets.

2. Acid-test (quick ratio)

$$\frac{\text{Cash + short-term investments} + \text{net current receivables}}{\text{Current liabilities}}$$

Shows ability to pay current liabilities from the most liquid assets.

Measuring the ability to sell inventory and collect receivables

3. Inventory turnover

$$\frac{\text{Cost of goods sold}}{\text{Average inventory}}$$

Indicates saleability of inventory.

4. Accounts receivable turnover

$$\frac{\text{Net credit sales}}{\text{Average net accounts receivable}}$$

Measures collectibility of receivable.

5. Days' sales in receivables

$$\frac{\text{Average net accounts receivable}}{\text{One day's sales}}$$

Shows how many days it takes to collect average receivables.

Measuring the ability to pay long-term debts

6. Debt ratio

$$\frac{\text{Total liabilities}}{\text{Total assets}}$$

Indicates percentage of assets financed through borrowing.

7. Times-interest-earned ratio

$$\frac{\text{Income from operations}}{\text{Interest expense}}$$

Measures coverage of interest expense by operating income.

Measuring profitability

8. Rate of return on net sales

$$\frac{\text{Net income}}{\text{Net sales}}$$

Shows the percentage of each sales dollar earned as net income.

9. Rate of return on total assets

$$\frac{\text{Net income + interest expense}}{\text{Average total assets}}$$

Gauges how profitably assets are used.

10. Rate of return on common shareholders' equity

$$\frac{\text{Net income} - \text{preferred dividends}}{\text{Average common shareholders' equity}}$$

Gauges how profitably the assets financed by the common shareholders are used.

11. Earnings per share of common stock

$$\frac{\text{Net income} - \text{preferred dividends}}{\text{Number of shares of common stock outstanding}}$$

Gives the amount of earnings per one share of common stock.

Analyzing stock as an investment

12. Price/earnings ratio

$$\frac{\text{Market price per share of common stock}}{\text{Earnings per share}}$$

Indicates the market price of one dollar of earnings.

13. Dividend yield

$$\frac{\text{Dividend per share of common stock}}{\text{Market price per share of common stock}}$$

Shows the proportion of the market price of each share of stock returned as dividends to shareholders each period.

14. Book value per share of common stock

$$\frac{\text{Total shareholders' equity} - \text{preferred equity}}{\text{Number of shares of common stock outstanding}}$$

Indicates the recorded accounting value of each share of common stock outstanding.

Self-Study Questions

Test your understanding of the chapter by marking the best answer for each of the following questions:

1. Net income was $240,000 in 19X4, $210,000 in 19X5, and $252,000 in 19X6. The change from 19X5 to 19X6 is a (an) *(p. 841)*
   a. Increase of 5 percent
   b. Increase of 20 percent
   c. Decrease of 10 percent
   d. Decrease of 12.5 percent

2. Vertical analysis of a financial statement shows *(p. 844)*
   a. Trend percentages
   b. The percentage change in an item from period to period
   c. The relationship of an item to the total on the statement
   d. Net income expressed as a percentage of shareholders' equity

3. Common-size statements are useful for comparing *(pp. 845–46)*
   a. Changes in the makeup of assets from period to period
   b. Different companies
   c. A company to its industry
   d. All of the above

4. The statement of changes in financial position is used for decision-making by *(p. 848)*
   a. Reporting where cash came from and how it was spent
   b. Indicating how net income was earned
   c. Giving the ratio relationships between selected items
   d. Showing a horizontal analysis of cash flows

5. Cash is $10,000, net accounts receivable amount to $22,000, inventory is $55,000, prepaid expenses total $3,000, and current liabilities are $40,000. What is the acid-test ratio? *(p. 852)*
   a. .25
   b. .80
   c. 2.18
   d. 2.25

6. Inventory turnover is computed by dividing *(pp. 852–53)*
   a. Sales revenue by average inventory
   b. Cost of goods sold by average inventory
   c. Credit sales by average inventory
   d. Average inventory by cost of goods sold

7. Capp Corporation is experiencing a severe cash shortage due to inability to collect accounts receivable. The decision tool most likely to help identify the appropriate corrective action is the *(pp. 853–54)*
   a. Acid-test ratio
   b. Inventory turnover
   c. Times-interest-earned ratio
   d. Day's sales in receivables

8. Analysis of Mendoza Ltd. financial statements over five years reveals that sales are growing steadily, the debt ratio is higher than the industry average and is increasing, interest coverage is decreasing, return on total assets is declining, and earnings per share of common stock is decreasing. Considered together, these ratios suggest that *(pp. 855–58)*
   a. Mendoza should pursue collections of receivables more vigorously
   b. Competition is taking sales away from Mendoza
   c. Mendoza is in a declining industry
   d. The company's debt burden is hurting profitability

9. Which of the following is most likely to be true? *(pp. 857–58)*
   a. Return on common equity exceeds return on total assets.
   b. Return on total assets exceeds return on common equity.
   c. Return on total assets equals return on common equity.
   d. None of the above

10. How are financial ratios used in decision-making? *(p. 860)*
    a. They remove the uncertainty of the business environment.
    b. They give clear signals about the appropriate action to take.
    c. They can help identify the reasons for success and failure in business, but decision-making requires information beyond the ratios.
    d. They are not useful because decision-making is too complex.

Answers to the Self-Study Questions are at the end of the chapter.

Accounting Vocabulary

accounts receivable turnover *(p. 853)*

acid-test ratio *(p. 852)*

book value per share of common stock *(p. 860)*

common-size statements *(p. 845)*

current ratio *(p. 851)*

days' sales in receivables *(p. 854)*

debt ratio *(p. 855)*

dividend yield *(p. 859)*

earnings per share (EPS) *(p. 858)*

earnings per share of common stock *(p. 858)*

efficient capital market *(p. 861)*

horizontal analysis *(p. 841)*

interest-coverage ratio *(p. 856)*

inventory turnover *(p. 853)*

leverage *(p. 858)*

long-term solvency *(p. 840)*

price/earnings ratio *(p. 859)*

quick ratio *(p. 852)*

rate of return on common shareholders' equity *(p. 857)*

rate of return on net sales *(p. 856)*

rate of return on total assets *(p. 857)*

return on assets *(p. 857)*

return on common shareholders' equity *(p. 857)*

return on sales *(p. 856)*

short-term liquidity *(p. 840)*

times-interest-earned ratio *(p. 856)*

vertical analysis *(p. 844)*

working capital *(p. 851)*

ASSIGNMENT MATERIAL _____

Questions

1. Identify two groups of users of accounting information and the decisions they base on accounting data.

2. What are three analytical tools that are based on accounting information?

3. Briefly describe horizontal analysis. How do decision-makers use this tool of analysis?

4. What is vertical analysis, and what is its purpose?

5. What use is made of common-size statements?

6. State how an investor might analyze the statement of changes in financial position. How might the investor analyze investing activities data?

7. Why are ratios an important tool of financial analysis? Give an example.

8. Identify two ratios used to measure a company's ability to pay current liabilities. Show how they are computed.

9. Why is the acid-test ratio called by this name?

10. What does the inventory-turnover ratio measure?

11. Suppose the days'-sales-in-receivables ratio of Gomez, Inc. increased from 36 at January 1 to 43 at December 31. Is this a good sign or a bad sign about the company? What would Gomez management do in response to this change?

12. Company A's debt ratio has increased from .50 to .70. Identify a decision-maker to whom this increase is important, and state how the increase affects this party's decisions about the company.

13. Which ratio measures the effect of debt on (a) financial position (the balance sheet) and (b) the company's ability to pay interest expense (the income statement)?

14. Company A is a chain of grocery stores, and Company B is a computer manufacturer. Which company is likely to have the higher (a) current ratio, (b) inventory turnover, and (c) rate of return on sales? Give your reasons.

15. Identify four ratios used to measure a company's profitability. Show how to compute these ratios and state what information each ratio provides.

16. The price/earnings ratio of Hollinger was 8.9, and the price/earnings ratio of Cominco was 30.6. Which company did the stock market favor? Explain.

17. Irwin Toy paid cash dividends of $.22 (22 cents) per share when the market price of the company's stock was $7.00. What was the dividend yield on Irwin's stock? What does dividend yield measure?

18. Hold all other factors constant and indicate whether each of the following situations generally signals good or bad news about a company:
   a. Increase in current ratio
   b. Decrease in inventory turnover
   c. Increase in debt ratio
   d. Decrease in interest-coverage ratio
   e. Increase in return on sales
   f. Decrease in earnings per share
   g. Increase in price/earnings ratio
   h. Increase in book value per share

19. Explain how an investor might use book value per share of stock in making an investment decision.

20. Describe how decision-makers use ratio data. What are the limitations of ratios?

Exercises

Exercise 19-1   *Computing year-to-year changes in working capital* **(L.O. 1)**

What was the amount of change, and the percentage change, in Lux Corporation's working capital during 19X4 and 19X5? Is this trend favorable or unfavorable?

	Year 5	Year 4	Year 3
Total current assets	$312,000	$260,000	$280,000
Total current liabilities................................	150,000	117,000	140,000

Exercise 19-2   *Horizontal analysis of an income statement* **(L.O. 1)**

Prepare a horizontal analysis of the following comparative income statement of LaPaz Incorporated. Round percentage changes to the nearest one-tenth percent (three decimal places):

LaPaz Incorporated **Comparative Income Statement** **years ended December 31, 19X9 and 19X8**		
	19X9	**19X8**
Total Revenue	$440,000	$373,000
Expenses		
Cost of goods sold	$202,000	$188,000
Selling and general expenses	118,000	93,000
Interest expense...	7,000	4,000
Income tax expense....................................	42,000	37,000
Total expenses..	369,000	322,000
Net Income..	$ 71,000	$ 51,000

Why did net income increase by a higher percentage than total revenues increased during 19X9?

Exercise 19-3   *Computing trend percentages (L.O. 1)*

Compute trend percentages for net sales and net income for the following five-year period, using year 1 as the base year:

	Year 5	Year 4	Year 3	Year 2	Year 1
			(amounts in thousands)		
Net sales	$1,510	$1,287	$1,106	$1,009	$1,043
Net income............................	127	114	93	71	85

Which grew more during the period, net sales or net income?

Exercise 19-4   *Vertical analysis of a balance sheet (L.O. 2)*

Quattlebaum Ltd. has requested that you perform a vertical analysis of its balance sheet to determine the component percentages of its assets, liabilities, and shareholders' equity.

Quattlebaum Ltd. Balance Sheet December 31, 19X3	
Assets	
Total current assets..	$ 62,000
Long-term investments..	35,000
Property, plant and equipment, net......................	227,000
Total assets..	$324,000
Liabilities	
Total current liabilities	$ 38,000
Long-term debt	118,000
Total liabilities...	156,000
Shareholders' Equity	
Total shareholders' equity......................................	168,000
Total liabilities and shareholders' equity	$324,000

Exercise 19-5   *Preparing a common-size income statement (L.O. 3)*

Prepare a comparative common-size income statement for LaPaz Incorporated, using the 19X9 and 19X8 data of Exercise 19-2 and rounding percentages to one-tenth percent (three decimal places).

Exercise 19-6   *Analyzing the statement of changes in financial position (L.O. 4)*

Identify any weaknesses revealed by the statement of changes in financial position of Tanglewood Home Centers, Inc.

Tanglewood Home Centers, Inc.
Statement of Changes in Financial Position
for the current year

Operating activities		
Income from operations		$ 12,000
Add (subtract) noncash items		
Depreciation..	$ 23,000	
Net increase in current assets other		
than cash...	(15,000)	
Net increase in current liabilities		
exclusive of short-term debt...............................	11,000	19,000
Net cash inflow from operating activities		31,000
Financing activities		
Issuance of bonds payable..	$114,000	
Payment of short-term debt..	(101,000)	
Payment of long-term debt...	(79,000)	
Payment of dividends	(12,000)	
Net cash outflow from financing activities		(78,000)
Investing activities		
Sale of property, plant and equipment.........................		81,000
Increase in cash...		$34,000

Exercise 19-7   *Computing five ratios (L.O. 5)*

The financial statements of Snyder Corp. include the following items:

	Current Year	Preceding Year
Balance sheet		
Cash..	$ 17,000	$ 22,000
Short-term investments......................	21,000	26,000
Net receivables	64,000	73,000
Inventory..	87,000	71,000
Prepaid expenses.................................	6,000	8,000
Total current assets............................	195,000	200,000
Total current liabilities.......................	121,000	91,000
Income statement		
Net credit sales	$444,000	
Cost of goods sold................................	237,000	

Required

Compute the following ratios for the current year: (a) current ratio, (b) acid-test ratio, (c) inventory turnover, (d) accounts receivable turnover, and (e) days' sales in average receivables.

Exercise 19-8   *Analyzing the ability to pay current liabilities (L.O. 5, 6)*

Holmes, Inc. has requested that you determine whether the company's ability to pay its current liabilities and long-term debts has improved or deteriorated during 19X5. To answer this question, compute the following ratios for 19X5 and 19X4: (a) current ratio, (b) acid-test ratio, (c) debt ratio, and (d) times-interest-earned ratio. Summarize the results of your analysis.

	19X5	19X4
Cash	$ 31,000	$ 37,000
Short-term investments	28,000	—
Net receivables	102,000	116,000
Inventory	226,000	263,000
Prepaid expenses	11,000	9,000
Total assets	553,000	519,000
Total current liabilities	205,000	241,000
Total liabilities	261,000	273,000
Income from operations	165,000	158,000
Interest expense	26,000	31,000

Exercise 19-9   *Analyzing profitability (L.O. 5, 6)*

Compute four ratios that measure ability to earn profits for Gaspé, Inc. whose comparative income statement appears below. Additional data follow.

Gaspé, Inc.
Comparative Income Statement
years ended December 31, 19X1 and 19X0

	19X1	19X0
Net sales	$174,000	$158,000
Cost of goods sold	93,000	86,000
Gross profit	81,000	72,000
Selling and general expenses	48,000	41,000
Income from operations	33,000	31,000
Interest expense	9,000	10,000
Income before income tax	24,000	21,000
Income tax expense	6,000	8,000
Net income	$ 18,000	$ 13,000

Additional data	19X1	19X0
a. Average total assets	$204,000	$191,000
b. Average common shareholders' equity	96,000	89,000
c. Preferred dividends	3,000	3,000
d. Shares of common stock outstanding	18,000	18,000

Did the company's operating performance improve or deteriorate during 19X1?

Exercise 19-10   *Evaluating a stock as an investment (L.O. 5, 6)*

Evaluate the common stock of Grand Banks, Inc. as an investment. Specifically, use the three stock ratios to determine whether the stock has increased or decreased in attractiveness during the past year.

	Current Year	Preceding Year
Net income	$ 58,000	$ 55,000
Dividends (half on preferred stock)	28,000	28,000
Common shareholders' equity at year end		
(100,000 shares)	530,000	500,000
Preferred shareholders' equity at year end	200,000	200,000
Market price per share of common stock at year end	$7.25	$5.75

Problems   *(Group A)*

Problem 19-1A   *Trend percentages, return on sales, and comparison with the industry* **(L.O. 1, 5, 6)**

Net sales, net income, and total assets for LeClerc Manufacturing, Inc. for a six-year period follow.

	19X6	19X5	19X4	19X3	19X2	19X1
			(amounts in thousands)			
Net sales	$327	$303	$266	$271	$245	$241
Net income	23	21	12	17	14	13
Total assets	286	244	209	197	181	166

Required

1. Compute trend percentages for 19X2 through 19X6, using 19X1 as the base year.
2. Compute the rate of return on net sales for 19X2 through 19X6, rounding to three decimal places. In this industry, rates above 5 percent are considered good, and rates above 7 percent are viewed as outstanding.
3. How does LeClerc's return on net sales compare to the industry?

Problem 19-2A   *Common-size statements, analysis of profitability and comparison with the industry* **(L.O. 2, 3, 5, 6)**

Top managers of Blanton & Bornhauser Ltd., a department store, have asked your help in comparing the company's profit performance and financial position with the average for the department-store industry. The accountant has given you the company's income statement and balance sheet, and also the following actual data for the department-store industry:

Blanton & Bornhauser Ltd.
Income Statement
Compared with Industry Average
year ended December 31, 19X3

	Blanton & Bornhauser	Industry Average
Net sales	$957,000	100.0%
Cost of goods sold	653,000	65.9
Gross profit	304,000	34.1
Operating expenses	287,000	31.1
Operating income	17,000	3.0
Other expenses	2,000	0.4
Net income	$15,000	2.6%

Blanton & Bornhauser Ltd.
Balance Sheet
Compared with Industry Average
December 31, 19X3

	Blanton & Bornhauser	Industry Average
Current assets	$448,000	74.4%
Fixed assets, net	127,000	20.0
Intangible assets, net	42,000	0.6
Other assets	13,000	5.0
Total	$630,000	100.0%
Current liabilities	$246,000	35.6
Long-term liabilities	124,000	19.0
Shareholders' equity	260,000	45.4
Total	$630,000	100.0%

Required

1. Prepare a two-column common-size income statement and a two-column common-size balance sheet for Blanton & Bornhauser. The first column of each statement should present Blanton & Bornhauser's common-size statement, and the second column should show the industry averages.
2. For the profitability analysis, compare Blanton & Bornhauser's (a) ratio of gross profit to net sales, (b) ratio of operating income (loss) to net sales, and (c) ratio of

net income (loss) to net sales. Compare these figures with the industry averages. Is Blanton & Bornhauser's profit performance better or worse than average for the industry?

3. For the analysis of financial position, compare Blanton & Bornhauser's (a) ratio of current assets to total assets and (b) ratio of shareholders' equity to total assets. Compare these ratios with the industry averages. Is Blanton & Bornhauser's financial position better or worse than the average for the industry?

Problem 19-3A *Using the statement of changes in financial position for decision-making* **(L.O. 4)**

You are evaluating two companies as possible investments. The two companies, similar in size, are in the commuter airline business. They fly passengers from Toronto to smaller cities in Ontario. Assume that all other available information has been analyzed, and that the decision on which company's stock to purchase depends on the information given in their statements of changes in financial position shown on the next page.

Required

Discuss the relative strengths and weaknesses of UC Air and Western Ontario Flight. Conclude your discussion by recommending one of the company's stocks as an investment.

Problem 19-4A *Effects of business transactions on selected ratios* **(L.O. 5, 6)**

Financial statement data of Goliad Corporation include the following items:

Cash	$ 47,000
Short-term investments	21,000
Accounts receivable, net	102,000
Inventories	274,000
Prepaid expenses	15,000
Total assets	933,000
Short-term notes payable	72,000
Accounts payable	96,000
Accrued liabilities	50,000
Long-term notes payable	146,000
Other long-term liabilities	78,000
Net income	119,000
Number of common shares outstanding	32,000

Required

1. Compute Goliad's current ratio, debt ratio, and earnings per share.
2. Compute each of the three ratios after evaluating the effect of each transaction that follows. Consider each transaction separately.
   a. Borrowed $56,000 on a long-term note payable.
   b. Sold short-term investments for $34,000 (cost $46,000); assume no tax effect of the loss.
   c. Issued 14,000 shares of common stock, receiving cash of $168,000.
   d. Received cash on account, $6,000.
   e. Paid short-term notes payable, $51,000.
   f. Purchased merchandise of $48,000 on account, debiting Inventory.
   g. Paid off long-term liabilities, $78,000.
   h. Declared, but did not pay, a $31,000 cash dividend on the common stock.

UC Air, Inc.
Statements of Chnages in Financial Position
for the years ended November 30, 19X9 and 19X8

	19X9	19X8
Operating activities		
Income from operations	$184,000	$131,000
Add (subtract) noncash items:		
Total	64,000	62,000
Net cash flow from operating activities	248,000	193,000
Financing activities		
Issuance of long-term notes payable	$ 131,000	$ 83,000
Issuance of short-term notes payable	43,000	35,000
Payment of short-term notes payable	(66,000)	(18,000)
Net cash inflow from financing activities	108,000	100,000
Investing activities		
Purchase of property, plant and equipment	$(303,000)	$(453,000)
Sale of property, plant and equipment	46,000	39,000
Sale of long-term investments	—	33,000
Net cash outflow from investing activities	(257,000)	(381,000)
Increase (decrease) incash	$ (99,000)	$ (88,000)
Cash summary from balance sheet:		
Cash balance at beginning of year	$116,000	$204,000
Increase (decrease) in cash	99,000	(88,000)
Cash balance at the end of year	$215,000	$116,000

Western Ontario Flight Corporation
Statements of Chnages in Financial Position
for the years ended November 30, 19X9 and 19X8

	19X9	19X8
Operating activities		
Income (loss) from operations	$ (67,000)	$154,000
Add (subtract) noncash items:		
Total	84,000	(23,000)
Net cash flow from operating activities	17,000	131,000
Financing activities		
Issuance of long-term notes payable	$ 122,000	$ 143,000
Issuance of short-term notes payable	(179,000)	(134,000)
Payment of cash dividends	(45,000)	(64,000)
Net cash outflow from financing activities	(102,000)	(55,000)
Investing activities		
Purchase of property, plant and equipment	$(120,000)	$ (91,000)
Sale of property, plant and equipment	118,000	39,000
Sale of long-term investments	52,000	4,000
Net cash inflow (outflow) from investing activites	50,000	(48,000)
Increase (decrease) incash	$ (35,000)	$ 28,000
Cash summary from balance sheet:		
Cash balance at beginning of year	$131,000	$103,000
Increase (decrease) in cash	(35,000)	28,000
Cash balance at the end of year	$ 96,000	$131,000

Use the following format for your answer:

Requirement 1		Current Ratio	Debt Ratio	Earnings per Share
Requirement 2	Transaction (letter)	Current Ratio	Debt Ratio	Earnings per Share

Problem 19-5A *Using ratios to evaluate a stock investment* **(L.O. 5, 6)**

Comparative financial statement data of Manatee Furniture Inc. are as follows:

Manatee Furniture Inc.
Comparative Income Statement
Years Ended December 31, 19X4 and 19X3

	19X4	19X3
Net sales	$667,000	$599,000
Cost of goods sold	378,000	283,000
Gross profit	289,000	316,000
Operating expenses	129,000	147,000
Income from operations	160,000	169,000
Interest expense	47,000	41,000
Income before income tax	113,000	128,000
Income tax expense	44,000	53,000
Net income	$69,000	$75,000

Manatee Furniture Inc.
Comparative Balance Sheet
December 31, 19X4 and 19X3
(selected 19X2 amounts given for computation of ratios)

	19X4	19X3	19X2
Current assets			
Cash	$ 37,000	$ 40,000	
Current receivables, net	188,000	151,000	$138,000
Inventories	372,000	286,000	184,000
Prepaid expenses	5,000	20,000	
Total current assets	602,000	497,000	
Property, plant and equipment, net	287,000	276,000	
Total assets	$889,000	$773,000	707,000
Total current liabilities	$286,000	$267,000	
Long-term liabilities	245,000	235,000	
Total liabilities	531,000	502,000	
Preferred shareholders' equity, $.80	50,000	50,000	
Common shareholders' equity	308,000	221,000	148,000
Total liabilities and shareholders' equity	$889,000	$773,000	

Other information:

a. Market price of Manatee common stock: $30.75 at December 31, 19X4 and $40.25 at December 31, 19X3.

b. Common shares outstanding: 20,000 during 19X4 and 19,000 during 19X3.

c. Preferred shares outstanding: 2,500 during both years.

d. All sales on credit.

Required

1. Compute the following ratios for 19X4 and 19X3:
   a. Current ratio
   b. Return on common shareholders' equity
   c. Inventory turnover
   d. Earnings per share of common stock
   e. Accounts receivable turnover
   f. Price/earnings ratio
   g. Times-interest-earned ratio
   h. Book value per share of common stock
   i. Return on assets

2. Decide (a) whether Manatee's financial position improved or deteriorated during 19X4, and (b) whether the investment attractiveness of its common stock appears to have increased or decreased.

Problem 19-6A *Using ratios to decide between two stock investments* **(L.O. 5, 6)**

Assume you are purchasing stock in a company in the grain business. Suppose you have narrowed the choice to AgriCorp and MultiGrains, Inc., and have assembled the following data:

Selected income statement data for current year

	AgriCorp	MultiGrains, Inc.
Net sales (all on credit)	$603,000	$519,000
Cost of goods sold	454,000	387,000
Income from operations	93,000	72,000
Interest expense	—	8,000
Net income	56,000	38,000

Selected balance sheet and market price data at end of current year

	AgriCorp	Multigrains, Inc.
Current assets		
Cash	$ 25,000	$ 39,000
Short-term investments	6,000	13,000
Current receivables, net	189,000	164,000
Inventories	211,000	183,000
Prepaid expenses	19,000	15,000
Total current assets	450,000	414,000
Total assets	974,000	938,000
Total current liabilities	366,000	338,000
Total liabilities	667,000	691,000
Preferred stock $4.00 (250 shares)		25,000
Common stock (150,000 shares)	150,000	
(20,000 shares)		100,000
Total shareholders' equity	307,000	247,000
Market price per share of common stock	$8	$47.50

Selected balance sheet data at beginning of current year

	AgriCorp	MultiGrains, Inc.
Current receivables, net	$142,000	$193,000
Inventories	209,000	197,000
Total assets	842,000	909,000
Preferred shareholders' equity, $4.00 (250 shares)		25,000
Common stock (150,000 shares)	150,000	
(20,000 shares)		100,000
Total shareholders' equity	263,000	215,000

Your investment strategy is to purchase the stocks of companies that have low price/earnings ratios but appear to be in good shape financially. Assume you have analyzed all other factors, and your decision depends on the results of the ratio analysis to be performed.

Required

Compute the following ratios for both companies for the current year and decide which company's stock better fits your investment strategy:

1. Current ratio
2. Acid-test ratio
3. Inventory turnover
4. Days' sales in average receivables
5. Debt ratio
6. Times-interest-earned ratio
7. Return on net sales

8. Return on total assets
9. Return on common shareholders' equity
10. Earnings per share of common stock
11. Book value per share of common stock
12. Price/earnings ratio

(Group B)

Problem 19-1B   *Trend percentages, return on common equity and comparison with the industry (L.O. 1, 5, 6)*

Net sales, net income, and common shareholders' equity for Nasdac Computing, Inc. for a six-year period follow:

	19X9	19X8	19X7	19X6	19X5	19X4
	(amounts in thousands)					
Net sales...	$781	$714	$621	$532	$642	$634
Net income..	51	45	42	38	41	40
Ending common shareholders' equity..	386	354	330	296	272	252

Required

1. Compute trend percentages for 19X5 through 19X9, using 19X4 as the base year.
2. Compute the rate of return on average common shareholders' equity for 19X5 through 19X9, rounding to three decimal places. In this industry, rates of 13 percent are average, rates above 16 percent are considered good, and rates above 20 percent are viewed as outstanding.
3. How does Nasdac's return on common shareholders' equity compare with the industry?

Problem 19-2B   *Common-size statements, analysis of profitability, and comparison with the industry (L.O. 2, 3, 5, 6)*

Middlebrook Sporting Goods Ltd. has asked your help in comparing the company's profit performance and financial position with the average for the sporting goods retail industry. The proprietor has given you the company's income statement and balance sheet, and also the following industry average data for retailers of sporting goods:

	Middlebrook	Industry Average
Middlebrook Sporting Goods Ltd.		
Income Statement		
Compared with Industry Average		
year ended December 31, 19X6		
Net sales	$781,000	100.0%
Cost of goods sold	497,000	65.8
Gross profit	284,000	34.2
Operating expenses	243,000	29.7
Operating income	41,000	4.5
Other expenses	5,000	0.4
Net income.........................	$36,000B	4.1%

	Middlebrook	Industry Average
Middlebrook Sporting Goods Ltd.		
Balance Sheet		
Compared with Industry Average		
December 31, 19X6		
Current assets	$350,000	70.9%
Fixed assets, net...................	74,000	23.6
Intangible assets, net...........	4,000	0.8
Other assets.........................	22,000	4.7
Total.....................................	$450,000	100.0%
Current liabilities.................	$230,000	48.1%
Long-term liabilities.............	62,000	16.6
Shareholders' equity............	158,000	35.3
Total.....................................	$450,000	100.0%

Required

1. Prepare a two-column common-size income statement and a two-column common-size balance sheet for Middlebrook. The first column of each statement should present Middlebrook's common-size statement, and the second column should show the industry averages.

2. For the profitability analysis, compute Middlebrook's (a) ratio of gross profit to net sales, (b) ratio of operating income to net sales, and (c) ratio of net income to net sales. Compare these figures to the industry averages. Is Middlebrook's profit performance better or worse than the industry average?

3. For the analysis of financial position, compute Middlebrook's (a) ratio of current assets to total assets and (b) ratio of shareholders' equity to total assets. Compare these ratios to the industry averages. Is Middlebrook's financial position better or worse than the industry averages?

Problem 19-3B   *Using the statement of changes in financial position for decision-making (L.O. 4)*

You have been asked to evaluate two companies as possible investments. The two companies, similar in size, buy computers, airplanes and other high-cost assets to lease to other businesses. Assume that all other available information has been analyzed, and the decision on which company's stock to purchase depends on the information given in their statements of changes in financial position shown on the next page.

Required

Discuss the relative strengths and weaknesses of each company. Conclude your discussion by recommending one company's stock as an investment.

Problem 19-4B   *Effects of business transactions on selected ratios (L.O. 5, 6)*

Financial statement data of Bylinski Corp. include the following items on p.880:

Lease Alberta, Inc.
Statements of Changes in Financial Position
for the years ended November 30, 19X5 and 19X4

	19X5	19X4
Operating activities		
Income from operations...........	$ 37,000	$ 74,000
Add (subtract) noncash items:		
Total...........................	14,000	(4,000)
Net cash flow from operating activities............	51,000	70,000
Financing activities		
Issuance of short-term notes payable.............	$ 73,000	$ 19,000
Issuance of long-term notes payable.............	31,000	42,000
Payment of short-term notes payable.............	(181,000)	(148,000)
Payment of long-term notes payable.............	(55,000)	(32,000)
Net cash outflow from financing activities.........	(132,000)	(119,000)
Investing activities		
Purchase of property, plant and equipment..........	$ (13,000)	$ (3,000)
Sale of property, plant and equipment..........	86,000	79,000
Sale of long-term investments...........	13,000	—
Net cash outflow from investing activites...........	86,000	76,000
Increase in cash............	$ 5,000	$ 27,000
Cash summary from balance sheet:		
Cash balance at beginning of year..............	$ 31,000	$ 4,000
Increase (decrease) in cash during the year.............	5,000	27,000
Cash balance at the end of year.....	$ 36,000	$ 31,000

Prairie Leasing Corporation
Statements of Chnages in Financial Position
for the years ended November 30, 19X9 and 19X8

	19X5	19X4
Operating activities		
Income from operations............	$ 79,000	$ 71,000
Add (subtract) noncash items:		
Total..........................	19,000	—
Net cash inflow from operating activities.............	98,000	71,000
Financing activities		
Issuance of long-term notes payable.................	$ 46,000	$ 43,000
Issuance of short-term notes payable.................	(15,000)	(40,000)
Payment of cash dividends................	(12,000)	(9,000)
Net cash inflow (outflow) from financing activities............	19,000	(6,000)
Investing activities		
Purchase of property, plant and equipment..............	$(121,000)	$(91,000)
Sale of long-term investments.................	13,000	18,000
Net cash outflow from investing activites.............	(108,000)	(73,000)
Increase (decrease) in cash............	$ 9,000	$ (8,000)
Cash summary from balance sheet:		
Cash balance at beginning of year.................	$ 72,000	$ 80,000
Increase (decrease) in cash during the year.............	9,000	(8,000)
Cash balance at the end of year.....	$ 81,000	$ 72,000

Cash	$ 22,000
Short-term investments	19,000
Accounts receivable, net	83,000
Inventories	141,000
Prepaid expenses	8,000
Total assets	657,000
Short-term notes payable	49,000
Accounts payable	103,000
Accrued liabilities	38,000
Long-term notes payable	160,000
Other long-term liabilities	31,000
Net income	71,000
Number of common shares outstanding	40,000

Required

1. Compute Bylinski's current ratio, debt ratio, and earnings per share.

2. Compute each of the three ratios after evaluating the effect of each transaction that follows. Consider each transaction separately.
   a. Issued 5,000 shares of common stock, receiving cash of $120,000.
   b. Received cash on account $19,000.
   c. Paid short-term notes payable, $32,000.
   d. Purchased merchandise of $26,000 on account, debiting Inventory.
   e. Paid off long-term liabilities, $31,000.
   f. Declared, but did not pay, a $22,000 cash dividend on common stock.
   g. Borrowed $85,000 on a long-term note payable.
   h. Sold short-term investments for $18,000 (cost, $11,000); assume no income tax on the gain.

Use the following format for your answer:

Requirement 1		Current Ratio	Debt Ratio	Earnings per Share

Requirement 2	Transaction (letter)	Current Ratio	Debt Ratio	Earnings per Share

Problem 19-5B   *Using ratios to evaluate a stock investment* **(L.O. 5, 6)**

Comparative financial statement data of Oaktree Realty Ltd. appear on the next page.

Required

1. Compute the following ratios for 19X7 and 19X6:
   a. Current ratio
   b. Inventory turnover
   c. Accounts receivable turnover
   d. Times-interest-earned ratio
   e. Return on assets
   f. Return on common shareholders' equity
   g. Earnings per share of common stock
   h. Price/earnings ratio
   i. Book value per share of common stock

2. Decide (a) whether Oaktree's financial position improved or deteriorated during 19X7, and (b) whether the investment attractiveness of its common stock appears to have increased or decreased.

Oaktree Realty Ltd.
Comparative Income Statement
years ended December 31, 19X7 and 19X6

	19X7	19X6
Net sales..	$462,000	$427,000
Cost of goods sold...	229,000	218,000
Gross profit..	233,000	209,000
Operating expenses...	136,000	134,000
Income from operations	97,000	75,000
Interest expense...	21,000	12,000
Income before income tax	76,000	63,000
Income tax expense...	30,000	27,000
Net income..	$46,000	$ 36,000

Oaktree Realty Ltd.
Comparative Balance Sheet
December 31, 19X7 and 19X6
(selected 19X5 amounts given for computation of ratios)

	19X7	19X6	19X5
Current assets			
Cash	$ 91,000	$ 97,000	
Current receivables, net	107,000	116,000	$103,000
Inventories	182,000	162,000	207,000
Prepaid expenses...	16,000	7,000	
Total current assets	396,000	382,000	
Property, plant and equipment, net	189,000	178,000	
Total assets	$585,000	$560,000	598,000
Total current liabilities....................................	$206,000	$223,000	
Long-term liabilities	119,000	117,000	
Total liabilities	325,000	340,000	
Preferred shareholders' equity, $6.00	100,000	100,000	
Common shareholders' equity.........................	160,000	120,000	90,000
Total liabilities and shareholders' equity.......	$585,000	$560,000	

Other information:

a. Market price of Oaktree common stock: $39 at December 31, 19X7 and $32.50 at December 31, 19X6.

b. Common shares outstanding: 10,000 during 19X7 and 9,000 during 19X6.

c. Preferred shares outstanding: 1,000 during both years.

d. All sales on credit.

Problem 19-6B *Using ratios to decide between two stock investments* **(L.O. 5, 6)**

Assume you are purchasing an investment and have decided to invest in a company in the air-conditioning and heating business. Suppose you have narrowed the choice to Linz Corp. and Hutton, Inc. You have assembled the following selected data:

Selected income statement data for current year

	Linz Corp.	Hutton, Inc.
Net sales (all on credit)...	$371,000	$497,000
Cost of goods sold	209,000	258,000
Income from operations...	79,000	138,000
Interest expense..	—	19,000
Net income...	48,000	72,000

Selected balance sheet and market price data at end of current year

	Linz Corp.	Hutton, Inc.
Current assets		
Cash	$ 22,000	$19,000
Short-term investments..	20,000	18,000
Current receivables, net	42,000	46,000
Inventories..	87,000	100,000
Prepaid expenses	2,000	3,000
Total current assets	173,000	186,000
Total assets	265,000	328,000
Total current liabilities...	108,000	98,000
Total liabilities	108,000	131,000
Preferred stock: $5.00 (200 shares)...................................		20,000
Common stock (10,000 shares)...	10,000	
(5,000 shares)...		12,500
Total shareholders' equity	157,000	197,000
Market price per share of common stock...........................	$51	$118

Selected balance sheet data at beginning of current year

	Linz Corp.	Hutton, Inc.
Current receivables, net...	$ 40,000	$48,000
Inventories..	93,000	88,000
Total assets..	259,000	270,000
Preferred shareholders' equity, $5.00 (200 shares)..........	—	20,000
Common stock (10,000 shares)	10,000	
(5,000 shares)		12,500
Total shareholders' equity...	118,000	126,000

Your investment strategy is to purchase the stocks of companies that have low price/earnings ratios but appear to be in good shape financially. Assume you have analyzed all other factors, and your decision depends on the results of the ratio analysis to be performed.

Required

Compute the following ratios for both companies for the current year and decide which company's stock better fits your investment strategy:

1. Current ratio
2. Acid-test ratio
3. Inventory turnover
4. Day's sales in average receivables
5. Debt ratio
6. Times-interest-earned ratio
7. Return on net sales
8. Return on total assets
9. Return on common shareholders' equity
10. Earnings per share of common stock
11. Book value per share of common stock
12. Price/earnings ratio

Extending Your Knowledge

Decision Problems

1. Identifying action to cut losses and establish profitability (L.O. 2, 5, 6)

Suppose you manage BiSports Ltd., a sporting goods and bicycle shop, which lost money during the past year. Before you can set the business on a successful course, you must first analyze the company and industry data for the current year in an effort to learn what is wrong. The data appear below.

Required

Based on your analysis of these figures, suggest four courses of action BiSports should take to reduce its losses and establish profitable operations. Give your reasons for each suggestion.

BiSports Ltd. Balance Sheet Data

	BiSports	Industry Average
Cash and short-term investments	2.1%	6.8%
Trade receivables, net	16.1	11.0
Inventory	64.2	60.5
Prepaid expenses	1.0	0.0
Total current assets	83.4	78.3
Capital assets, net	12.6	15.2
Other assets	4.0	6.5
Total assets	100.0%	100.0%
Notes payable, short-term, 12%	18.1%	14.0%
Accounts payable	20.1	25.1
Accrued liabilities	7.8	7.9
Total current liabilities	46.0	47.0
Long-term debt, 11%	19.7	16.4
Total liabilities	65.7	63.4
Common shareholders' equity	34.3	36.6
Total liabilities and shareholders' equity	100.0%	100.0%

BiSports Ltd. Income Statement Data		
		Industry
	BiSports	Average
Net sales	100.0%	100.0%
Cost of sales	(69.7)	(64.8)
Gross profit	30.3	35.2
Operating expense	(35.6)	(32.3)
Operating income (loss)	(5.3)	2.9
Interest expense	(6.8)	(1.3)
Other revenue	1.1	.3
Income (loss) before income tax	(11.0)	1.9
Income tax (expense) saving	4.4	(0.8)
Net income (loss)	(6.6)%	1.1%

2. *Understanding the components of accounting ratios (L.O. 5, 6)*

a. Harvey Drago is the controller of Hunan Industries Inc., whose year end is December 31. He prepares cheques for suppliers in December and posts them to the appropriate accounts in that month. However, he holds on to the cheques and actually mails them to the suppliers in January. What financial ratio(s) are most affected by the action? What is Drago's purpose in undertaking this activity?

b. Janet Wong has asked you about the stock of a particular company. She finds it attractive because it has a high dividend yield relative to another stock she is also considering. Explain to her the meaning of the ratio and the danger of making a decision based on it alone.

c. Limeridge Ltd.'s owners are concerned because the number of days' sales in receivables has increased over the previous two years. Explain why the ratio might have increased.

Ethical Issue

Krisler Corporation's long-term debt agreements make certain demands on the business. Krisler may not repurchase company stock in excess of the balance of Retained Earnings. Also, Long-term Debt may not exceed Shareholders' Equity, and the current ratio may not fall below 1.50. If Krisler fails to meet these requirements, the company's lenders have the authority to take over management of the corporation.

Changes in consumer demand have made it hard for Krisler to sell its products. Current liabilities have mounted faster than current assets, causing the current ratio to fall to 1.47. Prior to releasing financial statements, Krisler management is scrambling to improve the current ratio. The controller points out that an investment can be classified as either long-term or short-term, depending on management's intention. By deciding to convert an investment to cash within one year, Krisler can classify the investment as short-term (a current asset). On the controller's recommendation, Krisler's board of directors votes to reclassify long-term investments as short-term.

Required

1. What effect will reclassifying the investment have on the current ratio? Is Krisler Corporation's financial position stronger as a result of reclassifying the investment?

2. Shortly after releasing the financial statements, sales improve and so, then, does the current ratio. As a result, Krisler management decides not to sell the invest-

ments it had reclassified as short-term. Accordingly, the company reclassifies the investments as long-term. Has management behaved unethically? Give your reason.

Financial Statement Problems

1. Measuring profitability and analyzing stock as an investment (L.O. 5, 6)

Use the financial information in the Schneider Corporation financial statements in Appendix C to chart the company's progress through the fiscal years 1990 and 1991. Compute the following ratios that measure profitability and that are used to analyze stock as an investment:

a. Rate of return on net sales

b. Rate of return on total assets

c. Rate of return on common shareholders' equity

d. Earnings per share

   In the management discussion and analysis (MD&A), management indicates that the market values of common shares and Class A shares had improved from $21.50 to $24.50 and from $16.50 to $24.50 respectively from October 27, 1990 to October 26, 1991.
   Is this improvement in the stock price justified in light of the changes in the four ratios?

2. Measuring profitability and analyzing stock as an investment (L.O. 5, 6)

Obtain the annual report of an actual company of your choosing.
   Use the financial statements and the multi-year summary data to chart the company's progress during the three most recent years including the current year. Compute the following ratios that measure profitability and which are used to analyze stock as an investment.

Profitability Measure
a. Return on net sales

b. Return on common shareholders' equity

c. Return on total assets

Stock Analysis Measure
d. Price/earnings ratio (If given, use the average of the "high" and "low" stock prices for each year.)

Is the trend in the profitability measures consistent with the trend in the stock analysis measure? Evaluate the company's overall outlook for the future.

Comprehensive Problem for Part Six

In this problem you are to decide whether or not to lend $10 million to Schneider Corporation, whose financial statements appear in Appendix C. Examine the statements, Notes to the Consolidated Financial Statements, Ten Year Statistical Review, and the Reports of Management and the Auditors. In addition to the statements, you will need these data from Schneider's 1989, 1988, and 1987 annual reports:

	1989	1988	1987
		(thousands)	
Short-term investments	2,739	—	—
Accounts receivable	30,918	26,710	31,412
Inventories	50,524	47,823	46,636
Income taxes recoverable	995	116	590
Other	4,456	2,798	4,022
Total current assets	89,632	77,447	82,660
Total current liabilities	69,850	54,228	57,056
Cost of products sold	556,268	534,796	616,453

To help make your lending decision, compute or locate in the Schneider report the following ratios and other decision-relevant items for the year 1988 to 1991:

1. Current ratio
2. Acid-test ratio
3. Cash collections from customers
4. Inventory turnover
5. Day's sales in average receivables
6. Debt ratio (As the ten-year statistical review discloses both total assets and shareholders' equity, end of year, you can derive total liabilities.)
7. Times-interest-earned ratio
8. Gross margin percentage
9. Rate of return on total assets
10. Rate of return on shareholders' equity (Consider the two classes of shares equivalent.)
11. Earnings per share (Consider the two classes of shares equivalent.)
12. Book value per share (Consider the two classes of shares equivalent.)

Required

Analyze the trends in these ratios, and write a one-page memo (exclusive of the appendix, which would include such ratios as you refer to in the report) to the loan committee of the bank where you work as a credit analyst. Make a recommendation to the loan committee, giving the reasoning behind your conclusion.

Answers to Self-Study Questions

1. b $252,000 – $210,000 = $42,000; $42,000/$210,000 = .20
2. c
3. d
4. a
5. b ($10,000 + $22,000)/$40,000 = .80
6. b
7. d
8. d
9. a
10. c

Appendices

Appendix A

Accounting for the Effects of Changing Prices

We use accounting information for making economic decisions. Of course, these decisions can only be as good as the information we weigh in making them. Critics charge that accounting fails to provide the most accurate information possible because it fails to measure the effects of changing prices. How intelligent, then, can our economic decisions be?

We know that GAAP directs companies to assume the stable-monetary-unit concept when preparing financial statements. For accounting purposes, companies use the historical cost of the building throughout the building's lifetime. However, critics maintain that historical-cost accounting does not provide the necessary information to allow statement users to make intelligent decisions. Is it valid to assume a stable monetary unit when prices — and the dollar's value itself — change over time?

There are two forces simultaneously at work on the price of an asset over time. They are changes in the general price level and changes in specific prices of particular assets and liabilities. These are now discussed in turn.

Changes in the general price level, which is a weighted average of all the prices of goods and services in the economy, lead to changes in the purchasing power of the dollar. When the general price level increases and the purchasing power of the dollar decreases, we call it *inflation*; when the general price level decreases and the purchasing power of the dollar increases, we call it deflation. Since World War II, the world has seen almost steady inflation, that is, an almost continuous fall in the purchasing power of the dollar.

Changes in the general price level can be measured by a general price index that assigns a value of 100 to a base year. The price index tracks the movement of prices in the economy over time. A 6 percent price increase during year 1 would cause the price index to rise to a value of 106 (100×1.06) at the end of the year. A 50 percent increase in prices over a six-year period would result in a price index of 150 (100×1.50) at the end of six years.

The most widely used price index in Canada is the *Consumer Price Index* (CPI), published monthly by Statistics Canada. The CPI is based on a representative sample of food, clothing, shelter, transportation and other items purchased by an average consumer. The present base period for the CPI is 1981. Each month the average of these items' prices is compared to their prices the preceding month, and a new price index is computed. The CPI, based on 1981 as 100, was 33.1 in 1964, indicating that prices tripled from 1964 to 1981. The CPI was 154.3 at the end of 1989, an increase of 54.3 percent over 1981. Since 1989, the change in the CPI has slowed significantly and now is running at less than 2 percent a year.

As the CPI increases, the purchasing power of a dollar decreases, and it becomes more and more difficult to compare assets acquired in different years. For example, it is difficult to compare the cost of an asset bought in 19X1, when the CPI was at, say 120, with an asset that was purchased five years later in 19X6 when the CPI was at, say 140.

In order to make financial data comparable between years when inflation occurs, we restate amounts into *constant dollars*. We call dollars stated in terms of current purchasing power *nominal dollars*. We calculate constant dollars by using one year, for example, 19X1, as the base and deflating the dollars of the other year, for example, 19X6, by multiplying them by the CPI for 19X6 divided by the CPI for 19X1. Suppose Cathy Hanna bought 1 hectare of land for $2,000 in 19X1 (when the index was 120) and is considering buying a second hectare adjoining it in 19X6 (when the index is 140). The second hectare is for sale for $2,600. Hanna would compare the two prices by calculating the price of the second hectare in terms of constant or 19X1 dollars [$2,229 ($2,600 $\times$ (120/140))] and then comparing them; the first hecatre cost her $2,000 in 19X1 dollars.

Another way to describe inflation is in terms of decreases in the purchasing power of the dollar. A dollar today will buy less meat, less gasoline, less laundering for shirts and less of most other goods and services than a dollar would buy in 1981.

Changes in specific prices are caused by a variety of factors in addition to changes in the purchasing power of the dollar. The development of new technology can lead to falling prices for particular products. For example, computers and compact disc players have fallen in price over the past several years, in part, because of new technology. Market conditions can affect specific prices. A drought can lead to higher prices for grain because a shortage results, while a bumper crop can lead to a fall in prices.

The specific price of an asset may also be described as its current value. Specific prices can be measured in a variety of ways; two different ways that were suggested in Chapter 9 are *current replacement cost* and *net realizable value*. Current replacement cost is also called an entry or buying price, while net realizable value is an exit or selling price. An entry price is the amount of cash required to buy an asset that is similar to the asset being valued. An exit price is amount of cash that would be received from selling the asset, that is, the selling price less the cost of selling the asset.

Assume that Brehme Inc. bought land 20 years ago in June, 1970, for $500,000; the land was to be used for a planned expansion of the company's manufacturing facilities. Assume that inflation and an increase in demand for land have pushed the price of the land to $2,500,000. The specific price of the land increased by $2,000,000 ($2,500,000 – $500,000). The Consumer Price Index (based on 1981 as 100) was 41.0 in 1970 and is 157.8 in June, 1990.

The increase in the price of the land has two components: a *fictitious* component caused by inflation and a *real* component. The fictitious component is called fictitious because it is caused only by a decline in the purchasing power of the dollar; it represents no real change in the value of the asset. Thus you need $1.58 in 1990 dollars to buy what you could have bought for $.41 in 1970. The real increase is the difference between the increase in the specific price and the fictitious increase.

The fictitious gain is calculated by subtracting the historic cost from the inflation-adjusted cost:

$$[(\$500,000 \times (157.8/41.0)) - \$500,000] = \$1,424,390$$

The real gain is calculated by subtracting this amount from the increase in the specific price:

Specific price change..	$2,000,000
Fictitious gain caused by inflation.........................	1,424,390
Real Gain...	$ 575,610

By investing in the land in 1970, Brehme Inc. is $575,610, 1990 dollars better off in terms of general purchasing power than it was in 1970. Note that most of the specific price gain is illusory; it was caused by a decline in the purchasing power of the dollar.

Certain financial statement items, such as inventory, cost of goods sold, fixed assets and depreciation, are affected by changing prices more than others; providing information about the effects of changing prices on these items is helpful to users of the financial statements. However, not all assets, liabilities, revenues and expenses are affected by inflation to the same extent. For example, sales are made at a price that accurately reflects current value at the time of sale; the receivable arising from the sale reflects that same current value. Similarly, wages and salaries reflect the current value of the services performed at the time they are performed. For these financial statement accounts, current cost is historical cost.

In the remainder of this chapter, we discuss, first, issues related to the reporting of changing prices. Next, we illustrate the purchasing-power losses that accrue from holding net financial assets (and vice versa the gains from liabilities) when the purchasing power of the dollar is decreasing. The discussion concludes with a consideration of the components of the profit that arise from the sale of inventory when specific prices are increasing.

Reporting the Effects of Changing Prices

There are three issues that must be resolved when determining how to report the effects of changing prices:

1. Which attribute of the financial statement elements should be measured and reported?
2. Which capital maintenance concept should be followed?
3. What unit of measurement should be used?

The three issues are discussed below.

Attribute of Financial Statement Elements You learned in Chapter 12 that the elements of financial statements include assets, liabilities, revenue and expenses. The attribute to be measured could be, among others, the historical cost of the element or its current value. Remember that among the possible definitions of the current value of an asset are its buying price or its selling price. As you learned in Chapter 1 and again in Chapter 12, accountants usually use historical cost in preparing financial statements according to GAAP.

Capital Maintenance A company must maintain its capital (that is, owner's equity) if it is to continue in operation. In other words, it should not pay out to its owners more than it earns as income. This is especially true in a period of rapidly rising prices. As is illustrated below, the concept of *capital maintenance* suggests that income can be earned only after capital is maintained. In the three examples that follow we will consider measuring income under the three different capital maintenance concepts most commonly favored by accountants:

1. *Maintenance of financial capital in nominal dollars.* Financial capital is maintained in nominal dollars if the historical cost owner's equity is the same at the end of the period as it was at the beginning. Financial statements prepared under the historical cost principle are concerned with the maintenance of financial capital in nominal dollars. If they show owner's equity (ignoring dividends and capital transactions) at the end of the period is equal to owner's equity at the beginning of the period, financial capital has been maintained; if owner's equity at the end of the period is greater than owner's equity at the beginning of the period, income has been earned and is taken to be equal in amount to the increase.

   Suppose a company begins operations on January 1, 19X1 with cash of $10 and owner's equity of $10. The company buys one unit of product for $10 cash and sells the unit for $15 cash; income earned is $5. Following the historical cost principle, the company's balance sheet would be as follows after the transaction:

Assets		**Owner's Equity**	
Cash	$15	Owner's Equity	$15

   Opening owner's equity was $10 so income would be $5 ($15 – $10). A dividend of $5 could be paid and owner's equity would be maintained at $10. The company's income statement for the period would be as follows:

Sales..	$15
Cost of goods sold...	10
Income	$ 5

2. *Maintenance of financial capital in constant dollars.* The second capital maintenance concept is like the first except that the capital to be maintained is opening owner's equity adjusted for inflation during the period. If owner's equity (ignoring dividends and capital transactions) at the end of the period is equal to owner's equity at the beginning of the period adjusted for inflation during the period, financial capital has been maintained. If owner's equity at the end of the period is greater than owner's equity at the beginning of the period adjusted for inflation during the period, income has been earned and is equal in amount to the increase.

Suppose the Consumer Price Index (CPI) increased by 10 percent during 19X2. The price adjusted opening owner's equity would be $11 ($10 × 1.10). In order to maintain the purchasing power of its capital the company would have to retain $1 ($11 − $10) of the $5 excess of selling price over cost; the company's income would therefore be $4 ($5 − $1). The company's income statement for the period would be as follows:

Sales	$15
Cost of goods sold	10
Excess of sales over cost of goods sold	5
Amount required to maintain price-level-adjusted capital [($10 × 1.10) − $10]	1
Income	$ 4

3. *Maintenance of operating capability or capital.* This capital maintenance concept requires the entity to maintain its *operating capability* or capacity (that is, the same level of operations as the previous year) before income can be earned. Suppose the purchase price of the product increased to $12 per unit during 19X2. To maintain its ability to operate, the company must be able to replace the unit of product sold during 19X2 at a price of $12. In order to maintain the operating capacity of its capital, the company would have to retain $2 ($12 − $10) of the $5 excess of selling price over cost; the company's income would then be $3 ($5 − $2). The company's income statement for the period would be as follows:

Sales	$15
Cost of goods sold	10
Excess of sales over cost of goods sold	5
Additional amount required to maintain operating capability at one unit of inventory ($12–$10)	2
Income	$ 3

Income is earned only after operating capacity (in this case $12, the new cost of a unit of product) has been maintained. Note that the maximum amount the company will be able to pay out as a dividend and still maintain operating capacity is $3. The assumption underlying this discussion is that the company wishes to maintain the same level of operations.

The above illustrations are simple; the situation becomes more complex when the company's assets include other kinds of assets and when activities are financed by both debt and owner's equity.

Unit of Measurement   The information reported could be in nominal dollars or constant (price-adjusted) dollars. Recall that:

1. The attribute to be measured in historical cost financial statements is the historical cost of the asset, liability, revenue and expense.

2. The capital maintenance concept followed in historical cost financial statements is the maintenance of financial capital in nominal dollars.

Thus historical cost financial statements, which have been the kind traditionally compiled, use nominal dollars as the unit of measurement. Economists report national income accounts, for example, in both nominal and real or constant dollars.

After decisions have been made about the attribute to be measured, the capital maintenance concept to be adopted and the unit of measurement to be used, a decision must be made on what information should be reported and whether complete financial statements or elements from the financial statements should be reported taking into account changes in prices.

CICA Pronouncements on the Effects of Changing Prices __

Until January 1983, with the exception of a few Canadian companies, annual reports contained only historical cost financial information, financial statements were prepared using the historical cost model. On that date, Section 4510 "Reporting the Effects of Changing Prices" was added to the *CICA Handbook*. Section 4510 suggested that companies whose shares were publicly traded and who met a size test (had inventories and fixed assets before depreciation of $50 million and total assets of $350 million) should issue information supplementary to the audited financial statements reporting the effects of changing prices. The information could be but did not have to be audited.

Companies meeting the size test could, but were not required to, provide the supplementary information about the effects of changing prices. Most companies elected not to provide it while those that did initially later discontinued the disclosure. The reasons that the Section 4510 experiment was not successful are not clear; two reasons put forward are the decline in the rate of inflation and the cost of the additional disclosures. The seventeenth, eighteenth, and nineteenth editions of the CICA publication, *Financial Reporting in Canada*, which is a survey of the financial statement reporting practices of 300 Canadian companies, cover the years 1983 to 1991. During that period, the percentage of companies that were covered by Section 4510 and did report information about changing prices in some form decreased from 57 percent in 1983 to 0 percent in 1990.[1] Section 4510 was withdrawn in 1991.

Purchasing-Power Gain or Loss

A company may have a purchasing-power gain from holding net monetary liabilities (that is, monetary liabilities exceed monetary assets) in a period of rising prices; if the company held net monetary assets during the same period, it would suffer a purchasing-power loss. The gain occurs during inflation because the company is able to pay its liabilities with dollars that are cheaper than the dollars borrowed.

What does the purchasing-power gain mean? Suppose you borrow $5,000 to purchase a sailboat. You repay the loan after two years, during which time prices have risen 20 percent. If you are obligated to pay only $5,000 (ignoring interest for the moment), you experience a *purchasing-power gain* of $1,000 ($5,000 multiplied by the inflation rate of 20 percent). The creditor who loaned you the money in-

---

[1] *Financial Reporting in Canada*, 17th edition, Toronto: CICA, 1987, p. 79; 18th edition, Toronto: CICA, 1990, pp. 92–93; and 19th edition, Toronto: CICA, 1992, pp. 68–70.

curs the corresponding *purchasing-power loss* of $1,000 because the dollars the creditor receives when you repay the loan are worth less than the dollars lent in terms of their command over goods and services. Interest rates are intended to compensate for this purchasing-power gain or loss, but interest is accounted for separately.

The purchasing-power gain or loss depends on the company's monetary assets and monetary liabilities. *Monetary assets* are assets whose values are stated in a fixed number of dollars. This amount does *not* change, regardless of inflation. Examples include cash and receivables. Cash of $1,000 remains cash of $1,000 whether inflation occurs or not. If you hold $1,000 cash during a period of inflation, your $1,000 will buy fewer goods and services at the end of the period. The result is a purchasing-power loss. Likewise, if you sell $1,500 of merchandise on account and you receive the cash after a period of inflation, you receive only $1,500. Holding the receivable results in a purchasing-power loss.

Nonmonetary assets are those assets whose prices do change during inflation. Examples include inventory, land, buildings and equipment. Holding nonmonetary assets does not result in a purchasing-power gain or loss.

Monetary liabilities are liabilities that are stated in a fixed number of dollars. Most liabilities are monetary. As discussed above in the sailboat example, you have a purchasing-power gain if you have a monetary liability during inflation.

The computation of the purchasing-power gain or loss is based on the company's *net monetary position* (monetary assets minus monetary liabilities). If the company has more monetary assets than monetary liabilities, it has *net monetary assets*. If its monetary liabilities exceed its monetary assets, it has *net monetary liabilities*. Most industrial corporations have net-monetary-liability positions and experience purchasing-power gains. Most financial institutions, such as banks, trust companies and insurance companies, have net-monetary-asset positions. They usually incur purchasing-power losses during inflation. A company's monetary assets and liabilities can be determined from its historical-cost balance sheet.

Exhibit A-1 illustrates one way to calculate a purchasing-power gain or loss. Dajol Ltd. had monetary assets of $450,000 in 19X8 and $520,000 in 19X9 at December 31, its year end. Monetary liabilities were $640,000 at December 31, 19X8 and $812,000 at December 31, 19X9. The CPI was 146.1 at December 31, 19X8 and 153.5 at December 31, 19X9.

At December 31, 19X8 (the beginning of 19X9), Dajol had a net-monetary-liability position of $190,000. During 19X9 the company increased its net monetary liabilities by $102 and ended 19X9 with a net-monetary-liability position of $292,000. These amounts are in the Historical Cost column. The net-monetary-liability positions are not comparable because they are stated in dollars of different purchasing power. The beginning position is stated in December 19X8 dollars, which are not comparable to the ending position, which is stated in December 19X9 dollars. The reason is that the general price level and the CPI in Canada increased during 19X9, that is, inflation occurred. To compute Dajol's overall purchasing-power gain or loss, it is necessary to compare the beginning and ending positions in dollars of equal purchasing power.

The inflation adjustments of Dajol's net monetary liabilities are in Exhibit A-1 under the columns Conversion Factor and Average 19X9 Dollars. The conversion factors are used to restate the beginning and ending net-monetary-liability positions to dollars of constant purchasing power. The Consumer Price Index (CPI) is used for the conversion. At the beginning of 19X9, when Dajol had net monetary liabilities of $190,000, the CPI was 146.1. For 19X9, the average was 149.8.

The beginning historical-cost balance is restated into average constant dollars of 19X9 by multiplying the ratio of the current-year average index (149.8) by the beginning price index (146.1). The numerator of the price-index ratio is the

EXHIBIT A-1 *Purchasing-Power Gain*

Dajol Ltd.
Gain from Purchasing Power of Net Amounts Owed
(Purchasing-Power Gain)
for the year ended December 31, 19X9
(thousands of dollars)

	Historical Cost	Conversion Factor	Average 19X9 Dollars
December 31, 19X8			
Monetary liabilities............................	$640		
Monetary assets................................	450		
Net monetary liabilities	190	149.8	$194.8
		146.1	
Increase during year	102	149.8	102.0
		149.8	
			296.8
December 31, 19X9			
Monetary liabilities	$812		
Monetary assets	520		
Net monetary liability....................	292	149.8	285.0
		153.5	
Gain in general purchasing power from having net monetary liabilities during the year.			$ 11.8

Note: The change in dollar amount of net monetary liabilities during 19X9 is assumed to have occurred evenly over the year.

current-year average index, and the denominator is the price index that was in effect on the date of the balance. The adjustment of the beginning balance is (amounts rounded to the nearest thousand dollars):

$$
\begin{array}{ccccc}
\text{Beginning} & & \text{Current-Year Average} & & \text{Beginning Net Monetary} \\
\text{Net Monetary} & \times & \dfrac{\text{Consumer Price Index}}{\text{Beginning-of-Year}} & = & \text{Liabilities Stated in Average Constant} \\
\text{Liabilities} & & \text{Consumer Price Index} & & \text{Dollars of the Current Year}
\end{array}
$$

$$
\$190 \quad \times \quad \frac{149.8}{146.1} \quad = \quad \$194.8
$$

The change in net monetary liabilities during 19X9 ($102,000) is not adjusted because it occurred as the company transacted business all during the year. The average price index (149.8) is both the numerator and the denominator of the index ratio, resulting in a ratio of 1.

The subtotal in Exhibit A-1 ($296.8) is the sum of the adjusted beginning net monetary liabilities plus the increase (or minus the decrease) in net monetary liabilities that arose from the transactions of the year. During 19X9, Dajol increased its net monetary liabilities by $102,000. The subtotal of $295,000 is the amount of net monetary liabilities that Dajol would owe if the company's assets and liabilities had just kept pace with inflation during the year.

The ending historical-cost balance ($296.8) is restated into average constant dollars of 19X9 by multiplying it by the ratio of the current-year average index (148.9) to the ending price index (153.5). The adjustment of the ending balance is (amounts rounded to the nearest thousand dollars):

Ending Net Monetary Liabilities	×	Current-Year Average Consumer Price Index / End-of-Year Consumer Price Index	=	Ending Net Monetary Liabilities Stated in Average Constant Dollars of the Current Year
$292	×	$\dfrac{149.8}{153.5}$	=	$285.0

The purchasing-power gain can now be computed. Its amount is determined by subtracting the ending adjusted net-monetary-liability balance ($285,000) from the subtotal ($296,800). If Dajol had just kept pace with general inflation during 19X9, its net-monetary-liability position would have been $296,800. But at year end, the company's net monetary liabilities are only $285,000. The result is a purchasing-power gain of $11,800. Dajol's gain resulted primarily from (1) inflation during 19X9 and (2) the company's net-monetary-liability position during the year. If the company had had more monetary assets than liabilities during the year and there had been inflation, the company would have experienced a purchasing-power loss.

The purchasing-power gain computation is useful for determining how well the entity is managing its monetary position during inflation. Purchasing-power gain (or loss) can be applied to individual persons as well as businesses of all sizes.

Trading Gains and Holding Gains

In order to simplify the discussion in this section, we assume that there is no change in the purchasing power of the dollar in the illustrations provided below. In this way, we can focus on the trading gain and the holding gain.

A company that sells a unit of product for more than it paid for it in a period of rising prices earns a profit which has two components. Part of the profit arises from selling the product; it is called a *trading gain*. The balance of the profit arises from holding the product in inventory; it is called a *holding gain*. Todd's Cycle and Sports Ltd. buys one bicycle for $100, holds it for six months, and sells it for $180. During the six months, the cost to Todd of replacing the bicycle in inventory (or entry price) increases to $120; $120 is the amount Todd must pay to replace the bicycle that was sold. The total profit on the transaction was $80 ($180 − $100). The profit can be broken down as follows:

Selling price..........................	$180 ⎫	Trading gain	$60
Replacement cost..................	120 ⎬		
Original cost..........................	100 ⎭	Holding gain	20

The trading profit arose from the sale of the bicycle while the holding profit arose from holding the bicycle while its replacement cost price rose from $100 to $120. The total profit ($80) is the amount we normally would recognize on the income statement; it is not broken down into components as we have done in the example.

The notion of earning a profit from simply holding an item in inventory may be difficult to grasp. Imagine two companies that sell Big Boom portable stereos. Company A buys one stereo on January 1, 19X1, from the manufacturer for $300, while Company B buys the same model from the same manufacturer for $350 on June 30, 19X1 (the cost price has increased to $350 because of an increase in the cost of components of the stereo). Both companies sell their stereos to customers on July 1, 19X1 for $500. Company A earns a total profit of $200; $50 ($350 − $300) is a holding profit, while the trading profit is $150 ($500 − $350). Company B earns a total profit of $150 ($500 – $350); there is no holding profit because Company B did not hold (own) the stereo while its cost price increased. You have probably noticed that we have assumed that the selling price increased as the cost price increased so that both companies sold the stereos for $500.

Companies that expect an increase in the replacement cost of inventory may try to earn a holding gain by purchasing more than is immediately needed. Of course, there are costs to buying the extra inventory, extra insurance coverage, extra storage costs and, perhaps, borrowing costs. If the holding gain exceeds these costs, then the decision to buy the extra inventory is sound. The situation may be complicated by the fact that there may be a change in general prices (inflation) during the holding period that may erode the potential holding gain.

Appendix B

Present-Value Tables
and Future-Value Tables

This appendix provides present-value tables (more complete than those appearing in Chapter 16 and Chapter 26) and future-value tables.

Table B-1   *Present Value of $1*

Periods	1%	2%	3%	4%	5%	6%	7%	8%	9%	10%	12%
1	0.990	0.980	0.971	0.962	0.952	0.943	0.935	0.926	0.917	0.909	0.893
2	0.980	0.961	0.943	0.925	0.907	0.890	0.873	0.857	0.842	0.826	0.797
3	0.971	0.942	0.915	0.889	0.864	0.840	0.816	0.794	0.772	0.751	0.712
4	0.961	0.924	0.888	0.855	0.823	0.792	0.763	0.735	0.708	0.683	0.636
5	0.951	0.906	0.883	0.822	0.784	0.747	0.713	0.681	0.650	0.621	0.567
6	0.942	0.888	0.837	0.790	0.746	0.705	0.666	0.630	0.596	0.564	0.507
7	0.933	0.871	0.813	0.760	0.711	0.665	0.623	0.583	0.547	0.513	0.452
8	0.923	0.853	0.789	0.731	0.677	0.627	0.582	0.540	0.502	0.467	0.404
9	0.914	0.837	0.766	0.703	0.645	0.592	0.544	0.500	0.460	0.424	0.361
10	0.905	0.820	0.744	0.676	0.614	0.558	0.508	0.463	0.422	0.386	0.322
11	0.896	0.804	0.722	0.650	0.585	0.527	0.475	0.429	0.388	0.350	0.287
12	0.887	0.788	0.701	0.625	0.557	0.497	0.444	0.397	0.356	0.319	0.257
13	0.879	0.773	0.681	0.601	0.530	0.469	0.415	0.368	0.326	0.290	0.229
14	0.870	0.758	0.661	0.577	0.505	0.442	0.388	0.340	0.299	0.263	0.205
15	0.861	0.743	0.642	0.555	0.481	0.417	0.362	0.315	0.275	0.239	0.183
16	0.853	0.728	0.623	0.534	0.458	0.394	0.339	0.292	0.252	0.218	0.163
17	0.844	0.714	0.605	0.513	0.436	0.371	0.317	0.270	0.231	0.198	0.146
18	0.836	0.700	0.587	0.494	0.416	0.350	0.296	0.250	0.212	0.180	0.130
19	0.828	0.686	0.570	0.475	0.396	0.331	0.277	0.232	0.194	0.164	0.116
20	0.820	0.673	0.554	0.456	0.377	0.312	0.258	0.215	0.178	0.149	0.104
21	0.811	0.660	0.538	0.439	0.359	0.294	0.242	0.199	0.164	0.135	0.093
22	0.803	0.647	0.522	0.422	0.342	0.278	0.226	0.184	0.150	0.123	0.083
23	0.795	0.634	0.507	0.406	0.326	0.262	0.211	0.170	0.138	0.112	0.074
24	0.788	0.622	0.492	0.390	0.310	0.247	0.197	0.158	0.126	0.102	0.066
25	0.780	0.610	0.478	0.375	0.295	0.233	0.184	0.146	0.116	0.092	0.059
26	0.772	0.598	0.464	0.361	0.281	0.220	0.172	0.135	0.106	0.084	0.053
27	0.764	0.586	0.450	0.347	0.268	0.207	0.161	0.125	0.098	0.076	0.047
28	0.757	0.574	0.437	0.333	0.255	0.196	0.150	0.116	0.090	0.069	0.042
29	0.749	0.563	0.424	0.321	0.243	0.185	0.141	0.107	0.082	0.063	0.037
30	0.742	0.552	0.412	0.308	0.231	0.174	0.131	0.099	0.075	0.057	0.033
40	0.672	0.453	0.307	0.208	0.142	0.097	0.067	0.046	0.032	0.022	0.011
50	0.608	0.372	0.228	0.141	0.087	0.054	0.034	0.021	0.013	0.009	0.003

Table B-1   *(cont'd)*

| | | | | | Present Value | | | | | | |
14%	15%	16%	18%	20%	25%	30%	35%	40%	45%	50%	Periods
0.877	0.870	0.862	0.847	0.833	0.800	0.769	0.741	0.714	0.690	0.667	1
0.769	0.756	0.743	0.718	0.694	0.640	0.592	0.549	0.510	0.476	0.444	2
0.675	0.658	0.641	0.609	0.579	0.512	0.455	0.406	0.364	0.328	0.296	3
0.592	0.572	0.552	0.516	0.482	0.410	0.350	0.301	0.260	0.226	0.198	4
0.519	0.497	0.476	0.437	0.402	0.328	0.269	0.223	0.186	0.156	0.132	5
0.456	0.432	0.410	0.370	0.335	0.262	0.207	0.165	0.133	0.108	0.088	6
0.400	0.376	0.354	0.314	0.279	0.210	0.159	0.122	0.095	0.074	0.059	7
0.351	0.327	0.305	0.266	0.233	0.168	0.123	0.091	0.068	0.051	0.039	8
0.308	0.284	0.263	0.225	0.194	0.134	0.094	0.067	0.048	0.035	0.026	9
0.270	0.247	0.227	0.191	0.162	0.107	0.073	0.050	0.035	0.024	0.017	10
0.237	0.215	0.195	0.162	0.135	0.086	0.056	0.037	0.025	0.017	0.012	11
0.208	0.187	0.168	0.137	0.112	0.069	0.043	0.027	0.018	0.012	0.008	12
0.182	0.163	0.145	0.116	0.093	0.055	0.033	0.020	0.013	0.008	0.005	13
0.160	0.141	0.125	0.099	0.078	0.044	0.025	0.015	0.009	0.006	0.003	14
0.140	0.123	0.108	0.084	0.065	0.035	0.020	0.011	0.006	0.004	0.002	15
0.123	0.107	0.093	0.071	0.054	0.028	0.015	0.008	0.005	0.003	0.002	16
0.108	0.093	0.080	0.060	0.045	0.023	0.012	0.006	0.003	0.002	0.001	17
0.095	0.081	0.069	0.051	0.038	0.018	0.009	0.005	0.002	0.001	0.001	18
0.083	0.070	0.060	0.043	0.031	0.014	0.007	0.003	0.002	0.001		19
0.073	0.061	0.051	0.037	0.026	0.012	0.005	0.002	0.001	0.001		20
0.064	0.053	0.044	0.031	0.022	0.009	0.004	0.002	0.001			21
0.056	0.046	0.038	0.026	0.018	0.007	0.003	0.001	0.001			22
0.049	0.040	0.033	0.022	0.015	0.006	0.002	0.001				23
0.043	0.035	0.028	0.019	0.013	0.005	0.002	0.001				24
0.038	0.030	0.024	0.016	0.010	0.004	0.001	0.001				25
0.033	0.026	0.021	0.014	0.009	0.003	0.001					26
0.029	0.023	0.018	0.011	0.007	0.002	0.001					27
0.026	0.020	0.016	0.010	0.006	0.002	0.001					28
0.022	0.017	0.014	0.008	0.005	0.002						29
0.020	0.015	0.012	0.007	0.004	0.001						30
0.005	0.004	0.003	0.001	0.001							40
0.001	0.001	0.001									50

Table B-2 *Present Value of Annuity $1*

Periods	1%	2%	3%	4%	5%	6%	7%	8%	9%	10%	12%
1	0.990	0.980	0.971	0.962	0.952	0.943	0.935	0.926	0.917	0.909	0.893
2	1.970	1.942	1.913	1.886	1.859	1.833	1.808	1.783	1.759	1.736	1.690
3	2.941	2.884	2.829	2.775	2.723	2.673	2.624	2.577	2.531	2.487	2.402
4	3.902	3.808	3.717	3.630	3.546	3.465	3.387	3.312	3.240	3.170	3.037
5	4.853	4.713	4.580	4.452	4.329	4.212	4.100	3.993	3.890	3.791	3.605
6	5.795	5.601	5.417	5.242	5.076	4.917	4.767	4.623	4.486	4.355	4.111
7	6.728	6.472	6.230	6.002	5.786	5.582	5.389	5.206	5.033	4.868	4.564
8	7.652	7.325	7.020	6.733	6.463	6.210	5.971	5.747	5.535	5.335	4.968
9	8.566	8.162	7.786	7.435	7.108	6.802	6.515	6.247	5.995	5.759	5.328
10	9.471	8.983	8.530	8.111	7.722	7.360	7.024	6.710	6.418	6.145	5.650
11	10.368	9.787	9.253	8.760	8.306	7.887	7.499	7.139	6.805	6.495	5.938
12	11.255	10.575	9.954	9.385	8.863	8.384	7.943	7.536	7.161	6.814	6.194
13	12.134	11.348	10.635	9.986	9.394	8.853	8.358	7.904	7.487	7.103	6.424
14	13.004	12.106	11.296	10.563	9.899	9.295	8.745	8.244	7.786	7.367	6.628
15	13.865	12.849	11.938	11.118	10.380	9.712	9.108	8.559	8.061	7.606	6.811
16	14.718	13.578	12.561	11.652	10.838	10.106	9.447	8.851	8.313	7.824	6.974
17	15.562	14.292	13.166	12.166	11.274	10.477	9.763	9.122	8.544	8.022	7.120
18	16.398	14.992	13.754	12.659	11.690	10.828	10.059	9.372	8.756	8.201	7.250
19	17.226	15.678	14.324	13.134	12.085	11.158	10.336	9.604	8.950	8.365	7.366
20	18.046	16.351	14.878	13.590	12.462	11.470	10.594	9.818	9.129	8.514	7.469
21	18.857	17.011	15.415	14.029	12.821	11.764	10.836	10.017	9.292	8.649	7.562
22	19.660	17.658	15.937	14.451	13.163	12.042	11.061	10.201	9.442	8.772	7.645
23	20.456	18.292	16.444	14.857	13.489	12.303	11.272	10.371	9.580	8.883	7.718
24	21.243	18.914	16.936	15.247	13.799	12.550	11.469	10.529	9.707	8.985	7.784
25	22.023	19.523	17.413	15.622	14.094	12.783	11.654	10.675	9.823	9.077	7.843
26	22.795	20.121	17.877	15.983	14.375	13.003	11.826	10.810	9.929	9.161	7.896
27	23.560	20.707	18.327	16.330	14.643	13.211	11.987	10.935	10.027	9.237	7.943
28	24.316	21.281	18.764	16.663	14.898	13.406	12.137	11.051	10.116	9.307	7.984
29	25.066	21.844	19.189	16.984	15.141	13.591	12.278	11.158	10.198	9.370	8.022
30	25.808	22.396	19.600	17.292	15.373	13.765	12.409	11.258	10.274	9.427	8.055
40	32.835	27.355	23.115	19.793	17.159	15.046	13.332	11.925	10.757	9.779	8.244
50	39.196	31.424	25.730	21.482	18.256	15.762	13.801	12.234	10.962	9.915	8.305

Table B-2   *(cont'd)*

					Present Value						
14%	15%	16%	18%	20%	25%	30%	35%	40%	45%	50%	Periods
0.877	0.870	0.862	0.847	0.833	0.800	0.769	0.741	0.714	0.690	0.667	1
1.647	1.626	1.605	1.566	1.528	1.440	1.361	1.289	1.224	1.165	1.111	2
2.322	2.283	2.246	2.174	2.106	1.952	1.816	1.696	1.589	1.493	1.407	3
2.914	2.855	2.798	2.690	2.589	2.362	2.166	1.997	1.849	1.720	1.605	4
3.433	3.352	3.274	3.127	2.991	2.689	2.436	2.220	2.035	1.876	1.737	5
3.889	3.784	3.685	3.498	3.326	2.951	2.643	2.385	2.168	1.983	1.824	6
4.288	4.160	4.039	3.812	3.605	3.161	2.802	2.508	2.263	2.057	1.883	7
4.639	4.487	4.344	4.078	3.837	3.329	2.925	2.598	2.331	2.109	1.922	8
4.946	4.772	4.607	4.303	4.031	3.463	3.019	2.665	2.379	2.144	1.948	9
5.216	5.019	4.833	4.494	4.192	3.571	3.092	2.715	2.414	2.168	1.965	10
5.453	5.234	5.029	4.656	4.327	3.656	3.147	2.752	2.438	2.185	1.977	11
5.660	5.421	5.197	4.793	4.439	3.725	3.190	2.779	2.456	2.197	1.985	12
5.842	5.583	5.342	4.910	4.533	3.780	3.223	2.799	2.469	2.204	1.990	13
6.002	5.724	5.468	5.008	4.611	3.824	3.249	2.814	2.478	2.210	1.993	14
6.142	5.847	5.575	5.092	4.675	3.859	3.268	2.825	2.484	2.214	1.995	15
6.265	5.954	5.669	5.162	4.730	3.887	3.283	2.834	2.489	2.216	1.997	16
6.373	6.047	5.749	5.222	4.775	3.910	3.295	2.840	2.492	2.218	1.998	17
6.467	6.128	5.818	5.273	4.812	3.928	3.304	2.844	2.494	2.219	1.999	18
6.550	6.198	5.877	5.316	4.844	3.942	3.311	2.848	2.496	2.220	1.999	19
6.623	6.259	5.929	5.353	4.870	3.954	3.316	2.850	2.497	2.221	1.999	20
6.687	6.312	5.973	5.384	4.891	3.963	3.320	2.852	2.498	2.221	2.000	21
6.743	6.359	6.011	5.410	4.909	3.970	3.323	2.853	2.498	2.222	2.000	22
6.792	6.399	6.044	5.432	4.925	3.976	3.325	2.854	2.499	2.222	2.000	23
6.835	6.434	6.073	5.451	4.937	3.981	3.327	2.855	2.499	2.222	2.000	24
6.873	6.464	6.097	5.467	4.948	3.985	3.329	2.856	2.499	2.222	2.000	25
6.906	6.491	6.118	5.480	4.956	3.988	3.330	2.856	2.500	2.222	2.000	26
6.935	6.514	6.136	5.492	4.964	3.990	3.331	2.856	2.500	2.222	2.000	27
6.961	6.534	6.152	5.502	4.970	3.992	3.331	2.857	2.500	2.222	2.000	28
6.983	6.551	6.166	5.510	4.975	3.994	3.332	2.857	2.500	2.222	2.000	29
7.003	6.566	6.177	5.517	4.979	3.995	3.332	2.857	2.500	2.222	2.000	30
7.105	6.642	6.234	5.548	4.997	3.999	3.333	2.857	2.500	2.222	2.000	40
7.133	6.661	6.246	5.554	4.999	4.000	3.333	2.857	2.500	2.222	2.000	50

Table B-3 *Future Value of $1*

Periods	1%	2%	3%	4%	5%	6%	7%	8%	9%	10%	12%	14%	15%
1	1.010	1.020	1.030	1.040	1.050	1.060	1.070	1.080	1.090	1.100	1.120	1.140	1.150
2	1.020	1.040	1.061	1.082	1.103	1.124	1.145	1.166	1.188	1.210	1.254	1.300	1.323
3	1.030	1.061	1.093	1.125	1.158	1.191	1.225	1.260	1.295	1.331	1.405	1.482	1.521
4	1.041	1.082	1.126	1.170	1.216	1.262	1.311	1.360	1.412	1.464	1.574	1.689	1.749
5	1.051	1.104	1.159	1.217	1.276	1.338	1.403	1.469	1.539	1.611	1.762	1.925	2.011
6	1.062	1.126	1.194	1.265	1.340	1.419	1.501	1.587	1.677	1.772	1.974	2.195	2.313
7	1.072	1.149	1.230	1.316	1.407	1.504	1.606	1.714	1.828	1.949	2.211	2.502	2.660
8	1.083	1.172	1.267	1.369	1.477	1.594	1.718	1.851	1.993	2.144	2.476	2.853	3.059
9	1.094	1.195	1.305	1.423	1.551	1.689	1.838	1.999	2.172	2.358	2.773	3.252	3.518
10	1.105	1.219	1.344	1.480	1.629	1.791	1.967	2.159	2.367	2.594	3.106	3.707	4.046
11	1.116	1.243	1.384	1.539	1.710	1.898	2.105	2.332	2.580	2.853	3.479	4.226	4.652
12	1.127	1.268	1.426	1.601	1.796	2.012	2.252	2.518	2.813	3.138	3.896	4.818	5.350
13	1.138	1.294	1.469	1.665	1.886	2.133	2.410	2.720	3.066	3.452	4.363	5.492	6.153
14	1.149	1.319	1.513	1.732	1.980	2.261	2.579	2.937	3.342	3.798	4.887	6.261	7.076
15	1.161	1.346	1.558	1.801	2.079	2.397	2.759	3.172	3.642	4.177	5.474	7.138	8.137
16	1.173	1.373	1.605	1.873	2.183	2.540	2.952	3.426	3.970	4.595	6.130	8.137	9.358
17	1.184	1.400	1.653	1.948	2.292	2.693	3.159	3.700	4.328	5.054	6.866	9.276	10.76
18	1.196	1.428	1.702	2.026	2.407	2.854	3.380	3.996	4.717	5.560	7.690	10.58	12.38
19	1.208	1.457	1.754	2.107	2.527	3.026	3.617	4.316	5.142	6.116	8.613	12.06	14.23
20	1.220	1.486	1.806	2.191	2.653	3.207	3.870	4.661	5.604	6.728	9.646	13.74	16.37
21	1.232	1.516	1.860	2.279	2.786	3.400	4.141	5.034	6.109	7.400	10.80	15.67	18.82
22	1.245	1.546	1.916	2.370	2.925	3.604	4.430	5.437	6.659	8.140	12.10	17.86	21.64
23	1.257	1.577	1.974	2.465	3.072	3.820	4.741	5.871	7.258	8.954	13.55	20.36	24.89
24	1.270	1.608	2.033	2.563	3.225	4.049	5.072	6.341	7.911	9.850	15.18	23.21	28.63
25	1.282	1.641	2.094	2.666	3.386	4.292	5.427	6.848	8.623	10.83	17.00	26.46	32.92
26	1.295	1.673	2.157	2.772	3.556	4.549	5.807	7.396	9.399	11.92	19.04	30.17	37.86
27	1.308	1.707	2.221	2.883	3.733	4.822	6.214	7.988	10.25	13.11	21.32	34.39	43.54
28	1.321	1.741	2.288	2.999	3.920	5.112	6.649	8.627	11.17	14.42	23.88	39.20	50.07
29	1.335	1.776	2.357	3.119	4.116	5.418	7.114	9.317	12.17	15.86	26.75	44.69	57.58
30	1.348	1.811	2.427	3.243	4.322	5.743	7.612	10.06	13.27	17.45	29.96	50.95	66.21
40	1.489	2.208	3.262	4.801	7.040	10.29	14.97	21.72	31.41	45.26	93.05	188.9	267.9
50	1.645	2.692	4.384	7.107	11.47	18.42	29.46	46.90	74.36	117.4	289.0	700.2	1,084

Table B-4 *Future Value of Annuity of $1*

Periods	1%	2%	3%	4%	5%	Future Value 6%	7%	8%	9%	10%	12%	14%	15%
1	1.000	1.000	1.000	1.000	1.000	1.000	1.000	1.000	1.000	1.000	1.000	1.000	1.000
2	2.010	2.020	2.030	2.040	2.050	2.060	2.070	2.080	2.090	2.100	2.120	2.140	2.150
3	3.030	3.060	3.091	3.122	3.153	3.184	3.215	3.246	3.278	3.310	3.374	3.440	3.473
4	4.060	4.122	4.184	4.246	4.310	4.375	4.440	4.506	4.573	4.641	4.779	4.921	4.993
5	5.101	5.204	5.309	5.416	5.526	5.637	5.751	5.867	5.985	6.105	6.353	6.610	6.742
6	6.152	6.308	6.468	6.633	6.802	6.975	7.153	7.336	7.523	7.716	8.115	8.536	8.754
7	7.214	7.434	7.662	7.898	8.142	8.394	8.654	8.923	9.200	9.487	10.09	10.73	11.07
8	8.286	8.583	8.892	9.214	9.549	9.897	10.26	10.64	11.03	11.44	12.30	13.23	13.73
9	9.369	9.755	10.16	10.58	11.03	11.49	11.98	12.49	13.02	13.58	14.78	16.09	16.79
10	10.46	10.95	11.46	12.01	12.58	13.18	13.82	14.49	15.19	15.94	17.55	19.34	20.30
11	11.57	12.17	12.81	13.49	14.21	14.97	15.78	16.65	17.56	18.53	20.65	23.04	24.35
12	12.68	13.41	14.19	15.03	15.92	16.87	17.89	18.98	20.14	21.38	24.13	27.27	29.00
13	13.81	14.68	15.62	16.63	17.71	18.88	20.14	21.50	22.95	24.52	28.03	32.09	34.35
14	14.95	15.97	17.09	18.29	19.60	21.02	22.55	24.21	26.02	27.98	32.39	37.58	40.50
15	16.10	17.29	18.60	20.02	21.58	23.28	25.13	27.15	29.36	31.77	37.28	43.84	47.58
16	17.26	18.64	20.16	21.82	23.66	25.67	27.89	30.32	33.00	35.95	42.75	50.98	55.72
17	18.43	20.01	21.76	23.70	25.84	28.21	30.84	33.75	36.97	40.54	48.88	59.12	65.08
18	19.61	21.41	23.41	25.65	28.13	30.91	34.00	37.45	41.30	45.60	55.75	68.39	75.84
19	20.81	22.84	25.12	27.67	30.54	33.76	37.38	41.45	46.02	51.16	63.44	78.97	88.21
20	22.02	24.30	26.87	29.78	33.07	36.79	41.00	45.76	51.16	57.28	72.05	91.02	102.4
21	23.24	25.78	28.68	31.97	35.72	39.99	44.87	50.42	56.76	64.00	81.70	104.8	118.8
22	24.47	27.30	30.54	34.25	38.51	43.39	49.01	55.46	62.87	71.40	92.50	120.4	137.6
23	25.72	28.85	32.45	36.62	41.43	47.00	53.44	60.89	69.53	79.54	104.6	138.3	159.3
24	26.97	30.42	34.43	39.08	44.50	50.82	58.18	66.76	76.79	88.50	118.2	158.7	184.2
25	28.24	32.03	36.46	41.65	47.73	54.86	63.25	73.11	84.70	98.35	133.3	181.9	212.8
26	29.53	33.67	38.55	44.31	51.11	59.16	68.68	79.95	93.32	109.2	150.3	208.3	245.7
27	30.82	35.34	40.71	47.08	54.67	63.71	74.48	87.35	102.7	121.1	169.4	238.5	283.6
28	32.13	37.05	42.93	49.97	58.40	68.53	80.70	95.34	113.0	134.2	190.7	272.9	327.1
29	33.45	38.79	45.22	52.97	62.32	73.64	87.35	104.0	124.1	148.6	214.6	312.1	377.2
30	34.78	40.57	47.58	56.08	66.44	79.06	94.46	113.3	136.3	164.5	241.3	356.8	434.7
40	48.89	60.40	75.40	95.03	120.8	154.8	199.6	259.1	337.9	442.6	767.1	1,342	1,779
50	64.46	84.58	112.8	152.7	209.3	290.3	406.5	573.8	815.1	1,164	2,400	4,995	7,218

Appendix C

Published
Financial Statements

CORPORATE PROFILE

Schneider Corporation of Kitchener, Ontario is one of Canada's largest producers of premium quality food products. The Corporation was founded in 1890 by John Metz Schneider who began making pork sausage in his home. Today, as a publicly owned corporation, Schneider Corporation has over 3,300 employees manufacturing and selling a wide variety of meat, poultry, cheese and baked goods products. These products are sold throughout Canada, and to the United States, Japan and other foreign markets.

The majority of the Corporation's meat processing is done through its subsidiary, J.M. Schneider Inc. which operates plants in Winnipeg, Manitoba, and Kitchener, Ontario. Meat products are also manufactured by the Corporation's subsidiary, Charcuterie Roy Inc. in St-Anselme, Quebec and by a joint venture company, National Meats Inc. in Toronto, Ontario

Cheese products are manufactured at J.M. Schneider Inc. processing plants in Millbank and Winchester, Ontario.

The Corporation has a 50% joint venture interest in Horizon Poultry Products Inc. Operations include a major hatchery in Hanover, Ontario, and manufacturing and processing facilities in Paris, Ayr and Kitchener, Ontario.

Mother Jackson's Open Kitchens Limited, also a subsidiary of the Corporation, manufactures a variety of baked goods products at its facility in Port Perry, Ontario. Schneider products are warehoused and shipped through major distribution centres in Vancouver, British Columbia, Calgary, Alberta, Winnipeg, Manitoba and Kitchener, Ontario.

In 1991, Schneider Corporation had sales of $630,966,000 and assets of $175,466,000. The Corporation's most valuable asset is its reputation for providing consumers with the finest quality food products available in the marketplace.

MANAGEMENT'S REPORT

Management of Schneider Corporation is responsible for the integrity and objectivity of the financial statements and all other information contained in the Annual Report. The financial statemetns have been prepared in accordance with generally accepted accounting principles and are based on management's best information and judgments.

In fulfilling its responsibilities, management has devleoped internal control systems and procedures designed to provide reasonable assurance that the Corporation's assets are safeguarded, that transactions are executed in accordance with appropriate authorization and that accounting records may be relied upon to properly reflect the Corporation's business transactions. To augment the internal control systems, the Corporation maintains an internal audit department which evaluates company operations and formally reports on the adequacy and effectiveness of the controls and procedures to the Audit Committee of the Board of Directors.

The Audit Committee of the Board of Directors is composed of a majority of outside directors. The committee meets periodically and independently with management, the internal auditors and the shareholders' auditors to discuss the Corporation's financial reporting and interanl controls. Both the internal auditors and the independent external auditors have unrestricted access to the Audit Committee.

Management recognizes its responsibility for conducting the Corporation's affairs in the best interest of its shareholders. The responsibility is characterized in the Code of Conduct signed by each management employee which provides for compliance with laws of each jurisdiction in which the Corporation operates and for observance of rules of ethical business conduct.

Douglas W. Dodds
President and Chief Executive Officer

Gerald A. Hooper
Vice-President and Chief Financial Officer

AUDITORS' REPORT

To the Shareholders

We have audited the consolidated balance sheets of Schneider Corporation as at October 26, 1991 and October 27, 1990 and the consolidated statements of earnings, retained earnings and changes in financial position for the years then ended. These financial statements are the responsibility of the Corporation's management. Our responsibility is to express an opinion on these financial statements based on our audits.

We conducted our audits in accordance with generally accepted auditing standards. Those standards require that we plan and perform an audit to obtain reasonable assurance whether the financial statements are free of material misstatement. An audit includes examining, on a test basis, evidence supporting the amounts and disclosures in the financial statements. An audit also includes assessing the accounting principles used and significant estimates made by management, as well as evaluating the overall financial statement presentation.

In our opinion, these consolidated financial statements present fairly, in all material respects, the financial position of Schneider Corporation as at October 26, 1991 and October 27, 1990 and the results of its operations and the changes in its financial position for the years then ended in accordance with generally accepted accounting principles.

Peat Marwick Thorne

Chartered Accountants, Kitchener, Canada, November 29, 1991

CONSOLIDATED BALANCE SHEETS

October 26, 1991 and October 27, 1990
(in thousands of dollars)

Assets	1991	1990
		(restated)
Current assets:		
Accounts receivable	$33,379	$29,556
Inventories	38,811	44,163
Income taxes recoverable	—	1,872
Current portion of loans receivable	463	—
Other	2,405	2,739
Total current assets	75,058	78,330
Property, plant and equipment	89,352	81,077
Other assets:		
Loans receivable	2,606	1,173
Production licences and rights	3,800	2,825
Intangible assets	4,650	3,115
Total other assets	11,056	7,113
Total assets	$175,466	$166,520

Liabilities and Shareholders' Equity	1991	1990
		(restated)
Current liabilities:		
Bank advances	$4,894	$22,695
Outstanding cheques	4,578	8,462
Accounts payable and accrued liabilities	34,808	31,109
Income taxes payable	4,458	—
Principal due within one year on debentures and loans	5,569	3,496
Total current liabilities	54,307	65,762
Debentures and loans	44,900	30,490
Other liabilities:		
Deferred income taxes	5,893	8,102
Deferred gains	1,814	—
Deferred pension liability	1,038	943
Minority interest	568	—
Total other liabilities	9,313	9,045
Shareholders' equity:		
Capital stock	11,529	9,668
Retained earnings	55,417	51,555
Total shareholders' equity	66,946	61,223
Total liabilities and shareholders' equity	$175,466	$166,520

The accompanying notes are an integral part of these statements.

On behalf of the Board:

Director   Director

CONSOLIDATED STATEMENTS OF EARNINGS

Years ended October 26, 1991 and October 27, 1990
(in thousands of dollars, except per share amounts)

	1991	1990
		(restated)
Sales $630,966	$627,797	
Expenses:		
Cost of products sold	559,470	567,411
Selling, marketing, and administrative	46,091	44,726
Depreciation and amortization	9,419	9,661
	614,980	621,798
Earnings from operations	15,986	5,999
Interest expense	6,951	7,910
Earnings (loss) before income taxes	9,035	(1,911)
Income taxes (recovery)	3,971	(234)
Net earnings (loss)	$ 5,064	$ (1,677)
Earnings (loss) per share	$ 1.86	$ (.62)

CONSOLIDATED STATEMENTS OF RETAINED EARNINGS

Years ended October 26, 1991 and October 27, 1990
(in thousands of dollars)

	1991	1990
		(restated)
Balance, beginning of year:		
As previously reproted	$50,987	$54,414
Adjustment of prior year's earnings	568	—
As restated	51,555	54,414
Net earnings (loss)	5,064	(1,677)
	56,619	52,737
Dividends:		
Class A shares	1,037	1,017
Common shares	165	165
	1,202	1,182
Balance, end of year	$55,417	$51,555

The accompanying notes are an integral part of these statements.

CONSOLIDATED STATEMENTS OF CHANGES IN FINANCIAL POSITION

Years ended October 26, 1991 and October 27, 1990
(in thousands of dollars)

	1991	1990
		(restated)
Operating activities:		
Cash from operations	**$12,285**	$ 8,327
Net change in non-cash working capital balances relating to operations	**9,372**	2,624
Cash provided by operating activities	**21,657**	10,951
Investment activities:		
Acquisition of subsidiaries and joint venture, less cash received of $1,104	**(13,874)**	—
Additions to property, plant and equipment	**(5,475)**	(15,952)
Proceeds on sale of equipment	**168**	205
Cash used in investment activities	**(19,181)**	(15,747)
Financing activities:		
Proceeds from loans	**15,450**	3,738
Transfer of assets to joint venture, net of deferred gains	**3,060**	—
Proceeds from issue of shares	**1,861**	1,229
Decrease (increase) in loans receivable	**337**	(80)
Decrease in debentures and loans	**(4,181)**	(2,397)
Dividends	**(1,202)**	(1,182)
Cash provided by financing activities	**15,325**	1,308
Increase (decrease) in bank advances	**(17,801)**	3,488
Bank advances, beginning of year	**22,695**	19,207
Bank advances, end of year	**$ 4,894**	$22,695
Cash from operations is derived as follows:		
Net earnings (loss)	**$ 5,064**	$ (1,677)
Adjustment for non-cash items:		
Depreciation and amortization	**9,419**	9,661
Deferred income taxes (reduction)	**(2,692)**	46
Loss on sale of equipment	**387**	93
Deferred pension liability	**95**	204
Minority interest in earnings of subsidiary	**12**	—
	$12,285	$ 8,327

The accompanying notes are an integral part of these statements.

NOTES TO CONSOLIDATED FINANCIAL STATEMENTS

Years ended October 26, 1991 and October 27, 1990
(tabular amounts only in thousands of dollars)

1. **Significant accounting policies:**

    (a) Basis of consolidation:
    The consolidated financial statements include the accounts of the Corporation and all of its subsidiaries and the Corporation's proportionate share of the assets, liabilities, revenues and expenses of joint ventures.

    (b) Inventories:
    Products are valued at the lower of cost and net realizable value. Since most products can be sold at any stage in their production, it is not practical to segregate them into raw materials, work in process or finished goods. Cost includes laid down material cost, manufacturing labour and certain elements of overhead to the stage of production completion. Net realizable value is based on the adjusted wholesale trading price at the balance sheet date.

    Certain raw materials and supplies, which include packaging, maintenance and manufacturing materials, are valued at the lower of cost and replacement cost.

    (c) Property, plant and equipment:
    Property, plant and equipment are stated at cost which includes capitalized interest incurred on major projects during the period of construction. Depreciation is provided on a straight-line bais to amortize the cost of the assets over their estimated useful life with estimated useful lives not to exceed certain limits. Depreciation is not provided on assets under construction.

	Maximum useful lives	Annual rates of depreciation
Buildings of solid constuction	40 years	2.5% to 5%
Buildings of frame construction and im proved areas	25 years	4% to 25%
Machinery and equipment	15 years	7% to 25%

    (d) Other assets:
    Production licences and rights and intangible assets are being amortized on a straight-line basis over their estimated lives, such amortization period not exceeding forty years. The Corporation recognizes permanent impairment in the value of these assets by additional charges against earnings.

    (e) Other liabilities:
    Deferred gains, which relate to asset transfers to joint ventures, will be included in income when amounts receivable from a joint venture partner are repaid or through amortization over the remaining estimated useful lives of the transferred assets.

    Pension obligations are determined by independent actuarial valuation using the accrued benefit method. Pension costs related to current service are charged to earnings as services are rendered, and past service costs, as well as variations between fund experience and the actuarial estiamtes, are amortized over the expected average remaining service life of each employee group.

    (f) Earnings per share:
    Earnings per share are calculated on the weighted average number of all classes of shares outstanding during the year.

2.   **Acquisitions:**

During 1991, the Corporation increased its investment in Mother Jackson's Open Kitchens Limited to a 72% interest and made the following acquisitions directly or through a 50% owned joint venture company:

Company name	Nature of business	Effective accquisition date	Voting interest acquired
Chickens, Inc. and Saville Food Products Inc.	Poultry slaughter	November 30, 1990	50%
Charcuterie Roy Inc.	Processed and speciality meats	August 2, 1991	100%
National Meats Inc.	Ground meats	August 6, 1991	50%
Mother Jackson's Open Kitchens Limited	Baked goods	August 31, 1991	22%

The Corporation acquired a 50% interest in a joint venture company, National Meats Inc., by contributing assets with a book value of $6,120,000. In addition to the joint venture interest, the Corporation received assets from the joint venture partner consisting primarily of cash and notes receivable. The fair value of the joint venture interest and the assets received exceeded the Corporation's share of the book value of the assets contributed and this difference has been recorded in the financial statements as a deferred gain.

Details of other acquisitions are as follows:

Net assets acquired at assigned values:	
Property, plant and equipment	$15,586
Other assets	1,126
Net working capital	1,770
Other liabilities	(7,652)
Excess cost of shares over assigned values of net assets	1,644
	12,474
Less minority interest	556
	$11,918

Consideration given at fair value:	
Cash	$ 8,345
Loans payable within one year	2,000
65,534 Class A shares	1,573
	$11,918

The acquisitions have been accounted for by the purchase method with the results of operations included in these financial statements from the dates of acquisition.

The Corporation is committed to paying additional consideration for the shares of Charcuterie Roy Inc. in each of the next five years based on earnings of that company during the period, with total additional consideration not to exceed $4,750,000. The additional consideration will be recorded as an additional cost of the purchase as it becomes determinable.

3.   **Joint ventures:**

The Corporation's joint venture investments include Schneider Horizon Inc., Mother Jackson's Open Kitchens Limited to the date of acquisition of control on August 31, 1991, and National Meats Inc., from the date of acquisition on August 6, 1991.

NOTES TO CONSOLIDATED FINANCIAL STATEMENTS

Years ended October 26, 1991 and October 27, 1990
(tabular amounts only in thousands of dollars)

Consolidated financial statements for the Corporation include a proportionate share of the assets, liabilities, revenues and expenses of these joint ventures as follows:

	1991	1990
Assets	$20,909	$21,817
Liabilities	14,718	14,564
Sales:		
Intercompany	40,254	25,727
Other	10,893	9,609
	51,147	35,336
Expenses, excluding income taxes	52,625	33,738

4. Property, plant and equipment:

	Cost	Accumulated depreciation	1991 Net book value	1990 Net book value
Land and improved areas	$ 5,162	$ 606	$ 4,556	$ 4,643
Buildings and leasehold improvements	66,214	28,856	37,358	32,278
Machinery and equipment	100,048	57,727	42,321	36,042
Assets under construction	5,117	—	5,117	8,114
	$176,541	$87,189	$89,352	$81,077

Interest capitalized on major projects during the period of construction was $nil in 1991 (1990 - $595,000). The Board of Directors has approved capital expenditures on future projects of $5,355,000.

5. Loans receivable:

	1991	1990
Loan receivable, interest at bank prime less 1/4%, maturing August 6, 1996	$2,213	$ —
Non-interest bearing loans receivable from companies which are related by virture of common management with joint venture companies, due on demand but not expected to be repaid prior to October 31, 1992	856	1,173
	3,069	1,173
Principal included in current assets	463	—
	$2,606	$1,173

6. Debentures and loans:

	1991	1990
Loans payable, interest at 7.875% to 12.15%, maturing at dates from December, 1991 to August, 1996	$30,053	$13,380
12.3% Sinking fund debentures, maturing Aug. 15, 1995	8,500	9,800
Bank term loans, interest at bank prime rate, repayable in monthly principal instalments	5,576	5,256
10.75% Sinking fund debentures, maturing Feb. 1, 1997	4,500	4,950
Mortgages payable at lender's cost of borrowing plus 2.25%, maturing July, 1999	920	—
Mortgages payable at bank prime rate plus 1.25%, maturing November, 1994	920	—
8.5% Sinking fund debentures, repaid during the year	—	600
	50,469	33,986
Principal included in current liabilities	5,569	3,496
	$44,900	$30,490
Interest for the year	$ 4,957	$ 3,602

Principal due within each of the next five years is as follows:

1992	$ 5,569
1993	3,911
1994	16,231
1995	6,439
1996	14,676

The debentures are secured by fixed and specific charges on certain assets and floating charges on all assets of the Corporation.

A trust indenture securing the sinking fund debentures contains certain covenants some of which limit the creation of additional debt and the entering into of long-term leases and restricts the use of proceeds from the sale of a substantial part of the Corporation's property, plant and equipment. The Corporation has undertaken not to declare or pay dividends or otherwise make changes in its capital which would have the effect of reducing the Corporation's equity below $50,000,000. In addition, the Corporation is required to maintain certain other financial ratios.

Bank term loans and certain bank advances are secured by an assignment of accounts receivable of a joint venture company as well as first fixed charge debentures, of which the Corporation's proportionate share is $9,500,000, covering all assets of the joint venture.

Loans payable of $5,600,000 and certain bank advances are secured by a fixed charge debenture in the amount of $3,500,000 covering property and plant of a subsidiary company, as well as an assignment of short-term investments and a general security agreement covering all assets of the subsidiary.

7. **Capital stock:**

	1991	1990
Authorized:		
5,401,000 Class A non-voting shares		
373,627 common shares		
Issued:		
2,418,722 Class A shares (1990 - 2,341,188)	**$11,295**	$9,434
373,627 common shares	**234**	234
	$11,529	$9668

The holders of the Class A shares are entitled toa 24¢ cumulative annual dividend and equal participation with the holders of common shares in annual dividends in excess of 24¢ and in any distribution of assets of the Corporation to its shareholders.

The Class A shares are restricted shares in that they are generally non-voting and only vote in very limited circumstances on matters respecting the attributes of the class itself, or in relation to the common shares where class approval is specifically required.

A "coat-tail" provision has been attached to the Class A shares which is designed to ensure that all holders of the Class A shares have an equal opportunity toarticipate with the holders of the common shares in any premium paid on a take-over bid.

During the year, the Corporation issued 12, 000 Class A shares to participants of its employee Share Purchase Plan for cash consideration of $288,000 and 65,534 Class A shares in connection with the acquisition of a company for consideration of $1,573,000. In 1990, the Corporation issued 63,660 Class A shares to participants of its employee Share Purchase Plan for cash consideration of $1,229,000.

NOTES TO CONSOLIDATED FINANCIAL STATEMENTS

Years ended October 26, 1991 and October 27, 1990
(tabular amounts only in thousands of dollars)

8. Income taxes:

The Corporation's effective income tax rate on earnings (loss) is made up as follows:	1991 %	1990 %
Combined basic Canadian federal and provincial rate (recovery)	44.3	(44.3)
Adjustment in income tax rate resulting from:		
Manufacturing and processing deduction	(5.3)	4.3
Ontario manufacturing and processing current cost adjustment	(2.0)	(4.1)
Non-deductible expenses	2.9	12.5
Large corporations tax in excess of federal surtax	—	9.0
Other	4.0	10.4
Effective income tax rate (recovery)	43.9	(12.2)

9. Prior year's adjustment:

As a result of a ruling by the United States International Trade Commission during the year, countervailing duty charges on Canadian fresh, chilled and frozen pork exports to the United States were reversed. The effect of the change on the prior year, which has been included in retained earnings, amounted to $568,000, net of income taxes of $425,000. Comparative figures have been restated to reflect this change.

10. Pension plans:

The Corporation maintains defined benefit pension plans which provided pension benefits for most employees, based on years of service and contributions. The comparison of benefit obligations with assets of the pension plans is as follows:

	1991	1990
Pension plan assets at market value	$115,634	$ 96,667
Estimated present value of pension plan obligations	126,831	116,957

11. Commitments:

(a) The Corporation has issued letters of credit in the amount of $265,000 (1990 - $1,836,000).

(b) The following is a schedule of future rental payments required under operating leases as of the year end:

1992	$ 4,585
1993	2,380
1994	1,496
1995	803
1996	519
Later years	1,623
	$11,406

12. Segmented information:

The Corporation's principal business activity is the processing and distribution of meat and related food products. All of the Corporation's operations, employees and assets are located in Canada.

Sales to customers in foreign countries amounted to $47,520,000 in 1991 (1990 - $64,533,000).

13. Other information:

(a) The Corporation is incorporated under the laws of Ontario

		1991	1990
(b)	Depreciation	**$9,179**	$9,423
	Amortization	**240**	238

(c)   Certain 1990 figures have been reclassified to conform with those presented in the 1991 financial statements.

(d)   The Corporation has signed a letter of intent to study the feasibility of forming a national distribution joint venture with Maple Leaf Foods Inc. This study is now completed and is currently being reviewed by both companies.

TEN YEAR STATISTICAL REVIEW

(thousands of dollars except where noted)

	1991	*1990	1989	1988	1987	1986	1985	1984	1983	1982
Operations:										
Sales	$630,966	627,797	619,168	597,932	683,934	648,468	648,598	645,558	590,074	581,071
Depreciation and amortization	9,419	9,661	8,195	7,543	6,688	6,458	7,072	5,960	5,978	5,861
Salaries, wages and employee benefits	138,491	132,688	134,549	122,372	121,780	117,129	126,791	128,316	108,508	100,515
Interest expense	6,951	7,910	4,861	4,182	4,774	4,285	5,303	4,502	3,557	5,375
Income taxes (recovery)	3,971	(234)	516	1,790	4,502	883	832	4,245	4,222	2,238
Earnings (loss) before extraordinary items	5,064	(1,677)	20	2,007	5,612	1,102	2,009	5,766	5,272	2,887
Earnings (loss) before extraordinary items as a percent of sales	0.80	(0.27)	0.00	0.34	0.82	0.17	0.31	0.89	0.89	0.50
Net earnigns (loss)	5,064	(1,677)	20	2,007	5,612	1,102	(2,036)	5,766	5,272	2,887
Net earnings (loss) as a percent of sales	0.80	(0.27)	0.00	0.34	0.82	0.17	(0.31)	0.89	0.89	0.50
Cash flow:										
Cash from operations	12,285	8,327	8,291	11,160	16,484	5,357	8,053	11,067	10,834	8,337
Capital expenditures	5,475	15,952	16,722	10,249	8,001	5,072	6,983	5,254	5,741	3,329
Dividends paid	1,202	1,182	1,167	1,167	1,167	1,167	1,167	1,167	1,167	1,162
Financial position:										
Working capital	20,751	12,568	19,782	23,219	25,604	21,995	22,786	24,336	22,487	22,333
Working capital ratio	1.38	1.19	1.28	1.43	1.45	1.42	1.41	1.49	1.51	1.62
Total assets	175,466	166,520	171,749	144,338	146,942	137,245	143,814	136,811	126,867	119,715
Long-term debt	44,900	30,490	30,251	17,350	19,538	23,063	24,999	19,259	19,747	24,089
Shareholders' equity, end of year	66,946	61,223	62,853	64,000	63,160	58,715	58,780	61,983	57,384	53,279
Percent return on equity, beginning of year	8.27	(2.67)	0.03	3.18	9.56	1.87	(3.28)	10.05	9.90	5.62
Per share statistics, in dollars:										
Earnings (loss) before extraordinary items	1.86	(0.62)	0.01	0.76	2.12	0.42	0.76	2.17	1.99	1.10
Net earnings (loss)	1.86	(0.62)	0.01	0.76	2.12	0.42	(0.77)	2.17	1.99	1.10
Dividends paid	0.44	0.44	0.44	0.44	0.44	0.44	0.44	0.44	0.44	0.44
Equity, end of year	23.97	22.55	23.71	24.14	23.83	22.15	22.17	23.38	21.64	20.10

*1990 results restated

Glossary

Accelerated depreciation   See Declining-balance method (438)

Account   The detailed record of the changes that have occurred in a particular asset, liability or owner equity during a period (45)

Account format of the balance sheet   Format that lists the assets at the left with liabilities and owner equity at the right (160)

Account payable   A liability that is not written out. Instead, it is backed by the reputation and credit standing of the debtor (14)

Account receivable   An asset, a promise to receive cash from customers to whom the business has sold goods or services (14)

Accounting   The system that measures business activities, processes that information into reports and financial statements, and communicates the findings to decision-makers (2)

Accounting cycle   Process by which accountants produce an entity's financial statements for a specific period (138)

Accounting information system   The combination of personnel, records and procedures that a business uses to meet its need for financial data (256)

Accounting Standards Board (ASB)   The ASB issues Recommendations on accounting (Volume 1 of the *CICA Handbook*) which are the basis of generally accepted accounting principles (GAAP) (527)

Accounts receivable turnover   Ratio of net credit sales to average net accounts receivable. Measures ability to collect cash from credit customers (853)

Accrual-basis accounting   Accounting that recognizes (records) the impact of a business event as it occurs, regardless of whether the transaction affected cash (94)

Accrued expense   An expense that has been incurred but not yet paid in cash (103)

Accrued revenue   A revenue that has been earned but not yet received in cash (104)

Accumulated depreciation   The cumulative sum of all depreciation expense from the date of acquiring a capital asset (102)

Acid-test ratio   Ratio of the sum of cash plus short-term investments plus net current receivables to current liabilities. Tells whether the entity could pay all its current liabilities if they came due immediately. Also called the quick ratio (370, 852)

Adjusted trial balance   A list of all the ledger accounts with their adjusted balances (108)

Adjusting entry   Entry made at the end of the period to assign revenues to the period in which they are earned and expenses to the period in which they are incurred. Adjusting entries help measure the period's income and bring the related asset and liability accounts to correct balances for the financial statements (99)

Aging of accounts receivable   A way to estimate bad debts by analyzing individual accounts receivable according to the length of time they have been due (357)

Allowance for doubtful accounts   A contra account, related to accounts receivable, that holds the estimated amount of collection losses. Also called Allowance for uncollectible accounts (354)

Allowance for uncollectible accounts   Another name for Allowance for doubtful accounts (354)

Allowance method   A method of recording collection losses based on estimates prior to determining that the business will not collect from specific customers (354)

Amortization   The term the *CICA Handbook* uses to describe the systematic changing of the cost of a capital asset; it is often called depreciation when applied to property, plant and equipment and depletion when applied to wasting assets. Also the term used to describe the writing off to expense of intangible assets (449)

Appropriation of retained earnings   Restriction of retained earnings that is recorded by a formal journal entry (661)

Articles of incorporation   The document issued by the federal or provincial government giving the incorporators permission to form a corporation (611)

Asset   An economic resource a business owns that is expected to be of benefit in the future (14)

Auditing   The examination of financial statements by outside accountants, the most significant service that public accountants perform. The conclusion of an audit is the accountant's professional opinion about the financial statements (9)

Authorization of stock   Provision in the articles of incorporation of a corporation that gives the issuing jurisdiction's permission for the corporation to use (that is, to sell) a certain number of shares of stock (618)

Average cost method   Inventory costing method based on the average cost of inventory during the period. Average cost is determined by dividing the cost of goods available for sale by the number of units available (396)

Bad debt expense   Another name for Uncollectible accounts expense (353)

Balance sheet   List of an entity's assets, liabilities and owner equity as of a specific date. Also called the statement of financial position (19)

Balancing the ledgers   Establishing the equality of (a) total debits and total credits in the general ledger, (b) the balance of the accounts receivable control account in the general ledger and the sum of individual customer accounts in the accounts receivable subsidiary ledger, or (c) the balance of the accounts payable control account in the general ledger and the sum of individual creditor accounts in the accounts payable subsidiary ledger (277)

Bank collection   Collection of money by the bank on behalf of a depositor (311)

Bank reconciliation   Process of explaining the reasons for the difference between a depositor's records and the bank's records about the depositor's bank account (309)

Bank statement   Document for a particular bank account showing its beginning and ending balances and listing the month's transactions that affected the account (308)

Batch processing   Computerized accounting for similar transactions in a group or batch (260)

Beginning inventory   Goods left over from the preceding period (393)

Betterment   Expenditure that increases the capacity or efficiency of an asset or extends its useful life. Capital expenditures are debited to an asset account (452)

Board of directors   Group elected by the shareholders to set policy for a corporation and to appoint its officers (613)

Bond discount   Excess of a bond's maturity (par) value over its issue price (693)

Bond indenture   Contract under which bonds are issued (705)

Bond premium   Excess of a bond's issue price over its maturity (par) value (693)

Bond sinking fund   Group of assets segregated for the purpose of retiring bonds payable at maturity (705)

Bonds payable   Groups of notes payable (bonds) issued to multiple lenders called bondholders (691)

Bonus   Amount over and above regular compensation (485)

Book value of a capital asset   The asset's cost less accumulated amortization (or depreciation or depletion) (102)

Book value of stock   Amount of owners' equity on the company's books for each share of its stock (630)

Book value per share of common stock   Common shareholders' equity divided by the number of shares of common stock outstanding (860)

Budgeting   Setting of goals for a business, such as its sales and profits, for a future period (9)

Bylaws   Constitution for governing a corporation (613)

Callable bonds   Bonds that the issuer may call or pay off at a specified price whenever the issuer wants (706)

Canada (or Quebec) Pension Plan   All employees and self-employed persons in Canada (except in Quebec where the pension plan is the Quebec Pension Plan) between 18 and 70 years of age are required to contribute to the Canada Pension Plan administered by the Government of Canada (488)

Capital   Another name for the owner's equity of a business (14)

Capital asset   Long-lived assets, like land, buildings and equipment, wasting assets and intangible assets used in the operation of the business (101)

Capital cost allowance   Depreciation allowed for income tax purposes by Revenue Canada; the rates allowed are called capital cost allowance rates (438)

Capital deficiency   Debit balance in a partner's capital account (589)

Capital lease   Lease agreement that transfers substantially all of the benefits and risks of ownership from the lessor to the lessee (709, 711)

Capital stock   A corporation's capital from investments by the shareholders. Also called Share capital (614)

Cash-basis accounting   Accounting that records only transactions in which cash is received or paid (95)

Cash disbursements journal   Special journal used to record cash disbursements by cheque (271)

Cash equivalent   Highly liquid short-term investments that can be converted into cash with little delay (778)

Cash flows   Cash receipts and cash payments (disbursements) (778)

Cash receipts journal   Special journal used to record cash receipts (264)

Certified General Accountant (CGA)   A professional accountant who earns this title through a combination of education and experience and the passing of national exams in certain subjects. A member of the Certified General Accountants Association of Canada (5)

Certified Management Accountant (CMA)   A professional accountant who earns this title through a combination of education, experience, and acceptable scores on national written examinations. A member of the Society of Management Accountants of Canada (5)

Chartered Accountant (CA)   A professional accountant who earns this title through a combination of education, experience, and an acceptable score on a written four-part national examination. A member of the Canadian Institute of Chartered Accountants (5)

Chairperson of the board   Elected person on a corporation's board of directors, usually the most powerful person in the corporation (613)

Change in accounting estimate   A change that occurs in the normal course of business as a company alters earlier expectations. Decreasing uncollectible account expense from 2 percent to 1½ percent of sales and changing the estimated useful life of a capital asset are examples (539)

Change in accounting principle   A change in accounting method, such as from the FIFO method to the LIFO method for inventories and a switch from declining-balance depreciation to straight-line (538)

Chart of accounts   List of all the accounts and their account numbers in the ledger (60)

Cheque   Document that instructs the bank to pay the designated person or business the specified amount of money (308)

Cheque register   Special journal used to record all cheques issued in a voucher system (323)

Closing entries   Entries that transfer the revenue, expense, and owner withdrawal balances from these respective accounts to the capital account (152)

Closing the accounts   Step in the accounting cycle at the end of the period that prepares the accounts for recording the transactions of the next period. Closing the accounts consists of journalizing and posting the closing entries to set the balances of the revenue, expense, and owner withdrawal accounts to zero (152)

Collection method   Method of applying the revenue principle by which the seller waits until cash is received to record the sale. This method is used only if the receipt of cash is uncertain (534)

Commission   Employee compensation computed as a percentage of the sales that the employee has made (485)

Common-size statement   A financial statement that reports only percentages (no dollar amounts); a type of vertical analysis (845)

Common stock   The most basic form of capital stock. In describing a corporation, the common shareholders are the owners of the business (616-617)

Comparability principle   Specifies that accounting information must be comparable from business to business and that a single business's financial statements must be comparable from one period to the next (532)

Completed-contract method   Method of applying the revenue principle by a construction company by which all revenue earned on the project is recorded in the period when the project is completed (535)

Conservatism   Concept that underlies presenting the gloomiest possible figures in the financial statements (401)

Consignment   Transfer of goods by the owner (consignor) to another business (consignee) who, for a fee, sells the inventory on the owner's behalf. The consignee does not take title to the consigned goods (395)

Consistency principle   A business must use the same accounting methods and procedures from period to period (399)

Consolidated accounting   A method of combining the financial statements of two or more companies that are controlled by the same owners (743)

Consolidated statements   A combination of the balance sheets, income statements, and other financial statements of the parent company with those of the subsidiaries into an overall set as if the parents and its subsidiaries were a single entity (743)

Consolidation method for investments   A way to combine the financial statements of two or more companies that are controlled by the same owners (743)

Contingent liability   A potential liability (367)

Contra account   An account with two distinguishing characteristics: (1) it always has a companion account and (2) its normal balance is opposite that of the companion account (102)

Contra asset   An asset account with a credit balance. A contra account always has a companion account and its balance is opposite that of the companion account (102)

Contract interest rate   Interest rate that determines the amount of cash interest the borrower pays and the investor receives each year. Also called the Stated interest rate (694)

Control account   An account whose balance equals the sum of the balances in a group of related accounts in a subsidiary ledger (264)

Controlling (majority) interest   Ownership of more than 50 percent of an investee company's voting stock (743)

Convertible bonds   Bonds that may be converted into the common stock of the issuing company at the option of the investor (706)

Convertible preferred stock   Preferred stock that may be exchanged by the preferred shareholders, if they choose, for another class of stock in the corporation (627)

Copyright   Exclusive right to reproduce and sell a book, musical composition, film, or other work of art. Issued by the federal government, copyrights extend 50 years beyond the author's life (450)

Corporation   A business owned by shareholders that begins when the federal government or provincial government approves its articles of incorporation. A corporation is a legal entity, an "artificial person," in the eyes of the law (11)

Cost accounting   The branch of accounting that determines and controls a business's costs (9)

Cost method for investment   The method used to account for short-term investments in stock and for long-term investments when the investor holds less than 20 percent of the investee's voting stock. Under the cost method, investments are recorded at cost and reported at the lower of their cost or market value (738)

Cost of a capital asset   Purchase price, sales tax, purchase commission and all other amounts paid to acquire the asset and to ready it for its intended use (433)

Cost of goods sold   The cost of the inventory that the business has sold to customers, the largest single expense of most merchandising businesses. Also called Cost of sales (206)

Cost of sales   Another name for Cost of goods sold (206)

Cost principle   States that assets and services are recorded at their purchase cost and that the accounting record of the asset continues to be based on cost rather than current market value (533)

Coupon bonds   Bonds for which the owners receive interest by detaching a perforated coupon (which states the interest due and the date of payment) from the bond and depositing it in a bank for collection (692)

CPP   Abbreviation for Canada Pension Plan (488)

Credit   The right side of an account (48)

Credit memorandum   Document issued by a seller to indicate having credited a customer's account receivable account (273)

Creditor   The party to a credit transaction who sells a service or merchandise and obtains a receivable (352)

Cumulative preferred stock   Preferred stock whose owners must receive all dividends in arrears before the corporation pays dividends to the common shareholders (626)

Current asset   An asset that is expected to be converted to cash, sold, or consumed during the next 12 months, or within the business's normal operating cycle if longer than a year (159)

Current liability   A debt due to be paid within one year or one of the entity's operating cycles if the cycle is longer than a year (159)

Current portion of long-term debt   Amount of the principal that is payable within one year (479)

Current ratio   Current assets divided by current liabilities (161, 851)

Date of record   Date on which the owners of stock to receive a dividend are identified (625)

Days' sales in receivables   Ratio of average net accounts receivable to one day's sales. Tells how many days' sales remain in Accounts Receivable awaiting collection (371, 854)

Debentures   Unsecured bonds, backed only by the good faith of the borrower (692)

Debit   The left side of an account (48)

Debit memorandum   Business document issued by a buyer to state that the buyer no longer owes the seller for the amount of returned purchases (275)

Debt ratio   Ratio of total liabilities to total assets. Tells the proportion of a company's assets that it has financed with debt (161, 855)

Debtor   The party to a credit transaction who makes a purchase and creates a payable (352)

Declaration date   Date on which the board of directors announces the intention to pay a dividend. The declaration creates a liability for the corporation (625)

Declining-balance (DB) method of depreciation   A type of depreciation method that writes off a relatively larger amount of an asset's cost nearer the start of its useful life than does the straight-line method (438)

Default on a note   Failure of the maker of a note to pay at maturity. Also called Dishonor of a note (367)

Deferred revenue   Another name for Unearned revenue (479)

Deficit   Debit balance in the retained earnings account (615)

Defined benefits pension plan   Benefits to be paid to the employee upon retirement are specified (712)

Defined contribution pension plan   The contribution to the plan is defined and the benefits to be paid to the employee depend on what is available at retirement (712)

Depletion   That portion of a wasting asset's natural resource cost that is used up in a particular period. Depletion expense is computed in the same way as units of production depreciation (448)

Deposit in transit   A deposit recorded by the company but not yet by its bank (311)

Depreciable cost   The asset's cost minus its estimated residual value (435)

Depreciation   Expense associated with spreading (allocating) the cost of a capital asset over its useful life (101)

Direct method   Format of the operating activities section of the statement of changes in financial position that lists the major categories of operating cash receipts (collections from customers and receipts of interest and dividends) and cash disbursements (payments to suppliers, to employees, for interest and income taxes) (782)

Direct write-off method   A method of accounting for bad debts by which the company waits until the credit department decides that a customer's account receivable is uncollectible and then records uncollectible account expense and credits the customer's account receivable (359)

Disclosure principle   Holds that a company's financial statements should report enough information for outsiders to make knowledgeable decisions about the company (536)

Discounting a note payable   A borrowing arrangement in which the bank subtracts the interest amount from the note's face value. The borrower receives the net amount (475)

Discounting a note receivable   Selling a note receivable before its maturity (366)

Dishonor of a note   Another name for Default on a note (367)

Dissolution   Ending of a partnership (570)

Dividend yield   Ratio of dividends per share of stock to the stock's market price per share (859)

Dividends   Distributions by a corporation to its shareholders (616)

Dividends in arrears   Cumulative preferred dividends that the corporation has failed to pay (626)

Donated capital   Special category of shareholders' equity created when a corporation receives a donation (gift) from a donor who receives no ownership interest in the company (623)

Double taxation   Corporations pay their own income taxes on corporate income. Then, the shareholders pay personal income tax on the cash dividends that they receive from corporations (612)

Doubtful account expense   Another name for Uncollectible account expense (353)

Earnings per share (EPS)   Amount of a company's net income per share of its outstanding common stock (666)

Economic dependence   A company that is dependent on another company as its supplier or customer (544)

Effective interest rate   The rate that investors demand for loaning their money. Another name for market interest rate (694)

Efficient capital market   One in which the market prices fully reflect all information available to the public (861)

Electronic fund transfer   System that accounts for cash transactions by electronic impulses rather than paper documents (326)

Ending inventory   Goods still on hand at the end of the period (393)

Entity   An organization or a section of an organization that, for accounting purposes, stands apart from other organizations and individuals as a separate economic unit. This is the most basic concept in accounting (11-12)

EPS   Abbreviation of Earnings per share of common stock (666)

Equity method for investments   The method used to account for investments in which the investor can significantly influence the decisions of the investee. Under the equity method, investments are recorded initially at cost. The investment account is debited (increased) for ownership in the investee's net income and credited (decreased) for ownership in the investee's dividends (742)

Estimated residual value   Expected cash value of an asset at the end of its useful life. Also called Residual value, Scrap value and Salvage value (435)

Estimated useful life   Length of the service that a business expects to get from an asset; may be expressed in years, units of output, miles or other measures (435)

Expense Decrease in owner equity that occurs in the course of delivering goods or services to customers or clients (17)

Extraordinary item A gain or loss that is infrequent, not typical of the business and does not depend on a management decision (666)

FIFO The First-in, first-out inventory method (396)

Financial accounting The branch of accounting that provides information to people outside the business (10)

Financial statements Business documents that report financial information about an entity to persons and organizations outside the business (19)

Financing activity Activity that obtains the funds from investors and creditors needed to launch and sustain the business. A section of the statement of changes in financial position (780)

First-in, first-out (FIFO) method Inventory costing method by which the first costs into inventory are the first costs out to cost of goods sold. Ending inventory is based on the costs of the most recent purchases (396)

FOB destination Terms of a transaction that govern when the title to the inventory passes from the seller to the purchaser — when the goods arrive at the purchaser's location (394)

FOB shipping point Terms of a transaction that govern when the title to the inventory passes from the seller to the purchaser — when the goods leave the seller's place of business (394)

Foreign-currency exchange rate The measure of one currency against another currency (754)

Foreign-currency transaction gain or loss This occurs when the exchange rate changes between the date of the purchase on account and the date of the subsequent payment of cash (755)

Franchises and licenses Privileges granted by a private business or a government to sell a product or service in accordance with specified conditions (450)

Fringe benefits Employee compensation, like health and life insurance and retirement pay, which the employee does not receive immediately in cash (485)

Gain An increase in owner equity that does not result from a revenue or an investment by an owner in the business (547)

Generally accepted accounting principles (GAAP) Accounting guidelines, formulated by the CICA's Accounting Standards Committee, that govern how businesses report their financial statements to the public (6)

General journal Journal used to record all transactions that do not fit one of the special journals (262)

General ledger Ledger of accounts that are reported in the financial statements (262)

Going-concern concept Accountants' assumption that the business will continue operating in the foreseeable future (530)

Goods available for sale Beginning inventory plus net purchases (393)

Goodwill Excess of the cost of an acquired company over the sum of the market values of its net assets (assets minus liabilities) (451)

Gross margin Excess of sales revenue over cost of goods sold. Also called Gross profit (199)

Gross margin method A way to estimate inventory based on a rearrangement of the cost of goods sold model: Beginning inventory + Net purchases = Cost of goods available for sale. Cost of goods available for sale – Cost of goods sold = Ending inventory. Also called the Gross profit method (404-405)

Gross pay Total amount of salary, wages, commissions, or any other employee compensation before taxes and other deductions are taken out (485)

Gross profit Excess of sales revenue over cost of goods sold. Also called Gross margin (199)

Gross profit method Another name for the gross margin method of estimating inventory cost (404-405)

Hardware Equipment that makes up a computer system (259)

Hedging This means to protect oneself from losing by engaging in a counterbalancing transaction (757)

Horizontal analysis Study of percentage changes in comparative financial statements (841)

Imprest system A way to account for petty cash by maintaining a constant balance in the petty cash account, supported by the fund (cash plus disbursement tickets) totaling the same amount (320)

Income from operations Gross margin (sales revenue minus cost of goods sold) minus operating expenses. Also called Operating income (214)

Income statement List of an entity's revenues, expenses, and net income or net loss for a specific period. Also called the Statement of operations (19)

Income summary A temporary "holding tank" account into which the revenues and expenses are transferred prior to their final transfer to the capital account (152)

Incorporators Persons who organize a corporation (613)

Indirect method Format of the operating activities section of the statement of changes in financial position that starts with net income and shows the reconciliation from net income to operating cash flows. Also called the Reconciliation method (795-796)

Information system design Identification of an organization's information needs, and development and implementation of the system to meet those needs (9)

Installment method Method of applying the revenue principle in which gross profit (sales revenue minus cost of goods sold) is recorded as cash is collected (534)

Intangible asset An asset with no physical form, a special right to current and expected future benefits (449)

Interest The revenue to the payee for loaning out the principal, and the expense to the maker for borrowing the principal (363)

Interest-coverage ratio Another name for the Times-interest-earned ratio (856)

Interest period The period of time during which interest is to be computed, extending from the original date of the note to the maturity date (363)

Interest rate The percentage rate that is multiplied by the principal amount to compute the amount of interest on a note (363)

Internal auditing Auditing that is performed by a business's own accountants to evaluate the firm's accounting and management systems. The aim is to improve operating efficiency and to ensure that employees follow management's procedures and plans (9-10)

Internal control Organizational plan and all the related measures adopted by an entity to meet management's objectives of discharging statutory responsibilities, profitability, prevention and detection of fraud and error, safeguarding of assets, reliability of accounting records, and timely preparation of reliable financial information (257-258)

Inventory cost Price paid to acquire inventory — not the selling price of the goods. Inventory cost includes its invoice price, less all discounts, plus sales tax, tariffs, transportation fees, insurance while in transit, and all other costs incurred to make the goods ready for sale (395)

Inventory turnover Ratio of cost of goods sold to average inventory. Measures the number of times a company sells its average level of inventory during a year (853)

Investing activity Activity that increases and decreases the assets that the business has to work with. A section of the statement of changes in financial position (780)

Invoice Seller's request for payment from a purchaser. Also called a bill (201)

Issued stock The stock that the corporation has issued to shareholders (618)

Journal The chronological accounting record of an entity's transactions (50)

Last-in, first-out (LIFO) method Inventory costing method by which the last costs into inventory are the first costs out to cost of goods sold. This leaves the oldest costs — those of beginning inventory and the earliest purchases of the period — in ending inventory (396)

LCM rule The Lower-of-cost-or market rule (402)

Lease Rental agreement in which the tenant (lessee) agrees to make rent payments to the property owner (lessor) in exchange for the use of the asset (709)

Leasehold Prepayment that a lessee (renter) makes to secure the use of an asset from a lessor (landlord) (450)

Ledger The book of accounts (45)

Lessee Tenant in a lease agreement (709)

Lessor Property owner in a lease agreement (709)

Leverage Another name for Trading on the equity (858)

Liability An economic obligation (a debt) payable to an individual or an organization outside the business (14)

LIFO The last-in, first-out inventory method (396)

Limited liability No personal obligation of a shareholder for corporation debts. The most that a shareholder can lose on an investment in a corporation's stock is the cost of the investment (612)

Liquidation The process of going out of business by selling the entity's assets and paying its liabilities. The final step in liquidation of a business is the distribution of any remaining cash to the owners (586)

Liquidation value of stock Amount a corporation agrees to pay a preferred shareholder per share if the company liquidates (630)

Liquidity Measure of how quickly an item may be converted to cash (158-159)

Long-term asset An asset other than a current asset (159)

Long-term commitments Commitments that involve making payments that may be unequal in amount over a series of years (542)

Long-term investment Separate asset category reported on the balance sheet between current assets and capital assets (741)

Long-term liability A liability other than a current liability (159)

Long-term solvency The ability to generate enough cash to pay long-term debts as they mature (840)

Loss A decrease in owner equity that does not result from an expense or a distribution to an owner of the business (547)

Lower-of-cost-or-market (LCM) rule Requires that an asset be reported in the financial statements at the lower of its historical cost or its market value (current replacement cost or net realizable value) (402)

Mainframe system Computer system characterized by a single computer (259)

Maker of a note The person or business that signs the note and promises to pay the amount required by the note agreement. The maker is the debtor (363)

Management accounting The branch of accounting that generates confidential information for internal decision-makers of a business, such as top executives (10)

Market interest rate Interest rate that investors demand in order to loan their money. Also called the Effective interest rate (694)

Market value of stock Price for which a person could buy or sell a share of stock (629)

Marketable security Another name for short-term investment, one that may be sold any time the investor wishes (737-738)

Matching principle The basis for recording expenses. Directs accountants to identify all expenses incurred during the period, measure the expenses and match them against the revenues earned during that same span of time (96-97)

Materiality concept States that a company must perform strictly proper accounting only for items and transactions that are significant to the business's financial statements (545)

Maturity date The date on which the final payment of a note is due. Also called the due date (363)

Maturity value The sum of the principal and interest due at the maturity date of a note (363)

Microcomputer A computer small enough for each employee to have his or her own (259)

Minicomputer Small computer that operates like a large system but on a smaller scale (259)

Minority interest   A subsidiary company's equity that is held by shareholders other than the parent company (746)

Mortgage   Borrower's promise to transfer the legal title to certain assets to the lender if the debt is not paid on schedule (707)

Multiple-step income statement   Format that contains subtotals to highlight significant relationships. In addition to net income, it also presents gross margin and income from operations (217)

Mutual agency   Every partner can bind the business to a contract within the scope of the partnership's regular business operations (570)

Natural resources   Another name for wasting assets (432)

Net earnings   Another name for Net income or Net profit (17)

Net income   Excess of total revenues over total expenses. Also called Net earnings or Net profit (17)

Net loss   Excess of total expenses over total revenues (17)

Net pay   Gross pay minus all deductions, the amount of employee compensation that the employee actually takes home (485)

Net profit   Another name for Net income or Net earnings (17)

Net purchases   Purchases less purchase discounts and purchase returns and allowances (204)

Net sales revenue   Sales revenue less sales discounts and sales returns and allowances (206)

Nominal account   Another name for a Temporary account — revenues and expenses — that is closed at the end of the period. In a proprietorship the owner withdrawal account is also nominal (152)

No-par stock   Shares of stock that do not have a value assigned to them by the articles of incorporation (617)

Nonsufficient funds (NSF) cheque   A "hot" cheque, one for which the payer's bank account has insufficient money to pay the cheque (311)

Note payable   A liability evidenced by a written promise to make a future payment (14)

Note receivable   An asset evidenced by another party's written promise that entitles you to receive cash in the future (14)

NSF cheque   A nonsufficient funds cheque (311)

Off-balance-sheet financing   Acquisition of assets or services with debt that is not reported on the balance sheet (711)

On-line processing   Computerized accounting for transaction data on a continuous basis, often from various locations, rather than in batches at a single location (260)

Operating activity   Activity that creates revenue or expense in the entity's major line of business. Operating activities affect the income statement. A section of the statement of changes in financial position (779-780)

Operating cycle   The time span during which cash is (1) used to acquire goods and services and (2) those goods and services are sold to customers, who in turn pay for their purchases with cash. Usually a few months in length (159)

Operating expenses   Expenses, other than cost of goods sold, that are incurred in the entity's major line of business: rent, depreciation, salaries, wages, utilities, property tax and supplies expense (214)

Operating income   Another name for Income from operations (214)

Operating lease   Usually a short-term or cancelable rental agreement (709)

Organization cost   The costs of organizing a corporation, including legal fees, taxes and charges by promoters for selling the stock. Organization cost is an intangible asset (624)

Other expense   Expense that is outside the main operations of a business, such as a loss on the sale of capital assets (214)

Other receivables   A miscellaneous category that includes loans to employees and branch companies, usually long-term assets reported on the balance sheet after current assets and before capital assets. Other receivables can be current assets (352-353)

Other revenue   Revenue that is outside the main operations of a business, such as a gain on the sale of capital assets (214)

Outstanding cheque   A cheque issued by the company and recorded on its books but not yet paid by its bank (311)

Outstanding stock   Stock in the hands of a shareholder. Also referred to as Issued Stock (614)

Owner's equity   The claim of an owner of a business to the assets of the business. Also called Capital (14)

Par value   Arbitrary amount assigned to a share of stock (617)

Parent company   An investor company that owns more than 50 percent of the voting stock of a subsidiary company (743)

Participating preferred stock   Preferred stock whose owners may receive (that is, participate in) dividends beyond the stated amount or stated percentage (627)

Partnership   An unincorporated business with two or more owners (10)

Partnership agreement   Agreement that is the contract between partners specifying such items as the name, location and nature of the business, the name, capital investment and duties of each partner, and the method of sharing profits and losses by the partners (570)

Patent   A federal government grant giving the holder the exclusive right for 17 years to produce and sell an invention (450)

Payee of a note   The person or business to whom the maker of a note promises future payment. The payee is the creditor (363)

Payroll   Employee compensation, a major expense of many businesses (485)

Pension   Employee compensation that will be received during retirement (711)

Percentage of completion method   Method of applying the revenue principle by a construction company by which revenue is recorded as the work is performed (535)

Periodic inventory system   The business does not keep a continuous record of the inventory on hand. Instead, at the end of the period the business makes a physical count of the on-hand inventory and applies the appropriate unit costs to determine the cost of the ending inventory (406)

Permanent accounts   The assets, liabilities and capital accounts. These accounts are not closed at the end of the period because their balances are not used to measure income. Also called a Real account (152)

Perpetual inventory system   The business keeps a continuous record for each inventory item to show the inventory on hand at all times (407)

Petty cash   Fund containing a small amount of cash that is used to pay minor expenditures (319)

Postclosing trial balance   List of the ledger accounts and their balances at the end of the period after the journalizing and posting of the closing entries. The last step of the accounting cycle, the postclosing trial balance ensures that the ledger is in balance for the start of the next accounting period (154-155)

Posting   Transferring of amounts from the journal to the ledger (52)

Preferred stock   Stock that gives its owners certain advantages over common shareholders, such as the priority to receive dividends before the common shareholders and the priority to receive assets before the common shareholders if the corporation liquidates (617)

Prepaid expense   A category of miscellaneous assets that typically expire or get used up in the near future. Examples include prepaid rent, prepaid insurance, and supplies (99)

Present value   Amount a person would invest now to receive a greater amount at a future date (694)

President   Chief operating officer in charge of managing the day-to-day operations of a corporation (613)

Price-earnings ratio   Ratio of the market price of a share of common stock to the company's earnings per share (859)

Principal amount   The amount loaned out by the payee and borrowed by the maker of a note (363)

Prior period adjustment   Correction to retained earnings for an error of an earlier period is a prior period adjustment (669)

Private accountant   Accountant who works for a single business, such as a department store or Northern Telecom (5)

Promissory note   A written promise to pay a specified amount of money at a particular future date (363)

Proprietorship   An unincorporated business with a single owner (10)

Proxy   Legal document that expresses a shareholder's preference and appoints another person to cast the shareholder's vote (613)

Public accountant   Accountant who serves the general public and collects fees for work, which includes auditing, income tax planning and preparation, management consulting and bookkeeping (5)

Purchase discount   Reduction in the cost of inventory that is offered by a seller as an incentive for the customer to pay promptly. A contra account to purchases (203)

Purchase returns and allowances   Decrease in a buyer's debt from returning merchandise to the seller or from receiving from the seller an allowance from the amount owed. A contra account to purchases (203)

Purchases   The cost of inventory that a firm buys to resell to customers in the normal course of business (200-201)

Purchases journal   Special journal used to record all purchases of inventory, supplies and other assets on account (269)

Quantity discount   A purchase discount that provides a lower price per item the larger the quantity purchased (202)

Quick ratio   Another name for the Acid-test ratio (370, 852)

Rate of return on common shareholders' equity   Net income minus preferred dividends, divided by average common shareholders' equity. A measure of profitability. Also called Return on common shareholders' equity (857)

Rate of return on net sales   Ratio of net income to net sales. A measure of profitability. Also called Return on sales (856-857)

Rate of return on total assets   The sum of net income plus interest expense divided by average total assets. This ratio measures the success a company has in using its assets to earn a profit. Also called Return on assets (628-629, 857)

Real account   Another name for a Permanent account — asset, liability and capital — that is not closed at the end of the period (152)

Receivable   A monetary claim against a business or an individual, acquired mainly by selling goods and services and by lending money (352)

Reconciliation method   Another name for the indirect method of formatting the operating activities section of the statement of changes in financial position (795-796)

Redemption value of stock   Price a corporation agrees to pay for stock, which is set when the stock is issued (630)

Registered bonds   Bonds for which the owners receive interest cheques from the issuing company (691-692)

Relative-sales-value method   Allocation technique for identifying the cost of each asset purchased in a group for a single amount (434)

Reliability principle   Requires that accounting information be dependable (free from error and bias). Also called the Objectivity principle (532)

Repair   Expenditure that merely maintains an asset in its existing condition or restores the asset to good working order. Repairs are expensed (matched against revenue) (452)

Report format of the balance sheet   Format that lists the assets at the top, with the liabilities and owner equity below (160)

Repurchased capital stock   Stock purchased by a corporation from its shareholders (656)

Residual value   Same as Estimated residual value (435)

Retail method   A way to estimate inventory cost based on the cost of goods sold model. The retail method requires that the business record inventory purchases both at cost and at retail. Multiply ending inventory at retail by the cost ratio to estimate the ending inventory's cost (405)

Retained earnings A corporation's capital that is earned through profitable operation of the business. The sum of profits less losses and dividends (615)

Return on assets Another name for Rate of return on total assets (628-629, 857)

Return on common shareholders' equity Another name for Rate of return on common shareholders' equity (857)

Return on sales Another name for Rate of return on net sales (856-857)

Revenue Increase in owner equity that is earned by delivering goods or services to customers or clients (16)

Revenue Canada rate The maximum depreciation rate, also called the Capital cost allowance rate, that Revenue Canada allows a taxpayer to use in calculating depreciation expense, also called capital cost allowance, in determining taxable income (438)

Revenue principle The basis for recording revenues, tells accountants when to record revenue and the amount of revenue to record (96)

Reversing entry An entry that switches the debit and the credit of a previous adjusting entry. The reversing entry is dated the first day of the period following the adjusting entry (155)

Salary Employee compensation stated at a yearly, monthly or weekly rate (485)

Sales discount Reduction in the amount receivable from a customer, offered by the seller as an incentive for the customer to pay promptly. A contra account to Sales revenue (205)

Sales journal Special journal used to record credit sales (262)

Sales method Method of applying the revenue principle in which revenue is recorded at the point of sale. This method is used for most sales of goods and services (533-534)

Sales returns and allowances Decrease in the seller's receivable from a customer's return of merchandise or from granting the customer an allowance from the amount the customer owes the seller. A contra account to Sales revenue (205)

Sales revenue Amount that a merchandiser earns from selling inventory before subtracting expenses (205)

Salvage value Another name for Residual value or Estimated residual value (435)

Segment of a business A distinguishable component of a company (665)

Serial bonds Bonds that mature in installments over a period of time (692)

Service charge Bank's fee for processing a depositor's transaction (311)

Share capital Another name for Capital stock (614-615)

Shareholder A person who owns the stock of a corporation (11)

Shareholders' equity Owners' equity of a corporation (614)

Short-term investments The investor must intend either to convert the investments to cash within one year or to use them to pay a current liability (737-738)

Short-term liquidity The ability to meet current payments as they become due (840)

Short-term note payable Note payable due within one year, a common form of financing (474)

Single-step income statement Format that groups all revenues together and then lists and deducts all expenses together without drawing any subtotals (217)

Slide An accounting error that results from adding one or more zeros to a number, or from dropping a zero. For example, writing $500 as $5,000 or as $50 is a slide. A slide is evenly divisible by 9 (163)

Software Set of programs or instructions that cause the computer to perform the work desired (259)

Specific cost method Inventory cost method based on the specific cost of particular units of inventory (395-396)

Spreadsheet Integrated software program that can be used to solve many different kinds of problems. An electronically prepared work sheet (146)

Stable monetary unit concept Accountants' basis for ignoring the effect of inflation and making no adjustments for the changing value of the dollar (531)

Stated capital The value assigned by the board of directors of a corporation to a share of no-par stock at the time of its issue and thus its issue price (615)

Stated interest rate Another name for the Contract interest rate (694)

Statement of changes in financial position Reports cash receipts and cash disbursements classified according to the entity's major activities: operating, financing and investing (777-800)

Statement of financial position Another name for the Balance sheet (19)

Statement of operations (Also called Statement of earnings) Another name for the Income statement (19)

Statement of owner's equity Summary of the changes in the owner equity of an entity during a specific period (19)

Stock Shares into which the owners' equity of a corporation is divided (611)

Stock dividend A proportional distribution by a corporation of its own stock to its shareholders (653)

Stock split An increase in the number of outstanding shares of stock coupled with a proportionate reduction in the book value per share of stock (655)

Stock subscription Contract that obligates an investor to purchase the corporation's stock at a later date at a specified price (619)

Straight-line method Depreciation method in which an equal amount of depreciation expense is assigned to each year (or period) of asset use (436)

Strong currency The exchange rate of this type of currency is rising relative to other nations' currencies (755)

Subsequent event An event that occurs after the end of a company's accounting period but before publication of its financial statements and which may affect the interpretation of the information in those statements (539)

Subsidiary company An investee company in which a parent company owns more than 50 percent of the voting stock (743)

Subsidiary ledger Book of accounts that provides supporting details on individual balances, the total of which appears in a general ledger account (264)

Temporary accounts The revenue and expense accounts which relate to a particular accounting period are closed at the end of the period. For a proprietorship, the owner withdrawal account is also temporary. Also called a Nominal account (152)

Temporary investments Another name for Short-term investments (737-738)

Term bonds Bonds that all mature at the same time for a particular issue (692)

Time and a half Overtime pay computed as 150 percent (1.5 times) the straight-time rate (485)

Time period concept Ensures that accounting information is reported at regular intervals (530)

Times-interest-earned ratio Ratio of income from operations to interest expense. Measures the number of times that operating income can cover interest expense. Also called the Interest-coverage ratio (856)

Trademarks and trade names Distinctive identifications of a product or service (450)

Trading on the equity Earning more income than the borrowed amount, which increases the earnings for the owners of a business. Also called Leverage (858)

Transaction An event that affects the financial position of a particular entity and may be reliably recorded (14)

Transposition An accounting error that occurs when digits are flip-flopped. For example, $85 is a transposition of $58. A transposition is evenly divisible by 9 (163)

Trial balance A list of all the ledger accounts with their balances (55)

UI Abbreviation of Unemployment Insurance (489)

Uncollectible account expense Cost to the seller of extending credit. Arises from the failure to collect from credit customers (353)

Underwriter Organization that purchases bonds or stocks from an issuing company and resells them to its clients, or sells the bonds or stocks for a commission, agreeing to buy all unsold bonds or stocks (691)

Unearned revenue A liability created when a business collects cash from customers in advance of doing work for the customer. The obligation is to provide a product or a service in the future. Also called Deferred revenue (105)

Unemployment Insurance All employees and employers in Canada must contribute to the Unemployment Insurance Fund which provides assistance to unemployed workers (489)

Units-of-production (UOP) method Depreciation method by which a fixed amount of depreciation is assigned to each unit of output produced by the capital asset (436)

Unlimited personal liability When a partnership (or a proprietorship) cannot pay its debts with business assets, the partners (or the proprietor) must use personal assets to meet the debt (571)

Useful life Same as Estimated useful life (435)

Vertical analysis Analysis of a financial statement that reveals the relationship of each statement item to the total, which is the 100 percent figure (844)

Voucher Document authorizing a cash disbursement (321)

Voucher register Special journal used to record all expenditures in a voucher system, similar to but more comprehensive than the purchases journal (323)

Voucher system A way to record cash payments that enhances internal control by formalizing the process of approving and recording invoices for payment (321)

Wages Employees' pay stated at an hourly figure (485)

Wasting assets Capital assets that are natural resources (432)

Withheld income tax Income tax deducted from employees' gross pay (488)

Work sheet A columnar document designed to help move data from the trial balance to the financial statements (138)

Weak currency The exchange rate of this type of currency is falling relative to other nations' currencies (755)

Workers' compensation A provincially administered plan which is funded by contributions by employers and which provides financial support for workers injured on the job (490)

Working capital Current assets minus current liabilities, measures a business's ability to meet its short-term obligations with its current assets (851)

Index

Accelerated-depreciation
method. *See* Declining-
balance method of de-
preciation, 30
Account(s), 45
chart of, 60
closing of, 152-154
illustration of, 55-56, 68
normal balances of, 61-62
permanent (real), 152
temporary (nominal), 152
Accountants
private, 5
public, 5
Accountant's work sheet. *See*
Work sheet
Account format
"T," 48
Account format (balance sheet),
160
Accounting, 2
computers in, 111, 258-260
(*see also* Computer-as-
sisted accounting sys-
tems; Microcomputers)
conservatism in, 401, 545-
546
constraints on, 544
history of, 4
importance of, 2
profession of, 4-5
separation of custody of assets from, 306
separation of duties within,
306-307
separation of operations
from, 306
Accounting, areas of application in. *See* Consolida-
tion accounting;
Management account-
ing
Accounting basis. *See*
Measurement of busi-
ness income
Accounting changes, reporting
of, 538-539
Accounting cycle, 138

Accounting equation, 14
and balance sheet, 22
and debits/credits, 48-50
as fundamental, 68
and transaction analysis, 15
Accounting errors. *See* Errors
Accounting firms, "Big Six," 5
Accounting information (data)
analytical use of, 68-69
flow of, 53
as relevant/reliable/com-
parable, 529
users of, 2-4
Accounting information system,
256, 261
compatibility of, 258
and computer data processing, 258-260
control through, 257-258
cost/benefit relationship in,
258
design of, 257
flexibility of, 258
and information processing
model, 257
installation of, 256-257
Accounting organizations, 5-7
Accounting period, 95-96
and accounting cycle, 138
and bond interest expense,
698-699
Accounting policies, and disclosure principle, 536-544
Accounting principles. *See*
Principles and concepts
Accounting services, specialized,
9-10
Accounting Standards Board
(ASB) 6, 527
Accounts payable, 14, 474
as current liability, 159
in statement of changes in
financial position, 790
Accounts payable account, 46,
64
Accounts payable subsidiary
ledger, 271
Accounts receivable, 14, 353

internal control over collection of, 361-362
separation of authority to
write off, 306
Accounts receivable account,
45, 63
as control account, 264
credit balances in, 360
Accounts Receivable ledger,
264, 266-267
Accounts receivable turnover,
371, 853-854
Account titles, 62-64
Accrual-basis accounting, 94
and adjusting entries, 99,
150-151
Accrual entries, 531
Accrued expenses, 103-104, 479
Accrued revenue, 104-105
Accumulated deficit, 615
Accumulated depreciation, 102,
435
Accumulated depreciation account, 102
Acid-test (quick) ratio, 370, 852
Acquisitions, 781
in statement of changes in
financial position, 794-
795 (*see also* Consolidation accounting)
Adjusted bank balance, 312
Adjusted book balance, 312
Adjusted trial balance, 108-110
omission of, 211-212
preparing financial statements from, 108
Adjusting entries, 94, 99
for accrued expenses,
103-104
for accrued revenues,
104-105
in bank reconciliation, 314
computer for, 111
for depreciation and capital
assets, 101-103
for merchandising business,
215
posting of, 106-107

for prepaid expenses, 99-100
recording of, 150-51
for unearned revenues, 105
and work sheet, 139, 142
Advertising expense account, 64
Aging the accounts, 357
Aging of accounts method, 357-360
Allowance for Uncollectible Accounts (Allowance for Doubtful Accounts), 354
and bad-debt write-offs, 355-356
Allowance method, 354-355
Allowances, purchase, 203-204
Allowances, reporting of, 369-370
Allowances, sales, 205-206
Amortization, 449-451
for bonds, 697-698, 701-704
in statement of changes in financial position, 784, 797
Analysis of transactions. See Transaction analysis
Annuity
present value of, 730-732
Appropriations, 661
Articles of incorporation, 611
Assets, 14, 546
on balance sheet, 22
capital, 432 (see also Capital assets)
as credits or debits, 48
current, 159 (see also Current assets)
expired, 100
fixed, 432
fully depreciated, 445
intangible, 432, 449-451, 624
long-term, 159
obsolescence of, 435
in statement of changes in financial position, 785-786
Assets, personal, and partnership, 572-573
Asset accounts, 45-46, 63-64
normal balance for, 61
as permanent, 152
Auditing, 9
external, 304, 307
internal, 7, 304, 307
Authorization, as control provision, 305-306
Authorization for stock issue, 618, 619

Average cost method, 396-399
Bad debt expense, 353
Balance, 49
in ledger, 55
normal, 61-62
Balance sheet, 19-22
account titles for, 63-64
and adjusted trial balance, 108
and aging of accounts method, 357-359
CICA on elements of, 546
classified, 159-160
consolidated, 744-745, 746-748
and contingent liabilities, 482-483
dating of, 779
format of, 160
horizontal analysis of, 841-844
for merchandising vs. service entity, 215
and off-balance-sheet financing, 711
and postclosing trial balance, 154-155
and statement of owner's equity, 110, 111
shareholders' equity on, 614-616
vertical analysis of, 844-845
work sheet columns for, 140, 141, 143, 144, 145, 149
Balancing the ledgers, 277
Bank account
as control device, 308-314
payroll, 495
Bank collections, 311, 312
Bank reconciliation, 309-314
Bank statements, 308-309
Basic earnings per share, 668
Basis of accounting. See Measurement of business income
Basket (group) purchases of assets, 434
Batch processing, 260
Beginning inventory, 393
Betterments, 452
"Big Six" accounting firms, 5
Bill (invoice), 701
Board of directors, 613
Bond discount, 693, 694, 696-697, 701-703
Bond indentures, 705
Bond premium, 693, 694, 697-698, 703-704

Bond sinking fund, 705
Bonds payable, 691
amortizing for, 697-6908, 701-704
convertible, 706
coupon, 692
debenture, 692
interest expense on, 695, 696, 697, 698-699, 701-704
interest rates of, 694
issuing of, 694-698
mortgage, 692
present value of, 732-733
prices of, 692, 694
registered, 691-692
retirement of, 705-706
serial, 692, 707
term, 692
Bonus, 485
Bookkeeping, 2
double-entry, 4, 47-48
Book value, 102
and residual value, 439
of a capital asset 102
Book value per share of common stock, 860
Book value of stock, 630-631
Bottom line, 215
Budgeting, 9
Building account, 46, 64
Buildings
cost of, 433
in statement of changes in financial position, 794
see also Capital assets
Business
accounting and careers in, 4-5
importance of accounting to, 2
Business assets. See Assets
Business decisions. See Decision-making
Business documents. See Documents
Business income, measurement of, 94 (see also Measurement of business income)
Business organizations, types of, 10-11
Business segments, 540-542
Bylaws of corporation, 613
Callable bonds, 706
CA. See Chartered Accountant
CAmagazine, 6
Canadian Business Corporations

Act (CBCA), fn. 304, 615, 618, 619, 656
Canada (or Quebec) Pension Plan, 488-489
Canadian Academic Accounting Association (CAAA), 7
Canadian Institute of Chartered Accountants (CICA), 5
Capital, 14
  as credit/debit, 62
  donated, 623
  and working capital, 851-852
Capital account, 46
  in closing, 152, 154
  normal balance for, 63
  as permanent, 152
Capital asset 101
Capital asset ledger cards, 448
Capital assets, 101-103, 431
  control of, 447-448
  cost of, 433-434
  depreciation of, 434-435 (*see also* Depreciation)
  determining useful life of, 435
  disposal of, 445
  natural resources as, 448
  in statement of changes in financial position, 785, 794
  see also specific kinds of assets
  wasting assets as, 448
Capital cost allowance (CCA), 438
  rate, 438
Capital deficiency, 589
Capital leases, 709-711
  vs. operating leases, 711
  present value of, 733
Capital stock, 614-615 (*see also* Stock)
Career path, for accountants, 6
Cash
  and cash equivalents, 778
  as current asset, 159
  internal controls over, 307-308, 317-326 (*see also* Bank account)
  reporting of, 316-317
Cash account, 45, 63
  and adjusted trial balance, 108
Cash-basis accounting, 94-95
  and adjusting entries, 98
Cash disbursements
  internal control over, 318-326, 500-501

for payroll, 496-500
Cash disbursements journal, 269, 271-273, 274-275
Cash equivalents, 778
Cash flows. *See* Statement of Changes in Financial Position
Cash receipts
  internal control over, 317-318
  postal, 317
Cash receipts journal, 264-267
Cash Short and Over account, 318, 321
CCA. *See* Capital cost allowance
Certified General Accountant (CGA), 5
Certified General Accountants Association of Canada (CGAAC), 5
Certified Internal Auditor (CIA), 7
Certified Management Accountant (CMA), 5
CGA. *See* Certified General Accountant
CGA Magazine, 7
CGAAC. *See* Certified General Accountants Association of Canada
Chairperson of board of directors, 613
Change in accounting estimate, 539
Change in accounting principle, 539-539
Chart of accounts, 60-61
Chartered Accountant (CA), 5
Cheque (bank), 308
  as control, 318
  payroll, 495, 496
  returned to payee, 311
Cheque register, 323-325
CICA. *See* Canadian Institute of Chartered Accountants
CICA Handbook, 6, 525-527
Classification of assets and liabilities, 158-160
Classified balance sheet, 159, 160
Closing the accounts, 152-154
Closing entries, 152-153
  for merchandising business, 215, 217
  from work sheet, 151
CMA. *See* Certified Management Account
Codes of (professional) conduct, 8

"Collect cash on account," 18
Collection method, 534
Commission, 485
  broker's, 738
Commitment, 542-543
Common-size statement, 845-846
Common stock, 616-617
  dividends on, 625-626, 667-668
  issuing of, 618-621
Common Stock Dividend Distributable account, 654
Comparability principle, 532-533
Compatibility, of accounting information system, 258
Completed-contact method, 535
Computer-assisted accounting systems, 111
  in accounting for receivables, 371
  for current liabilities, 501-502
  and internal control, 326
  and inventory, 410
  as "journal-less," 69
  and microcomputers, 259, 260 (*see also* Microcomputers)
  and minicomputers, 259
  spreadsheet for, 146-147
  see also Microcomputers
Computer data processing, 258
Computerized data processing, 258
Computerized inventory records, 410
Computer spreadsheet. *See* Spreadsheet
Concepts. *See* Principles and concepts
Conservatism in accounting, 401, 545-546
Consignment, 395
Consistency principle, 399, 532
Consolidation accounting, 743-748
Consumer groups, as accounting users, 4
Contingent liabilities, 367, 482-483, 537-538
  on financial statements, 343
Contra account, 102
  netted parenthetical recording of, 208
Contra asset account, 102
Contract interest rate, 694, 702
Control
  through accounting system, 257-258

internal, 302-307 (*see also* Internal control)
Control account, 264
Controlling (majority) interest, 743
Convertible bonds or notes, 706-707
Convertible preferred stock 627, 668
Copyrights, 450
Corporate income tax, 664-665
and "double taxation," 612
see also Taxes
Corporation, 11, 529, 611-613
income statement of, 666-668
incorporation of, 623-624
organization of, 613-614
shareholder rights in, 616
statement of retained earnings for, 668-670
stock in 614-621 (*see also* Stock)
Correcting entry, 162-163
Cost(s), 433
historical, 13
transportation, 204-205
Cost accounting, 9
Cost and management, 7
Cost/benefit relationship for accounting system, 253
Cost of goods sold, 206-210, 393
control over, 318-319
in statement of cash flows, 790
Costing methods, inventory, 395-396
Cost method for investments, 738-739
Cost of capital asset, 433-434
Cost principle (historical cost), 13, 533
and partnership dissolution, 583-586
Cost of printed cheques, 311
Cost of sales, 206
Coupon bonds, 691-692
Credit, 48, 62
recording of, 48
Credit balance in Accounts Receivable, 360
Credit balance accounts, 61
Credit card sales, 360-361
Credit department, 353
Creditor(s), 14, 352
as accounting users, 3, 9
Credit memorandum (credit memo), 273-275

Credit ratings, 353
Credit sales, 352
bad debt expense of, 353-354
Credit sales journal, 262
Criminal business practices
and internal control, 302
see also Fraud; Theft
Cumulative preferred stock, 626-627
Current assets, 159
accounts receivable as, 159, 352
common-size analysis of, 846
notes receivable as, 353
Current liabilities, 159
computer accounting systems for, 501-502
to be estimated, 480-482
of known amount, 474-480
Current portion of long-term debt (current maturity), 479, 707
Current ratio, 161, 851-852
Current replacement cost, 402
Customer Deposits Payable, 480
Cycle
accounting, 138
operating, 159, 200-201
Data. *See* Accounting information
Data processing, 257
by computer, 258-261
Date of declaration, 625
Date of payment, 625
Date of record, 625
Days'-sales-in-receivables ratio, 371, 854-855
Debentures, 692
Debit, 48, 63
cash as, 785
recording of, 48-50
Debit-balance accounts, 61
Debit memorandum (debit memo), 275
for bank service charge, 311
Debt
long-term, 479, 707, 792
in statement of changes in financial position, 785, 792
Debtor, 352
Debt ratio, 161, 855
Decision-making
accounting information in, 161-162, 219-220, 370-371

complexity of, 860-861
using ratios, 850-851
statement of changes in financial position, 848-849
Declaration date, 625
Declining-balance methods of depreciation, 438-439
Default on bonds, 692
Default on a note, 367
Deferred revenues
as a liability, 479-480
and reversing entries, 191-193
Deficit, 615, 651
Defined benefits pension plan, 712
Defined contribution pension plan, 712
Depletion expense, 448
in statement of changes in financial position, 784, 797
Deposits in transit, 311
Deposit ticket, for banks, 308
Depreciable asset, change in useful life of, 444-445
Depreciable cost, 435
Depreciation, 101-103
accumulated, 102, 435
declining-balance method of, 438-439
double-declining-balance method of, 439-440
and income taxes, 442-443
and land, 432
measuring of, 435-436
for partial years, 443-444
of capital assets, 434-435
Revenue Canada rates, 438
in statement of changes in financial position, 784, 797
straight-line method of, 436, 440-442
units-of-production method of, 411-412, 436-437, 440-441
Dilution, of EPS, 668
Direct method (for statement of changes in financial position), 782-785
Direct write-off method, 359-360
Disclosure principle, 536-544
Discontinued operations, 665
Discount on bonds, 693, 694, 696-697, 701-703

Discounting a note payable, 475-476

Discounting a note receivable, 366-367

Discount from purchase price purchase, 203
  quantity 202

Discount from sales price, 205

Dishonor a note, 367

Disposal, of capital assets, 445-448

Disposal (scrap) value, 435-436

Dissolution of partnership, 570

Distributions to owners, 547

Dividend dates, 624-625

Dividends, 616, 625-626
  in arrears, 626
  cash receipts of, 783
  preferred, 625-626, 667-668
  recording of, 739
  and Retained Earnings/Cash, 652-653
  in statement of changes in financial position, 784, 796
  stock, 653-655, 739

Dividend yield ratio, 859-860

Documents
  as journals, 277
  prenumbering of, 307

Donated capital, 623

Double-declining-balance (DDB) method, 439-440

Double-entry bookkeeping or accounting, 4, 47-48
  financial statements produced by, 94

Double taxation, 612

Doubtful account expense, 353, 354

Duties, separation of. *See* Separation of duties

Earnings per share (EPS) (Earnings per share of common stock), 666-668, 858-859
  dilution of, 668

Earnings record, 497-500

Economic dependence, 544

Effective interest method of amortization, 701-703

Effective interest rate, 694, 703

Efficient capital market, 861

Electronically prepared work sheets, 142

Electronic funds transfer (EFT), 326

Electronic scanners, 410

Electronic spreadsheets. *See* Spreadsheets

Elimination entries, 745-746

Employee compensation, 485

Employee compensation, 485

Employee withheld Canada Pension Plan contributions payable, 488

Employee withheld Income Tax Payable account, 488

Employee withheld Unemployment Insurance Premiums payable, 489

Employees, payments to, 784, 791-792

Employees' Union Dues Payable account, 489

Employer payroll costs, 490

Ending inventory, 393-394

Entity, 11-12

Entity concept, 11-12, 18, 529

Equation, accounting. *See* Accounting equation

Equipment
  cost of, 433
  in statement of changes in financial position, 794
  see also Capital assets

Equipment, furnitures and fixtures account, 46, 63

Equity. *See* Owner's equity; Shareholders' equity

Equity method, 741-743

Errors, 162, 163
  inventory, 403-404
  in journal entries, 162, 163
  and normal balance, 62
  in posting, 163
  transpositions, 163
  slides, 163
  and trial balance, 55-56
  on work sheet, 147

Estimated residual value, 435-436

Estimated useful life, 435

Estimated Warranties Payable, 480-481

Exchanging, of capital asset, 446-447

Expenses, 17, 62, 546-547
  accrued, 103-104, 479
  as credit/debit, 63
  on income statement, 22

  matching principle for, 96-97
  operating, 214, 788-792
  other, 214
  prepaid, 99, 100, 159

Expenses account, 47, 64
  closing of, 152-154, 215
  normal balance for, 62
  as temporary, 152
  in work sheet, 146

External auditors, 304

Extraordinary gains and losses (extraordinary items), 665-666

Fidelity bond, 317

FIFO. *See* First-in, first-out method

Financial accounting, 10

Financial accounting standards, 6-7

Financial Executive, 7

Financial Executives Institute (FEI), 7

Financial ratios. *See* Ratios

Financial reporting, objective of, 529

Financial statement analysis, 839-840
  and common-size statements, 845-846
  horizontal, 841-844
  ratios in, 850-860
  vertical, 844-845

Financial statements, 2, 19-22
  and adjusted trial balance, 108-110
  CICA on elements of, 546-547
  and consolidation accounting, 743-751
  and contingent liabilities, 367
  and disclosure principle, 536-544
  as end product, 94
  essential features of, 108
  and estimates of uncollectibles, 356
  and industry comparisons, 846-847
  from information processing, 257
  information sources for, 847
  interim, 96, 151
  of merchandising business, 214
  net amounts for, 208
  order for preparation of, 108

for partnership, 590-592
preparing of, 149-150
relationship among, 111
responsibilities for, 303
and statement of changes in financial position, 848-849
and work sheets, 138-139
Financing activities, 780
    computing cash amounts of, 792-794
    noncash, 795
Firing policies, 500
Firms, public accounting, 4-5
First-in, first-out (FIFO) method, 395-396
    comparison of, 397-399
Fiscal year, 95
Fixed assets. *See* Capital assets
Flexibility, of accounting information system, 258
Flow of accounting data, 53
FOB (free on board), 204-205
FOB destination, 394
FOB shipping point, 394
Foreign-currency exchange rates, 754
Foreign-currency transaction gain or loss, 755
Forgery, failure to catch, 308
Format
    of balance sheet, 160
    of income statement, 215-219
Format, account. *See* Account format
Franchises, 450
    and installment method, 534-535
Fraud
    and cash receipts, 317-318
    and collusion, 307
    payroll, 500-501
Fringe benefits, 485, 492-493, 497
Fully depreciated assets, 445
Fully diluted earnings per share, 668
GAAP. *See* Generally accepted accounting principles
Gains, 547
General expenses, 214
General journal, 261, 262
General ledger, 262-263, 266
    and bank accounts, 309
Generally accepted accounting principles (GAAP), 6, 11-13, 525-529
    accrual basis required by, 95
    on bond amortization, 701

on bond gains and losses, 706
choice offered by, 532-533
and depreciation methods, 440-441
and standards, 525-527
on stock investments, 738
Going-concern concept, 530
Goods available for sale, 393
Goods and services tax (GST), 209-210, 476-477
Goodwill, 451
    and consolidation, 746
Government regulation, 3
Gross cost, in recording of purchases, 318-319
Gross margin, 199, 219
Gross margin method, 404-405
Gross margin rate, 405
Gross pay, 485
Gross profit, 199
Gross profit percentage, 844-845
Group (basket) purchases of assets, 434
Hardware (computer), 259-260
Health insurance, 485
Hedging, 757
Hiring policies, 500
Historical cost, 13
    see also Cost principle
Horizontal analysis, 841-844
Hot cheques, 311
Imprest system, 320
Improvements cost, land, 434
In arrears (dividends), 626
Income
    of consolidated entity, 748
    as tax concept, 4
    see also Net income
Income, measurement of. *See* Measurement of business income
Income from operations, 214
Income statement, 19, 22
    account titles for, 64
    and adjusted trial balance, 108
    common-size, 845-846
    consolidated, 748
    of corporation, 662-668
    dating of, 779
    formats for, 215-219
    horizontal analysis of, 841-844
    for merchandising entity, 214
    and percentage of sales method, 356-357

and statement of owner's equity, 111
    vertical analysis of, 844-845
    work sheet columns for, 138-146
Income Summary, 152, 215, 651
Income tax
    for corporations, 664-665
        (*see also* Corporate income tax)
    and depreciation, 442-443
    and partnership, 571
    withholding and quarterly payments for, 490-492
    see also Taxes
Income Tax Expense
    in income statement, 664-665
    in statement of changes in financial position, 784
Incorporation, 623-624
Incorporators, 613
Indirect method (for statement of cash flows), 795-798
Industrial Revolution, and accounting development, 4
Industry comparisons, 846-847
Information. *See* Accounting information
Information processing, 257, 258-261
Information sources, 847
Information system. *See* Accounting information system
Information systems design, 9
Installment method, 534-535
Intangible assets, 432, 449-451
    organization cost as, 624
    see also Goodwill
Interest, 363, 364-365
Interest-coverage ratio, 856
Interest Expense, 64, 214
    on bonds, 694, 695, 696, 697, 698-699, 701-703
    as operating activity, 779, 780
    in statement of changes in financial position, 783, 794
Interest Payable
    as current liability, 159
    as operating activity, 779-781
Interest period, 363
Interest rate, 363
Interest Revenue, 214
    accruing of, 368-369
    on chequing account, 311
Interim periods, 96

Interim statements or reports, 151, 531
Internal auditing, 9, 304, 307
Internal control, 257-258, 302
    bank account as, 308-314
    over cash disbursements, 318-326
    over cash receipts, 317-318
    and cash reporting, 316
    characteristics for effectiveness of, 304-307
    over collections of accounts receivable, 361-362
    and computers, 326
    over inventory, 409-410
    limitations of, 307-308
    over payroll, 500-501
    for capital assets, 447-448
International Accounting Standards (IAS), 527-528
Inventory, merchandise, 199, 393
    in calculating cost of goods sold, 207
    closing entries for, 215
    computerized system for, 501-502
    controlling cost of, 318-319
    as current asset, 159
    effect of errors on, 403-404
    estimating of, 404-406
    figuring cost of, 394-395
    internal control over, 409-410
    purchase of, 200-205
    selling of, 205-206
Inventory accounting systems
    periodic, 406-407
    perpetual, 207, 407-409
Inventory cost, 395
Inventory costing methods, 395-399
    average cost, 396-397, 398
    and consistency principle, 399
    first-in, first-out (FIFO), 396-397, 398
    last-in, first-out (LIFO), 396-397, 398
    and lower-of-cost-or-market rule, 403-404
    questions for judging of, 397-399
    specific cost, 395-396
Inventory profit, 398
Inventory records, computerized, 410
Inventory turnover ratio, 220, 852-853
Investee, 737

Investing activities, 780, 781
    computing cash amounts of, 794
    noncash, 795
    in statement of changes in financial position, 784-785, 794
Investment
    and consolidation accounting, 743
    long-term, 738, 741 (see also Long-term investments)
    in partnership, 572-573, 579-581
    short-term, 738-739, 739-741
    in stock, 737
Investment by owners, 547
Investor(s)
    as accounting users, 3, 9
    shareholders as, 737
Invoice, 201
    purchase, 201-202
    sales, 201
    in voucher system, 321-323
Journal, 50
    analysis without, 68
    cash disbursements, 262, 264-273
    cash receipts journal, 268, 264-267
    detailed information in, 58-59
    documents as, 277
    errors in, 162-163
    general, 261-262
    payroll, 493-495
    purchases, 262, 269-271
    sales, 262-264
Journalizing (recording transaction), 51
    of adjusting entries, 150-151, 217
    of closing entries, 152-154, 215
Journal reference
    in subsidiary ledgers, 263-264
    see also Posting reference
Labor unions, as accounting users, 4
Land
    cost of, 433
    and depreciation, 432
    in statement of changes in financial position, 794
Land account, 46, 64
Land improvements, cost of, 434

Last-in, first-out (LIFO)
    method, 396-397, 398
    comparison of, 397-399
LCM rule, 402-403, 545, 738-741
Lease, 70-9-711
Leasehold, 450-451
Ledger, 45
    Accounts Receivable ledger, 263-264, 266-267
    balancing (proving) of, 277
    detailed information in, 59, 60
    general ledger, 262-263, 266
    subsidiary ledger, 263-264, 266-267, 274-275
    usefulness of, 68
Lessee, 709
Lessor, 709
Leverage, 858
Liabilities, 14, 474, 546
    on balance sheet, 19, 21-22
    contingent, 367, 482-483 (see also Contingent liabilities)
    as credits or debits, 48, 62-63
    current, 159, 474 (see also Current liabilities)
    long-term, 159, 474, 691 (see also Long-term liabilities)
    pension, 711-713
    in statement of changes in financial position, 792
Liabilities accounts, 46, 64
    normal balance for, 61-62
    as permanent, 152
Licenses, 450
LIFO. See Last-in, first-out method
Limited liability, 612
Limited partnership, 570
Liquidation, 95, 530, 586
    of partnership, 578, 586-590
Liquidation value, 630
Liquidity, 158-159
Loans, in statement of changes in financial position, 795
Lock-box system, 311
Long-term assets, 159
Long-term debt
    current portion of, 479, 707
    in statement of changes in financial position, 792
Long-term investments, 741
    consolidation method for, 743-748
    cost method for, 741
    equity method for, 741-743

Long-term liabilities, 159
Long-term receivables, 353
Long-term solvency, 840
Losses, 547
 probable, 538
 see also Net loss
Lower-of-cost-or-market (LCM)
  rule, 402-403, 545
 with cost method, 738-741
Machinery, cost of, 433-434. *See
  also* Capital assets
Mail, internal control over, 317,
  361-362
Mainframe computer system,
  259
Maker of a note, 363
Management accounting, 10
Management consulting, 9
Management reports, 303-304
Manufacturing accounting. *See*
  Cost accounting for
  manufacturers
Margin
 gross, 199
Marketable securities, 737
market interest rate, 694
Market value of inventories, 402
market value of stock, 629
Matching principle, 96-97, 536
 and bad debt expense, 354
Materiality concept, 545
Maturity date (due date), 363
Maturity value, 363
 discount on, 366-367
Measurement of business income, 94
 accounting period in, 95-96
 accrual vs. cash basis in, 94-
  95 (*see also* Accrual-
  basis accounting;
  Cash-basis accounting)
 adjustment to accounts in,
  98-106 (*see also*
  Adjusting entries)
 revenue principle in, 96
Merchandise inventory. *See*
  Inventory, merchandise
Merchandising entity, 199
 adjusting and closing entries
  for, 215
 adjusting and closing
  process for, 211
 financial statements of,
  214-215
 operating cycle for, 200
 work sheet for, 211-214
Merchandising inventory. *See*
  Inventory, merchandise

Microcomputers, 111, 259
 see also Computer-assisted
  accounting systems
Microcomputer spreadsheet. *See*
  Spreadsheet
Minicomputers, 259
Minority interest, 746
Mistakes. *See* Errors
Monetary units, stability assumed for, 531
Mortgage, 692, 707
Multiple-step income statement
  format, 217
Mutual agency, 570
 absence of in corporation,
  612
 in partnership, 570
Natural resources. *See* Wasting
  assets
Net cost, in recording of purchases, 318-319
Net earnings, 17
Net income, 17, 62
 and statement of changes in
  financial position, 779
 on income statement, 19, 22
 and Income Summary, 152
 on statement of owner's
  equity, 19-20, 22
 and work sheet, 139, 146, 214
Net loss, 17
 closing of, 154
 on statement of owner's
  equity, 19-20, 22
 on work sheet, 139, 146, 214
Net pay, 485
Net profit, 17
Net purchases, 204
Net Realizable Value (NRV), 402
Net sales revenue (net sales),
  199, 206
Network (computer), 259
Nominal (temporary) accounts,
  152
Nonbusiness transaction, 18
Noncash investing and financing
  activities, 795
Noncumulative preferred stock,
  626
Nonprofit organizations, 529
 as accounting users, 4
Nonsufficient funds (NSF)
  cheque, 311
No-par stock, 617
Normal balances of accounts,
  61-62
Notes payable, 14
 bonds as, 691 (*see also* Bonds

  payable)
 convertible, 706-707
 as current liability, 159
 short-term, 474-476
Notes payable account, 46, 64
Notes receivable, 14, 353, 363
 computing interest on, 364-
  365
 contingent liabilities on, 367
 defaulting on (dishonor-
  ing), 367-368
 discounting of, 366-367
 maturity dates of, 363-364
 recording of, 365-366
Notes receivable account, 45, 63
NSF (nonsufficient funds)
  cheques, 311
Objective, of financial reporting,
  529
Objectivity principle, 12
Off-the-balance-sheet financing,
  711
Office equipment account, 46, 63
Office expenses, 214
Office furniture account, 46, 63
Office supplies account, 46, 63
On account, 16-17, 269
On-line processing, 260-261
Open account, 16
Opening the account, 50
Operating activities, 779-780
 cash flows from, 783-784
 computing cash amounts
  of, 789-792
Operating cycle, 159
 for merchandising business,
  200
Operating expense, 214
 vs. payments to suppliers,
  784
 in statement of changes in
  financial position, 791
Operating income, 214
Operating lease, 709
 vs. capital lease, 711
Operator, computer, 260
Ordinary repairs, 452
Organization chart, 305
Organization cost, 624
Organizations, accounting, 5-7
Other receivables, 353
Other revenue and expense, 214
Outstanding cheques, 311, 312
Outstanding stock, 614
Overpayment, as credit balance,
  360
Over-the-counter market
  (OTC), 692-693

Owner's equity, 14, 546
    on balance sheet, 19-20, 22
    CICA on elements of,
      546-547
    as credits or debits, 48-50
Owner's equity accounts, 46-47,
    64
    and adjusted trial balance,
      107-108
    normal balance for, 62
    in partnership, 571-573
    revenues and expenses in, 62
    in work sheet, 146
Owner withdrawals. *See*
      Withdrawals, owner
Owner withdrawal accounts. *See*
      Withdrawals account
Pacioli, Luca, 4
Paid voucher file, 321, 325-326
Parent company, 743
Participating preferred stock, 627
Partnership, 10-11, 568
    agreement, 570
    characteristics of, 569
    death of partner in, 586
    dissolution of, 578
    and entity concept, 529
    financial statements for,
      590-592
    and income tax, 571
    initial investment in, 572-573
    limited, 570
    liquidation of, 586-590
    partners' drawings in,
      577-578
    sharing profits and losses
      in, 573-577
    withdrawal of partner from,
      583-86
Partnership agreement, 570
Par value, 617, 620-621
Patents, 450
Pay
    gross, 485, 492, 493
    net, 485, 492, 493
Payables, and consolidation
    accounting, 746
Payee, 363
Payment date, 625
Payments to employees, in
    statement of changes in
    financial position, 784,
    791-792
Payments to suppliers, in state-
    ment of changes in fi-
    nancial position, 784,
    790-791
Payroll, 485

internal control over, 500-501
    recording cash disburse-
    ments for, 496-500
Payroll deductions, 488
    optional, 489
    required, 488-489
Payroll entries, 492-493
Payroll expense, reporting of,
    501-502
Payroll fraud, 500
Payroll liability, reporting of,
    501-502
Payroll system, 493-496
    bank account, 495
    cheques, 495-496
    register, 493-495
Pension, 711
Pension liabilities, 711-713
Percentage-of-completion
    method, 535-536
Percentages, trend. *See* Trend
    percentages
Percentage of sales method,
    356-357, 358, 359
Periodic inventory system,
    207-209, 406-407
Permanent (real) accounts, 152
Perpetual inventory system,
    207, 406, 407-409
Personal liability, in partnership,
    571
Personnel
    computer, 260
    and internal control, 304 (*see*
      also Internal control)
    petty cash, 319-321
Postal cash receipts, and internal
    controls, 317, 361-362
Postclosing trial balance,
    154-155, 211
Posting, 52, 60
    of adjusting entries, 106-
      107, 150-151
    of closing entries, 152-154,
      215
    errors in, 163
    illustrative problems in,
      53-55, 64-67
Posting period, and bank state-
    ment, 303-309
Posting reference
    account number as, 60
    in subsidiary ledgers,
      263-264
Potential liabilities. *See*
      Contingent liabilities
Preferred stock, 617
    convertible, 627

dividends on, 625-627
    issuing of, 621
    nonparticipating, 627
    participating, 627
Premium on bonds, 693, 694,
    697-698, 703-704
Prenumbering, 307
Prepaid expenses, 99-100
    as current asset, 159
    and reversing entries,
      188-191
Prepaid expenses account, 45-46
Present value, 693-394, 729-733
    of annuity, 730-732
    of bonds payable, 732-733
    of capital lease, 733
President of corporation, 613
Price/earnings ratio, 859
Prices of stocks, 736-737
Principal amount (principal),
    363, 691
Principles and concepts, 529, 532
    comparability, 532-533
    conservatism, 401-403,
      545-546
    consistency, 399, 532
    cost, 13, 533
    disclosure, 536-544
    entity, 11-12, 18, 529
    going-concern, 530
    matching, 96-97, 354, 536
    materiality, 545
    reliability, 12, 532
    revenue, 96, 533-536
    stable-monetary-unit, 531
    time-period, 530-531
    see also Generally accepted
      accounting principles;
      Rules
Prior period adjustments, 669-670
Private accountants, 5
Private accounting, 9-10
Probable losses, reporting of, 538
Proceeds, of note, 366
Profit-and-loss-sharing method,
    573-578
Profit percentage, gross, 844
Profits, 94
    gross, 199-200
Programmer, 260
Promissory note, 352, 363
Proper authorization, 305-305
Property tax expense account, 64
Proprietorship, 10, 529
Protection. *See* Internal control
Protest fee, 368
Provincial securities commis-
    sions, 3

Proving the ledgers, 277
Proxy, 613
Public accountants and accounting, 4-5, 9
Purchase discounts, 203
Purchase Discounts Lost account, 319
Purchase invoice, 201
Purchase order, 201
in voucher system, 321
Purchase request, in voucher system, 321
Purchase returns and allowances, 203-204, 275
Purchases, 200-201
Purchases journal, 269-271
Quantity discount, 202-203
Quick (acid-test) ratio, 370, 852
Rate of return on common shareholders' equity, 628, 857-858
Rate of return on net sales (return on sales), 856-857
Rate of return on total assets (return on assets), 628, 857
Ratios, 850-851
accounts receivable turnover, 371, 853-854
acid-test (quick), 370, 852
book value per share of common stock, 860
current, 851-852
days'-sales-in-receivables, 371, 854-855
debt, 855
dividend yield, 859-860
earnings per share of common stock, 858-859
inventory turnover, 220, 852-853
price/earnings, 859
rate of return on common shareholders' equity, 628, 857-858
rate of return on net sales, 856-857
rate of return on total assets, 628-629, 857
times-interest-earned (interest-coverage), 856
Real (permanent) accounts, 152
Receivables, 353
accounts receivable, 353 (see also Accounts receivable)
computers in accounting of, 371

and consolidation accounting, 745, 746
as current asset, 159
notes receivable, 352-353, 363 (see also Notes receivable)
reporting of, 369-370
Receiving report, in voucher system, 321
Reconciliation, bank. See Bank reconciliation
Reconciliation method (for statement of changes in financial position), 795-796
Records, prenumbering of, 307
Recoveries, of uncollectible accounts, 356
Redemption value, 629-630
Register, payroll, 493-495
Registered bond, 691-692
Regulatory agencies, government, 3
Related party transactions, 543-544
Relative-sales-value method, 434
Reliability (objectivity) principle, 12, 532
and cost principle, 533
Remittance advice, 317
Rent, prepaid, 99-100
Rent expense account, 64
Repairs, 452
Report format (balance sheet), 160
Reporting, of cash, 316-317
Repurchased capital stock, 656-659
Residual value, 435
estimated, 435-436
Responsibilities, and internal control, 306-307
See also Separation of duties
Retailing
inventory records system for, 410
see also Credit sales
Retail method, 405-406
Retained earnings, 614-616
appropriations of, 661
restrictions on, 661
statement of, 668-669
Retained Earnings account, 651-653
Return on assets, 628-629, 857
Return on common sharehold-

ers' equity, 628-629, 857-858
Return on sales, 856-857
Returns, purchase, 203-204
Returns, sales, 205-206
Revenue Canada, 432
Revenue Canada rate, 438
Revenue principle, 96, 533-536
Revenues, 16, 61, 546
accrued, 104-105
as credit/debit, 62
on income statement, 19, 21-22
other, 214
unearned (deferred), 105, 479-480 (see also Unearned revenue)
Revenues account, 46, 64
closing of, 152-154, 215, 217, 218
as temporary, 152
in work sheet, 146
Reversing entries, 155-158, 188-194
and prepaid expenses, 188-191
Rules
of debit and credit, 62
lower-of-cost-or-market (LCM), 402-403, 545, 738-741
see also Principles and concepts
Safeguards. See Internal control
Salaries Payable
as current liability, 159
in statement of changes in financial position, 791-792
Salary, 485
Salary or wage expense account, 64, 103-104
Salary or wage payable account, 64, 103-104
Sale(s)
of business segment, 665
of inventory, 205-206
net, 205
of capital asset, 445-446
Sale return, recording of, 273-275
Sales discounts, 205-206
Sales invoice, 201
Sales journal, 262-264
Sales method, 533-534
Sales return and allowances, 205-206
Sales revenue, net, 205

Sales revenue account, 64
Sales tax, 275-276, 476-78
Sales Tax Payable account, 476-478
Salvage value, 435
SCFP. *See* Statement of Changes in Financial Position
Scrap value, 435
Secured (mortgage) bonds, 692
Securities. *See* Bonds payable; Stock
Security (for loan), 352
Security measures. *See* Internal control
Segment of the business, 665
Selling expenses, 214
Separation of duties, 306-307
    for accounts receivable, 361-362
    for payroll disbursement, 500-01
    and capital assets, 447-48
    see also Internal control
Serial bonds, 692, 707
Service charge (bank), 311, 313
Service revenue account, 64
Share capital, 615
Shareholder rights, 161
Shareholders, 11, 611
Shareholders' equity, 614-616
Shareholders' rights, 616
Short-term investments, 737-738
    cost method for, 738-741
Short-term liquidity, 840
Short-term notes payable, 474-76
Short-term liquidity, 840
Short-term notes payable, 474-476
Signature card, for bank account, 308
Single-step income statement format, 217-219
Sinking fund, for bonds, 705
Slide (error), 163
SMAC. *See* Society of Management Accountants of Canada.
Software, 146, 259-260
Society of Management Accountants of Canada (SMAC), 5
Sole proprietorship, 10, 529
Special accounting journals, 261-262
    cash disbursements, 262, 271-273
    cash receipts, 262, 264

purchases, 262, 269-271
    sales, 262-264
Specific cost, 395-396
Spreadsheet, 146-147
Stable-monetary unit concept, 531
Standards. *See* Principles and concepts
Stated capital, 615
Stated interest rate, 694
Stated value, 618-619
Statement of accounting policies, 536-537
Statement of cash flows. *See* Statement of changes in financial position
Statement of changes in financial position, 778
    computing individual amounts for, 788-795
    in decision-making, 848-849
    direct method for preparation of, 782-785
    focus of, 785-786
    indirect method for preparation of, 795-798
    and noncash investing, 795
    purposes of, 778-779
Statement of earnings, 19
Statement of financial position, 19
Statement of operations, 19
Statement of owner's equity, 19-20, 22
    and adjusted trial balance, 108-111
    and balance sheet, 108-111
    and income statement, 108-111
    for merchandising and service entities, 215, 216
Statement of retained earnings
    for corporation, 669-670
    dating of, 779
Stock, 611, 614
    analyzing of as investment, 859-860
    common 616-617, 618-621, 625-626 (*see also* Common stock)
    dividends on, 616, 624-627 (*see also* Dividends)
    investments in, 737
    issuing of, 618-621
    no-par, 617
    par value, 617
    preferred, 617, 621, 625-627 (*see also* Preferred stock)

prices, 736-737
    repurchased, 656-659
    in statement of changes in financial position, 784, 792-793
    values of, 629-631
Stock dividend, 653-655
    and stock split, 655-656
Stock investment, 737-738
    and consolidation accounting, 743-748
    long-term (cost method), 741
    long-term (equity method), 741-743
    Short-term, 737-741
Stock prices, 736-737
Stock split, 655-656
Stock subscription, 619-620
Straight-line (SL) depreciation method, 436, 437, 440-441
Strong currency, 755
Subsequent event, 539-540
Subsidiary company, 743
Subsidiary ledger, 264, 266
    daily posting to, 274
Suppliers, payments to, 784, 790-791
Suppliers expense, 64
    as prepaid, 100-101
Systems analyst, 260
Tables of present values, 730, 731, 732
T-account, 48
    and journal, 52
    recording of debits and credits in, 49-50
Tax accounting, 9
Taxes
    and accounting, 3-4
    corporate, 612 (*see also* Corporate income tax)
    employee payroll, 485-489, 496-497
    employer payroll, 490, 493-495
    goods and services tax (GST), 209-210, 476-477
    sales, 275-276
TD1, 486, 488
Temporary (nominal) accounts, 152
Temporary investments, 737-738
Term bonds, 692
T4 Supplementary, 497, 499
Theft
    through accounting system, 256

of cash, 307
and cash disbursements, 258
fidelity bond against, 317
and postal cash receipts, 317
prenumbering against, 307
Time-and-a-half, 485
Time periods in accounting. *See*
Accounting period
Time-period concept, 530-531
Times-interest-earned ratio, 856
Time value of money, 693-694
Titles, account, 62-64
Trade Account Receivables, 353
(*see also* Accounts re-
ceivable)
Trade accounts payable, 474
Trademarks, 450
Trade names, 450
Trading on the equity, 858
"Trail" through accounting
records, 58
Transaction, 14
and account records, 50
categories of, 262
vs. intention, 96
nonbusiness, 18
recording of in journal, 50-52
Transaction analysis, 14-19
and cash account, 51
illustrative problems in,
53-55, 64-67
Transportation cost, 204-205
Transposition, 163
Trend percentages, 843-844
Trial balance, 55-56, 94
adjusted, 108

illustration of, 68
postclosing, 147-148, 154-
155, 211
unadjusted, 98
and work sheet, 138-139
Typical account titles, 62-64
UI. *See* Unemployment
Insurance
Unadjusted trial balance, 98
Uncollectible account expense,
353
Uncollectible accounts (bad
debts), 353
estimating of, 356-360
measuring of, 354-355
recoveries of, 356
writing off, 355-356
Underwriter, 618, 691
Unearned (deferred) revenue,
105, 479-480
as current liability, 159
Unemployment Insurance (UI),
488, 489, 490
Units-of-production (UOP)
method, 436-437, 440-
441
Unlimited personal liability, 571
Unpaid voucher file, 323
Unusual events. *See*
Extraordinary gains
and losses
Useful life, 435
change in, 444-445
determining of, 435
Utility expense account, 64
Vacation, as internal control, 304

Valuation, vs. depreciation,
434-435
Verifiability, and reliability
principle, 12
Vertical analysis, 844-845
common-size statement as,
845-846
Voucher, 321
Voucher register, 323, 324
Voucher system, 321-326
Wages, 485
Warranties Payable, 480-481
Wasting assets, 432, 448-449
Withdrawals,
vs. business expense, 19
as credits/debits, 62
from partnership, 577-578
on statement of owner's equity, 19-20, 22
Withdrawals account, 46
and adjusted trial balance,
108
closing of, 152-154
normal balance for, 62
as temporary, 152
Withheld income tax, 488
Working capital, 851
Work sheet, 138, 138-139, 138-146
closing entries from, 152-154
interim statements from, 151
for merchandising business,
211-214
use of, 149-155
Workers' Compensation, 490